Handbook of
SOCIAL STUDIES IN HEALTH AND MEDICINE

edited by

GARY L. ALBRECHT,
RAY FITZPATRICK,
AND SUSAN C. SCRIMSHAW

SAGE Publications

London • Thousand Oaks • New Delhi

This paperback edition first published 2003

First published 2000

 SAGE Publications Ltd
6 Bonhill Street
London EC2A 4PU

SAGE Publications Inc
2455 Teller Road
Thousand Oaks, California 91320

SAGE Publications India Pvt Ltd
B-42, Panchsheel Enclave
Post Box 4109
New Delhi 100 017

British Library Cataloguing in Publication data

A catalogue record for this book is available from the British Library

ISBN 0 7619 5617 4
ISBN 0 7619 4272 6 (pbk)

Library of Congress Control Number 2002114562

Typeset by Keyword Typesetting Services, Wallington, Surrey
Printed in Great Britain by The Cromwell Press, Trowbridge, Wiltshire

Handbook of
SOCIAL STUDIES IN

To our mentors

Contents

Contributors

Lu Ann Aday is Professor of Behavioral Sciences and Management and Policy Sciences at The University of Texas School of Public Health. She received her B.S. degree (1968) in economics from Texas Tech University, and her M.S. (1970) and Ph.D. (1973) degrees in sociology from Purdue University. Dr Aday's principal research interests have focused on the conceptual, empirical, and policy dimensions of equity of access to care for vulnerable populations. She has conducted major national and community surveys and evaluations of national demonstrations and published extensively in this area. She is the author of twelve books, including, most recently, *At Risk in America: The Health and Health Care Needs of Vulnerable Populations in the United States* (1993); *Designing and Conducting Health Surveys: A Comprehensive Guide* (1st edn, 1989; 2nd edn, 1996); and *Evaluating the Healthcare System: Effectiveness, Efficiency, and Equity* (1st edn, 1993; 2nd edn, 1998).

Gary L. Albrecht is Professor of Public Health and of Disability and Human Development at the University of Illinois at Chicago where he is Co-Principal Investigator of the Center for Emerging Disabilities and Principal Investigator of a National Institutes of Health-funded study of women with disabilities experiencing the menopausal transition. His current work focuses on the quality of life of persons with disabilities. He is past Chair of the Medical Sociology Section of the American Sociological Association and a member of the Strategic Planning Committee of the National Institute of Disability and Rehabilitation Research. He recently received the Award for the Promotion of Human Welfare and the Eliot Freidson Award for *The Disability Business: Rehabilitation in America*, a Switzer Distinguished Research Fellowship, the University of Illinois at Chicago Award for Excellence in Teaching, and was a Visiting Fellow at the University of Oxford and the Maison des Sciences de l'Homme, Paris.

David Armstrong is Reader in Sociology as Applied to Medicine at the University of London. He is based in the Department of Primary Care in the medical school attached to Guy's and St. Thomas's Hospitals. He has had a longtime interest in the work of Michel Foucault and has written several papers and a monograph on changes in medicine over the last few decades using a Foucaultian perspective. He is also qualified in medicine and is a specialist in public health medicine in the British National Health Service. This has led to an interest in health service research and publications in the area of primary health care, the primary–secondary interface, and clinicians' behavior.

Mary Boulton is Professor of Sociology, Oxford Brookes University. Her main research interests are in lay understandings and experience of health and health care. She has worked predominantly in the areas of genetic screening, where her attention has focused on issues relating to cystic fibrosis carrier screening, and of HIV and AIDS, where she has conducted a number of studies on the experience of gay and bisexual men and families of children with HIV infection. She is editor of *Challenge and Innovation: Methodological Advances in Social Research on HIV/AIDS* (Taylor & Francis, 1994) as well as a number of papers on qualitative methods in health services research.

Sarah Cant is a Senior Lecturer in the Faculty of Business and Sciences, Canterbury Christ Church University College. She has published extensively within medical sociology and has developed an interest in both private and alternative medicine. Her most recent books include *Complementary and Alternative Medicines. Knowledge in Practice* (Free Association Books, 1996), co-edited with Ursula Sharma, and *A New Medical Pluralism? Alternative Medicine, Doctors, Patients and the State* (UCL Press, 1999), co-authored with Ursula Sharma. Her current research interests cover social change, alternative medicine, and the sociology of the professions, and she is completing her Ph.D. on homeopathy and reflexive modernity.

Ralph Catalano is Professor of Public Health at the University of California, Berkeley. He holds a Ph.D. in social science from the Maxwell School of Syracuse University. He has served as Associate Vice Chancellor at the Irvine Campus of the University of California, as well as Vice Mayor of the City of Irvine. He has also been Head of the Division of Health Policy and Management at the School of Public Health at Berkeley. In addition to his work on the spatial distribution of illness, he continues his research program into the health and behavioral effects of unemployment.

Kathy Charmaz is Professor of Sociology and Faculty Writing Coordinator at Sonoma State University. Her books include two recent co-edited volumes, *The Unknown Country: Death in Australia, Britain and the USA* and *Health, Illness, and Healing: Society, Social Context and Self*, in addition to *The Social Reality of Death* and *Good Days, Bad Days: The Self in Chronic Illness and Time*, which won awards from the Pacific Sociological Association and the Society for the Study of Symbolic Interaction. She is editor-elect of *Symbolic Interaction* and will serve as President of the Pacific Sociological

Association for 1999–2000. Currently, Dr Charmaz is working on a study of the social psychology of suffering, explications of qualitative methods, and a handbook on writing for beleaguered social scientists.

Donald A. Cibula, Ph.D., has served as the Director of Surveillance and Statistics for the Onondaga County Health Department since 1992. In this capacity, he has designed, conducted, and analyzed results of epidemiologic research projects, including infant mortality, hepatitis A, occupational exposure to PCBs, and fetal drug exposures. Dr Cibula has authored periodic reports to assess the local status of TB, HIV/AIDS, syphilis and gonorrhea, teenage pregnancy, maternal and child health, and many other topics. He has contributed to developing the computer hardware and software infrastructure that facilitates research and public health monitoring within the health department he serves.

David Coburn is a sociologist and Professor in the Department of Public Health Sciences, University of Toronto. His research has mainly focused on the changing power structure in health care in Ontario. He has particularly analyzed 'the rise and fall of medicine' thesis, but he has also written on chiropractic, nursing, and naturopathy. His present interests lie in relating globalization and neo-liberalism to changes in health care. Recent publications include editorship of the third edition of *Health and Canadian Society: Sociological Perspectives* (University of Toronto Press, 1998) with Carl D'Arcy and George Torrance, a critique of 'population health' in *Social Science and Medicine*, and analysis of the 'restratification of medicine' thesis in *Sociology of Health and Illness*. With Ivy Bourgeault and Susan Rappolt he has written a series of papers on professional state relationships in Ontario, which will appear in the journal *Health and Canadian Society*.

Angela Coulter is Chief Executive of the Picker Institute Europe. A social scientist by training, she has a doctorate in health services research from the University of London. She is an Honorary Professor at the Royal Free and University College Schools of Medicine, a Visiting Fellow at Nuffield College, Oxford, and a Governor of Oxford Brookes University. Dr Coulter's research interests include user involvement in health care, primary care development, clinical effectiveness, women's health, public health, and evaluating health system reforms. She is editor of *Health Expectations,* a new international journal of public participation in health care and health policy.

Sarah Cunningham-Burley is Senior Lecturer in Medical Sociology, Department of Public Health Sciences, Medical School, University of Edinburgh. Her research interests span family and medical sociology, and she has conducted work on grandparenthood as well as the experience of health and illness at different stages of the lifecourse. Her research is informed by a commitment to understanding people's own interpretations of their experiences and of the factors which influence their lives. In recent years she has been investigating lay and professional views of the new genetics. She is especially concerned to develop sociological work in this crucial area and contribute to effective public debate of key issues. She has co-edited two volumes (with Neil McKeganey), *Enter the Sociologist* (Avebury, 1987) and *Readings in Medical Sociology* (Routledge, 1990), and has published widely in a range of journals.

Carroll L. Estes is the Director of the Institute for Health & Aging and Professor of Sociology in the Department of Social and Behavioral Sciences, School of Nursing, University of California, San Francisco. Dr. Estes (Ph.D., University of California, San Diego) conducts research on health and aging policy, long-term care, health and economic security of the aged, older women, fiscal crisis, and the impact of devolution on health and human services. She is the author of *The Decision-Makers: The Power Structure of Dallas* (SMU Press, 1963); *The Aging Enterprise* (Jossey Bass, 1979); co-author of *Fiscal Austerity & Aging* (Sage, 1983) with J. Swan; *Political Economy, Health and Aging* (Little Brown, 1984); *The Long Term Care of the Elderly* (Sage, 1984) with C. Harrington and R. Newcomer; *The Long Term Care Crisis* (Sage, 1993); co-editor of *The Nation's Health* (Jones & Bartlett, 1997) with P. Lee; *Health Policy & Nursing* (Jones & Bartlett, 1997) with C. Harrington; and *Critical Gerontology* (Baywood, 1998) with Meredith Minkler.

Ray Fitzpatrick is Professor of Public Health and Primary Care, Institute of Health Sciences, University of Oxford, and Fellow and Dean, Nuffield College, Oxford. His research interests focus on measurement of outcomes of health care, such as health status, quality of life, and patient satisfaction, and their use in clinical trials and evaluative research. With Gary Albrecht he edited *Quality of Life in Health Care* (JAI Press, Greenwich, Connecticut, 1994). With Stan Newman, Tracy Revenson, Sue Skevington, and Gareth Williams he wrote *Understanding Rheumatoid Arthritis* (Routledge, London, 1995). He co-edited with Nick Black, John Brazier, and Barnaby Reeves *Health Services Research Methods: A Guide to Best Practice* (BMJ Books, London, 1998). He is currently editing with colleagues a *Handbook of Methods of Health Technology Assessment* to be published by Sage.

Renée C. Fox, Ph.D. in sociology, Harvard University, 1954, is Professor Emerita at the University of Pennsylvania. She was a member of the Columbia University Bureau of Applied Social Research and a member of the faculty of Barnard College. At the University of Pennsylvania, she was Professor of Sociology with joint appointments in Psychiatry and Medicine and Nursing and held an interdisciplinary chair as the Annenberg Professor of Social Sciences. During the 1996–97 academic year, she was the George Eastman Visiting Professor at the University of Oxford.

Her research on the sociology of medicine, medical education, and medical ethics has involved her in first-hand, participant observation studies in Continental Europe, Central Africa, the People's Republic of China, and the United States. She is the author of seven books and numerous articles. Her best known books are *Experiment Perilous: Physicians and Patients Facing the Unknown*; *The Courage to Fail: A Social View of Organ Transplants and Dialysis*; *Spare Parts: Organ Replacement in American Society;* and *In the Belgian Château: The Spirit and Culture of a European Society in an Age of Change*.

Dr Fox is a member of the American Academy of Arts and Sciences and of the Institute of Medicine of the National Academy of Sciences, a Fellow of the American Association for the Advancement of Science, the holder of a Centennial Medal from the Graduate School of Arts and Sciences of Harvard University, and a recipient of the American Sociological Association's Leo G. Reeder Award for Distinguished Contributions to Medical Sociology. She holds six honorary degrees, and in 1995 she was named Chevalier of the Order of Leopold II by the Belgian government.

Byron J. Good is Professor of Medical Anthropology, Department of Social Medicine, Harvard Medical School. Professor Good has written widely about social theory and medical anthropology (with a special interest in phenomenology and narrative studies), cultural issues relevant to psychopathology and mental health services, and the implications of new and emerging biotechnologies for medical practice. He is currently conducting research in central Java, Indonesia. Professor Good is author of *Medicine, Rationality and Experience: An Anthropological Perspective* (Cambridge University Press, 1994), and co-editor of several books, including *Culture and Depression* (University of California Press, 1985) and *Pain as Human Experience* (University of California Press, 1992). Together with Mary-Jo Good, he is editor of the international journal, *Culture, Medicine and Psychiatry: A Journal of International and Cross-Cultural Research*.

Mary-Jo DelVecchio Good is Professor of Social Medicine at Harvard Medical School. Professor Good studies the culture and political economy of biomedicine in the United States and in international contexts. Her most recent work examines the worlds of research and clinical oncology and the influence of innovations in biotechnology on clinical narratives that physicians create with and for patients in cancer treatment. She is the author of *American Medicine: The Quest for Competence* (University of California Press, 1995, 1998); 'Cultural Studies of Biomedicine' in *Social Science and Medicine*, 1995; and 'L'Abbracio Biotecnico: Un Invito al trattamento sperimentale' in *Il sapere della quarigione* (Laterza, 1996); and author and editor of *Pain as Human Experience* (University of California Press, 1992, 1994), with P. Brodwin, A. Kleinman, and B. Good. She is co-editor in chief, with Byron Good, of *Culture, Medicine and Psychiatry: A Journal of International and Cross-Cultural Research*. She and Byron have collaborated for nearly three decades in medical anthropology research, writing, and teaching. In addition to this chapter, their most recent article is "'Fiction' and 'Historicity' in Doctors' Stories: Social and Narrative Dimensions of Learning Medicine" in *Narrative and the Cultural Construction of Illness and Healing* (University of California Press, 1999), and they have a new book in progress, *The Biotechnical Embrace*.

Steve Harrison is Reader in Health Policy and Politics at the University of Leeds Nuffield Institute for Health, where he has taught and researched since 1978. His main research interests are in the macropolitics of health care, including government decisions about funding and organising services, and in its micropolitics, especially medical–managerial relationships, NHS-user group politics, and public consultation. In 1997–98 he was Hallsworth Research Fellow in the Department of Government at the University of Manchester, and is currently studying the politics of 'evidence-based medicine.' He is author or co-author of ten books and over 200 other publications.

James S. House is Professor of Sociology and Director of the Survey Research Center in the Institute for Social Research at the University of Michigan, where he is also affiliated with the Department of Epidemiology and Institute of Gerontology. He received his Ph.D. in social psychology from the University of Michigan in 1972. His research has focused on the role of psychosocial factors in the etiology of health and illness, initially on occupational stress and health, later on social relationships, social support, and health, and currently on the nature and explanation of socioeconomic differences in health and the relation of age to health. He is an elected Fellow of the American Academy of Arts and Sciences and has been a Guggenheim Fellow and a member of the editorial boards of the *Annual Review of Sociology*, *Journal of Health and Social Behavior*, *Social Psychology Quarterly*, *Work & Stress*, and the *Journal of Behavioral Medicine*.

Mary Ann Jezewski, Ph.D., R.N., is Associate Professor at the University at Buffalo, School of Nursing. With a master's degree in nursing and a Ph.D. in anthropology, Dr Jezewski has focused her research on culture brokering in health care and patient/provider interactions during end-of-life decision making. She has studied migrant farmworkers and the homeless as part of her research on culture brokering.

Judith D. Kasper is Associate Professor in the Department of Health Policy and Management in the Johns Hopkins University School of Hygiene and Public Health. Her research and teaching interests include health policy in long-term care, expenditures and access to health care for vulnerable populations, and the development and application of data sources for health policy and health services research. She has extensive experience in the design, conduct, and analysis of population-based health surveys and has served on the National Committee on Vital and Health Statistics. She has published in numerous journals in the fields of health policy, health services research, and gerontology. Dr Kasper holds a Ph.D. in sociology from the University of Chicago.

Carl Kendall is Professor of Medical Anthropology and International Health at the London School of Hygiene and Tropical Medicine. He holds joint appointments at the Johns Hopkins University School of Hygiene and Public Health and the Tulane University School of Public Health and Tropical Medicine. He was the founder and first Director of the International Center for Community-Based Disease Control at Johns Hopkins. Professor Kendall is the author of more than sixty books and articles in general anthropology and in the field of applied medical anthropology. Professor Kendall has worked in more than forty countries in the areas of child health, women's reproductive health, AIDS, and community-based vector-borne disease control. His primary focus in this research has been the design, implementation, and evaluation of community-based interventions, with an eye to understanding why interventions work or fail. His current research focuses on health-seeking behaviors and using ethnographic models to explore the health transition.

Arthur Kleinman is the Maude and Lillian Presley Professor of Medical Anthropology in the Departments of Anthropology and Social Medicine at Harvard University. A psychiatrist and anthropologist, he has carried out intensive research on illness experience, other forms of suffering, and therapeutic practices in China, Taiwan, and North America since 1968.

Sandra D. Lane is a medical anthropologist/epidemiologist with a background in clinical nursing. She is currently Project Director of Syracuse Healthy Start and a behavioral scientist with the Onondaga County Health Department in Syracuse, New York. Dr Lane's research background includes work on behavioral factors in trachoma infection, the differential mortality of females in Egypt, the political, economic, and health consequences of unsafe abortion in Egypt, evaluation methods for media-based health education messages, and evaluation of the public health costs and benefits of needle exchange in North America. She has served as an expert consultant to the United Nations Population Program on rapid methods in program evaluation and as a member of an advisory committee on operations research for tuberculosis for the World Health Organization.

Steven Lewis received a B.A. and an M.A. in political science from the University of Saskatchewan (Canada). Since 1974 he has worked as a healthcare planner, researcher, program evaluator, and research administrator. He is currently Chief Executive Officer of the Health Services Utilization and Research Commission, Province of Saskatchewan, which includes responsibility for the province's extramural research granting programs. The Commission analyses the use of health services and develops recommendations to improve effectiveness and efficiency, and in general promotes evidence-based change. He is theme leader of HEALNet, a major national project linking research and evidence to decision making in health care, funded under the Networks of Centres of Excellence program. He has been a member of numerous provincial and national bodies, including the National Forum on Health chaired by Prime Minister Jean Chretien, the Advisory Committee on Health Services to the Federal/Provincial/Territorial Deputy Ministers of Health, the board of directors of the Canadian Nurses' Association, the board of the Saskatchewan Health Information Network, and the Health Services Research review committee of the Medical Research Council of Canada.

Donald W. Light does comparative research on health-care systems, markets, insurance, and the professions as a professor at the University of Medicine and Dentistry of New Jersey and at Rutgers University. In the past decade, he has been involved in the evolution of competitive health-care markets in both the United States and the United Kingdom, and he is editing a set of studies on how sociological and political forces interacted with policies advocating 'managed competition' in various countries. Professor Light majored in history at Stanford University before going on to do his graduate work at the University of Chicago and Brandeis University.

Karen W. Linkins, Ph.D., is a Research Specialist and Project Director at the Institute for Health & Aging, University of California, San Francisco. Currently, Dr Linkins is the co-investigator of two studies: an investigation of the impact of welfare reform on community-based nonprofit organizations serving the elderly and persons with disabilities in the San Francisco Bay area; and an evaluation of the effectiveness of substance abuse and mental health services for the elderly in a managed care setting. In addition, she is conducting a United States provider and payer analysis for drug therapies targeting the severely and persistently mentally ill, as well as a retrospective review of pharmacy and clinical databases to assess treatment patterns and quality of life in patients with psychosis or schizophrenia. Dr Linkins has written widely on the political economy of the health and social service systems in the United States.

Margaret Lock is Professor in the Department of Social Studies of Medicine and the Department of Anthropology at McGill University. She is the author of *East Asian Medicine in Urban Japan: Varieties of Medical Experience* (1980) and *Encounters with Aging: Mythologies of Menopause in Japan and North America* (1993), which won the J. I. Staley Prize, School of American Research, the Eileen Basker Memorial Prize, the Canada–Japan Book Award, the Berkeley Award, the Wellcome Medal of the Royal Anthropological Institute, and was a finalist for the Hiromi Arisawa Award. Both books were published by the University of California Press and have been translated into Japanese. Dr Lock has edited five other books and written over 100 scholarly articles. She was the recipient of a Canada Council Izaak Killam Fellowship for 1993–95, is a Fellow of the Royal Society of Canada, a member of the Canadian Institute of Advanced Research, Population Health Program, and was awarded the 1997 Prix Leon-Gerin by the government of Quebec. Dr Lock is currently a member of a strategic network grant team funded by the Social Sciences and Humanities Research Council of Canada and a member of the MELSI committee (Medical, Ethical, Legal and Social Issues) of the Canadian Human Genome Project (CGAT).

Deborah Lupton is Associate Professor in Cultural Studies and Cultural Politics and Deputy Director of the Centre for Cultural Risk Research, School of Social Sciences and Liberal Studies, Charles Sturt University, Australia. Her current research interests are in the sociocultural aspects of medicine and public health, the body, food, HIV/AIDS, sexuality, the media and commodity culture, parenthood, the emotions and risk. She is author/co-author of nine books on these topics, including *Medicine as Culture: Illness, Disease and the Body in Western Societies* (1994), *The Imperative of Health: Public Health and the Regulated Body* (1995), *Food, the Body and the Self* (1996) and *The New Public Health: Health and Self in the Age of Risk* (1996, with A. Petersen). Her latest book is *The Emotional Self: A Sociocultural Exploration* (1998).

Ann McElroy is an Associate Professor of Anthropology and Director of the Program in Applied Medical Anthropology at the State University of New York (SUNY) at Buffalo. She received her Ph.D. in anthropology from the University of North Carolina at Chapel Hill in 1973. Dr McElroy has served on the Executive Boards of the Society for Medical Anthropology and the Society for Applied Anthropology, has been the book review editor for the *Medical Anthropology Quarterly*, and has chaired the Social Sciences Human Subjects Review Committee at SUNY Buffalo since 1995. Her research interests include medical ecology, maternal and child health, migrant farm worker health, disability studies, and the political ecology of the Arctic. She is co-author with Patricia Townsend of *Medical Anthropology in Ecological Perspective* (3rd edn, 1996) and co-editor of *Making our Research Useful* (1989).

Colleen A. McHorney is a Professor of Medicine at Regenstrief Institute at Indiana University School of Medicine. She is also Director of the Health Services Research & Development Program at the Wm. S. Middleton Memorial VA Hospital. She is deputy editor for *Medical Care,* the official journal of the Medical Care Section of the American Public Health Association. Dr McHorney was Scientist at The Health Institute, New England Medical Center, and on the faculty at the Harvard School of Public Health. Dr McHorney's research focuses on outcomes research and health status assessment, with particular emphasis on quality of life and quality of care assessment. As the Picker/Commonwealth Scholars Program Finalist, Dr McHorney examined attitudinal and methodological barriers to the use of health status measures in clinical practice.

Michael Moran is Professor of Government at the University of Manchester, United Kingdom. A graduate of the Universities of Lancaster and of Essex, he has written widely on British politics and on comparative public policy. Among his publications are *The Politics of the Financial Services Revolution* (Macmillan, 1991) and *States, Regulation and the Medical Profession* (with Bruce Wood, OUP, 1993). He is presently completing a comparative study of health care policy, *Governing the Health Care State*, to be published in 1999 by Manchester University Press. Since 1993 he has been editor of *Political Studies*, the journal of the U.K. Political Studies Association.

Suzanne E. Morrissey is a Ph.D. candidate in the Department of Anthropology at Syracuse University. She is an Assistant Professor of Epidemiology at the State University of New York Health Science Center. She is also a research anthropologist working for the Onondaga County Health Department in Syracuse, New York, on an infant mortality prevention project funded through the Health Resources and Services Administration. Her dissertation field research examines the interplay of poverty and urban living among WIC-eligible women at risk for poor birth outcomes. She has conducted research in the Republic of Ireland on maternal health and breastfeeding patterns.

Lois LaCivita Nixon, Ph.D., M.P.H., is Professor of Ethics and Humanities in the College of Medicine and the College of Public Health at the University of South Florida. In addition to co-editing two books on health care and co-authoring one, Dr Nixon has published in *The Journal of Clinical Ethics, Law, Medicine & Health Care, The Journal of Medical Humanities, Pharos, The Journal of Aging and Identity*, and *Academic Medicine*. Her most recent articles are entitled 'Pyramids and Rhomboids in the Rationalist World of Medicine' and 'Emerging Issues in International Health Systems Organization.' Dr Nixon has graduate degrees from Rollins College (M.A.T.), Middlebury College (M.Litt.), and the University of South Florida (Ph.D., M.P.H.). For two years, she served as Chair of the Hillsborough County Hospital Authority and is currently a member of the Committee on Governance for the American Hospital Association and is active, as well, in the National Association of Public Hospitals. She is a former Peace Corps Volunteer (Togo), a three-time National Endowment for the Humanities Fellow, a Pew Trust Fellow, and a Fulbright Scholar in Jordan. Dr Nixon's areas of study include medical ethics and humanities, women's issues, and the impact of globalism on health care.

Karen E. Peters, M.P.H., is at the Health Research and Policy Centers at the University of Illinois at Chicago. Her dissertation research focuses on home health care providers' utilization of home care services and the outcomes of home care. She is currently Project Director of the Cooperative Actions for Health Program, Medicine and Public Health Initiative at the American Medical Association. Previously she served as project manager of two research efforts concerning health promotion interventions with diverse ethnic and racial older adult populations in Chicago at UIC's Prevention Research Center. Her main interest areas are health services research, program evaluation, ethnic aging studies, and organizational theory.

Kate E. Pickett is a doctoral student in the Division of Public Health Biology and Epidemiology, School of Public Health, University of California, Berkeley. She is conducting research on the effects of neighborhood social environments on risk of preterm birth. She holds masters' degrees in nutritional science from Cornell University and in anthropology from Cambridge University.

Thomas R. Prohaska is Professor and Director of the Division of Community Health Sciences of the University of Illinois at Chicago School of Public Health. He is also Co-Director of the University of Illinois Center for Research on Health and Aging. He has recently co-edited a book, *Public Health and Aging* (with T. Hickey and M. Speers), which focuses on behavioral health issues in older populations. His research interests focus on gerontological public health including health behavior, illness behavior in older adults, and the psychosocial factors associated with self care in older populations. His current research activities involve the investigation of psychosocial issues associated with recruitment and retention of minority older adults in group exercise activities, doctor–patient interaction studies, and dissemination of community-based collaborative research and health promotion interventions among diverse older populations.

Heléna Ragoné received her Ph.D. in anthropology from Brown University. *Surrogate Motherhood: Conception in the Heart* (1994), her first book, was the first ethnographic study of surrogate motherhood. In it, Dr Ragoné documents the experiences of women who choose to become surrogate mothers as well as those of two previously inaccessible populations: commissioning couples and surrogate mother program staff. She has since co-edited three collections, *Situated Lives: Gender and Culture in Everyday Life*, *Reproducing Reproduction: Kinship, Power, and Technological Innovation*, and *Ideologies and Technologies of Motherhood: Race, Class, Sexuality, and Nationalism*. Dr Ragoné frequently delivers guest lectures throughout the United States and Europe and is currently completing *Distant Kin: Gestational Surrogacy and Gamete Donation*, an ethnography that will explore the meteoric rise in the rates of gestational surrogacy and ovum donation in the United States. She is also completing *Riding Danger:*

Women in Horse Culture, an ethnography that highlights how and why women negotiate the risk of death and serious physical injury in the highly gendered sport of riding.

Marc Renaud is currently President of the Social Sciences and Humanities Research Council of Canada, a position he has occupied since September 1997. He received a B.A. from Collège Saint-Viateur (Montréal, 1966), a B.Sc. (1968) and an M.A. (1970) in sociology from the Université de Montréal, and a Ph.D. in sociology from the University of Wisconsin (1976). Dr Renaud has been, since 1975, a Professor in the Department of Sociology at the Université de Montréal. From 1991 to 1997, he was President of the Conseil québécois de la recherche sociale. He has been Vice-President and Fellow of the Canadian Institute for Advanced Research since 1991, and was Director of the Groupe de recherche sur les aspects sociaux de la santé et de la prévention (GRASP) from 1984 to 1991. Dr Renaud was an active member of the National Forum on Health chaired by the Prime Minister. In 1992, he was elected to the Royal Society of Canada.

Stephanie A. Robert is Assistant Professor of Social Work at the University of Wisconsin–Madison, where she is also affiliated with the Institute for Research on Poverty and the Institute on Aging. After receiving her joint Ph.D. in sociology and social work from the University of Michigan in 1996, Dr Robert spent two years as a Robert Wood Johnson Foundation Scholar in Health Policy Research at the University of California, Berkeley. Her primary research interest is in socioeconomic inequalities in health over the life course. She is also interested in community-based long-term care programs and policies for older adults. Her most recent research focuses on the impact of the socioeconomic characteristics of communities on the health, mortality, and well-being of community residents.

Robert A. Rubinstein is Professor of Anthropology and of International Relations and Director of the Program on the Analysis and Resolution of Conflicts at Syracuse University. He received a Ph.D. in anthropology from the State University of New York at Binghamton (1977) and an M.S.P.H. from the School of Public Health, University of Illinois at Chicago (1983). He specializes in medical anthropology and conflict resolution. He has conducted research in Egypt, Belize, Yucatan, and the urban United States. His research focuses on community-based health interventions for preventing infectious disease, on cross-cultural negotiation, and on multilateral peacekeeping. He has published over fifty articles and is author or editor of five books, including *Science as Cognitive Process: Towards an Empirical Philosophy of Science* (University of Pennsylvania Press, 1984), *Peace and War: Cross-Cultural Perspectives* (Transaction, 1986), *Fieldwork: The Correspondence of Robert Redfield and Sol Tax* (Westview, 1991), and *The*

Social Dynamics of Peace and Conflict: Culture in International Security (Kendall/Hunt, 1997).

Marcel Saulnier is a Senior Policy Analyst in the Social Policy Division, Department of Finance, Government of Canada. Prior to this posting, Mr Saulnier worked for the secretariat of the Prime Minister's National Forum on Health, a federally appointed task force which delivered its final report in early 1997. Mr Saulnier's career in the federal public service also includes several years as policy analyst in the federal Department of Health, as well as various other positions in federal government departments, including the Privy Council Office, the Treasury Board Secretariat, and the Department of Western Economic Diversification.

Susan C. Scrimshaw, Ph.D., Anthropology, Columbia University, 1974, is Dean, School of Public Health, and Professor of Community Health Sciences and Anthropology, University of Illinois at Chicago. Her research focuses on family planning and fertility decision making, improving pregnancy outcomes, child survival programs, violence prevention, and culturally appropriate delivery of health care. She has written extensively on quantitative and qualitative methodologies including the Rapid Anthropological Assessment Procedures (RAP) guidelines for nutrition and primary health.

Dr Scrimshaw is a member of the Institute of Medicine, a Fellow of the American Association for the Advancement of Science, a Fellow of the American Anthropological Association, and an appointed member of the Chicago Board of Health. Awards for her work include the 1985 Margaret Mead Award. Most recently, her appointments include the Centers for Disease Control and Prevention Task Force on Community Preventive Services, the Institute of Medicine's Committees on Cancer Research Among Minorities and the Medically Underserved, the National Institutes of Health Priority Setting Process, and President-Elect of the Association of Schools of Public Health.

Don Seeman is Lecturer in the Department of Sociology and Anthropology at The Hebrew University of Jerusalem. As an anthropologist, he has carried out research on the social context of infectious disease among migrants and on the relationship between illness experience, religion, and national identity in Israel.

Ursula Sharma trained in both sociology and social anthropology at the University of London. Recently, she has specialized in medical anthropology and has published extensively on complementary and alternative medicine. She is the author of *Complementary Medicine Today: Practitioners and Patients* (Routledge, 1995), and with Sarah Cant has co-authored *A New Medical Pluralism? Alternative Medicine, Doctors, Patients and the State* (UCL Press, 1999). She is Professor of Comparative Sociology at the School of Education and Science, University of Derby, United Kingdom.

Johannes Siegrist studied sociology, philosophy, and history and received his Ph.D. from the University of Freiburg, Germany, in 1969. From 1973 to 1992, Dr Siegrist was Professor of Medical Sociology at the University of Marburg. Since 1992, he has served as Professor of Medical Sociology and Director of the Postgraduate Training Program on Public Health in the Medical School at the University of Düsseldorf, Germany. Dr Siegrist is responsible for major scientific work in the social epidemiology of cardiovascular disease (psychosocial work environment) and in health-care evaluation research, and he is the author of some 200 original papers and several books, including a standard textbook on medical sociology. He has held Visiting Professorships at Johns Hopkins University, Baltimore, USA, and the Institute of Advanced Studies, Vienna, Austria. His honors include the Hans Roemer Award (German College of Psychosomatic Medicine), the Belle van Zuylen Chair, University of Utrecht, The Netherlands, and Honorary Membership, European Society of Health and Medical Sociology.

Robert T. Trotter, II, is Regent's Professor of Anthropology at Northern Arizona University. He has conducted research on cross-cultural health care and educational issues in the United States, Mexico, and Puerto Rico, as well as World Health Organization multinational studies of substance abuse, and with the International Classification of Impairments, Handicaps and Disabilities (ICIDH). His research interests include HIV risk prevention research, cross-cultural alcohol and drug studies, and traditional medicine. He has a long-term interest in ethnographic research methods and the use of computers to assist ethnographic research. He is also active in both graduate and postgraduate training in ethical practices for ethnographic research.

Bryan S. Turner is Professor of Sociology at the University of Cambridge. He has held professorial chairs in Australia, Britain, and The Netherlands, and was an Alexander von Humboldt Professorial Fellow at Bielefeld University, Germany (1986–87). He was the Morris Ginsberg Fellow at the London School of Economics in 1981. He is founding co-editor of the journal *Body & Society* and founding editor of *Citizenship Studies*. His current research interests include (1) voluntary associations and the privatization of the welfare state, (2) intimacy in old age, and (3) the lifestyle of postwar generations. He has published extensively in medical sociology, the sociology of religion, and political sociology. His recent publications include: *The Blackwell Companion to Social Theory* (1996) and *The Body & Society* (1996, 2nd edn). He is the series editor of *Politics & Culture* (Sage).

Lois M. Verbrugge, Ph.D., M.P.H., is Distinguished Senior Research Scientist, Institute of Gerontology, at the University of Michigan. A social demographer, Dr Verbrugge centers her current research on disability in mid- and late life. She is engaged in research projects on (1) the efficacy of personal and equipment assistance in relieving disability, using data from the National Health Interview Survey Disability Supplement, (2) multiplicities of disability in adults (patterns of ADL/IADL disabilities, duration, and severity) using the same data set, and (3) how musculoskeletal function (strength, endurance, range of motion) affects physical and social functioning, using primary data collected on persons ages 60+. Her research career has covered the topics of osteoarthritis and its disabling impacts, gender differences in health and mortality, health trends and future health prospects for American adults, multiple roles and physical health of women and men, and health diary methodology.

Dr Verbrugge has had several prominent awards: (1) a Research Career Development Award from the National Institute on Child Health and Human Development to work on sex differentials in health and mortality; (2) a Special Emphasis Research Career Award from the National Institute on Aging to secure biomedical training in the rheumatic diseases and develop collaborative research with rheumatology colleagues; and (3) the Distinguished Contribution to Women's Health Award from the American Psychological Association. In 1992, she was awarded the Distinguished Research Scientist title by the University of Michigan in recognition of her research achievements.

Jan S. Warren-Findlow is at the Health Research and Policy Centers at the University of Illinois at Chicago School of Public Health. She received an M.B.A from Lehigh University in 1983 and a B.A. in economics from Moravian College in 1981. She works at the Center for Research on Health and Aging and is currently the Project Manager on an Edward R. Roybal Center grant to study the effects of exercise on older adults with multiple chronic illnesses. Her research background envelopes the life span including: cardiovascular risk assessment in school-aged children, school-based health interventions for adolescents, health issues of older women, and needs assessments of older adults living in low-income, federally subsidized housing.

Deena White is Associate Professor of Sociology at the Université de Montréal, specializing in social policy, and Director of the Interdisciplinary Ph.D. in Applied Social Science. She is also a senior researcher at the Social Aspects of Health and Prevention Research Center. There, she leads an applied research team that, in partnership with regional health and social service boards, investigates questions of macro- and microregulation in the health domain, with study topics ranging from policy and planning to doctor–patient relations. Her work over the past ten years has addressed the dynamics of health and welfare reform, with a particular focus on state–civil society relations in the areas of occupational health, mental health, and social assistance. Dr White has published extensively in recent years on community involvement in the area of mental health, at the levels of intervention, planning, and policy development. She is currently examining the phenomenon of intersectoral cooperation in this field.

Linda M. Whiteford, Ph.D., M.P.H., a medical anthropologist, is Professor and Chair of the Department of Anthropology at the University of South Florida in Tampa, Florida. The focus of her research is infectious disease and international health, and much of her writing has focused on comparative health systems, particularly in the Caribbean and Latin America. Her publications related to comparative health systems are: 'Children's Health as Accumulated Capital: Structural Adjustment in the Dominican Republic and Cuba' in *Small Wars: The Cultural Politics of Childhood;* 'Sembrando El Futuro: Globalization and the Commodification of Health' in *Crossing Currents: Latin America in Transition;* 'Caribbean Colonial History and Its Contemporary Consequences: The Case of the Dominican Republic' in the *Journal of Social Science and Medicine*, 1992; and 'International Policies and Child Health' in the *Journal of Social Science and Medicine*, 1993. In addition to her work on comparative health systems, Dr Whiteford has also published on infectious and vector-borne diseases, such as cholera and dengue fever, and child–maternal health.

Evan Willis is Associate Professor of Sociology in the School of Sociology, Politics and Anthropology at La Trobe University in Melbourne, Australia. His research interests in the field of health sociology include technology assessment, demarcation disputes between health professions, occupational health and safety, and the social implications of the 'new' genetics. He has lived and worked in New Zealand and Canada in addition to Australia.

Sharla K. Willis is at the School of Public Health, Ohio State University. Her past research has included qualitative studies with Latino- and African-American populations looking at issues related to pregnancy and prenatal care. She is currently finishing her dissertation research on the impact maternal experience with a jaundiced infant has on breastfeeding. She holds an M.P.H in international population and family health and an M.A. in Latin-American studies from the University of California, Los Angeles.

Emily C. Zielinski Gutiérrez, M.P.H, is pursuing a doctorate in public health (DrPH) at the Tulane University School of Public Health and Tropical Medicine in the Department of International Health and Development. Her dissertation study is an evaluation of methods, outcomes, and sustainability of integrated, community-based dengue prevention in Guatemala. Ms Zielinski Gutiérrez has worked in the evaluation of HIV educational material, production of an HIV prevention print media series, and with young adult reproductive health programs in Latin America. She has also worked in HIV education and hospice care on the Texas–Mexico border and maintains a strong interest in border health issues.

Acknowledgments

The germination of the ideas for this handbook took place in lively discussions with colleagues and Sage Publishers in England, Germany, France, Switzerland, and the United States over a period of years. Chris Rojek and Stephen Barr provided the opportunity and encouragement to produce an international, multidisciplinary handbook reflective of the intellectual work being done in the social studies of health and medicine. We thank the reviewers from different countries who read and commented on the original book prospectus for their thoughtful ideas, suggestions, and constructive criticism. Listening to their comments broadened our horizons and made us appreciate the diverse viewpoints in the field across disciplines, countries, and intellectual traditions.

A sabbatical visit by Gary Albrecht to Nuffield College, the University of Oxford, and Centre de Recherche Medicine Maladie et Science Sociales (CERMES), Paris, provided the time and environment to conceive the project, discuss it with colleagues, and test ideas. David Cox and Anthony Atkinson were gracious hosts at Nuffield College, and the Fellows provided the intellectual stimulation that helped the book evolve. Claudine Herzlich, Isabelle Baszanger, Martine Bungener, Renée Waissman, Robert Castel, Serge Moscovici, Henri-Jacques Stiker, Jean-François Ravaud, Hans-Georg Brose, Harrison White, Aaron Cicourel, Jean-Luc Lory, and colleagues at the Maison des Sciences de l'Homme, Paris, engaged in lively discussions about social science and health which clarified the issues and content of the book. The administration and staff of the School of Public Health at the University of Illinois at Chicago were efficiently helpful in managing the production of the book. Special thanks go to our editorial assistant, Pamela Ippoliti, whose management skills, attention to detail, and cheerful reminders of deadlines made the idea of the book become a reality. Sharla K. Willis set up the original files, and Isabel Martinez helped to keep the project moving forward. Sandra Burkes provided secretarial and data processing assistance to help launch the project. Maggi Lunde handled many telephone calls, e-mail traffic, and express mail packages in an expeditious fashion which facilitated work on the book around the world. We also thank our technical editor, Phyllis Crittenden, who reviewed all chapter manuscripts for form and technical consistency.

The International Editorial Advisory Board members gave freely of their time to review the book outline, raise questions, suggest authors, and review manuscripts. Their collective wisdom and insights improved the conception of the book and individual chapters. In addition, many other colleagues graciously contributed their thoughts and reviewed individual manuscripts for the book.

Introduction

GARY L. ALBRECHT, RAY FITZPATRICK, AND
SUSAN C. SCRIMSHAW

Health is one of the most vital but taken-for-granted qualities of everyday life. Yet when jeopardized or diminished, an individual's health becomes a salient and central concern. Health and illness are universal elements of human life, which at different stages in the life cycle may go unnoticed, or alternately may appear in the foreground of consciousness. One of the defining aspects of the twentieth century has been that large sections of the world increasingly expect longer lives during which positive health can be largely assumed and anticipated. Almost paradoxically, this same century has appeared to render health problematic; something at risk, something requiring effort, and something precarious.

At the same time that health status has so dramatically improved for many sections of humankind, vastly more human resources have come to be invested in the provision of health care. In industrial and postindustrial societies, health care services have expanded in their scope, use of resources, and sheer visibility. Health care now is one of the largest sectors of most economies in more affluent societies. The very scale and ambitions of the health sector have provoked a counterreaction. Causal connections between improvements in health and increased investment in health services are far from obvious. The financial and social costs associated with highly technological medicine, managed care, and heroic efforts to fight disease in the last years of life do not seem to result necessarily in improved patient satisfaction or quality of life. Increasingly doubts are raised about the value and the effectiveness of the health-care services in which society has invested.

It is therefore no surprise that the social sciences have sought to make sense of health and illness both at the level of individual experience and perception and at the level of the institutionalized system. The social realities of health and illness are obvious areas of focus if we are to understand the distinctive features of modern life. The attention of the social sciences does not arise solely out of autonomous intellectual curiosity and the need to understand central experiences of the society of which they are a part. Governments, professions, consumer groups and other organized interests look to the social sciences for guidance in addressing fundamental questions about the nature and determinants of health and the value of health services. The so-called 'applied' role of the social sciences arises from institutional needs for evidence and advice regarding health policy.

The social sciences on which we have especially drawn in this volume, particularly sociology and anthropology, were impelled into the study of health for diverse reasons. In some cases the goal has been social theoretical analyses of the significance of modern medicine; for example, Parsons' analyses of the sick role and of the role of medical sciences arose out of theoretical concerns to unravel how society functions more generally. Equally important is ameliorative work to address 'real-world' problems such as social inequalities in health and access to health care, failures of health professionals to address patients' primary concerns, and the need to evaluate the impact of health services on populations' well-being. It is as essential that these different motivations and focuses in the social sciences of health, the desire analytically and theoretically to understand as well as the desire to contribute to change, are equally maintained and appreciated.

In planning and producing this volume of original work, we have been made acutely conscious of the huge challenges faced by the social sciences generally, and sociology and anthropology in particular, in their efforts to contribute to understanding the worlds of health and illness. Increasingly expected to provide a unique and pivotal framework of understanding of health, the social sciences often struggle to achieve such ambitions. This volume has provided us with an invaluable opportunity to think about some of the broader reasons for the difficulties that the social sciences sometimes have in achieving an impact upon wider public debates about health and illness.

In the first instance, one has to be struck by the challenges we confront arising from the very pace of change in health, health services, and, of course, the wider societies in which health and illness are experienced. The social sciences can sometimes seem to be struggling to stay abreast of developments and chasing others' formulations of issues rather than setting their own intellectual agenda. The pace of change in health care is hectic. Most obviously, Western biomedical sciences form one of the most dynamic components of modern society. Daily, the public is presented with news of breakthroughs in the causal understanding of the body and its malfunctions, of the building blocks of life, and, in their wake, the development of increasingly sophisticated interventions to tackle problems of health. More often than not, the social scientist is an outsider to this dynamic, an observer, struggling just as much as the journalist, the politician, or the patient to make sense of the complex and continuous process of innovation in biomedical knowledge. The models and explanatory frameworks of the social scientist struggle to stay in the slip-stream of biomedical change. For instance, as is argued in this volume, the human genome project promises fundamentally to transform the forms of health-care interventions provided and the ways in which individuals are identified as able to benefit from interventions.

Patterns of health and illness in populations, and our grasp of those patterns, are also constantly revised. To take a simple instance that is explored further in this volume, we have become used to thinking of the twentieth century as a period of epidemiological transition where the burden of disease due to infection was replaced by the chronic and degenerative diseases. At the very moment that such views became the conventional wisdom, new or newly resurgent infections have arisen to render notions of epidemiological transition simplistic. Our paradigms struggle to stay appropriate to the problems we attempt to address.

As another instance, one might cite the involvement of social scientists in debates about the relative advantages of institutional versus community care for the mentally ill. Some of the most outstanding contributions from the social sciences to the field of health have stemmed from humanitarian critiques of the damaging consequences of institutionalism. Yet even as this social scientific perspective enters the mainstream of thinking, society has begun to recognize the serious limitations of community care for the mentally ill. Compared with the biomedical sciences, we are compelled by the very nature of our subject matter to chase after phenomena the very definition and sense of which are rapidly transformed ahead of us. Society as a whole changes in ways we struggle sociologically to capture. The examples are legion. Rapid changes in the roles of men and women impact on the division of labour in health care. The dynamics of the economy, and of work processes, result in constantly shifting exposures to health hazards and changing groups at resulting risk. New and more sophisticated forms of imagery and representation ever change our understanding of bodies and bodily processes. Constantly changing information technology requires concomitant revision of ways to manage and integrate health services. A constant flurry of policies emerge to 'reform' the organization and deliver health care as a whole, whether in pluralist systems such as in the United States or in more unified systems such as exist in much of Europe. In common to all these illustrations is the sense that the pace of change will increasingly threaten our ability to stay focused on issues long enough to grasp and explain key social processes at work in the field of health.

A second challenge to our ability to contribute to understanding that is immediately sensed by anyone involved in the social sciences and health is the limited resource invested in the social compared with the biomedical sciences. Despite occasional and growing institutional scepticism about the capacity of biomedical sciences alone to deliver all that is promised, the allure to public and private funding sources of supporting the biomedical sciences is enormous. At the practical level, a staggering array of diagnostic, pharmaceutical, and surgical innovations are constantly presented as urgent and deserving cases requiring funding in order to contribute to more effective health care. At a more fundamental level, the biomedical sciences have accelerated in their capacity to shape public expectations of their capacity to translate generous levels of funding into deeper understanding of underlying biological processes that will, in turn and in the longer term, translate into practical interventions. For example, the human genome project will deliver a basic but complete description of the genetic structure of mankind. It can be expected with certainty that calls for a further explosion of basic biomedical research that flow from this achievement will be successful. Despite growing recognition of the need to complement biomedical with social scientific understanding of the nature of health and illness, the social sciences will always struggle to attract the scale of funding of their biomedical colleagues. With funds come glamour, attention, impact, and a voice to shape policy. The social sciences will continue to work with more modest resources and a limited voice.

A third challenge concerns the distinctive and defining nature of the social sciences in the health field and the two seemingly contradictory roles of social science. On the one hand, the social sciences have emerged as a semi-autonomous body of knowledge, thinking, and commentary on the world. Increasingly established as disciplines within universities and other institutions of learning, the social sciences have been able to provide analysis of the wider society to inform their own intellectual development and understanding and the understanding of those who chose to expose themselves to such disciplines. On the other hand, governments, health-care professionals, provider organizations, and consumer groups have steered the social sciences in another direction; to become a part of the problem-solving system that seeks to explain, prevent, cure, or manage disease. These two distinctive roles of the social sciences in the health arena have been expressed succinctly as two types of knowledge or enterprise; the sociology of medicine and sociology in medicine. To considerably simplify, the purpose of the former is to analyse and explain from without, consistent with an autonomous analytic discipline. The latter role is accepting of institutional and other frameworks within which the discipline attempts to contribute in an applied context as part of the direct process of change. To some extent, this distinction is artificial, simplified, and exaggerated, but some correspondence between the two distinct roles and underlying reality is apparent to all who work in this area.

We have considered these tensions between alternative roles for the social sciences as constituting a challenge largely because they seem to be viewed as such within the disciplines of medical sociology and medical anthropology. With some simplification, one can distinguish a tradition of social science whose primary contribution is to provide social, cultural, and political critiques and commentary on the nature of

health and health care from a tradition of applied research more typically attempting to provide useful evidence within the health-care system. It often appears that these traditions, far from forming a unitary corpus of work, tend toward either mutual avoidance and incomprehension or actual intellectual hostility. The first tradition accuses the second of uncritical acceptance of prevailing social definitions of the reality; the second tradition despairs of the failure of the first to engage with real-world problems. Such cleavages tend to become reinforcing. The growing risk is of mutual incomprehension between so called 'theoretical' and 'applied' branches of the social sciences in health.

The fourth challenge became apparent as a result of compiling a multinational set of contributions; it is the difficulty that the social sciences have in working with a common or universal frame of reference compared with other disciplines in the health-care field. It may be considered a naive concept even to postulate such a construct for the social sciences given our basic assumption of the social and cultural diversity of social groups. Nevertheless, it is clearly the case that the local, regional, and national specificity of ways of viewing health and health-care services, whilst a constant reinforcement of the value and rationale for social scientific analyses, also acts as a barrier to the internationalization of the social sciences for health. Moreover, whilst there are distinguished contributions to the comparative analysis of health-care systems represented in this volume, it is also striking how system- and culture-bound much of the evidence and analysis in the field generally tends to be. This is particularly frustrating when many health-care problems have a global scale and dimension and suggest that global analysis will require the development of more encompassing theory and paradigms.

RESPONDING TO THE CHALLENGE

This volume represents a concerted effort by many distinguished and experienced social scientists working together in the field of health to respond to the challenges facing them at the turn of a millennium. Considerable effort was invested by authors and editors in attempting to define and develop a social scientific agenda for health. First and foremost, we went to some lengths to identify the most appropriate authors to write on the subjects identified for the volume. The editorial board was actively involved from the beginning in advising as to the best authors to address each topic. The net was therefore cast wider than for most volumes of this nature to produce the most expert and most innovative of social scientists from around the world as contributors. We aimed for a mix of internationally distinguished scholars and those in mid-career who were making essential contributions to the field. We were fortunate that few potential contributors declined, and we have therefore been able to assemble our most preferred authors to write on their areas of expertise. There also was iteration between editors and the editorial board about topics needing to be covered and potential omissions of important areas. Secondly, we posed a challenge to authors. The invitation was to review a field in terms of its current state of play, but also to look over the horizon to where their field was going. Authors were encouraged to move beyond the immediate in time and place wherever possible to identify the most salient universal themes.

The volume has set out to be interdisciplinary in a particular way. Nowadays, interdisciplinary is a readily claimed feature of any venture in the field of health. In this instance our principal objective was to combine the forces of those disciplines that focus on the social, cultural, and political dimensions of health and health care, especially the disciplines of sociology and anthropology. In identifying themes, topics for chapters, and potential authors, it has been informative and stimulating for both disciplines to consider how exactly core constructs are defined and addressed by an adjacent discipline. Especially with regard to the analysis of health and health care as cultural processes, both disciplines have much to learn from each other. At the heart of this volume, therefore, is an ambitious effort to bring to bear these two basic social science disciplines in focusing on health. However, it will be apparent that many other important disciplines have also contributed in this volume to the analysis of health in cultural, social, and political terms, for example, political science, demography, health policy analysis, and psychology.

Influential in our planning and execution of the volume has been that the three editors pursue social science in the context of public health. In both Europe and North America, public health, the unique focus on health and health care at the level of populations, may be considered to be undergoing revival, and possibly renaissance. As it is increasingly recognized that society must make the most appropriate use of finite resources to achieve and promote health, the core disciplines of public health, such as clinical medicine, epidemiology, biostatistics, health economics, anthropology, and sociology become essential tools for identifying

and assessing health needs and evaluating alternative strategies for meeting these needs.

The volume has three overarching themes that govern its shape and the selection of topics and authors: social and cultural frameworks of analysis, the experience of health and illness, and health-care systems and practices. These themes point to the major distinctive contributions that we expect will continue to be the key foci of future development of sociology and anthropology in the context of health and illness.

By focusing the first section on social and cultural frameworks of analysis, we underline the convergence of these two pivotal emphases of sociology and anthropology, the social and the cultural. Concepts of health and illness are defining elements of how individuals view themselves and their bodies. These concepts are shaped by, and in turn shape, the particular society and culture in which they arise. Essential to social scientific analyses of concepts of health and illness is what is often termed the 'social constructivist' view that concepts of biology and disease are not neutral products of the clinic or the laboratory, but also emergent from social processes. The appearance of modern medical science, not just at the organizational level but at the level of scientific ideas, cannot be understood without reference to broader social, cultural, and economic processes. This constructivist perspective can be seen in several of the chapters in the first section to derive much of its original inspiration from the philosophical ideas of Foucault. More recently, this tradition has developed an influential impetus, independent of its philosophical origins, within the social sciences and serves constantly to remind us to examine the presuppositions and social consequences of even the most apparently neutral and esoteric of scientific ideas in modern medicine.

Sociology and anthropology also continue to contribute to evidence and thinking of the ways in which ill health is patterned by social factors and social processes. The social sciences now play a lead role in providing innovative research on the many ways in which socioeconomic status, region and location, gender, age, and other social structural properties determine risks of ill health. In particular, the emergence of sociology and anthropology as distinct disciplines within the health field has resulted in increased sophistication in research that goes beyond the documentation of associations between demographic and social variables to address questions of the intervening social processes mediating such associations. The unequal enjoyment of health within and between nations represents one of the most urgent of challenges to the disciplines of public health. Most recently, the social sciences have recognized that biological evidence of the role of the gene in contributing to risks of ill health does not preclude powerful analyses of the social shaping of genetic influences.

The first section therefore points to the dual and complementary role of the social sciences in relation to health, on the one hand, detailing the social processes whereby social position and social processes shape individuals' risks of ill health, and on the other hand, underlying the social and cultural factors that shape the perceptions of health and illness held by individuals, groups, and societies as a whole.

The second organizing theme of the volume is the experience of health and illness. From their origins, sociology and anthropology have played a pivotal role in theoretical and empirical work underlining the centrality of the individual's views, perceptions, and responses to the experience of health problems. This emphasis defines a territory that cannot be addressed by the biomedical sciences. Since the classical definition of illness behaviour by David Mechanic, research has delineated the mediating influence of individuals' perceptions in determining responses to symptoms, impairments, and disability. A wide and rich array of phenomenological, interpretative, and ethnographic methods unite sociology and anthropology in centering on the emergent meanings of health and illness. How individuals define and experience their health problems has immediate consequences for what forms of help are sought; how the individual, the family, and social networks cope with ill health; and how much benefit is obtained from interventions received. The health-care system is increasingly compelled to take account of patients' and caregivers' personal experiences and perceptions if it is to provide effective care. One of the most significant achievements of the social sciences has been to provide both qualitative evidence of this aphorism and also a quantitative framework of health status and quality-of-life measures that allow personal consequences of ill health to be more fully taken account of in the evaluation of health needs and health-care evaluation.

However, this interpretative focus has to be complemented with recognition of the constraining circumstances of the individual: limitations of income, place, and resource as well as of biology. Cultural frameworks of explanation, and prevailing informal and formal definitions of health and illness, are also both resource and constraint and may be independently analysed as channelling perception and behaviour.

The third strategic focus of the volume is upon health-care systems and practices. The level of analysis here shifts to the organizational and institutional arrangements for health care. Historically, the medical profession has been viewed as the crucial shaping force of health-care systems. Professionalization established their preeminent role. However, transformations in work processes in the health-care system and the increasing emphasis upon market competition, business ethos, or governmental supervision and accountability may jeopardize this dominance. Meanwhile, the practice of medicine continues to be influenced by the need to deal with new and old uncertainties; the very growth in the evidence base of medical knowledge often seems paradoxically to enhance the sense of medicine's epistemological insecurity. The social sciences continue to give particular attention to the scope for alternative health-care practices, if not to overcome the dominance of biomedicine, at least to find increasing numbers of roles in health care neglected or mishandled by biomedicine.

New forces have become more visible in the health-care system. This volume focuses on the growing centrality of the individual patient as the recognition of the need for the patient's active participation in decisions grows. The community and lay groups are also increasingly given voice to influence the direction of health-care policies at the local and national level. Whilst enhancing patients' and communities' voices, health-care systems also must address issues of equity and access, ethical desiderata that are undermined in all health-care systems by the capacity of the articulate and resourceful to obtain greater access. Mechanisms meanwhile emerge, varying from country to country, intended to enable the health-care system to manage the imbalance between supply and demand, aspirations and realities. The volume ends by sketching out the potential for radical reconfiguring of health policy. It is fitting that this reconfiguring is couched in terms of evidence from the public health and population health perspectives that we hope make this volume distinctive.

Sociology and anthropology are core conceptual and research-based disciplines in multidisciplinary public health. The constant imperative to extend populations' health requires the challenging contributions of the social sciences. It is to these disciplines that we must turn to question dominant definitions of health and illness, to evaluate alternative options for achieving health, and to assess the appropriateness of health-care systems for individuals and groups. Our hope is that the contributions in this volume inspire as well as inform readers about past achievements and possible future directions for the sociology and anthropology of health and illness.

Part One
SOCIAL AND CULTURAL FRAMEWORKS OF ANALYSIS

1.1

The History of the Changing Concepts of Health and Illness: Outline of a General Model of Illness Categories

BRYAN S. TURNER

INTRODUCTION: A TYPOLOGY OF HEALTH
CONCEPTS

Concepts of health and illness stand at the core of the social values of human society because they give expression to many of our fundamental assumptions about the meaning of life and death. A description of health, therefore, tends necessarily to offer a description of 'the good life' as a moral state of affairs. Although we attempt in the social sciences to avoid the confusion between the notions of 'norm' as a prescriptive standard and 'normal' as a description of an average state of affairs, in the everyday world these separate notions tend to merge because the description of an average provides a convenient measure of morality. In addition, the conception of illness as *dis-ease* is drived from the old French word *aise* meaning 'comfort,' and it indicates the fact that an illness involves discomfort or lack of ease; it is comfort as to strengthen or to fortify. The discomfort of disease is the loss of power we experience in situations that are otherwise comfortable or homely. Discomfort and disease both express our subjective sense of alienation, which follows the disempowerment of illness, while 'normal' provides a lay benchmark for things that are both healthy and moral (King 1982: 119).

Medical terms are frequently employed as metaphors to describe society, as in a 'sick society,' or to categorize deviancy in individuals, as in a 'sick mind.' Corporations or national economies that are financially sound are often referred to as being 'healthy.' It is hardly surprising, therefore, that concepts of health tend to be highly contested because they involve struggles over the moral significance of life. Conceptions of health tend to merge into or be based on fundamental religious and moral views about existence, and differences in orientations towards health tend to reflect or to express basic structural and cultural differences in power relations in society. The result is that there is little consensus about what constitutes 'health' and 'illness,' which are and remain 'essentially contested concepts.'

Given these basic conflicts in beliefs about health and illness, it is not possible to give an authoritative account of *the* history of these concepts. It would be more appropriate to talk in the plural about the *histories* of the many conceptualizations of human well-being and suffering. In order to simplify the problems, I shall start with a general model of the historical development of concepts of health and illness. My argument is that beliefs about health and illness in traditional or premodern societies were inextricably caught up with notions of religious purity and danger. As Mary Douglas (1966) has demonstrated, primitive notions of pollution and taboo were not about hygiene because there was simply no knowledge about such principles; concepts about scientific hygiene simply did not exist. The dietary prescriptions of the Old Testament are recommendations about religious not hygienic behaviour. In other words, medical concepts were directed at the health of the soul rather than the body.

A taboo, which for example divides the world into acceptable/not acceptable in terms of the couplet edible/not edible, is a conceptual mechanism for giving the world structure and meaning. People got sick, not because of a breach of hygienic regulations, but because they had transgressed a social norm or taboo that separated the sacred from the profane. Sickness and health were often associated with taboos about bodily fluids where contact, for example with menstrual blood, could cause illness in an individual or disaster for a tribe. For instance, Polar Eskimos explained personal misfortune, illness, and failure to catch food in terms of transgressions of taboos (typically surrounding ritualistic organization of menstruation). These misfortunes and sicknesses were treated through shamanistic practices such as seances, where a 'confession' took place to purify the individual and the group (Hepworth and Turner 1982: 71).

In such a system of meaning, sickness was associated with evil forces that attacked human beings through, for instance, the agency of witchcraft and demonic possession. Concepts of illness functioned within a cosmology of good and evil forces, and they were explanatory devices that described, and possibly justified, evil and misery. Notions of illness have typically been set within a general theodicy, namely a system of beliefs that attempts to explain and justify the presence of human disease and suffering. When people fall victim to disease and sickness, there is almost inevitably the question: Why me? Concepts of health and disease have typically provided an answer to that type of question. The dominant assumptions of disease were located within a discourse of sacred phenomena.

With the process of modernization, health and illness were transferred to more secular paradigms and eventually became embraced by various scientific discourses. In Western medicine, disease entities became increasingly differentiated and disease states more specified as the human body is itself differentiated into its component parts. Microbiology offered an account of minute viruses that invade the body and overtly have no connection with the moral or religious status of the individual. As scientific concepts of disease replaced traditional notions of the quasireligious state of illness, the status of the medical professional increased, and the status and role of traditional healers (medicine men, wise women, and midwives) decreased (Flint 1989). There was, in addition, a differentiation between physical and mental health which in turn relied on a basic division between mind and body. This mind/body dualism was associated with the empiricist revolution in philosophy, namely rationalist Cartesianism. The notions of 'mental illness' were subsequently elaborated by separate developments in clinical psychology, psychiatry, and psychoanalysis (Foucault 1971). Finally, the social sciences of health and illness were themselves part of the growing complexity of the contemporary model of sickness, where medical sociology, for instance, distinguishes among various levels, such as the illness experience in the individual, cultural categories of sickness at the social level, and finally health-care systems at the societal level (Turner 1995: 5).

The historical development of health and illness concepts is characterized by increasing secularization, the rise of scientific theories of health, the separation of mental and physical illness, the erosion of traditional therapies by scientific practices (a process that also involved the colonization of indigenous belief systems), and the differentiation of categories into specific micronotions. The domain assumptions of health and illness phenomena became predominantly secular, but medical notions continued to evoke and be connected with paradigms of moral behaviour. For example, there is still a strong professional and lay tendency to blame people for their illness, and thus attribute moral responsibility for health status. Western societies have often 'psychologized' cancer by believing that at least some specific cancers result from the fact that people cannot or will not express themselves emotionally; they are blamed for their cancer because they do not manage their emotions effectively (Sontag 1978).

This model provides a useful framework for the historical exploration of disease concepts. However, we should also note that there was, even in premodern medical systems, considerable complexity and dispute. For example, in his study of the history of anatomy, Andrew Cunningham (1997) notes that there were radical differences between Plato, Aristotle, Erasistratus, and Galen as to the nature of the human body, its functions and structure, and the purpose of medicine. There is also no neat point in history where secular views came to dominate. While the anatomical works of Versalius were believed to have paved the way towards scientific medicine, Versalius clearly retained a religious view that the ultimate role of medicine is to reveal the hand of God in Nature. These medical sciences remained an important part of Natural Philosophy, namely that branch of knowledge that exhibited the laws of God. As such, scientific medicine frequently carried a covert moral and religious message. The authority of doctors trained in secular and scientific medicine has not been passively accepted by the lay public, and alternative medical systems have always thrived alongside Western allopathic medicine. In the twentieth century, there has been a great revival of alternative systems of medicine and widespread criticism of the claims of allopathic medicine. There are considerable philosophical and ethical problems with the notion of 'scientific medicine,' which cannot be regarded as a single, unified, and complete account of disease. In short, we cannot accept a 'whig theory' of medical history as the heroic march of reason that resulted in the final triumph of rational science over magical or irrational systems of medicine. We can argue, however, that the overarching religious framework of medicine and disease concepts has gone, just as Natural Philosophy has disappeared from the curriculum of the modern university.

As a heuristic device to provide this chapter with a simple conceptual structure, I argue (see Figure 1) that health concepts can be analyzed along two dimensions, namely the sacred/profane domain and the collective/individual orientation to health and illness. First, the causes and treatment of disease can be set within a sacred framework in which the ultimate explanations of illness are sought in nonnatural causes (such as divine punishment), and being sick is seen in moral terms, where human beings are held to be responsible for their illness. Alternatively, human illness is explained in natural terms by reference to causal agents such as germs or viruses, and individual humans are not held morally responsible for viral infection. Second, disease can be seen in individual terms, or the causes of human suffering and disease are explained in collective terms by reference to poor environmental conditions, low educational provision, poverty, and so forth. By combining these two dimensions, we can produce a four-cell property-space to illustrate this approach.

The growth of collectivist and secular assumptions about health and illness was characteristic of the public health movements of the nineteenth century, when radicals like Friederich Engels, Edwin Chadwick, and Rudolf Virchow identified the causes of human disease in the deprivations and alienation of working-class slums in a rapidly expanding urban environment. Disease was a collective and secular condition of social existence in emergent capitalism, where morbidity and mortality rates were directly related to the quality of the food supply and income per capita. In the twentieth century, similar concepts of health and illness have been embraced by Marxist medical sociologists such as Howard Waitzkin (1983) and Vincente Navarro (1976), and by radical historians of medicine such as Henry E. Sigerist and his students (Fee and Brown 1997). While social reformers have treated disease as an effect of social deprivation, eugenics policies under national socialism in Germany and similar medical strategies in Stalinist Russia attempted to control the health of society by collective, secular approaches to reproduction to remove biological 'defects' from society (Weindling 1989). These approaches to disease are very different from the individualist/secular concepts that form the basis of the allopathic medical approaches of empiricist Cartesian medicine. Illness and disease in this paradigm are seen as consequences of malfunctions in the human organism that are produced by infections. Treatment is based on allopathic strategies that attempt to control these infections through medical interventions (drugs, rest cure, surgery, and so forth). Health is improved by personal hygiene, isolation from germs and viruses, and the presence of a highly trained cohort of professional doctors with the support system of universities, medical faculties, and general hospitals. Within this individualistic and specialized context, private health insurance is a crucial responsibility of the patient if he wants an effective response to his acute condition. By contrast, socialized medical health is thought to encourage a lack of responsibility on the part of the individual and to increase the burden of the 'undeserving poor' on the taxpayer and the state. Socialized medicine in the American context was regarded as a political threat to the fundamental values of individualism (Porter 1997). In terms of social Darwinism, the survival of the fittest was the only safe guide to public policy.

Medical paradigms, which operate on the basis of a religious belief system and from an individualistic perspective, would include the ascetic practices of monastic religious orders, where diet and abstinence were thought to be simultaneously beneficial to soul and body. Illness was linked to the fundamentally evil nature of fallen man in creation, but human beings were exhorted to strive against evil through a 'government of the body' (Turner 1992). Such medico-religious paradigms can also assume more collectivist forms. Taboos attempt to regulate human behaviour in the interests of society

Sacred	Profane	
Saintly Sickness	Allopathic Medicine	Individual
Sickness Taboos	Social Medicine	Collective

Figure 1 *Typology of domain assumptions*

as a whole, because individuals who disregard ritualistic prohibitions bring misfortune and disease upon the whole tribe. Shamanistic medical rituals are illustrations of this sacred and collectivist orientation.

This chapter proposes that in Western societies there has been a long historical trend, starting with the scientific revolution in the late sixteenth and early seventeenth centuries, away from collectivist/sacred conceptions towards individualistic/profane perspectives, which simultaneously charts the rise of scientific professional medicine. However, this dominant paradigm is constantly challenged by both collectivist/secular social medicine and by alternative medical paradigms that draw upon various religious legacies. At the level of both the individual and society, various paradigms can exist simultaneously. For example, it is not uncommon to find that a person dying of cancer may seek out both chemotherapy and exorcism in a desperate attempt to find a cure.

PRIMITIVE MEDICAL SYSTEMS

In primitive societies, disease is symbolic of the relationships between the sacred and the profane world. Diagnosis and healing are both undertaken within a sacred context. According to Emile Durkheim in *The Elementary Forms of the Religious Life* (1954), the belief systems of primitive society were based on a profound dichotomy between the everyday world of practical utilitarian activities and the sacred world, which is organized around religious phenomena that are set apart and forbidden. Human illness and disease provide a bridge between these two worlds because sacred values are revealed to humans via the extraordinary states of consciousness, which are associated with disease. Hence, according to Henry E. Sigerist (1951: 127)

'the primitive does not distinguish between medicine, magic and religion. To him they are one, a set of practices intended to protect him against evil forces. Spirits inhabit the objects of his environment. The ghosts of the dead are hovering over the village. The transcendental world is real to him, and he partakes in it when he dreams and his soul leaves the body temporarily and has intercourse with the spirits.'

While Sigerist's summary of the anthropological perspective is still valuable, there are real limitations to this account. First, as Sigerist himself acknowledged, even in so-called primitive society there was, alongside the religious belief system, a realm of practical medical practices based on experience and experiment. For example, in Egyptian medicine, while there was a strong dimension of religious cosmology, there was also an 'empirical–rational medicine,' which had been revealed by research in 1922 by James H. Breasted of the so-called 'Papyrus Edwin Smith.' These documents show, among other things, that Egyptian court physicians relied on elementary diagnostic and prescriptive practices that were grounded in observations, case studies, and pragmatic responses to illness through the use of herbs, diets, rest, and other mundane approaches. It suggests that, while religious belief systems were important, physicians did not confuse religious meaning with mundane medical interventions.

Similar conclusions can be drawn from the extensive anthropological debate about magic, religion, and science. For example, Bronislaw Malinowski (1948) argued on the basis of his fieldwork that Trobriand Islanders systematically distinguish between magic, which attempts to regulate the environment through ritual, and religion, which is an expression of belief. When Trobriand fishermen were involved in outer lagoon fishing – which was considered dangerous – they regularly resorted to magic. In primitive societies, magic functions to give some structure and predictability to uncertain and dangerous contexts. Religion, by contrast, is the cultural vehicle for general social values. Similar conclusions might be drawn from the work of E. Evans-Pritchard (1937), whose fieldwork showed that in primitive cultures human beings believe they are surrounded by threats. These dangers are often the products of social conflicts and tensions, wherein accusations of witchcraft, for example, indicate interpersonal conflicts. Divination, which is important in explaining illness, has the important social function of allocating blame and responsibility. Thus, 'disease categories' function in a context of social uncertainty as explanations of misfortunate.

GREEK MEDICINE

In Western philosophy, we often look back to Greek civilization as the cradle not only of democratic institutions, but also of natural science and rational inquiry. Certainly, Greek traditions have come to play a major role in shaping medical ethics and practice. The notion of the Hippocratic Oath itself has been fundamental to the evolution of professionalism in medical etiquette and practice. While the Greek tradition contained a mixture of rational scientific and religious perspectives and practices, generally speaking, Greek medicine represents a secular orientation to health and illness because health was seen as a consequence of natural causes. The humoral theory of disease, which survived into the modern period, was derived from the secular traditions of Hippocrates, Empedocles, and Galen. The world was conceived in terms of four basic elements (fire, water, air, and earth), four qualities (hot, cold, dry, and damp), four humours (blood, phlegm, yellow bile, and black bile), and four personality types (sanguine, phlegmatic, choleric, and melancholic). In this humoral theory, the body could be imagined as a hydraulic system in which illness represented a lack of balance (Turner 1996). For instance, melancholia was a consequence of an excess of black bile. Greek therapeutics consisted of bloodletting, diet, exercise, and bed rest, which were designed to restore the equilibrium of the system. In the Greek system, the reproductive processes that involved a sexual act were compared to a convulsion or fermentation; sex involved heating up the organism (Foucault 1986). These notions of balance also reflected the basic premise of Aristotle's ethics in which 'the good life' was one that avoided the excesses of both hedonism and asceticism. In these medical regimes, diet played an especially important role. The word 'diaita' indicated a way of life, a regimentation or regime, or a government. Medical prescriptions for good living covered a variety of activities, including leisure, nutrition, lifestyle, and sexuality. These regimes were based on secular assumptions about medicine and the role of the physicians, who attempted to distinguish themselves from popular medicine, which included leech craft and magic. For example, the Hippocratic treatise on *The Sacred Disease* argued that epilepsy was not brought about by sacred causes, but could be understood within the naturalistic framework of the four humours.

Greek medical tradition also revealed the tension between an individualistic and a collectivist approach. In his *Mirage of Health*, René Dubos (1959) recalls the struggle between Hygeia and Asclepius. The former was associated with the virtues of a rational life in a pleasant and healthy environment. In Rome she was known as Salus, or general well-being, from which we derive notions such as 'salubrious' and 'salutary.' Asclepius, the first physician, by contrast did not teach wisdom as a response to illness, but found therapies in the study of plants and herbs. As the mythology of these figures evolved, Asclepius eventually appears as a self-confident young god in the company of two maidens – Hygeia from whom we derive the notion of hygiene, and Panakeia from whom we derive the concept of panacea. From these gods, a division in medicine developed that I define in terms of a collectivist (hygienic) approach and an individualistic (Asclepian) perspective. Hygeia points towards a communal and preventive approach that identifies a rational lifestyle in a salubrious environment, whereas Asclepius promotes an interventionist medicine that restores health by directly treating the ailments of an individual.

MEDICINE AND THE WORLD RELIGIONS

While the Greek legacy of Galen (129–99 AD), Hippocrates, and Aristotle shaped medieval practice and laid the foundations for contemporary secular medicine, this Greek legacy often came to the West via the medium of Judeo-Christian beliefs. Islamic medicine was also an important conduit for this tradition, and Islamic science contributed significantly to optics and chemistry. In the Abrahamic faiths, there was often a tension between their Greek legacy and the prophetic monotheism of the Old Testament. Thus, early Christianity was a hellenizing force whose language was Greek, but whose basic notions of man and God were Hebraic (O'Leary 1949). These tensions were also present in Christian responses to health and illness.

This Judeo-Christian legacy was deeply ambiguous with respect to the importance and role of secular medicine. Pauline theology was based on an assumption about the punishment of the flesh. These attitudes were particularly prominent in the early Church's attitudes towards women and sexuality, where marriage was at best regarded as a necessary evil against the corrupting presence of sexual desire. We must also keep in mind that the early Church expected and hoped for the end of the world in a teleological system that predicted the Second Coming of Christ as an end to human suffering and sinfulness. Given the anticipation of the end of human history, there was no strong motivation to invest in human health and happiness, which were merely illusory chimera. As the anticipation of the Second Coming largely disappeared in the official position of the Roman Church, there emerged a clear division between lay people who lived in the world (and experienced its sinfulness) and those (monks and priests) who devoted their lives to God and His works. Hence, lay people married to reproduce, while religious people 'married' Jesus in order to obtain grace. This division of labour created a system of exchange whereby the charisma of grace, which was stored up in the Church and handed on to the religious, was transferred to the (sinful) laity through such means as baptism, communion, and confession.

There developed, therefore, a metaphorical parallel between health and grace, in which the healing grace of the body of Christ, for example, was transferred to the people through the Eucharistic feast. This metaphorical exchange of gifts 'traded' on an etymological similarity between salvation and *salus* (salutation and health). Christianity came to adopt a model in which the religious were responsible for both the health of the body and the salvation of the soul of its Flock.

The ascetic doctrines of Christianity treated the body as a means of human education through suffering. Disease and discomfort are inevitable in this world because the body, as the vessel of the soul, is corrupted by the Fall from Grace in the story of Adam's disobedience. However, through this suffering human beings can come, through humility and pain, to a better understanding of God and themselves. The lives of the saints revealed this ambiguity towards the sinfulness of human embodiment (Turner 1997a). Disease is a corruption that indicates the sinfulness of human kind, but also creates the occasions of insight and knowledge. However, since God is the author of nature, He must also 'send' disease into the world. Disease had a characteristically ambiguous status. It could simultaneously indicate charismatic status through divine election and indicate the sinfulness of the victim. These contradictions are summarized in Christian theology under the notion of theodicy, which is any attempt to explain and justify God as a merciful and all-powerful being, who both loves and punishes human beings.

This ambiguity was characteristic of the Church's response to plague and plague control. While the spread of plague was a sign of human sinfulness, religious institutions had an obligation to care for the sick and the poor. Christian houses for plague victims and leprosaria expressed this religious obligation through acts of charity. Medieval religious houses provided an institutional model of care from which evolved a secular means of poor relief and medical support. The word 'hospital' derives from the Latin adjective 'hospitalis,' relating to 'hospites' (guests). Early religious houses were 'hospices' (spitals) for pilgrims, and eventually evolved into hospitals in the modern sense. Between 1066 and 1550, 700 spitals were created in Britain, and spitals for leprosy emerged around 1078 as so-called 'lazar houses.' Leprosy declined after 1315 partly because of the Black Death (1346–50), which produced a profound crisis of theodicy in the West.

Christian asceticism and the institutions of charity were both responses to this profound theological condemnation of the human body as flesh and as the conduit of evil into the soul (Turner 1991). Because the Fall of Man was often blamed on the weakness of Eve, Christian theology was basically patriarchal, and its negative view of women was reinforced by the legacy of Greek philosophy and medicine. For example, Aristotle had noted that women may occasionally achieve orgasm, but their fluids were not seminal. The womb was simply a vehicle within which male sperm produced another human being. For Aristotle, there was a parallel between female blood in menstruation and male sperm in orgasm, but a woman was essentially a sterile man and her organs were merely a pale and inverted form of male organs. Greek medical manuals, which the Fathers of the Church inherited, were written to assist male fertilization and, by implication, control women's bodies. Christian patriarchy can be regarded as a continuation of the attitude of classical authors to women and reproduction in which Christianity contributed a more potent and far reaching doctrine of sinfulness (Rousselle 1988). The mortification of the flesh by the female religious became a form of 'holy anorexia' by which the saints could paradoxically accept the patriarchal authority of the Church and assert their own spirituality (Bell 1985).

As the Roman Church became established as part of the dominant political institutions of the medieval period, sin became both regulated and commercialized by the practice of confession and indulgences. Both sinfulness and illness were treated within this network of monetary exchanges, whereby sinful lay people bought a salvation in the next world and health in this world. It was this commercialization of the sacred that was challenged by Luther and Calvin. The Reformation retained a conception of the total depravity of man and took away the conventional means of grace (baptism, eucharist, and confession) by which that sinfulness had been managed. The consequences of this emphasis on the individual, the authority of the written word, and the criticism of conventional religion produced both uncertainty and individualism, which contributed to the rise of the seventeenth-century scientific revolution and the erosion of medieval visions of disease and depravity.

EMPIRICAL RATIONALISM AND THE GROWTH OF EXPERIMENTAL MEDICINE

In sociology, we are familiar with the argument (Weber 1930) that the ascetic and individualistic ethic of the Calvinistic sects had an 'elective affinity' with the emergent culture of competitive capitalism. Alongside the growth of rational capitalism in the seventeenth century, there was an elective affinity among the philosophy of Rene Descartes (1596–1650), Isaac Newton (1643–1727), and the growth of empirical and rational medicine. The growth of experimental medicine was founded on the rationalism of Descartes and Newton through the work of the physician Herman Boerhaave (1668–1738). Just as early capitalism assumed an individualistic and ascetic orientation, so the medical revolution of the seventeenth century assumed an individualistic, rational, and experimental ethos. There was an important convergence in values and practice between the religious Reformation and the scientific Renaissance.

Descartes created the basis of modern experimental rationalism by attempting, through a thought experiment, to exclude religious and irrational dimensions from philosophy. His rationalism attempted to find a point of certainty that was beyond further doubt. His solution was the famous individualist slogan, 'I think, therefore I am.' The force of this claim is to give a primacy to cognitive rationalism over emotions and feelings, but it also gives a focus to individual truths. Furthermore, it sets the foundation for the separation of mind and body, which has been characteristic of Western thought from the seventeenth century. Descartes was not entirely successful in establishing his own brand of rationalist philosophy in the universities, being replaced by an empirical philosophy that was probabilist, mechanical, and Newtonian. By the end of the seventeenth century, rationalist medicine was neo-Newtonian. However, Cartesian rationalism as a system remained a profoundly influential doctrine. Cartesian secularism became a potent aspect of medical belief. It required a simple and complete separation between mind and body. Indeed in Cartesianism, body is merely extension. However, Cartesian materialism was highly compatible with a mechanistic and materialist vision of reality.

Cartesian rationalism was combined with Newtonian physics in the quest for a mathematical system to express the laws that governed the processes of the human body. Physicians sought to create a medical system that would have the same elegance and simplicity as the Newtonian laws of gravity. In the seventeenth century, physicians such as Archibald Pitcairne (1652–1713) were part of a scientific network stretching from Edinburgh through Oxford to Leiden. This scientific network wanted to provide medical theory with mathematical precision (Guerrini 1989). This theory was referred to as 'principiia medicinae theoreticae mathematicae'; its influence was considerable. Newtonian ideas became influential in the work of George Cheyne (1671–

1743), whose publications on diet had considerable influence on the eighteenth-century London elite (Turner 1992). Cheyne offered medical advice to the London coffeehouse set who, like Cheyne, were victims of obesity. The principal causes of melancholy were connected with excessive consumption of food, drink, and tobacco.

The iatromathematicians of the period reduced God to a clockmaker who was in a general way responsible for the functioning of the Newtonian universe, but who did not intervene through revelation into the lives of human beings. There was little space here for a compassionate saviour on the cross. William Harvey (1578–1657) had discovered the principles of the circulation of the blood, validating the doctrine of circulation on Aristotelian and teleological grounds. His *De Circulatione* of 1649 gave further authority to this view of the human body as a mechanical pump whose flows and tides could be measured mathematically by exact calculation. The machine might need a soul to start the motor, but there was little room for a reflexive mind in this mechanical universe. We should not exaggerate the secular dimension of medical practice in the seventeenth century. Medical interventions were still typically set within a broader moral and religious framework. In prescribing a dietary regime in order to control the machine, Cheyne was following a long line of Christian physicians who sought to regulate the soul through a diet of the body. His views on a disciplined life to control the nerves appealed to the leader of Methodism John Wesley who, in his *Primitive Physick* of 1752, provided a methodistical version of the medical regime. In addition, the moral significance of the seventeenth-century anatomy lesson should not be underestimated. Comparative anatomy had always raised questions of conscience because it was either thought to spy on God's secret principles of the universe, or it was thought to be a vain and pointless quest for ultimate causes. From a Christian point of view, if the body is merely flesh, can the anatomical inquiry reveal anything of God's purpose? Anatomy had, as a result, remained a conservative area of medical science, where it continued to be dominated by, for example, Galen's text *On the Conduct of Anatomy*. Anatomy had begun to change radically with the work of Andreas Vesalius (1514–64) who, through experimentation on human beings, broke away from the scholastic conformity to the Galenic tradition.

In the seventeenth century the anatomy lesson continued to function as a moral lesson. In the work of anatomists such as Andreas Laurentius (1558–1609), the anatomy section encouraged the observer to 'know thyself' and to embrace the feeling that 'there, but for the grace of God, go I.' These sentiments are well illustrated in the famous painting by Rembrandt in 'The Anatomy Lesson of Dr Tulp' of 1632, which shows Dr Nicolaas Tulp in the Waaggebouw over the sectioned body of the criminal Aris Kint. The light and shadow employ the realism of Caravaggio, but the picture has many iconic features pointing to Christian truths about the frailty and finitude of man. For example, behind the figure of Tulp there is in the wall a Christian symbol of the shell. The anatomy lesson continued to be part of a moral discourse about sinfulness and judgement within the new framework of scientific experiment, which stood at the core of the seventeenth-century scientific revolution.

MENTAL HEALTH AND THE PANOPTIC GAZE

In this chapter I am primarily concerned with concepts of physical health, but it is important to touch briefly on the issue of mental health. Contemporary sociological analysis of medical systems has been profoundly influenced by the work of Michel Foucault (1926–84), who contributed to the study of madness, French post-revolutionary medicine, the medical responses to sexual deviance, and the history of Christian attitudes to health and illness. Foucault's work on systems of knowledge follows the tradition of Gaston Bachelard and George Canguilhem who, among other things, demonstrated that scientific revolutions often take the form of a violent break with the past (an 'epistemological rupture'), and that science is best understood in its practice rather than in its claims, which were typically inconsistent with, or not supported by, its practical applications. Both propositions tend to be critical of whiggish views of history as an evolutionary progress.

Foucault (1971) identified a break in the middle of the seventeenth century when large numbers of people were confined in detention in such places as the General Hospital in Paris. Because the definition of madness was broad and vague, detention functioned as a way of imposing government or regulations on the poor, needy, and incompetent. 'Madness' is a regulatory discourse for the management of large populations. A second break occurred in the eighteenth century when 'madness,' as an indefinite concept, began to give way to modern notions of 'mental illness.' Whereas madness as in the notion of 'folie' or foolishness in Shakespeare's *King Lear* was historically associated with divine insight and creativity, mental illness became a technical discourse that overtly attempts to distance itself from more traditional notions of possession, violence, and creativity. In 'folie,' reason and madness could communicate, but the modern notion of insanity has domesticated and neutralized the old forces of jest and foolishness. This new conception of mental illness required a new setting, and Foucault traced the evolution of psychiatry alongside the institutional growth of the modern asylum, which applied the principles of panoptic surveillance in Benthamite utilitarianism to the management of the mentally sick (Foucault 1977).

The point of Foucault's history of the categories of mental health was in fact to criticize the dominant ideology of psychiatry, which analyzed the history of its own profession as the triumph of reason over witchcraft. Foucault noted that, like medieval responses to witchcraft, psychiatry involved various forms of 'governmentality' to regulate individuals whose behaviour was in various ways 'deviant.' Foucault's approach directed attention to the function of concepts of disease and illness as components of a larger system of social regulation. Although his approach was very different in its assumptions and methods, there is some similarity between Foucault and, for example, Thomas Szasz (1961, 1970), who questioned the role of psychiatry in eroding individual and human rights. For Szasz, the differences between the liberal West and the communist East had been exaggerated because in both societies medical practices such as electroconvulsive therapy could be used to control political dissidents. The importance of writers like Foucault and Szasz in the social sciences of medicine raises fundamental questions about the alleged neutrality and reliability of scientific method and concepts in the management of human affairs because the medicalization of deviance often removed the right of an individual to rational debate. The attempt to treat homosexuality as a mental disease is a classic illustration.

THE NINETEENTH CENTURY: THE STRUGGLE WITH INFECTION

Although the nineteenth century is seen in official histories of medicine as the great triumph of the scientific revolution, it also disguised a profound struggle between individualistic allopathic medicine and social medicine. At the core of this debate was on the one hand, the great success in scientific responses to infection through such techniques as vaccination, and on the other, the great social needs of the urban population and the growth in social science responses through the development of town planning. It is the classic illustration in the historical conflict between human suffering and illness as the effects of environmental pollution and social degradation versus an individualistic medical response to the disease entities. These differences are particularly important in the historical analysis of such epidemics as tuberculosis (Szreter 1988). Were the major improvements in health a consequence of medical intervention to control disease through vaccination, or were the improvements in health a function of rising standards of living? The nineteenth century produced monumental social investigations on the conditions of the poor, which continue to influence social responses to health and illness.

Throughout Europe, there were major social attempts to control illness through the political manipulation of urban conditions to improve hygiene. For example, in The Netherlands the Hygienists were a group of medical practitioners who, between 1840 and 1890, embraced the view that the health of the nation was determined by public health (Houwaart 1991). The Hygienists rejected attempts to centralize public health at the level of the state and supported some devolution of health care. The movement illustrates the fact that medical and political reform tend to go together because the Hygienists were very much a product of the 1848 liberal revolutions, which were characteristic of Germany and France. In their medical views, they rejected the contagionistic assumptions and traditional methods of describing diseases by their external aspects, which characterized early nineteenth-century epidemiology. These concepts were focused on ontology. For the Hygienists, diseases were not entities that flourish and die following environmental changes, but were caused by anatomical and physiological relations in the body. By their standardization of disease classification, they were able to collect more effective statistical evidence on morbidity and mortality. After 1850, they came to accept the *Bodentheorie* (ground or soil theory) of Max von Pettenkofer (1818–1901), the professor of hygiene, who claimed that epidemics were caused by soil pollution. His reputation was based on his analysis of the south German cholera epidemic of 1854. The cholera germ was a product of the soil, not the human intestine, and von Pettenkofer offered a technical solution, namely a reconstruction of urban water systems in order to regulate water levels. The *Bodentheorie* was well suited to the political culture of postrevolutionary Europe because it implied a technical, rather than a political, response to epidemics.

This illustration of public health in the nineteenth-century Netherlands has to be located within the broader context of the debate about contagion. The notion that disease was passed from one person to another by infective organisms by contagion can be traced back to responses to pestilence in early societies. The author of *Leviticus* recognized that leprosy and gonorrhea were transmitted by contagion and had therefore to be quarantined – a name derived from *quarantina* or the 40-day period of isolation required of people entering Italian ports who were thought to be infected by disease. The alternative view of epidemics was that they are caused by atmospheric influence or 'epidemic miasma.' Epidemics are caused by bad air; *mal aria*. Although the notion of miasma has long been discredited, it pointed to the role of poor living conditions and lack of hygiene as a cause or condition of illness. However, miasma as a theory was destroyed in the nineteenth century by the discovery of the living organisms that produced many diseases. The theory of contagion by infective organisms also led, after much professional resistance, to the conclusion that disease was spread by doctors from one patient to another. The work of Ignaz Semmelweis, from the General Hospital in Vienna, in the 1860s on puerperal fever was significant in the development of hygienic practices in the treatment of pregnant women. Through observation, Simmelweis came to the conclusion that infection (in this case puerperal fever) was spread by his own students from dead infective material. Cleanliness and hand washing in a solution of chloride of lime reduced mortality rates by more than 6 per cent. The scientific principles behind these practical procedures were eventually supplied by Joseph Lister, for example, building on the tradition of Louis Pasteur and Robert Koch. These advances made possible a much safer environment for the practice of surgery and contributed to the containment of infections following hospitalization (Youngson 1979). Despite the resistance of the medical profession to the scientific discoveries of Semmelweis and Lister, the advances in medical science made possible the growth of the medical profession as a 'learned profession' driven by the cutting-edge of science. It also contributed to the 'mirage of health' as a Utopia of modern consciousness.

THE TWENTIETH CENTURY: THE RISE OF THE MEDICAL FACULTY

The twentieth century has been the context for radical changes in medicine. In these changes, one cannot separate transformations of the concepts of health and illness from the development of the role of professional medicine. Medical power and social knowledge are necessarily combined, and therefore the transformation of the university curriculum indicates shifting balances in authority between different professional groups and institutions. The reform of the medical curriculum is an important guide to these changes. The triumph of allopathic, individualist, and secular medicine over social or environmental medicine is symbolized by the publication of the Flexner Report on *Medical Education in the United States and Canada* in 1910. Abraham Flexner argued that scientific medicine required an intensive and protracted university-based training in the fundamental natural science curriculum. The immediate implication was that only students from the upper classes could achieve the lengthy university training necessary for professional entry into medical roles (Berliner 1984). The report had the consequence of limiting the flow of black students, women, and the working class into the medical faculty, and the recruitment of these groups into the profession showed no sign of revival in North America until after 1970 (Mumford 1983).

The Flexner Report recognized and authorized the social dominance of a research-oriented scientific medicine in which the biological sciences, along with laboratory training, provide the foundation of medical understanding. It also involved the triumph of allopathic over complementary medicine generally, and homeopathic medicine in particular. Medicine was increasingly specialized in terms of its knowledge base, and there was a division of labour around the separate organs of the body. The new breed of scientific doctors were specialists in the biological functioning of the human body.

This scientific corpus of medical knowledge was also associated with the evolution of the medical faculty within the university system as a separate, high cost, research faculty with its own unique authority and eventual dominance over the academic board. Medical faculties were increasingly separate in spatial and academic terms from the rest of the university. This physical separation reinforced the social solidarity of the medical faculty and effectively isolated the medical curriculum from other parts of the university. Specialization and subspecialization intensified the technical aspects of the scientific discourse of medicine, which was later associated with the rapid growth of physiology and pharmacology (Perrin and Perrin 1984). These curriculum changes laid the foundation of the golden age of twentieth-century scientific medicine from 1910 to 1950, in which Flexnerian reforms were dominant in North America and Europe. The growing importance of the general hospital was also associated with the rising social status of medicine. Improvements in

hygiene, sanitation, and nursing resulted in declining morbidity rates, thereby making hospitals safe for their middle-class clients. The growth of scientific medicine, the research medical faculty, and the evolution of the hospital were the context for a distinctive period of medical professionalism, where the medical associations controlled entry into the medical occupational cluster (Larson 1977). There were complementary processes of professionalism in dentistry, pharmacy, nursing, and many other paraprofessional groupings. These social changes ushered in the era of the medical–industrial complex (Ehrenreich and Ehrenreich 1970) and fostered a new wave of social criticism directed at the negative consequences of the 'medicalization' of society and the growth of iatrogenic illness (Illich 1976).

A variety of medical analysts have argued that since the 1970s there has been a profound transformation of health-care systems associated with a decline in the centrality of professional medicine and its professional autonomy (Starr 1982). The decline of medical dominance has also been associated with the erosion of social security schemes, centralized welfare states, and the commercialization of medical provision. As the insurance companies began to influence debates and policies about health funding, the professional autonomy of doctors became constrained. Governments have also turned to a mixture of preventive medicine, third-sector finance, and public health policies to support self-regulation. These fiscal crises in health care are closely related to the greying of the population. These political and economic changes have focused the attention of medical sociologists on what Foucault called 'governmentality' (Turner 1997b).

THE GREYING OF THE WEST

By the second half of the twentieth century, there was a general agreement that the great epoch of infectious disease had come to an end. Medical historians and epidemiologists such as Thomas McKeown (1979) could argue that the infectious scourges of the previous century (tuberculosis, measles, whooping cough, and venereal disease) had virtually disappeared with improvements in housing, water supply, food, and education. McKeown's thesis, which is not simply confined to the nineteenth century, demonstrated the importance of environmental and social causes in the decline of mortality rates. Tuberculosis was declining steadily from the 1830s before the use of bacillus Calmette–Guerin vaccination and the introduction of drug treatment such as streptomycin in 1944, paraaminosalicylic acid in 1946, and isoniazid in 1952. The drug treatment of TB had a profound impact on mortality rates. Whereas 900 girls died from TB in England and Wales in 1946, only 9 died in 1961. However, these improvements, according to McKeown, were the consequences of socioeconomic improvements that enhanced the general health status of the population.

Social inequality and poverty are now regarded as major determinants of individual health, with major differences in morbidity and mortality among social classes, as demonstrated in Great Britain by the publication of the *Black Report* (Townsend and Davidson 1982). Social medicine, as a result, has often been closely connected with political radicalism because it has concluded that poverty causes illness, and therefore the remedy has to be sought in social change, if necessary, of a revolutionary character. In Great Britain the new discipline of social medicine was advanced by radicals such as John Ryle, who in 1942 became the first professor of social medicine (Porter 1997). In North America, the debate about the social causes of illness and disease was promoted by medical sociologists such as Howard Waitzkin, who explored the notion of 'the second sickness' – a disease of the body produced by social injustice (Waitzkin 1983; Waitzkin and Waterman 1974).

As mortality rates declined, the populations of the industrial societies increased because birth rates remained high. Demographic transition was the result. However, as contraceptive devices became more common and there was a new emphasis on the family and motherhood, households sought to control their reproduction and birth rates began to decline. The conventional view is that modernization, in demographic terms, involves an s-shaped curve as societies pass from high death and birth rates to low death and birth rates. One further consequence, in the absence of migration, is the greying of the population and the epidemiological transition as deaths from infectious diseases are replaced by mortality determined by cancer, heart disease, and strokes. As Western societies became more affluent, geriatric illnesses such as diabetes came to dominate the demography of advanced societies. In terms of social knowledge, these changes were accompanied by the rise of social gerontology, which remains an incoherent domain of theory relating to both individual and cohort ageing (Green 1993).The greying of the population has also given rise to a general debate about the impact of age dependency on the capacity of societies to provide care for the elderly. The new social gerontology has begun to chronicle a wide range of new infirmities and

misfortunes waiting for human beings who have successfully survived into later life, in particular Alzheimer's disease, which is present in 20 per cent of the population over age 85.

Although geriatric illness has not enjoyed the same status as heroic medical intervention in acute diseases, there has been considerable interest in a range of degenerative conditions. For example, there has been a medicalization of 'women's complaints,' especially menopause. There has been considerable debate on the existence and consequences of premenstrual tension, the universality of menopause, and the existence of the sexual drive in old age. Some anthropologists have denied that menopause is universal, claiming that maturation for women in many societies, including Japan, is not accompanied by hot flashes, tension, and irritability (Lock 1993). Medical responses to the menopause, such as estrogen replacement therapy, have been equally controversial, with accusations that similar ageing processes in men have been ignored or neglected. Indeed many men's activist groups argue that, given the political importance of feminism, men's diseases such as prostate cancer have been neglected. Prostate cancer is the second leading cause of death from cancer for older men in the United States.

The greying of the population in the United States, where in 1990 more than 12 per cent were over age 65, has resulted in important political conflicts over illness categories. With medicalization there is a tendency to treat ageing as a disease which, with profound medical interventions (cosmetic surgery, hormone replacement therapy, organ transplants, and coronary bypass surgery), can be partially arrested. While the rich and famous have attempted to deny ageing and death, mainstream grey politics have challenged the assumption that immobility, memory loss, and an erosion of libidinal interest are inevitable consequences of ageing (Friedan 1993).

By the 1970s it was assumed that the conquest of disease in Western societies would require the development of drugs that would delay or manage old age. As medical attention moved from acute to chronic diseases, preventive medicine and health education would contribute to the containment of diabetes and heart disease. This complacency was shattered in the 1980s by the emergence of the HIV/AIDS epidemic, which was first reported in 1979–80 and which spread rapidly among the homosexual communities of North America, Europe, and Australia. The epidemic has, and will have, a major economic impact on Third World societies and in those communities (such as Islamic fundamentalist societies) that refuse to recognize the presence of HIV-positive communities in their midst.

The virus is now reported in 130 countries and carried by millions. In North America, it was originally confined to the homosexual communities of the West Coast and New York. In Australia, approximately 80 per cent of new cases are reported in Sydney, the gay capital of the continent. However, the virus spread to heterosexual couples and to hypodermic drug users who failed to observe the necessary etiquette of not sharing needles. The epidemic often gave rise to hostile moral condemnation of gay men, demonstrating once more the intimate connection between medical and moral discourses.

I refer to the HIV/AIDS phenomenon as an 'epidemic' partly to indicate its complexity. One does not die of AIDS but from the cluster of conditions (such as pneumonia) to which it gives occasion. AIDS is a medical condition that promotes a spectrum of illnesses and discomforts, so the categorization of AIDS requires other 'opportunistic infections.' The constellation of signs and symptoms in the context of HIV infection is termed the AIDS-related complex or ARC. In short, AIDS is socially constructed of the multiplicity of illnesses and malignancies that opportunistically flourish within a depleted immune system. Given the complexity of the condition, it is not surprising that a wealth of social metaphors also opportunistically multiplied. Susan Sontag (1989) suggests that AIDS shares with medieval plagues the notion of an invasion, but it is also organized around notions of pollution resulting from personal perversity.

Sexually transmitted diseases have forced society to rethink policies towards infectious disease, but they also demonstrated once more that medical understanding can never be easily separated from moral assumptions about normal behaviour. AIDS has also indicated that the future development of human health will inevitably and inextricably be part of a more general process of cultural globalization. In previous centuries, while plagues and epidemics were spread by migration and trade in the world, diseases were somewhat specific to geographical niches. With the growth of world tourism and trade, the global risk of infectious disease has spread rapidly. Influenza epidemics now spread almost instantaneously. There is widespread anxiety about the development of a variety of new conditions that are difficult to diagnose and to classify, complex in their functions and diffusion, and resistant to rapid or conventional treatments. The list of such conditions includes the eruption of newly discovered diseases such as hantavirus, the migration of diseases to new areas (such as cholera in Latin America), diseases produced by new technologies (such as toxic shock syndrome and Legionnaires'

Disease), and diseases transmitted from animals to humans. These problems have, along with ebola, Marburg virus, Lassa fever, and swine flu, generated a concern for 'the coming plague' (Garrett 1995).

These fears have been associated with the perception that we now face a new generation of hazards and risks that arise from the global pollution of the atmosphere and the environment. These global hazards gave rise to a new theory of society in the work of Ulrich Beck (1992), who argued that with modernization we have moved into an uncertain and precarious social condition called the 'risk society.' As society becomes more sophisticated, the potential risks from scientific experiment increase, especially where medical innovations are inadequately regulated. Indeed as societies become more deregulated and subject to market discipline, the scale of risks and hazards increases. Many critical commentators claim that the damage from the thalidomide drug, the spread of 'mad cow disease,' and the speculation surrounding the causes of Creutzfeldt Jacob's Disease (CJD) are evidence of the arrival of a risk society where medical interventions and experimentations are increasingly out of control. President Clinton's attempts to control the spread of cloning is simply further evidence for many that a 'brave new world' of secret medical experimentation is already upon us. The globalization of disease, the reproduction of people through new technologies, the degradation of the environment, the spread of cyborgs, and the mechanization of the domestic environment have given rise to speculation about postmodernization of the human body, which would become a hybrid phenomenon, precariously poised between nature, technology, and culture. In postmodern theory, human beings will no longer be metaphorically mechanical; they will, in fact, be mechanized.

CONCLUSION: THE PHILOSOPHY OF MEDICAL SCIENCE

To provide a history of medical concepts is automatically to raise questions about the ontological character of disease states; to indicate that any phenomenon has a history is to imply a relativistic view of reality. In this chapter, I have been concerned to trace, through a heuristic typology of disease concepts, the broad parameters of medical change in Western societies. In so doing, I have taken for granted a range of analytical issues concerning disease. It would be important in a more detailed approach to distinguish carefully among the experiences of sickness, the social behaviour associated with disease, the social roles that people are expected to perform in such circumstances, and the disease categories by which medical science describes a range of physical and mental malfunctions. In this history of concepts of health and illness, I have been primarily concerned with expert systems of knowledge and belief.

A weak program in the sociology of knowledge may simply argue that while lay perceptions of health and illness have a history because they are embedded in everyday understandings of reality, scientific concepts of health and illness may be either true or false, but they are not determined by the cultural context within which they emerge. Medical sociology has often embraced 'social constructionism' as a platform for its research. This perspective is said to entail three dimensions. First, the meanings of social reality are not fixed or intrinsic, but are the product of human interaction. The meanings of social reality emerge out of the constant flux of social exchange. Second, these meanings can never be taken for granted because they are constantly contested in everyday interactions. Third, human beings are self-reflexive about these meanings and constantly intervene to discuss and to change them (Levine 1992: 186). Such a perspective has been useful in studying the processes by and through which patients and doctors negotiate the meaning or significance of illness. This perspective also goes on to argue that these meanings of illness at the microsocial level are also conditioned by, and impact upon, the more general macrobelief systems that surround health and illness concepts. At this general level, concepts of health and well-being become inextricably connected to fundamental notions of self-identity (Herzlich and Pierret 1987).

Although from a sociological point of view this constructionist argument is persuasive, it is in many respects a limited view of scientific beliefs. A critic of this orientation might argue that, while lay beliefs and everyday assumptions about health and illness are indeed the products of everyday experiences of being sick, the clinical categories of disease that arise from close scientific inspection and doctors' observations of symptoms are not socially constructed and do not change significantly over time. One version of this argument would be to claim that some concepts of disease are more socially constructed than others (Turner 1992: 106). What people say or believe about a disease changes over time, but the clinical condition itself is relatively timeless. Thus, Ilza Veith (1981: 222) claims that Hippocrates' clinical description of mumps could easily be identified and confirmed by a contemporary general practitioner; she argues that 'what is unchanged is disease. What did change,

however, is the way in which disease was looked upon.' Our understanding of this contrast can be facilitated by Lester King (1982: 149), who suggests a useful distinction between a clinical entity and a disease entity. A clinical entity (from *kline* or bed) is a configuration or pattern that is observed by a doctor in (a bedside) interaction with a patient. The concept is thus linked to the practice of medicine. A disease entity is 'knowledge about' a condition that is produced by doctors' observations, statistical information, and laboratory tests. As a disease entity becomes scientifically established, it may well radically alter a clinical identity. A textbook of medicine is, in essence, a collection of theories of disease entities. Thus, if we compare Thomas Sydenham's seventeenth-century description of puerperal fever with Hippocrates' description, we find a remarkable convergence. What is being described (the clinical condition of the fever) is relatively constant, but the theory behind the description has changed considerably. Theories change over time because they are produced by changes in domain assumptions, reorganization of university curricula, professional competition between scientists, new discoveries from laboratory trials, and so forth.

It is not contradictory, therefore, to hold both that there is a clinical reality (fever or mumps) which is captured in the 'classic descriptions of disease' that doctors handed down over the centuries (King 1982: 152), and that theories and concepts of health and illness vary considerably over time, being influenced by general social values, fashion, and changing social circumstances. It is in the strong program of the sociology of knowledge and in the social studies of science tradition that one finds research that attempts to demonstrate that these fundamental concepts of science are socially produced. However, clinical entities are also socially produced by the fact that, for example, doctors are trained to recognize the signs and symptoms that announce the presence of fever or mumps. To say that fever is socially produced is not to say that it is a 'fiction,' or that it does not exist, or that it could be conjured up by the doctor as a magician pulls a rabbit from a hat. However, the signs and symptoms of fever in a clinical setting are mediated through and by the experiences and training of physicians, and these physicians are the products of specific and local medical cultures.

From a social science perspective, we can summarize the principal issues in contemporary understandings of the concepts of health and illness in the following manner. Regardless of the epistemological difficulties surrounding the notion of disease entities, there is widespread agreement that *conceptions* of disease have changed radically. It is no longer accepted that there is a universal taxonomy of disease or that medical categories are neutral. The general theories of health and illness that explain the medical condition of humanity are shaped and organized around the dominant ideologies and beliefs of a culture (its domain assumptions). Medical categories are not neutral because they typically carry and house the metaphors of a society by which praise and blame are allocated. In addition, the nineteenth-century search for the specific etiologies of every disease, in which each disease has its own cause, has been abandoned. Disease is now seen to have multiple, interactive causes and therefore no simple single cure is possible or desirable. As we have seen, the AIDS epidemic is a good illustration of this complexity. In this respect, Bachelard, Canguilhem, and Foucault have influenced social science approaches that generally accept some version of the argument that sciences develop through revolutionary paradigm shifts, and that scientific theories are socially constructed.

At the everyday level, social experiences of illness are equally shaped and constructed by cultural assumptions and social relationships. At this level of lay beliefs, there is a continuing tendency to see illness experiences within a moral framework of blame and responsibility, a framework that attempts to help individuals, in a predominantly secular environment, to answer questions about life and death. The growing literature, both lay and professional, on death and dying is one indication of the fact that despite, or because of, the erosion of the authority of traditional religious institutions, rituals, and beliefs, ordinary individuals need to find some meaning for the seemingly trivial nature of the passage from birth to the grave (Nuland 1994).

REFERENCES

Beck, U. (1992) *Risk Society. Towards a New Modernity*. London: Sage.

Bell, R.M. (1985) *Holy Anorexia*. Chicago and London: University of Chicago Press.

Berliner, H.S. (1984) 'Scientific medicine since Flexner', in J.W. Salmon (ed.), *Alternative Medicine, Popular and Policy Perspectives*. London: Tavistock. pp. 30–56.

Cunningham, A. (1997) *The Anatomical Renaissance. The Resurrection of the Anatomical Projects of the Ancients*. Aldershot: Scolar Press.

Douglas, M. (1966) *Purity and Danger. An Analysis of Concepts of Pollution and Taboo*. London: Routledge & Kegan Paul.

Dubos, R. (1959) *Mirage of Health. Utopias, Progress and Biological Change*. London: George Allen & Unwin.

Durkheim, E. (1954) *The Elementary Forms of the Religious Life*. London: Allen & Unwin.

Ehrenreich, B. and Ehrenreich, J. (1970) *The American Health Empire: Power, Profits and Policies*. New York: Random House.

Evans-Pritchard, E.E. (1937) *Witchcraft Oracles and Magic among the Azande*. Oxford: Oxford University Press.

Fee, E. and Brown, T.M. (eds) (1997) *Making Medical History. The Life and Times of Henry E. Sigerist*. Baltimore and London: The Johns Hopkins University Press.

Flint, V.J. (1989) 'The early medieval "Medicus," the saint – and the enchanter', *Social History of Medicine*, 2 (2): 127–46.

Foucault, M. (1971) *Madness and Civilization*. London: Tavistock.

Foucault, M. (1977) *Discipline and Punish. The Birth of the Prison*. London: Tavistock.

Foucault, M. (1986) *The Care of the Self*. New York: Random House.

Friedan, B. (1993) *The Fountain of Age*. New York: Simon & Schuster.

Garrett, I. (1995) *The Coming Plague. Newly Emerging Diseases in a World Out of Balance*. London: Virago.

Green, B.S. (1993) *Gerontology and the Construction of Old Age: A Study in Discourse Analysis*. New York: Aldine de Gruyter.

Guerrini, A. (1989) 'Isaac Newton, George Cheyne and the "Principia Medicinae"', in R. French and A. Weir (eds), *The Medical Revolution of the Seventeenth Century*. Cambridge: Cambridge University Press. pp. 222–45.

Hepworth, M. and Turner, B. S. (1982) *Confession. Studies in Deviance and Religion*. London: Routledge & Kegan Paul.

Herzlich, C. and Pierret, J. (1987) *Illness and Self in Society*. Baltimore and London: The Johns Hopkins University Press.

Houwaart, E.S. (1991) *De hygienisten. Artsen, staaat and volksgezondheid in Nederland 1840–1890*. Groningen: Historische Uitgeverij.

Illich, I. (1976) *Medical Nemesis. The Expropriation of Health*. New York: Random House.

King, L.S. (1982) *Medical Thinking. A Historical Preface*. Princeton, NJ: Princeton University Press.

Larson, M.S. (1977) *The Rise of Professionalism. A Sociological Analysis*. Berkeley: University of California Press.

Levine, M.P. (1992) 'The implications of the constructionist theory for social research on the AIDS epidemic among gay men', in G. Herdt and S. Lindenbaum (eds), *The Time of AIDS. Social Analysis, Theory and Methods*. Newbury Park: Sage. pp. 185–98.

Lock, M. (1993) *Encounters with Aging. Mythologies of Menopause in Japan and North America*. Berkeley: University of California Press.

Malinowski, B. (1948) *Magic, Science and Religion and Other Essays*. Glencoe: Free Press.

McKeown, T. (1979) *The Role of Medicine. Dream, Mirage or Nemesis?* Oxford: Basil Blackwell.

Mumford, E. (1983) *Medical Sociology. Patients, Providers and Policies.* New York: Random House.

Navarro, V. (1976) *Medicine under Capitalism.* New York: Prodist.

Nuland, S.B. (1994) *How We Die.* London: Random House.

O'Leary, D.L. (1949) *How Greek Science Passed to the Arabs.* London: Routledge & Kegan Paul.

Perrin, E.C. and Perrin, J.M. (1984) 'Anti-intellectual trends and traditions in academic medicine', in W.A. Powell and R. Robbins (eds), *Conflict and Consensus: A Festschrift in Honor of Lewis A. Coser.* London: Collier–Macmillan. pp. 313–26.

Porter, D. (ed.) (1997) *Social Medicine and Medical Sociology in the Twentieth Century.* Amsterdam: Rodopi.

Rousselle, A. (1988) *Porneia. On Desire and the Body in Antiquity.* Oxford: Basil Blackwell.

Sigerist, H.E. (1951) *A History of Medicine.* Oxford: Oxford University Press, Vol. 1.

Sontag, S. (1978) *Illness as Metaphor.* New York: Vintage.

Sontag, S. (1989) *AIDS and its Metaphors.* London: Allen Lane.

Starr, P. (1982) *The Social Transformation of American Medicine.* New York: Basic Books.

Szasz, T. (1961) *The Myth of Mental Illness.* London: Paladin.

Szasz, T. (1970) *The Manufacture of Madness.* New York: Harper & Row.

Szreter, S. (1988) 'The importance of social intervention in Britain's mortality decline c. 1850–1914: a reinterpretation of the role of public health', *Social History of Medicine,* 1(1): 1–37.

Townsend, P. and Davidson, N. (1982) *Inequalities in Health.* Harmondsworth: Pelican Books.

Turner, B.S. (1991) *Religion and Social Theory.* London: Sage (2nd edn).

Turner, B.S. (1992) *Regulating Bodies. Essays in Medical Sociology.* London: Routledge.

Turner, B.S. (1995) *Medical Power and Social Knowledge.* London: Sage (2nd edn).

Turner, B.S. (1996) *The Body & Society.* London: Sage (2nd edn).

Turner, B.S. (1997a) 'The body in Western society: social theory and its perspectives', in S. Coakley (ed.) *Religion and the Body.* Cambridge: Cambridge University Press. pp. 15–41.

Turner, B.S. (1997b) 'From governmentality to risk: some reflections on Foucault's contribution to medical sociology', in A. Petersen and Robin Bunton (eds), *Foucault, Health and Medicine.* London: Routledge. pp. ix–xxi.

Veith, I. (1981) 'Historical reflections on the changing concepts of disease', in A.L. Caplan, H.T. Engelhardt, and J.J. McCartney (eds), *Concepts of Health and Disease: Interdisciplinary Perspectives.* London: Addison-Wesley. pp. 221–30.

Waitzkin, H. (1983) *The Second Sickness: Contradictions of Capitalist Health Care.* New York: Free Press.

Waitzkin, H. and Waterman, B. (1974) *The Exploitation of Illness in Capitalist Society.* Indianapolis: Bobbs-Merrill.

Weber, M. (1930) *The Protestant Ethic and the Spirit of Capitalism.* London: Allen & Unwin.

Weindling, P. (1989) *Health Race and German Politics between National Unification and Nazism, 1870–1945.* Cambridge: Cambridge University Press.

Youngson, A.J. (1979) *The Scientific Revolution in Victorian Medicine.* Canberra: Australian National University Press.

1.2

Social Theorizing About Health and Illness

DAVID ARMSTRONG

INTRODUCTION

At the end of the eighteenth century a new explanatory model of illness emerged in Parisian hospitals (Ackerknecht 1967). This new model replaced the constantly shifting symptoms of humoral medicine with the novel idea that illness was a product of a specific localized pathological lesion within the body. The contemporary emergence of the clinical examination and autopsy with which to identify the lesion, and the hospital in which to capture it, represented the practical and institutional manifestations of the perception of illness. Over the subsequent two centuries this framework was extended and developed, culminating in the elaborate and sophisticated biomedical view of health and illness that exists today. The new model of disease and illness provided what must count as the most successful theory of health and illness, spreading over the last two centuries to become the major formal explanatory framework for illness in all countries of the world. As Foucault observed, for two centuries this theory has provided 'the dark, but firm web of our experience' (Foucault 1963).

The phenomenal success of the biomedical theory of illness has constituted the essential backdrop for social theorizing about health and illness. The pathological lesion has provided the critical context in which – and sometimes against which – social theorizing has developed. This chapter will therefore map social theorizing about health and illness in its relation to this overarching explanatory framework of pathological medicine. This chapter

examines this relationship in five of its principal forms, which also happen to follow a rough historical progression.

First, there is the position of almost total acceptance of the biomedical model that leaves a limited role for social theorizing. At best, social theory can offer conceptual support for the medical enterprise, attempting to provide a theoretical underpinning for wayward patient behaviour, for some of the social precursors of the biological lesion, and for some of its social consequences. The second form of the relationship is less subservient, seeking out an independent role for the social sciences, yet still failing to offer any fundamental challenge to the suzerainty of biomedicine. Nevertheless, in areas such as life events, labelling theory, and patient experience, social theorizing develops an understanding of illness that lies largely outside the dominant biomedical paradigm. The third type of relationship is one of challenge as social theorizing engages with some of the outward trappings of biomedicine such as the power of the profession, its increasing medicalization of the population, and the social values often encoded in seemingly neutral medical/scientific knowledge. Fourth, there comes the point when social theorizing questions the cognitive basis of biomedicine itself, a perspective that is underpinned by viewing biomedicine as historically and culturally located, as simply one way – albeit a very successful way – of modelling illness. Finally, reflecting the postmodern turn in late twentieth-century thought, the chapter offers a brief glimpse of a reflexive world in which social theorizing about illness becomes itself the object of social theorizing.

Inevitably, through space restrictions and the limitations of authorship, this chapter is not a comprehensive or total review of all social theorizing. Rather, it attempts to offer a map or framework for understanding the various forms of social theorizing that have emerged over the last few decades.

SOCIAL THEORIZING ABOUT HEALTH-RELATED PHENOMENA COMPLEMENTARY TO BIOMEDICAL SCIENCE

The cornerstone of the biomedical model is the belief that illness can be reduced to a pathological lesion, such as an inflammation or a cancer, within the confines of the body. This lesion has deleterious effects on neighbouring tissues, causing disruption to biological systems, negative experiences for the patient (most commonly pain), and sometimes the possibility of death.

The goal of clinical practice has therefore been the identification and treatment of the lesion. Because the lesion is held to have an effect on a patient's perceptions and experiences, these latter could be reported to the doctor (through taking the medical 'history') and interpreted as symptoms of the underlying lesion. Different diseases produced different patterns of symptoms so that the nature of the lesion could often be inferred from these patient reports. However, this inferential task was considerably aided by additional evidence about the lesion gained from identifying the biological disturbances caused by the lesion that were not directly accessible to patient experience. This other evidence came in the form of the signs of disease elicited by the physician during the clinical examination. (While in recent decades the latter search has been considerably augmented by the development of clinical investigations that, in effect, extend the doctor's senses.) Having identified the disease type, the physician could then initiate treatment that was focussed on removing the lesion and its potential dangers or, if that was not possible, ameliorating its negative effects in some way.

An additional component of the medical model, that was partially developed at first but subsequently enhanced its success and prestige, was the construction of an aetiological framework for disease that identified the precursors and causes of the underlying lesion. Importantly, these causal factors were mainly construed as biological in nature, perhaps the most famous being the germ theory of disease.

Given the extent and success of the biomedical model of disease, social science found itself constrained, at least in the early years, to working in its formidable shadow. The 'social' could only be introduced to the extent that it impinged in some way on the paradigm of biomedicine outlined above. In effect, the first contribution of social science to medicine, and the first opportunity for social theorizing, lay in offering complementary and supportive explanatory models for biomedicine. This contribution can be traced through three core elements of biomedicine, namely the process of identifying illness, assessment of the consequences of illness, and the discovery of the causes of illness.

Identifying Illness

The identification of illness relied partly on patients' accounts of their experience and partly on the doctor successfully eliciting the signs of illness. However, this clinical activity depended on the patient choosing to visit the doctor: the process of deciding to visit the doctor therefore became an early focus for social science enquiry.

The problem of patients not presenting themselves to health services first emerged with the failure of many people to respond to invitations to take part in population immunization programmes. For example, the Sabin and the Salk vaccines provided what appeared to be an effective and safe technique for guarding against poliomyelitis, yet many parents did not take up the invitation to bring their children for this simple procedure. An earlier age might have explained this behaviour in terms of fecklessness or ignorance, but the preventive medicine of the 1950s turned to psychosocial explanations. The major theory to emerge from this work was the Health Belief Model which, with various revisions, is still called upon to explain health-related behaviour (Rosenstock 1965). Essentially the Health Belief Model claimed that various measurable facets of an individual, such as their level of concern, motivation, and previous experiences, could be used to explain and predict behaviour with regard to preventing ill health. Later models such as the Theory of Reasoned Action (Fishbein 1967), the Theory of Planned Behaviour (Ajzen 1985), and the Health Action Process (Schwarzer 1992), developed and clarified these ideas but remained faithful to the original objective of identifying the intrapsychic factors that determined individual behaviour.

The Health Belief Model was primarily a psychological model of human behaviour and related mainly to preventive activities, but evidence began to accumulate of a parallel problem. To be sure, many people failed to use available preventive services, but of far greater

consequence – and apparently even more inexplicable – many patients chose not to seek medical attention when ill (Koos 1954). The search
for the reasons why patients chose not to take
their symptoms to the doctor ushered in a major
body of investigations around the problem of
what became known as 'illness behaviour'
(Mechanic, 1962; Mechanic and Volkart 1960).

Initial concerns focused on patients who failed
to use services despite needing preventive measures or attention for their illnesses. However,
this soon spread to embrace all patient behaviour, including those patients who attended
with apparently trivial complaints. Theories to
explain behaviour were relatively low level, often
taken from a social psychological background
with an emphasis on the 'triggers' and impediments to seeking medical attention (Zola 1973).
Above all, however, these theories of patients'
behaviour relied on the appearance of the symptom as the defining moment from which the process started. As such, the symptom was viewed
as a biological fact in exactly the same conceptual form as used by medicine, a biological poin-
ter to the underlying lesion. Certainly it was
believed that there could be psychological as
well as organic symptoms, but all related to an
underside, an illness that the trained medical
practitioner could infer. Later, with the realization that all symptoms were percepts, the way
would be open to reconstruct the process of
going to see the doctor and to locate its origins
in patients' more fundamental experiences and
cognitions.

If patients did not respond appropriately to
their symptoms, then their behaviour intruded
upon the smooth operation of clinical practice;
but medicine also expected patients to report
their symptoms accurately and take clear note
of medical explanation and advice. Early psychological studies of the consultation therefore
addressed the mechanics of the interaction and
of whether information had been accurately
relayed and acted upon (Ley 1988). Limits to
patient memory and advice on how doctors
could more effectively provide patients with
information were of great concern, as was the
apparently related 'problem' of noncompliance
with medical advice. In retrospect, the underlying model of human functioning reflected a
very mechanistic one.

The understanding of what has since become
known as help-seeking behaviour has remained
a thread running through social theorizing over
the last four or five decades. From its origins as
an adjunct to the biomedical process, it has
become a substantive area in its own right.
However, perhaps ironically, the topic has
tended to move outside the purview of social
theorizing as health psychologists searching for

the intrapsychic factors that drive behaviour
have taken it up with more alacrity. Help-seeking behaviour has also proved of interest in more
policy and utilization studies that now recognize
that health service use is not simply a product of
illness severity. More recent theorizing about
risk and risk-related behaviour may yet revive
this area of work within mainstream medical
sociology.

Social Factors in the Cause of Illness

Perhaps the longest relationship between social
science and medicine has been the joint project
to explore the role of social factors in the aetiology of disease. The traditional medical model
was largely concerned with identifying the
immediate biophysical insults that caused disease, but it could raise no objection to an analysis for investigating the social distribution of
those same factors. Indeed, attention to the distribution of aetiological factors had been a central concern of nineteenth- and twentieth-
century epidemiologists, so it might be better
to describe this area of social science as 'social
epidemiology.' This reflects not only its reliance
on traditional epidemiological methods, but also
the rather empirical and atheoretical nature of
the enquiry in that there was little need to go
beyond identification of the population 'pattern': the medical model provided the subsequent implications. In this sense, much of the
interwar epidemiological work and analyses of
mortality statistics might be termed social
science, although its theoretical sophistication
was very limited.

Even so, historically there was a theoretical
framework for the understanding of the distribution of biophysical threats, namely the Marxist,
that was revived in the 1960s (Doyal 1979;
Navarro 1976). In the nineteenth century,
Engels observed the close relationship between
the distribution of poverty and the distribution
of illness, and his observations were placed in a
powerful explanatory framework by his collab-
orator Marx. Of course, in the world of biomedicine there was little need for Marxism. It
was clear that the distribution of biophysical
threats was paralleled by that of poverty and
deprivation, but there was little interest in
whether it was due to exploitation of the working class or an inevitable part of human progress. In effect, biomedicine continued to
control the conceptual and research agenda in
that the central problem to be explained
remained the link between the noxious agent
and the pathological lesion; all else was an epi-
phenomenon. If this can be construed as a struggle between the theory of Marx and the theory

of biomedicine, there really was no contest. Marxism was to make more of an immediate critical impact on the organization and delivery of health services rather than on understanding the nature of health and illness.

Although it was sociology that claimed jurisdiction over mapping the social distribution of (biophysical) aetiological factors, some of the most significant developments in this area have come, perhaps ironically, from within medicine. On the one hand, the 'McKeown thesis,' which argued that health gains over the last two centuries could largely be explained by improving social conditions (McKeown 1979), and the foetal origins hypothesis, mostly associated with Barker (Barker 1992), which claimed it was early environmental conditions that determined later adult morbidity and mortality, have been very influential in both medical and social science in understanding the relationship between social environment and disease.

Although an overt Marxist theoretical framework might have had problems in asserting its claims against biomedicine, a more implicit and empiricist approach in the form of health inequalities research has proved a strong and fruitful line of enquiry. Inequalities in health status have remained a major feature of Western societies, despite increasing standards of living and health-care investment. A number of theories have emerged to explain these differences, ranging from the quasi-Marxist materialist explanation to a more cultural framework. A wealth of studies have tried to test and tease out the exact mechanisms through which deprivation in its many forms gets translated into compromised health status (Blane et al. 1996). There has also been a claim that the extent of the range of material inequality in any society predicts health status irrespective of the actual standard of living (Wilkinson 1996). Explaining this observation offers yet another challenge for social theorizing.

Social Consequences of Illness

For biomedicine, the consequences of disease were expressed in the biological disruption that it caused, and in as much as this might also affect the wider integrity of the patient, it remained a central focus. However, illness also marked a social status beyond the pathological lesion, and this too had implications for patients.

The classic account of the additional psychosocial impact of the lesion was developed by Parsons in his famous essay on the sick role (Parsons 1951). In effect, not only did the lesion damage the biological integrity of the patient, but it also compromised the patient's social status. Later, critics of Parsons – and there were many – rejected this narrow formulation of the sick role. Its assumptions of consensus and harmony have become less popular as an explanatory framework in sociological theory. Equally, it would seem that the sick role as described by Parsons ignored the plight of many patients with chronic illnesses who were unable to benefit from or fulfil one or more of its characteristics.

Nevertheless, for all its faults, the sick role still forms one of the conceptual building blocks of medical social science (and its theoretical ramifications have remained a topic of interest ever since (Gerhardt 1989)). The historical significance of Parsons' concept was that it recast the doctor/patient relationship from a therapeutic encounter to an engagement of wider 'social control' mechanisms. Illness was a deviant status, and without appropriate control mechanisms over patient behaviour and motivation there was a potential risk to social stability. Parsons also represented the main route through which psychoanalytic theory made its small impression on social theorizing. Parsons himself was influenced by psychoanalysis, and this perspective, as later commentators pointed out, was embedded in his notion of the sick role. Accordingly, the few attempts to bring the unconscious into medical sociology have been through rehabilitation of Parsons' original insights. Even so, the wealth of psychoanalytic perspectives remains largely marginal to the sociological enterprise (Figlio 1987; Lupton 1997).

The idea of the patient as a social actor corresponded well with the empirical problem of patients' behaviour that had been discovered in the early medico-social surveys. The notion of the sick role gave a conceptual basis for thinking about the apparent vagaries of patients' response to symptoms and medical intervention. The other themes in Parsons' original essay, namely the doctor's responsibilities in the medical encounter, were less well cited, although they too represented a novel theoretical line of enquiry which was further developed in ensuing decades in terms of the role of the medical profession in society.

SOCIAL THEORIZING ABOUT HEALTH-RELATED PHENOMENA IGNORED OR OVERLOOKED BY BIOMEDICAL SCIENCE

Biomedicine defines health and illness largely in terms of biologically based diseases. This means that causes, manifestations, and consequences of disease are expressed in biological terms. This perspective also treats the ill person, often by default, as a biological object. However, social theorizing identified and addressed the other more psychosocial dimensions of the ill person. The discovery of illness behaviour and the idiosyncrasies of patient behaviour in the consultation began to open up the possibility that the patient was more than an inefficient recording instrument for the underlying pathological lesion.

Two strands in social science represented this reconstruction of the patient. First, the external aetiological factors that medicine had conceptualized in terms of biological hazards (and social epidemiology had shown to be socially patterned) began to be perceived as themselves psychosocial in nature. Second, the impact of illness was extended beyond the individualized status of the sick role to the wider social identity of the patient. These two theoretical innovations involved a reconceptualization of the form of identity embedded in patienthood, from the limited well-behaved patient entering the sick role to the holistic experiencing person engaging with chronic illness.

Psychosocial Threats

Although the observation that biological hazards were socially distributed was not a central part of the medical model, the analysis of social patterning did not pose a challenge in that the aetiological factors remained essentially biological in nature. However, the components of an alternative aetiological framework already existed in the very heart of social theory. Earlier in the twentieth century, Durkheim analysed suicide rates to show that they were closely related to degrees of social integration and regulation (Durkheim 1952). Examining contemporary suicide statistics in tables of three variables, Durkheim developed a primitive form of multivariate analysis to show that suicide rates varied in different European societies in a manner that fitted his theory, and that the rate was indeed lower amongst 'integrated' groups such as the married and Catholics.

The idea that social integration could affect the rate of suicide was taken further with postwar community studies of mental illness. If social disintegration could affect suicide then why not mental illnesses in general (Leighton et al. 1963)? At first social integration was operationalized in terms of respondents' reports of the health of their community. Later the measure became a more individualized one involving on the one hand the disruptive stimulus of a negative life event, and on the other

the protective integration afforded by social support (Dohrenwend and Dohrenwend 1981). Following Durkheim's original insights, research has since attempted to establish whether social support, or lack of it, had a direct effect on health or acted as a buffer against negative experiences such as life events (Berkman and Syme 1979; Henderson 1980). Antonovsky (1979) provided a further theoretical development of these notions in his concept of sense of coherence that represents a more individualized version of social integrity.

In summary, the collaborative work between social epidemiologists and medical sociologists continued to explore the relationship between social factors and illness. Some of this research was directed at uncovering the links between various facets of lifestyle and their health correlates (Blaxter 1990), particularly as this integrated with the needs of the growing health promotion and illness strategies of the 1970s and 1980s, but another strand of research began to emphasize the importance of psychosocial factors. Psychologists had already reported on the effects of stress on health but, despite the initial promise, stress was proving remarkably difficult to define consistently across many studies. Life events, however, provided a more clearly defined personal 'insult' that could be operationalized more easily. Observations of bereavement reactions had shown the powerful immediate effects of a negative life event, and work was pursued to explore the role of life events in psychiatric illness, particularly depression, but also in organic illness (Brown and Harris 1978).

The overall result of these studies of psychosocial threats has been the creation of a conceptual field in which psychology, sociology, and clinical practice intersect. While largely accepting the biomedical definition of illness/disease, these studies have continued to assert the importance of the psychosocial environment against the more biological factors to be found in traditional models of disease aetiology.

Labelling

Parsons' notion of the sick role had shown that illness was expressed in social status as well as in biological disruption, and just as the work on aetiology had extended into a more psychosocial realm, the understanding of the social impact of illness was later enhanced. The labelling theory provided the important bridge between social aetiology and social pathology.

Labelling theory was developed in the 1960s as an explanation of why social reaction to a person could have important effects for that person (Becker 1963; Lemert 1967), but perhaps its most famous expression was in the work of Goffman. Drawing upon symbolic interactionism (Rose 1962), Goffman focussed on the everyday interactions between social actors. In later writing he was more explicit about his theoretical grounding (of frame analysis), but his texts on stigma and asylums are important statements in their own right that were to inform much later conceptualization of the impact of illness on patients (Goffman 1961, 1963). Labelling, particularly as inspired by Goffman, has proved important in the field of disability, allowing the psychosocial problems experienced by the mentally and physically impaired – mainly brought about through the reactions of others – to be identified and better understood (Higgins 1980; Scott 1969). Indeed, the WHO was sufficiently convinced of the importance of this perspective and introduced a now well-accepted classification of impairment, disability, and handicap. Impairment was classified as the patient's biological deficit, disability was the degree to which function was affected, and handicap the extent of social problems, mostly brought about through labelling or the fear of labelling (WHO 1980; Wood 1975).

There has been subsequent theoretical development of the labelling/stigma model. For example, the distinction between felt and enacted stigma has been a particularly useful one (Scambler and Hopkins 1986), but the theoretical insights of this approach have been more remarkable for becoming a taken-for-granted framework for understanding reactions to illness. This meant that the patient became more than a passive repository for the pathological lesion. During the 1970s, this latent sentient creature awoke further as social scientists began to recognize and measure cognitions and experiences.

Cognitions and Experiences

Research on illness behaviour, which had been such a potent force for defining a disciplinary space for medical sociology, began to run out of steam in the 1970s. The problem was a theoretical one. Understanding patients' responses to symptoms had failed to develop a coherent theory that would allow fruitful predictions; the result was a series of largely empirical studies offering at best a descriptive epidemiology of symptom prevalence. This framework was revolutionized by studies using an ethnographic/anthropological approach that argued that theorizing had to start from the patients' understanding of the symptom's meaning (Herzlich 1973; Kleinman 1980). This meant that health-related behaviour could be linked to patient's cognitions or lay explanatory models of illness. For example, biomedicine explained an upper respiratory tract infection in terms of a virus, whereas most lay people seem to have ideas about draughts, wet hair, cold feet, etc., together with appropriate 'folk' remedies (Helman 1978). It thus became possible to begin to explain the 50 per cent of patients who failed to comply with medical instructions in terms of a failure of the doctor to identify the real underlying problem. Sociologists could then advise doctors that part of the consultation should be spent eliciting and dealing with the patient's 'lay theories' (Tuckett et al. 1985).

The second aspect of patient functioning that, in parallel, became a focus for sociological work was patient experience. Rather than seeing illness as something patients 'had' or reacted to (especially in terms of help-seeking behaviour), it could be viewed as something patients experienced. There followed a great number of studies that explored patients' experiences of a variety of illnesses, particularly in the ways that patients 'made sense' of illness-related events (Anderson and Bury 1988; Fitzpatrick et al. 1984; Scambler and Hopkins 1986).

Ironically, while the emphasis on cognitions and experience represented an initial challenge to medicine, it was not long before these same themes began to find their way into medical practice. In this case it was medicine living in the shadow of social science rather than the other way round. Understanding the patients' view and experience of illness remains an important force in changing, even humanizing, clinical practice, and just as the old biomedical paradigm studied the clinical manifestations of the disease, modern social science writes a parallel text on the experiential manifestations of illness. However, this is largely empirical work, usually based on qualitative methods, and theoretical development has been limited.

In 1977, Engel advanced the notion of a biopsychosocial model of illness that combined the various elements of the classical biomedical model with the new researches of social scientists (Engel 1977). Despite its name, his model did not give equal priority to the different dimensions (how could it?), but offered the biomedical prime place. In effect, it can be seen as an attempt to consolidate social theorizing into biomedicine. Yet, despite frequent appeals for a biopsychosocial approach, social science had already begun to move beyond the cognitive constraints of biomedicine. Patients' explanatory models posed an alternative understanding of the nature of illness; true, it was 'lay' rather than professional, 'folk' rather than scientific, but in effect it mapped out the ground for later battles. Biomedicine no longer had a monopoly of theories of illness.

SOCIAL THEORIZING IN OPPOSITION TO MEDICAL SCIENCE

Writing in 1957, Straus made what has now become a classic observation: there was both a sociology *in* medicine and a sociology *of* medicine (Straus 1957). Sociology in medicine was concerned with offering support for the medical enterprise, in effect, a continuation of biomedical theory or an addendum to it. Certainly it seemed much more orientated towards the patient's perspective than traditional medical practice, but it was still essentially concerned with the improvement of health services and the further amelioration of illness and disease. The sociology of medicine promised much more, but against the overwhelming dominance of the biomedical model of illness progress was slow. Indeed, initial skirmishes were not directed against the medical citadel – at the time it seemed largely impregnable – but against the way that medicine was practised. If medical knowledge was unassailable, then the medical profession and the organization of health-care delivery offered a more tempting target.

Professions

Echoing Carr-Saunders and Wilson's 1933 classic interwar treatise on the medical profession (Carr-Saunders and Wilson 1933) and following Durkheim's supportive stance towards professional and guild groups (Durkheim 1933), social theorists at first saw the profession and its work as a form of ideal social organization. This view certainly informed Parsons' view and the place he reserved for the medical practitioner in his functionalist account of the doctor–patient relationship. Here was a group of people drawn together by a commitment to the welfare of the public and sharing a common expertise: these two characteristics, namely a service ideal and an esoteric knowledge base, were the basis of any profession in society (Goode 1960). Questions then arose about exactly which occupational groups could be defined as professions and, for those aspiring to professional status, the steps that might be taken to achieve it (Wilensky 1964). However, it was medicine that remained the archetypal profession against which all other

claims had to be compared during the 1950s and indeed for most of the 1960s.

From the Parsonian perspective, the medical profession had been seen as an important mechanism in the maintenance of social stability, but there was an alternative account of the profession's role in society that was less benign. This alternative view held that doctors existed because they had successfully wielded power in the marketplace to seize a virtual monopoly of control over health-care provision (Berlant 1975; Parry and Parry 1976). This enabled the profession's past 'altruistic' acts, particularly those around licensing and registration, to be seen as less intended to 'protect the public' and more to squeeze out competition.

Perhaps the most significant break with the old sociology of the professions – which was said to have simply accepted the profession's own definition of itself – was Freidson's claim that the medical profession's status was a product of political action in the widest sense (Freidson 1970). This thesis ushered in a series of new studies that 'exposed' the self-seeking aggrandisement of the profession. The backdrop for most of these studies was the realization that the medical profession had managed to pull off an amazing feat. By the mid-twentieth century the medical profession was extremely powerful but, unlike other commanding institutions of organized labour, the population had been largely persuaded that the profession's power was in the public interest. The roots of this achievement clearly went back to the nineteenth century, so sociologists turned to historiographical sources, many of them secondary, to support their explanations of how medicine had succeeded. Most of these analyses focused on the marketplace. Medicine had succeeded in cornering the market for health care and it had demonstrated skilful 'occupational closure' through which new recruits did so under the auspices of the profession and, at the same time, unqualified healers were driven out of business (Larson 1977).

The sociological exposure of the doctors' professionalizing tactics proved useful for understanding the ascendancy of the medical profession, but it has been argued more recently that the power of the profession may be in decline as clinical autonomy is restricted by third-party payers and medico-legal concerns. An alternative literature on de-professionalization has therefore emerged that tries to set professions within the wider health division of labour and health-care systems (Hang 1988). These new studies have yet to achieve the theoretical coherence of the earlier professionalization literature, but nevertheless properly situate health work within a wider occupational context.

Medicalization

The argument that the growth of biomedicine under the tutelage of the medical profession might have negative consequences also resonated with further developments in relating the notion of 'social control,' as laid out in Parsons' model of the doctor–patient relationship, to 'modern medicine.' Far from control being exercised for patient welfare and wider social well-being, medicine seemed to be extending its interest and involvement into the minutiae of social life. Not only were considerable medical resources available for the ill, but even the healthy were being persuaded that they were still 'at risk' and could usefully follow medical advice. The net effect was the increasing 'medicalization' of everyday life (Zola 1972) and of deviance (Conrad and Schneider 1980). Medicine was seen to be replacing the role of the church and the law in policing the boundary between normal and abnormal. At its mildest, 'experts' took responsibility away from people, thereby rendering them more docile; at its most extreme, people were being controlled and manipulated by a subtle and potentially dangerous force.

The thesis that society was becoming medicalized allowed a strong indictment of the way medical knowledge was used. Perhaps Illich's charge in his book *Medical Nemesis* that 'The medical establishment has become a major threat to health' represented an extreme but oft-cited illustration of this position (Illich 1975: 11), but this critique was essentially about how medical care was delivered. There was little comment on the 'validity' of so-called scientific biomedicine. This more fundamental analysis of medicine emerged in a series of studies that emphasized less the political/economic ascendancy of medicine and more its cognitive triumph. Nevertheless, the medicalization thesis has proved an important consideration in understanding the ever-increasing demands for more health-care provision.

Medical Knowledge

In 1972, Johnson published a short monograph entitled *Professions and Power* in which he described three historical phases of professional organization, namely, patronage, collegiate, and mediated (Johnson 1972). The basis for this division was his quasi-Marxist analysis of the relationship between professions as producers (of a service) and their clients as consumers. In any transaction between producers and consumers there is always an irreducible element of uncer-

tainty, or indeterminacy as he called it, that both sides struggle to control. In the eighteenth century, patients largely controlled this indeterminacy because they tended to hold a higher social and economic position. Thus, the medical profession was organized under a system of patronage. During the nineteenth century, the medical profession seized control of the indeterminacy contained in medical knowledge as their work shifted to the new hospitals and their clients were drawn increasingly from lower social and economic strata. This allowed medicine to organize itself along self-governing collegiate lines. During the twentieth century, governments and other third parties (particularly insurance companies) have become more and more involved with the funding of health care; these agencies have begun to claim the right to control the indeterminacy factor by monitoring and influencing what doctors actually do in clinical situations. This represents the third phase of professional organization, namely third-party mediation. According to a study by Starr of the medical profession in the United States, over the last 200 years this process may have almost reached the point where medicine has lost its former pre-eminence as an autonomous self-governing body able to define the nature of illness, and he asks what should be done about it (Starr 1982).

For Johnson, the key to professional organization was control over knowledge. Four years later his colleague Jewson extended this analysis by examining the form of the knowledge itself under these different regimes of professional organization (Jewson 1976). Medical knowledge had long seemed inviolable to sociological investigation; after all, it was highly technical and came under the trusteeship of 'science' as a form of 'privileged' knowledge. However, the exclusivity and epistemological superiority of scientific knowledge was itself under siege from the sociology of science, and the way was soon open for sociologists to invade the citadel of medicine.

SOCIAL THEORIZING ABOUT MEDICAL THEORIES

In the English-speaking world at least, it was Freidson's *Profession of Medicine*, subtitled 'a study of the sociology of applied knowledge,' that initially opened up a more cognitive approach to the study of medicine (Freidson 1970). Freidson tried to show that what medicine had achieved was the legitimate right to define who was ill and who was not, and what was biologically abnormal and what was normal. He also claimed that 'illness may or may not be based in biological reality, but it is always based in social reality.' Of course, this claim had resonance in Parsons' 20-year-old notion of the sick role that defined a social dimension for all illness. The strong implication that it was possible for illness to exist only in social reality, without any biological correlates, was also unexceptional in view of the rhetoric of the 1960s antipsychiatry movement: that was precisely their claim. Psychiatrists had used social judgements and not biological ones to identify/label mental illness (Sedgewick 1973).

However, there was also another more radical implication in Freidson's statement, namely that perhaps the biological reality of illness was actually irrelevant, and that it was possible to perceive all illnesses as social constructs. Such an argument appears counter-intuitive: illnesses, especially those that result in death, must be fundamentally biological in nature because individuals are fundamentally complex biological machines. On the other hand, perhaps the very claim of the fundamental nature of the physical and biological realms, particularly in its relation to human identity, was part of the problem that needed to be explained. At the very least, the essential medical distinction between normality and pathology could not be predicated in 'nature,' but must be dependent on social classification and judgement. This insight radically widened the possibilities for critically evaluating medicine.

During the early postwar years a new branch of sociology emerged that took scientific knowledge as its object of study. At first, it concentrated on identifying those social factors that influenced the timing and appearance of new scientific knowledge, but this approach was then transformed by the publication of Kuhn's *The Structure of Scientific Revolutions* in 1962 (Kuhn 1962). Kuhn argued that it was possible for social scientists to examine the internal cognitive structure of scientific knowledge. A decade or so later this insight began to be applied to medical knowledge.

Adopting a Marxist theoretical framework, Jewson examined the 'social forces of production' of medical knowledge (Jewson 1976). He suggested that the three phases of professional control, as identified by his colleague Johnson, could be used to explain the form of medical knowledge that emerged. First, under patronage, or bedside medicine, as Jewson referred to it, the patient controlled the relationship so that medical practice was primarily based on the patient's view as expressed through symptoms. It was therefore the client's view of the world, based on detailed recounting and classification of symptoms, that was embodied in late eighteenth century medical knowledge.

With the advent of a collegiate system of professional control, a regime of hospital medicine came to dominate. Patient's views, as expressed through symptoms, were then subordinated to the doctor's perspective on illness that was informed by pathology. A specific pathological lesion hidden within the body became the locus of illness, not the capricious movement of obscure symptoms. This meant that the patient had to defer to the doctor's knowledge of the true nature of illness that occurred beyond immediate lay perception. Thus, the relative relationship of activity and passivity between doctor and patient produced a system of medical knowledge in the form of pathological medicine or biomedicine – with its concomitant clinical examinations and autopsies – which, in its turn, reproduced the particular form of the doctor–patient relationship characterized by a subservient patient. According to Jewson, this process was further extended in the late nineteenth and early twentieth centuries by the increasing reliance on laboratory medicine, in which the 'sick man' became even further divorced from the immediate reality of his illness.

Jewson's account of the shifts in medical knowledge described an increasing alienation of the patient from her own illness through the imposition of the medical intermediary. His work thus belongs to that humanist (and at times Marxist) trend in medical sociology which has seen itself struggling for patients' rights in the face of medical domination. However, in parallel with this exposure of medical knowledge as both the product and producer of alienation, a different theoretical tradition proposed an alternative reading of the nature of medical knowledge. Foucault's *Birth of the Clinic*, first published in 1963 (Foucault 1963) (but long in translation and even longer in recognition), also explained the emergence of biomedicine, or the 'clinic' as he called it, at the end of the eighteenth century, but here the analysis (coupled with his later writing) portrayed not a negative alienating force but a creative one.

The fundamental difference between the Marxist and Foucautian perspectives lies in their views of the nature and identity of the individual. For Marx, human nature and identity (and presumably the human body) is a historical given. It is different modes of production that imprint themselves on those same bodies/identities and, as with biomedicine, objectify and alienate. For Foucault, however, there is no prior identity or body. Rather the processes of objectification as represented by biomedicine serve to construct the very nature of the body. In this sense, the current anatomical reading of the body is simply one way, neither the first nor the last, of making the body legible.

In this way, Foucault's work can be used to explore the emergence of the current dominant biomedical model that reduces illness to an intracorporal biological lesion. The disciplinary mechanism of power/surveillance, which Foucault contended has pervaded Western society since the end of the eighteenth century, can be used as a method of explaining the emergence of various facets of modern medical practice, particularly the hospital and autopsies and the clinical examination. These techniques were used in the nineteenth century to 'discover' the human body, and can be seen in the twentieth century as being used to construct ('discover') the human mind and social relations through analysis of patient's talk and relationships (Armstrong 1983). These techniques further extend surveillance to everyone through the monitoring of 'risk' status in total populations (Armstrong 1995; Arney and Bergen 1982). In this sense, the fundamental building blocks of the biomedical model are revealed to be cultural artefacts (Young 1995) and biomedicine, above all else, a social activity.

Taking its cue from the sociology of knowledge, the more recent forms of social theorizing treat biomedical theories as simply another form of knowledge, as a descriptive language for constructing what is held to exist. Becoming a doctor involves internalizing this descriptive language and then imposing it in clinical practice (Atkinson 1981). Because of its privileged status, this biomedical knowledge has therefore come to define and constitute the very nature of health and illness in modern society. In this way, exploration of biomedical theory opens up the possibility of fundamental theorizing about health and illness.

Social Theorizing About Social Theorizing...

Just as biomedical theories construct a reality about which social theorizing can engage, so social theorizing constructs a world that itself can be explored with a more reflexive perspective. There is a limited literature reflecting on theory (Gerhardt 1989; Scambler 1987), but it leaves considerable scope to develop, at a sort of metalevel, theories of theories. For example, the changes in social theorizing outlined in this chapter map not only a shifting conceptual framework for understanding health, illness, and the patient, but also successive reconstructions of those objects. There are several common 'patterns,' including the changing reality implied by successive theories of the nature of the patient (and to a lesser extent of the doctor) that have

shifted from positions of passivity and objectivity to ones of activity and subjectivity. Surely, social theorizing is not simply a passive activity in this process, monitoring the changes induced by forces beyond itself, but is an integral part of the process through which certain social objects are created. Did the concept of stigma not change the way that the disabled and handicapped were viewed, and in consequence the very experience of being in this social state? Did the emphasis on patient cognitions and experiences of illness not lead to the application of techniques, in research and in the clinic, that helped crystallize these very phenomena? A postmodern twist would suggest that social theory could become the material for further social theory in some virtual (and virtuous?) regression.

Conclusion

This chapter has attempted to provide a map of social theorizing about health and illness. A few conceptual roads have proved to be cul-de-sacs, many have emerged into important highways, and some of the most recent are little more than paths that need further exploration. Nevertheless, social theorizing in this area has proved fertile ground over the last few decades.

Any discussion of social theorizing in health and illness must necessarily draw boundaries around the topic. One such boundary is that which separates social theorizing about health and illness from social theorizing about other worlds, but these are not watertight compartments. Classical theorists such as Marx and Durkheim have been usefully deployed in the area of health and illness to further theoretical work, and some general conceptual schemata such as labelling have passed smoothly across the divide. Particular mention must also be made of the heterogeneous field of feminist theory and feminist writing that has had an important impact on almost all of the theoretical areas described above. In part, it has involved feminist theory simply using the health field as a suitable medium in which to develop and apply theory (Martin, 1987); in part it has been the importation and incorporation of feminist theory into social theorizing about health and illness (Lupton 1994; Stacey 1988).

Movement of theory in the opposite direction has been less noticeable. The reason why is given by the underlying thesis of this chapter: social theorizing has grown in the shadow of biomedicine and for much of its history has been tied to the core assumptions of that paradigm. It is only when it develops theoretical positions that transcend medicine will its creative output become more transferable.

In focussing on the different strands of social theorizing in health and illness, this chapter has perforce ignored the vast number of influential studies that have produced important empirical findings. It has also ignored the complex and fruitful relationship between theory and method. Arguably, the rise of qualitative methodologies over the last two decades has changed the form of social theorizing in that inductive processes rarely lead to high-level theory. Indeed, much of the output from qualitative research can only be described as descriptive, and at best offers only low-level theoretical understanding. This, of itself, would not be a problem if one study could build on the findings of another, but too often the 'field' simply produces another set of findings that produce yet another set of grounded concepts. Perhaps this proliferation of (conceptual) narratives is itself simply another component of the postmodern turn described above, but so long as theory remains constantly and deliberately grounded it impedes the development of the sort of social theorizing that is described in this chapter. This would be ironic, as it is theory that has provided in many different ways the facilitative framework that has enabled these empirical studies, both qualitative and quantitative, to become possible.

References

Ackerknecht, E. (1967) *Medicine at the Paris Hospital 1774–1848*. Baltimore: Johns Hopkins University Press.

Ajzen, I. (1985) 'From intention to actions: A theory of planned behaviour', in J. Kuhl and J. Beckman (eds), *Action-control: From Cognition to Behaviour*. Berlin: Springer-Verlag.

Anderson, R. and Bury, M. (eds) (1988) *Living with Chronic Illness*. Boston: Unwin Hyman.

Antonovsky, A. (1979) *Health, Stress and Coping: New Perspectives on Mental and Physical Well-Being*. San Francisco: Josey-Bass.

Armstrong, D. (1983) *Political Anatomy of the Body: Medical Knowledge in Britain in the Twentieth Century*. Cambridge: Cambridge University Press.

Armstrong, D. (1995) 'The rise of surveillance medicine', *Sociology of Health and Illness*, 17: 393–404.

Arney, W.R. and Bergen, B. J. (1982) *Medicine and the Management of Living: Taming the Last Great Beast*. Chicago: University of Chicago Press.

Atkinson, P. (1981) *The Clinical Experience: The Construction and Reconstruction of Medical Reality*. Farnborough: Gower.

Barker, D.J.P. (1992) *Fetal and Infant Origins of Adult Disease*. London: BMJ.

Becker, H.S. (1963) *Outsiders: Studies in the Sociology of Deviance*. London: Free Press.

Berkman, L.F. and Syme, S.L. (1979) 'Social networks, host resistance, and mortality: A nine year follow-up study of Alameda County residents', *American Journal of Epidemiology*, 109: 186–204.

Berlant, J.L. (1975) *Profession and Monopoly: A Study of Medicine in the United States and Great Britain*. Berkeley: University of California Press.

Blane, D., Brunner, E., and Wilkinson, R. (eds) (1996) *Health and Social Organization: Towards a Health Policy for the Twenty-First Century*. London: Routledge.

Blaxter, M. (1990) *Health and Lifestyles*. London: Routledge.

Brown, G.W. and Harris, T. (1978) *Social Origins of Depression: A Study of Psychiatric Disorder in Women*. London: Tavistock.

Carr-Saunders, A.M. and Wilson, P.A. (1933) *The Professions*. Oxford: Oxford University Press.

Conrad, P. and Schneider, J.W. (1980) *Deviance and Medicalisation: From Badness to Sickness*. St Louis: Mosby.

Dohrenwend, B.S. and Dohrenwend, B.P. (eds) (1981) *Stressful Life Events and their Context*. New York: Prodist.

Doyal, L. (1979) *The Political Economy of Health*. London: Pluto Press.

Durkheim, E. (1933) *The Division of Labour in Society*. New York: Macmillan.

Durkheim, E. (1952) *Suicide: A Study in Sociology*. London: Routledge and Kegan Paul.

Engel, G.L. (1977) 'The need for a new medical model: A challenge for biomedicine', *Science*, 196: 129–34.

Figlio, K. (1987) 'The lost subject of medical sociology', in Scambler, G. (ed.), *Sociological Theory and Medical Sociology*. London: Routledge.

Fishbein, M. (1967) 'Attitude and the prediction of behaviour', in M. Fishbein (ed.), *Readings in Attitude Theory and Measurement*. New York: Wiley.

Fitzpatrick, R. et al. (1984) *The Experience of Illness*. London: Tavistock.

Foucault, M. (1963) *The Birth of the Clinic: An Archaeology of Medical Perception*. London: Tavistock.

Freidson, E. (1970) *Profession of Medicine*. New York: Dodd Mead.

Gerhardt, U. (1989) *Ideas about Illness: An Intellectual and Political History of Medical Sociology*. London: Macmillan.

Goffman, E. (1961) *Asylums: Essays on the Social Situation of Mental Patients and other Inmates*. London: Penguin.

Goffman, E. (1963) *Stigma: Notes on the Management of Spoiled Identity*. London: Penguin.

Goode, W.J. (1960) 'Encroachment, charlatanism and the emerging profession: Psychiatry, sociology and medicine', *American Sociological Review*, 25: 902–14.

Haug, M. (1988) 'A re-examination of the hypothesis of deprofessionalization', *Milbank Quarterly*, Suppl. 2: 48–56.

Helman, C. (1978) '"Feed a cold, starve a fever" – folk models of infection in an English suburban community and their relation to medical treatment', *Culture Medicine and Psychiatry*, 2: 107–37.

Henderson, S.A. (1980) 'A development in social psychiatry: The systematic study of social bonds', *Journal of Nervous and Mental Diseases*, 168: 63–9.

Herzlich, C. (1973) *Health and Illness*. London: Academic Press.

Higgins, P.C. (1980) *Outsiders in a Hearing World: A Sociology of Deafness*. London: Sage.

Illich, I. (1975) *Medical Nemesis*. London: Caldar Boyars.

Jewson, N.K. (1976) 'Disappearance of the sick-man from medical cosmologies, 1770–1870', *Sociology*, 10(2): 25–44.

Johnson, T.J. (1972) *Professions and Power*. London: Macmillan.

Kleinman, A. (1980) *Patients and Healers in the Context of Culture*. Berkeley: University of California Press.

Koos, E. (1954) *The Health of Regionsville: What the People Felt and Did About it*. New York: Columbia University Press.

Kuhn, T.S. (1962) *The Structure of Scientific Revolutions*. Chicago: University of Chicago Press.

Larson, M. (1977) *The Rise of Professionalism*. Berkeley: University of California Press.

Leighton, D.C, Harding, J.S, Macklin, D.B. et al. (1963). *The Character of Danger*. New York: Basic Books.

Lemert, E. (1967) *Human Deviance, Social Problems and Social Control*. Hemel Hempstead: Prentice Hall.

Ley, P. (1988) *Communicating with Patients*. London: Croom Helm.

Lupton, D. (1994) *Medicine as Culture*. London: Sage.

Lupton, D. (1997) 'Psychoanalytic sociology and the medical encounter', *Sociology of Health and Illness*, 19: 561–79.

Martin, E. (1987) *The Woman in the Body*. Milton Keynes: Open University Press.

McKeown, T. (1979) *The Role of Medicine*. Oxford: Blackwell.

Mechanic, D. (1962) 'The concept of illness behaviour', *Journal of Chronic Diseases*, 15: 189–94.

Mechanic, D. and Volkart, E.H. (1960) 'Illness behaviour and medical diagnosis', *Journal of Health and Human Behaviour*, 1: 86–94.

Navarro, V. (1976) *Medicine under Capitalism*. New York: Prodist.

Parry, N. and Parry, J. (1976) *The Rise of the Medical Profession*. London: Croom Helm.

Parsons, T. (1951) *The Social System*. New York: Free Press.

Rose, A.M. (ed.) (1962) *Human Behaviour and Social Processes: An Interactionist Approach*. London: Routledge and Kegan Paul.

Rosenstock, I.M. (1965) 'Why people use health services', *Millbank Memorial Fund Quarterly*, 44: 95.

Scambler, G. (ed.) (1987) *Sociological Theory and Medical Sociology*. London: Tavistock.

Scambler, S. and Hopkins, A. (1986) 'Being epileptic: Coming to terms with stigma', *Sociology of Health and Illness*, 8: 26–43.

Schwarzer, R. (1992) 'Self-efficacy in the adoption and maintenance of health behaviours: Theoretical approaches and a new model', in R. Schwarzer (ed.), *Self-Efficacy: Thought Control of Action*. Washington, DC: Hemisphere.

Scott, R.A. (1969) *The Making of Blind Men*. London: Russell Sage.

Sedgewick, P. (1973) 'Mental illness *is* illness', *Salmagundi*, 20: 196–224.

Stacey, M. (1988) *The Sociology of Health and Healing*. London: Unwin Hyman.

Starr, P. (1982) *The Social Transformation of American Medicine*. New York: Basic Books.

Straus, R. (1957) 'The nature and status of medical sociology', *American Sociological Review*, 22: 200–4.

Tuckett, D. et al. (1985) *Meetings Between Experts: An Approach to Sharing Ideas in Medical Consultations*. London: Tavistock.

WHO (1980) *International Classification of Impairments, Disabilities and Handicaps*, Geneva: WHO.

Wilensky, H. (1964) 'The professionalisation of everyone', *American Journal of Sociology*, LXX: 137–58.

Wilkinson, R.G. (1996) *Unhealthy Societies: The Afflictions of Inequality*. London: Routledge.

Wood, P. (1975) *Classification of Impairments and Handicap*. Geneva: World Health Organization.

Young, A. (1995) *The Harmony of Illusions*. Princeton: Princeton University Press.

Zola, I.K. (1972) 'Medicine as an institution of social control', *Sociological Review*, 20: 487–504.

Zola, I.K. (1973) 'Pathways to the doctor: From person to patient', *Social Science and Medicine*, 7: 677–89.

1.3

Classification and Process in Sociomedical Understanding: Towards a Multilevel View of Sociomedical Methodology

ROBERT A. RUBINSTEIN, SUSAN C. SCRIMSHAW,
AND SUZANNE E. MORRISSEY

INTRODUCTION

The various social sciences that contribute to the understanding of health, illness, and health systems employ a variety of research methodologies. In this chapter we distinguish between methodology and methods. By methods, we mean the particular data collection tools – such as surveys, interviews, observations, and the like – and the techniques of data analysis – such as statistical manipulations, content analysis, or coding schemes. Methodology, in contrast, is concerned with the epistemological and ontological foundations of inquiry. Our main concern in this chapter is with methodology.

Methodologies include not only the methods used for data collection and ways of manipulating these data for analysis, but also their underlying theoretical and philosophical assumptions. Each discipline, such as sociology, anthropology, psychology, economics, and epidemiology, has its own favorite array of methods, which are the subject of debate, even within the discipline. Across disciplines, there has been a historical misunderstanding, and sometimes disrespect, regarding the methods of other fields, yet at the same time, disciplines borrow methods from each other, sometimes without recognizing their similarity to methods which they claim to disparage.

Increasingly, we see a convergence and combination of methods among the various social sciences. Shared theoretical approaches or philosophical commitments that underlie the methodologies do not always accompany this convergence in data collection and analysis strategies. In this chapter we explore the importance and implications of going beyond a multimethod strategy to take a multilevel and theoretically holistic approach towards sociomedical research, and relate the increasingly sophisticated methods of research that seeks a better understanding of the complex relationships between health, illness, and healing (which we call sociomedical research) to such an imperative. In this regard, sociomedical inquiry focuses not only on the biological, organic correlates of health and illness, but also on the roles played by social and cultural factors for the triggering of the onset of disease or for the role played by these factors in increasing the susceptibility of individuals and populations to disease.

We define holistic as an approach that takes the broader context into account. This includes the wider settings of both space and time. For example, an observed health system should be seen in the context of a wider community and culture, and the requirements of that health system may vary with seasonal variations in disease entities as well. We define multilevel in terms of the unit of analysis. For instance, health outcomes may be dependent on a combination of individual factors, provider behaviors, family setting, cultural factors, and the community context.

We take for granted that convergent validation from a single level of systemic organization, while serving well efforts to increase the sophistication of methods in sociomedical research, is an inadequate basis for the future development of sociomedical research. We discuss some of the continuities that our multilevel view has with previous work, mainly in anthropology. Then we discuss some cultural characteristics upon which sociomedical research has been based, and we suggest that these are in need of revision. Particular attention is paid to the role of expert knowledge, the valuing of technology, and the discounting of reports of experience.

Recent Historical Context

Problematic situations can only be dealt with effectively once they have been defined as problems (Rubinstein 1984; Rubinstein et al. 1984). Problematic situations are situations that ordinary persons find troublesome and for which they often seek help. For professional researchers, problematic situations are constituted by data that depart from the expected, anomalous results. Such anomalous results may be dismissed or taken as a site for profitable investigation (Kuhn 1970; Rubinstein et al. 1984; Ward and Werner 1984).

In most areas relying on specialized knowledge, the ability to construct problems from the analysis of troublesome experience develops through practice (Argyris 1980; Schon 1983), and is codified, more or less formally, in rules of methodology and classification. The methods used by sociomedical researchers give them ways of construing physical, psychological, and other 'difficulties' as particular kinds of problems to be explored and understood. Sociomedical categories thus reduce people's problematic experiences to relatively familiar patterns to which our methods can be applied. These methods and approaches are increasingly recognized as culturally and socially situated (Freund and McGuire 1999; Romanucci-Ross et al. 1991). This has the effect of introducing a cultural bias, or ethnocentricity, in these approaches and their results. The value and utility of the information that results from their use depends in part on the congruence or conflict between the meaning and significance ascribed to them by people and practitioners (Kottak 1991; Romanucci-Ross 1991).

In the early post-World War II years, a schism developed within the sociomedical research community between those who applied methods based on hypothetico-deductive techniques grounded in positivist philosophies of science, and those who applied more inductively defined techniques based in alternative visions of science, such as pragmatism (Hollis 1994; Schweizer 1998). Because these differences involved competition for resources and also for the definition of authoritative, useful knowledge, for some time these two traditions developed in antagonistic relation to one another (Diesing 1991). This antagonism was often expressed as a contest between qualitative and quantitative approaches to methods. For some time, hypothetico-deductive – quantitative – approaches achieved a certain dominance and set the terms of debates about sociomedical methods (Hempel 1965; Kuipers 1996; Schweizer 1998).

During the past two or three decades, qualitative methods associated with humanist approaches in the social sciences have gained authority as objectivity in science has been called into question and the implications contingent on scientific knowledge have been explored (Latour 1987). This exploration has created a greater recognition that the knowledge claims that result from hypothetico-deductive and inductive approaches are both contingent and incomplete. Considerable suspicion remains among many researchers about the usefulness of the representations produced by each method. Nonetheless, the epistemological difficulties shared by these approaches have resulted in a greater willingness among researchers to seek ways to reconcile them. The most obvious fruit of this rapprochement has been an increase in efforts to integrate qualitative and quantitative research methods (Brewer and Collins 1981; Janes et al. 1986; Scrimshaw 1990).

Perhaps the most basic principle underlying these efforts is the view that methods ought to increase the validity and reliability of our knowledge by using multiple measures of a phenomenon (Jenkins and Howard 1992; Pelto and Pelto 1996). The high value placed on this convergent validation, or triangulation, has been one area where qualitative and quantitative approaches have sought common ground.

Phenomena of interest to sociomedical researchers might be found on any of a number of levels of systemic organization (Figure 1). At the macrolevel, health policy researchers might find their attention directed to the societywide, behavioral artifacts of symbolically encoded information, while at the microlevel sociomedical researchers might focus on individual biological aspects of illness and disease. Sociomedical research typically involves the use

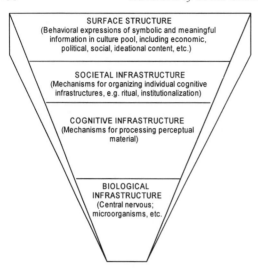

Figure 1   *Levels of systemic organization (after Laughlin and Brady, 1978)*

of multiple methods (measures or interpretive strategies) to achieve some form of convergent validation. In this chapter we propose that, while useful, such strategies are incomplete.

As we look toward the future, methods must, in addition to requiring convergent validation, also accommodate different levels of analysis. This is especially true in an era when the contingent nature of knowledge is increasingly evident. One general methodological position consistent with this view is the 'rule of minimal inclusion,' which states that an adequate account of behavior must include 'any and all levels of systemic organization efficiently present in the interaction between the system operating and the environment of that system. The rule of minimal inclusion will require the theoretical consideration of systemic levels at least one step below and one step above the level or levels appropriate to the phenomenon being explained' (Rubinstein et al. 1984: 93).

Multilevel Analysis and Anthropological Holism

It is worth noting that the valuing of multiple levels of organization in sociomedical research has a noble heritage. The founding of contemporary epidemiology is traced to John Snow's investigation of cholera in London. In spirit, if not by intentional design, the character of Snow's investigation of the complex relationships between social behavior and water, and

his supposition that fecal contamination played a role in the spread of the disease were multi-leveled. His famous 1854 removal of the Broad Street pump handle depended upon an understanding of the interactions of person, place, and time to conclude that individuals exposed to a single water pump on Broad Street were at far greater risk of infection than were others (Watts 1997). Despite this beginning, epidemiological work soon became less concerned with integrating multiple levels. Thus, in the face of the post-War dominance of hypothetico-deductive research, holism was found mainly in anthropological work.

Holism refers to the methodological and epistemological view that the proper understanding of human social behavior depends upon integrating information from all sectors of society and from all levels of empirical investigation relevant to the human experience.

Until about twenty-five years ago, the goal of 'traditional' ethnographic research in anthropology was to describe the social life and history of small well-bounded societies (Leach 1954; Malinowski 1992; Richards 1956). Ethnographers were likely to look for information from a variety of levels of organization in order to understand the people with whom they worked. Thus, anthropologists sought explanations that treated human biological, social, and cultural life as an integrated whole. Anthropologists came to strongly value *holistic* research. In fact, many people saw anthropology's unique contribution to the understanding of the human condition to be precisely in its application of a holistic perspective (Tax et al. 1953). In comparison with such earlier anthropological work, the rule of minimal inclusion is, perhaps, unremarkable. While it is clearly holistic in spirit, because it allows researchers to truncate their inquiry by considering just three levels of organization, the rule of minimal inclusion might be unacceptable to some holists (Phillips 1976).

During the past two decades, however, the context in which anthropological work is carried out has changed dramatically (Behar and Gordon 1995; Fox 1991; Gupta and Ferguson 1997; Kondo 1990). As a result there is increased anthropological concern with issues that derive from deductive hypothesis testing research design. This is an important development in the growth of the discipline (Bernard 1994; Pelto and Pelto 1996). Yet, as anthropologists have sought to adapt to the changing environment, the process of continuing inductive–deductive alternation that characterizes traditional ethnographic fieldwork, and from which the perspective of anthropological holism grew, has begun to erode in the face of specialization and the development of professionally adaptive niches such as medical anthropology.

As anthropologists have joined other socio-medical researchers in research that seeks to answer practical questions – 'problem oriented research' – there has been a discernible shift in the kinds of methods anthropologists report using (Gorman 1986; Lurie et al. 1993; Rubinstein and Perloff 1986). More frequently than before, for instance, anthropologists report research that relies on only one or a few indices of the phenomenon that they are investigating, whether these be increasingly well-bounded quantitative measures or reflexive analytical frameworks. Also reported are more results based on short-term ethnographic field-work (Manderson and Aaby 1992; Scrimshaw 1992; Scrimshaw and Gleason 1992; Zambrana et al. 1997a), or studies that focus so tightly on particular aspects of social life that other sources of data are lost or ignored (Chambers 1985; McGuire 1997; Ward and Werner 1984). As anthropological methods have converged with those more standard in sociomedical research, the commitment to holism has seemed to fade. There is some irony in this, as it was the anthropological penchant for holism that brought the work of early medical anthropologists to the notice of other sociomedical researchers (Paul 1955). It should be noted, however, that more tightly focused studies need not completely exclude holism. One important feature of anthropological holism is to remain alert to factors or influences that were not within the original scope of data to be collected, and to include these in the research if they seem important to the problem at hand. This, even a focused study, can change and expand in response to the researchers' willingness and ability to take the broad view. This change in the data to be collected, and sometimes in the view from which questions are asked and observations are made as the study progresses, is precisely what makes traditional quantitative researchers so nervous about qualitative work. It is also what helps to retain holism, because the researcher is continually open to the broadest possible influences on the phenomenon under investigation.

HOLISM AND 'CONVERGENT VALIDITY'

Despite its having faded in prominence, the holistic perspective remains in our view one of the most valuable developments in efforts to understanding the human condition. It is a perspective that is lamentably lacking from problem-oriented sociomedical research (Hall 1982; Penfold and Walker 1983; Simon 1983), despite the fact that it is precisely in the intersection of biological, psychological, and social aspects of health and illness that it might most naturally be found. To some degree, sociomedical research has drifted away from holism because such a move enabled well-bounded studies that could form the basis upon which claims for funding and other resources could rest, and because of the social organization of the grant-review process which disburses research support.

The resulting reward structure for research works against the kind of thoughtful interdisciplinary research required for holistic investigation. For instance, extensive publication records are taken as indications that a researcher is capable and 'productive,' which in turn encourages researchers to go to press with 'the least publishable bit' rather than with fuller and more integrative treatments of their topic. Also, the pressure for productivity frequently constrains researchers to report positive results – publication of null or negative results, even when such results might provide interesting clues about the dynamics of sociomedical phenomena, are discouraged, if only informally.

Indeed, before researchers face decisions about publication they must first find support for their research. In this regard they face challenges that also make holism in sociomedical research more difficult to achieve. For instance, grant proposals are directed to specialized review sections that rate highly work within the particular disciplinary paradigms of the members. Proposals that seek to integrate theory or methods from a number of disciplines thus fall between the institutional arrangements of the review process. Funding agencies, often in response to the public or boards of directors, shift their funding emphases periodically in order to stay on the 'cutting edge' of sociomedical knowledge. This allows the funding agencies to claim that they are pushing the development of knowledge. Wittingly or not, researchers respond to these 'fads and fashions' by altering their research, even, perhaps, before they have fully investigated the earlier problems upon which their work focused (Lane and Rubinstein 1996b).

One of the values of the holistic perspective is the recognition that scientific and technical knowledge are understood to be always incomplete, and thus fallible (Argyris 1980; Brewer and Collins 1981; Cantril 1967; Pacey 1983; Rubinstein et al. 1984; Schon 1983; Simon 1983). Because specialized knowledge is always constructed on the basis of incomplete information about phenomena, it must always be seen as provisional.

The contingency of knowledge is, of course, a fundamental insight of other perspectives that also emphasize the provisional nature and fallibility of our knowledge of the world. This principle is found, for instance, in the American Pragmatism of Peirce (Almeder 1980; Rescher 1978) and James (1978), in the skeptical philosophy of David Hume (Popper 1962; Salmon 1967), and in contemporary evolutionary epistemology (Brewer and Collins 1981; Campbell 1973, 1974). Given these diverse sources, the provisional nature and the fallibility of knowledge deserve to be taken most seriously.

Some of the methodological implications of this have been set out by epistemologists working in the tradition of 'evolutionary epistemology,' or 'critical hypothetical realism' (Campbell 1973; Naroll and Cohen 1973; Pinxten 1981; Rubinstein et al. 1984). This work emphasizes that because each way of collecting data carries a particular perspective, it is important to use multiple measures to assess a phenomenon. Problem-oriented work is equally limited in its perspective, and requires multiple disciplinary perspectives to be used if 'tunnel vision' (Pacey 1983) is to be avoided.

For instance, David Hufford (1982a) made a comprehensive review of studies of the 'sleep disorder' characterized by nightmare and paralysis and an incubus experience – which Hufford calls the Old Hag experience. Hufford shows that the accounts offered by researchers from each of the disciplines that studied the Old Hag experience are all characterized by a kind of tunnel vision. Thus, anthropologists, sociologists, and medical folklorists ascribe it to tradition, treating the phenomenon as culture-bound artifact. Sleep researchers attempt to characterize the phenomenon as a kind of sleep disorder associated with unusual patterns of REM sleep, and psychiatrists as a mental illness. None of the researchers are able to account fully for the phenomenology of the Old Hag experience, yet as Hufford (1982a: 116) points out, the effect of their disciplinary efforts 'has been to explain the phenomenon away while discouraging the development of a thorough description of it.'

In sociomedical research the prescription for avoiding tunnel vision has been to pursue a strategy of 'convergent validation' (Campbell and Fiske 1959) and 'multiple iteration' (Werner and Campbell 1973), and its proponents have been explicit in arguing that it is important to consider as legitimate many different 'ways of knowing' (Balshem 1993; Gifford 1986; Lieberson 1992).

Our call for multilevel research designs adds to these two methodological principles the requirement that the convergent validation be made from multiple levels. This is a necessary addition because precisely what aspects of the phenomena under study are salient to an investigation depend upon how the problem being investigated is framed (Albrecht 1989: 73; Diez-Roux 1998; Fienberg and Tanur 1989; Rubinstein et al. 1984; Schon 1983). Not only is our knowledge contingent because each of our measures provides only partial information (as critical hypothetical realism emphasizes), or because particular professional lore provides a limited range of solutions, but because, as Whitehead (1960) pointed out, the world is constructed of processes in an infinite concatenation of systems within systems. At any given time our models will capture only a small portion of reality.

Even if a phenomenon is well described with a variety of measures that come from a single-level, maintaining the authority of that single-level account requires very strong, and ultimately indefensible, 'as if' clauses in our explanations of social behavior (Humphrey 1984; Simon 1983). Convergent validation on a single level does not guarantee that the result is not fundamentally provisional. Accounts of phenomena are useful only when they capture those levels that are required to answer a particular set of questions (Holland 1987). By failing to recognize their essential multilevel nature, we are more likely to assume that the phenomena of concern are themselves stable over time, rather than to ask if the apparent stability is an artifact of the techniques of analysis used.

In addition to the critical hypothetical realist analysis which emphasizes that our knowledge is fallible because the ways of knowing with which we gather our data access only particular perspectives on reality, our knowledge is also tentative because every phenomenon has multilevel aspects, differing combinations of which are important for resolving different questions. The fluidity introduced by multiple levels of organization is as important for problem-defining sociomedical research as it is for research in general (Hufford 1982a, 1982b). Adequate problem-defining work must meet at least three essential methodological principles: (1) multiple measures, (2) multiple iterations, and (3) multiple levels in analysis.

Anyone recognizing the complex nature of sociomedical phenomena ought to concur with the intuitive requirements for complexity and multilevel accounts just outlined. However, it remains to specify how to decide which levels of organization need to be considered. It is inappropriate to propose decision rules for making that judgement at this time because these must be developed in the light of much more experience with research that explicitly attempts to meet this intuitive model of explanatory adequacy. There are, however, some 'basic research' analyses that can be drawn on for guidance, especially the analysis of ritual by d'Aquili et al. (1979), that of societal responses to resource deprivation by Laughlin and Brady (1978), and the analysis by Laughlin et al. (1990) of the biological basis of cognition, all of which provide empirical applications of the rule of minimal inclusion. However, there are few other studies that explicitly follow this rule. Moreover, the number of levels of organization that must be considered will vary depending upon the research question and the problem being considered.

In one project, induced abortion in Ecuador was studied by following individual women as they sought abortions, by conducting ethnographic work with women in sixty-five families on topics that included abortion, by survey research in the same community where more than 3000 women were interviewed on topics that included their views and experience regarding abortion, by observations of local family planning clinics, and by interviews with policy makers at the local and national level. The opposition of policy makers to abortion carried over into barriers to contraception, which translated into increased proportions of pregnancies terminating in induced abortions as the infant mortality rates declined (Scrimshaw 1985). In this case, many levels ranging from the individual to the national contributed to the understanding of the forces driving up the rates of induced abortion.

The rule of minimal inclusion instructs the researcher to examine factors on several levels of organization, and to learn how these factors interact within and between levels. At the very least, when we choose to work with factors and processes on only one level it is incumbent on us to ensure that the accounts we offer of that level are compatible with what is known of factors and processes operating on other levels.

Two Views of Sociomedical Categories

The process of converting observed evidence into named, understood categories of experience is at the heart of sociomedical research. For example, the *evidence* might consist of data obtained from examining a patient; the *analytic categories* in this case are conceptual entities that identify or explain constellations of experience that have been 'problematized' by sociomedical researchers. Sociomedical categories define the kinds of inferential processes or intervention strategies to which the evidence is referred, but the ontological and epistemological statuses of

sociomedical categories are open questions. As a result, particular sociomedical categories are subject to controversy because they can be interpreted from at least two contrasting perspectives.

One view holds that sociomedical categories provide the basis for the objective classification of human health behavioral activity and experience, thus allowing us to tell what functioning falls outside of the range of normal activity. In addition, this view holds that these categories are natural categories whose boundaries exist, only needing to be discovered. On this first view, sociomedical categories provide us with names for objectively identified real entities the functioning of which deviates from the norm.

A second view holds that sociomedical categories consist of culturally and socially grounded characterizations of human health behavioral activity and experience as healthy or unhealthy, normal or not. In addition, this view holds that the boundaries of sociomedical categories are always the result of consensual agreement and thus are to some degree socially constructed.

The first view takes a nonnormative–realist position: sociomedical categories define ontologically real, epistemologically neutral entities. In contrast, the second view describes a pragmatist–nominalist position: sociomedical categories are socially constructed and epistemologically relative classifications.

Following the first view, researchers spend considerable time and material resources devising sophisticated methods for sociomedical research that systematize their specialized knowledge. Based on the assumption that sociomedical categories index natural processes, each of these methods seeks to define what are important human health behavioral activities, and seeks to do so based on the convergent validation of social phenomena.

In contrast, the literatures of medical sociology and anthropology contain many case studies that support the latter, pragmatist–nominalist, position. This literature makes it clear that in practice sociomedical categories are used as explanatory systems for dealing with people's difficulties, and that this introduces biases that limit the types of data researchers will collect and consider when attempting to make sense of people's complaints.

Sociomedical categories get formed and reformed through processes of social construction that are themselves responsive to the social and cultural processes in the context of which that construction takes place (Conrad and Schneider 1980; Feinstein 1973a, 1973b, 1974; Hufford 1985; Lieberson 1985; Penfold and Walker 1983). Moreover, it is clear that the processes of social construction and relativization apply equally to 'strictly physical' difficulties – such as 'cerebral arteriosclerosis' (Feinstein 1974), 'neurasthenia' (Sicherman 1977), 'blindness' (Scott 1969), or 'dwarfism' (Ablon 1984) – as they do to psychological difficulties – such as 'depression' (Penfold and Walker 1983), 'personality disorders' (Kaplan 1983), or 'schizophrenia.'

Both approaches to sociomedical categories acknowledge that to deal effectively with people's difficulties they must be able to classify them according to some system, and thereby to understand problematic processes as problems. The point of debate between advocates of each view focuses on the status granted to those problems, which is important because it has implications for sociomedical research practice. On the one hand, the normative–realist interpretation of sociomedical categories leads to a world view the hallmarks of which are reliance on technology for 'objective' problem assessment, an emphasis on the role of expert knowledge, and a limited acceptance of the authenticity of people's reports of their experience. On the other hand, the pragmatist–nominalist approach supports a world view that sees technology as socially situated, expert knowledge as partial and tentative, and people's reports of their experience as authentic and important for problem construction. It is these, and other similar, features that form the cultural contexts of sociomedical research categories.

The Cultures of Sociomedical Research

The epistemological and ontological statuses accorded to sociomedical categories are important because they help to define the cultural context in which that sociomedical research practice is situated, and circumscribe what phenomena are researchable and why. While there is a considerable range among all practitioners, the realist view of sociomedical categories results from and supports a view of health care and behavior that is radically different from that underlying the pragmatist perspective. It is our view that the privileging realist views in the development of sociomedical research has had some untoward consequences. It is important to make explicit the consequences for sociomedical research of the dominance of realist views of research. We think this discussion suggests why it is especially important that sociomedical research be approached from multiple levels of analysis.

Here it may be useful to consider in a bit more depth one interesting example of these untoward effects of privileging a realist view of health and illness. An illustrative example is found in the search for the biological validation of 'hyperactivity,' and 'attention deficit' disorders. This untoward result occurs in the context of research that can be characterized by the application of multiple measures and multiple iteration – that is by convergent validation. About half-a-dozen different types of biological measures have been used to validate the 'disease.' As discussed below, the results have been equivocal – providing only tenuous support for the validation of a general difference between normal and troubled children, but not including specific support for subtypes like ADD and ADDH. Nonetheless, these research results are robust in indicating these nonspecific differences, and thus the clinical community continues to treat hyperactivity as though its status as a disease entity was well established. There have been five major approaches to the biological validation of hyperactivity as an entity. These are outlined below.

1 *Stimulant drugs manage hyperactivity.* Researchers have reasoned that if children who have been diagnosed as hyperactive respond to pharmacological therapy, this response is *prima facie* evidence that there is a physiological pathology underlying hyperactivity (Brown and Sleator 1979). In fact, treatment of hyperactive children with a stimulant is the therapy of choice for many clinicians, who in turn take it that hyperactivity is an objective, nonnormative disease. This is the case despite the fact that there is little clinical specificity in this response to drug therapy. Several studies report success using stimulant drug therapy to treat the entire spectrum of pediatric problems (Rutter 1983), and 'normal' children respond in ways that are similar to the responses of hyperactive children when they are administered stimulant drugs.

2 *Prenatal and perinatal difficulties are risk factors for hyperactivity.* Several investigators have tried to validate hyperactivity biologically by linking it to difficulties encountered during the pre- and perinatal periods. Some of these studies have demonstrated that such difficulties are related to early behavioral difficulties. However, it appears from the literature that these rapidly diminish in importance in relation to other factors in the environment, and that the influence of pre- and perinatal events on hyperactive behavior disappear by the diagnostically prescribed 'age of onset' of 3 years. In themselves, pre- and perinatal events do not

biologically validate hyperactivity. At best, pre- and perinatal measures might contribute to a multivariate notion of generalized risk, rather than to validating a specific disease entity.

3 *Abnormal neurological functioning and slow maturation accompany hyperactivity.* One position for biologically validating hyperactivity holds that maturation of hyperactive children lags behind that of their peers. Researchers following this view seek to validate hyperactivity by finding signs of abnormal neurological functioning (which they call 'soft signs') in these children. Confounding the usefulness of using soft signs to validate hyperactivity is that such signs occur among many children whose behavior and achievement is 'normal.' Moreover, the discovery of soft signs may have more to do with the interview context than with the child's physical condition (Collins 1981).

4 *Minor physical anomalies with hyperactivity.* Several researchers have proposed that the 'disease' of hyperactivity could be validated by finding minor physical anomalies in hyperactive children. While there is some evidence that children with anomalies do have more difficulties than children without, the relationship is a general one not specific to hyperactivity. Indeed screening for minor physical anomalies is not a particularly specific or useful indicator of hyperactivity.

5 *Genetic basis for hyperactivity.* Studies of the possible genetics of hyperactivity have not been successful in demonstrating a specific genetic link for hyperactivity.

Each of the approaches outlined above focuses on finding the biological pathology associated with the behaviors thought to represent hyperactivity, thus reducing the query to a single (biological) level. In so doing the category has been reified, an essentially multilevel process oversimplified, and the clinical community has developed a false sense that the identification of hyperactivity is actually very robust. In part this false sense has developed because many nonspecific data have been assembled from multiple biological measures to build up a consistent picture of differences between troubled and nonhyperactive children. Thus, despite a general lack of specificity in the biological findings, many clinicians and researchers conclude that hyperactivity is an independent entity. In this tradition, a recent advertisement proclaimed the new possibility of discovering this entity: 'Objective Evaluation of Attention Deficit Disorders in Just 8 minutes . . . the GDS changes subjective interpretation to objective, accurate analysis!' (Diagnostics 1984: 2).

Here we should consider (and for longer than 8 minutes!) Hufford's warning: 'Whenever a single theory or method is advanced as providing the complete explanation of a complex body of cultural or psychological data, we should be very skeptical' (Hufford 1982a: 172).

Another example of the problem of working with a single theory, method, or level can be found in the ongoing attempts to understand ethnic differences in pregnancy outcomes in the United States. In general, Latino women have better outcomes (unless they are from Puerto Rico) than do African–American women, and sometimes better than Caucasian women. Because Latino women have the least access to prenatal care (due in part to barriers created in relation to their immigration status), health officials and epidemiologists believed the better outcomes were suspect, and were due to poor data or women delivering at home or with midwives and concealing poor outcomes. We now know that positive pregnancy behavior (less smoking, drinking, and drugs, better diet, better social support) are important contributors to these better outcomes. This also explains why women from Mexico do better than women from Puerto Rico (Zambrana et al. 1996, 1997b). However, there is an additional biological factor of stress that is apparently mediated by better social support in the Latino women, and more 'environmental stress' (e.g., daily microinsults resulting from more overt racism) for African–American women. Thus, in addition to behavior during pregnancy, social–environmental factors appear to contribute to a biological process (Neter et al. 1995; Zambrana et al. 1997a, 1997b).

This is complicated by some possible genetic factors such as differences in susceptibility to diabetes or hypertension. This example underscores the need to include biological as well as social and behavioral factors in a complete analysis of complex problems.

The relationship between the status accorded to the sociomedical research procedures and the general culture within which this status is constructed is reflexive – the realist world view influences, and is influenced by, the uses to which sociomedical research is put. The underlying cultural assumption expressed through the realist approach to sociomedical categories is the belief that the problems are stable entities, including people's experience of their problematic situation. Thus, once discovered, problems are dealt with by the straightforward application of technical knowledge. This has several interrelated consequences for practice, three or four of which are highlighted below.

Set-Theoretic Metaphor

At the center of the dynamic system of meanings in which sociomedical research has been grounded is the belief that the difficulties dealt with by medical practitioners are a set of health behavioral activities, experiences, or physiological events. This 'set-theoretic metaphor' (Straight 1979) – which treats behavior as a set of discrete, stable 'things' to be discovered – allows researchers to assume that their job is to discover the elements of this set. Because this is a discovery process, not a process of evaluation and construction, this cultural assumption serves as a heuristic that allows researchers to carry out their work without reference to aspects of the problematic situation not included within their expert's technical knowledge. Moreover, this set-theoretic metaphor allows practitioners to assume a reductionist locus for causality and, by placing a premium on the internal elegance and parsimony of their theoretical systems, it pushes researchers to systematically oversimplify various asymmetries in the processes with which they deal, as for example when quantitative data are smoothed to exclude 'outliers,' or qualitative researchers take a narrow solipsistic reflective stance.

It is useful to recall that 'lay' and 'professional' understandings often differ. For example, in considering how various publics understood the risks associated with needle exchange programs, Lurie and his colleagues found that what people considered as relevant to calculating 'risk' varied depending on their position within the political, legal, or health professions, or the general population (Lurie et al. 1993). Such a finding is not unusual, as Mary Douglas and others have shown (Douglas and Wildavsky 1982; Ingham 1994).

All heuristics have biases (Piattelli-Palmarini 1994; Simon 1983; Wimsatt 1980). Among those introduced by the realist dominance of sociomedical research is the belief that the social structure of some settings (in this case, medical settings) allows us to take for granted the meanings of problematic (or other) activity. Contrary to this view, however, a number of researchers have shown that the meaning of human conduct is always 'established as a result of the conjoint adjustive responses of interacting and communicating individuals' (Maines 1977: 239).

Dominance of Expert Knowledge

In much of sociomedical research our expert knowledge is given a special status. In part, this follows from a view that expert knowledge

is stable and cumulative. In this view, 'professional practice is a process of problem *solving*. Problems of choice or decision are solved through the selection, from available means, of the one best suited to established ends' (Schon 1983: 39–40).

This view fosters a kind of 'scientism' that leads to an emphasis on dealing with problematic situations by means of technique alone. In the realist view, sociomedical categories are said to be objective and 'scientific.' This general perspective also underlies the realist view of the social arrangements of practice. Because the professional technology is taken to be neutral (or seeking ways to achieve neutrality), its use allows the introduction of the belief that problem definitions are objective, and that the technology for dealing with those objective problems is itself culturally neutral and value free (Martin 1987; Sibley 1995).

Following this conception of practice allows the practitioner to ignore the fact that the problem definition is negotiated, and that this negotiation process affects the ends to be achieved and the ways that these ends will be reached. The search for the single-level validation of research categories results in the use of just such an 'objective' technical fix.

The privileged position given to sociomedical categories, of the research methods developed to describe and account for these phenomena, and their derivative technology results in reinforcing the guild interests of sociomedical researchers (Balshem 1993; Gifford 1986; Lane 1994). By giving special, privileged status to information derived by sociomedical research methods, problematic situations are removed from public discussion and made into topics for expert treatment. The claim that these discussions are neutral and value-free elevates their status, and insulates the sociomedical research professionals from the consequences of their work.

Yet there is considerable debate about the status and adequacy of expert knowledge. In particular, there is considerable debate about how such knowledge develops. Does expert knowledge come from a smooth process, a process that consists of fits and starts, but in a structured fashion or does expert knowledge result from disjunctive and more haphazard processes (Diesing 1991)?

Discounted Experience

Treating the goal of sociomedical research as seeking to describe and account for health behavioral activities, and experiences and categories that are objectively discoverable entities, not only supports a privileged view of expert knowledge and of the uncritical use of research technology (as when researchers 'dredge' their data sets), it also supports discounting people's reports of their experience (Davis-Floyd 1996). We are not arguing that professional knowledge is wrong or that it is bad to use the research technologies developed in the past few decades, but that it is wrong to treat them as though they are not situated in cultural and social realities (Davis 1996; Fisher and Todd 1986; Sargent and Brettell 1996). To do so allows for the development of an artificially restricted sense of reality based upon narrow medical (academic) belief systems (Hufford 1982a, 1982b, 1983, 1985, 1987).

The tendency to discount people's reports of experience and to subordinate these to professional judgment is a general problem in social research. It is not that these reports are always accurate, but rather that it is wrong to dismiss them *a priori*. The critical issue is how to evaluate reports of experience in ways that equally respect expert and lay reports. Focusing on one kind of report to the exclusion of others always leads to the confounding of understanding rather than to its improvement (Newell 1973; Quine 1964).

Conclusion: Toward Multilevel Sociomedical Research

Whatever their perspective, all sociomedical studies incorporate particular views about the nature of the field of study. These assumptions include understandings about the characteristics of the phenomena under study and about how these phenomena ought to be investigated empirically. On one level, these assumptions privilege particular ways of making and supporting knowledge claims about social life and its relation to health and illness (Diesing 1991; Tesh 1988).

Sociomedical research yields judgments that are always based on incomplete information, and therefore will always be fallible. When we rely on multiple measures from a single level of organization, we can develop the mistaken impression that we have a better understanding of how to think about the problematic situations than we really do, and we develop a false sense of the adequacy of the resulting problem definitions. It is the development of models of analysis that is critical for future sociomedical research. Promising developments have been made in the difficult process of developing statistical and other analytic techniques of multilevel analysis. DiPrete and Forristal (1994) show that researchers have begun exploring ways to statistically analyze the links between levels of analysis. In

their review of these efforts, they show that micro- and macrolevel variables may usefully be incorporated into regression analysis. They also show how other forms of managing and interpreting multilevel data are being developed, including, for example, the elaboration of contingency table analysis. Such analytic developments promise to allow researchers to specify better the role of context and time in sociomedical research. It will also allow us to 'scaffold' (Rubinstein 1998) our understandings between micro- and macrolevel phenomena so that they are incorporated into a single interpretive framework.

Ignoring the importance of multilevel analysis as captured in the rule of minimal inclusion means that this information is going to be incomplete. Because we can only begin to deal with problematic situations once we have defined them as problems, the consequence of failing to strive to make our research multilevel in nature will mean that the definition of problems is always underspecified. It is important to understand that sociomedical research is a continuing process alternating between inductive and deductive work. Any research finding is a product of this process and is, in a fundamental sense, an artifact abstracted from ongoing activity. These research products can help to provide categories through which useful judgments about the world can be made, but the value of such categories depends upon their providing information that is useful for particular purposes. Therefore, it is also important to be conscious that, fundamentally, categories are reifications of processes and do not exist independently of the purposes for which they are developed. Sociomedical categories must always be treated as tentative and provisional.

Under these circumstances, Cantril's (1967: 93) advice that it is 'much more important to analyze crucial questions with whatever methods are available ... than ... to study trivial problems with precise methods' delivers a message that is of enduring importance.

What are the implications for sociomedical research of the view set forth in this chapter? Overall, as a research community we must refocus our efforts. If we are to make real progress in understanding health and illness during the next decades we need to focus not on tinkering with our methods so as to make them more sophisticated and reliable, but on directing our efforts towards improving our understanding of how better to comprehend and engage the dynamic, contingent nature of sociomedical phenomena.

The most important change we need to make in order to achieve this will be to find new metaphors for organizing and legitimating our work.

The recent history of methodological work in sociomedical research reaffirms the contingent and dynamic nature of our understanding of behavior, health, and illness. During the middle of the twentieth century, these contingencies temporarily receded in sociomedical research. As a result, the structuring metaphors of 'proof' and 'control' (as in disease control and eradication) came to dominate our efforts (Lane and Rubinstein 1995). Now it is clear that despite great technical advances and technical sophistication, our knowledge claims must be made with care; they must be made relative to the question at hand and made with a more modest tone. This is especially so because we now recognize that people's behavior and understanding associated with health and illness are always culturally situated (Lane and Rubinstein 1996a). To avoid committing the 'fallacy of detachable cultural descriptions' (Rubinstein 1992) and seeing homogeneity and stability instead of dynamic processes, it is essential that sociomedical researchers continue to learn from one another and draw upon the best their fields have to offer.

In order to achieve this, we must focus on realizing the integration of disciplines at the theoretical and methodological levels, not merely at the level of method and technique. This will require a re-evaluation of the kinds of data that ought to count as useful knowledge. That re-evaluation will necessarily place the treatment of meaning as equal to quantification (Scrimshaw 1990). This realignment is essential because it will lead to greater specificity in research and in our interpretation of sociomedical phenomena. It is, after all, on such interpretive acts that the quality and utility of our work ultimately depends.

Acknowledgments

We thank Gary Albrecht, Sandra D. Lane, Gretel Pelto, and H. Russell Bernard for their comments on earlier drafts of this chapter and Isabel Martinez for research assistance.

References

Ablon, J. (1984) *Little People in America: The Social Dimensions of Dwarfism*. New York: Praeger.

Albrecht, G. (1989) 'The intelligent design of AIDS research strategies', in L. Sechrest, H. Freeman, and A. Mulley (eds), *Health Services Research: A Focus on AIDS*. Washington, DC: NCHSR, pp. 67–74.

Almeder, R. (1980) *The Philosophy of Charles S. Pierce*. Totowa, NJ: Rowman and Littlefield.

Argyris, C. (1980) *Inner Contradictions of Rigorous Research*. New York: Academic Press.

Balshem, M. (1993) *Cancer in the Community: Class and Medical Authority*. Washington, DC: Smithsonian Institution Press.

Behar, R. and Gordon, D.A. (eds) (1995) *Women Writing Culture*. Berkeley: University of California Press.

Bernard, R. (1994) *Research Methods in Anthropology: Qualitative and Quantitative Approaches*. Thousand Oaks, CA: Sage.

Brewer, M. and Collins, B. (eds) (1981) *Scientific Inquiry in the Social Sciences*. San Francisco: Jossey-Bass.

Brown, R. and Sleator, E. (1979) 'Methylphenidate in hyperkinetic children: Differences in dose effects on impulsive behavior', *Pediatrics*, 64: 408–11.

Campbell, D. (1973) 'Natural selection as epistemology', in R. Naroll and R. Cohen (eds), *A Handbook of Method in Cultural Anthropology*. New York: Columbia University Press.

Campbell, D. (1974) 'Evolutionary epistemology', in P. A. Schilpp (ed.), *The Philosophy of Karl Popper*. La Salle, IL: Open Court Publishing Co.

Campbell, D. and Fiske, D. (1959) 'Convergent and discriminant validation by the multitrait–multimethod matrix', *Psychological Bulletin*, 56: 81–105.

Cantril, H. (1967) 'Sentio, ergo sum: "Motivation" Reconsidered', *Journal of Psychology*, 65: 91–107.

Chambers, E. (1985) *Applied Anthropology: A Practical Guide*. Englewood Cliffs, NJ: Prentice Hall.

Collins, B. (1981) 'Hyperactivity: Myth and entity', in M. Brewer and B. Collins (eds), *Scientific Inquiry and the Social Sciences*. San Francisco: Jossey Bass. pp. 385–412.

Conrad, P. and Schneider, J. (1980) *Deviance and Medicalization: From Badness to Sickness*. St. Louis: C.V. Mosby.

d'Aquili, E., Laughlin, C.D. and McManus, J. (1979) *The Spectrum of Ritual: A Biogenetic Structural Analysis*. New York: Columbia University Press.

Davis, D. (1996) 'The cultural constructions of pre-menstrual and menopause syndromes', in C. Sargent and C. Brettell (eds), *Gender and Health: An International Perspective*. Upper Saddle River, NJ: Prentice-Hall.

Davis-Floyd, R.E. (1996) 'The technocratic body and the organic body: Hegemony and heresy in women's birth choices', in C Sargent and C. Brettell (eds). *Gender and Health: An International Perspective*. Upper Saddle River, NJ: Prentice-Hall.

Diagnostics, C. (1984) *The Gordon Diagnostic System*. Golden, CO: Clinical Diagnostics.

Diesing, P. (1991) *How Does Social Science Work? Reflections on Practice*. Pittsburgh: University of Pittsburgh Press.

Diez-Roux, A. (1998) 'Bringing context back into epidemiology: Variables and fallacies in multilevel analysis', *American Journal of Public Health*, 88: 216–22.

DiPrete, T. and Forristal, J. (1994) 'Multilevel models: Methods and substance', *Annual Review of Sociology*, 20: 331–57.

Douglas, M. and Wildavsky, A. (1982) *Risk and Culture: An Essay on the Selection of Technical and Environmental Dangers*. Berkeley, CA: University of California Press.

Feinstein, A. (1973a) 'An analysis of diagnostic reasoning. 1. The domains and disorders of clinical macrobiology', *Yale Journal of Biology and Medicine*, 46: 212–32.

Feinstein, A. (1973b) 'An analysis of diagnostic reasoning. 2. The strategy of intermediate decisions', *Yale Journal of Biology and Medicine*, 46: 264–83.

Feinstein, A. (1974) 'An analysis of diagnostic reasoning. 3. The construction of clinical algorithms', *Yale Journal of Biology and Medicine*, 47: 5–32.

Fienberg, S. and Tanur, J. (1989) 'Combining cognitive and statistical approaches to survey design', *Science*, 243: 1017–22.

Fisher, S. and Todd, A.D. (eds) (1986) *Discourse and Institutional Authority: Medicine, Education, and Law*. New Jersey: Ablex.

Fox, R.G. (ed.) (1991) *Recapturing Anthropology: Working in the Present*. Santa Fe, NM: School of American Research Press.

Freund, P.E.S. and McGuire, M.B. (1999) *Health, Illness, and the Social Body: A Critical Sociology*. Upper Saddle River, NJ: Prentice Hall.

Gifford, S.M. (1986) 'The meaning of lumps: A case study of the ambiguities of risk', in C. Janes, S. Gifford and R. Stall (eds), *Anthropology and Epidemiology: An Interdisciplinary Approach to the Study of Health and Disease*. Dordrecht: Reidel.

Gorman, M.E. (1986) 'The AIDS epidemic in San Francisco: Epidemiological and anthropological perspective', in C. Janes, S. Gifford, and R. Stall (eds), *Anthropology and Epidemiology: An Interdisciplinary Approach to the Study of Health and Disease*. Dordrecht: Reidel.

Gupta, A. and Ferguson, J. (eds.) (1997) *Anthropological Locations*. Berkeley: University of California Press.

Hall, P. (1982) *Great Planning Disasters*. Berkeley: University of California Press.

Hempel, C.G. (1965) *Aspects of Scientific Explanation*. New York: Free Press.

Holland, D. and N. Quinn, (ed.) (1987) *Cultural Models in Language and Thought*. Cambridge: Cambridge University Press.

Hollis, M. (1994) *The Philosophy of Social Science*. Cambridge: Cambridge University Press.

Hufford, D.J. (1982a) *The Terror that Comes in the Night: An Experience-Centered Study of Supernatural Assault Traditions*. Philadelphia: University of Pennsylvania Press.

Hufford, D.J. (1982b) 'Traditions of disbelief', *New York Folklore*, 8: 47–56.

Hufford, D.J. (1983) 'The supernatural and the sociology of knowledge: Explaining academic belief', *New York Folklore Quarterly*, 9: 21–9.

Hufford, D.J. (1985) 'Reasons, rhetoric and religion: Academic ideology versus folk belief', *New York Folklore*, 11 , 177–94.

Hufford, D.J. (1987) Contemporary folk medicine', in N. Gevitz (ed.), *Unorthodox Medicine in American Society*. Baltimore, MD: Johns Hopkins University Press.

Humphrey, N. (1984) *Consciousness Regained: Chapters in the Development of Mind*. Oxford: Oxford University Press.

Ingham, R. (1994) 'Some speculations about the concept of risk', *Advances in Medical Sociology*, 4: 89–112.

James, W. (1978) *Pragmatism and the Meaning of Truth, Introduction by A. J. Ayer*. Cambridge, MA: Harvard University Press [originally 1907 and 1909].

Janes, C., Stall, R. and Gifford, S. (eds) (1986) *Anthropology and Epidemiology*. Boston: Reidel.

Jenkins, C. and Howard, P. (1992) 'The use of ethnography and structured observations in the study of risk factors for the transmission of diarrhea in Highland New Guinea', *Medical Anthropology*, 15: 1–16.

Kaplan, M. (1983) 'A women's view of DSM-III', *Amercan Psychologist*, 38: 738–92.

Kondo, D.K. (1990) *Crafting Selves*. Chicago: University of Chicago Press.

Kottak, C.P. (1991) 'When people don't come first: Some sociological lessons from completed projects', in M.M. Cernea (ed.), *Putting People First: Sociological Variables in Rural Development*. Washington, DC: World Bank.

Kuhn, T.S. (1970) *The Structure of Scientific Revolutions*. Chicago. IL: University of Chicago Press (2nd edn).

Kuipers, T.A.F. (1996) 'Truth approximation by the hypothetico-deductive method', in W. Balzer and C.U. Moulines (eds), *Structuralist Theory of Science*. Berlin: de Gruyter. pp. 83–113.

Lane, S.D. (1994) 'From population control to reproductive health: An emerging policy agenda', *Social Science and Medicine*, 39: 1303–14.

Lane, S.D. and Rubinstein, R.A. (1995) 'Public health iatrogenesis or scapegoating?: Reemergent tuberculosis and patient blaming', *Annual Meeting of the American Anthropological Association*, November.

Lane, S. and Rubinstein, R. (1996a) 'Judging the other: Responding to traditional female genital surgeries,' *Hastings Center Report*, 26: 31–40.

Lane, S.D. and Rubinstein, R.A. (1996b) 'International health: Problems and programs in anthropological perspective', in C. a. J. Sargent, T. (eds). Westport, CT: Greenwood. pp. 396–423.

Latour, B. (1987) *Science in Action*. Cambridge, MA: Harvard University Press.

Laughlin, C.D. and Brady, I.A. (eds) (1978) *Extinction and Survival in Human Populations.* New York: Columbia University Press.

Laughlin, C.D., McManus, J. and d'Aquili, E. (1990) *Brain, Symbol and Experience. Toward a Neurophenomenology of Human Consciousness.* Boston: New Science Library.

Leach, E.R. (1954) *Political Systems of Highland Burma.* London: Athlone.

Lieberson, S. (1985) *Making it Count. The Improvement of Social Research.* Berkeley, CA: University of California Press.

Lieberson, S. (1992) 'Einstein, Renoir, and Greeley: Some thoughts about evidence in sociology', *American Sociological Review,* 57: 1–15.

Lurie, P., Reingold, A., Bowser, B., Foley, J., Guydish, J., Kahn, J., Lane, S. and Sorensen, J. (1993) *The Public Health Impact of Needle Exchange Programs in the United States and Abroad.* San Francisco, CA, and Atlanta, GA: University of California at San Francisco and Centers for Disease Control and Prevention.

Maines, D.R. (1977) 'Social organization and social structure in symbolic interactionist thought', *Annual Review of Sociology,* 3: 235–59.

Malinowski, B. (1922) *Argonauts of the Western Pacific.* London: Routledge and Kegan Paul.

Manderson, L. and Aaby, P. (1992) 'An epidemic in the field? Rapid assessment procedures and health research', *Social Science and Medicine,* 35: 839–50.

Martin, E. (1987) *The Woman in the Body: A Cultural Analysis of Reproduction.* Boston: Beacon.

McGuire, W. (1997) 'Creative hypothesis generating in psychology: Some useful heuristics', *Annual Review of Psychology,* 48: 1–30.

Naroll, R. and Cohen, R. (eds.) (1973) *A Handbook of Method in Cultural Anthropology.* New York: Columbia University Press.

Neter, E., Colins, N.L., Lobel, M., and Dunkel-Schetter, C. (1995) 'Psychosocial predictors of post-partum depressed mood in socioeconomically disadvantaged women', *Women's Health,* 1: 15–71.

Newell, A. (1973) 'You can't play 20 questions with nature and win', in W. G. Chase (ed.), *Visual Information Processing.* New York: Academic Press.

Pacey, A. (1983) *The Culture of Technology,* Cambridge. MA: MIT Press.

Paul, B. (ed.) (1955) *Health, Culture and Community. Case Studies of Public Reactions to Health Programs.* New York: Russell Sage Foundation.

Pelto, P.J. and Pelto, G.H. (1996) 'Research designs in medical anthropology', in C. Sargent and T. Johnson (eds), *Medical Anthropology.* Westport, CT: Praeger.

Penfold, P.S. and Walker, G. (1983) *Women and the Psychiatric Paradox.* Montreal: Eden.

Phillips, D. C. (1976) *Holistic Thought in Social Science.* Stanford: Stanford University Press.

Piattelli-Palmarini, M. (1994) *Inevitable Illusions.* New York: Wiley.

Pinxten, R. (1981) 'Observation in anthropology: Positivism and subjectivism combined', *Communication and Cognition,* 14: 57–83.

Popper, K. (1962) *Conjectures and Refutations: The Growth of Scientific Knowledge.* New York: Basic Books.

Quine, W. (1964) 'On simple theories of a complex work', in G. A. Harris (ed.) *Form and Strategy in Science.* Dortrecht: Reidel.

Rescher, N. (1978) *Peirce's Philosophy of Science.* Notre Dame, IN: University of Notre Dame Press.

Richards, A. (1956) *Chisungu: A Girl's Initiation Ceremony Among the Bemba of Northern Rhodesia.* London: Faber and Faber.

Romanucci-Ross, L. (1991) 'Creativity in illness: Methodological linkages to the logic and language of science in folk pursuit of health in central Italy', in L. Romanucci-Rose, D. E. Moerman, and L. R. Tancredit (eds), *The Anthropology of Medicine.* New York: Bergin and Garvey. pp. 5–19, (2nd edn).

Romanucci-Ross, L., Moerman, D.E. and Tancredi, L.R. (eds) (1991) *The Anthropology of Medicine.* New York: Bergin and Garvey (2nd edn).

Rubinstein, R. (1992) 'Culture and negotiation', in E. Fernea and M. Hocking (eds) *The Struggle for Peace: Israelis and Palestinians.* Austin, TX: University of Texas Press. pp. 116–29.

Rubinstein, R.A. (1984) 'Epidemiology and anthropology: Notes on science and scientism', *Communication and Cognition,* 17: 163–85.

Rubinstein, R.A. (1998) 'Peacekeeping under fire: Understanding the social construction of the legitimacy of multilateral intervention', *Human Peace,* 11: 22–9.

Rubinstein, R.A. and Perloff, J.D. (1986) 'Identifying psychoscoial disorders in children: On integrating epidemiological and anthropological understandings', in C. Janes, S. Gifford, and R. Stall (eds), *Anthropology and Epidemiology: An Interdisciplinary Approach to the Study of Health and Disease.* Dordrecht: Reidel.

Rubinstein, R.A., Laughlin, C.D. and McManus, J. (1984) *Science as Cognitive Process: Toward an Empirical Philosophy of Science.* Philadelphia: University of Pennsylvania Press.

Rutter, M. (1983) 'Introduction: Concepts of brain dysfunction syndromes', in M. Rutter (ed.), *Developmental Neuropsychiatry.* New York: Guilford.

Salmon, W. (1967) *The Foundations of Scientific Inference.* Pittsburgh, PA: University of Pittsburgh Press.

Sargent, C.F. and Brettell, C.B. (eds) (1996) *Gender and Health: An International Perspective.* Upper Saddle River, NJ: Prentice-Hall.

Schon, D. (1983) *The Reflective Practioner.* New York: Basic Books.

Schweizer, T. (1998) 'Epistemology: The nature and validation of anthropological knowledge', in H.

R. Bernard (ed.), *Handbook of Methods in Cultural Anthropology*. London: Altamira. pp. 39–88.

Scott, R. (1969) *The Making of Blind Men: A Study of Adult Socialization*. New York: Russell Sage Foundation.

Scrimshaw, N.S. and Gleason, G.R. (eds) (1992) *RAP: Rapid Assessment Procedures: Qualitative Methodologies for Planning and Evaluation of Health-Related Programs*. Boston: International Nutrition Foundation for Developing Countries (INDFC).

Scrimshaw, S.C.M. (1985) 'Bringing the period down: Government and squatter settlement confront induced abortion in Ecuador', in P. J. Pelto and W. deWalt (eds), *Macro and Micro Levels of Analysis in Anthropology*. Boulder, CO: Westview Press.

Scrimshaw, S.C. (1990) 'Combining quantitative and qualitative methods in the study of intra-household resource allocation', in B. L. Rogers and N. P. Schlossman (eds), *Intra-household Resource Allocation: Issues and Methods for Development and Policy Planning*, Food and Nutrition Bulletin Supplement 15. Tokyo, Japan: United Nations University Press.

Scrimshaw, S., Carballo, M., Ramos, L., and Parker, R. (1990) *HIV/AIDS Rapid Assessment Procedures: Rapid Anthropological Approaches for Studying AIDS Related Beliefs, Attitudes, and Behaviours*. Geneva: World Health Organization.

Scrimshaw, S.C.M. (1992) 'The adaptation of anthropological methodologies to rapid assessment of nutrition and primary health care', in N. S. Scrimshaw and G. R. Gleason (eds), *RAP: Rapid Assessment Procedures: Qualitative Methodologies for Planning and Evaluation of Health-Related Programs*. Boston: International Nutrition Foundation for Developing Countries (INDFC). pp. 25–38.

Sibley, D. (1995) *Geographies of Exclusion*. New York: Routledge.

Sicherman, B. (1977) 'The uses of a diagnosis: Doctors, people and neurasthenia', *Journal of the History of Medicine and Allied Sciences*, 32: 33–54.

Simon, H.A. (1983) *Reasons in Human Affairs*. Stanford: Stanford University Press.

Straight, H.S. (1979) 'The set-theoretic metaphor versus the information-processing metaphor in the development of behavioral-science theory', in W. Callebaut, M. D. Mey, R. Pinxten, and F. Vandamme (eds), *Theory of Knowledge and Science Policy*. Ghent: Communication and Cognition Books.

Tax, S., Eiseley, L., Rouse, I. and Voegelin, C. (eds) (1953) *An Appraisal of Anthropology Today*. Chicago: University of Chicago Press.

Tesh, S. (1988) *Hidden Arguments. Political Ideology and Disease Prevention Policy*. New Brunswick, NJ: Rutgers University Press.

Ward, J.J. and Werner, O. (1984) 'Difference and dissonance in ethnographic data', in R. Rubinstein and R. Pinxten (eds), *Epistemology and Process: Anthropological Views*. Ghent: Communication and Cognition Books.

Watts, S. (1997) *Epidemics and History. Disease, Power and Imperialism*. New Haven, CT: Yale University Press.

Werner, O. and Campbell, D.T. (1973) 'Translating, working through interpreters, and the problem of decentering', in R. Narroll and R. Cohen (eds), *Handbook of Method in Cultural Anthropology*. New York: Columbia University Press.

Whitehead, A.N. (1960) *Process and Reality*. New York: Norton.

Wimsatt, W. (1980) 'Reductionistic research strategies and their biases in the units of selection controversy', *Scientific Discovery, Vol. 2. Historical and Scientific Case Studies*. Dordrecht: Reidel.

Zambrana, R.E., Scrimshaw, S.C., and Dunkel-Schetter, C. (1996) 'Prenatal care and medical risk in low income primiparous Latino and African American women', *Families, Systems and Health*, 14: 349–60.

Zambrana, R.E., Scrimshaw, S.C.M., Collins, N. and Dunkel-Schetter, C. (1997a) 'Prenatal health behaviors and psychosocial risk factors in pregnant women of Mexican origin: The role of acculturation', *American Journal of Public Health*, 87: 1022–26.

Zambrana, R.E. Scrimshaw, S.C. and Dunkel-Schetter, C. (1997b) 'Prenatal behaviors and psychosocial factors associated with substance use in low-income pregnant women', *Pediatric Nursing*, 23: 253–9.

1.4

The Social Construction of Medicine and the Body

DEBORAH LUPTON

INTRODUCTION

This chapter examines the social construction of ideas, knowledge, and individual's experiences of health and medicine in Western societies, using an interdisciplinary approach. The central argument of the chapter is that health, illness and disease, and health care may all be viewed as sociocultural products, and that it is therefore important to analyze the nature of their social and cultural representations and the symbolic meanings that surround them. In addressing these issues, the perspective of what may loosely be called 'social constructionism' is employed.

There is not the space here to cover the full range of social constructionist analyses of medicine, health, and illness, particularly as this perspective is found across a range of disciplines, including history, sociology, anthropology, gender studies, cultural studies, and social psychology. Instead, the chapter will focus on several key areas to which social constructionism has brought some interesting insights to bear on the nature of human embodiment in relation to health and medicine, thus serving to illustrate the epistemological and methodological tenets of this approach. The term embodiment is used here to describe the daily lived experience for humans of both having a body and being a body. Humans perceive the world as embodied subjects with particular arrangements of limbs, sensory organs, and so on, and all knowledge is therefore developed through the body (Leder 1992; Merleau-Ponty 1962). Our identities are interbound with the dynamic processes of embodiment, including incidents of pain, illness, and medical care.

For most social constructionists, the types of knowledges that are developed and brought to bear upon health, illness, and medical care may be regarded as assemblages of beliefs that are created through human interaction and preexisting meanings. This perspective contrasts with the traditional view of medicine, which sees disease as being located in the body as a physical object of physical state that can be objectively identified and treated as a physiological condition by scientific medical knowledge (Good 1994: 116). However, there are varying approaches along the social constructionist continuum. At the most extreme end of this continuum, it is believed that it is impossible to extricate physical bodily experiences from their sociocultural contexts, for the ways in which we think about, treat, and live our bodies are always and inevitably socially and culturally shaped. There is no such thing, therefore, as the purely 'natural' body, the body that may be separated from society and culture. This is not to argue that the material world or 'real' phenomena such as pain, disease, or death do not exist. Rather, it is to contend that we can only ever know, think about, and experience these realities through our specific location in society and culture. At the other end of the continuum social constructionism takes a weaker form, simply seeing human bodily experiences as influenced to some extent, and in some contexts, by social and cultural processes. The analyses reviewed in this chapter tend to be located more towards the 'strong' rather than the 'weak' versions of social constructionism. They also tend to adopt poststructuralist theoretical perspectives that emphasize the importance of discourse.

DISCOURSE AND POWER RELATIONS IN THE CONTEXT OF MEDICINE

The social constructionist perspective as applied to analyzing health, illness, and medicine was initially strongly influenced by writers on phenomenology, cultural anthropology, and the sociology of knowledge who addressed the questions of how shared notions of reality are created through acculturation and social relationships. The work of Berger and Luckmann (1967) on the social nature of knowledge and its role in constituting reality and social life has been particularly influential for social constructionism in sociology. They argued that humans and their social world exist in a dialectical relationship in which each creates the other. Although the material and social worlds are experienced by most individuals as objective, preexisting realities, Berger and Luckmann and others have pointed out that these realities involve the reproduction of meaning and knowledge through social interaction and socialization, and rely upon shared definitions. They emphasize that because of the continually constructed nature of reality, its meanings are precarious and subject to change.

Many of the more recent scholars taking a social constructionist approach have drawn upon the work of poststructuralist theorists, particularly the writings of Foucault on power, knowledge, and discourse. Poststructuralism builds upon the earlier work of writers like Berger and Luckmann. Like other 'strong' constructionist approaches, poststructuralism sees the social world, knowledge, meanings, and notions of reality as contingent and dynamic rather than fixed. It draws particular attention to the role played by language in constituting notions of reality, including our understanding and experience of embodiment. The concept of discourse brings together language, visual representation, practice, knowledge, and power relations, incorporating the understanding that language and visual imagery are implicated with power relations and the construction of knowledge and practices about phenomena. The term 'discourse' is commonly used in poststructuralist writings to denote the patterns of ways of thinking, making sense of, talking or writing about, and visually portraying phenomena such as the human body, medical and nursing practices, sexuality and reproduction, illness, disease, and death.

Discourse is viewed as a form of social practice; a mode of action as well as a mode of representation (Fairclough 1992: 63). Discourses may be said to be textual, or expressed in texts, or intertextual, drawing upon other texts and their discourses to achieve the meaning and context embedded in particular social, historical, and political settings. The word 'text' as used here does not mean simply a product of writing, but more broadly refers to verbal interactions, visual images, built structures, physical actions, and practices. For some writers, the human body itself is seen as a text that is 'written' upon by discourses. Grosz, for example, refers to the body as an 'inscriptive surface,' which various adornments, practices, and actions mark more or less permanently (Grosz 1994: 138).

Cultural analysts adopting a poststructuralist perspective argue that there is an inescapable relationship between power, knowledge, discourse, and what counts as 'truth.' Discourses are both delimiting, structuring what it is possible to say or do, and productive. Discourses bring into being, make visible, render malleable, useful, functional, or dysfunctional, and differentiate between various types of bodies – the female and the male body, the young and the old body, the normal and the deviant body, the homosexual and the heterosexual body, the thin and the obese body, the healthy and the ill or diseased body, the sane and the mad body – to name a few. Specific discourses relating to phenomena may be identified, such as a discourse of hope in relation to cancer, a discourse of activism in relation to HIV/AIDS politics, a discourse of nature in relation to alternative therapies, a discourse of science in relation to medicine. These discourses may be articulated and acted upon in a range of contexts, from patients' lay explanations and beliefs about their illness, to mass media coverage of an illness or disease, to medical textbooks and curricula.

A discourse, however, is sited within a broader matrix of sociocultural and historical meaning and thus extends beyond its context. For example, the discourse of science, as it is expressed in relation to medicine in contemporary Western societies, has a long history, developing over the last few centuries as science and medicine has – as systems of knowledge emerged and developed. A number of underlying assumptions derived from a broader Western tradition of thought contribute to the discourse of science in medicine. These include the assumptions that the mind is separate from the body, nature is separate from society and culture, nature/truth is universal, individuals are distinct from society and culture, and illness is a threat to rationality (Gordon 1988; Kirmayer 1988; Stein 1990). At the end of the twentieth century, in which notions of fate have largely been replaced by modernist ideals of order and certainty over the chaos of illness and disease, the discourse of science in medicine has a particular resonance, as it appeals to contemporary beliefs in the efficacy of the rationalist approach to containing disorder.

Those discourses that tend to dominate over others are those emerging from powerful individuals or social groups, helping to further their interests in shaping the ways in which phenomena are represented. The discourse of science in medicine relies, in part, on the assumption that it is politically and culturally neutral, unlike some other knowledge, such as that articulated in lay or alternative therapy discourses. As Rapp asserts: 'The language of biomedical science is powerful. Its neutralizing vocabulary, explanatory syntax, and distancing pragmatics provide universal descriptions of human bodies and their life processes that appear to be pre-cultural or non-cultural' (Rapp 1990: 29). The discourse of science serves to underpin the powerful and high status role of orthodox medical practitioners, who claim that their system of knowledge is superior to that of other health-care providers. Dominant discourses, however, are constantly subject to challenge. While, for example, the discourse of science may currently dominate understanding of the body and health states in Western societies, it may be challenged by the counter discourses expressed by proponents of alternative therapies, who use the discourse of beneficent nature to oppose what they see as being the objectifying nature of scientific approaches in medicine. As this suggests, 'Power struggle occurs both in and over discourse' (Fairclough 1992: 56), and this struggle is an important feature of social change.

The methods of research that are typically employed in constructionist analyses are qualitative and interpretive. All social constructionist analyses are directed at uncovering, or 'deconstructing,' the underlying values, meanings, and discourses in systems of knowledge and practice such as biomedicine. There is no single or main source of data used in social constructionist investigations. For those researchers interested in medical and health topics, in-depth interviews or focus group data, mass media texts, diaries and letters, articles in medical or public health journals, medical textbooks, conversations between patients and doctors, death records, statistical tables, and medical case notes are some of the sources of data that have been 'deconstructed' for their underlying sociocultural meanings. Some of these data are preexisting (for example, articles on diseases in medical journals), while others are created by the researcher especially for the purposes of the research project, such as interviews conducted by the researcher with research participants about the topic he is investigating. Once gathered or selected by the researcher, these data become 'texts' for the purposes of analysis.

In one analysis, Prior (1997) used a variety of preexisting texts, mainly those constructed by health-care workers, to examine the ways in which 'Freddie,' a particular patient he observed, was 'constructed' as a psychiatric case. Certain aspects of Freddie's demeanour, physical attributes, and state of mind were recorded on such documents as the medical file produced by his psychiatrist from clinical interactions and test results. Other documents included nursing care notes from when Freddie was hospitalized and social work records from when he was under the care of social workers. Prior notes that:

> In each case the discourse that describes him is drawn together from different threads. Thus, the psychiatrist, in large part, draws his threads from the vade-mecum knowledge contained in psychiatric texts. Nurses draw on one of their many 'models of nursing' and social workers draw their threads from their professional texts. (Prior 1997: 77)

Such written texts, following Freddie wherever he went for health care, came to constitute him in certain defined ways that in some situations proved more influential than his actual behaviour. Prior notes, for example, meant that because Freddie was labelled as schizophrenic on his medical records, he was constantly referred to as such by health-care and social workers even when none of the symptoms of this condition were present at the time.

As well as using written or audio texts, analysts may adopt an ethnographic approach. This is similar to the fieldwork of anthropologists, and involves spending an extended period of time observing the practices and noting the verbal exchanges of social actors in a specific setting, such as a hospital, clinic, patient self-help group, or medical consumer organization. Atkinson (1995), for example, conducted an observation study of haematologists working in the United States and Britain, with a particular focus on identifying and analyzing the medical discourses that were employed as part of these specialists' everyday working practices. In doing so, he followed the haematologists on their routine hospital rounds and attended their in-house conferences, tape-recorded proceedings, and observed them taking fieldnotes. He also recorded individual interviews with staff members. Atkinson analyzed the transcribed data produced by focusing on such aspects as how the medical discourses he identified were reproduced from senior to junior staff and students, how they affirmed the participants' membership of a professional culture, and how they served to construct particular narratives about patients as 'cases.'

In recent social and cultural theory, an interest in the ways in which place and space operate to shape practices and notions of selfhood and embodiment has developed. These writings go beyond a focus on language in acknowledging the importance of physicality, motion, and the material world. Space and place are understood as constructed through sociocultural processes rather than as objective and given. Kearns and Joseph (1993: 712) refer to this approach as a sociospatial rather than a geometric view of space. These perspectives have been adopted in medical geography and the sociology and anthropology of health and illness to explore how spatial and temporal dimensions interact in producing and reproducing the discourses and practices and, thus, the meanings and experiences of health, illness, and medical care. Again, the writings of Foucault have been influential here, particularly in relation to his writings on the role played by a specific form of architecture (the panopticon) in monitoring the inmates of public buildings such as prisons, schools, and hospitals, thus bringing them into a specific field of visibility. Such features of medical care as the architecture of the clinic or hospital, the physical layout of operating theatres, and the bodily movements and interactions of medical staff and patients within the bounded spaces of the clinic/hospital have been studied (see, for example, Armstrong 1988; Fox 1997; Hirschauer 1991).

THE BODY AND NOTIONS OF HEALTH AND ILLNESS

Recent writings in the sociology, anthropology, philosophy, and history of the human body have made important contributions to understanding the ways in which embodied experience changes across historical periods and social and cultural contexts (see, for example, Armstrong 1983; Good 1994; Grosz 1994; Herzlich and Pierret 1987; Leder 1992; Scheper-Hughes and Lock 1987; Shilling 1993; Turner 1992, 1996). As such, they have insights to offer sociocultural analysis of health, medicine, and illness. Like other writers adopting the constructionist perspective, these scholars view the body as both 'natural' and 'cultural,' acknowledging that there is no clear boundary between the two categories.

The term 'body image' has been used to denote the ways in which the lived experience of the body is brought together with sociocultural meaning in the ways in which we think about and imagine our bodies. The body image is central to ways of experiencing and conceptualizing states of health, illness, and health care. An individual's body image is developed throughout her lifetime, and is dynamic, and constantly subject to revision and transformation. 'The body image establishes the distinctions by which the body is usually understood – the distinctions between its outside or skin, and its inside or inner organs; between organs and processes; between active and passive relations; and between the positions of subject and that of object' (Grosz 1994: 84). It is embedded within social, cultural, and historical settings as well as responsive to everyday embodied experience. Thus, dominant discourses circulating within the sociocultural context in which an individual lives are important to how he constructs his body image. Individuals' own experiences of the body – the sensations they feel, the perceptions they make through their bodies – are also important, however. The body is not simply passively inscribed by discourses. Rather, bodily experience and perception themselves contribute to the production and reproduction of discourses, just as discourses shape the ways in which bodies are thought about and experienced.

Distinct changes, as well as congruities, in ways of thinking about and representing the body, health, and illness have been identified by cultural analysts. In medieval and Renaissance Europe, for example, very little was known about the internal constituents and workings of the body, for dissections were banned as blasphemous (Muchembled 1985: 26). It was thought that illness and disease entered the body through the skin and bodily orifices. People took care not to allow water – especially hot water – to touch the body, for this was thought to open the skin to unhealthy miasmas, or vapours, bearing disease. They believed that the body could best be protected against such vapours by wrapping oneself in tightly woven clothing, reinforcing the 'closed' nature of the body (Thomas 1997; Vigarello 1988). Care was taken not to allow vapours in through one's bodily orifices, and a set of taboos existed in relation to disposal of bodily fluids as a protection against this (Muchembled 1985). Urine was believed to be a particularly potent bodily fluid, thought to bear the essence of a person and to be a conduit between the inside of the body and the outside world, and therefore the path of possible contamination. Among the peasantry of medieval France, it was believed that urinating against the same wall that a leper had urinated upon could result in contracting leprosy oneself (Muchembled 1985: 72).

Concepts of body image as they relate to health have shifted significantly even within the past half century, incorporating centuries-old ideas as well as bringing in new ideas often introduced by scientific or medical discoveries about the body. Martin (1994) has identified signs of a change since the 1940s and 1950s in popular and medical accounts of the body in relation to the immune system and its effects on health. In her analysis of interviews with lay people and of popular representations of the body, she found that conceptualizations of the inside of the body frequently made references to the immune system. According to Martin, in the 1940s and 1950s concepts of health in American society tended to represent the body as a castle or fortress, with distinct openings that required protection from external invaders. Hygiene was a dominant strategy for defending the body from the 'germs' that sought to enter through its orifices and subsequently cause disease. During the 1960s and 1970s, however, the notion of the body as harbouring an interconnected immune system developed, drawing on changing biomedical knowledge about immune response. This resulted in a shift in emphasis from the outside of the body, with its envelope of protective skin, to what was happening on the inside. By the early 1990s, discourses on the immune system had become central to body image in relation to health and illness. People were now exhorted to take care of their immune system as a means of protection against ill health and disease.

Contemporary notions of the body and health states, as Martin's work demonstrates, combine centuries-old ideas relating to body openings and hygiene with newer ideas concerning the microlevel of bodily function. The body image, therefore, may be understood as a complex intertwining of traditional and novel understandings of the ways in which the body functions and relates to other bodies, objects, and spaces that produces possible ways of thinking about and living in the body.

As noted earlier in the chapter, the discourses of scientific medicine are very dominant in contemporary understanding of, and practices related to, the body, health, illness, and disease. The result of this dominance is that the ways in which individuals in Western societies tend to think about health, illness, health care, and their own bodies is very much influenced by the discourses and practices of scientific medicine. Medical knowledge, however, is just as subject to change and variation as are other systems of knowledge, including lay knowledge. Comparative analyses of medical discourses

and practices in different cultural settings often reveal the ways in which the same knowledge system (in this case, scientific medicine) is understood and practiced in strikingly different ways. For example, one detailed analysis of the practices of French and American physicians treating patients with HIV/AIDS and engaging in HIV/AIDS research (Feldman 1995) noted strong differences in approach between doctors in the two countries. Feldman notes that 'AIDS in France is a different disease than AIDS in the United States' (1995: 236). This is not only because of the different health-care funding systems (the French socialized system versus the American privatized system), but also because of underlying assumptions about the nature of patienthood and the doctor–patient relationship. In France, she found a more paternalistic model of the doctor–patient relationship, in which trust is privileged, accepted, and supported by both patients and doctors. In contrast, American doctors and patients tend to highlight the importance of patient 'empowerment' and the provision of information to patients. Often, French patients are not told of their diagnosis of AIDS by their doctors, while American doctors almost always inform their patients. French patients tend to rely on their doctors for more emotional support and advice than do American patients, rarely questioning prescribed treatments or suggesting alternatives, as HIV/AIDS patients in the United States often do.

According to Feldman, medical treatment is also different in the French and American settings, based on differing concepts of disease and the body. In the United States, 'aggressive' medical treatment for HIV/AIDS and other illnesses is supported: health is seen to be regained through immediately attacking the disease 'invader' and removing it through surgery or drug therapy. For the French physicians, argues Feldman, protecting and improving patients' overall constitution and resistance is viewed as important. Therefore, French physicians tend to be more reticent about the early use of toxic drugs to treat HIV/AIDS. Good (1995) has identified similar differences between American physicians' treatment of cancer, on the one hand, and the approach of Italian and Japanese physicians. She notes that American doctors are far more ready to inform their patients about their disease than are Italian and Japanese doctors, and place much more importance on patient autonomy. The Italians and the Japanese, in contrast, subscribe more strongly to a paternalistic and protective model of care and are less supportive of the notion of patient autonomy.

Rather than see biomedicine as a singular entity, therefore, it has been argued that it should be viewed as 'a plurality of biomedicines that are socially and culturally situated' (Good 1995: 462). While a series of overarching paradigms that serve to unite biomedicine may be identified, it is taken up in a variety of different cultural contexts, in which such factors as the economic system, assumptions about the doctor–patient relationship, and ideas about health and illness, among other elements, shape its manifestations.

THE MEDICAL GAZE AND THE ROLE OF TECHNOLOGY

The discourses and practices of medical knowledge produce and work on specific kinds of bodies. One way in which they do so is through the use of spatial and temporal dimensions. In the context of the clinic or hospital, the body of the patient becomes subject to the medical gaze. For Foucault (1975), it is through the medical gaze that the patient's body is constructed as a particular archetype of illness. The medical gaze is a product of a dominant discourse in scientific medicine that champions the importance of expert medical practitioners using visual cues to assess and monitor patients' bodies. This approach to diagnosing and treating the ill body is a result of changes that took place in the late eighteenth and early nineteenth centuries, in which scientific medicine, reliant on systematic measurement and identification of visible signs of disease and comparison, emerged. The fields of pathology and anatomy, employing the hitherto taboo practice of dissection of human bodies, began to underpin medical knowledge, opening to the medical gaze what was previously hidden (Armstrong 1983; Foucault 1975). Where once physicians relied on a patient's account of his symptoms to diagnose illness, they now used technologies such as stethoscopes and X-rays to construct their knowledge of the body by seeing or listening to what was going on inside it: 'The core task of medicine became not the elucidation of what the patient said but what the doctor saw in the depths of the body.' (Armstrong 1984: 738)

As part of the processes of medical examination, diagnosis, and treatment, patients are brought into a visibility that differentiates and judges them, comparing them to a norm and attempting to restore them to that norm. Medical surveillance and treatment practices, therefore, perform a disciplinary function upon the body of the patient, reading the body as docile and productive, the product of medical discourse and power. The use of the term 'disciplinary' in this context does not necessarily imply an interaction that involves punishment or coercion, but rather conveys the sense that patients' bodies, usually voluntarily, conform to and are shaped by medical practices and knowledge. So, too, are patients incited by medical practitioners and other health-care workers to reveal their experiences and feelings as part of diagnostic and treatment routines. This is a dominant aspect of the discourse of 'patient-centred medicine,' which has become viewed as the most appropriate approach for health-care workers to interact with their patients (Osborne 1994). This transfer of knowledge about one's body and one's self, however, is very much one-way: doctors and other health-care workers do not reveal their bodies to patients, and rarely do they reveal their private feelings and thoughts. The medical gaze, therefore, is not reciprocated.

Individuals become constituted as particular subjects through the discourses and practices of medicine and other health or welfare professions. For example, the ritual procedures carried out on patients when they are being prepared for surgery – such as rendering the patient unconscious through general anaesthesia, using linen to cover certain parts of the body, painting other parts orange-brown with disinfectant and obscuring the patient's face – turn the patient's body into a particular object for the examination and use of the health-care workers (Hirschauer 1991).

In the clinic, a range of medical technologies is brought to bear to monitor and measure bodily signs, to diagnose and 'bring into visibility' the body of the patient. This is the apotheosis of the extension of the medical gaze into the interior of the body. The various technologies available to survey and visually document aspects of the human body – such as magnetic resonance imaging, X-rays, ultrasounds, CT scanners, nuclear tracing, and electrocardiograms – present different nuances and representations of the body. These accounts are subject to expert interpretation, as are diagnostic tests of sample tissue (Atkinson 1995). Novice clinicians and clinical pathologists must learn to look for and see these images and specimens that are fragments of bodies and then to interpret and name what they see to make sense of them. This comes through a gradual process of acculturation into the 'ways of seeing' of the clinic (Atkinson 1995: 74). In some situations, the data produced by the medical technologies hooked up to the patient come to stand for the patient's body, while the fleshly body itself may be largely ignored by doctors and nurses monitoring the patient's progress (Hirschauer 1991). Atkinson notes that via such practices of bodily segmentation, representation, and interpretation, the body of the patient is dispersed and even disembodied, and read at different sites: 'The patient thus may have a multiple existence within the clinic' (Atkinson 1995: 89).

The medical gaze may itself be internalized by patients in some cases, changing their perceptions of their bodies. The cultural theorist Jackie Stacey wrote of her changed perceptions of her own body and that of others following an operation to remove a cancerous growth when she awoke feeling as if she had actually witnessed the operation:

> The clear sense of my internal body occupied my mind, and indeed, remained with me for several months. I felt sure I had seen inside myself and thus had an awareness of my body as 'flesh and blood' in a more literal way that was quite new. On leaving hospital, I began to see everyone through this physiological lens... I began to see everyone through these new X-ray eyes: the woman in front of me in the supermarket queue suddenly comprised skin, intestine, bladder, liver, lungs and kidneys. (Stacey 1997: 97–8)

While Stacey did not, of course, witness her own operation, it is evident from her description that she is drawing upon medicalized or anatomical images of the inside of the body she had previously seen in constructing her new image of her own body, and the bodies of others, through a new lens of perception – the medical gaze. Her preexisting knowledge of the inside of the body (perhaps drawn from such texts as documentaries on surgical techniques, television dramas showing simulations of surgical procedures, or biology textbooks) had risen to prominence over other ways of seeing the body, catalysed by the traumatic embodied experience of undergoing a serious operation.

As Stacey's observations suggest, lay people may come to see themselves differently via their interaction with medical technologies. The experience of interacting with medical technologies may lead to a sense of disruption of body image that is distressing. For example, those who undergo a diagnostic screening test, such as for HIV, or prostate, cervical, or breast cancer, often find themselves entering a liminal state when waiting for the result. When previously they may have had no signs or symptoms of disease, once having undertaken the diagnostic test they are forced to reconsider the notion of themselves as 'healthy' (Lupton 1994: 98–100). The notion that diseases that require a diagnostic test are 'hidden' and 'secret' within the body, giving no clear sign of their presence except via a diagnostic test, may lead people to feel anxious about the integrity of their own knowledge of their bodies.

Technologies may also be productive of bodily capacities. When hooked up to medical (and other) technologies, the patient's body becomes a cyborg, a juncture of human flesh and machine. These technologies become part of the individual's body image, extending the body in space (Grosz 1994: 80). In Western societies we feel extremely ambivalent about our relationships with technologies, disliking the idea that we should be dependent upon machines or have some sort of symbiotic relationship with them that blurs the boundaries between self and other (Lupton 1995a). The idea of having a prosthesis may inspire feelings of disquiet, or even horror, disgust, and revulsion for its 'unnatural' and liminal character, its location somewhere between human and machine, its constant reminder of the failings of one's body (Wilson 1995). Nonetheless, the potential offered by technologies and their ability to give us knowledge of our bodies, alleviate the failings or sufferings of the body, and fend off senescence and death, at least for a time, are seductive.

The capacities of the human body may be extended or even replaced by technologies, as in the case of spectacles or contact lenses, artificial respirators, heart pace-makers, cochlear implants, and artificial limbs, for example. Sobchack has written vividly about having a prosthetic limb fitted after her leg was amputated and of adapting a mechanical device into her body image and embodied experience:

> I love my prosthesis with its sculpted foam cosmetic cover – particularly the thigh which has no cellulite and is thinner than the thigh on my so-called 'good' leg. With much effort, I have learnt to walk again, the stump first thrust into the socket of a leg held on by a suspension belt and now into what is called a 'suction' socket of a leg that – when it or I am working right – almost feels like 'me.' This new socket has also allowed me a kind of experience with 'artificial orifices' that has none of the pain of surgery and all of the erotic play of technology. (Sobchack 1995: 207–8)

Such accounts demonstrate the ways in which notions of the 'natural' and the 'cultural' body, of self and nonself, come to blur in relation to medical technologies.

THE CIVILIZED BODY AND THE LOGIC OF CONTROL

One of the most dominant logics organizing ways of thinking and acting in Western societies at the end of the twentieth century is that of control. Individuals constantly engage in activities in the quest for control over their lives. It is believed that most aspects of life are malleable and amenable to the exertion of will. We see ourselves as a continuing unfinished project, requiring work and effort to shape and improve, seeking to impose order and certainty upon what is perceived to be a chaotic, uncertain, disorderly world. Foucault (1988) referred to such practices as the 'technologies of the self.' The 'technologies of the self' involve the voluntary internalization of norms governing appropriate behaviour in the interests of achieving the best possible self, including the quest for self-knowledge, self-mastery, and self-care (Lupton 1995b; Rose 1996). Engaging in the 'technologies of the self' involves seeking out and employing knowledge and the constant making of choices.

Nowhere is this desire for control more evident than in the ways in which people conceptualize embodiment, health, and illness. For the late-modern individual, the body is viewed as signifying the self and demonstrating one's capacity for self-knowledge, self-mastery, and self-care. The ideal body is that which is tightly contained, its boundaries stringently policed, its orifices shut, kept autonomous, private, and separate from other things and other bodies (Bordo 1993; Shilling 1993). Good health and 'normal functioning' of the body is commonly viewed in contemporary Western societies as the product of careful self-regulation and self-discipline. Behaviours that are seen to be linked to 'lifestyle' choices and therefore under the control of individuals, such as alcohol consumption, cigarette smoking, diet, physical exercise, and sexual activity, have been singled out in public health campaigns. Such campaigns exhort members of the 'target' audience to engage in 'body maintenance' activities (Featherstone 1991). Under the discourse of self-control, citizens are urged to turn the medical gaze upon themselves, and engage in such technologies of the self as monitoring their own bodies and health states and taking preventive action in accordance with medical and public health directives (Herzlich and Pierret 1987; Lupton 1995b; Petersen and Lupton, 1996).

The notion of the 'civilized' body, emerging in early modern Europe, is particularly important to contemporary understandings about the ideal body (Elias 1978; Shilling 1993). The 'civilized' body is understood to be that which is self-controlled, which is autonomous and self-regulated. Its boundaries are kept contained from the outside world and from others. In contrast to this ideal notion is the 'grotesque' or 'uncivilized' body, the body that lacks self-control and self-discipline and is constantly breaching its boundaries. The body that is suffering pain or illness, that is deformed or disabled, that is dying, tends to conform far more closely to the 'grotesque' body than the 'civilized' body.

A further perspective drawn from anthropological and psychoanalytic theory is that which acknowledges the ways in which individuals construct a sense of body boundaries and define themselves as self in opposition to 'other.' This perspective has provided insights for those scholars who are interested in how such notions as 'health,' 'illness,' and 'risk' are used to deal with central anxieties and fears about contamination, the blurring of bodily boundaries and death. The work of anthropologist Mary Douglas has been highly influential in our understanding of the symbolic role played by body image and notions of the body boundaries. In her book *Purity and Danger* (1966), Douglas argued that the human body serves a conceptual means of distinguishing between self and 'other.' Just as the body is seen to have defined boundaries between 'inside' and 'outside,' with rules regulating what matter comes in, what comes out, and in which ways, all human societies construct understandings of which people and things belong 'inside' and which should be maintained 'outside.'

All humans, as they are socialized into their cultures, learn the appropriate cultural norms about how to police and control their bodily boundaries. Douglas pointed out the anxieties that cohere around the margins of boundaries and the subsequent rules for control that have been developed to control margins at the level of the individual body and at the broader level of the body politic:

> All margins are dangerous. If they are pulled this way or that the shape of fundamental experience is altered. Any structure of ideas is vulnerable at its margins. We should expect the orifices of the body to symbolise its specially vulnerable points. Matter issuing from them is marginal stuff of the most obvious kind. Spittle, blood, milk, urine, faeces or tears by simply issuing forth have traversed the boundary of the body. So also have bodily parings, skin, nail, hair clippings and sweat. The mistake is to treat bodily margins in isolation from all other margins. (Douglas 1966: 121)

The orifices of the body constantly present a challenge to individuals to exert control over the movement of bodily fluids from 'inside' to 'outside.' In Western societies, we are particularly disgusted by notions of the inside of the body and the slimy viscera, organs, and fluids it contains. Actions or accidents that expose this inside matter break down the boundaries between 'inside' and 'outside' that we are exhorted since early childhood to preserve as part of our accomplishment and maintenance of the 'civilized' body. Hence, 'The disgust that arises when the body is sliced open with a knife or pierced with a bullet is more than just a function of the muck that pours out, it is a function primarily of the inappropriateness of destroying the integrity of the body's seal' (Miller 1997: 58).

In infancy and extreme old age and in illness or some forms of disablement, these bodily boundaries are constantly breached. Other bodily changes, such as pregnancy and menopause, may also involve loss of control over the body. Menopause, for example, confronts some women with shame, embarrassment, and anxiety in relation to unexpected flushing of the face, sweating, or uterine bleeding. The loss of control that women in mid-life feel when they experience these symptoms can be profoundly distressing and challenging of their sense of self (Lupton 1996). The appearance of reviled body fluids at socially 'incorrect' times or places demonstrates a frightening and disturbing loss of such rational control, signalling a return to a state of bodily chaos of infancy. The dribbling, incontinent elderly or disabled body is a nightmarish vision for its childishness and its supposed loss of humanity. Unlike the ideal of the 'civilized' body, the ill or dying body, the body in pain, the deformed or disabled body is that which lacks control. It is also that which lacks autonomy because it is dependent on others, and that which constantly threatens to breach its boundaries through pain, spasms, or the expulsion of bodily fluids at 'inappropriate' times. Such bodies arouse disgust because they bring the 'inside' of the body 'outside.' Ill, disabled, or dying people are the 'other,' those from whom the healthy, young, and able-bodied seek, often unconsciously, to differentiate themselves because of the fears, anxieties, revulsion, and dread they harbour of the incipient chaos and dissolution of their own bodies.

Grosz (1994) has taken up both Douglas' writings to analyze the symbolic nature of bodily fluids, with a particular focus on gender implications. She claims that because the female body is conceptualized as more marginal, indeterminate, fluid, borderline, and liminal, as seeping fluids that are considered to be 'dirty' and therefore as less controlled, it is viewed as more dangerous, defiling, and diseased than the male body (Grosz 1994; see also Heywood 1996). Indeed, femininity has been strongly associated with both embodiment and disease. Women's bodies have been traditionally portrayed in medical and other discourses as inferior to men's bodies: as smaller, frailer, weaker, and more disorderly, and as more defective and more prone to illness (Bordo 1993; Ehrenreich and English 1974).

So, too, other types of bodies have been typically represented, both in medical and more popular discourses, as 'inferior' because they are regarded as being unable to properly regulate their body boundaries. These include black or brown bodies, homosexual bodies, ageing bodies, and working-class bodies. Comaroff (1993) has shown, for example, how nineteenth-century British colonialist and medical discourses in South Africa portrayed black Africans as inherently dirty and diseased, as 'savage' rather than 'civilized,' and as both morally and physically degenerate. In describing black Africans as 'dirty' and 'greasy,' the British portrayed the black body as porous, odorous, and damp, and therefore as potentially contaminating to those who came into contact with it, in stark contrast to the ideal of the white European as clean, contained, and controlled (Comaroff 1993: 316). Standing for normality and self-discipline is the white, heterosexual, youthful, middle-class, masculine body. The male body is culturally represented as ideally invulnerable, disciplined, strong, contained, healthy, and physically able, and therefore as more 'civilized' than other bodies (Petersen and Lupton 1996).

MORAL MEANINGS AND BODY REGULATION

The emphasis that is currently placed in Western societies on the importance of the regulation and disciplining of the self and the body has implications for how ill people are conceptualized in moral terms. In the 'new morality' of preventive health, falling ill has become viewed as a sign of moral failure, a source of blame. States of health, therefore, are inherently associated with moral meanings and judgements (Crawford 1994; Greco 1993; Herzlich and Pierret 1987; Lupton 1994, 1995b; Stein 1990). Not to engage in risk-avoiding behaviour is considered 'a failure of the self to take care of itself – a form of irrationality, or simply a lack of skilfulness' (Greco 1993: 361).

These ways of representing the ideal human body are themselves the products of notions that have emerged over the course of Western history and intensified in recent centuries. There is a long history in Western societies of the association of moral meanings with health states. Since antiquity, those who have fallen ill have often been judged to be morally culpable for allowing illness into their bodies by failing to conform to cultural regulations and taboos. Sinfulness has been linked to illness for centuries (Thomas 1997). In early modern England (spanning the sixteenth, seventeenth, and eighteenth centuries), for example, Christian thought regarded sinners as being ultimately punished by God for their sins. Each of the seven deadly sins was associated with its own embodied pathology. Pride was thought to cause swellings such as tumours and inflammations, sloth was believed to result in dead flesh and palsy, and gluttony in dropsy and a large belly. Lust led to fluxes and discharges, leprous skin and the pox, avarice was associated with gout or dropsy, envy with jaundice, venom, and fever, and wrath with spleen, frenzy, and madness. It was common at this time for individuals who had fallen ill to examine the conduct of their lives to determine how they might have brought this condition upon themselves (Thomas 1997: 16-17).

Susan Sontag wrote about the contemporary moral meanings of illness in her important essay *Illness as Metaphor*, first published in 1978. She points out that 'Nothing is more punitive than to give a disease a meaning – that meaning being invariably a moralistic one' (Sontag 1989: 58). As she observes, cancer is commonly viewed as being caused by the repression of emotion, 'afflicting those who are sexually repressed, inhibited, unspontaneous, incapable of expressing anger (1989: 21). Like leprosy in medieval times, cancer evokes the meanings of horror, contamination, corruption, and blame. Sontag argues that these meanings also influence the type of treatment given to cancer patients and the words used to describe both the disease and its treatment. Cancer treatment is 'aggressive,' used to 'attack' the cancer that has 'invaded' the body, 'bombarding' the body with radiation. With the use of these military metaphors, the patient's body becomes thought of, and treated, as a battleground (1989: 64–5).

In the two decades since Sontag's essay was first published, cancer has also become strongly linked to such activities as cigarette smoking, a diet high in animal fat, sun exposure, and in the case of breast cancer, bearing children late in life or not at all. As Stacey (1997) notes in her more recent book on the cultural meanings of cancer, because the disease is that of one's own body cells 'turning against' the body and multiplying out of control, it is viewed as autopathogenic, caused in some way by the individual who has it. It is now very difficult for a person diagnosed with cancer not to feel as if they have in some way played a part in bringing the illness upon themselves. Many go through a process whereby they search their past behaviours to identify what might have caused the disease. As one woman who survived treatment for breast cancer wrote: 'The guilt of responsibility – could I have wished this on myself...What did I do wrong? Can I make it up again?' (Malchiodi 1997: 53)

People with cancer often seek to regain control of the uncertainties associated with cancer treatment, for example, by seeking out information voraciously. People with cancer (and other illnesses) are also expected to be 'heroes' and to 'battle' with their illness and exert will-power to overcome it. Not to do so is considered to 'give in' to the 'enemy,' relinquishing the attempt to regain the 'civilized' body from the chaotic ill body. In this discourse championing 'fighting' one's illness, 'dying is a defeat, a sign that individuals cannot transform themselves' (Coward 1989: 86).

Since the early 1980s, HIV/AIDS has become one of the most reviled and dreaded diseases in Western societies. Because the routes of transmission of HIV are associated with behaviours that are considered by many people to be socially 'deviant,' such as homosexuality, sexual promiscuity, and intravenous drug use, the syndrome itself and those who have it have become labeled 'deviant.' Sontag herself recognized the power of the cultural meanings of HIV/AIDS and wrote a sequel to *Illness as Metaphor* entitled *AIDS and its Metaphors* (1989). She and other cultural critics have drawn attention to the ways in which HIV/AIDS is strongly associated with blame and shame, particularly in the distinctions that are routinely drawn between 'innocent' and 'guilty' people with HIV/AIDS. Those who are deemed to be 'innocent' are typically seen to have become infected with HIV through no 'fault' of their own (for example, infants who were infected in their mothers' womb or haemophiliacs infected through contaminated blood transfusions). Those who are viewed as 'guilty' are seen to have somehow invited the virus into their body by engaging in risky activities.

Some alternative medicine approaches emphasize the responsibility of the person with illnesses such as cancer and HIV/AIDS even more than do orthodox medical and public health discourses, focusing particularly on 'destructive' inner feelings and thoughts that have been repressed, linking cancer to certain personality types (Coward 1989; Stacey 1997). Alternative therapies, in general, have a strong focus on lay people 'taking control' of their health by engaging in activities deemed to prevent illness. Many alternative therapies draw strongly upon the discourse of 'nature' in representing illness as an imbalance within the body (Coward 1989). A dominant assumption in the self-help discourses of many alternative therapies is that good health is a product of strength of will, and 'wrong attitudes' are punished by illness. A healthy body becomes a sign of personal achievement; illness is the sign of failure and weakness. In many ways, therefore, alternative medicine shares with scientific medicine the tendency to cast moral judgement upon those who are ill, positioning them as having failed to engage properly in self-regulation. Indeed, it has been argued that the discourses of alternative medicine broaden the 'pathogenic sphere' and in doing so extend the medicalization of everyday life into areas that are currently left largely untouched by biomedicine (Coward 1989; Lowenberg and Davis 1994; Rosenberg 1997).

Notions of 'healthiness' also often appear in the popular media in the context of selling commercial products. Such media as advertising and other forms of publicizing commodities often elide distinctions between 'healthiness' and 'attractiveness.' Thus, for example, advertisements for 'low fat' food frequently portray the product as desirable both because it is 'good for you' in terms of promoting health and because it contributes to a slim body shape. As this suggests, while health discourses are directed primarily at the 'inner body' in their emphasis on function and disease, prevention and consumer culture discourses are directed at the 'outer body' in terms of its appearance (Featherstone 1991: 171). These discourses intersect with each other in significant ways. Both public health media campaigns and commercial advertising campaigns address the same ideal of the body: as conforming to current notions of attractiveness as youthful, vital, and healthy. While health and medical discourses may involve limiting consumption of some commodities (those deemed to be 'unhealthy'), they encourage the consumption of other commodities (for example, exercise shoes and clothing, diet foods, vitamins). Both are directed at the notion of the individual who is keen to engage in activities to care for, work upon, and improve the self and the body as well as indulging herself. As Featherstone has argued: 'Within this logic, fitness and slimness become associated not only with energy, drive and vitality but worthiness as a person; likewise the body beautiful comes to be taken as a sign of prudence and prescience in health matters' (1991: 183). The suggestion is that the pleasures of consumption are heightened by improved health and physical capacity for hedonism.

In contemporary Western societies, therefore, notions of the ideal body conflate health, beauty, youth, and normality. Health tends to be culturally linked to beauty, erotic attraction, and truth as well as morality, and illness and death to ugliness, grotesquerie, falsity, repulsion, and immorality. As Gilman argues 'We experience the body as seemingly in control through the world of the visual. We censor out the association with the world of the ugly and of decay – the mark of our own decay, our own gradual collapse' (Gilman 1995: 179). Very old bodies, ill bodies, disabled bodies, and obese bodies are either stigmatized in mass media representa-

tions, or else are simply absent, treated as unworthy of portrayal because they are deemed to be deviant, unsightly, or dependent (Davis 1995; Featherstone and Wernick 1995).

Presenting realistic images of the diseased, mutilated, or dying body in the popular media often results in controversy. When, for example, a self-portrait of the artist Matuschka displaying her mastectomy scar was published on the cover of the *New York Times Magazine* in 1993, some readers were offended, although some women who themselves had breast cancer were supportive of such images receiving public attention (Malchiodi 1997: 56–7). In creating this self-image, Matuschka was setting out to demonstrate that a woman's body, lacking one or both breasts, need not be considered ugly, diseased, or deformed, noting of her purpose that: 'When men come home from war bandaged and broken, they are considered symbols of strength, even sexy. Could I actually show a mastectomy woman who looks beautiful, who has pride and dignity? A picture evoking not self-indulgence, but power and strength?' (Malchiodi 1997: 58).

Others with conditions such as HIV/AIDS, cancer, and disabilities have sought what they consider to be oppressive images of the condition in popular or medical representations, replacing them with more positive images. HIV/AIDS activists have become well known for their challenges to mainstream representations of people with HIV/AIDS. By identifying features of the politics of representation of HIV/AIDS, they have worked to 'resist the AIDS mythology' (Boffin and Gupta 1990), countering images of people with HIV/AIDS that represent them as passive, grotesque, living out an inevitable death sentence, and as deviant outsiders deserving of their fate (see, for example, the essays and images in Boffin and Gupta 1990; Crimp 1989; Klusacek and Morrison 1992). Crimp (1989) has referred to these activities as 'cultural activism,' based in cultural analysis.

Similarly, photographer and activist David Hevey (1992) mounted a strong critique of the images of people with disabilities that appear in such forums as charity advertising. He argued that in attempting to arouse pity for disabled people, such advertisements tend to be patronizing, supporting the notion that the disabled are freaks, pathetic, marginalized, and dependent on others' help. As he notes, apart from charity advertising, images of people with disabilities are rare in the popular media. They are 'admitted in culture,' Hevey argues, 'only as symbols of fear or pity' (1992: 54). His own photographic work with disabled people set out to achieve 'positive disability imagery,' allowing them to project their own perspective on the world in ways that sought to go beyond the clichéd 'brave battler' or 'helpless, dependent victim' portrayals.

CONCLUDING COMMENTS

As this chapter has demonstrated, much research and scholarship relating to the socio-cultural representations and meanings of health, medicine, and the body has been published in recent times. It has been particularly invigorated by the incorporation of poststructuralist perspectives and a growing interest in the sociology and history of the human body. One of the most important insights of sociocultural analyses is the identification of the link between knowledge, discourse, power, and notions of reality. Their value lies in challenging the status quo by deconstructing taken-for-granted perspectives and representations, and in the process producing new ways of seeing, thinking, and acting.

Critics of social constructionism and post-structuralism have criticized those who adopt these perspectives for taking a relativistic and nihilistic approach, avoiding attempts at reform and achieving improvements in health status for disadvantaged groups. They ask that if all knowledge is a social product, what are we to take as 'truth,' and whose view should we accept as valid? In response to these critiques, advocates of social constructionism and poststructuralism contend that it is important to be aware that any knowledge claim is underpinned by the desire to shape a debate, and that no such claim can be accepted as politically neutral. They argue that while the project of deconstructing taken-for-granted assumptions may be seen as destabilizing and challenging, this is precisely one of its achievements. As Leder put it: 'If we are to understand the strengths and limits of our medicine and envision its alternatives, we must come to grips with the world-view it assumes' (1992: 17).

Constructionist inquiries need not reject political causes or avoid any adherence to values such as democracy, equality, and social justice. As this chapter has shown, for example, feminist writers and advocates for people with cancer, HIV/AIDS, and disabilities have fruitfully employed deconstructionist analyses to challenge taken-for-granted meanings that they see as being oppressive or stigmatizing. Their intention is to demonstrate the ways in which the voices and activities of the members of certain social groups constantly take precedence over, and subjugate, the voices and activities of marginalized groups. Identifying discourses and showing how the use of discourses contribute to assumptions about social groups, including assumptions that contribute to their disadvantaged status, is not in itself a strategy for dealing with social inequity. It is a vital starting point, however, for attempts to 'do something,' for deconstruction serves to destabilize unifying assumptions that themselves are part of the establishment and maintenance of social inequality.

Social constructionist analyses conducted thus far have provided a richness of material that challenges the objectivist perspective on medicine and the body that reigns in medicine. Much scope remains for further inquiries into how lay people understand their bodies in relation to the dominant discourses emerging from such influential institutions as medicine, public health, and the mass media. The relationship between these preexisting discourses and the meanings developed through individuals' own life experiences of embodiment, illness, and medical care has yet to be fully explored and understood. There is much potential for future empirical studies that seek to identify aspects of this relationship and investigate the different perspectives and experiences relating to embodiment, health and illness of subcultural groups in society.

REFERENCES

Armstrong, D. (1983) *Political Anatomy of the Body: Medical Knowledge in Britain in the Twentieth Century*. Cambridge: Cambridge University Press.

Armstrong, D. (1984) 'The patient's view', *Social Science and Medicine* 18: 737–44.

Armstrong, D. (1988) 'Space and time in British general practice', in M. Lock and D. Gordon (eds), *Biomedicine Examined*. Dordrecht: Kluwer. pp. 207–25.

Atkinson, P. (1995) *Medical Talk and Medical Work: The Liturgy of the Clinic*. London: Sage.

Berger, P. and Luckmann, T. (1967) *The Social Construction of Reality: A Treatise in the Sociology of Knowledge*. London: Allen Lane.

Boffin, T. and Sunil G. (eds) (1990) *Ecstatic Antibodies: Resisting the AIDS Mythology*. London: Rivers Oram.

Bordo, S. (1993) *Unbearable Weight: Feminism, Western Culture, and the Body*. Berkeley, CA: University of California Press.

Comaroff, J. (1993) 'The diseased heart of Africa: Medicine, colonialism, and the black body', in S. Lindenbaum and M. Lock (eds), *Knowledge, Power and Practice: The Anthropology of Medicine and Everyday Life*. Berkeley, CA: University of California Press. pp. 305–29.

Coward, R. (1989) *The Whole Truth: The Myth of Alternative Health*. London: Faber and Faber.

Crawford, R. (1994) 'The boundaries of the self and the unhealthy other: Reflections on health, culture and AIDS', *Social Science and Medicine*, 38: 1347–65.

Crimp, D. (ed.) (1989) *AIDS: Cultural Analysis, Cultural Activism*. Cambridge, MA: MIT Press.

Davis, L. (1995) *Enforcing Normalcy: Disability, Deafness, and the Body*. London: Verso.

Douglas, M. (1966) *Purity and Danger: An Analysis of Concepts of Pollution and Taboo*. London: Routledge and Kegan Paul.

Ehrenreich, B. and English, D. (1974) *Complaints and Disorders: The Sexual Politics of Sickness*. London: Compendium.

Elias, N. (1978) *The Civilizing Process*. New York: Urizen.

Fairclough, N. (1992) *Discourse and Social Change*. Cambridge: Polity Press.

Featherstone, M. (1991) 'The body in consumer culture', in M. Featherstone, M. Hepworth, and B. Turner (eds), *The Body: Social Process and Cultural Theory*. London: Sage. pp. 170–96.

Featherstone, M. and Wernick, A. (1995) 'Introduction', in M. Featherstone and A. Wernick (eds), *Images of Aging: Cultural Representations of Later Life*. London: Routledge. pp. 1–15.

Feldman, J. (1995) *Plague Doctors: Responding to the AIDS Epidemic in France and America*. Westpoint, CT: Bergin and Garvey.

Foucault, M. (1975) *The Birth of the Clinic: An Archaeology of Medical Perception*. New York: Vintage.

Foucault, M. (1988) 'Technologies of the self', in L. Martin, H. Gutman, and P. Hutton (eds), *Technologies of the Self*. London: Tavistock. pp. 16–49.

Fox, N. (1997) 'Space, sterility and surgery: Circuits of hygiene in the operating theatre', *Social Science and Medicine*, 45: 649–57.

Gilman, S. (1995) *Health and Illness: Images of Difference*. London: Reaktion.

Good, B. (1994) *Medicine, Rationality and Experience: An Anthropological Perspective*. Cambridge: Cambridge University Press.

Good, M.-J.D. (1995) 'Cultural studies of biomedicine: An agenda for research', *Social Science and Medicine*, 41: 461–73.

Gordon, D. (1988) 'Tenacious assumptions in Western medicine', in M. Lock and D. Gordon (eds), *Biomedicine Examined*. Dordrecht: Kluwer. pp. 19–56.

Greco, M. (1993) 'Psychosomatic subjects and the "duty to be well": Personal agency within medical rationality', *Economy and Society*, 22: 357–72.

Grosz, E. (1994) *Volatile Bodies: Toward a Corporeal Feminism*. Sydney: Allen and Unwin.

Herzlich, C. and Pierret, J. (1987) *Illness and Self in Society*. Baltimore: Johns Hopkins University Press.

Hevey, D. (1992) *The Creatures Time Forgot: Photography and Disability Imagery*. London: Routledge.

Heywood, L. (1996) *Dedication to Hunger: The Anorexic Aesthetic in Modern Cultures*. Berkeley, CA: University of California Press.

Hirschauer, S. (1991) 'The manufacture of bodies in surgery', *Social Studies of Science*, 21: 279–319.

Kearns, R. and Joseph, A. (1993) 'Space in its place: Developing the link in medical geography', *Social Science and Medicine*, 37: 711–17.

Kirmayer, L. (1988) 'Mind and body as metaphors: Hidden values in biomedicine', in M. Lock and D. Gordon (eds), *Biomedicine Examined*. Dordrecht: Kluwer. pp. 57–94.

Klusacek, A. and Morrison, K. (eds) (1992) *A Leap in the Dark: AIDS, Art and Contemporary Cultures*. Montreal: Véhicle Press.

Leder, D. (1992) 'A tale of two bodies: The Cartesian corpse and the lived body', in D. Leder (ed.), *The Body in Medical Thought and Practice*. Dordrecht: Kluwer. pp. 17–35.

Lowenberg, J. and Davis, F. (1994) 'Beyond medicalisation-demedicalisation: The case of holistic health', *Sociology of Health and Illness*, 16: 579–99.

Lupton, D. (1994) *Medicine as Culture: Illness, Disease and the Body in Western Societies*. London: Sage.

Lupton, D. (1995a) 'The embodied computer/user,' *Body and Society*, 1(3–4): 97–112.

Lupton, D. (1995b) *The Imperative of Health: Public Health and the Regulated Body*. London: Sage.

Lupton, D. (1996) 'Constructing the menopausal body: The discourses on hormone replacement therapy', *Body and Society*, 2: 91–7.

Malchiodi, C. (1997) 'Invasive art: Art as empowerment for women with breast cancer,' in S. Hogan (ed.), *Feminist Approaches to Art Therapy*. London: Routledge. pp. 49–64.

Martin, E. (1994) *Flexible Bodies: Tracking Immunity in American Culture from the Days of Polio to the Age of AIDS*. Boston, MA: Beacon Press.

Merleau-Ponty, M. (1962) *Phenomenology of Perception*. London: Routledge and Kegan Paul.

Miller, W. (1997) *The Anatomy of Disgust*. Cambridge, MA: Harvard University Press.

Muchembled, R. (1985) *Popular Culture and Elite Culture in France, 1400–1750*. Baton Rouge, LA: Louisiana State University Press.

Osborne, T. (1994) 'Power and persons: On ethical stylisation and person-centred medicine', *Sociology of Health and Illness*, 16: 515–35.

Petersen, A. and Lupton, D. (1996) *The New Public Health: Health and Self in the Age of Risk*. Sydney and London: Allen and Unwin/Sage.

Prior, L. (1997) 'Following in Foucault's footsteps: Text and context in qualitative research', in D. Silverman (ed.), *Qualitative Research: Theory, Method and Practice*. London: Sage. pp. 63–79.

Rapp, R. (1990) 'Constructing amniocentesis: Maternal and medical discourses', in F. Ginsburg and A. Tsing (eds), *Uncertain Terms: Negotiating Gender in American Culture*. Boston, MA: Beacon Press. pp. 28–42.

Rose, N. (1996) *Inventing Our Selves: Psychology, Power, and Personhood.* Cambridge: Cambridge University Press.

Rosenberg, C. (1997) 'Banishing risk: Continuity and change in the moral nanagement of disease', in A. Brandt and P. Rozin (eds) *Morality and Health.* London: Routledge. pp. 35–52.

Scheper-Hughes, N. and Lock, M. (1987) 'The mindful body: A prolegomenon to future work in medical anthropology', *Medical Anthropology Quarterly*, 1: 6–42.

Shilling, C. (1993) *The Body and Social Theory.* London: Sage.

Sobchack, V. (1995) 'Beating the meat/surviving the text, or how to get out of this century alive', *Body and Society*, 1(3–4): 205–14.

Sontag, S. (1989) *Illness as Metaphor/AIDS and its Metaphors.* New York: Anchor.

Stacey, J. (1997) *Tetrologies: A Cultural Study of Cancer.* London: Routledge.

Stein, H. (1990) *American Medicine as Culture.* Denver, CO: Westview.

Thomas, K. (1997) 'Health and morality in early modern England', in A. Brandt and P. Rozin (eds) *Morality and Health.* London: Routledge. pp. 15–34.

Turner, B. (1992) *Regulating Bodies: Essays in Medical Sociology.* London: Routledge.

Turner, B. (1996) *The Body and Society.* London: Sage (2nd edn).

Vigarello, G. (1988) *Concepts of Cleanliness: Changing Attitudes in France since the Middle Ages.* Cambridge: Cambridge University Press.

Wilson, R. (1995) 'Cyber(body)parts: Prosthetic consciousness', *Body and Society*, 1(3–4): 239–60.

1.5

A Taxonomy of Research Concerned with Place and Health

RALPH CATALANO AND KATE E. PICKETT

INTRODUCTION

Interest in how and why illness varies in geographic space is hardly new. Epidemiologists, geographers, sociologists, and others have written sporadically on the topic for a least a century and a half. However, contributors have rarely shown an awareness of the history and breadth of the work concerned with place and health. The result is that the field thrives for a period, stagnates, and begins again by duplicating much of what has gone before.

A new generation of social scientists is interested in the spatial distribution of illness. They, like their predecessors, may fail to discover earlier or related work and waste time and effort covering old ground. We hope to reduce the chances of this happening by surveying the breadth of work concerning place and health. This is done by providing a taxonomy of the literature. This may also help start new lines of research in that empty cells in the taxonomy suggest opportunities to make seminal contributions.

ORGANIZING THE RESEARCH ON PLACE AND HEALTH

We believe that most researchers serendipitously discover the literature on place and health while seeking an answer to a narrow question raised by other literature or lines of inquiry. The researcher finds a work that may or may not answer the original question, but which piques his or her curiosity about the spatial distribution of a health-related phenomenon. The discovered work refers to related literature. The researcher pursues these and subsequent references in a more or less unguided search. This process continues through iterations of identifying work that may or may not satisfy an evolving and deepening curiosity. For those who persist, the reward is a realization of the considerable breadth and depth of the field.

We want to accelerate this process and make it more efficient. We believe that this is best done by organizing the literature such that a newcomer can find the path through it that best matches his evolving curiosity.

We offer a taxonomy based on four questions. The answers to these questions combine to form a table with twenty-four cells to which literature in the field can be assigned. Branching through the questions should lead newcomers to the cell most closely related to their original interest. Two persons may arrive at the same original cell, but go on to different subsequent cells. Understanding the structure of the table will allow each easily to identify the literature most closely related to their evolving interests. This structured inquiry can lead newcomers to literature that might otherwise go unnoticed or take much effort to find.

The first question is whether the dependent variable is physical or mental illness. Lay persons, clinicians, and scholars continue to separate illness into these two broad categories. We will do likewise.

The second question is which of the following better describes the outcome in which you are interested?

1 True prevalence or incidence of the illness in the population.
2 The prevalence or incidence of diagnosis or treatment of the illness.

Both of these phenomena are important and they are obviously related. They are not, however, interchangeable. Treated illness is often presented as a surrogate for true prevalence without a discussion of the social processes that separate undiagnosed from treated illness.

The third question that shapes our taxonomy is which of the following do you want to explain or understand?

1 Variation in the rates of illness across places.
2 Variation in illness across people as a function of the places in which they live.

We will call the first interest 'geographic' because the unit of analysis in any test will be space and the dependent variable will be a characteristic of spatial units. We refer to the second interest as 'etiologic' because the unit of analysis in tests will be the individual and the dependent variable will be a characteristic of individuals.

Researchers interested in one of these issues will likely be interested in both because empirical information gained from one line of inquiry might inform the other. Ultimately, however, these issues are not the same and the explanation of one will not axiomatically explain the other (Barrett 1986). The fact that distance from medical services is inversely related to the rate of treated psychoses (e.g., Jarvis 1852), for example, helps explain geographic variation in mental illness. This fact, however, adds nothing new to our understanding of the etiology of psychoses.

Understanding the difference between these two issues should help contributors to the field deal with the ecological fallacy. The fallacy is the inference that an association between two characteristics of population aggregates generalize to the same characteristics measured among individuals (Morgenstern 1982). Concern over this fallacy has led some researchers to dismiss any study in which an association between characteristics of population aggregates is measured. The geographic issue, however, is appropriately addressed by ecological data. This is because the theory being tested describes ecological units and not individuals. The fallacy occurs only when the result is generalized to individuals.

The fourth dimension of the taxonomy is defined by the theory that is explicit or implicit in the work. More specifically, the dimension is defined by the following question. Which mechanism do you assume accounts for spatial variation in the outcome? We have used three categories of mechanisms for our classification.

1 Environmental hazards.
2 Resources available to help individuals cope with threats without exhibiting symptoms.
3 Tolerance of society for coping strategies.

The first category in the mechanism dimension includes work that assumes that environmental hazards, or the dose of these experienced by individuals, varies over space. Dose is the combination of exposure and virulence. Exposure varies across encounters and is the amount of a hazard actually experienced. Virulence varies across hazards and can be intuitively gauged as the number of persons in a random sample of the population that will be ill if all had the same exposure. The more that are ill, the greater the virulence. Dose of a hazard, therefore, can vary with either or both virulence or exposure.

Hazards can be roughly separated into four groups. These are infectious toxins, noninfectious toxins, hazards for trauma, and stressful life events. The last of these alludes to the notion that coping with adverse experiences requires us to adapt both physically and behaviorally.

The second category in the mechanism dimension includes work concerned with spatial variation in individual ability to cope with hazards. This ability is both genetic and acquired. In the case of infectious hazards, for example, our likelihood of coping without symptoms is a function of our genetically endowed immune response and how much of that response is available at the time of the exposure. The fraction of our potential capacity that we can use is a function of our past and recent interactions with the environment. Some of these interactions are beneficial in that they make more of our capacity available, while others are disadvantageous because they deplete available capacity. Examples of beneficial interactions are healthful diets, exercise, rest, and intentional and unintentional 'inoculations.' Interactions that can deplete the fraction of our potential available at any exposure include the load of other hazards with which we are dealing. These can include other infectious agents, noninfectious toxins, nutritional deficiency, fatigue, and other stressful events that draw from our capacity to respond without appearing disabled.

The extremes of genetic endowment are often noted in the mass media. The centenarian who smokes and never exercised is often celebrated. The child with no immune response who lives in total isolation is often pitied. A person genetically endowed with average or less than average immune response may, however, be no more likely to succumb to a hazard than someone with a better than average genetic endowment. This is so because the former may have encountered fewer hazards and had more salutary interactions with the environment than the latter.

Responding to noninfectious toxins is at least metaphorically like responding to infectious toxins. Individuals are known to vary in their likelihood of exhibiting physical or behavioral disability in response to noninfectious toxins. That likelihood is often age-specific and can be mediated by exposure to other hazards or protective agents.

Our ability to cope with hazards for trauma is a function of our genetically determined physical dexterity and experiences that can increase (i.e., training, exercise) or reduce (i.e., fatigue, alcohol use) the fraction of that dexterity that we enjoy at a particular time. Our ability to cope with stressful life events is also a function of genetic factors (e.g., personality, penchant to depression) as well acquired resources (e.g., social support, professional therapy).

The third, and least intuitive, category of mechanisms that may vary in space is tolerance for coping behavior. This construct is derived from a sociological understanding of illness. A person is ill only if others judge her response to a hazard as illness. This label is usually applied to responses that reduce a person's ability to function in jobs, families, and social networks. Diagnosis is, therefore, a function of the group's tolerance or willingness to allow someone to continue in her roles even if performance is reduced by coping with hazards. Groups with high tolerance would allow persons coping with hazards to continue functioning, while those with low tolerance might not. Groups with high tolerance may adjust obligations so that the person can continue to function. Those with low tolerance expect the individual to do what is necessary to 'recover' and meet performance expectations.

Tolerance can be thought of as a function of the interest a group has in applying the label 'ill' to one of its members, as well as of the group's power to have the label 'stick.' Interests can range from those of family members who would be psychologically or financially hurt or helped by a member being diagnosed as ill, to those of employers, to those of providers of medical or other services. The issue of whose interests will be served comes down to how much power each participant has to influence the final decision and how they coalesce around the issue. Intuition may suggest that the interest of the patient, or perhaps the doctor, will always prevail, but this is not necessarily the case. We know that children, for example, have little power to influence the course of their diagnosis. We also know that the interests of employers and insurers can override those of physicians.

Interest, at least as a construct, may be easier to comprehend and measure than power. The former could, for example, be measured by interviewing individuals, since they should be able to report their perceived interests and because their perceptions will probably guide their behavior. The latter, however, cannot be reported in interviews because it is, by definition, estimated from the effect of one person's will on the behavior of others. The power of an individual, therefore, has to be estimated from observed attempts to exercise it.

A simple version of the tolerance effect assumes that identical twins exhibit the same response to the same hazard before two different groups. In one group the sum of the power among those interested in a diagnosis exceeds the power of those who are not served by such a label. In the other group, the power is held by those not wanting a label of ill. The inference is that the person in the first group will be labeled as ill whereas the person in the second group will not.

We could have had many more dimensions in our taxonomy but adding them made the result unwieldy and, in our opinion, less informative. We included only those that were useful in demonstrating the breadth of the field and those for which we could devise decision rules for assigning a work to one or another category.

The four questions discussed above yield the taxonomy shown in Figure 1. The next section of this chapter provides examples of work in cells for which there is literature.

EXAMPLES OF LITERATURE IN THE FIELD

We limited the number of studies in any cell to two. The first rule guiding our selections was to pick work that was seminal regardless of when it was first published. We did this because, as noted at the outset, we believe the field has a tendency to wane and then repeat work that went before. Older studies were, when possible, balanced with recent work. We also tried to pick work that demonstrated the breadth of the literature from which we sampled. We avoided studies that were so medical or technical as to be, in our judgment, opaque to most social scientists. On the other hand, we tried to find studies that might 'stretch' the social scientist toward a more epidemiologic perspective. We also included studies of violent behavior because violence has become widely perceived as a threat to public health.

The discussion that follows is organized by the columns of Figure 1. For the sake of coherence,

Mental or Physical Illness?	True or Treated Prevalence?	Geographic or Etiologic Inquiry?	Examples of Studies by Presumed Mechanism		
			Hazard	Coping Resources	Tolerance for Coping
Physical Illness	True Prevalence	Geographic	1 Sampson et al. 1997 Hart et al. 1998	2 O'Brien and Dean 1997 Wilkinson 1996	3
		Etiologic	4 Roberts 1997 Haan et al. 1987	5 Jehlik and McNamara 1952 Nesbitt et al. 1997	6
	Treated	Geographic	7 Cleek 1979 Cliff and Haggett 1988	8 Shannon and Dever 1974 Jenkins 1983	9 Wennberg and Gittelsohn 1973 Dartmouth Medical School 1996
		Etiologic	10 Krieger 1992 Morgan and Chinn 1983	11 Mayer 1979 Mandelblatt et al. 1994	12
Mental Illness	True Prevalence	Geographic	13 Leighton et al. 1963 Kleinman and Cohen 1997	14 Doyle 1995	15
		Etiologic	16 Ettner 1997 Evans et al. 1984	17 Hauenstein and Boyd 1994	18 Catalano et al. 1993
	Treated	Geographic	19 Mayhew 1862 Shaw and McKay 1942	20 Jarvis 1852 Sohler and Thompson 1970	21 Faris and Dunham 1939
		Etiologic	22	23 Cuffel 1994	24 Rost et al. 1993 Rost et al. 1994

Figure 1   *A taxonomy of the empirical literature concerning space and health*

we decided to discuss the columns for physical health and then proceed to those for mental health.

PHYSICAL ILLNESS: HAZARDS (COLUMN 1)

Cell 1

We were surprised to find so few examples of research that use true prevalence to estimate the role of hazards in the spatial distribution of illness. We expected that assessments of population health such as the National Health Information Survey would have yielded research in which the dependent variable was derived from representative samples of geographically defined populations. We found no such analyses.

Mortality is the dependent variable in both examples cited in Cell 1. We accepted mortality as a measure of true prevalence because we have no reason to believe that epidemiologic surveys would have yielded better estimates.

The first article included in Cell 1 is that of Sampson et al. (1997), which is concerned with spatial variation in homicide in Chicago. In the tradition of the Chicago School of Human Ecology (Park and Burgess 1925) Sampson et al. attribute the spatial variation in violent behavior and homicide to 'collective efficacy.' This construct is derived from the Chicago School's notion of social disorganization in that its referent is the degree to which the residents of an area cooperate to preserve or improve the quality of their shared spaces, amenities, and services. The authors measure the frequency of these behaviors through household surveys.

Sampson et al. report, among other findings, that areas with high collective efficacy had fewer homicides than those with lower collective efficacy, controlling for the characteristics of persons who live in the areas. Among the control variables were measures of residential stability and of the concentration of poverty and immigrants.

Among the other findings reported by the authors is that individuals are more likely to suffer violence if they live in areas of low collective efficacy. This inference was based on individual-level analyses in which characteristics of the individuals were controlled. This analysis and the findings imply that the work of Sampson et al. could also be included in Cell 4. We included it in Cell 1 because we found so few examples of work in which true prevalence was used as a dependent variable across spatial units.

Our second example of work that could fill this cell (Hart et al. 1998) is an ecological analysis of age-adjusted mortality among African Americans across standard metropolitan statistical areas (SMSAs) with populations larger than 200 000. The authors claimed to be testing the degree to which residential segregation affects death rates. The argument for why segregation would be associated with higher death rates is not well developed. The implied mechanism is that African Americans in highly segregated areas are less able to move away from hazardous environments than are those who live in less segregated SMSAs. The results supported the notion that segregation was positively related to death rates for African Americans.

We suspect that Cell 1 is sparsely populated because researchers interested in explaining spatial variation in illness, as opposed to the role of place in the etiology of illness, are more likely to be geographers or sociologists than epidemiologists. Therefore, they are not likely to be expert at measuring true prevalence and will tend to use archival data. This poses problems if the researcher assumes that archival records of diagnosed illness is an unbiased indicator of true prevalence. For reasons alluded to above in our discussion of tolerance, and described in more detail below, spatial variation in diagnosed illness may result from circumstances other than variation in true prevalence.

Cell 4

Cell 4 includes much of the work by the emerging group of social scientists interested in place

and well-being. Among the frequently cited authors are Aneshensel (Aneshensel and Sucoff 1996), Jones (Jones and Duncan 1995), Kaplan (1996), Macintyre (Macintyre et al. 1993), and Meyer and Jencks (1989). The works we describe as examples for the cell are less likely to be known to social scientists because they appear in the public health literature and focus on physiological outcomes.

Roberts' (1997) work is an example of research that uses spatial variation in a presumed hazard to shed light on the etiology of a particular pathology. The pathology in this case is low birth weight and the hazard is residing amid economic hardship. The analysis was based on all (i.e., 112 327) live births in the Chicago metropolitan area in 1990. Each birth was characterized by the dimensions of the mother as well as by those of the neighborhood in which the mother lived. Among the individual-level characteristics were race/ethnicity, age, marital status, education, use of prenatal care, cigarette and alcohol consumption, and parity. The neighborhood characteristics included unemployment rates, proportion of families in poverty, measures of community socioeconomic status, median rent, crowding, racial makeup, and age composition. The primary analysis was a logistic regression in which the dependent variable was the odds of a low weight birth (i.e., < 2500 g) among each group formed by combinations of the independent variables. Results supported the 'a priori' expectation that neighborhood hardship would contribute to the odds of low birth weight controlling for individual-level variables and other community characteristics.

Haan et al. (1987) used cohort data from Alameda County, California, to study the effect of living amid poverty on mortality. The cohort consisted of 1800 persons aged thirty-five or older selected at random in 1965. The authors had access to survey data describing the socioeconomic and demographic characteristics as well as the health status of individuals in the cohort 9 years before the tests conducted for the article. Haan et al. modeled the risk of mortality in the 9 years as a function of the individual characteristics as well as of living in federally defined poverty areas. The results were that living in a poverty area significantly increased the risk of mortality.

The primary objective of the Roberts and Haan studies was to illuminate the etiology of illness in individuals. The contribution of the work to understanding the spatial distribution of illness is secondary. This places the work squarely in Cell 4.

Cell 7

The third cell in the hazard column includes the atlases of disease and much of the work of medical geography. These atlases include the classic works of the nineteenth century (e.g., Hirsch 1886) as well as the work of Rodenwaldt and Jusatz (1952), May (1955), and Howe (1963). These, and the related work of such eminent medical geographers as McGlashan (McGlashan and Blunden 1983), Pyle (1986), and Shannon (1977; Shannon and Pyle 1993), are all impressive presentations of the spatial distribution of disease and causes of disease. The emerging cohort of social scientists interested in the spatial distribution of illness would be well served by becoming familiar with the substance (e.g., Dahl 1984) and methods of this work.

As implied by the above, there are many seminal (e.g., Hirsch 1886) and recent (e.g., Myaux et al. 1997) examples of this work that could have been cited in this cell. The two we chose are informative both substantively and methodologically. The first is the *Atlas of Disease Distributions* by Cliff and Haggett (1988). This is a particularly good introduction for social scientists to the material in Cell 7. The work includes classic examples of spatial epidemiology (e.g., cholera in London in the eighteenth century) as well as of contemporary methods (e.g., time–space methods). In fact, the volume is less an atlas than an introduction to the methods of studying the spatial array of hazards and their presumed effects. The section on the eradication of smallpox (Section 6.3) is particularly helpful for its demonstration of how work in Cell 7 can have a major effect on health without contributing insights into the etiology of a disease.

The second piece we selected for Cell 7 (Cleek 1979) deals with the problem of spatial aggregation that can confound any work assigned to this cell. Cleek focuses on the association between environmental hazards and rates of cancer in spatially defined units. The argument is that the scale of aggregation greatly affects the measured association, and that this should cause both epidemiologists and geographers to be careful in their inferences. The most obvious concern is that the spatial unit should be consistent with what is known about variation in the presumed environmental cause. Air sheds, for example, are better spatial units for testing the effect of air pollution than are political units (e.g., states). Other matches of spatial unit with hazard may not be so intuitive and may require more knowledge of environmental science than either geographers or epidemiologists typically have.

Cell 10

Work in Cell 10 is very similar to that in Cell 4 in that both types of work use the individual as the unit of analysis. They are also similar because both intend to make a contribution to understanding the etiology of disease rather than the spatial variation in illness. The work in Cell 10, however, uses treated disorder rather than true prevalence. This fact raises an issue that we discuss after describing two articles typical of work in the cell.

Krieger (1992) studied the records of 14 420 members of a large health maintenance organization to determine if the socioeconomic characteristics of the individual's census block were related to likelihood of, among other outcomes, being diagnosed with hypertension. She was able to control for individual characteristics including age, weight, height, smoking, and occupation. The results were that subjects in low socioeconomic census blocks were more likely to be diagnosed with hypertension than other subjects. Krieger inferred that the findings supported her suspicion that living in lower socioeconomic neighborhoods was a hazard for hypertension.

Morgan and Chinn (1983) used data describing the hospital and physician contacts among 4900 children (aged 5–11 years) residing in twenty-two enumeration districts in England and Scotland to measure the association between neighborhood characteristics and help-seeking. The neighborhoods were scored on a scale of desirability derived from forty census characteristics. Children in less desirable neighborhoods were more likely to use medical services than those in better neighborhoods, controlling for household socioeconomic status. Like Krieger, the authors infer that living in less desirable neighborhoods is a hazard for illness.

Studies in Cell 10 support the notion that some places are more hazardous that others, but the fact that the dependent variable is diagnosed illness weakens the etiologic evidence. It is possible that the presumed hazard, or some correlate of it, affects the decision to seek help rather than the onset of illness. The findings in Cell 4, which estimate true prevalence, are therefore more compelling evidence of the etiologic role of the presumed hazard.

PHYSICAL ILLNESS: RESOURCES FOR
COPING (COLUMN 2)

Cell 2

Cell 2 includes work that attempts to explain variation in true prevalence of illness (or mortality) across geographic areas as a function of similar variation in the coping resources of the populations. The resources available for coping with hazards can be either genetically endowed or acquired from the environment. Places can therefore vary in illness because they vary in the genetic or acquired capacity of the population to cope with hazards.

An important distinction needs to be made between two classes of acquired coping resources. The first are those that were acquired earlier at a place other than that currently occupied by the individual or individuals. Places can, in other words, vary in the capacity of their resident population to cope because migration has spatially combined persons with very different coping resources that were acquired elsewhere (Marmot 1994). This circumstance is similar to the spatial distribution of genetically endowed coping resources in that the influence of the currently occupied place on such coping might be small. The current spatial distribution of genetically endowed coping is attributed primarily to migration patterns from places at which natural selection had historically more time to work.

The second type of acquired coping resources includes those acquired from the place currently occupied. Examples of these resources include social support and medical care.

The literature alluded to below rarely makes a distinction between these two types of acquired coping resources. Differences in acquired coping resources are typically attributed to the place currently occupied.

Work concerned with the spatial distribution of genetically endowed immunity or vulnerability is, with the possible exception of sickle cell anemia (e.g., Kulozik et al. 1986), rare. The example we chose for Cell 2 is the recently reported and provocative work on genetically endowed resistance to AIDS (O'Brien and Dean 1997). It appears that there is a type of HIV resistance that is genetically endowed. The geographic distribution of the resistance is such that it is virtually nonexistent in Africa and eastern Asia and more common in Europe and western Asia. Current speculation is that the distribution is a product of an HIV-like epidemic that swept Europe and western Asia approximately 4000 years ago. One effect of such an epidemic would have been to favor,

through natural selection, any genetic characteristic that increased the chances of successful coping with the organism. The current geographic pattern of the endowed resistance is believed to be a function of migration from the areas that suffered the original epidemic.

For Cell 2 we chose a similarly provocative example of work concerned with the spatial distribution of acquired coping resources. The research focuses on the effect of relative income distribution on mortality. The argument, although not always clear in the literature, is that the maldistribution of income corrodes the social unity of a population and this, in turn, reduces social support and, to invoke Sampson's construct alluded to earlier, 'collective efficacy.' The loss of these coping resources supposedly puts the population at increased risk of illness.

This argument has been repeated in one form or another by several authors in recent years (e.g., Kaplan 1996; Waldmann 1992), but its best known advocate is probably Wilkinson. In his 1996 book, Wilkinson overviews his earlier work and that of others and provides a summary of his argument. The empirical work he describes tends to be measurements of the association between income distribution and life expectancy across countries or subnational units. The work cited typically controls for other variables that might account for the association (e.g., per capita wealth, education levels). The most common inference from the work is that communities that distribute wealth more evenly (e.g., the Scandinavian countries and Japan) exhibit better health than similarly wealthy communities that distribute wealth less equitably (e.g., the United States and United Kingdom). The health benefits of greater equality of wealth supposedly accrue not only to the relatively poor but also to the relatively rich.

Wilkinson's and related work has been criticized on several grounds including the vagueness of his 'a priori' arguments (e.g., Catalano 1998; Fiscella and Franks 1997; Gravelle 1998). However, the work remains appealing to many in the mainstream of public health who believe that social justice is a precursor of population health.

Cell 5

Cell 5 includes work that uses individual-level data to determine if the spatial distribution of coping resources helps explain the spatial distribution of illness. We have chosen two examples in which the principal issue is whether distance from medical care providers can explain excess morbidity among persons in rural areas.

The study of illness among rural families by Jehlik and McNamara (1952) is a seminal piece in distance-to-care research. The authors' most controversial dependent variable was the prevalence of 'bed illness' among families in their sample. The data showed that the further a family resided from a medical care provider, the more likely its members were to suffer illness that required loss of normal functioning. The authors also reported that more distant families were less likely to use preventive care. They concluded that this circumstance accounted, in part, for the greater amount of bed illness among the more rural families. Jehlik and McNamara attempted to control for such other factors as socioeconomic status, but acknowledged that this and related factors could have confounded their work.

The Jehlik and McNamara study has been replicated many times. The object of this replication has been to control for confounding demographic and socioeconomic variables. Among the best known of the replications is a large study of the Finnish population (Purola 1968) that allowed for control of an extensive array of potential confounding variables. The results were very similar to those of Jehlik and McNamara.

Our second example is a contemporary replication of the Jehlik and McNamara study conducted in rural Washington. Nesbitt et al. (1997) studied the hospital records for approximately 30 000 births over a 3-year period (i.e., 1987–1989) in rural areas to determine if access to care was associated with adverse outcomes. Among the dependent measures was whether the neonate was characterized as 'nonnormal' for billing purposes, and whether the length of stay exceeded 5 days. The principal independent variable was whether the mother lived in areas in which local facilities allowed delivery in the community, or the lack of facilities required delivery in another community. Controlling for many characteristics of the mother and the gestation (e.g., nulliparous, parity > 4, gestational age, cesarean section), the distance-to-care variable remained a significant predictor of whether a neonate would be normal. The data also indicated that mothers who were privately insured and who resided at a greater distance from hospitals were more likely to have stays greater than 5 days.

Nesbitt et al. were not able to control directly for income or education. Their control for public or private insurance, marital status, and race, however, adds strength to their claim that socioeconomic status was not likely to have induced their results.

Cell 8

Work in Cell 8 measures the spatial association between coping resources and health using prevalence or incidence of treated disorder. The unit of analysis is the place rather than the individual, and the health data typically come from archives of health-care providers rather than from assessments of representative samples of the population.

The first study we chose for this cell is Jenkins' (1983) frequently cited analysis of cancer mortality rates across thirty-nine mental health catchment areas in Massachusetts. Cancer deaths in 1972 and 1973 were combined, and their association with 130 socioeconomic and demographic characteristics of the catchment areas was measured. The results suggested that female cancer mortality was not related beyond chance with any area characteristics, but that mortality among males was associated with many. Jenkins claims that environmental exposures could not explain the associations, and infers that the predictors were a measure of 'social connectedness.' He argued that survival among ill men was a function of social support, and that neighborhoods low on this coping resource had high mortality.

Jenkins clearly intended to contribute to our understanding of the natural history of cancer. He acknowledged, however, that the ecological nature of his work made it suggestive at best. It fact, the work is more a contribution to medical geography, in that it made arguments for explaining spatial variation in cancer mortality as a function of social coping resources, rather than of environmental hazards.

The second work we chose for Cell 8 is the well-known volume by Shannon and Dever (1974) on health-care delivery. The book includes a chapter in which they not only review much literature on the spatial distribution of healthcare resources but also provide original maps describing the distribution. Among the differences in health care that they document is that between rural and other areas. Citing several studies they conclude that this lack of adequate health care is reflected in the health statistics of rural areas. This is particularly true, they argue, for the chronic sequelae of trauma.

Work typified by what we cite in Cell 8 is clearly important to medical geography because it may help explain why the prevalence or incidence of diagnosed illness varies from place to place. The work is also important to health services and to understanding how place of residence can affect real and perceived quality of life. Its contribution to our understanding of the etiology of illness is, however, less obvious. This is true because spatial variation in treated illness can be influenced by the decision to seek help as much as, if not more than, the prevalence or incidence of illness.

Cell 11

The work in Cell 11 differs from that in Cell 8 because it uses individual-level data and is typically intended to make a contribution to the etiologic literature. The fact that the dependent variable is treated disorder makes the caveat offered immediately above more salient than in Cell 8. However, we have tried to select work that does not confuse prevalence of treatment with prevalence of illness, and which makes a contribution to our understanding of the course, if not cause, of disease.

The work of Mayer (1979) describing paramedic treatment for cardiac arrest is a clear example of how individual-level research using spatial data can further our understanding of the course of an important illness. Using data from Seattle, WA, he studied the effect of time elapsed between dispatch of paramedics and arrival at the scene of a cardiac arrest on several outcomes. A total of 525 incidents met the strict inclusion criteria for the study period (i.e., 1 year beginning 1 September 1977). Mayer found that the longer the time from dispatch to arrival, the lower the odds that the patient would survive long enough to get to the hospital and would eventually be discharged from the hospital. He concluded that persons at greater distance from dispatch centers were at greater risk of death. This was particularly true for those in rural areas.

Mandelblatt et al. (1995) studied the incidence of late-stage discovery among 24 500 breast tumors registered in New York City from 1980 through 1985. The authors were able to characterize each tumor by the demographic and socioeconomic characteristics of the patient as well as by the socioeconomic characteristics of the patient's neighborhood. Access to mammography screening in the neighborhoods was also scored. The results were that, after controlling for patient characteristics, being in a neighborhood with better access to mammography reduced the odds that a tumor would be discovered late rather than early.

The Mandelblatt et al. study clearly has implications for services planning and cancer treatment. It also confirms that coping resources, medical screening in this case, play an important role in the etiology of breast cancer mortality. For our purposes, it also demonstrates that spatial variation in coping resources affects spatial variation in mortality.

PHYSICAL ILLNESS: TOLERANCE FOR COPING (COLUMN 3)

The construct of tolerance is made operational at the simplest level as societal opinion on whether some characteristic of individuals is sufficiently stigmatizing to label it an illness. Most of the literature on tolerance for coping is concerned with behavioral and mental illness, but the concept applies, albeit less intuitively, to physiological coping as well. Society decides which physiological reactions to hazards are 'normal' (i.e., not appropriately subjected to treatment) and which are not. An extreme example of this is the recent tendency to view small children as candidates for treatment with growth hormones (Voss 1995). Is being short an illness? Are we less tolerant of short persons than we were historically? If so, why?

Other less obvious examples include the reduction in tolerance for properly aligned teeth. The rapid expansion of orthodontics in the United States in particular cannot be explained by an increased incidence of badly aligned teeth (Johnson 1996). It is clearly due to society's reduced tolerance for the circumstance.

The best example of increased tolerance for what was once labeled an illness is psychiatry's reversal on homosexuality. There are, however, physiologic examples as well. Among these is the condition traditionally referred to as being 'crippled' or 'disabled.' The political movement to provide full access to the 'disabled' has led to the notion that what was once considered a chronic illness is actually the circumstance of having to function in environments designed for persons with different physical characteristics. Legislation such as the Americans with Disability Act makes being physically and behaviorally different from the norm a circumstance dealt with by politicians and lawyers as much as by medical personnel (Bonnie and Monahan 1997).

Places can vary in their incidence of illness because they vary in tolerance. There is, however, little empirical work dealing with spatial variance in tolerance for physiological coping. The only literature in the column deals with treated disorder measured over units of space. Cells 3, 6, and 12 in Figure 1 are empty. The empty cells imply an opportunity for new researchers in the field to make seminal contributions.

Cell 9

Cell 9 includes two related studies. The first is the classic study of spatial variation in frequency of medical procedures by Wennberg and Gittelsohn (1973). The authors used archival data to characterize thirteen health service planning areas in Vermont by socioeconomic and demographic characteristics as well as by availability of medical services and utilization of those services. Wennberg and Gittelsohn found large differences in the age-adjusted rates of surgery across the planning areas. Tonsillectomy, for example, varied from a rate of 13 per 10 000 persons to 151! The area with a rate of 151, moreover, was surrounded by areas with rates that did not exceed 40. Other surgical procedures, such as hysterectomy (age-adjusted rates from 20 to 60 years), showed similar, albeit less extreme, distributions. The authors concluded that the variation could not possibly be entirely due to variation in the true prevalence of illness. Instead they attribute much of the difference to the interest of physicians and medical care providers. Areas with high concentrations of specialists and populations covered by fee-for-service medical insurance will, they conclude, have more of the procedures for which the specialists are trained.

The findings of Wennberg and Gittelsohn are consistent with the theory that tolerance is a function of interest and power. Physicians are very powerful in the decision to pursue medical procedures and it is often in their economic interest to deliver the procedure. Tolerance for the illness treated by the procedure will therefore be low in areas with a high concentration of specialists and fee-for-service financing.

The second example in Cell 9 is an outgrowth of the seminal work of Wennberg and Gittelsohn. The work is referred to as the *Dartmouth Atlas of Health Care* (Dartmouth Medical School 1996) and has appeared in several editions in which maps of the spatial distribution of medical procedures are updated. The maps are based on data such as that from the Medicare program which allow accurate rates of treatment to be computed. The program has nationally consistent definitions of procedures, and enrolment data allow the population eligible for the procedures to be accurately estimated. The maps show variations in all major procedures, and the authors attribute much of this to availability of services and financing of treatment.

Although both works in Cell 9 are concerned with the power and interest of medical care providers, it is increasingly clear that tolerance for illness is influenced by a larger ecology of actors. The interest and power of families and social support networks is clearly important in that the decision to seek medical care has to be made before providers can pursue their interests.

The power of who pays for medical care has been made dramatically clear in recent years. As cost containment has become a principal objective of medical care management, tolerance for physiological coping may be increasing. This is true because medical care is increasingly financed via 'capitation,' or a set payment per year for each person eligible for service. Providers therefore make more money if the patient is treated less than if he is treated more. This circumstance changes the providers interest in treatment and may increase tolerance for coping. It appears, for example, that cataract surgery is much less common among Medicare recipients in capitated systems than among those in fee-for-service systems.

MENTAL ILLNESS: HAZARDS (COLUMN 1)

Cell 13

Works in Cell 13 study the association across places between environmental hazards and what is believed to be true prevalence of mental illness. The prevalence of mental illness is typically measured via population surveys.

The first example in the cell is the classic work by Leighton et al. (1963) based on survey and other data collected in Sterling County, Canada in the early 1950s. The principal contribution of the work was its integration of psychiatry, sociology, and epidemiology. The Leighton team assumed that the social environment in which individuals lived affected the odds of exhibiting abnormal behavior. More specifically, they hypothesized that salutary environments were ones in which families and institutions met most of the physical and emotional needs of their members. Meeting the needs of members empowered institutions to reinforce behavior which was consistent with rules and to discourage deviance. This made the community more orderly and, in turn, allowed institutions to prosper and meet yet more needs.

This pattern of cohesion could be disrupted by exogenous events such as physical disasters or rapid economic growth or decline. These events disrupted the capacity of families and institutions to support their members, or introduced rapid in or out migration that overwhelmed or depopulated institutions. In any case, the result was 'social disintegration' that confused and disoriented the young and dispirited others. This circumstance leads to affective disorders and related behaviors such as alcohol abuse and vice.

The Leighton team tested their hypothesis with great care and found the associations they expected. Areas of Sterling County with a history of disintegrating events had higher rates of mental illness. The Leighton group, of course, anticipated the issue of reverse causation. Leighton concluded that:

> The historical sequence of the depressed areas ...suggests that they first became impairing places to live and then, as a result of this impairment to personality, abetted by later drifting in of other impaired individuals, became self-perpetuating systems of both social and psychological pathology. (Leighton et al. 1963: 369)

The Sterling County studies fit the criteria for Cell 13 in that they use estimates of true prevalence of disorder to gauge the effect of environmental hazards on mental illness. The contribution is primarily toward answering the geographic question of why the prevalence of illness varies across places. There are individual-level analyses in the study, but these typically deal with individual risk factors of mental illness and do not address spatial distribution.

The second article chosen for Cell 13 is a contemporary attempt to demonstrate that the social environment influences mental illness. Kleinman and Cohen (1997) argue that cross-cultural differences in the true prevalence of mental illness are due to more than biological factors. They cite large differences in the rate and mix of diagnoses from different countries as evidence that two common assumptions made by psychiatric epidemiologists are wrong. The first assumption is that the rate of mental illness is relatively constant across places; the second is that the social environment provides only the cultural nuances of illnesses that are basically biological.

Kleinman and Cohen offer no specific formulation as to how the social environment affects mental health, but they implicate maldistribution of power and wealth as well as the social disruption that comes with political struggle and economic development. The victims of war and economic collapse are mentioned, as well as the fact that mainland Chinese women suffer nine times the rate of neurotic disorder among men. They note that a biological explanation is not compelling given that women on Taiwan do not exhibit such high rates.

Cell 16

Works in Cell 16 use surveys of true prevalence to study the role of environmental hazards in the etiology of mental illness among individuals. Place is important only in that it provides variation in the hazard.

The first article in the cell is a test of the hypothesis that not working is a risk factor for alcohol consumption and abuse. Ettner (1997) used data from the National Health Information Survey to empirically pit two rival hypotheses against each other. The first was the income theory which argues that persons who are not employed should drink less because they have less money to spend on alcohol. The second is the provocation theory that assumes that persons who are not working drink more as a means to cope with the anxiety and stress of economic uncertainty.

The results suggested that the income effect described persons who were not working, but that the provocation effect better described those who were involuntarily not working. Ettner analyzed the relationship between state unemployment rates and the odds of not working, and concluded that respondents who were unemployed in states with high unemployment were probably not unemployed because they drank alcohol. The implication is that among the reasons for state-to-state variation in alcohol abuse is probably a variation in the number of persons involuntarily without work.

The second article in this cell deals with the effect of air pollution on mental health. Evans et al. (1987) hypothesized that ozone is likely to interact with stressful life events to affect the onset of psychological symptoms. They used survey data from Los Angeles County describing the psychological status and life experiences of 6000 subjects interviewed in the late 1970s. The likelihood of respondents reporting symptoms of disorder was modeled as a function of their socioeconomic and demographic characteristics as well as of their recently experienced life stressors and ambient ozone levels measured at the air pollution measuring station (fourteen stations in all) closest to their home. The surveys were conducted over 3 years, allowing for time and space variation in ozone exposure. The test was conducted with cross-sectional as well as panel data. The latter allowed the researchers to control for psychological status before the experience of stressful events or high levels of ozone. The results suggested that there was a main effect for stressful life events and an interaction effect of life events and ozone levels on disorder.

The implication of the Evans et al. finding is that a variation in symptoms of psychological disorder across Los Angeles County could be accounted for, at least in part, by exposure to ozone. Individuals who had experienced stressful life events and high ozone were at elevated risk. This was true controlling for socioeconomic and demographic characteristics of the individuals.

Cell 19

Research in Cell 19 would measure the association across spatial units between treated disorder and some presumed hazard for mental illness. There are many classic ecological studies that could be assigned to this cell. We have chosen the seminal work of Henry Mayhew (1862) and the frequently cited studies of Shaw and McKay (1942).

Mayhew's classic study of London in the mid-nineteenth century should be of interest to new researchers in place and health for many reasons. Among these is that Mayhew spent much time interviewing convicted and active criminals to understand the processes by which they became deviant. He was aware that many commentators of his day attributed criminal behavior to mental defects indicated by cranial and other physical abnormalities. The reason for chronically high rates of criminal and other deviant behavior in several neighborhoods of London was presumed to be social selection (i.e., drift) of mental defectives into low-rent areas of the city.

Mayhew combined his mapping of court and hospital data with the information gained through the hours of interviewing alluded to above. His conclusion was that:

Crime, we repeat, is an effect with which the shape of the head and form of the features appear to have no connection whatever...the great mass of crime in this country is committed by those who have been born and brought up in the business, and who make regular trade of it, living systematically by robbery or cheating as others do by commerce or the exercise of intellectual or manual labour. (Mayhew 1862: 413)

His work set the stage for much of the spatial analysis of deviant behavior that continues to this day. While his spatial analysis is often cited as influential, few commentators appear to be aware of his seminal notion that place of residence is important in understanding the prevalence of deviant behavior because such behavior is learned. A full century before the learning theorists devised the conditioning model of deviance, Mayhew had posited it as an explanation of the spatial distribution of crime in London.

The second work chosen for the cell is also frequently cited. In fact, Sampson et al. (1997), whose work is listed in Cell 1, cite the studies of Shaw and McKay among the antecedents of their own. Shaw and McKay are known primarily for their original presentation and frequent replication of maps showing that delinquency was distributed 'ecologically,' in that rates were greatest near the center of metropolitan areas and decreased with distance from the center (Shaw and McKay 1942). This distribution had been suggested by researchers in the Chicago School of Human Ecology (e.g., Park and Burgess 1925), who showed that the poorest neighborhoods were near the historic centers of metropolitan areas, and that the socioeconomic status of neighborhoods generally increased with distance from the center. Crime, illness, delinquency, mental illness, and many other phenomena were shown to be distributed similarly. Shaw and McKay's contribution to the Chicago School literature was the mapping of delinquency.

Shaw and McKay's early work was virtually without theory. They eventually embraced Sutherland's (1939) notion of differential association to explain their maps. This notion held that adolescents' attitudes toward the social contract were learned from the preponderance of those with whom they associated. Growing up in an area with many deviants, therefore, supposedly put children at risk of developing attitudes that led to deviant behavior.

Differential association and the theoretical component of Shaw and McKay's work went out of favor when psychologists rejected the notion that attitudes predicted behavior. The spatial distribution of delinquency was more parsimoniously explained as a function of conditioning. The mapping component of Shaw and McKay's work, however, is still widely cited as an example of the Chicago School's interest in the spatial distribution of deviance.

Cell 22

As indicated by the empty cell in Figure 1, we know of no research that uses survey measures of spatial distribution in treated disorder to test the general hypothesis that an environmental stressor causes mental illness. The closest work to this type that we know of is concerned with the much-reported association over time between economic contraction and use of mental health services (Dooley and Catalano 1984). The work was designed to determine if the association was due to new episodes of disorder (i.e., the provocation hypothesis) or to increased help-seeking by those who were chronically disordered (i.e., the uncovering hypothesis). Help-seeking was measured in representative samples surveyed over several years in Los Angeles County. The results supported both provocation and uncovering.

The findings have spatial implications in that places with relatively poor economies should, controlling for other factors, consume more mental health services than places with stable or growing economies.

MENTAL ILLNESS: COPING RESOURCES (COLUMN 2)

Cell 14

Cell 14 includes work that measures the true prevalence across places to test the possibility that spatial variation in coping resources account for spatial variation in mental illness. We found one study that could fit the cell, and then only if true incidence could be expanded to include reported suicide. We accept that it could because there is no reason to believe that other methods of counting suicide would produce better estimates of incidence.

The one study is Doyle's (1995) mapping of suicide rates across US counties for the years 1979–1992. Doyle cites several factors that could account for the observed pattern. The one that led to our assigning the work to the column concerned with coping resources was 'lack of family and community support.' Doyle notes (1995: 22), 'It is not surprising, therefore, that the proportion of divorced people follows, in rough fashion, the regional pattern depicted by the map.'

Doyle's analyses are squarely in Cell 14 because he does not suggest that the spatial distribution contributes any new insights into the etiology of suicide. In fact, he is quite explicit that he looks to the etiologic literature for explanations of the spatial distribution.

Cell 17

Work in Cell 17 uses measures of true prevalence to determine if the spatial variation in mental illness is attributable to available coping resources. The only piece we found to fit these criteria was the analysis by Hauenstein and Boyd (1994) of depression in rural areas. They report that there are higher rates of depression in rural than in other areas. This was particularly true for young persons, the unemployed, and poorly educated women. Among the explanations offered for the difference was the relative lack of services available to these persons in rural areas.

There is no dispute over the relative paucity of mental health services in rural areas (Rohland 1995). There is, however, disagreement over its effects on the prevalence of illness (Kessler et al. 1994). The Hauenstein and Boyd findings should be viewed with this controversy in mind.

Cell 20

Cell 20 is defined by work that explains spatial variation in treated disorder as a function of similar variation in coping resources. Among the pieces that could be assigned to the cell is one of the truly seminal works in medical geography. The piece is the report by Jarvis (1852) that the prevalence of treated disorder decreases with distance from mental hospitals. Jarvis carefully documented the rates of treatment for several American communities and noted that his 'law' (i.e., people in the vicinity of 'lunatic hospitals' send more people to them than do people at greater distance) applied to all of them. Jarvis rejected the notion that the phenomenon reflected a similar distribution of true prevalence. Instead, he argued that simple impedance made it less likely that people at greater distance would use mental health facilities. The benefit of treatment was not viewed as being as great as the cost of getting the patient to the hospital. He further noted that the perceived benefit of treatment might be distributed so that those closer to mental health facilities were more optimistic about the effectiveness of treatment.

Jarvis' basic empirical finding has been replicated many times. Perhaps the most impressive of these is the analyses by Sohler and Thompson (1970) of admissions to mental health facilities in Connecticut. The state was divided into districts and each was scored by its rate of hospitalization, distance from facility, socioeconomic and demographic characteristics, metropolitan or nonmetropolitan status, and availability of other traditional and nontraditional mental health service providers. The results of the analyses were similar to those of Jarvis. Distance predicted utilization for all types of diagnoses controlling for all the above confounds.

The work on Jarvis' law is the best example of that which asks geographic as opposed to etiologic questions. The work assumes that the spatial distribution of treated disorder is not related to true prevalence, and looks for theory from fields entirely separate from those concerned with the etiology of illness. The work also falls clearly in the coping resources column in that the explanation it offers assumes that the distribution of treated disorder is a function of access to medical care.

Cell 23

Research in Cell 23 uses treated disorder measured in individuals as a means of understanding the role of coping resources in the etiology of a behavioral problem. We found only one study that came close to matching these criteria. Cuffel (1994) studied the determinants of violence and disruptive behavior among persons admitted to the state mental hospital in Arkansas. He surveyed the records of those admitted with and without violence, and discovered that those from rural areas were, controlling for diagnosis, more likely to be disruptive. Further study of the conditions preceding the criterion admission led Cuffel to conclude that persons from rural areas were more likely to be violent upon admission because their communities had fewer formal and informal services available to stabilize patients before their transfer to the state hospital.

MENTAL ILLNESS: TOLERANCE FOR COPING (COLUMN 3)

As has been noted above, much of the theoretical and empirical work concerned with tolerance for coping with hazards has focused on behavioral coping (e.g., Gove 1975, 1980, 1982; Link et al. 1992; Rosenfeld 1997). Unfortunately, this issue of how and why tolerance for behavioral coping varies over space has not been much explored. We have found examples of work that comes close to matching the criteria for each cell in the tolerance column, but few of the examples are satisfying. Cell 15, for example, is empty. This suggests that new researchers could make a seminal contribution by addressing whether and why tolerance for coping varies in space.

Cell 18

To fit Cell 18 squarely, research would use survey measures of true prevalence of mental disorder to assess the role of tolerance at the onset of illness. The closest fit we know of is work that tests the theory that economic contraction makes a community less tolerant of behavioral deviance, and that the punishment this intolerance forebodes reduces the incidence of such behavior. Catalano et al. (1993) tested the theory using survey data that measured, among other disorders, clinically significant alcohol abuse and dependence in a panel of Americans living in four different labor markets. The initial and follow-up (i.e., 1 year later) surveys were conducted at different times across the communities, giving the authors temporal and spatial variation in labor market conditions.

The results were that persons who remained employed between interviews but worked in contracting labor markets were less likely to move from having no disorder at first interview to being clinically dependent or abusive of alcohol at their second interview than persons who remained employed in stable or growing labor markets. The authors inferred support for the theory that growing intolerance for deviance reduced the incidence of deviance.

The implication of the work for space and health is that the incidence of behavioral deviance in communities may vary as a function of their economies. Other work has added support to this possibility (e.g., Catalano et al. 1993, 1997).

Cell 21

Cell 21 includes work concerned with the role of tolerance in the distribution of treated disorder across spaces. We know of only one piece that meets the criteria for inclusion, but it is among the truly seminal works in the field. The study by Faris and Dunham (1939) of the spatial distribution of mental illness in Chicago is frequently cited as the beginning of the modern inquiry into the effects of space on mental health. Essentially they found that most types of treated disorder exhibited an 'ecological gradient.' This means that the prevalence of diagnosis was greatest in the areas closest to the center of the city, and decreased with distance from the center. The exception to this rule was manic depression, which appeared to be randomly distributed throughout the city.

Faris and Dunham offered several explanations for their maps. These are truly seminal because they were the first to posit the tension between the social selection and social causation hypotheses. They noted that the strongest correlate of the ecological gradient was socioeconomic status of residents. They invoked the work of Thomas and Znaniecki (1920) that had earlier argued that the experiences of the poor and migrant in American cities was so aversive that it caused behavioral disorder. Faris and Dunham also noted, however, that it was demonstrably true that many disordered persons who had been seriously ill from childhood had 'drifted' into the poorest part of the city. The authors prophetically suggested that differentiating between these two explanations was a topic for further research.

Their interpretation of the findings for manic depression leads to their assignment to this cell. They report having spoken to psychiatrists in Chicago who reported that it was common practice in private hospitals to diagnose behaviorally disordered persons as manic depressive regardless of 'true' disorder. This was done because the families of patients did not want the more stigmatizing label of schizophrenia to be applied to their relatives. Psychiatrists also reported that poor persons seen in public hospitals were routinely given the schizophrenia label because it would entitle the patient to more treatment. Being sent home was less desirable, the psychiatrists believed, because poor families had little understanding of diagnostic differences and few resources with which to cope with an ill member. The effect of these diagnostic biases would be to over-diagnose schizophrenia among the poor and under-diagnose it among the better off. The opposite would be true for manic depression. Faris and Dunham acknowledge that these differences in tolerance by class may have induced an unknown fraction of the ecological gradient in their maps.

Another characteristic of Faris and Dunham's work that places it squarely in this cell is their speculation that part of their findings could be due to the 'isolation effect' (Castle and Gittus 1957). They hypothesized that migrants living in areas in which their cultural group is the majority are less likely to be diagnosed as behaviorally ill than similar persons living in areas in which their cultural group is in the minority. The reasoning for the hypothesis is that coping strategies are more likely to be tolerated by those who would cope similarly. Migrants in areas in which they are the minority are, conversely, more likely to be diagnosed as ill because their coping strategies are more likely to be viewed as deviant.

Cell 24

Our last cell is defined by using treated disorder among samples of individuals to shed light on how tolerance across places may affect the etiology of mental illness. We found two examples of such work. Both deal with urban/rural differences in tolerance for mental illness.

The first study (Rost et al. 1993) was a survey of attitudes toward mental illness among rural persons who had themselves used mental health services. The number of respondents who negatively characterized persons who sought help for depression was higher than expected by the authors and higher than among urban samples. The implications for etiology were that rural persons with depression were probably deterred from treatment by the intolerance of their communities for help seeking.

The second study (Rost et al. 1994) reports that the stigma in rural areas of seeking help from mental health professionals leads to a greater use of primary care practitioners for mental health problems than in urban areas. Physicians in rural areas, moreover, are less likely to refer patients with mental health problems to mental health professionals than are primary care physicians in urban areas. The authors imply that the effect of low tolerance for mental illness in rural areas on the course of treatment probably affects the nature of the disease in those areas.

Enduring and Emerging Themes

The universe of research from which the above sample was selectively drawn is diverse. So much so that the reader might wonder if the work has anything in common other than an interest in the distribution of illness in space. We believe that most of the literature shares at least two other important themes. The first is the largely implicit but enduring theme that the distribution of wealth affects the spatial distribution of health and illness. The second is an emerging yet more explicit motif. This is that research on place and health can and should lead to more humane social and economic policies.

The implicit theme that wealth affects the spatial distribution of illness assumes that the economy is a generator of hazards as well as a resource for coping. The connection of the economy to coping resources is intuitive. Households with more money can procure more of the coping resources distributed by the market. Communities with more money are more able to provide services for people with health and behavioral problems than are communities with less money. The notion that personal and commonly held wealth are means to enhance coping is not new, and is developed in the work of Robert (in this volume) as well as in many other works (e.g., Black et al. 1982)

The connection of economic policy to the spatial distribution of hazards is perhaps less intuitive than the connection of policy to coping resources. The dynamism of the economy is, however, experienced by individuals as demands to cope behaviorally and physiologically with stressful life events, infectious and noninfectious toxins, and safety hazards.

The stressful life events research is considerable and has been reviewed in depth elsewhere (Dohrenwend and Dohrenwend 1974). It should be sufficient to note here that the research supports the hypothesis that many life experiences that can be specified 'a priori' are risk factors for subsequent physiological and behavioral disorder. Undesirable experiences are apparently more likely to elicit symptoms than desirable events (Ross and Mirowsky 1979). The association between these undesirable life experiences and illness is typically weak, and is thought to be mediated by coping resources, including social support (Rook and Dooley 1985).

It has also been argued that physiologic coping resources, whether genetic or acquired, can be temporarily depleted with use and permanently depleted with age (Selye 1952; Taylor et al. 1997). We supposedly regain much, but not all, of the capacity to cope if we are not required to cope too soon with other hazards. The capacity lost with each adaptation may increase, and the proportion of the capacity regained, may, moreover, decrease with age.

As has been noted elsewhere (Catalano et al. 1987), the typical list of undesirable events that have been found to be risk factors for disorder can be separated into several groups. Among these groups are job and financial events. The incidence of these events has been empirically linked to the performance of local economies (Dooley and Catalano 1984). These events have been found to be risk factors for both physiological and behavioral disorder. These findings withstand controlling for other undesirable events and for other variables that intuition and theory imply could confound the relationship (e.g., age, gender, and socioeconomic characteristics) (Catalano and Dooley 1983; Dooley et al. 1987).

The experience of an undesirable job and financial events by a principal wage earner has also been reported to be a risk factor for disorder for her spouse (Rook et al. 1991). Undesirable job and financial experiences, moreover, are apparently risk factors for subsequent nonjob, nonfinancial experiences (Catalano et al. 1987). The performance of a local economy can, in other words, increase the experience of undesirable job and financial events that in turn increase the risk of experiencing yet other undesirable experiences not intuitively related to the economy. These undesirable events raise the risk of disorder not only among those who experience them, but also among spouses and perhaps other members of the family.

The experience of undesirable job and financial events also apparently increases the likelihood that an individual will seek help for behavioral problems controlling for his or her symptoms of such problems. In fact, the perception of job insecurity, controlling for symptoms and for the experience of undesirable events of all kinds, is enough to increase the likelihood of seeking help (Catalano et al. 1986). As one would expect, the perception of job insecurity is related to objective economic indicators (Catalano et al. 1986).

A population exposed to a high frequency of economic stressors may well be at elevated risk of succumbing to future stressors whether those are economic in nature or not (Catalano 1989).

In fact, research done on those who experienced the great depression of the 1930s suggests that economically induced stressors can affect behavior into the long-term future (Elder 1974).

In addition to increasing the number of stressful life experiences with which a population must cope, economic policy can also influence the type of infectious and toxic substances, as well as the safety hazards, to which a population is exposed. As Hippocrates (Jones 1923) noted, the industries upon which a community is based predict the epidemic diseases to which the community is exposed. This is true primarily because the microorganisms that are necessary, if not sufficient, for infectious illness are frequently brought to, and circulate within, a community through economic connections (Pyle 1986).

The type of noninfectious toxins to which a population is exposed can also be influenced by the local economy (McMullen 1976; Ozolins 1966; Welson and Stevens 1970). These toxins are usually classed as ambient (e.g., air or water pollution) or local (e.g., work site). Much of both types of these toxins can be attributed to the industries a community chooses to permit within its boundaries.

Safety hazards are also ambient (e.g., road hazards) and local (e.g., work-site risks). The type of vehicles using the road system of a community, as well as the time distribution of that use, is a function of the industries present. Work-site safety hazards are, moreover, obviously associated with the types of industries a community harbors. Less intuitive is the possibility that the stressful events induced in a population by economic dynamics will cause fatigue and distraction that interact with safety hazards to yield spatial variability in the incidence of accidental injury. Research has demonstrated that stressful life events are risk factors for accidental injury (Selzer 1969; Selzer and Vinokur 1974). The incidence of auto- and work-related accidents has been found to be associated with changes in the economy (Catalano and Serxner 1987; Wagenaar 1984).

The economy may affect the prevalence of disorder as much through tolerance for coping as through the actual incidence of symptoms. The literature in this field has come to accept illness as the label society applies to adaptations that reduce a person's ability to perform day-to-day functions. How great changes in performance, the 'just noticeable difference,' must be before a community notices them becomes an important determinant of how many among those who are coping will be labeled ill. Moreover, the difference may not be the same for everyone. Those who are, or who have been in the past, deviant may be held to a different standard of performance. Minorities and those with histories of behavioral problems, for example, may be scrutinized more carefully and held to a more difficult standard than others.

The just noticeable difference from performance standards has been studied by both sociologists and psychologists, and has been found to vary in ways that may connect it to the economy. The ecological psychologists have, for example, noted that overstaffed organizations (i.e., those with more participants than roles) tend to be less tolerant of deviance than understaffed organizations (Barker and Shoggen 1973). The assumption is that maintaining an understaffed organization requires its members to be tolerant of the idiosyncrasies of those available to perform needed functions. Members of an overstaffed organization, on the other hand, must choose among several candidates for a role, and can therefore set higher standards for what is acceptable functioning. Those in overstaffed organizations who are adapting to undesirable events, infectious or noninfectious toxins, or safety hazards are therefore at a disadvantage because they are not as likely to be performing at their best as are those without such stressors.

The notion that organizations can be understaffed or overstaffed and that this can affect tolerance for deviance has been expanded by sociologists to apply to communities (Catalano et al. 1986). The economy of a community affects staffing in a profound sense. If the economy is contracting, the community is probably overstaffed. If, on the other hand, the economy is expanding, many firms are probably understaffed. These dynamics imply the hypothesis that, controlling for symptoms, workers in communities with contracting economies are more likely to seek help for illness than workers in expanding economies. The hypothesis has been supported for help-seeking for behavioral disorder (Catalano et al. 1986).

The emerging, more explicit, theme is that research into space and health can and should move economic policy toward a narrower distribution of wealth. Jones and Duncan (1995) make the connection between the old and new theme explicit:

> In substantive terms, there appears to be good evidence that health outcomes cannot be simply reduced to individual characteristics. There is an ecology of chronic illness that remains after a wide range of demographic, socio-structural and behavioral variables are included in the models. This ecology is related to measures of deprivation and income variation. In general, and irrespective of individual characteristics, places with a low income or deprivation suffer the worst health on a range of measures. (Jones and Duncan 1995: 38)

Sampson et al. (1997) listed in Cell 1, move the argument beyond its empirical base into the realm of politics. They note:

> As shown, what happens within neighborhoods is in part shaped by socioeconomic and housing factors linked to the wider political economy. In addition to encouraging communities to mobilize against violence through 'self-help' strategies of informal social control...strategies to address the social and ecological changes that beset many inner city communities need to be considered. (Sampson et al. 1997: 923)

Roberts (1997), listed in Cell 4, goes further. He writes,

> Much of the social differentiation of the city that we see today is the result of powerful individuals and groups actively working to divert resources and maintain segregation in the ongoing oppression that occurred over most of the 20th century. (Roberts 1997: 598)

Wilkinson (1996), listed in Cell 2, takes the theme to its logical extension:

> As research on the socioeconomic determinants of health progresses, and public understanding of the issues increases, the demand for social reform will become unstoppable. Growing knowledge changes both the morality and the rationality of the status quo. It turns excusable official inaction into culpable negligence. (Wilkinson 1996: 25)

The emerging theme in the research appears to be based on the following reasoning.

1   The aspect of being poor that elicits the most sympathy from those who are not poor is relative bad health.
2   Research shall show that the health problems of the poor are reinforced, if not caused, by the unequal spatial distribution of hazards, coping resources, and tolerance.
3   Those who are not poor would support making the environments of the poor less hazardous, richer in coping resources, and more tolerant if more research on the spatial distribution of illness were conducted and disseminated.

We use 'shall' rather than 'will' in the second paragraph above because we do not assert that the new researchers in the field cause their work to produce the politically useful finding. Rather, they appear to trust that such a finding will emerge from their science. Whether this trust unintentionally affects the research is, of course, difficult to determine. The possibility that it might, however, warrants consideration as we move forward in this important line of research.

REFERENCES

Aneshensel, C. and Sucoff, C. (1996) 'The neighborhood context of adolescent mental health', *Journal of Health and Social Behavior*, 37: 293–310.

Barker, R. and Shoggen, P. (1973) *Qualities of Community Life*. San Francisco: Jossey Bass.

Barrett, A. (1986) 'Medical geography: Concept and definition', in Michael Paccione (ed.), *Medical Geography: Progress and Prospect*. London: Croom Helm. pp. 1–34.

Black, D. Morris, J., Smith, C. and Townsend, P. (1982) *Inequalities and Health: The Black Report*. New York: Penguin.

Bonnie, R. and Monahan, J. (1997) *Mental Disorder, Work Disability, and the Law*. Chicago: University of Chicago Press.

Castle, I. and Gittus, E. (1957) 'The distribution of social defects in Liverpool', *Sociological Review*, 5: 43–64.

Catalano, R. (1989) 'Ecological factors in illness and disease', in H. Freeman and S. Levine (eds), *Handbook of Medical Sociology*. New York: Prentice-Hall. pp. 87–101.

Catalano, R. (1998) Review of Wilkinson, R. G., 'Unhealthy Societies: The Afflictions of Inequality'. London: Routledge, 1996. In *Journal of Community and Social Psychology*, 8: 165–68.

Catalano, R. and Dooley, D. (1983) 'Health effects of economic instability: A test of the economic stress hypothesis', *Journal of Health and Social Behavior*, 24: 46–60.

Catalano, R. and Serxner, S. (1987) 'Time-series designs of potential interest to epidemiologists', *American Journal of Epidemiology*, 126: 724–31.

Catalano, R., Rook, K., and Dooley, D. (1986) 'Labor markets and help-seeking: A test of the employment security hypothesis', *Journal of Health and Social Behavior*, 27: 277–87.

Catalano, R., Dooley, D., and Rook, K. (1987) 'A test of reciprocal risk between undesirable economic and noneconomic life events', *American Journal of Community Psychology*, 15: 633–51.

Catalano, R., Dooley, D., Wilson, G., and Hough, R. (1993) 'Job loss and alcohol abuse: A test using data from the Epidemiologic Catchment Area Project', *Journal of Health and Social Behavior*, 34: 215–26.

Catalano, R., Novaco, R., and McConnell, W. (1997) 'A model of the net effect of job loss on violence', *Journal of Personality and Social Psychology*, 72: 1440–47.

Cleek, R. (1979) 'Cancers and the environment: The effect of scale', *Social Science and Medicine*, 13D: 241–47.

Cliff, A. and Haggett, P. (1988) *Atlas of Disease Distributions*. Oxford: Blackwell.

Cuffel, B. (1994) 'Violent and destructive behavior among the severely mentally ill in rural areas: Evidence from Arkansas' Community Mental Health System', *Community Mental Health Journal*, 30: 495–504.

Dahl, R. (ed.) (1984) *The Geography of Disease*. London: Churchill Livingstone.

Dartmouth Medical School (1996) *The Dartmouth Atlas of Health Care*. Chicago, IL: American Hospital Publishing.

Dohrenwend, B. and Dohrenwend, B. (1974) *Stressful Life Events: Their Nature and Effects*. New York: Wiley.

Dooley, D. and Catalano, R. (1984) 'Why the economy predicts help-seeking', *Journal of Health and Social Behavior*, 25: 160–75.

Dooley, D., Rook, K., and Catalano, R. (1987) 'Job and non-job stressors and their moderators', *Journal of Occupational Psychology*, 60: 115–32.

Doyle, R. (1995) 'Suicide', *Scientific American*, 273(6): 22.

Elder, G. (1974) *Children of the Great Depression*. Chicago, University of Chicago Press.

Ettner, S. (1997) 'Measuring the human cost of a weak economy: Does unemployment lead to alcohol abuse?' *Social Science and Medicine*, 44: 251–60.

Evans, G., Jacobs, S., Dooley, D., and Catalano, R. (1987) 'The interaction of stressful life events and chronic strains on community mental health', *American Journal of Community Psychology*, 15: 23–34.

Faris, R. and Dunham, W. (1939) *Mental Disorders in Urban Area: An Ecological Study of Schizophrenia and Other Psychoses*. Chicago, IL: University of Chicago Press.

Fiscella, K. and Franks, P. (1997) 'Poverty of income inequality as predictor of mortality: Longitudinal cohort study', *British Medical Journal*, 314: 724–28.

Gove, W. (1975) *The Labeling of Deviance*. New York: Sage.

Gove, W. (ed.) (1980) *Labeling Deviant Behavior*. Beverly Hills: Sage.

Gove, W. (ed.) (1982) *Deviance and Mental Illness*. Beverly Hills: Sage.

Gravelle, H. (1998) 'How much of the relation between population mortality and unequal distribution of income is a statistical artifact?' *British Medical Journal*, 316: 382–85.

Haan, M., Kaplan, G., and Comacho, T. (1987) 'Poverty and health: Prospective evidence from the Alameda County Study', *American Journal of Epidemiology*, 125: 989–98.

Hart, K., Kunitz, S., Sell, R., and Mukamel, D. (1998) 'Metropolitan governance, residential segregation, and mortality among African Americans', *American Journal of Public Health*, 88: 434–38.

Hauenstein, E. and Boyd, M. (1994) 'Depressive symptoms in young women of the Piedmont: Prevalence in rural women', *Women and Health*, 21: 105–23.

Hirsch, A. (1886) *Handbook of Geographical and Historical Pathology*. London: New Sydenham Society.

Howe, G. (1963) *National Atlas of Disease Mortality in the United Kingdom*. London: Nelson.

Jacobs, S., Evans, G., Catalano, R., and Dooley, D. (1984) 'Air pollution and depressive symptomatology', *Population and Environment*, 7: 260–71.

Jarvis, E. (1852) 'On the supposed increase in insanity', *American Journal of Insanity*, 8: 331–61.

Jehlik, P. and McNamara, R. (1952) 'The relation of distance to the differential use of certain health personnel and facilities and to the extent of bed illness', *Rural Sociology*, 17: 261–65.

Jenkins, D. (1983) 'Social environment and cancer mortality in men', *New England Journal of Medicine*, 308: 395–98.

Johnson, C. (1996) 'Orthodontia'. *American Journal of Orthodontics and Dentofacial Orthopedics*, 110: 111–16.

Jones, K. and Duncan, C. (1995) 'Individuals and their ecologies: Analyzing the geography of chronic illness within a multilevel modeling framework', *Health and Place*, 1: 27–40.

Jones, W. (1923) *Hippocrates*. Cambridge, MA: Harvard University Press.

Kaplan, G. (1996) 'People and places: Contrasting perspectives on the association between social class and health', *International Journal of Health Services*, 26: 507–19.

Kessler, R., McGonagle, K., Zhao, S., Brown, R., and Broman, C. (1994) 'Lifetime and 12-month prevalence of DSM-III-R psychiatric disorders in the US: Results from the National Comorbidity Survey', *Archives of General Psychiatry*, 51: 8–19.

Kleinman, A. and Cohen, A. (1997) 'Psychiatry's global challenge', *Scientific American*, 276: 86–91.

Krieger, N. (1992) 'Overcoming the absence of socioeconomic data in medical records: Validation and application of a census-based methodology', *American Journal of Public Health*, 82: 703–10.

Kulozik, A., Wainscoat, J., Serjeant, G., Kar, B., Al-Always, B., Essan, G., Falusi, A., Haque, S., Hilali, A., and Kate, S. (1986) 'Geographical survey of BS-globin gene haplotypes: Evidence for an independent Asian origin of the sickle cell mutation', *American Journal of Human Genetics*, 39: 239–44.

Leighton, D., Harding, J., Macklin, D., Macmillan, A., and Leighton, A. (1963) *The Character of Danger*. New York: Basic Books.

Link, B., Cullen, F., Mitrotznik, J., and Struening, E. (1992) 'The consequences of stigma for persons with mental illness: Evidence from the social sciences', in P. J. Fink and A. Tasman (eds). *Stigma and Mental Illness*. Washington, DC: American Psychiatric Press. pp. 87–96.

Macintyre, S., MacIver, S., and Sooman, A. (1993) 'Area, class and health: Should we be focusing on places or people?' *Journal of Social Policy*, 22: 213–34.

Mandelblatt, J., Andrews, H., Kao, R., Wallace, R., and Kerner, J. (1995) 'Impact of access and social context on breast cancer stage at diagnosis', *Journal of Health Care for the Poor and Underserved*, 6: 342–51.

Marmot, M. (1994) 'Changing places and changing risks: The study of migrants', *Public Health Reviews*, 21: 185–95.

May, J. (1955) *Atlas of Disease*. New York: American Geographical Society.

Mayer, J. (1979) 'Paramedic response time and survival from cardiac arrest', *Social Science and Medicine*, 13: 267–71.

Mayhew, H. (1862) *The Criminal Prisons of London and Scenes of Prison life*. London: C. Griffen Bohn.

McGlashan, N. and Blunden, J. (1983) *Geographic Aspects of Health*. London: Academic Press.

McMullen, T. (1976) 'Air quality and community characteristics'. Paper presented to the Annual Meeting of the Air Pollution Control Association.

Meyer, S. and Jencks, C. (1989) 'Growing up in poor neighborhoods: How much does it matter', *Science*, 243: 1441–5.

Morgan, M. and Chinn, S. (1983) 'ACORN group, social class, and child health', *American Journal of Epidemiology*, 37: 196–203.

Morgenstern, H. (1982) 'Uses of ecological analyses in epidemiologic research', *American Journal of Public Health*, 72: 1336–44.

Myaux, J., Ali, M., Felsenstein, A., Chakraborty, J., and de Francisco, A. (1997) 'Spatial distribution of watery diarrhoea in children: Identification of "risk areas" in a rural community in Bangladesh', *Health & Place*, 3: 181–6.

Nesbitt, T., Larson, E., Rosenblatt, R., and Hart, G. (1997) 'Access to maternity care: Its effect on neonatal outcomes and resource use', *American Journal of Public Health*, 87: 85–90.

O'Brien, S. and Dean, M. (1997) 'In search of AIDS-resistance genes', *Scientific American*, 277(3): 44–51.

Ozolins, G. (1966) *Rapid Survey Technique for Estimating Community Air Pollution Emissions*. Cincinnati: US Department of Health, Education, and Welfare.

Park, R. and Burgess, E. (eds) (1925) *The City*. Chicago: University of Chicago Press.

Purola, T. (1968) *The Utilization of the Medical Services and Its Relationship to Morbidity, Health Resources and Social Factors. A Survey of the Population of Finland Prior to the National Sickness Insurance Scheme*. Helsinki: Research Institute for Social Security.

Pyle, G. (1986) *The Diffusion of Influenza*. Totowa NJ: Rowman and Littlefield.

Roberts, E. M. (1997) 'Neighborhood social environments and the distribution of low birthweight in Chicago', *American Journal of Public Health*, 87: 597–603.

Rodenwaldt, E. and Jusatz, H. (1952) *Atlas of Epidemic Diseases*. Hamburg: Falk.

Rohland, B. (1995) 'A survey of utilization of psychiatrists in community mental health centers in Iowa', *Psychiatric Services*, 46: 81–3.

Rook, K. and Dooley, D. (1985) 'Applying social support research: Theoretical problems and future directions', *Journal of Social Issues*, 41: 5–28.

Rook, K., Catalano, R., and Dooley, D. (1991) 'Stress transmission: The effects of husband's job stressors on the emotional health of their wives', *Journal of Marriage and the Family*, 53: 165–77.

Rosenfield, S. (1997) 'Labeling mental illness: The effects of received services and perceived stigma on life satisfaction', *American Sociological Review*, 62: 660–72.

Ross, C. and Mirowsky, J. (1979) 'A comparison of life-event weighting schemes', *Journal of Health and Social Behavior*, 20: 166–77.

Rost, K., Smith, G., and Taylor, J. (1993) 'Rural–urban differences in stigma and the use of care for depressive disorders', *Journal of Rural Health*, 9: 57–62.

Rost, K., Humphrey, J., and Kelleher, K. (1994) 'Physician management presences and barriers to care for rural patients with depression', *Archives of Family Medicine*, 2: 409–17.

Sampson, R., Raudenbush, S., and Earls, F. (1997) 'Neighborhoods and violent crime: A multilevel study of collective efficacy', *Science*, 277: 918–24.

Selye, H. (1952) *The Story of Adaptation*. Montreal: Acta.

Selzer, M. (1969) 'Alcoholism, mental illness, and stress in 96 drivers causing fatal accidents', *Behavioral Science*, 14: 1–10.

Selzer, M. and Vinokur, A. (1974) 'Life events, subjective stress, and traffic accidents', *American Journal of Psychiatry*, 131: 903–6.

Shannon, G. W. (1977) 'Space, time and illness behavior', *Social Science and Medicine*, 11: 683–9.

Shannon, G. and Dever, A. (1974) *Health Care Delivery: Spatial Perspectives*. New York: McGraw Hill.

Shannon, G. and Pyle, G. (1993) *Disease and Medical Care in the United States: A Medical Atlas of the Twentieth Century*. New York: Macmillan.

Shaw, C. and McKay, H. (1942) *Juvenile Delinquency and Urban Areas*. Chicago: University of Chicago Press.

Shevky, E. and Bell, W. (1955) *Social Area Analysis: Theory Illustrative Applications and Procedures*. Stanford, CA: Stanford University Press.

Sohler, K. and Thompson, J. (1970) 'Jarvis' law and the planning of mental health services', *Public Health Reports*, 85: 503–10.

Sutherland, E. (1939) *Principles of Criminology*. Philadelphia: Lippincott.

Taylor, S., Repetti, R., and Seeman, T. (1997) 'Health psychology: What is an unhealthy environment and how does it get under the skin?' *Annual Review of Psychology*, 48: 411–47.

Thomas, W. and Znaniecki, F. (1920) *The Polish Peasant in Europe and America*. New York: Alfred A Knopf.

Voss, L. D. (1995) 'Short stature: Does it matter? A review of the evidence', *Journal of Medical Screening*, 2: 130–2.

Wagenaar, A. (1984) 'Effects of macroeconomic conditions on the incidence of motor vehicle accidents', *Accident Analysis and Prevention*, 16: 191–205.

Waldmann, R. (1992) 'Income distribution and infant mortality', *Quarterly Journal of Economics*, 107: 1283–302.

Welson, J. and Stevens, B. (1970) *Air Quality and its Relationship to Economic, Meteorological, and Other Structural Characteristics of Urban Areas in the United States*. Philadelphia: Regional Science Research Institute.

Wennberg, J. and Gittelsohn, A. (1973) 'Small area variations in health care delivery', *Science*, 182: 1102–8.

Wilkinson, R. (1996) *Unhealthy Societies: The Afflictions of Inequality*. London: Routledge.

1.6

The Globalization of Health and Disease: The Health Transition and Global Change

EMILY C. ZIELINSKI GUTIÉRREZ AND
CARL KENDALL

DEFINING GLOBALIZATION

'Globalization' is a diffuse construct used to denote the growing perceived spread of a capitalist world system and its integration with systems of trade, communication, transportation, patterns of urbanization, cultural influence, and migration throughout the world. Kearney defines globalization as the movement of people, '...information, symbols, capital and commodities in global and transnational spaces' (Kearney 1995: 547). Quoting Giddens, Kearney notes that globalization in his usage is '...the intensification of worldwide social relations which link distant localities in such a way that local happenings are shaped by events occurring many miles away and vice versa' (Giddens 1990).

There is nothing particularly new about these phenomena. However, authors who use the construct argue that there is something different about the velocity of these changes that has created a qualitatively new set of economic and social forces. Some authors use the construct as a portmanteau that encompasses any economic, cultural, or social phenomena with extra-national links, while others argue for appreciating the synergistic integration of finance, trade, economics, politics, and culture that they mean by globalization.

These multiple meanings, and the enormous range of phenomena glossed, make a review of the globalization construct difficult if not impossible. Although there is no denying the sense of 'connectedness' – both psychological and physical – that permeates the contemporary world, the consequences of this for politics, economics, society, and culture, let alone for health and disease, are difficult to predict and sometimes even to trace.

In the case of the globalization of disease, the reviewer must appreciate both the globalization of disease in terms of epidemiology, and the impact of globalization *on* disease. A complete account of these two topics is not attempted here. What is attempted is an exploration of recent literature on health and globalization, including the roles of economic linkages, transportation and systems of communication, and the impacts of environmental change and urbanization on health. This chapter will review exemplary global health problems, several social processes that are embedded in globalization, and finally, medical and public health responses in a world where health must be 'globally' considered. Without committing to either the argument that the world is qualitatively or only incrementally different, the construct of globalization can be worthwhile to explore as an example of new public health thinking (Yach and Bettcher, 1998: 735 ff). Identifying social constructs that help to explain patterns of disease is an increasingly important goal for a public health community that is seeking a broad-based understanding of the current health transition and how to influence it.

The 'globalization of disease' functions as a deliberately provocative term, in both the health and economic sectors. Jonathan Mann states that, 'the world has rapidly become much more vulnerable to the eruption and, most critically, to the widespread and even global spread of both new and old infectious diseases'. (Mann in Garrett 1994: xv). This vulnerability means that infectious diseases are no longer isolable in dangerous tropical locales, and this fact has been used to regenerate interest – sometimes approaching panic – in infectious diseases in economically advantaged countries. However, what is less well reported is how the economic and social processes associated with globalization (often originating within these 'more developed' countries) visit diseases on the developing world.

Convergence and Divergence: Health in a Connected World

Examining the globalization of disease often involves appreciating patterns of convergence made clearer by advances in measurement. Murray and Lopez (1996) draw on their research in the Global Burden of Disease (GBD) study, and the derived composite measure of disability-adjusted life years (DALYs: 'the sum of years of life lost becaue of premature mortality and years of life lived with disability, adjusted for severity of disability') (Murray and Lopez 1996: 740) to project global mortality and disability burdens between the years 1990 and 2020. Their baseline projection anticipates ischemic heart disease, unipolar major depression, road traffic accidents, and cerebrovascular disease becoming the top four causes of mortality and disability, positions currently (1990) occupied by lower respiratory infections, diarrheal disease, and perinatal conditions. Demographic shifts and trends (many attributable to the increased use of tobacco) are cited as the main causes for these changes (Murray and Lopez 1996). In these projections we see the rising proportional effects of noninfectious disease, with increasing numbers of persons in both higher income and 'developing' nations being affected by noncommunicable conditions. Murray and Lopez cite that nearly 9 per cent of the GBD in 2020 may be due to tobacco-related mortality and disability; global marketing, transportation, and communication are all implicated in tobacco's spread. Additionally, as strides are made against infectious diseases, these survivors in lower-income regions will become candidates for chronic conditions.

There are also important dynamics of *divergence* in the impacts stemming from globalization. The above projections do not mean that communicable diseases cease to be a problem. Murray and Lopez note, 'there is a dramatic difference in the distribution of deaths between established market economies (EMEs) and the formerly socialist economies of Europe and the developing regions' (Murray and Lopez 1996: 741). Communicable diseases, maternal and perinatal causes, and nutritional deficiencies accounted for 65 per cent of deaths in sub-Saharan Africa, and they were implicated in just over 15 per cent of deaths in EMEs (Murray and Lopez 1996: 741). It is the *relative* burden of disease that is anticipated to shift, more than a large-scale reduction in the absolute number of people affected by infectious disease. In Murray and Lopez's baseline projection, HIV would rise from twenty-eighth to tenth in its share of the GBD, and tuberculosis would retain its current rank, although increasing its share of DALYs, from 2.8 to 3.1 per cent. While the maxim holds true that anyone *can* be infected, the reality is that the toll is higher among the poor in all regions.

Globalization has led, in some respects, to more awe and fear of the microbial world – and its human and animal hosts – than during preceding generations of medicine and public health. After all, with the advent of modern technology a sense of security overcame native caution (Lappé 1995). The complex interweaving of the health effects of globalization and the responses to it can be demonstrated when examining malaria as a long-known infectious disease that still defies control.

Although heading toward control in the 1960s, malaria has reemerged as a first-order health problem in the tropical regions of the globe. Approximately 300–500 million people are infected with malaria each year, making it the fifth most common cause of ill health worldwide and the cause of an estimated 1.5–2.7 million deaths per year. Nearly one million of these deaths are among children under 5 years old, some of whom succumb to malaria in combination with nutritional deficiencies and respiratory disease (WHO 1998a).

Several waves of control strategies have been attempted, none achieving definitive success: environmental alteration, prophylactic use of antimalarials, vector control with insecticides, and, since the early 1980s, vaccine development (NIAID, 1998). Treatment has, in fact, played a role in the new threat that malaria poses (Oaks et al. 1991: 67). In many places, mass chemoprophylaxis led to the presumptive treatment of all fevers with chloroquine, the biological effect of which has likely played a great role in the doubly deleterious effect of promoting resistance to chloroquine and reducing naturally gained immunity in populations. Population movement further enhanced this process. Many villagers have learned to use chloroquine as a universal fever remedy. Helitzer-Allen et al. (1994) and others have demonstrated that a broad range of illnesses is now popularly associated with malaria. As the term 'malaria' replaces local language terms for 'fever,' this heightens the difficulty of using fever as a signal for mothers to bring young infants and children to clinics for other treatment. If fever = malaria, then treatment = chloroquine in the local lexicon. Thus, not only is chloroquine being used inappropriately for malaria, but also to treat other diseases. Part of the globalization of disease is the diffusion of biomedical nosology, even if it remains incomplete.

Financial crisis in malaria-endemic countries impedes the utility of many scientific advancements against the parasite. Second-line drugs are beyond the economic reach of most residents in chloroquine-resistant areas. Although reliable rapid diagnostic tests for malaria exist (Makler et al. 1998), at their present cost the expense of one test outspends many countries' per person yearly health allocation (Verle et al. 1996). Without means of delivery, medical breakthroughs cannot reach those in severest need.

While much credit for historical malaria control successes has been attributed to the use of DDT, malaria was also successfully controlled with environmental interventions and rural development initiatives in many parts of Southern Europe, Latin America, and Asia (Brown 1984; Kere et al. 1996; Litsios 1997). Recent research in Kenya, the Gambia, Ghana, and Burkina Faso suggests that bed nets may be more successful in preventing deaths from malaria than current candidate vaccines (Economist 1998a). In combination with new discoveries about the role of vitamin A and zinc in promoting the body's own immune response, community-based interventions may be more feasible (Economist 1998b).

Community-based interventions that demonstrate the need for an integrated approach to health appear to offer great promise. Such programs, however, require close collaboration across health, economic, and social sectors, and broad population adherence achieved through significant participation and education. Such 'development-focused' and fine-tuned interventions are less predictable, more laborious, and do not lend themselves to the development of commercial products. As a result, they become less likely to be promoted in this global environment.

'A WEB OF INTERCONNECTEDNESS?'

There can be no denial that the benefits of global trade are distributed unevenly, while the economic and social costs associated with rapid change fall more heavily on poorer countries. Developing regions of the world provide raw materials, cheap labor, and vast new markets, and there are no social safety nets to protect vulnerable populations of women, children, and adolescents. This lack of balance in global costs and benefits is also true in terms of health systems and technology. Although some authors argue that globalization promises a more equitable development of the health sector in the future, one can also speculate that these economic changes will only further polarize wealthier and poorer countries.

While this convergence of economic interests has been well noted, the effects of such integration on local health have not always been so clearly in focus. Globalization has fueled the mobilization of groups – from US and European factory workers to indigenous groups in rural Mexico and mass uprisings in Indonesia. People recognize that they are not sharing equitably in the benefits of a global economy (Navarro 1998). Economic growth affects numerous physical exposures to risk factors, but additionally it determines access to resources and investment in infrastructure within a country. These factors have clear implications for current health conditions, and for the emerging patterns of disease. As Navarro states, 'One consequence of public policies that benefit globalization has been an unprecedented growth of inequalities in today's world' (Navarro 1998: 742).

Yach and Bettcher (1998), in a notably positive review, state that expectations regarding globalization have been mixed. Optimists have written of 'a web of... [interconnectedness]... from which our sense of commitment to the other half is strengthened' (Yach and Bettcher 1998). Yet who are the 'other half' spoken of here? If it is the poor, there are several points of error. First, the proportions are not even so well divided, and second, the response to the appreciation of poverty is not necessarily to correct the condition. In fact, awareness without identification can make the poor seem more, not less, remote. As a justifying ideology for globalization, this theory falls short.

Globalization has primarily been the project of just a few countries in Europe and North

America during the twentieth century: although they have been fueled by capitalism and technological development, they are inextricably linked to cultural baggage, such as an ethic of 'acquisitive individualism' and growth without limit (Lasch 1991: 15). The popular recognition that growth and expansion can have negative as well as positive consequences has come as a relatively recent revelation to the developed world. Other countries have felt the impact of incipient globalization and pandemics of imported disease since the sixteenth century, and have had diverse, but often negative, reactions to it (Diamond 1997; Wolf 1982).

Ironically, globalization is a process in which national boundaries – the construction of which appears to have been the work of nineteenth and twentieth century capitalism – recede in importance (Kalekin-Fishman 1996). While 'internationalization' heightens the degree of cooperation among states, globalization refers to processes that act in a separate arena, thereby 'undermining or eroding sovereignty' (Fidler 1996: 77). This process is repeated at many other institutional levels, and can result in an intensification of personal relationships at the expense of social, political, and economic institutional ties. As a result, any individual's lifecourse appears more contingent on personal networks than on any institutional features. 'Personhood,' or the valorization of the individual social and biological personae, is also a Eurocentric project, and illness, identifying as it does the individual sufferer, grows in importance in this scheme.

The most common meaning associated with globalization is economic, especially the 'internationalization of finance' (Navarro 1998). Global factors play an increasing role in local economies, as is manifest in the huge volume of goods and services that move across national borders each day. Production facilities in the developing world take advantage of low local wages, gender inequity, and other social, political, and cultural differences to produce cheap goods for distant markets. International investment can move toward the maximization of profits largely heedless of national borders, with currency and market speculation at times blamed for significant trauma to local economies. This financial globalization takes advantage of the relative absence of social, political, and cultural globalization.

The Institute of Medicine has characterized the result of economic globalization as a transfer of risks due to the 'movement of people,' 'exchange of toxic products' (both intentional and unintentional), 'variance in environmental and occupational safety standards,' and 'the indiscriminate spread of medical technology,'

(Institute of Medicine 1997). The United Nations Development Fund, in its 1998 World Development Report, frames 'underconsumption' as a major constraint to better health and livelihood conditions in the developing world. The need to increase the availability, and equitable distribution, of goods and services conforms well to a model of global propagation of consumption and economic expansion. Solutions under such a paradigm are clearly placed within the hands of producers rather than the public sector (United Nations 1998a).

While most attention to economy has focused on the role of capital, at times as a rather disembodied element acting in financial markets, the 1998 Nobel Prize for Economics marked a change when it was awarded to Amartya Sen (Sachs 1998). Sen's focus on welfare economics and redefinition of poverty not by income but according to one's welfare and capability moves toward the realization that measurement must adjust to the local reality (Sen 1997).

Globalization, of course, has institutional features beyond the movement of capital. Giddens refers to a 'time–space grid' that is laid over the planet as one characterization of globalization (Giddens 1990). While the accomplishment of such a linkage is honored, its effect, as mentioned above, can be to dismember local institutions and to devalue local meanings. Globalization results in the confrontation of the local and global; global forces, be they economic, political, technological, or biological, penetrate local environments at such a pace and intensity that 'local' ceases to have a clear referent. Although Redfield was quick to critique his own notion of the small-scale, isolated community in the sociology of the 1930s, this model made sense to many, as both descriptor and goal (Redfield 1989).

It is precisely this quality of overpowering the local context that tempers enthusiasm for globalizing tendencies as a positive force. The local community – Bhopal, India, for example – is not equipped to respond to global forces that manifest as a 'local' health event. Catastrophes constitute only a small part of the potentially dangerous situations that are a result of the spread of technology to new social and cultural environments. Mundane objects out of context can prove dangerous; for example, the recycling of insecticide and herbicide sacks for the storing of food and seed grains in rural Central America has grave consequences for health. The changes in local economies due to international market influences, a redefinition of local medicine according to cosmopolitan medical standards, and the influx of new risks – social, behavioral, and biological – appear to have overwhelmed the local ability to adapt and cope.

At the same time, at the global level, the conceptual tools used to capture information about health and changes in health have not kept pace with the accelerating effects of globalization. The next section reviews several key concepts – epidemiological transition, epidemiological polarization, and health transition – and examines their relevance in the light of globalization's influence.

GLOBALIZATION AND THE EPIDEMIOLOGICAL TRANSITION

The transformation of health conditions, including the decline of infectious childhood diseases, first in the developed world at the beginning of this century and then accelerating throughout the world in the latter half of this century, has been termed the epidemiological transition. Under this paradigm, societies, responding to improvements in health and agricultural technologies, pass from conditions of high infectious disease mortality in children to concern about chronic diseases of aging, such as coronary heart disease. This apparent transition led to a naïve and simplistic belief in the power of health technologies: '... as nations moved out of poverty and basic food and housing needs were met, scientists could use the pharmaceutical and chemical tools at hand to wipe out parasites, bacteria and viruses. [Leaving] ... the slower chronic diseases that primarily struck in old age' (Garrett 1994: 32). This supports the argument for the convergence of health problems discussed earlier.

Although medical and technological advances have tempted belief in the linear and irreversible character of health development, no society has made this transition completely. At the end of the twentieth century, one-third of all deaths in the United States are due to infectious disease, and infectious diseases are still the leading cause of death in the developing world. Even some of the so-called chronic diseases of aging or 'lifestyle induced' health problems are linked to infectious causes, such as the role found for the infectious agent *Helicobactor pylori* in producing ulcers.

The concept of epidemiologic polarization (Mosley et al. 1993) is key to understanding the divergent effects of globalization. This concept describes a dual dynamic of increasing chronic disease and entrenchment of infectious disease among lower-income populations in both developed *and* developing countries. Some mechanisms of globalization, such as the diffusion of new technologies, allow rapid 'development' within subsectors of a population and

subsequent improvements in health indicators. However, the dilemma is not only that a restricted enclave is benefiting from this technology, but rather that other economic dislocations accompany these processes, creating a marginalization and impoverishment that contributes to disease, either through new exposures to pathogens, the creation of new disease-enhancing environments, dislocations of land tenure and traditional food supplies, or several other effects.

While the epidemiological transition focuses solely on changing patterns of morbidity and mortality, the *health transition* embeds the demographic and epidemiological transition in a construct that refers simultaneously to the social and economic factors that produce them (Caldwell 1990). The health transition, as elaborated in the work of Caldwell, Frenk, Bobadilla, and others (q.v. Jamison et al. 1993), is deliberately self-conscious of the complex interaction between health and interacting forces that propel social change. Conflating the epidemiological and the health transition produces a difficulty – while the epidemiological transition can be understood through exploration of fairly proximate disease variables (Mosley and Chen 1984), the health transition recognizes that its effects are produced through changes in social, economic, and political factors such as globalization. The construct of the health transition to date, however, provides few clues in understanding the multiple pathways that interconnect these sectors, predicting the impact of changes in one sector on another, or directly influencing health in the future.

A SHRINKING WORLD: OUR PHYSICAL AND ELECTRONIC CONNECTIONS

The mechanical connection between the globalization of certain diseases and advances in travel and the transportation of people and goods is clear. During 1994, more than 97 million passengers traveled by air between the United States and other countries (United States Department of Transportation 1998). A commentator noted, 'The protective effect of clipper ship travel is long gone' (Ginzburg 1996), although certainly the slow speed of transport did not prevent the devastation of the New World either. The volume and accessibility of air travel literally means that, at least as far as the microbes are concerned, the global village is here. Policy makers, as well as the public, have seized on transportation as an explanation of a world at risk. This is evidenced by stories about a 'patient-zero,' a widely traveled, 'promiscuous' airline steward who is cited as the origin of the worldwide AIDS epidemic. It is hard to imagine a more perfectly crafted social parable to support discrimination and the erection of community barriers. There is an easily imagined fear of an undiagnosed hemorrhagic fever patient arriving from Africa to a major North American or European transportation hub, the vividness of which is as likely to be responsible for prompting attention and funding for disease surveillance and reporting as countless carefully considered scientific reports (Hamilton 1995; Institute of Medicine 1992).

Despite the important role of increased air travel, other trajectories of movement are even more vital in determining disease. Massive migration takes place in response to political, military, and social unrest. The factors surrounding large-scale migration are often associated with the inability of local authorities or communities to control violence or provide adequate means for subsistence. Such massive migration sets the stage for epidemic infectious disease. The exodus of millions from Rwanda in 1994 gave witness to one of the most devastating and deadly cholera epidemics in recent history (Kristof 1997). A quick review of the rising numbers of refugees and internally displaced persons, especially on the African continent, reveals the gravity of the situation. In 1997, figures for Africa note 4.3 million refugees, 1.7 million 'returnees,' and 16 million internally displaced persons (United Nations 1998b). If change and instability are the footholds for disease, these numbers speak volumes about the entrenchment of disease on the globe's largest continent. Worldwide, the number of refugees, returnees, and internally displaced persons has increased more than four-fold, from 5.4 million in 1980 to 22.7 million in 1997 (United Nations 1998b).

Migration is important in less dramatic circumstances as well, contributing, for example, to the introduction of multiple dengue serotypes in new regions, a factor implicated in the development of dengue hemorrhagic fever. Migrant workers can suffer from their lack of immunity to diseases such as malaria when they travel looking for work. Economic migration has played a key role in the spread of HIV (Lurie et al. 1995). While the decision to migrate and resultant disease are local manifestations, they are often in response to distant factors.

Threats to health can also move directly in trade. Adopting the use of hazardous products such as tobacco and alcohol is discussed in depth below, but concern also centers on the unintentional export of health-threatening materials. Numerous incidents, such as the discovery BSE (bovine spongiform encephalopathy)-infected beef and cyclospora-infected raspberries, verify the urgency of cooperation between governments to adapt to the global trade in food produced by consumer-driven markets fed by multinational agroindustry.

Communication

Although global transportation has been transformed, the sweep of communication technology and content has even broader implications for health. Our capabilities in communication epitomize the ever-shrinking world evoked by the term 'globalization.' Global cash and culture transfer ride on the 'time–space grid' of communication technologies. Communication does not carry the same readily apparent threat of disease that is present in travel and transportation; digital information is (organic) virus free. Yet, for many in the developing world, communication technology brings disembodied contact with patterns of living that must stand in surreal contrast to local realities. A vivid anecdote from one of the authors is a late afternoon visit to a rural *pulperia* (store) in Honduras in 1985. Rather than lounging outdoors after a long day's work, men crowded inside a dark house. The rubber-booted and straw-hatted farmers, machetes dangling from their hands, stared at a 12-inch black and white TV powered by an automobile battery. In a country with a GNP per capita of less than $500, these grindingly poor farmers were watching the Mexican telenovela, *Los ricos tambien lloran* (The Rich Cry Too). In response to the question 'what's going on here?' the author got a plot synopsis.

Global mass media and other forms of communication lead to a transnationalization of culture. Certainly there is greater recognition, and celebration, of the rich cultural legacy of many parts of the world and an internationalization of many major metropolitan areas. The effects on health, though, come from less benign messages and stem more from growing effects of sedentarism and consumerism. Murray predicts that 8.4 million deaths in the year 2020 will be attributed to tobacco (Murray and Lopez 1996). The effects of dietary change, increased access to alcohol, tobacco, and other drugs, and violence will take a high toll even in countries with the infrastructure to treat them. The effects can be devastating in areas still struggling under high burdens of infectious disease, low disposable income, and high levels of malnutrition.

A few countries may deflect the satellite-borne images that waft the globe and discourage viewing in a thoroughly futile attempt to restrict access, but the effect of communication is not necessarily negative. The presence of electronic devices and materials in even the most inaccessible locales demonstrates the power available through communication for improved health and education, and, of course, disease surveillance. Failure to invest in information technology and the supporting infrastructure can only widen the disparity between industrialized and nonindustrialized countries. Communication creates new agendas for health, and produces social and cultural construction of health, as evidenced by the worldwide prioritization of child health. Although there are clear ethical reasons for reducing disparities in the use of technology for surveillance and health, it is also in the best interests of the developed world to truly 'globalize' communication. The most sophisticated technical surveillance abilities in industrialized countries can be rendered useless by the weakest communications links in developing countries.

One example of the promising use of technology is provided by Pro-MED, an Internet-based newsgroup begun by the Federation of American Scientists, which gathers worldwide reports of human, plant, and animal disease outbreaks (http://www.healthnet.org/programs/promed.html). Moderated to maintain the quality of submissions, this system bypasses traditional academic journals, opening a communication channel through which more voices can be heard and can communicate with one another with unprecedented rapidity. Clinicians and public health professionals are able to poll their global peers for insight and instruction through this technology, demonstrating how knowledge is truly able to serve a global public. Although limited to those lucky enough to have access to a computer and an Internet connection, it is step in the right direction.

Although an untapped potential exists to harness technology and incorporate it into health programs, global communication continues to deliver less benign messages. Widely disseminated messages have enormous ramifications for health. Advertising for tobacco and alcohol products in developing countries, as well as in low-income US neighborhoods (Hackbarth et al. 1995; Moore et al. 1996), aids in the penetration and promotion of these goods in vulnerable areas. At the same time, new, biomedically defined diseases and lifestyles relatively free from infectious diseases have become better known through the media, challenging local constructs. Coupled to this is the spread of commercial pharmaceuticals, which are both more expensive than their local counterpart and often inappropriately used. This phenomena affects conceptions of health throughout the world.

At the same time, the evolution of the concept of emerging diseases provides an example of how alliances can be formed between science and the public through communication. However, the reader should bear in mind that visions of the 'other' are easily distorted through the media. Messages are not transmitted as pure 'information,' but rather act as packets of cultural knowledge that are squirted around the world. Recognizing the cultural content of messages is as important for understanding communication (or the lack of it) as the scientific content.

GLOBAL ENVIRONMENT IMPACT

A major area of current and potential convergence of risk is connected to environmental change. These processes are clearly independent of national boundaries, yet attempts to control the factors influencing environmental change and degradation remain bound to national politics and policies despite numerous attempts to bridge such differences through multinational negotiation. John Last, in his text *Public Health and Human Ecology*, notes numerous phenomena encompassed by the term 'global change,' including global warming, stratospheric ozone depletion, environmental pollution, species extinction, reductions in biodiversity, and desertification; all of which represent a 'new scale of human impact on the world...' (Last 1998: 395).

The unfolding of globalization has changed the basic relationship of communities to the environment, with an impact that is impossible to fully quantify or predict. Forces such as migration and expanding production can carry negative consequences, especially when production is not restricted to the service of local needs and may not be managed according to local wishes. Expanding economies and populations also have an impact on the earth that is impossible to fully quantify or to predict. Much of the ongoing debate regarding global climate change acknowledges that our human history of record keeping, and even the predictions interpreted from other natural sources, can mean little in the light of long-term trends. In the long term, environmental degradation may come to play the largest role in determining global health.

Several current examples can be provided. The introduction of vector and rodent species into new areas is linked to habitat destruction and weakened regional biodiversity. Accounts that relate disease to shifts in local land use are legion. Lyme disease in the northeastern United States was a reaction to changed housing patterns and forest incursion that enhanced human exposure to deer-borne ticks (Institute of Medicine 1992). Outbreaks of Lassa fever in Africa, hantavirus in the southwestern United States, and Bolivian hemorrhagic fever were linked to increased rodent–human interaction (Garrett 1994; Ryan 1997). These 'emerging' threats are, at least in part, responses to human activity.

As global climate change occurs, the spread of vectors beyond current tropical areas is likely. The presence of a vector alone, of course, does not predict the spread of disease. Epidemiologic modeling involves the reproductive rate of a vector-borne disease ('number of new cases of the disease that will arise from one current case given an entirely susceptible population') which is produced by a number of factors including rainfall and temperature. A high reproductive rate among a disease-naïve population could bring epidemic spread of disease (Rogers and Packer 1993).

Border Economics, Environment, and Health

Economic policies that are at odds with local control of resources interact with environmental issues to heighten health problems. An example lies in the privatization of government-held land previously used by '*ejidos*' (organized groups of farmers and peasants) and individual farmers in Mexico. Partly, this was a response to the need for investment in irrigation and new agricultural technology in a desiccating environment. The sale of land reinforced rural-to-urban migration. This trend provided abundant low-wage employees to the thriving *maquiladora* industry (foreign-owned factories at the heart of Mexico's 1965 'Border Industrialization Program'). On one hand, the dynamics of migration and plant employment undermine family, community, and economic structures in both urban and rural areas and bring their own consequences. On the other hand, urban land resources are taxed with vast *colonias* (shantytowns) that spring up to accommodate urban migrants with no local identification, opening up new ecologies for disease. The sheer scale of industrial development and agricultural runoff from both sides of the border have, at times, turned the Rio Grande into one of the most polluted waterways in North America, and ineffective environmental protection has raised deep concern over the dumping of toxic waste.

While such change may be inevitable and necessary under the operating economic paradigm, the rapidity of change outpaces local ability to adapt, threatening the environment and traditional lifestyles as well as health. There is great reluctance among national politicos and legislatures to confront issues that may present boundaries to economic development. While decisions to migrate are made locally, they are responses to global forces that converge to determine the choices of action available on the local level (see DeWalt et al. 1994; Interhemispheric Research Center 1998a, 1998b).

URBANIZATION: A CONFLUENCE OF MIGRATION AND ECONOMIC CHANGE

Urbanization as a social process exemplifies the simultaneously physical and cultural phenomenon that is globalization. This discussion posits urbanization as a major by-product of globalization. Economic development and investment fuels the growth of cities, which draw increasingly larger populations. Population growth, however, outpaces investment in infrastructure and overwhelms the local capacity to accommodate new urban dwellers. These large populations become proletarianized, threatening both the state and the economy if their needs are not met, as events in Jakarta during 1998 demonstrated.

This century has seen an explosion of 'megacities': urban centers with populations greater than 10 million, the vast majority of which are in developing countries. Such cities include Bangkok, Beijing, Bombay, Buenos Aires, Cairo, Calcutta, Delhi, Jakarta, Karachi, Lagos, London, Los Angeles, Manila, Mexico City, Moscow, Paris, Rio de Janeiro, Sao Paulo, and Tokyo. Never before in history have people gathered with such density; as a species prone to 'herd' diseases, the implicit danger is clear, yet the effects of urbanization on health are complex.

The history of health in cities provides a mixed picture. In England in the nineteenth century the infant and child mortality rates of the rural poor were lower than those rates among the urban poor and even the middle class. Data from England as recently as 1910–1912 indicate that mortality from several of the most common diseases of the time was lower among farm laborers than among better-paid urban professional and salaried workers (Collins 1926). Yet the twentieth century, especially post-World War II, did demonstrate improved health in urban centers. Poor access to health and educational services and the lack in variety and quantity of foods available in rural areas enhanced infant and child health.

Despite their modern conveniences, urban centers are once again creating greater risk: air, water and environmental pollution, high population densities with consequent opportunities for infectious disease spread, and lifestyle changes in sexuality, diet, and exercise that are conducive to disease (United Nations 1996a). Cities have been called 'the dynamo driving infection' (Horton 1996). Today, in both developed and developing countries, the urban poor have the highest health risks (WHO 1995). Urbanization appears to be driven by two highly interrelated factors: inadequate distribution of infrastructure, resources, and opportunities in rural areas, and the concentration of industrial activity within megacities, factors certainly not divorced from other patterns considered in this chapter and intimately related to the project of globalization.

Urban dwellers may have remarkably different patterns of risk. While the wealthy and middle classes have better access to tertiary care, the poorest groups have little or no access to such services. Rapidly growing squatter and shanty settlements usually have no services of any kind, and residents may be barred or discouraged from using those in nearby neighborhoods. Even emergency services, which are generally in town centers, may not be readily available to the many who live in settlements on the outskirts.

Urban settings serve as laboratories for examining how poverty differentials determine health. In Porto Allegre, Brazil, the infant mortality rate (IMR) in squatter settlements is three times that of nonsquatter areas, more than 75 deaths per thousand live births (Fischmann and Guimaraes 1986), with further evidence of the association of low income and childhood mortality provided by Victora et al. (1992). In Quito, Ecuador, in the early 1980s, the IMR in upper-class districts was 5 per 1000 live births, comparable to the most developed countries today. At that same time, manual workers in Quito's squatter settlements saw their children die at a rate of 129 per 1000 live births, a rate slightly below the global average at that time for the least developed countries. Similarly, large differentials have been observed in the Philippines, Sri Lanka, England, Wales, and elsewhere.

Although official poverty levels used in national studies are suspect, even these studies estimate that half of urban inhabitants in developing countries are living in poverty (Hamid and Fouad 1993). In 1990 'at least 600 million urban dwellers in Africa, Asia, and Latin America live in "life and health-threatening" homes and neighborhoods because of the very poor housing and living conditions and the inadequate provision for safe and sufficient water supplies and for sanitation, drainage, the removal of garbage, and health care' (Satterthwaite 1995).

The impact of crowding, poor access to care, and high population densities can be seen in a number of diseases. Tuberculosis is responsible for approximately 3 million deaths per year, and 'is the single largest cause of adult death in the world' (WHO, 1998b). Acute respiratory infections take the lives of 4–5 million infants and children annually. These diseases tend to be more prevalent in urban areas, with the highest incidence seen in the poorest, most-crowded areas. Air quality deteriorates as well. Mexico City and São Paulo, for example, are afflicted with excessive levels of carbon monoxide, ozone, and particulates that lead to increases in respiratory and cardiovascular diseases (UN 1996b).

Urban environments provide epicenters for the transmission of multiple-drug-resistant tuberculosis, allowing for interactions between various risk populations. Predictably, high rates of tuberculosis often correlate with high AIDS prevalence in an area, with the additional twist that TB is the one AIDS-related opportunistic infection that can impact the general population (WHO 1998c).

Cholera, long absent from Latin America, has reestablished itself due to poor sanitation and hygiene, failure to protect water sources and food supplies, and global trade and travel (WHO 1998d). Urban environments, particularly sections without adequate water, sanitation, and solid waste services, and where many people handle food before it reaches the consumer, provide ideal circumstances for transmission. A host of other diseases abound, such as dengue fever, which can thrive in trash-strewn urban landscapes (Gubler and Clark 1996). Parasitic diseases such as Chagas fever is transmitted to humans by the *T. cruzi*-infected triatomine bug, which has now adapted to life in the housing that typifies the sprawling periurban shanty towns of Latin America (Coura et al. 1995; Walsh et al. 1993). This disease is controllable when discovered early, but is difficult to diagnose and has seriously debilitated many sufferers, particularly in Brazil. In general, malaria is less common in urban areas, but in South Asia the vector mosquitoes have adapted to urban life (Hati 1997). The future may see further emergence of malaria proximate to urban areas and the rapid spread of drug-resistant strains of the parasite, helped by increased contact between urban and rural populations and travel between countries (Moore et al. 1994).

The intense social dynamics created by urbanization contribute to rising disease rates, as demonstrated by HIV. HIV/AIDS thrives in urban settings, which initially demonstrated the highest levels of HIV incidence in both developed and developing countries. Urban areas create new opportunities for mixing populations and spreading the risk of sexually transmitted disease (STD) and HIV infection. The groups at highest risk, particularly in the earliest stages of the epidemic, are present in disproportionate numbers in urban populations. Even small groups of people who engage in high-risk sexual behaviors in urban centers – such as intravenous drug use, commercial sex work, and transport workers, and their sexual contacts – may suffice to fuel successive waves of the infection into the population at large (Way and Stanecki 1995). STDs, including HIV, account for more than 10 per cent of the disease burden for both men and women worldwide (United Nations 1996). The World Health Organization (WHO) recognizes that STDs are most frequent in sexually active young people aged 15–24 years, with the peak age of infection lower in girls than in boys. Young women are among those most at risk for HIV and STDs, often being taken as desirable sexual partners by older male members of high-risk groups. It is estimated that half of all HIV infections in developing countries have been contracted by people younger than 25 years of age. Up to 65 per cent of infections in females are believed to occur by age 20 (WHO 1995). The reasons for this are many. Traditional barriers to early sexual activity and limiting sexual partners are more likely to have broken down in urban settings. At the same time, wide disparities in income are created, prompting resort to desperate income-generating activities such as prostitution. In sub-Saharan African samples, estimates suggest that as many as half of all female migrants are involved in prostitution at one time or another. In Thailand, there is a large proportion of urban migrants who are young women participating in prostitution, either voluntary or coerced. While this activity has been historically tolerated, attitudes appear to be changing rapidly (Hanenberg and Rojanapithayakorn 1998).

The social, political, and economic links tied to HIV stretch across the globe. Migratory patterns connected to global trade, urbanization, and the movement of labor and goods help explain the trajectory of this epidemic. Structural adjustment policies in Africa intended to encourage free-market economic development and the consequent decline of government-provided health services (Lurie et al. 1995) created an ideal environment for the transmission of STDs (Felman 1990). The basic circumstances are not improving, 'thus deepening the social crisis in which HIV breeds' (Epstein 1992).

In addition to 'conventional' disease threats, huge urban populations are vulnerable to natural disasters that are, to all intents and purposes, inevitable. It is, in fact, unknown whether large megacity populations can be sustained within finite areas. Events that killed hundreds in centuries past may kill thousands in the future due to the economic and social forces that create these megacities. Paradoxically, globalization spreads linkages widely over the globe but contributes to the dynamics of local urban concentration. The continuing demands of economic growth, and the desires of people to access education and the limited infrastructure, will doubtless sustain patterns of urbanization.

THE FUTURE OF GLOBAL RESPONSE TO HEALTH AND DISEASE

The growth and hegemony of biomedicine have characterized health policy and intervention during the twentieth century. Lappé states, 'the superficial success of modern medicine has created an illusion of human supremacy over the natural world' (Lappé 1995: ix). Advances in biochemistry imply a knowledge and manipulation of cellular mechanisms, with a promise to change the basis of prevention and therapy and to improve the clinical control of disease in the twenty-first century. Vast areas of the world, particularly Africa, were once off-limit to globalizing processes due to disease. Vaccines, antimalarials, and other treatments have opened many of these regions to an influx of expatriates and tourists (while the benefits from these advances have not been available to local residents to the same extent). Yet many successful disease control interventions were not the products of laboratory research, but of epidemiological investigation, and the interventions were revolutions in the organization and management of health programs more than new technical 'fixes.'

What is billed as the single greatest public health achievement of this century, the eradication of smallpox, is often misinterpreted. Disease eradication is usually regarded as the epitome of technological intervention. Smallpox eradication, however, was not the product of new technology (although a new, more heat-stable vaccine was made available, a vaccine for smallpox has been available for 200 years), but rather the combination of the disease's special epidemiological characteristics, a new, vertical strategy that focused on enhanced surveillance and disease outbreaks (rather than overall immunization coverage) and skillful international management (Baxby 1995; Hopkins 1983: 305). Enhanced surveillance and communication recognized outbreaks while there was still time to do something about them. Taking advantage of improved transportation, the program could arrive with enough vaccine to surround and arrest the outbreak. Fear of smallpox and the prestige, political support, and promise of the program drove even skeptical communities and individuals to be immunized. The eradication effort demonstrated the accomplishments possible with the new global tools.

While certain other diseases such as polio and measles may be susceptible to eradication, the vast majority of diseases are not (CDC 1993; Olive et al. 1997). The model of focus on disease, epidemiological prioritization, and enhanced delivery strategies has been the model for other selective primary health-care interventions as well. How relevant is this model today? Smallpox eradication occurred at a particular historical moment: fueled by Cold War dollars, the program operated through the World Health Organization and national ministries of health. It led to the epidemiological mapping of the world. We currently retain a fairly detailed picture of global disease control priorities that permits the recognition of the role of major childhood diseases such as diarrheal disease, acute respiratory infection (ARI), and malaria in the quest for global health.

However, the response to the identification of this global burden of disease has not been straightforward. The primary health care (PHC) declaration 'health for all by the year 2000' was to be a response to the health infrastructure and disease control needs for the developing world. These health programs were intended to function with very limited resources, promote prevention and the use of appropriate technology, and rely on health education and community participation. Health was seen as inextricable from development, and was recognized as being tied to the ability of the population to sustain itself and as a reflection of the total 'health' of a community. However, these communities were identified as distant and foreign – not part of the developed world's community – and even this program was soon deemed too ambitious.

A more targeted, 'selective' primary health care (SPHC) approach was devised that biomedicalized 'prescriptions' for the most severe diseases affecting large numbers of people. The focus was on diseases that were more amenable to discreet interventions and were the most attractive to international donors. Medical and technological treatments – immunizations, oral rehydration therapy, pesticide application, and access to antimalarials – are measurable and often highly effective means to intervene rapidly in disease. They lend themselves to vertical, targeted, and limited programs that may or may not ultimately enhance the capacity of that village or community to deal with continuing threats to its overall health.

These types of programs have only been sustainable with large external inputs. At the same time, they provide interventions that are at odds with tertiary solutions available in the private sector and in hospitals, but rather illustrate the fact that these medical interventions demonstrate the contradictions inherent in considering globalization as a unified and beneficial phenomenon. Tools from the same global surveillance kit demonstrate both the health needs and the economic shortfall in realizing health for all, transforming the question 'How much health is enough?' (not an economic question, but a global one) into 'How much health care can be bought for x dollars?' misses the point, puts economics before health, and produces very different answers in different parts of the world.

What Does it Mean if Health Is a Commodity?

Under an economic paradigm, decisions are made to maximize economic benefit. As the world is brought into a more coordinated economic system, it is valuable to examine how the decisions that affect health are made, and who is affected. To the extent that the global economic system mirrors processes in advanced capitalist countries, the American experience may be instructive. The commodification of health influences the debate over health costs, and leads to a confusion between 'health' and 'health care.' If 'health' is a good that can be purchased by an individual consumer, then the model for decision making is the marketplace. Yet, this perspective is clearly inadequate. Children must be vaccinated regardless of their wishes and the wishes, or ability, of their parents' to pay. The public is forced to pay, both financially and in terms of disease, when others choose less healthy lifestyles, or are forced to go without adequate health care. Even if consumers could purchase health, the cost of new technology puts it out of the reach of all but a handful of individuals. Standing astride this debate, medicine finds that professional autonomy and high-quality health care is difficult to achieve within the institutions that have been developed to awkwardly bridge consumer needs and population health needs.

To translate this template to the global market is certainly a recipe for disaster (see Navarro 1993). Decisions have already been made about the levels of health that may be achieved in different countries. Often without the benefit of formal economic analysis, policy makers in both the health and other sectors often presumptively exclude programs and investments in health. Contamination of drinking water in Peru due to the failure to expand and maintain water systems in Lima, Callao, and Trujillo, for example, factored into the reintroduction of cholera in the Americas (Swerdlow et al. 1992). Declining environmental surveillance and the failure to control trade in tires containing mosquito eggs led to the introduction of *Aedes albopictus* in the United States and contributed to concerns about the transmission of encephalitis and imported dengue fever (Francy et al. 1990). Trade in used tires from the United States played a major role in the reintroduction of *Aedes aegypti* to Latin America in the 1960s.

How should governments and international organizations consider the trade-off among investments in health and investment in other sectors? At both national and international levels, health is distilled into quantifiable indicators of success or failure, but these figures are difficult to interpret and often fail to influence policy. Current health may be attributable to investments made long ago or to temporary economic success. At the same time, short-term political influences may demand investment for disasters or emergencies that far outpace development assistance. The pattern of continuing crises creates an unending series of demands for programs that leave little behind for the next crisis.

The commodification of health has contributed to the widespread availability of antibiotics, which are often seen as an inexpensive and easily dispensed remedy, and they are substantially misused. Although the widespread use of antibiotics has contributed to better health in the past 40 years, these drugs have been increasingly abused. Patterns of adherence are poor, and patients stop taking the expensive drugs when symptoms disappear or when side effects, such as gastric disturbance, begin. In addition, these drugs are often self-prescribed and one or two may be taken at a time. Parents, accustomed to some 'tangible' health treatment, may insist on antibiotics for a child's treatment, and overworked, harried physicians may concede to the demands, despite the knowledge that the infection could be viral or not require medication. The culture of medicine in which antibiotics represent 'purchasable health' has contributed to the rapid evolution of drug-resistant strains of infections (Demissie et al. 1997; Rapkin 1997).

Finally, in considering commodification, it must be recognized that biomedicine is a huge industry. Potential profits and eager markets drive drug development. While developing countries represent huge markets, the relative returns are low due to the use of generic drugs and poor populations that are unable to pay high prices regardless of the utility offered by a drug

(Trouiller 1996). Research for malaria treatment – one of the most important causes of infectious mortality in the world – must be covered under 'orphan drug' protection, with little commercial support for development. The global diffusion of biomedicine is displacing local knowledge of remedies that could have enormously enhanced the pharmaceutical armamentarium. While some local remedies may be nonefficacious, their use constitutes a coping strategy for dealing with misfortune. Now, deaths from pneumonia, diarrhea, malaria, and even AIDS are reduced to 'outside' social, economic, and political explanations. Although locally meaningful remedies have existed, they are simply no longer being provided.

There are, however, far-sighted companies, such as Merck and Smith Kline, which have found ways to support drugs for orphan diseases. The free distribution of Merck's Ivermectin for onchocerciasis control in Africa and Latin America is subsidized by its sale for veterinary use in the United States. The partnership between WHO's Tropical Diseases Research Program, these companies, and the country disease programs is a model of enlightened corporate multinationalism (TDR 1998).

CONCLUSION

This examination of globalization reminds us that, whether or not one believes in an inevitable drive toward a more unified economic, social, and technological world, there are terrific costs being paid, both in human and environmental terms, in the current world system. International health and medicine must play an active role in considering these issues and structuring responses as we lurch towards the millennium.

While both human population growth and the development of medical technology in the twentieth century have been staggering, ill health still plagues much of mankind. The very young, children and adolescents, women, the elderly, and the poor of all ages are still vulnerable. The ability of pathogens to adapt and new pathogens to develop must challenge our faith in uniquely technological solutions. To fully accept the concept of the globalization of disease demands that we view our expansion as a social, cultural, and ecological project as well as an economic one.

The Institute of Medicine's 1992 report on emerging infections acknowledges that the 'factors in emergence' of emerging infectious disease are inherently social in nature. Members of the panel identified six sets of factors, specifically focusing on human demographics and behavior, technology and industry, economic development and land use, international travel and commerce, the breakdown of public health measures, and microbial adaptation and change. These social factors also work in describing the patterns that are tied to globalization dynamics and the spread of disease, both infectious and chronic.

Popular questions concerning the globalization of disease ask whether a new, lethal, worldwide epidemic is likely. The argument of this chapter is that such considerations are only a small part of the globalization and health picture. Without large-scale change beyond the health sector, infectious and chronic disease burdens will continue to grow among those who are most vulnerable. Under a system where the numbers of people in poverty and poor health greatly outweigh the number of people with high incomes, the challenges seem clearly laid out. There is no indication of a reversal in these trends.

This chapter would be incomplete without an effort to address potential solutions to the issues outlined above. The patterns of the global economy, mobility, communication, and urbanization provide opportunities as well as problems. Although these comments will seem utopian, the reader must realize that they are perceived as goals, a utopian realism, as Giddens (1991) would put it.

- Health must remain, and become more of, a public/private partnership. Funding of public investments in health must recognize the role that the global economy, including consumerism, trade, and transport, plays in disease. Although a variety of medical services will be increasingly available throughout the world, and rising economic circumstances will continue to improve health in many parts of the world, the cost for this expansion should not be borne solely by public investments in health infrastructure. Part of the cost of this must be shouldered by the institutions of global economic expansion.
- Differences in the cost of labor and goods fuel global expansion; however, the ethics of this expansion demand more equitable levels of investment in health. Initial global economic penetration fuels rapid urbanization and taxes existing infrastructure. The argument that certain areas of the world need to 'accept' certain levels of disease on the road to development when these risks are well known is unethical and simply acquiesces to current practice. At the very least, these decisions need to be debated in the open and involve the populations concerned. The enhanced expectations explicit in global growth, communication, and urbanization

are as real as the economic facts. These expectations and priorities in development need to be negotiated in a multisector forum where health as well as economic development is considered an outcome.
- Globalization offers opportunities to build systems of disease surveillance. An effective system of surveillance for disease can and should be constructed, linking sentinel national institutions where available, and providing direct assistance for the construction and support of sentinel sites in areas that do not yet, or no longer, have the infrastructure for effective surveillance of disease. Remote sensing technology is able to provide enormous detail about large areas of the world. We have the technology to develop a significant global network, and we have institutions, such as the WHO, available to implement and coordinate these functions. This surveillance should include not only traditional disease categories, but also substance abuse and violence, human rights violations, and violation of environmental laws.
- Multilateral institutions have not prospered in the global expansion. The mandate of these institutions, such as the United Nations, the World Health Organization, and the lending institutions needs to be changed to meet new priorities or, if unable to adapt, new institutions should be designed in their place. A new reorganization of the WHO demonstrates the recognition of these needs and promises new innovative approaches. However, to fully address these needs will require implementation, as well as coordination, which will require expanded budgets and authority.
- International, 'global' institutions should not be created at the expense of national institutions, many of which have suffered as a result of economic restructuring. A mechanism is required not only to sustain but also to encourage local training and research. Developed country institutions should be encouraged to build real partnerships with their counterpart institutions, and provide the long-term support and mutual benefit that are essential for careers in research programs.
- The Global Burden of Disease study and Sen's approaches to defining poverty provide models for improving the science of health, disease, and welfare measurement. Challenges to conventional notions of determining risk must continue in order to provide data that are useful in weighing intervention options.
- A tremendous global communication industry exists. This infrastructure should be put to

use for educational as well as commercial purposes. The newly created urban environments create great need for education about health risks and appropriate treatment. The learning deficits on both sides of the equation are large.

- Global authority is required to control travel during epidemics. This requires the active participation of the transportation sector and a truly global authority with the ability to take forceful action when necessary. Such global authorities might also be mandated to participate in the control of biological weapons and weapons of mass destruction and to assist in complex emergencies.

What the 'globalization of disease' best offers is an enhanced paradigm for understanding health. The health transition consists of social processes such as globalization that directly affect health and investment in the health sector. Globalization demands attention to changing vulnerabilities and recognition of the multifaceted outcomes of 'development' and technological advances. Surveillance and intervention, both preventive and curative, require a rethinking of institutions and strategies. The patterns of economic and social change outlined here are only going to intensify. Automation, global communication, and a focus on production have allowed many societies to reach the future that they have been defining, but the by-products of these same mechanisms can further entrench the health problems that we once thought were surmountable through technology. Certainly technical solutions, health communication, and policy dialogue are needed. However, the new challenge is to use the promises and realties of globalization, not just to respond to crises, but to take responsibility for and shape our future.

REFERENCES

Baxby, D. (1995) 'Myths in medicine. Surveillance-containment is key to eradication of smallpox', *BMJ*, 310(6971): 62.

Brown, P. (1984) 'Socioeconomic and demographic effects of malaria eradication: A comparison of Sri Lanka and Sardinia', *Social Science Medicine*, 22: 847–59.

Caldwell, J. (1990) 'Introductory thought on health transition', in J. Calwell, S. Findley, and P. Caldwell (eds), *What We Know About Health Transition: The Cultural, Social and Behavioural Determinants of Health*, series 1, vol. 1, The Health Transition Series. pp. xi-xiii.

CDC (Centers for Disease Control and Prevention) (1993) 'Recommendations of the International Task Force for Disease Eradication', *MMWR*, 42 (Rr-16): 1–38.

Collins, S.D. (1926) 'Economic status and health: A review and study of the relevant morbidity and mortality data,' *Public Health Bulletin*, No. 165, Treasury Department, US Public Health Service. Washington, DC: US Government Printing Office in Kunitz, Stephen J. and Engerman, S. L. (1992) 'The ranks of death: Secular trends in income and mortality', *Health Transition Review*, No. 2 (suppl.).

Coura J.R. et al. (1995) '"Chagas" disease in the Brazilian Amazon. III. A cross-sectional study', *Revista do Instituto de Medicina Tropical de Sao Paulo*, 37: 415–20.

Demissie, M., Gebeyehu, M., and Berhane, Y. (1997) 'Primary resistance to antituberculosis drugs in Addis Ababa, Ethiopia', *International Journal of Tuberculosis & Lung Disease*, 1: 64–7.

Dewalt, B.R., Rees, M.W., and Murphy, A.D. (1994) *The End of Agrarian Reform in Mexico: Past Lessons, Future Prospects. Transformation of Rural Mexico, No. 3*, San Diego: University of California Center for US–Mexican Studies.

Diamond, J. (1997) *Guns, Germs and Steel: The Fates of Human Societies*. New York: W.W. Norton.

Economist (1998a) 'Jamming the net work', 1 August 1998.

Economist (1998b) 'Diet and disease. Lost without a trace', 1 August 1998.

Epstein, P. (1992) 'Commentary: pestilence and poverty – historical transitions and the great pandemics', *American Journal of Preventive Medicine*, 8(4): 263–5.

Felman, Y.M. (1990) 'Recent developments in sexually transmitted diseases: Is heterosexual transmission of human immunodeficiency virus a major factor in the spread of acquired immunodeficiency syndrome?' *III: AIDS in Sub-Saharan Africa*. Cutis 46: 204–6.

Fidler, D.P. (1996) 'Globalization, international law, and emerging infectious diseases', *Emerging Infectious Diseases*, 2(2): 77–84.

Fischmann, A. and Guimaraes, J.J. (1986) 'Risk of dying in the 1st year of life among slum and non-slum residents in the municipality of Porto Alegre, RS (Brazil), in 1980', *Revista de Saude Publica*, 20(3): 219–26.

Francy, D.B., Moore, C.G., and Eliason, D.A. (1990) 'Past, present and future of *Aedes albopictus* in the United States', *Journal of the American Mosquito Control Association*, 6(1): 127–32.

Garrett, L. (1994) *The Coming Plague: Newly Emerging Diseases in a World out of Balance*. New York: Penguin.

Giddens, A. (1990) *The Consequences of Modernity*. Stanford, CA: Stanford University Press.

Ginzburg, H. (1996) 'Needed: Comprehensive response to the spread of infectious diseases', EID,

April–June 1996, 10 November 1997: http://www.cdc.gov/ncidod/EID/vol2no2/ginzbrg.htm

Gubler, D.J. and Clark, G.G. (1996) 'Community involvement in the control of *Aedes aegypti*', *Acta Tropica*, 61: 169–79.

Hackbarth, D.P., Silvestri, B., and Cosper, W. (1995) 'Tobacco and alcohol billboards in 50 Chicago neighborhoods: Market segmentation to sell dangerous products to the poor', *Journal of Public Health Policy*, 16: 213–30.

Hamid, T. and Fouad, M. (1993) *The Incidence of Poverty in Developing Countries: An ILO Compendium of Data. A World Employment Programme Study*. Geneva: International Labour Organization.

Hamilton, J.O. (1995) 'The point man in germ warfare', *Business Week*, August: 72–3.

Hanenberg, R. and Rojanapithayakorn, W. (1998) 'Changes in prostitution and the AIDS epidemic in Thailand', *AIDS Care*, 10: 69–79.

Hati, A.K. (1997) 'Urban malaria vector biology', *Indian Journal of Medical Research*, 106: 149–63.

Helitzer-Allen, D.C., Kendall, A., Macheso, A. and Wirima, J. (1994) 'Interventions to improve adherence to malaria chemoprophylaxis in pregnant women in Malawi', *Acta Tropica*, 58: 255–66.

Hopkins, D.R. (1983) *Princes and Peasants: Smallpox in History*. Chicago: University of Chicago Press.

Horton, R. (1996) 'The infected metropolis', *Lancet*, 347: 134–5.

Institute of Medicine (1992) J. Lederburg, R.E. Shope, and S.C. Oaks, Jr (eds), *Emerging Infections: Microbial Threats to Health in the United States*. Washington, DC: National Academy Press.

Institute of Medicine (1997) *America's Vital Interest in Global Health*. Washington, DC: National Academy Press.

Interhemispheric Research Center (1998a) 'Community health in the borderlands: An overview', *Borderlines* (newsletter), 6 (4).

Interhemispheric Research Center (1998b) 'Hazardous waste management on the border: Problems with practices and oversight continue', *Borderlines* (newsletter), 6 (5).

Jamison, D.T., Mosley, W.H., Measham, A.R., and Bobadilla, J.L. (eds) (1993) *Disease Control Priorities in Developing Countries*. New York: Oxford Medical Publications.

Kalekin-Fishman, D. (1996) 'The impact of globalization on the determination and management of ethical choices in the health arena', *Social Science Medicine*, 43(5): 809–22.

Kearney, M. (1995) 'The local and the global: The anthropology of globalization and transnationalism', *Annual Review of Anthropology*, 24: 547–65.

Kere, N.K., Arabola, A., Bakote'e, B., Qalo, O., Burkot, T.R., Webber, R.H., and Southgate, B.A. (1996) 'Permethrin-impregnated bednets are more effective than DDT house-spraying to control malaria in Solomon Islands', *Medical and Veterinary Entomology*, 10(2): 145–48.

Kristof, N.D. (1997) 'Rwandans, once death's agents, now its victims', *New York Times* (Late New York Edition) 13 April (Sect. 1): 1.

Lappé, M. (1995) *Breakout: The Evolving Threat of Drug-Resistant Disease*. San Francisco: Sierra Club Books.

Lasch, C. (1991) *True and Only Heaven: Progress and its Critics*. New York: W.W. Norton.

Last, J. (1998) *Public Health and Human Ecology*, Stamford, CT: Appleton & Lange, (2nd edn).

Litsios, S. (1997) 'Malaria control, the cold war, and the postwar reorganization of international assistance', *Medical Anthropology*, 17: 255–78.

Lurie, P., Hintzen, P., and Lowe, R.A. (1995) 'Socioeconomic obstacles to HIV prevention and treatment in developing countries: The roles of the International Monetary Fund and the World Bank', *AIDS*, 9: 539–46.

Makler, M.T., Palmer, C.J., and Ager, A.L. (1998) 'A review of practical techniques for the diagnosis of malaria', *Annals of Tropical Medicine Parasitology*, 92: 419–33.

Moore, D.J., Williams, J.D., and Qualls, W.J. (1996) 'Target marketing of tobacco and alcohol-related products to ethnic minority groups in the United States', *Ethnic Disease*, 6: 83–98.

Moore, T.A. et al. (1994) 'Imported malaria in the 1990s. A report of 59 cases from Houston, Texas', *Archives of Family Medicine*, 3: 130–6.

Mosley, W.H. and Chen, L.C. (1984) 'An analytical framework for the study of child survival in developing countries', *Population Development Review*, 10 (suppl).

Mosley, W.H., Bobadilla, J.L., and Jamison, D.T. (1993) 'The health transition: Implications for health policy in developing countries' in D.T. Jamison, W.H. Mosley, A.R. Measham, and J.L. Bobadilla, (eds), *Disease Control Priorities in Developing Countries*. New York: Oxford Medical Publications. pp. 673–99.

Murray, C.J.L. and Lopez, A.D. (1996) 'Evidence-based health policy – Lessons from the global burden of disease study', *Science*, 274: 740–3.

Navarro, V. (1993) *Dangerous to Your Health: Capitalism in Health Care*. New York: Monthly Review Press.

Navarro, V. (1998) 'Comment: Whose globalization?' *American Journal of Public Health*, 88: 742.

NIAID Fact Sheet (1998) 'Summary of the blue ribbon panel on malaria vaccine development', located at: URL: www.niaid.nih.gov/dmid/panel.htm

Oaks, Jr., S.C., Mitchell, V.S., Pearson G.W. and Carpenter, C.C.J. (eds) (1991) *Malaria: Obstacles and Opportunities*. Washington, DC: National Academy Press.

Olive, J.M., Aylward, R.B., and Melgaard, B (1997) 'Disease eradication as a public health strategy: Is measles next?' *World Health Statistics Quarterly*, 50: 185–7.

Rapkin, R. (1997) 'Bacterial resistance to antibiotics: It's our problem', *Pediatric Dentistry*, 19: 374.

Redfield, R. (1989) *The Little Community and Peasant Society and Culture.* Chicago: University of Chicago Press (reprint edn).

Rogers, D.J and Packer, M.J. (1993) 'Vector-borne diseases, models and global change', *Lancet*, 342 (8882): 1282–4.

Ryan, F. (1997) *Virus X: Tracking the New Killer Plagues of the Present and into the Future.* Boston: Little, Brown.

Sachs, J. (1998) 'The real causes of famine', *Time*, 26 October 1998: 69.

Satterthwaite, D. (1995) 'Rapid urbanization and the urban environment', paper presented at the Seminar on Demography and Poverty, International Union for the Scientific Study of Population, Liège.

Sen, A. (1997) *On Economic Inequality.* Oxford: Clarendon Press (enlarged edn).

Swerdlow, D.L., Mintz, E.D., Rodriguez, M., Tejada, E., Ocampo, C., Espejo, L., Greene, K.D., Saldana, W., Seminario, L., and Tauxe, R.V. (1992) 'Waterborne transmission of epidemic cholera in Trujillo, Peru: Lessons for a continent at risk', *Lancet*, 340 (8810): 28–33.

TDR (1998) UNDP/World Bank/WHO, Special Programme for Research and Training in Tropical Diseases (TDR), 'TDR: How does it work? What are its advantages?' URL: www.who.int/tdr/about/works_oncho.htm (3 July 1998).

Trouiller, P. (1996) 'Research and pharmaceutical development on the subject of communicable diseases in the intertropical region', *Sante*, 6: 299–307.

United Nations (1996a) United Nations, Population Division, Department for Economic and Social Information and Policy Analysis. 'Trends in urbanization and the components of urban growth', paper prepared for the Symposium on Internal Migration and Urbanization in Developing Countries: Implications for Habitat II, New York.

United Nations (1996b) United Nations Centre for Human Settlements/Habitat. *An Urbanizing World: Global Report on Human Settlements*, New York: UN Publications.

United Nations (1998a) United Nations Development Program. Overview of *Human Development Report 1997*, located at URL: www.undp.org/undp/hdro/e98ober/htm (24 September 1998).

United Nations (1998b) United Nations High Commissioner for Refugees URL: www.unhcr.ch/sowr97/statsum.htm (23 October 1998).

United States Department of Transportation. URL: www.bts.gov/oai/international/calyr94.htm (23 October 1998).

Verle, P., Binh, L.N., Lieu, T.T., Yen, P.T., and Coosemans, M. (1996) 'ParaSight-F test to diagnose malaria in hypo-endemic and epidemic prone regions of Vietnam', *Tropical Medicine and International Health*, 1: 794–96.

Victora, C.G., Barros, F.C., Huttly, S.R., Teixeira, A.M., and Vaughan, J.P. (1992) 'Early childhood mortality in a Brazilian cohort: The roles of birthweight and socioeconomic status', *International Journal of Epidemiology*, 21: 911–15.

Walsh, J.F., Molyneux, D.H., and Birley, M.H. (1993) 'Deforestation: Effects on vector-borne disease', *Parasitology*, 106: S55-S75.

Way, P.O. and Stanecki, N. (1995) *Transmission of HIV/AIDS in Sub-Saharan Africa.* Washington, DC: US Bureau of the Census.

WHO (1995) *The World Health Report: Bridging the Gap.* Geneva: World Health Organization.

WHO (1998a) WHO: Division of Control of Tropical Diseases, Malaria Prevention and Control, Burdens and Trends. URL: www.who.int/ctd/html/malaria burtre.html (26 October 1998).

WHO (1998b) Fact Sheet 112: June 1996, Cities and Emerging or Re-Emerging Diseases in the XXIst Century. URL: www.who.int/inf-fs/en/fact122.html (23 October 1998).

WHO (1998c) URL: www.unaids.org/highband/document/epidemio/june98/global_report/slides/slide2.html (19 August 1998).

WHO (1998d) Press release WHO/18, 29 January 1998: 3 Billion people worldwide lack sanitation facilitates: WHO strategy on sanitation for high risk communities, URL: www.who.int.inf-pr-1998/on/pr98-18.html (11 February 1999).

Wolf, E. (1982) *Europe and the People Without History.* Berkeley: University of California Press.

Yach, D. and Bettcher, D. (1998) 'The globalization of public health I: Threats and opportunities', *American Journal of Public Health*, 88: 735–8.

1.7

The Social Causation of Health and Illness

JOHANNES SIEGRIST

INTRODUCTION

Sociology as a science is concerned with the description and explanation of societal phenomena and processes as they affect human populations and individuals. To a large extent, scientific progress in this field is dependent on input from specialized subdisciplines that deal with particular areas of societal life in a systematic way. Health and illness and the societal reactions towards them define the scope of one such subdiscipline, termed sociology of health, or medical sociology (Cockerham 1992; Mechanic 1978; Suchman 1963). The focus of this chapter is restricted to the first one of the two mainstream lines of health-related sociology, the study of social factors that determine well-being and health, and precipitate ill health, illness, and disease. Traditionally, this field was termed sociology in medicine (Straus 1957), but obviously this definition is too narrow given the fact that health and disease are not simply biological entities, but are often intertwined with social and psychological processes. As suggested by the title, sociology is expected to contribute to our understanding of the causation of health and illness. Most scientists today agree that this is basically an interdisciplinary task calling for an integration of biomedical and social science information. Therefore, it is crucial to discuss the different notions of 'social causation' of human health and disease to some extent (first section). On this background, an attempt is made to highlight crucial developments in the history of health-related sociology, a history that dates back to the late nineteenth century

(second section). In the main part of this chapter (third section), selected current theoretical concepts are described and illustrated, and the final section discusses policy implications and possible future developments in this field of scientific inquiry. It goes unsaid that this is a selective review whose focus is put on in-depth analysis and exemplification rather than on comprehensive breadth.

NOTIONS OF SOCIAL CAUSATION

Although an epistemiologic debate on the scientific nature of sociology and the problems of developing and testing theories in this field is ongoing (Mayntz 1985), it is commonly believed that the notions of 'regularity' and 'causality' of phenomena under study, the crucial assumptions of any type of scientific inquiry, can be successfully applied to the discipline of sociology as well (Nagel 1961; Popper 1959). For instance, some basic principles of organizing societal exchange, of developing and maintaining social order and social systems, and of socializing individual persons into society were identified by social scientists (e.g., Berger and Luckmann 1966; Blau 1977; Luhmann 1984; Parsons 1951). Thus, there is strong evidence of the existence of some regularity operating at different levels of societal life. Whereas several patterns of regularity governing the social dimension of human life were identified by sociological theories, additional ones remain to be detected. It may well be that the study of phenomena at the intersection of the social, the psychological, and the biological dimension of human life, such as health and illness, offers new insights in this regard.

It is probably less easy to agree on an appropriate use of the term 'causality' in sociological thinking. 'Causality' implies two notions: temporal antecedence and determination. Depending on the time scale underlying social processes, there is good reason to believe that longitudinal, observational studies provide an appropriate frame of reference for analyzing the temporal sequence of many of the social phenomena of interest, but how can we prove that one social phenomenon under study determines another phenomenon? In particular, if this second phenomenon is of a social nature too it may be difficult to escape tautological explanations. In the case of health and illness, the phenomenon under study is a characteristic of an individual person to be analyzed in biological or psychological terms, although it is admitted that the study of disease patterns at the aggregate level ('population health') offers important insights as well. (Some authors still talk about 'healthy societies,' but in this case, the term refers to an analogy rather than to a testable concept (e.g., Wilkinson 1996).)

The question then, is: What do we mean by social causation of health and illness? Three different types of answer were given to this question. The first, most provocative type of answer was proposed by labeling theorists, referring to some forms of mental illness. According to this theory, mental illness is produced by societal reactions to a person exhibiting strange, unexpected, or inappropriate behavior. Medical decision making, by assigning a diagnosis of mental illness to such a person, is interpreted as an act of social control, confirming the validity of a socially constructed normality (Scheff 1966). This approach has the merit of having sensitized a broader public against the dangers inherent in certain processes of social control by which deviant individuals are stigmatized. Moreover, labeling theorists critically emphasize the power and responsibility of psychiatrists, who have the exclusive right of defining mental illness (Szasz 1974). Up to now, however, empirical support in favor of the labeling approach is poor, leaving little room for a social production hypothesis of health and illness (Cockerham 1992).

A second type of answer refers to intergenerational processes of social 'heritage' acting as enabling, as well as selective, forces of health and illness. For instance, it is well known from genetic epidemiology that short height is more prevalent among people in lower socioeconomic groups (Marmot et al. 1984). Short height, in turn, is associated with excess risk of certain types of chronic disease, such as cardiovascular disease, and thus, might 'confound' to some extent the association of low socioeconomic status with elevated morbidity and mortality (Barker 1994; Marmot et al. 1984). Another example concerns the 'programming' of a person's health risk in adult life by unfavorable circumstances of his mother's health during pregnancy. One study even reported unfavorable effects on adult health produced by severe social deprivation of the grandmother's generation (Lumey 1992). Although the parents' reduced health may be associated with adverse social circumstances, these circumstances 'cause' poor health mainly by means of biological processes that are transmitted from one generation to the next one during pregnancy or early infancy.

Some scholars maintain that the paradigm of social heritage needs to be expanded to include transgenerational transmission of health-related lifestyles where early socialization and mechanisms of model learning operate within the family (e.g., Baumrind 1991). Yet we should keep in mind that significant attitudes and behaviors that shape a person's health-related lifestyle are acquired in extrafamilial social contexts later in childhood and in adolescence (Jessor and Jessor 1977).

While the explanatory power of the two paradigms of 'social production' and of 'social heritage' is limited, a third paradigm of social causation of health and illness must be considered most important: the paradigm of 'exposure and resource.' This approach maintains that society determines the health of individuals mainly by exposing them to specific health-detrimental risks in their social environment. Moreover, individuals may have acquired different resources to cope with these health risks, and processes of resource acquisition are assumed to be socially patterned as well.

Today, two versions of the 'exposure and resource' paradigm are distinguished, the 'material' and the 'psychosocial' versions, although there exists substantial interaction between them. Evidence on the first version of the exposure paradigm is widespread: in this perspective, a health-damaging social environment includes poor housing, air pollution, heavy traffic and associated risk of accident, inappropriate sanitation, and noxious work places, among others. Poverty not only increases the risk of being exposed to these health-adverse conditions, but also reduces the opportunity of having adequate coping resources at one's disposal. Important coping resources such as healthy diet or access to health care are unequally distributed across society (Blane et al. 1996; see also Chapter 1.8). Explanations of a social causation of illness in this material version of the 'exposure and resource' paradigm usually refer to known physical, chemical, or biological risk factors. In related explanatory models, social factors are important to the extent that they determine exposure prevalence, duration, and intensity. This is quite different in explanations that are based on the psychosocial version of this paradigm. Here, stressful experience in terms of cognitive and emotional input to the brain is considered the crucial process. Exposure to specific social environments in the long run impairs a person's health by eliciting recurrent stressful experience in terms of negative emotions (e.g., threat, anxiety, anger, and helplessness) and of autonomic nervous system activation (Lazarus 1991). Again, successful coping with stressful experience is contingent on available resources, and psychosocial resources include the availability of social support as well as distinct psychological skills (e.g., self-efficacy; Bandura 1992).

After a long period of scientific stagnation, modern stress research more recently provided us with powerful evidence on a causal chain of events linking exposure to stressful social circumstances with subsequent illness susceptibility, as moderated by poor coping resources (Weiner 1992). Thus, a majority of theories of social causation of health and illness today refer to modern stress theory, at least in conjunction with the more conventional 'material' paradigm.

At this stage of the argument, some caution is needed. First, when talking about causal pathways we need to keep in mind that respective evidence, to a large extent, relies on probabilistic statistical associations derived from observational population studies. Experimental evidence of health-detrimental effects of stressful experience in humans is limited, due to ethical constraints, and results derived from more rigorous social stress experimentation in animals cannot easily be extrapolated to the human situation (Kaplan and Manuck 1997). Second, the complexities of human health and illness are overwhelming (Weiner 1992). While analytical distinctions and strategic reductions of complexity are inherent in any scientific approach, the multiple interactions of genetic and environmental conditions, of material, behavioral, and psychosocial influences, nevertheless need to be taken into account. This situation provides ongoing challenges to theory development and testing in sociomedical research. Nevertheless, a number of criteria were developed by epidemiologists to test whether a statistical association can be interpreted in terms of a causal link. These criteria are listed below.

1 Temporality of events (exposure to a risk factor precedes disease outcome).

2 Strength of association (as measured, for instance, by the magnitude of relative risks or odds ratios).

3 Consistency of associations (independent replication of findings).

4 Biological gradient and biological plausibility (higher exposure to risk is followed by higher risk of disease; pathogenic processes linking exposure to disease are evident).

5 Coherence of findings (evidence derived from different types of observational and experimental studies points in the same direction).

6 Specificity of outcome (if the effects of risk factor exposure are specific for a particular disease, the likelihood of causality is increased).

7 Interventional evidence (reduction of exposure to risk is followed by reduction of disease vulnerability).

It is probably appropriate to state that little, if any, definite evidence exists to date on specific social circumstances causing a specific physical disease or mental illness. Nevertheless, rapid progress is being made in this area of research, as will be discussed later. Before doing so, a brief look at the history of sociological studies dealing with the social causation of health and illness is needed.

HISTORICAL DEVELOPMENTS

Interestingly, the scientific study of social causes of health and illness originated from one of the most profound revolutions in the history of mankind, the double revolution of industrialization and democratic developments in the late eighteenth and early nineteenth centuries, especially in the United Kingdom, France, and somewhat later, Germany and the United States (Rosen 1979). Official statistics were established collecting administrative data on epidemics and their geographical and socioeconomic distribution; occupational health provided evidence on the pathogenic role of specific working conditions. For the first time, mental illness was studied in a socioenvironmental perspective, and most researchers were directly involved in the health policy implications of their findings. Yet the scientific quality of this research was rather modest, as it was restricted to descriptive and correlational information, and as the underlying pathogenic models (e.g., the miasma theory of infectious diseases) were misconceived, as demonstrated by scientific breakthroughs in cellular pathology, virology, and related disciplines (Loomis and Wing 1990).

While the scientific discipline of sociology also originated from the industrial revolution, the two activities converged only a couple of decades later. In 1897, French sociologist Emile Durkheim published his landmark study on suicide (Durkheim 1951). This was the first investigation to test a set of sociological propositions dealing with an important cause of death that was observed to be unequally distributed across the French society. According to Durkheim, the risk of suicide is elevated among social groups that are characterized by a weakening or loss of social norms and values guiding interpersonal life. As a consequence, egoistic or anomic tendencies manifest themselves, precipitating socioemotional crisis, distress and, ultimately, despair. Thus, suicide is interpreted as a socially triggered event, not as an action based on individual motives. It is important to mention that, in methodologic terms, Durkheim describes suicidal episodes as social facts that are generated at a societal rather than at an individual level. Therefore, the social patterning of health and disease is studied using aggregate data as a distinct source of information.

Both seminal insights provided by Durkheim, the critical role of social anomie in explaining health and illness, and the methodologic emphasis on social facts as a distinct category of analysis, were developed further by American sociologists earlier this century. For instance, Faris and Dunham (1939), among others, demonstrated the use of ecological analysis in studies dealing with adverse effects of urban development, including mental illness. Hollingshead and Redlich (1958) were the first to detect a clear-cut association between the prevalence of certain types of treated psychiatric illness and social class membership, as defined by an index of relevant socioeconomic characteristics. Perhaps even more important in theoretical terms, the concept of social anomia was specified in two landmark studies of mental illness, the Midtown Manhattan and the Stirling County Studies (Leighton et al. 1963; Srole et al. 1962).

Srole et al. analyzed social anomia – a person's sense of normlessness, powerlessness, and helplessness – as a consequence of Midtown's 'partial breakdown in the person-to-person private lines of communication' (Srole et al. 1962: 119). Its adverse effects on mental health become evident in the presence of critical life events and lack of group support that are more prevalent in lower socioeconomic groups (these core notions, not necessarily the appropriate terms, are already present in this interesting study!).

Carrying further these ideas, Langner and Michael (1963) demonstrated the cumulative effects of deprived childhood and of stressful working and living conditions in adulthood on mental illness, thus pioneering in an area that is currently of growing interest, the life course perspective of social epidemiology. In a similar approach, Leighton et al. (1963) advanced the idea of a pathogenic role of sociocultural disintegration in explaining the prevalence of psychiatric disturbances.

While these studies still owe a lot to the Durkheimian paradigm of illness as a social rather than an individual fact, they increasingly refer to a concurrent sociological approach, the paradigm of 'social action' developed most convincingly by Max Weber (Weber 1978). Social action theory claims that the ultimate unit of sociological analysis – the pattern of social interaction among persons – combines sociostructural (e.g., economic, historical) and individual (motivations, cognitions, emotions) information. In particular, different types of mismatch may arise between a society's structure of opportunities or constraints, and socially patterned individual aspirations and needs (Merton 1938). In this sociological perspective, conflicts and pressures resulting from this mismatch are considered major causes of impaired health and well-being. Concepts such as social integration/disintegration, social support, social anomia, or social stress implicitly or explicitly refer to this paradigm.

During the early 1960s a number of socioepidemiologic studies were undertaken with cardiovascular risk factors and coronary heart disease morbidity or mortality as outcome criteria. The two most important consequences of this shift from mental to physical disease were (1) the advancement of stress-theoretical approaches integrating sociological and biological information, and (2) the development of a cross-cultural, comparative research tradition within social epidemiology and medical sociology. This latter tradition provided us with a number of seminal insights into pathogenic effects on the cardiovascular system produced by rapid sociocultural change (Henry 1997; Henry and Cassel 1969; Scotch 1968; Tyroler and Cassel 1964), lack of stable sociocultural assets (Bruhn et al. 1966; Marmot and Syme 1976; Syme et al. 1964), poor social network and support (Berkman and Syme 1979), social status incongruence (Shekelle et al. 1969) and job loss (Kasl and Cobb 1970). Although at this stage of development the field suffered, to some extent, from conceptual inconsistency, the two decades ranging from the late 1950s to the late 1970s must be considered the founding period of a sociologically driven epidemiology of chronic diseases.

In 1977, Henry and Stephens published their book on *Stress, Health, and the Social Environment*. With this publication, for the first time, the crude links that existed between sociological constructs and disease endpoints were substantiated by physiological and pathophysiological evidence derived from social stress research in animals. Meanwhile, a growing number of investigations were performed that use psychophysiologic, neuroendocrinologic, and psychoneuroimmunologic techniques as part of experimental or observational studies of psychosocial risk groups (Weiner 1992). This type of transdisciplinary research conducted in a biopsychosocial perspective holds great promise for an advancement of our understanding of how societal life contributes to the causation of bodily disease.

This development was paralleled by the formation of a highly consistent body of evidence on an inverse social gradient of mortality. Information was obtained from official administrative data and from socioepidemiologic field studies. The basic finding was as follows: the lower a group's socioeconomic status, the higher its overall mortality. It is important to stress that this result challenges the traditional notion of an underprivileged, disadvantaged social group at the bottom of society, as there exists a linear relationship of socioeconomic indicators (level of education, occupational position, household income) with mortality. In other words, relative rather than absolute social deprivation is the critical condition.

Following early studies conducted by Hinkle et al. (1968), Antonovsky (1967) and Kitagawa and Hauser (1973) provided powerful results on the social patterning of mortality, based on national administrative data from the United States. In the United Kingdom, Marmot et al. (1978) demonstrated a social gradient of morbidity and mortality due to cardiovascular disease and some other conditions of chronic disease according to occupational standing in the now famous Whitehall I and II Studies (Marmot et al. 1991). This latter study is still ongoing, and more recently has offered promising explanations of the social gradient of health and disease in middle adulthood (see below). The publication of the so-called Black Report on social inequalities in health in the United Kingdom (Department of Health and Social Services 1980) must be considered a major event in the more recent history of medical sociology and social epidemiology in Europe and beyond. For the first time, sociological explanations of a pressing public health problem became part of the official health policy. This fact had, and still has, far-reaching implications for research policy and the formation of a cumulative sociological research paradigm (Evans et al. 1994; Fox 1989; Kunst 1997; Lahelma and Rahkonen 1997; see also Chapter 1.8).

In summary, the history of research on social causes of health and illness documents an intellectually appealing and empirically well-grounded body of sociological knowledge where two major analytical approaches, the Durkheimian and the Weberian paradigms, were successfully applied to human health and well-being. In the following section, a few more recent theoretical contributions are discussed that carry further some of the core notions developed in this field.

SELECTED THEORETICAL CONCEPTS

Theory development in the social sciences is a difficult task. This is due to the variabilities, dynamics, and complexities of its object, the human societies. For instance, it is widely accepted that there are three levels of sociological analysis: the macro, the meso, and the microsociological level. Research findings generated at each level are significant, but we hardly know how to link them within a comprehensive theoretical framework. Moreover, in epistemiologic terms, societal life at the same time is experienced as an objective (intersubjective) reality and as a subjectively defined, symbolically meaningful reality.

Therefore, it was proposed that the development of sociological theories may be restricted to so-called middle-range theories whose level of generalization is limited in time and space (Merton 1957). When using the term 'theory,' we expect an analytical scheme or model to be able to produce new explanatory or predicting information and, by doing so, to exclude other, concurrent explanations. We also expect a theoretical model to be successfully applied to a wider range of phenomena under study. In fact, the wider its explanatory range and the more economic its formulations, the more advanced and powerful a theory is.

The concepts of social causation of health and illness to be discussed here are all examples of such middle-range theories. Moreover, the selection of concepts favors the mesosociological level of analysis that links socioenvironmental conditions of everyday life to the actions, cognitions, and emotions of individuals (the Weberian paradigm). This emphasis on the mesosociological level of analysis and its focus on core social roles by which the individual person meets the demands and takes the opportunities of societal life does not preclude a similarly important macrostructural analysis of social determinants of illness, such as social class (Amick et al. 1995), income distribution (Wilkinson 1996), or the structure of the labor market (Brenner 1997) (the Durkheimian paradigm). Yet, ultimately, these determinants need to be linked to the illness susceptibility of individuals, and this is exactly why an analytical approach is given preference that combines sociostructural (sociological) and personal (psychological, biological) information.

Social Stressors and Resources: The Model of Life Events, Vulnerability Factors, and Cognitive Coping Responses

Most theoretical frames developed in studies on social causes of health and illness deal with associations between stressful socioenvironmental contexts and the resources mobilized by exposed individuals to mitigate the threats of stressful experience. Concepts differ according to the types and time structure of stressors under study (e.g., focus on a particular period in life vs. focus on life course, focus on stressful circumstances in family/nonwork vs. working life, focus on chronic vs. acute stressors, such as life events) and according to the delineation of coping resources. In most currently discussed theories, resources are classified into two broader categories: external (material or interpersonal) and internal (personal traits, skills, etc.) resources. In both cases, resources are assumed to moderate the stressor–strain relationship. Yet the causal models that specify this relationship differ, as does the emphasis put on pathogenic vs. salutogenic components of the stress process.

Examples of theories that put their main emphasis on the role of resources in the stressor–strain association are Antonovsky's concept of 'sense of coherence' (Antonovsky 1987), Hobfall's theory of resource conservation (Hobfall 1998), and the 'buffer' model of social support (House 1981). Moreover, several socialpsychological theories of self-regulation (e.g., Bandura's theory of self-efficacy (1992), and theories of attributional style and internal control (Weiner 1985)) are examples of this line of analysis. Other theories stress the cumulative effects on health produced by the presence of social stressors and the absence of strong external or internal resources (or the presence of distinct vulnerability factors (see below)), pointing to 'cycles of disadvantage' that precipitate a person's illness susceptibility and adaptive breakdown (Mirowsky and Ross 1989; Rutter and Madge 1976).

A discussion of single concepts is beyond the scope of this chapter. Rather, a few specific theoretical models are selected to review the current evidence of sociological explanations of mental and physical illness.

One of the most elaborate theoretical formulations of the relation between stressors, resources, or vulnerability factors and illness susceptibility was developed and tested by sociologist George W. Brown and colleagues in their studies on social causes of affective disorders (Brown and Harris 1978; Brown et al. 1990a). Starting from the paradigm of life event research, they specified a model in which stressful life events or chronic difficulties adversely influence a person's affective health and well-being if at least one of the following two 'vulnerability factors' is present: (1) lack of a confidant or lack of crisis support, and (2) negative evaluation of self (poor self-esteem). This latter vulnerability factor is more often present in persons who experienced loss of a parent in childhood. Moreover, a person's cognitive coping response to crises is of relevance (e.g., self-blame or helplessness vs. optimism).

The model was tested by Brown et al. in a more recent follow-up study of 353 mothers with a child under the age of 18 years living at home (Brown et al. 1985). Onset of depression was best predicted by a combination of three variables: (1) negative cognitive coping (denial, self-blame, pessimism), (2) personal vulnerability, and (3) lack of crisis support in the face of experienced life events or chronic difficulties.

In this psychosocial high-risk group, 69 per cent of the women (20 out of 29) developed depression compared with 9 per cent in the psychosocially less stressful or even protective constellations. Multivariate analysis using logistic regression techniques indicated that each variable produced a separate effect on the likelihood of experiencing the onset of depression (Bifulco and Brown 1996). Yet, interestingly, further detailed data analysis revealed that these factors interact in a dynamic way. For instance, women who reported self-blame and pessimism more often experienced discontinued support as a direct result of their own failure to confide. Thus, the presence of a distinct attributional style in a person may increase the likelihood of experiencing additional amounts of chronic distress, which in turn triggers generalized feelings of hopelessness and related symptomatology of affective disorders.

Brown's work on the social origins of affective disorders must be considered as definite progress in this area of sociological research, not only because of its elaborate theoretical formulations, but also because the data collection is based on newly designed, carefully elaborated assessment methods, such as the life events and difficulties schedule (LEDS (Brown and Harris 1978)), and

the self-esteem and social support schedule
(SESS (Brown et al. 1990b)).

Control and Reward in Core Social Roles in Mid-life: Models of the Psychosocial Work Environment

There are at least four reasons that account for the centrality of work and occupation in adult life in all economically advanced societies. First, having a job is a principal prerequisite for continuous income opportunities. Level of income determines a wide range of life chances. Second, training for a job and achievement of occupational status are the most important goals of primary and secondary socialization. It is through education, job training, and status acquisition that personal growth and development are realized, that a core social identity outside the family is acquired, and that intentional, goal-directed activity in human life is shaped. Third, occupation defines the most important criterion of social stratification in advanced societies. Furthermore, type and quality of occupation, and especially the degree of self-direction at work, strongly influence personal attitudes and behavioral patterns (Kohn and Schooler 1983). Finally, occupational settings produce the most pervasive continuous demands during one's lifetime, and they absorb the largest amount of time in adult life. Exposure to stressful job conditions carries the risk of ill health by virtue of the amount of time spent and the quality of demands faced at work. At the same time, occupational settings provide unique opportunities to experience reward, success, or satisfaction, and thus to promote health and well-being by eliciting strong positive emotions.

The paradigm of psychosocial exposure and resource has guided – and continues to guide – most of the sociological studies on salutogenic and pathogenic effects of the work role. Whereas in the 1960s and early 1970s the Michigan school provided most significant contributions to this development, in particular by proposing and testing the 'person–environment-fit-model' (French et al. 1982) as an analytical perspective, more recent research focuses on two conceptions that, due to dynamic research developments in this particular field, are discussed in some detail. These two conceptions are: the demand–support–control model, and the model of effort–reward imbalance at work. Both have the potential of being extended beyond the context of paid work to identify additional areas of socially patterned stressful experience in mid-life.

Originally, the first concept was designed as a two-dimensional model of job characteristics by sociologist Robert A. Karasek (1979). Based on evidence derived from psychophysiology (Frankenhaeuser 1983) and occupational sociology (Kohn and Schooler 1983), the demand–control–support model claims that the combined effects of low control over one's job tasks (low decision latitude or low level of skill discretion) and of high demands (e.g., mental load due to work pressure) produce a state of 'strain' that inhibits learning and triggers emotional tension. Exposure to 'strain jobs,' that is, jobs defined by high demands and low task control, increases the risk of ill-health and bodily disease in the long run via two mechanisms: (a) continued autonomic nervous system activation and stress-related pathophysiologic developments; (b) enhanced health-adverse behaviors such as cigarette smoking or unhealthy diet. 'Active jobs,' on the contrary, stimulate psychological growth and emotional well-being (for an extensive discussion see Karasek and Theorell 1990).

Adverse effects on health are intensified if a third dimension is introduced into the model: the presence or absence of social support at work. Workers exposed to high demands, low control, and a high degree of social isolation on their job (so-called 'iso-strain groups') experience relatively high health risks, whereas strong support at work moderates these effects (Johnson and Hall 1988).

Figure 1 gives an example of socioepidemiological research based on this three-dimensional model of 'job strain.' Findings are derived from a follow-up study of a large sample of randomly selected Swedish working men where the association between age and cardiovascular morbidity is analyzed according to the degree of 'iso-strain' demands × lack of support × lack of control). The 20 per cent with the highest scores, the 20 per cent with the lowest scores, and the middle 60 per cent are compared (Johnson et al. 1989). As can be seen from this figure, an elevated probability of cardiovascular disease manifestation is observed among workers who are exposed to 'iso-strain' jobs compared with the remaining two groups, at all age levels, but particularly beyond age 45.

Up to now, a number of prospective, cross-sectional, and experimental studies had been performed to test the hypothesis of adverse health effects produced by exposure to strain jobs (for a recent review see Theorell and Karasek 1996). Few sociological models of social causation of health and illness in recent past were analyzed to a comparable extent. Taken together, the currently available empirical support can be summarized as follows.

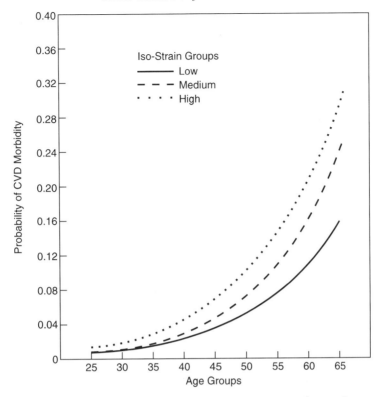

Figure 1 *The combined effects of job strain and social isolation on cardiovascular disease (randomly selected Swedish working males, N = 7219). Source: Johnson, J.V., Hall, E.M., and Theorell, T. (1989).*

1. A majority of studies report independent effects of either single components or of some combination of components of the model on health outcomes, mostly on cardiovascular health. However, relatively the highest consistency of findings is observed with respect to the component 'low job task control.' Few studies document a multiple interaction term, as postulated by the original model, and even fewer studies have so far explored the three-dimensional as compared with the two-dimensional model.

2. Relative risks (or odds ratios) of 'job strain' or 'low job control,' although varying according to study population, country, gender, and age, as well as according to the measurement approach, usually range between 1.5 and 3.0. Again, most evidence relates to cardiovascular disease. In view of the rather high prevalence of 'strain jobs' in advanced economies, this result is significant both in terms of interdisciplinary chronic disease epidemiology and of policy implications. For instance, it was pointed out that, based on these findings, up to 10 per cent of all coronary events occurring in the workforce

could be prevented if 'strain jobs' were absent. Moreover, the economic costs of work-related stress are of a critical magnitude (Levi and Lunde-Jensen 1996).

3. Additional adverse effects on health caused by 'job strain' are documented for behaviorally induced risk factors such as cigarette smoking, and for risk factors whose levels are influenced, among others, by stress-physiological mechanisms, as is the case for high blood pressure, atherogenic lipids, and elevated fibrinogen. Moreover, experimental studies indicate elevated blood pressure levels and elevated levels of stress hormones secreted into blood or urine as well as reduced immune function, in individuals exposed to 'job strain.' More recently, other health risks were also studied, including musculoskeletal disease, mental illness, subjective health, and absenteeism from work.

While this summary of current evidence is impressive, several conceptual and methodological criticisms were raised. The following two theoretical arguments are particularly challenging. First, as the model concentrates on exposure, it neglects the resources of the individual person, and thus bypasses a substantial body of research highlighting the role of coping processes and of individual differences in the stress response (Cooper and Payne 1991; Lazarus 1991). Second, it is not clear whether 'job strain,' and in particular 'job task control,' is an explanatory construct in itself or whether it is a powerful indicator of stressful conditions associated with, but not identified by, the model. Examples of stressful conditions in this context are low job security, lack of promotion prospects, or economic hardship. In view of current challenges to the labor market caused by economic globalization, these latter conditions are of growing concern for health.

An alternative model of stressful experience at work, the model of effort–reward imbalance (Siegrist 1996; Siegrist et al. 1986), addresses these latter criticisms to some extent while focussing on the reward structure of working life. The model maintains that the work role defines a crucial link between the self-regulatory needs of a person (e.g., self-esteem, self-efficacy) and the social opportunity structure. In particular, availability of an occupational status is associated with recurrent options of contributing and performing, of being rewarded or esteemed, and of belonging to some significant group (e.g., work colleagues). Yet these potentially beneficial effects are contingent on a basic prerequisite of exchange in social life, that is, reciprocity. Effort at work is spent as part of a socially organized exchange process to which society at large contributes in terms of rewards. Rewards are distributed by three transmitter systems as scarce resources: money, esteem, and career opportunities. The model of effort–reward imbalance claims that lack of reciprocity between costs and gains (i.e., high-cost/low-gain conditions) defines a state of emotional distress with special propensity to autonomic arousal and neuroendocrine stress responses. For instance, having a demanding but unstable job, achieving at a high level without being offered any promotion prospects, are examples of a particularly stressful working context.

Contrary to the expectancy value theory of motivation (Schönpflug and Badmann 1989), this model predicts continued high effort under the conditions listed below.

- Lack of alternative choice in the labor market may prevent people from giving up even unfavorable jobs as the anticipated costs of disengagement (e.g., the risk of being laid off or of facing downward mobility) outweigh the costs of accepting inadequate benefits.
- Unfair job arrangements may be accepted for a certain period of one's occupational trajectory for strategic reasons; by doing so

employees tend to improve their chances for career promotion and related rewards at a later stage.

- A specific personal pattern of coping with demands and of eliciting rewards, characterized by excessive work-related overcommitment, may prevent people from accurately assessing cost–gain relations. Owing to the cognitive–motivational dynamics underlying this pattern of coping, individuals who score high on a scale measuring work-related overcommitment tend to misjudge demanding stimuli (i.e., underestimate demands, overestimate own coping resources (Matschinger et al. 1986)).

A graphic representation of the effort–reward imbalance model is given in Figure 2. This figure highlights the main differences from the demand–support–control model. First, the model assumes that threats to the reciprocity of exchange in core social role relations, and in particular in the work role, elicit recurrent and sustained stressful experience, and thus impair health and well-being in the long run. Second, three dimensions of reward experience or expectancy are distinguished where money and career opportunities link the individual job situation with macrostructural labor market conditions that are of growing concern for health (in particular job instability, forced mobility, and low-salary jobs). Third, the model explicitly distinguishes between extrinsic (situational) and intrinsic (personal) components of effort–reward imbalance. It is assumed that a combination of both sources of information provides a more accurate estimate of experienced stress at work than a restriction to one of these two sources (either situational or personal).

Compared with the 'job strain' model, fewer studies have been performed using measures of effort–reward imbalance. However, current evidence indicates that high effort/low reward conditions at work predict cardiovascular morbidity with odds ratios that are comparable in size to the ones reported for 'job strain' or 'job control' (Siegrist 1996). In addition, the model explains the prevalence of important cardiovascular risk factors such as hypertension, atherogenic lipids, or a high level of fibrinogen, after adjusting for biobehavioral confounders (Siegrist et al. 1997). Most recent research documents consistent effects of effort–reward imbalance at work on subjective health, symptom experience, and the risk of imminent psychiatric illness. Interestingly, one study found differential prediction of health outcomes according to whether the full model or only part of it was included in the analysis. Whereas the full model explained the prevalence of cardiovascular risk factors

Figure 2   *The model of effort–reward imbalance at work*

such as hypertension, the presence of low reward only (absence of high extrinsic or intrinsic effort) explained conditions of passive coping and withdrawal, such as the prevalence of short-term sickness absence (Peter and Siegrist 1997). In a recent analysis based on data from the Whitehall II study, independent effects on coronary heart disease of the two alternative job stress models, the effort–reward imbalance model and the job strain model (job control only), were reported (Bosma et al. 1998). It may well be that the combined study of these models and their extension beyond occupational life offers new insights into the social patterning of health. For instance, conditions of low control and of high cost/low gain may characterize stressful experience in groups that are excluded from paid work (e.g., homemakers). Another application concerns the further elucidation of reported associations of income inequality with mortality (see also Chapter 1.8).

In conclusion, current psychosocial exposure–resource models of social causation of health and illness offer some promise in advancing our understanding of how the social, psychological, and biological dimension of human health are interrelated. Nevertheless, we should keep in mind that most evidence reported so far concerns modern Western societies, and that the role of ethnicity and culture needs to be explored more vigorously. Moreover, the models discussed so far are biased towards the productive life span in adulthood, leaving little room for understanding the social causes of illness in the elderly. In view of major sociodemographic changes, this bias is critical, and despite the fact that biological influences may override the psychosocial impact on morbidity in older age, this topic deserves substantial attention in future research. A similar argument can be made with

respect to young age, strengthening a life course approach towards studying the social causes of illness. This approach is briefly discussed in the following section.

Social Causes of Illness in a Life Course Perspective: The 'Pathways' Model

At least since the Midtown Manhattan Study (Langner and Michael 1963), socioepidemiologic researchers have been interested in understanding the links between adverse social conditions in childhood, relative social deprivation in adult life, and subsequent illness susceptibility. Answers to this question require data that are obtained from longitudinal birth cohort studies. By now, several prospective studies of birth cohorts have been established, and results covering at least the first thirty years of a life span are currently available from some of these studies (Kuh and Ben-Shlomo 1997; Power et al. 1996). In theoretical terms they challenge traditional sociological thinking as they call for a dynamic rather than a static conceptualization of the relations between sociostructural conditions and individual behavior, well-being, and health. Answers to the question mentioned above that result from these birth cohort studies usually refer to one of two explanatory frameworks: the so-called 'latency' model and the so-called 'pathways' model.

The latency model postulates early programming of impaired health, either by genetic, intrauterine, or perinatal conditions. These conditions are assumed to exert a strong independent effect on health that manifests itself after a long period of latency some decades later in life (see above, 'social heritage').

The pathways model emphasizes the cumulative effect on adult health produced by social stressors that occur along developmental trajectories from childhood through adolescence into adulthood. In this model, the transmission of parent's deprived socioeconomic and sociocultural conditions to offspring's well-being, or in other words the transmission of continued social disadvantage, receives special attention.

The latency model is well established as a paradigm of genetic epidemiology. Furthermore, it was confirmed by a series of studies demonstrating that adult cardiovascular disease was strongly influenced by biological programming occurring in utero or early infancy (Barker 1994). More specifically, inappropriate placental size and metabolic dysfunction in the pregnant mother 'set' the regulation of the infant's key biological parameters such as blood pressure or lipid metabolism during the fetal period. Early manifestations of this dysregulation include low birth weight and inappropriate growth in the first year, but later, after decades of latency, hypertension, hyperlipidemia, overweight, or diabetes manifest themselves and contribute to an acceleration of cardiovascular pathology.

In this approach, socially deprived parental life circumstances exert an indirect effect on children's health only, an effect that is largely mediated by maternal biological health during pregnancy. Yet more recent research indicates that associations between parent's socioeconomic status, offspring's birth weight, and their subsequent health status are more complex, calling for an application of the 'pathways' framework. For instance, low birth weight babies were found to be at higher risk of later social disadvantage, in terms of education and employment, even after controlling for parent's socioeconomic status (Paneth 1994). Conversely, children at developmental risk arising from complications during delivery enjoyed normal mental developmental after 24 months if they were born into middle-class or upper-class families, but suffered from substantial developmental deficits if born into lower-class families (Werner and Smith 1992). Thus, biological risks established in early life may be exacerbated or attenuated by the consequences of subsequent socioeconomic conditions.

In summary, as a recent review suggests, 'work on the effect of early life environment on health in adulthood promises fresh insights into the shaping of adult health and disease, because it may be that later life events do not tell the whole aetiological story. However, it is necessary to take account of intervening factors, since the early life–adult disease relationship could be partly attributable to the later socio-economic circumstances with which birth weight is associated. Longitudinal data...provide evidence that a link between birth weight and socioeconomic circumstances exists in childhood and through to age 33. In other words, low birth weight may be acting as a marker of a particularly disadvantaged life trajectory' (Power et al. 1996: 201).

First results from one of these birth cohort studies indicate that subjective health at age 33 is best predicted by a combination of social 'heritage' factors (parent's socioeconomic status, low birth weight, height), offspring's own socioeconomic position, the amount of her chronically stressful experience at work, and offspring's health-adverse behavior, in particular cigarette smoking (Power 1997, personal communication). As postulated by the pathways model, the emergent trend is one of differential accumulation of risk factors occurring at different stages according to social position at birth. These preliminary results illustrate the potential explanatory power of a life course ('pathways') approach towards studying social causes of health and illness.

POLICY IMPLICATIONS AND FUTURE DEVELOPMENTS

The demonstration of an inverse social gradient of morbidity and mortality within and between populations in a large number of advanced societies must be considered one of the most consistent and most important findings of modern social epidemiology and medical sociology. The policy implications of these results are far-reaching, especially so since the contribution of health-care factors to an explanation of the social gradient is rather modest (Marmot 1994). Other explanations pointing to social selection or genetic risk were also shown to be of minor relevance. However, health-damaging behaviors and unfavorable exposure–resource conditions play a crucial role in explaining the social gradient of chronic disease, at least in middle adulthood (Bobak and Marmot 1996; Marmot 1994). This also holds true for the psychosocial exposure–resource approach in general, and the models of chronically stressful experience at work in particular (Lynch et al. 1997; Marmot et al. 1997). Based on the most recent findings from the Whitehall II study, Michael Marmot and colleagues conclude that much of the inverse social gradient in coronary heart disease reports can be attributed to unfavourable psychosocial working conditions (Marmot et al. 1997).

Provided this line of explanation is further substantiated, its policy implications point to the relevance of structural primary prevention in three distinct social environments: the family, the school, and the work place. Whereas the first two social environments need to be addressed by structural measures in order to improve health-promoting behaviors and underlying psychosocial skills and competences in children and adolescents, the work place environment offers options to reduce the pathogenic effects of chronically stressful experience at work and to enhance its salutogenic potentials in adults.

First, results from psychosocial intervention studies in family and school settings are promising, as they underline some favorable long-term effects of these measures (for an instructive review, see Hertzman and Wiens 1996). This also holds true for work-site intervention studies in adult populations based on the models discussed. For instance, favorable effects of enlarged decision latitude and improved support on sickness absence, subjective health, and reduction in atherogenic lipids were found (Karasek 1992; Orth-Gomer et al. 1994; Theorell and Karasek 1996). Furthermore, reinforced social skills and improved esteem contributed to well-being by reducing a critical level of work-related overcommitment (Aust et al. 1997).

In conclusion, policy implications of advanced, theory-based sociological knowledge on social causes of illness are considerable, and it is hoped that these findings receive more attention in future political debates, especially so as the direct and indirect health costs of chronic stress at work were recently shown to be substantial (Levi and Lunde-Jensen 1996).

Despite these preliminary successes, much remains to be done to further improve the scientific quality of sociological research in this area. Future developments most probably include the development of more sophisticated measures of existing concepts in the field of psychosocial exposure–resource models, the exploration of biological pathways mediating chronically stressful experience to bodily dysfunction and disease, and the exploration of beneficial effects obtained from theory-based interventions. Moreover, existing concepts need to be integrated into a life course perspective that is better suited to deal with dynamic processes of social heritage, cumulative exposure to stressful social circumstances, and lack of, or weakening of, available coping resources in triggering illness susceptibility.

Finally, the question arises whether this research has the potential of advancing our knowledge beyond the boundaries of middle-range theories on social life, and thus to contribute to the development of general sociological theory. It became clear from the content of this chapter that emotions play a powerful role in maintaining health and in triggering disease, and that the intensity of individual emotional experience, both positive and negative, is critically enhanced by exposure to, and coping with, particular social contexts. Knowledge on the intrinsic effects of socio-emotional experience on human health and well-being to some extent may challenge, or at least enrich, cognitively biased sociological theories.

One possible line of further theory development in this perspective concerns a broader conceptualization of the health effects generated by control and reward experiences in core social roles. As argued elsewhere (Siegrist 1998), a balance between the demands and rewards of the social opportunity structure on the one hand, and an individual's need for successful self-regulation in terms of social role functioning on the other, is needed to promote well-being and health. Socially approved experience of successful self-regulation includes self-esteem, self-efficacy, and self-integration (i.e., a sense of belonging to a significant interpersonal or spiritual community). Threats to this fragile balance of sociostructural contexts of demands and rewards, of everyday social role functioning, and of emotional benefits obtained from successful self-regulation are particularly stressful if core expectations of reciprocity in social exchange are violated. This may be due to the fact that our evolutionary brain structures are 'imprinted' by a basic grammar of social exchange, the grammar of reciprocity and fairness (Cosmides and Tooby 1992). Under these conditions, resource management becomes difficult, and profound experiences of injustice, unfairness, and relative social deprivation are expected to trigger illness susceptibility. Such an analytical perspective might to some extent bridge the gap between macrosociological information, for example, on the adverse health effects of income inequality, or of disruption and loss of intimate social ties, and social-psychological information on the adverse health effects of an individual's impaired self-regulation.

References

Amick, B.C., Levine, S., Tarlov, A.R., and Chapman, W.D. (eds) (1995) *Society and Health*. Oxford: Oxford University Press.

Antonovsky, A. (1967) 'Social class, life expectancy, and overall mortality', *Milbank Memorial Fund Quarterly*, 45: 31–73.

Antonovsky, A. (1987) *Unraveling the Mystery of Health: How People Manage Stress and Stay Well*. San Francisco: Jossey Bass.

Aust, B., Peter, R., and Siegrist, J. (1997) 'Stress management in bus drivers: A pilot study based on the model of effort–reward imbalance', *International Journal of Stress Management*, 4: 297–305.

Bandura, A. (1992) 'Exercise of personal agency through the self-efficacy mechanism', in R. Schwarzer (ed.), *Self-Efficacy: Thought Control of Action*. Washington, DC: Hemisphere. pp. 3–38.

Barker, D.J.P. (1994) *Mothers, Babies and Disease in Later Life*. London: British Medical Journal.

Baumrind, J. (1991) 'The influence of parenting style on adolescent competence and substance use', *Journal of Early Adolescence*, 11: 56–95.

Berger, P.L. and Luckmann, T. (1966) *The Social Construction of Reality*. New York: Basic Books.

Berkman, L.F. and Syme, S.L. (1979) 'Social networks, host resistance, and mortality: A nine year follow-up study of Alameda County residents', *American Journal of Epidemiology*, 109: 186–204.

Bifulco, A. and Brown, G.W. (1996) 'Cognitive coping response to crises and onset of depression', *Social Psychiatry and Psychiatric Epidemiology*, 31: 163–72.

Blane, D., Brunner, E., and Wilkinson, R. (eds) (1996) *Health and Social Organization*. London: Routledge.

Blau, T.M. (1977) *Inequality and Heterogeneity*. New York: Free Press.

Bobak, M. and Marmot, M. (1996) 'East-West mortality divide and its potential explanations: Proposed research agenda', *British Medical Journal*, 312: 421–25.

Bosma, H., Peter, R., Siegrist, J., and Marmot, M. (1998) 'Two alternative job stress models and the risk of coronary heart disease', *American Journal of Public Health*, 88: 68–74.

Brenner, M.H. (1997) 'Heart disease mortality and economic changes, including unemployment, in Western Germany 1951–1989', *Acta Physiologica Scandinavica*, 161, Suppl. 640: 149–52.

Brown, G.W. and Harris, T.O. (1978) *Social Origins of Depression*. London: Tavistock.

Brown, G.W., Craig, T.K.J., and Harris, T.O. (1985) 'Depression: Disease or distress? Some epidemiological considerations', *British Journal of Psychiatry*, 147: 612–22.

Brown, G.W., Andrews, B., Bifulco, A., and Veiel, H. (1990a) 'Self-esteem and depression. I. Measurement issues and prediction of onset', *Social Psychiatry and Psychiatric Epidemiology*, 25: 200–9.

Brown, G.W., Bifulco, A., and Andrews, B. (1990b) 'Self-esteem and depression. III. Aetiological issues', *Social Psychiatry and Psychiatric Epidemiology*, 25: 235–43.

Bruhn, J.G., Chandler, B., Lynn, T.N., and Wolf, S. (1966) 'Social characteristics of patients with coronary heart disease', *American Journal of Medical Sciences*, 251: 629–37.

Cockerham, W.C. (1992) *Medical Sociology*. Englewood Cliffs: Prentice Hall. 5th edn.

Cooper, C.L. and Payne, R. (eds) (1991) *Personality and Stress: Individual Differences in the Stress Process*. Chichester: Wiley.

Cosmides, L. and Tooby, J. (1992) 'Cognitive adaptations of social exchange', in J. H. Barkow, L. Cosmides, and J. Tooby (eds), *The Adapted Mind: Evolutionary Psychology and the Generation of Culture*. New York: Oxford University Press. pp. 163–228.

Department of Health and Social Security (1980) *Inequalities in Health: Report of a Working Group chaired by Sir Douglas Black*. Department of Health Statistics and Surveys London.

Durkheim, E. (1951) The Suicide. New York: Free Press (original in French, 1897).

Evans, R.G., Barer, M.L., and Marmor, T.R. (1994) *Why are Some People Healthy and Others Not? The Determinants of Health of Populations*. New York: Aldine deGruyter.

Faris, R.E. and Dunham, H.W. (1939) *Mental Disorders in Urban Areas*. Chicago: University of Chicago Press.

Fox, J. (ed.) (1989) *Health Inequalities in European Countries*. Aldershot: Gower.

Frankenhaeuser, M. (1983) 'The sympathetic-adrenal and pituitary-adrenal response to challenge', in T.M. Dembroski, T.H. Schmidt, and G.Blümchen (eds), *Biobehavioral Base of Coronary Heart Disease*. Basel: Karger. pp. 91–105.

French, J.R., Kaplan, R.D., and Harrison, R.V. (1982) *The Mechanisms of Job Stress and Strain*. Chichester: Wiley.

Henry, J.P. (1997) *Cultural Change and High Blood Pressure*. Münster: Lit.

Henry, J.P. and Cassel, J.C. (1969) 'Psychosocial factors as risk factors in essential hypertension: Recent epidemiologic and animal experimental evidence', *American Journal of Epidemiology*, 90: 171–200.

Henry, J.P. and Stephens, P.M. (1977) *Stress, Health, and the Social Environment*. New York: Springer.

Hertzman, C. and Wiens, M. (1996) 'Child development and long-term outcomes: A population health perspective and summary of successful interventions', *Social Science and Medicine*, 43: 1083–96.

Hinkle, L.E. Jr., Whitney, L.H., Lehman, E.W., and Dunn, J. (1968) 'Occupation, education and coronary heart disease: Risk is influenced more by education and background than by occupational experiences, in the Bell system', *Science*, 161: 238–46.

Hobfall, S.E. (1998) *Stress, Culture and Community: The Psychology and Philosophy of Stress*. New York: Plenum.

Hollingshead, A.B. and Redlich, F.C. (1958) *Social Class and Mental Illness*. New York: Wiley.

House, J.S. (1981) *Work Stress and Social Support*. Reading, MA: Addison Wesley.

Jessor, R. and Jessor, S. L. (1977) *Problem Behavior and Psychosocial Development: Longitudinal Study of Youth*. New York: Academic Press.

Johnson, J.V. and Hall, E.M. (1988) 'Job strain, work place social support, and cardiovascular diseases', *American Journal of Public Health*, 78: 1336–42.

Johnson, J.V., Hall, E.M., and Theorell, T. (1989) 'Combined effects of job-strain and social isolation on cardiovascular disease morbidity and mortality in a random sample of the Swedish male working population', *Scandinavian Journal of Work Environment and Health*, 15: 271–9.

Kaplan, J.R. and Manuck, S.B. (1997) 'Using ethological principles to study psychosocial influences on coronary atherosclerosis in monkeys', *Acta Physiologica Scandinavica*, 161 (Suppl. 640) 96–9.

Karasek, R.A. (1979) 'Job demands, job decisions latitude, and mental strain: Implications for job redesign', *Adminstration Science Quarterly*, 24: 285–307.

Karasek, R.A. (1992) 'Stress prevention through work reorganization: A summary of 19 international case studies', *Conditions of Work Digest*, 11: 23–41.

Karasek, R.A. and Theorell, T. (1990) *Healthy Work: Stress, Productivity, and the Reconstruction of Working Life*. New York: Basic Books.

Kasl, S.V. and Cobb, S. (1970) 'Blood pressure changes in men undergoing job loss: A preliminary report', *Journal of Chronic Disease*, 22: 259–78.

Kitagawa, E.M. and Hauser, P.M. (1973) *Differential Mortality in the United States. A Study in Socioeconomic Epidemiology*. Cambridge: Harvard University Press.

Kohn, M. and Schooler, C. (1983) *Work and Personality: An Inquiry Into the Impact of Social Stratification*. Norwood: Ablex.

Kuh, D. and Ben-Shlomo, Y. (1997) *A Life Course Approach to Chronic Disease Epidemiology*. Oxford: Oxford Medical Publications.

Kunst, A. (1997) *Cross-National Comparisons of Socio-Economic Differences in Mortality*. Rotterdam: Erasmus University Press.

Lahelma, E. and Rahkonen, O. (eds) (1997) 'Health inequalities in modern societies and beyond', *Social Science and Medicine*, 40 (Special Issue): 721–910.

Langner, T.S. and Michael, S.T. (1963) *Life Stress and Mental Health: The Midtown Manhattan Study*. New York: Free Press.

Lazarus, R.S. (1991) *Emotion and Adaptation*. New York: Oxford University Press.

Leighton, D.C., Harding, J.S., Macklin, D.B. et al. (1963) *The Character of Danger: Psychiatric Symptoms in Selected Communities*. New York: Basic Books.

Levi, L. and Lunde-Jensen, B. (1996) '*A Model for Assessing the Costs of Stressors at National Level*'. Dublin: European Foundation for the Improvement of Living and Working Conditions.

Loomis, D. and Wing, S. (1990) 'Is molecular epidemiology a germ theory for the end of the twentieth century?', *International Journal of Epidemiology*, 19: 1–3.

Luhmann, N. (1984) *Soziale Systeme (Social Systems)*. Frankfurt: Suhrkamp.

Lumey, L.H. (1992) 'Decreased birthweights in infants after maternal in utero exposure to the Dutch famine of 1944–45', *Pediatric and Perinatal Epidemiology*, 6: 240–53.

Lynch, J., Krause, N., Kaplan, G.A. et al. (1997) 'Workplace conditions, socioeconomic status, and the risk of mortality and acute myocardial infarction: The Kuopio ischemic heart disease risk factor study', *American Journal of Public Health*, 87: 617–22.

Marmot, M.G. (1994) 'Social differentials in health within and between populations', *Daedalus*, 123: 197–216.

Marmot, M.G. and Syme, S.L. (1976) 'Acculturation and coronary heart disease in Japanese Americans', *American Journal of Epidemiology*, 104: 225–47.

Marmot, M.G., Adelstein, A.M., Robinson, N., and Rose, G.A. (1978) 'Changing social-class distribution of heart disease', *British Medical Journal*, 2: 1109–12.

Marmot, M.G., Shipley, M., and Rose, G. (1984) 'Inequalities in death – specific explanation of a general pattern?' *The Lancet*, 1: 1003–6.

Marmot, M.G., Davey Smith, G., Stansfield, S. et al. (1991) 'Inequalities in health twenty years on: The Whitehall II study of British civil servants', *The Lancet*, 337: 1387–93.

Marmot, M.G., Bosma, H., Hemingway, H. et al. (1997) 'Contribution of job control and other risk factors: To social variations in heart disease', *The Lancet*, 350: 235–9.

Matschinger, H., Siegrist, J., Siegrist, K., and Dittmann, K.H. (1986) 'Type A as a coping career: Towards a conceptual and methodological redefinition', in T.H. Schmidt, T.M. Dembroski, and G. Blümchen (eds) *Biological and Psychological Factors in Cardiovascular Disease*. Berlin: Springer. pp. 104–26.

Mayntz, R. (1985) 'On the use and non-use of methodological rules in social research', in U. Gerhardt and M.E.J. Wadsworth (eds), *Stress and Stigma*. Frankfurt: Campus. pp. 39–52.

Mechanic, D. (1978) *Medical Sociology*. New York: Free Press.

Merton, R. K. (1938) 'Social structure and anomie', *American Sociological Review*, 3: 672–82.

Merton, R.K. (1957) *Social Theory and Social Structure*. New York: Free Press.

Mirowsky, J. and Ross, L.E. (1989) *Social Causes of Psychological Distress*. New York: Aldine deGruyter.

Nagel, E. (1961) *The Structure of Science*. New York: Free Press.

Orth-Gomer, K., Eriksson, I., Moser, V. et al. (1994) 'Lipid lowering through work stress reduction', *International Journal of Behavioural Medicine*, 1: 204–14.

Paneth, N. (1994) 'The impressionable fetus – fetal life and adult health', *American Journal of Public Health*, 84: 1372–4.

Parsons, T. (1951) *The Social System*. New York: Free Press.

Peter, R. and Siegrist, J. (1997) 'Chronic work stress, sickness absence and hypertension in middle managers: General or specific sociological explanations? *Social Science and Medicine*, 45: 1111–20.

Popper, K. (1959) *The Logic of Scientific Discovery*. London: Oxford University Press.

Power, C., Bartley, M., Davey Smith, G. et al. (1996) 'Transmission of social and biological risk across the life course', in D. Blane, E. Brunner, and R. Wilkinson (eds), *Health and Social Organization*. London: Routledge. pp. 188–203.

Rosen, G. (1979) 'The evolution of social medicine', in H.S. Freeman, S. Levine, and L. Reeder (eds), *Handbook of Medical Sociology*. Englewood Cliffs: Prentice Hall. pp. 23–45.

Rutter, M. and Madge, N. (1976) *Cycles of Disadvantage*. London: Heinemann.

Scheff, T. (1966) *Being Mentally Ill*. Chicago: Aldine.

Schönpflug, W. and Badmann, W. (1989) 'The costs and benefits of coping', in S. Fisher and J. Reason (eds), *Handbook of Stress, Cognition and Health*. Chichester: Wiley. pp. 699–714.

Scotch, N.A. (1968) 'Sociocultural factors in the epidemiology of Zulu hypertension', *American Journal of Public Health*, 53: 1205–13.

Shekelle, R.B., Osterfeld, A.M., and Paul, O. (1969) 'Social status and incidence of coronary heart disease', *Journal of Chronic Diseases*, 22: 381–94.

Siegrist, J. (1996) 'Adverse health effects of high effort–low reward conditions at work' *Journal of Occupational Health Psychology*, 1: 27–43.

Siegrist, J. (1998) 'Reciprocity in basic social exchange and health: Can we reconcile person-based with population-based psychosomatic research?', *Journal of Psychosomatic Research*, 45: 99–105.

Siegrist, J., Siegrist, K., and Weber, I. (1986) 'Sociological concepts in the etiology of chronic disease: The case of ischemic heart disease', *Social Science and Medicine*, 22: 247–53.

Siegrist, J., Peter, R., Cremer, P., and Seidel, D. (1997) 'Chronic work stress is associated with atherogenic lipids and elevated fibrinogen in middle-aged men', *Journal of Internal Medicine*, 242: 149–56.

Srole, L., Langner, T.S., Michael, S.T. et al. (1962) *Mental Health in the Metropolis: The Midtown Manhattan Study, Vol. 1*. New York: McGraw-Hill.

Straus, R. (1957) 'The nature and status of medical sociology', *American Sociological Review*, 22: 200–4.

Suchman, E.A. (1963) *Sociology and the Field of Public Health*. New York: Russell Sage.

Syme, S.L., Hyman, M.M., and Enterline, P.E. (1964) 'Cultural mobility and coronary heart disease in an urban area', *American Journal of Epidemiology*, 82: 334–46.

Szasz, T. (1974) *The Myth of Mental Illness*. New York: Harper and Row.

Theorell, T. and Karasek, R.A. (1996) 'Current issues relating to psychosocial job-strain and cardiovascular disease research', *Journal of Occupational Health Psychology*, 1: 9–26.

Tyroler, H. and Cassel, J. (1964) 'Health consequences of cultural change. II. The effect of urbanization and coronary heart mortality in rural residents', *Journal of Chronic Diseases*, 17: 167–77.

Weber, M. (1978) *Economy and Society*. Berkeley: University of California Press.

Weiner, B. (1985) 'An attributional theory of achievement motivation and emotion.' *Psychological Review*, 92: 548–73.

Weiner, H. (1992) *Perturbing the Organism. The Biology of Stressful Experience*. Chicago: Chicago University Press.

Werner, E.E., and Smith, R.S. (1992) *Overcoming the Odds: High Risk Children from Birth to Adulthood*. Ithaca: Cornell University Press.

Wilkinson, R. E. (1996) *Unhealthy Societies*. London: Routledge.

1.8

Socioeconomic Inequalities in Health: Integrating Individual-, Community-, and Societal-Level Theory and Research

STEPHANIE A. ROBERT AND JAMES S. HOUSE

INTRODUCTION

Socioeconomic inequalities in health have been observed persistently over the course of human history. These differences are manifest across individuals, communities, and societies, and recent analyses suggest that for the most part they have increased over the past century, and even in the past few decades (Marmot et al. 1987; Pappas et al. 1993; Preston and Haines 1991). The nature and size of these inequalities make them arguably *the* major problem of population and public health in America and many other societies for reasons that will become clearer below. Hence, socioeconomic inequalities in health have increasingly become a focus of health policy (Department of Health and Human Services 1990) as well as health research.

We still do not well and consensually understand, however, why socioeconomic inequalities in health exist and persist, nor what policies are most likely and necessary to reduce these inequalities. In seeking such understanding, research has increasingly focused on socioeconomic differentials in health at the level of communities and societies as well as at the level of individuals. Yet, there has been little integration of our substantial knowledge of the relationship between *individual*-level socioeconomic position and health with our growing understanding of the relationship between *community*-level socio-economic position and health. Thus, this chapter seeks to focus on: (1) what we have learned from studies of socioeconomic inequalities in health at the levels of individuals, communities, and societies, (2) whether and how the information from such multiple levels of analysis helps us to understand better the nature and explanations for socioeconomic inequalities in health at all levels, and (3) how social and health policy might address socioeconomic inequalities in health.

A comprehensive review of the literature on individual- and family-level socioeconomic inequalities in health is beyond the scope of this or any single chapter or paper of moderate length. There are, however, sources that have reviewed much of the literature, and we will refer readers to these while highlighting only the major theories, findings, and issues relevant to our discussion. We will first summarize major findings of individual- and family-level research on socioeconomic differentials in health, so that our later discussion of community-level research will indicate: (1) how findings from research on individual- and family-level socioeconomic position might inform research and theory at the level of communities or societies on socioeconomic differentials in health, and (2) how multilevel research on socioeconomic differentials in health may answer some of the questions that have previously been left unanswered in individual- and family-level research.

The Relation of Individual- and Family-Level Socioeconomic Position to Health: Major Findings and Issues

A large body of research, well-reviewed elsewhere (Adler et al. 1994; Antonovsky 1967; Feinstein 1993; Kaplan and Keil 1993; Krieger and Fee 1994; Marmot et al. 1987; Townsend and Davidson 1982; Williams 1990; Williams and Collins 1995), has documented the higher rates and risk of mortality and morbidity from most causes, as well as of functional limitations, among persons who have lower socioeconomic position – people with lower levels of education, income, occupation, material possessions and/or wealth, or people who are part of marriages or households with such characteristics. There remains a number of issues and factors that may qualify this generalization and which deserve to receive increasing attention in research.

Variations Across Measures of Socioeconomic Position

A good deal has been written on how to measure socioeconomic position, which are the best indicators of socioeconomic position, and whether some indicators are more predictive of health in different populations (e.g., Berkman and Macintyre 1997; Krieger et al. 1997; Liberatos et al. 1988). To a considerable degree these questions remain unanswered, and perhaps unanswerable in a generic sense. There is often considerable variation in the extent to which different indicators of socioeconomic position can be measured in different populations and in the precision and reliability of such measures. European research makes heavy use of occupational indicators, while research in the United States relies more heavily on income and education, the last being the most widely used indicator in underdeveloped nations. Wealth or permanent income is now being used more in health research in the United States and Canada (e.g., Kington and Smith 1997; Robert and House 1996; Schoenbaum and Waidmann 1997; Wolfson et al. 1993). Material circumstances (such as car ownership or housing tenure) have been additional indicators used primarily in British research (e.g., Arber and Ginn 1993; Marmot et al. 1987).

We support the position of Krieger et al. (1997) that composite indices of socioeconomic position are generally to be avoided in favor of using a variety of separate indicators. Education and income, if measured reasonably well, have the virtues of being applicable to all individuals and being relatively continuous in nature, and the same is true of wealth and material possessions, although these are more difficult to measure well. Occupation, in contrast, works well for employed populations, but becomes increasingly difficult or even inappropriate to apply to those not or never in the labor force. Researchers should try to use multiple measures of socioeconomic position, as there is evidence that:

1　Different measures have both common and independent pathways linking them to health (e.g., education affects health both through and independent of its impact on income (Reynolds and Ross 1998));

2　Some measures of socioeconomic position may be particularly salient for specific populations or subgroups (e.g., wealth may increasingly rival or surpass income as a measure of the socioeconomic position of the elderly (Robert and House 1996));

3　Different socioeconomic factors may affect different health outcomes in different degrees and ways (e.g., education may be more important for health outcomes and risk factors such as cardiovascular disease or smoking that have their origins earlier in life (Blane et al. 1997; Davey Smith et al. 1998a)).

Temporality and Causality

In addition, care needs to be given in several ways to conceptualizing and measuring what role *time* plays in measuring socioeconomic position and its relationship to health. First, rather than measuring socioeconomic position at one point in time and assessing its relationship to health and mortality, we need to understand how stability and change in socioeconomic position relate to health and mortality (Lynch et al. 1997b). For example, McDonough et al. (1997), using a longitudinal panel study of adults ages 45 and older in the United States, found that persistent low income was a particularly strong determinant of mortality, but that income *instability* was also an important predictor of mortality among middle-income adults.

Second, research needs to clarify the complex relationships among childhood socioeconomic position, childhood health, adult socioeconomic position, and adult health. Do socioeconomic conditions of childhood have a profound effect on health in adulthood, or are socioeconomic conditions in adulthood the primary determinants of health in adulthood? Measuring the association between adult socioeconomic position and health ignores the potential role of childhood socioeconomic position on both adult socioeconomic position and health, and may thereby overstate the role of adult socioeconomic position and/or understate the role of childhood socioeconomic position. Recent research from Power and colleagues (Power and Matthews 1997; Power et al. 1996, 1998) suggests that occupational class differences in health at age 33 in Great Britain result from the accumulation of conditions and experiences throughout both childhood and early adulthood. Other studies generally conclude that childhood socioeconomic conditions are related to adult health and mortality both through and independent of adult socioeconomic conditions. However, childhood socioeconomic conditions are not fully, or even primarily, responsible for the robust association between adult socioeconomic position and health (Blane et al. 1996; Brunner et al. 1996; Elo and Preston 1992; Kaplan and Salonen 1990; Kuh and Ben-Shlomo 1997; Lynch et al. 1994, 1997a; Peck 1994; Reynolds and Ross 1998). Again, childhood socioeconomic position appears to be more consequential for health outcomes and risk factors with long-term etiologies, whereas adult socioeconomic position may be more consequential for other health outcomes and risk factors (Davey Smith et al. 1997, 1998b). Further research measuring socioeconomic inequalities in health at different points in the life course can help us understand the pathways linking socioeconomic position to health. It can also help us better understand at what point in the life course different types of interventions might be most beneficial (Bartley et al. 1997; Kuh and Ben-Shlomo 1997).

Third, and related to the prior discussion, we need to better understand the causal relationship between socioeconomic position and health. Some suggest that it is the effects of poor health on restricting or reducing socioeconomic position that drives the overall socioeconomic inequalities in health. Such claims rely primarily on research in economics showing that extreme levels of ill health constrain the ability of individuals or whole populations to engage in productive work roles (Fogel 1991; Fuchs 1983; Shaar et al. 1994; Smith and Kington 1997). In contrast, most sociologists and social epidemiologists, though recognizing that health must play some role in affecting socioeconomic position, view the causal direction as running primarily from socioeconomic position to health. Such conclusions are usually based on research that (a) shows a prospective effect of socioeconomic position on health and mortality while adjusting for health at baseline (e.g., House et al. 1994; Marmot et al. 1997; Mirowsky and Hu 1996),

(b) probes in various ways the ability of selection effects to explain the association between socioeconomic position and health and finds that selection effects of health on socioeconomic position cannot be the major explanation (Blane et al. 1993; Fox et al. 1985; Lichtenstein et al. 1993; Lynch et al. 1997b; Power et al. 1996; Wolfson et al. 1993), and (c) indicates that actual patterns of downward and upward mobility work to constrain rather than cause overall patterns of socioeconomic inequalities in health (Bartley and Plewis 1997). Research is still needed to estimate more precisely the relative effects of socioeconomic position on health and vice versa.

Gradient Effects?

An intriguing finding of some research on socioeconomic inequalities in health is that it is not just those who are in the lowest socioeconomic groups that have poorer health than those in the higher socioeconomic groups. Rather, a relationship between socioeconomic position and health has been observed across the socioeconomic hierarchy, with even those in relatively high socioeconomic groups having better health than those just below them in the socioeconomic hierarchy (Adler et al. 1994; Marmot et al. 1991). Perhaps the most important implication of this finding is that it is not just the material, psychological, and social conditions associated with severe deprivation or poverty (such as lack of access to safe housing, healthy food, and adequate medical care) that explain socioeconomic inequalities in health among those already at relatively high levels of socioeconomic position.

Despite evidence for gradient effects of socioeconomic position on health, it is also important to note that many studies indicate that the relationship of socioeconomic position to health is monotonic but not a linear gradient, particularly when socioeconomic position is indexed by a measure of income. Although increasingly higher levels of socioeconomic position may be associated with increasingly higher levels of health, there are also substantially diminishing returns of higher socioeconomic position on health. For example, studies have found diminishing and even nonexistent relationships between income and mortality (Backlund et al. 1996; Chapman and Hariharan 1996; McDonough et al. 1997; Wolfson et al. 1993) and morbidity (House et al. 1990, 1994; Mirowsky and Hu 1996) at higher levels of income (e.g., above the median). This trend partially reflects a health 'ceiling effect' caused by the fact that people in the upper socioeconomic strata maintain overall good health until quite late in life, leaving little opportunity for improvements in health among these groups throughout much of adulthood (House et al. 1994). Thus, it is most important to understand what accounts for socioeconomic inequalities in health across the broad lower range (e.g., the lower 40–60 per cent) of socioeconomic position, rather than focusing mainly or only on factors that might explain this relationship across the gradient or at higher levels.

Race Differences

In the United States, race and socioeconomic position are intertwined in complex ways, making it crucial that research on race differentials in health consider the role of socioeconomic position, and that research on socioeconomic inequalities in health consider the role of race. Regarding the former, a sizable and growing number of studies find that much, but not all, of race differences in health in the United States are explained by socioeconomic factors (Clark and Maddox 1992; Kington and Smith 1997; Krieger and Fee 1994; Krieger et al. 1993; Lillie-Blanton and LaVeist 1996; Mendes de Leon et al. 1997; Mutchler and Burr 1991; Rogers et al. 1996; Schoenbaum and Waidmann 1997; Williams and Collins 1995). However, these studies on race differences in health have not included a full range of socioeconomic measures – most notably excluding community-level socioeconomic measures. Many have argued that simply controlling for individual- and family-level socioeconomic position when looking at race differences in health overlooks the significant race differences in the types of neighborhoods that whites and non-whites live in, even at similar levels of individual- and family-level socioeconomic position (Anderson and Armstead 1995; Lillie-Blanton and LaVeist 1996). For example, in metropolitan areas in 1990, only 6.3 per cent of poor white people lived in high poverty areas, compared with 33.5 per cent and 22.1 per cent of poor black and poor Hispanic people, respectively (Jargowsky 1997). Thus, the socioeconomic characteristics of the community may further explain observed race differences in health, a point we return to in discussing community-level socioeconomic effects on health.

Often research focusing on socioeconomic inequalities in health does not investigate whether this relationship differs by race, and what little research there is has found inconsistent results. Krieger et al. (1993) summarize work showing that education does not have the same economic return (e.g., actual salary, non-

wage benefits, or occupational status) for blacks as it does for whites, raising the question of whether there might also be differential socioeconomic returns to health by race. Some research does find that education has less of an effect on measures of self-rated health (Mutchler and Burr 1991; Reynolds and Ross 1998), coronary heart disease (Diez-Roux et al. 1995), and infant mortality (Din-Dzietham and Hertz-Picciotto 1998; Schoendorf et al. 1992) among blacks compared with whites, whereas other research finds virtually no race differences in the effects of income (Diez-Roux et al. 1995; Hahn et al. 1996; McDonough et al. 1997; Mutchler and Burr 1991) and occupation (Gregorio et al. 1997) on health and mortality. Gillum et al. (1998) found that both education and income predict coronary heart disease incidence in white men, white women, and black men, but neither predict coronary heart disease incidence in black women.

In sum, race and socioeconomic position are inextricably related to each other and to health, and hence one cannot be considered without the other. Socioeconomic position is a major explanation of race differences, but not the full one. Other experiences associated with race in our society, such as discrimination (Hummer 1996; Krieger and Sidney 1996; Krieger et al. 1993; Williams 1997; Williams and Collins 1995) and residential segregation (Jargowsky 1997; Massey and Denton 1993), may also account for some race effects on health. Finally, the relation of different indicators of socioeconomic position to health may vary across racial/ethnic populations due to the differential importance or sensitivity of different socioeconomic measures across these populations.

Gender Differences

Despite the fact that women are more likely than men to have lower socioeconomic position and higher morbidity, socioeconomic inequalities in health have often been found to be stronger in men than in women. This finding has resulted in much debate about whether standard measures of socioeconomic position are equally appropriate for men and women, particularly whether married women should be classified according to their own socioeconomic position, that of their husbands, or both. Although some research finds that measuring socioeconomic position at the individual or at the family level makes little difference in patterns of socioeconomic inequalities in health for women (Arber and Ginn 1993), other research suggests that measuring socioeconomic position at both the individual and family level may be important to understanding the full association between socioeconomic position and health – for both women and men (Krieger et al. 1993; Pugh and Moser 1990). For example, Krieger et al. (1993) suggest that individual-level socioeconomic position may be most directly related to working conditions, whereas family-level socioeconomic position may be most directly related to one's overall standard of living. Community-level socioeconomic conditions might be considered additional measures of a family's overall standard of living, and one that may be particularly salient for women who do not work and who spend a substantial amount of time in their community environment.

Other research suggests that the issue of gender differences in the relationship between socioeconomic position and health goes beyond determining how to classify the socioeconomic position of married women and homemakers. Gender differences in labor force participation and in the structure and quality of occupations themselves may play a role in explaining gender differences in the relationship between socioeconomic position and health (Arber 1991; Arber and Lahelma 1993; Stronks et al. 1995). For example, Arber and Lahelma (1993) compared Finland and Britain and found that socioeconomic inequalities in health are strong for both women and men in Finland, but only for men in Britain. However, housewives in Britain were found to have particularly poor health. The researchers suggest that in countries with a high degree of female labor force participation, socioeconomic position may be strongly related to health for both men and women, whereas in countries with less female labor force participation, women's family roles and housing characteristics may play more of a role than socioeconomic position in affecting women's health. Other research in The Netherlands suggests that the more pronounced relationship between socioeconomic position and health in men compared with women may partially reflect the poor working conditions of men with low socioeconomic position (Stronks et al. 1995).

In sum, research generally demonstrates a stronger relationship between socioeconomic position and health for men compared with women, which challenges us to consider: (1) whether *community*-level socioeconomic conditions may play an additional role in affecting health, particularly for women who do not work; (2) how gender differences in labor force participation and in family roles both directly affect and interact with socioeconomic position to ultimately affect health; (3) what role gender differences in working conditions may play in explaining gender differences in

the relationship between socioeconomic position and health.

Age Differences

Despite the strong overall relationship between socioeconomic position and health, this relationship varies by age. Socioeconomic differences in prenatal, neonatal, and infant health and mortality are large (Aber et al. 1997; Singh and Yu 1996), but there are strikingly diminished socioeconomic differences by adolescence (Ford et al. 1994; West 1997; West et al. 1990). With few exceptions (Ross and Wu 1996), research suggests that socioeconomic inequalities in adult health and mortality are generally small in early adulthood, increasingly larger through middle and early old age, and then smaller again in later old age (Elo and Preston 1996; Haan et al. 1987; House et al. 1990, 1994; Kaplan et al. 1987; Kitagawa and Hauser 1973; McDonough et al. 1997; Sorlie et al. 1995; Wilkins et al. 1989). This age variation in the relationship between socioeconomic position and health challenges researchers to discover why such age variation exists. Robert and House (1994) have described some of the potential explanations for this diminished relationship between socioeconomic position and health at older ages. (1) Health and social policies targeted to older people (such as Medicare and social security benefits) might help equalize access to care and resources at older ages. (2) Only the hardiest and healthiest people with low socioeconomic position may survive infancy and into older ages, making their health increasingly similar with age to that of people with higher socioeconomic position. (3) There may be age variation in how socioeconomic position affects exposure to and impact on mediating psychosocial, behavioral, and environmental factors that are known to help explain socioeconomic inequalities in health. (4) Standard measures of socioeconomic position may be less applicable to older adults, thereby showing a diminished relationship between socioeconomic position and health at older ages that reflects poor measurement rather than a true relationship. (5) The biological robustness of late adolescence/early adulthood and the frailty of later old age may somewhat limit the ability of socioeconomic position to affect health at these ages. To date, there is some evidence for each of these explanations, although we are still far from understanding the relative importance of these and other explanations. Yet, if we can better understand why age variations in the relationship between socioeconomic position and health exist, we will certainly be much closer to having a more comprehensive understanding of the overall relationship between socioeconomic position and health.

EXPLANATIONS FOR SOCIOECONOMIC INEQUALITIES IN HEALTH

The Central Mediating Role of Psychosocial Risk Factors

As other reviews have pointed out (Feinstein 1993; Krieger et al. 1993), the literature has been more successful at documenting the existence and patterns of socioeconomic inequalities in health than in explaining why these inequalities persist. Recent work, however, suggests an emerging consensus. Research indicates that people in lower socioeconomic strata tend to be disadvantaged in a broad array of biomedical, environmental, behavioral, and psychosocial risk factors for health, which mediates the relationship between socioeconomic position and health (see Chapter 1.9 in this volume for more extensive discussion of mechanisms by which this occurs). Central among these are health behaviors (Berkman and Breslow 1983), chronic and acute stress in life and work (Karasek and Theorell 1990; Theorell 1982), hostility and depression (Scheier and Bridges 1995), lack of social relationships and supports (House et al. 1988), and lack of control, efficacy, or mastery (Rodin 1986). While any single or small subset of these risk factors (e.g., medical care, health behaviors such as smoking, drinking, eating, and exercise, or biomedical risk factors such as blood pressure and cholesterol) can account for only a small fraction (10–20 per cent) of the association between socioeconomic position and health (e.g., Feldman et al. 1989; Lantz et al. 1998; Marmot et al. 1984), a broad array (12–25 or so) of such risk factors can explain 50–100 per cent of the relationship between socioeconomic position and various measures of health, functional status, and mortality (House et al. 1992, 1994; Lundberg 1991; Lynch et al. 1996; Marmot et al. 1991, 1997; Power et al. 1998; Ross and Wu 1995). For example, Lynch et al. (1996) found that an array of 23 biological, behavioral, psychological, and social risk factors accounted for much of the income differentials in mortality. For men in the lowest income quantile, adjusting for the set of risk factors reduced the excess relative risk of all-cause mortality by 85 per cent, the risk of cardiovascular mortality by 118 per cent, and the risk of acute myocardial infarction by 45 per cent. Although no study has been able to include a full range of

environmental, psychosocial, and behavioral factors, it is likely that including a full range of these factors might consistently account for the relationship between socioeconomic position and health at one point in time. However, determining which factors mediate the relationship between socioeconomic position and health at one point in time is just that – a snapshot of current relationships. Since the mechanisms linking socioeconomic position to health may evolve and change over time (House et al. 1990; Link and Phelan 1995; Williams 1990), research must continue examining which factors become more or less crucial in perpetuating the relationship between socioeconomic position and health.

In addition, some studies suggest that it is not only differential exposure to these mediating factors that lead to poorer health among people with lower socioeconomic position, but that differential vulnerability to those exposures may also help explain social inequalities in health (Krieger et al. 1993). The strongest evidence for this comes from studies of racial, gender, and socioeconomic differences in mental health, with more suggestive evidence for physical health (House et al. 1992; McLeod and Kessler 1990).

Research on the gradient relationship between socioeconomic position and health suggests that we pay less attention to mediating factors associated with extreme material deprivation, such as unsanitary or inadequate material living conditions, and focus primarily on the psychosocial factors that may be more directly related to relative deprivation across the entire socioeconomic scale (Adler et al. 1994). However, a recent analysis by Cohen et al. (forthcoming) found that psychosocial factors were of equal or even greater importance in explaining socioeconomic inequalities in self-rated health among people in the *lowest* socioeconomic categories, rather than being more important among people in the higher socioeconomic categories. There is also speculation that gradient effects of socioeconomic position on health are seen because there may be something about simply being lower in any hierarchy that may be detrimental to health (Adler et al. 1994). Despite a number of suggestive findings from animal studies about physical reactions to social ordering or hierarchical status (Sapolsky 1992), studies on the potential direct effects of socioeconomic inequality or relative deprivation on health among humans are essentially nonexistent at this time.

Moreover, excessive focus on the mediating environmental, psychosocial, and behavioral pathways that help to 'explain' socioeconomic inequalities in health can lead to ignoring or downplaying the role of socioeconomic position as a fundamental cause of health (House et al. 1990, 1994; Link and Phelan 1995; Williams 1990). Focusing on the mediating factors may lead policy makers to conclude that these factors are the more important causes of ill health that should be targeted in efforts to improve health. In contrast, by recognizing the primary importance of socioeconomic position in affecting a broad range of health outcomes through multiple pathways, attention may be focused on more broad-based interventions, such as altering social and economic policies, which may more effectively improve health. This argument is particularly compelling in view of the fact that although the factors mediating the relationship between socioeconomic position and health have changed over time, the association between them has persisted (House et al. 1990; Link and Phelan 1995; Williams 1990).

Importance of Medical Care

Most research suggests that access to medical care plays a relatively minor role in explaining socioeconomic inequalities in health. Such conclusions have been made for three primary reasons. First, cross-national research indicates that socioeconomic inequalities in health have persisted or increased even in countries that have initiated national health programs that somewhat equalize access to health care (Adler et al. 1993; Roos and Mustard 1997; Townsend and Davidson 1982; Wilkins et al. 1989). Second, socioeconomic differences are seen both in diseases that are amenable to medical treatment and in diseases that are not amenable to medical treatment (Adler et al. 1993), with deaths from diseases amenable to treatment representing only a fraction of all deaths in any case (Marmot et al. 1987; Poikolainen and Eskola 1986). Third, some studies have controlled for factors related to health care (such as health insurance, number of visits to doctors) and found that these factors do not account for much of the association between socioeconomic position and health (Marmot et al. 1987; Ross and Wu 1995; Williams 1990).

However, we should not be too quick to dismiss the role of access to and quality of medical care. First, even countries that are supposed to have more equal access to health care have found that differential access to and quality of care still exist (Katz and Hofer 1994). Also, large socioeconomic position and race differences in health, mortality, and health care exist even among participants in the Medicare program in the United States (Gornick et al. 1996). Second, studies that investigate the role of mediating factors in explaining the association

between socioeconomic position and health have had inadequate controls for the many aspects of access to medical care (e.g., adequate transportation, prescription coverage) and quality of medical care (e.g., continuity of care, access to preventive care) that may be distributed unevenly by socioeconomic position (Feinstein 1993). The downplaying of the role of medical care is consistent with findings that medical care plays only a minor role in the overall health of populations in more developed countries (Bunker et al. 1994; McKeown 1976), but a more careful look needs to be taken at whether particular aspects of medical care may still explain some of the impact of socioeconomic position on health.

Summary

In sum, although it was once hoped and believed that socioeconomic differentials in health would wither away with increasing economic development and improvements in the technology, practice, and availability of medical care, several decades of research in the most developed countries (and increasingly in the developing countries as well) indicate that this has not come to pass in the United States and most other developing countries. This has led to a veritable explosion of research (Kaplan and Lynch 1997), largely at the level of individuals and families, which has not only documented the persistence, pervasiveness, and even perhaps increase of socioeconomic inequalities in health, but has also substantially advanced our understanding of the processes producing them.

We now know that these inequalities exist across a wide range of dimensions of socioeconomic position, though we still need to understand better how these interrelate in affecting health. We have substantial evidence that temporal and causal priority flows from socioeconomic position to health in a process that may cumulate over the life course, but which is driven most strongly by the current and recent socioeconomic positions of individuals in families, though again more research is needed in this area. We know that the relationship between income, and probably many or most other socioeconomic dimensions, and health is monotonic but nonlinear (following a path of diminishing impact, especially at levels above the mean or median), though again further research is needed to refine our understanding, and we know that the effects of socioeconomic position on health may vary by race, age, and gender in ways not yet well understood. There is a great need for more research on how socioeconomic inequalities combine with inequalities by race, gender, and age in affecting health.

We have evidence that the impact of socioeconomic position on health is mediated by our exposure to a very broad range of psychosocial and behavioral, as well as physical–chemical–biological risk factors to health. However, we also increasingly understand that these factors can never fully explain or eliminate socioeconomic differences in health because, as new risk factors emerge, exposure to them ultimately comes to be differentiated by socioeconomic position. In this regard, the role of medical care, especially in the forms of both prevention and advanced treatment, needs to be reexamined, even as we know that medical care is at best a minor part of the explanation of existing socioeconomic inequalities in health. Finally, the role of socioeconomic position as a fundamental cause of health suggests a need to look not only at how these socioeconomic effects may be understood or explained on the individual and family levels or more microscopic ones (e.g., psychophysiology), but also how broader community, state, and national contexts may affect and interact with individual- and family-level socioeconomic position in affecting individual and population health.

The Health Impact of Community- and Societal-Level Socioeconomic Conditions

An emerging focus of the study of socioeconomic inequalities in health is the potential health impact of the socioeconomic characteristics of communities and other large social aggregates (e.g., states, regions, and countries). Two types of studies involving community socioeconomic conditions offer new perspectives and information about socioeconomic inequalities in health. One investigates the health impact of the socioeconomic *level* of communities, whereas the other investigates the health impact of socioeconomic *inequality* within and between communities, counties, states, and countries. These new lines of research, however, must both inform and be informed by research on individual- and family-level socioeconomic position.

Socioeconomic Level of Communities

Research consistently shows that communities with lower average levels of income, education, etc., have higher rates of morbidity and mortality than communities with higher socioeconomic levels (Crombie et al. 1989; Guest et al. 1998).

However, because these findings derive from ecological data, it is unclear to what extent communities with worse socioeconomic conditions have worse overall health. This is because (1) people with lower socioeconomic position in those communities have poor health, or (2) living in communities with worse socioeconomic conditions is detrimental to the health of all residents, in addition to (or interacting with) their individual- or family-level socioeconomic position. That is, is the aggregate relation at the community level simply reflecting the relationship at the individual or family level discussed above, or is there an effect of community socioeconomic level on individual health that is over and above the effect of individual- or family-level socioeconomic position? Few studies have actually tested this question, primarily because most existing data sets do not contain adequate information about the socioeconomic characteristics of respondents, their families, *and* their communities, as well individual health information.

With few exceptions (Ecob 1996; Reijneveld 1998; Sloggett and Joshi 1994), extant studies do find that community socioeconomic conditions are associated with various measures of health status (Diez-Roux et al. 1997; Hochstim et al. 1968; Jones and Duncan 1995; Kaplan et al. forthcoming; Krieger 1992; Morgan and Chinn 1983; O'Campo et al. 1997; Reijneveld 1998; Robert 1998; Sloggett and Joshi 1998) and mortality (Anderson et al. 1997; Davey Smith et al. 1998c, 1997; Haan et al. 1987; LeClere et al. 1997, 1998; Waitzman and Smith 1998a), over and above the impact of individual- and family-level socioeconomic position.

For example, early work by Haan et al. (1987) showed that, in a population of adults age 35 and older living in Oakland, California, in 1965, the effects of residence in a poverty area on 9-year mortality persisted after controlling separately for individual-level measures of socioeconomic position, age, sex, and race, and even after adjusting for mediating behavioral factors. A more recent study by Waitzman and Smith (1998) found that residence in a poverty area predicted mortality among individuals aged 25–54 years across thirty-three metropolitan areas, after adjusting for age, race, sex, marital status, household income, formal education, poverty status, baseline health, and multiple behavioral and biological risk factors. Similarly, focusing on health status rather than mortality in a national sample of adults in the United States in 1986, Robert (1998) found that the percentage of families earning $30 000 or more and the percentage of adult unemployment in respondents' census tracts each had an independent association with the number of chronic conditions, over and above the effects of respondents' individual- and family-level education, income, and assets, and their age, race, and sex. Similarly, the percentage of households receiving public assistance had independent associations with self-rated health, after controlling for the same individual- and family-level variables.

Although such multilevel studies indicate an independent role of community socioeconomic conditions in predicting health and mortality, most of the community-level effects have been relatively small in size, tempering any grand conclusions that can be made about the importance of community-level socioeconomic effects. For example, Robert (1998) found that not all measures of community socioeconomic conditions were associated with all measures of health, after controlling for individual- and family-level socioeconomic position and demographic variables. In addition, all the observed community socioeconomic effects were substantially smaller in size than individual- and family-level socioeconomic effects. Contextual or multilevel analyses in other areas of research have similarly found relatively weak independent community-level effects (Brooks-Gunn et al. 1997; Elliott et al. 1996; Jencks and Mayer 1990).

Many of the multilevel studies have also had limitations that further temper conclusions about the existence or strength of community-level socioeconomic effects on health. For example, some studies (Anderson et al. 1997; Haan et al. 1987; Hochstim et al. 1968; O'Campo et al. 1997) have had few or inadequate individual- and family-level socioeconomic controls, making it difficult to conclude that observed community-level socioeconomic effects were not just picking up unmeasured individual- or family-level socioeconomic effects. Alternatively, community socioeconomic characteristics might just be proxies for a person's 'usual' or 'permanent' socioeconomic position – balancing out the short-term variability of reported income, assets, or occupation that is inherent in a one-time cross-sectional survey (Davey Smith et al. 1996; Krieger et al. 1997). Some other methodological and substantive criticisms of multilevel analyses include (Blalock 1984; Diez-Roux 1998; Duncan et al. 1997; Hauser 1970, 1974; Krieger et al. 1997): not considering the existence and impact of stability and change in community characteristics; not considering length of time respondents lived in their communities; not fully accounting for factors affecting selection into and out of certain types of communities; not having measured 'community' in any meaningful way since the focus is primarily on census areas rather than more subjective community boundaries. Other criticisms include not using appropriate statistical methods that account for the multilevel nature of the data, and not taking into account potential differences in measurement error at the individual vs. aggregate level. Every existing multilevel analysis of the effects of socioeconomic position on health has been characterized by a number of these and other problems that could bias the effects of community variables either upward or downward, both absolutely and relative to individual- or household-level effects. As a result, making generalizations about findings in this area is still tentative.

Comparisons with and Contributions to Studies on Individual- and Family-Level Socioeconomic Position

Nevertheless, multilevel research on socioeconomic inequalities in health has the potential to amplify and clarify the complex pathways through which socioeconomic position affects health, if this multilevel research simultaneously informs and is informed by individual- and family-level socioeconomic research. Just as studies on individual- and family-level socioeconomic position have noted gradient effects on health, some of the community-level studies suggest that not only does living in a poverty area have an independent impact on health and mortality, but there also seem to be gradient effects of community socioeconomic conditions on health as well, such that those living in the highest socioeconomic communities have better health even than those living in communities just below them on the socioeconomic scale (e.g., Jones and Duncan 1995; LeClere et al. 1997; Robert 1998). It may be that the impact of community socioeconomic conditions on health helps to *explain* the moderate gradient effects seen at higher levels of socioeconomic position in some studies at the individual and family level. That is, these individual-level gradient effects may reflect the fact that those with similar high income levels may nevertheless reside in different types of communities that vary by socioeconomic profile. If so, the gradient association between individual- or family-level socioeconomic position and health may weaken or disappear once community socioeconomic conditions are controlled for.

Research on community-level socioeconomic effects on health may also help us better understand how socioeconomic inequalities in health vary by race, gender, and age. Regarding race, as discussed earlier, research on race differences in health often controls for individual- or family-level socioeconomic position to see how much of the race effects are explained by individual- or family-level socioeconomic position. However, community socioeconomic conditions may further explain the relationship between race and health, since nonwhites are more likely to live in lower socioeconomic communities than whites of the same individual socioeconomic position (Jargowsky 1997). In a national sample of adults in the United States in 1986, race differences (black vs. nonblack) in number of chronic conditions persisted after controlling for age, sex, income, education, and assets, but disappeared after controlling further for community socioeconomic characteristics (Robert 1998). Similarly, Haan et al. (1987) found that the association between race and mortality (controlling for individual-level socioeconomic position) was virtually eliminated after controlling for residence in a poverty area in Alameda County, California. In contrast, LeClere et al. (1997) found that in a sample of adults in the United States, the effect of race on mortality (controlling for individual-level socioeconomic position) was not entirely eliminated by adding community median income, but was eliminated after including community-level measure of racial minority concentration. Although generally consistent with theories about the role of residence in explaining racial disadvantage (Jargowsky 1997; Massey and Denton 1993; Wilson 1987), such ideas have gone relatively untested, particularly as they relate to health outcomes.

Further, the relationship between community socioeconomic conditions and health may vary by race. Diez-Roux et al. (1997) found that for African–American men living in poor neighborhoods in Jackson, Mississippi, in the late 1980s, the prevalence of coronary heart disease actually decreased as neighborhood characteristics worsened. However, Collins et al. (1997) found that both African–American and white infants born in Chicago were less likely to be very-low-birth-weight infants if their parents had lived in communities with a higher income level than their own. Anderson et al. (1997), similarly found no race differences in the association between community-level median income and all-cause mortality after controlling for family income in a national sample of adults. Kaplan et al. (forthcoming) found no race differences in the impact of living in a poverty area on 9-year incidence of disability in a sample of adults in Oakland, California.

With respect to age, research has found smaller or nonexistent associations between community socioeconomic conditions and health for people 65 years and older (Anderson et al. 1997; Haan et al. 1987; Waitzman and Smith 1998a). In contrast, Robert (1996) found that community socioeconomic characteristics were better predictors of adult health at middle and older ages compared with younger ages, and that community socioeconomic characteristics were sometimes better predictors of health than individual- or family-level socioeconomic measures at these middle and older ages.

As discussed earlier, community socioeconomic characteristics might be particularly salient to the lives and health of women compared with men, particularly for women who do not work outside the home. Diez-Roux et al. (1997) found increased odds for coronary heart disease among white women living in more disadvantaged communities, even after controlling for individual-level socioeconomic measures, with much weaker effects for white men. In contrast, LeClere et al. (1997) found that community socioeconomic indicators were better predictors of mortality for men than for women (after controlling for measures of individual-level socioeconomic position). Anderson et al. (1997) found no gender differences in the association between community-level median income and all-cause mortality (after controlling for family income).

At this point, evidence for race, age, and gender differences in the relation of community socioeconomic characteristics to health is contradictory, but the potentially complex interactions between race, age, gender, individual-level socioeconomic position, community-level socioeconomic characteristics, and residential segregation need to be explored in more detail to help us understand how they work to affect health.

Studies on the multilevel effects of socioeconomic position on health also allow us to test for possible health effects of interactions between individual- and community-level socioeconomic position, and thus to test theories about double jeopardy and relative deprivation. The double-jeopardy hypothesis suggests that living in a lower socioeconomic community would be particularly detrimental to individuals with low socioeconomic position themselves. Alternately, living in a higher socioeconomic community could be worse for the health of people with lower socioeconomic position than living in a lower socioeconomic community because people with lower socioeconomic position would experience greater relative deprivation in higher socioeconomic communities. Diez-Roux et al. (1997) found no interactions between community-level and individual-level socioeconomic position when predicting coronary heart disease among white adults. However, other results from Britain (Jones and Duncan 1995) and the United States (Kaplan et al. forthcoming; O'Campo et al. 1997) also suggest that interactions between individual- and community-level socioeconomic position do exist, although they are complex and difficult to interpret.

Problems in determining explanations for the independent association between community socioeconomic characteristics and health are similar to problems determining explanations for the association between individual- and family-level socioeconomic position and health. Explanations for the association that are caused by methodological limitations (such as reverse causality or selection problems) need to be excluded before substantive or theoretical explanations for the association can be verified. Further, the mechanisms proposed to mediate this relationship are so varied (Macintyre et al. 1993; Robert 1998) that one study is unlikely to be able to explore the mediating effects of all explanations at once, necessitating a cumulative approach to building our knowledge base in this area, and we are only beginning to assemble and analyze the complex, multilevel data sets needed for such studies. Finally, even if we could fully understand which characteristics of the physical, social, and service environments of communities account for the relationship between community socioeconomic conditions and health, this would not preclude debate about how to use this information to improve health. As with individual- and family-level research, the question arises as to whether one can improve health best by addressing the characteristics of the physical, social, and service environments of communities, or by more directly improving the socioeconomic profiles of communities.

Socioeconomic Inequality Within and Between Societies and Communities

Another line of research suggests that it is not just the absolute level of income or deprivation of communities that is associated with the health and mortality of residents. Income inequality within communities or societies is also associated with health and mortality, and may even be more important than level of income for developed countries. Cross-national comparisons indicate that country-level measures of average socioeconomic levels (e.g., per capita income) are associated with population health (e.g., life expectancy), although this relationship is nonlinear (Preston 1975; Wilkinson 1996). Per capita income is strongly and linearly associated with health among less developed countries, but as per capita income rises, the relationship weakens and becomes almost nonexistent among more developed countries. For example, among OECD countries in 1990, there was virtually no

association between gross domestic product per capita and life expectancy (Wilkinson 1996).

However, although some remain to be convinced (e.g., Judge 1995), a growing body of research over two decades indicates that among developed countries, and to a lesser degree developing countries as well, the degree of income *inequality* within a country is strongly and linearly associated with differences in life expectancy between countries. This is the case even after controlling for average level of income within each country (Rodgers 1979; van Doorslaer et al. 1997; Wilkinson 1992, 1996). Simply put, among developed countries, the bigger the gap in income between the rich and poor, the poorer the health of the population. In addition, comparing areas within single countries rather than between countries, studies in England (Ben-Shlomo et al. 1996) and the United States (Kaplan et al. 1996; Kennedy et al. 1996; Lynch et al. 1998) suggest that differences in income inequality across local authorities in England and across states and metropolitan areas in the United States are strongly related to mortality rates (see Lynch and Kaplan 1997 for an excellent review and appraisal of this body of research and critiques of it).

Reactions to this new line of research range from extreme excitement to extreme caution. The idea that income inequality in itself may be bad for health is congruent with other arguments that the large and growing income inequality in the United States and other countries should be reversed. For those who argue that socioeconomic position be considered a 'fundamental cause' of health (Link and Phelan 1995), the idea that income inequality at the country and community levels may be important to health helps draw attention to socioeconomic position as an important force in itself at the macrolevel. Discussions about the importance of macrolevel income inequality also resonate with those who have been grappling with the idea that there are gradient effects on health at the more microlevel. Perhaps there is something similar between the processes that create gradient effects of socioeconomic position on health at the microlevel and processes linking income inequality to health at the macrolevel. Finally, this research suggests some new ways of thinking about inequality and how it might work to affect health. In particular, Wilkinson (1996) and others (Kawachi et al. 1997) suggested that income inequality may work to affect health through mechanisms of social cohesion and social trust. Wilkinson (1996) points out that those countries with the least income inequality are the most socially cohesive countries, and suggests that it is this social cohesion that may affect health. The melding of two resurgent research traditions – that on socioeconomic inequalities in health with that on social cohesion and social capital – promises intellectual challenges as well as potentially useful and novel policy implications.

Yet caution must also be used in interpreting these new findings on the aggregate relation of income inequality to health between countries and between subunits (i.e., states, counties, and wards) within countries. There are many potential explanations for this empirical finding, with both competing and complementary implications for how to improve health. Some recent research has explored the potential role of aggregate measures of social capital, such as social cohesion and trust, as mediators in the relationship between socioeconomic inequality and health between countries and between subunits (i.e., states, counties, and wards) within countries (Kawachi and Kennedy 1997; Kawachi et al. 1997; Wilkinson 1996). We will argue that this type of argument is neither logically necessary to make sense of the relationship between socioeconomic inequality and health at the aggregate level, nor logically or empirically consistent with and related to known empirical relationships at the individual level. We will first briefly describe some of the potentials and pitfalls (both theoretical and methodological) of current research investigating the role of social cohesion or capital in explaining the relationship between aggregate measures of socioeconomic inequality and health. Then we will suggest an alternative theoretical argument that might also explain the relationship between aggregate measures of socioeconomic inequality and health by integrating what we know at both the individual and aggregate levels about the relationship between income (and perhaps other dimensions of socioeconomic position) and health.

Socioeconomic Inequality, Social Capital, and Health

The basic argument of Wilkinson (1996) and others (Kawachi and Kennedy 1997; Kawachi et al., 1997) is that income inequality somehow affects population health via a variable at the societal or aggregate level – social cohesion and trust. Wilkinson, however, has never directly measured this variable or assessed its empirical relationship to health. Kawachi et al. (1997) measured trust at the level of the United States via the mean levels of trust reported by residents of those states represented in the General Social Survey. They show that adjusting for this variable weakens or eliminates the relationship across these same states between

income inequality and population life expectancy, consistent with both their theories and those of Wilkinson.

There are ambiguities, however, about the interpretation of Kawachi et al. (1997) and others that growing income inequality leads to a lack of trust in people, which then affects population mortality. Lacking longitudinal data, they concede that lack of trust in people may also lead to income inequalities that then affect population mortality, or even that unmeasured societal attitudes or characteristics affect both lack of trust in people and tolerance of income inequality (Kawachi et al. 1997). However, even beyond these problems in testing causation, these interpretations suffer from more important problems of failing to theoretically or empirically link aggregate properties of communities to the experiences of individuals. How does inequality at the aggregate level actually affect attitudes of trust at the individual and aggregate levels, and how do these attitudes actually impact the health of individuals? The complex multilevel approach necessary to answer these questions has been missing from both the theoretical and methodological analyses.

In fact, without controlling for individual-level socioeconomic position in a multilevel analysis, it is not clear that socioeconomic inequality at the country or community levels actually has an independent effect on the health of individuals. Fiscella and Franks (1997) found that although community income inequality (at approximately the county level) relates to individual-level mortality in the United States (just as it does to aggregate life expectancy), once family income is controlled, the relation between community income inequality and individual mortality becomes minimal and nonsignificant. Because Fiscella and Franks derive their aggregate inequality measures from the data on their survey respondents, rather than an independent (e.g., census) source, their results have been criticized as overly conservative (e.g., Soobader and LeClere, forthcoming; Waitzman and Smith 1998b). These critics and others (e.g., Daley et al. 1998) are increasingly demonstrating effects of socioeconomic inequality at the level of counties or metropolitan areas on morbidity and mortality in multilevel analyses with appropriate adjustment for individual or household income. However, even these studies indicate that the substantial majority of the impact of aggregate income equality on individual morbidity and mortality, and hence population life expectancy, operates through individual income, not via some independent effect of aggregate-level inequality or derivatives/correlates of it such as social cohesion or trust.

Integrating Individual- and Community-Level Research on Income Inequality

Arguments linking country or community socioeconomic inequality to health through mechanisms of social cohesion or trust virtually ignore how country or community socioeconomic inequality may relate to individual- or family-level socioeconomic position to produce health outcomes. Yet, it is the very link between socioeconomic inequality at these aggregate and individual levels that helps to explain how and why socioeconomic position relates to health at both levels.

A number of authors, beginning with Preston (1975) and especially Rodgers (1979) and most recently Gravelle (1998), demonstrate that the relationship between country or community income inequality and health is necessarily implied by the curvilinear relationship between income and health seen at the individual level. Countries or communities with higher aggregate income inequality will always have worse aggregate health than communities or countries with lower aggregate income inequality, even if they have the same average aggregate levels of income. This effect occurs because an increase in community income inequality will always disproportionately hurt the health of the poor more than it will benefit the health of the rich, which is because there is a greater impact of income on health at lower levels of individual- or family-level income. Gravelle (1998) and others (Fiscella and Franks, 1997) argue that it is the relationship between individual- or family-level income and health that determines the relationship between country or community income inequality and health. In essence, the relationship between country or community income inequality and health is simply an artifact of individual-level processes.

We find this statistical argument compelling, and believe that it and available data suggest that the relationship between country or community income inequality and health is primarily due to the curvilinear relationship between socioeconomic position and health at the individual level, rather than to effects of aggregate measures of social capital, which do not operate through individual socioeconomic position. However, we do not agree with Gravelle that this means the impact of country or community income inequality should be seen as simply a statistical artifact. Nor do we conclude that the relationship between country or community income inequality and health is necessarily totally explained by relationships at the individual level.

First, rather than seeing the relationship between country (or community) income inequality and health simply as an artifact of relationships at the individual level, as Gravelle implies, aggregate income inequality may instead be seen as the major macroeconomic force driving the levels and distribution of individual income, which then more directly affect health. Given the curvilinear relationship between income and health, any reduction in community-level income inequality that raises income levels of the poor will improve the health of both the poor and the total population.

Second, existing theory and data both suggest that characteristics of communities or societies, including both their average income and level of income inequality, have an effect on individual and population health net of individual or household socioeconomic position, although the bulk of the effects of these community or societal income levels or inequalities must and do operate via individual and household socioeconomic positions. However, the other mechanisms through which community- or societal-level socioeconomic characteristics affect health remain to be elucidated, both theoretically and empirically.

We agree with Lynch and Kaplan (1997) that there are, in fact, two rather different variants of the 'social capital' hypothesis linking income inequality to health. Wilkinson (1996) and Kawachi and Kennedy (1997) espouse one based on the psychological perceptions and feelings of individuals in response to collective levels of 'social cohesion' or 'trust.' Alternatively, Kaplan and Lynch and their colleagues (Kaplan et al. 1996, Lynch et al. 1998) and others (Davey Smith 1996) suggest that income inequality is associated with and shapes levels of public investment in education, health care, housing, transportation, public safety, environmental quality, and other human and social capital. These more tangible forms of social capital then impact the health of individuals, independent of their socioeconomic position, although probably most importantly among persons of lower socioeconomic position. Kaplan et al. (1996) show that income inequality correlates across states with many such indicators of tangible social capital. Such tangible social capital seems to us a more plausible and likely explanation of the effects of income inequality (not mediated via individual or household socioeconomic position) than the somewhat 'miasma-like' constructs of social cohesion and trust. Such cohesion and trust may be necessary conditions for public actions to moderate or reduce income inequality and to invest in tangible social capital.

Comparisons with and Contributions to Studies on Individual- and Family-Level Socioeconomic Position

Research on country and community income inequality and health can increasingly be integrated with research at the individual level, but it also shares many of the same problems. Issues of causal direction arise just as they do with individual-level research. Rather than looking at how aggregate socioeconomic characteristics impact health, economists have emphasized the effects of health as a form of human capital on macroeconomic growth and performance (Fogel 1991; Fuchs 1983). Issues of causation among community-level measures of socioeconomic position, income inequality, and health need to be explored, as well as causal pathways linking community- and individual-level processes. In addition, research on community socioeconomic inequality has focused to date on *income* inequality with little attention to whether aggregate inequality in education, assets, etc., impact health beyond their average levels within and between countries and communities.

As already indicated, the curvilinear (vs. linear gradient) nature of the relationship between income and health is important in making sense of socioeconomic inequalities in health at the aggregate as well as individual levels, and relations among them. In addition, much more analysis is needed on the impact of age, race, and gender on socioeconomic inequalities in health at aggregate as well as individual levels, and on the relations between them (see discussion of sex, race, and gender variation in the effects of community characteristics on health). In particular, we need to consider how racial inequality, in general, and racial residential segregation, in particular, affects and is affected by the relationship between community income inequality and health. In cross-national studies, those countries with a greater proportion of racial minorities are the same countries with more income inequality. In the United States, those states with a higher proportion of racial minorities are the same states with more income inequality (Kaplan et al. 1996). Conceptualizing and testing the complex relationships between race, racial residential segregation, community-levels and distribution of socioeconomic position, individual-level socioeconomic position, and health will certainly be important, particularly in the United States where it is clear that race and socioeconomic position are related in complex ways (Williams and Collins 1995).

SUMMARY AND IMPLICATIONS FOR RESEARCH AND POLICY

The last two decades have seen a virtual explosion of research on socioeconomic differences in health (Kaplan and Lynch 1997), with all results demonstrating that socioeconomic inequalities in health are large, pervasive, and persisting even in the face of major improvements in overall levels of population health and attendant improvements in the quality and availability of modern medical care. At this point, socioeconomic and related racial and gender differences in health are arguably the major public health problem of many developed societies (and developing ones as well). The upper socioeconomic strata of these societies are increasingly experiencing levels of life expectancy and health over the life course that approximate Fries' (1980, 1984) utopian scenario of the compression of morbidity, and approach the biological limits of human longevity and health. Such limits may be gradually extendable, but the greatest opportunity for improving population health in these societies lies in bringing the life expectancy and life course trajectory of health of the lower socioeconomic strata closer to that of the upper socioeconomic strata, trends that seem to be occurring in those societies with the highest levels of population health (e.g., Sweden and Japan).

If we are to reduce socioeconomic inequalities in health and hence improve overall population health, we need to better understand the forces that generate and explain the existence and persistence of these inequalities. Many suggest that this implies better understanding of the mechanisms or pathways through which the socioeconomic position of individuals comes to affect their health. This is an important scientific objective, but one on which we believe substantial progress has been made, although more remains to be done.

This chapter suggests that research also needs to move in another more upstream direction: a direction of understanding how health is affected not only by a person's own socioeconomic position, but also by the level and distribution of socioeconomic variables in the communities, states/provinces, and nations within which individuals and families live and work. The research must also address how these aggregate-level indicators of socioeconomic position combine with individual- and family-level socioeconomic indicators to affect health. At this point, however, what we have are often parallel analyses at the individual and aggregate levels rather than the multilevel research that is necessary for understanding how and why the socioeconomic characteristics of individuals, families, communities, states/provinces, and nations are so profoundly related to their health.

Such complex multilevel analyses require not only more theoretical development and clarity in proposing models and hypotheses, but also more methodological sophistication as well. First, it will be necessary to find new ways of combining individual-level information about socioeconomic position and health with community-level information about socioeconomic level, socioeconomic inequality, and other community-level characteristics. Geocoding large data sets to combine with census data is one way of accomplishing this, although we will also ultimately want more detailed information about community characteristics that cannot be obtained from the census (e.g., availability of transportation, physical environment quality, etc.). We will also want to reconsider how we conceptualize 'communities,' both in terms of how we measure them (e.g., census tract vs. self-reported community boundaries) and of how we expect different processes to occur at different levels (e.g., individual, family, group, community, county, state, or national levels). We will want to find or collect multilevel longitudinal data that can track an individual's movement in and out of different communities, changes in community profiles over time, and changes in individual-level socioeconomic position, health risk factors, and health status. Furthermore, when analyzing multilevel data, we need to use appropriate statistical techniques and software that take into account the multilevel nature of the data (e.g., Hierarchical Linear Models, Bryk and Raudenbush, 1992).

Implications for Policy

Asking questions about the potential impact of community socioeconomic conditions on the health of individuals does not necessarily mean that resulting policy implications will or should focus on community-level interventions. Rather, studying the potential impact of these aggregate socioeconomic conditions should force us to consider more closely which levels of intervention – at the individual, family, community, county, state, or national levels – might best achieve our goals of improving and maintaining health.

For example, although research has found an independent association between community socioeconomic conditions and health and mortality over and above the effects of individual- and family-level socioeconomic position, this research nevertheless suggests that individual-

and family-level socioeconomic position is still more strongly linked to health and mortality than are community-level socioeconomic characteristics (Robert 1998). Therefore, directing interventions to lower socioeconomic communities would ignore the many people with lower socioeconomic position who live in higher socioeconomic communities (Berk et al. 1991). On the other hand, directing interventions to lower socioeconomic communities might be both an efficient way of reaching many people with low socioeconomic position, and necessary to alleviate the particular detrimental health effects of living in a lower socioeconomic community. Studying the multilevel effects of socioeconomic position on health should encourage us to think about complementary intervention strategies at different levels.

The evidence of the deleterious impact of country and state income inequality on population health indicates that socioeconomic forces at those levels drive the levels and distribution of income and other socioeconomic resources at the level of families and individuals. There is increasing consensus that improving population health requires reducing socioeconomic inequality. It is important to recognize that it is not inequality per se that is the primary culprit here, but rather the greater absolute and relative deprivation of *lower* socioeconomic strata in more unequal societies (e.g., the United Kingdom and the United States) versus societies that are less unequal (e.g., Sweden or Japan). Direct comparison of socioeconomic differences in infant mortality and adult health for the United Kingdom and Sweden show reduced socioeconomic inequalities in infant mortality in Sweden, produced primarily by the better health of the lower socioeconomic strata in those societies (Vågerö and Lundberg 1989). Although socioeconomic inequality matters to health, reducing income inequality solely by reducing the income levels of the richest members of society is not likely to improve individual or population health. However, reducing income inequality by increasing the income levels of the poorest members of society is likely to improve individual and population health.

Thus, reducing the absolute and relative deprivation of the bottom 25–50 per cent of the socioeconomic hierarchy in societies such as the United States, rather than reducing inequality per se, is the policy goal. We know of policy mechanisms for doing this (e.g., earned income tax credits, adequate minimum wage levels, full employment policies, and adequate support systems for those, especially women and children, not employable), if we have the will to apply them (Ellwood, 1988). These are likely to require reductions in income inequality, although the extent of such reductions depends on the overall level of economic and income growth in a society or region. Both government (e.g., welfare reform) and market forces are constantly producing policy changes affecting income inequality and the absolute and relative socioeconomic position of the less 'well off.' We must do more to evaluate the effects of these policy changes on health as well as other outcomes.

There will probably always be a residual socioeconomic gradient in health in all societies, but the magnitude of it can and should be moderated if the United States and other societies that have mediocre and worsening levels of population health relative to other developed societies are to achieve levels of population health commensurate with their overall economic level. Health policy alone cannot now, nor could it ever, solve our problems of population health. Socioeconomic policy is equally or more important, and should be evaluated in terms of its consequences for health as well as other desirable goals.

ACKNOWLEDGMENTS

This work was partially supported by the Scholars in Health Policy Research Program (Robert and House) and Investigator Awards in Health Policy Research Program (House), both supported by the Robert Wood Johnson Foundation. We would like to thank Felicia LeClere, Paula Lantz, Marc Musick, and especially John Lynch for helpful comments on an earlier draft.

REFERENCES

Aber, J.L., Bennett, N.G., Conley, D.C., and Li, J. (1997) 'The effects of poverty on child health and development', *Annual Review of Public Health*, 18: 463–83.

Adler, N.E., Boyce, T., Chesney, M.A., Folkman, S., and Syme, S.L. (1993) 'Socioeconomic inequalities in health: No easy solution', *JAMA*, 269(24): 3140–5.

Adler, N.E., Boyce, T., Chesney, M.A., Cohen, S., Folkman, S., Kahn, R.L., and Syme, S.L. (1994) 'Socioeconomic status and health: The challenge of the gradient', *American Psychologist*, 49: 15–24.

Anderson, N.B. and Armstead, C.A. (1995) 'Toward understanding the association of socioeconomic status and health: A new challenge for the biophysical approach', *Psychosomatic Medicine*, 57: 213–25.

Anderson, R.T., Sorlie, P., Backlund, E., Johnson, N., and Kaplan, G.A. (1997) 'Mortality effects of community socioeconomic status,' *Epidemiology*, 8: 42–7.

Antonovsky, A. (1967) 'Social class, life expectancy and overall mortality', *The Milbank Memorial Fund Quarterly*, 45: 31–73.

Arber, S. (1991) 'Class, paid employment and family roles – making sense of structural disadvantage, gender and health status,' *Social Science and Medicine*, 32: 425–36.

Arber, S. and Ginn, J. (1993) 'Gender and inequalities in health in later life', *Social Science and Medicine*, 36: 33–46.

Arber, S. and Lahelma, E. (1993) 'Inequalities in women's and men's ill-health: Britain and Finland compared', *Social Science and Medicine*, 37 (8): 1055–68.

Backlund, E., Sorlie, P.D., and Johnson, N.J. (1996) 'The shape of the relationship between income and mortality in the United States', *AEP*, 6: 12–20.

Bartley, M. and Plewis, I. (1997) 'Does health-selective mobility account for socioeconomic differences in health? Evidence from England and Wales, 1971 to 1991', *Journal of Health and Social Behavior*, 38: 376–86.

Bartley, M., Blane, D., and Montgomery, S. (1997) 'Health and the life course: Why safety nets matter', *British Medical Journal*, 314: 1194–6.

Ben-Shlomo, Y., White, I.R., and Marmot, M. (1996) 'Does the variation in the socioeconomic characteristics of an area affect mortality?' *British Medical Journal*, 312: 1013–14.

Berk, M.L., Cunningham, P., and Beauregard, K. (1991) 'The health care of poor persons living in wealthy areas,' *Social Science and Medicine*, 32(10): 1097–103.

Berkman, L.F. and Breslow, L. (1983) *Health and Ways of Living*. New York: Oxford University Press.

Berkman, L.F. and Macintyre, S. (1997) 'The measurement of social class in health studies: Old measures and new formulations', in M. Kogevinas, N. Pearce, M. Susser and P. Boffetta (eds), *Social Inequalities and Cancer*. Lyon: International Agency for Research on Cancer. pp. 51–63.

Blalock, H.M. (1984) 'Contextual-effects models: Theoretical and methodological issues', *Annual Review of Sociology*, 10: 353–72.

Blane, D., Davey Smith, G., and Bartley, M. (1993) 'Social selection: What does it contribute to social class difference in health?' *Sociology of Health and Illness*, 15: 1–15.

Blane, D., Hart, C.L., Davey Smith, G., Gillis, C.R., Hole, D.J., and Hawthorne, V.M. (1996) 'Association of cardiovascular disease risk factors with socioeconomic position during childhood and during adulthood', *British Medical Journal*, 313(7070): 1434–8.

Blane, D., Bartley, M., and Davey Smith, G. (1997) 'Disease aetiology and materialist explanations of socioeconomic mortality differentials', *European Journal of Public Health*, 7: 385–91.

Brooks-Gunn, J., Duncan, G.J., and Aber, J.L. (1997) *Neighborhood Poverty: Context and Consequences for Children*. New York: Russell Sage Foundation.

Brunner, E., Davey Smith, G., Marmot, M., Canner, R., Beksinska, M., and O'Brien, J. (1996) 'Childhood social circumstances and psychosocial and behavioural factors as determinants of plasma fibrinogen', *Lancet*, 347(9007): 1008–13.

Bryk, A.S. and Raudenbush, S.W. (1992) *Hierarchical Linear Models*. London: Sage.

Bunker, J.P., Frazier, H.S., and Mosteller, F. (1994) 'Improving health: Measuring effects of medical care', *Milbank Quarterly*, 72: 225–58.

Chapman, K.S. and Hariharan, G. (1996) 'Do poor people have a stronger relationship between income and mortality than the rich? Implications of panel data for health–health analysis', *Journal of Risk and Uncertainty*, 12: 51–63.

Clark, D.O. and Maddox, G.L. (1992) 'Racial and social correlates of age-related changes in functioning', *Journal of Gerontology*, 47(5): S222–32.

Cohen, S., Kaplan, G.A., and Salonen, J.T. (forthcoming) 'The role of psychological characteristics in the relation between socioeconomic status and perceived health', *Journal of Applied Social Psychology*.

Collins, J.W., Herman, A.A., and David, R.J. (1997) 'Very-low-birthweight infants and income incongruity among African American and white parents in Chicago', *American Journal of Public Health*, 87: 415–17.

Crombie, I.K., Kenicer, M.B., Smith, W.C.S., and Tunstall-Pedoe, H.D. (1989) 'Unemployment, socio-environmental factors, and coronary heart disease in Scotland', *British Heart Journal*, 61: 172–7.

Daly, M.C., Duncan, G.J., Kaplan, G.A., and Lynch, J.W. (1998) 'Macro-to-micro links in the relation between income inequality and mortality', *Milbank Quarterly*, 76: 315–39.

Davey Smith, G. (1996) 'Income inequality and mortality: Why are they related?' *British Medical Journal*, 312: 987–8.

Davey Smith, G., Neaton, J.D., Wentworth, D., Stamler, R., and Stamler, J. (1996) 'Socioeconomic differentials in mortality risk among men screened for the Multiple Risk Factor Intervention Trial. I. White men', *American Journal of Public Health*, 86: 486–96.

Davey Smith, G., Hart, C., Blane, D., Gillis, C., and Hawthorne V. (1997) 'Lifetime socioeconomic position and mortality: Prospective observational study', *British Medical Journal*, 314: 547–52.

Davey Smith, G., Hart, C., Hole, D., MacKinnon, P., Gillis, C., Watt, G., Blane, D., and Hawthorne, V. (1998a) 'Education and occupational social class: Which is the more important indicator of mortality risk?' *Journal of Epidemiology and Community Health*, 52: 153–60.

Davey Smith, G., Hart, C., Blane, D., and Hole, D. (1998b) 'Adverse socioeconomic conditions in childhood and cause specific adult mortality: Prospective observational study', *British Medical Journal*, 316: 1631–51.

Davey Smith, G., Hart, C., Watt, G., Hole, D., and Hawthorne, V. (1998c) 'Individual social class, area-based deprivation, cardiovascular disease risk factors, and mortality: The Renfrew and Paisley study', *Journal of Epidemiology and Community Health*, 52: 399–405.

Department of Health and Human Services (1990) *Healthy People 2000: National Health Promotion and Disease Prevention Objectives Summary*. Washington, DC: US Government Printing Office.

Diez-Roux, A.V. (1998) 'Bringing context back into epidemiology: Variables and fallacies in multilevel analysis', *American Journal of Public Health*, 88: 216–22.

Diez-Roux, A.V., Nieto, F.J., Tyroler, H.A., Crum, L.D., and Szklo, M. (1995) 'Social inequalities and atherosclerosis', *American Journal of Epidemiology*, 141: 960–72.

Diez-Roux, A.V., Nieto, F.J., Muntaner, C., Tyroler, H.A., Comstock, G.W., Shahar, E., Cooper, L.S., Watson, R.L., and Szklo, M. (1997) 'Neighborhood environments and coronary heart disease: A multilevel analysis', *American Journal of Epidemiology*, 146: 48–63.

Din-Dzietham, R. and Hertz-Picciotto, I. (1998) 'Infant mortality differences between whites and African Americans: The effect of maternal education', *American Journal of Public Health*, 88: 651–6.

Duncan, G.J., Connell, J.P., and Klebanov, P.K. (1997) 'Conceptual and methodological issues in estimating causal effects of neighborhoods and family conditions on individual development', in J. Brooks-Gunn, G.J. Duncan, and J.L. Aber (eds), *Neighborhood Poverty: Context and Consequences for Children*. New York: Russell Sage. pp. 219–50.

Ecob, R. (1996) 'A multilevel modelling approach to examining the effects of area of residence on health and functioning', *Journal of the Royal Statistical Society A*, 159: 61–75.

Elliott, D.S., Wilson, W.J., Huizinga, D., Sampson, R.J., Elliott, A., and Rankin, B. (1996) 'The effects of neighborhood disadvantage on adolescent development', *Journal of Research in Crime and Delinquency*, 33: 389–426.

Ellwood, D.T. (1988) *Poor Support: Poverty in the American Family*. New York: Basic Books.

Elo, I.T. and Preston, S.H. (1992) 'Effects of early-life conditions on adult mortality: A review', *Population Index*, 58: 186–212.

Elo, I.T. and Preston, S.H. (1996) 'Educational differentials in mortality: United States, 1979–85', *Social Science and Medicine*, 42: 47–57.

Feinstein, J.S. (1993) 'The relationship between socio-economic status and health: A review of the literature,' *Milbank Quarterly,* 71: 279–322.

Feldman, J.J., Makuc, D.M., Kleinman, J.C., and Cornoni-Huntley, J. (1989) 'National trends in educational differentials in mortality', *American Journal of Epidemiology,* 129(5): 919–33.

Fiscella, K. and Franks, P. (1997) 'Poverty or income inequality as a predictor of mortality: Longitudinal cohort study', *British Medical Journal,* 314: 1724–7.

Fogel, R.W. (1991) 'The conquest of high mortality and hunger in Europe and America: Timing and mechanisms', in D. Landes, P. Higgonet, and H.R. Rosovsky (eds), *Favorites of Fortune: Technology, Growth, and Economic Development Since the Industrial Revolution.* Cambridge, MA: Harvard University Press.

Ford, G., Ecob, R., Hunt, K., Macintyre, S., and West, P. (1994) 'Patterns of class inequality in health through the lifespan: Class gradients at 15, 35 and 55 years in the west of Scotland', *Social Science and Medicine,* 39(8): 1037–50.

Fox, A.J., Goldblatt, P.O., and Jones, D.R. (1985) 'Social class mortality differentials: Artefact, selection or life circumstances?' *Journal of Epidemiology and Community Health,* 39: 1–8.

Fries, J.F. (1980) 'Aging, natural death, and the compression of morbidity', *New England Journal of Medicine,* 303: 130–5.

Fries, J.F. (1984) 'The compression of morbidity: Miscellaneous comments about a theme', *Gerontologist,* 24: 354–9.

Fuchs, V.R. (1983) *How We Live.* Cambridge, MA: Harvard University Press.

Gillum, R.F., Mussolino, M.E., and Madans, J.H. (1998) 'Coronary heart disease risk factors and attributable risks in African–American women and men: NHANES I epidemiologic follow-up study', *American Journal of Public Health,* 88(6): 913–17.

Gornick, M.E., Eggers, P.W., Reilly, T.W., Mentnech, R.M., Fitterman, L.K., Kucken, L.E., and Vladeck, B.C. (1996) 'Effects of race and income on mortality and use of services among Medicare beneficiaries', *New England Journal of Medicine,* 335(11): 791–9.

Gravelle, H. (1998) 'How much of the relation between population mortality and unequal distribution of income is a statistical artefact?' *British Medical Journal,* 316: 382–5.

Gregorio, D.I., Walsh, S.J., and Paturzo, D. (1997) 'The effects of occupation-based social position on mortality in a large American cohort', *American Journal of Public Health,* 87 (9): 1472–5.

Guest, A.M., Almgren, G., and Hussey, J.M. (1998) 'The ecology of race and socioeconomic distress: Infant and working-age mortality in Chicago', *Demography,* 35: 23–34.

Haan, M., Kaplan, G.A., and Camacho, T. (1987) 'Poverty and health: Prospective evidence from the Alameda county study', *American Journal of Epidemiology,* 125(6): 989–98.

Hahn, R.A., Eaker, E.D., Barker, N.D., Teutsch, S.M., Sosniak, W.A., and Krieger, N. (1996) 'Poverty and death in the United States', *International Journal of Health Services,* 26: 673–90.

Hauser, R.M. (1970) 'Context and convex: A cautionary tale', *American Journal of Sociology,* 75: 645–64.

Hauser, R. (1974) 'Contextual analysis revisited', *Sociological Methods and Research,* 2: 365–75.

Hochstim, J.R., Athanasopoulos, D.A., and Larkins, J.H. (1968) 'Poverty area under the microscope', *American Journal of Public Health,* 58: 1815–27.

House, J.S., Landis, K.R., and Umberson, D. (1988) 'Social relationships and health', *Science,* 241: 540–5.

House, J.S., Kessler, R.C., Herzog, A.R., Mero, R.P., Kinney, A.M., and Breslow, M.J. (1990) 'Age, socioeconomic status, and health', *Milbank Quarterly,* 68: 383–411.

House, J.S., Kessler, R.C., Herzog, A.R., Mero, R.P., Kinney, A.M., and Breslow, M.J. (1992) 'Social stratification, age, and health', in K.W. Schaie, D. Blazer, and J.S. House (eds), *Aging, Health Behaviors, and Health Outcomes.* Hillsdale, NJ: Lawrence Erlbaum Associates. pp. 1–32.

House, J.S., Lepkowski, J.M., Kinney, A.M., Mero, R.P., Kessler, R.C., and Herzog, A.R. (1994) 'The social stratification of aging and health', *Journal of Health and Social Behavior,* 35: 213–34.

Hummer, R.A. (1996) 'Black–white differences in health and mortality: A review and conceptual model', *Sociological Quarterly,* 37: 105–25.

Jargowsky, P.A. (1997) *Poverty and Place: Ghettos, Barrios, and the American City.* New York: Russell Sage Foundation.

Jencks, C. and Mayer, S.E. (1990) 'The social consequences of growing up in a poor neighborhood', in L.E. Lynn Jr. and M.G.H. McGeary (eds), *Inner-City Poverty in the United States.* Washington, DC: National Academy Press. pp. 111–86.

Jones, K. and Duncan, C. (1995) 'Individuals and their ecologies: Analysing the geography of chronic illness within a multilevel modelling framework', *Health and Place,* 1: 27–40.

Judge, K. (1995) 'Income distribution and life expectancy: A critical appraisal', *British Medical Journal,* 311: 1282–5.

Kaplan, G.A. and Keil, J.E. (1993) 'Socioeconomic factors and cardiovascular disease: A review of the literature', *Circulation,* 88: 1973–98.

Kaplan, G.A. and Lynch, J.W. (1997) 'Editorial: Whither studies on the socioeconomic foundations of population health?' *American Journal of Public Health,* 87(9): 1409–11.

Kaplan, G.A. and Salonen, J.T. (1990) 'Socioeconomic conditions in childhood and ischaemic heart disease during middle age', *British Medical Journal,* 301(6761): 1121–3.

Kaplan, G.A., Seeman, T.E., Cohen, R.D., Knudsen, L.P., and Guralnik, J. (1987) 'Mortality among the elderly in the Alameda County study: Behavioral and demographic risk factors', *American Journal of Public Health*, 77: 307–12.

Kaplan, G.A., Pamuk, E.R., Lynch, J.W., Cohen, R.D., and Balfour, J.L. (1996) 'Inequality in income and mortality in the United States: Analysis of mortality and potential pathways', *British Medical Journal*, 312: 999–1003.

Kaplan, G.A., Shema, S.J., Balfour, J.L., and Yen, I.H. (forthcoming) 'Poverty area residence and incidence of disability', *American Journal of Public Health*.

Karasek, R. and Theorell, T. (1990) *Healthy Work*. New York: Basic Books.

Katz, S.J. and Hofer, T.P. (1994) 'Socioeconomic disparities in preventive care persist despite universal coverage. Breast and cervical cancer screening in Ontario and the United States', *JAMA*, 272(7): 530–4.

Kawachi, I. and Kennedy, B.P. (1997) 'Health and social cohesion: Why care about income inequality?' *British Medical Journal*, 314: 1037–40.

Kawachi, I., Kennedy, B.P., Lochner, K., and Prothrow-Stith, D. (1997) 'Social capital, income inequality, and mortality', *American Journal of Public Health*, 87(9): 1491–8.

Kennedy, B.P., Kawachi, I., and Prothrow-Stith, D. (1996) 'Income distribution and mortality: Cross-sectional ecological study of the Robin Hood index in the United States', *British Medical Journal*, 312: 1004–7.

Kington, R.S. and Smith, J.P. (1997) 'Socioeconomic status and racial and ethnic differences in functional status associated with chronic diseases', *American Journal of Public Health*, 87(5): 805–10.

Kitagawa, E.M. and Hauser, P.M. (1973) *Differential Mortality in the United States: A Study in Socioeconomic Epidemiology*. Cambridge, MA: Harvard University Press.

Krieger, N. (1992) 'Overcoming the absence of socioeconomic data in medical records: Validation and application of a census-based methodology', *American Journal of Public Health*, 82: 703–10.

Krieger, N. and Fee, E. (1994) 'Social class: The missing link in US health data', *International Journal of Health Services*, 24: 25–44.

Krieger, N. and Sidney, S. (1996) 'Racial discrimination and blood pressure: The CARDIA study of young black and white adults', *American Journal of Public Health*, 86(10): 1370–8.

Krieger, N., Rowley, D.L., Herman, A.A., Avery, B., and Phillips, M.T. (1993) 'Racism, sexism, and social class: Implications for studies of health, disease, and well-being', *American Journal of Preventive Medicine*, 9(6): 82–122.

Krieger, N., Williams, D.R., and Moss, N.E. (1997) 'Measuring social class in US public health research: Concepts, methodologies, and guidelines', *Annual Review of Public Health*, 18: 341–78.

Kuh, D. and Ben-Shlomo, Y. (1997) *A Lifecourse Approach to Chronic Disease Epidemiology*. Oxford: Oxford University Press.

Lantz, P.M., House, J.S., Lepkowski, J.M., Williams, D.R., Mero, R.P., and Chen, J. (1998) 'Socioeconomic factors, health behaviors, and mortality', *JAMA*, 279(21): 1703–8.

LeClere, F.B., Rogers, R.G., and Peters, K.D. (1997) 'Ethnicity and mortality in the United States: Individual and community correlates', *Social Forces*, 76(1): 169–98.

LeClere, F.B., Rogers, R.G., and Peters, K. (1998) 'Neighborhood social context and racial differences in women's heart disease mortality', *Journal of Health and Social Behavior*, 39: 91–107.

Liberatos, P., Link, B.G., and Kelsey, J.L. (1988) 'The measurement of social class in epidemiology', *Epidemiologic Reviews*, 10: 87–121.

Lichtenstein, P., Harris, J.R., Pedersen, N.L., and McClearn, G.E. (1993) 'Socioeconomic status and physical health, how are they related? An empirical study based on twins reared apart and twins reared together', *Social Science and Medicine*, 36: 441–50.

Lillie-Blanton, M. and LaVeist, T. (1996) 'Race/ethnicity, the social environment, and health', *Social Science and Medicine*, 43: 83–91.

Link, B.G. and Phelan, J. (1995) 'Social conditions as fundamental causes of disease', *Journal of Health and Social Behavior*, (Extra Issue): 80–94.

Lundberg, O. (1991) 'Causal explanations for class inequality in health – an empirical analysis', *Social Science and Medicine*, 32: 385–93.

Lynch, J.W. and Kaplan, G.A. (1997) 'Understanding how inequality in the distribution of income affects health', *Journal of Health Psychology*, 2: 297–314.

Lynch, J.W., Kaplan, G.A., Cohen, R.D., Kauhanen, J., Wilson, T.W., Smith, N.L., and Salonen, J.T. (1994) 'Childhood and adult socioeconomic status as predictors of mortality in Finland', *Lancet*, 343: 524–7.

Lynch, J.W., Kaplan, G.A., Cohen, R.D., Tuomilehto, J., and Salonen, J.T. (1996) 'Do cardiovascular risk factors explain the relation between socioeconomic status, risk of all-cause mortality, cardiovascular mortality, and acute myocardial infarction', *American Journal of Epidemiology*, 144: 934–42.

Lynch, J.W., Kaplan, G.A., and Salonen, J.T. (1997a) 'Why do poor people behave poorly? Variation in adult health behaviours and psychosocial characteristics by stages of the socioeconomic lifecourse', *Social Science and Medicine*, 44: 809–19.

Lynch, J.W., Kaplan, G.A., and Shema, S.J. (1997b) 'Cumulative impact of sustained economic hardship on physical, cognitive, psychological, and social functioning', *New England Journal of Medicine*, 337: 1889–95.

Lynch, J.W., Kaplan, G.A., Pamuk, E.R., Cohen, R.D., Heck, K.E., Balfour, J.L., and Yen, I.H. (1998) 'Income inequality and mortality in metropolitan areas of the United States', *American Journal of Public Health*, 88: 1074–80.

Macintyre, S., Maciver, S., and Sooman, A. (1993) 'Area, class and health: Should we be focusing on places or people?' *Journal of Social Policy*, 22: 213–34.

Marmot, M.G., Shipley, M.J., and Rose, G. (1984) 'Inequalities in death-specific explanations of a general pattern?' *Lancet*, 1(8384): 1003–6.

Marmot, M.G., Kogevinas, M., and Elston, M.A. (1987) 'Social/economic status and disease', *Annual Review of Public Health*, 8: 111–35.

Marmot, M.G., Smith, G.D., Stansfeld, S., Patel, C., North, F., Head, J., White, I., Brunner, E., and Feeney, A. (1991) 'Health inequalities among British civil servants: The Whitehall II study', *Lancet*, 337(8754): 1387–93.

Marmot, M., Ryff, C.D., Bumpass, L.L., Shipley, M., and Marks, N.F. (1997) 'Social inequalities in health: Next questions and converging evidence', *Social Science and Medicine*, 44: 901–10.

Massey, D.S. and Denton, N.A. (1993) *American Apartheid: Segregation and the Making of the Underclass*. Cambridge, MA: Harvard University Press.

McDonough, P., Duncan, G.J., Williams, D., and House, J. (1997) 'Income dynamics and adult mortality in the United States, 1972 through 1989', *American Journal of Public Health*, 87: 1476–83.

McKeown, T.J. (1976) *The Role of Medicine: Dream, Mirage, or Nemesis*. London: Nuffield Provincial Hospitals Trust.

McLeod, J.D. and Kessler, R.C. (1990) 'Socioeconomic status differences in vulnerability to undesirable life events', *Journal of Health and Social Behavior*, 31: 162–72.

Mendes de Leon, C.F., Beckett, L.A., Fillenbaum, G.G., Brock, D.B., Branch, L.G., Evans, D.A., and Berkman, L.F. (1997) 'Black–white differences in risk of becoming disabled and recovering from disability in old age: A longitudinal analysis of two EPESE populations', *American Journal of Epidemiology*, 145: 488–97.

Mirowsky, J. and Hu, P.N. (1996) 'Physical impairment and the diminishing effects of income', *Social Forces*, 74(3): 1073–96.

Morgan, M. and Chinn, S. (1983) 'ACORN group, social class, and child health', *Journal of Epidemiology and Community Health*, 37: 196–203.

Mutchler, J.E. and Burr, J.A. (1991) 'Racial differences in health and health care service utilization in later life: The effect of socioeconomic status', *Journal of Health and Social Behavior*, 32: 342–56.

O'Campo, P., Xue, X., Wang, M.-C., and Caughy, M.O.B. (1997) 'Neighborhood risk factors for low birthweight in Baltimore: A multilevel analysis', *American Journal of Public Health*, 87(7): 1113–18.

Pappas, G., Queen, S., Hadden, W., and Fisher, G. (1993) 'The increasing disparity in mortality between socioeconomic groups in the United States, 1960

and 1986', *New England Journal of Medicine*, 329: 103–9.

Peck, M.N. (1994) 'The importance of childhood socio-economic group for adult health', *Social Science and Medicine*, 39: 553–62.

Poikolainen, K. and Eskola, J. (1986) 'The effect of health services on mortality: Decline in death rates from amenable and non-amenable causes in Finland, 1969–81', *Lancet*, 1(8474): 199–202.

Power, C. and Matthews, S. (1997) 'Origins of health inequalities in a national population sample', *Lancet*, 350(9091): 1584–9.

Power, C., Matthews, S., and Manor, O. (1996) 'Inequalities in self-rated health in the 1958 birth cohort: Lifetime social circumstances or social mobility?' *British Medical Journal*, 313(7055): 449–53.

Power, C., Matthews, S., and Manor, O. (1998) 'Inequalities in self-rated health: Explanations from different stages of life', *Lancet*, 351(9108): 1009–14.

Preston, S.H. (1975) 'The changing relation between mortality and level of economic development', *Population Studies*, 29: 231–48.

Preston, S.H. and Haines, M.R. (1991) *Fatal Years*. Princeton, NJ: Princeton University Press.

Pugh, H. and Moser, K. (1990) 'Measuring women's mortality differences', in H. Roberts (ed.), *Women's Health Counts*. London: Routledge. pp. 93–112.

Reijneveld, S.A. (1998) 'The impact of individual and area characteristics on urban socioeconomic differences in health and smoking', *International Journal of Epidemiology*, 27: 33–40.

Reynolds, J.R. and Ross, C.E. (1998) 'Social stratification and health: Education's benefit beyond economic status and social origin', *Social Problems*, 45: 221–47.

Robert, S.A. (1996) 'The effects of individual-, family-, and community-level socioeconomic status on health over the life course', PhD Dissertation, University of Michigan, Ann Arbor.

Robert, S.A. (1998) 'Community-level socioeconomic status effects on adult health', *Journal of Health and Social Behavior*, 39: 18–37.

Robert, S.A. and House, J.S. (1994) 'Socioeconomic status and health across the life course', in R.P. Abeles, H.C. Gift, and M.G. Ory (eds), *Aging and Quality of Life*. New York: Springer. pp. 253–74.

Robert, S. and House, J.S. (1996) 'SES differentials in health by age and alternative indicators of SES', *Journal of Aging and Health*, 8: 359–88.

Rodgers, G.B. (1979) 'Income and inequality as determinants of mortality: An international cross-section analysis', *Population Studies*, 33: 343–51.

Rodin, J. (1986) 'Aging and health: Effects of sense of control', *Science*, 233: 1271–6.

Rogers, R.G., Hummer, R.A., Nam, C.B., and Peters, K. (1996) 'Demographic, socioeconomic, and behavioral factors affecting ethnic mortality by cause', *Social Forces*, 74(4): 1419–38.

Roos, N.P. and Mustard, C.A. (1997) 'Variation in health and health care use by socioeconomic status in Winnipeg, Canada: Does the system work well? Yes and no', *Milbank Quarterly*, 75: 89–111.

Ross, C.E. and Wu, C. (1995) 'The links between education and health', *American Sociological Review*, 60: 719–45.

Ross, C.E. and Wu, C. (1996) 'Education, age, and the cumulative advantage in health', *Journal of Health and Social Behavior*, 37: 104–20.

Sapolsky, R.M. (1992) *Stress, the Aging Brain, and the Mechanisms of Neuron Death*. Cambridge, MA: MIT Press.

Scheier, M.F. and Bridges, M.W. (1995) 'Person variables and health: Personality predispositions and acute psychological states as shared determinants for disease', *Psychosomatic Medicine*, 57: 255–68.

Schoenbaum, M. and Waidmann, T. (1997) 'Race, socioeconomic status, and health: Accounting for race differences in health', *Journal of Gerontology*, 52B: 61–73.

Schoendorf, K.C., Hogue, C.J., Kleinman, J.C., and Rowley, D. (1992) 'Mortality among infants of black as compared with white college-educated parents', *New England Journal of Medicine*, 326(23): 1522–6.

Shaar, K.H., McCarthy, M., and Meshefedjian, G. (1994) 'Disadvantage in physically disabled adults: An assessment of the causation and selection hypotheses', *Social Science and Medicine*, 39: 407–13.

Singh, G.K. and Yu, S.M. (1996) 'US childhood mortality, 1950 through 1993: Trends and socioeconomic differentials', *American Journal of Public Health*, 86: 505–12.

Sloggett, A. and Joshi, H. (1994) 'Higher mortality in deprived areas: Community or personal disadvantage?' *British Medical Journal*, 309: 1470–4.

Sloggett, A. and Joshi, H. (1998) 'Deprivation indicators as predictors of life events 1981–1992 based on the UK ONS longitudinal study', *Journal of Epidemiological Community Health*, 52: 228–33.

Smith, J.P. and Kington, R. (1997) 'Demographic and economic correlates of health in old age', *Demography*, 34(1): 159–70.

Soobader, M. and LeClere, F.B. (forthcoming) 'Aggregation and the measurement of income inequality affects on morbidity', *Social Science and Medicine*.

Sorlie, P.D., Backlund, E., and Keller, J.B. (1995) 'US mortality by economic, demographic, and social characteristics: The National Longitudinal Mortality Study', *American Journal of Public Health*, 85: 949–56.

Stronks, K., van de Mheen, H., van den Bos, J., and Mackenbach, J.P. (1995) 'Smaller socioeconomic inequalities in health among women: The role of employment status', *International Journal of Epidemiology*, 24: 559–68.

Theorell, T.G.T. (1982) 'Review of research on life events and cardiovascular illness', *Advance Cardiology*, 29: 140–7.

Townsend, P. and Davidson, N. (1982) *Inequalities in Health: The Black Report*. Harmondsworth, England: Penguin.

Vågerö, D. and Lundberg, O. (1989) 'Health inequalities in Britain and Sweden', *Lancet*, 2: 35–6.

van Doorslaer, E., Wagstaff, A., Bleichrodt, H., Calonge, S., Gerdtham, U.-G., Gerfin, M., Geurts, J., Gross, L., Hakkinen, U., Leu, R.E., O'Donnell, O., Propper, C., Puffer, F., Rodriguez, M., Sundberg, G., and Winkelhake, O. (1997) 'Income-related inequalities in health: Some international comparisons', *Journal of Health Economics*, 16: 93–112.

Waitzman, N.J. and Smith, K.R. (1998a) 'Phantom of the area: Poverty-area residence and mortality in the United States', *American Journal of Public Health*, 88: 973–6.

Waitzman, N.J. and Smith, K.R. (1998b) 'Separate but lethal: The effects of economic segregation on mortality in metropolitan America', *Milbank Quarterly*, 76: 341–73.

West, P. (1997) 'Health inequalities in the early years: Is there equalization in youth?' *Social Science and Medicine*, 44: 833–58.

West, P., Macintyre, S., Annandale, E., and Hunt, K. (1990) 'Social class and health in youth: Findings from the west of Scotland twenty-07 study', *Social Science and Medicine*, 30: 665–73.

Wilkins, R., Adams, O., and Brancker, A. (1989) 'Changes in mortality by income in urban Canada from 1971 to 1986', *Health Reports (Statistics Canada Catalogue 82–003)*, 1: 137–74.

Wilkinson, R.G. (1992) 'Income distribution and life expectancy', *British Medical Journal*, 301: 165–8.

Wilkinson, R.G. (1996) *Unhealthy Societies: The Afflictions of Inequality*. New York: Routledge.

Williams, D.R. (1990) 'Socioeconomic differentials in health: A review and redirection', *Social Psychology Quarterly*, 53(2): 81–99.

Williams, D.R. (1997) 'Race and health: Basic questions, emerging directions', *Annals of Epidemiology*, 7: 322–33.

Williams, D.R. and Collins, C. (1995) 'US socioeconomic and racial differences in health: Patterns and explanations', *Annual Review of Sociology*, 21: 349–86.

Wilson, W.J. (1987) *The Truly Disadvantaged: The Inner City, the Underclass, and Public Policy*. Chicago: University of Chicago Press.

Wolfson, M., Rowe, G., Gentleman, J.F., and Tomiak, M. (1993) 'Career earnings and death: A longitudinal analysis of older Canadian men', *Journal of Gerontology*, 48: S167–79.

1.9

Gender and Health

SANDRA D. LANE AND DONALD A. CIBULA

INTRODUCTION

This chapter addresses the influence of gender on health from both social science and public health perspectives. The major organizing theme is the interplay of the cultural patterning of gender *and* the biomedical outcomes that result. Gender influences life-cycle roles and choices, notably reproduction, but it also influences less obvious phenomena such as aging and survival. Rather than an exhaustive listing of the available data, the chapter utilizes case studies, both international and domestic, to illustrate many of the ways that gender influences health. An important caveat is that cross culturally and within individual cultures, tremendous variation is the norm.

APPROACHES TO THE STUDY OF GENDER AND HEALTH

Gender studies have proliferated enormously in the past decade, but this wealth of published literature has produced more questions than definitive answers. In part, this confusion results from the different premises that scholars bring to the subject. Two main approaches characterize the study of gender and health. The first seeks to understand how culture shapes gender roles, and therefore health perceptions, policy, and research questions; the second relies on epidemiological or clinical measurements of health status, morbidity, and mortality.

Beginning with Mead's (1935) landmark study, *Sex and Temperament in Three Primitive Societies*, anthropological studies have demonstrated how sex roles vary greatly in human societies, and that there is little that we can say is universally feminine or masculine in terms of behavior. Feminist scholarship since the 1970s took this perspective further by examining the social disadvantage of females, particularly women and girls, in the West (di Leonardo 1991).

Within the analysis of how culture shapes gendered health experiences are several overlapping areas of concern. A number of authors address the influence of culturally defined sex roles on health-promoting behavior, illness roles, health-seeking behavior, and health risks. Women's responsibility, in most societies, for the nutrition, health promotion, and hygiene of their families may influence them to take better care of their own health. In a Canadian study, for example, women engaged more frequently and in a wider range of health-promoting behaviors than men did, although the male/female differences were not large (Kandrack et al. 1991). Women's more frequent hygienic behavior may not always be health-promoting, however. Among the infertile women in Inhorn's (1993) study, the cultural emphasis on genital cleanliness, expressed by frequent manual douching, was associated with decreased fertility. In rural Egypt, gender and age were found to influence women's sick-role behavior and access to costly biomedical care (Lane and Meleis 1991; Morsey 1978). McGrath et al. (1992) demonstrated that in Uganda, where norms dictate a single partner for women but allow multiple partners for men, culturally patterned sexual behavior exposes women to the risk of HIV transmission.

A number of scholars are concerned with women's voices. Jenkins (1996) makes extensive use of narrative to understand Salvadoran women's lived experience of political violence. Egyptian *baladi* women's illness stories, as recounted by Early (1993), bring to life the women's struggles to obtain health care for themselves and for their children.

Critical medical anthropology assesses biomedicine as a cultural system, dissecting biomedical discourse and questioning both the categories into which biomedical knowledge is sorted and the increasing use of technology to control women's bodies. Martin (1987) analyzes the language in medical textbooks, in which the female reproductive cycle is described in terms of failure, waste, and loss, whereas male reproductive function is depicted in robustly positive terms. An edited volume on *Gender and Health: An International Perspective* presents articles on the cultural construction of premenstrual and menopausal syndromes (Davis 1996) and the hegemony of technology in women's birth choices (Davis-Floyd 1996). As the editors describe in their introduction, much of the reproductive processes in the female life cycle – especially menstruation, childbirth, and menopause – have been medicalized (Sargent and Brettell 1996). Once transformed into pathologies, their treatment becomes an economic boon to drug companies and physicians.

Another critical perspective, political economy, weighs the impact of gender on health in the context of local, national, or international resource struggles (Singer et al. 1988; Whiteford 1996). Bruce's (1989) analysis of the gendered division of household goods is a corrective to economists who naively assumed an equitable allocation of food and finances within households. Morsey (1993) shows how the female research subjects in the internationally funded Egyptian Norplant trials were denied removal of the implanted contraception devices, which caused them considerable discomfort, despite their frequent requests. The study by Lane et al. (1998) of Egyptian women's access to induced abortion demonstrated how, even where abortion is severely restricted, safety can be purchased. Poor women, who cannot afford safety, risk injury and death in ending their unwanted pregnancies.

The second main approach to the study of gender and health attempts to quantify the magnitude of morbidity and mortality afflicting males and females. In the past decade, a wealth of information has been compiled to describe women's health status worldwide (United Nations 1991, 1995). With this quantitative data comes the ability to make comparisons between males and females, or between females of different geographical areas. The public recognition of these statistical findings has pushed policy makers to consider more seriously the welfare of women and girls. The Programme of Action, for example, adopted at the 1994 International Conference of Population and Development in Cairo, addresses the higher rates of preventable mortality among young girls and maternal mortality, two issues that became officially 'visible' only after the publication of the tragically high rates of their occurrence (United Nations 1995a: 19, 42.)

Yet, aggregate statistics often do not provide the kinds of information with which to fashion effective interventions, and even the categories in which the data are collected can be misleading. For example, since the beginning of the Safe Motherhood initiative in 1987, the World Health Organization (WHO) and the United Nations Population Fund (UNFPA) have alerted the international community to the tragedy of 500 000 women dying each year of pregnancy-related causes. The leading clinically defined causes of this preventable death – hemorrhage, infection, hypertensive disorders of pregnancy, obstructed labor, and unsafe abortion – were also disseminated at conferences and in published material (AbouZahr and Royston 1991). However alarming, this information insufficiently outlines the steps to be taken to remedy the situation. A four-country study (Egypt, Bangladesh, Indonesia, and India) on the severe and life-threatening morbidities that women suffer during pregnancy did point to possible remedies because it combined epidemiological measurements with in-depth analyses of how and why these morbidities occurred (Fortney and Smith 1997). The study found that inadequate transportation and other impediments to access to emergency services were more salient causes of maternal morbidity (and a predictor of mortality) than the oft-cited clinical diagnoses.

Another hotly contested distinction in gender research is whether a trait or risk factor is biologically/genetically driven or environmentally/culturally shaped. Of course this nature/nurture argument is not at all new, but it has taken on renewed force with recent developments in genetics and on the role of sex hormones and disease risk (Khachaturian 1998). Studies on the genetic component to gender largely began with Wilson's (1975) *Sociobiology: The New Synthesis*, which addressed the evolution of sex roles. This approach looks to nonhuman primate and other animal or even insect behavior to predict what is genetically hard-wired, and thus possibly universal, in gendered human behavior (Townsend 1998). As Sperling has argued, however, many of these studies rely on functionalist models of primate – usually baboon – behavior in captivity to claim a scientific basis for male dominance (Sperling 1991). In fact, as Sperling demonstrates, non-human primates in their natural environments exhibit a great deal more diversity in gendered behavior than many sociobiologists credit. In contrast, Ehrenreich (1997) suggests that the Paleolithic human experience – and the non-human primate experience in the 'wild' – was probably more as the prey of carnivores than as triumphant male hunters bringing home their kill. Our behavioral inheritance from millennia of being hunted as food may thus be more a propensity to anxiety than to a nineteenth-century gendered division of labor. Yet these socio-biological assumptions about what is natural about men and women influence policy on child-care, reproductive health, and women's work. In a speech on 'Renewing American Civilization,' for example, Speaker of the House Newt Gingrich bolstered his arguments about the proper roles for males and females in combat with the following: 'If combat means living in a ditch, females have biological problems staying in a ditch for thirty days because they get infections, [whereas] males are biologically driven to go out and hunt giraffes' (cited in the Gingrich Poll 1998).

In much of the social science literature, it has become commonplace to distinguish between *sex* and *gender*, with sex referring to the biological categories of male and female and gender to the roles into which societies socialize men and women (Los Rios and Gomez 1991; Whitehead and Conaway 1986). This distinction has heuristic value in feminist scholarship, particularly in the many studies of women's social roles that have proliferated in the past decade (see, for example, Bonvillain 1998 and Morgen 1989). In terms of health, however, it is less easy to separate those aspects governed by women's and men's social roles from those intricately tied to biomedical health risks. Culturally patterned gender expectations – such as the drive to be thin – influence health behavior and health status; for example, some 90 per cent of anorexia nervosa sufferers are female (Leutwyler 1998). Social gender norms also shape the context in which individual health behaviors are enacted and range of choices available, as in access to abortion services (Lane and Millar 1987). Some authors have tried to tease apart the bio-medical and cultural risks by controlling for pregnancy-related morbidity and mortality. However, if, as the four-country study (Fortney and Smith 1997) cited above suggests, pregnancy-related risks are increased by inadequate transportation, then these risks are less than entirely biologically governed. It seems at least possible that if men could die of pregnancy risks, emergency transportation might be more available to prevent such tragedies.

Clearly, both culturally patterned gender behavior and biologically based risks interact to produce health or illness. Very few studies, however, link the examination of the cultural and political construction of gender with rates of actual morbidity and mortality. Two landmark studies that do link the sociocultural, political, epidemiological, and clinical aspects of gender and health are Lock's work on menopause in Japan and in the United States (Lock 1986, 1993) and Inhorn's analysis of infertility in Egypt (Inhorn 1993, 1996). Lock shows that many of the salient features of menopause in the United States, notably hot flashes, do not even have linguistic correlates in Japanese. Inhorn demonstrates that the cultural imperative to have children becomes a quest for infertile women, who undergo expensive and risky treatments in their hope of conceiving. Unfortunately, many of the practitioners – physicians and indigenous healers – whom the women seek out do more to damage than to help the women's fragile fertility.

POWER AND POLICY

Discussions of gender's influence build upon critical assumptions about the power imbued in, or available to, a given gender – almost universally male – and the lesser power to which females have access. As Inhorn (1996: 10) asserts in her review of the multiple scholarly usages of both power and patriarchy, however, the terms are variously and often loosely applied. (In this discussion of power and gender, I draw on Inhorn's analysis of patriarchy and power.) Largely taking an imperialist perspective, Weber views power as involving prestige and the authority to impose one's will (Gerth and Mills 1958: 160). In addition to his claim of the hegemonic power of discourse, Foucault sees power as interwoven in kinship, family, and sexuality relations (Gordon 1980). Handwerker's more materialist argument defines power as access to resources (1990: 1). Nelson (1974) suggests that in the Arab world female deference to male authority is publicly demonstrated, but in the privacy of the family power is often negotiated.

All of these definitions of power can be found in the examination of gender and health. Idealized visions of women's bodies that proliferate in magazines and on television, combined with advice on how to achieve the look, represent a hegemonic discourse involving the creation of abnormalities that can be corrected through medical intervention – liposuction for cellulite, breast augmentation, or pharmaceutical diet aids. The widespread prohibitions against women and girls consuming protein-rich meat, described by Simoons (1967) in *Eat not this Flesh,* represent significant barriers of female access to health-promoting resources. The high fertility rate in societies where women's status depends at least in part on the number of children, especially sons, to whom she gives birth, is a bid for power. Among Palestinian women in the West Bank, high fertility contributes toward nationalist aspirations as well (Peteet 1991: 185). The high value placed on sons over daughters, combined with the technology to detect and abort female fetuses, has resulted in some areas in measurable decreases in the number of girls born. In five of China's 30 provinces in 1992, for example, for every 100 female births there were 120 male births rather than the biologically expected number of 105–6 boys for every 100 girls (Kristof 1993). Women in gender-stratified societies often actively seek to enhance their access to power and resources – for themselves, their children, or their families – thorough reproductive strategies. While the women may not be passively acted upon, nor uniformly compelled into obedience by their men, the restrictions on female gender severely constrain their options. The personal health consequences of their strategies, moreover, may be disability or death from pregnancy-related risks. The societal consequences of the skewed sex ratios present among Chinese children may be dramatically increased crime rates as those 'excess' males reach late adolescence.

Power and efforts to enhance authority are key elements in local, national, or international policy debates involving gender concerns. Indeed, the contesting of social policy becomes most acute regarding issues of reproduction, sexuality, and gender. Ethical, human rights, and governmental policies all evolve out of political milieu in which assumptions about what is natural, or even divinely ordained, about men and women take precedence. In a recent edited volume on *Nationalisms and Sexualities,* authors writing on Latin America, Europe, and Africa persuasively argue that the enactment of ethnic, national, or religious identity is expressed importantly through the articulation of norms governing sexual and reproductive behavior (Parker et al. 1992). It is not surprising, then, that policy on sexuality and reproduction – for example, adolescent pregnancy or abortion – elicits heated, contentious debate because it touches on core issues of 'who we are' as a people. While it might be argued that water rights or military spending have a greater impact on quality of life, family planning, abortion, and female sexuality are much more likely to inspire vehement, even violent, protest.

A recent shift in national and international policy in the field of reproductive health came about only after a critical mass of women achieved positions of influence as health professionals, researchers, and policy makers (Lane 1994). From the beginning of the public funding of family planning programs in the 1960s, through the 1980s, the dominant metaphor guiding these efforts was population control. The thrust of this development work was aimed at controlling what was perceived to be the unruly fertility behavior of poor women, at home and abroad (Ward 1986). Reproductive health – a women- and family-centered approach to research, policy, and programs – focuses instead on quality of care, access to services, choice, confidentiality, dignity, and comfort (Germain and Ordway 1989). Accordingly, the Population Council's Middle East Working Group defines reproductive health as, 'The ability of women to live through reproductive years and beyond with reproductive choice, dignity, and successful childbearing and to be free of gynecological disease and risk' (Zurayk 1991). A major accomplishment of these efforts was the hard-won acceptance of reproductive health as the dominant paradigm at the 1994 International Conference on Population and Development, held in Cairo, Egypt.

In the United States as well, the critical mass of women gaining power has resulted in policy changes. Through the efforts of Representative Patricia Shroeder, National Institutes of Health (NIH) Director Dr Bernadine Healy, and others, NIH created the Office of Research on Women's Health in 1990. The goal of this new agency is to redress inattention to women's health needs, in part through an allocation of $500 million over 10 years to the Women's Health Initiative study (Cotton 1992; Pinn 1994).

MORBIDITY AND SURVIVAL

In most areas around the world, and in most subgroups that have been studied, females report greater morbidity than males, yet they have lower rates of mortality and live longer lives. In the United States women more often restrict their activities and stay in bed for illness than men (Verbrugge 1985). Studies on US middle-class adolescents (Goodman et al. 1997), the homeless (Ritchey et al. 1991), and the elderly in the United States, Jamaica, Malaysia, Bangladesh, and the United Kingdom (Arber and Ginn 1993; Rahman et al. 1994) all found that women more frequently report illness symptoms.

A United States national survey demonstrated that between the ages of 17 and 44 years, and excluding reproductive conditions, women utilize 30 per cent more health care than men (Verbrugge 1985). A recent Canadian survey, however, found that controlling for pregnancy and other reproductive-based services resulted in nearly equal levels of health-care expenditure for males and females (Mustard et al. 1998). An accompanying editorial in the *New England Journal of Medicine* argued, however, that because Canadian women outlive men by on average 6.4 years, equal levels of care may not be equitable (Haas 1989).

A major portion of the nonreproductive causes of women's excess morbidity is emotional distress and depression. The World Health Organization found depression to be women's major 'disease burden,' affecting some 20 per cent of women worldwide (Liebenluft 1998). In the United States, women receive twice as many prescriptions for psychotropic drugs as men (Verbrugge 1985). These findings have inspired numerous studies that attempt to provide explanations. Gove's (1984) finding that married women have poorer mental health than married men led him to speculate that women's many-role stresses affect them negatively. Verbrugge (1989) subsequently demonstrated that employed women have much less risk of affective and psychological disorder. Support for Verbrugge's findings were provided by a four-country study (Denmark, Finland, Norway, and Sweden) indicating that in families where women are full-time housewives, their morbidity was about 150 per cent that of men; in families where women worked for pay, their morbidity rates were more nearly equal (Haavio-Mannila 1986). The study also found that morbidity and anxiety were inversely related; employed women more frequently reported feelings of anxiety than did full-time housewives. Still,

selection bias may play a role in healthier employed wives, and not all of the studies found significant male/female differences. Popay et al. (1993) express their frustration that the available measures, which do not adequately account for the lived experiences of women and men, insufficiently explain the differences in affective disorders and minor physical morbidity. More recent work in Scotland, England, and the Czech Republic claims that male/female differences in reported malaise and psychological and physical symptoms are much less prevalent than earlier reported, particularly when demographic variables are well controlled (Arber 1991; Hraba et al. 1996; MacIntyre et al. 1996).

At every age, in most regions, males have consistently higher mortality than females (Verbrugge 1985). American males die at considerably higher rates than females from homicide, lung cancer, suicide, chronic obstructive pulmonary disease, accidents, liver cirrhosis, and heart disease (Perls and Fretts 1998). The female advantage in survival is being somewhat eroded, however, as more women smoke cigarettes. The World Development Report examined the years of life lost by premature death, combined with the loss of healthy life from disability, in a disability-adjusted life years analysis (DALYs) (World Bank 1993). With the exception of India and China, where for reasons that will be addressed later in this chapter female death rates are higher, male death and disability is higher than female, as shown in Table 1.

Why the Male Disadvantage in Survival?

A key element in many of the studies on gender and health is the role that power plays in influencing access to resources, particularly for females. As yet unresolved, however, is the extent to which the cultural aspects of male

Table 1   *DALYs lost per 1000 population*

Region	Male	Female	Male/female ratio
Sub-Saharan Africa	606	542	1.12
India	331	359	0.92
China	177	178	0.99
Latin America and Caribbean	258	205	1.26
Middle East	288	285	1.01
Formerly Socialist Economies	201	138	1.45
Established Market Economies	133	102	1.30
World	269	248	1.08

Source: World Bank 1993: 215.

gender impact men's survival. As mentioned, when compared with females, males in most populations have higher mortality at each age and shorter life expectancies. Is males' poorer survival a biological vulnerability, a product of male socialization, or, perhaps most likely, some combination of both factors? Some of the causes of female protection and male excess mortality are biologically based. Genetic diseases carried on the X-chromosome (such as hemophilia) and the protective effect of female sex hormones for heart disease are fairly clear examples. Other causes of male excess death – accidents, suicides, homicides, lung cancer, chronic obstructive pulmonary disease, liver cirrhosis, and some heart disease – are associated with health-risk behaviors that are at least in part culturally mediated. Although there is considerable cross-cultural and intercultural variation, a number of generalizations hold for male/female differences in risk-taking in Western countries, and possibly in other countries as well (Verbrugge 1985; Waldron 1994). Men tend to work at occupations that involve more physical risk and to pursue leisure activities that also involve risk. Males have higher rates of cigarette smoking than females, although this difference is narrowing. Males drive cars more often than females, and have higher rates of accidents than females for comparable hours of driving. Males drink alcohol more frequently, and more males use illicit drugs than do females. These risky behaviors are intrinsic to the masculine role in many societies, where less adventuresome males may be stigmatized as weak, or even effeminate. Indeed, it has been suggested that learning to adopt the masculine gender role is in itself a source of psychosocial stress (Eisler et al. 1988).

Whether these behaviors are the product of culturally shaped male gender roles or are genetically hard-wired is the source of extensive debate. The cross-cultural evidence for male physical risk-taking and violence provides substantial support for a male genetic vulnerability to risky behavior (Blum 1997). What is not at all clear, however, is how much of this propensity is reinforced by culture, or how it might be reined in by deliberate attempts to minimize its harm. Both authors of this chapter serve on the Onondaga County Child Death Review Committee. We have reviewed the case reports of many males between the ages of 12 and 17 years whose deaths resulted from bicycle and automobile accidents. Because part of the committee's mandate is to suggest educational or policy interventions to prevent such occurrences in the future, the question of how to protect adolescent males from their own reckless behavior is one with which we continue to wrestle.

Comparing Females in Developed and Developing Countries

Important differences exist between women in industrialized countries and those in less developed areas with regard to morbidity and mortality (Lane and Meleis 1991; Okojie 1994). The demographic transition in which lower rates of mortality were followed by lower fertility occurred in Europe and North America during the nineteenth century and is currently occurring in many developing countries (Vlassof 1994). Birth rates worldwide are falling; since the mid-1960s social, political, and economic changes – and access to modern contraceptives – have led to a decline in the average number of children born to women in the world from six to four (Robey et al. 1993). Still, wide differences exist between countries, and between the rich and poor within countries. In most of sub-Saharan Africa, many Middle Eastern states, and parts of Asia, total fertility rates range from 5 to more than 7. In these regions a leading – or in many cases *the* leading – cause of death in adult women is pregnancy-related mortality. Insight into the lived experience of such high fertility can be dramatically illustrated by the following anecdote. A middle-aged rural Egyptian woman, interviewed by one of the authors (SL), reported not ever having experienced a menstrual period. The woman was married before menarche and became pregnant before her first menstruation. Thereafter, for some two decades, she was either pregnant or lactating.

High fertility is part of a complex picture that generally includes low educational attainment and illiteracy and high maternal mortality as illustrated in Table 2.

An important aspect in the discussion of total fertility rates is the below-replacement fertility (less than 2.1) facing many European countries and Japan (Cowell 1994; Kinzer 1994). In these areas the population structure is dramatically changing. The growth of the older population, including those over age 85, combines with such declines in birth rates that there are serious questions about whether there will soon be sufficient workers in the productive life stages to support their elders. Also, because women outlive men, as described above, these societies are becoming even more predominantly female.

The epidemiologic transition also differentiates developed and developing regions. This transition involves a shift from infectious disease as a primary cause of morbidity and mortality to such noninfectious causes as heart disease, cancer, diabetes, liver cirrhosis, and accidents. Of

Table 2   *The impact of lived experiences on fertility rate*

Country	Total fertility rate	Female literacy rate (%)	Maternal mortality ratio (per 100 000 live births)
Uganda	7.3	35	300
Sudan	6.1	12	550
Pakistan	6.2	21	500
Egypt	4.2	34	270
Tunisia	3.5	56	70

Source: UNICEF 1994.

course, this model's assumption that infectious disease was conquered is no longer entirely tenable, as evidenced by the AIDS epidemic and the resurgence of tuberculosis in the developed world. Nevertheless, in many less developed countries only about half of the population has access to safe drinking water and less than half has access to adequate sanitation, causing frequent diarrheal disease and compromising nutritional status (UNICEF 1994). Growing resistance to antimicrobials to treat tuberculosis, malaria, and bacterial infections and to control insect vectors has led to increased infection rates and infections that are more difficult to treat (Sommerfeld 1994). While these problems affect both males and females in developing regions, women may be particularly vulnerable during their reproductive years. Anemia, for example, caused by hookworm, schistosomiasis, or malaria, makes women much less able to survive hemorrhage during childbirth (AbouZahr and Royston 1991). Malaria, furthermore, can be devastating to a pregnant woman, whose own resistance is decreased by pregnancy (AbouZahr and Royston 1991).

Howson et al. (1996) used a life-span approach in their comprehensive review of women's health in sub-Saharan Africa. This approach is particularly helpful in planning for interventions, because it encompasses both *when* and *how* particular disease risks or conditions occur. It also accounts for cumulative risk that increases with exposures to risks at each age. Two examples illustrate the utility of a life-span approach: vesico-vaginal fistula in adolescent mothers and the health risks facing widows. In both of these examples, a woman's life stage, her previous life experiences, and her limited access to resources influence her health risks.

Vesico-Vaginal Fistula (VVF)

Vesico-vaginal fistula (VVF) an opening between the bladder and anterior vagina, results most frequently from pressure necrosis due to prolonged obstructed labor. In Nigeria, an important secondary cause is the traditional 'gishiri' cut, in which the anterior vagina is cut with a razor blade as an indigenous treatment for a wide variety of reproductive problems. While it is not possible to determine the frequency of the condition in the general population, in a University Hospital in Zaria, Nigeria, more than 140 women per year undergo reconstructive surgery to repair their VVFs (Nnatu 1983, cited in AbouZahr and Royston 1991). The risk of fistula is highest among adolescents who are younger than age 16 when they give birth. These young women are often short, with contracted pelvises that are a legacy of childhood malnutrition. Cephalo-pelvic disproportion, caused at least in part by the women's narrowed pelvises – combined with extreme distance to, reluctance to utilize, or other barriers to access to emergency care – mean that the women experience prolonged obstructed labor. Frequently, both mother and fetus die. Women who survive with VVF leak urine and are often divorced by their husbands, who return the women to their families in disgrace (AbouZahr and Royston 1991). The surgical repair of VVF requires a great deal of technical skill, and even so is frequently unsuccessful because the wound left from a necrotic pressure injury heals very poorly.

Widows

The custom of husbands being older than their wives – in some cultures considerably older – combined with women outliving men means that many women survive their husbands by decades. In areas where her husband controls a woman's economic resources, and in societies where wives inherit little or nothing of their husband's estate, women may be impoverished when their husbands die. Howson et al. describe how, in parts of sub-Saharan Africa, economic hardship, particularly under current structural adjustment conditions, has led to widows being abandoned by their relatives (Howson et al. 1996: 37). Without traditional family protection, and lacking marketable skills, the widows face violence and may resort to commercial sex for survival.

DIFFERENTIAL MORTALITY: CASE STUDIES

The health risks, or health benefits, associated with gender are part of a complex picture in which poverty and ethnic or racial discrimination also interact to influence health status. As will be described, in certain developing societies females have greater rates of malnutrition and less access to health care, resulting in excess female death (McGee 1984). The interaction of male gender, social class, and racial discrimination may also negatively influence health status. In the United States, for example, the interaction of gender and the pervasive social disadvantage facing African–Americans, results in measurable mortality disparities among African–American men.

Egypt: Female Gender and Poverty as Synergistic Risks

Amartya Sen, in looking at the disparity in female mortality in Asia and North Africa, claims that, 'failure to give women medical care similar to what men get and to provide them with comparable food and social services results in fewer women surviving than would be the case if they had equal care' (Sen 1990: 61). Based on an analysis of aggregate national sex ratios, Sen claims that 100 million women and girls are 'missing' worldwide. This section uses Sen's approach with demographic data from Egypt to illustrate the potential mortality effects of gender stratification that favors the survival of males.

As mentioned earlier, more boys than girls are conceived and born, but after that at every age from birth to old age, given equal care, females have better survival rates than males (Sen 1990; United Nations 1989: 19, 1991: 11). In countries where male and female infants receive apparently equal care, for example in Eastern Europe and in Japan, Sweden, and The Netherlands, male infants have between 10 and 30 per cent higher mortality than female infants (Turner 1991).

Where females receive fairly equal food and medical care, researchers generally expect them to outnumber males in population census counts as well. For example, in sub-Saharan Africa there are estimated to be 102 females for every 100 males (United Nations 1991: 12). In North America and Europe the gender ratio is even more weighted in favor of females at about 105 females for every 100 males (United Nations 1989: 50). The North American and European ratios show a greater preponderance of females, however, because of the generally older ages of the bulk of the population and the fact that women tend to outlive men.

In areas where it appears that males receive more food and health care than females, the expected gender ratio is reversed, as shown in Table 3.

The conditions favoring the survival of males over females are not simply a result of general poverty. On the contrary, sub-Saharan Africa, cited above, is one of the world's poorest geographical areas. Although poverty plays a role, in cultures where male children and adult males are favored in terms of food, education, health care, and social support, girls and women have higher death rates during childhood and during the childbearing years (Bekele 1980; Chen et al. 1981; Kamel 1983; Pebley and Amin 1991). In contrast, where women have higher education status and greater economic and reproductive autonomy, they and their children have greater survival rates (MacCormack 1988; Williamson and Boehmer 1997).

In Egypt, in every year from 1953 to 1985, female infants had higher mortality rates than male infants, although with increasing development subsequent to 1985 this trend has reversed (CAPMAS/UNICEF 1988). Mortality rates for children under age 5 show a similar pattern. Through tremendous effort, Egypt has lowered its overall infant and child mortality in recent years. In rural locations and among the urban poor, however, poverty and male preference still results in excess female death.

When we examine the population in Egypt by gender, there is a preponderance of males. The 1986 Egyptian census enumerated 95.5 females for every 100 males, or 23 549 752 women out of a total population of 48 205 049 (CAPMAS 1987: 4, 47). If Egyptian gender ratios were

Table 3   *Gender ratios in areas where males receive greater care*

Country	Females per 100 males
Bangladesh	94
India	94
Pakistan	92
Tunisia	98
Libya	92
China	95

Source: Compiled from United Nations 1995a.

similar to those of sub-Saharan Africa, where 50.5 per cent of the population is female, then we would expect there to be 24 343 549 women in Egypt. Subtracting the actual number of women in the Egyptian census from the expected number yields a total of 793 797 'missing' women. Coale (1991) analyzed the same data, but used a more conservative method that compared Egypt's population with a stable 'model' population. Coale found the number of 'missing' females in Egypt's population to be 600 000 and the total number of missing females worldwide to be some 60 million. More research is needed to examine mortality by gender in Egypt and elsewhere, but a likely explanation for this disparity in gender ratios is differential mortality of females.

There are, however, other potential explanations for missing females in census data that must be considered. It is possible that some women were simply not counted. In the rural Egyptian hamlet where one of the authors (SL) conducted fieldwork, if one asked a father how many children he had he would often respond by enumerating only his sons. It was necessary to phrase the question to include daughters as well. Similarly, when interviewing one of the two co-wives of a polygamous man, she would not usually include the other wife or her co-wife's children in her responses. While this may account for some inaccuracies in reporting, it seems unlikely that it would result in large differences. Another possible explanation is selective migration of women. In rural Ireland or in the Philippines, two countries where women leave in search of work abroad; this explanation might make sense. In Egypt, however, women represent a very small percentage of labor migrants. It is usually the women who stay home, in fact, and the men who leave in search of work.

While a proportion of the overall difference between the numbers of males and females in Egypt might therefore be due to inaccuracies in enumeration, the most likely explanation for the preponderance of men is preventable mortality of girls and women. Figure 1 presents a population census, compiled by Rubinstein and his colleagues (Rubinstein 1992), for a rural Egyptian hamlet. In the breakdown of age and gender it is clear that in every age except 20–30 years old (when males are in the military or working abroad as migrant laborers) males outnumber females.

Studies have found that among poor rural and urban Egyptian families, males have greater access to care than females. In a random sample of 25 rural Egyptian households, women were interviewed to determine sources of therapy for eye disease and reasons for choice of therapy (Lane and Millar 1987). A number of variables (education, innovation, socioeconomic status, belief in microbes as a source of disease, gender, and age) were cross-tabulated with sources of

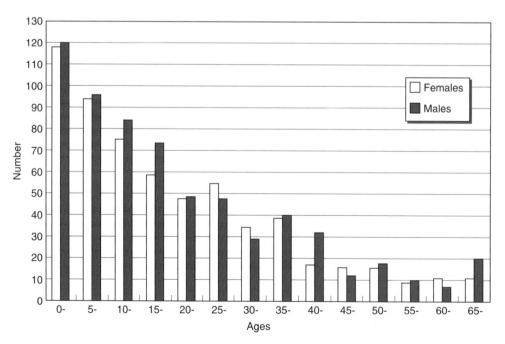

Figure 1   *Population distribution Spring 1991, Ei Youni, Beheira, Egypt*

therapy for eye disease. Only two variables, gender and age, were associated with type of therapy. Females were more likely to receive treatment with home remedies only; males were more likely to progress to second-step therapy (treatment by either a traditional or biomedical practitioner). Adults were more likely to receive therapy from a private physician than were children, and adult women who received such therapy were most often mothers of sons. Logistic regression indicated that both gender and age were independently predictive of access to therapy. Thus, the status associated with male gender and advanced age seems to have influenced access to therapy for eye disease. Despite the fact that the most common eye disease in the area, trachoma, is highest among children, and its long-term sequelae overwhelmingly affect women, these groups received the least biomedical therapy.

In poorer Egyptian families, limited food supplies are often directed preferentially toward the boys and men in the family. A study of child health in a squatter settlement outside Cairo found significantly more malnutrition among girls as compared with boys ages 2 and 3 (Tekce 1990). Research conducted in villages in the Qalyubeya governorate among children from birth to age 6 found that one of the risk factors for protein-energy malnutrition was being female (Hemid et al. 1978). A number of leading Egyptian experts in nutrition summed up the data on food distribution within rural and poor Egyptian households as: male wage earners receive the largest share, women and children receive a smaller share, and young girls are given the least of all (Galal et al. 1984). Adequate nutrition is the cornerstone of good health and, as these studies make clear, many Egyptian females of all ages suffer from gender-linked undernutrition.

In Egypt, data on the number of deaths are relatively accurate, but population-based data on the causes of death are less reliable because so many people die at home, and family members report the causes of death to the authorities. Therefore, there are insufficient data on the causes of excess female mortality, with the exception of certain conditions such as those affecting child survival and pregnancy related mortality. The data that are available illustrate that access to care, and probably predisposing malnutrition, play a role in female deaths. In 1982, for example, there were 14 girls for every 10 boys under age 5 who died of diarrheal disease and acute respiratory infection – two conditions for which medical care can be lifesaving (CAPMAS/UNICEF 1988: 54–5). For the categories of 'complications of pregnancy' and 'congenital anomalies,' however, in which medical care might not be as clearly lifesaving, females have lower or nearly equal levels of mortality compared with males.

Syracuse, New York: Male Gender and African–American Race as Synergistic Risks

In most of the published literature, 'gender' means female. Male gender is either assumed to be the norm from which female gender differences are derived, or is ignored altogether. Yet, as mentioned earlier, where gender and social disadvantage intersect, minority males have disproportionate mortality over nonminority males (Heckler 1985). In Syracuse, New York, a demographic analysis, based on vital records data from the 1990 census, of the white and African–American populations illustrates what appears to be a considerable disparity in survival between the two groups, particularly among males. Syracuse has a population of just over 160 000, with 25 per cent being African American and less than 5 per cent other minority groups. Coale (1991) has said that in all populations, given the larger number of males born and their poorer survival, there is a point of 'crossover' at which time females outnumber males. As illustrated by Figure 2, the Syracuse African–American population crossover to fewer males than females begins at age 15. In the Syracuse white population, the crossover occurs at age 39. Figure 3 presents a comparison of Syracuse African–American and white populations. In populations with a younger age structure (higher fertility, lower survival in the older ages), such as that of Syracuse African Americans, the crossover would be expected to occur later. Therefore, the Syracuse African–American population exhibits the opposite of what would be expected.

Because the white population has much greater survival past age 65 and the African–American population has higher fertility, it would be inaccurate to compare their total populations of males and females. A comparison of the two groups between the ages of 20 and 59 controls somewhat for this bias. Moreover, this age category has social meaning, in that those between these ages are the primary productive and caretaking members of society. For every 100 white males there are 105 females; for every 100 African–American males there are 127 females. This analysis shows that there is a 16.5 per cent difference in the proportion of males among the African–American and white populations

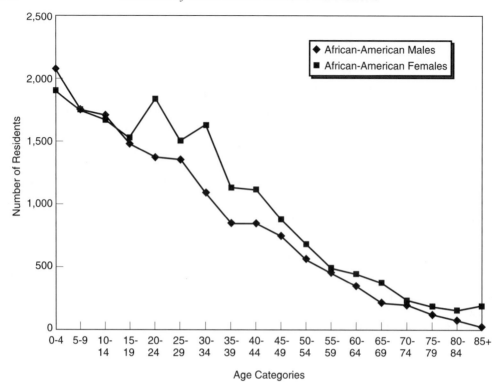

Figure 2   *Syracuse African–American population by age and gender*

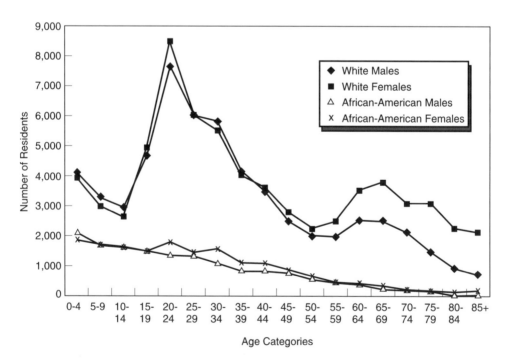

Figure 3   *Syracuse population by age and gender. African–American and white populations*

in Syracuse. If we calculate the 'expected' number of males, based on the proportion of white males (48 per cent), then there are 712 'missing' African–American men in Syracuse.

As with the missing Egyptian females, the African–American males in the Syracuse study may have been undercounted by census takers, they may have migrated, they may be incarcerated, or they may have died. Recent concerns have been raised about the under enumeration of minorities in census counts, so this may account for a portion of the missing males. While differential migration of males away from Syracuse does not seem likely, incarceration is a possible reason for a portion of the missing males. The US Bureau of Justice estimates that 28 per cent of African–American males will enter state or federal prisons in their lifetimes versus 4.4 per cent of white males (Gagnon 1998). However, an examination of the vital records data on 1994–1996 deaths in Onondaga County (the county in which Syracuse is located) indicates that not only do African Americans as a group have much earlier rates of death than the white population, but also African–American males have a much steeper rate of death, beginning at about age 20, than either white males or females of either race (Figure 4). From these data it seems evident

that a portion of the 'missing' African–American males have died.

A Health and Human Services report on US national data found that 42.3 per cent of African–American deaths before the age of 70 would not have occurred if African Americans had the same age–sex mortality rates as whites (Heckler 1985: 70). While a great deal of the disparity occurred during infancy, a large part of the excess African–American deaths occurred during the productive adult years (age 24–64). Comparing African–American males and females, the report concluded that more males than females died between the ages of 25 and 44 years, whereas more females than males died between 45 and 69 years. More than 40 per cent of the excess African–American male deaths was due to homicide and accidents, and about 20 per cent to infant mortality, followed by heart disease, cancer, liver cirrhosis, and diabetes. A possible contributing factor in the male deaths is that 23 per cent of African Americans lack health insurance, compared with 13 per cent of whites (Martinez and Lillie-Blanton 1996). Moreover, since Medicaid provides coverage to low-income women with children, African–American men are likely to have less health insurance coverage than African–American women.

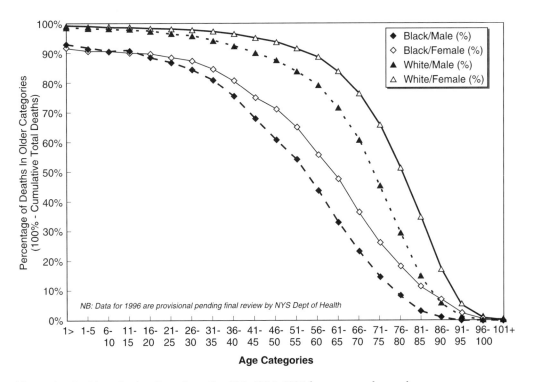

Figure 4   *Resident deaths, Onondaga Co, NY, 1994–1996 by race, gender, and age at death*

GENDER-LINKED HEALTH RISKS

In many societies worldwide, the enactment of gender roles, rites of passage, or gendered behavior exposes women and girls to considerable harm or death. Two examples of gender-linked health risks will be examined: (1) family and sexual violence, and (2) female genital mutilation. An important caveat is that males also experienced gender-linked harm, such as the primary responsibility to fight in wars. This cause of male disability and death is sufficiently well documented elsewhere, however, and is not addressed in this chapter.

Family and Sexual Violence

Domestic violence is a major cause of women's disability and death worldwide. In the United States approximately two million women are beaten per year and four to five women are killed *every day* by their male partners (Gagnon 1998). Domestic violence accounts for more than 40 per cent of female homicides in the United States. (Sanfilippo and Smith 1998). Some 16 per cent of adult pregnant women and 22 per cent of pregnant teens report being hit during their pregnancies by a male partner. Among battered women, 25–45 per cent are abused during their pregnancies (Sanfilippo and Smith 1998).

Internationally, domestic violence also occurs at alarming rates. In Canada, a nationwide survey indicated that 29 per cent of women had been beaten by a male partner (Heise 1994). In Costa Rica, half of the 1388 women attending a primary care clinic, reported being physically abused (Heise 1994). In Bangkok, Thailand, 50 per cent of married women report regular physical abuse from their husbands (United Nations 1995a). The United Nations reports that surveys in Africa, Latin America, and Asia indicate that more than half of the women interviewed report having been assaulted by their male partners (United Nations 1995a).

In certain areas family violence takes culturally patterned forms. In India, for example, 'bride burning' or 'dowry deaths' are a significant concern (Bumiller 1990). Among many groups in India a prerequisite for marriage is that the bride's family provide her with furnishings, electronic equipment, jewels, and/or cash. In recent years this dowry has been affected by inflation and is often quite difficult for families of daughters to afford. In some cases, the husband's family's unhappiness with his bride's dowry is the motive behind their dowsing her with kerosene and setting her ablaze. While the custom is probably not new, it has come to public attention since the 1970s through the social action of Indian feminists. Because kerosene is a ubiquitous cooking fuel and fires are common, these deaths are seriously under reported. Nevertheless, in 1987 the Indian government documented 1786 dowry deaths, which was higher than the death toll due to terrorism in Punjab that year (Bumiller 1990).

'Honor killing' in the Arab world is another culturally specific type of family violence. Females whose reputations have been compromised by premarital or extramarital relations, even if these are only rumored to have occurred, or by an illegitimate pregnancy, may be killed by the males of her own family – father, brothers, cousins, or paternal uncles – to restore the family's honor. The Egyptian Ministry of the Interior reported that nationally there were 775 cases of homicide in 1988, 49 of which were to 'wipe out shame,' a euphemism for honor killing (*Asharq al-Awsat* 1989).

Sexual coercion and rape is a second type of gender-linked health risk that is predominantly perpetrated on females. As with domestic violence, the reported figures are a serious underestimate because of the stigma still attached to being a victim of sexual assault. A five-country survey (Canada, the United States, Republic of Korea, New Zealand, and the United Kingdom) found that between 8 and 15 per cent of female college students had been raped and between 20 and 27 per cent were victims of attempted rape (United Nations 1995a). Forced sex is a factor in STD transmission (Heise 1994) and adolescent pregnancy (Guttmacher 1994). Scholars at the Alan Guttmacher Institute found that in the United States 74 per cent of girls who began intercourse before age 13 had involuntary sex (Guttmacher 1994: 28).

Female Genital Mutilation

Female genital mutilation (FGM), or female circumcision, denotes a set of traditional surgeries, usually performed in childhood, that remove part or all of the external genitalia and are conducted primarily on African and some Middle Eastern and Asian women. Toubia's (1993) two-part scheme of classification divides the procedures into (1) reduction and (2) covering operations. Reduction operations include partial or total clitoridectomy, in some cases with excision of the labia minora. Covering operations (infibulation and pharonic circumcision) involve clitoridectomy, excision of the labia minora, removal of part of the labia majora, and approximation of the wound edges of the remaining labia majora, which heal to form a sheet of skin and scar tissue. The wound edges are held together while healing by suturing (often with indigenous thorn sutures) or by binding the girl's legs together for up to 40 days (El Dareer 1982). In some cases, a small object is placed in the wound to maintain a small opening for the flow of urine and menstrual blood (El Dareer 1982). The resulting 'hood of skin' covers the urinary meatus and most of the vagina (Toubia 1993: 10). Depending on the resulting size, the vaginal opening may need to be widened after marriage to allow sexual intercourse. Deinfibulation, or anterior episiotomy, to release the scar must be performed for childbirth. Women are then reinfibulated, or resutured, after childbirth.

Traditional female genital surgeries are performed on an estimated 80–114 million women in 27 Eastern and Western African countries, parts of Yemen, and scattered groups in India and Malaysia (Minority Rights Group International 1992; Toubia 1993: 5). Available data show that 85 per cent of the procedures worldwide involve clitoridectomy, while infibulation accounts for about 15 per cent of all procedures (Toubia 1993: 10).

FGM is often a prerequisite for marriage. Concerns with virginity, marriageability, and the husband's sexual pleasure are also commonly stated reasons for performing female circumcision (El Dareer 1982; SHDS 1991). Infibulation provides physical evidence of virginity, and the diminution of a woman's sexual response, caused by removal of clitoris and labia minora, is valued because it is believed that she will then be much less likely to act in a manner that would compromise her family's honor. Many rural and poor urban Egyptians also believe that if a girl is not circumcised her clitoris will grow long like a penis, and thus removal of this potentially masculine organ makes a girl more completely female (Early 1993; Lane and Rubinstein 1996). In areas where different ethnic groups live in close proximity, the tradition can be an important marker of group identity (Gruenbaum 1991). Also common is the belief that female circumcision is required by religion (El Dareer 1982; SHDS 1991). In Egypt and Sudan, both Christians and Muslims (Assaad 1980; SHDS 1991) and in Ethiopia, the Falashas, a Jewish group, have all circumcised young girls (Toubia 1993). Perhaps the most important rationale is that because it is such an ancient and commonly practiced tradition, reduced or infibulated genitals are simply considered normal. Indeed, when villagers in Sudan, Egypt, or Mali have discussed the custom with female Western researchers, they have been shocked to discover that the female researchers have not themselves been circumcised (Dettwyler 1994; Gruenbaum 1982; Lane and Rubinstein 1996).

In a great number of cases, the surgery is performed without anesthesia or sterile instruments. The immediate direct adverse health effects include hemorrhaging, shock, infection, pain, urinary retention, and damage to the urethra or anus (Toubia 1994). Septicaemia, tetanus, and urinary infections result, as well as acute urinary retention due to fear of the pain of urinating through the open wound. The range of long-term physical complications and health effects due to the procedures are considerably more severe with covering operations than with reduction operations, and include repeated urinary tract infections, urethral or bladder stones, excessive scar tissue formation, dermoid cysts, and obstructed labor (Toubia 1994). After infibulation the urinary meatus is covered by the 'hood' of skin, making urination occur more slowly, which makes a woman more prone to urinary tract infection and to the formation of stones (El Dareer 1982). Among infibulated women, scaring and the need for an anterior episiotomy for childbirth and frequently resulting tears, fistulae, and chronic pelvic infections, are likely contributors to infertility and the very high rates of maternal mortality in Sudan and Somalia (Toubia 1985). Sexual and psychological problems include dyspareunia or painful intercourse, diminished sexual response, depression, and anxiety.

Pelvic inflammatory disease from chronic infection, and blockage of the fallopian tubes by scar tissue can cause infertility. In a study conducted in Khartoum Hospital, Rushwan (1980) found that infibulation is an important cause of pelvic inflammatory infection in Northern Sudan. As mentioned earlier, vesico-vaginal fistulae and recto-vaginal fistulae are potentially disabling consequences of childbirth (AbouZahr and Royston 1991; Toubia 1985). The prolonged obstructed labor from which these fistulae result can be due to the extensive scar tissue caused by infibulation.

CONCLUSION

The data in this chapter make it clear that gender influences health status, social roles, culturally patterned behavior and access to both nutrition and health care. The biological aspects of risk are so intertwined with the social, cultural, political, and economic life experiences that to separate these factors seriously distorts the analysis.

It is clear that the widespread gender stratification favoring males negatively affects the health of females in many societies, and on many levels in society. On a macro/policy level, allocation of resources for women's health concerns is influenced not only by cultural assumptions about gender, but also by the number of women in positions of authority. On the family level in many countries, unequal distribution of food and resources critically affects the health of women and girls.

Yet, despite having less access to power, and despite the disproportionate numbers of women in poverty, women have lower mortality and greater longevity than men do in most countries. A significant cause of the excess male mortality is risk behavior (reckless driving, substance abuse, and intentional injury) that is at least in part a product of male socialization, and a large cause of female death and disability is male violence. These findings suggest that policies that address male risk-taking and violence as a root cause of many types of poor health outcomes are warranted.

The cultural aspects of gender combine synergistically with economic disadvantage and racism to dramatically increase health risks among some groups. The vast differences in health status between the citizens of developed and developing countries result in large measure from economic disparities. Even in less developed areas such as Egypt, however, where gender stratification favors male survival, girls and women from wealthier families are much less affected. Similarly, among African Americans in Syracuse, poverty exacerbates the social disadvantage in ways that hit hardest on men in their productive years. Gender concerns must therefore be assessed in the context of resource allocation, resource equity, and ethnic and racial discrimination.

Acknowledgments

The authors are grateful to Stacy Barone, Joyce Moore-Dawson, May Dimeson, and Suzanne Morrissey for research assistance.

References

AbouZahr, C. and Royston, E. (1991) *Maternal Mortality: A Global Factbook*. Geneva: World Health Organization.

Arber, S. (1991) 'Class, paid employment, and family roles: Making sense of structural disadvantage, gender and health status', *Social Science and Medicine,* 32: 425–36.

Arber, Sara, and Ginn, J. (1993) 'Gender and inequalities in health in later life', *Social Science and Medicine*, 36: 33–46.

Asharq al-Awsat (1989) (this is a London-based weekly Arabic language newspaper.) 1 March 1989.

Assaad, M. B. (1980) 'Female circumcision in Egypt: Social implications, current research, and prospects for change', *Studies in Family Planning* 11: 3–16.

Bekele, M. (1980) 'Social and economic factors affecting women's health', *Assignment Children*, 49/50: 63–79.

Blum, D. (1997) *Sex on the Brain: The Biological Differences between Men and Women*. New York: Viking.

Bonvillain, N. (1998) *Women and Men: Cultural Constructs of Gender*. Upper Saddle River, NJ: Prentice Hall.

Bruce, J. (1989) 'Homes Divided', *World Development*, 17: 979–92.

Bumiller, E. (1990) *May you be the Mother of a Hundred Sons*. New York: Ballantine.

CAPMAS (Central Agency for Public Mobilization and Statistics) (1987) Annual Report. Cairo.

CAPMAS/UNICEF (1988) *The State of Egyptian Children*. Cairo: CAPMAS/UNICEF.

Chen, L. C., Huq, E., and D'Souza, S. (1981) 'Sex bias in the family allocation of food and health care in rural Bangladesh', *Population and Development Review*, 7: 55–70.

Coale, A. (1991) 'Excess female mortality and the balance of sex in the population: An estimate of the numbers of "missing females"', *Population and Development Review*, September: 517–23.

Cotton, P. (1992) 'Women's health initiative leads way as research begins to fill gender gaps', *Journal of the American Medical Association*, 267: 469–73.

Cowell, A. (1994) 'In an affluent Europe, the problem is graying', *The New York Times*, 8 September 1994.

Davis, D. (1996) 'The cultural constructions of the premenstrual syndromes', in C.F. Sargent and C.B. Brettell (eds), *Gender and Health: An International Perspective*. Upper Saddle River, NJ: Prentice Hall.

Davis-Floyd, R. (1996) 'The technocratic body and the organic body: Hegemony and heresy in women's birth choices', in C.F. Sargent, and C.B. Brettell (eds), *Gender and Health: An International Perspective*. Upper Saddle River, NJ: Prentice Hall.

Dettwyler, K. (1994) *Dancing Skeletons: Life and Death in West Africa*. Prospect Heights, IL: Waveland Press.

di Leonardo, M. (1991) *Gender at the Crossroads of Knowledge: Feminist Anthropology in the Postmodern Era*. Berkeley: University of California Press.

Early, E. (1993) *Baladi Women of Cairo: Playing with an Egg and a Stone*. Boulder, CO: Lynne Rienner.

Ehrenreich, B. (1997) *Blood Rites*. New York: Metropolitan Books, Henry Holt.

Eisler, R., Skidmore, J., and Ward, C. (1988) 'Masculine gender-role stress: Predictor of anger, anxiety and health-risk behaviors', *Journal of Personality Assessment*, 52: 133–41.

El Dareer, A. (1982) *Woman, Why do you Weep?* London: Zed Press.

Fortney, J. and Smith, J. (1997) *The Base of the Iceberg: Prevalence and Perceptions of Maternal Morbidity in Four Developing Countries*. Triangle Park, NC: Family Health International.

Gagnon, M. (1998) 'Police departments unresponsive to domestic violence complaints', *Crime Victims' Litigation Quarterly*, (cited in www.nvc.org/).

Galal, O., Dakroury, M.A., Hussein, F., El Nahry, M., El Ghorab, M., and Shaheen, F. (1984) 'The state of food and nutrition in Egypt', in O. Galal and E.K. Amine (eds) *Nutrition Workshop on Identification and Prioritization of Nutritional Problems in Egypt*. Cairo: UNICEF and Egyptian Ministry of Health.

Germain, A. and Ordway, J. (1989) *Population Control and Women's Health: Balancing the scales'*, New York: International Women's Health Coalition and the Overseas Development Council.

Gerth, H.H. and Wright Mills, C. (1958) *From Max Weber: Essays in Sociology*. New York: Oxford University Press.

Gingrich Poll (1998) 'Renewing American civilization', Lecture given at Reinhardt College, 7 January, 1995. www: msae.wisc.edu.

Goodman, E., Amick, B., Rezendes, M., Tarlov, A., Rogers, W., and Kagan, J. (1997) 'Influences of gender and social class on adolescents: Perceptions of Health, *Archives of Pediatrics and Adolescent Medicine*, 151: 99–104.

Gordon, C. (1980) *Power/Knowledge: Selected Interviews and Other Writings 1972–1977: Michel Foucault*. New York: Pantheon.

Gove, W.R. (1984) 'Gender differences in mental and physical illness: The effects of fixed roles and nurturant roles', *Social Science and Medicine* 19: 77–91.

Gruenbaum, E. (1982) 'The movement against clitoridectomy and infibulation in the Sudan: Public health and the women's movement', *Medical Anthropology Newsletter*, 13: 4–12.

Gruenbaum, E. (1991) 'The Islamic movement, development, and health education: Recent changes in the health of rural women in central Sudan', *Social Science and Medicine*, 33: 637–45.

Guttmacher, A. (1994) *Sex and America's Teenagers*. New York and Washington, DC: Alan Guttmacher Institute.

Haas, J. (1989) 'The cost of being a woman', *New England Journal of Medicine*, 338(23): 1694–5.

Haavio-Mannila, E. (1986) 'Inequalities in health and gender', *Social Science and Medicine*, 22: 141–9.

Handwerker, W.P. (1990) 'Politics and reproduction: A window on social change', in W. Penn Handwerker (ed.), *Births and Power: Social Change and the Politics of Reproduction*. Boulder, CO: Westview Press. pp. 1–38.

Heckler, M.M. (1985) 'Black and minority health: Report of the secretary's task force', Bethesda, MD: US Department of Health and Human Services.

Heise, L.L. (1994) 'Gender-based violence and women's reproductive health', *International Journal of Gynecology and Obstetrics*, 46: 221–9.

Hemid, G.A. El-Mougy, M., El-Badrawy, F., and El-Mosallami, M.A. (1978) 'An epidemiological study of energy protein malnutrition in a rural community in Egypt', *Journal of the Egyptian Medical Association*, 61: 9–10.

Howson, C., Harrison, P., Hofna, D., and Law, M. (1996) *In Her Lifetime: Female Morbidity and Mortality in Sub-Saharan Africa*. Washington, DC: National Academy Press.

Hraba, J., Lorenz, F., Lee, G., and Pechacova, Z. (1996) 'Gender differences in health: Evidence from the Czech Republic', *Social Science and Medicine*, 43(10): 1443–51.

Inhorn, M. (1993) *Quest for Conception*. Philadelphia: University of Pennsylvania Press.

Inhorn, M. (1996) *Infertility and Patriarchy: The Cultural Politics of Gender and Family Life in Egypt*. Philadelphia: University of Pennsylvania Press.

Jenkins, J.H. (1996) 'The impress of extremity: Women's experience of trauma and political violence', in C.F. Sargent and C.B. Brettell (eds), *Gender and Health: An International Perspective*. Upper Saddle River, NJ: Prentice Hall.

Kamel, N. (1983) 'Determinants and patterns of female mortality associated with women's reproductive role', in *Sex Differentials in Mortality: Trends, Determinants, and Consequences*. Miscellaneous Series No. 4, Department of Demography, Australian National University, Canberra.

Kandrack, M.-A., Grant, K., and Segall, A. (1991) 'Gender differences in health-related behavior: Some unanswered questions', *Social Science and Medicine*, 32: 579–90.

Khachaturian, Z.S. (1998) 'At more risk for Alzheimer's?' *Women's Health*, 9: 110–13.

Kinzer, S. (1994) '$650 a baby: Germany to pay to stem decline in births', *The New York Times*, 25 November 1994. p. A3.

Kristof, N. (1993) 'Peasants of China discover new way to weed out girls', *The New York Times*, 21 June 1993. pp. A1, A4.

Lane, S.D. (1994) 'From population control to reproductive health: An emerging policy agenda', *Social Science and Medicine*, 39: 1303–14.

Lane, S.D. and Millar, M.I. (1987) 'The "hierarchy of resort" reexamined: Status and class differentials as determinants of therapy for eye disease in the Egyptian delta', *Urban Anthropology* 16: 151–82.

Lane, S.D. and Meleis, A. (1991) 'Roles, work, health perceptions and health resources of women in rural Egypt', *Social Science and Medicine*, 33: 1197–1208.

Lane, S.D. and Rubinstein, R.A. (1996) 'Judging the other: Responding to traditional female genital surgeries', *Hastings Center Report*, 26 (3): 31–40.

Lane, S.D., Jok, J.M., and El-Mouelhy, M.T. (1998) 'Buying safety: The economics of reproductive risk and abortion in Egypt', *Social Science and Medicine*, 47(8): 1089–99.

Liebenluft, E. (1998) 'Why are so many women depressed?' *Women's Health*, 9(2): 30–37.

Leutwyler, K. (1998) 'Dying to be thin', *Women's Health*, 9(2): 16–19.

Lock, M. (1986) 'Ambiguities of aging: Japanese experience and perceptions of menopause', *Culture, Medicine and Psychiatry*, 10: 23–47.

Lock, M. (1993) *Encounters with Aging: Mythologies of Menopause in Japan and North America*. Berkeley: University of California Press.

Los Rios, R. and Gomez, E. (1991) 'Women in health and development: An alternative approach', Paper presented at the University of Rochester, New York Fourth International Women's Conference, 10 April, 1991.

MacCormack, C. (1988) 'Health and the social power of women', *Social Science and Medicine*, 26: 677–83.

MacIntyre, S., Hunt, K., and Sweeting, H. (1996) 'Gender differences in health: Are things really as simple as they seem?' *Social Science and Medicine*, 42: 617–24.

Martin, E. (1987) *The Women in the Body: A Cultural Analysis of Reproduction*. Boston, MA: Beacon Press.

Martinez, R.M. and Lillie-Blanton, M. (1996) 'Why race and gender remain important in health services research', *American Journal of Preventive Medicine* 12: 316–18.

McGee, L. (ed.) (1984) 'Child survival and sex differentials in the treatment of children', *Medical Anthropology*, 8 (2).

McGrath, J., Schumann, D., Pearson-Marks, J., Rwabukwali, C., Mukasa, R., Namande, B., Nakayiwa, S., and Nakyobe, L. (1992) 'Cultural determinants of sexual risk behavior for AIDS among Baganda women', *Medical Anthropology Quarterly*, 6: 153–61.

Mead, M. (1935) *Sex and Temperament in Three Primitive Societies*. New York: Morrow.

Minority Rights Group International (1992) *Female Genital Mutilation: Proposals for Change*. London: Minority Rights Group International.

Morgen, S. (ed.) (1989) *Gender and Anthropology: Critical Reviews for Research and Teaching*, Washington, DC: American Anthropological Association.

Morsey, S. (1978) 'Sex roles, power, and illness in an Egyptian village', *American Ethnologist*, 5: 137–50.

Morsey, S. (1993) 'Bodies of choice: Norplant experimental trials on Egyptian women', in *Norplant: Under her Skin*. Amsterdam: Women's Health Action Foundation.

Mustard, C., Kaufert, P., Kozyrsky, A., and Mayer, T. (1998) 'Sex differences in the use of health care services', *New England Journal of Medicine*, 338(23): 1678–83.

Nelson, C. (1974) 'Public and private politics: Women in the Middle-Eastern world', *American Ethnologist* 1: 551–63.

Okojie, C. (1994) 'Gender inequalities of health in the Third World', *Social Science and Medicine*, 39: 1237–47.

Parker, A., Russo, M., Sommer, D., and Yaeger, P. (eds) (1992) *Nationalisms and Sexualities*. New York: Routledge.

Pebley, A. R. and Sajeda, A. (1991) 'The impact of public health interventions on sex differentials in childhood mortality in rural Punjab, India', New York: Population Council Research Division Working Papers No. 24.

Perls, T. and Fretts, R. (1998) 'Why women live longer than men', *Women's Health*, 9: 100–3.

Peteet, J.M. (1991) *Gender in Crisis: Women and the Palestinian Resistance Movement*. New York: Columbia University Press.

Pinn, V. (1994) 'The role of the NIH's office of research on women's health', *Academic Medicine*, 69: 698–702.

Popay, J., Bartley, M., and Owen, C. (1993) 'Gender inequalities in health: Social position, affective disorder and minor physical morbidity', *Social Science and Medicine*, 36: 21–32.

Rahman, O., Strauss, J., Gertler, P., Ashley, D., and Fox, K. (1994) 'Gender differences in adult health: An international comparison', *Gerontologist*, 34: 463–9.

Ritchey, F., La Gory, M., and Mullis, J. (1991) 'Gender differences in health risks and physical symptoms among the homeless', *Journal of Health and Social Behavior*, 32 (March): 33–48.

Robey, B., Rutstein, S., and Morris, L. (1993) 'The fertility decline in developing countries', *Scientific American*, 60 (December).

Rubinstein, R. (1992) 'Household and behavioral factors affecting the prevalence of blinding trachoma in the Egyptian delta', A paper presented at the annual American Anthropological Association meeting, San Francisco, CA, 6 December 1992.

Rushwan, H. (1980) 'Etiological factors in pelvic inflammatory disease in Sudanese women', *American Journal of Obstetrics and Gynecology*, 136: 877–9.

Sanfilippo, J.S. and Smith, R.P. (eds) (1998) *Primary Care in Obstetrics and Gynecology*. New York: Springer.

Sargent, C.F. and Brettell, C.B. (eds) (1996) *Gender and Health: An International Perspective*. Upper Saddle River, NJ: Prentice Hall.

Sen, A. (1990) 'More than 100 million women are missing', *New York Review of Books*. 20 December 1990: 61–6.

SHDS (1991) *Sudan Demographic and Health Survey 1989/1990*. Khartoum, Sudan and Columbia, MD: Department of Statistics, Ministry of Economic and National Planning and Institute for Resource Development.

Simoons, F. (1967) *Eat not this Flesh: Food Avoidances from Prehistory to the Present*. Madison: University of Wisconsin Press.

Singer, M., Davidson, L., and Gerdes, G. (1988) 'Culture, critical theory, and reproductive illness behavior in Haiti', *Medical Anthropology Quarterly*, 2: 370–85.

Sommerfeld, J. (1994) 'New diseases: A challenge for medical anthropological research', *International Health and Infectious Disease Study Group Newsletter* 1: 1.

Sperling, S. (1991) in M. di Leonardo (ed.), *Baboons with Briefcases vs. Langurs in Lipstick: Feminism and Functionalism in Primate Studies. Gender at the Crossroads of Knowledge: Feminist Anthropology in the Postmodern Era*. Berkeley: University of California Press.

Tekce, B. (1990) 'Households, resources, and child health in a self-help settlement in Cairo, Egypt', *Social Science and Medicine*, 30: 929–40.

Toubia, N. (1985) 'The social and political implications of female circumcision: The case of Sudan', in E. Fernea (ed.), *Women and the Family in the Middle East*. Austin: University of Texas Press. pp. 148–59.

Toubia, N. (1993) *Female Genital Mutilation: A Call for Global Action*. New York: Women Ink.

Toubia, N. (1994) 'Female circumcision as a public health issue', *New England Journal of Medicine*, 331: 712–16.

Townsend, J. (1998) *What Women Want, What Men Want. Why the Sexes Still See Love and Commitment so Differently*. Syracuse: Syracuse University Press.

Turner, R. (1991) 'Over the past 30 years, most developed countries have had substantial declines in infant mortality', *Family Planning Perspectives*, 23: 139–40.

UNICEF (1994) *The State of the World's Children*. New York: UNICEF.

United Nations (1989) *World Population Prospects 1988*. New York: United Nations.

United Nations (1991) *The World's Women 1970–1990: Trends and Statistics*. New York: United Nations.

United Nations (1995a) *The World's Women 1995: Trends and Statistics*. New York: United Nations.

United Nations (1995b) *Population and Development: Programme of Action adopted at the International Conference on Population and Development, Cairo, 5–13 September 1994*. New York: United Nations.

Verbrugge, L. (1985) 'Gender and health: An update on hypotheses and evidence', *Journal of Health and Social Behavior*, 26 (September): 156–82.

Verbrugge, L.M. (1989) 'The twain meet: Empirical explanations of sex differences in health and mortality', *Journal of Health and Social Behavior*, 30: 282–304.

Vlassof, C. (1994) 'Gender inequalities in health in the Third World: Uncharted ground', *Social Science and Medicine*, 39: 1249–59.

Waldron, I. (1994) 'What do we know about causes of sex differences in mortality? A review of the literature', *The Sociology of Health and Illness*. New York: St. Martin's Press.

Ward, M. (1986) *Poor Women, Powerful Men: America's Great Experiment in Family Planning*. Boulder, CO: Westview Press.

Whiteford, L. (1996) 'Political economy, gender and the social production of health and illness', in C.F. Sargent, and C.B. Brettell (eds), *Gender and Health: An International Perspective*. Upper Saddle River, NJ: Prentice Hall.

Whitehead, T.L. and Conaway, M.E. (1986) 'Introduction', in T.L. Whitehead and M.E. Conaway (eds), *Self, Sex, and Gender in Cross-Cultural Fieldwork*. Urbana and Chicago: University of Illinois Press. pp. 1–14.

Williamson, J.B. and Boehmer, U. (1997) 'Female life expectancy, gender stratification, health status, and level of economic development: A cross-national study of less developed countries', *Social Science and Medicine*, 45: 305–17.

Wilson, E. O. (1975) *Sociobiology: The New Synthesis*. Cambridge, MA: Belknap.

World Bank (1993) *World Development Report 1993: Investing in Health*. New York: Oxford University Press.

Zurayk, H. (1991) 'Reproductive health and reproductive morbidity', A paper presented at a Seminar on Measurement of Maternal and Child Mortality, Morbidity, and Health Care: Interdisciplinary Approaches. International Union for the Scientific Study of Population, Committee on Population and Health, and the Center for Applied Demography, Institute of Statistical Studies and Research, Cairo University, 4–7 November 1991.

1.10

Critical Perspectives on Health and Aging

CARROLL L. ESTES AND KAREN W. LINKINS

INTRODUCTION: WHAT IS THE FIELD OF CRITICAL HEALTH AND AGING?

Critical approaches to health and aging employ a variety of theoretical perspectives including political economy, feminist theories, and humanistic gerontology (Minkler and Estes 1998; Phillipson 1996). These perspectives examine social issues in ways that challenge dominant or mainstream thinking, and reveal underlying ideological justifications of existing structural arrangements and resource distributions that affect health and aging. As such, these perspectives are open to multiple and alternative accounts of social processes, such as current concerns and debates regarding the aging population and the impact this will have on societies around the world.

As social and health policy interests regarding the aging of the population have intensified in Europe and the United States over the last decade, aging and old age have been constructed and regarded as a problem of the welfare state. Thus, much of the policy focus in many countries has centered on the role of the welfare state in the financing of care and support for the elderly. The field of critical health and aging is concerned with the cause and effect of this policy focus that reduces the experience of aging in all societies to a problem of dependency of the elderly and overlooks other issues associated with aging. As such, many issues of import and consequence to research and policy regarding the condition of aging in societies are underexplored. These issues are at the heart of critical health and aging, and include the meaning and lived experience of aging, the heterogeneity of (differences in race, class, and gender) and inequalities within the aging population, and how the state and the economy influence health and aging.

MAJOR THEORETICAL PERSPECTIVES CONSTITUTING THE FIELD

The critical approach is founded on an array of intellectual traditions, including Marx, Weber, Gramsci, the Frankfurt School, and more recently Habermas, state theorists such as Offe and O'Connor, psychoanalytic perspectives (Biggs 1997), and the contemporary work of Giddens. Building on these theoretical seeds, the field of critical health and aging has coalesced over the past decade with work in the United States and Europe. In general, three major theoretical areas constitute and inform the field: political economy, feminist theories, and humanistic gerontology.

A central and unifying tenet among these theories is the notion that aging and the problems faced by the elderly are socially constructed and result from societal conceptions of aging and the aged (Estes 1979a). This process occurs at both the macro- and microlevel. The state and economy can be seen as influencing the experience and condition of aging, while individuals also actively construct their worlds through their interactions with their social worlds and society.

Political Economy

The political economy approach offers an important approach to understanding the condition of health and aging in society. Beginning with the work of Estes (1979a,b), Guillemard (1983), Phillipson (1982), and Walker (1981), these theorists initiated the task of describing the role of ideology in systems of domination and marginalization of the aged. The political economy perspective can be distinguished from pluralist and other political approaches in that it gives greater importance to social structures and social forces other than the government as shaping and reproducing the prevailing power structure of society. Social policies pertaining to issues such as income, health, and social service benefits and entitlements are seen as resulting from economic, political, and sociocultural processes and forces interacting at any given sociohistorical period (Estes et al. 1995). As such, policy is considered an outcome of the social struggles, conflicts, and dominant power relations of the period. Policy represents the structure and culture of advantage and disadvantage as reflected in class, race, gender, and age relations. Concurrently, policy stimulates these struggles, and as such, social policy is a powerful determinant of the life chances and conditions of population groups such as the elderly.

A central assumption of the political economy perspective is that aging and old age are directly related to the nature of the society in which they are situated, and therefore cannot be considered or analyzed in isolation from other societal forces and characteristics. The power of the state, business, and labor, and the role of the economy, are central concerns. The operating framework of this approach comprises at least four conceptual levels that facilitate an understanding of the various ideological views and stakes regarding perspectives on aging and the structure and organization of health and aging services: (1) the global level of financial and industrial capital (e.g., multinational corporations with financial stakes in health, medical care, insurance, pharmaceuticals); (2) the activities of the capitalist state within and among countries; (3) the level of the 'aging enterprise' (Estes 1979a) and the health-care industry; (4) the public level (McKinlay 1984). Explicitly recognized in this framework are the structural influences on the aging experience and the role of societal institutions and social relations in understanding how aging and old age are defined and treated in society. The major problems facing the elderly, such as dependency, are understood as socially constructed as a result of societal conceptions of aging and the aged (Estes 1979b).

Feminist Theories

Another set of theories constituting the critical approach to health and aging are feminist theories. Feminist theories, which are complementary and often related to or included in the political economy perspective, emphasize the importance of gender by examining the gender biases in social science research on health and aging and within social policy. Gender is seen as an organizing element of social life throughout the life course that influences and shapes the experience of aging (Calasanti 1993; Diamond 1992; Estes 1998b; Ginn and Arber 1995) and the distribution of resources in old age to men and women.

Feminist approaches to aging offer an important angle for addressing differences in the health and aging experiences of the population, as well as how social, cultural, and structural factors influence and shape social conditions (Calasanti 1993). Gender is a crucial organizing principle in economic and power relations and societal institutions. This perspective builds a more robust picture of the aging population (which is mainly female) by identifying and challenging the dominant, male-centered biases in society (Arber and Ginn 1991; Calasanti 1996). When integrated into the political economy perspective, feminist approaches argue that there are fundamental, gender-based differences in the accessibility of material (e.g., income), health, and caring resources that influence the aging experience for men and women.

Humanistic Gerontology

Humanistic gerontology adds still another dimension to critical approaches to health and aging, especially insofar as it seeks to critique existing theories and to construct positive models of aging based on research by historians, ethicists, and other social scientists (Bengtson and Allen 1993; Cole 1992; Cole et al. 1993). Moody (1993) identifies several goals for the critical humanistic perspective in gerontology. These include: (1) developing theories that emphasize and reveal the subjective and interpretive dimensions of aging, (2) committing to praxis and social change, and (3) producing emancipating knowledge. Consistent with and complementary to both the political economy and feminist theories, this approach centers on the concepts and relations of power, social action, and social meanings as they pertain to aging. Central to this approach is concern regarding the absence of meaning in the lives of the elderly, and the sense of doubt and uncertainty that is thought to permeate and influence their day-to-day lives and social relations (Moody 1992).

Prevailing Gerontological Theories and Their Limitations

Since its inception in 1945, the field of gerontology has evolved into a formal interdisciplinary science involving biology, clinical medicine, and the behavioral and social sciences. While researchers, practitioners, policy makers, and the lay population agree that aging is a part of the life course, there is substantial disagreement among and within these groups regarding the definition of old age, the perception of what constitutes normal and successful aging, and the extent and scope of public/private responsibility in the promotion of 'successful' aging. This disparity in perspectives is reflected in the broad and fragmented body of theory that constitutes the field of gerontology, where '. . . there is no common thread or tie to a common core of disciplinary knowledge to unify the field' (Estes et al. 1991: 50). Another aspect of this fragmented body of work on aging stems from the larger social science debate of micro versus macro, in which the leading theories of aging are seen as emphasizing either the individual actor or the structure of society as the primary object of study. A small group of theoretical strands attempt to bridge both micro and macro perspectives (Bengtson et al. 1997).

Many of the leading theories of aging, especially those that approach the study of aging from the perspectives of biology and social psychology, focus on the individual as the primary unit of analysis. As such, the aging process is viewed and assessed in terms of the biological breakdown of the individual, or in terms of the individual personality and process, and the presumed concomitant dependency, loss, and requisite adjustment to these states of being.

Two examples of aging theories developed by social psychologists that focus on the individual are disengagement theory and activity theory. Disengagement theory (Cumming and Henry 1961) holds that old age is a period in which the aging person and society engage in mutual separation (e.g., retirement). The process of disengagement is treated as a natural, biologically based, and normal part of the life course. This assertion also fits into the broader functionalist paradigm that was dominant at the time of its development insofar as disengagement is presumed to be 'functional' from the standpoints of both the individual and society. Although disengagement theory is no longer widely accepted among researchers in aging, its influence is still apparent in the policy arena (e.g., Social Security and Medicare) as well as in the retirement policies of corporations. In fact, this theory can be seen as a basis for the trend in implementing incentives for early retirement evident in corporations, universities, and public sector institutions over the past decade.

Activity theory developed in opposition to the assumptions of disengagement theory, asserting that people in old age continue the roles and activities they developed over the course of life, including maintaining the same needs and values present at earlier points in their lives. The basic assumption of this theory is that the more active people are, the more likely they are to be satisfied with their lives. Activity theory stimulated the development of a whole host of social psychological theories of aging, including continuity theory (Costa and McCrae 1980) and successful aging (Abeles et al. 1994; Baltes and Baltes 1990; Rowe and Kahn 1987). Continuity theory asserts that aging persons have the tendency and need to maintain the same personalities, habits, and perspectives on life that they developed over their life course. As such, decreases in activity or social interaction are viewed as related more to changes in health and physical function than to an inherent need for a shift in, or relinquishment of, previous roles.

More recently developed theories of successful aging expand the basic framework of activity and continuity theory to three fundamental components: low probability of disease and disease-related disability, high cognitive and physical functional capacity, and active engagement with life (Rowe and Kahn 1997). Successful aging is seen as involving more than the absence of disease and more than the maintenance of functional capacities. Rather, these two components combine and interact with the active engagement with life.

On the surface, activity theory and its later derivations promote the eradication of ageist stereotypes of the elderly and create opportunities for individual empowerment and quality of life in later years. Nevertheless, these theories rarely account for the influence of structural factors on individual outcomes; nor do they examine or treat race, gender, and class as individual attributes or social mediators of the aging experience. In addition, they provide little insight into understanding the broader (and unequal) division of labor and allocation of resources in society. Therefore, policies and programs developed from these theories frequently do not account for or address the diversity and heterogeneity of the aging experience. As such, these policies and programs do not hold much promise for remedying social inequalities or promoting social change.

From the early days of development, a major focus of inquiry for gerontology concerned not only the adaptation of aging persons in society, but also the consideration of health, economic, and social problems related to aging. With regard to elders' health, there has been a strong emphasis on the biomedical aspects of aging (Estes and Binney 1989), with early work treating aging as a disease and the prescription of medical services as the primary intervention. Aging, defined and treated largely by physicians and biologists, was described as decremental, and both unidirectional (inevitable loss of function and adaptability) and negative in terms of outcome.

While the early social and behavioral work focused on individual aging and the factors in 'successful aging,' life satisfaction, adaptation, disengagement, and adjustment with advancing years, more recent studies focus on understanding the process of aging from the perspective of the life course and its relationship to coping, social support, personal control, self efficacy, and the behavioral dimensions of aging. This work acknowledges the malleability and reversibility of various biological and behavioral phenomena previously thought to be inevitable (Rowe and Kahn 1987, 1998) and increasingly recognizes the influence of social, behavioral, and environmental factors in the explanation of the processes of aging and of health in old age (House et al. 1990). This work is consistent with a substantial body of literature affirming the importance of social, behavioral, and environmental factors in both individual and population health (Adler et al. 1993; Hahn and Kaplan 1985; Navarro 1990; Syme and Berkman 1976). In particular, the work of Rowe and Kahn and Bortz and Bortz (1996) suggests a declining significance of medical and biological factors in health with advancing age. Attention to the interplay of social structures (structural opportunities in schools, offices, families, communities, social networks, and society at large) and structural change in explaining healthy and successful aging is highlighted by Riley and Riley (1994, 1998). Other recent work calculates the proportion of health (mortality and morbidity) that may be accounted for by biological in contrast to social, environmental, and behavioral factors. The latter factors are seen as carrying the most weight (ranging from 50 per cent or more of the explanations for health outcomes).

More recently, aging has been viewed from the life-course perspective, which situates aging of individuals and cohorts as one phase of the entire lifetime and is shaped by factors (historical, social, economic, and environmental) that occur at earlier ages (Bengtson and Allen 1993;

George 1993). An important contribution of life-course theory is the commitment to bridging the macro–micro levels of analysis. Nevertheless, there is a tendency within this perspective to focus more on the micro, with an emphasis on how macrolevel phenomena influence individuals.

Another macrolevel approach is the age stratification perspective, which analyzes the role and influence of social structures on the process of individual aging and the stratification of age in society (Riley and Riley 1994, 1988). This perspective looks at the differential experiences of age cohorts across time, as well as what Riley and Riley (1994) call the interdependence of changes in lives and changes in social structures. A more recent dimension of this theory is the concept of structural lag, wherein social structures (e.g., policies of retirement at age 65) do not keep pace with changes in population dynamic and individual lives (such as increasing life expectancy). One of the major limitations of the age-stratification approach is its relative inattention to issues of power and social class relationships, especially insofar as these factors influence the social structure and the policies constituted by it.

Critical perspectives on aging and health emerged in response to the limitations of traditional theorizing in aging. Critical analysis of traditional aging theories reveals how these theories avoid questioning the very social problems and conditions facing the elderly (Estes 1979a) and therefore have the tendency to reproduce rather than change the conditions of the elderly. At a basic level, theories such as disengagement and activity can be seen as reinforcing ageist attitudes about the elderly and legitimating policies that reinforce dependency at the expense of empowerment. In addition, the association of age with disease and inevitable decline can be reframed such that aging is seen as a social, rather than a biological process. This alternative view, which is central to the critical perspective, reveals that many experiences related to aging result from socioeconomic conditions and inequalities experienced over the life course.

In attempting to bridge some of the issues of concern about many of the aforementioned aging theories – namely fragmentation and the macro–micro problem – the critical approach to aging considers the multilevel relationships among social structure, social processes, and the population. Within this frame, the recursive relationship among levels of analysis are emphasized (Giddens 1984), which provides an avenue for extending and further synthesizing this micro–macro linkage. As such, issues of aging are not perceived as beginning with the individual, the generation, institutions or organizations, or society. Instead, all levels are viewed in terms of mutual dependency, rather than in opposition.

Although the field of critical approaches to health and aging has grown over the past decade, the promise of the field – namely its incorporation of a variety of disciplinary perspectives – also contributes to the difficulty that the field faces in realizing its potential. For one, as both Baars (1991) and Phillipson (1999) note, critical health and aging is a very broad field concerned primarily with questions and analyses that fall outside the mainstream of gerontology and other disciplines in the social sciences. These questions and analyses range from understanding the role of the state and capital in managing the aging process (e.g., Estes 1979a, *The Aging Enterprise*) to questions regarding the meaning and purpose of aging in the context of postmodern societies (Cole 1992).

THE CHANGING CONTEXT OF HEALTH AND AGING

Two major elements of the larger context of health and aging are the ongoing market-driven restructuring of the delivery system and changes in the welfare state.

Delivery System Restructuring, Privatization, and Devolution

A critical perspective on health and aging addresses health policy developments in terms of the changing roles and resources of the state and corporate enterprise, respectively, with a particular interest in the consequences for society and the public's needs and access to care and the distribution of inequalities therein. Attention is also given to the uses of ideology (e.g., the superiority of the market) in advancing the interests of dominant economic and political forces. The critical framework points to power struggles and social conflicts as central processes through which resources are distributed that either maintain the status quo or alter disparities in health status and health care by race, class, gender, and age. The medical industrial complex and the aging enterprise are seen as 'products' of the relations of the state, capital, the sex/gender system, and the public (Estes 1998b). Simultaneously, these entities and the businesses that comprise them influence, reflect, and benefit from the definition and treatment of old age and the aging as a medical-techno rather than a social problem (Estes 1979a).

Since the 1930s, the federal government has played an influential role in the development of health and long-term care through policies supporting an expansion of the federal welfare state, such as Social Security, Old Age Assistance, the Hill–Burton statute, the Kerr–Mills program, Medicare and Medicaid, and other policies and regulations.

In the United States, the state's role has been and continues to be one of complementing and subsidizing, rather than competing with the private sector. The passage of Medicare for the elderly in 1965 was the first major public health insurance program for the nation aimed at citizens aged 65 and older. Medicare supported private fees for service physician care and hospital payments based on retrospective billing – both of which provided incentives for doctors and hospitals to bill more and often. Barbara and John Ehrenreich aptly described this as the beginning of the 'American Health Empire.' Furthering the process that began with the passage of Medicare and Medicaid in 1965, Reagan Administration policies in the 1980s fueled the growth in the for-profit service sector and health care costs (Fuchs 1990). Although 40 per cent of the cost of US health care is financed by a largely private sector medical–industrial complex, the state has limited its own activities in the public health and social services arena to those that maintain and assist the development of the private market through limited public financing programs of health insurance. These programs are primarily for the aged (Medicare) and the poor, who cannot afford to pay for private insurance (Medicaid) (Estes 1991).

State policy also provides opportunities for private capital through civil law and regulation by protecting the market and encouraging the participation of proprietary health entities (e.g., the Omnibus Reconciliation Act of 1980), including more than $30 billion in federal tax subsidies for the purchase of private health insurance. Over time, government tax cuts for business, combined with the promotion of for-profit medical care, have acted in a contradictory fashion to exacerbate the fiscal problems of the state (Estes 1991).

Direct attacks on the welfare state, including Social Security and Medicare, surfaced early in the 1980s as part of President Reagan's first term of office. Subsequently, Reagan, with the support of a rattled but democratically controlled Congress, produced both a recession and a major federal deficit due to increased military expenditure and deep tax cuts for the wealthy. The financing of the deficit then generated major interest payments by the federal government, which further increased the deficit. In the late 1980s and early 1990s there was grave political concern and exhortation over the size of the federal deficit. President Clinton was elected on the mantra of 'It's the economy stupid' and the promotion of deficit reduction as a major policy, which has contributed to intensified power struggles over the commitments and jurisdiction of the Federal government. These concerns have prompted the passage of multiple policies aimed at (1) reducing the federal deficit, (2) stimulating market competition and containing costs in the health-care sector (e.g., legislation promoting managed care and prospective payment), (3) transferring a greater cost burden and risks of out-of-pocket medical payments to patients (e.g., the 1997 Balanced Budget Amendment for Medicare), and (4) re-directing responsibility to the state and local levels (e.g., the 1996 Welfare Reform Act) and the private sector.

Between the time that President Reagan took office and the present, there has been more than a threefold increase in US health expenditure, which now exceeds one trillion dollars annually. The Reagan administration created a watershed in promoting state policies that would increase market involvement in medical care, accompanied by ideologically laden rhetoric extolling the superiority of the market and excoriating the inferiority of government. As a result, a series of developments over the past two decades have converged to shape and transform the health and long-term care industries in the United States (Estes 1986; Estes et al. 1984 1993; Relman 1980; Starr 1982).

The magnitude and profundity of this restructuring have been described as the medical equivalent of the industrial revolution, in which health-care entities moved from small entrepreneurial operations to large, powerful, and increasingly concentrated capital enterprises. Three key characteristics of these changes are: (1) the overpowering strength of the ideology of the market, (2) the expansion and near-domination (in influence if not dollars) of proprietary organizations into every aspect of health care, and (3) an increasingly contested but continuing role of government as a major revenue source supporting the growth of the medical industrial complex and as a payer of care for the elderly, the disabled, and the poor. While the roles of federal and state governments in the health-care system are challenged, there has been a shift away from the federal government and an increase in the responsibility and discretion given to the states. Such a shift is particularly consequential for the elderly, given that the federal–state Medicaid program is the largest public funding source for long-term care for the elderly.

Beginning with the passage of the 1983 Medicare Prospective Payment System (PPS),

which gives hospitals financial incentives to discharge patients earlier, and the dramatic reductions in hospital lengths of stay (LOS), the sector of postacute and ambulatory care services increasingly assumed an important role in the health-care delivery system (Estes 1986, 1988; Estes and Binney 1988; Estes et al. 1993). For the elderly who have been discharged from hospitals 'quicker and sicker' (with millions of days of the caregiver time formerly provided via hospital care transferred to the home and community), the demand for skilled nursing and home health care increased (Heinz 1986). New forms of care emerged, such as hospitals branching into home health services, inpatient posthospital services, and hospice and hospital swing beds (Guterman et al. 1988). Access to nursing home care became more limited as the illness acuity levels of patients discharged earlier from hospitals increased, thus requiring more complex treatment from highly trained health-care professionals (Hing 1987; Shaughnessy et al. 1990). In addition, regulatory policies, such as the 1987 Omnibus Budget Reconciliation Act (OBRA), introduced a number of changes to organizations that provide community-based long-term care (CBLTC). These include new training and reporting requirements, more strict reimbursement standards, and other forms of oversight and utilization review.

One significant change that occurred during the Reagan administration was the initiation of what has become a sustained attack on the non-profit sector in health (Estes and Alford 1990). President Reagan's approach reversed the prior state policy (in effect from the mid-1960s to the 1980s) in which preference had been given to nonprofit health and social service agencies as President Johnson intentionally supported the development of the nonprofit service sector. The attack on nonprofits occurred through the deregulation and encouragement, as well as the direct financing, of for-profit providers of medical care and social services. In this way, state policy under Reagan clearly augmented and stimulated market investment opportunities for private capital in areas that had been traditionally the domain of nonprofit health entities (Marmor et al. 1987). The medical market has advanced in areas that promised the greatest likelihood of profit (e.g., managed care, hospital, and home health services).

With all of the state financing and the high and growing government and private sector costs for health care, there has been (1) a deepening of divisions in the *de facto* rationing system of US health care based on ability to pay (Darling 1986), and (2) a largely unchecked rise in federal health-care costs (Estes et al. 1995: 354; Reinhardt 1988). Beginning in the early

1980s and continuing to the present, the state intensified funding constraints for social and community care services, which was of great concern to the elderly (Abramson and Salomon 1986; Estes and Linkins 1997; Salomon 1987). These services are among the most needed by the elderly because they are not funded by Medicare and are provided largely in nonprofit service organizations that have had a high degree of dependency on government funding. These social and supportive services experienced the most severe cuts by the Reagan administration (and are underdeveloped today). Also, these services tend to be less attractive for business investment because there is less certainty of profitability due to the bias in reimbursements in favor of medical and skilled care and against the social and supportive services needed for the chronically ill and for the elderly. Additional impediments to for-profit investments in social services concern their relative labor intensity, lower technological content, and their unpredictability in terms of demand and scope (Estes 1986; Estes et al. 1993).

All of the government's promotion of market forces and competition from the 1980s to the present has failed to realize either the goal of containing the rising costs of health and long-term care services or the goal of increasing access to care. Based on research by Himmelstein, Woolhandler, and Carrasquillo, the nation's uninsured exceeded one in six, or 43.2 million in 1997 (PCHRG 1998: 11–12), while an even higher number of Americans are underinsured for health care. The failure of President Clinton's national health insurance reform efforts shifted the initiative for health policy reform to the discretion (and direction) of the market. The resulting structural changes have further accelerated the privatization and rationalization (Weber 1946) of medical care through the growth of large, complex, multi-facility systems (Fennell and Alexander 1993; Shortell et al. 1990). State tax subsidies, the lure of high profit margins, and state policies to promote competitive bidding practices have continued to encourage and stimulate proprietary sector involvement of ever larger and more complex organizational health-care entities, conglomerates, and subsidiaries that may have few community ties. The continuing consolidations, mergers, and conversions of nonprofit health entities to for-profits have greatly strengthened and emboldened the hand of the insurance and managed care industries (Bergthold et al. 1990; Berliner 1987; Estes et al. 1993) Institute of Medicine 1986; Light 1986; Salomon 1987).

Regarding public financing of health care, compared with other developed countries, the United States spends significantly more on health care in absolute dollars and as a percentage of gross domestic product (approximately 14 per cent of the GDP in 1998, which is two to three times the expenditure of other comparable nations). Yet the United States remains the only Western industrialized nation without national health insurance. Historically, US health costs rise well above general inflation. In terms of health care for the elderly, the United States lags behind other Western industrial nations in the provision of long-term care.

Medicare

Medicare, the US program of health insurance for the elderly, covers nearly all nonworking persons over age 65. Although Medicare is a program primarily for the elderly, 13 per cent of its beneficiaries are younger than 65 and disabled; 300 000 are covered for kidney dialysis. In 1994, Medicare represented 12 per cent of the federal budget, with growth projections to 16 per cent by 2002 (Feder 1995/1996). In 1996, Medicare spent about $169 billion for elderly beneficiaries, or $4875 per elderly person. By 1998, Medicare expenditures exceeded $217 billion ($5600 per person). In the early years of the program, Medicare represented 11 per cent of total health-care expenditure. By 1993 and continuing to the present, Medicare has accounted for about 20 per cent of total health-care expenditure (Davis and Burner 1995; Kaiser Family Foundation 1998). In 1998, Medicare accounted for 2.6 per cent of the economy, and it is expected to more than double to 5.9 per cent in 2030. The Medicare Trust Fund faces a shortfall in the next decade, which is being addressed by 1997 legislation that promotes HMOs and increases the costs of care to beneficiaries. In addition, a federal Medicare commission is debating options that are expected to augment elements of privatization and rationalization of the Medicare program for the elderly through additional means of market stimulation and proposals to privatize Medicare through vouchers and/or medical savings accounts.

Medicare barely covers half of the total health-care expenditures incurred by people over age 65. The bulk of Medicare payments (79 per cent of 1998 benefit payments) are for hospital (inpatient and outpatient), physician, and managed care costs (CBO in Kaiser Family Foundation 1998: 4). The most significant exclusions from Medicare coverage are long-term care and prescription drug coverage (44 per cent and 18 per cent of out-of-pocket costs, respectively).

Medicaid

For two distinct groups of elders that comprise about 15 per cent of the total Medicare population (Kaiser Family Foundation 1998), Medicaid augments Medicare coverage. The first group includes the below-poverty-level elderly. The second group includes elders who 'spend down' to Medicaid eligibility later in life, typically as a result of expenditure on medical and long-term care services not covered by Medicare. Some of these services include custodial nursing home care, prescription medications, and nonskilled home health services. Medicaid typically covers a wide range of uncovered services for both groups of eligible elderly. Medicaid's most important coverage for the elderly is nursing home coverage.

Privatization and Devolution

Two social processes are strongly linked with struggles over labor and the economic fortunes of increasingly large (now global) capital enterprises. During the 1970s and 1980s, the United States was joined by other industrial societies in pursuing policies to promote the sale of public goods at an escalating rate (Esping-Andersen 1996). Privatization, or the administrative transfer of public goods and services to the private sector, became an acceptable approach for governments to fend off fiscal crises and to delegate down (devolve) or even outright to divest their responsibilities to their citizenry (Estes and Linkins 1997).

The process of privatization in health and long-term care is the subject of a great deal of debate and controversy, and raises major questions about the proper role of government and the existence of citizenship rights and entitlements. Nevertheless, there is limited empirical data about the human and social costs and consequences of the multiple ways in which governments are privatizing health services.

A number of scholars working from the critical perspective view privatization in terms of a new form of class war (Piven and Cloward 1997), where privatization and globalization are both seen more as ideological weapons in the struggle of workers and citizens against big business, rather than as economic requisites. Privatization is not seen as an inevitable response to the fiscal crisis of the state, nor does it inevitably stem from some conspiracy to roll back the welfare state. Instead 'health services privatization depends on the specific nature of conflict among the state, the private sector, health care consumers, and capital' (Scarpaci 1989: 2).

Current interest in privatization intersects with a climate increasingly disposed toward market solutions and devolution. The dominant and deep-seated view in the United States is that the market and business sectors can administer programs more efficiently than politicians and bureaucrats. Public opinion polls indicate that the public believes the market system is fairer than the political system. 'They prefer the market's criteria of earned desserts to the polity's criteria of equality and need, and believe that market procedures are more fair than political procedures' (Lane 1986: 386).

The market-generated discourse of cost-effectiveness, downsizing and rightsizing, and fiscal restraint now permeate the government and virtually all elements of the welfare state, health care, and even the social services. However, the application of these principles in welfare state and health and social service activities reveals the contradictions of capitalism with regard to how two value structures conflict or blend together – the market forces of postindustrial capitalism and the more socialistic traditions of industrial capitalism (Nelson 1995). Although the welfare state is currently incurring formidable attacks, it is unlikely that it will be eliminated entirely (O'Connor 1973; Piven and Cloward 1997). 'Health, welfare, education, security – these are considered to be "rights" and are not easily dismissed' (Nelson 1995: 137).

What is emerging through the processes of privatization is an altered form of the welfare state in which the context is shifted from the public sector to a sector coordinating public–private linkages. The private sector, including a gigantic trillion-dollar medical industrial complex, represents major stakeholders in this emerging new form. Social welfare expenditure, broadly defined with Social Security included, are relatively large expenditures at all levels of government. Privatization breaks the constraints on the use of public resources and puts them to multiple ends: to provide welfare and secure profits (Nelson 1995). The fundamental principle driving the development of the welfare state was for economic development to feed social development and, in so doing, to minimize inequality. Privatization is an example of an economic development strategy that potentially escalates inequality, as has occurred in the United States. The altered resources associated with privatization result in a new principle of economic growth.

For the elderly, a fundamental question is whether privatization will lower (or increase) costs (and efficiency) in health care and long-term care in accord with the prevailing rationale undergirding the drive toward more privatization. The high costs associated with health and long-term care reflect the pluralistic financing, complexity, and fragmentation of these domains of service delivery. The political and economic stakes render cost-cutting procedures difficult. From a pluralistic perspective, the costs associated with health and long-term care stem less from the inefficiencies and lack of competitiveness of government than from (1) expenses associated with health-care professionals, (2) the difficulty and extensive use of diagnosis for problem evaluation, (3) costly technology at the edge of innovation, and (4) the growth of care needs associated with the aging population. There is little evidence that for-profit institutions and mechanisms will lead to lower costs associated with the delivery of health care and long-term care. Instead, as Brad Gray asserts:

> Studies of hospitals provide no evidence to support the common belief that investor-owned organizations are less costly or more efficient than are not-for-profit organizations . . . [Available] studies that have controlled for many confounding factors including distinguishing investor-owned from independent proprietary hospitals show the opposite to be true. (Gray 1994: 1525)

From a critical perspective, the rising costs associated with health and long-term care are attributed primarily to the waste and excess resources squandered in the drive for profits, the costs of marketing, and the extraordinary costs of administration and regulation of the highly varied corporate activities and entities. Such entities continually seek to avoid the risks of a sick population and to dump those who cannot be profitably treated on the state or the nonprofit sector. The fact that the United States continues to pursue its current course, in view of very high costs (which are variously estimated at 40 per cent or more of the health-care dollars spent), signals the power of corporations in health (Navarro 1993), particularly when contrasted with the consistent positive evidence that the alternative publicly administered single-payer system has higher administrative efficiency and lower cost (Himmelstein and Woolhandler 1992). An additional and very high price is the inability of the current US health-care system to provide health insurance coverage for more than 43 million persons. Vicente Navarro notes:

> . . . the popular demand for allocating health care resources according to need has always conflicted with the capital logic of putting profits first and people's needs second. Every inch of human space in the capitalist order has been won after enormous struggle carried out by working people against the powerful and rich. (Navarro 1993: 98)

The Welfare State and Aging: A Critical Perspective

According to Gosta Esping-Andersen (1996: 27), the 'welfare state has been a mechanism of attaining the goals of social integration, the eradication of class differences, and nation building including solidarity and citizenship.' From the late 1970s to the present, the politics of aging have been fought in the political context of 'crisis' (Estes 1979a). Esping-Andersen (1996) confirms that the phenomenon of demographic aging is part of the present welfare state debate. He identifies three categories of contemporary theorizing about the welfare state 'crisis' in which scholars alternatively attribute the problems of the welfare state to (1) distortions of the market, (2) the cataclysmic effects of population aging, or (3) the consequences of the new global economy, which is punishing governments that spend and those that are not economically competitive.

Indeed, the social construction of, and the political uses of, crisis definitions have been – and remain – central to the struggles over social policy for the aging (Estes 1991). Today the question is whether it is possible for the United States to continue to afford to support such bedrock social programs for the elderly as Social Security and Medicare. Beginning with the Reagan administration, increasing attention has been given to the elderly as the source of problems in larger US society and the economy, particularly in creating the necessity for great 'tradeoffs' for the society. Actual and projected demographic changes associated with population aging have been ballyhooed as a major crisis. The elderly have been widely and negatively portrayed by the media as 'greedy geezers' getting rich at the expense of their children. The media is also reporting that US welfare policy will have to be changed due to the inability of the nation to afford the growing number of elders as the baby boomers reach age 65 and older.

The construction of population aging as a crisis reflects ideological dimensions of the larger sociopolitical struggle in US society (Estes 1979a 1996), which is of particular import for older women, people of color, and those who earn low incomes. The concept of the 'demographic imperative' is a rallying point for those who argue that the elderly are living too long, consuming too many societal resources, and robbing the young, which is an argument used to justify rollbacks of state benefits for the aged. It is an inescapable fact that the majority of these elders are female, and the majority who are most dependent upon the welfare state are female, low income, and members of racial and ethnic minority groups.

Some of the most persuasive critical approaches to understanding national health policy have focused on social class and the status cleavages that have split the power of workers by 'granting . . . different levels of benefits to different types of workers and the use of means tests [by which] the capitalist class sought to break working-class solidarity' (Navarro 1993: 86). For health policy, Navarro's point would be the crucial import of retaining universality of coverage and provision as contained in the social insurance principles underlying US retirement (Social Security) and health (Medicare) programs for the aging. Navarro (1993: 86–87) identifies eight conditions on which working-class power depends, including degree and type of unionization, unity of the labor movement, links between labor and political parties, alliances with other classes, and the unity of the capitalist class.

Welfare state theories seek to explain the patterns of social provision adopted by different nations. Research attends to the relations of the state, corporate interests, and labor in producing different types of welfare state programs (Esping-Andersen 1996). Work on the state and the life course focuses on the 'impact of the state on the structuring of the life course' (Mayer and Schoepfin 1989), highlighting 'overarching and integrative mechanisms for institutionalizing the life course' including old age, childhood, public employment, education, military service, and wars. Applied to aging, welfare state theories have acknowledged the importance of both the demographic aging and social class (particularly the strength of labor) in producing more rather than less generous welfare state programs (e.g., Social Security for the elderly) (Pampel 1994; Street and Quadagno 1993). These theories have been successfully used to illuminate the varying health and welfare spending patterns for the elderly in different nations. Particularly important developments for understanding the welfare state and aging are in the incorporation of gender into theories of state–market relations. Two additional dimensions are proposed to capture the effects of state social provision on gender relations: access to paid work and capacity to form and maintain an autonomous household (Orloff 1993: 303).

MAJOR ISSUES RAISED BY A CRITICAL PERSPECTIVE

A critical perspective on health and aging draws attention to the importance of social inequality and gender in understanding the life chances and life experience of older persons. Key individual and structurally linked attributes that explain the experience of aging are one's social location according to race, ethnicity, social class, and gender.

Social Inequality, Health, and Aging

Over the life course, a variety of social and economic factors interact to shape the trajectory of disease development, treatment, and health outcomes. The critical approach to health and aging considers social class, broadly defined to include wealth, status, and power, as one of the most significant factors influencing the experience of aging in all societies. The inequality of wealth, status, and power evident between racial and gender groups has an impact of health status, and in old age this effect is seen as an issue of accumulated advantage or disadvantage experienced over the life course. Crystal and Waehrer (1996) show that inequalities among groups depend upon and intensify with age. These and other findings (Burkhauser and Smeeding 1994) highlight the ineffectiveness of state policy in compensating for the discrimination (e.g., wage) and disadvantage that one may experience earlier in the life course. Retirement income from all sources is appreciably less for older women than older men (averaging 75 per cent or less the retirement income of men, see Hartman 1998), while nearly three-quarters of the elderly below the poverty level are women. Women are much more dependent on Social Security for their subsistence than are men. Half of older unmarried women rely on Social Security for 80 per cent or more of their income, while one-fifth (20 per cent) of all women rely on it for 90 per cent or more of their income. Fifty-five per cent of women aged 75 and older and 45 per cent of those 65–74 years old are below the poverty line (Stone and Griffith 1998).

The concept and measurement of social class has been addressed and measured in a variety of ways. A frequently used proxy for social class is socioeconomic status (SES), which is widely recognized as a strong predictor of morbidity and premature mortality, and a linear mortality gradient has been demonstrated at all socioeconomic levels with a variety of diseases (Adler et al. 1993). Recent research demonstrates that SES, measured in terms of education or income, is a major predictor of health status because persons with lower SES are at greater risk of exposure to a range of psychosocial risk factors to health, primarily in middle and early old age (House et al. 1994).

With regard to race and health status, data consistently show the African–American elderly to be disadvantaged compared with whites in life expectancy, chronic illness rates, and levels of disability. While the health disparity between blacks and whites declines with advancing age on some health indicators, including mortality rates, African–American elderly as a group are less healthy and more disabled than white elderly. Some suggest that the health gap between white and black elderly will widen due to increased rates of diabetes and hypertension (Wallace et al. 1998: 331). Older African–Americans and Latinos have two to three times the poverty rate of white elderly, and many do not have health insurance. Thus, access to care is a serious problem to many minority elders. Because minority elderly are 'projected to comprise over one-third of all persons age sixty-five and older' (Wallace et al. 1998: 331) in 2050, racial disparities in health status and access to care will be a serious concern. Although it is often assumed that access to health care is a major determinant of health status, international comparative research on SES and health reveals that correction of data for access to health care (e.g., through the availability of universal health insurance) does not eliminate SES as a risk factor (Adler et al. 1993). Therefore, social and environmental factors have persistent and direct effects on health outcomes and on the health status and life expectancy of elderly individuals.

Differences and disparities in life expectancy by race and gender offer another window into the issue of inequality in health and aging. Overall, elders of color experience more health problems than whites because of problems accessing adequate medical care, high poverty rates, and relatively low participation rates in Social Security. These factors contribute to morbidity and mortality differences across populations. For example, research shows that the most important factor contributing to the widening gap in life expectancy between whites and African–Americans is the slower decline in heart disease mortality experienced in the African–American population in recent decades (American Health Line 1998; Papas 1994).

In the United States, population trends reveal a 'female advantage' in terms of overall life expectancy; however, this trend is offset by the disability rates occurring among older women. Women at age 65 can expect to live approximately 10 years free of disability and 7 years with disability. In contrast, older men can expect to live 8 disability-free years and 7 years with disability. Therefore, the proportion of disability-free remaining years at age 65 is greater for men, while the absolute number of years of life is less than that for women. Women are also much more likely to be the primary long-term care-givers, to live alone, and to need caregiving assistance themselves.

Inequality related to social class, gender, race, and ethnicity also tend to be related to and reinforce each other, creating a situation that many call double or multiple jeopardy (Bengtson and Dowd 1980–81; Dressel et al. 1998; Minkler and Stone 1985).

Gender, Health, and Aging

Based on demographics alone, with older women outliving and outnumbering older men 3 to 2 (and with the gap growing larger with advancing age), aging is appropriately defined as a gender issue. In important respects, aging is a women's issue. Corroborating this view, Dr Robert Butler, former director of the National Institute on Aging (NIA), recently described the US health programs for the elderly, Medicare and Medicaid, as 'women's programs' for the very old (Butler 1996).

Gender dependence on the state and the consequences of state policy for older persons in general, and older women in particular, are essential elements of a critical analysis of public policy and health and aging (Estes 1998a). A pivotal element in the critical analysis of health and aging from a gender perspective is an examination of the 'interlocking systems of oppression' and inequality (Collins 1990) that are contained within, and result from, the social relations of gender, social class, and racial and ethnic status. Social class, race, and gender are directly related to the health resources (e.g., Medicare policy, private insurance, and access) upon which older men and women may draw through systems of public and private sector provision. There is an important life-course dimension to these intertwined systems of inequality and oppression (gender, race and class), resulting in multiple and triple jeopardies in old age. Feminist analysis, race, and class must not simply be used in an 'add and stir' approach, but one that recognizes the compounding and interacting effects of the relative disadvantages and advantages of these three attributes of stratification (Dressel et al. 1998).

Women and Health Insurance over the Life Course

Public and private sector policy discriminates against women in terms of health insurance. It also rewards the traditional nuclear family in which married women do not live alone and economically depend on a working male spouse. This is in spite of societal trends of increasing divorce, single motherhood, and attenuated work careers.

Mature women are more likely to be insured as wives than as workers, but that safety net is only available to married women. Unmarried women are 2 to 3 times as likely to be uninsured or to rely on public programs such as Medicaid, and because they are significantly less likely to be married to a covered worker, black women are 2 to 3 times more likely to be uninsured or to rely on public programs. Given rising instability in both employment and marital status across the life course, stable health insurance coverage can only be attained by universal rather than employment-based or family-based schemes (Meyer 1990: 553). Women comprise a significant proportion (18 per cent) of the 'near elderly' (those aged 55–64) who are not insured for health care.

Women, Social Policy, Health, and Aging

Analysis of the role of the state in social provision for the aging, issues of gender dependence on the state, and the consequences of state action are significant elements of the study of the political economy of aging. A feminist critical perspective seeks to understand how state policy actually 'constructs' the experience of older women, including their economic status and/or dependency (e.g., through Social Security policy) (Estes 1979a). In the United States, both health and retirement policy contribute to the dependency of older persons and women. Older women's dependency is produced as a result of women's roles in the family, the labor market, and the state (Estes et al. 1984). Multiple sources of older women's dependency include:

- wage inequality and sex discrimination that exists throughout the life course, with cumulated results in old age;
- Social Security policy predicated on the traditional nuclear family and a wife's dependency on her husband for economic security;
- women's informal caregiving labor that is not compensated or counted toward retirement income credits;
- age discrimination in employment and early retirement necessitated by caregiving work;
- health policy (e.g., the provision of private health insurance through employment) and retirement policy (e.g., Social Security) that rewards married women and penalizes unmarried women;
- the projected cumulative negative economic effects for women over the life course of the 1996 Welfare Reform for single mothers.

Women, the State, and Long-Term Care

The treatment of older women by state policies is particularly important because women are more dependent on the welfare state than are men (Butler 1996; Estes 1998b). Older women are particularly vulnerable as a result of the absence of government financing for long-term care.

- Medicare (the nation's universal elder health policy) does not cover long-term care (LTC), necessitating women to provide these services, largely without assistance.
- Reimbursement incentives through public policy (e.g., Medicare) have widened the gap between medical and social services. Acute care services are paid for under Medicare, while long-term chronic care services are not. This is one form of the 'medicalization' of aging (Estes and Binney 1989), with negative social and financial cost shifts to older women.
- The effects of the government's refusal to adopt a publicly financed universal LTC policy are borne unequally by gender. As the majority of care providers, women do most of the LTC work, and they are also more likely to outlive anyone to care for them (thus, to need formal LTC assistance). Women are more likely than men to have to 'spend down' all of their resources to poverty in order to qualify for public assistance for nursing home care through Medicaid.
- A higher number of risk factors for both health and economic insecurity exist for older women than for men (e.g., living alone, chronic illness, low income). Also a higher proportion of income is required for older women to pay for LTC services.
- Devolution and increased state responsibility place long-term care policy (and the women who need it) at the effect of 50 state governors and legislatures, which are increasingly conservative (more than 30 with Republican governors). The result is the continuation and deepening of a fragmented and unequal policy for similar women across different states.

Arguments against a universal long-term care policy reside in the unfounded contention that it would encourage the abdication of family (i.e., women's) responsibility for providing care to the aging and cost the state. The debate is whether the public provision of social services will diminish private care services by family members (Sharlach and Kaye 1997). Such reasoning legitimates the state's refusal to either provide or pay for long-term care beyond that for the poor under Medicaid. Thus, the state reinforces the ideology that such care is, and must continue to be, the responsibility of women and their 'free' labor.

A reasonable question is whether the continuing denial of responsibility for long-term care by government, with the support of business, is attributable to the unnamed gender content of aging – female.

CRITICAL HEALTH AND AGING: THREE DEBATES

Two basic *organizing principles* on which public (state) policy may be based are (1) citizenship and entitlement, and (2) the market. The first principle accords formal recognition in the national community of social rights of citizenship, while the second principle recognizes individual responsibility and the rights of private property. They refer, respectively, to citizen-based or state-based rights *versus* class-based or property-based rights. A key question concerns the basic organizing principle for a society and state policy and how it affects age relations, and within these, class, race, and gender relations.

As we approach the new millennium, macro- or policy-level issues surrounding the topic of health and aging command attention not only of scholars but also of the media, the public, and policy makers. It is a time of hotly debated controversies that are both highly politicized and polemic. Three significant examples are: (1) the challenge to entitlements and the potential privatization of Social Security and Medicare; (2) the debate surrounding long-term care policy as a universal program versus one provided through commercial private insurance; (3) the pros and cons of Medicare managed care for the elderly.

Understood from a critical perspective, each of these issues involves enormous economic and political stakes, with struggles over profits and control of financial resources and the organization and delivery of medical care in the private sector that have profound consequences for the elderly and their health and well-being. To the extent that steps toward privatization and the curtailment of public programs are realized, the consequences will be most severe for those who are least powerful in society and most economically vulnerable. The media emphasis on the viability of (and preference for) the privatization of entitlements reflects the strength of the market ideology and the reality of the threat of transforming social policy from a communal and universal basis to a class basis that is sim-

ultaneously gender- and race-biased. Similar stratified and deleterious consequences are associated with commercial health insurance for long-term care in lieu of a public plan.

The Challenge to Citizen Entitlements: Privatizing Social Security and Medicare

Social policy debate concerning the elderly has, for almost two decades, been permeated by the rhetoric of crisis and increasing attacks on the entitlement and social insurance programs that are the backbone of support for older persons in the United States. These social struggles are profoundly important in health policy and in the provision of health care to the elderly.

The 'model of citizenship entitlements,' in which 'benefits accrue to individuals independently of need or labor force participation' (Myles 1996: 126) is rare in the United States, but the near-universal coverage of Medicare for those over age 65 (regardless of need or labor market contributions) and to a lesser extent Social Security retirement programs, reflect such a principle.

The late 1990s are characterized by an increasingly divisive contest between corporate and conservative political forces aimed at privatization and those moderates and citizen activists seeking to preserve the existing entitlement-based provisions under Medicare and Social Security.

The privatization of Medicare could be accomplished through the replacement of this federal insurance program with private commercial health insurance. Capitated managed care plans will effectively eradicate the *defined benefits* of the current Medicare system and replace them with *defined contributions* and tax subsidies that encourage the purchase of private plans. This would shift the financial risk from the Medicare program to individual elders. Included among privatization strategies are policies to promote private savings to pay for the costs of medical care through medical retirement accounts (MRAs) and vouchers for the purchase of medical care insurance.

The means testing of Medicare is another means of eliminating the universal entitlement to the program, while simultaneously eliminating the universal broad base across all social strata of public support for the program. With means testing, Medicare would become a poor people's welfare program (and with all the liabilities of diminished public support of welfare programs). The large majority of elders whose incomes exceed Medicare means-tested eligibility levels would be forced to purchase private insurance to cover their medical care.

From a critical perspective, pressures for the privatization of health care for the elderly inhere in the private profits to be made and the corporate control that can be imposed via such policy change. Privatization proponents argue that the rising costs of health care and the Medicare program mean that government (i.e., taxpayers) cannot afford it with the demographic expansion of the aging. Further, the market ideology holds that the private insurance market is more efficient. Opponents of privatization contend that privatizing Medicare does not address the factors that increase the costs of medical care (the fragmented, highly inefficient, and expensive for-profit system that promotes provider- and technology-induced cost increases and service demand). In addition, policies of privatization are class-based policies that disadvantage the already vulnerable (women, minorities, the poor and near poor, and the oldest old).

Commercial Private Insurance versus Universal Public Insurance for Long-Term Care

Given the state's reluctance to pay for long-term care (LTC) costs under Medicare and its existing and limited LTC coverage, the primary public coverage for LTC is available under Medicaid only for those who are poor or near poor (depending on the state in which a person lives). Advocates for commercial private LTC insurance argue that public insurance is too costly and that LTC should be insured privately, with some subsidy by the government. Opponents of private insurance for LTC argue that only a small percentage of the elderly are ever likely to be able to afford private LTC insurance (10–20 per cent), and that lower cost LTC insurance products do not provide enough benefits or inflation protection to make them attractive even to those who could afford them (Estes and Bodenheimer 1994; Wiener 1997).

With the limited ability of most elders to afford private insurance and the design of LTC insurance policies themselves, less than 10 per cent of the costs of LTC will ever be covered (or saved) by private insurance. Private LTC insurance will still leave the major financing responsibility of paying for LTC to the individual and to the government for those who 'spend down' to the poverty level and have Medicaid eligibility for LTC. Wiener (1997) notes that,

> virtually no one argues that the sick or . . . terminally ill should use all of their income and assets to

pay for hospital or physician care, yet doing so is routine in long term care. (Wiener 1997: 51)

Universal health care advocates contend that the public financing of LTC is a reasonable extension of the already universal Medicare program. Such a

> social insurance approach explicitly recognizes LTC as a normal risk of growing old. There is no cogent reason why LTC should be financed primarily through a welfare program [Medicaid], whereas acute care and income support for the elderly are financed through the non-means-tested programs of Medicare and Social Security. (Wiener 1997: 54)

Universal social insurance programs have the political advantage of

> including more middle and upper income beneficiaries as part of their constituency. . . [and] to be more politically stable than programs for the poor. (Wiener 1997: 54)

Managed Care for the Elderly

Lynch and Estes (1997), Feder and Moon (1998), and others have raised a number of issues concerning the benefits of managed care for the elderly. First, HMOs provide 'managed money, not managed care' and at a higher cost than does Medicare (Feder and Moon 1998). HMOs have administrative costs of 12–20 per cent off the top before paying providers, compared to the 2–3 per cent costs to administer Medicare. Second, certain groups of elderly and disabled fare worse in HMOs compared to fee-for-service (FFS) medical care. Research on Medicare HMOs show that they enroll a more healthy population than the average, and although research is sparse on how elders with chronic diseases and disabilities fare in HMOs, the studies that do exist point to problematic results. Access to home health care and chronic care services is more limited in HMOs. For example, elders in Medicare HMOs receive 50 per cent less home health care (Brown et al. 1993). Other access problems identified include that for Alzheimer's diagnostic and treatment centers and comprehensive services (Safran et al. 1994).

As Medicare shifts billions of public dollars to for-profit HMOs with few strings attached, the following items fuel the managed care debate.

1 The potential and real tradeoffs between (lower) out-of-pocket costs (in HMOs) for (higher) quality and satisfaction (with fee-for-service non-HMO plans). As health care restructuring and competition squeezes the easy profits out, consumers face rising

HMO rates and curtailed benefits – elevating questions about the possible loss of the HMO advantage in providing more benefits than Medicare fee-for-service options.

2   The lack of incentives (contrary to rhetoric) to provide preventive care because of annually generated plan redesign and enrollment changes (e.g., disenrollments).

3   The public accountability and consumer involvement issues attendant to for-profit insurance companies that comprise the large majority of HMOs.

The Future

From a critical health and aging perspective, some of the most important issues for future empirical and theoretical work are given below.

• Tracking the origins and consequences of the dramatic acceleration in social inequality (e.g., the gap between rich and poor) in society between Americans of all ages and its rise within the older generation. Particular attention needs to be given to the consequences of the high social inequality for the health and quality of lives of older women, minorities, and poor and middle-class people, and the effects of social inequality on health inequality between generations and within the older generation, by race, class, and gender.

• The effects of devolution and privatization on the elderly, including changes in social policy that 'trade off' federal universal social provision for decentralized state and locally determined policy and provision. Attention needs be given to the effects on the health and health care of the aging, particularly of those most vulnerable (women, minorities, the poor, the oldest old, and the unmarried).

• Whether devolution promotes a 'race to the bottom' in which states compete to reach the lowest common denominator.

• The changing role of the welfare state and its effects on the economic and health security of the elderly under conditions of postindustrial capitalism and globalization. One issue is whether in health and retirement programs for the elderly, the United States will become part of a solely market-determined 'class state' or a citizen rights-based 'universal state' – and with what effects on older persons of color, and by gender and social class.

• The future of Medicare and Medicaid in the short and long term, and the consequences for program beneficiaries in subgroups of elders of policies to promote cost contain-

ment, managed care, and privatization initiatives.

• The success of different stakeholders (capital, the state, labor, women, minorities) in advancing policy and/or pro-entitlement and pro-privatization social movements.

Conclusion

To address the pressing research questions facing the field, there is a need for both the development of new and the reconceptualization of existing methodologies. There is a clear need for more research and theory development that is informed by the social, political, and economic factors that converge and interact to produce significant differences among the elderly. As a field, gerontology and studies of health and aging need to acknowledge the value of multiple methodological and theoretical approaches. There is a great need for systematic meta-analytic and retrospective work in the field, particularly that which addresses the meso- and macro-level of explanation in the critical examination of health and aging. To address the need for research that accounts for the differential effects of phenomena occurring at different levels of analysis, there are several analytic methods, such as hierarchical linear modeling, that would allow this type of assessment. Finally, the debate and resultant false dichotomy between quantitative and qualitative methods needs to be put to rest in favor of studies that incorporate both.

In addition to the need for alternative and creative methods, there is also an ever-present need for data, and particularly projects in the tradition of the Frankfurt School that are multi-disciplinary and that attend to the structural factors and institutional forces and processes that are important in any critical examination of health and aging in society and globally. Attention must be given to re-balancing studies of the individual aspects of health and aging with the 'social', including the examination of the political, economic, and cultural processes underlying public policy and the social provision that materially affects the health of the different elements of the population in significantly and unequal ways. The historic and relative disciplinary funding advantage of psychology, biology, and economics over sociology has diminished the prevalence of more critical studies while reproducing the knowledge structure of the field through the funding of positivistic research approaches that are perceived as more 'scientific.'

REFERENCES

Abeles, R.P., Gift, H.G., and Ory, M.G. (eds) (1994) *Aging and Quality of Life.* New York: Springer.

Abramson, A. and Salomon, L. (1986). *The Nonprofit Sector and the New Federal Budget,* Washington, DC: The Urban Institute, p. 70.

Adler, N.E., Boyce, T., Chesney, M.A., Folkman, S., and Syme, L. (1993) 'Socioeconomic inequalities in health: No easy solution', *Journal of the American Medical Association,* 269: 3140–5.

American Health Line (1998) *Black Mortality Widens.* November 1998.

Arber, S. and Ginn, J. (1991) *Gender and Later Life.* London: Sage.

Baars, J. (1991) 'The challenge of critical studies', *Journal of Aging Studies,* 5: 219–43.

Baltes, P.B. and Baltes, M.M. (1990) 'Psychological perspectives on successful aging: The model of selective optimization and compensation', in P.B. Baltes and M.M. Baltes (eds), *Successful Aging: Perspectives from the Behavioral Sciences.* New York: Cambridge University Press. pp. 1–34.

Bengtson, B.E. and Allen, J.T. (1993) 'Sociological functionalism: Exchange theory and life-cycle analysis', in P.G. Boss, W.J. Doherty, R. LaRossa, W.R. Schum, and S.K. Steinmetz (eds), *Sourcebook of Family Theories and Methods: A Contextual Approach.* New York: Plenum Press.

Bengtson, V. and Dowd J.J. (1980–81) 'Sociological functionalism: Exchange theory and life cycle analysis. A call for more explicit theoretical bridges', *International Journal of Aging and Human Development* 12: 55–73.

Bengtson, V. E., Burgess, O., and Parrott, T. M. (1997) 'Theory, explanation, and a third generation of theoretical development in social gerontology', *Journal of Gerontology: Social Sciences,* 52B(2): S72–88.

Bergthold, L.A., Estes, C.L., and Villanueva, A.M. (1990). 'Public light and private dark: The privatization of home health services for the elderly in the US', *Home Health Care Services Quarterly,* 11: 7–33.

Berliner, H.S. (1987). 'Walk-in chains: The proprietarization of ambulatory care', *International Journal of Health Services,* 17: 585–594.

Biggs, S. (1997) 'Choosing not to be old? Masks, bodies and identity management in later life', *Aging and Society,* 17: 553–70.

Bortz, W.M. IV and W.M. Bortz II (1996) 'How fast do we age? Exercise performance over time as a biomarker', *Journal of Gerontology: Medical Sciences,* 51A(5): M223–M225.

Brown, R., Clement, D., Hill, J., Retchin, S., and Bergeron, J. (1993) 'Do HMOs work for Medicare?', *Health Care Financing Review,* 15: 7–23.

Burkhauser, R.V. and Smeeding, T. (1994) 'Social security reform: A budget neutral approach to reducing older women's disproportionate risk of poverty', *Policy Brief.* Maxwell School Center for Policy Research, 2, Syracuse, NY.

Butler, R. (1996) 'Medicare and women', *New England Journal of Medicine,* 334: 794–6.

Calasanti, T. (1993) 'Introduction: A socialist–feminist approach to aging', *Journal of Aging Studies,* 7: 107–9.

Calasanti, T. (1996) 'Incorporating diversity: Meaning, levels of research, and implications for theory', *Gerontologist,* 36: 147–56.

Cole, T. (1992) *The Journey of Life.* Cambridge: Cambridge University Press.

Cole, T., Achenbaum, A., Jakobi, P., and Kastenbaum, R. (eds) (1993) *Voices and Visions of Ageing: Toward a Critical Gerontology.* New York: Springer.

Collins, P.H. (1990) *Black Feminist Thought.* London: Unwin-Hyman.

Costa, P.T. and McCrae, R.R. (1980) 'Still stable after all these years: Personality as a year to some issues in aging', in P.B. Baltes and O.G. Brim (eds), *Life-Span Development and Behavior.* Vol. 3. New York: Academic Press. pp. 65–102.

Crystal, S. and Waehrer, K. (1996) 'Later-life economic inequality in longitudinal perspective', *Journal of Gerontology,* 51(B): S307–S318.

Cumming, E. and Henry, W.E. (1961) *Growing Old: The Process of Disengagement.* New York: Basic Books.

Darling, H. (1986) 'The role of the federal government in assuring access to health care', *Inquiry,* 23: 286–95.

Davis, M.H. and Burner, S.T. (1995) 'Three decades of Medicare: What the numbers tell us', *Health Affairs,* 14: 236–41.

Diamond, T. (1992) *Making Gray Gold: Narratives of Nursing Home Care.* Chicago: University of Chicago Press.

Dressel, P., Minkler, M., and Yen, I. (1998) 'Gender, race, class and aging: Advances and opportunities', in M. Minkler and C. L. Estes (eds), *Critical Gerontology: Perspectives from Political and Moral Economy,* Amityville, NY: Baywood. pp. 275–94.

Esping-Andersen, G. (ed.) (1996) 'After the golden age? Welfare state dilemmas in a global economy' and 'Positive sum solutions in a world of trade-offs?' in *Welfare States in Transition: National Adaptations in Global Economies.* Thousand Oaks, CA: Sage. pp. 1–31, 256–67.

Estes, C. L. (1979a) *The Aging Enterprise.* San Francisco: Jossey Bass.

Estes, C. L. (1979b) 'Toward a sociology of political gerontology', *Sociological Symposium,* 26: 1–18.

Estes, C.L. (1986) 'The aging enterprise: In whose interests?', *International Journal of Health Services,* 16: 243–51.

Estes, C.L. (1988) "Cost-containment and the elderly: Conflict or Challenge?" *Journal of the American Geriatrics Society,* 36: 68–72.

Estes, C.L. (1991) 'The Reagan legacy: Privatization, the welfare state, and aging in the 1990s', in J. Myles and J. Quadagno (eds) *States, Labor Markets and the Future of Old Age Policy*. Philadelphia: Temple University Press. pp. 59–83.

Estes, C.L. (1996) 'Crisis, the welfare state and aging', Presidential Address, Annual Meeting of the Gerontological Society of America, Washington, DC.

Estes, C.L. (1998a) 'Critical gerontology and the new political economy of aging', in M. Minkler and C. L. Estes (eds), *Critical Gerontology: Perspectives from Political and Moral Economy*. Amityville, NY: Baywood.

Estes, C.L. (1998b) 'Patriarchy, the welfare state, and women', Paper presented at a Conference on Autonomy and Aging, Kingston University, Kingston on Thames.

Estes, C.L. and Alford, R. (1990) 'Systemic crisis and the nonprofit sector: Toward a political economy of the non-profit health and social services sector', *Theory and Society*, 19: 173–98.

Estes, C.L. and Binney, E.A. (1988) 'Towards transformation of health and aging policy', *International Journal of Health Services*, 18: 69–82.

Estes, C.L. and Binney, E.A. (1989) 'The biomedicalization of aging: Dangers and dilemmas', *Gerontologist*, 29: 587–96.

Estes, C.L. and Bodenheimer, T. (1994) 'Paying for long term care', *Western Journal of Medicine*, 160: 64–9.

Estes, C.L. and Linkins, K.W. (1997) *Decentralization, Devolution . . .* , Washington, DC: Gerontological Society of America.

Estes, C.L., Gerard, L., and Clarke, A. (1984) 'Women and the economics of aging', *International Journal of Health Services*, 14: 55–68.

Estes, C.L., Binney, E.A., and Culbertson, R.A. (1991) 'The gerontological imagination: Social influences on the development of gerontology 1945–present', *Journal of Aging and Human Development*, 35: 49–67.

Estes, C.L., Swan, J.H., and Associates. (1993) *The Long Term Care Crisis: Elders Trapped in the No-Care Zone*. Newbury Park, CA: Sage.

Estes, C.L, Linkins, K. and Binney, E.A. (1995) 'The political economy of aging', in L. George and R. Binstock (eds), *Handbook of Aging and the Social Sciences*. 4th edn. San Diego: Academic Press. pp. 346–61.

Feder, J. (1995/96) 'Thoughts on the future of Medicare', *Inquiry*, 32: 376–8.

Feder, J. and Moon, M. (1998) 'Managed care for the elderly: A threat or a promise?' *Generations*, xxix, (2): 6–10.

Fennell, M.L. and Alexander, J.A. (1993) Perspectives on organizational change in the US medical care sector', *Annual Review of Sociology*, 19: 89–113.

Fuchs, V.R. (1990) 'The health sector's share of the gross national product', *Science*, 247: 534–8.

George, L.K. (1993) 'Sociological perspectives on life transitions', *Annual Review of Sociology*, 19: 353–73.

Giddens, A. (1984) *The Constitution of Society: Outline of the Theory of Structuration*. Berkeley: University of California Press.

Ginn, J. and Arber, S. (1995) 'Only connect: Gender relations and aging', in S. Arber and J. Ginn (eds), *Connecting Gender and Aging: A Sociological Approach*. Philadelphia: Open University Press.

Gray, B. (1994) 'Ownership matters: Reform and the future of nonprofit health care', *Inquiry*, 30: 352–61.

Guillemard, A.-M. (ed.) (1983) *Old Age and the Welfare State*. New York: Sage.

Guterman, S., Eggers, P.W., Riley, G., Greene, T.F., and Terrell, S.A. (1988) 'The first 3 years of Medicare prospective payment: An overview. *Health Care Financing Review*, 9: 67–77.

Hahn, M. and Kaplan, G.A. (1985) 'The contribution of socioeconomic position to minority health', in M. Heckler (ed.), *Report of the Secretary's Task Force on Black and Minority Health*. Washington, DC: US Department of Health and Human Services.

Hartman, H. (1998) *Women and Social Security*. Washington, DC: Institute for Women's Policy Research.

Heinz, J. (1986). 'The effects of DRGs on patients', *Business and Health*, 20: 17–20.

Himmelstein, D. and Woolhandler, S. (1992) *The National Health Program Chartbook*. Cambridge, MA: The Center for National Health Program Studies, Harvard Medical School.

Hing, E. (1987) 'Use of nursing homes by the elderly: Preliminary data from the 1985 National Nursing Home Survey', *NCHS Advancedata*, 135: 1–11.

House, J.R., Kessler, C., and Herzog, A. R. (1990) 'Age, socioeconomic status, and health', *Milbank Quarterly*, 68: 383–411.

House, J.R., Lipkowski, J., Kinney, A.M., Mero, R., Kessler, R., and Herzog, A.R. (1994) 'The social stratification of aging and health', *Journal of Health and Social Behavior*, 35: 213–34.

Institute of Medicine (IOM) (1986) *For-Profit Enterprises in Health Care*. Washington, DC: National Academy Press.

Kaiser Family Foundation (1998) *Medicare: The Basics*. Menlo Park: Kaiser Family Foundation.

Lane, R. (1986) 'Market justice, political justice', *American Political Science Review*, 80: 383–402.

Light, D. (1986) 'Corporate medicine for profit', *Scientific American*, 255: 38–45.

Lynch, M. and Estes, C. L. (1997) 'Is managed care good for older persons?' in A. E. Scharlach and L. W. Kaye (eds), *Controversial Issues in Aging*. Boston: Allyn & Bacon. pp. 114–25.

Marmor, T.R., Schlesinger, M, and Smithey, R.W. (1987) 'Nonprofit organizations and health care', in W.W. Powell (ed.), *The Nonprofit Sector: A Research Handbook*. New Haven, CT: Yale University Press. pp. 221–39.

Mayer, K. and Schoepfin, U. (1989) 'The state and the life course', *Annual Review of Sociology*, 15: 187–209.

McKinlay, J.B. (ed.) (1984) 'Introduction', *Issues in the Political Economy of Health*. New York: Methuen–Tavistock.

Meyer, M.H. (1990) 'Family status and poverty among older women: the gendered distribution of retirement income in the US', *Social Problems*, 37: 551–63.

Minkler, M. and Estes, C.L. (1998) *Critical Gerontology: Perspectives from Political and Moral Economy*. Amityville, NY: Baywood.

Minkler, M. and Stone, R. (1985) 'The feminization of poverty and older women', *Gerontologist*, 25: 351–7.

Moody, H. (1992) 'Gerontology and critical theory', *Gerontologist*, 32: 294–5.

Moody, H. (1993) 'Overview: What is critical gerontology and why is it important', in T. Cole, A. Achenbaum, P. Jakobi, and R. Kastenbaum (eds), *Voices and Visions of Ageing: Toward a Critical Gerontology*. New York: Springer.

Myles, J. (1996) 'When market fails: Social welfare in Canada and the United States', in G. Esping-Anderson (ed.), *Welfare States in Transition: National Adaptations in Global Economies*. London: Sage. pp. 116–40.

Navarro, V. (1990) 'Race or class versus race and class: Mortality differentials in the US', *Lancet*, 336: 1238–40.

Navarro, V. (1993) *Dangerous to Your Health: Capitalism in Health Care*. New York: Monthly Review Press.

Nelson, J.I. (1995) *Post-Industrial Capitalism: Exploring Economic Inequality in America*. Thousand Oaks, CA: Sage.

O'Connor, J. (1973) *The Fiscal Crisis of the State*. New York: St. Martin's Press.

Orloff, A.S. (1993) 'Gender and the social rights of citizenship: The comparative analysis of gender relations and welfare states', *American Sociological Review*, 58: 303–28.

Pampel, F.C. (1994) 'Population aging: Class context and age inequality in public spending', *American Journal of Sociology*, 100: 153–9.

Pappas, G. (1994) 'Elucidating the relationship between race, socioeconomic status and health', *American Journal of Public Health*, 84: 892–3.

Phillipson, C. (1982) *Capitalism and the Construction of Old Age*. London: Macmillan.

Phillipson, C. (1996) 'Interpretations of ageing: Perspectives from humanistic gerontology', *Ageing and Society*, 16: 359–69.

Phillipson, C. (1999) *Reconstructing Old Age: New Agenda in Social Theory and Social Practice*, London: Sage.

PCHRG (Public Citizen Health Research Group) (1998) 'Number of Americans without health insurance jumps to 43.2 million', *Health Letter*, 14: 11–12.

Piven, F.F. and Cloward, R.A. (1997) *The Breaking of the American Social Compact*. New York: New Press.

Reinhardt, U. (1988). The battle over medical costs isn't over. *The Wall Street Journal*, 22 October 1988.

Relman, A.S. (1980) 'The new medical–industrial complex', *New England Journal of Medicine*, 303: 963–70.

Riley, M. W. and Riley, J. W. (1994) 'Structural lag: Past and future', in M.W. Riley, R. L. Kahn, and A. Foner (eds), *Age and Structural Lag*. New York: Wiley. pp. 15–36.

Riley, M. W. and Riley, J. W. (1998) 'Letters to the editor', *Gerontologist*, 38: 151.

Rowe, J. W. and Kahn, R. L. (1987) 'Human aging: Usual and successful', *Science*, 237: 143–9.

Rowe, J.W. and Kahn, R.L. (1997) 'Successful aging', *Gerontologist*, 37: 433–40.

Rowe, J. W. and Kahn, R. L. (1998) *Successful Aging*. New York: Pantheon Random House.

Safran, A. Tarlov, A.R., and Rogers, W.H. (1994) 'Primary care performance in fee-for-service and prepaid health care system', *JAMA*, 271: 1579–86.

Salomon, L.A. (1987) 'Of market failure, voluntary failure, and third-party government: Toward a theory of government–nonprofit relations in the modern welfare states, in S.A. Ostrander, S. Langton, and J. Van til (eds), *The Shifting Debate: Public/Private Sector Relations in the Modern Welfare State*, New Brunswick, NJ: Transaction Books. pp. 29–49.

Scarpaci, J.L. (1989). 'The theory and practice of health services privatization', in J.L. Scarpaci, (ed.), *Health Services Privatization in Industrial Societies*. New Brunswick: Rutgers University Press. pp. 1–23.

Sharlach, A. and Kaye, L. W. (eds) (1997) *Controversial Issues in Aging*. Boston: Allyn & Bacon. pp. 114–25.

Shaughnessy, P.W., Schlenker, R.E., and Kramer, A.M. (1990) 'Quality of Long-term care in nursing homes and swing-bed hospitals', *Health Services Research*, 25: 65–96.

Shortell, S.M., Morrison, E.M., and Friedman, B. (1990). *Strategic Choices for America's Hospitals*. San Francisco: Jossey-Bass.

Starr, P. (1982) *The Social Transformation of American Medicine*. New York: Basic Books.

Stone, A. and Griffith, J. (1998) *Older Women: The Economics of Aging*. Washington, DC: Women's Research and Education Institute. p. 26, Table 2-11.

Street, D. and Quadagno, J. (1993) 'The state, the elderly, and the intergenerational contract: Toward a new political economy of aging,' in K.W. Schaie and W. A. Achenbaum (eds), *Societal Impact on Aging*. New York: Springer.

Syme, L. and Berkman, L. F. (1976) 'Social class, susceptibility and sickness', *American Journal of Epidemiology*, 104: 1–8.

Walker, A. (1981) 'Towards a political economy of old age', *Ageing and Society*, 1: 73–94.

Wallace, S., Enriquez-Haass, V., and Markides, K. (1998) *Stanford Law Review.* p. 331.

Weber, M. (1946) *From Max Weber: Essays in Sociology.* (H.H. Gerth & C.W. Mills, Translation and eds). New York: Oxford University Press.

Wiener, J. (1997) 'Are private sector solutions to long term care financing preferable to expansion of public long term care programs?' in A. E. Scharlach and L. W. Kaye (eds), *Controversial Issues in Aging.* Boston: Allyn & Bacon. pp. 51–6.

1.11

The Social Context of the New Genetics

SARAH CUNNINGHAM-BURLEY AND
MARY BOULTON

INTRODUCTION

Developments in human genetics, especially when related to health and disease, are discussed and debated in a range of contexts – in the media, in policy arenas, and through various forms of public debate. A range of professional and lay groups are involved in such discussions, including scientists, clinicians, bio-ethicists, social scientists, patient and interest groups, and industry. This suggests that the knowledge and applications arising from genetic research are expected to have considerable impact on our social institutions as well as on individuals themselves, and thus should be openly debated. Concerns are profound, for genetic research will influence the way in which we define, prevent, and treat disease, organize health and social care, and manage insurance and employment. Issues around discrimination, stigma, and eugenics all evoke anxiety and raise questions about how we regulate science and clinical practice. The presence of such far-reaching concerns, operating at every level in society, demand that the social context of the 'new genetics' is thoroughly understood. Such an analysis needs to consider both the social shaping of genetic science, that is, how and why it develops in the way it does, as well its social consequences and impact, which themselves may influence future developments. This chapter offers an overview of some of the key areas that describe this context.

A consideration of the social context of the new genetics must start from a position that characterizes science as a social activity. This effectively challenges the view that science is the objective accumulation of value-free knowledge, suggesting instead that science should be understood as reflexively related to society and culture. Science is conducted with reference to interests and goals (Barnes et al., 1996), and scientists will seek to protect their interests, often by demarcating science from non-science, and their expertise from that of the non-specialist (Barnes et al. 1996; Gieryn 1983, 1995; Kerr et al. 1997). Lay people, on the other hand, are in much less powerful positions, and their interests may be determined rather than protected by science. However, a sociological understanding of lay experience must not start from a position of privileging scientific knowledge. Rather, it should treat lay people as knowledgeable, and able to engage with science in a range of ways, in order to make sense of its relevance to their daily lives and decision making. These two elements to understanding the social context of the new genetics, essential to informed sociological inquiry, underlie the contribution of this chapter.

The first part of the chapter considers the development of genetic science by providing a sociohistorical overview of the growth of genetics over the twentieth century. This embraces a consideration of genetics' early link with the eugenics movement, and how genetics came to be reinstated as a viable science with something to offer in terms of understanding and ameliorating human disease. The Human Genome Project is a high-profile manifestation of the central place accorded to genetics in the life sciences and medicine. (The term 'genome' refers to all the genetic material in the chromosomes of an organism; the human genome is contained in 23 pairs of chromosomes.) In describing genetic science, the chapter then focuses on current significant clinical applications, namely genetic testing and screening, and considers the potential and problems associated with these. The second part of the chapter broadens the discussion to include lay responses to these clinical developments, and then moves on to consider the wider social issues and concerns raised by current and future research. Finally, the chapter examines the role of public involvement in debates about genetics, and considers the range of expertise that needs to be harnessed to ensure democratic and inclusive science and health care. In conclusion, suggestions are made for areas of future development and the role that social scientists have in continuing active and meaningful debate in this important area of scientific, medical, and social concern.

The term the 'new genetics' refers specifically to the body of knowledge and techniques arising since the invention of recombinant DNA technology in 1973. It involves research into the genetic components of human disease and behaviour, which may have clinical applications through the provision of genetic testing or screening for disease or risk factors for disease, and through treatments such as gene therapy or new pharmaceuticals. Although the chemical structure of DNA was discovered in 1953, it was not until the development of polymerase chain reaction (PCR) techniques, which made possible the rapid production of many copies of a particular DNA sequence, that it became possible to isolate single human genes and to identify their function. The ability to produce and manipulate DNA in the laboratory hastened developments in the field and led to the identification of genes, and markers for genes, for a range of diseases (such as cystic fibrosis in 1989). Indeed, in 1995 alone, some 60 disease genes were isolated (Yates 1996). These discoveries are often portrayed as breakthroughs by scientists and the media alike, but the associated promise of cures for disease deriving from such research has been matched by concerns about emergent risks to current and future generations and a slippery slope to eugenic practice. Clinical applications currently include genetic testing and screening; gene therapy is developing more slowly than first anticipated, although the development of new pharmaceuticals is proceeding rapidly. While some diseases are caused by a single gene, most disease is likely to be polygenic (caused by a number of genes), or multifactorial (the product of the interaction between genes and environmental factors, both during foetal development and onwards throughout the life course). Despite uncertainty and caution, developments in genetics are clearly having, and will

continue to have, considerable impact on individuals seeking health-related advice and treatment, the institutions within which such activities are embedded, and the wider social and cultural processes that influence them.

GENETIC SCIENCE AND ITS CLINICAL APPLICATIONS

The Rise of Genetic Science

Genetics has now moved to centre stage in the life sciences and into the arena of 'big science,' with its new alliances between venture capital and academia (Rose 1994). However, throughout the first half of this century, it was very much a marginal science, making few significant inroads into either biology or medicine. Its varied and mixed relationship to eugenics throughout the early part of this century has meant that its marginality as a science has become somewhat overshadowed by its prominence as the scientific backdrop to the eugenics movement. This legacy has important implications for current genetics, which has to seek a new public support and scientific authority after the atrocities of Nazi Germany during World War II. However, at the start of the century, an alliance with eugenics was a way of ensuring public support for genetics, by linking it with significant social interventions. Concern persists today about the eugenic potential of genetic interventions, although cast in different contexts.

Although Mendel's work on pea plants in the nineteenth century led to the identification of dominant and recessive factors in heredity, it was not until the start of the twentieth century that these rules were rediscovered (Judson 1992). The developing fields of cell biology and statistics led to further work on heredity, much focusing on the fast-breeding fruit fly, but also including the transmission of diseases in humans. Although Kevles (1992) suggests that some of these scientists were motivated by the potential relationship with medicine, and by the quest for knowledge for its own sake, he identifies eugenics as the driving force in these early scientific endeavours in relation to understanding human inheritance. Eugenics, he states, was 'the cluster of ideas and activities that aimed at improving the quality of the human race through the manipulation of its biological heredity' (Kevles 1992: 4). This 'modern eugenics' originated with Galton, who pursued the idea that improvement of the human race might be attained through selective breeding, whereby the 'undesirable' could be eliminated (negative eugenics) and the 'desirable' multiplied (positive eugenics). This became a popular movement across the United States and Europe, embracing many professional groups, although most policies were aimed at negative, not positive, eugenics – for example, through sterilization laws, some of which were only repealed as recently as the 1970s. Crucially, the eugenics movement included geneticists 'for whom the science of human biological improvement offered an avenue to public standing and usefulness' (Kevles 1992: 5). In pursuit of this science, and motivated by eugenic applications, an emphasis was placed on studying medical and social disorders – the latter including the public concerns of the day such as criminality, prostitution, and alcoholism. The study of 'feeblemindedness' was of particular concern. Although the nature of the eugenics movement, and the relationship of genetics to it, changed and reconfigured across the century (Paul 1992), the emphasis of these early investigations, reflecting the wider popular movement with which genetics was associated, resonates in more recent claims. The genetic basis of mental illness, intelligence, and a range of behavioural traits considered socially undesirable, re-emerged as topics for investigation throughout the 1970s, and research continues today. Similarly, a concern for disease, although much more prominent today in the new genetics, finds some continuity with the past (Kerr et al. 1998b). Science clearly cannot be set apart from the social values with which it is infused.

The commonplace assumption that all eugenics was based on bad science, often promoted by geneticists today (Kerr et al. 1998b), has been challenged. For example, there has been a lasting impact in terms of statistical techniques still used today (MacKenzie 1978). However, from the 1930s onward, many scientists disassociated themselves and their scientific work away from mainline eugenics (Kevles 1995). Weaknesses in the science became obvious: it neglected the role of the environment, did not eliminate bias from studies, and focused on traits that could not easily be measured. These concerns, along with the blatant class and race biases of the early eugenics movement and its increasing association with Nazism, discredited genetics. By the mid-twentieth century, human genetics was not an attractive discipline, nor one that seemed particularly useful in social or medical arenas. However, over the next few decades, it was to develop and become the strong force in biological and medical science that it is today. Increasingly, it came to align itself with clinical medicine and to study well-defined traits that could be measured accurately. Its eugenic links were at once severed yet subtly reconfigured as a 'reform eugenics,' that focused on preventive and therapeutic medicine (Kevles 1995). Here, biology or nature was considered important in explaining human difference, but the environment or nurture was also accorded some significance.

Although the eugenic potential of genetics and the power attributed to genes declined in acceptability from the 1930s, Keller (1992) argues that geneticists then set about separating their science and its knowledge from its use or abuse, and distinguished human from nonhuman genetics and physiology from behaviour. This helped to preserve the integrity of the developing science and to firmly entrench it as valuable to medicine. The biochemical and molecular biological advances since the discovery of the structure of DNA created a body of knowledge and techniques that had some useful application in clinical genetics and avoided association with any overt eugenicist goals. Yoxen (1982a) argues that clinical geneticists were a new professional group and had to negotiate a position within the profession of medicine as a whole. Their expertise derived from knowledge of many rare disorders that came to be defined as genetic diseases. As Kevles notes, the emphasis became the family not the whole population, and the science became seen as valuable in its own right as well as for its contribution to understanding genetic disease (1992: 16).

As this brief overview shows, the development of genetics is not simply a story of scientific progress, but is also linked to particular actions and activities of scientists as they seek to promote approval and funding for their work. New boundaries and alliances are created: recent research in the United Kingdom demonstrates the persistence and power of this boundary work, where the new genetics is effectively separated from old eugenics through a range of rhetorical strategies. The new genetics is portrayed as based on good science, as opposed to the bad science of eugenics. It is said to produce neutral knowledge that may be used or abused by society; eugenics is described as being to do with totalitarian regimes, not liberal democracies. The new genetics emphasizes disease not behaviour, and individual choice rather than coercion (Kerr et al. 1998b). This serves to make legitimate the knowledge gained through genetic research and the authority of both scientists and clinicians (Kerr et al. 1997). This can deflect criticism of both science and scientists and encourage a conceptual separation of science from its applications. However, the aim of providing new understandings of the complex role of heredity in the aetiology of disease in order to improve diagnosis and treatment, which may be beneficial, has only the appearance of being value free. Definitions of disease are socially shaped and historically contingent. The interweaving of scientific and medical concerns cannot displace these processes. Genetic counseling may involve implicit or explicit values favouring particular actions and decisions that conform to dominant cultural values. Medicine itself is in a powerful position to, at least partly, determine the nature of clinical practice and what are deemed appropriate choices and interventions. This all suggests that any understanding of the new genetics must embrace this broader context. As Duster (1990) argues, although the 'front door' to eugenics is closed, the 'back door' of disease prevention remains powerfully present, all the more so for being taken for granted by those with the power to decide (scientists, clinicians, and biotechnology and pharmaceutical industries). Relatedly, the potential expansion of genetics from families at risk of rare disorders to larger populations at risk of common, multifactorial conditions, increases its 'clinical gaze' (Foucault 1989). Similarly, the influence of molecular genetics now extends into many areas of medical research and practice, from genetic testing and screening, to the development of new pharmaceuticals, such as those relating to the treatment of HIV and AIDS (Bell 1998).

The reconfiguration of human genetics, primarily as a medical concern from the 1950s onwards, provides the context upon which subsequent technological and scientific innovations developed. This alignment, although preceding any substantial advances in genetic technology, contributed to a powerful and winning discourse – that genetics, through medicine, can alleviate suffering and eliminate disease (Rose 1994). The medical receptivity to genetic explanations, and the utility of testing in clinical contexts, heralded the slower reinstatement of genetic explanations for a range of other behaviours and traits after their dismissal (post-World War II) in favour of a far greater emphasis on psychological and social explanations (Keller 1992; Nelkin 1992). Keller (1992) argues that this involved both a resurgence and transformation of genetic determinism: biology, by being more thoroughly understood, could be controlled. The promotional strategies of scientists offered the promise of genetic interventions aimed at improving the lives of individuals long before this became technologically feasible (Nelkin 1994). Support for genetic research could be assured, and the anticipation that genetics would significantly influence the experience of disease itself helped shape both research

and rhetoric. The Human Genome Project embodies these developments, placing genetic research firmly in the centre of cultural, economic, and health-related arenas.

The Human Genome Project: Mapping and Sequencing the Human Genome

The idea of a human genetic map was raised as early as the 1930s, with considerable prescience given the status of genetics and technology at that time. By the 1980s, the methods and technology were advancing so that such a venture could become a reality. The Human Genome Project, initiated in the late 1980s in the United States, is now an international, multimillion-dollar endeavour. It will result in the mapping of the 100 000 genes and the sequencing of the 3500 million base pairs that make up the whole human genome (although representing no one human being). It involves the hitherto unlikely alliance of the US Department of Energy (interested initially in genetic mutations caused by radiation) and the National Institutes of Health, traditional federal funders of the life sciences. However, the formation of the project, although reaching some scientific consensus, was neither uncontested nor uncontroversial. Some prominent molecular biologists were critical of blind sequencing, of the possibility of funds being diverted from other important projects, and for the centralizing of science into a few large centres because this might stifle creativity (Kevles 1992; Tauber and Sarkar 1992). However, the momentum for the project meant that it was unlikely to be abandoned. Eventually it involved new money and an agreed division of labour between the DOE and the NIH. The former would do the sequencing and develop associated technology, and the latter would concentrate on the mapping, which was to have initial priority, with a particular focus on disease. Cultural, economic, political, and technological processes shape the context of knowledge production, and the development of the human genome project, with its links to capital and the state, was both contingent and contested. However, in the end, as Kevles pointed out, 'The most compelling reality was the consequences of remaining out of the human genome sweepstakes' (1992: 29). Scientists, despite reservations, would have to become involved in order to get their work funded, and the nature of future research became at least partially determined.

The Human Genome Project became possible because of the association of genetics with understanding disease (Keller 1992). This made it an acceptable venture, or indeed an imperative, as health and the prevention of disease are taken-for-granted values. Protagonists actively promoted the project by stressing its usefulness in the area of health care, disease prevention, diagnosis, and treatment. However, the hyperbole of the rhetoric extended beyond this to include metaphors likening the project to the Holy Grail: it promised 'to teach us what it is to be human.' As discussed, scientists need to ensure public support for their work, and Yoxen (1982b) has noted how the development of molecular biology was a public process, involving scientists using the media to disseminate their message. The promises pronounced to justify the mapping and sequencing of the human genome operate as hopeful predictions of future scientific successes, yet can powerfully shape the direction of research (Keller 1992). They can also raise hopes and expectations within the public and influence a range of policy arenas. This is evident, most immediately and directly, in the provision of genetic testing and screening for disease.

Clinical Applications of the New Genetics: Genetic Tests and Screening

The identification of genes associated with both rare and common disorders has very rapidly led to the development of clinical tests for these genes in individuals. A gene is simply a 'string' of nucleotides at a defined location on a chromosome that has been associated with a specific trait and its variants. Each gene encodes a specific functional product (usually a protein). The sequence of nucleotides in the gene, that is, the order in which the nucleotides appear in the 'string,' may vary slightly between individuals, and consequently the protein products encoded by the genes may also vary, contributing to the variations in the trait that can be observed in the population. The different variants of genes are known as alleles and are the variants that produce disease as disease mutations. Genetic tests involve the examination of the sequence of nucleotides in a gene, either by direct methods to detect the sequence or indirectly through the use of gene probes or through the analysis of their protein products. By establishing whether one or both copies of an individual's particular gene harbour a known disease mutation, genetic tests potentially offer the ability to explain or predict the development of clinical disorders.

In practice, however, the predictive value of genetic tests is more uncertain. Knowing the allele of a gene may provide some prognostic information. For example, an individual identified as having the gene mutation associated with Huntington's Disease (HD) will almost certainly develop the slowly progressive dementia and uncontrollable body movements characteristic of the disorder. However, considerable uncertainty remains about the manner in which the disease will develop, for example, when symptoms will begin, the form they will take, and their severity and progression. For some conditions, this uncertainty may be so great that the information gained from identifying the gene variant is of little practical value.

Uncertainty arises primarily because there is no simple or straightforward relationship between the sequence of nucleotides identified by a genetic test and the manifestation of disease in an individual. For example, individuals with the same disease mutation may experience different clinical symptoms and show different pathological processes. Hubbard and Lewontin (1996) cite the example of autosomal dominant retinitis pigmentosa, a condition in which cells in the eye degenerate over time: 'In one family containing two sisters with the same mutation, however, one is blind whereas the other (the older one) drives a truck even at night' (Hubbard and Lewontin 1996: 1192). Conversely, individuals with different gene mutations may experience the same clinical symptoms. For example, it is estimated that there may be as many as 500 disease-producing variants of the gene associated with cystic fibrosis (CF), a disorder that involves severe digestive and lung problems and substantially reduces life expectancy. Some variants are associated with specific symptoms, but most are associated with symptoms that are indistinguishable from one another. This complex and highly variable relationship between the variants of genes identified by genetic tests and the development of clinical symptoms and disease in the individual makes it very difficult to interpret the significance or precise predictive meaning of a genetic test.

This difficulty is further complicated by the limitations imposed by cost and other practical considerations in genetic screening. Given the vast number of individual variants of genes, genetic screening may not seek to identify which particular alleles an individual carries, but look only for the presence of specific disease mutations that are known to be common in a given population. This inevitably means that a percentage of those who receive a negative test result do in fact carry a disease mutation. In Britain, for example, past CF carrier screening programmes have looked for only four to seven of the common mutations, with the result that about 15 per cent of those who carried a disease mutation might have been given a negative test result. Thus, while a positive test result may have some predictive value, the meaning for an individual of a negative test result is more difficult to interpret.

The value of programmes that offer genetic testing to populations or defined groups within populations is also unclear. Benefits are more likely to be derived from programmes for single-gene disorders. CF, for example, is a single-gene, autosomal recessive disorder, which means that those who carry one 'normal' allele and one disease mutation – that is, heterozygous carriers – are themselves healthy. However, if their partner is also a carrier, they have a one in four chance of having a child who inherits a mutation from each parent – that is, a child who is homozygous for the mutation and experiences the disease. Population screening makes it possible to identify heterozygous carriers who are not generally aware of their risk of having an affected child. Through counseling to explain their reproductive options, including prenatal diagnosis, such carriers may be offered the possibility of avoiding the birth of a baby with a severe chronic disease. Huntington's Disease, described above, provides another example. HD is a single-gene autosomal dominant disorder that means those who inherit the mutation from just one parent are likely eventually to develop the disease. It does not develop until later in life, however, so individuals with a family history of the disease live for a considerable time with uncertainty about whether they will eventually develop the condition. By identifying at an earlier age those who do and those who do not carry the disease mutation, genetic testing can reduce this uncertainty and provide individuals with information they need to plan their lives.

What is less convincing, however, is the value of screening programmes for genes that 'predispose' individuals to disease. In contrast to single-gene disorders, most common chronic diseases with a genetic component, such as diabetes, heart disease, and various forms of cancer, have a complex aetiology, involving interactions amongst many genes and between genes and the environment (social, psychological, biological, infectious, and physical). Genetic epidemiology has developed as a discipline to explore the contribution of genes and gene/environment interactions to the occurrence of disease in a population (Khoury et al. 1993). However, only a start has been made on the vast amount of research that will be required to identify significant polymorphisms (variants of genes found in more than 1 per cent of the population that are passed on to the next generation) and to establish the extent of their contribution, on their own and in interaction with environmental factors, to the production of dis-

ease. In the meantime, there is limited value in screening to identify mutations of only one or two genes that may 'predispose' an individual to a disease with a complex aetiology.

This is well illustrated in relation to breast cancer, in which the identification of two genes, BRCA1 and BRCA2, has created the possibility of genetic testing programmes for those with a strong family history of the disorder. The disease mutations for these genes confer on a woman a lifetime risk of developing breast cancer of up to 85 per cent, and a lifetime risk of developing ovarian cancer of 45 per cent. However, over a hundred variants of the BRCA1 gene have already been identified, and only a few are associated with cancer tumours. Moreover, only a small proportion of breast cancers (about 5 per cent) is associated with the identified mutations: the vast majority of breast cancers arise from more complex interactions of genetic and environmental factors. It is therefore very doubtful whether women will gain much benefit from tests for these two predisposing genes. Only a few women would be regarded by clinical geneticists as having an inherited risk, but even for these women, given the high prevalence of breast cancer in the general population of women, a negative test result (showing she does not carry a mutation associated with tumour growth) would offer little reassurance of avoiding breast cancer. For those who receive a positive test result, the benefits are again of limited value. Learning that she carries a gene predisposing for breast cancer reduces only one form of uncertainty; it does not predict exactly which tumour she may develop or when, or even whether a cancer might occur at all. Moreover, as Collins (the director of the Human Genome Project) warns, 'We are still profoundly uncertain about the appropriate medical care of women with these mutations' (Collins 1996: 187). This means that a positive test result may simply increase a woman's anxiety and condemn her to years of surveillance, or drastic prophylactic measures such as bilateral mastectomy and oophorectomy. With so little to be gained from testing, it is not surprising that many doctors have reservations about offering or recommending it (Hubbard and Lewontin 1996).

Despite the rhetoric of promise in relation to preventing and treating disease, clinical applications derived from the new genetics are limited. However, the rapid pace of research suggests that the potential of new pharmaceuticals and gene therapy will continue to offer the promise of future clinical interventions. Doctors, scientists, and lay people express ambivalence and concerns about current and future developments. The experience of the latter in relation to testing and screening will now be examined.

Lay Responses to Genetic Testing and Screening

Uncertainties relating to the predictive ability of genetic tests and their benefits are mirrored in the ambivalence of lay responses. People may take information on genetic risk into account, but it is interpreted and evaluated in the context of their individual values and concerns. These may differ considerably from the essentially utilitarian values that underpin screening and testing programmes. Although surveys conducted in a number of countries have reported that most people regard developments in medical genetics in positive terms and have an essentially optimistic view of the benefits that genetic testing can bring (Green 1992; Hietala et al. 1995), such acceptance has not been reflected in decision making in practice. Where screening and testing programmes have actually been offered, lay responses have been considerably more sceptical than these attitudes would suggest, and rates of acceptance of tests are considerably less than proponents had expected. This has been the case across a wide range of conditions. Early surveys conducted amongst individuals with a family history of HD, for example, indicated that two-thirds wanted to have a genetic test for the condition (Kessler et al. 1987). When testing became available, however, less than 15 per cent of those who initially expressed interest came forward for testing (Craufurd et al. 1989). Similarly, community surveys suggested that between two-thirds and three-quarters of individuals would want to be tested for CF carrier status (Williamson et al. 1989). When screening programmes were introduced, however, interest in them outside the context of pregnancy and antenatal care was almost negligible (Bekker et al. 1993; Tambor et al. 1994). Responses to breast cancer screening appear to be developing in a similar direction. Interest in genetic screening amongst women with a family history of breast cancer has been widespread (Julian-Reynier et al. 1996; Lerman et al. 1995). However, where women who belong to known high-risk families have been offered testing through research programmes, only a minority have ultimately accepted it (Lerman et al. 1996). It appears that, while the lay public may acknowledge the benefits of advances in genetics in principle, in practice they are less convinced of their value.

Why has screening been rejected on such a large scale? One factor is the influence of lay understandings of heredity and inherited disease. Heredity plays an important role in lay explanations of illness, and research is beginning to tease out the complex sets of rules and conditions that shape perceptions of risk and vulnerability (Richards 1996). Central to these is the commonsense assumption that you can pass on to future generations only those conditions that have been present in past generations. For recessive conditions such as CF, the great majority of carriers (for whom community carrier screening is specifically intended) have no family history of the condition and generally feel at little risk of having an affected child (Loader et al. 1996; Watson et al. 1991). The pre-test information on population risk provided in screening programmes may make little sense to individuals in the context of their existing beliefs and assumptions and, despite educational materials, many continue to feel that screening is of little relevance to them.

A second and perhaps more significant factor, however, is the recognition that the 'costs' of testing may outweigh its 'benefits.' Where effective treatments are available for genetic disorders, the benefits of testing are clear and include release from surveillance programmes (often involving invasive procedures) for those identified as not having the relevant gene mutation. For example, the identification of the gene associated with polyposis colii, a form of inherited colon cancer, means that children of known suffers can be tested to establish whether they have inherited the disease mutation. Those who have may then be offered regular colonoscopy to identify early symptoms and surgical treatment when they appear, while those who are identified as not having inherited the disease mutation can be free of further screening. In circumstances such as these, it is more common for individuals identified as 'at risk' by their family history to accept genetic testing (Evans et al. 1997).

However, it is a feature of genetic disorders that the increasing ability to identify them accurately is not matched by the ability to treat them effectively. Where effective treatment does not follow, individuals may perceive no obvious benefit from testing. Women with a family history of breast cancer who declined genetic testing, for example, indicated that whatever their test result, they would continue to see themselves as at risk and to have regular breast screening (Julian-Renier et al. 1996; Lerman et al. 1995). Where the result has no practical implications, there may seem little point in having the test. Conversely, where the potential costs of receiving a positive result are perceived to be very high, costs may become an insurmountable barrier to testing. For example, amongst individuals with a family history of HD who were offered presymptomatic testing, many were concerned about the psychological difficulties of living with the knowledge that they would develop HD if they tested positive, and with the guilt they would feel if they found they had passed on the disease mutation to their children (Quaid and Morris 1993). For these individuals, ambiguity and uncertainty were welcomed for the broader possibilities they embraced, and resisting a definitive genetic label became important in its own right.

Other costs of a positive test result have been described by those who are not themselves ill but who are identified as carriers of a recessive disorder. These include feelings of stigma and anxieties about discrimination in relation to employment and insurance, as well as concern about the implications of being 'at risk' of having an affected child. These costs may be brought into greater focus simply by the offer of genetic testing. For example, for those who are not currently pregnant, the potential costs of being identified as a CF carrier have been found to loom much larger in their assessment of screening than any potential benefits that it might bring (Clayton et al. 1996). For those who are pregnant, even the 'benefits' of screening often appear of limited value. While in theory the reproductive choices available to carriers include adoption and various forms of assisted reproduction, those who are already pregnant are limited to prenatal diagnosis and the option to terminate an affected pregnancy. Where abortion is unacceptable, or the individuals do not want to be put in a position where they would have to make such a decision, the 'benefits' of screening could be perceived as another form of 'costs.' In these circumstances, individuals may feel it is better to remain ignorant of their genetic status, particularly when the momentum of the medical process may be difficult to resist once screening has been accepted. It is this crescendo of intervention and surveillance that gives force to wider concerns about the social aspects of the new genetics.

Broader Social Concerns

While genetic testing raises very specific issues at the level of the individual, his family, and social institutions such as health-care organizations and welfare services, there are broader concerns raised about genetic research. Three main areas of critique relate to genetic determinism, including where genetic explanations are accorded too great an emphasis, the associated process of geneticization where disease is increasingly seen in genetic terms (Lippman 1992a,b), and the limitations of a reductionist approach. Duster

(1990) has argued that there is increasing appropriation of genetic explanations, whereby a causal role is given to genetics for a range of socially derived categories (for example, criminality and intelligence). The 1970s witnessed a move away from sociological and psychological explanations towards biological ones. Although this did not come from molecular biology itself, but from psychology, psychiatry, and physical anthropology, this shift paved the way for a prioritizing of genetic explanations in medicine (Keller 1992). However, interest is now resurging into the genetic basis of a range of behavioural traits and disorders, including mental illness. Several commentators, from within genetics and elsewhere, have raised concerns that genetic determinism may result in a neglect of environmental factors, also important in disease aetiology (Clarke 1995; Duster 1990; Muller-Hill 1993; Willis 1998). The narrowing definitions of disease resulting from genetic research also results in the narrowing of interventions, causing an expansion of services such as testing and treatments, ever more tailored to specific genotypes.

Geneticization, where more traits and diseases are identified as having a genetic component, is particularly evident in the clinical setting through the expansion of prenatal testing (Lippman 1992a,b). In the United States this is coupled by a strong legal imperative, where doctors may be sued for wrongful birth. Through prenatal testing, a parent may be identified as a carrier of a recessive or dominant condition, and the foetus may be tested if necessary. Although more and more people and their unborn children can be identified as potentially diseased, there remains little prospect of intervention other than via selective abortion. The powerful rhetorics associated with preventive medicine take an especially potent form in genetics, particularly because they maintain an emphasis on individual choice. Of course, the choices available to someone are always limited, and the range of appropriate actions is similarly constrained.

Most obviously, the rhetoric of disease prevention and cure directly affects the lives of disabled people. Shakespeare (1995) has stressed that the taken-for-granted assumptions about impairment and quality of life should be more openly contested. The new genetics, he argues, affects disabled people by undermining the authenticity of their lives, reinforcing the hegemony of biomedicine through eugenic elimination of impairment, and through the active promotion of biological determinism. More generally, genetic determinism can reduce social problems to individual pathology. A language of individual rights masks strong cultural pressures to make particular decisions, and to hold individuals responsible for their own health and for the genetic health of their offspring.

Other criticisms of the new genetics and the Human Genome Project focus on the scientific limitations of reductionism (Eisenberg 1995; Rose 1997; Tauber and Sarkar 1992). The link between genotype (genetic makeup) and phenotype (physical characteristics and symptoms) is complex; the range of genetic diversity and the complex action of genes and their interaction with the environment challenge the usefulness of a reductionist approach, as evidenced in the limitations of genetic testing described earlier. The quest to map and sequence the whole human genome will not necessarily help with explaining complex biological interactions, and thus may not answer questions significant to biology. Shuster has noted that 'The leaders of the Human Genome Project have thus created, through their world views, a "paradigm shift" in genetics and an aggressive, simplifying, reductionist perception of genetic knowledge and of humans. Their immediate success in research strategy has enabled them to pass persuasively from science to social implications and to express powerfully their views in the form of reductionist and deterministic generalization in advance of experimental evidence' (Shuster 1992: 121). That this paradigm finds a powerful position in popular culture has been well documented by Nelkin and Lindee (1995).

Science and its applications, then, do not operate in a vacuum but reflect and influence wider social and cultural processes. The social and cultural changes in late modernity suggest a reification of the individual (Giddens 1990, 1991) concerned with planning his or her future. There is also a growing emphasis on health as something that an individual can and should have some control over. This may contribute to an imperative of health as something that individuals, with the support of medical technology and surveillance, should seek to attain. Genetic interventions may reinforce this emphasis on individual responsibility for health. Any difference between health and beauty or perfection may be conflated, potentially blurring a distinction between interventions that enhance human potential and those that ameliorate disease. There are concerns that developments in cloning and gene therapy may lead inexorably down this road, both because of limited regulation and through some acceptance of therapeutic potentials. The negative values attributed to disease and impairment are often taken for granted, rather than openly discussed. However, definitions of health and disease are socially produced, involving cultural values as well as political and economic processes (Petersen 1998). However,

an emphasis on the promotion of health, the prevention of disease, and the amelioration of suffering may be used to dismiss eugenic concerns about engineering genetic improvement and mask the values underpinning definitions of disease and how those thus identified are treated. Society is hierarchically organized; people have differential access to health-care resources, and indeed inequalities in health are at least in part socially derived. Genetic interventions may reinforce inequalities if only those who have sufficient resources are able to access the relevant technology. This may lead to a genetic underclass, consisting of those unable to make use of genetic interventions, or those excluded from mainstream society because of their genetic makeup.

The link between biotechnology companies and genetic research and practice adds further impetus to genetic determinism and geneticization. Industry is directly involved in the race to complete the mapping and sequencing of the human genome because of the lucrative patenting this will bring. The invention of tests for a range of genetic conditions, both common and rare, or for genetic predisposition to disease (even though still of dubious practical value to patients), is proving profitable for these companies. Such interventions reinforce dependence by doctors and patients on high-technology diagnostics and create definitions of disease based on genotype not phenotype. Genetic tests are also proving particularly useful in the United States, where both insurance companies and employers may use genetic information to screen out individuals at risk of genetic disease. The implications of this may be the creation of an uninsurable genetic underclass, and of the onus of responsibility for workplace-induced ill health being placed on the individuals themselves. Medicine, the biotechnology industry, and insurance companies are powerful lobbyists, all of whom may benefit from increasing the range of medical interventions, dependent on ever more complex technologies, aimed at predicting, diagnosing, or treating disease at the level of the individual. A powerful alliance between medicine and the biotechnology industry will shape the choices available to individuals and divert attention away from the social processes that shape inequalities, the experience of ill health, and the human condition.

However, neither science nor culture is monolithic, and dissension and diversity are present in both. The Human Genome Project, although rapidly progressing in its aim to map and sequence the whole human genome, has not met its early promise; it has its ardent critics both within and outside biology. Popular culture, while embracing and reinforcing genetic determinism, does not necessarily reflect the lives of ordinary people, for whom scepticism and ambivalence towards science in general, and genetics in particular, may lead to a more critical engagement with the new genetics (Kerr et al. 1998c). Public debate involving a range of people may help to generate critical and useful discussion on the direction of research and acceptable applications. This may enable a more creative dialogue to be achieved at the level of research and policy.

Public Debate and Public Involvement

Because many different commentators, professionals, and lay groups agree that the new genetics has significant social implications, public debate may flourish, forging new paths in democratic science and health-care policy. For example, in an unprecedented acceptance by scientists of the implications of their work for society, the Human Genome Project has devoted roughly 3 per cent of its budget to consider ethical, legal, and social issues. Acceptance of some responsibility for the social impact of science is clearly important, although this can also protect the authority of science in an increasingly ambivalent and sceptical environment (Beck 1992; Gieryn 1983; Kerr et al. 1997). Scientists play a key role on committees charged with considering the social, ethical, and legal implications of genetics research and applications and are thus in a powerful position to frame the ensuing debates; this may serve to limit the nature of public involvement.

Public debate is often cited as an appropriate way of restraining the potential 'abuse' of genetics. However, the tendency is to use calls for public debate to promote the need for better public understanding of science (Nuffield Council on Bioethics 1993), rather than for inclusive and critical engagement with policy decisions. This discourse rests on the twin assumptions that the public is generally not well informed about the scientific foundations of the new genetics, and that such scientific knowledge is essential for meaningful debate and decision making. In Britain, for example, a prominent clinical geneticist has pointed to the 'poor state of education of the public regarding science in general and genetics in particular' as limiting the possibilities for public debate about future developments (Harper 1992: 721). In North America, too, scientists and clinicians have bemoaned the fact that 'the public is grossly ignorant of the discoveries of science and of the way science works' (Griffiths 1993: 230). Public response to the first wave of services developed from the new genetics has been seen

as evidence of the poor state of public understanding, rather than reflecting active decision making. Knowledge questionnaires, often administered in conjunction with screening or testing, have been taken as providing further confirmation of public ignorance. In many ways this reflects the views of the public itself. When asked in population surveys, only a minority of respondents report 'a great deal of knowledge' or 'a clear understanding' of genetics or genetic screening (Durant et al. 1996). Even in more informal contexts, lay people express anxieties about their lack of relevant knowledge and competence in discussing issues associated with the new genetics (Kerr et al. 1998a). Such self-deprecation may be another barrier to effective public engagement with science.

However, the characterization of public mistrust and resistance to genetic testing and screening, as based on popular ignorance of scientific facts, can be challenged. As Turney (1995) has noted, much less attention is paid to why people might want to understand genetics or what it is that they might wish to know. Knowledge, of various kinds, will be taken up and used in different ways by different people, in different contexts, depending on both relevancy and social opportunity (Lambert and Rose 1996; Parsons and Atkinson 1992; Wynne 1991). The 'deficit model' of public understanding is challenged once lay accounts are analyzed in their rich complexity. For example, Kerr et al. (1998a) found that the general public was able to draw on a range of knowledge that they could mobilize to produce sophisticated and discerning arguments about the social and ethical issues raised by the new genetics – the very area in which scientists and others demand public debate. Moreover, their knowledge extended well beyond the 'technical' information of concern in traditional studies of the public understanding of science to incorporate knowledge in a range of other domains, including knowledge of the methods of science, of the institutional processes of science, and cultural knowledge. The 'factual accuracy' of their knowledge varied, reflecting the range of personal and professional experience on which individuals could draw. However, Kerr et al. argue that factual accuracy was of limited significance, as information that was strictly accurate or technically correct was not necessary for people to be able to discuss issues around the new genetics and health in a competent and sophisticated manner.

There are dangers in putting too great an emphasis on work that assesses the public's ability to reproduce a set of scientific 'facts' at a level deemed appropriate by scientists or medical professionals. The static mastery of 'facts' *per se* is of limited value to the lay public, and the way in which people seek out and use those facts is more important. Standardized questionnaires derived from textbook accounts of genetics inevitably document gaps in lay knowledge of scientific information. By contrast, research methods that put lay knowledge at centre stage are able to reveal the extent of expertise amongst the general public. Even those who claim not to know about 'medical science' generally demonstrate considerable scientific knowledge in explaining their condition to others. As Lambert and Rose suggest, 'specific medical knowledge is often implicit and perhaps what lay people themselves know, they do not regard as scientific' (Lambert and Rose 1996: 78). The status attributed to a lay person's knowledge is also sensitive to the context in which it is elicited. Where lay knowledge is not perceived or accepted as relevant (as is generally the case in clinical encounters or research studies) and where power relations devalue their perspective, individuals are less likely to regard themselves as possessing any expertise (Kerr et al. 1998a).

There is considerable misunderstanding of the public by scientists and care-providers, who tend to over emphasize a knowledge deficit and denigrate 'lay expertise' (Kerr et al. 1998a). Indeed, Macintyre (1995) has called for the need for a better scientific understanding of the public. It should be remembered that scientific knowledge itself is not a static set of facts that can be correctly grasped once and for all. Medical science, in particular, is contested and provisional, with competing disciplines providing alternative explanations for diseases, and recommendations from each discipline subject to continuous revision. Some of this debate takes place within the public domain, as risks and retractions are covered in the media. Lay people are aware of the provisional nature of scientific knowledge, which may engender appropriate ambivalence and scepticism (Kerr et al. 1998c; Lambert and Rose 1996). As well as misrepresenting the extent of expertise amongst the lay population, the emphasis on the poor state of the public's understanding of science in general, and genetics in particular, may be misleading in another way. That is, there is a risk that in stressing the poor understanding on the part of the lay population, the gap between lay and medical understanding may be exaggerated (Boulton and Williamson 1995). This can maintain a divide between lay and expert knowledge, which reinforces the legitimacy of the latter and preserves the privileged position of science and medicine in framing the social impact of the new genetics. While education remains important, a mutual recognition of expertise should help pave the way for open dialogue and debate across professional groups and the public. Informed discussion

must recognize lay experience of the new genetics, as it is applied in health-care settings in particular. Nuanced understanding, which embraces responses of ambivalence and contestation, may contribute positively to the social shaping of genetic practice. Both proponents and critics of the new genetics must engage with the views and lived experience of those drawn into contact with genetic services. Failure to do so can lead to a reliance on professional expertise and its hegemonic discourse, and also to a tendency to view the lay public as cultural dupes, willingly embracing the promotional rhetoric of genetic determinism and the power of the gene.

CONCLUSION

The new genetics has the potential to fundamentally alter the way in which disease is defined, understood, and managed. It raises profound issues within health care and beyond. The values associated with the new genetics, especially the prevention and treatment of disease, both reflect and take for granted a range of social and cultural processes. The implications of ever more narrowly defined disease categories and ever more complex treatments and interventions may lead to an expansion of health-care services aimed at the individual and his or her genetic make-up. The costs to society of these developments will be vast, and may lead to greater inequalities in both health and health-care provision. At a wider level, the inclusion of a range of other traits within the genetic gaze may incite eugenic intervention aimed at improving the human condition. Although genetic testing and screening has limited value, and has not always been taken up enthusiastically, wider use of testing for insurance or employment purposes remains likely. Research continues apace, and developments in cloning techniques, gene therapy, pharmaceuticals, and xenotransplantation all suggest that genetic science will remain at the forefront of health-care debates and thus demand the critical attention of social scientists interested in health and medicine.

Understanding these issues requires a consideration of the social contexts that shape genetic research and medical practice, as well as individual and cultural responses to these developments. It is important to recognize that scientific knowledge is socially produced, and that there are strong cultural, economic, and political reasons why research takes the direction it does (Barnes et al. 1996). In relation to genetics, a close association with biomedicine – with the rhetoric of the ability to detect and cure disease – offers what may be a culturally acceptable form of genetic determinism. This can help protect scientific authority, enable ever more developments in medical interventions, and serve the interests of the biotechnology industries. Although some improvements in health will almost certainly derive from genetic interventions, the discourse of promise is matched by one of concern both within and outside science and medicine. The way in which genetics and genetic services develop is not uncontested, and is shaped by the interplay of interests of a range of competing groups. These groups are themselves diverse, containing proponents and critics alike. A recognition of this contestation and the differential power associated with different groups' positions is a necessary first step towards the possibility of a social shaping of science and technology that may be truly inclusive of the range of interests of those affected by, or concerned with, such developments.

Although it has been recognized that vigorous public debate may serve to constrain potential abuses of genetics, the underlying discourses of such pleas tend to preserve a lay–expert divide, with the public construed as ignorant. They also tend to separate science from its application, with an emphasis only on the social context and implications of the latter. At the present time, the debates that take place around the new genetics, and the committees and regulatory bodies involved, tend to be dominated by scientists and clinicians. Their discourse embraces an important but limited set of ethical concerns (Kerr et al. 1997). This may indeed suppress more critical discussion, especially around the role of industry in a free market (Paul 1992) and around issues relating to definitions of disease and quality of life (Shakespeare 1995). The emphasis on individual choice, so fundamental to the current debates about the new genetics and health, fails to recognize the structural limitations on choice and casts issues of health and disease in individual and medical terms (Petersen 1998).

Current developments in genetics are shifting away from an emphasis on testing for the prevention of disease towards ever more sophisticated classifications of disease, diagnostics, and treatments (Bell 1998). This trend seems to generate much less public debate than, for example, the use of prenatal testing, or the use of genetic information by insurance companies. However, the implications are also far-reaching: disease may become increasingly defined by technology not patient experience, yet also become an attribute of an individual patient in terms of their unique genetic make-up, lifestyle, and social location. Research into the social causes of disease may take an increasingly genetic turn, although this may also promote understanding of the complex relationship between genes and the environment. However, industry, in terms of developing pharmaceutical and diagnostic tools, will be much more interested in promoting interventions aimed at the level of the individual rather than at the amelioration of the social factors known to contribute to inequalities in health.

A social scientific understanding of the social context of the new genetics should embrace not only an understanding of the behaviour of individuals and groups in response to scientific developments, but also a broader analysis of these developments themselves. Social science, through its emphasis on social relations, has a crucial role to play in promoting an understanding of scientific and technological developments as rooted in social action and cultural values. Its contribution can help to develop a reflexive awareness of the context within which research and its applications are developed. By analyzing what is often taken for granted, and by challenging traditional boundaries – for example, the distinction between experts and lay people, or health and disease – social scientists are well placed to move discussion forward. In this way society, in the form of its social institutions as well as through the behaviour of individuals and groups, will be ready for the applications arising from the new genetics because it has been openly involved in determining the direction of research and practice. Social science also has a particular part to play in ensuring that the social factors that influence health, illness, and disease remain on the research and policy agenda. By working with geneticists and others to develop holistic and sophisticated understanding of the range of processes that make up human experience, complex models of human society and behaviour can be developed. Such analyses from social scientists, along with the range of lay expertise present in different public groups, and the diversity of views amongst scientists and clinicians themselves, should form the core of all debates and policies around the new genetics. As Duster observes: 'In a heterogeneous mix, the public forum for this debate needs to be vigorous and informed, not just by modest levels of technical knowledge about genetic or molecular biological developments, but about the role of power and the relative social locations of key actors in the determination of the knowledge and its application' (1990: 128).

REFERENCES

Barnes, B., Bloor, D., and Henry, J. (1996) *Scientific Knowledge. A Sociological Analysis.* London: Athlone Press.

Beck, U. (1992) *Risk Society: Towards a New Modernity.* London: Sage.

Bekker H., Modell, M., Nenniss, G., Silver, A., Mathew, C., Bobrow, M., and Marteau, T. (1993) 'Uptake of cystic fibrosis testing in primary care: Supply push or demand pull?' *British Medical Journal,* 306: 1584–6.

Bell, J. (1998) 'The new genetics: The new genetics in clinical practice', *British Medical Journal,* 36: 618–20.

Boulton, M. and Williamson, R. (1995) 'General practice and the new genetics: What do general practitioners know about community carrier screening for cystic fibrosis?' *Public Understanding of Science,* 4: 255–67.

Clarke, A. (1995) 'Population screening for genetic susceptibility to disease', *British Medical Journal,* 311: 35–8.

Clayton, E., Hannig, V., Pfotenhauer, J., Parker, R., Campbell, P., and Phillips, J. (1996) 'Lack of interest by nonpregnant couples in population-based cystic fibrosis carrier screening', *American Journal of Human Genetics,* 58: 617–27.

Collins, F. (1996) 'BRCA1 – Lots of mutations, lots of dilemmas', *New England Journal of Medicine,* 18: 186–8.

Craufurd, D., Dodge, A., Kerzain-Storrar, L., and Harris, R. (1989) 'Uptake of presymptomatic predictive testing for Huntington's disease', *Lancet, ii:* 603–5.

Durant, J., Hansen, A., and Bauer, M. (1996) 'Public understanding of the new genetics', in T. Marteau and M. Richards (eds), *The Troubled Helix: Social and Psychological Implications of the New Human Genetics.* Cambridge: Cambridge University Press.

Duster, T. (1990) *Backdoor to Eugenics.* New York/London: Routledge.

Eisenberg, L. (1995) 'Medicine – Molecular, monetary, or more than both?' *Journal of the American Medical Association,* 274: 331–4.

Evans, D., Maher, E., Macleod, R., Davies, R., and Craufurd, D. (1997) 'Uptake of genetic testing for cancer predisposition', *Journal of Medical Genetics,* 34: 746–8.

Foucault, M. (1989) *The Birth of the Clinic.* London: Routledge.

Giddens, A. (1990) *The Consequences of Modernity.* Cambridge: Polity Press.

Giddens, A. (1991) *Modernity and Self-identity. Self and Society in the Late Modern Age.* Cambridge: Polity Press.

Gieryn, T.F. (1983) 'Boundary-work and the demarcation of science from non-science: Strains and inter-ests in Professional ideologies of scientists', *American Sociological Review,* 48: 781–95.

Gieryn, T.F. (1995) 'Boundaries of science', in S. Jasanoff, G. Markle, J. Petersen, and T. Pinch (eds), *Handbook of Science and Technology.* London: Sage. pp. 393–443.

Green, J. (1992) 'Principles and practicalities of carrier screening: Attitudes of recent parents', *Journal of Medical Genetics,* 29: 313–19.

Griffiths, A. (1993) 'What does the public really need to know about genetics?' *American Journal of Human Genetics,* 52: 230–2.

Harper, P. (1992) 'Genetics and public health', *British Medical Journal,* 340: 721.

Hietala, M., Hakone, A., Ro, R., Nimble, P., Peltonen, L., and Aula, P. (1995) 'Attitudes towards genetic testing among the general population and relatives of patients with severe genetic disease: A survey from Finland', *American Journal of Human Genetics,* 566: 1493–500.

Hubbard, R., and Lewontin, R.C. (1996) 'Pitfalls of genetic testing', *New England Journal of Medicine,* 334: 1192–4.

Judson, H.F. (1992) 'A history of the science and technology behind the gene mapping and sequencing', in D.J. Kevles, and L. Hood (eds), *Scientific and Social Issues in the Human Genome Project.* Cambridge, MA: Harvard University Press.

Julian-Reynier, C., Eisinger, F., Vennin, P., Chabal, F., Aurran, Y., Nogues, C., Bignon, Y.-J., Machelard-Roumagnac, M., Maugard-Louboutin, C., Serin, D., Blan, B., Orsoni, P., and Sobol, H. (1996) 'Attitudes towards cancer predictive testing and transmission of information to the family', *Journal of Medical Genetics,* 33: 731–6.

Keller, E.F. (1992) 'Nature, nurture, and the Human Genome Project', in D.J. Kevles and L. Hood (eds), *Scientific and Social Issues in the Human Genome Project.* Cambridge, MA: Harvard University Press. pp. 281–99.

Kerr, A., Cunningham-Burley, S., and Amos, A. (1997) 'The new genetics: professionals' discursive boundaries', *Sociological Review,* 45: 279–303.

Kerr, A., Cunningham-Burley, S., and Amos, A. (1998a) 'The new genetics and health: Mobilising lay expertise', *Public Understanding of Science,* 7: 41–60.

Kerr, A., Cunningham-Burley, S., and Amos, A. (1998b) 'Eugenics and the new genetics in Britain: Examining contemporary professionals' accounts', *Science, Technology and Human Values,* 23: 175–98.

Kerr, A., Cunningham-Burley, S., and Amos, A. (1998c) 'Drawing the line: An analysis of lay people's discussions about the new genetics', *Public Understanding of Science,* 7: 113–33.

Kessler, S., Field, T., Worth, L., and Mosbarger, H. (1987) 'Attitudes of persons at risk for Huntington's disease towards predictive testing', *American Journal of Medical Genetics,* 26: 259–70.

Kevles, D.J. (1992) 'Out of eugenics: The historical politics of the human genome', in D.J. Kevles, and L. Hood (eds), *Scientific and Social Issues in the Human Genome Project*. Cambridge, MA: Harvard University Press. pp. 3–36.

Kevles, Daniel J. (1995) *In the Name of Eugenics. Genetics and the Uses of Human Heredity*. Cambridge, MA: Harvard University Press.

Khoury, M., Beaty, T., and Cohen, B. (1993) *Fundamentals of Genetic Epidemiology*. Oxford: Oxford University Press.

Lambert, H. and Rose, H. (1996) 'Disembodied knowledge? Making sense of medical science,' in A. Irwin and B. Wynne (eds), *Misunderstanding Science? The Public Reconstruction of Science and Technology*. Cambridge: Cambridge University Press. pp. 65–83.

Lerman, C., Seay, J., Balshem, A., and Audrain, J. (1995) *American Journal of Medical Genetics*, 57: 385–92.

Lerman, C., Narod, S., Schulman, K., Hughes, C., Gomez-Caminero, A., Bonney, G., Gold, K., Trock, B., Main, D., Lynch, J., Fulmore, C., Snyder, C., Lemon, S., Conway, T., Tonin, P., Lenoir, G., and Lynch, H. (1996) 'BRCA1 testing in families with hereditary breast–ovarian cancer', *Journal of the American Medical Association*, 275: 1885–92.

Lippman, A. (1992a) 'Led (astray) by genetic maps: The cartography of the human genome and health care', *Social Science and Medicine*, 35: 1469–76.

Lippman, A. (1992b) 'Prenatal genetic testing and screening: Constructing needs and reinforcing inequities', *American Journal of Law and Medicine*, 17: 15–50.

Loader, S.P., Caldwell, A., Kozyra, J., Levenkron, C., Boehm, H., and Kazazian, P.R. (1996) *American Journal of Human Genetics*, 59: 234–47.

Macintyre, S. (1995) 'The public understanding of science or the scientific understanding of the public? A review of the social context of the 'new genetics', *Public Understanding of Science*, 4: 223–32.

MacKenzie, D. (1978) 'Eugenics in Britain', *Social Studies of Science*, 6: 499–532.

Muller-Hill, B. (1993) 'The Shadow of Genetic Injustice', *Nature*, 362: 491–2.

Nelkin, D. (1992) 'The Social Power of Genetic Information', in D.J. Kevles, and L. Hood (eds), *Scientific and Social Issues in the Human Genome Project*. Cambridge, MA: Harvard University Press. pp. 177–90.

Nelkin, D. (1994) 'Promotional metaphors and their popular appeal', *Public Understanding of Science*, 3: 25–31.

Nelkin, D. and Lindee, S.M. (1995) *The DNA Mystique. The Gene as a Cultural Icon*. New York: Freeman.

Nuffield Council on Bioethics (1993) *Genetic Screening Ethical Issues*. London: Nuffield Council on Bioethics.

Parsons, E. and Atkinson, P. (1992) 'Lay constructions of genetic risk', *Sociology of Health and Illness* 14: 437–55.

Paul, D. (1992) 'Eugenic anxieties, social realities, and political choices', *Social Research*, 59: 663–83.

Petersen, A. (1998) 'The new genetics and the politics of public health', *Critical Public Health*, 8: 59–71.

Quaid, K. and Morris, M. (1993) 'Reluctance to undergo predictive testing: The case of Huntington Disease', *American Journal of Medical Genetics*, 45: 41–45.

Richards, M. (1996) 'Families, kinship and genetics', in T. Marteau and M. Richards (eds), *The Troubled Helix*. Cambridge: Cambridge University Press. pp. 249–73.

Rose, H. (1994) *Love, Power and Knowledge. Towards a Feminist Transformation of the Sciences*. Cambridge: Polity Press.

Rose, S. (1997) *Lifelines. Biology, Freedom, Determinism*. Harmondsworth, Allen Lane: Penguin.

Shakespeare, T. (1995) 'Back to the future? New genetics and disabled people', *Critical Social Policy*, 44/45: 22–35.

Shuster, E. (1992) 'Determinism and reductionism: A greater threat because of the human genome project?' in G.J. Annas, and E. Sherman (eds), *Gene Mapping. Using Law and Ethics as Guides*. Oxford: Oxford University Press.

Tambor, E., Bernhardt, B., Chase, G., Faden, R., Geller, G., Hofman, K., and Holtzman, N. (1994) 'Offering cystic fibrosis carrier screening to an HMO population: Factors associated with utilization', *American Journal of Human Genetics*, 55: 626–37.

Tauber, A.I. and Sarkar, S. (1992) 'The Human Genome Project: Has blind reductionism gone too far?' *Perspectives in Biology and Medicine*, 35: 220–35.

Turney, J. (1995) 'The public understanding of genetics – where next?' *European Journal of Genetics and Society*, 1: 5–20.

Watson, E., Mayall, E., Chapple, J., Dalziel, M., Harrington, K., Willams, C., and Williamson, R. (1991) 'Screening for carriers of cystic fibrosis through primary health care services', *British Medical Journal*, 303: 504–7.

Williamson, R., Allison, M., Bentley, T., Lim, S., Watson, E., Chapple, J., Adam, S., and Boulton, M. (1989) 'Community attitudes to cystic fibrosis carrier testing in England: A pilot study', *Prenatal Diagnosis*, 9: 727–34.

Willis, E. (1998) 'Public health, private genes: The social consequences of genetic biotechnologies', *Critical Public Health*, 8: 131–9.

Wynne, B. (1991) 'Knowledges in context', *Science, Technology and Human Values*, 19: 1–17.

Yates, J.R.W. (1996) 'Medical genetics', *British Medical Journal*, 312: 1021–5.

Yoxen, E. (1982a) 'Constructing Genetic Diseases', in P. Wright and A. Treacher (eds) *The Problem of Medical Knowledge. Examining the Social Construction of Medicine*. Edinburgh: Edinburgh University Press. Chapter 7, pp. 144–61.

Yoxen, E. (1982b) 'Giving life a new meaning: The rise of the molecular biology establishment', in N. Elias, H. Martins, and R. Whitley (eds), *Scientific Establishments and Hierarchies. Sociology of the Sciences*, VI: 123–43.

Part Two
THE EXPERIENCE OF
HEALTH AND ILLNESS

2.1

Cultural Variation in the Experience of Health and Illness

ANN McELROY AND MARY ANN JEZEWSKI

INTRODUCTION

Prevention of suffering underlies most therapeutic systems, but paradoxically, as Dostoevsky reflects, 'man will never renounce real suffering . . . [which] is the sole origin of consciousness' (1955: 140). Awareness of distress, in oneself or others, is a universal human trait, and the fundamental dichotomy of wellness versus illness may have deep evolutionary roots. Fábrega (1997: 46) argues that responses to affliction emerged in protocultural primate groups and were retained through natural selection in human evolution, leading to a sickness–healing adaptation that underlies all medical systems.

Although the capacity to respond to distress is biogenetic, criteria of abnormality, and the signs and symptoms that denote suffering, vary culturally (Csordas and Kleinman 1996). We define culture as a system of learned and shared codes or standards for perceiving, interpreting, and interacting with others and with the environment (Jezewski 1990). As a normative framework for decision making and behavioral strategies, culture is an integral component in defining and achieving a state of health, maintaining health, and treating illness.

Definitions of health are inherently subjective, influenced by the dialectic between the body and the self. Criteria of health usually include instrumental components such as the ability to work and to fulfill expected roles. For many people, environmental parameters – the ability to procure nourishing food and other resources and to live without undue hardship – also define

health. Spiritual components of health are central in many cultures.

Recognizing a wide spectrum of illness and wellness definitions, and the fact that professional criteria differ from lay concepts, anthropologists find it helpful to distinguish three categories: *disease* (deviations from a biomedical norm), *illness* (the lived experience of culturally constructed categories), and *sickness* (patients' roles). While disease is a central focus of biomedical practitioners, factors affecting illness and sickness, and the transformative power of illness and disability, are more pivotal concerns of social scientists.

The phenomenology of illness, focusing on the person's experience, offers a valuable alternative to studies of disease. *Phenomenological* refers to 'perspectives that are concerned with the natives' point of view, with meaning, subjectivity, and consciousness – perspectives that account for "the phenomenon" under investigation as irreducible and autonomous in its own right' (Kaufmann 1988: 340). In addition to eliciting the individual's experience of health or illness, phenomenology accounts for the transformations of consciousness and self-identity that can occur in illness, disability, or trauma.

The illness experience is inextricably intertwined with the self and others across time. The responses of others are as important in the illness experience as is the interpretation of the one who is ill. 'Illness is not only a self experience but a social, community experience. Communities affect the one who is ill just as the one who is ill affects community' (Estroff 1993: 258). Despite the emphasis in this chapter on individual experience of health and illness in different cultures, the role of culture cannot be explained solely by studies of the self, and our level of analysis cannot be solely individual. Contextual factors are important in accounting for variation in illness experience. Class, gender, ethnicity, educational level, age, and social support especially influence risk of illness, access to care, and the probability of resolving a health problem (Harwood 1981). Environment, economic constraints, and political structures also influence health and illness (Bair and Cayleff 1993; McElroy and Townsend 1996).

This chapter focuses primarily on the personal experience of health and illness, but also links the individual level of analysis to broader community and cultural levels. We focus on multiple behavioral environments and the multiple networks that individuals form in preventing or dealing with health problems, as well as on economic and ecological factors that influence the well-being of whole communities. Methods and models traditionally used to explore personal experiences of health and illness will also be reviewed, as well as newer, multifaceted methods of research.

A Stratigraphy of Health/Illness

The experience of illness and health may be studied on several analytical levels: the *individual* (personal identity; biogenetic/ontogenetic traits), the *microcultural* (interpersonal roles and interactions; household and group traditions), and the *macrocultural* (cultural and transcultural systems) (cf. Figure 1).

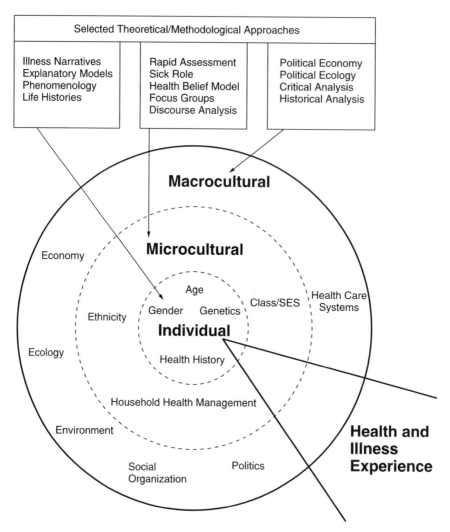

Figure 1   *Analytic domains in the experience of health and illness*

The triangle representing illness experience cuts across three levels to denote that people individually and collectively respond to health problems through multiple systems. The boundaries are permeable. Communicating through 'idioms of distress,' culturally distinctive ways of symbolizing and imaging illness and injury, symptoms become 'grounded in the social and cultural realities of individual patients' (Good and Good 1980: 166–69). As people in the microcultural domain (family members, the community, health professionals) become aware of an individual's distress through these symptoms, they try to define the problem and to effect healing. The meaning of distress also resonates into political and economic arenas when it is interpreted as related to lack of power, inadequate resources, or discriminatory policies. It is this extension of linkages, when personal suffering becomes redefined in social and political terms, that is of particular interest in medical anthropology.

Culture brokering serves as a useful heuristic to link the levels of health experience shown in Figure 1. Culture brokering is defined as the act of bridging, linking, or mediating between groups or persons of differing cultural systems for the purpose of reducing conflict or producing change. The culture broker serves as a bridge between the patient and others she encounters during the course of making sense of an illness.

The concept of culture brokering has a long history in anthropology, beginning with the work of Wolf (1956) and Geertz (1960) and continuing into the 1970s and early 1980s with the Health Ecology Project in Miami, Florida (Weidman 1975, 1982). Jezewski's culture brokering model (Jezewski et al. 1993; Jezewski 1995; Jezewski and Finnell 1998) consists of a three-stage process whereby problems in the health-care encounter are identified and strategies are implemented to resolve the problems (Figure 2). The third stage results in a resolution

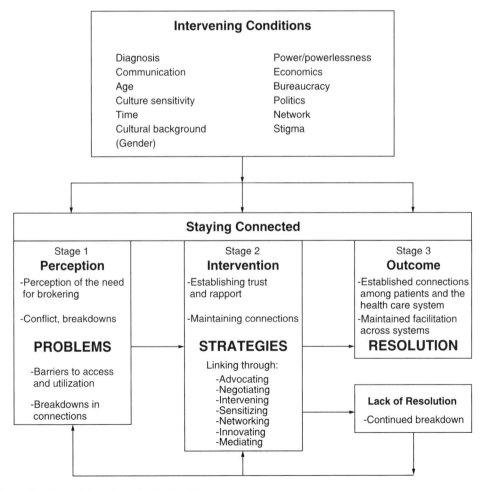

Figure 2   *Jezewski's culture brokering theory*

of the problem or a return to previous stages to attempt again to resolve the problem.

The intervening conditions in the culture brokering model consider micro- and macrosocial variables that influence the personal experience of illness. Culture brokering can serve as the bridge between the patient's personal experience of illness and the broader environmental, community, political, and economic constraints that affect the way patients seek and receive care within the biomedical health-care system.

History of Studies of Illness Experience

No single discipline can claim intellectual ownership of the phenomenology of illness. Sociology, anthropology, nursing, and psychiatry are among the major fields that focus on experience as an alternative to the depersonalized focus on disease characteristic of biomedicine. Kaplan (1964: viii) writes: '. . . too often psychiatry has not listened carefully enough to its patients, choosing instead to take seriously only what it could observe and verify . . . [but] the reality of the person, psychologically speaking, lies in his action and his experiencing.'

Unifying these disciplines is use of subjective, personal accounts in place of the objective case studies. The 'privileged position' of these texts reveals that patients identify with their illnesses. 'Although they suffer . . . , there is also gratification, excitement, and meaning' (Kaplan 1964: viii, x).

First-person accounts by patients are a rich resource for understanding the process of becoming ill and then recovering. In addition to analysis of personal accounts, the ethnographic method of participant-observation has revealed the 'inner world' of mental illness. Estroff's *Making it Crazy*, a study of 'persons grappling with psychiatric disorder' as well as of their care providers (Estroff 1981: 3), is an outstanding example. Reynolds and Farberow's *The Family Shadow* (1981) describes the day-by-day pressures experienced by a young, suicidal man as he attempts to adjust to his home environment after being released from a psychiatric hospital.

Studies at the Individual Level

Viewing 'illness as residing "within the individual" and connected with that person,' medical sociologists have focused on the *identity* of the sick person (Herzlich and Pierret 1987: 118).

Through historic and clinical studies of how individual patients seek understanding of the cause and the meaning of their condition, contextual analysis can illuminate notions of the self and the body. For example, the novelist Kafka saw his tuberculosis as reflecting his good self and his bad self 'doing battle with one another' (quoted in Herzlich and Pierret 1987: 118). Some patients see their condition as 'illness spawned by the self,' implying that illness represents failure (p. 124). Other patients feel less alienated from their illnesses; one noted 'my subconscious calls the illness and takes refuge in it' (p. 122). Despite his discomfort, the patient may enjoy being cared for and being free of responsibility. A French patient writes about a childhood illness: 'I remember the deep pleasure of snuggling in my bed, knowing that . . . I would not have to make any effort or bear responsibility for anything' (Herzlich and Pierret 1987: 124).

Others experience progressive illness not as refuge, but as a series of challenges. Anthropologist Robert Murphy's struggle to continue working and writing, to 'make an extra effort to establish status as an autonomous, worthy individual' as a tumor gradually causes paralysis is vividly documented in *The Body Silent* (Murphy 1987, 1995: 146). Illness accounts of the progression of multiple sclerosis provide a sense of disease trajectory for others coping with similar or earlier stages of the disease (Monks and Frankenberg 1995).

Explanatory and Cognitive Models

Beliefs and perceptions held by patients and their families constitute an important reality, not only for ethnographers, but also for practitioners. Good and Good (1980: 166) advocate a meaning-centered approach to clinical practice that 'recognizes all illness realities to be fundamentally semantic,' that is based on explanatory models and illness narratives. Kleinman's concept (1980, 1986, 1988) of *explanatory models* (EMs) has stimulated a large body of research on individual and microcultural constructions of health and illness. Being informed about the popular health-care sector (that is, lay persons' beliefs and models) and listening to the patient's narrative 'is central to the work of doctoring' (Kleinman 1988: 96) as well as obviously central to the anthropological task. Kleinman's negotiation model, which includes eliciting patient and provider EMs of illness, is also useful for health-care providers and applied researchers.

The explanatory model framework is directed primarily at patient–provider interaction in health-care settings. The utility of this model stems, in part, from the ease with which it can be used in a clinical setting. In a relatively short time, health-care providers can elicit patients' perspectives of their illness in their own words. Patients' perspectives provide the health-care provider with a means to compare the provider's EM with patients' personal explanation of their illness. A comparison of similarities and disparities in patient and provider explanations can result in better understanding, and particularly more effective negotiation of disparities. Negotiation of differences between patient and provider explanatory models of illness affords the opportunity for a treatment plan that is mutually agreeable, relevant, and most importantly one that considers the personal experience of the patient in the stabilization of illness or the healing process.

Blumhagen's (1980) study of 'hyper-tension' among African Americans is a classic example of the importance of patients' explanatory models in directing treatment plans for a particular population. Twenty years later, eliciting explanatory models of illness remains an important tool for both researchers and clinicians. For example, Heurtin-Roberts and Reisin (1992) look at the cultural influence of lay models of hypertension on compliance with treatment. Handelman and Yeo (1996) use explanatory models to understand chronic symptoms in Cambodian refugees. Likewise, Gray (1995) uses Kleinman's explanatory model perspective to examine parents' beliefs about autism in their children.

Kleinman's negotiation model, including the clinical technique of eliciting explanatory models, is not without its critics. Young (1982) has called for greater emphasis on social relations within a framework of critical analysis. Good (1994) takes a more temperate approach, accepting the concept of EMs but suggesting that interpretive research should be informed by a critical stance. Kleinman (1995) himself discusses increasing discomfort with the concept of medical systems. He has shifted from focus on explanatory models to narratives, in part because of his professional shift from clinical practice to academia and his intellectual movement from symbolic anthropology to phenomenology and from symbolic forms and social structures to subjectivity and intersubjectivity. Nevertheless, eliciting explanatory models serves as a useful heuristic for health-care professionals attempting to understand the personal experiences of their patients, and the negotiation model directs providers toward a more collaborative relationship with patients.

Cognitive models held by biomedical practitioners and by patients who seek their services may create barriers that impede patients' movement toward wellness, and it is in such multi-

cultural settings that culture brokerii effective. McElroy and Jezewski's (19 of a pediatric clinic illustrates problems munication when patients and provider differing ethnic backgrounds. Those pι traverse language and demonstrate the b ..iers to understanding in clinical encounters. The barriers are due not only to terminology, but also to differing premises, backgrounds, and roles.

The values and assumptions of physicians and other care providers have been understudied, although Hahn and Gaines' *Physicians of Western Medicine* (1985) is a useful beginning; see especially Hahn's portrait (1985a) of an internist's world view. Hahn (1985b) has also analyzed fifteen first-person accounts by doctors of their own illnesses, surgery, and trauma, describing the often transformative effect of discovering the 'world of patienthood' (p. 94). A more recent effort to address cognitive patterns of physicians as well as of patients is Hunt and Mattingly's (1998) collection on varieties of reasoning in clinical encounters. Hunt's account (1998) of the heavy use of moral reasoning by Mexican physicians in explaining cancer is especially illuminating.

Studies at the Microcultural Level

The concept that illness and wellness is best studied at the level of the individual reflects a particularly Western bias about the autonomy of the individual (Lock and Scheper-Hughes 1996). This atomistic approach may not be valid in some cultural systems. Not all societies hold a concept of personhood, and many merge individual and social identities. The egocentric experience of bodily changes and interpretation of their meaning (e.g., as signs of personal failure or weakness) has little parallel in societies that interpret affliction through sociocentric terms.

Medical sociologists and anthropologists have long sought meaning and purpose in illness interactions, recognizing that beyond the clinical domain of individual care lies the psychosocial, microcultural realm of relationships transformed by illness. The individual level and the microcultural level interconnect and mutually influence sickness behavior, as suggested by Parsons' concept (1948, 1951) of *sick role*. This role includes behaviors the sick person adopts in response to the expectations of others, especially the expectations of care providers. In Parsons' model, sickness is viewed as deviance or dysfunctional behavior, yet paradoxically the patient is not usually held to be morally responsible for the illness and is excused from normal role expectations as long as he seeks care and attempts to regain health. Ethnographic studies by Fox (1959) of hospitalized patients with degenerative illnesses have refined the sick role concept, showing that patients without hope of cure nevertheless felt responsibility to function as competently as possible.

Like many seminal concepts, Parson's sick role idea has received its share of criticism. The major objection is that it does not account for intracultural variation by gender, age, and class, nor for interethnic variation. Zborowski's study (1952) of ethnic differences in expression of pain illustrates considerable variability in sick-role behavior. In addition, some stigmatized illnesses, such as AIDS and lung cancer, do evoke concepts of moral responsibility.

That illness and disability lead to interactions profoundly marked by stigma (Goffman 1963), that is spoiled or discredited identity, which in turn lead to a 'moral career' in which negative or deviant self-identity is pivotal, has been influenced by the symbolic interactionism theory of the self (Cooley 1964). Ethnographic studies of stigma (e.g., Edgerton's 1967 study of mentally retarded people) have demonstrated the power of negative public stereotypes to discredit people and create barriers to their well-being. Nevertheless, the stigma concept, like sick role and explanatory models, has been subject to considerable revisionism. Critics point out that many individuals and families can be more resilient than stigma theory suggests, developing coping strategies and positive identities in spite of (or because of) negative public reactions. Becker's (1980) ethnography of elderly deaf people shows that although stigma clearly deprived and disturbed deaf people during their childhoods, by the time they reached middle age and beyond they had developed many positive strategies, including a strong peer support system within a deaf community.

Community and Family Studies

Clinicians and epidemiologists often use Western (allopathic or biomedical) diagnostic systems as the gold standard when studying illness behavior and comparing disease rates. However, these systems may be regarded as a product of culture itself (Kleinman et al. 1978). Indigenous illness categories (*emic* categories) not recognized in Western diagnostic systems are frequently discovered in medical anthropology research. In fact, some researchers consider all illness categories to be emic, that is, culturally specific, while disease categories are thought to be *etic* or universal. The argument between empiricists (who claim that disease can be observed and is therefore real in an etic sense)

and the social construction of health theorists (that even diseases are cultural, emic categories) remains a serious controversy (Browner et al. 1988).

Studies of folk illnesses can easily combine ethnographic and clinical methodology, merging emic and etic analyses (cf. Foulks 1972; Rubel et al. 1984). One of the earliest and most influential medical ethnographies of illness behavior and experience was Clark's *Health in the Mexican–American Culture* (1970), which explored Chicano health and illness in California. Early studies of illness in Navajo culture by Leighton and Leighton (1944) is another pioneering work.

One difficulty with early medical ethnographies was the tendency to describe cultural systems homogeneously. As a corrective, Harwood (1981) emphasized the diversity of ethnomedical beliefs and practices within a population related to educational level, class, and degree of assimilation into mainstream culture. Janzen's study (1978) of therapeutic options in Lower Zaire also corrects some of the weaknesses of earlier studies that tended to describe ethnomedical systems as homogeneous.

Medical anthropologists and nurse-anthropologists have found that the individual's illness experience cannot be separated fully from the experience of other family members, especially caregivers. Social units – families, peers, and communities – carry the cultural meanings of the illness and control many resources to deal with it. Nursing has contributed significantly to phenomenological research in studies of family support systems. Morse and Johnson view illness 'as an experience that affects the sick person *and* his or her significant others' (1991: 317, emphasis in original). Their illness–constellation model focuses on the meaning of illness as the individual and significant others move through four stages of managing illness. This diachronic, dynamic model reminds us that illness varies in meaning over time, and the identities of the sick change depending on the particular stage or point in the illness trajectory.

Anthropological studies of life transitions have shown considerable variation in definitions of life-cycle events such as menopause. Despite North American medical views emphasizing loss, decline, atrophy, and increased health risk, menopause is experienced as normal in many societies. It fits the domain of health, not illness. Lock's research (1993) shows that hot flashes, headaches, difficulty in concentrating, or depression typical among menopausal European and North American women are not universal. The key physical marker of menopause for Americans, the cessation of menses, carries different meaning and significance for Japanese women. Conversely, North Americans rarely link typical symptoms of menopause among Japanese women (shoulder pain, for example) with menopause.

Cultural variation in the experience of menopause indicates the need for a phenomenology of the healthy body. Steps toward this approach have been taken in the genre of 'embodiment' studies (Csordas 1994) which go beyond individual consciousness of illness or culturally reinforced meanings of illness events. Reaching toward an understanding of the body not as a natural, biological entity, but as the 'existential ground of culture and self' (Csordas 1994: 4) focuses on how the self performs and is displayed, how the body and mind experience acts of violence and torture, and how metaphors and symbols evoke and/or give meaning to physical sensations. Studies of the body have been, for the most part, in the genre of critical and feminist studies (for example, Emily Martin's *The Woman in the Body* (1987)), although some rather inaccessible publications (e.g., Scott's 1978 cross-ethnic study of concepts of menstruation and well-being) represent more applied studies.

Studies at the Macrocultural Level

Research on health and illness at the macrocultural level encompasses a range of theoretical approaches including political economy, political ecology of health (Baer 1996), and critical analysis (Singer 1995). Research focusing on environmental change and policy (Follér and Hansson 1996) and disease history (Farmer 1992) contextualize health problems as part of large global and regional systems rather than as isolated, individualized issues. Kunitz's (1994) account of impacts of colonialism on the epidemiology and demography of New World populations is a particularly excellent example of macrocultural analysis.

An earlier study by Levy and Kunitz (1974) illustrates how macrocultural, microcultural, and individual analysis can be integrated. This project, focusing on alcohol use by Navajos, Hopis, and White Mountain Apaches, uses a wide range of research techniques: historical analysis, epidemiology, survey research, study of clinical records, and personal interviews. Based on these data, the authors questioned stereotyped assumptions held by non-Indian care providers, administrators, and educators. For example, the assumption that alcohol use led to violence was not supported; suicide and homicide rates did not vary with alcohol-use patterns. Levy and Kunitz (1974: 193) found that the majority of Navajos who drank excessively did so for normal, cultural reasons rather

than pathological ones such as addiction. The 'disease model' of alcohol use was not prevalent in Native American communities at the time of this study, and it is probable that even today treatment programs for indigenous communities function better with other therapeutic models, for example, spiritual healing and restoration of community harmony.

Macrocultural studies of health have recently been subject to considerable controversy as medical anthropologists struggle to develop theory and appropriate methodologies. The debate between advocates of the political economy of health approach and medical ecologists has been particularly divisive (McElroy 1996). While neither approach has a particularly strong claim to study of *experience*, each gives differing priority to economic, political, and ecological frameworks. One compromise is the *political ecology* of health (Baer 1996). The two case studies that follow illustrate political ecology approaches.

IMPLEMENTING THE MODEL: TWO CASE STUDIES

This section discusses two populations in relation to macrocultural and microcultural variables that affect the individual's experience of health and illness. The cases demonstrate variability in the way that the larger societal infrastructure affects the lived experience of health and illness in complex societies.

Migrant Farmworkers

There is a wide variation in the estimation of the number of migrant farmworkers in the United States, from one to five million (Slesinger 1992). In 1991, agriculture surpassed mining as the most hazardous occupation in the United States. In addition to farm accidents from using heavy machinery, health hazards include herbicides and pesticides, and repeated exposure to the sun. Noise-related hearing loss, pulmonary diseases, musculoskeletal problems, skin diseases, and stress-related illnesses affect migrant farmworkers and their families in disproportionate numbers compared with the rest of the US population (National Coalition for Agricultural Safety and Health 1989). Chronic health conditions such as diabetes and hypertension are higher in the migrant population than in the rest of the US population. In one study, migrant farmworker clinic visits for diabetes were 338 per cent higher than the national average

(Dever 1991). Rates of diabetes in Mexican Americans are 110-120 per cent higher than in non-Hispanic whites (Harris 1991).

The average yearly income for a migrant farmworker family of four is estimated as being between $6000 and $8000 per year, well below the national poverty level (Slesinger 1992). Migrants often live in crowded conditions with poor sanitation, including lack of clean running water, which puts them at risk of infectious and parasitic illnesses.

The work ethic among migrant farmworkers is strong, as is the importance of family. One study characterized the work ethic as pragmatic survivalism; migrants work in the fields regardless of illness because 'no work means no pay' and perhaps no food for themselves and their families (O'Brien 1982). O'Brien states that only when a farmworker is too sick to work in the fields will she seek health care, especially when health services hours conflict with work hours.

An example from Jezewski's (1989) study illustrates how migrant farmworkers wait to seek care until illness prevents them from working. A Mexican farmworker sustained a gash on his lower leg but did not seek care for 2 weeks. Only when the injury became infected and he was having trouble bearing weight on his leg did he come to the clinic. He was afraid that the clinic staff would notify the grower that he should not be working because of the injury and infection. Negotiating treatment was an important aspect of the clinical encounter with this patient. Under ideal circumstances, the staff would recommend he remain out of work with his leg elevated for 7–10 days. This was not acceptable or feasible for the farmworker. After talking with the physician and receiving an antibiotic, the man agreed to keep off his leg and elevate it when he was not working. The lifestyle of the migrant farmworker was an important consideration in understanding the personal experience of this man's illness.

Access and use of health services is a major problem for migrant farmworkers. Despite the passage of the Migrant Health Act (Public Health Service Act, Sec. 310) in 1962, which authorized funds to establish health centers to deliver primary health service to migrant farmworkers and their families, recent estimates suggest that these centers serve less than 20 per cent of the targeted population (Dever 1991). Lack of health insurance, including Medicaid, is a major barrier to access and use of health services (Slesinger and Ofstead 1993). Other barriers to health care include clinic hours during times when migrants must work, lack of transportation to health services, and language and cultural barriers, as well as the stigma of the label

'migrant farmworker' within the communities where they work (Jezewski 1990).

Barriers to health care often emanate from language and cultural differences between patients and providers of care. Staff in a migrant farmworker primary care clinic (Jezewski 1989) related the story of a young Haitian woman whose newborn needed to remain in the hospital for several days after birth. When the baby was ready to leave the hospital, the mother came to the hospital with only a clean towel to wrap the baby. Hospital staff would not release the baby to the mother's care because she did not bring baby clothes. The staff perceived that she was not a 'good' mother and that the baby was in danger of being neglected when, in fact, Haitian mothers do not routinely dress their newborn babies but wrap them loosely in light blankets or toweling. Clinic personnel intervened on behalf of this mother, who did not speak English, thus preventing further misunderstanding and a charge of child neglect (this illustrates the culture brokering role). The mother was behaving according to her Haitian cultural tradition and the hospital staff was evaluating the mother's behavior based on their cultural beliefs about child care. Language barriers further confounded the interaction.

Political and economic issues work against migrant farmworkers' health as well as their ability to access and use health services. Continuity of health care, a sense of community involvement, employment, and family life are disrupted on a regular basis. Because they are essentially an uncounted population and seldom recognized as a separate entity in health services research, legislation enacted to facilitate care for the general population and special populations like the urban poor seldom aid the migrant population. Migrant farmworkers are truly one of the invisible populations in the United States, an ethnically diverse population who are among the most vulnerable and powerless populations in the United States.

Modernizing Inuit in Northern Canada

Once a nomadic, foraging people, about 15 000 Canadian Inuit live today in small settlements in the Northwest Territories. Many are wage-employed, and they live in modern houses with electricity, television, phones, and plumbing. They drive cars, motorcycles, snowmobiles, and all-terrain vehicles. Children attend local and regional schools. Government health care has been available since the 1950s, when polio, tuberculosis, measles, and other infectious diseases reached epidemic levels. Despite this care, health statistics were not favorable. In 1965 the infant mortality rate was 124 per 1000 in Iqaluit, on Baffin Island. In 1976 the tuberculosis rate was 137.8 per 100 000 (the all-Canada rate was 13 per 100 000; Muir 1991). The high incidence of death and injury due to alcohol has led some communities to pass liquor-control ordinances. The majority of adults and many teenagers smoke, and lung cancer has become a leading cause of death.

Traditionally, Inuit were foragers of marine and terrestrial animals. In the last few decades, consumption of native foods has diminished. Dog teams are rarely used for hunting, and gasoline for snowmobiles or for boat motors is expensive. Those who can afford gasoline are often too busy to hunt daily, confining subsistence activities to weekends and summer holidays. In addition, the market for seal skins has declined due to European and US boycotts and trade restrictions (Wenzel 1991). With the collapse of the export trade, the economies of northern settlements have suffered.

Decline in meat consumption is a great loss for Inuit. Land foods, the foci of food-sharing networks, collaborative hunting teams, rituals celebrating first kills by children, and community feasts are viewed by many Inuit as health-giving. Seal meat offers important nutrients: three to seven times as much iron as beef, twice as much protein, five times as much calcium, and twenty times as much vitamin A (Mackey 1988; Wenzel 1991: 121). However, Inuit preferences are not based on pragmatic grounds, but rather on a strong identification with seals and other mammals. 'Seal blood gives us our blood. Seal is life-giving' (Borré 1991: 54). Seal meat is thought to cause a person's blood to become fortified and to flow faster, giving warmth and strength. One respondent explained: 'when the body is warm with seal blood, the soul is also protected from illness . . . [and] when [people] are deprived of seal or other country foods, they become physically, then mentally sick' (Borré 1991: 54). Further, seal meat nourishes the soul. In order to maintain health, the body and soul must be unified through proper social actions, including hunting rituals, certain food preparation methods, and sharing of food. If the soul–body linkage becomes weak, illness may follow (Borré 1991: 53).

The shortage of land food has real physical and emotional consequences, as do proposed policies to impose quotas on hunting of beluga whales and other marine mammals. PCBs (polychlorinated biphenyls) from industrial waste have been found in the tissues of seals, walruses, caribou, and narwhals. About one-fifth of the people of Broughton Island, on Baffin Island, had higher than acceptable daily intakes of PCBs. Among children, 63 per cent had PCB blood levels above acceptable contaminant levels (Kinloch and Kuhnlein 1988).

Inuit have been denied control of their land and resources, but this may change in 1999, when the Nunavut territory, encompassing one-fifth of the landmass of Canada, is established. Compensation of Can$580 million will be paid to Inuit over 15 years, and the territorial government will be largely run by native people. 'Nuna' means more than territory. It signifies the ecosystem in which Inuktitut culture is rooted and in which health is experienced as a set of relationships with a harsh environment, with the life-giving animals of the habitat, and with spiritual elements existing in every entity and action.

Discussion of the Cases

The macrocultures in which they live and work puts both the migrant farmworkers and the Inuit at risk of poor health. They have little power to control their environment. Except for central California and the Midwest, migrant farmworker laborers are not organized and have little political influence. Their housing is temporary, usually substandard and crowded. Sanitation is a problem both in the fields and in their living quarters. They are disenfranchised from the larger population, essentially unseen by the communities in which they work or the metropolitan areas for whom they provide the produce found in supermarkets. Poor housing and working conditions, along with a poverty subsistence level, cause increased stress, physical and emotional, in migrant workers and their families. Ethnic identity is strong in the Mexican migrant farmworkers, but the sense of community is fractured because of long intervals away from their extended families and community home bases.

The Inuit case represents the political ecology of health of a population transformed through cultural contact and economic development. The twenty-first century may be an opportunity to come full circle, as Inuit attempt to restore the connectedness of their work, of their social relations, and of their place in the natural order. Restoration of the ecosystem means restoration of health. The experience of illness for Inuit, whether malnutrition, infection, or addiction, has become embedded in politics and a changed ecology. This is not simply an etic model imposed on emic explanatory models. Inuit explanatory models themselves link food, politics, economics, and well being. A political ecology of health model is especially salient among young, activist adults who look to Nunavut to address some of the most serious health challenges they face.

VARIATIONS IN THE EXPERIENCE AND DEFINITION OF ILLNESS

This section deals with social interactions in the experience of illness in various ethnic populations. We view social systems as transmitters of information about the meanings and significance of health, sickness, and care. Following Rubel and Garro's concept (1992) of 'health culture,' 'sick people use their health culture to interpret their symptoms, give them meaning, assign them severity, organize them into a named syndrome, decide with whom to consult, and for how long to remain in treatment' (Rubel and Garro 1992: 627).

Most illnesses are managed and resolved in the household without recourse to professional care. Symptoms are discussed and interpreted by family members, particularly those who typically provide lay diagnoses and home remedies. Decisions are made whether to seek professional care and from whom. Of course, if professional care is sought, family involvement does not end. Compliance with prescriptions and prohibitions depends in part on family comprehension and support of therapeutic regimens, and should the condition not be resolved, leading to disability or to chronic or terminal illness, management again usually becomes localized in the domestic sphere. Consequently, understanding variations in household management is essential.

Family Influences

Breast cancer, the second leading cause of cancer mortality in US women, is a disease in which stigma creates barriers to early detection. Black women in North America are usually diagnosed at a later stage than white women and have twice the risk of dying from breast cancer (Wardlow and Curry 1996). Black women studied in Atlanta, Georgia, in a cancer screening project mostly viewed cancer as invariably fatal. They considered mammograms to be messengers of terminal illness, or worse, believing that mammography itself could damage the breast through pressure and bruising. They also believed that any activity, including sexual activity or abuse, causing bumps or bruises could lead to potentially malignant 'knots' in the breast (Wardlow and Curry 1996: 322–23).

Despite fears of mammography, interviewees felt strong responsibility for their health. Seventy per cent did get regular mammograms and practised frequent, sometimes daily, breast self-examinations. They also shared information (both accurate and erroneous) about breast cancer risks with older and younger women in the family, functioning as teachers and even as managers, helping female kin to keep track of medical appointments (including annual mammograms), medication refills, and self-examination routines (Wardlow and Curry 1996: p. 333). In this case, although the connotations of cancer are negative, mother–daughter support systems and information sharing help reduce stigma and facilitate responsible care seeking.

Undoubtedly social support affects decision making about illness management. In a study of drug-using HIV-positive women in the Bronx, New York, Pivnick (1994) found that pregnancy decisions were associated with personal histories, particularly experiences of loss. Most of the women were Latina or African–American; all were poor, and two-thirds were addicts. Many of them believed they had been abandoned by their own mothers, described as cold and unsupportive. Being diagnosed with HIV is just another chapter in a history of deprivation, abandonment, economic hardship, and addiction. Many saw themselves as victims, believing that HIV is a form of germ warfare to eliminate people of color, drug users, homosexuals, and other 'undesirables' (Pivnick 1994: 49). Of 115 women who had previously borne children, 63 per cent had lost or surrendered custody of at least one child. This fact was strongly correlated with the decision not to undergo abortion despite the risk of vertical transmission of HIV to the fetus. Women who had lived with at least one child continuously were more likely to agree to abortion. Some of these women saw their pregnancies as a chance to redeem themselves, to make one positive contribution, and to have a loving relationship with one child before they became terminally ill. Children were perceived as 'saviors,' as 'rescuers,' providing 'a constructive focus in a woman's life' (p. 51).

Community Influences

Culture-bound syndromes (CBSs), also called folk illnesses, represent disorders that communicate distress to arenas beyond the household. The symptomatology of a CBS often embodies various levels of meaning about the person's status (or change in status), about troubled relationships with family members and the wider community, and about the disorienting effects of biochemical disorder. Appropriately called 'idioms of distress' in anthropological literature

(Nichter 1981), folk illnesses offer insight into cultural dynamics.

Among Latinos, including Puerto Ricans and Dominicans, the syndrome *ataques de nervios* (attacks of nerves) has been interpreted as a 'culturally meaningful way to express powerful emotions' such as anger or deep sadness (Guarnaccia et al. 1989: 47). To understand the meaning of ataques de nervios, Guarnaccia emphasizes that it is important to focus on the themes and structure of the narratives of patients, who usually describe stressful life experiences, family crises, the disruption of migration, losses, and abandonment. The symptoms refer not only to family tensions, but also to larger contexts, especially for political refugees and migrants who have left family members behind in difficult and possibly dangerous situations (Guarnaccia et al. 1989: 60).

While anthropological analysis of nerves focuses on social tensions, the individual's experience of emotional distress is actual symptoms; a process called somatization (Kleinman and Kleinman 1985). This concept has been widely used in analyses of the meaning of illness behavior, including neurasthenia in Chinese culture (Kleinman 1980), comparisons of 'nerves' in various cultures (Davis and Guarnaccia 1989; Low 1985), and of culture-bound syndromes in general (Simons and Hughes 1985).

Variations in Pain Perception and Experience

Culture mediates pain and disability as well as illness, and perception of pain intensity varies depending on how one has learned to interpret pain. Tolerance thresholds may vary by cognitive as well as by neurological factors.

'The world of the chronic pain sufferer is a lonely one,' writes Bates (1996: xv), whose study of ethnic groups in New England and Puerto Rico focused on variation in pain perception and management in patients, most with low back pain due to degenerated and herniated disks. The loneliness comes because others find it difficult to comprehend the draining nature of intractable pain. When medication or surgery do not bring lasting relief, family members may question the authenticity of the pain. Frustration about inability to return to normal roles often leads to depression. The psychosocial issues are as important as the medical ones.

The patient's degree of ethnicity, or 'heritage consistency,' is associated with differences in reported pain intensity. In most ethnic groups (except Anglo-Americans), patients with high heritage consistency reported lower intensities

of back pain. Another factor is 'locus of control,' a measure of whether one feels internal responsibility for health problems or feels that control is external and not a question of personal responsibility. In all ethnic-groups studies, except Anglo-Americans and Polish, those with internal locus of control also reported lower pain intensity.

Bates found major differences between ethnic groups in communication styles. Latinos and Italians, who rated their pain as highest in intensity, tended to be highly expressive about discomfort. Polish, Irish, and Anglo-Americans, who reported lower intensities, were relatively restrained in expressing pain. A woman of Polish background in her 70s stressed the importance of hiding her pain from others. With high pain intensity, she described herself, nevertheless, as 'generally healthy with a slight disability' (Bates 1996: 73). Many of her friends were not aware of her medical problems.

The characteristic responses of Latino patients differed. Latino men in pain were very expressive, 'wincing, grimacing, and groaning more often than most of the non-Latino patients' (Bates 1996: 50). One patient, unable to work even after back surgery, defined himself as unhealthy and disabled, unable to carry out the normal male provider role for his family. He said that the pain controlled his life. A Latina woman with degenerative joint disease of the spine also moaned and cried frequently. Her complaints made her unpopular with the pain center's staff, who preferred patients to be stoic and as cheerful as possible. Whether pain is regarded as physical pathology rather than psychosomatic (that is, as 'real' rather than 'just in the head') is an issue that chronic-pain patients must face in communicating with staff as well as with family members, friends, and employers.

Chronic Illness

The realness or legitimacy of chronic illness is particularly important in poorly understood conditions such as chronic fatigue syndrome (Ware 1992). Interviews of 50 chronic fatigue sufferers in the United States showed that others often defined the problem as not real, as being 'in the head,' called *delegitimation* by Ware. Symptoms such as exhaustion, depression, muscle pain, and poor concentration are trivialized and dismissed by others as being problems of everyday life. Some patients are not taken seriously because they do not look sick enough. Because physicians cannot find definitive signs of disease, the problem is defined as psychosomatic. One respondent said, 'They [doctors] would say things like, "You can't be experiencing what you are experiencing. You need to see a psychologist. You aren't as sick as you think you are" ' (Ware 1992: 351).

Loss of a sense of realness, of legitimacy, also affects individuals disabled by spinal cord injury, traumatic brain injury, or stroke. The body's physical limitations after stroke, for example, and the extreme dependence on others during rehabilitation, are experienced as an assault on the self (Kaufmann 1988: 342). One patient said: 'You can't imagine how frustrating it is when you are dependent on all these people for your every move.' (p. 343). The sense of being constrained by the body, and the inability of the self to master the body, is experienced as failure. Feelings of dependence, and frustration with a medical system that is supposed to cure but cannot in cases of stroke, are particularly salient when patients live in a culture that values autonomy and trusts medical competence.

In rare cases stroke brings on almost total paralysis of the body. It is instructive to consider what happens to the sense of self when the body is incapable of movement and when communication is limited to eyeblinks. Such was the condition of Jean-Dominique Bauby, who relied on blinking to dictate *The Diving Bell and the Butterfly* (1997) while hospitalized for 'locked-in syndrome.' Attempting to maintain his relationship with his children through hospital visits and outings by wheelchair to the beach, Bauby feels he is 'something of a zombie father' (p. 69). 'Grief surges over me . . . . my son Théophile sits patiently waiting – and I, his father, have lost the simple right to ruffle his bristly hair, clasp his downy neck, hug his small, lithe body tight against me' (p. 71). He decides to dictate the book, describing how fantasy and dreams help maintain his sense of self, to prove that he has not become a 'vegetable' and that his mind is intact. Yet in his relations with others, and in his own memories of the past, Bauby senses that he is fading away. 'I watch my past recede. My old life still burns within me, but more and more of it is reduced to the ashes of memory' (p. 77).

Terminal Illness

Patients with terminal cancer also experience a sensation of 'fading away,' a transition that involves redefining the self in respect to the reality of illness, weakness, and impending death. As family members note physical decline in the patient, they begin to realize that he or she will probably not recover. In a study of palliative care in western Canada, interviewees described the transition 'as starting to disappear' or 'feeling eroded' (Davies et al. 1995: 4). One woman

said, 'The physical me is no longer here as I was . . . it seems that I'm trapped in this sort of helpless little carcass. But my mind and my soul, I think, are the same' (p. 9). Here the redefinition of self involves accepting the physical limitations of the disease while emphasizing that the mind, and hence the self, remains intact.

Part of redefinition comes from searching for the meaning of the illness. Patients reflect on their lives, their values and priorities, and the beauty of nature as they look for the spiritual meaning of the illness. Spouses often focus on their relationship, and despite the pain of the situation may perceive the last months or weeks together as 'a beautiful time in our lives' (p. 45).

Family dynamics, either negative or positive, are crucial elements in the experience of illness. Lyles (1993) describes an argument with her father that occurs after her mother's mastectomy. Infuriated with her father's seemingly callous attitude toward her mother's needs, Lyles breaks her years-long role of keeping peace in this African–American family. 'My mother is going, and with her the standard of conduct that has kept a vise on my lips. If she is going to die, I need not try to act quiet, tame, and ladylike any more . . . I am miserable at my mother's dying, but fiercely content and the realization that with that terrible event, my deepest self has begun to be born' (Lyles 1993: 280). Growth of the self is often part of the experience of losing a parent.

When the cancer patient is a child, family dynamics become even more crucial as layers of deception or denial filter communication about treatment and the long-term prognosis. An ethnographic study of children with leukemia and their families showed the centrality of 'mutual pretense' in communication about the child's state of health (Bluebond-Langner 1978). The pretense in this case involves communication that suggests that the child is *not* dying, despite all evidence to the contrary. In fact, even young children become aware of the changes in their health status, learning from other children on the ward and by observing subtle cues in their parents and in hospital staff. A 5-year-old boy, for example, notes: 'See my mommy's red nose, that's from me. Everybody cries when they see me. I'm pretty sick' (Bluebond-Langner 1978: 8), but this child will not necessarily discuss his leukemia directly with the mother. By not disclosing that he knows how sick he is, he maintains some degree of normalcy in the relationship.

Parents in turn may not discuss the illness because they wish to protect the child from knowledge of the prognosis or awareness of the impending 'irrevocable separation' (p. 216). In addition, hospital staff practice mutual pretense with children. Bluebond-Langner found that staff were uncomfortable around the parents who practiced 'open awareness' and disclosure with their children, believing that such parents increased the child's difficulties.

While it is clear that the fear of loss and separation creates difficulties in communication in families when one member is critically or terminally ill, illness also creates a binding interdependency that is both enriching and stifling. Murphy, writing of his progressive paralysis, observes that his wife is 'tied down by me, her actions are severely limited by me, and my needs are never absent from her mind . . . we are both held in thrall by my condition – we are each other's captives' (Murphy 1987: 199). He notes that this degree of dependence is associated with debased status in American society, where autonomy is expected of adults and dependence is considered childish (p. 201).

UNRESOLVED ISSUES

Bioethical Dilemmas

Marshall (1992) presents a thoughtful discussion pertaining to the real and potential contributions of anthropology to bioethics. She emphasizes the importance of a hermeneutic interpretive approach to understanding the personal experience of bioethics. Importantly, ethics and values cannot be separated from social, cultural, and historical determinants that regulate both the definition and resolution of moral quandaries. 'Of critical importance is the inherent complexity of individual and cultural values concerning the nature of illness, the management of medical care and the use of medical technology' (1992: 62).

Within health-care delivery there exists the conundrum of cultural sensitivity/competence and clinical standards and professional ethics. Clinicians and social scientists alike wrestle clinically and academically with medical issues that are strongly influenced by cultural values and beliefs as well as by professional ethics of biomedicine. The resolution of these dichotomies has no easy solution. What is needed is a broad spectrum of methods and investigators to study the personal experiences of health and illness.

Increasingly, social scientists are providing important insight into the discipline of bioethics. Kleinman, in *Writing at the Margins* (1995), critiques bioethical approaches that ignore the social and cultural components in ethical discourse and those who do not address the

personal experience in ethical decision making. Examples of anthropologists studying bioethical issues from an ethnographic perspective include Lock and Honda's (1990) study of the meaning of death in Japanese society in relation to the concept of brain death and the medical harvesting of organs for transplantation. In a society with a modern medical system, technological advances and the centuries old Japanese moral and cultural meaning of death often clash.

The illness narratives of the dying process of elderly parents, as experienced by their middle-aged daughters, illustrate the personal experiences of ethical decision making and the powerful influence of medicine in controlling the dying experience for both patients and families (Rubinstein 1995). Rubinstein's study describes the importance of considering the values of society and the insidiousness of stigmatization (ageism), the irreducible subjectivity of illness for families, and the complex ethical dilemmas surrounding end-of-life decisions.

Legislative decisions impose widespread mandates on ethical decision making. Sometimes these political decisions have serious consequences on the personal experience of illness. Carrese and Rhodes' (1995) interdisciplinary, focused ethnography of bioethics on a Native American reservation presents one such dilemma. The Patient Self Determination Act (PSDA), enacted by Congress in 1991, mandates that any health-care facility receiving Medicare or Medicaid reimbursement must inform its patients about advance directives and the patient's right to self determine end-of-life decisions based on individual state laws. The Indian Health Service is under the mandate to comply with the provisions of the PSDA. The results of Carrese and Rhodes' study demonstrate that biomedicine's principles of autonomy and patients' rights of self determination sometime conflict with the Navajo belief that language shapes reality. Negative information (discussion of death, poor prognosis, and end of life decisions) conflicts with the Navajo concept of *hozho* and is viewed by Navajo as potentially harmful. The researchers concluded that because 86 per cent of their Navajo informants considered advance care planning a dangerous violation of Navajo values, policies complying with the Patient Self Determination Act are ethically troublesome and warrant reevaluation. This study not only illustrates the incongruence between cultural beliefs and government policy, but also the applied potential of the study for changing policy.

Jezewski (1993) explored the complexity of end-of-life decisions based on the narratives of nurses. The study focuses on nurses' experiences with patients and families, as those patients and families made decisions about do-not-resuscitate (DNR) status for the patient. The findings describe the complexity of end-of-life decisions, and the importance of considering the personal experiences of patients, families, and staff in the decision-making process of consenting to a DNR status. Jezewski's study also explores the conflict that arises when the personal experiences of patients, families, and staff differ. Interpersonal conflict (conflict between patients, families, and/or staff) centered on differences in personal experiences and cultural values. In one narrative, a nurse described in detail an experience with a young woman, a Jehovah's witness, who was seriously ill and needed a blood transfusion. The woman refused to consent to a blood transfusion because of her religious beliefs. The physician tried to coerce the woman into the transfusion or a DNR status because he did not want to be responsible if the woman died or coded because she refused the transfusion. The interaction between the physician and the patient created a crisis situation for both. The woman felt intimidated with the decisions she was being asked to make; one option which was against her religious beliefs, and the other, which in her perception, indicated that the medical team was giving up on her care. The woman was treated without a transfusion and was eventually discharged from the hospital, but the personal struggle for the patient and the family added stress to their illness experience.

chemicals (Levine 1982). Missing from these studies is assessment of the psychosocial impacts of living in communities labeled as contaminated. Fitchen's ethnographic research (1989) on the symbolism of the home, and how the meaning of home changes for those whose groundwater becomes contaminated, represents the approach we are advocating.

Edelstein's work (1988) also offers a model. Edelstein notes that toxic exposure affects people's *lifescape*, that is, 'their shared social and personal paradigms used for understanding the world' (Edelstein 1988: 11). In the communities of Love Canal (evacuated after discovery that homes and schools were built on chemical waste dumps) and Legler (with drinking water contaminated by nearby waste dumps), people found their lifescapes transformed as the level of toxicity in their neighborhoods became clear. Trust in the environment, in other people, and especially in the government diminished, and a sense of personal control was lost. Health seemed far less attainable over the long run, and people felt vulnerable. Past health problems, miscarriages, and deaths were re-interpreted in reference to new information and the new perception of the environment as disease-causing (p. 51). Children became especially sensitized to fear of contact with water, to awareness of the strain on their parents, and to generalized anxiety. Edelstein's study demonstrates a methodology that should serve medical anthropology well into the next century.

FUTURE DIRECTIONS

Interdisciplinary Research on Perceptions of the Environment

Multiple perspectives allow us to look productively at health phenomena at the macrocultural level. Study of ecology and health especially warrants the input of several disciplines (Follér and Hansson 1996). Medical ecology, medical geography, and epidemiology are inherently multidisciplinary, integrating clinical, statistical, and social science concepts. Nevertheless, these approaches often rely on quantitative methods, and research in the ecology of health needs to emphasize qualitative, experiential understanding of the meanings of risk and pollution.

Clinical findings in studies of Love Canal and other 'contaminated communities' (Edelstein 1988) have been ambiguous. There is some effect of toxic exposure on children's growth patterns (Paigen et al. 1987). Self-reported incidence of a wide range of health problems is greater in the areas with the greatest exposure to landfill

Multiple Methods Approach to Studying the Personal Experience of Illness

The traditional survey and broad-based ethnographic studies of the social sciences are evolving into more sophisticated methods of data collection and analysis. Triangulation in social science research is becoming the norm. Denzin (1978) describes four different types of triangulation in research – methodological, data, investigator, and theoretical. Triangulation refers to the use of several means of verifying, confirming, and enriching the findings of a study. Triangulation in research involves using multiple investigators, more than one means of data collection, and/or multiple methodologies or theories within one study. Janesick (1994) adds a fifth type of triangulation – interdisciplinary triangulation, in which investigators from multiple disciplines conduct studies together to give a richer context to the findings. Multidisciplinary research is becoming more prevalent, as are increased numbers of articles in the social science literature on methodology.

Social scientists are increasingly advocating multiple methods to study the personal experience of illness/wellness. Emphasis on a broader, more holistic decision model for the study of illness beliefs and behaviors dictates a change in the way help seeking is investigated. Pelto and Pelto (1997) suggest a methodology that falls between traditional study of cultural belief systems and the quantitative survey that emphasizes knowledge, attitude, and practices. They call for a more comprehensive investigation, including intracultural variation and the effect of macrosocial variables, such as economic influences and political structure, on decisions regarding the seeking of treatment. The research protocol known as focused ethnographic studies (FES) was developed by the Acute Respiratory Infection (ARI) Programme of the World Health Organization (WHO 1993). Pelto and Pelto state, 'the research approach is designed to explore the systematic patterns of cultural knowledge concerning specific illness categories in relation to actual behaviors involving those illnesses and accompanying symptoms to obtain operationally important information and insights on specific health problems' (1997: 155).

The FES method is focused on collection of emic data (explanatory models) as well as collecting data on actual episodes of illness so that cultural statements of participants can be compared to their actual behaviors as the illness unfolds. Questions asked of informants are loosely based on Kleinman's concept of eliciting explanatory models. The study by Gittelsohn, et al. (1991) of ARI in Gambia, and that of Hudelson et al. (1995) of ARI in Bolivia are examples of the application of the WHO/ARI focused ethnographic study protocol. FES is particularly useful for researchers in the Third World as well as in industrialized health-care systems, and may be integrated with the rapid assessment procedures developed by Scrimshaw and Hurtado (1987) for brief ethnographic surveys of primary health-care services.

In general, focused ethnography promises to be an effective tool for social and health-related studies of particular illnesses. As an applied method with a broad ecological framework, it is an important method because of its emphasis on the personal experience of illness, the decision-making context, and the macrosocial variables that affect personal decisions surrounding illness. Studies of migrant farmworker communities in the northeast United States, with particular focus on health-care-seeking behavior, illustrate this approach (Jezewski 1990).

Data collection in social science, particularly studies that explore the personal experiences of health and illness, is becoming more sophisticated as well. Certainly in-depth interviewing and participant observation have been, and will continue to be, the focal point of data collection in anthropology and other social sciences, but more recently, social scientists are turning to other qualitatively oriented methods of collecting data. Focus groups have long been used in the business/marketing world and more recently in academia. Many useful resources (Greenbaum 1997; Krueger 1994; Morgan 1997a, 1997b;) are available to help researchers become familiar and adept at group interviewing. Coreil (1995) provides an extensive historical account of the use of focus group interviews in research as well as discussion of the strengths and weaknesses of conducting group interviews in social science research. Coreil prefers the term group interviews, and she outlines four different types of group interviews, with focus groups as one type. Coreil's distinction between different types of group interviews is most helpful to the social scientist by providing the scope of possibilities for those who are new to the concept of group interviews as a method of data collection.

The use of multiple research methods within any one study minimizes the danger of focusing only on either the microcultural or macrocultural levels of illness. Studies of personal experiences conducted by social scientists and others outside the traditions of anthropology and ethnography need to acknowledge the concept of culture and to make the influence of culture explicit in their data collection and analysis.

CONCLUSION

In *Medicine, Rationality and Experience*, Byron Good (1994) discusses and critiques what he labels the four orienting approaches in medical anthropology: empiricist, cognitive, meaning centered/interpretive, and critical. He states that although each approach has strengths and weaknesses, disease and human suffering cannot be comprehended from a single perspective. These approaches should not be viewed as a dialectic to be resolved through synthesis, but rather as multiple lenses to study core issues facing medical anthropology. Good's ideas can be taken a step further. Not only should social scientists embrace multiple theoretical approaches, but of necessity they must also embrace the multiple research methodologies that are best suited to the theoretical approaches guiding issues crucial to understanding human experience.

Perhaps because it fits poorly into quantitative research, phenomenology has as yet gained few supporters in medicine or in biocultural anthropology. Many researchers and clinicians are ambivalent about the value of the personal narrative as the primary source of data. It is difficult to compare narratives or to generalize from their subjective content. The sample of narratives often seems small, precluding easy cross-cultural or cross-national comparisons.

A second reason that phenomenology meets resistance in the clinical sciences is that it involves an 'experience-near' methodology. The clinician must listen empathetically to the patient, a labor-intensive and potentially emotionally draining interaction for most practitioners, especially since the information conveyed is thought to be tangential to the 'real' problem. We are reminded of the example described by Lock and Scheper-Hughes (1996: 46) of a case presented to medical students by a woman suffering from headaches. She described domestic abuse by an alcoholic husband, the burden of caring for her senile mother-in-law, and her worries about her difficult son. Sympathetic but impatient, a student interrupted, ' "But what is the real cause of the headaches?" ' When rich interpersonal details are considered extraneous, we know that a narrow biomedical model dominates.

Health and illness are broad, multifaceted domains, but we are not training our students to appreciate the complexity of these domains. The person's feelings of strength or weakness, joy or depression, energy or exhaustion are usually omitted from case studies. Self-awareness of changes in puberty, pregnancy, menopause, progressive illness, and aging (and self-assessment of what physical signs are normal or abnormal or threatening to one's physical and emotional integrity) are too rarely probed in clinical or ethnographic interviews. For a profession that claims to know much about the spectrum of human existence, medical anthropology still knows too little about the experience of wellness and illness, of birth and death, of grief and comfort, of terror and ecstasy.

In this chapter we have taken the position that the study of illness and wellness experiences is of value in its own right. Our argument is not that study of individual experience should replace objective study, but rather that the two approaches can be complementary. We have also advocated an integrative, multivariate model that links the individual, the community, and larger political and economic forces. This model will be of use not only to anthropologists, but also to clinicians, public health researchers, and medical ecologists.

References

Baer, H. (ed.) (1996) 'Critical and biocultural approaches in medical anthropology: A dialogue', *Medical Anthropology Quarterly*, 10: 451–522.

Bair, B. and Cayleff, S.E. (eds) (1993) *Wings of Gauze: Women of Color and the Experience of Health and Illness*. Detroit: Wayne State University Press.

Bates, M.S. (1996) *Biocultural Dimensions of Chronic Pain*. Albany: State University of New York Press.

Bauby, J.-D. (1997) *The Diving Bell and the Butterfly* (Translated J. Leggatt). New York: Alfred A. Knopf.

Becker, G. (1980) *Growing Old in Silence*. Berkeley: University of California Press.

Bluebond-Langner, M. (1978) *The Private Worlds of Dying Children*. Princeton: Princeton University Press.

Blumhagen, D. (1980) 'Hyper-tension: A folk illness with a medical name', *Culture, Medicine, and Psychiatry*, 4: 197–205.

Borré, K. (1991) 'Seal blood, Inuit blood, and diet: A biocultural model of physiology and cultural identity', *Medical Anthropology Quarterly*, 5: 48–62.

Browner, C.H., Ortiz de Montellano, B., and Rubel, A. (1988) 'A methodology for cross-cultural ethnomedical research', *Current Anthropology*, 29: 681–702.

Carrese, J. and Rhodes, L. (1995) 'Western bioethics on the Navajo reservation', *JAMA*, 274: 826–9.

Clark, M. (1970) *Health in the Mexican–American Culture*. Berkeley: University of California Press.

Cooley, C.H. (1964) *Human Nature and the Social Order*. New York: Schocken.

Coreil, J. (1995) 'Group interview methods in community health research', *Medical Anthropology*, 16: 193–210.

Csordas, T.J. (ed.) (1994) *Embodiment and Experience: The Existential Ground of Culture and Self*. New York: Cambridge University Press.

Csordas, T.J. and Kleinman, A. (1996) 'The therapeutic process', in C.F. Sargent and T. M. Johnson (eds), *Medical Anthropology: Contemporary Theory and Method (revised edn)*. Westport, CN: Praeger. pp. 3–20.

Davies, B., Reimer, J.C., Brown, P., and Martens, N. (1995) *Fading Away: The Experience of Transition in Families with Terminal Illness*. Amityville, NY: Baywood.

Davis, D.L. and Guarnaccia, P.J. (1989) 'Health, culture and the nature of nerves: Introduction', *Medical Anthropology*, 11: 1–13.

Denzin, N. (1978) *The Research Act: A Theoretical Introduction to Sociological Methods* (2nd edn). New York: McGraw-Hill.

Dever, G.E. (1991) *Migrant Health Status: Profile of a Population with Complex Health Problems*. Austin, TX: National Migrant Resource Program.

Dostoevsky, F. (1955) 'Notes from the underground', in *The Best Short Stories of Dostoevsky* (Translated D. Magarshack). New York: The Modern Library. pp. 107–240.

Edelstein, M.M. (1988) *Contaminated Communities: Social and Psychological Impacts of Residential Toxic Exposure*. Boulder, CO: Westview.

Edgerton, R.B. (1967) *The Cloak of Competence: Stigma in the Lives of the Mentally Retarded.* Berkeley: University of California Press.

Estroff, S. (1981) *Making it Crazy: An Ethnography of Psychiatric Clients in an American Community*. Berkeley: University of California Press.

Estroff, S. (1993) 'Identity, disability, and schizophrenia: The problem of chronicity', in S. Lindenbaum and M. Lock (eds), *Knowledge, Power and Practice*. Berkeley: University of California Press.

Fábrega, H. (1997) *Evolution of Sickness and Healing*. Berkeley: University of California Press.

Farmer, P. (1992) *AIDS and Accusation: Haiti and the Geography of Blame*. Berkeley: University of California Press.

Fitchen, J. (1989) 'When toxic chemicals pollute residential environments: The cultural meanings of home and home ownership', *Human Organization*, 48: 313–24.

Follér, M.-L. and Hansson, L.O. (1996) *Human Ecology and Health*. Göteborg, Sweden: Göteborg University, Section of Human Ecology.

Foulks, E. (1972) *The Arctic Hysterias of the North Alaskan Eskimo*. Anthropological Studies No. 10, Washington, DC: American Anthropological Association.

Fox, R. C. (1959) *Experiment Perilous: Physicians and Patients Facing the Unknown*. Glencoe, IL: Free Press.

Geertz, C. (1960) 'The Javanese Kijaji: The changing role of a cultural broker', *Comparative Studies in Social History*, 2: 228–49.

Gittelsohn, J., Sillah, B., and Sanneh, K. (1991) 'Ethnographic study of acute respiratory infections in the Gambia', Department of International Health, Johns Hopkins School of Hygiene and Public Health, Baltimore, MD. Cited in Pelto, P. and Pelto, G. (1997) 'Studying knowledge, culture, and behavior in applied medical anthropology', *Medical Anthropology Quarterly*, 11: 147–63.

Goffman, E. (1963) *Stigma*. Englewood Cliffs, NJ: Prentice-Hall.

Good, B. (1994) *Medicine, Rationality, and Experience*. London: Cambridge University Press.

Good, B. and Good, M.-J. (1980) 'The meaning of symptoms: A cultural hermeneutic model for clinical practice', in L. Eisenberg and A. Kleinman (eds), *The Relevance of Social Science for Medicine*. Boston: Reidel. pp. 165–96.

Gray, D. (1995) 'Lay conceptions of autism: Parents' explanatory models', *Medical Anthropology*, 16: 99–118.

Greenbaum, T. (1997) *The Handbook for Focus Group Research*. Thousand Oaks, CA: Sage.

Guarnaccia, P.J., De La Cancela, V., and Carillo, E. (1989) 'The multiple meanings of ataques de nervios in the Latino community', *Medical Anthropology*, 11: 47–62.

Hahn, R. A. (1985a), 'A world of internal medicine: Portrait of an internist', in R.A. Hahn and A.D. Gaines (eds), *Physicians of Western Medicine: Anthropological Approaches to Theory and Practice*. The Netherlands: Reidel. pp. 51–111.

Hahn, R. A. (1985b), 'Between two worlds: Physicians as patients', *Medical Anthropology Quarterly*, 16(4): 87–98.

Hahn, R. and Gaines, A. (1985) *Physicians of Western Medicine: Anthropological Approaches to Theory and Practice*. The Netherlands: Reidel.

Handelman, L. and Yeo, G. (1996) 'Using explanatory models to understand chronic symptoms of Cambodian refugees', *Family Medicine*, 28: 271–6.

Harris, M. (1991) 'Epidemiological correlates of NIDDM in Hispanics, whites, and blacks in the US population', *Diabetes Care*, 14 (Suppl. 3): 639–48.

Harwood, A. (ed.) (1981) *Ethnicity and Medical Care*. Cambridge, MA: Harvard University Press.

Herzlich, C. and Pierret, J. (1987) *Illness and Self in Society* (Translated E. Foster). Baltimore: Johns Hopkins University Press.

Heurtin-Roberts, S. and Reisin, E. (1992) 'The relation of culturally influenced lay models of hypertension to compliance with treatment', *American Journal of Hypertension*, 5(11): 787–92.

Hudelson, P., Huanca, T., Charaly, D., and Cirpa, V. (1995) 'Ethnographic studies of ARI in Bolivia and their use by the national ARI programme', *Social Science and Medicine*, 41(12): 1677–83.

Hunt, L.M. (1998) 'Moral reasoning and the meaning of cancer: Causal explanations of oncologists and patients in southern Mexico', *Medical Anthropology Quarterly*, 12: 298–318.

Hunt, L.M. and Mattingly, C. (eds) (1998) 'Special collection: Rationality in the real world. Varieties of reasoning in illness and healing', *Medical Anthropology Quarterly*, 12(3).

Janesick, V. (1994) 'The dance of qualitative research design', in N. Denzin, and Y. Lincoln (eds), *Handbook of Qualitative Research*. Thousand Oaks, CA: Sage.

Janzen, J. (1978) *The Quest for Therapy in Lower Zaire*. Berkeley: University of California Press.

Jezewski, M. (1989) 'Using a grounded theory method to develop a model of culture brokering in a migrant farmworker health care setting', PhD Dissertation, SUNY Buffalo. Ann Arbor, MI: UMI Dissertation Information Service #8913517.

Jezewski, M. (1990) 'Culture brokering in migrant farmworker health care', *Western Journal of Nursing Research*, 12: 497–513.

Jezewski, M. (1995) 'Staying connected: The core of facilitating health care for homeless persons', *Public Health Nursing*, 12: 203–10.

Jezewski, M.A. and Finnell, D. (1998) 'The meaning of DNR: Oncology nurses' experiences with patients and families', *Cancer Nursing*, 21: 212–21.

Jezewski, M.A., Scherer, Y.K., Miller, C., and Battista, E. (1993) 'Consenting to DNR: Critical care nurses' interactions with patients and families', *American Journal of Critical Care*, 2: 302–9.

Kaplan, B. (ed.) (1964) *The Inner World of Mental Illness: A Series of First-Person Accounts of What It Was Like*. New York: Harper and Row.

Kaufmann, S.R. (1988) 'Toward a phenomenology of boundaries in medicine: Chronic illness experience in the case of stroke', *Medical Anthropology Quarterly*, 2: 338–54.

Kinloch, D. and Kuhnlein, H. (1988) 'Assessment of PCBs in Arctic foods and diets – a pilot study in Broughton Island, Northwest Territories (NWT), Canada', in H. Linderholm et al. (eds), *Circumpolar Health 87*. Umea, Sweden: Nyheternas Trycheri. pp. 159–62.

Kleinman, A. (1980) *Patients and Healers in the Context of Culture*. Berkeley: University of California Press.

Kleinman, A. (1986) *Social Origins of Distress and Disease*. New Haven, CT: Yale University Press.

Kleinman, A. (1988) *The Illness Narratives*. New York: Basic Books.

Kleinman, A. (1995) *Writing at the Margins*. Berkeley: University of California Press.

Kleinman, A. and Kleinman, J. (1985) 'Somatization: The interconnections in Chinese society among culture, depressive experiences, and the meanings of pain', in A. Kleinman and B. Good (eds), *Culture and Depression*. Berkeley: University of California Press. pp. 429–90.

Kleinman, A., Eisenberg, L., and Good, B. (1978) 'Culture, illness and care: Clinical lessons from anthropological and cross-cultural research', *Annals of Internal Medicine*, 88: 251–8.

Krueger, R. (1994) *Focus Groups: A Practical Guide for Applied Research*. Thousand Oaks, CA: Sage.

Kunitz, S. (1994) *Disease and Social Diversity*. New York: Oxford University Press.

Leighton, A. and Leighton, D. (1944) *The Navaho Door: An Introduction to Navaho Life*. Cambridge, MA: Harvard University Press.

Levine, A. (1982) *Love Canal: Science, Politics, and People*. Lexington, MA: Lexington Books.

Levy, J.E. and Kunitz, S.J. (1974) *Indian Drinking: Navajo Practices and Anglo-American Theories*. New York: Wiley.

Lock, M. (1993) *Encounters with Aging: Mythologies of Menopause in Japan and North America*. Berkeley: University of California Press.

Lock, M. and Honda, C. (1990) 'Reaching consensus about death: Heart transplants and cultural identity in Japan', in G. Weisz (ed.), *Social Science*

Perspectives on Medical Ethics. Philadelphia: University of Pennsylvania Press. pp. 99–120.

Lock, M. and Scheper-Hughes, N. (1996) 'A critical–interpretive approach in medical anthropology: Rituals and routines of discipline and dissent', in C.F. Sargent and T.M. Johnson (eds), *Medical Anthropology: Contemporary Theory and Method* (revised edn). Westport, CN: Praeger. pp. 41–70.

Low, S. (1985) 'Culturally interpreted symptoms or culture-bound syndromes: A cross-cultural review of nerves', *Social Science and Medicine*, 21: 187–96.

Lyles, L. (1993) 'Cancer in the family', in B. Bair and S.E. Cayleff (eds), *Wings of Gauze: Women of Color and the Experience of Health and Illness*. Detroit: Wayne State University Press. pp. 273–80.

Mackey, M. (1988) 'The impact of imported foods on the traditional Inuit diet', *Arctic Medical Research*, 47 (Suppl. 1): 128–33.

Marshall, P. (1992) 'Anthropology and bioethics', *Medical Anthropology Quarterly*, 6: 49–73.

Martin, E. (1987) *The Woman in the Body*. Boston: Beacon.

McElroy, A. (1996) 'Should medical ecology be political?' *Medical Anthropology Quarterly*, 10: 519–22.

McElroy, A. and Jezewski, M. (1986) 'Boundaries and breakdowns: Applying Agar's concept of ethnography to observations in a pediatric clinic', *Human Organization*, 45: 202–11.

McElroy, A. and Townsend, P.K. (1996) *Medical Anthropology in Ecological Perspective* 3rd edn. Boulder, CO: Westview Press.

Monks, J. and Frankenberg, R. (1995) 'Being ill and being me: Self, body, and time in multiple sclerosis narratives', in B. Ingstad and S. Whyte (eds), *Disability and Culture*. Berkeley: University of California Press. pp. 107–34.

Morgan, D. (1997a) *The Focus Group Guidebook*. Thousand Oaks, CA: Sage.

Morgan, D. (1997b) *Focus groups as qualitative research*. Thousand Oaks, CA: Sage.

Morse, J. and Johnson, J. (1991) 'Toward a theory of illness: The illness-constellation model', in J. Morse and J. Johnson (eds), *The Illness Experience: Dimensions of Suffering*. Newbury Park: Sage.

Muir, B. (1991) *Health Status of Canadian Indians and Inuit – 1990*. Ottawa: Indian and Northern Health Services, Medical Services Branch, Health and Welfare Canada.

Murphy, R. (1987) *The Body Silent*. New York: Henry Holt.

Murphy, R. (1995) 'Encounters: The body silent in America', in B. Ingstad and S. Whyte (eds), *Disability and Culture*. Berkeley: University of California Press. pp. 140–58.

National Coalition for Agricultural Safety and Health (1989) *Agriculture at Risk: A Report to the Nation*. Iowa City: University of Iowa Press.

Nichter, M. (1981) 'Idioms of distress', *Culture, Medicine and Psychiatry*, 5: 379–408.

O'Brien, M. (1982) 'Pragmatic survivalism: Behavior patterns affecting low-level wellness among minority group members', *Advances in Nursing Science*, 4: 13–26.

Paigen, B. et al. (1987) 'Growth of children living near the hazardous waste site, Love Canal', *Human Biology*, 59: 489–508.

Parsons T. (1948) 'Illness and the role of the physician', in C. Kluckhohn and H. Murray (eds), *Personality in Nature, Society, and Culture*. New York: Alfred A. Knopf.

Parsons, T. (1951) *The Social System*. Glencoe, IL: Free Press.

Pelto, P. and Pelto, G. (1997) 'Studying knowledge, culture, and behavior in applied medical anthropology', *Medical Anthropology Quarterly*, 11: 147–63.

Pivnick, A. (1994) 'Loss and regeneration: Influences on the reproductive decisions of HIV-positive, drug-using women', *Medical Anthropology*, 16: 39–62.

Reynolds, D.K. and Farberow, N. L. (1981) *The Family Shadow: Sources of Suicide and Schizophrenia*. Berkeley: University of California Press.

Rubel, A. and Garro, L. (1992) 'Social and cultural factors in the successful control of tuberculosis', *Public Health Reports*, 107: 626–36.

Rubel, A., O'Nell, C., and Collado-Ardon, R. (1984) *Susto: A Folk Illness*. Berkeley: University of California Press.

Rubinstein, R. (1995) 'Narratives of elder parental death: A structural and cultural analysis', *Medical Anthropology Quarterly*, 9: 257–76.

Scott, C.S. (1978) 'The theoretical significance of a sense of well-being for the delivery of gynecological health care', in E.E. Bauwens (ed.), *The Anthropology of Health*. St. Louis: C.V. Mosby. pp. 79–87.

Scrimshaw, S. and Hurtado, E. (1987) *Rapid Assessment Procedures for Nutrition and Primary Health Care: Anthropological Approaches to Improving Program Effectiveness (RAP)*. Los Angeles, CA: UCLA Latin American Center Publications.

Simons, R. and Hughes, C. (eds) (1985) *The Culture Bound Syndromes*. Boston: Reidel.

Singer, M. (1995) 'Beyond the ivory tower: Critical praxis in medical anthropology', *Medical Anthropology Quarterly*, 9: 80–106.

Slesinger, D. (1992) 'Health status and needs of migrant farm workers in the United States: A literature review', *Journal of Rural Health*, 8: 227–34.

Slesinger, D. P. and Ofstead, C. (1993) 'Economic and health needs of Wisconsin migrant farm workers', *Journal of Rural Health*, 9: 138–48.

Wardlow, H. and Curry, R. (1996) ' "Sympathy for my body": Breast cancer and mammography at two Atlanta clinics', *Medical Anthropology*, 16: 319–40.

Ware, N. (1992) 'Suffering and the social construction of illness: The delegitimation of illness experience in chronic fatigue syndrome', *Medical Anthropology Quarterly*, 6: 347–65.

Weidman, H. (1975) *Concepts as Strategies for Change: A Psychiatric Annals Reprint*. New York: Insight Communications.

Weidman, H. (1982) 'Research strategies, structural alterations and clinically applied anthropology', in N. Chrisman and T. Maretzki (eds), *Clinically Applied Anthropology*. Boston, MA: Reidel.

Wenzel, G. (1991) *Animal Rights, Human Rights: Ecology, Economy, and Ideology in the Canadian Arctic*, Toronto: University of Toronto Press.

WHO (World Health Organization) (1993) *Focused Ethnographic Study of Acute Respiratory Infections*. Geneva: WHO/ARI.

Wolf, E. (1956) 'Aspects of group relations in a complex society: Mexico', *American Anthropologist*, 58: 1065–78.

Young, A. (1982) 'The anthropologies of illness and sickness', *Annual Review of Anthropology*, 11: 257–85.

Zborowski, M. (1952) 'Cultural components in responses to pain', *Journal of Social Issues*, 8: 16–30.

2.2

Ethnography and Network Analysis: The Study of Social Context in Cultures and Societies[1]

ROBERT T. TROTTER, II

INTRODUCTION

People consistently reflect their primary values and beliefs through the people they associate with and the people they avoid or are in conflict with. The immediate social world is made up of family and friends, work partners, and acquaintances. It then extends outward in a web of relationships through the organizations and communities that form the more distant structures in people's lives. The social structure in human culture reduces problems by producing predictability in relationships. The process is not perfect, and there are other purposes for cultural systems, but at least three elements of culture allow humans to live together and interact comfortably. One is cultural knowledge. This is the information, such as language, knowledge, values, and beliefs, that allows people to communicate and share both emotion and experience. Without this symbolic portion of culture, predictable behavior would be impossible and life would be incomprehensible. A second element of culture that produces predictability is the interaction between cultural knowledge and the environment. This element produces technology and lifestyles adapted to available resources. The third area is the human need for structure and organization in interpersonal and community relationships. Humans live their lives by interacting with small groups that are the organizational fabric of their existence. These groups include family and kinship groups, friends and work acquaintances, the political and power groups they associate with, and all of the other relationships and organizations that have an impact on them. This element of culture focuses on the people's interactions within the context of their cultural knowledge and their environment.

While anthropologists have used the idea of social networks both as a metaphor and as a theory for analysis (Johnson 1994: 125), this chapter explores the specific approaches, and the findings, that come from the techniques available through formal social network studies of human behavior. These studies allow anthropologists to find and define cultural differences in the ways that humans organize themselves into the small groups that handle the issues of daily life. Social network analysis is an attempt to identify the structure and meaning of relationships, explain their impact, and predict how they will affect the future of individuals, organizations, and societies. The social network approach allows anthropologists to ask and to answer very different questions than the ones that are focused on individual knowledge, behavior, or personal values. This approach allows us to move out into the broader important structures of society and to understand the forces beyond the individual level that shape the lives of people.

SOCIAL NETWORK APPROACHES TO HUMAN CULTURE

Early in the history of anthropology, researchers found that the cultures they encountered organized critical relationships differently. Cross-cultural studies identified unexpected differences that led to the first studies of kinship groups, marriage patterns, and social and political organizations in small societies. These were critical findings, and are still a part of the overall information that is important for understanding cultural differences in people's daily lives.

As ethnographic research progressed, two different approaches to understanding cultural networks were explored. Pasternak (1976) summarized the initial systematic approaches to the exploration of kinship groups, and Elizabeth Bott (1971) produced an ethnographic exploration of social networks in England. These works represent two theoretical and methodological anchor points for anthropologically driven social network analysis. Pasternak describes methods for collecting and then comparing the ways that different cultures identify, label, and understand the genealogical relationships that are part of their culture. The Bott study provides an in-depth exploration of the intimate support networks that most people use to survive in their culture, and provides a model for exploring these relationships across cultures. Following these studies, anthropologists conducted and systematically refined their examinations of informal and formal human groups and associations, in conjunction with work going on in sociology, social psychology, and political science (Galaskiewicz and Wasserman 1993; Johnson 1994; Wasserman and Faust 1994). The combined approaches expand our knowledge of the effects and dynamics of both kinship and nonkin networks in all parts of human culture. This research ranges from purely qualitative descriptions of groups and associations, to quantitative social network schemas that create network descriptions based on the algorithms of both graph theory and matrix algebra. Each approach provides valuable insights into human cultures. In combination, they provide powerful explanations for the ways that humans think, act, and organize their daily lives within their personal cultural context.

Social network research describes relationships. These relationships include physical contact with other people (sex, violence, supportive touch, healing), social contact (friendship, work relations, social events), symbolic contact (communication, emotional impact, e-mail), or even imaginary interactions. Different types of relationships produce different cultural contexts in people's lives. Social network analysis defines specific relationships (such as kinship or friendship, power or influence, communication, physical contact, or social support), and then determines how those relationships are orga-

nized or structured, and how that structure has an impact on individual lives. They describe the structural environment of individuals, organizations, and societies.

There are three primary anthropological approaches to network studies. These are ethnographic descriptions of social networks (Bernard and Killworth 1973; Morrill 1991), personal network studies or ego-centered networks (Hammer 1983; Shelley 1992), and the analysis of whole networks (e.g., Hage and Harary 1991).[2]

The social network approach has changed rapidly during the last ten years, due to the development of sophisticated data collection and analysis techniques, especially the development of new statistical approaches to understanding complex relationships.[3] Wasserman and Faust (1994) provide an excellent introduction to both the descriptive and the probabilistic statistical methods used to analyze social relationships. All of these techniques are based on an attempt to find order in the relationships that people create. The variety of important questions asked in different social science research paradigms (anthropology, sociology, geography, political science, and psychology) have resulted in the social network approaches described in this chapter. The authors provide examples of a wide range of fruitful research questions answered by a social network approach, including studies of occupational mobility, the impact of urbanization on individual well-being, world political and economic systems, community elite power and decision making, social support research, group problem solving, the diffusion and adoption of innovations, interlocking corporate directorates, cognition and social representation, markets, exchange relationships, social influence, and the formation of coalitions, among others (Wasserman and Faust 1994: 5-6).

There are three levels of analysis that can be simultaneously applied to social networks. These are analyses of the individual, the subgroup, and the whole system characteristics. At the individual level, the analysis consists of describing the relationships, position, and roles of the individual in relation to other people in the network. Each individual can be described in terms of how his relationships connect him with other people, how information and influence can flow to or from him (or through him to others), and how his place in the network affects his life by making him similar to, or different from, others in similar or different kinds of roles and positions in his own or other networks. Individuals can also be described in terms of their membership in subgroups in the network, and their closeness or distance to other individuals. Analysis of the subgroup structure of the network consists of discovering, describing, and analyzing the effect of subgroups in the network and the connection of those subgroups to other groups and individuals. In larger networks, people tend to cluster into smaller groups. An example would be an extended family. Kinship ties connect the entire family to each other. Each nuclear family would tend to have the closest ties in our culture, but would still maintain contact with other nuclear families. The adults would tend to have the most direct connections and the most frequent direct contacts, while their children would be connected to the rest of the group through indirect ties (their mother lets them know what is happening to their cousins, aunts, and uncles) with much less frequent direct contact (family reunions). Network analysis allows researchers to identify these subgroups within larger connected networks, and to analyze the impact that these groups have on people's lives. Finally, a network can be characterized as a whole and compared with other networks. Network density (the number of connections between people compared with the number of potential connections), network centrality measures, and transitivity measures (a measure of whether the connections of one individual are also connected with each other) are some of the technical measures of total network conditions.

APPROACHES TO STUDYING RELATIONSHIPS

Social network theory has commonly developed from the analysis of relationships, rather than an *a priori* theory of relationships. Anthropologists noted differences in family structure in different cultures, and developed theory to account for those differences, rather than having the theory first, and finding the difference afterwards. The same condition applies to many network approaches, where researchers first focused on describing relationships, and then created methods and theories to make those descriptions and analyses stronger over time.

This observation-based approach to social relationships has produced different but complementary methodological approaches that are used in network analysis. These are the exploration of personal networks, egocentric networks, chained or snowball network studies, and the analysis of whole networks. These approaches are summarized in Table 1.

Each of these types of study has its own theory, methods, and appropriate research instruments attached to it. The basic approaches are described in the following sections.

Table 1 *Approaches, foci, and methods of network analysis*

Approach	Focus	Methods, Instruments
Personal network	Questions about personal networks and relationships from the perspective of the informant (Burt and Minor 1983)	Standard questions about relationships (McCallister and Fischer 1983)
Egocentric	Description of individuals in personal networks and the relationships of both ego and the individuals named by them to each other (Sarason et al. 1983)	Name generators and questions about interactions of those named (Burt, 1984; Marsden 1990, 1993)
Chained or snowball	Descriptions of linked and overlapping personal networks and the relationships between individuals and the whole population drawn from snowball samples, random walk designs (Klovdahl 1989)	Survey instruments and name generators tied to chained sampling designs (Palmore 1967)
Full network	Identification of relationships in a bounded community (Knoke and Kuklinski, 1982)	Relationship matrix, membership lists, questions about relationships between all members of the community (Wasserman and Faust, 1994)

Personal Networks

The personal network approach focuses on individual informants and their personal relationships. The focus of this type of study is to identify similarities and differences in individual relationship environments. This is often called ego-centered network analysis. Each individual is assumed to exist in a structured social context. That context may have very similar effects for individuals who have the same type of contextual environment, and be very different for individuals who have significant differences in their personal networks. Anthropologists (Bott 1971; Kapferer 1973; and other British social anthropologists) who were studying urban systems pioneered this approach. The approaches used in personal network analysis fit very nicely into the small community, ethnographic interview, key informant format of ethnographic research designs (Johnson 1994: 135), and it works well with participant observation conditions. This approach allows the ethnographer to collect personal network data both through interviews and by directly observing the behavior of individuals in key social settings.

Personal network analysis concentrates on asking questions or recording observations about individual behaviors, attitudes, and beliefs. It is an attempt to introduce information about the context of individual lives into survey approaches to understanding culture and society. Early on, the theoretical underpinning of this approach came from the rational choice theory or structural functionalism, or a combination of both these approaches (Galaskiewicz and Wasserman 1993). These approaches assume that humans are actors in a larger social setting, and that the actors can be assumed to have autonomy and independence. Individuals are also treated as solitary or relatively solitary in these situations. This means that individual relationships are discounted as having an important impact on behavior or culture. However, research on personal relationships and interactions showed these approaches to be far too limited in describing and predicting patterns in peoples lives. The personal network approach was expanded to encompass influence patterns in addition to autonomy, multiple and multiplex relations in addition to solitary conditions, and influenced actions, in addition to independence of action.

Personal network research approaches have relied on asking two types of questions about relationships. One type of question asks the person to describe her personal networks, just as she would describe other personal characteristics such as gender, age, preferences, or knowledge. The second approach, the egocentric question-naire, collects additional information from the informant's perspective about the relationships between the other people mentioned by the informant, as part of the informant's personal network. These two approaches, combined or singly, answer many important questions about cultural conditions beyond the individual level.

Personal Network Questions

One of the easiest and most productive ways of finding out about the social context of an informant is to ask a series of questions about his relationships with the people around him (McCallister and Fischer 1983). Personal network analysis provides information from the perspective of the person providing the information. This creates an important strength to this approach and a weakness. Two people who are in a relationship may have widely different views of the relationship. One may be in love with the other, while the other may merely like the first person. Based on their perceptions, the assumptions that each one makes and the decisions they make about ways to follow through with the relationship can be very different. The strength in the personal network approach is that the questions asked allow the researcher to discover the individual perspective of each person interviewed. However, the weakness is that this method cannot resolve differences of opinion about a relationship. It can only identify those differences because it is focused on individual perceptions and how those perceptions are related to behavior, life events, or the predictability of some type of social interaction, for the individual. Within this limitation, the approach can produce very important insights into individual lives.

Personal network questions identify an informant's social context from a structural perspective and a role or meaning perspective. The structural questions focus on the size, shape, and organizing principles of the person's relationships. These include information about the size of the person's personal network, the strength of her relationship to other individuals, the closeness or intimacy of the relationships, and the overall shape of her connections to different kinds of people as well as different individuals. The role or meaning questions ask about the cultural labels and meanings of the relationships, such as kinship roles, gender roles, status questions, and the like. The combined questions are analyzed to produce a description of each informant's personal network. This information can then be aggregated to determine if there are patterns to personal networks that are closely related to the critical questions that the researcher is trying to uncover. For example, does the size of an individual's personal network have an important impact on his influence or power in a community? Do people in different cultures have different average size networks or different networks on the basis of their composition (roles, demographics)? Are personal networks made up mostly of family members more supportive than ones that are made up exclusively of friends and acquaintances? If someone wanted to get a job, what is the best kind of personal network to have? Do the structure and the role relationships in a personal network determine the success of an individual in business, love, or longevity of life? Each of these questions can be answered by asking people about their personal networks and then comparing those network answers to answers about the critical life experiences of the informant.

Egocentric Network Questions

The egocentric approach collects judgements about relationships among the people in ego's personal network, from the informant's perspective. This changes the data from a view of how the informant sees her relationship to each person she identifies in her network, to her perceptions of other people's relationships to one another and to herself. Some of the questions that could be answered with this approach include the following. Do networks where everyone knows everyone else provide better social support for ego than networks where the only connection among members is directly to ego, not to anyone else? What effect does dividing up your social life into several different tight subgroups (cliques) have on a person's success in business, compared with having one homogeneous network? If the people in ego's network are in conflict with each other, how does that affect the strength or the longevity of their relationship with ego? Are members of ego's network more likely to be connected with each other if they are the same gender, ethnicity, social status, or religion, and if so, what impact does that have on ego's success, happiness, or future health? How do personal networks form and how stable are they over time?

Asking informants about their relationships without the cross check of asking the people named about the same relationship raised a critical question for anthropologists engaged in personal network analysis. The primary question, if this approach is used for any type of critical decisions, is: 'are informants accurate when they provide information about their relationships?' One potential problem with this

approach arises from the ways people remember things. Memory is sometimes affected by emotion, bias, and biological processes (injury, aging). Reporting is affected by all of these issues plus social pressures to hide embarrassing or harmful information or to lie about relationships by bragging or exaggerating. Asking a person who has had a traumatic experience to remember that experience may produce only partially accurate memory, and asking a person who is married to name all of his sex partners may produce an incorrect list, due to lying. Yet, there are times when this information is the only information that can be collected about important relationships.

This issue produced a very powerful discussion and analysis of elements of informant accuracy (Johnson 1994: 122–7). The early experimental research (Bernard and Killworth 1973, 1977; Killworth and Bernard 1976, 1979–80) called into question the general accuracy of self-report data when people's reports about their contacts were compared with actual observations (also Bernard et al. 1980, 1982a, 1982b, 1984). As other scholars conducted further analysis on the original data sets, or conducted further experiments, it became clear that this complex question of accuracy had a number of answers, ranging from conditions that produce very little accurate information, through conditions that produce accurate information if certain biases are taken into account, to situations in which the aggregated information from inform-ants produces very accurate data (cf. Johnson and Miller 1983; Romney and Faust 1983; Romney and Weller 1984). These studies found that the accuracy of an informant depends on the level or intensity of the informant's participation in a group. It also showed that informants who have similar backgrounds and experiences tend to exhibit regular or predictable biases in accuracy depending on the characteristics of the informant (Freeman et al. 1987a, 1987b). It also found a range of accuracy in any group of informants which correlated with the informant's ability to describe a consensual model of the relationships being studied (Romney and Weller 1984; Romney et al. 1986). Finally, researchers discovered that the ability of individuals to describe some social interactions, compared with behavioral observations, produced the most accurate picture when it was analyzed by aggregating individual reports, rather than looking at the reports singly (Bernard et al. 1982a, 1982b; Freeman et al. 1988). This indicates that the most accurate pictures of social interactions often come from an aggregate group view, rather than from an individual perspective. The related question of how people remember, not just what they report, was also explored (Boster 1986a 1986b; Killworth and Bernard 1976), followed by explorations of the impact of an individual's social positions on his recall and reporting of social relationships (Boster et al. 1987; Michaelson and Contractor 1992). These studies on the relation between social position in a network and reporting indicate that there are regularities in perception of networks and interactions based on similarities in the roles that people have in a community. People's position in social networks influences the accuracy of their reports. Personal network data also show that the networks reported by individuals, whether they are accurately measured against another form of data or not, are a key condition for understanding the social world of any given informant, from that informant's perspective. These portrayals are useful in both understanding and predicting the behavior of individuals beyond the information that an informant gives us about herself alone.

Personal and Egocentric Data Collection

Personal or ego-centered network data is collected in the form of questionnaires or interviews. Individuals are asked a series of questions about the structure, composition, and relationships they have with a defined personal network. The most common way that data are collected is to ask a set of questions about the size and composition of a personal network, to ask the person to list the names of the people in that network, and to answer questions about the person's relationship with each of those people and the relationship between those people and each other (cf. Bernard et al. 1990) (Figure 1). In many cases, the actual names are not asked because of ethical considerations and legal issues, but each personal network member is identified by a label or nickname, so the persons answering the questions do not get confused about whom they are describing, and can easily talk about the relationships.

Personal Network Questionnaire
1. How many people have you been in regular contact with in the last 30 days? _____

2. Of the people you had regular contact with in the last 30 days, how many
     a. are relatives or kin?   _____
     b. are sex partners?   _____
     c. do you use drugs with? _____
     d. can be counted on to
       give you support   _____

3. Please name the people you had regular contact with in the past 30 days.

1.	6.	11.	16.
2.	7.	12.	17.
3.	8.	13.	18.
4.	9.	14.	19.
5.	10.	15.	20.

4. In the attached matrix, please indicate the age, gender, ethnic affiliation, and any kinship relationships for each of the people named above.

5. In the attached matrix, please indicate which of the individuals you have named have been in regular contact with any and all of the other individuals you have named.

(Other questions specific to the study would then follow.)

Figure 1   *Personal, egocentric questionnaire*

Analytical Strategies for Personal and Egocentric Data

There are four broad analytical strategies used to describe personal networks. The first provides composite views of the personal network characteristics of different groups of people. The most common descriptions are the size, age composition, gender composition, socioeconomic characteristics, and other demographics of the networks, compared by key subgroups, such as differences between the personal networks of different ethnic groups, gender differences, age, or socioeconomic differences. This allows the researcher to determine if men or women have the same average size of personal networks, or if young people have networks that are predominantly only people their own age, or if the rich have much contact with the poor. The average profile of personal networks can be compared with the profiles found in contrasting social groups.

If there are significant differences in the personal networks found in a research population, then the researcher can create a typology of personal networks and can describe the similarities and differences in the cultural context of people's lives by comparing and contrasting the individuals who are involved in each type of personal network.

The data that describes each person's relationship with each other person can be analyzed to determine the structure of each relationship set. Some personal networks are dense and tightly connected, with everyone knowing and interacting with everyone else, while others are very loosely connected or only connected by the informant. These structural differences are likely to change the way that the informant lives, loves, and takes care of himself and others. The structural analysis of networks, described in more detail below, includes connections among people, the subgroups, and the overall structure of personal networks.

Because personal network data are normally collected along with lots of other data about individual informants, it is possible to correlate the network data with other individual variables. This allows questions to be asked about the relationship between personal networks and other life outcomes. One very interesting example of this approach combines personal network analysis and the concept of the small world experiment, described in the next section. It is called a reverse small world experiment (Bernard et al. 1989; Killworth and Bernard 1978). This approach uses assumptions from several other forms of network analysis. It assumes that everyone is ultimately connected (small world phenomenon) and therefore it is possible accurately to determine the impact of events that affect everyone by collecting a random sample of data from informants in a society. The second assumption is that there is regularity in personal networks; everyone knows a relatively narrow range of people, depending on the type of relationship that is being studied (knows someone, has contact with someone, has someone in their home). The result is that if you know the size of the population, know the average connections between people, and know the average size of personal networks for a particular relationship, you can accurately estimate the impact of a specific event (Bernard et al. 1989; Freeman and Thompson 1989; Freeman et al. 1989; Killworth et al. 1990). The reverse small world experiments have been conducted to estimate the number of people infected with the HIV virus, the number of people who died in natural disasters (such as earthquakes, where the death toll is so high that there is no way to get an accurate account), and for events (such as rape) for which the actual occurrence is under-reported for social and cultural reasons.

Examples of Personal Network Studies

The most common studies of personal networks have been social support studies (Cohen and Syme 1985; Hays et al. 1990; Ostrow et al. 1991; Williams 1993) and diffusion of innovation studies (Coleman et al. 1966; Palmore 1967; Valente 1993, 1995, 1996). In recent times, egocentric network studies have been very valuable in helping prevent AIDS and other infectious diseases (Latkin 1995; Latkin et al. 1996; Trotter et al. 1995a, 1995c, 1996). The personal network studies for these projects have focused on 'risk networks.' Risk networks are the personal networks of individuals who are at risk for some kind of problem. The HIV risk networks of drug addicts include the sex partners and the needle-sharing partners of the drug addicts. Both of these groups put the drug addict at risk of being infected by HIV. The personal network studies in this area have been valuable for identifying the most common problems associated with HIV transmission in networks, and have provided evidence that it is possible to change both individual and network behavior and slow the AIDS epidemic (Needle et al. 1995).

Ego-centered personal network information allows anthropologists to quickly establish some of the important traits of the social context found in a given culture. These traits, such as the size of networks, the closeness and duration of relationships, and the impact of peer norms, can be collected from each person or a selected sample of persons in a community or a culture. This is normally reported in the form of tables such as Table 2, which comes from the Flagstaff Multicultural AIDS Prevention Project (FMAPP). This table compares the people who provided the information (respondents or egos) with the people whom they named in their personal network (alters). In this case, they were asked about people who were part of their network for the past 30 days and people who were present the last time they used drugs with other people.

The analysis of the personal network data for the FMAP Project demonstrated that the respondents belong to relatively small networks that commonly include both users and nonusers, some kin relations, and close friends. Only 25 per cent responded that all of the people they spend time with use drugs. The ego network data indicated that the majority of drug networks are relatively stable in their composition. The data also indicates that the majority of risks, such as needle sharing activities or sexual relationships, occur with the first three people named by ego as members of their network. This provides a very targeted group for a successful intervention strategy. A smaller portion of the needle sharing and sexual encounters occur with people outside of ego's close personal network, but the data also indicate that these encounters, called 'weak ties,' are the highest risk contacts for the majority of drug users. Based on these data, part of the FMAPP HIV prevention and education effort was directed at helping individuals break, reduce, or decrease the risks associated with the 'weak tie' types of relationships, while the other efforts were directed at changing relationships in the closest network group.

The project also explored the usefulness of finding proxy measures of network structural relationships (such as percentage of kin in the network, or percentage of sex partners in the network) to determine if it is possible to identify conditions that linked individual social networks to the individual's risk of spending time in jail, or becoming infected with HIV through drug use. This process allowed us to use relatively simple and nonthreatening questions that could be asked about individuals' social relationships (Trotter et al. 1995b). We assumed that risk taking is a generalized, rather than specific, activity for an individual. If they take risks in one area of their life, they are much more likely to take risks in other areas. Therefore, the individuals who accepted early recruitment into the FMAPP program were hypothesized to be more likely to be higher risk takers than the individuals recruited from the same network later in the process. Because these individuals did not know the project well, it was as much a risk for them to participate (and possibly be caught up in a drug sting) as it was for them to interact with other strangers. We believed that coming into the project as one of the first members of a network to be recruited (that is, acting as bridging individuals) would be a proxy measure for individual influence or centrality in the network. We were

Table 2   *Gender, age, and ethnic distribution of respondents, and respondent's 30-day and recent-use networks*

	Respondent (ego) (N = 52)	People (alters) in respondents' 30-day network (N = 127)	Alters Present in most recent drug-use episode (N = 90)
Gender			
Male	34 (67%)	81 (63%)	62 (68%)
Female	18 (33%)	46 (37%)	28 (31%)
Age			
10–19[4]	12 (23%)	36 (28%)	28 (31%)
20–29	14 (26%)	38 (29%)	25 (27%)
30–39	23 (44%)	43 (33%)	30 (33%)
40–49	3 (5%)	9 (7%)	7 (7%)
50–59	0 (0%)	1 (1%)	0 (0%)
Ethnicity			
African American	10 (19%)	22 (17%)	16 (17%)
Hispanic	19 (36%)	64 (50%)	42 (46%)
Anglo	18 (34%)	35 (27%)	27 (30%)
Native American	5 (9%)	6 (4%)	5 (5%)

able to show that the program recruitment order data (the rank order in which individuals were recruited into the project for their network) not only correlated with network structure measures (how they were connected or to which subgroup they belonged), but they were also related to increased risk taking (Trotter et al. 1994, 1995c, 1996) and correlated with higher risk behavior. Early arrivals in each network were more likely to have tried a drug treatment program than the subsequent recruits in the same network, while later arrivals were less likely to have injection drug user sex partners. Those recruited earlier in networks were very likely to have sex partners who were also injection drug users (that is, they participated in double-risk relationships).

We also hypothesized that participation in two or more networks involved more potential risk and risk taking than membership in a single network. Most of the people in the project (321) only participated in one drug network (66.5 per cent), while 162 individuals (33.5 per cent) were members of two or more drug networks. Our data indicated that simply asking individuals to self identify either single or multiple network membership provided a direct indication of both their types of risks and the levels of risks that the individual was most likely engaged in, within their personal drug-using networks. As a result, this type of personal, or ego-centered network data collection was very useful for revealing important facts about the most common personal groups (network of individuals) in our projects. The same type of information could easily be collected for educational programs, economic development conditions, or participation in any other form of cultural programs that would be enhanced by understanding the cultural context of people's lives.

CHAINED OR SNOWBALLED NETWORKS

The second approach to network analysis was created to move beyond the individual and to attempt to study larger social structures in a culture. In this approach, relationships are studied by following a trail of connections from each selected key informant outward into the larger society. The approach is similar to a chain letter or to snowball sampling. Each person leads the researcher to another person or a set of persons who are all connected by a particular kind of relationship. There are several forms of this sequential collection of data on relationships, each with its own advantages and disadvantages. The advantages are the relative ease of recruit-

ment of each chain, and the ability to demonstrate actual connections among the people being studied.

In general, the problems with this approach include running into a social box canyon and problems generalizing to the rest of the culture. The box canyon effect occurs when the chains or snowballs start with too few points and become trapped in social loops, while the real relationships actually extend much further out into the community. The problem of generalizability is produced by the sampling methods that need to be used for this type of research. If the respondents are discovered through a biased selection process, or a process that only identifies part of the full range of people who should be interviewed, then the researcher cannot generalize to the community as a whole. New methods associated with probabilistic sampling (Wasserman and Faust 1994), new approaches for generalizing from snowball samples (Frank 1979; Snijders 1992), and sequenced data collection (Klovdahl 1989; Klovdahl et al. 1994) help avoid some of the common snowball pitfalls. They also help to make the information more easily generalizable to the population as a whole.

Chained or Snowball Network Examples

The small world experiment (Poole and Kochen 1978) is the classic example of a chained or snowball type of social network research approach. In this type of experiment, individuals are asked to find the best way to get a message (or an object) to a randomly chosen person somewhere in the world. The only things typically known about the target person are his name, the town he lives in, and his occupation. The rules are that the person must pass on the message to someone he or she has personal contact with, with the request to keep passing it along until it reaches the target person. Then, the number of links between the original person and the target person are counted and described. The average number of links between people is used to define the difficulty of any one person in the world contacting any other person through direct social connections. The types of links used (a friend in the town, an acquaintance with the same occupation) allow the researcher to describe the type of strategies that work, and the ones that do not work, for carrying out the linkage task. The experiments have shown that a successful attempt at this type of contact takes an average of about five links within a specific cultural or racial group, about six links if cultural or racial boundaries are being crossed in a single society, and about seven links if significant international boundaries are being crossed.

There is some variation in the number of links found, depending on the importance given to the message, but these approximate averages appear to be fairly stable. The broken chains, ones that did not complete the linkage, also provide very important information about the size of the world and the fact that while everyone is theoretically connected, there are lots of ways that people can be isolated or kept out of the picture.

Kinship analysis is another interesting form of chained network analysis. The description of a kinship network begins with a central character (ego) and that person's kinship relationships. From that point, individuals connected to ego are interviewed (often sampled) and more connections are added to the original, forming first a chain of relationships, and ultimately a model of both individual and complete kinship systems in a community. Early attempts to create an overlap between sociometric network analysis and kinship analysis were unsuccessful, but in more recent studies, the two types of approach to network data have been both complementary and have added new dimensions to our understanding of kinship networks and the impact of kinship on larger social networks (Barnes 1980; Hage and Harary 1991; Plattner 1978; Schweizer 1988; Seidman and Foster 1978; White and Jorain 1992).

Chained Network Data Collection

The basic model for chained data collection is the same in each type of snowball or chained network. One person, or a small number of persons, is chosen as the starting point. This person can be chosen randomly from a community, or chosen because of some special characteristic that makes him or her a good starting point for the study. These individuals are asked to name and describe their relationships with individuals in their personal social network. In some cases, they are asked to name everyone they can think of, and in other cases they are asked to name individuals with whom they have a specific relationship or a specific set of relationships. The next person or persons to be interviewed can be either randomly selected from ego's original personal network (random walk approach) or can be nominated by the first person interviewed, based on their relationship to ego (snowball or referral approach).

Each person to be interviewed is chosen from the personal network of the last person interviewed. This process is followed for as long as needed, allowing more and more people to be nominated and then interviewed. The data set includes a set of interviewed people (known direct connections) and a set of persons described by them (alters or personal network members of those interviewed, some of whom will also be named in other networks). The first persons can be called the seeds for the chain. The people they identify are their personal networks. The person chosen to move the chain or snowball out one level can be considered a link. Since each person interviewed identifies a personal network, it is both possible and likely that the same person or persons will be identified by more than one of the people who are interviewed. This means that even though the data collection is moving from one person to the next, the overall data sets will have network linkages between both the interviewed individuals and the alters that they name. The analysis of these data can then show a large number of connections between individuals in the community, even though only a small number of people were directly interviewed. Good sampling strategies and statistical analysis allow the researcher to describe a much larger segment of the community than just the people who were interviewed about their networks.

Sampling and Chained Networks

Choosing the starting point or points for network studies (i.e., sampling) and then interviewing all of the people named, or sampling from the persons named by the network seed, has become a critical consideration for both collecting and analyzing all forms of network data, but especially chained or snowball data. Anthropologists have begun to pay increasing attention to the selection of ethnographic informants (cultural consultants) in their research (Johnson 1990; Werner and Schoepfle 1987). Johnson (1994) points out that for many network studies, the sampling frame must be extended beyond individuals to include places, events, and subgroups as points for beginning both observational network studies and interviews.

Chained Network Analysis

The analysis of chained network data can be accomplished in a number of ways. It can involve an attempt to discover how far the chains extend before they truncate. This analysis provides information about how people are connected in a community, and how far those connections go before they disappear, based on some critical kind of relationship. Through this type of research, you could ask how far a community health educator's influence extends, or you could determine how health promotion ideas or values diffuse through a social system. Another analytical strategy attempts to discover how the characteristics of a network chain change as the chain proceeds outward from its source. For example, if you start a chain with an active group of drug users, how far along a chain of connections do you have to go before the impact of that behavior is no longer visible or felt by the people who are ultimately connected with the first segment of the chain? The small-world experiment indicates that everyone is connected in the world, but it is also obvious that not every single line of relationships can or will extend from any one individual to any other in the world. Sometimes the connections run out, or are deliberately chopped off by persons using their role as a 'gatekeeper' to limit contact with the people they are protecting. This happens when parents prevent their children from seeing, hearing, or reading things that they think are harmful, such as sex education material or violent television shows. Therefore, one line of research is to determine all of the different lengths of chains between people, based on specific types of relationships, and to determine what causes those chains to be maintained and to be broken.

One of the interesting issues that can be studied through chain types of network research is how networks form, how stable they remain over time, and how they disintegrate or change. Several researchers have investigated the reasons why people get to know certain people and not others, and why they form network relationships (Bernard et al. 1982a, 1982b; Killworth and Bernard 1979). These and other studies include an analysis of cross-cultural variation in the size and characteristics of networks, how people respond to different kinds of network or relationship questions (giving different answers for the size of network for the same individual), and attempts to estimate the size of personal networks. This type of information would be very valuable in trying to understand why people join or leave self-help organizations, or participate in charitable groups that are trying to find cures for problems such as leukemia, cystic fibrosis, or genetic disorders.

Another line of analysis is to use the chained or snowball data as an approximation of the distribution of critical problems or relationships in a total population. This is common in research on hidden populations and on rare conditions such as HIV infection or specific genetic disorders. Because it is hard to find all instances of a rare or hidden condition, snowball and chained network approaches can provide data that are analyzed through statistical estimations for the culture or community as a whole, finding one or a small number of people who are affected and chaining out to other people who have the same condition or problem.

Whole Network Studies

The third approach to network studies attempts to describe and analyze the reciprocal relationships among all of the members of a social group. Many of these studies have focused on small communities or organizations. It takes time and effort to ask each person about her relationships with every other person in the group. There is a limit to patience that must be accommodated by these studies but, within that methodological boundary, there have been a large number of important discoveries about the nature of communities, businesses, self-help organizations, social clubs, and interlocking power groups that make this approach very valuable.

Full Reciprocal Networks

The research questions that are important for whole network studies require that everyone in the network (or virtually everyone, given the problems of real-life data collection) can be asked and can answer questions about every other member of the network. Sometimes the answers are about relationships and sometimes about the absence of relationships, but both kinds of information are needed. Once the relationship questions have been asked of everyone, it is possible to identify a large number of conditions that have an important impact on the network.

Whole Network Questions

Whole network questions can cover a wide variety of contextual relationships. Some of the questions focus on person-to-person relationships. They include asking people if they have physical ties, such as sexual relationships, or physical contact. Other questions investigate emotional or social relationships by asking people how much they are influenced by or influence other people's decisions, or how often they meet socially or communicate with one another. Whole network studies have significantly contributed to our knowledge about the AIDS epidemic and how to combat it (Needle et al. 1995). Whole network questions can also focus on geographical networks by asking everyone if, or how often, they visit locations (businesses, museums, organizations) or are at the same social events (parties, visits), where the location is the focus for identifying the social context. Whole network analysis can also be extended to organizations or even societies. Instead of focusing on the individual, these whole network studies ask how organizations are related to one another. Some studies have looked at the overlap in the membership of corporate boards of directors, and have shown how these supposedly separate companies are actually interlocked systems with advantages that individual corporations do not have. Other studies have shown how companies that produce parts or services for other companies can be made more efficient and profitable depending on the types and frequency of contacts between the organizations that all lead toward the completion of a final product.

Whole Network Data Collection Techniques

Whole network data can easily be collected in the form of a matrix. Each person is given a questionnaire or interviewed about his or her relationships with everyone else in the network. In one of our studies about HIV transmission risks, we asked people to fill out a matrix questionnaire about the people in their drug-using network. Figure 2 is an example of the questions we used in that study, and an example of the types of answers that were given. Respondents answered the questions using a scale that was labeled appropriately for each question, with zero being the low end of the scale and five being the high end. The blank lines in the ques-

	Jim	Jenny	Tom	Cille	Marge
How honest is __ with you?	0	5	1	3	3
How close a friend is __?	2	5	3	4	3
If you had AIDS, how willing would you be to tell __?	1	0	2	4	4
How often do you use drugs with __?	0	3	0	5	3
How comfortable would you feel discussing AIDS with __?	1	3	1	4	3

Figure 2   *Matrix-style questionnaire about Drug and Trust Relationships*

tion were used to indicate that the respondent should answer the question about each person represented by the names in the columns.

This form of data is then transferred to a set of matrices (one for each question) for analysis. Each question (or relationship) matrix consists of rows and columns that identify all of the people in the network. Each person is identified with both a row and a column. The square (cell) that is the intersection of a row (one person) with a column (another person) is used to record the answer to the question given by the first person, about the second person. The row and column intersection between the second person and the first is used to record the response in the other direction. Each final matrix represents a single type of relationship, so if data is being collected on multiple relationships like the example above, multiple final matrices are needed.

The data recording is easier to understand with a simple example. If we wanted to understand the relationships between five teenage friends, we might want to ask how often they call each other on the phone during the week. This would provide us with information about calling patterns that may also indicate other characteristics of their relationships. The five friends consist of two males and three females. They all know each other, but their social relationships are different, so they have different calling patterns. If we asked each person how often he or she had called each of the other four people in the past week, we might get a grid that looked like Table 3. In this example, Jim was asked 'how many times in the last week did you call Jenny?,' and then asked the same question for the other three people. He called Jenny, who is his girlfriend, five times, Tom once, and did not call either Cille or Marge, who are very good friends of Jenny's. When Jenny was asked the same question for the other four, she had called Jim, Cille and Marge (probably to talk about Jim), but not Tom, who is Cille's boyfriend. The three girls all called each other during the week, several times. In this example, Marge also called both boys, in addition to her girlfriends. In both cases, she was trying to help her friends get information, and

was acting as a go-between, which is very common in teenage relationships. This is typical whole network data, and when it is recorded as a matrix, can be analyzed to show a large number of important characteristics about the group.

Matrix data has two important attributes that are part of the data recording process. The data can be either binary or valued, and it can be either symmetrical or asymmetrical. Binary data indicates only the presence or absence of a relationship. It is recorded as a one or a zero. Sometimes the questions that are asked in network analysis only focus on whether a relationship exists, not how often or how forcefully something happens. The alternative is to record a value for the relationship. In the previous example, the value represents the number of phone calls in a week. Instead of numbers, the informants could have been asked to rate how important the call was (from unimportant to very important) or they could have been asked to rank the five people in terms of the frequency they call the other person. Each of these is recorded as a value, rather than a one or zero. The statistics that help analyze network structures often require one or the other type of data. The same is true of symmetrical and asymmetrical data. Some relationships automatically involve both individuals, so the data are identical for the pair (the top half and the bottom half of the matrix are identical). In other cases, like the example above, the relationship exists between the two people, but more things are happening in one direction than in the other direction. Jim calls Jenny more than Jenny calls Jim, even though they both participate in all of the telephone calls. This produces a matrix where the number in any cell may be different from any other cell. This helps identify asymmetrical relationships and conditions. For example, there may be a million calls each day that go to New York City, and only a thousand that go to a small town in Arizona. This means that the structure of the phone network will need far more connections into one place and fewer into another. The same structural differences happen in social networks.

Table 3 *Phone-call patterns among five friends*

	Jim	Jenny	Tom	Cille	Marge
Jim	0	5	1	0	0
Jenny	2	0	0	3	3
Tom	1	0	0	6	0
Cille	0	3	0	0	3
Marge	1	3	1	3	0

Whole Network Data-Analysis Techniques

The simple-looking data described in the last section can produce very complex and interesting results. Network relationships can be analyzed from several major perspectives. These include an analysis of every person's interaction pattern, place, and role in the network, as well as an analysis of the overall structure of the network.

The first part of any network analysis is to look at the relationships between each individual in the network and all other individuals. These relationships are often called actor interactions. Formal descriptions of the way these network elements are analyzed are available in methodological books, such as *Social Network Analysis* (Wasserman and Faust 1994). These analytical processes can describe how each actor in a network is connected with each other actor, how each person can or cannot be reached through other people, how much influence each person has in the network, and how central, powerful, or well connected a person is. A second part of the actor analysis allows the researcher to determine if there are subgroups in the network, and if certain positions and/or roles that people take on have an important impact on people's lives. These elements of network analysis are often called social cohesion measures, structural equivalence measures, and regular equivalence measures. The final analysis looks at the overall characteristics of networks.

The possibilities for different types of whole network analysis, along with some specific measures of key relationships, are shown in Table 4.

Each of these types of analysis may be important in answering different kinds of questions that researchers may be asking about the relationships within a community. For example, if a person is very central in a network, is that person more likely to be infected by a communicable disease that is moving through the network than a person who is peripheral to the group? How long does it take tobacco prevention information to saturate a network from any given starting point? If you can only talk to one person in a network and you want that person to change everyone else's eating behavior, who is the best person to talk to? If there are two factions in a network, and you want to separate them to keep them from fighting, which bridges in the network allow you to split the groups by eliminating the smallest number of connections? If you have a community that is made up of many different networks (such as teenage gangs), are there certain positions or roles in each of the networks that allow you to predict that people in those positions will have very similar life conditions and be more like each other than they are like other members of their gang? You might be able to predict, and prevent, fatalities by knowing the conditions attached to each position in the gang.

One key strategy for analyzing a whole network data is to create both a visual and a statistical display of the presence and absence of key relationships. One of the two most common visual displays is a sociometric diagram where individuals (actors) are represented by symbols, such as circles for females and squares for males, and lines or arrows represent the relationship or

Table 4 *Examples of network measures from matrix data sets*[5]

Focus	Analytical strategy	Examples of measures
Relationship between actors	Graph connections	Geodesic distance, reach, flow, volume, walks, influence
Relationship between actors	Centrality, power and prestige measures	Degree centrality, closeness centrality, betweenness, flow betweenness, information, Bonacich power
Subgroups	Social cohesion	Cliques, components, *K*-cores, *n*-cliques, *n*-clans, *K*-plexes, factions, connectivity sets
Roles and positions	Structural equivalence	Profile similarity, tabu search, CONCOR, CATIJ, automorphic equivalence
Roles and positions	Regular equivalence	Categorical, continuous, tabu search
Whole network characteristics	Structural measures	Density, network centrality, transitivity

connection between them. The thickness of the line may represent the strength of the relationship (for valued data) and arrowheads may represent the direction of the relationship (for directional or potentially asymmetrical) data. The second most common display is to provide a data matrix that indicates the relationships by numbers in a person-by-person matrix. Finally, each type of relationship can be described by accompanying statistics, including such approaches as cluster analysis and multidimensional scaling, as well as summary statistics.

Figure 3 is an example of a sociometric representation of the relationships described in a network where the lines represent sharing drugs. An arrow indicates one way sharing, while a line without a point indicates sharing in both directions. The thickness of the lines represents the frequency of sharing.

In this diagram, Aida (#7) is a nonuser, clearly represented in her lack of connections with the group. Anita (#13) shares the primary influence in the drug network with her son, Marcos (#5), and with Jaime (#9), who is central because he is a bilingual communication bridge between the Spanish (only) and the English (only) portions of the network. Marcos (#5) scores drugs for this network, keeps track of drug-related conditions, and influences the network through his mother's close connections with everyone else. The relationship chosen for this display was sharing drugs. Other data we collected indicated that #4 and #5, who are married to each other, are strongly tied by social relationships but are not connected by drug use. The kinship ties between #9 and #2 (living as married) are not visible in the drug relationship diagram either, nor is the aunt–niece connection between #6 and #7. This

points out the need to understand multiple relationships in a group, not just a single relationship, if you want a full understanding of a group.

The overall structure of the group is also important when compared with the structure of other drug-using networks. In this case, the comparative data showed that this is a tighter than normal network, due to the kinship ties among members, and that it has a better structure for solving social and drug-use problems than networks that are based on friendship and acquaintanceship alone. It is more stable and has resisted change longer than other types of drug networks. This condition makes this type of network harder to change, for HIV risk reduction, than networks where people can more easily be isolated from the influence of their peers.

THE FUTURE OF NETWORK STUDIES

The future of network studies in anthropology, and in the other social sciences, combines the continual exploration of the questions asked above with some new areas for the expansion of the paradigm. Anthropologists have not come close to exhausting the limits of the three network paradigms (personal, chained, or whole network approaches) in their studies, either from a geographical or a subdisciplinary focus. Medical anthropology, cognitive anthropology, and economic anthropology have made the most substantial uses of this approach (Johnson 1994). However, political anthropology and educational anthropology have neglected this area of investigation, as have anthropologists who are interested in expression and symbol, in the impact of different schools of anthropological theory on one another, and in the impact of graduate programs on the structure and development of the disciple, to name just a few.

There is a need to re-explore and provide further information on informant accuracy. Policy decisions are being made on a daily basis, with global impact, based on what our informants tell us. While we know more than we did before, there are still areas of both memory and reporting that make this information more vulnerable and less predictable than is desirable.

The diffusion of information and innovation has held the anthropological imagination for decades, and promises to have very important implications for future studies, at the personal and at the whole network level. More needs to be done to define the impact of networks on

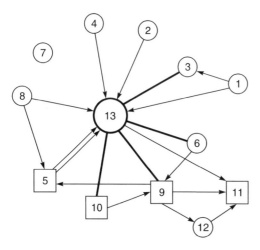

Figure 3   *Sociometric diagram of relationships in a drug-using network*

contagious diseases (Klovdahl 1985), on social support for victims of all types of problems (Sarason et al. 1986), and for directing power, influence, and information. This is an area where ethnography, mass media, and social network theory can be combined for very powerful findings.

There is still the need to understand the relationship between anthropological kinship analysis and network analysis. The importance of understanding kinship systems in a global geopolitical economy has been highly underrated and needs to be revisited. The news is full of stories about developing countries where kinship plays the key role in distributing power and influence over important sectors of the national economy, the national armed forces, and the national political system. The news is also full (sometimes only on the society page) of indications that the rich, famous, and powerful marry their children to people from their own social networks, further controlling power and fame in the next generation. The impact of kinship on social forces has a great deal of potential for further analysis.

On the other hand, there are some gaps in our knowledge that should be closed or addressed, even though they do not have the historical importance of those above. There is a great deal that we do not know about the boundaries of networks, or the impact of the borders of nations. There has been a lengthy debate on the definition of the term 'community,' and all of its associated terms and processes. Social network approaches can make a significant contribution not only to identifying rational boundaries, but also to showing how those boundaries change depending on the nature of relationships and the level of analysis that is being undertaken. We are still struggling with concepts of power, information sharing, shared governance, and other forms of social interaction. Social network approaches should be applied to these critical, political, and philosophical conditions.

Another neglected area is understanding and predicting the changes that occur in networks over time, from the micro-level personal network to macro-networks of society and the world. Evolutionary theory in anthropology potentially has a great deal to contribute in this area, and the issues of studying change through time are central to the discipline. Most networks are analyzed on the basis of a one-time picture, even though we know that our personal friends have changed over time, just as global alliances have changed. We need to know the mechanisms that cause the formation of networks, allow them to be stabilized and maintained, and cause their disruption and regeneration or their dissolution. What expectations should someone have in terms of knowing people as adults that they knew as children? How many friends from grade school do you still talk to? When and how should organizations or corporations, cities, states, or nations create alliances or change alliances, and when should they avoid them?

Finally, there is a very important unexplored area in social network research. This is the area of research ethics and the ethics of research. From one direction, we know very little about the impact of social networks on ethical conduct or ethical reasoning. This is an area that could be explored combining network methods, ethical inquiry, and anthropological theory. An important parallel issue is the exploration of the ethical conditions that need to be applied to conducting network research. Most of our ethical principles for research, such as the rules for the formation of institutional review boards or the Belmont Report (which sets out the basic principles of ethical research in the United States), are based on assumptions that may be either violated by, or in conflict with, the kinds of relationships and interconnections that exist in social networks. One of the three principles of research ethics is autonomy. Single individuals are assumed to be capable of deciding whether it is appropriate for them to participate in a research project, based on their being informed about the nature of the research and its risks (informed consent). However, this autonomy is potentially violated at the network level, when people are identified as part of a social network and information is given about them by the other members of the network, even if they themselves refuse to participate. Their participation may not achieve full autonomy, due to the influence of the network. The other primary principles, justice and beneficence, can also be challenging to apply when research is directed at a group, rather than at individuals. These conditions raise questions such as, 'Who should make the decision for a community to participate in a vaccine trial, individuals who want the vaccine, or community leaders who have an appreciation of the needs and the vulnerability of the community?' Who should benefit most from research on a group? Should it be individuals, the community, society at large, or the researchers? How do we make ethical choices to conduct or not to conduct research that will benefit society as a whole, but will be destructive to individuals or to small groups? How do we make judgements about research that will potentially harm a community (destroy its positive reputation, create stereotypes) but will be extremely beneficial to all of the individuals in the community who need certain services or need to know the dangers that confront them? How do we handle the ethical dilemmas posed by research that is viewed as positive, needed, and wanted by one subgroup in a culture, and viewed as negative, unwanted, and unneeded by another subgroup? There have been a number of studies that have benefited males but not females, one cultural group over another, and so on. Research, reporting, evaluating, and defining ethics beyond the level of the individual has been seriously underrepresented in the literature and deserves attention in the future along with the other questions raised above.

NOTES

1 Funding for some of the research reported in this chapter was provided by two grants from the National Institute on Drug Abuse (NIDA). These two grants were Grant #U01-DA07295, the Flagstaff Multicultural AIDS Prevention Project, and Grant #R01 DA09965, Small Town Drug Networks and HIV: Transmission Dynamics.

2 There are several reviews of social network theory that are important historical accounts of the theories and methods used in these studies and which form the backdrop for this chapter, but are not reviewed here. These include: Boissevain 1974; Burt 1980; Burt and Minor 1983; Harary 1965; Johnson 1994; Knoke and Kuklinski 1982; Marsden 1990; Marsden and Lin 1982; Rogers and Kincaid 1981; Scott 1991; Wasserman and Faust 1994; Wellman and Berkowitz 1988.

3 Some of the basics are reviewed or identified by Freeman (1979), and details are provided in Wasserman and Faust (1994). While not close to an exhaustive list, some of the seminal approaches that are of interest in anthropology, sociology, psychology, and political science are discussed in: Barnes 1980; Barnes and Harary, 1983; Bernard et al. 1990; Faust 1988; Freeman et al. 1989; Hage and Harary 1983, 1991; Hammer 1980; Johnson 1986, 1994; Johnson et al. 1989; Wellman 1988.

4 In order to participate, individuals had to be 18 years of age or older, could not have been in treatment in the past 12 months, and had to have a positive urine screen for cocaine or heroin, or needle marks (tracks) and a positive urine screen for some other injectable illicit drug. Therefore, this category includes only 18- and 19-year-olds.

5 This table, and the accompanying chapter, ignores dyadic and triadic network methods. These methods are rarely used in anthropology, although they do form a well-established area of social network analysis. These methods are discussed in detail in Part V, *Dyadic*

and Triadic Methods, and in Part VI, *Statistical Dyadic Interaction Models*, by Wasserman and Faust (1994).

REFERENCES

Barnes, J. (1980) 'Kinship studies: Some impressions of the current state of play', *Man*, 15: 293–303.

Barnes, J.A. and Harary, F. (1983) 'Graph theory in network analysis', *Social Networks*, 5: 235–44.

Bernard, H.R. and Killworth, P.D. (1973) 'On the social structure of an ocean-going research vessel and other important things', *Social Science Research*, 2: 145–84.

Bernard, H.R. and Killworth, P.D. (1977) 'Informant accuracy in social network data II', *Human Communications Research*, 4: 3–18.

Bernard, H.R. Killworth, P.D., and Sailer, L. (1980) 'Informant accuracy in social network data. IV. A comparison of clique-level structure in behavioral and cognitive network data', *Social Networks*, 2: 191–218.

Bernard, H.R., Killworth, P.D., and McCarty, C. (1982a) 'Index: An informant defined experiment in social structure', *Social Forces*, 61: 99–133.

Bernard, H.R., Killworth, P.D., and Sailer, L. (1982b) 'Informant accuracy in social network data. V. An experimental attempt to predict actual communication from recall data', *Social Science Research*, 11: 30–66.

Bernard, H.R., Killworth, P.D., Sailer, L., and Kronenfeld, D. (1984) 'On the validity of retrospective data', *Annual Review of Anthropology*, 13: 495–517.

Bernard, H.R., Johnsen, E.C., Killworth, P.D., and Robinson, S. (1989) 'Estimating the size of an average personal network and of an event subpopulation', in M. Kochen (ed.), *The Small World*. Norwood, NJ: Ablex. pp. 159–75.

Bernard, H.R., Johnsen, E.C., Killworth, P.D., Shelley, G.A., McCarty, C., and Robinson, S. (1990) 'Comparing four different methods of measuring personal social networks', *Social Networks*, 12: 179–215.

Boissevain, J. (1974) *Friends of Friends: Networks, Manipulators and Coalitions*. Oxford: Basil Blackwell.

Boster, J.S. (1986a) 'Selection for perceptual distinctiveness: Evidence from Aguaruna Jivaro varieties of *Manihot esculenta*', *Economic Botany*, 39: 310–25.

Boster, J.S. (1986b) 'Exchange of varieties and information between *Aguaruna manioc* cultivators', *American Anthropologist*, 88: 429–36.

Boster, J.S., Johnson, J.C., and Weller, S. (1987) 'Social position and shared knowledge: Actors' perception of status role and social structure', *Social Networks*, 9: 375–87.

Bott, E. (1971) *Family and Social Network: Roles, Norms, and External Relationships in Ordinary Urban Families*. London: Tavistock.

Burt, R.S. (1980) 'Models of network structure', *Annual Review of Sociology*, 6: 79–141.

Burt, R. (1984) 'Network items and the general social survey', *Social Networks*, 6: 293–339.

Burt, R. and Minor, J. (1983) (eds) *Applied Network Analysis*. Beverly Hills, CA: Sage.

Cohen, S. and Syme, S.L. (eds) (1985) *Social Support and Health*. San Francisco, CA: Academic Press.

Coleman, J.S., Katz, E., and Menzel, H. (1966) *Medical Innovation: A Diffusion Study*. New York: Bobbs Merrill.

Faust, K. (1988) 'Comparison of methods of positional analysis: Structural and general equivalences', *Social Networks*, 10: 313–41.

Frank, O. (1979) 'Estimation of population totals by use of snowball samples', in P. Holland and S. Leinhards (eds), *Perspectives on Social Network Research*. New York: Academic Press. pp. 319–47.

Freeman, L. (1979) 'Centrality in social networks: Conceptual clarification', *Social Networks*, 1: 215–39.

Freeman, L.C. and Thompson, C.R. (1989) 'Estimating acquaintanceship volume,' in M. Kochen (ed.), *The Small World*. Norwood, NJ: Ablex. pp. 147–58.

Freeman, L.C., Romney, A.K., and Freeman, S.C. (1987a) 'Words, deeds and social structure', *Human Organization*, 201–19.

Freeman, L.C., Romney, A.K., and Freeman, S.C. (1987b) 'Cognitive structure and informant accuracy', *American Anthropologist*, 89: 310–25.

Freeman, L.C., Freeman, S.C., and Michaelson, A.G. (1988) 'On human social intelligence', *Journal of Social and Biological Structure*, 11: 415–25.

Freeman, L.C., Freeman, S.C., and Michaelson, A. (1989) 'How humans see social groups: A test of the Sailer–Gaulin models', *Journal of Quantitative Anthropology*, 1: 229–38.

Galaskiewicz, J. and Wasserman, S. (1993) 'Social network analysis: Concepts, methodology, and directions for the 1990s', *Sociological Methods & Research*, 221: 3–22.

Hage, P. and Harary, F. (1983) *Structural Models in Anthropology*. London: Cambridge University Press.

Hage, P. and Harary, F. (1991) *Exchange in Oceania: A Graph Theoretic Analysis*. New York: Clarendon.

Hammer, M. (1980) 'Predictability of social connections over time', *Social Networks*, 2: 165–80.

Hammer, M. (1983) ' "Core" and "extended" social networks in relation to health and illness', *Social Science and Medicine*, 17: 405–22.

Harary, F., Norman, R.Z., and Cartwright, D. (1965) *Structural Models*. New York: Wiley.

Hays, R.B., Chauncy, S., and Tobey, L.A. (1990) 'The social support networks of gay men with AIDS', *Journal of Community Psychology*, 18: 374–85.

Johnson, J.C. (1986) 'Social networks and innovation adoption: A look at Burt's use of structural equivalence', *Social Networks*, 8: 343–64.

Johnson, J.C. (1990) *Selecting Ethnographic Informants*. Newbury Park, CA: Sage.

Johnson, J.C. (1994) 'Anthropological contributions to the study of social networks: A review', in S. Wasserman and J. Galackiewicz (eds), *Advances in Social Network Analysis*. Beverly Hills: Sage. pp. 113–47.

Johnson, J.C. and Miller, M.L. (1983) 'Deviant positions in small groups: The relation between role and individual', *Social Networks*, 5: 51–69.

Johnson, J.C., Boster, J.S., and Holbert, D. (1989) 'Estimating relational attributes from snowball samples through simulation', *Social Networks*, 11: 135–58.

Kapferer, B. (1973) 'Social network and conjugal role in urban Zambia: Toward a reformulation of the Bott hypothesis', in J. Boissevain and J.C. Mitchell (eds), *Network Analysis: Studies in Human Interaction*. The Hague: Mouton. pp. 83–110.

Killworth, P.D. and Bernard, H.R. (1976) 'Informant accuracy in social network data', *Human Organization*, 35: 269–86.

Killworth, P.D. and Bernard, H.R. (1978) 'The reversal small-world experiment', *Social Networks*, 1: 159–92.

Killworth, P.D. and Bernard, H.R. (1979) 'A pseudo-model of the small world problem', *Social Forces*, 58: 477–505.

Killworth, P.D. and Bernard, H.R. (1979–1980) 'Informant accuracy in social network data. III. A comparison of triadic structures in behavior and cognitive data', *Social Networks*, 2: 19–46.

Killworth, P.D. and Bernard, H.R. (1982) 'A technique for comparing mental maps', *Social Networks*, 3: 307–12.

Killworth, P.D., Johnsen, E.C., Bernard, H.R., Shelly, G.A., and McCarty, C. (1990) 'Estimating the size of personal networks', *Social Networks*, 12: 289–312.

Klovdahl, A.S. (1985) 'Social networks and the spread of infectious diseases: The AIDS example', *Social Science Medicine*, 21: 1203–16.

Klovdahl, A.S. (1989) 'Urban social networks: Some methodological problems and possibilities', in M. Kochen (ed.), *The Small World*. Norwood, NJ: Ablex.

Klovdahl, A.S., Potterat, J.J., Woodhouse, D.E., Muth, J.B., Muth, S.Q., and Darrow, W.W. (1994) 'Social networks and infectious disease: The Colorado Springs study', *Social Science and Medicine*, 38: 79–88.

Knoke, D. and Kuklinski, J.H. (1982) *Network Analysis*. Newbury Park, CA: Sage.

Latkin, C.A. (1995) 'A Personal Network Approach to AIDS Prevention', in R.H. Needle, S.L. Coil, S. Genser, and R.T. Trotter, II (eds), *Social Network Analysis, HIV Prevention and Drug Abuse*. NIDA

Monograph 151, Bethesda, MD: National Institute on Drug Abuse. pp. 181–95.

Latkin, C.A., Mandell, W., Vlahov, D., Oziemkowska, M., and Celentano, D.D. (1996) 'The long-term outcome of a personal network-oriented HIV prevention intervention for injection drug users: The SAFE study', *American Journal of Community Psychology*, 24: 341–64.

Marsden, P.V. (1990) 'Network data and measurement', *Annual Review of Sociology*, 16: 435–63.

Marsden, P.V. (1993) 'Reliability measurement', *Social Networks*, 16: 435–63.

Marsden, P.V. and Lin, N. (eds) (1982) *Social Structure and Network Analysis*. Newbury Park, CA: Sage.

McCallister, L. and Fischer, C. (1983) 'A procedure for surveying personal networks', in R. Burt and J. Minor (eds), *Applied Network Analysis*. Beverly Hills, CA: Sage.

Michaelson, A. and Contractor, N.S. (1992) 'Structural position and perceived similarity', *Social Psychology Quarterly*, 55: 300–10.

Morrill, C. (1991) 'The customs of conflict management among corporate executives', *American Anthropologist*, 93: 871–93.

Needle, R.H., Coyle, S.L., Genser, S.G., Trotter, R.T., II (eds) (1995) Social Networks, Drug Abuse, and HIV Transmission. NIDA Research Monograph Series, No. 151.

Ostrow, D.G., Whitaker, R.E.D., Frasier, K., Cohen, C., Wan, J., Frank, C., and Fisher, E. (1991) 'Racial differences in social support and mental health in men with HIV infection: A pilot study', *AIDS Care*, 3: 55–62.

Palmore, J.A. (1967) 'The Chicago snowball: A study of the flow and diffusion of family planning information', in D.J. Bogue (ed.), *Sociological Contributions to Family Planning Research*. Chicago: University of Chicago Press. pp. 272–63.

Pasternak, B. (1976) *Introduction to Kinship and Social Organization*. Englewood Cliffs, NJ: Prentice Hall.

Plattner, S.M. (1978) 'Occupation and kinship in a developing society', *Human Organization*, 37: 77–83.

Poole, I. De S. and Kochen, M. (1978) 'Contracts and influence', *Social Networks*, 1: 5–51.

Rogers, E.M. and Kincaid, D.L. (1981) *Communication Networks: A New Paradigm for Research*. New York: Free Press.

Romney, A.K. and Faust, K. (1983) 'Predicting the structure of a communications network from recalled data', *Social Networks*, 4: 285–304.

Romney, A.K. and Weller, S.C. (1984) 'Predicting informant accuracy from patterns of recall among individuals', *Social Networks*, 4: 59–77.

Romney, A.K., Weller, S.C., and Batchelder, W.H. (1986) 'Culture as a consensus: A theory of culture and informant accuracy', *American Anthropologist*, 88: 313–38.

Sarason, I.G., Leveine, H.M., Basham, R.B., and Sarason, B.R. (1983) 'Assessing social support:

The social support questionnaire', *Journal of Personality and Social Psychology*, 44: 127–39.

Sarason, I., Sarason, B., and Shearin, E.N. (1986) 'Social support as an individual difference variable', *Journal of Personality and Social Psychology*, 50: 845–55.

Schweizer, T. (1988) 'Detecting positions in networks: A formal analysis of loose social structure in rural Java', *American Anthropologist*, 90: 944–53.

Scott, J. (1991) *Network Analysis: A Handbook*. Newbury Park, CA: Sage.

Seidman, S.B. and Foster, B.L. (1978a) 'A note on the potential for genuine cross-fertilization between anthropology and mathematics', *Social Networks*, 1: 65–72.

Seidman, S. and Foster, B. (1978b) 'A graph theoretic generalization of the clique concept', *Journal of Mathematical Sociology*, 6: 139–54.

Shelley, G.A. (1992) The social networks of people with end-state renal disease: Comparing hemodialysis and peritoneal dialysis patients. Unpublished Doctoral Dissertation, University of Florida, Department of Anthropology.

Snijders, T.A.B. (1992) 'Estimation on the basis of snowball samples: How to weight', *Bulletin de Methodologie Sociologique*, 36: 59–70.

Trotter, R.T. II, Potter, J.M., Bowen, A.M., and Jiron, D. (Tradduction Arturo Ortiz) (1994) Enfoques Etnograficos y analisis de las redes sociales, para la creacion de programs de prevencion del uso de drogas y de VIH, en ursarios activos. In Las Adicciones: Hacia un Enfoque Multidisciplinario. Consejo Nacional contra las Adicciones. Secrataria de salud, Mexico. Mexico, DF: pp. 45–54.

Trotter, R.T. II, Bowen, A.M., and Potter, J.M. (1995a) 'Network models for HIV outreach and prevention programs for drug users', in R.H. Needle, S.L. Colle, S. Genser, and R.T. Trotter, II (eds), *Social Network Analysis, HIV Prevention and Drug Abuse*. NIDA Monograph 151, Bethesda, MD. National Institute on Drug Abuse. pp. 144–80.

Trotter, R.T., II, Rothenberg, R.B., and Coyle, S. (1995b) 'Drug abuse and HIV prevention research: Expanding paradigms and network contributions to risk reduction', *Connections*, 18: 29–46.

Trotter, R.T. II, Baldwin, J.A., and Bowen, A.M. (1995c) 'Network structure and proxy network measures of HIV, drug and incarceration risks for active drug users', *Connections*, 18: 89–104.

Trotter, R.T., Bowen, A.M., Baldwin, J.A., and Price, L.J. (1996) 'The efficacy of network-based HIV/ AIDS risk reduction programs in midsized towns in the United States', *Journal of Drug Issues*, 26: 591–606.

Valente, T.W. (1993) 'Diffusion of innovations and policy decision-making', *Journal of Communication*, 43: 30–45.

Valente, T.W. (1995) *Network Models of the Diffusion of Innovations*. Cresskill, NJ: Hampton.

Valente, T.W. (1996) 'Social network thresholds in the diffusion of innovations', *Social Networks*, 18: 69–89.

Wasserman, S. and Faust, K. (1994) *Social Networks Analysis: Methods and Applications*. Cambridge: Cambridge University Press.

Wellman, B. (1988) 'Structural analysis: From method and metaphor to theory and substance', in B. Wellman and S.D. Berkowitz (eds), *Social Structures: A Network Approach*. Cambridge: Cambridge University Press. pp. 19–61.

Wellman, B. and Berkowitz, S.D. (eds) (1988) *Social Structures: A Network Approach*. Cambridge: Cambridge University Press.

Werner, O. and Schoepfle, G.M. (1987) *Systematic Fieldwork* (2 vols). Newbury Park, CA: Sage.

White, D.R. and Jorian, P. (1992) 'Representing and computing kinship: A new approach', *Current Anthropology*, 33: 454–63.

Williams, H.A. (1993) 'A comparison of social support and social networks of black parents and white parents with chronically ill children', *Social Science and Medicine*, 12: 1509–20.

2.3

Personal Experience of Illness

ARTHUR KLEINMAN AND DON SEEMAN

INTRODUCTION

'They need to understand that we don't live in a health clinic.' These are the words of an Ethiopian–Israeli political activist, protesting his country's public health policy with respect to the prevention of HIV infection. In particular, he objected to the routinized (but unpublicized) destruction of blood donations made by Ethiopian immigrants, which he believed had stigmatized his community in a way that would have important social and health consequences (Seeman 1997). Indeed, the two can hardly be separated. As experience in the United States and elsewhere has shown, serious consequences can derive from depicting an ethnically defined segment of the population primarily as a vector of risk for infectious disease without an equal degree of concern for their own pressing health needs, or for the political and economic conditions that help to put them at increased risk.

In this case, bureaucratic taxonomies that kept particular groups of potential immigrants languishing in Addis Ababa transit camps for 5 years or more can be correlated with high rates of HIV infection, which were then deployed in arguments for the further restriction of immigration. For the ill and their families, this contributes to an already heavy burden of ostracism within their own ethnic community as well as the general society. The experience of illness becomes overlaid with concern for the collective authenticity of immigrants as citizens and their perceived rebuff by medical institutions. Haitians demonstrating over blood bank policies in New York (Farmer 1992) and Ethiopians demonstrating over blood bank policies in Jerusalem represent important local variations on a set of themes that appear increasingly international in scope, defined by a language of technical efficiency and cost effectiveness, which may leave little room for the concern with experience that we are advocating in this chapter.

The accusation that public health experts and government officials had acted as if the world they inhabited was one devoid of social meanings and free of the structural violence which systematically exposes some groups to risk while denying social responsibility for that risk represents a simplified diagnosis of a specific local problem, but it is a problem that can be heard echoing through many other settings. Whether the specific illness complaint is one of chronic pain whose contours are shaped by the traumatic political upheavals of revolutionary China (Kleinman and Kleinman 1994), or one of the 'emerging infectious diseases' whose paths of devastation can be shown to converge with those of impoverishment and international economic exploitation (Farmer 1996), the message that emerges from careful ethnographic research is that illness has a determinative social context and course (see Kleinman et al. 1995). 'We don't live in a health clinic' is a reminder that the *social course of illness* and the *personal experience of illness* are analytically inseparable.

Those whose lives are most directly touched by illness – the sick, their families, and members of their social networks (including in some cases their immediate care providers) – can often be heard resisting the reductionistic categories into which their experience is sometimes parsed by both medical professionals and social scientists. The aim of this chapter, therefore, is to suggest a more experientially valid and morally engaged mode of analysis. A useful conception of illness experience must bear sufficient theoretical weight to allow for the sustained analysis of its moral and social bases. It should also speak to the need for deepening both clinical care and research paradigms. The 'personal experience of illness' necessarily connects with a broad world of theoretical and practical concern.

Consider the anger of Mavis Williams, mother of a 23-year-old son in the United States who suffers from muscular dystrophy. When she was asked to fill out a questionnaire concerning the effect of her son's illness on her family, she responded instead with rage towards the investigator: 'There is a little voice in me which, if I knew you better, would scream at you: Doctor, [my son's illness] has murdered this family! There is no stability; we can't work it through . . . Before Andrew's disaster we were like everyone else: some days good, some bad . . . Now we are burning up. I sometimes think we are all dying, not just Andy. Even my parents and brothers and sisters have been more than "affected" . . . '

She proceeds to tell the tale of her family; of a husband who collapsed under the burden of his son's sickness, began to drink, and then disappeared; of two other children whose lives have been framed by the twin specters of guilt ('because they are normal') and intense (yet inexpressible) anger towards their mother, who has been absorbed with Andrew's care. As for Mavis Williams, she is morally and physically spent, and blames herself for much of her family's demise. 'You look around you, look!' she pleads. 'This, what you see, this tomb, our family's tomb.'

This is only a brief vignette of a story that has been told in greater detail elsewhere (Kleinman 1988: 183–4), but it confirms an important presupposition of our analysis. *The experience of illness is not bounded by the bodies or consciousness of those who are ill.* It reaches out to encompass a household, a family, or a social network. It reaches deep into the inner world of patients, yet is decidedly transpersonal. Where is the suffering located in the case of Mavis Williams and her son? In Andrew, dying of a progressively debilitating disorder? In his mother? His siblings? Obviously, the illness experience affects each of them, not in isolation, not always in the same way, but in relation to one another. A questionnaire can ask about symptoms and evaluate disability, but it cannot get at the qualities of experience that are so deeply at stake in this family tragedy.

It is the irreducible 'sociosomatic' quality of illness experience, rooted in the infrapolitics of everyday life as well as the more encompassing political, economic, and cultural realities of the societies we live in, which should be of deep concern to both social scientists and medical professionals. When we describe 'illness experience,' therefore, we mean something other than the stories of individuals, robbed of social context, cultural mooring, or personal agency and exigency. Illness experience as we are using that term here needs to be recognized for something that is not necessarily transparent to the categories of traditional biomedicine or social science, but more responsive to the contradiction, indeterminacy, and moral weightiness – in the sense of something being desperately at stake – which opens out to us from our encounter with Mavis Williams and her family. For a family such as hers, or for an immigrant group protesting the 'rational and necessary' measures taken by public health experts, the experience of illness takes on a wider significance than the view from the clinic might at first suggest.

What do we Mean by Illness?

One early contribution of medical anthropology, which, with some revision, remains crucial to our discussion of illness experience in this chapter, is the analytic distinction between illness and disease (Kleinman 1980: 72–80). Stated simply, 'disease' has been defined in medical anthropology as the practioner's construction of patient complaints in the technical terminology of a particular healing system. Thus, for biomedicine, 'disease' refers to 'abnormalities in the structure and/or function of organs and organ systems; pathological states whether or not they are culturally recognized; the arena of the biomedical model' (Young 1982: 264). This is not to say that other professional and folk healing systems (Aryuvedic, traditional Chinese, etc.) do not maintain their own technical concepts of disease, although the term has been less widely used in this context.

'Illness,' on the other hand, has been deployed as an 'experience-near' category, within which room can be found for the culturally patterned social and personal elements of sickness, which are often excluded as a matter of course from the technically constrained discourse on disease. As Allan Young wrote in his 1982 review article, 'Anthropologies of Illness and of Sickness,' 'illness refers to a person's perceptions and experiences of certain socially disvalued states, including, but not limited to, disease' (Young 1982: 265). In this conception, 'muscular dystrophy' would be considered by physicians of biomedicine a disease of the central nervous system. Its powerful and destructive ripple effect on the life-world of the Williams family, and on the bodily and emotional health of its members, constitutes the corresponding illness that is often excluded from consideration.

Part of the reason that the dichotomy between illness and disease was so fruitful for medical anthropology – but also perhaps limiting in certain ways – was that it mirrored a defining feature of contemporary biomedicine; namely, the self-avowed reductionism which is typically invoked in the name of instrumental rationality and, with growing urgency today, economic efficiency as well. A particularly striking example, as Byron Good has shown, is the systematic training of American medical students to locate the essence of disease not in the interpersonal context of social and political life, nor even within the contingent life trajectories of particular individuals, but in the ostensibly irreducible cellular and molecular processes which are the subject of increasing technical manipulation (Good 1994). This is a powerful local knowledge feature of contemporary biomedicine (cf. Geertz 1983), and we should not gainsay its contribution to the tremendous international prestige and efficacy of some biomedical interventions.

On the other hand, anthropologists and others have been painfully aware of what can get left out of accounts in this reductionist tradition, which pervades not only the training of medical students, but clinical practice and research as well. The limits of reductionist models are evident in at least three areas, each of which provides a special challenge to medical and social science paradigms, which we hope the study of illness experience can help to address. It is worth remembering, however, that while the distinction between illness and disease described above was originally conceived as an alternative to narrow and exlusionary biomedical accounts, it has not been useful to an equal degree in addressing each of these three areas of concern.

1. *Reductionist accounts may contribute to a regime of knowledge in which the social roots and distribution of disease as well as of resources for care are misrecognized.* This occurs when disease is treated as a property of individuals outside of meaningful social and political context. It has been argued convincingly, for instance, that poverty is *the* major worldwide risk factor today for mortality due to infectious disease (Farmer 1996). However, contemporary social science and medical accounts alike often focus on pathologies of individual choice and 'risk behavior' as if these were self-evident and untheorized constructs. Reference to the powerful and historically conditioned constraints on choice in precisely those settings where the burden of disease has been greatest tends to be avoided. Few accounts, for instance, note that poor women in many societies are at special risk for sexually transmitted disease. This is so, not because of their pathological inability to make appropriate behavioral choices, but because existing structures of power and economic inequality render them incapable of refusing the sexual demands of male partners, including their husbands (Farmer et al. 1996).

The perception of injustice, so often a component of illness experience, accurately reflects the structual violence that contributes to differential risk for sickness in many settings. Yet, this feature of social reality is typically absent from biomedical and public health narratives, and it is frequently (although by no means as systematically) absent from alternative professional and folk accounts of disease as well (Leslie and Young 1992). To the extent that we rely on stylized cultural narratives of illness therefore, there is a risk that anthropological accounts will parallel those of biomedicine in this regard. Investigation of the illness experience should always lead back to a consideration of the shifting political, historical, and physiological realities in which it is rooted. The analytic distinction between illness and disease ought not preclude an investigation of their subtle interlinkages.

2. *Reductionist accounts may overlook or exacerbate the disruptive and morally ramified effects of illness on the life-worlds of sufferers.* This is one of the problems that the illness model in medical anthropology was explicitly designed to ameliorate. Indeed, it is the contingent depiction of suffering in particular life-worlds that is most often identified with this approach. Not confronting the domain of illness can lead to a serious dehumanization of medical care. A physician who does not attend to the demoralizing effects of life with chronic pain, for example, its ability to drown out those qualities that make life seem worthwhile, and its tendency to raise suspicions of malingering or insincerity by the sufferers, will not adequately respond to the sufferer's needs (see Good et al. 1992). Worse, the physician may be drawn subtely into the chorus of doubting and frustrated voices which add to sufferers' misery (Scarry 1985: 4). Attending to the illness, and not just the disease, means taking the socially embedded person seriously. The late philosopher Emmanuel Levinas (1988) suggested that the call of medicine is the call to respond to sufferers' 'originary cry for help,' which includes, but is not limited to, the biomedically defined 'presenting symptoms' alone. Biomedical and other cultural idioms enter the stream of illness experience in complex and unpredictable ways, and should be approached not abstractly, but rather phenomenologically, as they appear from within and help to shape that lived context.

3. Medical anthropology, perhaps more than any other discipline, has shown that biomedi-

cine's striking (and perhaps unique) attempt to disengage healing from the realm of moral meaning may *allow cultural realities, which have great bearing on the course of illness and disease, to be made peripheral to its concern* (Kirmayer 1992; Kleinman 1980, 1988). There is by now an extensive literature on the ways in which illness is embedded in particular local systems of meaning and discourse (e.g., Brodwin 1996; Good 1976; Rubel et al. 1984; Taylor 1992). In one study, Karen Pliskin (1987) showed that doctors' inability to come to terms with the somatized rhetoric of complaint among Iranian immigrant patients led to frustration on the part of doctors and misdiagnosis of some patients as mentally ill.

In the field of mental health, cultural specificity has even attained a level of formal recognition, through the notion of 'culture bound syndromes,' which has been adopted within the diagnostic canons of DSM-IIIR and DSM-IV. While some authors have gone so far as to collapse the distinction between illness and disease completely in this setting, claiming that all mental illness is, in effect, culture-dependant and specific (Obeyesekere 1985), we prefer a more nuanced approach. It is by now increasingly well documented that social and cultural factors play a significant role in the presentation and course of mental illness, including those disorders whose etiologies are considered to have a strong biogenetic component (Ware and Kleinman 1992). Ethnography has been recognized by international bodies like the World Health Organization as an important tool in the design and analysis of successful strategies for intervention in the area of mental health (Desjarlais et al. 1995).

What these developments suggest, however, is a reconsideration of any dualism that may have been implied by the analytic distinction between illness and disease (Kleinman 1988; Schweder 1988). Biomedical and psychotherapeutic perspectives are now increasingly subject to the kind of sustained cultural and social analyses that have long been applied to so-called vernacular idioms of illness and healing (e.g., Bosk 1979; Conrad and Gallagher 1993; Martin 1987; Young 1995). The claims made by some practitioners of these disciplines to an acultural and transparent objectivity have been called seriously into question by studies in the anthropology, sociology, and history of science and medicine.

At the same time, current research has seen a renewal of interest in the deep interconnection between human psychophysiology and the social world. Researchers in medical anthropology, for instance, have been moving towards a conception of 'local biologies,' by which is meant the flexible interaction of social, cultural, and biological realities to produce locally distinctive patterns of bodily response (Kleinman and Becker, forthcoming; Kleinman and Kleinman 1994; Lock 1993a, 1993b). In a sense, the culture concept has become an even more powerful analytic tool than it was once thought. The realm of biomedical disease, previously bracketed from anthropological concern, is now being relinked with illness in a more subtle and less dualistic fashion.

Medical anthropology's impressive success with the culture concept has not, however, been matched by an equal concern with the *experiential* dimension of illness, which is the key to any nondualist conception. There are relatively few ethnographies of experience to match the thick description of culture that has characterized anthropological writing. This is a serious gap, because as sophisticated as our theories of culture may come to be, they will never grant a sufficient theoretical purchase on the complex illness experience of a woman like Mavis Williams, whose life is embedded within, but not determined by, her cultural repertoire. Cultural knowledge alone will never allow us to predict, or even to describe, the outcomes of medical and policy interventions in the lives of real people and communities.

In some cases, a focus on culture may even obscure more than it reveals, allowing the heavy hand of the interpreter to rob lived experience of its forcefulness and contingency by forcing it to conform with preconceived cultural categories. Recourse to these typically timeless categories may involve a denial or depoliticization of fluid social and political experience, which typically includes real struggle over both meaning and material resources. In the case of the Ethiopian–Israeli protesters with which we began this chapter, public health experts, politicians, and anthropologists all tended to reduce immigrant anger to an expression of the symbolic importance of blood 'in their culture.' By doing so, they ignored the politically ramified deployment of that symbolism in ways that could not have been predicted through a purely 'cultural' reading. *At stake* for these immigrants was not just the cultural symbolism of blood or of 'honor,' but their threatened membership in a national collective, and the right to a voice in the shaping of public health policies whose implementation would certainly have life and death consequences for their community. Culture, in the sense in which it is often invoked in public discourse, is an essential but insufficient component of this discussion.

Even a sensitive and compelling cultural analysis such as that of Anne Fadiman (1997), in her account of tragic miscommunication between a

Hmong refugee family in Merced, California, and their American doctors, relies on a totalizing framework of cultural difference, to the extent that other aspects of social life are neglected. A concern with experience, by contrast, would force us to challenge the sovereignty of cultural models, and to dispense with the false sense of predictability that they may help to generate. Despite frequent anthropological critiques, we maintain that the experience of illness is just as irreducible to the theoretical categories of cultural analysis as it is to those of biomedicine (Kleinman and Kleinman 1991). Experience itself must be subject to sustained analysis.

WHAT DO WE MEAN BY EXPERIENCE?

One of the great challenges facing medical anthropology today is the definition of experience in a useful and consistent way. In this chapter, we are using experience to represent the intersubjective, felt flow of events, bodily processes, and life trajectory which always takes place within a social setting. Experience is 'the outcome of cultural categories and social structures interacting with psychophysiological processes such that a mediating world is constituted' (Kleinman and Kleinman 1991: 277). This stands in contrast to commonplace assumptions in everyday usage, which treat 'experience' as a property of deep and individual subjectivity. When we say that experience is 'intersubjective,' we mean that it is constituted in social space; we call attention to the link between the social world, subjectivity, and psychophysiological processes, which becomes most apprehensible – and for sufferers most intractable – through the experience of illness itself.

Take the case of Huang Zhenyi, a worker from a rural town who was in his late twenties when he was first interviewed. (This account is paraphrased from that published in Kleinman 1986). Huang Zhenyi suffered from depression, and from chronic headaches and dizziness that he attributed to a traumatic childhood experience during the Chinese Cultural Revolution, about which he was able to talk only with his wife. As a child, he had found a piece of paper in his schoolyard with the message 'Throw down Chairman Mao' written in bold characters. A friend convinced him to turn the sign in to commune leaders, who responded by calling in public security agents who accused him of the crime. Huang Zhenyi was threatened during a long interrogation that he would not be allowed to go home or to the toilet unless he confessed.

He told his interrogators, however, that he had not written the slogan, and was angry at his friend for not backing up the story. Eventually, he was allowed to return home, and assured his distraught mother that he had done nothing wrong.

This was not, however, the end of Huang Zhenyi's ordeal. He was arrested again the next morning, and told that this time he would never leave the interrogation room without a confession. Terrified, he signed the confession, but decided not to tell his mother the truth, fearing it would only cause her trouble. Instead, he told her that he had written the slogan himself. 'If I knew you'd end up like this,' she said amidst curses and tears, 'I wouldn't have wanted you.' Huang Zhenyi remembers weeping, but found himself unable to tell his mother the truth. 'I felt like a coward. I couldn't tell her.'

This experience is not without precedent in Huang Zhenyi's autobiographical narrative. In fact, it recalls earlier incidents both in terms of the moral meaning that it conveys and the particular nexus of bodily and emotional complaints with which it is identified. At the age of 8, for instance, Huang Zhenyi had played truant from school with some friends. The angry teacher punished them by locking them in a small room, but they escaped. Huang Zhenyi recounts his experience of being searched for by his outraged teacher: 'I was so frightened, I froze in my place. I could not move.' When he returned to school the next day, in fact, the teacher ordered him to do menial work around the school rather than study. When he refused, he was criticized severely in front of other teachers. Recounting this event many years later, and in the light of his subsequent experience, Huang Zhenyi reports: 'My liver became small, and I became frightened, cowardly.' From this time on, he felt 'paralyzed' whenever he had to 'stand up' for himself before adults, a bodily symptom of an essentially moral failure.

Because of his admission of guilt in writing the anti-Maoist slogan 12-year-old Huang Zhenyi (again feeling 'paralyzed') was marched through the town wearing a dunce's cap, carrying a sign around his neck on which he had written a self-criticism. He was cursed and spat at by local people, and then sent to do the work of an adult as a peasant on a local production team. In addition, he had to undergo public self-criticism each day, and at one such session he felt himself go numb and mute, unable to scream out the truth he so desperately wanted to tell. Even later, when he returned to school and then resettled in a town where nobody knew his background, he remained unwilling to confess the full story to his mother, and so she died without knowing of his innocence. Huang Zhenyi returns to this fact again and again as a palpable explanation for his later feelings of desperate shame and self-hatred and for his physical symptoms. He felt a searing sense of injustice and anger, which he associated with a burning sensation in his head, dizziness, and exhaustion: all culturally salient symptoms of *shenging shuziruo*, or neurasthenia. He remained fearful that the events of his youth would return to cause him problems in his current life.

This story cannot be understood without recourse to key cultural idioms of distress and complaint in China, which have already been explored at length elsewhere (Kleinman 1986; Kleinman and Kleinman 1991). It is important to emphasize, however, that cultural analysis alone would be insufficient for the task at hand. Illness experience connects the social and cultural context and the biography of a person – not any person, but a highly specific one – to the disease process. Illness experience is given a shape and pattern by the shared categories of culture, gender, ethnicity, social position, and age cohort, but it is also unique in each particular case. The illness experience is as complex and subtle as the composition of a symphony organized around the simple structure of movements and a basic recurrent theme. Individual perception, interpretation based in past experience, learned patterns of coping, and local explanatory models, as well as the personal virtuosity of metaphor are all brought to bear on the experience of illness. Thus, *illness experience becomes a site for the infolding of the social world onto the body – but in a way that interacts complexly with, rather than effacing, the contingency of individual lives.*

WHAT IS AT STAKE?

While experience remains a difficult and somewhat elusive subject of inquiry, one of the approaches that has proven most useful has been the use of ethnography to elucidate what is at stake for people and groups in particular local settings. 'What is at stake?' is a gloss for attempts to explore the link between culturally patterned and personally contingent elements of experience as they impose themselves on people's lives. In Huang Zhenyi's story, part of what was at stake was the culturally interpreted 'dizziness' of moral and social disorder that he had been forced to endure. These social conditions continued to express themselves through the embodied symptoms of his illness even many years after the events in question. Huang Zhenyi's vertigo was (among other things) an

expression of stylized meanings carried by that symptom in classical Chinese moral and physiological theory, and cannot be readily understood without reference to them.

At the same time, however, Huang Zhenyi's story participates in that of an entire generation who lived through the Cultural Revolution. The collective experience of his generation gives Huang Zhenyi's complaint a resonance that contributes to its lived, phenomenological quality – its reception within a local social network, and its moral meaning for both Huang and others with whom he might share it. Finally, there is a resolutely personal quality to this story that cannot be replicated, and which resonates within a specific life trajectory of loss, disappointment, and the inability to speak at crucial junctures. Failure to attend to any of these levels – the personal, the collective historical, or the broadly cultural – would be to misrepresent the illness experience in its complexity. We will return to this tripartite model at the end of this chapter.

Reflecting on what is at stake for people is one way to avoid the reductionist determinisms to which both medicine and culture theory may sometimes fall prey. In Bali, for example, the typically placid and unemotional demeanor of many who have suffered personal loss led a generation of ethnographers to suggest that grief in its Western sense was foreign to Balinese sensibilities – an imposition of foreign cultural and moral values on an incommensurate cultural reality. Uni Wikan, however, has employed the ethnography of experience to argue that Balinese poise and emotional calm in the face of loss is actually a strategy for avoiding the harm to self and community which are associated with extreme negative emotion (Wikan 1988, 1990). Through her ethnography of what is at stake for particular people in particular life contexts (which is something very different from the ethnography of Balinese 'culture' in a generalized and abstract sense), Wikan shows that Balinese are characterized less by a lack of powerful emotion than by a social concern for the devastating power of emotional turmoil. This revision of received wisdom was made possible because Wikan looked beyond the cultural stereotypes in which informants and anthropologists had both sometimes traded, in order to explore what was deeply at stake for a particular young woman in her own long struggle with grief over the death of a lover. The focus on what is at stake in emotional life has special relevance for an ethnography of illness experience, which is often characterized (and in the case of depression, clinically defined) by its powerful affective dimension (cf. Lutz and White 1986; Rosaldo 1989).

Furthermore, the stakes of experience almost inevitably include political and socioeconomic concerns. These may range from considerations of belonging and exclusion for migrants moving through the bureaucratic labyrinths of state medical and immigration services (Ong 1995; Seeman 1997), to the 'search for respect' by young men in one of America's devastated inner cities (Bourgois 1995), or the desire to attain a degree of culturally validated autonomy from crippling chronic pain through employment (Good 1992). The stakes of experience involve whatever is most intractably 'given' in a local setting; that which imposes itself upon consciousness and informs social interaction because of its overwhelming importance to the people involved. The stakes are culturally patterned and interpreted, but often of literally life and death significance. As researchers, a concern with the stakes of experience also forces us to consider noncognitive features of social and cultural life: not just how people interpret, categorize, or impose meaning on the world, but how they 'struggle along' (Desjarlais 1994), strategize, or just make do with the social, cultural, and material resources at hand. The stakes of experience represent a *moral* engagement with the social world, which is never more stark than in our encounter – as researchers, healers, witnesses or sufferers – with illness.

ETHNOGRAPHY AND THE EXPERIENCE OF ILLNESS

Explanatory Models

'Ethnography,' understood here in an anthropological mode, includes participant observation, interviewing, historical interpretation, use of focus groups, and related qualitative methods, and is a set of key methodological tools available for the engagement with, and analysis of, illness experience. While it may be complemented (and should ideally be informed by) epidemiological, biomedical, and quantitative sociological data (see Inhorn et al. 1990), it is ethnography that primarily lends itself to exploration of the ways in which illness intersects with a particular culturally constructed life-world and a particular life trajectory to produce a unique and irreducible constellation of experience. Of course, there are still various ways in which this tool can be applied.

Some of the early work in medical sociology, associated especially with the work of Talcott Parsons, modelled the illness experience as a 'sick role.' The sick role represented the abridge-

ment of social functions and the imposition of social obligations based on a social actor's recognized illness. The person occupying the sick role would be temporarily freed from the responsibility of normal social duties (in the workplace, or in the family, for instance), but would be expected in return to cooperate with culturally valorized regimes of treatment, and to demonstrate a desire to 'get better' in certain culturally specific ways. The unspoken pact between ill person and community is important for its foundational role in negotiating the terms of interpersonal illness experience in a local world. Parson's student, Reneé Fox, demonstrated in several classical accounts that uncertainty was central to the sick role, its social positioning, and the management of experience in medical care (see Fox 1959).

The perception, conceptualization, and expression of symptoms and coping responses received further development in the work of medical sociologist David Mechanic (1982). Mechanic's work enabled researchers to operationalize and study particular elements of the experience of sickness, such as how cognitive processes of attending, perceiving, labeling, and interpreting symptoms were influenced by cultural orientations or by the social experience of severe economic constraints. This led, in turn, to research by numerous scholars on the choice-making patterns of those who are ill or seeking treatment, and on patients' evaluations of their relationships with clinicians and the quality of care they received. These sociological approaches helped to focus attention on the microprocesses of the social construction of illness and healing in particular social and cultural settings, which are an important part of illness experience.

Another means for assessing the influence of cultural and social factors upon a given episode of sickness has been the 'explanatory model' approach, which provides a structure for rapid and highly focused ethnographic investigation, and has been of interest to both social science researchers and clinicians for this reason (Kleinman et al. 1978). As the term implies, explanatory models (EMs) concern the ways in which an illness episode is interpreted and understood by patients, healers (including, of course, medical practitioners), and other members of the local social world. It includes notions of etiology, expected course, and predicted outcome, and ideas about appropriate treatment. In addition, EMs may be either shared or contested by differently positioned social actors, and may appear partially incohate or incompletely systematized. Patient EMs may include religious ideas of causality (i.e., karmic retribution or divine judgement), culturally specific understandings of bodily processes (i.e., maladies such as 'semen-loss,' 'tainted blood,' 'nervios,' etc.), and moral committments as to what constitutes an acceptable outcome for treatment, all of which may sometimes be at odds with the EMs brought to bear by physicians, family members, or other interested parties.

It is important, in fact, to resist the conception that EMs are fixed and static, and removed from the continual negotiations that characterize most social life. It is the *negotiability* of explanatory models that actually helps to impart their clinical usefulness, once identified by a caregiver. The doctor who understands his patient's explanatory model may be better able to negotiate a shared understanding with that patient as to the requirements and possibilities for treatment (Kleinman 1988). He may also be in a better position to empathize with that patient, and to bridge incommensurate understandings. There are, therefore, several basic questions that will always need to be asked in assessing the explanatory model, which is operative for any social actor at a given time. These questions include those listed below.

1 What is the problem? Is it an illness? If so, what kind of an illness?
2 How does it affect the body-self?
3 What can be expected to happen next?
4 What will be the long-term outcome? Will it get better or worse?
5 What is most to be feared about this condition?
6 What treatment is most appropriate?
7 What is most to be feared about the treatment?

The EM is designed to help caregivers attain relatively rapid access to the experience of illness on the part of patients, and cannot substitute for more comprehensive explorations of the social history of illness and the life histories of the persons involved. It is, however, a start, and in the context of extreme time–space compression (cf. Harvey 1990) that characterizes so much of medical care today, it is an important alternative to the anonymous and increasingly homogenized approach which systematically pushes cultural, moral, and biographical meaning in the illness experience aside. In addition, it is to be hoped that the EM will be understood as two-directional, which is to say that clinicians will learn to apply the analysis of explanatory models to the culture of science and biomedicine, and to the local cultures of their own clinics – and not just to the ostensibly less rational 'folk beliefs' and assumptions made by patients.

The self-reflexiveness presumed by this conception of explanatory modelling requires genuine respect for alternative ways of thinking, feeling, and being ill in different local worlds. EMs are inseparable from considerations of what is most at stake for participants in illness encounters, which means that they are inherently moral formulations and should not be ranked with regards to supposed rationality or degree of correspondance to 'objective' medical understanding. EMs may or may not square with current scientific understandings and may be infused with moral and explanatory significance drawn from different healing traditions, religious cosmologies, theodicies, and teleologies. In short, *the EM should be viewed as a point of entry into the life-world of the sufferer and not mistaken for a way of categorizing people, or explaining away their 'cultural' beliefs*. It is not enough to identify patient EMs within a fixed and culturally determined repertoire; the EM is an abstraction for much more dynamic social, personal, and moral processes.

Illness Narratives

Despite the usefulness of explanatory models, they are relatively constrained and artificial when compared with the 'illness narrative,' as this concept has been developed by medical anthropologists. Compared with EMs, the illness narrative is a more open-ended approach to the stories that always surround episodes of illness and healing for those who live through them. Huang Zhenyi's illness narrative, told as an adult suffering from dizziness and headaches, began with stories from his early childhood and adolescence which were, for him, intimately bound up with his current malady. The illness narrative may relate more broadly than the explanatory model to the interpersonal context and effects of illness. It may, in fact, extend to whatever the teller of the narrative considers to be at stake for herself in that episode. Whereas the EM may be constructed on the basis of a relatively narrow set of questions and takes an abstract form, illness narratives require a less structured form of interview technique. The hopes, fears, personal history, and cultural tradition of the ill person are all brought to bear, and it is up to the listener to adopt an analytic stance that is broad enough to accommodate these.

In addition, there are important narrative strategies and poetic conventions that need to be taken into account: voice, genre, master metaphors, and rhetorical strategies are all essential to the way in which illness narratives are constructed. Illness narratives do not simply recount a series of disconnected events, they tell a story that is typically, as in the case of Huang Zhenyi or Mavis Williams, a moral one. Illness is located within the autobiography of the person or community in question. It often contains implicit or explicit teleologies and moral cosmologies that may transcend or lie at odds with rationalized biomedical conventions. If this approach seems to require a developed literary sensitivity as well as personal empathy from the researcher or clinician, that impression may not be inappropriate. The listener needs to be able to hear the story that is *really* being told and to trace the ways in which widely shared cultural conventions are taken up as the embodied metaphors of some person's life or illness.

Towards this end, medical sociologist Arthur Frank (1995) has suggested that illness narratives in North America can be divided into four typical genres, the identification of which is essential to determining the meanings that underly a given narrative. As some historians have argued (White 1978), the choice of narrative genre that a writer or storyteller adopts may be broadly determinative of the kind of story he is likely to be able to tell. Frank's narrative genres are described below.

1   The *restitution narrative* emphasizes positive responses and outcomes; it is a story of coping with illness, rebuilding the body-self, and remoralization. It may also be evoked in the construction of patients or, even more, of doctors as heroes of the illness experience. These are stories with happy real or projected endings.

2   The *chaos narrative*, like that of Mavis Williams, tells a story of disorder, distortion, and fragmentation. Anguish, threat, and uncontrollability are the characterisitcs of this type of story. In her ethnography of the victims of ethnic violence in India, anthropologist Veena Das (1994) suggested that this type of narrative will tend to be chosen by those groups in society who actually have lost (or, more correctly, been denied) control over the events that define their lives and deaths. Those in power, argues Das, including localized power over family members and the like, are more likely to invoke systems of meaning in which those who suffer can be made to bear some measure of responsibility for their own suffering, especially when this deflects criticism from structures of social oppression. It is unlikely that this will always be the case, of course; guilty parties may also invoke chaos and meaninglessness to cover the tracks of their concupiscence. Still, it is good to keep Das's analysis in mind, and to remember that choices of narrative genre may be grounded in the power

politics of local settings, and cannot always be taken at face value.

3   *Quest narratives* emphasize either the search for cure (sometimes expressed through the turn towards experimental treatment or non-biomedical alternatives) or the search for meaning and transcendance within and through illness. The quest narrative is powerfully represented in contemporary North American film and literature, and in many first-person accounts by the ill or by doctors and other healers.

4   *Testimony* is an explicitly moralized form of story that seeks to bear witness, or to give voice to, those who suffer. Testimony may be organized around the special meaning that a person finds within illness or healing, or the special message to others that their experience is thought to bear. Some narratives of religious healing in the charismatic tradition are especially clear in this regard (Csordas 1994), but testimony may also take the more prosaic form of witnessing to family, friends, and caregivers what it is that has mattered most to a person during his or her illness, or during his or her life. This is a form of narrative that clinicians and caregivers are likely to hear when they elicit illness narratives from those who suffer extreme, or chronic pain, but who may never before have been asked to share their experience of suffering (Kleinman 1988).

These four categories should be understood as guideposts rather than rules to which every narrative must conform. Individuals' narratives may even participate in different genres at different points in their telling. In addition, it is important to understand that this shifting emplotment of different narrative genres may actually help to tranform illness experience over time (see Garro 1992; Good et al. 1994; Mattingly 1994). From a clinical perspective, it is important to understand what conventions of genre a patient may be presuming and how that may affect her outlook. A tendency to employ quest narrative strategies may, for instance, encourage doctor-shopping or unrealistic demands for experimental and unorthodox treatments.

At the same time, clinicians should realize that their own stories about illness and healing – the stories that they tell themselves, each other, and patients or their families – are also emplotted in crucial ways. The idea that patients should always be hopeful, that physicians should always be heroic, or conversely that 'realism' requires a matter-of-fact stoicism on the part of the families of the terminally ill, are all narrative strategies that have bearing on the ways in which care is organized, resources distributed, and meanings either allowed or disallowed from the clinical encounter. Illness narratives are scripted in negotiation between clinicians, patients, and others in a complex interplay that may be compared with literary creation, and which admits of different voices not just for different individuals, but for actors differently placed with regard to gender, ethnicity, or social and political position (Morris 1991).

Each type of illness narrative, furthermore, may hold coded political meanings in a local social field. Illness narrative as testimony may call attention, implicitly or explicitly, to abuses and injustice that exacerbate or are thought to lie at the heart of embodied psychosocial distress (Kleinman and Kleinman 1994). A narrative of restitution, by contrast, may carry messages that include the power of the individual to transcend suffering by following culturally approved rules of action, or the power of the collective (as in nationalist narratives of regeneration) to heal the social body which has been rent asunder. The clinician, like the social scientist, needs to be sensitive to the broad range of meanings at different levels that may be conveyed through illness narratives, or packed tightly within deceptively simple explanatory models of illness, suffering, and healing.

While most clinicians will not be able, given the constraints on their time and resources, to elicit a full illness narrative from each patient, the sensitivity developed through doing so occasionally may help to balance the tremendous pressures placed on caregivers in many settings to spend as little time as possible with each sick person, and to rely on narrowly biomedical categories. Such categories may be highly replicable across life-worlds, but they often, for that very reason, lack the validity that can only be attained through critical knowledge of some particular setting and set of life trajectories. Therefore, even a relatively rapid 'mini-ethnography' geared toward the elucidation of explanatory models may be useful in broadening one's therapeutic approach. As mentioned above, it can lead to enhanced negotiation with patients over models for care that will meet the requirements of treatment without undue violence to the life-world of the sufferer. It can also improve the quality of care by allowing cultural and biographical realities to be taken into account in determining treatment strategies. Perhaps most importantly, this strategy can help us to avoid the dehumanization – of clinician, researcher, or patient – that comes from treating those who suffer as if they have nothing to say of any relevance to their own lived context.

CONCLUSION

Representation and analysis of illness experience remains a challenge for theory in medical anthropology. Recently, Kleinman (1997) has suggested a model that can be represented in the form of a triangle: along one side lies *cultural representation* – the collective patterns of meaning that inform art, theodicy, and other cultural forms. Along the second side of this triangle lies *collective experience* – the events and social processes that help to define the lives of whole generations of people: World War I, the Cultural Revolution, and the kinds of events that led historian Eric Hobsbawm (1994) to describe the twentieth century as an age of 'catastrophes and extremes.' However, collective experience also represents the local events and processes that come to define important elements of the life-worlds of small social networks. The illness narrative of Huang Zhenyi represents these two kinds of collective experience – local and global – in their powerful intertwinement and indeterminacy.

Finally, the third side of this triangle is that of *subjectivity*, the somato-moral dimension where the expression of illness typically occurs. These three dimensions – cultural representation, collective experience, and subjectivity – exercise a reciprocal influence. Transformation in any one of them affects each of the others, so that observable changes in collective experience during this century, and in collective representations of suffering through the unprecedented commercialization of images of suffering which takes place through mass media (Kleinman and Kleinman 1996), lead us to consider the possible transformations in subjectivity to which these may be linked. The 'personal experience of illness' is thus inextricable from the pull of social and cultural change that takes place on every level, from the distinctively local to the increasingly global. It certainly cannot be limited to the health clinic, or to the sickbed of the individual patient alone. It is also a moral experience, and therefore a social one.

The ethnographic focus on experience which we have advocated here suggests these emotional–moral processes that link what is at stake in collective life with what matters in the inner life of patients, and allows us to describe a domain that co-determines the moral content of medical practice together with the institutional and personal constraints of doctoring. This makes illness experience an essential component in any consideration of medical ethics, from which it has too often been excluded or ignored (Kleinman 1995: 41–67). Illness experience, which takes place in the interpersonal spaces of social life, can help to inform ethical deliberation concerning the diversity of possible or actual ways of being in the world and, no less importantly, forces our attention on the powerful constraints – economic, political, and cultural – that stand ready to frustrate the builders of abstract ethical systems among us. Critical analysis of the relationship between human diversity and constraints on human life-worlds should represent an important future contribution by medical anthropology to the consideration of clinical contexts and their ethical, as well as socio-moral, ramifications.

We have argued that illness experience leads simultaneously to an exploration of broad social contexts and embodied states. Ethnography has already done a great deal to document and describe the links between the two, and to suggest theoretical perspectives for understanding that link. Our choice is no longer between narrow culturalist accounts and objectifying medical narratives. Indeed, both of these trends tend to obscure what is really at stake in lived experience and so create a false (in some cases dangerously false) object of analysis. On the other hand, the actual processes through which collective experience, cultural representation, and embodied subjectivity are joined remain relatively opaque; they are easier to trace through careful ethnography than to explain discursively, and this has been frustrating to many. We can only encourage other disciplines, besides medical anthropology, to turn their energies toward the unravelling of this problem. We would suggest though, that any attempt at explanation must follow close along the contours suggested by analysis of complex and personally ramified social experience, wherever it may draw particular disciplinary inspiration. Moral experience cannot be removed from the equation, and least of all from the equation of illness. For clinicians and researchers alike, moral experience is the fulcrum of body, self, and social world where illness matters most.

REFERENCES

Bosk, C. (1979) *Forgive and Remember: Managing Medical Failure.* Chicago: University of Chicago Press.

Bourgois, P.I. (1995) *In Search of Respect: Selling Crack in El Barrio.* New York: Cambridge University Press.

Brodwin, P. (1996) *Medicine and Morality in Haiti.* Cambridge: Cambridge University Press.

Conrad, P. and Gallagher, E. (eds) (1993) *Medicine Across Societies.* Philadelphia: Temple University Press.

Csordas, T. (1994) *The Sacred Self: A Cultural Phenomenology of Charismatic Healing.* Berkeley: University of California Press.

Das, V. (1994) 'Moral orientations to suffering: Legitimation, power and healing', in A. Kleinman, N. Ware, and L.C. Chen (eds.) *Health and Social Change in International Perspective.* Cambridge, MA: Harvard University Press.

Desjarlais, R. (1994) 'Struggling along: The possibilities for experience among the homeless mentally ill', *American Anthropologist*, 96: 886–901.

Desjarlais, R., Eisenberg, L., Good, B., and Kleinman, A. (1995) *World Mental Health: Problems and Priorities in Low Income Countries.* New York: Oxford University Press.

Fadiman, A. (1997) *The Spirit Catches You and You Fall Down.* New York: Farrar, Strauss and Giroux.

Farmer, P. (1992) *AIDS and Accusation: Haiti and the Geography of Blame.* Berkeley: University of California Press.

Farmer, P. (1996) 'Social inequalities and emerging infectious diseases', *Emerging Infectious Diseases*, 2: 259–69.

Farmer, P., Connors, M., and Simmons, J. (eds) (1996) *Women, Poverty and AIDS.* Monroe, ME: Common Courage.

Fox, R.C. (1959) *Experiment Perilous: Physicians and Patients Facing the Unknown.* New York: Free Press.

Frank, A. (1995) *The Wounded Storyteller: Body, Illness, and Ethics.* Chicago: University of Chicago Press.

Garro, L. (1992) 'Chronic illness and the construction of narratives', in M.-J.D. Good, P. Brodwin, B. Good, and A. Kleinman (eds), *Pain as Human Experience: An Anthropological Perspective.* Berkeley: University of California Press. pp. 100–37.

Geertz, C. (1983) *Local Knowledge: Further Essays in Interpretive Anthropology.* New York: Basic Books.

Good, B.J. (1976) 'The heart of what's the matter: The semantics of illness in Iran', *Culture, Medicine, and Psychiatry*, 1: 25–58.

Good, B.J. (1994) *Medicine, Rationality and Experience: An Anthropological Perspective.* Cambridge: Cambridge University Press.

Good, M.-J.D. (1992) 'Work as a haven from pain', in M.-J.D. Good, P. Brodwin, B. Good, and A. Kleinman (eds), *Pain as Human Experience: An Anthropological Perspective.* Berkeley: University of California Press. pp. 49–76.

Good, M.-J.D., Brodwin, P.E., Good, B.J., and Kleinman, A. (eds) (1992) *Pain as Human Experience: An Anthropological Perspective.* Berkeley: University of California Press.

Good, M.-J.D., Munakata, T., Kobayashi, Y., Mattingly, C., and Good, B.J. (1994) 'Oncology and narrative time', *Social Science and Medicine*, 38: 855–63.

Harvey, D. (1990) *The Condition of Postmodernity: An Enquiry into the Origins of Cultural Change.* Cambridge, MA: Blackwell.

Hobsbawm, E. (1994) *The Age of Extremes: A History of the World 1914–1991.* New York: Random House.

Inhorn, M.C. and Brown, P.J. (1990) 'The anthropology of infectious disease', *Annual Review of Anthropology,* 19: 89–117.

Kirmayer, L.J. (1992) 'The body's insistence on meaning: Metaphor as presentation and representation in illness experience', *Medical Anthropology Quarterly,* 6: 323–46.

Kleinman, A. (1980) *Patients and Healers in the Context of Culture.* Berkeley: University of California Press.

Kleinman, A. (1986) *Social Origins of Disease and Distress: Neurasthenia, Pain, and Depression in Modern China.* New Haven: Yale University Press.

Kleinman, A. (1988) *The Illness Narratives.* Boston: Beacon.

Kleinman, A. (1995) *Writing at the Margin: Discourse Between Anthropology and Medicine.* Berkeley: University of California Press.

Kleinman, A. (1997) ' "Everything that really matters": Social suffering, subjectivity, and the remaking of human experience in a disordering world', *Harvard Theological Review,* 90: 315–35.

Kleinman, A. and Becker, A., (eds) (1998) Special Issue 'Cross-cultural research', *Psychosomatic Medicine,* 60: July/August.

Kleinman, A. and Kleinman, J. (1991) 'Suffering and its professional transformation: Toward an ethnography of interpersonal experience', *Culture, Medicine and Psychiatry,* 5: 275–301.

Kleinman, A. and Kleinman, J. (1994) 'How bodies remember: Social memory and bodily experience of criticism, resistance, and delegitimation following China's cultural revolution', *New Literary History,* 25: 707–23.

Kleinman, A., and Kleinman, J. (1996) 'The appeal of experience: The dismay of images. Cultural appropriations of suffering in our times', *Daedalus,* 125: 1–24.

Kleinman, A., Eisenberg, L., and Good, B. (1978) 'Culture, illness and care', *Annals of Internal Medicine,* 88: 251–58.

Kleinman, A., Wang, W.-Z., Li, S.-C., Cheng, X.-M., Dai, X.-Y., Li, K.-T., and Kleinman, J. (1995) 'The social course of epilepsy: Chronic illness as social experience in interior China', *Social Science and Medicine,* 40: 1319–30.

Leslie, C. and Young, A. (eds) (1992) *Paths to Asian Medical Knowledge.* Berkeley: University of California Press.

Levinas, E. (1988) 'Useless suffering', in R. Bernasconi and D. Wood (eds), *The Provocation of Levinas: Rethinking the Other.* London: Routledge. pp. 156–67.

Lock, M. (1993a) *Encounters with Aging: Mythologies of Menopause in Japan and North America.* Berkeley: University of California Press.

Lock, M. (1993b) 'Cultivating the body: Anthropology and epistemologies of bodily practice and knowledge', *Annual Review of Anthropology,* 22: 133–55.

Lutz, C. and White, G.M. (1986) 'The anthropology of emotions', *Annual Review of Anthropology,* 15: 405–36.

Martin, E. (1987) *The Woman in the Body: A Cultural Analysis of Reproduction.* Boston: Beacon.

Mattingly, C. (1994) 'The concept of therapeutic emplotment', *Social Science and Medicine,* 38: 811–23.

Mechanic, D. (1982) *Symptoms, Illness Behavior, and Help Seeking.* New York: Prodist.

Morris, D.B (1991) *The Culture of Pain.* Berkeley: University of California Press.

Obeyesekere, G. (1985) 'Depression, Buddhism, and the work of culture in Sri Lanka', in A. Kleinman and B. Good (eds), *Culture and Depression.* Berkeley: University of California Press. pp.134–52.

Ong, A. (1995) 'Making the biopolitical subject: Cambodian immigrants, refugee medicine and cultural citizenship in California', *Social Science and Medicine,* 40: 1243–57.

Pliskin, K. (1987) *Silent Boundaries: Cultural Constraints on Sickness and Diagnosis of Iranians in Israel.* New Haven: Yale University Press.

Rosaldo, R. (1989) 'Grief and a headhunter's rage', *Culture and Truth: The Remaking of Social Analysis.* Boston: Beacon.

Rubel, A., O'Nell, C., and Collado-Ardon, R. (1984) *Susto: A Folk Illness.* Berkeley: University of California Press.

Scarry, E. (1985) *The Body in Pain: The Making and Unmaking of the World.* Oxford: Oxford University Press.

Schweder (1988) 'Suffering in style', Review of Kleinman, A. 'Social Origins of Disease and Distress', *Culture, Medicine and Psychiatry,* 12: 479–97.

Seeman, D. (1997) Religious Conversion, Public Health, and Immigration as Social Experience for Ethiopian-Israelis. Doctoral Dissertation, Harvard University.

Taylor, C. (1992) *Milk, Honey and Money: Changing Concepts in Rwandan Healing.* Washington, DC: Smithsonian Institute Press.

Ware, N. and Kleinman, A. (1992) 'Culture and somatic experience: The social course of illness in neurasthenia and chronic fatigue syndrome', *Psychosomatic Medicine,* 54: 546–60.

White, H. (1978) *Tropics of Discourse: Essays in Cultural Criticism.* Baltimore: Johns Hopkins University Press.

Wikan, U. (1988) 'Bereavement and loss in two Muslim communities: Egypt and Bali compared', *Social Science Medicine,* 27: 451–60.

Wikan, U. (1990) *Managing Turbulent Hearts: A Balinese Formula for Living*. Chicago: University of Chicago Press.

Young, A. (1982) 'The anthropologies of illness and sickness', *Annual Review of Anthropology*, 11: 257–85.

Young, A. (1995) *The Harmony of Illusions: Inventing Post-Traumatic Stress Disorder*. Princeton, NJ: Princeton University Press.

2.4

Clinical Narratives and the Study of Contemporary Doctor–Patient Relationships

MARY-JO DELVECCHIO GOOD AND BYRON J. GOOD

INTRODUCTION

In a series of essays published in *JAMA*, David Mechanic, one of the major medical sociologists of our era, addressed the contemporary eroding of traditions of 'trust' that has characterized ideal relationships between American physicians and their patients over much of the second half of the twentieth century (Mechanic 1997; Mechanic and Schlesinger 1996). The recent reorganization of American health services as capitated managed care systems, the shift in the balance of physicians' fiduciary responsibilities from individual patients to larger patient populations or stockholders in managed care groups, and shifts in professional relationships resulting from newly emerging biotechnologies have fostered public controversy and professional unrest (Gray 1997). From an international perspective, these changes in American medicine seem to reflect broader global changes in biomedical therapeutics, the medical profession, and relationships among doctors, patients, and the public. In this chapter, we explore analytic approaches to the physician–patient relationship that have relevance for understanding the contemporary turmoil in medicine in the United States and around the world. We also address those dimensions that reflect deeper cultural and professional forms that appear – as of this writing – to persist despite the radical changes in the organizational structure of health-care services.

The analytic framework we propose here suggests that 'clinical narratives' – stories of therapeutic activities created by physicians for and with patients over time – lie at the heart of doctor–patient communications, and that analysis of clinical narratives provides a means of exploring key dimensions of therapeutic relationships. We draw on recent ethnographic work in American and international biomedicine to analyze how young doctors learn particular narrative forms as they gain professional competence in clinical training, how physicians create and shape patient experience over time through clinical narratives, and how concepts such as clinical narratives have cross-cultural relevance in comparative studies of physician–patient relationships.

The globalization of biomedical cultures and political economies of medicine has had a profound influence on local and cosmopolitan cultures of clinical medicine world-wide. Nevertheless, although biomedicine is fostered through an international political economy of biotechnology and by an international community of medical educators and bioscientists, it still is taught, practiced, organized, and consumed in local contexts. It is our contention that contemporary studies of doctor–patient communications should focus attention on how relationships between clinicians and their patients mediate larger relations of culture, knowledge, and power, globalized political economies of medicine, and local and cosmopolitan dimensions of biomedical cultures. It is our argument that attention to clinical narratives provides one important approach to the study of these mediating processes.

ANALYTIC PERSPECTIVES ON THE DOCTOR-PATIENT RELATIONSHIP

Since social scientists began writing about medicine, the doctor–patient relationship has been the site of highly diverse and contested interpretations. In a literature most remarkable for its sheer mass, sociologists and anthropologists, sociolinguists, bioethicists, historians, popular writers, physicians, and more recently management specialists have analyzed and evaluated doctor–patient communications. Researchers have investigated this particular form of communication as conversation, often poorly executed (West 1984), as flawed exchanges of information (DiGiacomo 1987; Gordon 1990; Waitzkin and Stoeckle 1972, 1976), as interrupted narrative performances, with the 'voice of medicine' overwhelming the 'voice of the life world' (Mishler 1986), and as affective exchanges, fraught with transference and counter-transference (Balint 1957). Doctor–patient communications have been interpreted as contributing to the cultural construction of disease (Kleinman 1980), the commoditization of health and healing (Nichter and Nordstrom 1989), and the professional appropriation of suffering (Kleinman 1997; Kleinman and Kleinman 1991). They have been characterized as contributing to the medicalization of oppressive social relations and social suffering (Scheper-Hughes 1992; Taussig 1980) and to social control (Zola 1972), as providing a site for domination and exploitation (Pappas 1990; Waitzkin 1981, 1991), a setting for 'struggle and combat in the very heart of physician-controlled territory' (Singer 1989), and one context for gendered conflict between 'intimate adversaries' (Todd 1989). Despite its contentious and unequal nature, the relationship between clinicians and patients has been viewed as a setting for sustained witnessing of human suffering (Kleinman 1988) and for medicine's soteriological practices (Good 1994). It is through such relationships that physicians are expected to employ medical knowledge in a competent fashion and uphold fiduciary responsibility (Parsons 1978) and, through a variety of medical practices and biotechnologies, to convey hope and shape patient experience of disease and therapeutic processes (Good 1995a, 1995b).

Although medical sociologists, psychologists, and health services researchers have carried out sustained research on 'doctor–patient communi-

cations' since the 1950s, anthropologists are relative late-comers to the study of doctors, patients, and biomedical institutions. In their introduction to *Physicians of Western Medicine* in 1985, Hahn and Gaines called attention to the paucity of ethnographic research on physicians – in contrast to anthropological writing on traditional healers or healing rituals, and in contrast to sociological writing on medicine. Their collected volume was one of the first to draw together a group of studies by anthropologists working in diverse North American health-care settings. However, since the early 1980s, there has been a virtual explosion of anthropological writing about contemporary biomedicine. Collected volumes (e.g., Gaines 1992; Hahn 1995; Kleinman 1996; Lindenbaum and Lock 1993; Lock and Gordon 1988), review essays (e.g., Rhodes 1996), and articles and monographs (e.g., Good 1995a; Gordon 1988; Kaufman 1993; Marshall and Koenig 1996; Martin 1987, 1994; Rapp 1988; Rhodes 1991) have addressed 'biomedicine' in general, as well as particular medical subspecialties or clinical issues – oncology, psychiatry, reproductive technologies, immunology, genetic counseling, bioethics – in the United States or internationally.

Although relatively little anthropological writing focuses narrowly on doctor–patient communications, medical anthropology is relevant to the study of doctor–patient or clinician–client relationships in several ways. Medical anthropology places studies of doctors and patients in the context of comparative studies of medical systems. Since the 1970s, with the development of the study of Asian medical systems (Leslie 1976; Leslie and Young 1992), anthropologists have focused explicitly on pluralistic medical systems. From Kleinman's earliest, seminal formulation of medical systems as cultural systems composed of popular, folk, and professional domains (Kleinman 1980), to more recent studies of medical pluralism (e.g., Brodwin 1996; Good et al. 1993; Nichter 1989), patients are seen as having access to diverse strands of medical knowledge, explanatory systems, and healing traditions. Biomedicine is one form of medical knowledge among many, and transactions between doctors and their patients are complex transactions among systems of meaning, technologies, and power (cf. Rhodes 1996).

Diverse interpretive theories have been developed within medical anthropology to analyze these transactions. In his earliest work, Kleinman described clinical conversations as transactions across explanatory models, leading to the clinical construction of reality (e.g., Kleinman 1980; Kleinman, et al. 1978). In our own early work, we focused on the hermeneutic or interpretive dimensions of such transactions (Good and Good 1981a, 1981b; cf. Good 1994). Others have analyzed medical knowledge as hegemonic, portraying social inequalities as arising naturally from human nature or biology, and have gone on to interpret doctor–patient communications as an important site for making the hegemonic appear real to those seeking medical care (e.g. Martin 1987).

In addition to conducting studies of doctors and patients in the context of comparative research on pluralistic medical systems, medical anthropologists have also written about doctor–patient communications in a critical and normative literature directed explicitly to clinicians and educators. One goal of such writing has been to make explicit 'the relevance of social science for medicine.' In an edited book of this title published in 1981, Eisenberg and Kleinman gathered together a series of essays aimed at demonstrating 'the relevance of social science concepts, and the data derived from empirical research in those sciences, to problems in the clinical practice of medicine' (1981: ix). The book included explorations of 'cultural influences on illness behavior' (Lewis 1981), illness 'attributions' (Stoeckle and Barsky 1981), 'social labeling' (Waxler 1981), and other concepts which could be translated for clinical research and teaching. Our own essay in that volume – 'The meaning of symptoms: A cultural hermeneutic model for clinical practice' (Good and Good 1981a) – outlined a critique of empiricist or positivist epistemologies of clinical medicine and argued for rethinking medical practice in interpretive or hermeneutic terms. Grounded in the broad tradition of hermeneutic philosophy and interpretive social sciences (Ricoeur 1981a), the paper argued that clinical interactions should be understood as belonging to the world of meaning, aesthetics, and experience, rather than narrowly to the world of biology and instrumental communications about physical symptoms and diseases. Although theoretical in vein, the paper aimed at making explicit the relevance of a cultural interpretation of medical knowledge and clinical transactions for teaching medical students and residents alternative approaches to interviewing patients. The paper belonged to a genre of medical anthropology, which included empirical studies in 'clinically applied' anthropology (Chrisman and Maretzki 1982) as well as studies of 'the politics of medical encounters' (Waitzkin 1991), that aimed explicitly to criticize aspects of clinical medicine and to translate social science concepts and research into tools for clinical teaching and practice.

The decade of the 1990s has seen the emergence of new modes of anthropological analysis of medical knowledge, medical institutions, and clinical transactions. These are a result of both the sheer magnitude of changes in the world of medicine and changes in anthropological theory. Advances in molecular biology, investigations of the human genome and its role in disease, and the development of new biotechnologies – from reproductive technologies to imaging devices to new therapeutics – raise issues hardly conceived as recently as a decade ago. In addition, the rise to dominance of the for-profit managed care sector of the health-care system – particularly in the United States – has increased demands for efficiency, brought economic considerations into clinical transactions, and involved management specialists in clinical decisions, thus, dramatically altering relations between doctors and patients. Also, the transnational production and exchanges of medical knowledge, standards of care, and therapeutics have added global dimensions to medicine and medical practice in ways seldom imagined by earlier medical anthropologists. These changes have radically altered the world of clinical medicine, provoking new questions and offering new challenges for anthropological writing about 'doctor–patient relations.'

At the same time, the theoretical landscape for medical anthropology has also shifted. More than ever, anthropologists reject any account of doctor–patient relationships and communications that fails to link them systematically to broader social, political, economic, and cultural processes. Diverse forms of critical theory are now a part of any discussion of medical knowledge and clinical practice. Anthropologists routinely explore how medical systems reproduce hegemonic views of the body, the person, gender, and social relations. At the same time, new forms of poststructuralist theorizing have moved beyond exclusive attention to hegemony as an analytic approach. Medical anthropology has also come into conversation with 'science studies,' with anthropologists, sociologists, and historians carrying out innovative studies of late-twentieth-century science. Theoretical developments in the study of culture – in interpretive anthropology, subaltern studies, theories of the body, feminist writing – have all changed the way medical anthropologists write about 'the clinic,' and recent theories of transnationality and globalization, as well as new 'multisited' approaches to ethnographic research, provide diverse and innovative theoretical resources to study 'doctor–patient communications.'

Rather than attempt a broad review of this highly diverse field, our goal in this chapter is to outline a specific approach to the study of doctor–patient communications from the perspective of 'clinical narratives.' After providing a brief account of this analytic framework, we draw on small pieces of data from larger ethnographic studies to address three sets of questions. First, how do physicians in training enter into the world of medicine? How is medicine learned as a set of narrative practices? How does the learning of doctor–patient communications mediate entry into a complex set of social, political, economic, and biotechnical relations? Second, in cases of high-technology medicine and the treatment of serious medical conditions, how do relations between doctors and patients mediate emerging technologies and new political economies of research, biotechnologies, and health services? How are clinical narratives developed and sustained in such settings? How are issues of suffering and soteriology engaged via elaborate advanced technologies? Third, how do these issues translate cross-nationally? How do doctor–patient communications mediate local and global flows of knowledge and bio-technologies in low-income societies? How is the essence of doctoring threatened in societies that combine overwhelming disease problems with terrible scarcity of resources? The goal of these analyses will be to illustrate, rather than fully develop, an approach to analyzing doctor–patient communications consistent with current theoretical and analytic concerns of medical anthropology.

CLINICAL NARRATIVES: AN ANALYTIC APPROACH

In a series of studies, we have explored the idea that doctor–patient communications may be investigated as 'clinical narratives.' That is, stories created by physicians, for and with patients over time, about the course of disease and the progression of therapeutic activities (Good 1995b, 1998; Good et al. 1994; cf. Good and Good 1994; Good 1994). This approach focuses attention on on-going narrative processes that lie at the heart of clinical communications, thus making analytic concepts from literary criticism and narrative approaches to the social sciences relevant to the study of doctor–patient communications. At the same time, it provides a means for analyzing how larger social and cultural processes are made relevant to the experience of patients, suggesting that clinical conversations are a form of traffic not only among doctors and patients, but also among diverse local and global sites that produce biomedical knowledge, therapeutic technologies, and the scientific imaginary.

Studies of clinical narratives begin with the basic notion that physicians, in conversation with patients, 'emplot' disease and its treatment,

constructing meaningful stories linking the past and the present to potential futures and plotting courses of action.[1] In high-technology medical settings, physicians are nodal, directing the story, shaping patients' experience of treatment and disease course, and managing the treatment team. Clinicians establish therapeutic plots for patients, as a course of treatment is set in action, and they 'read' the unfolding 'medical plot' determined by disease process and patient response. Although clinical narratives are given directionality by physicians, and the 'voice of medicine' (Mishler 1986) and biomedical actions dominate, patients are also critical 'readers' and 'interpreters' of treatment plots, directing – often in collaboration with their clinicians – how the shifts in therapeutic course will affect their lives.

Physicians, even within the same subspecialty, hold a variety of opinions about how best to devise appropriate clinical narratives that are 'therapeutic,' caring, and productive of desired responses from patients. As creators of clinical narratives, physicians also develop multiple and parallel subplots, each tailored to specific actors. These include stories formulated for professional colleagues, the treatment team, and patients and patients' families, and also for the research groups and scientific communities to which they belong. The dimensions of temporality, outcome, and ending may differ for each audience and subplot of the clinical story (Good 1995b, 1998). A single, clear plot or theme seldom characterizes a clinical narrative; multiple and alternative readings, contributing to 'subjunctivity' and an openness to unexpected sources of healing, are the norm (Good 1994; Good and Good 1994; Good 1995b, 1998). Institutional forces, irrationalities in a health-care system, and fraud in research medicine can disrupt and fragment the progression of a clinical story and wreak havoc with professional intent. In addition, patients may choose to step out of a professionally devised 'plot,' to abandon treatment or seek alternative medical care.

Physicians are readers not only of the stories of their patients and the partially hidden course of the 'disease' as it is clinically manifest, but of the cultural flow from the biosciences. Bioscience narratives are occasionally brought into clinical practice through rank and file clinicians; more often they are introduced through clinician-investigators and teachers who conduct clinical trials and set standards of competence in specialty medicine. Such definitions of standards influence how competence is regarded in the evaluation of physicians' work as well as in physicians' construction of clinical narratives. Narratives of bioscience and technological expertise parallel even as they inform clinical narratives designed for patients, and many patients, at least in the American context, are aware of biomedical innovations and treatments (through television, science news articles, and even the fiction and films that feed Americans' insatiable interest in biomedicine). Nevertheless, bioscience narratives often introduce 'facts,' ambiguities, and uncertainties that are selectively employed by clinicians depending on the clinical culture in which they work. Thus, physicians articulate not only local cultural values, but the sciences and therapeutics that create standard frameworks for specialty narratives.

The teaching and practice of medicine and the production of clinical narratives draw from both global and local political economies and cultures of biomedicine. What happens in clinical contexts among patients (and their kin) and physicians (and other health-care workers) may be profoundly local, shaped by cultural assumptions about the appropriate role of physicians and their obligations to patients and by dominant conceptions of the person. How – and how long – physicians speak with patients in clinical contexts and how they construct clinical narratives varies across cultures and in different treatment settings. Nevertheless, comparative studies of patient–doctor communication document how even the more culturally resilient patterns of medical practice, such as assumptions about professional obligations, modes of disclosure of information about disease state and treatment, and the bases for trust, are affected by rapid changes in the biosciences and in the organiz-

ation of health-care delivery. Thus, medical culture and the political economies of biotechnology and health-care fuel constant shifts in definitions and meanings of clinical competence, standards of care, and ethical behavior. Such changes influence the physician–patient relationship as choices of therapeutic options and the use of new biotechnologies introduce unforeseen ethical and economic dilemmas, even as they alter the narrative strategies physicians employ in the treatment of patients.

Figure 1 provides an overall schema of the approach outlined here, suggesting ways in which the patient–doctor relationship and clinical narratives are influenced by domains beyond the actual dyadic interaction in clinical settings. The approach suggests a number of questions for the study of doctor–patient communications. For example, how do physicians learn to create competent clinical narratives that are meaningful for patients? How do they come to treat patients as partners in the creation of these clinical stories? How do parallel plots – for other clinicians or for bioscientists and researchers – influence the jointly constructed stories of physicians and patients? How are therapeutic stories set in motion? In what ways do various forms of clinical narratives shape patient experience? How, in the face of serious illness, does the doctor–patient relationship mediate new knowledge and biotechnologies and bring them into clinical practice? How does the 'political economy of hope' influence clinical interactions? What are the aesthetic structures of scientific images,

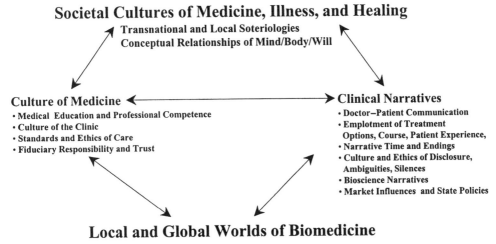

Societal Cultures of Medicine, Illness, and Healing

Transnational and Local Soteriologies
Conceptual Relationships of Mind/Body/Will

Culture of Medicine

- Medical Education and Professional Competence
- Culture of the Clinic
- Standards and Ethics of Care
- Fiduciary Responsibility and Trust

Clinical Narratives

- Doctor–Patient Communication
- Emplotment of Treatment
  Options, Course, Patient Experience,
- Narrative Time and Endings
- Culture and Ethics of Disclosure,
  Ambiguities, Silences
- Bioscience Narratives
- Market Influences and State Policies

Local and Global Worlds of Biomedicine

Political Economy of Health Services
Equity, Access, Limited Resources, and Scarcity
Political Economy of Hope
Biomedical Research, Pharmaceutical, and Biotechnical Products

Figure 1

such as statistics, data from clinical trials, and other knowledge forms through which clinicians bring the world of research medicine and bio-technology into everyday clinical conversations, and how are these received and interpreted by patients? What does 'treatment choice' and 'decision making' mean in emotionally charged contexts of serious and life-threatening illness? What remains unspoken, masked, actively silenced, or ambiguous within the clinical narra-tives? In what ways do clinicians and patients encounter the ultimate limits of lifetime and engage soteriological issues through the techno-logical treatments offered?

These and other questions provide a broad agenda for research on clinical narratives, reshaping classical approaches to studying 'doc-tor–patient communications.' In what follows, we provide brief examples from our research, illustrating how this analytic approach may be employed in several settings. We begin with research on medical education that asks how students learn to construct clinical narratives, and how such learning mediates entry into a complex set of medical relationships.

STUDIES IN MEDICAL EDUCATION: ENTERING THE WORLD OF CLINICAL NARRATIVES

Learning to interview patients is a critical step for American medical students entering the world of medicine. Early encounters with patients are often among the 'primal scenes' of medical education, and stories of these encoun-ters are retold with great emotion. One medical student told us:

> I never anticipated what a terrifying experience it was emotionally to see patients. I couldn't believe it! I'd even seen patients before [when he was a research interviewer]. But I was frightened. It was as if a woman came in a room you were in and started taking her clothes off! This time I was going to have to do the exam. I was the only one who was going to do it, and it happened too fast. I didn't get anything that I needed. I couldn't believe how anxiety-producing it was.

In American medical schools, enormous energy is devoted to teaching interviewing, and efforts to reform or 'humanize' medical practice often focus on teaching communications skills to doc-tors in training. Why then do both popular and social science reports continue to criticize physi-cians for their communications skills – for their failure to listen to, or provide adequate explana-tions to, patients?

Our research with Harvard medical students (see Good 1994: Ch 3; Good 1995b: Ch. 6–7. Good and Good 1989; Good and Good 1993) suggests that conversations between doctors and patients and the clinical narratives they con-struct mediate a complex set of social, cultural, economic, and biotechnical relations, and that learning to 'interview' and interact with patients is one means of entry into this complex set of relations. These broader structures are resistant to reform, and thus constrain the best-intended efforts to reform doctor–patient communica-tions. What is the basis for this argument? How does the learning of a distinctive form of constructing clinical narratives mediate entry into the medical life world?

In early encounters with patients, medical stu-dents are often taught to listen in a common sense way, to encourage patients to tell their stories and to learn to hear what patients tell them. However, these 'interview skills' are quickly linked to a larger set of speaking and writing practices, particularly as medical stu-dents enter their clinical rotations and the social relations associated with joining a medical team. Students learn to interview patients, to take a medical history along with doing a physical exam, in order to provide data for presenting patients to other physicians during rounds and for writing-up patients in medical charts. These practices – presenting patients and writing charts – precede and provide the structure for learning to interview.

Case presentations are organized as a distinc-tive form of medical narrative. A medical stu-dent we interviewed described it as follows:

> Telling a story is definitely one of the things, I mean that's often what you're kind of told . . . you have to organize things into some kind of a story, whether you choose to do it chronologically or whether you choose to do it from the basis of one particular dis-ease process or something, even though it might not be exactly a chronological progression or something, but definitely you're often told to, encouraged to tell a story in some way.

Students enter the world of medicine by learning narrative practices – by learning to tell patients' stories to other doctors. These stories are not simple reports of patients' narratives. 'They [other doctors on rounds] don't want to hear the story of the person. They want to hear the edited version,' a student told us. Patients' stor-ies are edited and retold as diagnostic stories, or as stories of the progress of a disease or treat-ment. They are stories that construct the patient as a medical project – a problem to be solved, a condition to be treated medically. Thus, clinical narratives are first learned as a form of stories told to other physicians.

Medical students are taught to construct clinical narratives in the context of diagnostic and therapeutic procedures. A case presentation or reporting on a patient in a chart leads directly to other medical acts, to interventions. By learning to construct clinical narratives, students enter the medical world as active participants. One student described a rotation in a pediatric emergency room.

> After a while you just become totally at home because you have to, walking into a room, introducing yourself to a complete stranger, doing a history and physical and trying to make sense of the situation, and come up with a diagnosis, and come up with a treatment plan and write it up very concisely on one sheet of paper because that's the way the ER works, deciding whether they need to be admitted or not, what tests to order.

In such settings, medical students learn to tell prototypical disease stories, to act upon those stories, and to observe the consequences. Narrative, diagnostic, and therapeutic practices are closely intertwined, and clinical narratives are seen to be linked to practical effects in the real world. Learning to produce clinical narratives is experienced, in turn, as a sign of increasing maturity and competence on the part of the student.

These narrative practices position medical students in a complex set of medical relationships. Case presentations situate medical students among a hierarchy of physicians during rounds. Writing in a chart constitutes the medical student as an authorized actor, even as it constitutes the patient as a medical project. As one student told us,

> To a large extent, you're authorized through your writing. That's sort of what justifies everything else, is you are actually now communicating important information, and that entitles you to poke and prod, . . . spiritually, verbally, and physically.

More than that, this set of speaking and writing practices situates the medical student in a complex social field of physicians, nurses, case managers, hospital administrators, and, potentially, lawyers. It also situates students in a field of biotechnologies, of imaging and diagnostic tools and a wide variety of therapeutic technologies. Learning the most fundamental narrative practices of communicating with patients thus draws medical students into the medical world, into this complex set of relationships, in ways that are highly constrained. Indeed, such constraints are what constitute this world as a medical world, even as they resist efforts to reform styles of doctor–patient communications.

Research on how medical students communicate with patients thus leads directly to investigations of how students learn to communicate clinical narratives to other physicians, and how this, in turn, shapes their relations with patients. It also reveals a process of maturation, a growing competence that is linked to an ability to construct complex clinical narratives in their interactions with both patients and other physicians. Our research in high-technology cancer treatments has focused specifically on such complex clinical narratives and their role in mediating broader social and biotechnical relations.

CLINICAL NARRATIVES IN HIGH-TECHNOLOGY MEDICINE: EXAMPLES FROM ONCOLOGY

The following examples are drawn from a recently completed study on clinical narratives and the treatment of breast cancer. We followed forty American women through their course of treatment at a major teaching hospital. Taped observations of clinical interactions, discussions with oncologists about therapeutic intent, interviews with patients about their interpretations of these interactions during and after their course of treatment, and interviews with the academic oncologists who care for these patients about their clinical science provided the basic ethnographic elements of the study.

Setting the Story in Motion

An interview with a female surgical oncologist.

> If it's malignant, I want them to have enough information so that they have the truth, but also so that they have some hope. They know that there are things that can be done that will help them. I think the hardest thing is uncertainty, and also I think it's extremely hard if you begin to think that your doctors are not telling you things. Then you don't know if you can ever believe them. So, I find being very frank, but not discouraging, from the beginning seems to be best. . . . Women are adults, women can deal with breast cancer, and . . . you start out with that assumption and you deal with them that way. . . . When patients start out being involved from the beginning and being in *control* from the beginning, it's much better. The whole way. And treating breast cancer is a long process these days.

Setting the clinical story in motion and beginning the therapeutic process are paramount to an oncologist's clinical task, and this 'beginning' engages most patients intensely. The surgical oncologist quoted above remarked how she deliberately shapes the therapeutic story for patients, consciously designing early clinical interactions to give patients the experience of control over their treatment course and ultimately over their illness. These early interactions, she contends, influence how patients cope with the lengthy process of therapy. In the example noted below, one of the patients in our study discusses how she chose her treatment team in response to the clinical narratives set forth in initial meetings with this surgeon and her colleagues.

Oncologists have long debated how best to carry out their clinical and informational tasks with patients. Conscious consideration of how to shape patient experience has become an expected part of clinical work. Although contemporary clinical standards vary in patient care, oncologists invest a high degree of professional attention to this aspect of their work, as evidenced by journal articles, essays, books, and interviews.

In a complex and uncertain field like contemporary American oncology, much more than a good 'bedside manner' is at stake. Given the current state of knowledge and available therapeutics, patients must rely on the clinical judgment and skilled actions of their physicians. However, in many situations, several alternative courses of action may be appropriate. Good care includes not only helping patients select a therapeutic option but also helping patients feel that a chosen course constitutes the best possible care for them. This work is accomplished through the medium of clinical narratives, and it is through this medium that clinicians mediate emerging technologies and protocols for patients.

Skilled clinicians are often quite conscious of the importance of this aspect of their work, especially women oncologists who treat breast cancer patients. This awareness reflects the challenges for this specialty; a challenge to treat life-threatening disease, often over long periods of time, in a context of high-technology medicine fraught with the uncertain efficacy of diverse therapeutic modalities and an unfolding array of treatment pathways, which at times appear to patients to be part of a never-ending journey.

Most patients in our study were aware of their diagnosis of breast cancer when they made their initial appointments at the Massachusetts General Hospital (MGH). Primary care physicians had often found cause – through routine mammograms or because of suspicious lumps – to order biopsies. Patients then began the search for a treatment setting and treatment team. Of those who agreed to participate in our study, many had sought opinions elsewhere. In the following example, we find that patients too set the

therapeutic story in motion. The choice of a treatment pathway is often entwined with choosing a team and a place that engender particular feelings about the therapeutic journey, and its many challenges, upon which patients are about to embark. It also is a choice of a particular kind of clinical story.

Choosing an Affect, Choosing a Team

In this first example, the patient chooses a team, and a comforting and calming feeling is conveyed by members of the team, rather than an explicit and bounded treatment plan. Mrs M's initial therapeutic decision – to have a mastectomy – is overridden by the particular team she has chosen. She recounted to us:

> I found my lump May 14, at 1:32 p.m. and went the following day to the clinic, where I have been treated for other things. And I – they confirmed the fact that I had a lump . . . and then I think it was the next day, I had a fine needle aspiration, and they called while I was in my car and told me I had cancer – that's how I found out I had cancer, I was driving my car . . . we went back . . . we had a meeting with a surgeon, and oncologist, and a radiation person and they described the course of treatment, and we decided that we needed a second opinion, so my husband called up everyone he knew. . . .

Although Mrs M. thought she would have a mastectomy, after having read 'all those books . . . maybe easier, getting rid of the cancer,' and remarked that 'I've had that phobia, for chemotherapy for a long time because I've seen a lot of people take it and be very sick and die after going through all that,' she entered a treatment path that began with breast conserving surgery, went on to 6 months of chemotherapy, followed by hormonal therapy, and concluded with 6 weeks of radiation. She selected the third medical group she 'interviewed' for 'opinions.' All three surgeons interviewed at each of the hospitals were women, all noted she was a candidate for 'lumpectomy.' Yet Mrs M., a lively primary school teacher, told us what led her to choose the MGH team.

> When I went into that room, I said "That's it," I said to my husband and daughter, "That's what I'm having. I'm going to have a mastectomy." And when we left, I said "All right, I'll have a lumpectomy." [laughs].

She scheduled the surgery that day. What Mrs M. chose was the effect conveyed by the treatment team. She commented about her surgeon:

> I found her very soft-spoken . . . she had a very calming effect on me. She could tell – she told

me – bad news, and the way she tells you, she has a wonderful manner about her and her credentials I thought were great. And as soon as I spoke to her, even though the other surgeons I had spoken to – I was so impressed with at the other hospitals. I just felt very comfortable with Dr S.

Regarding her medical oncologist:

I had very negative thoughts about chemotherapy, so when she came in, I had this wall. . . . She was very good at calming me also. She said, "I'll get you through this." And she assured me that it wasn't as bad as I thought it would be, and I believe her. I still believe her. I'll let you know next week. . . .

Her radiation oncologist:

He's young, probably in my children's age group, and I really don't have a lot of thoughts about him . . . he explained very well, and he explained how he would do it, and I figure that's off in the future, if I get through chemo I'll worry about that.

She concluded, 'I was happy to have two women on the team. Very happy.' She may also have chosen a team unassociated with the initial disclosure of the diagnosis, told to her as she was driving in her car (cf. Lind et al. 1989).

As we followed Mrs M. through a course of chemotherapy ('I'm off to chemotherapy,' she sang for us to the tune of *"I'm off to see the Wizard, the Wonderful Wizard of Oz"*) – followed by radiation treatments – a course that took over 9 months, she continued to question her oncologists about the reasons for each new treatment decision. The clinical narratives of her team not only addressed the 'why' of therapeutic decisions, but also gave scientific legitimacy to the biotechnical embrace within which Mrs M. lived for over a year. 'Why do radiation?' she asked her young radiation therapist. He justified the choice through the story of clinical evidence – the three arms of the famous and infamous clinical trials – legitimizing his recommendation in statistical terms '40 per cent recurrence without radiation, only 8 per cent recurrence with radiation, as good as mastectomy.' No mention was made of the scandal and research fraud that had momentarily cast the trials in questionable light at that time (Angell and Kassirer 1994; Rennie 1994).

Emergent Technologies and Experimental Treatment 'Rules Change': ABMT and High-Dose Chemotherapies

High-dose chemotherapy with autologous bone marrow transplantation and stem cell rescue

(HDC/ABMT/ASCR) is one of the emergent technologies and therapeutic options that patients with metastatic disease are now frequently offered (Kelly and Koenig 1998). As one medical oncologist noted in 1993 at the very beginning of our project, this expensive 'salvage therapy' had dubious therapeutic credentials. She recalled at the time that in clinical trials patients who initially responded positively to transplants 'were all relapsing at six or eight months after the transplant' (Good et al. 1995: 148). Yet in 1994, a now infamous suit brought by a California Kaiser patient who was refused coverage for ABMT helped to establish this 'experimental treatment' as a standard of care by 1995–96 (Good 1995b: Ch. 8). The chief of surgery for one of the large networks in Boston noted in 1996, 'No HMO would be able to refuse coverage now because of that suit.' In addition, the cost of providing autologous stem cell/bone marrow transplants declined dramatically – from approximately $150 000 in 1993 to $60–75 000 in 1995 to as low as $50 000 in 1997. As costs declined, promoters of the procedure (HDC/ABMT/ASCR), such as Dr William Peters, who directed the Duke University Bone Marrow Transplantation Program, sought to normalize the experimental work. At a 1994 hearing of the Federal Insurance Commission in New Orleans (5 December 1994), Dr Peters argued:

As our famous philosopher once said: 'the future just ain't what it used to be' – this is what most people think of bone marrow transplants as being – a high technology facility with isolation procedures, use of high-tech equipment, multiple supportive care efforts, and so on. What is really happening is that, in the last few years, this is occurring more frequently. Two women from our institution – [one] on Day 2 and [one] on Day 6 of their bone marrow transplants – are waiting for coffee to be delivered to the hotel where they are staying during their bone marrow transplant. [Shows two slides of women; how routine, how normal, how unremarkable.] We now essentially do all our bone marrow transplants as outpatient procedures. If one looks at the 100-day mortality in patients undergoing transplants, you can see that, back in the mid-1980s, the therapy-related mortality in the first 100 days was at over 30 per cent. Now, it is down in the range of about 3 per cent. In fact, if you look at the 30-day mortality shown here, again, from 15 per cent down to the 3–4 per cent realm. This represents massive change in therapy-related mortality.' (Federal Insurance Hearing transcript, New Orleans, 5 December 1994)

Even as this technological fix became increasingly efficient and standardized, and as treatment locales shifted from hospital to outpatient services, many oncologists continue to question the procedure's therapeutic efficacy. As the biotechnological activities alter and decisions to choose competing therapeutic options become ever more complicated, especially given the uncertain efficacy of many treatments and the potential for serious clinical error, clinical narratives have to be carefully orchestrated. Yet, even with questionable efficacy, we see how the traffic between research medicine and clinical practice leads to a kind of 'biotechnical embrace' which captures and enthuses both patients and physicians in imagining the possibilities of the therapeutics of the experimental (Good 1996).

When patients enter the embrace of the high-technology world of clinical oncology, choice of treatment often recedes and choice of place, of the culture of clinical oncology, predominates. In our study, several patients with advanced or metastatic disease who were 'good candidates' were offered ABMT and high-dose chemotherapy by 1994. Invitations to experimental treatment often appeared to hold 'no choice' if one was to take the only 'chance' for cure.

The following example illustrates how patients encounter the dilemma of 'choice, no choice' and how, through the clinical narrative, clinicians create meanings of 'hope' and 'chance' through the aesthetics of medical statistics. A 54-year-old patient, Mrs R., with metastatic disease, who appeared to 'be doing quite well' according to her medical oncologist, was offered the ABMT/HDC option.

> I guess if I had a concern, my concern is – is it going to damage my immune system so that it's going to make things worse? It seems like a very archaic sort of technique. . . .

Thus, Mrs R. described her worries to her medical oncologist after meeting with the transplant specialist. As she debated whether to take up the invitation to undergo experimental treatment ('an opportunity' as she and her husband labeled it), she remarked that perhaps she should not go on vacation as planned. She remarked with irony and humor on the statistical odds given for the success of the recommended treatment: 'I don't want to jeopardize this great 15–20 per cent chance.' As she continued her discussion with her oncologist, she asked, 'I really don't have a choice, do I?' Her oncologist, in her gentle educator voice, but again employing the irony of life-span talk responded:

> Dr: Yes, you do have a choice. You don't have a choice if you're only focusing on the big picture and 10 years down the road. Then you don't have a choice because only one of these choices can give

you a chance. But if you are focusing on the next five years. . . .
> Mrs R.: Five years is nothing.
> Dr: So you don't have a choice, It's your choice.
> Mrs R.: He [the transplanter] said that it's not a choice. . . .

In a subsequent interview with us, Mrs R. noted that the specialist 'gave me all the details. He was excellent. What he wasn't able to give me is the patient's perspective, only the medical perspective.'

Mrs R. is remarkably articulate, aware of the uncertain efficacy and cognizant of the potential toxicity of this experimental treatment. Yet, similar to most patients who participated in our study, she accepted the invitation with enthusiasm, albeit tempered with fear and what she noted was an underlying depression. As she proceeded to ABMT treatment (6 months after the initial invitation), she engaged her physicians with high humor, participating in the strangeness of the medical imagination and the irony of statistical odds and chances (questionably construed given the lack of clinical trials) – wondering whether she would make it into the '20 per cent success rate.' To the interviewer on her first day when stem cells were taken from her hip, she joked, 'why the hell did I decide to do this, this is stupid. Besides, the whole thing is Twilight Zone.' As her specialist entered her room, she went on, 'He's kind of got that Frankenstein look. What are we going to make today?' The discussion between patient, interviewer, and clinician evolves from the clinical event to soteriological issues of the life world and concerns with the ultimate outcome.

> Mrs R.: You know what the hardest part – not even the hardest part, but – I guess the irony of the whole thing is to go through all this and have absolutely not only no guarantee at the end, but not even an indication. . . . No way to have any idea whether it worked or didn't work. When you think about it, it seems like at the end they should be able to say, 'it looks good,' or 'it doesn't look good.'
> Interviewer: What did they say about that?. . . .
> Patient: If I'm alive and well in 5 years they'll call it a success, and I'll follow the 20 per cent success rate. It's a hindsight thing. And it's funny, one of the things that we did do initially that we've gotten off that we have to get back on, I think, was to go on a diet and become vegetarian. (She was referring to Tamoxifen and soy being a natural tamoxifen.) . . . You listen to the medical profession but you've gotta do your own thing. So I'll keep eating tofu. So, I'll keep eating tofu. So, I don't know. It's all so interesting. The teachers gave me a huge party. Very nice, a surprise party. And they sent out invitations

and they called it a shower. They had a shower for me, a shower of friendship, they called it.

Several weeks later, Mrs R. returned for a follow-up treatment just after news articles revealed that the esteemed Dana–Farber Cancer Center (a competing hospital) had inadvertently poisoned two women during high-dose chemotherapy when four times the dosage of the highly toxic drug Cytoxan was administered. One woman died of heart failure directly caused by the treatment; she was 39 years old, a mother, wife, and a health and medical columnist for the *Boston Globe*, and Dana–Farber was placed on probation by the Joint Commission on Accreditation of Hospitals (JCAH). These events influenced the interpretation of cancer caregivers and patients by the community, suggesting that indeed the treatment Mrs R. was undergoing could be 'in the Twilight Zone.'

At a clinical-research related visit 3 months later, Mrs R. evaluated for her oncology nurse her physicians' skill at extracting bone marrow (not only for therapeutic purposes but for a clinical observation study). She scored each of the three 'a five, a seven, a three!'

Nurse: 'Not a ten?'
Mrs R.: 'Ten does not exist, nobody can get a ten' – just as no ABMT patient can be assured of a cure.

She continued to reflect on her very lengthy treatment experience over the course of 22 months:

Mrs R: 'I decided that [cancer] it can be a chronic disease. It doesn't have to be a – I always believed it was a death sentence. . . . Now my next big decision is, they did the second bone marrow for their research, and their research is to see if there's any breast cancer cells in the bone marrow. So do I want to know that answer to that?'
Nurse: 'I don't think they can tell you the answer to that.'
Mrs R.: 'Yeh, he said he could.'
Nurse: 'Right . . . and you don't know what to do with the information . . . he shouldn't have even told you there was an option.'
Mrs R.: 'I'll have to think about that.'

Their conversation concluded with the difficulties of the uncertainty, the ambiguity, the not-knowing conveyed in the statistics and odds of a '15–20 per cent' cure rate and in the silences surrounding the clinical observational studies.

Hope in terms of odds and statistics dominates oncology narratives and becomes part of physician, patient, and family talk. Husbands in particular appear to try to master the odds talk;

patients, such as Mrs R., who are well educated, play with the odds talk, and buffer fear with the ironic humor that we observed over and over again in interactions with physicians and in our research interviews. The oncologists in the study note that at times, when alone with patients, the humor drops, the fear and tears and ultimate questions flow. In taped clinical interactions when no researcher was present, emotions were often intensely expressed, as they were in many of the one-on-one research interviews as well. Yet, hope and irony, odds and chances – these themes are not only present in many of our conversations with patients and physicians, but they arise very frequently in the clinical narratives physicians and oncology nurses use to justify and explain treatment recommendations. This deployment of clinical statistics is markedly 'American,' perhaps most characteristic of oncology narratives in American teaching hospitals.

As we examine the exchanges over time between oncologists and their patients, we find that concluding treatment appears to be one of the most difficult chapters in the unfolding clinical story. Cancer patients speak about being 'thrown from the nest,' of the sense of loss and anxiety they feel when they are no longer able to 'do anything.' Oncologists, reflecting on this concluding stage, acknowledge it as one of the classic and most difficult phases of treatment. Good clinicians reassure their patients that they will continue to see their physicians, seeing them in 'follow-up' appointments. Some patients choose to set the experience in their past, to simply 'get on with their lives'; others not only wish to 'get on with their lives,' but also seek continued connections to the clinicians who have shaped so much of their life experiences through lengthy treatment journeys, many of which have exceeded 2 years. Patients who have relapses or who are not cured of disease remain actors in the clinical stories, embraced by the experimental or salvage treatments offered, participating in a slowly unfolding treatment pathway that is marked by the uncertainty of endings.

Clinical narratives in high-technology cancer care thus mediate relations between patients and their caregivers. However, as suggested in Figure 1, they also mediate a broader set of cultural and technological relations. Newly emerging technologies and therapeutics, data from clinical trials, popular culture, and the 'technoscientific imaginary' all flow through the conversations between doctors and patients and are played out in the bodies of the patients.

CLINICAL NARRATIVES IN TRANSNATIONAL PERSPECTIVE

The perspective outlined in this chapter is intentionally comparative. Doctor–patient communications are analyzed in societal context – as embedded in distinctive cultures of the body and medicine, in particular organizational structures of health-care and biomedical research, in political economies that have powerful influences throughout the health-care system. Doctor–patient communications are also analyzed as belonging to a transnational field, as a site for the flows of knowledge, technologies, and practice forms through which local and global elements enter into conversation and conflict. How then do these issues translate cross-nationally? How do doctor–patient communications mediate local and global flows of knowledge and biotechnologies in low-income societies? How is the essence of doctoring threatened in societies that combine overwhelming disease problems with scarcity of resources? The study of clinical narratives provides a means for cross-national comparisons and analysis of high-technology medicine, as well as research on the influence of economic scarcity and disease patterns on the ways doctors and patients relate and communicate in poor societies.

Recent research on the practice of oncology in countries other than the United States provides an example of comparative studies of high-technology medicine and doctor–patient communications. Gordon and Paci's work in Italy (1997), Tana Nilchaikovit's studies in Thailand (Nilchaikovit 1998; Nilchaikovit et al. 1993), Hunt's work in Mexico (1992, 1994), our comparative work with colleagues in Japan, Indonesia, and the Philippines (Good 1995a; Good et al. 1993, 1994; Kusumanto et al. 1997; Ngelangel et al. 1995), and studies of ethnic differences within national medical cultures (Kagawa-Singer et al. 1997) document a wide variation in the culture and ethics of clinical practice, in particular in the way physicians shape clinical narratives for their patients throughout the lengthy course of treatment. More recently, essays written by clinicians from around the world and assembled by editors from the Memorial Sloan–Kettering Cancer Center have examined the diversity of the ethics of doctor–patient communications in different medical cultures (Surbone and Zwitter 1997). These essays wrestle with the difficulties and ethics of communicating information and 'truth' to patients, and with how 'truth' is defined in particular cultural contexts. However, it is not only explicit disclosure practices that vary widely. Ambiguity and silences are maintained and information is conveyed in culturally distinctive ways. Therapeutic choices and patient experiences are also diverse, dependent upon clinical culture and the resources available to pay for advanced treatments. Access to the latest chemotherapies or innovative treatments may be limited by government policy (e.g., in Norway bone marrow transplants are restricted according to patient age as well as health status) or by the economic situation of a country and members of its population. Current research in Indonesia provides one example of the latter (Good, forthcoming). In the pediatric oncology center in Yogyakarta, Indonesia, protocols for treating childhood leukemia (ALL) are in place. Yet, the cost of cycles of chemotherapy and of the antibiotics necessary to handle the infectious load is very high, often several times the cost of the same chemotherapies in The Netherlands (Kusumanto et al. 1997). Thus, responses to anticancer therapy are characterized by pediatric residents in training in Yogyakarta as governed by 'the economic gene.' However, levels of utilization of aggressive therapies do not depend on income levels alone. Japanese oncologists have long preferred treatments with minimal side effects (Good et al. 1993). Nilchaikovit et al. (1993) have noted, for example, that cancer patients in Europe and Asia seek care at later disease stages than do patients in the United States. This affects therapeutic options and thus the type of clinical narrative oncologists may develop for their patients.

Clinical narratives in high-technology medicine are a curious mix of local and cosmopolitan cultures. They are driven by what we have previously labeled 'the political economy of hope' (Good 1995b) and by advances in anticancer therapies, which are shared by the global community of cancer specialists and researchers through pharmaceutical markets and participation in clinical trials and new protocols. Clinical narratives are also shaped by local professional cultures, including the ethics of doctoring and patient care. Local and transnational political economies also have profound influences on clinical practice that give rise to distinctive clinical narratives and forms of communications between treatment teams and cancer patients and their families.

ANTINARRATIVE AND THE LIMITS OF ANALYSIS

The analytic concept of the clinical narrative makes sense in medical systems in which physicians are expected to communicate with patients or with family members, over time, about diagnostic, prognostic, and therapeutic processes. Whether cultures of disclosure are more open partnerships or ambiguous, protective, and paternalistic, the relationship of patients with physicians is at least partially grounded upon an assumption of professional responsibility, a trust that one's physician will recommend an optimal treatment pathway given a particular disease and the limits of available therapeutics. However, when scarcity and disease entities overwhelm ideals of clinical practice and the basic ethics of patient care, even minimalist communication with patients may be compromised. A Kenyan physician colleague recently noted that in his teaching hospital, the ideals of the profession of medicine in the HIV era have been 'overwhelmed by disease entity.' Remarking on the difficulties of teaching medicine and patient–doctor communication when medicine wards are populated with as many as 60 per cent HIV patients, he worried about a 'numbing' that afflicts the clinical faculty and medical students and distances them from their patients. Silence and withdrawal rather than narrative come to the fore when patient care appears hopeless and potentially dangerous to the caregiver. He argued that the effects of the AIDS plague are of a different magnitude than that of poverty, economic scarcity, or shortage of medical resources.

> Not only is there scarcity, but the essence . . . the principle of [doctoring] is to save life. So it comes to it that lives are no longer being saved. You have people dying much more than they used to and I really do not know how it affects me. . . . You don't get so bothered that you had a ward which was just full . . . and then at the end of the week it has been reduced . . . due to people who have died, and death no longer becomes a very serious affair. Before you would get worried when one of your patients died, but now it seems to be a usual thing. When AIDS comes in, death [regardless of cause] is so encompassed in the AIDS deaths, so that death looks the same. Even sometimes deaths you used to get so worried about – for example a young person dying – it is no longer having that amount of impact.
>
> Scarcity in the context of whether you can do something [is different from this] – even if I gave you everything, how much of a difference would it really make? People come, and they are just dying, it is just impossible to try to comprehend what to do.

HIV obliterates, he argues, what medicine is supposed to be about and what energizes teaching and professional practice.

> It makes you feel you may lose your proficiency [in your own specialty] and even your particular [ability at] solving diseases. Because you have one pattern

that comes all the time . . . diarrhea, cough, fever . . . and that pattern is all over. Even in ward rounds, it is no longer interesting because there is nothing challenging. Because medicine is supposed to challenge your mind – OK, this may be this disease, that disease, and lead to some kind of discussion. Now it goes to the extent where you arrive at the door and the diagnosis is obvious. . . . Now patients, who are in sight but . . . you don't really see them . . . *like so much wheat you don't see the other important crops for that.*

> Students fear – their biggest worry is that they will not be recognized (as competent physicians with requisite skills acquired in patient care). The recognition is more frightening – doing something for somebody is no longer the norm. And when you come out of the system, you are so numbed at that initial level because there should be an ideal – so you are seeing the worst. And the people complain that new doctors don't care about their competence and training.

These comments are exceptionally frank. Although our colleague and his fellow physicians in East Africa are combating the professional 'numbing' (the 'antinarrative' response of physicians to HIV patients) by teaching students how to counsel AIDS patients and families, the point made highlights the limits of narrative analysis of doctor–patient communications.

CONCLUSION

We began this chapter on doctor–patient communication with reference to the question of trust. The issue is central in current discussions of the financing of American health care. 'Many contend,' Gray (1997: 34) argues, 'that [the] intimate dynamic of the relation between physicians and their patients has been forever altered by managed care,' but the issue of trust is hardly limited to American discussions. Kenyan physicians, as we have seen, discuss the threat to the essential fiduciary qualities of medical practice that results from their being 'overwhelmed by the disease entity.' The appropriateness of disclosing the diagnosis of cancer in societies such as Italy and Japan is debated in terms of maintaining patients' trust in their physicians. Our most basic claim in this chapter has been that fundamental aspects of doctor–patient relations, such as trust, cannot be adequately understood using models of a former era of research that focused narrowly on conversational aspects of doctor–patient communications. Any analysis of doctor–patient relations opens immediately onto discussions of managed care, the global AIDS epidemic, the appropriateness of advanced and experimental treatments, the meanings of illness, and cultural norms for developing truthful and trusting relationships.

We have suggested a model of clinical narratives for addressing such issues. The model focuses on narrative dimensions of clinical communications, on the role of story-making in giving meaning to life-threatening experience and medical efforts to respond to a changing course of illness experience. At the same time, it views such narratives as a site that mediates broader, transnational relations of social class, gender and ethnicity, of biotechnologies, professional cultures, and political economies of health care. We believe such a model has importance for comparative studies of medicine, as well as for social science interventions aimed at improving the human quality of medical care.

ACKNOWLEDGMENTS

This study was funded by the Nathan Cummings Foundation, and carried out with the assistance of Rita Linggood, Irene Kuter, Simon Powell, Susann Wilkinson, and Martha Fuller.

NOTE

1 Literary theorists have argued that plot provides the underlying structure of narrative, constructing 'meaningful totalities out of scattered events' (Ricoeur 1981b: 278). Reader response theorists, such as Iser (1978) and Eco (1994), have focused attention on the activity of 'emplotment,' on the response of a reader or hearer of a story who engages imaginatively in making sense of a story. Readers try to 'uncover the plot' to determine what is really going on, what is likely to happen as the story progresses (Bruner 1986). 'Narrative time' is also a central dimension of all plots, with a sequential dimension of beginnings and endings, a directionality, an outcome or conclusion that bestows sense on what has occurred (Brooks 1984). Concern about how the story will turn out, about how the present will be seen retrospectively from the vantage of the ending, is present as a structuring quality in all storytelling and emplotment. Mattingly introduced the notion 'therapeutic emplotment' (1994) and has gone on to develop full analysis of the relevance of the literature on narrativity to therapeutic encounters (1998). See Mishler (1986) for an early statement of these issues. See Good and Good (1994) for a development of these ideas as we use them here.

REFERENCES

Angell, M. and Kassirer, J. P. (1994) 'Setting the record straight in the breast cancer trials', *New England Journal of Medicine*, 330: 1448.

Balint, M. (1957) *The Doctor, His Patient, and the Illness*. New York: International University Press.

Brodwin, P. (1996) *Medicine and Morality in Haiti: The Contest for Healing Power*. Cambridge: Cambridge University Press.

Brooks, P. (1984) *Reading for the Plot: Design and Intention in Narrative*. New York: Vintage Books.

Bruner, J. (1986) *Actual Minds, Possible Worlds*. Cambridge, MA: Harvard University Press.

Chrisman, N.J. and Maretzki, T.W. (1982) *Clinically Applied Anthropology: Anthropologists in Health Science Settings*. Dordrecht: Reidel.

DiGiacomo, S. (1987) 'Biomedicine as a cultural system: An anthropologist in the kingdom of the sick', in H. Baer (ed.), *Encounters with Biomedicine*. New York: Gordon and Breach. pp. 315–46.

Eco, U. (1994) *Six Walks in the Fictional Woods*. Cambridge, MA: Harvard University Press.

Eisenberg, L. and Kleinman, A. (eds) (1981) *The Relevance of Social Science for Medicine*. Dordrecht: Reidel.

Gaines, A.D. (1992) *Ethnopsychiatry: The Cultural Construction of Professional and Folk Psychiatries*. Albany: State University of New York Press.

Good, B.J. (1994) *Medicine, Rationality and Experience*. Cambridge: Cambridge University Press.

Good, B.J. and Good, M.-J.D. (1981a) 'The meaning of symptoms: A cultural hermeneutic model for clinical practice', in L. Eisenberg and A. Kleinman (eds), *The Relevance of Social Science for Medicine*. Dordrecht: Reidel. pp. 165–96.

Good, B.J. and Good, M.-J.D. (1981b) 'The semantics of medical discourse', in E. Mendelsohn and Y. Elkana (eds), *Sciences and Cultures. Sociology of the Sciences, Vol. V*. Dordrecht: Reidel. pp. 177–212.

Good, B.J. and Good, M.-J.D. (1993) '"Learning medicine": The constructing of medical knowledge at Harvard Medical School', in S. Lindenbaum and M. Lock (eds), *Analysis in Medical Anthropology*. Berkeley: University of California Press.

Good, B.J. and Good, M.-J.D. (1994) 'In the subjunctive mode: epilepsy narratives in Turkey', *Social Science and Medicine*, 38: 835–42.

Good, M.-J.D. (1995a) 'Cultural Studies of Biomedicine: An Agenda for Research', *Social Science and Medicine*, 41: 461–73.

Good, M.-J.D. (1995b) *American Medicine: The Quest for Competence*. Los Angeles: University of California Press.

Good, M.-J.D. (1996) 'L'Abbraccio Biotecnico: Un Invito al trattamento sperimentale', in P. Donghi (ed.) *Il sapere della guarigione*. Spoleto: Laterza. pp. 25–62.

Good, M.-J.D. (1998) *American Medicine: The Quest for Competence*. Los Angeles: University of California Press. (paperback edn).

Good, M.-J.D. (forthcoming) 'Do different health care systems make different doctors?' Article prepared from Plenary Lecture, Norwegian Medical Association Conference: The Physician Role in Transition: Is Hippocrates Sick? Oslo, 14 May 1997.

Good, M.-J.D. and Good, B.J. (1989) '"Disabling practitioners": Hazards of learning to be a doctor on American medical education', *Journal of Orthopsychiatry*, 59: 303–9.

Good, M.-J.D., Hunt, L., Munakata, T., and Kobayashi, Y. (1993) 'A comparative analysis of the culture of biomedicine: Disclosure and consequences for treatment in the practice of oncology', in P. Conrad and E. Gallagher (eds), *Sociological Perspectives in International Health*. Philadelphia: Temple University Press.

Good, M.-J.D., Munakata, T., Kobayashi, Y., Mattingly, C., and Good, B. J. (1994) 'Oncology and narrative time', *Social Science and Medicine*, 38: 855–62.

Good, M.-J.D., Kuter, I., Powell, S., Hoover, H. C. Jr., Carson, M. E., and Linggood, R. (1995) 'Medicine on the edge: Conversations with oncologists', in G. Marcus (ed.), *Technoscientific Imaginaries: Conversations, Profiles, and Memoirs*. Chicago: University of Chicago Press. pp. 129–52.

Gordon, D.R. (1988) 'Tenacious assumptions in western medicine', in M. Lock and D. Gordon (eds), *Biomedicine Examined*. Dordrecht: Kluwer. pp. 11–56.

Gordon, D.R. (1990) 'Embodying illness, embodying cancer', *Culture, Medicine and Psychiatry*, 14: 275–97.

Gordon, D.R. and Paci, E. (1997) 'Disclosure practices and cultural narratives: Understanding concealment and silence around cancer in Tuscany, Italy', *Social Science and Medicine*, 44: 1433–52.

Gray, B.H. (1997) 'Trust and trustworthy care in the managed care era', *Health Affairs*, 16: 34–49.

Hahn, R.A. (1995) *Sickness and Healing: An Anthropological Perspective*. New Haven: Yale University Press.

Hahn, R.A. and Gaines, A. (eds) (1985) *Physicians of Western Medicine*. Dordrecht: Reidel.

Hunt, L.M. (1992) 'Living with cancer in Oaxaca, Mexico: Patient and physician perspectives in cultural context', PhD Dissertation, Harvard University.

Hunt, L.M. (1994) 'Practicing oncology in rural Mexico: A narrative analysis', *Social Science and Medicine*, 38: 843–53.

Iser, W. (1978) *The Act of Reading. A Theory of Aesthetic Response*. Baltimore: Johns Hopkins University Press.

Kagawa-Singer, M.A., Wellisch, D.K., and Durvasula, R. (1997) 'Impact of breast cancer on Asian American and Anglo American women', *Culture, Medicine and Psychiatry*, 21: 449–80.

Kaufman, S.R. (1993) *The Healer's Tale: Transforming Medicine and Culture*. Madison: University of Wisconsin Press.

Kelly, S.E. and Koenig, B.A. (1998) '"Rescue" technologies following high-dose chemotherapy for breast cancer: How social context shapes the assessment of innovative, aggressive, and lifesaving medical technologies', in P.J. Boyle (ed.), *Getting Doctors to Listen: Ethics and Outcomes Data in Context*. Washington, DC: Georgetown University Press. pp. 126–52.

Kleinman, A. (1980) *Patients and Healers in the Context of Culture. An Exploration of the Borderland between Anthropology, Medicine, and Psychiatry*. Berkeley: University of California Press.

Kleinman, A. (1988) *The Illness Narratives: Suffering, Healing and the Human Condition*. New York: Basic Books.

Kleinman, A. (1996) *Writing at the Margin: Discourse between Anthropology and Medicine*. Berkeley: University of California Press.

Kleinman, A. (1997) '"Everything that really matters": Social suffering, subjectivity, and the remaking of human experience in a disordered world', *Harvard Theological Review*, 90: 315–35.

Kleinman, A. and Kleinman, J. (1991) 'Suffering and its professional transformation: Towards an ethnography of interpersonal experience', *Culture, Medicine and Psychiatry*, 15: 275–301.

Kleinman, A., Eisenberg, L., and Good, B. (1978) 'Culture, illness and care: Clinical lessons from anthropologic and cross-cultural research', *Annals of Internal Medicine*, 88: 251–8.

Kusumanto, Y.H., Huisman, J., Sutaryo, C., and Veerman, A.J.P. (1997) 'Psychosocial implications of childhood leukemia in a non-Western country', *International Journal of Pediatric Hematology/Oncology*, 4: 193–200.

Leslie, C. (1976) *Asian Medical Systems: A Comparative Study*. Berkeley: University of California Press.

Leslie, C., and Young, A. (eds) (1992) *Paths to Asian Medical Knowledge*. Berkeley: University of California Press.

Lewis, G. (1981) 'Cultural influences on illness behavior: A medical anthropological approach', in L. Eisenberg and A. Kleinman (eds), *The Relevance of Social Science for Medicine*. Dordrecht: Reidel.

Lind, S.E., Good, M-J.D., Seidel, S., Csordas, T., and Good, B.J. (1989) 'Telling the diagnosis of cancer', *Journal of Clinical Oncology*, 7: 563–89.

Lindenbaum, S. and Lock, M. (1993) *Knowledge, Power and Practice: The Anthropology of Medicine and Everyday Life*. Berkeley: University of California Press.

Lock, M. and Gordon, D. (1988) *Biomedicine Examined*. Dordrecht: Kluwer.

Marshall, P.A. and Koenig, B.A. (1996) 'Bioethics in anthropology: Perspectives on culture, medicine, and morality', in C.F. Sargent and T.M. Johnson (eds), *Medical Anthropology: Contemporary Theory and Method*. Westport, CT: Praeger.

Martin, E. (1987) *The Woman in the Body. A Cultural Analysis of Reproduction*. Boston: Beacon.

Martin, E. (1994) *Flexible Bodies: Tracking Immunity in American Culture from the Days of Polio to the Days of AIDS*. Boston: Beacon.

Mattingly, C. (1994) 'The Concept of therapeutic "emplotment"', *Social Science and Medicine*, 38: 811–22.

Mattingly, C. (1998). *Healing Dramas and Clinical Plots*. Cambridge: Cambridge University Press.

Mechanic, D. (1997) 'Managed care as a target of distrust', *Journal of the American Medical Association*, 277: 1810–11.

Mechanic, D. and Schlesinger, M. (1996) 'The impact of managed care on patients' trust in medical care and their physicians', *Journal of the American Medical Association*, 275: 1693–97.

Mishler, E. (1986) *The Discourse of Medicine: Dialectics of Medical Interviews*. Norwood, NJ: ABLEX.

Ngelangel, C.A., Ramiro, L.S., Perez, E.S., Ramos, M.S., Lacaya, L., Agbanlog, T.P., Talaver, B.C., Martinez, F.-G., and Good, M.-J.D. (1995) 'The process of disclosure in Philippine oncological practice', University of the Philippines Working Paper.

Nichter, M. (1989) *Anthropology and International Health: South Asian Case Studies*. Dordrecht: Kluwer.

Nichter, M. and Nordstrom, C. (1989) 'A question of medicine answering: Health commodification and the social relations of healing in Sri Lanka', *Culture, Medicine and Psychiatry*, 13: 367–90.

Nilchaikovit, T. (1998) 'Cancer patients in Thailand: Illness experience in a changing social context', paper presented at the Conference on Health and Social Change in Asia, Harvard Medical School, Boston, MA, 1 May.

Nilchaikovit, T., Hill, J., and Holland, J. (1993) 'The effects of culture on illness behavior and medical care: Asian and American differences', *General Hospital Psychiatry*, 15: 41–50.

Pappas, G. (1990) 'Some implications for the study of the doctor–patient interaction: Power, structure, and agency in the works of Howard Waitzkin and Arthur Kleinman', *Social Science and Medicine*, 30: 199–204.

Parsons, T. (1978) 'The sick role and the role of the physician reconsidered', in T. Parsons (ed.), *Action Theory and the Human Condition*. New York: Free Press.

Rapp, R. (1988) 'Chromosomes and communication: The discourse of genetic counseling', *Medical Anthropology Quarterly*, 2: 143–57.

Rennie, D. (1994) 'Breast cancer: How to mishandle misconduct', *Journal of the American Medical Association*, 271: 1205.

Rhodes, L.A. (1991) *Emptying Beds: The Work of an Emergency Psychiatric Unit*. Berkeley: University of California Press.

Rhodes, L.A. (1996) 'Studying biomedicine as a cultural system', in C.F. Sargent and T.M. Johnson (eds) *Medical Anthropology: Contemporary Theory and Method*. Westport, CT: Praeger.

Ricoeur, P. (1981a) *Hermeneutics and the Human Sciences*. J.B. Thompson (editor and translator). Cambridge: Cambridge University Press.

Ricoeur, P. (1981b) 'Narrative time', in W.J.T. Mitchell (ed.), *On Narrative*. Chicago: University of Chicago Press. pp. 165–86.

Scheper-Hughes, N. (1992) *Death Without Weeping: The Violence of Everyday Life in Brazil*. Berkeley: University of California Press.

Singer, M. (1989) 'The coming of age of critical medical anthropology', *Social Science and Medicine*, 28: 1193–203.

Stoeckle, J. and Barsky, A.J. (1981) 'Attributions: Uses of social science knowledge in the "Doctoring" of primary care', in L. Eisenberg and A. Kleinman (eds), *The Relevance of Social Science for Medicine*. Dordrecht: Reidel.

Surbone, A. and Zwitter, M. (eds) (1997) *Communication with the Cancer Patient: Information and Truth*. Annals of the New York Academy of Science, 809, 20 February.

Taussig, M.T. (1980) 'Reification and the consciousness of the patient', *Social Science and Medicine*, 14B: 3–13.

Todd, A. (1989) *Intimate Adversaries: Cultural Conflict between Doctors and Women Patients*. Philadelphia: University of Pennsylvania Press.

Waitzkin, H. (1981) 'The social origins of illness: A neglected history', *International Journal of Health Services*, 11: 77–103.

Waitzkin, H. (1991) *The Politics of Medical Encounters: How Patients and Doctors Deal with Social Problems*. New Haven: Yale University Press.

Waitzkin, H. and Stoeckle, J. (1972) 'The communication of information about illness', *Advances in Psychosomatic Medicine*, 8: 180–215.

Waitzkin, H. and Stoeckle, J. (1976) 'Information control and the micropolitics of health care: Summary of an ongoing research project', *Social Science and Medicine*, 10: 263–76.

Waxler, N.E. (1981) 'The social labeling perspective on illness and medical practice', in L. Eisenberg and A. Kleinman (eds), *The Relevance of Social Science for Medicine*. Dordrecht: Reidel.

West, C. (1984) *Routine Complications: Troubles with Talks between Doctors and Patients*. Bloomington, IN: Indiana University Press.

Zola, I.K. (1972) 'Medicine as an institution of social control', *Sociological Review*, 20: 487–504.

2.5

Accounting for Disease and Distress: Morals of the Normal and Abnormal

MARGARET LOCK

INTRODUCTION

Consideration of normality and abnormality in connection with health and illness inevitably raises questions for social scientists about just how this distinction is conceptualized and then reproduced in social practices. Further, how does the labeling of body states, or the behavior of individuals or groups of individuals as 'normal' or 'abnormal' affect their lives? Alternatively, how does the idea of being designated 'at risk' for future abnormalities affect daily life? Of even more interest is why the creation of a moral discourse is so often associated with ideas about normal and abnormal, even when the language and practices of biomedicine are usually assumed to be predominantly rational and free of censure? In this chapter, by drawing on examples from around the world, I will show how ideas about normality and abnormality are culturally constructed and intimately associated with the social, political, and moral order, with profound consequences for individual well-being, and frequently for the allocation of responsibility in connection with the onset or persistence of disease and illness.

A brief example at the outset will illustrate some of the complexities with which we must grapple when discussing this subject. The process of labor and birth has become progressively regulated over the past 20 years, so that this supremely subjective experience has been transformed into a statistically constructed process whereby the duration of the stages of delivery and the timing of the transitions from one stage to another must occur within medically established parameters. Almost all hospital births, in EuroAmerica at least, now carry out an 'active management of labor' based on the Friedman curves. The result of this normalization of birth has been increased pressure placed on many women, particularly Caucasian women, to 'speed up' the process of birth. By contrast, in the Canadian north, common knowledge, shared both by Inuit women and health-care professionals familiar with that environment, has it that 'normal' labor among the Inuit is remarkably rapid. Inuit women themselves take a certain pride in quick deliveries, to which diet and lifestyle may well contribute.

In an effort to try to reduce infant mortality, the Canadian government implemented a policy in the early 1980s whereby all Inuit women were to be 'evacuated' and flown south to give birth. This policy caused great unrest, not only because women were isolated from their families, but also because they were systematically subjected to technological interventions in hospitals in the Canadian south, where it became regular practice to slow down what were designated as abnormal labor experiences. These practices quickly led to disputes and active resistance on the part of women to the evacuation policy. In the intervening years, some policy modifications have been made, and increasingly, well-trained midwives work across northern Canada, but for a large number of Inuit women the process of giving birth commences with an aeroplane flight of more than 1000 miles so that labor and birth may be technologically managed in the tertiary care hospitals of urban Canada, where, more often than not, management is dominated by efforts to prolong labor and birth (Kaufert and O'Neil 1990).

This example illustrates a situation with which we have become familiar over the course of this century, namely an increase in interventions, both medical and psychological, into various stages of the life cycle by health-care professionals (Conrad 1992). As is well known, birth was one of the first life cycle events to be medicalized, and there is no doubt that this process has lowered both infant and maternal mortality rates to some extent, although changes in lifestyle factors have made a greater contribution to these improved statistics (Macfarlane and Mugford 1984).

What I want to emphasize here is not only the discrepancy between authoritative and subjective accounts about what constitutes a 'normal' birth, but further, the assumption made on the part of the majority of obstetricians that their knowledge can be applied without modification to all births, regardless of marked cultural, social, and economic differences among pregnant women. This assumption persists even though there is considerable evidence to suggest that cultural and lifestyle factors influence pregnancy, the process of birth, and its outcomes (see McClain 1982). Can this 'boxification' (Kaufert 1990) of birth into normal and abnormal cases based on a systematic setting aside of all apparent variation be justified? Do we have any evidence as to what might constitute 'normal' variation in the process of birth, wherever its location worldwide? Should the 'average' Caucasian body be taken as the standard around which variation is established, whether this be in connection with birth or other health-related events?

Inventing the Normal

Until well into the last century, use of the term normal was virtually limited to the fields of mathematics and physics. It was not until certain ideas about pathology took hold in the 1820s that arguments about the relationship between normal and abnormal biological states were seriously debated for the first time. Auguste Comte, writing in 1851, noted a major shift in conceptualization that had taken place 30 years previously, when the physician Broussais had first argued that the phenomena of disease are essentially of the same kind as those of health, and thus health and disease differ from each other only in 'intensity.'

Before Broussais, the dominant approach to disease in Europe had been one in which it was conceptualized as regulated by entirely different laws from those that govern health. Although the early Galenic idea of a healthy body being one of balance among excesses and deficiencies, hot and cold states, and so on remained important, in the late eighteenth century, a notion of pathological organs was superimposed on earlier thinking, and medicine became preoccupied with a study of sick organs, rather with variations in the condition of individual patients, which had previously been the case (see also Canguilhem 1991; Hacking 1990)

Although clinical medicine, until the present time, has remained focused on organ pathology, and Broussais himself was deeply immersed in theories about organ pathology (Porter 1998), he nevertheless postulated that normality could be understood as being on a continuum with pathology, and further that the 'normal' is the center from which all deviation departs (Hacking 1990: 164). This theme was taken up and expanded upon by several influential thinkers during the course of the nineteenth century, among them Auguste Comte and Claude Bernard. In the 1960s, Georges Canguilhem, in writing a synthesis of the work of the previous century in connection with normality, concluded that 'strictly speaking . . . there is no biological science of the normal. There is a science of biological situations and conditions called normal' (1991: 228). Canguilhem concluded that normality can only be understood in context, 'as situated in action,' and moreover, diversity does not infer sickness, nor does 'objective' pathology exist.

The systematization of disease categories and the ordering by governments, public health officials, and others of information on disease incidence became a social preoccupation from the end of the last century (Foucault 1979). In the interests of the 'surveillance' of society, what formerly had been an interest in variation around the norm was gradually reformulated so as to make categorical, classifiable distinctions between normal and pathological. Normal and abnormal were now conceptualized as a dichotomy.

The philosopher Ian Hacking, less interested than the physician Canguilhem in clinical medicine, seeking to document the formation of the science of probability, and influenced to some extent by Foucault, argues that our present understanding of the idea of normal is a key concept in what he labels 'the taming of chance.' Hacking notes that for a good number of years use of the normal/pathological continuum postulated by Broussais was confined to medicine, but then towards the end of the nineteenth century, 'it moved into the sphere of almost everything. People, behavior, states of affairs, diplomatic relations, molecules: all these may be normal or abnormal' (Hacking 1990: 160). Hacking argues that we talk freely today about 'normal' people, and, of even more importance, we often go on without a second thought to suggest that this is how things ought to be. Thus, the idea of normality is frequently used to close the gap between 'is' and 'ought,' and so has a moral quality built into it. Hacking traces our current expanded understanding of normal directly back to Comte. He describes the way in which Comte, perhaps inspired by a personal brush with mental illness, moved normality out beyond the clinic into the political sphere, at which point 'normal ceased to be the ordinary healthy state; it became the purified state to which we should strive, and to which our energies are tending. In short, progress and the normal state became inextricably linked' (Hacking 1990: 168), and further, not only individuals, but aggregates of individuals could be labeled as normal or otherwise.

Thus, a fundamental tension was introduced into the idea of normal that currently contains both the meaning of an existing average and a state of perfection towards which individuals or societies can strive. Both the idea of a deviation by degree from a norm and the idea of a perfect state are encapsulated in the one term. Following Durkheim, normal can be understood as that which is right and proper. In this case, efforts to restore normality entail a return to a former equilibrium, to a status quo, but taken further, normal can be interpreted as only average, and hence is something to be improved upon. In its most extreme form, argues Hacking, this interpretation can lead all too easily to eugenics. Two ideas, therefore, are contained in the one concept of normal: one of preservation, the other of amelioration. As Hacking aptly puts it: 'Words have profound memories that oil our shrill and squeaky rhetoric'; the normal now stands at once, 'indifferently' for what is typical, the 'unenthusiastic objective average, but it also stands for what has been, good health, and for what shall be, our chosen destiny' (1990: 169). Hacking concludes that this benign and sterile-sounding word, normal, has become one of the most powerful [ideological] tools of the twentieth century.

DISEASE AND THE NORMAL

It is generally agreed that the idea of disease as deviation from a biological norm dominates medical thinking and practice at the present time. Although social and cultural contributions

to the incidence of disease may be acknowledged, their effect is usually understood simply as contributing either directly (through diet and individual behavior) or indirectly (through a lack of sanitation, a polluted work environment, or stress, for example) to a 'final common pathway' leading to pathological changes in biology wherein lies the 'real' disease. Factors extraneous to the body are made accessories before the fact of disease.

In recent years, many social scientists and psychiatrists have taken a critical stance about this type of argument; one in which they question the epistemologically neutral claims inherent to the biomedical sciences. Mishler et al., for example, in tune with Canguilhem, made it clear long ago that there is no way to define a biological norm or deviations from that norm without reference to specific populations and their sociocultural characteristics (1981: 4). They cite Redlich, who insists that one must ask 'normal for what?' and 'normal for whom?' In other words, assertions about the normality of biological functioning, or about the normal structure of an organ, must be based on the relationship between the observed instance and its distribution in a specified population (Redlich 1957). Further, implicit to any specified norm is a set of presupposed standard conditions with regard to when, how, and on whom measurements are made.

A major difficulty arises because the average value for a variable of some specified population may not correspond to an ideal standard, ensuring that '[s]pecific characteristics of populations and their life situations are critical to understanding and interpreting the significance of average values and of 'deviations' from universal or idea standards of health (Mishler et al. 1981: 4). A classic study carried out by Ryle illustrates this difficulty. In a clinical and epidemiological study of adolescents in populations living on different diets, he found considerable variability in the size of thyroid glands. Ryle (1961) concluded that the presence of 'visible glands' in a population where this phenomenon is common cannot be interpreted as a meaningful clinical sign or precursor of a goitre in later life, as physicians are taught to believe. Ryle argues that this 'symptom' may represent a normal adaption to a specific environment rather than a deviation from a universal standard of healthy thyroid function.

A classic anthropological study supports Ryle's argument. While working among the Subanum of Mindanao, in the Philippines, Charles Frake, an ethnolinguist, made a classification of diseases using the local taxonomy (1977). He found that the Subanum have an exceedingly elaborate taxonomy of skin conditions based on their astute observation of the numerous skin changes commonly visible on their bodies, changes intimately associated with life in a damp, tropical environment. Frake, following the lead of his informants, interpreted the majority of these changes as 'normal,' even though they might at times need medication. To a biomedically trained dermatologist virtually all of these changes would no doubt have signalled disease, although it is likely that very few dermatologists would have great facility with either making specific diagnoses of these conditions or with treating them.

Yet, another classic study published in the 1930s, this time from the United States, provides evidence of the extent to which subjective assessment and prior expectations can be involved in making judgments about what is normal and abnormal. More than 1000 American schoolchildren were examined by physicians to determine whether they should have their tonsils removed. It was found that 600 children had already had this surgical procedure, and they were therefore removed from the study. Of the remaining 400, it was recommended that 45 per cent of them have a tonsillectomy, implying that the other 55 per cent fell within the bounds of normal. However, when these 'normal' children were examined by a second set of physicians, they recommended that 46 per cent of this group have their tonsils removed. A third group of physicians, who were not informed of the earlier recommendations, examined the children who had survived the first two rounds, and they recommended that 44 per cent of them have their tonsils removed. In all, after three successive rounds of examinations, only 44 children out of the original 1000 had not had a tonsillectomy recommended for them (Wennberg and Gittelsohn 1982: 130). When we recall that today tonsillectomies are avoided if at all possible, this telling example suggests two things. First, how the decisions about diagnosing pathology made by individual physicians can be highly subjective, and therefore by implication ideas about normal are also subjective. Second, in addition to variation in assessments among individual physicians, fashions in surgical and medical procedures also contribute to interpretations of normality.

SITUATING THE ABNORMAL

The examples cited thus far involve value judgements about physical signs and symptoms that are visible, or can be made visible, and are then subjected to assessment and measurement. However, it is in cultural psychiatry and cross-cultural studies in connection with issues relating to mental health that concepts of the normal have been most systematically challenged. One impetus from the outset for this kind of research has been the question of cultural relativism, and whether major mental disorder is the result of universal biological abnormalities or, alternatively, whether culture makes such a major contribution that certain diseases familiar to biomedicine do not occur in all settings. An extension of this approach, following labeling theory, argues that if certain types of behavior are neither labeled as abnormal nor stigmatized, then this may serve as a major form of protection against the appearance of serious or chronic pathology.

In her careful study among both the Bering Sea Eskimo (Inuit) and the Yoruba of Nigeria, Jane Murphy (1976) concluded that virtually all symptoms that would be labeled by a psychiatrist as signs of schizophrenia would, under certain conditions, similarly be regarded as abnormal in both these cultural settings, that is, as signs of 'craziness.' However, local responses to crazy people often buffered the effects of the illness. Murphy went further, and pointed out that certain classical symptoms of schizophrenia, such as dissociation, would not be recognized as abnormal if the affected individual could 'control' the episodes at will, especially if these episodes were integral to religious or sacred activities. On the contrary, they would probably be highly valued as essential to cultural continuity. Murphy's work was among the first of numerous anthropological studies that demonstrated enormous difficulties in attempting to translate concepts of mental disorder and ideas about abnormality across cultures (see also Field 1960; Rivers 1924).

In recent years, a more critical approach has been taken by a number of social scientists working in this area, one in which the disease categories of biomedicine are no longer assumed to be above epistemological scrutiny. The emphasis has shifted away, therefore, from the exoticisms of other cultures to a more balanced approach in which all knowledge about normal and abnormal is interpreted in cultural context. Good and Kleinman pose the problem as follows:

> How are we to know whether the clinical syndromes identified in research in the United States and Europe are universal diseases, linked to discrete biological disorders, or culture-specific forms of illness behavior resulting from complex interactions among physiological, psychological, social and cultural variables? Are they universal patterns, representing 'final common pathways' to be identified through studies of neurotransmitters and neuroendocrinol-

ogy, or are they culture-specific syndromes, linked to underlying psychophysiological processes but produced as final common ethnobehavioral pathways (Carr 1978). (Good and Kleinman 1985: 297)

Good and Kleinman reviewed research that reveals that anxiety disorders are present, as far as can be ascertained, in all societies, but that the phenomenology of such disorders, 'the meaningful forms through which distress is articulated and constituted as social reality' varies in significant ways across cultures (1985: 298). These authors argue that we must take care not to fall into the trap of creating a 'category fallacy' in which the nosological categories developed for particular EuroAmerican populations are then applied indiscriminately to all human populations (Kleinman et al. 1977).

Robert Barrett takes up the challenge of interpreting the disease of schizophrenia as it is understand today as, in effect, a culture-specific syndrome, a product of the recent history of EuroAmerican thought about mind and body, individualism, and modernity. In a review article he shows how the institutional practices of psychiatry first created in the nineteenth century made possible the production of a new category of knowledge – schizophrenia. Prior to institutionalization, the kind of 'crazy' behavior involving disorders of cognition and perception that we now associate with schizophrenia would have elicited a range of responses, not all of them indicating that pathology was involved. As with the Inuit and Yoruba, the specific circumstances would have been crucial in passing judgement. Barrett interprets schizophrenia as we know it today as a 'polysemic symbol' in which various meanings and values are condensed, including stigma, weakness, inner degeneration, a diseased brain, and chronicity. Without this associated constellation of meanings, schizophrenia as we understand it would not exist. Barrett goes on to argue that the individualistic concept of personhood, so characteristic of EuroAmerica, has also contributed to our understanding of this disease. He shows how a theme of a divided, split, or disintegrated individual runs through nineteenth century psychiatric discourse and continues to the present day. Of course, schizophrenia is not the only disease associated with splitting and dissociation, but it has also been the prototypical example of such a condition. The perceived loss of autonomy and boundedness taken as characteristic of schizophrenia are signs of the breakdown of the individual, and thus of the person. Further, the classification and treatment of schizophrenic patients as broken people with 'permeable ego boundaries'

profoundly influences the subjective experience of the disease (Barrett 1988).

Barrett, himself a psychiatrist, argues that categorizing patients as suffering from schizophrenia implies a specific ideological stance that may highlight, problematize, and reinforce certain experiences, such as auditory hallucinations, for example. Barrett's argument is neither one of simple social construction, nor of schizophrenia as a myth, but a much more subtle argument in which he does not dispute at all the reality of symptoms, or the horror of the disease. He points out, however, that a careful review of the cross-cultural literature indicates that some of the constitutional components of what we understand as schizophrenia may be virtually absent in certain non-Western settings: 'Thus, in some cultures, especially those which do not employ concept of "mind" as opposed to "body," the closest equivalents to schizophrenia are not concerned with "mental experiences" at all, but employ criteria related to impairment in social functioning or persistent rule violation' (Barrett 1988: 379). Craziness need not be conceptualized, therefore, as a state of mind, but as a loss of a capacity to be effectively social. In other words, where there is less of a focus on individual autonomy and the splitting of personality, and where symptoms of what, in psychiatry, is classified as dissociation is not necessarily regarded a priori as pathological, the meaning of symptoms will be interpreted differently, and carry a different moral valence, with implications for patient well-being. In cultural settings where schizophrenia-like symptoms are not stigmatized, for example, chronicity has been shown to be less severe (Waxler 1979).

Similar arguments to that of Barrett have been developed for clinical depression as we currently define it, that is, as being a psychiatric ethnocategory characteristic of EuroAmerica society, and further particularly associated with middle and higher socioeconomic groups. Translation of meaning in connection with depressive emotional states is extremely problematic both within and across cultures (Kleinman and Good 1985, see also Kirmayer 1984).

NEGOTIATING INTERPRETATIONS OF NORMAL AND ABNORMAL

Susan Sontag (1977) warned us, when she contracted breast cancer more than a decade ago, about the 'punitive and sentimental fantasies' concocted in connection with certain illnesses. She was concerned about the way in which images about illnesses are put to social use, and about the various stereotypes and moralizing that are associated with certain images throughout history. Sontag insisted that the 'most truthful way of regarding illness – and the healthiest way of being ill – is the one most purified of, most resistant to, metaphoric thinking.' She was particularly concerned, not surprisingly, with certain research, current at that time, that claimed to have established a statistically significant association between a given personality type and the incidence of breast cancer.

Sontag's exhortation to confine our interpretations about illness to the material is, it seems, easily justifiable as a means to eliminate stigmatization and to make disease morally neutral. However, failure to pay attention to the moral discourse associated with illness usually forces premature closure about the social dimensions of suffering (Kleinman et al. 1997). Further, and not unrelated to social suffering, this approach leaves unproblematized interpretations of the normal and abnormal. This is where the meaning-centered approach characteristic of much medical anthropology comes into its own; an approach that takes the lived experiences and local knowledge of involved individuals as its point of departure, and then situates this data in cultural and political context. Many researchers then go further, to reflect on the unexamined assumptions present in biomedicine, in light of the findings obtained from meaning-centered research projects.

While doing research among Greek immigrants in Montréal in the late 1980s, I found that the complaint most commonly expressed by women, particularly those working in the notoriously exploitative garment industry, was of nevra (nerves). Nevra is associated with a frightening loss of control, and is described as an experience of powerful feelings of 'bursting out,' 'breaking out,' or 'boiling over,' in other words, a sense of disruption of normal body boundaries. Once the condition becomes chronic, headaches, chest pain, and other pains radiating out from the back of the neck also characteristically become part of nevra symptomatology. This experience is so common that at least one major Montréal hospital uses nevra as a diagnostic category. Some women, when they visit a doctor, are diagnosed as clinically depressed and given antidepressants, but the majority do not meet the usual criteria for depression, and a tendency exists for certain physicians to dismiss the patient's complaints as being 'all in her head' (Lock and Dunk 1990).

The Greek concept of nevra is part of a larger family of similar conditions commonly experienced in the Arab world, the southern Mediterranean, and in Central and Latin America (where it appears to have been transported from Europe). The condition is also present in isolated parts of North America, including the Appalachians and Newfoundland (Low 1985), suggesting that it was formerly widely spread throughout Europe. Further, nevra or nervios (in Spanish) is just one among many 'culture-bound' or 'culturally interpreted' syndromes located around the world. Byron Good (1977) formulated the concept of a 'semantic illness network' in which popular categories of illness, including the culture-bound syndromes, can be understood as representing 'congeries of words, metaphors, and images that condense around specific events. These conditions are frequently characterized in the medical literature as 'somatization' and treated as evidence of a psychological disorder that manifests itself physically.

Among Montréal immigrants it is considered normal to experience nevra in daily life; it is only when symptoms become very disabling that a woman will visit her doctor. If episodes become very frequent or oscillate rapidly back and forth between stenohoria, in which an individual feels confined and depressed, and agoraphobia, in which one feels overwhelming anxiety at the thought of going out, then the condition is assumed to have become an illness. Some women are believed to be more constitutionally vulnerable to attacks than others, and men are not entirely immune from them. Further, nevra is associated by all women with the immigrant experience, and many of them, when interviewed, linked it explicitly to the abusive working conditions they were subjected to in Montréal.

This ever present stress is punctuated by precipitating events, ranging from crises such as being fired or laid off from to work, to family quarrels, or at times spousal abuse (Lock 1990). It is in situations such as these that the term nevra is used to describe a conjunction of destructive social events, uncontrollable emotional responses, and culturally characteristic disabling physical symptoms. In order to better appreciate the cultural significance of nevra, a brief digression into the structure of Greek family life, as it was until recently, is necessary.

In common with many other societies of the world (Griaule 1965; Hugh-Jones 1979), Greeks relate a healthy and 'correct' human body to a clean and orderly house, and this is, in turn, associated with moral order in society at large. The house is the focus of family life, not only because it furnishes all the physical and social needs of family members, but also because it is a spiritual center, replete with icons and regular ritual activity, where family members seek to emulate the Holy Family (DuBoulay 1986). Management of the house is the special responsibility of the woman, who is both functionally and symbolically associated with it (Dubisch 1986). Cleanliness and order in the house are said to reflect the character of the housewife, and a discussion of private, inside family matters should not cross the threshold into the threatening domain of the outside world. Ideally, a woman should never leave the house for frivolous or idle reasons or venture outside where dirt and immorality abound. A woman who spends too much of her time outside of the house can be accused of damaging the all-important social reputation of her family.

Just as a distinction is made between inside and outside the house, so too is a distinction made between the inner and outer body (Dubisch 1986). Contact between what enters the body and what leaves it must be avoided. Dirty clothes and polluting human products must be strictly segregated from food preparation. Although fulfillment of male sexual needs is considered imperative, a woman's life is hedged with taboos around menstruation, marriage, the sexual act, and childbirth, all designed to confine any elicit desires she may have, and contain the polluting nature of her bodily products.

A woman's task is to bind the family together, to keep it ritually pure, and to protect it from the potentially destructive outside world. This task, together with the raising of children, has traditionally been the prime source of self-esteem for Greek women. While men must protect the family honor in the outside world, women have been required to exhibit modesty at all times, and their bodies were symbols of family integrity and purity as a whole. Emotional stability is valued in this situation, and any signs of loss of control on the part of women is worrisome.

This is the normative state, an idealized situation that in daily life is, of course, often not lived up to, or alternatively may be deliberately flouted. Nevertheless, this has been the value system – the standard – against which Greek women have measured their lives until recently. As is usual among immigrant populations, values, particularly those pertaining to family life, tend to persist after migration; the uncertainties produced by a new way of life may actually promote and harden them. In Montréal, Greek immigrant women complain that they seldom have an opportunity to go out of the house unaccompanied by their husbands unless it is to go to work. A Greek–Canadian physician described many of his patients as suffering from what he called the 'hostage syndrome,' the results of vigilant husbands protecting their family honor in unfamiliar surroundings.

Abiding by traditional codes of conduct, once a source of pride for Greek women, can become

crippling after immigration. When a harsh climate, cramped apartment life with few friends or relatives nearby, language difficulties, and debilitating working conditions are taken into account, it is hardly surprising that so many women experience acute isolation, physical suffering in the form of nevra, and serious doubts about the worth of their lives. However, because a negative moral discourse is closely associated with nevra, women are often ambivalent about a frank discussion of symptoms. It is clear that many of those women who visit a doctor for medication do so with the hope that their physical distress will be legitimized, at the same time it is relieved, through medicalization. Like Sontag, the majority of these women want their illness purified of metaphoric thinking and recognized as thoroughly material, thus ensuring that their suffering is both individualized and depoliticized. When activists among immigrant women in Montréal have focused on the social and political origins of nevra and other illness states, their plea usually falls on stony ground, but this is not because the women do not explicitly recognize that bouts of nevra may be directly related to working conditions or near-poverty. Their financial insecurity and status as immigrants means that these women cannot risk even contemplating political action. Above all, they want prompt and effective action taken to relieve their individual suffering, and they want it made quite clear to husbands and other involved observers that their suffering is both 'real' and painful.

The literature of medical anthropology is replete with similar telling examples in which, at the most fundamental level, arguments about bodily ills are essentially moral disputes about the boundaries between normal and abnormal and their social significance. Ong (1988), for example, interpreted attacks of spirit possession on the shop floors of multinational factories in Malaysia as complex and ambivalent but not abnormal responses of young women to violations of their gendered sense of self, difficult work conditions, and the process of modernization. The psychologicalization and medicalization of these attacks by consultant medical professionals permitted a different moral interpretation of the problem by employers: one of 'primitive minds' disrupting the creation of capital.

Similarly, the refusal of many Japanese adolescents to go to school is labeled by certain psychiatrists in that country (but not all) as deviant, but this behavior can also be understood as an individualized, muted form of resistance to manipulation by families, peers, and teachers. Japanese themselves debate in public as to whether this behavior is indeed abnormal, or, on the contrary, positively adaptive, given the highly competitive, exhausting school system, in which bullying is a frequent, characteristic of their society today. Such a situation is noted by many to be one result of the heavy price of Japanese modernization (Lock 1991). Similarly, the Kleinmans have analyzed narratives about chronic pain in China as, in effect, normal responses to chaotic political change at the national level. These changes are associated with collective and personal delegitimation of the daily life of thousands of ordinary people, and the subjective experience of physical malaise, that in the clinical situation are interpreted as and reduced to physical disorder. Swartz and Levett note that, not surprisingly, 'psychological sequelae' have frequently been reported in connection with the impact of massive long-term political repression of children in South Africa. They go on to argue that this psychologicalization is too narrowly defined, and that 'the costs of generations of oppression of children cannot be offset simply by interventions of mental health workers' (Swartz and Levett 1989: 747) Further, these researchers argue, 'it is a serious fallacy to assume that if something is wrong within the society, then this must be reflected necessarily in the *psychopathological* make-up of individuals' (1989: 747, emphasis added). In common with those authors cited above, Swartz and Levett oppose the normalization and transformation of political and social repression into individual pathology and its management solely through medical interventions. They are particularly concerned that even when certain patients are labeled as 'victims,' and thus a moral and political component in addition to 'pathology' is in theory acknowledged, societal dynamics working to repress memories of the past ensure that the bodies of individuals rather than the body politic is made the focus of attention (see also Melish 1998, in connection with slavery in the United States). Furthermore, the plight of thousands of children whose suffering is chronic, but not exemplified by major traumatic episodes that bring them to the attention of mental health workers, goes largely unnoticed.

Allan Young, researching the invention of post-traumatic stress disorder, shows just how powerful is the current psychiatric model in the creation of this new disease. Psychiatrists assume that the uncovering and reliving of a single traumatic episode during the course of therapy will open the door to relief from chronic debilitating stress, and postulated pathological changes in the neuroendocrinological system (Young 1995). Thus, even the atrocities of the Vietnam War, and moral condemnation of them, are individualized and depoliticized. The violent and repressive behavior of powerful forces in society is rarely labeled as abnormal, nor is its long-lasting effect on the daily lives of millions of people explicitly acknowledged, but rather the physical manifestations of distress in those relatively few individuals who come to the attention of the medical world are interpreted as pathologies that must be purged.

MAKING HEALTH A MATTER OF MORALS

Historical and anthropological research suggests that all societies create concepts about what constitutes a well-functioning social, political, and moral order. These concepts are intimately associated with what is assumed to be the health and well-being of the individuals who form any given society (Janzen 1981). It must be kept in mind, of course, as Marx (1967), Mumford (1963), and more recently Comaroff (1985), Fanon (1967), Lock and Kaufert (1998), Scheper-Hughes (1992), and others have shown, with special emphasis on ethnicity and gender differences, that the well-being of some individuals may be exploited in any given society for the sake of those with power, and that this may, in effect, go unnoticed and be considered normal. Further, within any given society, dominant values and ideologies are contested, and they change over time. Nevertheless, a close association between the moral order and ideas about the health or ill health of society and of the individuals who compose that society persists in one form or another. By extension, a 'sick society' is one in which the moral order is thought to be under threat.

The dominant metaphor for more than 2000 years in China and for many hundreds of years in Korea and Japan, for example, has been that of harmony, implying the selfconscious contribution by individuals to a harmonious social and political order. Health is understood in the East Asian philosophical and medical system as being in a continuum with illness, and not diametrically opposed to it. Moreover, individuals are recognized as having relative amounts of health, depending on such factors as the season of the year, their occupation, their age, and so on, as opposed to a finite presence or absence of health. Thus, health can only be understood with respect to the location of the microcosm of the individual in the macrocosm of the social order, and the physical and mental condition of individuals is conceptualized as inextricable from that of their surroundings, social and environmental (Lock 1980).

East Asian medicine is often described as holistic by its aficionados, but in practice, it is the bodies of individuals that are manipulated, and not facets of the social order. Thus, in early Chinese history the health of the entire polity, for which the Emperor's body was a living synecdoche, was dependent upon the moral and healthy behavior of his subjects (similar knowledge was evident in medieval Europe). Individual concerns and interests are by definition suppressed in a Confucian ideology for the sake of society, and this attitude extends to the management of bodies. Thus, individuals are expected to 'bend' to fit the standards of society and, should illness occur, resort is made to herbal medication, acupuncture, and other therapies to bring the mind/body back into harmony with the macrocosm. The objective of such efforts is returning the individual to active participation in society. This system is therefore inherently conservative, and locates responsibility for the occurrence of health and illness firmly with individuals. Even though the demands posed by society on individual health are freely acknowledged, and it is sometimes recognized that they induce illness, they are nevertheless considered unavoidable and remain essentially unchallenged.

Turning to another example, the concept of health widely used by the majority of indigenous peoples of North America, prior to colonization, was one in which a healthy person was understood as inseparable from his relationship to the land. The Cree concept, 'being-alive-well,' suggests that individuals must be correctly situated with respect to the land; a 'sense of place' is inherent to the continuance of health in both the family and the community, and therefore to individual health (Adelson 1991). This concept is, of course, an abstract ideal, one that is currently being selfconsciously rethought among the Cree, in part as a response to the massive disruptions caused in their communities by, most recently, the building of the James Bay hydroelectric dam, followed by the threat for many years of the building of a second dam. The mobilization of tradition is also part of a movement across North America, among aboriginal peoples, to take back full control of their communities, and to eradicate the postcolonial situation of forced dependence and discrimination so evident for many years.

These two examples can be compared with the emergence of what Becker has described as the 'new health morality' (1986) in North America. Becker described an exceedingly individualized approach to health, produced by our historical and philosophical heritage and fostered by both governments and the medical profession (Lock 1998a), that has transformed individual 'health

into the moral' (Conrad 1994). Wellness, the avoidance of disease and illness and the 'improvement of health,' has become a widespread 'virtue,' especially among the middle classes, and for some appears to take on the aura of a secular path to salvation. Preservation of individual health has thus become an end in itself rather than a means to some other objective, an objective often understood, as with the East Asian and Cree examples, as contributing to society at large.

On the basis of empirical research, Crawford (1984) constructed a 'cultural account of health' as constituted in contemporary middle-class North America. The results of open-ended interviews carried out in the Chicago area with 60 adults, female and male, revealed two oft-repeated themes in the accounts of respondents. One theme was of self-control and a cluster of related concepts including self-discipline, self-denial, and will power. A second complementary set of themes were grouped around the idea of release and freedom. Individuals repeatedly expressed the idea that working out, eating well, giving up smoking, alcohol use, and so on, are essential to good health and a normal life, and moreover, such activities were taken to be evidence of willpower and self-control. Making time to be healthy was spontaneously ranked highly by the majority of informants, who also noted that such behavior exhibited an active refusal to be coopted by the unhealthy, pathological society in which they found themselves. Crawford summed his findings up as follows:

> The practical activity of health promotion, whereby health is viewed as a goal to be achieved through instrumental behaviors aimed a maintaining or enhancing biological functioning, is integral to an encompassing symbolic order. It is an order in which the individual body, separated from mind and society, is 'managed' according to criteria elaborated in the biomedical sciences. Medical knowledge, internalized and reproduced in our everyday discourse, represents a distinct, although by no means universal, way of experiencing our 'selves,' our bodies and our world. (Crawford 1984: 73)

One of the master symbols of contemporary medicine and of North American society as a whole is, of course, that of control. Crawford argues that by taking personal responsibility for health we are displaying not only a desire for control, but an ability to seize it and enact it. We cooperate in the creation of normal, healthy citizens, thus validating the dominant moral order. He goes on to suggest that in this time of severe economic cut-backs, individual bodies – 'the ultimate metaphor' – refract the general mood, as we attempt to control what is within our grasp (Crawford 1984: 80). Although it is the economically deprived who are the most affected by budget constraints, Crawford argues that the middle class reaffirm their relatively protected status through personal discipline designed, above all, to maintain health.

When interviewed by Crawford, many people expressed the idea that control must be tempered by release, usually through the fulfillment of instant desire and consumption. Crawford argues that it is not surprising, therefore, that bulimia, characterized by alternating behaviors of gorging and purging, has emerged as one of the most common eating disorders of our time. The body is not only a symbolic field for the reproduction of dominant values and conceptions, 'it is also a site for resistance to and transformation of those systems of meaning' (Crawford 1984: 95; see also Lock 1990, 1993a). In sickness, this struggle may be expressed (often unconsciously) in forms that replicate the tensions present in society at large. Crawford concludes his study by considering what political implications might be drawn from the current fitness movement. Is the taking of individual control and responsibility for health indeed a step to personal 'empowerment,' as many fitness advocates claim, or is it only part of the answer? Are individual lifestyle changes precisely what 'power' requires of us at this historical moment, while little is done about the social determinants of ill health, in particular about discrimination and poverty? Is well-being as virtue being transformed into a dangerous fetish as Illich has suggested (1992), while governments limit their domain of responsibility to economic development, frequently ignoring the cost to the well-being of large segments of society?

THE PROTEAN NATURE OF ABNORMALITY: GENDER AND AGING

I will return now to medicalization of the life cycle and, in particular, its linkage to the 'aging society,' in which the economic burden that the elderly are assumed to pose is currently a cause for great concern (Lock 1993b). In recent years we have witnessed the medicalization of aging on an unprecedented scale. The very process of aging has been widely reinterpreted as deviation from the normal, a process against which individuals and their physicians should take major precautions.

In North America, and in Europe to a slightly lesser extent, discourse about women as they approach the end of their reproductive years, whether that of the medical world or popular accounts, focuses obsessively on menopause and the supposed long-term consequences of an 'estrogen-starved body' to health in later life. Medical literature, with only a few exceptions, is overwhelmingly concerned with pathology and decrepitude associated with aging (although recently the strident tone characteristic of earlier decades has been modified). Thus, the end of menstruation is described as the consequence of 'failing ovaries' (Haspels and van Keep 1979: 59), or the 'inevitable demise' of the 'follicular unit' (London and Hammond 1986: 906). There are other, more positive ways, to interpret these biological changes (Wentz 1988), but the dominant discourse is about loss, failure, and decrepitude (Martin 1987) and menopause is widely understood as a deficiency disease, one in which depleted estrogen supplies should be replaced to attain the levels found in younger, fertile women.

Why should there be such an emphasis on female decrepitude? Surely, aging is an unavoidable, 'normal' process common to both men and women. Clearly, the increased proportion of the elderly in society is one source of concern. An article by Gail Sheehy gives us a clue as to why this concern is so worrying to us. Sheehy states: 'At the turn of the century, a woman could expect to live to the age of forty-seven or eight' (Sheehy 1991: 227), a sentiment widely expressed not only in popular literature but also in scientific articles. Gosden, for example, writing a text for biologists, is explicit that the very existence of 'post-menopausal' women is something of a cultural 'artifact,' the result of our 'recent mastery of the environment' (Gosden 1985: 2). Although the majority of authors who create arguments like Sheehy and Gosden believe that their conclusions are unbiased, it is clear that their reading of the evidence is selective. Demographers have convincingly shown that high rates of infant and maternal mortality have served until well into this century to keep mean life expectancies low, thus masking the presence of older people in all societies. When remaining life expectancy, once aged 45 or older, is examined, it is evident that people aged 60 and over have been part of all human groups for many hundreds and possibly thousands of years. It is the case, of course, that a greatly increased number of people live to old age than was formerly the case, and a concern about their health is clearly justified, but to talk of older women as artifacts or as 'unnatural', as does Gosden, is misleading, especially when claims such as his are then used to justify the administration of medication to all women on a life-time basis once they approach menopause.

Coupled with this inattention to demography by those who support the cultural artifact of aging as abnormality hypothesis, is a second assertion, namely that the human female is the only member of the class Mammalia to reach reproductive senescence during her lifetime. As the gynecologist Dewhurst puts it:

> The cessation of menstruation, or the menopause, in the human female is . . . a relatively unique [sic] phenomenon in the animal kingdom. With increasing longevity modern woman differs from her forebears as well as from other species in that she can look forward to 20 or 30 years . . . after the menopause. (Dewhurst 1981: 592)

This type of argument corroborates the ones based on false demography estimates in creating an image of older women as going against nature's purpose, whose very existence is, in effect, abnormal. An assumption embedded in arguments that compare women to apes and other animals who continue to menstruate until they die would seem to be that female life is about the reproduction of the species, and that the nonreproductive post-menopausal woman is a perambulating anomaly. However, biologists whose specialty is aging make the claim that the maximum human life-span potential is somewhere between 95 and more than 100 years. Further, all the systems of the human body, with the exception only of the female reproductive organs, age in order that they may survive to 80 years of age or older, unless pathology strikes (Leidy 1994). In addition, an emerging literature in biological anthropology argues that menopause in human females evolved approximately one and a half million years ago, most probably as a biological adaptation to the long-term nurturance necessary for highly dependent human infants, a dependency not found in apes. The hypothesis is that it is biologically more advantageous to the survival of human offspring to have both the mother and the grandmother providing care. Only under these circumstances could helpless infants be comparatively safe and weaned successfully onto solid foods that had to be collected by foraging (Peccei 1995). Investment in numerous infants produced by all women over the entire life span, probably proved to be less biologically advantageous than intense investment placed in fewer infants, the majority of whom survived (a situation in which mothers and grandmothers cooperated rather than competed with each other). If this was the case, then women who ceased to menstruate early would have been selected for over the course of evolutionary time.

Despite these data from the basic sciences, middle-aged women are explicitly contrasted with the animal world, and found wanting, by many members of the health-care profession. They are also compared with younger, fertile women whose bones and hearts show few signs of degeneration and who are taken as the standard for women of all ages (Lock 1993b: 38). Of even more significance, perhaps, is that women's bodies differ from those of men. Simone De Beauvoir argued that woman is constructed as 'other,' and Haraway, writing about nineteenth-century Europe and North America, asserts that 'the "neutral," universal body was always the unmarked masculine' (Haraway 1989: 357). Obviously, older people, both men and women, are at an increased risk for various diseases associated with aging, but there has been a tendency to conflate women's aging with the end of menstruation. Given the climate created by the arguments outlined above about older women as anomalies, it is not surprising that female aging has come to be understood primarily as inevitable pathology.

THE MANAGEMENT OF AGING

It has been postulated since classical times that ovarian secretions produce a profound effect on many parts of the female body, and although explanations have changed over the years as to just how this effect is produced, this interpretation is not disputed (Oudshoorn 1994). However, medical interest in failing ovaries and dropping estrogen levels is no longer confined, as was formerly the case, to what is often thought of among physicians as the rather inconsequential symptoms usually associated with menopause, in particular that of the hot flash. Interest has turned to the post-menopausal woman, her 30 years of remaining life, and the 'management' of her deviant body necessitated by being at an increased risk of broken bones and a failing heart. Recently, the estrogen deficiency of post-menopause has also been associated with an increased risk of Alzheimer's disease by certain researchers.

Some of the current literature goes further and describes medicalization with hormone replacement therapy not merely as a prophylactic against future disease, but as a positive enhancement to well-being and longevity (Utian and Jacobowitz 1990). Normality is not simply the mean, but also something that can be improved upon. The assumption is that virtually all women will benefit from replacement therapy, and any individuals who may be placed 'at risk' by taking this medication are thought of as 'outlyers' and as so much variation around the norm. It is not surprising, therefore, that it is recommended in professional journals that virtually all women of menopausal age be considered as candidates for replacement therapy, with the possible exception of those who are considered to be at high risk of breast cancer (SOGC Policy Statement 1995).

Of course, this discourse for medicalized health maintenance has been challenged by individual women, by organizations such as the National Women's Health Network in Washington (1989, 1995), by social scientists (Palmlund 1997), by a good number of physicians (Love 1997; Price and Little 1996), and by certain feminists (Freidan 1993; Greer 1991). An assumption could have been made that a decline in estrogen levels is 'normal' and that this decline functions as a protective device against cancer and other diseases associated with aging, as a few professionals have argued, but this suggestion barely sees the light of day. The pathology of deficiency associated with aging dominates.

Palmlund has studied the marketing of estrogens and progesterones over the past three decades. Following Bourdieu (1977), he argues that economic, cultural, and social capital have all been invested in creating the construction of menopause as abnormal, as a condition of risk for which hormones are marketed to subvert that risk (Palmlund 1997). Promotion of the long-term use of replacement therapy is in large part a reflection of the relationship between the medical profession and the major pharmaceutical companies, but concern about the economic 'liability' of an aging female population is also evident. In the medical and epidemiological literature on menopause, it is common to start out with a rhetorical flourish that sets the stage for coming to terms with the superfluity of older women and their potential cost to society if their health should fail:

> It is estimated that every day in North America 3500 new women experience menopause and that by the end of this century 49 million women will be post-menopausal. (Reid 1988: 25)

In recent years, the medicalization of the aging male has commenced (Oudshoorn 1997), indicating just how powerful are the economic incentives to commodify the latter part of the life cycle. This second wave of medicalization suggests that economic gain, rather than a patriarchal ideology, is perhaps the principal force driving this megaindustry, but it remains based on unexamined assumptions about the universality of aging, that part of the life cycle inextricably associated with pathology.

Extensive survey research carried out in the mid-1980s shows that, compared with Americans and Canadians, Japanese women experience remarkably few symptoms at the end of menstruation, including those considered to be universally characteristic of menopause, namely hot flashes and night sweats (Lock 1993b). It is notable that there is no word that specifically signifies a 'hot flash' in Japanese. On the basis of these findings, I have argued for a recognition of 'local biologies' (Lock 1993b). In other words, sufficient variation exists among biological populations that the physical effects of lowered estrogen levels on the body characteristic of the female mid-life transition are not the same in all geographical locations. There is evidence from other parts of the world, in addition to Japan, of considerable variation in symptom reporting at menopause (Beyene 1989; Lock 1994). This variation, to which genetics, diet, environment, and other cultural variables no doubt contribute, accounts for marked differences in subjective experience and associated symptom reporting at this stage of the life cycle. The differences between North American and Japanese women are sufficient to produce an effect on (but not determine) the creation of knowledge, both popular and professional, about this life cycle transition. *Konenki* (the term in Japanese glossed as menopause) has never been thought of as a disease-like state, nor even equated closely with the end of menstruation, even by Japanese medical professionals. The symptoms most closely associated with *konenki* are shoulder stiffness and other similar culturally specific sensations, including a 'heavy' head (Lock 1993b).

Japanese physicians keep abreast of the medical literature published in the West, and so one could expect them, living as they do in a country actively dedicated to preventive medicine, that there might be some incentive to make use of hormone replacement therapy (HRT), as is the case in EuroAmerica. However, this is not so because first, as we have seen, symptom reporting is different and very few women go to see gynecologists at this stage of the life cycle. In addition, local biology plays a part in other ways: mortality from coronary heart disease for Japanese women is about one-quarter that of American women (WHO 1990), and it is estimated that although Japanese women become osteoporotic twice as often as do Japanese men, nevertheless, this is approximately half as often as in North America (Ross et al. 1991). These figures, combined with a mortality rate from breast cancer about one-quarter that of North America and the longest life expectancy in the world for Japanese women, has meant that there is relatively little pressure for Japanese gynecologists to enter into the international arena of debate about the pros and cons of long-term medication with HRT, something about which many of them are, in any case, decidedly uncomfortable because of a pervasive concern about iatrogenesis. When dealing with healthy middle-aged women, the first line of resort of Japanese doctors is usually to encourage good dietary practices and plenty of exercise. For those few women with troubling symptoms, herbal medicine is commonly prescribed, even by gynecologists (Lock 1993b). Increasing use of HRT has taken place in Japan over the past few years, but not to the extent that is common in Europe or North America.

These findings, necessarily presented in a rather superficial fashion here, suggest that it is important to decenter assumptions about biological universalism. The margins between nature and culture and normal and abnormal are cultural constructs. Obviously, aging cannot be avoided, but the power of both biology and culture to shape the experience of aging and the meanings – individual, social, and political – attributed to this process demand fine-grained, contextualized interpretations in which we must reconsider that which we take to be normal and abnormal.

ELIMINATING THE MISTAKES OF NATURE

With the development of molecular genetics and the mapping of the human genome, genes have become knowable entities, subject to manipulation. This knowledge permits us to think in entirely new ways about what is to be taken as normal with respect to human bodies and behavior. Mapping the human genome has been likened to the Holy Grail of biology; one scientist declared in the mid-1980s that the Human Genome Project was the ultimate response to the commandment, 'Know thyself' (Bishop and Waldholz 1990). While certain members of the scientific community have been actively opposed to the genome project, in large part because it consumes a vast amount of resources that would otherwise be used for other kinds of research, many scientists have been very vocal about the benefits that society will receive by completing this project. Daniel Koshland, until recently the editor of Science, stated, for example, that withholding support from the Human Genome Project is to incur, 'the immorality of omission – the failure to apply a great new technology to aid the poor, the infirm, and the underprivileged' (Koshland 1989). Robert Plomin, in supporting the project, notes that, 'Just fifteen years ago, the idea of genetic influence on complex human behavior was anathema to many behavioral scientists. Now, however,

the role of inheritance in behavior has become widely accepted, even for sensitive domains such as IQ' (Plomin 1990).

The historian of science Edward Yoxen points out that we are currently witnessing a conceptual shift that has not been present in the language of geneticists prior to the advent of molecular genetics. While the contribution of genetics to the incidence of disease has been recognized throughout this century, it has only been in the past two decades that the notion of 'genetic disease' has come to dominate discourse such that other contributory factors are often obscured from view (Yoxen 1984). Fox Keller argues that it was this shift in discourse that made the Human Genome Project both reasonable and desirable in the minds of many researchers involved (Fox Keller 1992). In mapping the Human Genome, the objective is to create a baseline norm for our shared genetic inheritance. However, the map that will be produced, based almost completely on samples taken from a Caucasian population, with a few Asian samples included, will correspond to the actual genome of no living individual, and we will all, in effect, be deviants from this norm (Lewontin 1992).

Moreover, with this map in hand, the belief is that we will then rapidly move into an era in which we will be able to 'guarantee all human beings an individual and natural right, the right to health' (Fox Keller 1992: 295). Fox Keller cites a 1988 report put out by the Office of Technology Assessment in the United States in which it is argued that 'new technologies for identifying traits and altering genes make it possible for eugenic goals to be achieved through technological as opposed to social control.' The report discusses what is described as a 'eugenics of normalcy,' namely 'the use of genetic information . . . to ensure that . . . each individual has at least a modicum of *normal genes*' (1988: 84, emphasis added). This report concludes that 'individuals have a paramount right to be born with a normal, adequate hereditary endowment' (1988: 86).

The suggestion that emerges from this report is that for at least certain advocates of the new genetics, the idea of amelioration, of improving the quality of the gene pool, is looming large on the horizon. However, as Fox Keller and others have pointed out, the language used is no longer one that supports the implementation of eugenics via government-supported social policies for the good of society, the species, or even of the collective gene pool, as was the case earlier this century (1992: 295). We are now in an era dominated by the idea of individual choice in connection with decisions relating to health and illness. Thus, genetic information will simply furnish the knowledge that individuals need in order to realize their inalienable right to health. 'Geneticization' is the term coined by Lippman (1992) to capture this tendency to distinguish people one from another on the basis of genetics, and increasingly to define disorders, behaviors, and physiological variation as wholly or in part due to genetic abnormalities.

One major disadvantage with this utopian type of talk to date, aside from the fact that it is inherently eugenic, blatantly reductionistic, and often wildly inaccurate, is that as yet we do not have therapeutic techniques available to manipulate the genes of individuals, although the time is rapidly approaching when experiments in utero with gene therapy may be implemented. Further, we have definitive diagnostic capabilities for only those relatively uncomplicated (although often devastating) diseases that follow Mendelian inheritance patterns. We are not able to predict with any certainty how and when multifactorial diseases such as breast and prostate cancer and Alzheimer's disease (some forms of which are now associated with genetics) will occur. We know even less about the so-called behavioral disorders such as addictions or attention deficit disorder. Scientists critical of the hubris so often associated with the new genetics are careful to point out that only those with a mind set that assumes human behavior is determined by genetics could entertain the idea that we will soon be able to make diagnoses about the presence or absence of certain genes that determine individual behavior (Lewontin 1997).

Given the present level of knowledge in the new genetics, it takes little insight to realize that the burden of decision making in connection with genetic testing and screening, for the immediate future at least, will fall on women of reproductive age and their partners, and that the 'choice' they will be expected to make is in connection with abortion. The only alternative at present is to undergo expensive IVF treatment and select those fertilized embryos for implantation into the woman's uterus that have been 'screened' for certain diseases. It is clear that even when labeled as being 'at risk' of carrying a fetus with a major genetic disorder, not all women are willing to avail themselves of new reproductive technologies (Beeson and Doksum 1999; Lock 1998b). It is equally clear that women are already making decisions about pregnancies and abortion on the basis of information that they have been given by genetic counselors and geneticists, and that this information is couched in the language of risk and probabilities (Lock 1998c; Rapp 1988, 1990).

Mary Douglas has characterized the idea of 'risk' as a central cultural construct of our time (Douglas 1990), a construct that did not exist in a technical sense prior to the end of the last century. The 'philosophy of risk,' as Ewald notes, incorporates a secularized approach to life, where God is removed from the scene, leaving the control of events entirely in human hands. This approach is a logical outcome of understanding life as a rational enterprise to be actively orchestrated by societies and individuals (Ewald 1991). Obviously, a rational approach to the management of disease is not at issue here, and nor is the enormous advantages that have been incurred by the systematization of disease categories and by research into the abnormal and pathological. However, understanding disease in terms of risk inevitably raises some difficulties. Douglas argues that use of the word 'risk' rather than 'danger' or 'hazard' has the rhetorical effect of creating an aura of neutrality, of cloaking the concept in scientific legitimacy. Paradoxically, this permits statements about risk to be readily associated with moral approbation. Danger, reworded as risk, is removed from the sphere of the unpredictable, the supernatural, and the divine, and is placed squarely, in EuroAmerica at least, at the feet of responsible individuals, as the research of Crawford has shown. Risk becomes, in Douglas's words, 'a forensic resource' whereby individuals can be held accountable (1990). However, as Francis Collins, the current director of the National Center for Human Genome Research in Washington, points out, in the world of genetics 'we are all at risk for something,' and thus we are all, in effect, potentially abnormal (Beardsley 1996: 102).

Dorothy Nelkin has recently documented a case of what she describes as the 'growing practice of genetic testing in American society,' in this instance for the gene for Fragile-X syndrome associated with certain physical and behavioral disorders among children (Nelkin 1996). Guidelines for testing were issued in 1995 by the American College of Human Genetics, and included a recommendation that those asymptomatic individuals deemed to be 'at risk' from this disease should be tested, in addition to children already exhibiting characteristic symptoms. The incidence of this disease, associated with mental impairment among other things, is estimated to be about one per 1500 males and one per 2500 females. In common with a good number of other so-called genetic diseases, the genes involved exhibit 'incomplete penetrance,' that is, not all individuals with the genotype will manifest the disease. It is estimated that about 20 per cent of males and 70 per cent of females with the mutation express no symptoms, making the designation of 'at risk' extremely problematic. Moreover, the severity of symptoms varies enormously and cannot be predicted.

The first testing program, developed by an industry–university consortium, was organized in 1993 in the Colorado public school system as a prototype for developing a national program. The project was funded by Oncor, a private biotechnology company, and was explicitly designed to save later public expenditure on children with behavioral problems. The research team tested selected children and developed a checklist of 'abnormal' behavioral and physical characteristics associated with the disease, including hyperactivity, learning problems, double-jointed fingers, prominent ears, and so on. After 2 years, the program failed to turn up the anticipated number of cases, was deemed uneconomic, and suspended (Nelkin 1996: 538). Nelkin notes that testing was not done in a clinical setting. It was driven by economic and entrepreneurial interests, and there are no known therapeutic means to change the condition of the children identified. However, the impact on the lives of those children who tested positive was significant, not the least of which was discrimination against them by health insurance companies. Nelkin points out that many involved parents not only cooperated but actively encouraged the promotion of testing for the Fragile-X gene. She goes on to state that a significant number of parents, in particular mothers, experienced relief once their child's so-called behavioral problem was identified as genetic because the mothers could no longer be found wanting for the condition of their child.

CONCLUSION

The final two examples in this chapter, of the medicalization of menopause and of the move toward widespread genetic testing and screening, both clearly indicate that political and entrepreneurial interests are, above all, driving what is to be defined as abnormal today. In our present mood we are not willing to tolerate individuals who are liable, as we understand it, to place a financial burden on society, and their condition of being 'at risk' is treated as though pathological. Georges Canguilhem's maxim that normality can only be understood 'as situated in action,' and moreover, that diversity does not infer sickness nor does 'objective' pathology exist, has been entirely abandoned. We are no longer in a mood where normal means average;

we are in an era of amelioration, enhancement, and progress through increasing intervention into the 'mistakes' of nature. However, in this climate, the environmental, social, and political factors that, rather than genes, contribute to so much disease, are eclipsed, and tend to be removed from professional and public attention. Research in connection with these factors remains relatively underfunded. Basic medical science has made enormous strides and brought about insights in connection with any number of diseases, but when, under the guise of health promotion, individual bodies and individual responsibility for health are made the cornerstone of health care, moral responsibility for the occurrence of illness and pathology is often diverted from where it belongs (on perennial problems of inequality, exploitation, poverty, sexism, and racism) and inappropriately placed at the feet of individuals designated as abnormal or at risk of being so because of their biological make-up.

REFERENCES

Adelson, N. (1991) ' "Being alive well": The praxis of Cree health', in B. Postl et al. (eds), *Circumpolar Health 90: The Proceedings of the 8th International Congress on Circumpolar Health.* Winnipeg: University of Manitoba Press. pp. 226–8.

Barrett, R.J. (1988) 'Interpretations of Schizophrenia', *Culture, Medicine and Psychiatry,* 12: 357–88.

Beardsley, T. (1996) 'Vital data', *Scientific American,* 274: 100–5.

Becker, M.H. (1986) 'The tyranny of health promotion', *Public Health Reviews,* 14: 15–25.

Beeson, D. and Doksum, T. 'Family values and resistance to genetic testing', in B. Hoffmaster (ed.), *Bioethics in Context: Social Science Contributions to Moral Understanding.* Cambridge: Cambridge University Press.

Beyene, Y. (1989) *From Menarche to Menopause: Reproductive Lives of Peasant Women in Two Cultures.* Albany: State University of New York Press.

Bishop, J. and Waldholz, M. (1990) *Genome: The Story of the Most Astonishing Scientific Adventure of our Time – The Attempt to Map all the Genes in the Human Body.* New York: Simon and Schuster.

Bourdieu, P. (1977) *Outline of a Theory of Practice.* Cambridge: Cambridge University Press.

Canguilhem, G. (1991) *The Normal and the Pathological.* New York: Zone Books.

Carr, J.E (1978) 'Ethno-behaviorism and the culture-bound syndromes: The case of Amok culture', *Medicine and Psychiatry,* 2: 269–93.

Comaroff, J. (1985) *Body of Power: Spirit of Resistance. The Culture and History of a South African People*. Chicago: University of Chicago Press.

Conrad, P. (1992) 'Medicalization and social control', *Annual Review of Sociology*, 18: 209–32.

Conrad, P. (1994) 'Wellness as virtue: Morality and the pursuit of health', *Culture, Medicine and Psychiatry*, 18: 385–401.

Crawford, R. (1984) 'A cultural account of health: Self control, release and the social body', in J. McKinlay (ed.), *Issues in the Political Economy of Health Care*. London: Tavistock. pp. 60–103.

Dewhurst, J. (1981) *Integrated Obstetrics and Gynecology for Postgraduates*. Oxford: Blackwell Scientific.

Douglas, M. (1990) 'Risk as a forensic resource', *Deadalus*, 119: 1–16.

Dubisch, J. (1986) 'Culture enters through the kitchen: Women, food and social boundaries in rural Greece', in J. Dubisch (ed.), *Gender and Power in Rural Greece*. Princeton: Princeton University Press. pp. 195–214.

DuBoulay, J. (1986) 'Women: Images of their nature and destiny in rural Greece', in J. Dubisch (ed.), *Gender and Power in Rural Greece*. Princeton: Princeton University Press. pp. 139–68.

Ewald, F. (1991) 'Insurance and risk', in G. Burchell, C. Gordon, and P. Miller (eds), *The Foucault Effect: Studies in Governmentality*. Hempel Hempstead: Harvester, Wheatsheaf. pp. 197–210.

Fanon, F. (1967) *Black Skin, White Masks*. New York: Grove.

Field, M. (1960) *Search for Society: An Ethnographic Study of Rural Ghana*. Evanston, IL: Northwestern University Press.

Foucault, M. (1979) *Discipline and Punish: The Birth of the Prison*. New York: Vintage.

Fox Keller, E. (1992) 'Nature, nurture and the human genome project', in D.J. Kevles and L. Hood (eds), *The Code of Codes: Scientific and Social Issues in the Human Genome Project*. Cambridge, MA: Harvard University Press. pp. 281–99.

Frake, C.O. (1977) 'The diagnosis of disease among the Subanun of Mindanao', in D. Landy (ed.), *Culture, Disease and Healing: Studies in Medical Anthropology*. New York: Macmillan. pp. 183–95.

Freidan, B. (1993) *The Fountain of Age*. New York: Simon & Schuster.

Good, B.J. (1977) 'The heart of what's the matter: The semantics of illness in Iran', *Culture, Medicine and Psychiatry*, 1: 25–58.

Good, B.J. and Kleinman, A.M. (1985) 'Culture and anxiety: Cross-cultural evidence for the patterning of anxiety disorders', in H. Tuma and J. Mazur (eds), *Anxiety and the Anxiety Disorders*. New York: L. Earlbaum. pp. 297–323.

Gosden, R.R. (1985) *The Biology of Menopause: The Causes and Consequences of Ovarian Aging*. London: Academic Press.

Greer, G. (1991) *The Change: Women, Ageing and the Menopause*. Auckland: Harnish Mailton.

Griaule, M. (1965) *Conversations with Ogotemmeli*. Oxford: Oxford University Press.

Hacking, I. (1990) *The Taming of Chance*. Cambridge: Cambridge University Press.

Haraway, D. (1989) *Primate Visions: Gender, Race, and Nature in the World of Modern Science*. New York: Routledge.

Haspels, A.A. and Van Keep, P.A. (1979) 'Endocrinology and management of the peri-menopause', in A.A. Haspels and H. Musaph (eds), *Psychosomatics in Peri-Menopause*. Baltimore: University Park Press. pp. 57–71.

Hugh-Jones, C. (1979) *From the Milk of the River: Spacial and Temporal Process in Northwest Amazonia*. Cambridge: Cambridge University Press.

Illich, I. (1992) *In the Mirror of the Past: Lectures and Addresses 1978–1990*. New York: Marion Boyars.

Janzen, J. (1981) 'The need for a taxonomy of health in the study of African therapeutics', *Social Science and Medicine*, 15B: 185–94.

Kaufert, P. (1990) 'The boxification of culture', *Santé, Culture, Health*, 7: 139–48.

Kaufert, P. and O'Neil, J. (1990) 'Cooptation and control: The reconstruction of Inuit birth', *Medical Anthropology Quarterly*, 4: 427–42.

Kirmayer, L. (1984) 'Overview: Culture, affect and somatization', *Transcultural Psychiatric Research Review*, Part I, 21: 159–88, Part II, 21: 237–62.

Kleinman, A. and Good, B. (1985) *Culture and Depression: Studies in the Anthropology and Cross-cultural Psychiatry of Affect and Disorder*. Berkeley: University of California Press.

Kleinman, A., Veena, D., and Lock, M. (1997) *Social Suffering*. Berkeley: University of California Press.

Koshland, D. (1989) 'Sequences and consequences of the human genome', *Science*, 146: 189.

Leidy, L.E. (1994) 'Biological aspects of menopause: Across the lifespan', *Annual Review in Anthropology*, 23: 231–53.

Lewontin, R. (1992) The Dream of the Human Genome. *The New York Review of Books*, 28 May.

Lewontin, R. (1997) 'The confusion over cloning', *The New York Review of Books*, 44 (16) October.

Lippman, A. (1992) 'Prenatal genetic testing and screening: Constructing needs and reinforcing inequities', *American Journal of Law and Medicine*, 17: 15–50.

Lock, M. (1980) *East Asian Medicine in Urban Japan: Varieties of Medical Experience*. Berkeley: University of California Press.

Lock, M. (1990) 'On being ethnic: The politics of identity breaking and making in Canada, or Nevra on Sunday', *Culture, Medicine and Psychiatry*, 14: 237–54.

Lock, M. (1991) 'Flawed jewels and national dis/order: Narratives on adolescent dissent in Japan. Festschrift for George DeVos', *The Journal of Psychohistory*, 18: 507–31.

Lock, M. (1993a) *Encounters with Aging: Mythologies of Menopause in Japan and North America*. Berkeley: University of California Press.

Lock, M. (1993b) 'Ideology, female mid-life and the greying of Japan', *Journal of Japanese Studies*, 19: 43–78.

Lock, M. (1994) 'Menopause in cultural context', *Journal of Experimental Gerontology*, 29: 307–17.

Lock, M. (1998a) 'Situating women in the politics of health', in S. Sherwin (ed.), *The Politics of Women's Health: Exploring Agency and Autonomy*. Philadelphia: Temple University Press. pp. 48–63.

Lock, M. (1998b) 'Perfecting society: Reproductive technologies, genetic testing, and the planned family in Japan', in M. Lock and P. Kaufert (eds), *Pragmatic Women and Body Politics*. Cambridge: Cambridge University Press.

Lock, M. (1998c) 'Breast cancer: Reading the omens', *Anthropology Today*, 14: 7–16.

Lock, M. and P. Kaufert (1998) *Pragmatic Women and Body Politics*. Cambridge: Cambridge University Press.

Lock, M. and Wakewich-Dunk, P. (1990) 'Nerves and nostalgia: The expression of distress among Greek–Canadian immigrant women', *Canadian Family Physician*, 36: 253–8.

London, S. and Hammond, C. (1986) 'The climacteric', in D. Danforth and J. Scott (eds), *Obstetrics and Gynecology*. Philadelphia: J.B. Lippencott. pp. 905–26.

Love, S.M. (1997) *Dr Susan Love's Hormone Book: Making Informed Choices About Menopause*. New York: Random House.

Low, S. (1985) 'Culturally interpreted symptoms or culture-bound syndromes? A cross cultural review of nerves', *Social Science and Medicine*, 21: 187–97.

Macfarlane, A. and Mugford, M. (1984) *Birth Counts: Statistics of Pregnancy and Childbirth*. London: Her Majesty's Stationery Office.

Martin, E. (1987) *The Woman in the Body: A Cultural Analysis of Reproduction*. Boston: Beacon.

Marx, K. (1967) *Capital: A Critique of Political Economy*. 3 vols. New York: International.

McClain, C. (1982) 'Toward a comparative framework for the study of childbirth: A review of the literature', in M. A. Kay (ed.), *Anthropology of Human Birth*. Philadelphia: F.A. Davis. pp. 25–59.

Melish, J.P. (1998) *Disowning Slavery*. Ithaca: Cornell University Press.

Mishler, E.G., Amarasingham, L.R., Osherson, S.D. Hauser, S.T., Waxler, N.E. and Liem, R. (1981) *Social Context of Health, Illness, and Patient Care*. Cambridge: Cambridge University Press.

Mumford, L. (1963) *Technics and Civilization*. London: Harcourt Brace Jovanovich.

Murphy, J.M. (1976) 'Psychiatric labeling in cross-cultural perspective', *Science*, 191: 1019–28.

National Women's Health Network (1989) *Taking Hormones and Women's Health*. Washington, DC: National Women's Health Network.

National Women's Health Network (1995) *Taking Hormones and Women's Health: Choices, Risks and Benefits*. Washington, DC: National Women's Health Network.

Nelkin, D. (1996) 'The social dynamics of genetic testing: The case of fragile-X', *Medical Anthropology Quarterly*, 10: 537–50.

Office of Technology Assessment US Congress (1988) *Mapping our Genes*. Washington, DC: Government Printing Office.

Ong, A. (1988) 'The production of possession: Spirits and the multinational corporation in Malaysia', *American Ethnologist*, 15: 28–42.

Oudshoorn, N. (1994) *Beyond the Natural Body: An Archeology of Sex Hormones*. London: Routledge.

Oudshoorn, N. (1997) 'Menopause, only for women? The social construction of menopause as an exclusively female condition', *Journal of Psychosomatic Obstetrics and Gynecology*, 18: 137–44.

Palmlund, I. (1997) 'The marketing of estrogens for menopausal and postmenopausal women', *Journal of Psychosomatic Obstetrics and Gynecology*, 18: 158–64.

Peccei, J.S. (1995) 'A hypothesis for the origin and evolution of menopause', *Maturitas*, 21: 83–9.

Plomin, R. (1990) 'The role of inheritance in behaviour', *Science*, 248 (13 April): 187.

Porter, R. (1998) *The Greatest Benefit to Mankind*. New York: W.W. Norton.

Price, L. and Little, K. (1996) 'Women need to be fully informed about risks of hormone therapy', *British Medical Journal*, 312: 1301.

Rapp, R. (1988) 'Chromosomes and communication: The discourse of genetic counselling', *Medical Anthropology Quarterly*, 2: 143–57.

Rapp, R. (1990) 'Constructing amniocentesis: Maternal and medical discourses', in F.D. Ginsberg and A.L Tsing (eds), *Uncertain Terms: Negotiating Gender in American Culture*. Boston: Beacon.

Redlich, F.C. (1957) 'The concept of health in psychiatry', in A.H. Leighton, J.N. Clausen and R.N. Wilson (eds), *Explorations in Social Psychiatry*. London: Tavistock. pp. 3–22.

Reid, R.L. (1988) 'Menopause. Part I. Hormone replacement', *Bulletin of the Society of Obstetricians and Gynecologists*, 10: 25–34.

Rivers, W.H.R. (1924) *Medicine, Magic, and Religion*. London: Kegan, Paul, Trench, Trubner and Co.

Ross, P.D., Norimatsu, H., Davis, J.W., Yano, K., Wasnick, R.D., Fukiwara, S., Hosoda, Y., and Melton, L.J. (1991) 'A comparison of hip fracture incidence among native Japanese, Japanese–Americans and American Caucasians, *American Journal of Epidemiology*, 133: 801–9.

Ryle, J. (1961) 'The meaning of normal', in B. Lush

(ed.), *Concepts of Medicine*. New York: Pergamon. pp. 5–22.

Scheper-Hughes, N. (1992) *Death without Weeping: The Violence of Everyday Life in Brazil*. Berkeley: University of California Press.

Sheehy, G. (1991) 'The silent passage: Menopause', *Vanity Fair,* 10: 223–63.

SOGC Policy Statement (1995) 'The Canadian menopause consensus conference', *Society of Obstetricians and Gynecologists of Canada*, Statement Number 34, March.

Sontag, S. (1977) *Illness as Metaphor*. New York: Farrar, Straus and Giroux.

Swartz, L. and Levett, A. (1989) 'Political repression and children in South Africa: The social construction of damaging effects', *Social Science and Medicine*, 28: 741–50.

Utian, W.H. and Jacobowitz, R.S. (1990) *Managing your Menopause*. New York: Prentice Hall.

Waxler, N.E. (1979) 'Is outcome for schizophrenia better in nonindustrial societies?' *Journal of Nervous and Mental Disease*, 167: 144–58.

Wennberg, J. and Gittelsohn, A. (1982) 'Variations in medical care among small areas', *Scientific American*, 246: 120–33.

Wentz, A.C. (1988) 'Management of the menopause', in H.W. Jones, A.C. Wentz and L.S. Burnett (eds), *Novak's Textbook of Gynecology (11th edn)*. Baltimore: Williams & Wilkins.

WHO (World Health Organization) (1990) *World Health Statistics Annual*. Geneva.

Young, A. (1995) *The Harmony of Illusions: Inventing Posttraumatic Stress Disorder*. Princeton: Princeton University Press.

Yoxen, E. (1984) 'Constructing genetic diseases', in T. Duster and K. Garett (eds), *Cultural Perspectives on Biological Knowledge*. Norwood, NJ: Ablex.

2.6

Experiencing Chronic Illness

KATHY CHARMAZ

INTRODUCTION

Social scientific research on experiencing chronic illness focuses directly on pivotal players in health care – people who are sick. Health researchers, practitioners, and policy makers may claim to represent patients' concerns. However, they seldom obtain systematic 'in-depth' views of patients' experience of health care, much less of what it means to live with continued illness. The research on experiencing chronic illness emphasizes how people come to view themselves as chronically ill, and how illness affects their lives. Hence, this literature provides a significant corrective to knowledge about health and illness: it delineates patients' perspectives instead of practitioners' views that dominate both the institution of medicine and social scientific research (Mishler 1994). Understanding patients' perspectives brings fresh insights to three crucial levels of analysis: (1) the individual level of assumptions, attitudes, and actions toward health and illness, (2) the interactional level within and beyond health care, and (3) the institutional level of health policy and health-care reform.

Consistent with Peter Conrad (1987), I define illness as the person's experience; disease constitutes a bodily disorder as agreed upon by physicians. Some people do not experience illness when they have a diagnosed disease. Other people experience illness before receiving a diagnosis or being believed to have a disease. A chronic illness can be episodic or endless; it may have long plateaus or continual progression. It is at once subjective and social; it includes experiencing inchoate emotions and bodily sensations as well as making such experiences meaningful and responding to imagined or actual social responses.

Chronic illness poses more social, interactional, and existential problems than acute illness because it lasts. However, preconceptions of acute illness permeate ideas about chronic illness and pervade institutionalized practices for handling it. Through analyzing the experience of chronic illness, we learn what chronically ill people's actions mean, when and how they come into conflict with practitioners, and what it means to face loss and reconstruction of self. This field advances social studies of health and illness by accumulating facts about the empirical world and by building theoretical analyses from empirical data.

Experiencing chronic illness means much more than feeling physical distress, acknowledging symptoms, and needing care. It includes metaphor and meaning, moral judgments and ethical dilemmas, identity questions and reconstruction of self, daily struggles and persistent troubles. Experiencing serious illness challenges prior meanings, ways of living that have been taken for granted, and ways of knowing self. Life is now uncertain. The self has become vulnerable, and thus problematic. Its vulnerability derives, in part, from potential disapproval and devaluation, for continued illness has a profoundly moral cast. Moral meanings of illness arise through interactions in local worlds and specific lives (Das 1994; Kleinman 1994; Williams 1993). Whether, when, and how people might acknowledge and act upon illness is embedded in culture and context.

To understand the experience of chronic illness, we must study what ill people think, feel, and do in their natural settings. I begin by noting how the field emerged in response to structural analyses that did not account for patients' actions. Then I describe how people experience becoming and being ill, and suggest how culture shapes meanings. Throughout this and subsequent sections, I synthesize major ideas from the literature. Diverse researchers have discovered remarkably similar themes: ambiguity and uncertainty, autonomy and control, stigma and shame, isolation and connection, and loss and reconstruction of self. How and when these themes are played out varies. Despite the consistent themes, this research reveals some surprising results, as I show in the sections on managing illness and stigma control. Next, I outline ways that people with chronic illness handle and reconstruct a now problematic self. Last, I conclude by suggesting how the preceding analysis affects future policy problems and prospects and can direct further research.

EMERGENCE OF THE SUBJECT

Social scientific studies of illness gained momentum almost 40 years ago. At that time, sociological ethnographers discovered that structural theories did not account for how people lived with and made sense of conditions such as tuberculosis (Roth 1963), poliomyelitis (Davis 1963), blindness (Scott 1968), visible disability (Goffman 1963), and dying (Glaser and Strauss 1965, 1968). The subject of the experience of illness emerged as ethnographers moved from the structural toward the subjective. This move initiated new inductive analyses reasoning from individual and interactional levels to institutional levels of analysis. These ethnographers responded to Talcott Parsons' (1951) structural concept of the sick role which assumed recovery, passive patients, and active physicians who decided treatment on scientific criteria (Charmaz in press; Charmaz and Olesen 1997; Gerhardt 1989). The sick role temporarily exempted patients from usual adult responsibilities but obligated them to seek medical help and to comply with treatment. The sick role did not explain how people with chronic conditions managed their illnesses and their lives. As Roth (1963) discovered in the tuberculosis hospital, patients actively negotiated their roles, rather than passively following behavioral prescriptions. Being ill resembled a career with direction, goals, paths, and turning points.

Later works addressed chronically ill people's everyday worlds. *Chronic Illness and the Quality of Life* (Strauss 1975; Strauss et al. 1984) spawned research on how people managed illness and regimen. *Having Epilepsy* (Schneider and Conrad 1983) advanced sociological understanding of stigma management and stigma potential. Ray Fitzpatrick et al. (1984) brought further attention to the field with *The Experience of Illness*, and Peter Conrad (1987) and others defined it in the collection, *Research in the Sociology of Health Care: The Experience and Management of Chronic Illness* (edited by Roth and Conrad). Increasingly, medical anthropologists address the experience of illness (Desjarlais 1992) and study their own societies (Kaufman 1992; Kleinman 1988; Lock and Dunk 1987; Plough 1986). The experience of illness has gained interest among psychologists (Mishler 1981; Radley 1988, 1991, 1993; Radley and Billig 1996; Smith, 1996). Furthermore, leading researchers in health and illness have also explicated interpretive methods, thus providing tools for studying experience (Coffey and Atkinson 1996; Glaser and Strauss 1967; Hammersley and Atkinson 1983; Strauss 1987; Strauss and Corbin 1990). A research literature that began with role structure and deviance moved on to patient career and negotiation, then to managing illness and stigma, followed by increased emphasis on self and identity. With each shift, the literature came closer to the experiencing subject.

BECOMING AND BEING ILL

Prior Assumptions about Health and Illness

Michael Bury (1988: 90) states, '[M]uch of the experience and meaning of illness is emergent in nature.' True – within limits. However, everyone already has some notions of health and illness, although they differ among groups and societies. People with illnesses draw upon cultural meanings for metaphors to describe their bodily feelings, and from those feelings derive new meanings (Kirmayer 1988; Scheper-Hughes and Lock 1987). Bodily and illness metaphors consist of subtle descriptions and are applied as if they were concrete reality, rather than as a portrayal of this reality. Illness metaphors make inchoate experience comprehensible (Lock and Dunk 1987; Low 1994). Metaphors offer more than reductionist or comparative views; they illuminate, enliven, and evaluate experience (Radley 1993). Common Western metaphors of illness as 'an odyssey,' 'a challenge,' 'a personal failure,' 'a destroyer,' 'an occupation,' 'the enemy,' and 'a battle' shape beliefs (Charmaz 1991; Herzlich 1973; Williams 1981a, 1981b).

Beliefs about health and illness are ideological (see Calnan 1987; Crawford 1984; Fitzpatrick et al. 1984; Radley and Billig 1996). These beliefs provide individual and collective reasons for acting, justify prior actions, and call for future actions. Cultural variation in beliefs generally, and about illness specifically, gives rise to different ideologies about how to handle illness. Such ideologies bridge levels of individual beliefs and institutionalized practices. For example, Nancy E. Waxler (1981) argues that Ethiopians responded to having leprosy in consistent ways with the fatalism of the Ethiopian peasant. They often abstained from sex, left their families and homes, initiated divorces, and withdrew. Waxler states that situations making leprosy visible, its highly stigmatized status, and pervasive beliefs about its incurable nature led Ethiopians to adopt expected stigmatized identities voluntarily. In contrast, she finds that North Americans with leprosy fight back in almost a caricature of American values. They take action, organize, and educate others about the disease. Cultural meanings form the backdrop on which individuals develop their stance toward illness.

Medical practitioners' beliefs about health and illness also confer ideological meanings upon patients, and moreover, control structuring their treatment. Whether or not practitioners define a particular physical state as an illness profoundly affects individual and collective life. First, reducing a social problem to an individual's illness masks its social roots. For example, Nancy Scheper-Hughes (1992) contends that Brazilian institutionalized medicine has appropriated *nervos*, a folk concept explaining relationships between mind, body, and social context. *Nervos* results from nervous hunger of starving people. However, the medical establishment transforms it into a personal and psychological disorder requiring medications such as tranquilizers, vitamins, and sleeping pills. Scheper-Hughes states, '[H]unger is isolated and denied, and an individualized discourse on sickness comes to replace a more radical and socialized discourse on hunger' (1992: 169). Second, if epidemiological distribution of symptoms alone indicates a collective illness, then medical rejection of these symptoms also negates this illness and keeps sufferers marginalized and deviant, as occurred for years with sick Gulf War veterans. Such sufferers lack legitimacy as *bona fide* patients. Third, they suffer personal, economic, and social consequences – identity losses, financial hardships, stigma, and isolation. To improve their circumstances, receive medical legitimacy, and obtain help, they must organize collectively and struggle to prove that this illness is real and that they themselves have it (Brown 1996; Dumit 1997).

Individual accounts of health and illness reflect identity and reality claims for specific audiences and purposes (Charmaz 1987, 1995; Radley and Billig 1996). Joyce Cornwall (1984) had to persuade working-class East London adults that participating in a study of health would not brand them as 'ill.' She observes that people give different public and private accounts of illness: public accounts are selective and partial. East Londoners talk with doctors about information, ideas, and experiences that they believe doctors will respect. Cornwall suggests that private accounts are fuller, more fluid, and factual. Some East Londoners who first described themselves as healthy later revealed a litany of chronic conditions. Mildred Blaxter and Elizabeth Patterson (1982) argue that working-class English women avoid talking about symptoms and troubles because they believed 'thinking it so, makes it so.' They reduced causation of and moral responsibility for illness to individuals (see also Calnan 1987; McGuire and Kantor 1987).

Accounts of health and illness draw upon cultural values and individual intentions in response to particular circumstances. People take for granted that their views reflect the true, objective reality and build 'shoulds' and 'oughts' into them. For example, Blaxter's (1983) working-class women thought of illness as a 'leveler,' and as a natural consequence of age. To them, it affected rich and poor alike despite having experienced poverty and ill health in childhood themselves that precipitated lifelong health problems. Their view muted their social class disadvantage of having greater incidence of illness than middle- or upper-class people. Their view also shows how shared beliefs serve to keep understandings of illness within the individual level of analysis. These British studies point to the need for further research that compares health meanings and actions between social class groups and demonstrates differential institutional effects upon them.

Illness as Biographical Disruption vs. Continuity

A chronic illness often disrupts a person's life (Bury 1982), particularly so when it occurs during young or middle adulthood to working and middle-class people in affluent Western societies (see, for example, Brooks and Matson 1982; Bury 1982, 1988; Charmaz 1991; Herzlich and Pierret 1987; Robinson 1988; Schneider and Conrad 1983). Themes of disruption and loss of control permeate the Western literature on illness. Bury (1982, 1988) conducted two or more interviews with thirty working-class people with rheumatoid arthritis including twenty-five English women, two-thirds of whom were between 25 and 54 years old, and five men aged 45–64; most of them were young or middle-aged working adults. Locker (1983) interviewed twenty-four Londoners with arthritis twice, sixteen of whom range from 53 to 64 years old. Herzlich and Pierret (1987) illustrate their historical analysis of illness and French society with interview excerpts compiled for over 20 years. Corbin and Strauss (1988) analyzed published autobiographies and interviews of sixty California couples; at least one partner had a chronic illness or disability. My evolving study (Charmaz 1991, 1995) included informal interviews with caregivers, written personal accounts, and 140 in-depth interviews of middle- and working-class adults (two-thirds middle-aged and older; two-thirds women); sixteen respondents were followed from 5 years to more than a decade. I draw upon these studies in the subsequent discussions.

Chronically ill people lose their previously taken-for-granted continuity of life. Becoming ill poses three major problems to them: (1) making sense of bewildering symptoms, (2) reconstructing order, and (3) maintaining control over life (see also, Kirmayer 1992; Kleinman 1988). Making sense of symptoms spurs a diagnostic quest to define illness. Reconstructing order leads to efforts to manage illness and regimen, which I discuss in the next section. Maintaining control over life derives from concrete daily actions and regaining continuity and coherence of self and one's world. Experiencing bewilderment may be a luxury of societies in which people expect good health throughout long lives. Bewilderment spreads through families. It can lead to feeling overwhelmed once family members see what illness and care involves (Bluebond-Langner 1996; Lillrank 1998; Scambler and Hopkins 1988). Age may not ease a patient's bewilderment despite doctors' beliefs to the contrary, as Ruth Pinder (1992) reports of English practitioners and patients with Parkinson's Disease. Common illnesses such as a heart attack can also come as a shock and result in bewilderment (Cowie 1976; Johnson 1991; Speedling 1982). One of Bill Cowie's Scottish interviewees described his heart attack as 'quite out of the blue . . . It was completely unexpected' (Cowie 1976: 89). Bewilderment may shade into feeling betrayed by one's body, god, or physician (Charmaz 1995). Bewilderment dissolves when ill people have sustained contact with similar others and compare themselves accurately with them. Myra Bluebond-Langner (1978) shattered the assumption that small children have no concept of death. She demonstrated that little children with cancer learned of their imminent deaths by comparing themselves with their dying peers' illness and treatment.

Through understanding how people experience illness, problems at the interactional level become comprehensible. Beliefs and actions may become contested as practitioners and patients attempt to make sense of emerging symptoms. The path between discomfort and diagnosis is neither always smooth, nor direct. Definitions of illness may be rejected, challenged, negotiated, and redefined. Defining illness and being diagnosed occurs in several ways: (1) having a crisis, (2) comparing self with sick people, (3) redefining feelings or behavior as symptoms, and (4) receiving test findings or medical pronouncements. A crisis may not be initially identified as such. People normalize their symptoms for as long as possible (Johnson 1991; Stewart and Sullivan 1982). Seeking a diagnosis can turn into an onerous task (Corbin and Strauss 1988; Pinder 1992). If a prospective patient does not fit practitioners' images of someone who contracts a particular disease, then they may discount or minimize her symptoms. Age, appearance, sex, and race can all affect such judgments. For example, doctors discounted a woman's chest pains because they saw her as too young (51), healthy, and of the wrong sex for having heart disease. They told her, 'You don't look like there could be anything wrong' (Charmaz 1995: 666). These physicians' saw authentic illness as premature and unlikely. Perhaps more often it seems premature to the patient (Pinder 1992; Singer 1974; Weitz 1991). Shock results when the illness is unknown and symptoms are silent, nonexistent, or seemingly minor. Defining illness often results from other people's insistence that the person seek help. They observe changes or note a bizarre symptom unknown to the individual. For example, a little boy alarmed his mother when he complained that he could not mimic her contorted smile. When symptoms have long been intrusive, sufferers may welcome a serious diagnosis, especially if they had questioned their own veracity or had felt discredited.

Having an unmistakable health crisis imposes definitions of illness. What makes an episode a crisis, when it occurs, and how it is explained depends upon location, situation, and resources. Crises throw people out of ordinary life – order becomes disorder, the controllable becomes uncontrollable, the understandable becomes unfathomable (Charmaz 1991; Pinder 1992; Scarry 1985). The surge of extraordinary events usurps an ordinary flow. Life is out of control. When people already live in uncontrollable worlds filled with deprivation, disease, and crime, crises are constant and life is fragile (Scheper-Hughes 1992). Adding the wrenching incoherence of sickness and pain to lives already numbed by crises results in minimizing misery, individually and collectively.

During a crisis, the distance between symptom and calamity shrinks, if noted at all. Crises are filled with uncertainty; they swoop the ill person and helpers into the present (Charmaz 1991; Davis 1963). Ellen Idler observes, 'The experience of pain roots one in the present . . . Sickness creates and measures its own time' (Idler 1979: 727). The exigencies of the moment consume everyone, although they may have nothing to do but wait – and wait. Crises force the individual into the sick role in societies with access to medical care (Parsons 1951). Events topple upon each other so quickly that redefining self as critically ill may not occur (Charmaz 1991; Speedling 1982). Redefining self as 'chronically' ill is even more unlikely. Because a crisis turns life upside down, people can define it as an extraordinary episode while not necessarily realizing its lasting consequences (Charmaz 1991; Davis 1963). Later, a crisis can be long talked about, but kept contained in time and place. The teller can claim a heroic self who emerged victorious despite poor odds. A good story of a past crisis does not pollute the present – at least for a while or until audiences are exhausted, both in interest and in number. Such stories must be carefully constructed lest negative meanings from the past seep into the present. Both practitioners and patients may concentrate on past crises and thereby avoid dealing with present uncertainty, impaired bodies, and changed lives. However, when practitioners believe patients should face reality (i.e., disability), they may find patients unwilling to do so if they continue to define earlier crises as acute episodes.

Health crises reinforce viewing chronic illness as series of acute episodes, if some semblance of normal life follows each crisis (Charmaz 1994; Radley and Billig 1996). For example, a heart attack or a flare-up of myasthenia gravis may be defined as temporary crises. Other experiences and certain conditions do not lead to such definitions. If, for example, a person suffers a severe heart attack with irreversible disabilities, this crisis marks a changed life. Sharon Kaufman (1992) asked elders who had had strokes if they had recovered and if their lives were back to normal. She found that they invariably answered 'no' to both questions, even when they did not have visible disabilities. These people saw themselves as physically, emotionally, or cognitively changed.

In contrast to serial crises, creeping symptoms disrupt life less although they may cause logistical and social psychological problems. Finding out that something is wrong and what it is can become a long, tedious process (Pinder 1992; Stewart and Sullivan 1982). Ill people and their families usually adapt to early symptoms before they piece them together as meaningful signs of illness. How gradual symptoms are defined depends on cultural, familial, and situational contexts. To a degree, diffuse creeping symptoms such as fatigue, shortness of breath, and difficulty in concentrating can be confused with aging (see also Bury 1988). Yet, such symptoms are more likely to be dismissed in certain milieux, but not others. Stewart and Sullivan tell the tale of one man who was later diagnosed with multiple sclerosis. He had dismissed fleeting numbness in his ankles, clumsiness, and double vision because he saw them as 'a side effect of my work. I did precision work in cramped spaces in airplanes and it had always been hard on my legs and eyes. All the guys who did this complained of the same types of things' (1982: 1399). If coworkers have similar sensations, who would not dismiss early symptoms?

Lay beliefs about health and illness may compete with practitioners' views of a person's presenting symptoms. If so, people may experience symptoms long before seeking conventional care. Mathews et al. (1997) found that African–American women in North Carolina viewed lumps in their breasts as resulting from 'bad blood' trying to get out of the body. Impurities from bad blood are believed to cause a variety of diseases in African and Afro-Caribbean cultures. One woman said:

> If you have a lump and it's not bothering you, leave it alone. You don't want to get it started. That's why I don't hold with this idea of poking around to look for lumps. Why look for trouble? When that doctor wanted me to have the X-ray on my breast, I told him he was crazy. There's no telling what those X-rays might stir up. (Mathews et al. 1997: 53)

If practitioners or social scientists separate these women's experience from their indigenous understandings of health and illness, their delays and responses to treatment look like fatalism. However, Balshem (1991) and Mathews et al. (1997) point out that such attributions make fatalism itself a disease and discount stories through which patients comprehend their situations.

Common sense interpretations such as stress, depression, or weight changes may provide reasons for diffuse symptoms for both ill people and their practitioners in the early stages of some disease processes. Even considerable public discourse about the disease may not offer sufficient clues to those who have early symptoms. For example, when Rose Weitz's (1991) interviewees did not know of their HIV infection, they invoked other plausible explanations for their symptoms – the Arizona heat caused night sweats and exhaustion; drug use or withdrawal resulted in weight loss, sweating, and diarrhea. These examples indicate that laypersons (and sometimes practitioners) can explain distress in other ways than a disease process. The current rhetoric of stress combined with busy lives and over-burdened jobs encourage people to make sense of their bodily sensations in alternative ways. However, taken out of the context, it might seem that the person denies real and serious symptoms.

Chronically ill people seldom want to be invalids; they wish to be accepted as valid adults (Charmaz 1987; Locker 1983). Their self-doubts rise if other people imply that they wanted to get sick or harbor questionable motives for seeking care and claiming special needs: 'Are my symptoms real or all in my head?' (Bury 1988; Charmaz 1991). Their symptoms may be intermittent or gradually increase until they interfere with everyday life (Bury 1988; Charmaz 1991; Locker 1983; Robinson 1993). The person cannot meet obligations, keep up with coworkers, maintain their households, or handle daily child care. Esoteric and invisible illnesses often prove elusive. Then, symptoms may become pronounced before they are recognized as such. Yet, ill people do delay seeking help if it poses risk of further loss. Social purposes rather than health needs take priority. People delay seeking help when they risk losing valued roles, responsibilities, and images of self. For example, a parent who resists relinquishing child-care duties may defer seeking help.

Recognition of diminished function or inexplicable symptoms spurs a diagnostic search (Dingwall 1976; Kotarba 1983; Robinson 1971; Stewart and Sullivan 1982; Telles and Pollak 1981). Stewart and Sullivan (1982) found that patients with multiple sclerosis began their diagnostic search when they could no longer explain their symptoms. However, physicians and relatives typically did not affirm their symptoms as real until after diagnosis more than 2 years later. During this time, ill people live in 'diagnostic limbo' (Corbin and Strauss 1988) suspended in time. These patients often seek multiple physicians when their complaints are discounted and dismissed (see also Baszanger 1989; Kotarba 1983; Robinson 1988, 1990). Discounting and dismissal also may occur after a problem has been defined as chronic but practitioners cannot ameliorate it, such as chronic back pain (Baszanger 1989 1998; Kotarba 1983).

Diagnostic shock follows an announcement of serious illness that shows up in testing – cancer, multiple sclerosis, and diabetes – before patients either note symptoms or grant them any significance. From the patient's viewpoint, diagnostic shock occurs without warning, such as during a routine physical. Part of the shock means having reality disconfirmed. Not only are the person's suppositions about his body shaken, but also to the extent that a diagnosis has foreboding meaning, prior reality is disconfirmed as this diagnosis is confirmed. Subsequently, prior identities are also disconfirmed. When people do not anticipate bad news, have little knowledge and few symptoms of their confirmed diagnosis, the disparity between diagnosis and self-concept is greatest. Then the person needs time, bodily experiences, social encounters, and self-definitions to redefine self and identity. Meanwhile, the diagnosis confirms being catapulted into a patient role (Mairs 1989; Sourkes 1982). A new label, a new identity has been applied and given. Yet even the most dreaded and seemingly known diseases such as AIDS, leprosy, and cancer require learning what being ill means.

MANAGING ILLNESS

Learning what Illness Means

In order to be ill, someone has to feel sick. Merely being informed that one has a disease seldom suffices. Until a person defines changes in bodily feeling or function, she may postpone dealing with a diagnosis, even a serious one, and subsequently ignore medical advice and regimen. Illness does not seem real. Then the person may claim that the diagnosis is wrong, secondary, or inconsequential, and relations with practitioners suffer accordingly.

People learn what illness is through their experience of it (Charmaz 1991; Davis 1963). Lessons in chronicity come in small everyday experiences such as difficulty in opening a can, bending over to pick up a newspaper, folding bedsheets, and weeding the garden. Comparisons with past effortless performance can be shocking. Such jolts later become measures explicitly sought and then assessed. A man with heart disease who used to stride across a golf course now shuffles half way across the company parking lot. A present reality jolt can be reinvoked as a future measure. Measures include time – the person can only get through part of the work day, rest requirements become apparent to coworkers, fulfilling work standards takes hours or days longer. Indicators become measures when they are impossible to gloss over or to have someone else camouflage. A person may invoke measures, or other people may supply them. These measures can multiply and form a general standard against which to judge self.

Historical, cultural, social, and situational contexts influence meanings of illness. Waxler (1981) argues that in every society, the sick person learns to take a role that society expects. Waxler's work on leprosy presages moral meanings of AIDS. She shows how moral meanings of illness are pinned on certain groups, but not others. After 1850 in Hawaii, leprosy became associated with Chinese immigrants, although missionaries had recognized it earlier and health records indicated that the Chinese were not an important source of the disease.

Normalizing Illness and Regimen

Normalizing illness and regimen means making them routine, and treating whatever changes and improvisations are created as ordinary. For some people, normalizing means letting past plans and projects go and scaling life down. For others, it means struggling with illness and regimen to make life manageable so a valued future is possible. In both cases, normalizing means adapting to the situation at hand. It also means proceeding with activities '*as if* normal' (Wiener 1984: 91). Normalizing means finding ways to minimize the impact of illness, disability, and regimen on daily life, including their visibility (Drummond and Mason 1990; Robinson 1993). It constitutes an attempt to contain illness to personal experience and not intrude upon interaction. Thus, chronically ill people cover up limitations and keep up normal appearances and activities (Wiener 1984). They normalize a certain amount of discomfort when they can still function in ordinary ways. Such strategies become hazardous if a person over-extends his capacities and perhaps harms an already compromised body.

However, when ill people normalize symptom control and regimen, they may increase their capacities and maintain their health. This kind of normalizing means making new routines the norm and the normal. What earlier seemed bizarre becomes customary and comfortable. Hence, a man with balance problems pulls on his undershorts and pants while lying in bed. Many people jettison activities as their stamina decreases and illness increases. Women often dispense with hose, skirts, and heels; occasionally they dispense with underwear when it takes too much energy and too long to don. As innovations and changes become routine and accepted, they feel normal and allow the ill person to view the self as normal and the way of living now as natural (Kelleher 1988).

Normalizing reduces disruption. It softens the impact of frailty and disability. Through normalizing, ill people take their way of being and the changes they have endured for granted. As their lives become more restricted, their world shrivels, frame of reference shrinks, and self con-

tracts. As Oliver Sacks said of his convalescence for a broken leg:

> I had no sense, no realization of how contracted I was, how insensibly I had become contracted to the locus of my sickbed and sickroom – contracted in the most literal physiological terms, but contracted too, in imagination and feeling . . . It was an unavoidable, natural shrinking down of existence, made bearable and untreatable because not realizable – not directly realizable. How could one know that one had shrunk, if one's frame of reference had itself shrunk? (Sacks 1984: 156)

Illness Management Strategies

Chronically ill people learn ways to handle their physical symptoms through various strategies ranging from withdrawal to innovation (Charmaz 1991; Mitteness 1987b; Pinder 1988; Reif 1975; Schneider and Conrad 1983; Strauss et al. 1984). Strategies for managing illness also require strategies for effective negotiations. People in lengthy marriages make managing illness a coupled affair (see Corbin and Strauss 1984, 1988; Johnson 1985; Peyrot et al. 1988; Radley 1988). Visible disability drives other adult relatives away (Albrecht 1992). What people need to manage depends on their illness, its progression, and its meaning to them, as well as their situation and their responsibilities. One person juggles and paces work to get through the workday without collapsing. Another tries to survive from day to day on a minimal disability pension.

Younger and middle-aged people often make concerted efforts to manage their illness. They maintain hopes and plans, reasons, and responsibilities. They have not given up or given in. They become innovators. To do so they listen to their bodies and stay in tune with them in ways that they had not and in ways that Western culture discourages. They may make use of indigenous support groups, newsletters, and computer networks independent of professionals. The groups and methods provide collective information and shared community. They may constitute the only community for people who have become isolated in their homes. Members compare stories, gain information, learn about treatment successes and failures, and offer encouragement to continue to struggle with illness and not to sink into invalidism. They may keep daily logs to refine and extend data for working with their professionals (Barrett 1997).

Shared comparisons give support group members measures of where and who they are now. Certain chronic conditions such as kidney failure and treatment programs such as cardiac rehabilitation bring people into sustained contact with others with similar problems. A collective spirit may develop in these situations that either supports patients remaining involved in prior pursuits, or confirms that the world of illness now dominates their lives.

Some chronically ill people become so adept at monitoring and managing their illness that they break through textbook definitions, create individualized regimens, and construct new ways of living with their illness; but medical professionals may not welcome their innovations. Alonzo Plough (1986) argues that patients who know too much use medical terms and request specific treatments that anger their practitioners. Practitioners sometimes push these patients back into the sick role when challenged by their growing expertise. Chronically ill patients sometimes find that their practitioners hold an ambivalent stance toward them. Their practitioners want them to take responsibility for themselves but on professionals' terms, not on their own. When these ill people step outside or beyond medical authority, their practitioners resort to medical paternalism and authoritarian demands. Consequently, ill people's strategies for managing illness can require strategies for effective negotiations with professionals to minimize conflict.

Conflict between practitioners and patients can arise from unstated assumptions such as guiding metaphors. Kirmayer (1992, p. 326) shows how a man on renal dialysis assumed the metaphor of pollution and refused to receive a blood transfusion. His physician, however, assumed the metaphor of vision in which the eye sees the real, objective world of facts and the brain represents or mirrors it. Technology extends vision and available facts. If this patient would 'see' things accurately, then he would come to the same conclusion. However, patients have their own metaphors, values, and sentiments. Assumed values and unspoken priorities are played out in the ways that people live with illness.

STIGMA AND STIGMA CONTROL

Experiencing stigma is a common consequence of chronic illness and a constant threat in some ill individuals' view. If so, stigma makes a person vulnerable to negative social identifications and self-definitions. Stigma results from being identified as flawed, discredited, or spoiled (Goffman 1963; Jones et al. 1984). A defined difference from ordinary peers separates a person and confers an actual or potentially devalued identity.

That difference often becomes a master status, such as 'disabled person,' 'leper,' or 'AIDS victim,' that floods all statuses and identities. The stigmatizing label defines the person *and* every other defining characteristic she possesses. Thus, a woman who uses a wheelchair because of multiple sclerosis becomes a disabled mother, handicapped driver, disabled worker, and wheelchair dancer.

The labels are attached to the person, but stigma arises in interaction and within relations. Social scientists, like lay people, have treated some conditions such as AIDS, epilepsy, and leprosy as if inherently stigmatizing. Other conditions may elicit more neutral responses on the surface, but their consequences such as symptoms, disabilities, unemployment, or reduced performance elicit stigmatizing definitions of difference. Often other people dissociate the 'understandable' reason for an ill person's difference from his behavior eliciting the stigmatized response. Then blame is turned back upon this person, who is made morally culpable for the stigmatized response itself (Jackson 1992). In essence, the individual is blamed for the behavior and blamed again for being stigmatized for it.

Whether the person experiences being stigmatized arises in interaction. Scambler (1984) and Scambler and Hopkins (1988) distinguish between enacted and felt stigma in their study of ninety-four adults with diagnosed epilepsy in the London area. Enacted stigma means instances of discrimination against people because they are defined as different. Felt stigma derives from fear of discovery of this difference and shame about having it. Felt stigma reflects a person's internalized social values about her condition or difference. Scambler and Hopkins (1986) report that their interviewees act upon felt stigma, and thus limit possibilities for enacted stigma to occur, but actually experience little enacted stigma. Schneider and Conrad (1983) describe more experiences of enacted stigma in their interviews of eighty self-selected young Mid-Western Americans. Essayist Nancy Mairs (1996) suggests that unlike in the United States, the English assume that persons with disability neither seek nor exploit their situations. Following such cues with systematic comparative research would refine notions of stigma and yield insights about how cultural rules shape responses to illness.

Schneider and Conrad portray how visual images of epilepsy become taken as objective evidence of fundamental disreputability in this woman's statement:

It's one of those fear images; it's something that people don't know about and has strong negative connotations in people's minds. It's a bad image, something scary, sort of like a beggar; it's dirty, the person falling down and frothing at the mouth and jerking and the bystanders not knowing what to do. It's something that happens in public which isn't nice. (1983: 154)

Fear, guilt, and shame comprise felt stigma. Questions of 'Why me?' and 'What did I do to deserve this?' reveal how individuals accept the moral accountability imbedded in collective images of illness. Meredith B. McGuire and Debra J. Kantor (1987) studied three healing groups; each one emphasized individual responsibility for illness, albeit in different ways. The occult group saw illness as cleansing and pain as being present when a person 'needed' it, the metaphysical group saw health as the normal human condition and illness as error in thought, and the Christian group viewed illness as caused by sin. Many people may reject the language of sin while upholding views of the sick person as guilty or devalued for being ill, views that he or she may share. Guilt and shame last when the person faces daily consequences of not being able to function as before – a spouse's distancing, children's belligerence about added tasks . . . impoverishment.

Guilt and shame increase when chronically ill people view themselves as socially incompetent. Inability to uphold basic social rules about cleanliness, bodily functioning, and sociability evokes shame, particularly when visible transgressions occur in public. Gerhard Nijhof (1995) states that his respondents with Parkinson's disease felt shamed by their inability to control their excessive saliva, impassive faces, bent bodies, involuntary jerks and tremors, and clumsy table manners. Linda S. Mitteness (1987a, 1987b) and Lea MacDonald (1988) show how potential public shame, due to urinary or bowel incontinence, leads to withdrawal.

Because enacted stigma dramatizes difference, it magnifies loss. Discovering how others view one's self can be shocking. Such events live on in the minds of those who felt marked by them. When possible, the ill person will henceforth try to conceal or limit potentially discrediting views of self. What to tell, when to tell, how to tell and how much to tell all pose ethical dilemmas to a chronically ill person (Charmaz 1991; Schneider and Conrad 1980, 1983). Relationships, resources, control, and especially risks figure in the calculus of telling, and fateful telling occurs at points within the life course. In my study (Charmaz 1991), young and middle-aged adults risked losing acceptance and elders risked losing autonomy. Telling prospective partners too early sent them running. Telling too late was bad faith. Morgan (1982) states that elderly resi-

dents in a retirement center with multiple levels of care did not tell nursing staff of their increasing frailty because they risked losing their apartments and their independence.

Understanding such actions can aid families and professionals to remain sensitive to the person's feeling of vulnerability, and not to increase it through their response. They can easily lose sight of the person's sense of heightened vulnerability if he acts upon it without talking about it. Scambler and Hopkins (1988) find that people with epilepsy handle felt stigma by maintaining secrecy, which reduces enacted stigma but does so at the cost of disrupting their lives. Other studies indicate that felt stigma leads to limiting social relations and restricting involvements (Charmaz 1991; MacDonald 1988; Mitteness 1987a, 1987b). Susan Hopper (1982) describes an interviewee whose diabetes first cost him his job and then his girlfriend because he no longer could 'give service.' Afterwards the interviewee kept to himself.

Invisible and visible disabilities pose several different problems in which stigmatizing definitions can emerge. People with invisible disabilities are judged by conventional standards and blamed accordingly when they transgress them. Thus, they suffer public accusations of usurping the rights of the handicapped (such as when they occupy handicapped subway seats or parking spaces), imputations that their poor performance reflects a sick mind, not an impaired body, and private doubts as to what is real. These people seek acknowledgment and empathy. Nonetheless, they can still choose to conceal their disability. People with visible disabilities cannot. Visible disability can elicit rude intrusions and judgments of difference whenever in public. Ostentatious unsolicited help as well as scorn may be showered upon people with obvious disabilities. In either case, disability marks the person as flawed (Jones et al. 1984). Corbin and Strauss (1988) interviewed a woman who used a walker because of rheumatoid arthritis. She said:

> People so often treat you like you are deaf, dumb, blind, and retarded. [P]eople's attitudes . . . as a company we belong to a trade association and some of those people! I was asked to be on a committee and when a man found out I had a walker, he was very concerned because I was to be one of the hostesses. What difference does it make when all I have to do is stand there and talk to people? (Corbin and Strauss 1988: 213)

This woman acknowledged her disability, worked around it, and rejected stigmatizing definitions. Her routines allowed her to maintain her activities and a view of herself as whole. Until and unless routinized, a visible disability constantly reminds self and others of one's changed health and life. Visibility itself varies. Conditions such as mastectomy or impotence can cause someone to feel fundamentally flawed despite their relative lack of visibility. For example, one of Fallowfield and Clark's (1991) interviewees said of the breast prosthesis: 'I hate it so much – last week I just felt so angry that they'd taken off my breast and given me that awful alien thing – I threw it across the room and cried' (1991: 66). After a lumpectomy another woman remarked, 'When he said they'd remove a little lump, I felt relieved. I mean no one really wants to lose a breast, do they? But when I look at what's left, I wonder if it was worth it. I mean, I'm still a freak aren't I?' (1991: 68).

Any illness that sets a person apart as different and diminished has stigma potential and thus can affect interaction. The following characteristics increase stigma potential: a high incidence within disparaged groups, compromised adult status, loss of bodily control, sexual transmission, possible pollution, odor, and uncleanliness. MacDonald (1988) writes that fear of offending other people with noise and odors led rectal cancer patients to restrict their lives. Similarly, Mitteness (1987a, 1987b) finds that elders who had urinary incontinence commonly restricted their outings and interactions.

Davis (1963) argues that efforts toward prior identity preservation fail in direct proportion to the degree and extent of visible disability. Both enacted and felt stigma contribute to difficulties in preserving prior identity. The disability rights movement has made significant recent changes in the lives of its proponents. However, many ill people still find themselves responsible for preserving or reconstructing their identity after losses – whether their disability is visible or invisible. Concealment of an invisible but potentially stigmatizing mark of difference allows the person to preserve prior identities for a time and under specific conditions. Many disabilities do not remain completely invisible to a discerning observer. Partners or parents may perceive cues more readily than a professional who does not have steady contact. Fatigue, flare-ups, or distress may render symptoms visible. Disabling illnesses such as arthritis or multiple sclerosis grow in severity and thus shift from invisible to visible. If, in the interim, a person exerts substantial effort to keep illness secret, it takes on enlarged meaning for personal identity and self-concept. As Jones et al. (1984) contend, the person cannot put this aspect of self into perspective because normal social comparisons have been precluded. When invisible disability undermines fundamental ways of defining self, the person is isolated, and social comparisons are not possible. Then coherence and stability of self-concept is at risk.

SELF AND SOCIAL IDENTITY

Stigma can wreak havoc upon the self for it forces unwelcome new ways of conceiving self and situation. Still, serious chronic illness alone can render social identity and self problematic (Mathieson and Stam 1995). For months and years, people may try to forestall illness from touching the self. Valued roles and pursuits preserve continuity and coherence of self. People may acknowledge that illness affects their lives but resist its effects upon the self. They conceptualize it as a 'condition, not an illness,' 'just aging,' or 'a spell' and therefore maintain a sense of continuity and coherence of self (Charmaz 1991). They put it into the past by saying they 'had cancer' or 'had lupus' and decree that it will remain in the past. They also redefine criteria for crucial indicators of illness. As Mitteness (1987b) discovered, elders redefined incontinence to fit the way their bodies now functioned. For one elder, it was not incontinence if no accident occurred in public. For another, it was not incontinence if she made it to the bathroom, but did not get as far as the toilet. For others, it was not incontinence as long as the pads sufficed.

People with serious chronic illnesses must repeatedly rethink how they live and who they are becoming (Charmaz 1995). Self and social identities are intertwined in daily actions and endeavors. Chronically ill people seek to reestablish their legitimacy after disruption and devaluation makes them vulnerable. However, they may not go about it in ways of which their practitioners and families approve (Bury 1991). As life narrows, the ingredients shrivel for constructing a valued self and legitimate social identity. Their quality of life becomes problematic (Albrecht and Fitzpatrick 1994). Social, economic, and psychological resources expand possibilities and options. Without such resources, possibilities and options rapidly contract. Using available resources may be fraught with risks and increase vulnerability. Taking sick leave can result in increased scrutiny of an employee's performance. Filing an insurance claim might contribute to raising the business's group insurance rates. Social resources mean that commitments, assistance, and back-up are available – as long as caregivers do not wear out. Concrete assistance smoothes problems and reduces anxieties. Commitments keep the ill person within a web of relationships – from commitments that permit returning to work to commitments to visit or to run errands. Economic resources allow an individual to purchase objects and services that make life easier – a car with an automatic shift, a one-story home, household help. The more resources available, the more latitude the person has to take time-outs for illness and then return to earlier pursuits. Identity questions and change of self are muted or occur over long periods of time. As resources dwindle, identity questions and changes of self may be forced much earlier.

Experiencing chronic illness can mean embarking on an odyssey apart from the busyness of other adults' lives. Chronic illness separates the person from the social body, but also gives rise to a story that brings this individual back to reintegrate self on a different level. Someone may leave old identities behind but gain deeper meanings. Long stretches of time allow the person to reflect upon jarring images of self and to make sense of loss. Loss of self and social identity do comprise a fundamental form of suffering among chronically ill people (Charmaz 1983). Still, they may come to believe that facing such losses moves them toward transcending loss. Earlier vulnerability becomes a source of strength as they redefine illness as a time for reflection, reassessment, and redirection (Charmaz 1991, 1994; Frank 1991, 1993).

IMPLICATIONS OF STUDYING THE EXPERIENCE OF ILLNESS

What are the implications of this growing research literature? Two major areas are prominent: (1) ideas for institutional changes and health policy reform, and (2) directions for further research and development of the field. Insights from the individual and interactional levels of the illness experience recast institutional and policy levels in new light. A new model for chronic care with strong participatory and educational components would shift the medical model of acute care from its individual bias and basis to the social realm. This new model could change both the experience of illness and the effectiveness of care. A social model for chronic care means an *integrated* set of varied services and sustained patient involvement for *giving* as well as receiving services.

The current medical model of acute care fragments treatment, isolates patients, and individualizes their experience of chronic illness. Managed care has intensified these processes through curtailing and cutting services. Patients and caregivers' responsibility for care has therefore increased. Simultaneously, the graying of contemporary societies means that more people everywhere can expect to live with a serious chronic illness and its resulting disabilities. This prospect poses dilemmas for societies and health-care systems – particularly if the assumptions of the medical model remain essentially unchallenged. Currently, care is meager, at best, in developing societies and deteriorating in many developed nations. Concerns about the quality of life necessitate comprehensive support services for people with chronic illnesses. They often live independently in a frail state for protracted periods. Fragmented, limited, or stopgap services organized on an acute-care model do not meet the needs of average and impoverished citizens. These structural problems of care increase their *physical* as well as social, psychological, and economic vulnerability.

Studies of the experience of chronic illness reveal gaps in the medical model of acute care. Rather than reducing services, the prospect of more chronically ill people requires more services. The reductionist acute-care model assumes one atomized individual as the unit of care, separates this person from her world, views problems with illness as inhering in this individual, and addresses those problems amenable to medical interventions (Charmaz and Paterniti 1999). As evident above, patients currently also make these assumptions and assume recovery. Patients need time to learn what their illnesses mean and to have tools for the lessons. These tools include sustained community education *before* individuals become sick, a collective context of care and thus of shared knowledge among patients, and continued partnerships with patients and families.

Knowing a diagnosis seldom translates into realizing what it means to live with it. Including experienced patients as teachers and mentors to new patients would show them what their illness means and suggest ways to live with it. New patients might then adapt to their conditions more quickly than otherwise. Should adaptation be slow, this approach provides another, likely more neutral, way for professionals to learn about patients' expectations and level of knowledge than occurs within the treatment clinic or examining room. By learning more about metaphors their patients invoke, professionals can understand their patients' difficulties in coming to terms with their illnesses. As understanding increases, blame and conflict decrease.

Chronic illness points to collective problems of living; it occurs within a social context and it poses problems that go beyond medical management and the individual patient. Managing a life can become as problematic as keeping symptoms quiescent, and that requires other people. The effects of serious chronic illness of one person reverberate through the home. As illness progresses in severity and disability, it spreads out and devours other people's time, effort, and concern. The medical model of acute care – both in traditional or stripped-down managed care forms – fails to address these points. A social, community-based model of care would begin by taking the chronically ill person's *situation* as the fundamental unit of concern, not the disease process within that person.

People with chronic illnesses can and do become knowledgeable about their conditions; these individuals are not always the unsophisticated passive patients the medical model assumes. Nor do they have something within them that treatment can readily ameliorate. They need services to help them make, and moreover to *maintain*, gains. Leaving people on their own fosters their retreat into isolated private worlds and subsequently increases the likelihood that they will discount, ignore, or misunderstand medical mandates. Complications and setbacks follow.

Reorganizing care to keep patients involved has practical consequences. Such involvement would reduce noncompliance and medical mishaps, maintain optimal health with chronic illness, and enhance quality of life. A collective organization of care with and for patients furthers their involvement. Adopting principles from activist support groups can break down the isolation chronically ill people often experience and break up the reductionist medical model. These principles foster developing mutual information exchanges, offering caregiver assistance, and involve patients as active participants, all within a supportive network of patients and professionals.

Experiencing chronic illness at times seems incomprehensible. Vulnerability increases when people are isolated; it decreases when ill people learn that others have weathered their illnesses and can give voice to that experience. Active patients involved in their own treatment feel less vulnerable because they are taking control.

My analysis in this chapter lays out central directions of past research on the experience of illness. Which directions should our studies take next? The body of research in this area points the way to go deeper into the subjective and further outward into the social. This literature has contributed to theoretical and empirical interest in the body and emotions (Olesen 1994) and promises more significant developments in these areas – we are embodied beings and we do have feelings. Past social scientific emphasis on rationality has channeled vision away from these two significant dimensions of human experience. This area of study brings them back with challenges to create nuanced analyses not only of crisis, suffering, and loss, but also of renewal, hope, and transcendence.

Chronically ill people's stories mediate between their bodies and emotions because their stories make sense of their altered lives and limited bodies. These people's stories converge with the current narrative turn in the social sciences for their stories are filled with turning points, epiphanies, and reflections, and thus give narrative analysts grist for discovering change and transformation in adult life. These stories resonate because they are *our* stories, albeit writ bold and condensed in time. They tell of change and transition, of beginnings and endings throughout adult life. Yet stories alone do not cover the experience. Not everyone can find words to express inchoate feelings; not every culture condones the subjective story. The researcher's methods must fit the problem studied and the people observed. Interviews provide a means of going deep into the story. Because they frame discourse in a rational account, however, interviews may mask feelings just beneath the surface (see also Lillrank 1998). As reconstructions of the past, interviews never replicate experience, they render it. Stories in interviews serve new and different purposes than when originally experienced and first told.

To go deeper into the subjective story, we need to see and hear how it develops as it is lived. Stories from single interviews are partial and may isolate moments rather than relate the life course. Both researcher and reader may freeze responses in time and place, and thus reify the results as objective truth (Williams 1984). Longitudinal studies following people throughout the course of their illness can yield nuanced analyses of the ebb and flow of experience. Such studies provide context and meaning and illuminate shifts and changes. These studies may also refine current conceptions of responses to illness and frailty. For example, age and social class are confounded in research about the most elderly generation. Many of these elders did not receive advanced education, and thus their thoughts, feelings, and actions toward illness and disability may later be discovered to reflect social class more than age.

A hazard of any kind of research is inaccessible subjects. The earlier research focused on individuals has largely left out precisely those individuals who are difficult to trace – those who are isolated and impoverished. People without families or sustained help slip through the medical system and slip out of our studies. What happens when these individuals lose their livelihoods in addition to their health? Their stories might illuminate problems in the institution of medicine and, moreover, the larger society.

Although the field has started with the subjective, it can move into the realm of social interaction. The research can move to attend to all crucial participants in the scene, rather than maintain the current unitary foci on ill persons, couples, or caretakers. Further research directions include: (1) situating research within home and community, as *worlds* to study, (2) evaluating the relative significance of support group and/or social movement participation (Maines 1991; Sandstrom 1990), and (3) conducting comparative research of the experience of people with similar conditions within different social classes and between different societies to illuminate how social, structural, and cultural conditions shape meanings and actions toward illness.

This area of inquiry also has rich potential for continuing the development of theoretical analyses initiated by its progenitors. Social scientists can take their analyses of the experience of illness beyond narrow empirical data to shape theoretical understandings. At present, theories of suffering and loss are emerging in part from studies of illness. In the past, theoretical development may have been most apparent in analyses of construction and development of self and of the significance of stigma. However, other fruitful theoretical links can be made between individual experience and collective life, such as within social movement or community participation. Any theorizing arising from this area has the advantage of grounding in actual life, and therefore, gains analytic precision and practical applicability.

Finally, studying the experience of illness brings research subjects into social science narratives without abandoning our narratives to them (Charmaz in press). Social scientists bring an analytic focus to our subjects' stories and synthesize their experience. Despite our scientific allusions and narrative claims, our subjects remain the best judges of whether we provide a useful analytic handle on their oft elusive experience.

ACKNOWLEDGMENTS

Thanks are due to Judith Abbott, Gary L. Albrecht, Catherine Nelson, and two anonymous reviewers for their comments on an earlier version of this chapter.

REFERENCES

Albrecht, G.L. (1992) 'The social experience of disability', in C. Calhoun and G. Ritzer (eds), *Social Problems*. New York: McGraw-Hill. pp. 1–18.

Albrecht, G.L. and Fitzpatrick, R. (1994) 'A sociological perspective on health-related quality of life', in G.L. Albrecht and R. Fitzpatrick (eds), *Advances in Medical Sociology, Vol. 5. Quality of Life in Health Care*. Greenwich, CT: JAI. pp. 1–22.

Balshem, M. (1991) 'Cancer, control and causality: Talking about cancer in a working-class community', *American Ethnologist*, 18: 152–71.

Barrett, D. (1997) 'Making "invisible" illness visible through social science', Paper presented at Seeing 'Invisible' Illness: Transforming the Medical Gaze Through Lived Experience: An Interdisciplinary Workshop, Emory University, Atlanta, GA, 1 November.

Baszanger, I. (1989) 'Pain: Its experience and treatments', *Social Science and Medicine*, 29: 425–34.

Baszanger, I. (1998) *Inventing Pain Medicine: From the Laboratory to the Clinic*. New Brunswick, NJ: Rutgers University Press.

Blaxter, M. (1983) 'The cause of disease: Women talking', *Social Science and Medicine*, 17: 59–69.

Blaxter, M. and Patterson, E. (1982) *Mothers and Daughters: A Three Generation Study of Health Attitudes and Behavior*. London: Heinemann.

Bluebond-Langner, M. (1978) *The Private Worlds of Dying Children*. Princeton, NJ: Princeton University Press.

Bluebond-Langner, M. (1996) *In the Shadow of Illness*. Princeton, NJ: Princeton University Press.

Brooks, N.A. and Matson, R.R. (1982) 'Social psychological adjustment to multiple sclerosis', *Social Science and Medicine*, 16: 2129–35.

Brown, P. (1996) 'Popular epidemiology and toxic waste contamination: Lay and professional ways of knowing', in P. Brown (ed.), *Perspectives in Medical Sociology*. Prospect Heights, IL: Waveland. pp. 173–96.

Bury, M. (1982) 'Chronic illness as disruption', *Sociology of Health and Illness*, 4: 167–82.

Bury, M. (1988) 'Meanings at risk: The experience of arthritis' in R. Anderson and M. Bury (eds), *Living with Chronic Illness*. London: Unwin Hyman. pp. 89–116.

Bury, M. (1991) 'The sociology of chronic illness: A review of research and prospects'. *Sociology of Health and Illness*, 13: 451–68.

Calnan, M. (1987) *Health and Illness: The Lay Perspective*. London: Tavistock.

Charmaz, K. (1983) 'Loss of self: A fundamental form of suffering in the chronically ill', *Sociology of Health and Illness*, 5: 168–95.

Charmaz, K. (1987) 'Struggling for a self: Identity levels of the chronically ill' in P. Conrad and J.A. Roth (eds), *Research in the Sociology of Health Care: The Experience and Management of Chronic Illness*. Vol. 6. Greenwich, CT: JAI Press. pp. 283–321.

Charmaz, K. (1991) *Good Days, Bad Days: The Self in Chronic Illness and Time*. New Brunswick, NJ: Rutgers University Press.

Charmaz, K. (1994) 'Discoveries of self in illness', in M.L. Dietz, R. Prus, and W. Shaffir (eds), *Doing Everyday Life: Ethnography as Human Lived Experience*. Mississauga, Ontario: Copp Clark, Longman. pp. 226–42.

Charmaz, K. (1995) 'The body, identity, and self: Adapting to impairment', *The Sociological Quarterly,* 36: 657–80.

Charmaz, K. (In press) 'From the "Sick Role" to stories of self: Understanding the self in illness', in R.D. Ashmore and R.A. Contrada (eds) *Self and Identity. Vol. 2. Interdisciplinary Explorations in Physical Health*. New York: Oxford University Press. pp. 209–39.

Charmaz, K. and Olesen, V. (1997) 'Ethnographic research in medical sociology: Its foci and distinctive contributions', *Sociological Methods and Research,* 25: 452–94.

Charmaz, K. and Paterniti, D.A. (1999). 'Introduction to Section 3: Caretaking and caregiving relationships', in K. Charmaz and D.A. Paterniti (eds), *Health, Illness, and Healing: Society, Social Context and Self.* Los Angeles: Roxbury. pp. 145–7.

Coffey, A. and Atkinson, P. (1996) *Making Sense of Qualitative Data: Complementary Research Strategies*. London: Sage.

Conrad, P. (1987) 'The experience of illness: Recent and new directions,' in J.A. Roth and P. Conrad (eds), *Research in the Sociology of Health Care: The Experience and Management of Chronic Illness.* Vol. 6. Greenwich, CT: JAI. pp. 1–32.

Corbin, J.M. and Strauss, A. (1984) 'Collaboration: Couples working together to manage chronic illness', *Image,* 4: 109–15.

Corbin, J.M. and Strauss, A. (1988) *Unending Work and Care: Managing Chronic Illness at Home.* San Francisco, CA: Jossey-Bass.

Cornwall, J. (1984) *Hard-earned Lives: Accounts of Health and Illness from East London.* London: Tavistock.

Cowie, B. (1976) 'The cardiac patient's perception of his heart attack', *Social Science and Medicine,* 10: 87–96.

Crawford, R. (1984) 'A cultural account of "health": Control, release, and the social body', in J.B. McKinlay (ed.), *Issues in the Political Economy of Health Care.* New York: Tavistock. pp. 60–106.

Das, V. (1994) 'Moral orientations to suffering: Legitimation, power, and healing', in L.C. Chen, A. Kleinman, and N.C. Ware (eds) *Health and Social Change in International Perspective.* Boston, Harvard University Press. pp. 139–67.

Davis, F. (1963) *Passage Through Crisis: Polio Victims and Their Families.* Indianapolis: Bobbs-Merrill.

Desjarlais, R.R. (1992) *Body and Emotions: The Aesthetics of Illness and Healing in the Nepal Himalayas.* Philadephia, University of Pennsylvania Press.

Dingwall, R. (1976) *Aspects of Illness.* New York: St. Martin's.

Drummond, N. and Mason, C. (1990) 'Diabetes in a social context: Just a different way of life in the age of reason', in S. Cunningham-Burley and N.P. McKeganey (eds), *Readings in Medical Sociology.* London: Tavistock. pp. 37–56.

Dumit, J. (1997) 'Illnesses you have to fight to get: Social movements and the biomedical economy', Paper presented at 'Seeing "Invisible" Illness: Transforming the Medical Gaze Through Lived Experience: An Interdisciplinary Workshop.' Emory University, Atlanta, GA, 1 November.

Fallowfield, L. and Clark, A. (1991) *Breast Cancer.* London: Tavistock.

Fitzpatrick, R., Hinton, J., Newman, S., Scambler, G., and Thompson, J. (eds) (1984) *The Experience of Illness.* London: Tavistock.

Frank, A. (1991) *At the Will of the Body.* New York: Houghton-Mifflin.

Frank, A. (1993) 'The rhetoric of self-change: Illness experience as narrative', *Sociological Quarterly,* 34: 39–52.

Gerhardt, U. (1989) *Ideas about Illness: An Intellectual and Political History of Medical Sociology.* New York: New York University Press.

Glaser, B.G. and Strauss, A.L. (1965) *Awareness of Dying.* Chicago: Aldine.

Glaser, B.G. and Strauss, A.L. (1967) *The Discovery of Grounded Theory.* Chicago: Aldine.

Glaser, B.G. and Strauss, A.L. (1968) *Time for Dying.* Chicago: Aldine.

Goffman, E. (1963) *Stigma.* Englewood Cliffs, NJ: Prentice Hall.

Hammersley, M. and Atkinson, P. (1983) *Ethnography: Principles in Practice.* London: Tavistock.

Herzlich, C. (1973) *Health and Illness: A Sociological Analysis.* London: Academic Press.

Herzlich, C. and Pierret, J. (1987) *Illness and Self in Society.* Baltimore: Johns Hopkins University Press.

Hopper, S. (1982) 'Diabetes as a stigmatized condition', *Social Science and Medicine,* 15B: 11–19.

Idler, E.L. (1979) 'Definitions of health and illness and medical sociology', *Social Science and Medicine,* 13A: 723–31.

Jackson, J.E. (1992) ' "After a while no one believes you": Real and unreal pain', in M.-J.D. Good, P.E. Brodwin, B.J. Good, and A. Kleinman (eds), *Pain as Human Experience: An Anthropological Perspective.* Berkeley: University of California Press. pp. 138–68.

Johnson, C.L. (1985) 'The impact of illness on late-life marriages', *Journal of Marriage and the Family,* 47: 165–72.

Johnson, J.L. (1991) 'Learning to live again: The process of adjustment following a heart attack', in J.M. Morse and J.L. Johnson (eds), *The Illness Experience.* Newbury Park, CA: Sage. pp. 13–88.

Jones, E.E., Farina, A., Hastrof, A., Markus, H., Miller, D.T., and Scott, R.A. (1984). *Social Stigma: The Psychology of Marked Relationships.* New York: W.H. Freeman.

Kaufman, S. (1992) 'Illness, biography, and the interpretation of self following a stroke', in J. Gubrium and K. Charmaz (eds), *Aging, Self and Community*. Greenwich, CT: JAI. pp. 71–81.

Kelleher, D. (1988) 'Coming to terms with diabetes: Coping strategies and non-compliance', in R. Anderson and M. Bury (eds), *Living with Chronic Illness*. London: Unwin Hyman. pp. 155–87.

Kirmayer, L. (1988) 'Mind and body as metaphors', in M. Lock and D. Gordon (eds), *Biomedicine Examined*. Dordrecht: Kluwer. pp. 57–94.

Kirmayer, L. (1992) 'The body's insistence on meaning: Metaphor as presentation and representation in illness experience', *Medical Anthropological Quarterly*, 6: 323–46.

Kleinman, A. (1988) *The Illness Narratives*. New York: Basic Books.

Kleinman, A. (1994) 'An anthropological perspective on objectivity: Observation, categorization, and the assessment of suffering', in L.C. Chen, A. Kleinman, and N.C. Ware (eds), *Health and Social Change in International Perspective*. Boston: Harvard University Press. pp. 129–38.

Kotarba, J.A. (1983) *Chronic Pain: Its Social Dimensions*. Beverly Hills, CA: Sage.

Lillrank, A. (1998) *Living One Day at a Time: Parental Dilemmas of Managing the Experience and the Care of Childhood Cancer (Research Report 89)*. Helsinki: Stakes.

Lock, M. and Dunk, P. (1987) 'My nerves are broken', in D. Coburn, C. D'Arcy, G. Torrance, and P. New (eds), *Health and Canadian Society: Sociological Perspectives*. Toronto: Fitzhenry and Whiteside. pp. 295–313.

Locker, D. (1983) *Disability and Disadvantage: The Consequences of Chronic Illness*. London: Tavistock.

Low, S.M. (1994) 'Embodied metaphors: Nerves as lived experience', in T.J. Csordas (ed.), *Embodiment and Experience: The Existential Ground of Culture and Self*. New York: Cambridge. pp. 295–313.

MacDonald, L. (1988) 'The experience of stigma: Living with rectal cancer', in R. Anderson and M. Bury, (eds), *Living with Chronic Illness*. London: Unwin Hyman. pp. 177–202.

Maines, D.R. (1991) 'The storied nature of health and diabetic self-help groups', in G. Albrecht and J. Levy (eds), *Advances in Medical Sociology*. Vol. 5. Greenwich, CT: JAI. pp. 35–45.

Mairs, N. (1989) *Remembering the Bonehouse: An Erotics of Place and Space*. New York: Harper & Row.

Mairs, N. (1996) *Waisthigh in the World*. Boston: Beacon.

Mathews, H.F., Lannin, D.R., and Mitchell, J.P. (1997) 'Coming to terms with advanced breast cancer: Black women's narratives from Eastern North Carolina', in G.E. Henderson, N.M.P. King, R.P. Strauss, S.E. Estroff, and L.R. Churchill (eds), *The Social Medicine Reader*. Durham, NC: Duke University Press. pp. 43–61.

Mathieson, C.M. and Stam, H.J. (1995) 'Renegotiating identity: Cancer narratives', *Sociology of Health and Illness*, 17: 283–306.

McGuire, M.B. and Kantor, D.J. (1987) 'Belief systems and illness experiences: The case of non-medical healing groups', in J.A. Roth and P. Conrad (eds), *Research in the Sociology of Health Care: The Experience and Management of Chronic Illness*. Vol. 6. Greenwich, CT: JAI pp. 221–48.

Mishler, E.G. (1981) 'The social construction of illness', in E.G. Mishler, L.R. Amara Singham, S.T. Hauser, R. Liem, S.D. Osherson, and N. Waxler (eds), *Social Contexts of Health, Illness & Patient Care*, New York: Cambridge University Press. pp. 141–68.

Mishler, E.G. (1994) 'The struggle between the voice of medicine and the voice of the lifeworld', in P. Conrad and R. Kern (eds) *The Sociology of Health and Illness: Critical Perspectives*. New York: St. Martin's. pp. 288–300.

Mitteness, L.S. (1987a) 'The management of urinary incontinence by community-living elderly'. *Gerontologist*, 27: 185–97.

Mitteness, L.S. (1987b) 'So what do you expect when you're 85?: Urinary incontinence in late life', in J.A. Roth and P. Conrad (eds), *Research in the Sociology of Health Care: The Experience and Management of Chronic Illness*. Vol. 6. Greenwich, CT: JAI. pp. 177–219.

Morgan, D.L. (1982) 'Failing health and the desire for independence: Two conflicting aspects of health care in old age', *Social Problems*, 30: 40–50.

Nijhof, G. (1995) 'Parkinson's disease as a problem of shame in public appearance', *Sociology of Health and Illness*, 17: 193–205.

Olesen, V.L. (1994) 'Problematic bodies: Past, present and future', *Symbolic Interaction*, 17: 231-37.

Parsons, T. (1951). *The Social System*. Glencoe, IL: Free Press.

Peyrot, M., McMurry, J.F. Jr., and Hedges, R. (1988) 'Marital adjustment to adult diabetes: Interpersonal congruence and spouse satisfaction', *Journal of Marriage and the Family*, 50: 363–76.

Pinder, R. (1988) 'Striking balances: Living with Parkinson's Disease', in R. Anderson and M. Bury (eds) *Living with Chronic Illness*. London: Unwin Hyman. pp. 67–88.

Pinder, R. (1992) 'Coherence and incoherence: Doctors' and patients' perspectives on the diagnosis of Parkinson's Disease', *Sociology of Health and Illness*, 14: 1–22.

Plough, A.L. (1986) *Borrowed Time: Artificial Organs and the Politics of Extending Lives*. Philadelphia: Temple University Press.

Radley, A. (1988) *Prospects of Heart Surgery: Psychological Adjustment to Coronary By-Pass Grafting*. New York: Springer.

Radley, A. (1991) *The Body and Social Psychology*. New York: Springer.

Radley, A. (1993) 'The role of metaphor in adjustment to chronic illness', in A. Radley (ed.), *Worlds of Illness*. New York: Routledge. pp. 109–23.

Radley A. and Billig, M. (1996) 'Accounts of illness: Dilemmas and representations', *Sociology of Health and Illness*, 18: 220–40.

Reif, L. (1975) 'Ulcerative colitis: Strategies for managing life', in A.L. Strauss (ed.), *Chronic Illness and the Quality of Life*. St. Louis: Mosby. pp. 81–8.

Robinson, C.A. (1993) 'Managing a life with a chronic condition: The story of normalization', *Qualitative Health Research*, 3: 6–28.

Robinson, D. (1971) *The Process of Becoming Ill*. London: Routledge.

Robinson, I. (1988) *Multiple Sclerosis*. London: Tavistock.

Robinson, I. (1990) 'Personal narratives, social careers and medical courses: Analysing life trajectories in autobiographies of people with multiple sclerosis', *Social Science and Medicine*, 30: 1173–86.

Roth, J.A. (1963) *Timetables*. New York: Bobbs-Merrill.

Sacks, O. (1984). *A Leg to Stand On*. New York: Summit.

Sandstrom, K.L. (1990). 'Confronting deadly disease: The drama of identity construction among gay men with AIDS', *Journal of Contemporary Ethnography*, 19: 271–94.

Scambler, G. (1984) 'Perceiving and coping with stigmatizing illness', in R. Fitzpatrick, J. Hinton, S. Newman, G. Scambler and J. Thompson, *The Experience of Illness*. London: Tavistock. pp. 203–26.

Scambler, G. and Hopkins, A. (1988) 'Accommodating epilepsy in families', in R. Anderson and M. Bury (eds) *Living with Chronic Illness*. London: Unwin Hyman. pp.156–76.

Scarry, E. (1985) *The Body in Pain: The Making and Unmaking of the World*. New York: Oxford University Press.

Scheper-Hughes, N. (1992) *Death Without Weeping*. Berkeley, CA: University of California Press.

Scheper-Hughes, N. and Lock, M. (1987) 'The mindful body: A prolegomenon to future work in medical anthropology', *Medical Anthropology Quarterly*, 1: 6–41.

Schneider, J.W. and Conrad, P. (1980) 'In the closet with illness: Epilepsy, stigma potential, and information control', *Social Problems*, 28: 32–44.

Schneider, J.W. and Conrad, P. (1983) *Having Epilepsy*. Philadelphia: Temple University Press.

Scott, R.A. (1968) *The Making of Blind Men*. New York: Russell Sage.

Singer, E. (1974) 'Premature social aging: The social–psychological consequences of a chronic illness', *Social Science and Medicine*, 8: 143–51.

Smith, J.A. (1996) 'Beyond the divide between cognition and discourse: Using interpretative phenomenological analysis in health psychology', *Psychology and Health*, 11: 261–71.

Sourkes, B.M. (1982) *The Deepening Shade*. Pittsburgh: University of Pittsburgh Press.

Speedling, E.J. (1982) *Heart Attack: The Family Response at Home and in the Hospital*. New York: Tavistock.

Stewart, D.C. and Sullivan, T.J. (1982) 'Illness behavior and the sick role in chronic disease', *Social Science and Medicine*, 16: 1397–404.

Strauss, A. (ed.) (1975) *Chronic Illness and the Quality of Life*. St. Louis: Mosby.

Strauss, A. (1987) *Qualitative Analysis for Social Scientists*. New York: Cambridge University Press.

Strauss, A. and Corbin, J.M. (1990) *Basics of Qualitative Research*. Newbury Park, CA: Sage.

Strauss, A.L., Corbin, J., Fagerhaugh, S., Glaser, B.G., Maines, D., Suczek, B., and Wiener, C.L. (1984) *Chronic Illness and the Quality of Life*. (2nd edn). St. Louis: Mosby.

Telles, J.L. and Pollak, M.H. (1981) 'Feeling sick: The experience and legitimation of illness', *Social Science and Medicine*, 15: 243–51.

Waxler, N.E. (1981) 'Learning to be a leper: A case study in the social construction of illness', in E.G. Mishler, L.R. Amara Singham, S.T. Hauser, R. Liem, S.D. Osherson, and N. Waxler (eds), *Social Contexts of Health, Illness & Patient Care*. New York: Cambridge University Press. pp. 169–94.

Weitz, R. (1991) *Life With AIDS*. New Brunswick, NJ: Rutgers University Press.

Wiener, C.L. (1984) 'The burden of rheumatoid arthritis', in A.L. Strauss, J. Corbin, S. Fagerhaugh, B.G. Glaser, D. Maines, B. Suczek, and C.L. Wiener, (eds) *Chronic Illness and the Quality of Life* (2nd edn). St. Louis: Mosby. pp. 88–98.

Williams, G. (1984) 'The genesis of chronic illness: Narrative reconstruction', *Sociology of Health and Illness*, 6: 175–200.

Williams, G.H. (1993) 'Chronic illness and the pursuit of virtue in everyday life', in A. Radley (ed.), *Worlds of Illness: Biological and Cultural Perspectives on Health and Disease*. London: Routledge. pp. 92–108.

Williams, R.G.A. (1981a) 'Logical analysis as a qualitative method. I. Themes in old age and chronic illness', *Sociology of Health and Illness*, 3: 140–64.

Williams, R.G.A. (1981b) 'Logical analysis as a qualitative method. II. Conflict of ideas and the topic of illness', *Sociology of Health and Illness*, 3: 165–87.

2.7

The Global Emergence of Disability

GARY L. ALBRECHT AND LOIS M. VERBRUGGE

INTRODUCTION

Disability is a major contemporary theme in health policy and programs, and a commonplace experience in people's lives. Its rise in public attention and personal experience is due to several factors: increases in life expectancy and thus rising lifetime chances of chronic illness and dysfunction, interventions that extend the lives of disabled persons, environmental exposures and unhealthy lifestyles, organized advocacy on behalf of disabled persons, and expanded social and political definitions of disability (Institute of Medicine, Board on International Health 1997; LaPlante and Carlson 1995). In contrast to several decades ago, people are likely to encounter disabled persons in public places, to have a disabled family member or friend, and to experience disability themselves. The financial and social welfare burdens of disability are rising for many communities and countries (DeParle 1997; Georges 1997). Disability has seized the attention of government officials, is prompting scientific research in disciplines from medicine to sociology, and is generating interest in the lay population.

This chapter addresses disability in a global context. It considers disability in its worldwide presence, noting differences in definitions, social acceptance, and political impetus across countries. First, we discuss the multiple definitions of disability that exist in any society and across societies. Second, we discuss causes and prevalences of disability across countries. Third, we note how sociocultural forces help produce disability. Fourth, we discuss the main kinds of societal response to disability in the world, and

fifth, the ensuing personal and interpersonal meanings of disability. Sixth, we turn to features of disability policy in modern and developing economies. Lastly, we suggest future trends in disability advocacy, policy, and research.

DISABILITY DEFINITIONS

What is disability? Like the concepts of health and illness, disability is difficult to define and operationalize. A generic feature is a person's difficulty in performing a task or activity because of an underlying physical or mental dysfunction. However, the particular difficulties and the specific tasks are varied, and the ways of evaluating difficulty are diverse as well. In the disability literature, there are many theoretical models, legal definitions, health and social service agency definitions, and politically correct and socially common terminologies (Albrecht 1997a). All of these refer to the same general concept (disability), but they vary considerably from each other depending on ideology, cultural setting, and intended use (Bury 1997).

In this section, we consider several arenas of definitions: historical and traditional, modernist, professional, government, statistical, and scholarly.

Historical and Traditional

Historical definitions of disability emphasized abnormality, deviance, and the inability of people to fit into society or perform expected roles. Disability was a defining social status. It was intertwined with being poor, marginal, deviant, sick, and jobless. It was a terrible thing, and people with it were to be ignored and exiled from regular society.

As modern medicine emerged in the nineteenth century, what we will call the traditional view replaced the historical one and became dominant. The traditional definition stated that disability came about because of illness or other organic abnormality. Disability was thus 'inside' the person. It was a personal characteristic in the same way as age or socioeconomic status. Diseases and injuries with very high chances of disability were named 'disabilities.'

In countries with modern medical establishments, acceptable disabilities were spinal cord injury, cerebral palsy, multiple sclerosis, deafness, blindness, congestive heart failure, schizophrenia, and severe depression. This focus on a limited set of conditions (with typically severe dysfunctions) penetrated the thinking of many countries, especially those associated with European cultures. The frequently disabling conditions of sub-Saharan Africa, India, China, and the Middle East – malnutrition, diarrhea, malaria, tuberculosis, communicable childhood diseases – were excluded from the roster. Gradually, the Western view has broadened to include a larger list of conditions, with moderate chances of and degrees of dysfunction. However, little room is still allowed for dysfunctions due to conditions deemed ambiguous by the medical profession, such as multiple chemical sensitivities, undetermined low back pain, severe stuttering, chronic fatigue, and psychological stress (Crossley and Crossley 1998; Hydén and Sachs 1998), and the tendency to name disability by its instigating disease or injury, as opposed to on its own terms, persists.

Modernist

In the Western world, dissatisfaction with the medical model has risen in recent decades. New premises for disability emerged, emphasizing the importance that minority group membership, social attitudes, rehabilitation, environmental, and political economics have in the definition and experience of disability. Societal causes of disability became the focus (and sometimes the sole focus, discounting any medical origins at all). New models concentrate on the social construction of disability, personal experiences of disability, consumer empowerment, types and availability of government benefits, and the effects of physical and cultural environment on the individual (Albrecht 1997b, Finkelstein 1993; Oliver 1990). These models stress the power of forces external to

the individual (that is, extrinsic rather than intrinsic) for defining disability and shaping disabled persons' lives.

Proponents of social models are often publicly forceful; they are suspicious that nondisabled persons have no suitable notions or perceptions on the topic. How can people without the personal experience of disability be sensitive to the disability world? Debates that counterpose medically oriented and socially oriented models are often very heated, not just for reasons of intellectual difference, but also for reasons of experience credentials.

Professional

No matter what definitions researchers and scholars are debating, it is physicians and policymakers whose definitions most influence the lives of persons with disabilities. Physicians are the first (and sometimes sadly the last) professionals to see and evaluate disabled people and make recommendations about therapies. Further, physicians decide a patient's official disability status for government disability programs, and thus the denial of or access to benefits for them (Albrecht 1992; Blaxter 1976; Stone 1984). The physician is given and maintains these powers because the medical, inside-the-individual model of disability is the paradigm still accepted by most governments. Our real-world programs still operate on medical terms.

Government

Governmental definitions align closely with the medical model. Eligibility criteria for work disability benefits are now based mainly on a person's medical status, with secondary attention to job-relevant dysfunctions. Historically, disability benefits were provided first to those members of society deemed to be most valuable, such as veterans of foreign wars, merchant seamen, railroad workers, and those employed in nationally important industries. Contemporary government programs have expanded from these categorical definitions to broader ones based on health conditions, their expected duration, and their severity.

In any particular country, one will find a potpourri of government definitions. They are tailored to fit particular programs and their political or financial agendas. Program definitions are made and modified in isolation from other programs. The United States government has about fifty specific definitions of disability attached to social programs (Bickenbach 1993; Domzel 1995; Percy 1992). For example, the

Americans with Disabilities Act of 1990 states that: 'The term "disability" means, with respect to the individual – (a) a physical or mental impairment that substantially limits one or more of the major life activities of such an individual, (b) a record of such an impairment, or (c) being regarded as having such an impairment (42 USC 12101(2)). The Internal Revenue Service code reads: 'An individual is permanently and totally disabled if he is unable to engage in any substantial gainful activity by reasons of any medical determinable physical or mental impairment which can be expected to result in death or which has lasted or can be expected to last for a continuous period of not less than 12 months. An individual shall not be considered to be permanently disabled unless he furnishes proof of the existence thereof in such form and manner, and at such times, as the Secretary may require' (28 USC &22(e)(3)). In Great Britain, under the Disability Discrimination Act of 1995, 'a disability is defined as either a physical or a mental impairment, which has a substantial and long-term adverse effect on a person's ability to carry out normal day-to-day activities' (s. 1 (1) (Gooding 1996: 10). Governmental definitions are very sticky because they are stated in laws and statutes. Even when interagency groups proclaim the need for more consistency and integration of definitions, it rarely happens.

Governments in developing countries face the tough problem of developing definitions suitable to their own societies and needs. Disability models developed in the West were transported to the rest of the world without much attention to different health problems and cultural viewpoints. For example, spinal cord injury (SCI) programs are a prominent feature in Western countries and are promoted elsewhere, but they seldom exist in developing countries. The reasons are compelling: the services are prohibitively expensive; people with SCI usually die within several years because of pressure sores and urinary tract infections; they are kept entirely at home by their families. In this setting, spinal cord injury is not judged to be a disability warranting prominent national attention. As another example, some conditions rare in the West are common elsewhere. In the Brazilian Amazon where malaria is endemic, having serious malaria symptoms does not excuse one from the performance of daily roles because 'everyone has it' (World Resources Institute 1998). Lastly, activities that figure so strongly in disability evaluations in the West, such as reduced ability to work, inability to brush one's teeth, or need for help dressing, lose their relevance and heft in rural and developing economies. Without options for government

assistance, workers with low back pain may continue working without complaint despite great pain. Personal cleanliness may have lower value, and having someone's assistance for disability may be expected and nonembarrassing. It is easy for Western health officials and scholars to forget that most of the world's population lives under very different circumstances than their own. What other societies consider socially important dysfunctions may be quite different than those in EuroAmerica.

Statistical

Despite the imbedded stance of government policies, the importance of social factors is percolating into government thinking and statistics! The transformation is very evident in the disability classification scheme sponsored by the World Health Organization (WHO). The International Classification of Impairments, Disabilities and Handicaps (ICIDH) framework was developed to encourage medical professionals and health statisticians to pay more attention to disability in client data and published statistics. The first version, published in 1980, considered health problems as the launching point of disability, but paid detailed attention to classifying types of disabilities and disadvantages that can ensue (World Health Organization 1980; see also Grimby et al. 1988). In ICIDH 1980, impairment is defined as structural or functional abnormality resulting from injury or disease. Disability is restriction in an individual's ability to perform activities of daily living like washing, eating, bathing, walking, and lifting objects. Here at last, disabilities are named by the task/role problem people have, not by the condition they have. Handicap refers to social disadvantage that can occur due to impairment or disability. Bringing the notion of disadvantage into equal status with impairment and disability was an especially bold step.

However, ICIDH 1980 ran into swift trouble with social-model advocates, who said the scheme still kept disability 'inside' the individual, insinuating that it belongs to and is caused within the person. They claimed it did not pay sufficient attention to constraints in the external environment such as steep steps, transportation barriers, job discrimination, and negative public attitudes. The sharpest critics of ICIDH 1980 said that disability is entirely a social or community product, and that features of social, physical, and cultural environment are the sole causes of disability. By excluding medical causes altogether, they set the battle lines tightly 'for' and 'against' use of the classification. Furthermore, there were obvious inconsistencies, overlaps, and omissions in ICIDH 1980, and this diminished its appreciation in professional and scientific circles.

An international group is preparing a new version of ICIDH in the 1990s. The worldwide enterprise assures that the product will have good cultural coverage of disabilities and broadly acceptable terminology. Following strong opinions that disability should not have negative or pejorative terms, the ICIDH-2 is named International Classification of Impairments, Activities, and Participation (World Health Organization 1997). Its approach is to maintain impairments as functional and structural problems at the body/mind level, to delineate activities as simple tasks and abilities at the person level, to have participation reflect engagement in social roles, and to name contextual factors (environment) that facilitate or impede participation. Inconsistencies that peppered the first version are being remedied. In short, ICIDH-2 is a sophisticated classification that takes both medical and social factors into account. By the year 2000, there will be a fine-quality classification scheme with worldwide relevance available for use in public health statistics, research, and client records.

Scholarly

Disability theory is also moving towards a blend of medical and social perspectives. A theoretical stance that is rapidly gaining scholarly ground is that disability is the gap between personal capabilities and environmental demands (Brandt and Pope 1997; Verbrugge 1990; Verbrugge and Jette 1994). This mismatch makes it difficult or impossible for someone to do a particular activity. Is the person the cause of disability? No. Is environment the cause of disability? No. The cause lies in their interaction for a given activity, but if it is an 'interaction' or 'gap', is disability then unmeasurable? No, it is very measurable. Asking people about their difficulty in doing a task or measuring their performance objectively, or asking a professional, spouse, or other person to evaluate it, are all apt techniques to measure disability. A great contribution of the person–environment approach is its balanced perspective of remedies for disability. Remedies can aim at fixing the person (medical orientation), or fixing the environment (social orientation), or both. Medical strategies aim to boost capability and environmental ones to reduce demand. Success of either sort reduces disability, making it easier to accomplish a task.

Scholars note that definitions of disability are complicated by the nature of disability itself. Disability is often multiple and usually dynamic.

Multiplicity

It is unusual to find someone with a single, static disabling condition or just one enduring activity limitation. Disabilities occur in sets of inter-related physical and mental conditions that mutually affect each other. In established market economies, for example, people with low vision may also have diabetes, congestive heart failure, and a high level of personal stress resulting from living with the other conditions. In less developed economies, people with low vision often also have malnutrition, diarrheal diseases, heart disease, malaria, or major depression (Murray and Lopez 1996a). The cause of low vision may be different (macular degeneration or an accident in the first case, and river blindness in the second), and the environments and resources to deal with the disability may be quite dissimilar.

Dynamics

Degree of difficulty performing a task can rise or fall over time due to flare-ups of the underlying condition, therapeutic and rehabilitation success, reduction in personal standards for doing the task, and plenty of other factors. In the short run, disability is often characterized by an ebb and flow of good days and bad days (Charmaz 1991). Chronic illnesses and disability are also life course events. They demand social transitions that behaviorally alter and redefine activities, self-definition, and goals. A life course view of disability focuses attention on personal and disease trajectories, timing, critical events, and sequences in the disability process (Albrecht and Levy 1991; Strauss and Glaser 1975). In this context, aging and disability are two inter-related social experiences. The time of onset and the present stage in the life course also dramatically affect the impact of the condition (Verbrugge and Jette 1994).

CAUSES AND DISTRIBUTION OF DISABILITY

Disability has always existed in human society, but it is more publicly apparent today because of mass media, increasing numbers of laws, the presence of disabled people in public places, and growing awareness of disability in Asia, Africa, Latin America, and the Middle East.

Until recently, there was no truly global presentation of the epidemiology of disability. Most statistical literature was country-specific or had comparisons of several Western nations

(Osmond and Barker 1991; Pope and Tarlov 1991; Shiraishi and Arimoto 1982). This situation changed when the World Health Organization and World Bank recognized that the burden of disability in emerging and developed nations had serious implications for worldwide economic development, human rights, and quality of life. In 1992, the two agencies launched the Global Burden of Disease Study, designed to (a) develop internally consistent estimates of mortality from 107 major causes of death for the world and eight geographic regions, (b) estimate the incidence, prevalence, duration, and case fatality for 483 disabling sequelae resulting from those causes of death, (c) ascertain the fractions of mortality and disability attributable to ten major risk factors, and (d) generate projection scenarios of mortality and disability for the year 2020 (Murray and Lopez 1996b: 740). All calculations were prepared by age, sex, and region. To have comparable findings across regions, the research group developed a composite measure called the disability-adjusted life year (DALY). It is the sum of years of life lost from premature mortality plus years of life with disability, adjusted for severity of disability (Murray and Lopez

1996a). The DALY work is part of a larger movement among epidemiologists, economists, and demographers to characterize active life years and health-related quality of life. These concepts were proposed to estimate the expected remaining years of functional well-being, independence, or general well-being in an individual or population (Katz et al. 1983). The architects of these concepts and measures argue that healthful environments and behaviors can postpone disability and compress it into the last years of life (Vita et al. 1998). In this context, DALYs measure the years of active life lost to disability.

In the world overall, the three leading causes of DALYs in 1990 were lower respiratory infections, diarrheal diseases, and conditions related to the perinatal period (Table 1). The study is attentive to the importance of not just physical health problems, but also mental health ones – unipolar major depression proves to be a prominent cause of disability. With respect to risk factors, it is remarkable that the global burden of disease attributable to physical inactivity, especially in Western countries, is nearly equal to that of hypertension (Murray and Lopez 1996b). Projections were made about shifts in

Table 1   Change in rank order of DALYs for the fifteen leading causes, World 1990–2020

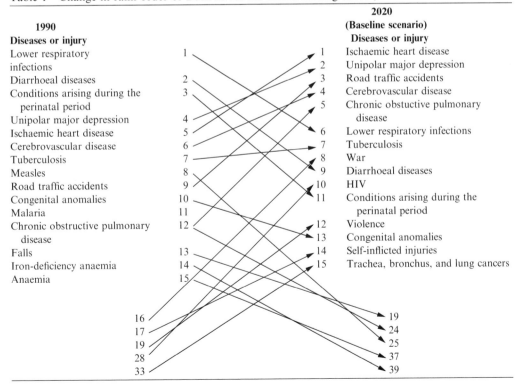

Source: Murray and Lopez (1996a), p. 375.

disability causes from 1990 to 2020. Infectious and communicable diseases, malnutrition, and poor sanitary conditions are expected to come increasingly under control, so the top five causes of DALYs in 2020 are anticipated to be ischemic heart disease, unipolar major depression, road traffic accidents, cerebrovascular disease, and chronic obstructive pulmonary disease. The pulmonary and respiratory conditions will be the outcome of this century's epidemic of tobacco-related diseases. Extrinsic conditions (road traffic accidents, war, violence, and self-inflicted injuries) are expected to play a larger role in disability, as well as this century's newest major disease, HIV/AIDS.

There are considerable differences across regions in the prevalence and causes of disability. Disability prevalence is highest in sub-Saharan Africa and lowest in market economies, without large differences between men and women in either instance (Murray and Lopez 1997). In wealthy regions, almost 90 per cent of disability is caused by noncommunicable diseases and injuries. The chances of disability increase with age and cumulative risk exposure (see also Guralnik et al. 1996; Vita et al. 1998). In poorer regions, however, nearly half of disability is due to infectious and childhood diseases and injuries. In these countries there is a high risk of disability for the young as well as the old.

Depending on how disability is measured, about 12–15 per cent of the world's population is disabled (Albrecht 1997b; United Nations 1992). This means that 846 million people will be disabled in the year 2000, with 80 per cent of them living in developing countries (300 million in Asia, 50 million in Africa, 34 million in Latin America). The number will continue to rise due especially to aging populations, environmental exposure, and social violence.

Disability is not a desirable social feature, and many countries strive to export it. Corporations and governments have moved much of their 'dirty work' off shore, so that risks of occupational illness and injury are shifted to persons in developing countries. For example, Nike athletic shoes are made in factories in Indonesia and Vietnam where wages are low and work conditions are often disabling (Bloomberg News 1998). The chemical release in Bohpal that killed and disabled hundreds of workers and community residents is an instance of dangerous production facilities being located in nonmodern economies. Further, international pharmaceutical companies and national medical research institutes of Western countries have often undertaken their more risky clinical trials in the Third World, where death or disability will not produce the same outcry and lawsuits as they will at home (Angell 1997; Barry and Molyneux

1992; Wardman 1997). When these pharmaceutical companies do develop vaccines, antibiotics, and prophylactic drugs for conditions like malaria, HIV/AIDS, diphtheria, and sexually transmitted diseases, they often price them at unaffordable levels or insist on pre-payment in hard currency (Garrett 1994; Scripps Howard News Service 1998). Such actions virtually guarantee that disability risk and experience is thrust upon the Third World or on those who cannot pay for treatment.

Within countries, known disability risks are also aimed toward the working classes, illegal immigrants, undocumented workers, and the poor. Disability is often associated with powerlessness, disenfranchisement, and poverty (Handler and Hasenfeld 1997). In the United States, garment sweatshops discovered recently in Manhattan and South Carolina were staffed with undocumented deaf Mexican workers. Immigrants from the Magreb (in France) and from Turkey (in Germany) work at risky jobs that nationals will not take; women and children are often found in the highest-risk and lowest-pay jobs. In all of these instances, wealthy people with influence have moved disability risk to poor people without it.

DISABILITY AS A SOCIAL AND CULTURAL PRODUCT

A nation's culture, political economy, environment, social structure, and history affect the kinds of disabilities that are produced, defined, and dealt with (Albrecht 1992).

- In the Western world, where strenuous recreation is fashionable, news of disabling injuries from mountain climbing, car racing, and long distance running is common. Sports medicine and sports rehabilitation facilities are found throughout the United States and other recreation-avid countries. Consider how different the next example is.
- Until recently, Kenyans were more likely to suffer disabling injuries from elephants and other wild animals than from automobile or industrial accidents; this was viewed as a high disability risk. By contrast, dysfunctions due to malaria (endemic in the rural countryside) were discounted because they were so commonplace, and no matter what disabilities and causes pertained, the nation lacked an accessible, integrated rehabilitation system to treat and support disabled people.
- Throughout the world, the causes and definitions of disability keep changing as risks, social roles and leisure pursuits, and public

attitudes change. Landmine accidents and civil/regional wars have become a significant cause of disability for people in Iran, Iraq, Afghanistan, Cambodia, Vietnam, and Sri Lanka. Reduced lung function due to smoking, diabetes, and heart conditions is a rising cause of restricted work, social life, and leisure in Great Britain, Germany, and the United States.

Three specific ways in which society and its participants powerfully shape disability are now discussed: social inclusion, social distancing, and the built and physical environment.

Social Inclusion

Disability has long been linked with social inclusion and exclusion (Bessis 1995). Stiker (1982) discusses how these forces operated in France over the past three centuries. Who is a citizen and who is not? Who should be allowed to live a regular social life and who should be taken away? In eighteenth-century France, disabled persons were those with leprosy, deformity, and profound mental illness. Disabled persons were also migrants, gypsies, vagabonds, and homeless persons, who were seen as a threat to the established social order. Strongly influenced by the Catholic Church, French health authorities institutionalized these people in large Parisian hospitals and released them only when they were no longer deemed as social threats. The authorities' power was illustrated by their insistence that *les exclus* renounce Protestant or Jewish beliefs and convert to Catholicism before receiving treatment. Castel (1995) points out that disaffiliation from established communities and economic vulnerability – for whatever reason – puts people at high risk of being labeled 'disabled' and a member of *les exclus*. In France, the ultimate issue was full citizenship, and disabled persons were not eligible. This historical background colors how *les handicapés* are defined and treated today in France. Disabled people often have adequate social welfare benefits but still feel treated as something other than members of their society (Ravaud et al. 1997).

Social Distancing

Interactions of nondisabled persons with disabled persons are influenced by diverse motives (Moscovici 1997). Why do people give money to disabled persons? Studies of helping behavior found that Italians give money to the poor and disabled to avoid a curse or the 'evil eye,' or with the belief that such gifts prevent having disability themselves. In the United States, people give money to keep disabled persons at a distance, achieve income tax relief, and reaffirm their moral values. Thus, a particular behavior toward disabled persons can spring from diverse cultural motivations.

Built and Physical Environment

Public architecture is a powerful, ostensibly impersonal way to permit disabled persons entry to some places and to impede their entry to others (Imrie 1996). Governments, schools, businesses, and factories all make decisions about initial design and later renovation that influence access. For example, social security and welfare offices, medical and rehabilitation facilities, and some public transportation are accessible, but court houses, high government officials, and educational institutions are often flanked by architectural barriers that serve literally and symbolically to distance disabled people from opportunities for advancement. The built environment is a visible arena for access, but the physical environment can cause just as much impediment. The miserable air quality in airplanes reduces the ability of persons with lung conditions, multiple chemical sensitivities, and immune system problems to travel, and compromises their well-being and health if they do. Cold dry winters can 'ground' people with chronic obstructive lung disease, and dryness in their residences can jeopardize breathing and reduce activity.

RESPONSES TO DISABILITY

Four general societal approaches to disability have emerged worldwide: social exclusion, financial constraint, medical causation, and social causation. The list is in order of traditional to modern stances; emphases on finances, medicine, and social construction represent ever-more-modern views. Several approaches can coexist in a country, but one of them tends to have preeminence. In any era and society, it is hard to eliminate the first approach (social exclusion) entirely, but fine legislation, mass media, and advocacy can lessen it.

Social Exclusion

The social exclusion ('out of sight, out of mind') approach is still very prevalent in the world. Historically, in Western societies, disabled people were cared for in their homes by their families, or they lived on the streets as beggars and homeless (Bungener 1995). Social exclusion remains prevalent in resource-poor countries of all kinds. In others, with modern economies, architectural barriers and social distaste still impede access for persons with physical or mobility problems. In Paris, individuals with spinal cord injury (SCI) are infrequently seen on the streets or at worksites because they often live on upper floors of buildings without elevators. Despite receiving disability benefits from the state and living on their own, they cannot easily go out or find jobs in accessible places. In Mexico, social access for SCI persons is even more constricted because of lower social benefits and family 'protection.' In many ways social exclusion is economical to a society. If disabled people are publicly invisible they are seldom in others' consciousness or moral landscape. This fundamental economy has given exclusion its enduring heft across time and space.

Financial Constraint

The financial constraint ('we cannot afford to recognize disability') approach appears in many different forms. Although disability has public knowledge and sympathy, there are inadequate financial and capital resources to help. (a) In poor agricultural countries disabled people are found in every village, but the local government has no resources to assist them. Disabled people either subsist on the support of their families and villagers or become sick and die. In larger towns and cities there are insufficient jobs, and this prevents government officials from developing employment programs for disabled persons. (b) Even in countries with well-established disability benefits programs, government officials watch the 'rolls' carefully to avoid swelling clienteles and expenses. Eligibility criteria are kept as-is unless legal action forces expansion. Disabilities due to new diseases (viruses, environmental exposures, protracted stress) wait in the wings for decades before being accepted as legitimate criteria for benefits (Studdert and Brennan 1997). (c) In all countries, refugees and illegal immigrants are the last to be considered for formal assistance, yet they often enter with disabilities or work and live in milieux that pose high risks (Choquet and Richard 1990). In short, public awareness may seem like a step forward from social exclusion, but the two approaches stick together very well and provide a double-barreled rationale (one social, the other governmental) for inattention to disabled persons.

Medical Causation

The medical causation approach emerged in countries with national monetary resources and modern medical structures. Physicians are trained to detect and diagnose pathologies and to provide therapies that reduce or halt them. Rehabilitation is less preferred (being slower in its effects), dependent on long-term patient motivation, and requiring interaction with other professionals (such as physical therapists). As medical specialization increased, the emphasis on medical therapies became entrenched. For individuals with chronic problems and dysfunctions expected to last many years or even a lifetime, the medical approach proved frustrating and demeaning. Disabled people felt viewed as biological material rather than whole social individuals. Insightful physicians have pointed out the dehumanizing aspects of modern medicine to their peers for a long time (see Blackwell (1890) 1995), but to no widespread avail. New diagnostic techniques (genetic screening, DNA mapping, HIV testing) are praised for their sophistication, but that sophistication is solely biological and provides no indication of disease consequences for the individual (Nelkin and Tancredi 1989). This is troublesome enough for persons with acute conditions and short-term limitations, but deeply awry for those with long-standing disabilities. They need a person-centered approach with comprehensive evaluation and care for physical, mental, and psychosocial aspects of their lives (Barbour 1995).

The medical approach has indeed dramatically altered the lives of disabled persons by reducing pain, averting common sequelae (secondary conditions), and extending life. Several medical specialties have even emerged that concentrate on disability (e.g., rehabilitation medicine) or whole-person treatment (e.g., geriatrics), but overall, the medical model has kept power in the hands of professionals who underplay the personal knowledge and insights disabled persons have, their needs for respect and social integration, and their wholeness of body, mind, and spirit.

Social Causation

The social causation model is a reaction to the medical one. In its purest form, activists and scholars claim that disability has nothing to do with a person's disease or impairment, but instead is entirely created by societal barriers and attitudes. Social causation models are evolving with variant forms in Great Britain, North America, Europe, and Australasia (see Barnes and Mercer 1996; Barton and Oliver 1997; Davis 1997; Ferguson et al. 1992; Hales 1996). The social model is proving to be an important political tool for mobilization and public action and also serves as the foundation for the academic field of disability studies. This model represents a paradigm shift from emphasis on an individual's disease, illness, and impairment to focus on social, cultural, political, and economic factors that produces exclusion, physical and social barriers, discrimination, and powerlessness for disabled people (Priestly 1998). Social models of disability are constructed on the principle that 'disability is a socially mediated state not a fixed attribute of the individual' (Gill 1998: 8). The goal is not to intervene to correct individual impairments and defects, but instead to alter social, built, and physical environments so that disabled people can achieve their goals and have autonomy. Political emphasis is on the rights of disabled people to participate in all domains of social life, and to modify environments and attitudes to achieve that.

A blend of medical and social models is advocated by many public health officials and scientists. They say that similar attention must be paid to environmental/societal and medical factors for both the causes and remedies of disability. This blending is respectful to all professions engaged in disability evaluation and remedy, and it offers a wider base for scholarship and public health programs. Disability studies programs are being created in universities, with strong social sciences emphasis, but also with ties to clinical medicine and allied health.

Personal and Interpersonal Meanings of Disability

Disability is a master status. It is a personal identity, which if recognized, shapes entire social worlds for individuals and their family, friends, and acquaintances. Demographic characteristics, such as sex, race/ethnicity, marital status, and social class, can add additional burdens to the disability experience by creating multiple restrictions in resources and opportunities. Women, minorities, and poor persons have far more difficulty than others in dealing with disability, because of less education, lower income, fewer job opportunities, less health insurance, and discrimination. For example, women in India and Bangladesh suffer downward mobility if they are household head and/or disabled (Charlton 1998). Self-respect is hard to develop for youngsters with early-onset disability, and difficult to maintain for middle-aged and older persons with late-onset disability. Self-help groups are a fine buttress and can be a launching place for new assertive identity. Advocacy groups demand that disabled people be called on by organizations to help define disability and design programs (Oliver 1992).

What is, or is not, considered a disability influences how disabled people view themselves and are treated by others (Bérubé 1997). In most countries and communities, some disabilities are more acceptable than others. For example, in the former Soviet Union, being a male veteran with spinal cord injury from the Battle of Leningrad is more acceptable than a woman with AIDS due to prostitution. In Great Britain, having a traumatic brain injury is more acceptable than longtime undiagnosable chronic fatigue syndrome. Even when a disability (disabling condition) is generally acceptable, there is considerable confusion about expectations for the disabled persons and general public who encounter them. A key problem is that evaluations in professional settings rarely tap critical details of real life. People may pass functional tests for home-based activities in a clinic setting, but be unable to do tasks at home because of structural barriers. Similarly, they may pass tests of work-based activities but be unable to work for an 8-hour stretch or from one day to the next. Exacerbating this matter, disabled persons often report they are held to higher standards and monitored more closely for performance than nondisabled persons!

Cultural representations of disabled people are reflected in language. There is considerable current debate in international and national settings about the terminology for referring to people with disabilities. In Britain, many people in the disability community and wider public use 'disabled people' to signify the social nature and community context of disability. In France, *les handicaps* is used to emphasize the corporeal integrity of the individual, environmental limitations, and ability to work. In the United States, 'persons with disabilities' is preferred to underscore that the individual has whole worth and integrity; he happens to have a disability, but this does not mean incompleteness. In this chapter, we follow the prevalent convention used in Britain, 'disabled people,' to accentuate the social model of disability. Overall, a common goal of current discussion is replacement of negative wordings with neutral or positive ones. This is sometimes almost infeasible to accomplish linguistically, but the forces of 'political correctness' are immense at this point of history.

DISABILITY POLICY

Key themes of social policies and programs developed by governments to address disability are: income support benefits, rehabilitation programs, provision of technical and personal assistance, special residences or educational programs, and civil rights. (a) Western countries have developed and modified policies throughout the twentieth century, and theirs are now extensive and detailed. Western countries watch each others' experience with disability programs closely, hoping to learn things that can make their own programs more efficient and economical. Occasionally, major overhauls are made (for example, recently in the work disability programs of Great Britain and The Netherlands) without much empirical or comparative basis, but driven by intense needs for reduced costs and efficient evaluations. (b) Rural agriculture-based countries have a small portfolio of policies and programs, often simpler forms of Western ones, but sometimes very distinctive to their own culture and history. Those with a strong ethos of family responsibility tend to have small-scale disability programs, existing as a last resort for disabled persons without family supports.

Disability policies and programs are hard to maintain in situations of social chaos. Regional and ethnic wars predictably result in many disabled persons, not only from the conflict itself, but from ensuing malnutrition, communicable diseases, and remnant war devices (landmines, bombs). The increased population of disabled persons consists of civilians, combatants, and refugees. They face compromised systems of care. Such swollen needs for disability support can sink an otherwise adequate program. In short, peace and economic stability buttress disability policies and programs, allowing them to do their job and carefully change. Wars have the opposite effect, especially in countries with weaker social program infrastructure and resources.

From the perspective of disabled persons, interventions are best when based on local realities and culture. (a) Low-technology devices have had great success in developing countries. An example is the Jaipur foot prosthesis (McGirk 1997). This artificial limb is light and durable, is suitable for use in rice paddies, and is acceptable in societies where people are barefoot indoors. It can be made for $28 and in 45 minutes with scrap metal and vulcanized rubber. The prosthesis is now seen throughout Afghanistan, giving mobility to persons who lost limbs from landmine explosions. (b) Disability prevention in developing countries probably takes its best shape in literacy, general education, and job training programs. Education increases opportunities for choice and social advancement, and it steers people away from exposure to risks in low-pay jobs and from involvement in civil unrest. Bringing jobs to local areas reduces people's urge to migrate to crowded, unsanitary conditions in large cities.

In the West and former socialist countries of Europe, three policy issues now have the attention of the public and government: the environment, the shape and future of social welfare systems, and migration.

Environment

Responsibility for prevention and treatment of disability, and efficacy of interventions, are the essential environmental issues. Is primary prevention of disability a responsibility of the government at all, or is it the sole responsibility of individuals, who (apparently) 'choose' their own risks? Which is more economical for public expenditure; altering physical, built, and social environments to enhance access for disabled persons, or expanding rehabilitation programs for them? Does universal design – designing things to help all persons, whether nondisabled or disabled – have a good pay-off for preventing disability? These issues inspire not just scholarly and policy debate, but also professional self-interest (Ratzka 1992). The medical profession is a powerful, large business in Western countries, and is becoming more so in the former socialist ones (Percy 1992). Reimbursement potential is increasing medicine's interest in disability despite its longstanding reluctance to deal with functional consequences of disease. But for-profit milieux still limit health professionals' commitment to disability, pushing them to treat specific episodes rather than planning for holistic and continuous care. A disabled person's ability to pay (either directly with income or insurance, or indirectly through government health and welfare benefits) still figures in quality of rehabilitation care and assistance in integrating into the community.

Social Welfare

The structure of social welfare systems is a topic of great debate in most advanced economies. While most of the countries are democratic, the flavor of democracy varies considerably from one to another. At issue is the perceived social contract between citizens and government. The 'rugged individualist' value system of the United States relies heavily on individual insurance and charitable contributions from the private sector, in contrast to France, where government's fundamental responsibility to its citizens is a deeply held value. Many Americans think that the French are naïve in avoiding the consequences of free market realities. By contrast, the French think that American democracy brutalizes the poor and needy and deprives part of its population from basic human rights while preaching such values to other countries. Both perspectives highlight critical issues in disability policy. What is the social contract between government and citizens, and who is willing to pay for it? What is the minimum standard that every individual can expect, and how much support is morally enough? Should benefits serve as income supports or simply pay for medical/rehabilitation services? Should benefits be coupled with incentives or requirements for rehabilitation to draw disabled persons toward productive social activity? Should employers be encouraged or required to reserve jobs for disabled persons (especially in economies with high unemployment rates)? What is a reasonable accommodation in public places and worksites? These are immense questions that pit social values against public finances, and whose answers have long-term implications for taxes borne by individuals, families, and businesses.

Migration

Persons in need often move to a country, state, or region with better social benefits and work opportunities than their origin place. This occurs both in stable societies (because national programs often permit specific local implementations) and in unstable ones (disrupted by wars and droughts at home or nearby). This rational decision can have a backlash. Discrimination often results when the newcomers are numerous and perceived as freeloaders. Those with privilege frequently react to such migration by discriminating against and excluding newcomers, especially the poorest. Stresses on the public purse and public attitudes end up changing disability policies and rehabilitation (Bickenbach 1993). The French debate over exclusion of undocumented workers, foreigners on welfare, and disabled persons is indicative of this process (Gros-Jean and Padieu 1995). In the United States, the minority group and civil rights arguments behind the Americans with Disabilities Act, and more recent discussions of disability as 'human variation,' reflect attempts to bring disabled people into public places and consciousness (Scotch and Schriner 1997).

In sum, disability policy is a litmus test for a society's overarching human values. It is one signal of how a nation values and treats its minority and disadvantaged groups (Walzer 1997). Written policies do speak louder than fine rhetoric and espoused values.

THE FUTURE OF GLOBAL DISABILITY

As the world population continues to grow in size and to age, the pressures of disability will rise in advanced market economies and still more in developing countries, where aging occurs rapidly when birth rates fall. Disability poses a variety of political problems for governments such as using public resources, managing welfare programs, controlling population flows, and accepting high-risk businesses. In developed countries, the main issues now are the eligibility rules for disability benefits programs to keep current and future payments in tow, the civil rights of disabled persons and programs to enhance access, regional/state differences in welfare benefits, and illegal and legal immigration of persons for low-paying high-risk jobs. In developing countries, the main issues are control of infectious and communicable diseases that cause long-term disability, reduction of inhumane work conditions, management of land resources and drought, and reduction of ethnic and regional wars.

We discuss seven themes that will influence disability policies and experience in coming decades: technology, community residence of disabled persons, advocacy, social acceptance, links between aging and disability, open discussion of moral issues, and research.

Technology

The importance of technology for alleviating disability is of rising interest throughout the world. Business and governments are taking greater interest in the development and widespread availability of low-cost prosthetic and mobility-enhancing devices. While development of high-technology rehabilitation is important for helping profoundly disabled persons, it is unaffordable for most countries and helps few rather than many disabled persons. Emphasis on universal design in architecture and community planning will increase, justified by the fact that it lets everyone operate in a more user-friendly environment.

Community Residence

The concepts of independent living and autonomy for disabled persons will increase, first in developed countries where public resources can assist these values, and later in developing countries. Tailored individual care programs will also increase. Services for older persons and disabled persons will gradually be integrated, both for cost-savings and because the great majority of disabled persons are/will be elderly. National policies and commitments will be important to these efforts, but local communities will provide great creativity. Teamwork of community groups, local government officials, and local employers will fashion community-wide programs that suit the specific needs and goals of disabled residents.

Advocacy

The disability community is becoming increasingly united, visible, and international. The impetus generated by the British and American disability communities in successfully advocating human-rights-oriented disability legislation will be influential in stimulating advocates in other nations to push for similar laws and programs. Information access and communication ease via the Internet and World Wide Web is rapidly helping disability scholars and officials develop international ties and discuss ideas.

Social Acceptance

As more people experience disability themselves, public attitudes towards disabled people are likely to change towards increased acceptance, and as more disabled people go about their business in public and live longer, disability will become a public rather than cloistered experience. Encountering disabled persons will be commonplace and comfortable, rather than infrequent and distressing to the general public. Jobs will remain an issue of contention. Discrimination against disabled people in the labor force will continue, and perhaps even intensify in regions where unemployment rates are high. Legislation and business incentives can help, but the best solution is changes in employer attitudes and in workplace accommodation.

Aging and Disability

Population aging is now a worldwide phenomenon, swift for persons aged 65 and older in developing countries, and for persons aged 85 and older in developed countries (which have experienced aging throughout the twentieth century). Falling birth rates and falling late-life mortality rates both provide momentum to population aging. Older persons have higher risks of incurring (incidence) and having (prevalence) chronic illnesses and associated disabilities. Thus, the bulk of disability will increasingly be among older persons. Health and disability policies aimed at older persons must always think about disability and vice versa. The two will be intertwined for a very long time.

Moral Issues

Critical moral issues will persist and will be answered variously across countries; how can disabled persons' freedom and self-worth be enhanced, and how can burdens on families and government be kept moderate and manageable? Who is a genuine citizen of a society, and what are the basic rights of citizens? What are a society's obligation to assure human rights to anyone in their country? How will support for disabled people be paid for, and what are the minimum kinds of support that are fair and necessary? Who or what is responsible for disability's creation and who is responsible for its treatment? What strategies in approaching the global disability problem are cost-effective, alleviating disability for many at acceptable cost? A country has better chances of making well-considered decisions now, because these issues are discussed in worldwide arenas.

Research

Scientific research and scholarship on disability are increasing in amount and improving in quality. They serve as good buttresses for government policies, rehabilitation programs, and technology development. Some key contemporary topics are defining disability in the global context, studying disability as person–environment fit, tracing the disablement process for specific conditions or population groups, measuring the efficacy of specific interventions, and evaluating policy options. Exiting from the long-standing medical perspective is difficult, no matter how intelligent and desirous researchers are. Further work is needed to develop integrative models that take into account all of these factors: organic bases of body and mind impairments, societal 'framing' of disability, the causal importance of physical and built environments, the nature of discrimination, and the force of political economy. Achieving this will require the interdisciplinary collaboration of social scientists, physicians, engineers, and ethicists, and to make models truly worldwide in relevance requires discourse among international scholars.

Conclusion

With or without anyone's attention, global disability will be on the rise for many decades to come, fueled by population aging, environmental degradation, and social violence. As disability grows, communications and thinking by government officials and scholars are also becoming worldwide. Programs and ideas advanced in one place can be known swiftly and considered elsewhere. The 'emergence of global disability' really refers to the contemporary springing forward of public advocacy and government programs on behalf of disabled persons. It is in good time and greatly to be encouraged by each of us in our roles as citizen and professional.

Acknowledgment

Preparation of this chapter was supported in part by a Mary E. Switzer Distinguished Research Fellowship, National Institute on Disability and Rehabilitation, US Department of Education, awarded to Dr Albrecht.

References

Albrecht, G.L. (1992) *The Disability Business: Rehabilitation in America*. Thousand Oaks, CA: Sage.

Albrecht, G.L. (1997a) 'The emergence of disability in society', *Footnotes*, 25: 6. Washington, DC: American Sociological Association (newsletter).

Albrecht, G.L. (1997b) 'The health politics of disability', in T.J. Litman and L.S. Robins (eds), *Health Politics and Policy* (3rd edition). Albany, NY: Delmar. pp. 367–89.

Albrecht, G.L. and Levy, J.A. (1991) 'Chronic illness and disability as life course events', *Advances in Medical Sociology*, (2): 3–13.

Angell, M. (1997) 'The ethics of clinical research in the Third World', *The New England Journal of Medicine*, 337: 847–9.

Barbour, A.B. (1995) *Caring For Patients: A Critique of the Medical Model*. Stanford, CA: Stanford University Press.

Barnes, C. and Mercer, G. (eds) (1996) *Exploring the Divide: Illness and Disability*. Leeds: Disability Press.

Barry, M. and Molyneux, M. (1992) 'Ethical dilemmas in malaria drug and vaccine trials: A bioethical perspective', *Journal of Medical Ethics*, 18: 189–92.

Barton, L. and Oliver, M. (eds) (1997) *Disability Studies: Past, Present and Future*. Leeds: Disability Press.

Bérubé, M. (1997) 'The cultural representation of people with disabilities affects us all', *Chronicle of Higher Education*, 30 May, xl: B4–B5.

Bessis, S. (1995) *From Social Exclusion to Social Cohesion: A Policy Agenda*, Paris: UNESCO.

Bickenbach, J. (1993) *Physical Disability and Social Policy*. Toronto: University of Toronto Press.

Blackwell, E. ((1890) 1995) 'The influence of women in the profession of medicine', in D.J. Rothman, S. Marcus, and S. A. Kiceluk (eds), *Medicine and Western Civilization*. New Brunswick, NJ: Rutgers University Press. pp. 282–7.

Blaxter, M. (1976) *The Meaning of Disability*. London: Heinemann.

Bloomberg News (1998) 'Nike set to improve factory conditions,' *Chicago Tribune*, 13 May.

Brandt, Jr., E. and Pope, A.M. (eds) (1997) *Enabling America: Assessing the Role of Rehabilitation Science and Engineering*. Washington, DC: National Academy Press.

Bungener, M. (1995) *Trajectoires brisées familles captives: La maladie mental à domicile*. Paris: Les Editions INSERM.

Bury, M. (1997) 'Defining and researching disability: Challenges and responses', in C. Barnes and G. Mercer (eds), *Exploring the Divide: Illness and Disability*, Leeds: Disability Press.

Castel, R. (1995) *Les métaphorphoses de la question sociale*. Paris: Fayard.

Charlton, J.I. (1998) *Nothing About Us Without Us*. Berkeley, CA: University of California Press.

Charmaz, K. (1991) *Good Days, Bad Days: The Self In Chronic Illness and Time*. New Brunswick, NJ: Rutgers University Press.

Choquet, M.-C. and Richard, B. (1990) *Leur silence est un cri*. Paris: Fayard.

Crossley, N. and Crossley, M.L. (1998) 'HIV, empowerment and the sick role: An investigation of a contemporary moral maze', *Health*, 2: 157–74.

Davis, L.J. (ed.) (1997) *The Disability Studies Reader*. New York: Routledge.

DeParle, J. (1997) 'Half the states unlikely to meet goals on welfare', *The New York Times* 147, (1 October): 1, 14.

Domzel, C. (1995) *Federal Statutory Definitions of Disability*. Washington, DC: National Institute on Disability and Rehabilitation Research, US Department of Education.

Ferguson, P.M., Ferguson, D.L., and Taylor, S.J. (eds) (1992) *Interpreting Disability*. New York: Teachers College, Columbia University.

Finkelstein, V. (1993) 'The commonality of disability', in J. Swain, V. Finkelstein, S. French, and M. Oliver (eds), *Disabling Barriers – Enabling Environments*. London: Sage. pp. 9–16.

Garrett, L. (1994) *The Coming Plague: Newly Emerging Diseases in a World Out of Balance*. New York: Farrar, Straus and Giroux.

Georges, C. (1997) 'A youngster has HIV, poor attention span; Is he really disabled?' *The Wall Street Journal*, No 65 (1 October), C1, 12.

Gill, C. (1998) 'Disability studies: Looking at the FAQ's', *Alert*, 9: 6–9,14–16.

Gooding, C. (1996) *Blackstone's Guide to the Disability Discrimination Act of 1995*. London: Blackstone.

Grimby, G., Finnstram, J., and Jette, A. (1988) 'On the application of the WHO handicap classification in rehabilitation', *Scandinavian Journal of Rehabilitation Medicine*, 20: 93–8.

Gros-Jean, C. and Padieu, C. (1995) 'Les exclus: Comment sortir de l'approche en catègories?' *Revue Française des Affaires Sociales*, 49: 5–28.

Guralnik, J.M., Fried, L.P., and Salive, M.E. (1996) 'Disability as a public health outcome in the aging population', *Annual Review of Public Health*, 17: 25–46.

Hales, G. (ed.) (1996) *Beyond Disability*. London: Sage.

Handler, J.F. and Hasenfeld, Y. (1997) *We The Poor People*. New Haven, CT: Yale University Press.

Hydén, L.-C. and Sachs, L. (1998) 'Suffering, hope and diagnosis: On the negotiation of chronic fatigue syndrome', *Health*, 2: 173–93.

Imrie, R. (1996) *Disability and the City: International Perspectives*. New York: St. Martin's.

Institute of Medicine, Board on International Health (1997) *America's Vital Interest in Global Health*. Washington, DC: National Academy Press

Katz, S., Branch, L.G., Branson, M.H., Papidero, J.A., Beck, J.C., and Greer, D.S. (1983) 'Active life expectancy', *The New England Journal of Medicine*, 309: 1218–24.

La Plante, M. and Carlson, D. (1995) *Disability in the United States, Prevalence and Causes*. Washington, DC.: National Institute on Disability and Rehabilitation, Department of Education.

McGirk, T. (1997) 'The $28 foot', in Time Editors (eds), *Heroes of Medicine*, New York: Time, pp. 23–7.

Moscovici, S. (1997) *Chronique des années égarées*. Paris: Editions Stock.

Murray, C.J. and Lopez, A.M. (eds) (1996a) *The Global Burden of Disease*. Boston, MA: Harvard University Press.

Murray, C.J. and Lopez, A.M. (1996b) 'Evidence-based health policy – lessons from the global burden of disease study', *Science*, 274: 740–3.

Murray, C.J. and Lopez, A.M. (1997) 'Regional patterns of disability-free life expectancy and disability-adjusted life expectancy: Global burden of disease study', *Lancet*, 349: 1347–52.

Nelkin, D. and Tancredi, L. (1989) *Dangerous Diagnostics*. New York: Basic Books.

Oliver, M. (1990) *The Politics of Disablement*. New York: St. Martin's.

Oliver, M. (1992) 'Changing the social relationships of research production', *Disability, Handicap and Society*, 7: 101–14.

Osmond, C. and Barker, D. J. (1991) 'Ischemic heart disease in England and Wales around the year 2000', *Journal of Epidemiology and Community Health*, 45: 71–1.

Percy, S.L. (1992) *Disability, Civil Rights, and Public Policy*. Tuscaloosa, AL: University of Alabama Press.

Pope, A.M. and Tarlov, A.R. (eds) (1991) *Disability In America: Toward a National Agenda for Prevention*. Washington, DC: National Academy Press.

Priestly, M. (1998) 'Constructions and creations: Idealism, materialism and disability theory', *Disability and Society*, 13: 75–94.

Ratzka, A.D. (1992) *Access Legislation and Design Solutions*. Stockholm: Royal Institute of Technology.

Ravaud, J.F., Didier, J.P., Aussilloux, C., and Aymé, S. (1997) *De la déficience à la réinsertion*. Paris: Les Editions INSERM.

Scotch, R.K. and Schriner, K. (1997) 'Disability as human variation: Implications for policy', *Annals of the American Academy of Political and Social Science*, 549: 148–59.

Scripps Howard News Services (1998) 'Drug giant tells Russia, Asia: Pay up front', *Chicago Sun–Times*, 21 October, p. 74.

Shiraishi, M. and Arimoto, H. (1982) 'Prediction of the future incidence of cancer in Japan', *Japanese Journal of Clinical Oncology*, 12: 65–72.

Stiker, H.-J. (1982) *Corps infirmes et sociétés*. Paris: Aubier Montaigne.

Stone, D.A. (1984) *The Disabled State*. Philadelphia, PA: Temple University Press.

Strauss, A. and Glaser, B. (1975) *Chronic Illness and the Quality of Life*. St. Louis, MO: C.V. Mosby.

Studdert, D.M. and Brennan, T.A. (1997) 'HIV infection and the Americans With Disabilities Act: An evolving interaction', *Annals of the American Academy of Political and Social Science*, 549: 84–100.

United Nations (1992) *Human Rights and Disabled Persons*. Geneva.

Verbrugge, L.M. (1990) 'The iceberg of disability', in S.M. Stahl (ed.), *The Legacy of Longevity*. Newbury Park, CA: Sage. pp. 55–75.

Verbrugge, L.M. and Jette, A.M. (1994) 'The disablement process', *Social Science and Medicine*, 38: 1–14.

Vita, A.J., Terry, R.B., Hubert, H.B., and Fries, J.F. (1998) 'Aging, health risks, and cumulative disability', *New England Journal of Medicine*, 338: 1035–41.

Walzer, M. (1997) *On Toleration*. New Haven, CT: Yale University Press.

Wardman, M. (1997) 'Controversy flares over AIDS prevention trials in the Third World', *Lancet*, 389: 894–8.

World Health Organization (1980) *International Classification of Impairments, Disabilities and Handicaps*. Geneva.

World Health Organization (1997) *International Classification of Impairments, Activities and Participation*. Beta-1 Draft for Field Trials. Geneva.

World Resources Institute (1998) *1998–1999 World Resources: A Guide to the Global Environment*. New York: Oxford University Press.

2.8

Reproduction and Assisted Reproductive Technologies

HELÉNA RAGONÉ AND SHARLA K. WILLIS

INTRODUCTION

During this century the world has become rapidly more technological. Technology is generally viewed as a positive and vital force in our lives, allowing us to become more developed as a society and live a higher quality of life. Nowhere is this view more apparent than in the field of health and medicine. Rapid advances in medical knowledge and technology call into question commonly held and accepted beliefs concerning the body, illness, and disease. This is especially true in the area of reproductive technology, where advances over the past decades have changed the biological and social meaning of reproduction. Fertility and infertility have moved into the realm of the controllable, raising questions of rights, responsibility, and ethics.

This chapter examines the impact of medical knowledge and medical technology on reproduction, particularly as it affects women. It begins with a review of the theory of medicalization and its relationship with reproduction to provide the context for further discussion. An increasing body of literature has documented and addressed the move from unassisted to medicalized ways of dealing with once 'natural' processes across a woman's reproductive life cycle, such as menses, conception, pregnancy, childbirth, and menopause. Specific examples are given in this chapter from the perinatal period and the menstrual cycle. Childbirth is discussed first because the medicalization of reproduction began with the birth process. The process of medicalization has now moved to encompass the prenatal period as well, which is discussed in the next section. The

medicalization of the menstrual cycle, specifically the development of the concept of premenstrual syndrome and menopause as diseases, is reviewed in the next two sections. The newest area of reproduction and reproductive technology is discussed next and in more depth. Assisted reproductive technologies have redefined concepts of family and motherhood by increasing the number of players involved in conception. The impact on those who participate is discussed in this section, as well as issues of secrecy and kinship. The chapter concludes by moving from what we have learned to a discussion of the implications of reproductive technology and the medicalization of reproduction on individuals and society, and the direction that social scientists should take from here.

MEDICALIZATION

Increasingly, human experiences have come under medical care, leading to what Illich called the 'medicalization of life' (Illich 1976). The process of medicalization occurs on at least three different levels, conceptually, institutionally, and within the doctor–patient interaction (Conrad and Schneider 1980). Conceptually, medicalization occurs when a process or condition is defined as a medical problem. Institutionally, it occurs when medical professionals legitimize the problem at hand as a medical issue. Within the doctor–patient relationship, medicalization occurs when an individual is diagnosed and treated for a problem.

Medicalizing an issue requires that the subject under consideration be defined as deviating from the norm. Once a condition is recognized as departing from the norm it then becomes obligatory for the illness to be addressed. It is important to consider that science, as well as illness, is ultimately a social construction that helps to reinforce social norms (Riessman 1983). Women and women's bodies have been particularly vulnerable to the process of medicalization due in part to Western gender-biased ideologies that view women primarily as reproductive beings (King 1992; Martin 1987). The male body, on the other hand, has been held up as the standard for the proper function of the human body from which women deviate, having obvious physical and hormonal differences (Gurevich 1995). Medicalization of the female reproductive process has led to the female body being viewed 'as a medical problem from the cradle to the grave' (Gijsbers van Wijk et al. 1996: 708).

Medicalization has occurred over time within the context of cultural, political, and social changes. While differences of opinion on the cause of medicalization abound, the majority of authors have focused on the expansion of the medical profession and medicine's influence on lay people, specifically their reliance on medical practitioner's 'expertise' (Riessman 1983; Williams and Calnan 1996). In the case of reproduction, this reliance has given physicians a power and mastery over women's reproductive experiences, often questioning or even replacing a woman's own knowledge and understanding of her experience. Jordan and other researchers have developed this idea in the area of pregnancy and childbirth specifically as it pertains to 'authoritative knowledge' (see Davis-Floyd and Sargent 1997a). Jordan explains authoritative knowledge in the following way: 'for any particular domain, several knowledge systems exist, some of which, by consensus, come to carry more weight than others, either because they explain the state of the world better for the purposes at hand (efficacy) or because they are associated with a stronger power base (structural superiority), and usually both' (Jordan 1997: 56).

In part, the medicalization of reproduction has occurred because of the Western reliance on technology. Data produced by technological devices are seen as being more accurate than subjective signs and symptoms (King 1992), and the increasing technical complexity of society has augmented society's reliance on the expertise of medical professionals (Zola 1972, 1975). Like science, technology is not value-free. Medical technology reflects the values and beliefs of its creators and is influenced by politics

as well as science, generating power and social control by accepting physicians and medical care institutions as the brokers of knowledge (King 1992). Banta (1983) defines medical technology as 'the drugs, devices and medical and surgical procedures used in medical care and the organisational and support systems within which such care is provided.' As will be discussed below, technology has played a critical role in the medicalization of reproduction from early developments such as the use of forceps in delivering infants to more recent developments in assisted reproductive technologies.

THE PERINATAL PERIOD

Childbirth

In America, and to a lesser degree in England, the historical shift of childbirth from a social event to a medical process has been well documented (Arms 1975; Leavitt 1986; Oakley 1984; Shaw 1974; Wertz and Wertz 1989). Researchers have discussed the roles that the medical profession as well as women have played in facilitating this shift. Physicians sought to strengthen their new claim as a profession, while women sought to be relieved from the fear and discomfort that accompanied the childbirth process. What was once carried out at home with the assistance of a female support group, and occasionally a midwife, evolved into a medical model of labor and delivery as a potentially pathological occurrence requiring the supervision of trained medical professionals in a hospital equipped with all of the latest technologies.

'Childbirth is a culturally defined act set within the universals of a common human evolutionary heritage' (Michaelson 1988: 8). The Western birth process is defined within the culture of technology, a type of 'technomedicine' that characterizes the way birth is viewed (Davis-Floyd and Sargent 1997b). In the obstetrical literature (Barker 1998; Wertz and Wertz 1989) women and childbirth have been likened to ships that must be piloted and cars that must be fixed by skilled mechanics (obstetricians). Most women generally assume that some form of technology will play a part in their birth experience, which requires them to depend on the physicians, or 'technicians', who possess the authoritative knowledge to interpret this technology (Davis-Floyd 1988; Davis-Floyd and Sargent 1997b).

Reproductive technologies, such as forceps, anesthesia, fetal monitoring, episiotomies, and cesarean sections, have been instrumental in the medicalization process. Medicalization should be viewed as having both positive and negative consequences for childbirth. It has reduced the risks of birth by providing the technology to deal more effectively with high-risk births and complications. Unfortunately, the use of many of these technologies has become routine, with little evidence that they improve birth outcomes in general. They have become part of the American 'birth ritual,' and can serve to distance women from their health-care providers if the technology becomes the focal point during labor rather than the women (Davis-Floyd 1988). The knowledge that these technologies provide can be used to negate women's own understanding of their bodies and birth experience, and may blind both patient and provider to the possibility of nontechnological interventions (Michaelson 1988). While more women are exploring 'natural childbirth' with limited medical intervention, the majority of women in the United States and many other countries still are dependent primarily upon the knowledge and expertise of the medical professional (Wertz and Wertz 1989).

Pregnancy

Since prenatal care is still primarily viewed as relatively low technology, women feel more free to choose which prenatal advice to accept depending on how well it fits within their own knowledge of pregnancy and the reality of their lives (Browner and Press 1996). As prenatal technology, such as ultrasounds, amniocentesis and other diagnostic tests, become more utilized, however, pregnancy becomes more medicalized. An example is the alpha feta protein (AFP) prenatal diagnostic blood test for neural tube defects, now required to be offered in California. Even those women who had the test were uncertain of what it is, but they nonetheless wanted the test, the most common reasons cited being to be reassured, to be prepared, or to comply with doctor's instructions (Browner and Press 1995).

Until as recently as the mid-1980s, ultrasounds were only used in high-risk pregnancies. Since that time, they have become more prevalent and a standard part of prenatal care in much of the world. In Greece, three ultrasounds are done, on average, per pregnancy (Georges 1996). While women often want and request these ultrasounds, the information learned from this technology can also be used to reinforce medical authority and the superiority of technological knowledge. Georges (1996) provides several examples of how women's knowledge of their pregnancy is denied in favor of the 'reality' of pregnancy dates available to physicians through ultrasounds.

All technology requires individuals to choose whether they will utilize the technology. One is forced, however, to ask whether this choice is always free, or can be coerced. In Western society, great value is placed on making informed and conscious decisions (Rothman 1988). As Browner and Press point out, 'Once a prenatal diagnostic technology becomes widely available it cannot be refused neutrally because refusal can be construed as a lack of responsibility on the part of the pregnant woman' (Browner and Press 1996: 153). There is 'no right not to know' (Michaelson 1988: 16), and many women accept new technologies because they do not want to risk 'blame for the failures that result from the inefficiencies of natural reproduction' (King 1992). In her study of women's decisions to have or not to have amniocentesis, Rothman (1988) found that when women were at risk and chose the unexpected, not to have the test, they were more prepared to defend their actions and explain.

Prenatal diagnostic testing is an area in which a dialogue must be opened allowing women to share their experiences. Unlike other aspects of pregnancy, it is deeply personal and there is a silence surrounding this medical event that separates it from the common maternal experience (Rapp 1988). There is a unique pressure on women not only to avail themselves of the technology, but to then face the question of what they are to do with the information provided (Browner and Press 1995; Rapp 1988; Rothman 1988).

Menstrual Cycle

Premenstrual Syndrome

Premenstrual syndrome (PMS) was first defined as a medical problem in 1931 and since has been the subject of considerable research, although the etiology and appropriate treatment still remain unresolved. Gurevich (1995) points to the cultural nature of this 'disease' in her discussion of comparative research, which has shown that PMS is much more prevalent in the US and other Western societies than in other cultures. Martin (1987) illustrates the role of social construction in the science of PMS research in the US throughout the period from the 1930s to the 1970s. Research on the menstrual cycle was originally concerned with the impact on women as employees. The pattern of findings on menstruation related to social changes, such as wars and the feminist movement, and the need for women in the workforce or the need for them to relinquish their jobs to men. If men needed the jobs, research findings tended toward the conclusion that PMS was detrimental to a woman's ability to work. If women were needed, such as during the war, researchers tended to find that women should not be allowed to use their menstrual cycles as an excuse as it had no bearing on their functionality as employees.

Once PMS was medicalized it led not only to the need for diagnosis, but for treatment as well, as it does for all diseases. Riessman (1983) suggests that market forces have played a role in the increase of PMS. She proposes that physicians, specifically obstetrician/gynecologists, need new problems to treat as their numbers increase and birth rates decline. Pharmaceutical companies have also played a pivotal role, since numerous drug therapies have been developed to treat premenstrual symptoms, with treatments ranging from over-the-counter medications and self-help books to progesterone therapy and PMS clinics (Gurevich 1995).

Just as with the medicalization of childbirth, this process has not been devoid of the participation of women or completely without benefit to women. Women have been actively involved in searching for answers to premenstrual syndrome as they seek out relief from menstrual discomfort (Riessman 1983). Gurevich (1995) suggests that PMS affords women an opportunity of maintaining culturally defined femininity, generally seen as passive, while allowing them a medically sanctioned release for emotionality. Unfortunately, it also reinforces the belief that women are controlled by their reproductive systems, or their 'raging hormones,' and redefines hormonal changes during the menstrual cycles as pathological rather than natural (Riessman 1983). Riessman points to several problems arising from this redefinition: medical treatments may become the norm, previously asymptomatic women may perceive symptoms simply because a medical explanation exists, and it reduces attention to women's complaints by explaining them away as 'simply PMS.'

Menopause

Conceptually, the medicalization of menopause began in the 1930s and 1940s when it was labeled a deficiency disease caused by a lack of estrogen (Bell 1987). In the 1960s, synthetic estrogen became widely available, increasing the focus on menopause and the need for it to be treated (McCrea 1983). Much of the focus on menopause in the 1960s, though, was, interestingly enough, on the impact of menopause on the

woman's husband and others around her rather than on the woman herself. Some practitioners advised that women be treated whether they realized they needed to be or not, emphasizing the point that the knowledge that counted was not with the women, but with the physicians. Gynecologist Robert A. Wilson, prominent advocate of estrogen, even suggested that women be given estrogen from 'puberty to grave' (Wilson and Wilson 1963).

Menopause, like all 'diseases,' is culturally dependent, as women from different cultures, ethnic groups, and class backgrounds experience symptoms differently (Flint and Samil 1990; Kaiser 1990). There is a pressing need to understand how women perceive menopause and to understand why women present certain symptoms. The biomedical model of menopause needs to encompass a biopsychocultural model and multidisciplinary research that includes both biomedical and social/behavioral inquiry (Flint and Samil 1990), as does research on all aspects of reproduction.

As with PMS and other areas of reproduction, the medicalization of menopause has had mixed effects. While it has legitimized women's menopausal complaints, it has also reinforced traditional stereotypes of aging women. Ironically, Bell (1987) points out that the disease orientation of menopause was introduced to reassure women that most often menopause was a normal and natural physiological event, but it has instead served to increase the cultural authority of medicine by overriding the importance of women's experiences. 'By individualizing the problems of menopause, the physician turns attention away from any social structural interpretation of women's conditions. The focus of the solution then becomes the doctor–patient interaction in which the physician is active, instrumental, and authoritative, while the patient is passive and dependent' (McCrea 1983: 113).

CONCEPTION

In recent years a plethora of studies exploring assisted reproduction technologies and infertility has emerged in the field of anthropology (Cannell 1990; Franklin and Ragoné 1998; Ginsburg and Rapp 1995; Inhorn 1994, 1996; Modell 1989; Ragoné 1994, 1996, 1998; Sandelowski 1993; Strathern 1991, 1992). In 1995, 6.2 million women aged 15–44 in the United States alone reported impaired fecundity; 44 per cent of these women had sought medical help for fertility problems (Chandra and Stephen 1998). There are a number of treatment options available to those who are diagnosed with fertility problems, ranging from hormonal to more invasive techniques (Hamberger and Janson 1997). Of course the act of defining infertility as a medical problem and the development of assisted reproductive technologies (ARTs) has helped lead to its medicalization. 'Once infertility is medically designated as a disease, both patients and practitioners pursue a "cure" through a well-delineated pattern of medical treatment, despite any risks such treatment may entail' (Becker and Nachtigall 1994: 516).

The existence of a technology to address infertility places pressure on infertile patients to seek out treatment. As Donchin (1996), in her review of feminist studies of the topic, points out, what was once accepted with resignation, the inability to conceive, is now viewed as a surmountable obstacle. Infertile patients cannot stop trying, because with today's technological options there is no problem that cannot be solved (Sheth and Malpani 1997). Treatment for infertility is generally a process of 3 years or more in length, often involving a progression of treatments. There are risks involved, but women take these risks because treatment is viewed as a socially responsible behavior for those who wish to conceive and to fulfil the cultural norm of motherhood (Becker and Nachtigall 1994).

With the introduction of assisted reproductive technologies (ARTs), seemingly simple yet nonetheless culturally bound assessments concerning what constitutes a 'family,' 'motherhood,' and 'fatherhood' can no longer be taken for granted. Reproductive technologies have served to defamiliarize what was once understood to be the 'natural' basis of human procreation and relatedness. In essence, ARTs have served, as the Comaroffs so eloquently said of ethnography, 'to make the familiar strange and the strange familiar, all the better to understand them both' (Comaroff and Comaroff 1992). Perhaps no other area of study in contemporary EuroAmerican culture is so charged with meaning, emotion, and contestation at this time as that of assisted reproduction.

In recent history, there have been three profound shifts in the Western conceptualization of the categories of conception, reproduction, and parenthood. The first occurred in response to the separation of intercourse from reproduction through birth control methods (Snowden et al. 1983). A second shift occurred in response to the emergence of assisted reproductive technologies and the subsequent fragmentation of the unity of reproduction, when it became possible for pregnancy to occur without necessarily having been 'preceded by sexual intercourse' (Snowden et al. 1983: 5). The third shift occurred in

response to further advances in reproductive medicine that called into question the 'organic unity of fetus and mother' (Martin 1987: 20).

It was not until the emergence of reproductive medicine that this fragmentation of motherhood became a reality. With that historical change, what was once the 'single figure of the mother is dispersed among several potential figures, as the functions of maternal procreation – aspects of her physical parenthood – become dispersed' (Strathern 1991: 32). It has called into question the EuroAmerican definitions of kinship and family, which are based primarily on biological relationships. Assisted reproduction effectively disperses kinship as well as conception, including not only those who produce a child with assistance, but those who assist (Strathern 1995). With the development of new fertility technologies, the social pressure to produce biologically related children intensifies (Donchin 1996). The issue of relatedness is of paramount importance in assisted reproductive technology research, since individuals who avail themselves of these technologies are often engaged in a desperate search for a genetic link.

This has ramifications not only for the relationships between those involved in the new forms of procreation, but also for the option of adoption. Adoption may increasingly be viewed as a last resort by couples after efforts to reproduce themselves genetically (Donchin 1996; Strathern 1995). The inherent problems individuals and couples face in the adoption process has been discussed elsewhere, including age-based criteria, religion, shortages of healthy EuroAmerican children, and cost (Ragoné 1994, 1996). Other controversial aspects of adoption include transnational and transracial adoption, both of which have caused a growing number of individuals and couples to turn to assisted reproduction.

Assisted reproduction encompasses a wide spectrum that ranges from a couple using their own sperm and ova carried to term in the woman's uterus, to the extreme end of the spectrum where a couple provides neither sperm nor ova and contracts with another woman to carry the child in her uterus. Each situation has varying degrees of acceptability for practitioners and for those involved, as will be discussed below (Dans 1992). The following section addresses the issues of kinship and relatedness at the end of the spectrum which is most problematic genetically – gamete donation and surrogacy.

Gamete Donation

Gamete donation refers to the process whereby men donate semen and/or women donate ova in order to assist infertile couples/individuals in their quest for children. Sperm donation has a long and checkered history in the annals of Western medicine. The first recorded case of donor insemination (DI) occurred in 1884 when a physician inseminated an unconscious and uninformed patient, a procedure clearly at odds with contemporary perspectives on donation.[1]

Although sperm donation is now positively valued and somewhat commonplace, in the 1940s and 1950s it was considered a deviant practice calling into question both the donor's and mother's motivations. Britain's Feversham Committee, for example, considered that it 'might be expected to attract more than the usual proportion of psychopaths' (Report of the Departmental Committee on Human Artificial Insemination 1960: 58). The Archbishop of Canterbury's Commission viewed the motivations of the woman who desired to enter motherhood through 'the seed of a man not her husband' as a pathological desire for motherhood (1948: 25). As late as 1948, the Archbishop of Canterbury's Commission recommended that a donor's semen be 'collected from the donor's wife's vagina' to remove the troublesome act of masturbation, and to include the 'donor's wife' so that 'she too was contributing to donation' (Haimes 1993a: 87). Over time, many of the beliefs and attitudes that equated sperm donation with social deviance have receded. In contemporary EuroAmerican culture, sperm donation is seen as a straightforward process of collection and insemination. The process has been predicated consistently on anonymity and, with a few notable exceptions, has remained devoid of cultural interpretation.

While sperm donation was the first successful attempt to extract gametes from the human body for the treatment of infertility, advances in reproductive medicine, specifically in vitro fertilization (IVF), now allow women the option of donating ova. The first recorded case of ova donation was in Australia in 1983, and since then there has been a meteoric rise in the rates of ovum donation. Ovum donation provides both agonadal women and women who fear passing on sex-linked diseases to their potential offspring with an opportunity to experience pregnancy and birth. Although ovum donation is certainly a great deal more medically complicated, risky, and intrusive than sperm donation, ovum donation also remains largely bereft of cultural analysis.

Gamete Donors and Surrogates

Gender is a crucial if understudied variable in any assessment of gamete donation. Studies on sperm donation have revealed that donors are primarily motivated by remuneration, but have found other motivations including altruism and assessing their own fertility (Daniels 1989; Handelsman et al. 1985; Mahlstedt and Probasco 1991; Purdie et al. 1994; Schover et al. 1992). While sperm donors report a feeling of 'specialness' while donating, they may come to reconsider their donor status (Baran and Pannor 1989). As one former sperm donor in a study examining the long-term impact of targeting students as donors expressed, 'he wished he had had the foresight to know that one day, twenty-five years later, he would regret that period in his life' (Baran and Pannor 1989: 90). Such reassessments appear to be influenced by the experience of becoming a father and realizing that they may have unknown offspring (Myers 1990) and 'a role devoid of any responsibility to the children they produce' (Baran and Pannor 1989: 96). In contrast to prevailing American views, France and Sweden encourage donation from older, married men, who are already fathers (Haimes 1993a).

Most surrogates and ovum donors deny the importance of remuneration in their decision-making process, but the fact remains that many of these women acknowledge that they find the financial incentive attractive. The issue of remuneration/altruism is a complicated one; women who choose to participate in surrogacy do so for a host of compelling reasons (Ragoné 1994, 1996, 1998). Surrogates continually assert that the importance of remuneration decreases as the process progresses, and this pattern may be repeated with ovum donors and sperm donors. Of all the surrogates' stated motivations, remuneration is the most problematic. On a symbolic level, of course, remuneration detracts from the idealized cultural image of women/mothers as selfless, nurturing, and altruistic, an image that surrogates and, quite likely, ovum donors do not wish to lose.

In one study of an oocyte donation program, the screening process for prospective ovum donors insists that the 'primary reason for participation . . . [be] a desire to help an infertile woman have a baby' (Sauer and Paulson 1992b: 727). In spite of this policy which does not permit women who express financial incentive to serve as ovum donors, 76 per cent of the 'women who had gone through at least one aspiration stated that compensation was important for their continued participation' (Sauer and Paulson 1992b: 727). Although the authors conclude that oocyte donors differ from men donating sperm, who routinely state the importance of remuneration (Sauer and Paulson 1992a), their conclusion seems odd when the majority of their ovum donors appear to value compensation. Such assessments conflate commonly accepted yet engendered and essentialist ideas about women and men.

The increasing demand for ova coupled with the routinization and naturalization of the procedure has created amongst infertility clinics the practice of targeting reproductively inexperienced young women as ovum donors (using the model of sperm donation in which college-aged men and medical students are the target audience). Acting on the questionable assumption that women in college have 'smarter' ova, clinics seek ova from these young women using financial incentives (the woman earns a fee of $10 000 for four ovulatory cycles). Competition among infertility clinics is increasing, and the prospect of making enormous profits coupled with weak regulatory policies (Reame 1998) is creating a volatile environment. Although a great deal has been written about infertility clinics' practice of inflating their 'success rates,' little has been written on the practice of advertising for ova donors in college newspapers. In contrast, the largest ovum donation program in the United States requires prospective donors to have had at least one child in order to be accepted into the program (also the policy in French programs).[2]

Extensive research on gestational surrogates revealed that they routinely report feeling 'unprepared' for the rigors and discomfort of self-administering shots during the course of their pregnancies (Ragoné 1998). Surrogates, however, commonly reformulate their expectations to include the near sacrifice of their lives and 'readily embrace the idea of meaningful suffering, heroisim, or sacrifice,' even when their experiences of surrogacy are at odds with their expectations (Ragoné 1996: 354). Perhaps this will also prove true for ovum donors.

An additional issue, aside from the reported physical discomfort ovum donors feel during the period surrounding retrieval (Rosenberg and Epstein 1995), is the risk of cervical cancer associated with ovulating-induction drugs (Rosen et al. 1997). While studies have consistently demonstrated the willingness of infertile women to accept the risks associated with infertility treatments (Modell 1989; Sandelowski 1993), they are making an informed decision, whereas when a young, fertile woman agrees to subject herself to the same risks it is not a comparable situation. Statistically we know that a percentage of ovum donors will join the ranks of the infertile, and they may come to regret deeply their decision to donate ova, a decision made at a time when they had minimal or no reproductive experience or knowledge. Do infer-

tility clinics provide their prospective ovum donors with adequate information concerning drug protocols, and do these young women process this information in a meaningful and informed way?

Gamete Recipients

Although sexual mores have changed since the 1940s and 1950s, contemporary studies on male infertility have yet to explore fully the emotional and/or psychological issues faced by infertile men and sperm donors (Pedersen et al. 1994). One of the most significant problems facing infertile men is the association between male infertility and impotence, although the two are not necessarily linked. Gender stereotyping, which assigns to males the role of 'initiators,' defines infertile men as 'powerless' or passive, unable to undertake successfully that which is considered 'appropriate masculine behavior' (Snowden et al. 1983: 121), further complicating the issue of infertility. A lack of medical knowledge and effective treatment programs (Snowden et al. 1983) also contributes to the stigma attaching to male infertility. The fact that 40 per cent of infertility is male (30 per cent female and 30 per cent unknown and/or shared) makes the lack of male infertility research puzzling. Furthermore, research on the exact number of children born through donor insemination (estimated at 30 000 births per year in the United States) (Barratt et al. 1990) has been impeded because records are routinely destroyed, information denied, and secrecy widely practiced by physicians (Baran and Pannor 1989: 5).[3]

In the 1950s, physicians were known to permit a husband to inseminate his wife with the 'actual syringe containing the donated semen so that he could say, "I impregnated my wife" ' (Fletcher 1955: 125). Physicians routinely mixed donor semen with the semen of the intending father well into the mid-1980s in an attempt to intentionally obscure the issue of paternity, and some continue to recommend to couples who request such mixed semen to engage in sexual intercourse prior to insemination (thus mixing semen on their own). Although the practice of mixing semen has been discontinued, it nonetheless reveals the highly engendered beliefs surrounding male infertility. Of profound interest is the current unreflective practice of mixing ova and embryos in a newfound attempt to confuse the issue of maternity and/or parenthood, respectively.

Women in committed relationships with infertile men/husbands are, through donor insemination (DI), able to sustain a pregnancy which further contributes to the secrecy model, because many individuals agree that no one else needs to know about the husband's sterility.[4] Although gender-role stereotyping may heighten the stigma associated with male infertility, it may conversely lessen the stigma associated with female infertility in that the characteristics associated with infertility, such as powerlessness, are more readily considered part of the spectrum of 'appropriate feminine behavior' (Snowden et al. 1983: 142). This theory is supported in part by the fact that many women with infertile husbands who participate in DI allow others to believe that they, rather than their husbands, are infertile (Snowden et al. 1983).

This strategy has been viewed as a means to shield men from potential shame or ridicule. In addition, when a DI wife feigns infertility, she is aware that any stigma associated with her infertility will be removed once she becomes pregnant, and that her infertility can thus be understood as a transient form of infertility, whereas his would not be so understood (Ragoné 1994). Perhaps even more important it is also a means by which the wife compensates for the fact that the resultant child will be biologically related to her and not to her husband. As Baran and Pannor's research (based upon an admittedly small sample) has revealed, some men whose wives have conceived through DI have reported a lifelong struggle to come to terms with their infertility and the fact that they lack a genetic tie to their children (Baran and Pannor 1989). With traditional surrogacy, in which a surrogate donates an ovum as well as the use of her womb, the intending mother must grapple with her lack of a genetic tie to the child which also requires that all the individuals negotiate their relationship to the child and to one another (Ragoné 1994, 1996, 1998).

In spite of attempts to cast sperm/ovum donation as equivalents, Haimes has argued that there are notable differences in sperm donation and egg donation and the issue of secrecy (1993). In general, anonymity appears to be preferred (especially for sperm donation), because a 'sense of danger' is attached to semen donation/donors that is not attached to egg donors (Haimes 1993a: 87). The fact that treatment with donor eggs 'was more acceptable than donor spermatozoa to both men and women in the fertile as well as the infertile population' (Kazem et al. 1995: 1547) seems to reinforce this position.[5] As Lessor et al. (1990) has suggested, perhaps paternity may be viewed as more important in cultures with patrilineal systems of inheritance. Additionally, with ovum donation both wives and husbands feel that 'they have contributed to the birth of the child' (Kazem et al. 1995: 1547).

Fragmentation and Reunification of the Body

The fragmentation of motherhood and the negotiation of relationships within this novel experience of assisted reproduction require a redefining of motherhood for those involved. Not surprisingly, this differs according to the role the participants choose to play. For example, with traditional surrogacy in which a surrogate donates an ovum, the overwhelming majority of surrogates devalue their own genetic/physical contribution. They do this while highlighting the 'pseudopregnancy' of the adoptive mother and the importance of the latter's role as nurturer. In this way, motherhood is reinterpreted as primarily a social role in order to avert problematic aspects of the surrogate's genetic relationship to the child and the adoptive mother's lack of a genetic link. A 39-year-old surrogate reflects this focus upon intention and nurture by both surrogates and adoptive mothers in the following statement:

> Parents are the ones who raise the child. I got that from my parents who adopted children. My siblings were curious and my parents gave them the information they had and they never wanted to track down their biological parents. I don't think of the baby as mine; it is the parents, the ones who raise the child that are important.

In the process of emphasizing the value of nurture, surrogates describe motherhood as a role that one can either adopt or refuse, and this concept of nurture as choice is for them the single most important defining aspect of motherhood. Traditional surrogates believe that motherhood is comprised of two separable aspects: first, the biological process (insemination, pregnancy, and delivery), and second, the social process (nurture). They reason that a woman can choose to nurture, that is, to accept the role of social mother, or choose not to nurture, thereby rejecting the role of social mother. A traditional surrogate explains her perception of surrogacy in the following way, 'It was an egg I wasn't going to be using.'

Ovum donors also embrace this position. On the other hand, they find it more difficult to contemplate serving in the capacity of surrogate, citing their belief that their husband would have difficulty accepting surrogacy, a history of problem pregnancies, and/or the fear that they might bond with the child they were gestating for the couple. Interestingly, they are, however, able to part with their ova and potentially their genetic child.

At odds with these perspectives is the gestational surrogate's view of the relationship. As a whole, women who elect to become gestational surrogates tend to articulate the belief that traditional surrogacy, even though less medically complicated, is not an acceptable option for them because they are uncomfortable with the prospect of contributing their own ovum (or ova) to the creation of a child. They also cannot readily accept the idea that someone else would raise a child who is genetically related to them. In other words, they explicitly articulate the opinion that in traditional surrogacy (where the surrogate contributes an ovum) the surrogate is the mother of the child, whereas in gestational surrogacy (where she does not contribute an ovum) she is not.

Couples are attracted to ovum donation for different reasons: husbands for the genetic link, wives for the experience of pregnancy, and both wives and husbands are able to gain prenatal control. Prenatal control is also important to couples who pursue gestational surrogacy whether it is the couples' embryos or embryos produced through ovum donation. Couples who choose gestational surrogacy using donor eggs/husband's semen/gestational surrogate are still ending up with the same degree of relatedness to the child as they would with traditional surrogacy, i.e., a child who is genetically related only to the husband. It appears, though, that some couples chose this arrangement for its ability to sever the surrogate's genetic tie to the child (Ragoné 1996, 1998). Adding to the complexity of these arrangements is the couple who will use donated eggs and, in some cases, donor semen, and the intending mother gestates the embryo(s). The intending mother, through the process of gestation, forms her bond to the child, a bond that, as we have seen, the gestational surrogate intentionally de-emphasizes.

In a study of the experiences of recipient couples in the context of ovum donation, 90 percent of couples in the program used anonymous donation and 9.7 percent used known, i.e., sister, donation (Applegarth et al. 1995). The authors concluded that only a 'small percentage,' 10 percent of husbands and 26 percent of wives, 'expressed the desire to meet their ovum donor' (Applegarth et al. 1995: 577). The fact that over one-quarter want to meet their donors seems highly significant.

Individuals typically attest to their satisfaction with ovum donation by thanking 'God,' 'the wonders of modern medical miracles,' 'medical science,' and 'fantastic technology.' In only one case does a recipient state that she is 'thankful for my donor' (Applegarth et al. 1995: 580). The acceptance and subsequent implementation of anonymity in both ovum donation programs and sperm banks contributes not only to the further fragmentation of reproduction and the

body but, as the above quotes aptly demonstrate, to the fact that in practice gamete donation involves disembodied gametes (rather than persons). The ovum donor coordinator at the largest ovum donation program stated that they often interview couples who are seeking total anonymity. As she said, 'Some couples don't want any contact, they want to see her [ovum donor] as genetic material!'

The complexity of these relationships and the difficulty of reinterpreting our definitions of motherhood are evident in the questions raised by the courts as they attempt to clarify the roles of the players. Current legal opinion in both Britain and Australia is that 'when a child is born to a woman following the donation of another's egg the women giving birth should, for all purposes, be regarded in law as the mother of that child' (Shalev 1989: 117). Does this apply equally to a woman who receives a donor egg that she gestates herself and a woman who contracts another to be a gestational surrogate through in vitro fertilization? It is interesting to note that this opinion contradicts the views expressed by gestational surrogates who choose gestational surrogacy precisely because it eliminates the issue of genetic relatedness for them. This effort to expand our definition of relatedness runs contrary to the EuroAmerican emphasis on genetic relatedness, in which genetic parents are legally and socially considered the 'real' parents. The fragmentation or dispersal of parenthood, a byproduct of reproductive technologies, has resulted in the 'claims of one kind of biological mother against other kinds of biological and nonbiological mothers' (Strathern 1991: 32) and biological and nonbiological fathers.

In the precedent-setting case in California, *Anna Johnson v. Mark and Crispina Calvert*, Case #SO23721, a gestational surrogate and a couple both filed custody suits. Under California law, both of the women could claim maternal rights: Johnson by virtue of being the woman who gave birth to the child, and Calvert, who donated the ovum, because she is the child's genetic mother. In rendering its decision, however, the court in a sense circumvented the issue of relatedness and focused instead on the 'intent' of the parties as the ultimate and decisive factor in determining parenthood. Specifically, Justice Edward Penelli wrote: 'It is not the role of the judiciary to inhibit the use of reproductive technology when the legislature has not seen fit to do so. Any such effort would raise serious questions in light of the fundamental nature of the rights of procreation and privacy.' In addition, the court concluded that compensation to the surrogate is understood not as the New Jersey Supreme Court ruled – as baby selling or selling the rights to her child – but rather as payment for her services of gestation and labor. The court ruled that surrogacy contracts are enforceable and consistent with prevailing public policy. To date, no egg donor has attempted to claim maternal rights.

Constructing Family – Secrecy and Anonymity

Psychological directives that reiterate the importance of informing children of their birth origins and the deleterious consequences of secrecy continue to be ignored for the most part, just as the importance of the genetic basis of relatedness in EuroAmerican kinship ideology is ignored. In EuroAmerican culture the 'blood relationship cannot be lost' (Schneider 1968: 24) nor can one have an ex-blood relative (Schneider 1968). The literature on gamete donation suggests tacitly that the acceptance of anonymity is predicated on the belief that the family must be protected from the potential disruption posed by known donors. With ovum donation (unlike with sperm donation), however, there is some precedent for known donors, namely sisters, but its impact on the overall practice of ovum donation appears at this point to be somewhat negligible.

Purdie et al. recommend that DI 'move away from the animal husbandry model (with the selection of highly fertile donors to service many recipients) to a social model where a donor (and his family) "adopt" one or a few infertile couples' (Purdie et al. 1994: 1358), a recommendation that seems to be a radical departure from gamete donation policies in the United States. Implementation of a disclosure policy would require a rethinking of the issues of secrecy and privacy, and a reeducation of recipients (and donors) which would require programs to encourage individuals to accept their infertility and also their worst fear, namely that the donor, the only person that can ameliorate their childlessness, is also the person who may want to take back the child (also a common fear with surrogacy). It should be noted that anonymous donation not only requires a significantly less developed infrastructure, but it also does not place demands on the paying client.

The Glover Report, in a radical departure from anonymous models of donation, has advocated an experimental approach in which children produced through DI would be given information and access to their donors upon reaching 18 years of age (Haimes 1993a: 88). However, despite the growing body of literature on adoptees and their often frustrating attempts

to locate their biological parents (a search that is often confined exclusively to mothers), they continue to be denied access to the identity of their biological parents and, most importantly, to their own sense of identity. Using a small sample of adults who were conceived through sperm donation, Baran and Pannor (1989) concluded that many of these individuals are 'angry' about the secrecy surrounding their birth origins and their biological father's identity, and they are joining traditional adoptees in searching for their biological parents. While Sweden and Australia have passed legislation to permit DI children access to identifying information about their donors when they have reached 18 years of age (Weil 1997), and Austria and The Netherlands are 'moving in this direction' (Haimes 1993b), the issue of disclosure remains controversial in the United States. At the largest sperm bank in the United States, though, there is now a policy that the bank will contact the donor to ask him if he would be willing to relinquish his anonymity if a DI child requests information. They have found that donors are more likely to agree to the request after they have had their own children.

The policy at the largest and most well-established surrogate program is predicated on disclosure and openness. Having entered ovum donation, they too now permit anonymous donation. It is not, however, anonymous in the strictest sense in which donors know little if anything about their couples. For example, one 28-year-old ovum donor whose first donation was completely anonymous (facilitated by a physician) described her negative experience: 'It made me feel like a prostitute. It was disgusting. I left there crying. In the end, I said, "I will never do this again"; it was a horrible experience.' Interestingly, she donated two additional times in a program that encourages openness. One of the psychologists at the largest program explained her decision to donate again as an action that was 'helping her to heal.' Her ability to participate a second and third time was because in an open program the ovum donor and prospective couple meet and are free to accept or reject one another, which accords agency to both commissioning couples and donors.

It seems likely that individuals who have gestational surrogates may be tempted not to inform the child of her origin. This appears to be especially true for couples who engage in gestational surrogacy contracts independent of programs. Research on gestational surrogacy reveals that many couples view their surrogates as 'carriers,' and emphasize the remunerative aspect of their relationship as the defining factor.[6] This view stands in stark contrast to couples enrolled in open programs who have ready access to guidelines and counselors who continually advocate openness and disclosure.

In the open surrogacy programs, which require surrogates and commissioning couples to meet and interact with one another throughout the process, couples are strongly encouraged to inform their child of his birth origins, and it appears that most couples take this admonition seriously. However, as Hilary Hanafin, the psychologist at The Center for Surrogate Parenting and Egg Donation, reasoned, IVF surrogacy (when it is the couple's embryos) can be reduced to a reproductive act since the couple ends up with the same child they would have had through traditional reproduction. As a consequence, the motivation for couples to inform their children about their gestational surrogate is lessened.

Information on children produced through gamete donation (whether by ovum or sperm donation) is sparse. In the handful of studies that have examined third-party reproduction, the pattern has been that when children were informed of their birth origins it was usually because 'the system . . . had broken down and the practice of secrecy had failed' (Baran and Pannor 1989: 71).[7] Researchers have concluded that children conceived by third-party reproduction and not informed of their birth origins appear to be well adjusted; parenting in these families also appears to be superior (Golombek et al. 1993). The psychosocial development of these children appears to be the same as that of children conceived through traditional means and adoptees (Kovacs et al. 1993). Based upon the only longitudinal study on DI, which points to the ongoing secrecy of these arrangements and the continued resistance of parents to the idea of informing their children about their birth origins (Snowden et al. 1983), we have little reason to expect disclosure with ovum donation. At present, there are no available data on the long-term effects of either anonymous or open ovum donation.

In preliminary interviews with ovum donors who were in semi-anonymous relationships, all five interviewees expressed similar sentiments when questioned about not being able to meet their couples. They all reported that they felt the need to 'respect their couple's wishes,' a position not at all dissimilar to that of surrogates who were enrolled in anonymous or 'closed' relationships (Ragoné 1994). One component of the constellation of altruistic motives expressed by surrogates, which may also apply to gamete donors, is the courteousness of donors toward recipients.

With surrogate motherhood, as greater numbers of prospective surrogates learned of surrogate mother programs that encouraged interaction between surrogates and commissioning couples, it became increasingly more difficult for programs to enlist the services of surrogates who would agree to anonymous arrangements. At the largest ovum donation program, some of their ovum donors insist upon meeting their recipient couples, and those donors are matched with couples who want to meet their donors. The donor coordinator also said that 'All donors are told of a birth; it creates closure for them. We believe they are entitled to that.'

CONCLUSION

Franklin (1995) points out that there has been a shift in the cultural meaning and organization of reproduction. Reproductive technologies, however routinized and naturalized, are culturally constructed. The ability to separate gametes from their 'owners' has yet to be sufficiently unproblematized, although it has met with a plethora of complex litigation.[8] Advances in reproductive medicine have far-reaching implications and consequences not only for individuals who avail themselves of the procedures, but also for the donors and the children born via them. Continued failure to consider the ways in which individuals must grapple with their decisions to partake in reproductive technologies and beliefs about what constitutes family and relatedness in EuroAmerican kinship ideology (an ideology that bespeaks to the centrality of blood tie) will continue to produce studies, policies, and positions that neglect to take full account of technology's complicated intersections with culture and social values.

The control of reproduction has led to a need for a greater understanding of the impacts of this control, not only on the individuals involved, but also on society. The emotional, social, and economic consequences of choices leading to the use of reproductive technology must be calculated. Questions arise that must be addressed. For example, Does everyone have the right to choose to give birth when and under the circumstances that they want? How do reproductive technologies impact a woman's and couple's right and responsibility to produce a healthy child and member of society? Does society have a say in these decisions? Are women being led to feel that they are somehow responsible for 'quality control' through reproductive technology as Rapp (1988) suggests? Questions related to the economic costs should include the following: Who should pay for reproductive technology and its consequences? Should only those individuals who can afford to pay be given the opportunity to conceive through ARTs? Should society bear the cost of the technology needed to ensure a successful pregnancy for those whose personal choices place them at greater risk to require more technological interventions?

This raises the issue of balancing personal freedom in choices with accountability for those decisions. Cultural values and norms, which can vary between generations, interplay with biological processes to influence fertility. For example, childbearing later in life due to a desire to focus on establishing one's career or to a desire to have additional children in a second marriage can result in decreased fertility, making the need for technological intervention more likely. The desire to ensure a healthy pregnancy when one does get pregnant can lead toward overutilization of technology and the need to address the decisions necessitated by the information provided. The choices made earlier in life, including the use of reproductive technologies such as contraceptives or fertility drugs, can have repercussions throughout the reproductive cycle and beyond. As the postmenopausal population continues to grow, more attention must be focused on the health needs of this cohort, as is being done with the Women's Health Initiative (WHI), a large, US clinical trial assessing the health consequences of nutritional and hormonal interventions for postmenopausal women (Rossouw et al. 1995; WHI Study Group 1998).

Advances in reproductive technology have further contributed to the process of medicalization and continue to influence interactions between women and health-care providers. In all areas of reproduction, the tendency has been a move toward 'technomedicine,' and the knowledge most valued increasingly has become that of the physician trained to interpret the technology. As Jordan (1997: 58) explains, 'the power of authoritative knowledge is not that it is correct, but that it counts.' Because health-care providers often act as arbiters of the knowledge provided by reproductive technology, it is important to study their experiences with, and perceptions of, technology as well as their interactions with patients. While this has been somewhat accomplished in the area of childbirth, there remains a need for more studies of health-care interactions in other domains of reproduction. For example, the acknowledgment that clinicians are 'highly influential' in 'creating the overall atmosphere . . . in which donors and recipients experience gamete donation' (Hamies 1993b: 1518). The role of infertility clinics in the acceptance of anonymity and the structuring of donors and recipients' perceptions, expectations, and

experiences deserves further study, as does the influence of health-care providers on women's decisions to undergo prenatal diagnostic testing and their understanding of, and reactions to, those tests.

As discussed, women have been far from passive in the various processes involved in the medicalization of reproduction. Additional studies on whether women are satisfied with the prices and results of medicalization, or if in fact other models could be developed to deal more effectively with women's concerns about their reproductive health. Women must be given a voice in the discourse of reproduction and reproductive technology because they are the ones whose lives are impacted, both positively and negatively, by the use of reproductive technologies. Their individual perspectives and understandings of the issues surrounding specific areas such as prenatal diagnosis and assisted reproduction are necessary, as is an understanding of the social context within which they live. As seen in the examples provided in this chapter, cultural and medical views about women must also be taken into account when studying reproduction and reproductive technology. As Reissman (1983) illustrates in her analysis of PMS, it is important that the conceptual medicalization of an issue, i.e., naming it a disease, does not hinder an examination of the social etiology. How does medicalizing an issue, such as menopause or infertility, affect the women who are diagnosed with the 'disease'?

The importance of examining differences in women's reproductive experiences based upon such variables as socioeconomic class and ethnicity cannot be overstated. For example, Gabe and Calnan (1989) found that lower-class women were less accepting of medical technology than were middle-class women. Ethnicity also affects the availability of ovum donors and surrogates: specifically, Asian American and Jewish women will participate with great frequency in ovum donation, but it is extremely difficult to find women from these ethnic groups who are willing to serve as surrogates (Ragoné 1998). Further studies are needed to determine how race, culture, and religion influence reproduction in its technological atmosphere.

The sociocultural aspects of reproduction and reproductive technology must be taken into consideration, as well as biomedical aspects. There is a need to work in multidisciplinary teams employing a variety of data collection and analysis methods. The perspective of a broad range of scholars, anthropologists, sociologists, feminists, and cultural historians, as well as clinicians and epidemiologists, is necessary if we are to fully appreciate the complexities of reproduction and reproductive technologies.

NOTES

1 The patient and her husband were not told of the procedure. She gave birth to a son who they raised as their own. The first case of husband insemination occurred in 1775 in London.

2 In 1994, France implemented laws addressing the bioethical and legal aspects of ovum donation and included a proviso that 'donors will never know which couple received their oocytes, the outcome, whether a pregnancy occurred, and what the result was' (Weil 1997: 369).

3 Because DI does not require the expertise of an infertility specialist, accurate documentation on the number of children born is difficult to obtain.

4 Exactly what, if any, differences occur in the rates of disclosure between men who voluntarily chose DI so as not to pass on sex-linked diseases to their offspring and other infertile men is as yet unknown, but worthy of study.

5 Care must be taken when extrapolating since Sweden, noted for its liberal reproductive policies, banned ovum donation as anathema to the 'natural process of life,' while sperm donation is regarded as being more 'natural' (Haimes 1993a: 88), reflecting another policy decision reflective of culturally specific engendered ideas about women, men, and family.

6 The increase in the rate of couples pursuing IVF surrogacy without the assistance of a surrogate program reveals that some couples may view IVF surrogacy as unproblematized since it mimics the biogenetic relationship attained through traditional reproduction.

7 For example, divorce, or in one disturbing case when the children were denied their inheritance since their paternal grandfather reasoned that they were not part of the genetic family (Baran and Pannor 1989).

8 The cases range from a divorced couple's custody battle over 'their' frozen embryos, grandparents seeking a surrogate to gestate their deceased daughters' embryos (none of the transfers were successful), and sperm that was removed from deceased individuals. All of these cases serve as testimony to the importance of acknowledging the inviolability of the blood tie in EuroAmerican culture.

REFERENCES

Applegarth, L., Goldberg, N., Cholst, I., McGoff, N., Fantini, D., Zeller, N., Black, A., and Rosenwaks, Z. (1995) 'Families created through ovum donation: A preliminary investigation of obstetrical outcome and psychosocial adjustment', *Journal of Assisted Reproduction and Genetics*, 12 (9): 574–80.

Arms, S. (1975) *Immaculate Deception: A New Look at Women and Childbirth in America*. Boston: Houghton-Mifflin.

Banta, H.D. (1983) 'Social science research on medical technology, utility and limitations', *Social Science and Medicine*, 17: 1363–9.

Baran, A. and Pannor, R. (1989) *Lethal Secrets: The Psychology of Donor Insemination*. New York: Amistad.

Barker, K.K. (1998) 'A ship upon a stormy sea: The medicalization of pregnancy', *Social Science and Medicine*, 47: 1067–76.

Barratt, C.L., Chauhan, M., and Cooke, I.D. (1990) 'Donor insemination – a look to the future', *Fertility and Sterility*, 54: 375–87.

Becker, G. and Nachtigall, R.D. (1994) '"Born to be a mother": The cultural construction of risk in infertility treatment in the U.S.' *Social Science and Medicine*, 39: 507–18.

Bell, S.E. (1987) 'Changing ideas: The medicalization of menopause', *Social Science and Medicine*, 24: 535–42.

Browner, C.H. and Press, N.A. (1995) 'The normalization of prenatal diagnostic screening', in F.D. Ginsburg and R. Rapp (eds), *Conceiving the New World Order: The Global Politics of Reproduction*. Berkeley: University of California Press. pp. 307–22.

Browner, C.H. and Press, N. (1996) 'The production of authoritative knowledge in American prenatal care.' *Medical Anthropology Quarterly*, 10: 141–56.

Cannell, Fenella (1990) 'Concepts of parenthood: The Warnock Report, the Gillick debate and modern myths', *American Ethnologist*, 17: 667–86.

Chandra, A. and Stephen, E.H. (1998) 'Impaired fecundity in the United States: 1982–1995', *Family Planning Perspectives*, 30: 34–42.

Comaroff, J. and Comaroff, J. (1992) *Ethnography and the Historical Imagination*. Boulder and Oxford: Westview.

Conrad, P. and Schneider, J.W. (1980) 'Looking at levels of medicalization: A comment on Strong's critique of the thesis of medical imperialism', *Social Science and Medicine*, 14A: 75–9.

Daniels, K.R. (1989) 'Semen donors: Their motivations and attitudes to their offspring', *Journal of Reproductive, Infant Psychology*, 7: 121–7.

Dans, P.E. (1992) 'Reproductive technology: Drawing the line', *Obstetrics and Gynecology*, 79: 191–5.

Davis-Floyd, R.E. (1988) 'Birth as an American rite of passage', in K.L. Michaelson (ed.), *Childbirth in America: Anthropological Perspectives*. South Hadley, MA: Bergin and Garvey. pp. 153–72.

Davis-Floyd, R.E. and Sargent, C.F. (eds) (1997a) *Childbirth and Authoritative Knowledge: Cross-Cultural Perspectives*. Berkeley: University of California Press.

Davis-Floyd, R.E. and Sargent, C.F. (1997b) 'The anthropology of birth', in R.E. Davis-Floyd and C.F. Sargent (eds), *Childbirth and Authoritative*

Knowledge: Cross-Cultural Perspectives. Berkeley: University of California Press. pp. 1–51.

Donchin, A. (1996) 'Feminist critiques of new fertility technologies: Implications for social policy', *Journal of Medicine and Philosophy*, 21: 475–98.

Fletcher, J. (1955) *Morals and Medicine*. London: Victor Gollancz.

Flint, M. and Samil, R.S. (1990) 'Cultural and subcultural meanings of the menopause', *Annals of the New York Academy of Science*, 592: 134–48.

Franklin, S. (1995) 'Postmodern procreation: A cultural account of assisted reproduction', in F.D. Ginsburg and R. Rapp (eds), *Conceiving the New World Order: The Global Politics of Reproduction*. Berkeley: University of California Press. pp. 323–45.

Franklin, S. and Ragoné, H. (eds) (1998) *Reproducing Reproduction: Kinship, Power, and Technological Innovation*. Philadephia: University of Pennsylvania Press.

Gabe, J. and Calnan, M. (1989) 'The limits of medicine: Women's perception of medical technology', *Social Science and Medicine*, 28: 223–31.

Georges, E. (1996) 'Fetal ultrasound imaging and the production of authoritative knowledge in Greece', *Medical Anthropology Quarterly*, 10: 157–75.

Gijsbers van Wijk, C.M.T., van Vliet, K.P., and Kolk, A.M. (1996) 'Gender perspectives and quality of care: Towards appropriate and adequate health care for women', *Social Science and Medicine*, 43: 707–20.

Ginsburg, F. and Rapp, R. (eds) (1995) *Conceiving the New World Order: The Global Politics of Reproduction*. Berkeley: University of California Press.

Golombek, S., Cook R., Bish, A., and Murray, C. (1993) 'Quality of parenting in families created by the new reproductive technologies: A brief report of preliminary findings', *Journal of Psychosomatic Obstetrics and Gynecology*, 14 (17):

Gurevich, M. (1995) 'Rethinking the label: Who benefits from the PMS construct?', *Women and Health*, 23 (2): 67–98.

Haimes, E. (1993a) 'Issues of gender in gamete donation', *Social Science and Medicine*, 36: 85–93.

Haimes, E. (1993b) ' Do clinicians benefit from gamete donor anonymity?', *Human Reproduction*, 8: 1518–20.

Hamberger, L. and Janson, P.O. (1997) 'Global importance of infertility and its treatment: Role of fertility technologies', *International Journal of Gynecology and Obstetrics*, 58: 149–58.

Handelsman, D.J., Dunn, S.M., Conway, A.J., Boylan, L.M., and Jansen, R.P.S. (1985) 'Psychological and attitudinal profiles in donors for artificial insemination', *Fertility and Sterility*, 43: 95–101.

Illich I. (1976) *Medical Nemesis: The Expropriation of Health*. New York: Pantheon.

Inhorn, M. (1994) *Quest for Conception: Gender, Infertility, and Egyptian Medical Traditions*. Philadelphia: University of Pennsylvania Press.

Inhorn, M. (1996) *Infertility and Patriarchy: The Cultural Politics of Gender and Family Life in Egypt*. Philadelphia: University of Pennsylvania Press.

Jordan, B. (1997) 'Authoritative knowledge and its construction', in R.E. Davis-Floyd and C.F. Sargent (eds), *Childbirth and Authoritative Knowledge: Cross-Cultural Perspectives*. Berkeley: University of California Press. pp. 55–79.

Kaiser, K. (1990) 'Cross-cultural perspectives on menopause', *Annals of the New York Academy of Science*, 592: 430–2.

Kazem, R., Thompson, L.A., Hamilton, M.P.R., and Templeton, A. (1995) 'Current attitudes towards egg donation among men and women', *Human Reproduction*, 10: 1543–8.

King, C.R. (1992) 'The ideological and technological shaping of motherhood', *Women and Health*, 19: 1–12.

Kovacs, G.T., Mushin, D., Kane, H., and Baker, H.W. (1993) 'A controlled study of the psycho-social development of children conceived following insemination of donor semen', *Human Reproduction*, 8: 788.

Leavitt, J.W. (1986) *Brought to Bed: Childbearing in America, 1750–1950*. New York: Oxford University Press.

Lessor, R., Reitz, K., Balmaceda, J.H., and Asch, R. (1990) 'A survey of public attitudes toward oocyte donation between sisters', *Human Reproduction*, 5: 889–92.

Mahlstedt, P.P. and Probasco, K.A. (1991) 'Sperm donors: Their attitudes toward providing medical and psychological information for recipient couples and donor offspring', *Fertility and Sterility*, 56: 747–53.

Martin, E. (1987) *The Woman in the Body: A Cultural Analysis of Reproduction*. Boston: Beacon.

McCrea, F.B. (1983) 'The politics of menopause: The "discovery" of a deficiency disease', *Social Problems*, 31: 111–23.

Michaelson, K.L. (1988) 'Childbirth in America: A brief history and contemporary issues', in K.L. Michaelson (ed.), *Childbirth in America: Anthropological Perspectives*. Massachusetts: Bergin & Garvey. pp. 1–32.

Modell, J. (1989) 'Last chance babies: Interpretations of parenthood in an in vitro fertilization program', *Medical Anthropology Quarterly*, 3: 124–38.

Myers, M.F. (1990) 'Male gender-related issues in reproduction and technology', in N.L. Stotland (ed.), *Psychiatric Aspects of Reproductive Technology*. Washington, DC: American Psychiatric Press. pp. 25–35.

Oakley, A. (1984) *The Captured Womb*. Oxford: Blackwell.

Pedersen, P., Neilsen, A., and Lauritsen, J. (1994) 'Psychosocial aspects of donor insemination', *Acta Obstetrica et Gynecologica Scandinavica*, 73: 701–5.

Purdie, A., Peek, J., Adair, V., Graham, F. and Fisher, R. (1994) 'Attitudes of parents of young children to sperm donation – implications for donor recruitment', *Human Reproduction*, 9: 1355–8.

Ragoné, H. (1994) *Surrogate Motherhood: Conception in the Heart*. Boulder and Oxford: Westview.

Ragoné, H. (1996) 'Chasing the blood tie: Surrogates, adoptive mother, and fathers', *American Ethnologist*, 23: 352–65.

Ragoné, H. (1998) 'Incontestable motivations', in S. Franklin and H. Ragoné (eds), *Reproducing Reproduction: Kinship, Power, and Technological Innovation*. Philadelphia: University of Pennsylvania Press. pp. 118–31.

Rapp, R. (1988) 'The power of "positive" diagnosis: Medical and maternal discourses on amniocentesis', in K.L. Michaelson (ed.), *Childbirth in America: Anthropological Perspectives*. Massachusetts: Bergin and Garvey. pp. 103–16.

Reame, N. (1998). 'Unintended consequences: What America should do about assisted reproduction', Health Policy Report to the American Academy of Nursing and Institute of Medicine, Washington, DC.

Report of the Departmental Committee on Human Artificial Insemination (1960) (The Feversham Report), Cmnd. 1105. Her Majesty's Stationery Office, London.

Riessman, C.K. (1983) 'Women and medicalization: A new perspective', *Social Policy*, pp. 3–18.

Rosen, B., Irvine, J. Ritvo, P. et al. (1997) 'The feasibility of assessing women's perceptions of the risks and benefits of fertility drug therapy in relation to ovarian cancer risk', *Fertility and Sterility*, 68: 90–4.

Rosenberg, H. and Epstein, Y. (1995) 'Follow-up study of anonymous ovum donors', *Human Reproduction* 10: 2741–7.

Rossouw, J.E., Finnegan, L.P., Harlan, W.R., Pinn, V.W., Clifford, C., and McGowan, J.A. (1995) 'The evolution of the Women's Health Initiative: Perspectives from the NIH', *Journal of the American Medical Women's Association*, 50 (2): 50–5.

Rothman, B.K. (1988) 'The decision to have or not to have aminocentisis for prenatal diagnosis', in K.L. Michaelson (ed.), *Childbirth in America: Anthropological Perspectives*. Massachusetts: Bergin and Garvey. pp. 90–102.

Sandelowski, M. (1993) *With Child in Mind: Studies of the Personal Encounter with Infertility*. Philadelphia: University of Pennsylvania Press.

Sauer, M. and Paulson, R. (1992a) 'Understanding the current status of oocyte donation in the United States: What's really going on out there?', *Fertility and Sterility*, 58: 16–18.

Sauer, M. and Paulson, R. (1992b) 'Oocyte donors: A demographic analysis of women at the University of Southern California', *Human Reproduction*, 7: 776–8.

Schneider, D. (1968) *American Kinship: A Cultural Account*. Chicago: University of Chicago Press.

Schover, L.R., Rothman, S.A., and Collins, R.I. (1992) 'The personality and motivation of semen donors: A comparison with oocyte donors', *Human Reproduction*, 6: 1487–91.

Shalev, C. (1989) *Birth Power: The Case for Surrogacy*. New Haven: Yale University Press.

Shaw, N.S. (1974) *Forced Labor: Maternity Care in the United States*. New York: Pergamon.

Sheth, S.S. and Malpani, A.N. (1997) 'Inappropriate use of new technology: Impact on women's health', *International Journal of Gynecology and Obstetrics*, 58: 159–65.

Snowden, R., Mitchell, G., and Snowden, E. (1983) *Artificial Reproduction: A Social Investigation*. London: Allen and Unwin.

Strathern, M. (1991) 'The pursuit of certainty: Investigating kinship in the late twentieth century', Paper Presented at the 90th American Anthropological Association Annual Meeting, Chicago.

Strathern, M. (1992) *Reproducing the Future*. New York: Routledge.

Strathern, M. (1995) 'Displacing knowledge: Technology and the consequence for kinship', in F.D. Ginsburg and R. Rapp (eds), *Conceiving the New World Order: The Global Politics of Reproduction*. Berkeley: University of California Press. pp. 346–63.

Weil, E. (1997) 'Privacy and disclosure: The psychological impact on gamete donors and recipients in assisted reproduction', *Journal of Assisted Reproduction and Genetics*, 14: 369–71.

Wertz, R.W. and Wertz, D.C. (1989) *Lying In: A History of Childbirth in America*. New York: Free Press.

Williams, S.J. and Calnan, M. (1996) 'The "limits" of medicalization?: Modern medicine and the lay populace in "late" modernity', *Social Science and Medicine*, 42: 1609–20.

Wilson, R. and Wilson, T. (1963) 'The fate of non-treated post-menopausal woman: A plea for the maintenance of adequate estrogen from puberty to the grave', *Journal of the American Geriatrics Society*, 11: 347–61.

WHI (Women's Health Initiative) Study Group (1998) 'Design of the Women's Health Initiative clinical trial and observational study', *Controlled Clinical Trials*, 19: 61–109.

Zola, I.K. (1972) 'Medicine as an institution of social control', *Sociological Review*, 20: 487–504.

Zola, I.K. (1975) 'In the name of health and illness: On some socio-political consequences of medical influence', *Social Science and Medicine*, 9: 83–7.

2.9

Health-Care Utilization and Barriers to Health Care

JUDITH D. KASPER

INTRODUCTION

Attributes of both individuals and societies contribute to the health of populations. Among these, the relative contribution of health-care services provided by trained professionals and aimed at preventing or curing disease is viewed by some as inflated. Rene Dubos observed 40 years ago that:

> The greatest strides in health improvement have been achieved in the field of diseases that responded to social and economic reforms after industrialization. (Dubos 1959: 139)

More recently, Evans and Stoddart have argued that 'the factors which affect health . . . go well beyond health care *per se.*' (1990: 1350).

While the prominence of health-care services as a feature in the broader landscape of population health is subject to debate, there is widespread acceptance of the view that individuals should be able to obtain health services when illness strikes, and should have access to certain proven health-care interventions known to prevent or reduce the risk of disease. Most developed industrialized societies have implemented systems that guarantee basic health care as a right of citizenship. This is not the case in the United States, where financial barriers and the existence of a large number of uninsured people in particular remain central facts in any discussion of health-care utilization or barriers to care. Following the failure of large-scale health system reform in the first Clinton administration, political consensus around improving opportunities for coverage among uninsured children

gradually developed, resulting in the State Children's Health Insurance Program in the Balanced Budget Act of 1997. Other such government-sponsored efforts, for example, expanding Medicare eligibility to those 55–64 years old, face major political obstacles, however. Financial barriers to care have dominated concerns about access in the United States, and set this country apart from other industrialized nations in the health care area. One consequence has been diminished awareness of other barriers that are found not only in the United States but also in countries that have removed payment as an obstacle to care.

This chapter provides an overview of the state of knowledge concerning barriers to health care, drawing on literature from health services research and the social sciences. The scope is limited to Western developed nations, primarily the United States, United Kingdom, and Canada. Barriers to health care in developing nations are frequently only one of many challenges facing the public and private infrastructures of these countries. A recent report on health inequalities in South Africa (Hirshowitz and Orkin 1995), for example, noted that in addition to scarcity of medical clinics and providers, and access problems related to costs, distance, and waiting time, the majority African population was 'worse off' in almost every aspect of their lives, including lack of electricity and clean drinking water, poor sanitation, and overcrowded housing. While some of the findings on barriers to care in countries with well-developed and sophisticated health systems may be applicable to Third-World countries, the form barriers take and priorities among them are apt to differ substantially. Rural health problems in the US or Canada, for example, are of a different order from those in a country like South Africa, where half of the African population is rural and one-third relies on walking as their principal means of transportation.

The term 'health care' will be used to encompass preventive in addition to medical services. This overview begins with a brief historical perspective followed by a discussion of current definitions of access and barriers to care. Empirical research is reviewed relating to barriers to entry to care, and barriers that arise once the care process is underway. Finally, new conceptual and methodological developments are discussed.

A HISTORICAL PERSPECTIVE ON BARRIERS TO CARE: EARLY CONCERNS AND CONCEPTUAL MODELS

Early Concerns About Whether People were Getting Needed Care

In the United States, the initiation of the Committee on the Costs of Medical Care is often depicted as the point of origin for a population perspective on health-care use, as well as concern about whether people were able to obtain medical care when needed (Anderson 1990; Committee on the Costs of Medical Care 1932; Roemer 1985). The population surveys conducted by the Committee found lower-income people, although in poorer health, received less medical care than those with higher incomes (Committee on the Costs of Medical Care 1932). The United States did not implement a national health insurance program in the wake of the Committee's report, a pattern of inaction that persists (for comprehensive studies of the politics of health care in the United States, see Anderson 1990; Weissert and Weissert 1996). Today, only those aged 65 and older, under the Medicare program established in 1965, enjoy universal entitlement to physician and hospital care, although continued increases in beneficiary cost-sharing over the years have led some to argue these pose a financial barrier for those with low incomes (American Association of Retired Persons 1995).

In other developed countries, recognition of the need to 'protect, promote and restore' (Canada Health Act 1984) the health of citizens through access to health services led to government-funded national systems of health care. The goals of these programs have been to promote 'equal treatment for equal need' (Smaje and Le Grand (1997) on the British National

Health Service), and provide 'access to health-care services without financial or other barriers' (Canada Health Act 1984). The organizational approaches to these goals differ. In the UK, the establishment of the National Health Service in 1948 linked each patient to a general practitioner who could be consulted as needed at no cost to the patient, both ensuring a point of entry to the health-care system and eliminating financial barriers. The Canadian health-care system, established under the Canada Health Act of 1984, is administered at the provincial level. It guarantees coverage to all and prohibits direct charges to patients. While direct access to hospital-based physicians is restricted, as in the UK, access to community practitioners is not limited to a single practitioner.

Empirical research on access and barriers to care has been a major focus of health services research in the United States. Resources in the form of government-sponsored health survey data and federal research funding have fostered such research. Equally important, perhaps, is that access has remained in the forefront of US health policy issues because of the lack of universal coverage. Even in Great Britain and Canada, however, there continue to be evaluations of equity in access to health services (cf. Badgley 1991; Benzeval and Judge 1996; Birch and Abelson 1993; Eyles et al. 1995; O'Donnell and Propper 1991; Smaje and Le Grand 1997), with attention focused on noneconomic barriers such as social class and education.

Research Developments – Population-Based Surveys and Behavioral Models for Care-Seeking

Empirical research on access and barriers to care has been fostered by two developments: (1) conceptual models which provided a framework for understanding determinants of health behavior, and service use specifically, and (2) the availability of population-based data, usually in the form of large national surveys, which made it possible to conduct empirical analyses and produce national estimates of interest to health policymakers. Andersen was explicit about this linkage, stating that the behavioral model of health services use he and others developed 'was intended to assist in the analysis of national survey data' (1995: 1).

Today in the United States, there are two ongoing federally funded national population-based surveys that are routinely used to evaluate access and barriers to care, among other issues – the National Health Interview Survey sponsored by the National Center for Health

Statistics (cf. Bloom et al. 1997; Cohen et al. 1997; Simpson et al. 1997), and the Medical Expenditure Panel Survey sponsored by the Agency for Health Care Policy and Research (cf. Weinick et al. 1997). In addition, there are surveys specifically designed to monitor access to care, such as those sponsored by the Robert Wood Johnson Foundation (see Aday et al. 1980, 1984; Berk et al. 1995; Freeman et al. 1987, for results). While health surveys are more numerous in the United States, similar national databases are available in many other developed countries (cf. General Social Surveys in Canada; General Household Survey in Great Britain).

Although various conceptual frameworks and models have been employed in studying access and barriers to care, two of the most widely-used are discussed here – the behavioral model of health services use (Aday and Andersen 1975; Andersen 1968, 1995) and the health belief model (Rosenstock 1966; Strecher and Rosenstock 1997). The origins and objectives of these models have been described elsewhere by their developers (Andersen 1995; Strecher and Rosenstock 1997), and critical appraisals are not lacking (see Good (1994) on the health belief model; see Pescosolido and Kronenfeld (1995) on utilization models such as Andersen's). Briefly, the health belief model deals with the process by which individuals assess their risk from disease or poor health habits, evaluate the seriousness of the risk, weigh the benefits of action, and grapple with barriers to action such as pain, costs, and inconvenience. This model has been applied to a broad spectrum of health behavior that includes differences in willingness to change poor health habits or adopt healthy ones, compliance with medical regimens, and some types of health service use, preventive care in particular (see Janz and Becker (1984) for a review of findings). Andersen's behavioral model of health services was from the outset intended to address use of health-care services; the bulk of studies using this model have concentrated on physician care. The basic model, although still evolving, consists of factors that predispose service use (e.g., demographic, social structure, health beliefs), enable use (e.g., personal/family/community financial resources, service availability), and indicate need for care. As Pescosolido and Kronenfeld (1995) have noted, these models have components in common but different points of emphasis. For example, health beliefs are disaggregated into several discrete elements (e.g., perceived susceptibility, perceived severity, perceived benefits) in the health belief model which has social psychology underpinnings, but constitute

only one of several characteristics predisposing service use in Andersen's model, which draws on a sociological prospective.

From the perspective of studies of access and barriers to care, the Andersen model has been more influential. Andersen's model is more narrowly targeted on health services use, while the health belief model is applicable to a broad array of help-seeking behavior. Furthermore, Andersen and colleagues (Aday and Andersen 1975; Andersen 1968, 1995) suggested that a key application of the model was to evaluate equity in health service use. Because health services are intended to address needs for care, if characteristics other than need, such as insurance coverage (enabling) or race (predisposing or, to the extent it correlates with poverty, enabling) are predictors of use, these relationships suggest inequities in access. The influence of enabling characteristics in particular, such as insurance coverage and income, in empirical analyses of physician use have been a major focus of access studies that employ this model. Finally, as Mechanic (1979) observed, Andersen's model when applied to data from large surveys has been more successful in accounting for variance in service utilization than models that emphasize psychosocial factors.

The role of 'need for care' in the two models is very different. In the health belief model need is not addressed directly, although the end result of various 'calculations' that a person undertakes to form a decision to change behavior or seek treatment could be characterized as a determination of need for care. Such 'calculations' include: Am I at risk? What are the consequences of inaction? How effective is the course of action being considered? How difficult will it be to implement? Andersen and colleagues distinguish between 'perceived need,' a self-evaluation of health such as overall health, symptoms, or functional difficulty, and 'evaluative need,' a professional judgement concerning health status and need for care such as diagnoses. Measures of need in empirical analyses using Andersen's model, whether perceived or evaluative, generally reflect degrees of good or ill health. These have been shown repeatedly to correlate with illness-related care, but are of less relevance in understanding use of preventive services or health promoting/damaging behavior. In the health belief model, on the other hand, determination of need equates with a willingness to act, which provides a framework for understanding behavior that is not driven by illness or poor health, but by the desire to avoid these states. These different perspectives on need may explain why Andersen's model has largely been applied to access to illness-related services, while the health belief model has found broader application in studies of access to preventive health services and screening behavior.

CURRENT DEFINITIONS OF ACCESS AND BARRIERS TO CARE

Defining Access and Barriers to Care

Access to care and barriers to care are often used interchangeably, and will be here. Reference to barriers to care seems to be gaining currency, however. According to a recent Institute of Medicine (Institute of Medicine) report, access is:

> A shorthand term for a broad set of concerns that center on the degree to which individuals and groups are able to obtain needed services from the medical care system. (1993: 4)

In a reformulation of Andersen's model, the same report recasts predisposing and enabling characteristics as various barriers to care – personal (e.g., attitudes, education, cultural), financial (e.g., poverty, insurance coverage), and structural (e.g., service availability, transportation). Another report on access issued recently by the Robert Wood Johnson (RWJ) Foundation (1993) also attributes lack of access to specific types of barriers – economic, supply and distributional, and sociocultural.

While this shift is not entirely new (see Aday 1975), a Medline literature review since 1960 shows greater use of the 'barriers' terminology in the last decade. Describing factors that affect service use as barriers to care may stem from several factors. First, analyses of access, using Andersen's model in particular, identified certain characteristics, such as lack of insurance coverage or presence of a usual source of care, as influences that facilitated or interfered with access. Later studies have focused on identifying determinants or correlates of the presence or absence of these 'barriers.' Secondly, the Institute of Medicine report expresses the view that 'the most important consideration' in access to health services is:

> Whether *opportunities* for good health outcomes are systematically denied to groups in society. (1993: 4)

A focus on barriers to care that deny such opportunities logically follows, and as already noted, the Institute of Medicine report identifies several. It is noteworthy that the Institute of Medicine statement proposes health outcomes rather than equal service use as the measure of whether access is adequate. As Birch and Abelson (1993) point out in discussing the

goals of the Canadian health system, achieving equity may depend on some types of inequality, for example allocating more health resources to those with greater needs for care. While equality of health outcomes cannot be guaranteed by equitable access alone, considering barriers to care that influence health outcomes represents a shift from prior models that focused on barriers to unequal utilization.

Finally, the emphasis on barriers to care reflects the policy orientation of many researchers engaged in analyzing the health-care system. 'Barriers' provide targets for policy intervention. For example, stating that poverty is a barrier to utilization makes the target for action clear; noting that service use decreases with income, does not. Empirical analysis of large data sets, particularly those that provide national estimates, has also been compatible with producing policy-relevant findings that demonstrate the size and scope of access problems. The health belief and utilization models were offspring of the social sciences and informed by the desire to understand human behavior within the context of health-care use and help-seeking generally. As Gray and Phillips (1995) suggest, drawing policy implications from such perspectives presents a challenge. In general, policymakers are more interested in knowing which actions to take to address problems, than in the complexities of human behavior.

Barriers to Entry, Barriers in the Care Process, and Barriers from the Consumer's Perspective

Much of the research on barriers to care has focused on entry to services, usually measured by contact with a physician. A focus on entry to physician care has dominated research on access, in part because physicians are key points of entry to the health-care system. Initiation of preventive care, such as cancer screening or well-child visits, are specialized services where interest in factors affecting entry to care has also generated considerable research. As research on population subgroups, such as the severely mentally ill and those with chronic physical illness, has grown, so has recognition of the need to consider other service sectors such as specialty mental health care and long-term care.

More recently, barriers at other phases of the care process, following entry to care, have emerged as important. This is particularly true in the United States, where the spread of managed care has sparked interest in the effects on access of such organizational policies as putting physicians at financial risk for patient care and restricting specialty referrals. Characteristics previously established as barriers to care entry are still of interest as possible influences on whether a patient receives appropriate care within health-care systems. For example, in a study of health outcomes among Medicare-covered elderly people in managed care, Ware et al. (1996) found worse health outcomes for the poor elderly relative to those better off over a 4-year period.

A renewed interest in quality of care has also generated more studies that evaluate access to services considered standard, or appropriate treatment for specific diagnoses or health problems. Examples include receipt of ophthalmological exams by diabetics (Weiner et al. 1995), and access to certain types and appropriate doses of medications by schizophrenics (Lehman et al. 1998). Such studies often emphasize variations among providers in delivering services, ignoring, for the most part, the patient's role in the process.

Finally, some access studies are including measures that reflect the consumer's perspective on problems, such as difficulty or delays in obtaining care. Interest has grown in the consumer point of view in the United States (Knickman et al. 1996) as managed care has disrupted established relationships with doctors and introduced a new layer of bureaucracy to the process of seeking health care. This line of inquiry might be viewed as a much pared-down version of the 'perceived barriers' component of the health belief model. Results are usually interpreted in the context of the Andersen model, however; reported difficulty or delays due to costs are seen as alternative measures of financial or other barriers. Findings are also interpreted as indicating 'unmet need for care.' Berk et al. (1995) reported unmet needs from the 1994 Robert Wood Johnson Foundation access survey, for example, using questions about not getting needed medical services including prescription drugs, dental care, and mental health care in addition to general physician care.

BARRIERS TO ENTRY TO CARE

Characteristics of Individuals and their Social Environment

Poverty and Socioeconomic Status

There is extensive literature on the relationship of socioeconomic status to health and the pernicious effects of poverty on health (see Haan et al. 1989; Marmot et al. 1997; Robert and House, Chapter 1.8 in this volume; Williams and Collins 1995). Despite skepticism about the ability of health services to significantly intervene in this relationship (Evans and Stoddart 1990; Williams 1990), the extent to which poverty or low socio-economic status contributes to problems in obtaining care has been a major focus of access studies and remains a key test of health system equity. Measures of socioeconomic status vary in definition and use (see Williams and Collins (1995) for a discussion). Access studies in the United States tend to use income and/or education. Studies in other countries often focus on social class.

National data from the United States, prior to the implementation of public programs for the elderly and poor documented that 71 per cent of high-income people, but only 56 per cent of low-income people saw a doctor in a year (Andersen et al. 1976). Coverage of the elderly and many of the poor, through Medicare and Medicaid, has reduced income differences in likelihood and volume of physician contacts in the US population. However, between 1991 and 1993, while average physician contacts per person in a year were similar, or slightly higher, for poor compared with nonpoor men and women, among those reporting their health as fair or poor, average contacts for the poor were much lower. Average contacts for the poor were 13 per cent and 15 per cent for men and women, respectively, versus 17 per cent and 23 per cent, respectively, for the nonpoor.

In Canada and the UK, where the introduction of universal coverage and public financing of care has largely eliminated the relationship between income and utilization (Badgley 1991; Eyles et al. 1995), the continued influence of 'class position' has been noted (Badgley 1991). Based on a comparison of family physician use in Canada in 1985 and 1991, Eyles et al. (1995) suggest that although needs among poorer income groups have increased relative to richer groups, utilization has not increased correspondingly. Furthermore, while the relationship between use and income has been shown to disappear in various analyses, these authors still find relationships with other measures of socioeconomic status, including education and region of residence 'which would appear to represent nonincome based barriers to access' (Eyles et al. 1995: 638).

Andersen et al. (1976) included one preventive service in a health survey done in the early 1960s and found:

> The low income population was least likely to have had a physical within a year and most likely to report never having had an examination. (1976: 8)

Recent data on preventive services document continued disparities by income. Vaccination levels for children 19–35 months of age in the United States are higher for nonpoor compared with poor children. Recent data indicated that only 59 per cent of poor children in this age group had been immunized against preventable childhood illnesses such as polio, measles, and diphtheria, compared with 71 per cent of non-poor children (National Center for Health Statistics 1995). In 1990, among adult women, 73 per cent of poor compared with 84 per cent of nonpoor women were found to have received a pap test in the previous 3 years. Similarly, although breast cancer screening among women over 50 has increased dramatically, in 1990, only 22 per cent of poor women compared with 46 per cent of nonpoor women had received a mammogram in the previous year. For both cervical and breast cancer, which screening tests are designed to detect at an early stage, women living in low-income areas were more likely to be diagnosed after metastasis than women living in high-income areas – 14 per cent and 5 per cent, respectively, for cervical cancer, and 22 per cent versus 46 per cent, for breast cancer (Robert Wood Johnson Foundation 1993). It is tempting to attribute income differences in preventive service use solely to lack of insurance coverage, but differences persist even when these services are financed. Among the elderly on Medicare, for example, a higher percentage of the nonpoor have received the one-time immunization for pneumococcal pneumonia (Robert Wood Johnson Foundation 1993).

Despite the effectiveness of implementation of universal coverage as a remedy for socioeconomic differences in many types of utilization, evidence from other countries shows differences by social class in the use of preventive services. Benzeval et al. (1995) note findings of lower immunization rates among lower social classes in the UK and 'an inverse class gradient in relation to attendance at health checks and other preventative services' (1995: 166). As reported by MacIntyre (1997), the Black Report also took note of 'inequalities in use of health services, particularly and most worryingly of the preventive services' (1997: 727). MacIntyre observes that social class is too often simply a control variable in analyses of health-related behavior, and infrequently the subject of investigation – a charge reminiscent of criticisms of the use of race in many analyses of access of health-care use in the United States. Benzeval et al. (1995) echo the need for more research on factors that underlie treatment-seeking behavior which may account for social class differences.

Ethnic and Racial Minorities

The use of race as an explanatory variable in health services research has been challenged recently on the grounds that it often functions merely as a proxy for other characteristics, primarily socioeconomic status (LaVeist 1994; Schulman et al. 1995). Greater efforts to differentiate the effects of socioeconomic status from race are also called for (LaVeist 1994; Nickens 1995; Schulman et al. 1995; Williams 1994). In addition, race and ethnic group membership also 'proxy' for culture, which can incorporate attitudes, beliefs, and preferences. This perspective on race is usually not explicit, but emerges as analysts attempt to interpret results that indicate effects of race/ethnicity independent of socioeconomic status. Despite conceptual fuzziness about what race represents, Williams (1994) and Williams and Collins (1995) point to one key reason to continue to focus on racial differences – the existence of discrimination in the health-care system as in other segments of society. He suggests:

> The failure of socioeconomic indicators to completely account for racial differences in health (also results from) the failure of most studies to consider the effects of racism on health. (Williams and Collins 1995: 366)

Race and ethnic differences in patterns of care have been documented repeatedly for physician use, and for many other services as well, including prenatal care (LaVeist et al. 1995), mental health care (Wells et al. 1987), nursing home use (Mui and Burnette 1994), interventions for coronary artery disease (Ford and Cooper 1995) and emergency room use (White-Means 1995).

Disentangling the effects of race/ethnicity from socioeconomic status and other factors influencing service use is difficult. Stein et al., (1991) studied mammography use among white, black, and Hispanic women and found that cost concerns exerted the largest effect on mammography use among Hispanic women. Although impoverishment was greater among the Hispanic women, the authors suggest that this was partly a result of acculturation, specifically inability to speak English. In addition, use by both black and Hispanic women was related to perceptions of the examination as painful and fears about radiation levels. It appears from this study that eliminating financial barriers might eliminate a significant portion of the difference in mammogram use by race/ethnicity, but clearly not all.

Acculturation is sometimes advanced as an explanation for the effects of ethnic group membership on access, particularly in studies that include Hispanic subgroups. Results are mixed, in part because measures of acculturation are not consistent across studies. Chesney et al. (1982) and Wells et al. (1987) found effects; Marks et al. (1987) and Markides et al. (1985)

did not. Solis et al. (1990), using national survey data with large samples of three Hispanic sub-groups, examined several preventive services, including a routine physical examination, a dental checkup, vision testing, blood pressure testing, pap test, and breast examination. They found lower use of services by Mexican Americans, than by Puerto Ricans or Cuban Americans, but attributed these differences to insurance coverage and having a regular source of care. Only one measure of acculturation, language, was associated with recency of screening examinations; several others were not, including country of origin, contact with homeland, and parental expectations of children.

The persistence of race differences in utilization despite removal of financial barriers is illustrated by studies of the elderly population. A recent report by the agency that administers the Medicare program showed that 22 per cent of elderly blacks received a flu shot in 1995 compared with 43 per cent of whites (Health Care Financing Administration 1996). Another study examined 32 procedures and tests, that included services for cardiac, cerebrovascular, and orthopedic procedures and mammograms, and found that whites were more likely than blacks to receive services for 23 procedures and had a particular advantage in access to higher technology or newer services (Escarce et al. 1993). The authors offer a variety of hypotheses for further investigation: differences in prevalence and severity of clinical conditions; financial barriers associated with more and better private supplemental coverage for whites; the reliance of blacks on different providers (neighborhood health centers and hospital outpatient departments rather than private physicians); the effect of race on physician and institutional decision making; patient preferences and health beliefs. These correspond to already familiar explanations for race/ethnic differences in patterns of utilization – inadequate measurement of health differences and effects of SES related to race, quality of care differences, racism, and psychosocial factors that reflect culture or education. Efforts to explore these explanations are few, however, in part because the data that are the mainstay for many analyses of access to care, national surveys and administrative claims, are inadequate to the task.

Smaje and Le Grand (1997) point out that in the UK:

> Ethnicity is a dimension of possible inequity . . . that has received much less attention than that arising from other forms of social stratification such as social class or income. (1997: 485)

However, their study found few differences in service use among Indian, African, Pakistani, Bangladeshi, and Chinese people compared with whites. Only the Chinese displayed consistently lower utilization, which the authors attribute to possible differences in cultural views of health, as well as residential patterns.

Culture

In Chapter 2.1 of this volume, McElroy and Jezewski define culture as 'a normative framework for decision making and behavioral strategies.' Studies on access to care that derive conceptually from the Andersen model and make use of large surveys have demonstrated that socioeconomic status and race/ethnicity influence patterns of use, but have had little success in measuring the impact of more elusive concepts such as culture. About 20 years ago, Mechanic (1979) noted the 'gap between [the] two literatures dealing with physician utilization' regarding the importance of psychosocial factors – one based on more theoretical, small sample studies focusing on illness behavior, and the other using multivariate statistical techniques to analyze large samples.

Attention to culture, and psychosocial factors, such as health beliefs and attitudes that derive in part from culture, remains an underrepresented area in the literature on access and barriers to care. One striking example of the importance of this type of research comes from outside the field. A recently published book by Anne Fadiman (1998), *The Spirit Catches You and You Fall Down: A Hmong Child, her American Doctors and the Collision of Two Cultures,* describes the inability of Western physicians and a Cambodian family to find common ground in the treatment of a young girl with epilepsy, given their conflicting perspectives on the meaning of illness and the roles and responsibilities of patients and doctors. Two other recent studies are useful illustrations of the importance of addressing culture and health beliefs if we are to move beyond mere speculation about the effects of noneconomic variables on access to care.

Using a large national survey sample, Fiscella et al. (1998) examined skepticism toward medical care which they describe as:

> The final common pathway for disparate socioeconomic and cultural forces that generate doubts about the relative ability of conventional medical care to improve one's health. (1998: 181)

Multivariate analyses confirmed a relationship between a four-item scale measuring skepticism and several behaviors: not having health insurance, not having a regular source of care, uniformly lower health-care utilization, and unhealthy behaviors such as smoking and not using a seatbelt. The study also indicated that certain demographic characteristics were associated with skepticism – being male, younger, lower income, less educated, and white. One motivation for this study was to raise awareness among the medical and health services community of attitudinal factors in patient behavior. The authors argue that efforts to hold physicians and health plans accountable for performance by measuring various indicators of patient health or compliance with preventive care guidelines do not consider the limits of provider influence over patient attitudes and behavior. The study clearly emphasizes the importance of some of the psychosocial factors in health behavior that have received short shrift in many access and utilization studies. Interestingly, references from the body of work on health beliefs in the social science literature are not cited. The authors do note, however, that in their study, skepticism toward medical care explains only a modest amount of variation in utilization:

> Consistent with previous studies (Mechanic 1979 is cited) that have examined the effect of multiple psychosocial factors (Fiscella et al. 1998: 188)

This lack of explanatory power in multivariate analyses has clearly worked against attention being given by those in health services research to psychosocial and cultural factors in studies of access and barriers to care. White-Means (1995), a health economist, notes that 'empirical models typically exclude measures of culture and attitudes' (1995: 219). However, in a study of emergency medical use, she shows that race may represent cultural and attitudinal differences that affect utilization of care, and should not be viewed as 'simply correlated with a subset of economic variables' (1995: 210). Using as a measure of culture a tradition of use of home remedies, and as a measure of attitudes a trust in the traditional medicine system, she demonstrates that both are related to emergency room use by black elders, although neither is a factor in use by whites.

Characteristics of Health-Care Organization and Financing

Insurance Coverage

The literature regarding the deleterious impact of being uninsured on access to care and utilization is extensive. Two lines of research continue to be pursued. The first is the continued monitoring of the size and scope of the uninsured population in the United States. Declines in employment-based coverage (Holahan et al. 1995), and gaps in Medicaid eligibility that leave many poor people without coverage (Davis 1997), remain central issues in policy research. Among the major objectives of many national population-based health surveys is to provide data on insurance coverage for purposes of characterizing the numbers and characteristics of those without coverage. The second and more recent research initiative is to document the consequences of being without coverage by linking perceptions of unmet needs or poor health outcomes to inadequate access among the uninsured. Davis, addressing the Association for Health Services Research, called for more studies of this type, noting that there are only a few studies that document the health consequences of being uninsured and 'as a result, many believe that the uninsured are able to get care when they need it' (1997: 645).

Other aspects of insurance coverage in the United States, and effects on access, have also been the focus of research, including reductions in use as insurance co-payments increase (Newhouse et al. 1981; Simon et al. 1996), lower use among Medicare beneficiaries without supplemental private coverage (Blustein 1995), and the consequences of less comprehensive private insurance benefits (Short and Banthin 1995). As long as variations in coverage and multiple types of coverage and plans characterize US health care, the extent to which these variations represent barriers and the determinants of variations in coverage – employment, family composition, income, disability – will be a focus of health policy and health services research.

Regular Source of Care

The importance of a regular source of care (usually a specific physician, but including health-care organizations such as clinics) was proposed as a key enabling characteristic affecting utilization in Andersen's initial model. In the words of the Institute of Medicine report, having a regular source of ambulatory care 'has traditionally been viewed as a *sine qua non* for access to medical care' (1993: 159). Having a point of contact for care is seen as facilitating both illness-related and preventive care. Studies show that lacking a regular source of ambulatory care is associated with not seeing a physician (Aday et al. 1984), not receiving recommended medical care and receiving less preventive care (Hayward et al. 1991), less continuity of care (Becker et al. 1974), and delays in seeking care (Sox et al. 1998).

In the United States, the proportion of the population with no usual source of care ranges from 10 to 15 per cent. Elderly people and very young children are more likely to have a usual source of care than others, as are higher-income people, and white compared with black or Hispanic individuals (Aday et al. 1984; Kasper and Barrish 1982). Not surprisingly, a much higher percentage of people without health insurance report no usual source of care. Among poor and nonpoor children, for example, 87 per cent of those under age 4 without insurance and 74 per cent of those 5–17 years old were without a usual source of care, compared with 94 per cent and 89 per cent, respectively, of those with public coverage (Robert Wood Johnson Foundation 1993).

There also has been investigation of the effects of types of usual source of care, in particular seeing a specific physician versus obtaining care at a regular site with no specific doctor, or at sites such as hospital outpatient departments and emergency rooms (Cornelius et al. 1991; Kasper 1987). One recent study found that having a regular doctor, compared with a regular site but no regular doctor, improved the likelihood of a physician visit for people in poor health, but made no difference for mammography among women over 50 or childhood immunizations (Lambrew et al. 1996).

In the United States, reliance on hospital outpatient departments or emergency rooms as a regular source of care has been associated with low income, minority ethnic status, public insurance coverage, and lack of coverage (Aday et al. 1984). For example, in 1982, 27 per cent of poor nonwhites indicated this type of regular source of care. This pattern seems likely to change dramatically as states enroll Medicaid populations into managed care plans that restrict direct access to emergency rooms. One recent study (Shah-Canning et al. 1996) suggests, however, that altering the heavy reliance of inner-city poor families on the hospital emergency room may be difficult. While 95 per cent of families seeking pediatric ER care reported a usual source of care, most did not attempt to contact their regular source prior to visiting the ER.

Some analysts question a uniform interpretation of lack of a usual source of care as an access barrier because the majority of those with no usual source indicate they feel no need for one (Hayward et al. 1991). Lambrew et al. (1996) argue that this perception is at odds with reality, since individuals with no usual source of care consistently appear 'at risk of receiving less timely and appropriate care' (1996: 148). Other criticisms relate to the inability of this construct to reflect more complex patterns of provider relationships. Persons with chronic disease, for example, make use of multiple regular providers, and access to nonphysician providers may be equally critical.

Lack of a usual source of care is an access indicator that appears largely irrelevant to studies of the British or Canadian health systems. In Great Britain, individuals are explicitly linked to a general practitioner. In both countries the supply of primary care physicians is greater and the distribution more even than in the United States. Furthermore, direct access to hospital-based practitioners is quite limited (requiring a referral from a general practitioner), so reliance on hospital outpatient departments or ERs as regular sources of care is precluded. Even in the United States, as the percentage of Americans in managed care continues to climb, absence of a regular source of care may diminish in value as an access indicator at least among the insured because most plans require selection of a primary provider or clinic as the first point of contact.

Service Availability

Early studies of access indicated significant regional and rural/urban differences in access to care in the United States. Data from 1963, for example, showed the rural farm population was less likely to have a physical examination, and that central city dwellers and the rural farm population were least likely to see a doctor and most likely to report having no usual source of care (Andersen et al. 1976). At present, however, residence has declined in importance in considerations of access, in part because large residential differences have disappeared. In a study from the 1980s, Freeman et al. (1987) noted that:

> After many years of national attention to achieving a more equitable geographic distribution of health resources, rural Americans, on average, appear to be receiving as much medical care as urban residents. (1987: 17)

Designation of certain areas as medically underserved for purposes of augmenting physician supply was introduced in the mid-1970s, although there is skepticism about how well this designation reflects access problems (Berk et al. 1983; Kleinman and Wilson 1977). Community Health Centers, subsidized by various levels of government, were also established in the 1960s to provide primary care services in inner cities and rural areas. A review by Blumenthal et al. (1995) of studies on the impact of these centers, by and large showed improvements in access to services.

Disparities in the distribution of physicians remain. For example, the distribution of providers continues to be associated with population income. In 1990, there were 75 pediatricians per 100 000 children under age 19 in high-income counties in the United States, and 33 per 100 000 in low-income counties. The distribution of internists followed a similar pattern (Robert Wood Johnson Foundation 1993). However, the implications of physician supply for access to care are not clear. Grumbach et al. (1997), using data from urban areas in California, found physician supply to be unrelated to access once insurance status, income, and race/ethnicity were taken into account. They argue that:

A more geographically equitable distribution of physicians in the US is unlikely to compensate for a less than egalitarian system of health insurance. (1997: 82)

They also suggest that greater attention to race and ethnicity, rather than to numbers of physicians, may go further toward addressing unmet needs, since minority physicians are more likely to care for minority patients.

In the United States there are still concerns about the distribution of providers and services. As managed care networks develop, which potentially exclude community health centers and urban hospitals, there are fears about the availability of 'safety net' providers for vulnerable populations, such as the inner-city poor and the seriously mentally ill. Data on geographic differences in treatment patterns, attributed to a variety of factors including physician practice patterns and supply, have also led to concerns about high, and possibly unnecessary, utilization, in addition to whether lower levels of use indicate access problems (cf. Chassin et al. 1987).

BARRIERS WITHIN SYSTEMS OF CARE OR TREATMENT EPISODES

There is growing concern in the United States about the ability to obtain needed and appropriate care, independent of concerns about gaining entry. Managed care organizations attempt to reduce utilization of high-cost, specialty, and hospital-based care, and some fear these reductions will mean poorer quality care or will fall disproportionately on those who are sickest and most vulnerable. The development of 'outcomes research' has also focused attention on the care process. Concerns about barriers to care have expanded beyond physician access to include whether specialty care is available, and whether care is provided appropriately, for example,

according to recognized treatment guidelines and standards of care.

The distinction between studying quality of care and studying barriers or access is not always clear in outcomes research. Some investigators start from observed variations in practice or treatment modalities, and attempt to determine whether these affect outcomes, and if so, why; others start from a known outcome, such as hospitalizations that are considered medically unnecessary, and attempt to identify predictors or correlates of these events. In the first type of study, the role of access relative to other forces that affect outcomes can not always be clearly identified. A study by Ware et al. (1996), for example, found differences in health outcomes for elderly, and poor, chronically ill patients treated in a Health Maintenance Organization (HMO) and fee-for-service systems over a 4-year period. In interpreting their results, the authors raise several areas for future exploration that may explain these differences, including clinical factors, and variations in quality of care such as comprehensiveness, service coordination, treatment queues, and continuity. While noting that HMOs reduce utilization, the authors do not speculate on whether differences in access to services is a causal factor in their findings, although some of the process measures suggested for future research, specifically comprehensiveness and treatment queues, may reflect access differences. Another study of this type is that by Shaughnessy et al. (1994), who explored differences in outcomes for home health patients in Medicare fee-for-service and HMO care. The reduced levels of disability in fee-for-service patients were, in this instance, linked to a higher volume of home health visits.

The second type of study seems more likely to reflect directly on access issues in the process of care. Two recent articles that focus on hospitalizations which could be prevented by access to primary care illustrate this approach. The first, by Bindman et al. (1995), calculated hospitalization rates for five chronic conditions (asthma, hypertension, congestive heart failure, chronic obstructive pulmonary disease, and diabetes) for different zip code areas in urban California. Interviews were conducted with random samples of adults living in these areas who were asked about access to care, chronic medical conditions, and propensity to seek care. Controlling for various characteristics, the authors found that within zip codes, rates of preventable hospitalizations for these chronic diseases were inversely related to access to care. A second article, by Pappas et al. (1997), focused on 'potentially avoidable hospitalizations' using a list of twelve diagnoses for which hospitalization 'can be avoided if ambulatory care is provided in a timely and effective manner' (1997: 811). These authors reported higher rates of potentially avoidable hospitalizations for persons living in middle- and low-income compared with high-income areas, and for blacks compared with whites, among people under age 65. Hospitalizations for ambulatory care-sensitive conditions such as asthma, severe ear/nose/throat infections, and bacterial pneumonia have also been shown to vary between children living in low- and high-income areas (Robert Wood Johnson Foundation 1993). These studies represent efforts to demonstrate that poor access to good quality primary care leads to subsequent utilization that is costly and unnecessary, bringing access considerations directly into the stream of research concerned with quality and outcomes of care.

Where Is Research on Access and 'Barriers to Care' Heading, and What Methods are Needed to Answer New Questions?

Conceptual Issues

New Access Indicators

Interest in health outcomes and the role of access to specific types of services at appropriate stages of treatment will likely grow. Several factors will influence the development of access indicators that are meaningful in terms of health or treatment outcomes. At present there are a limited number of diseases and conditions for which access to specific services or treatments have been proposed as significant influences on health outcomes. These include access to primary care in childhood asthma to prevent emergency care and hospitalizations (Robert Wood Johnson Foundation 1993), cancer screening for early detection of breast and cervical cancer (Institute of Medicine 1993; Robert Wood Johnson Foundation 1993), and office-based blood tests and eye examinations for diabetics to prevent health declines (Weiner et al. 1995). Highly prevalent or costly diseases and conditions are the most likely candidates for further development of such indicators because there is greater interest in monitoring health conditions that affect large numbers of people or consume significant resources. For conditions that do not meet these criteria, however, research and policy interest may be more limited. Secondly, these types of indicators require knowledge about the relationship of service use to health or treatment outcomes that at present is limited to

selected conditions and diseases. For example, preventable hospitalizations for angina or hypertension among chronically-ill adults have been suggested as indicators of inadequate primary care, reflecting poor access or quality (Institute of Medicine 1993). For other diseases of the elderly, such as arthritis or dementia, for example, too little is known about the relationship between service use and outcomes to suggest an indicator that would measure the consequences of good or poor access. In these instances, hospitalization cannot be interpreted as indicating either one. Finally, the development of indicators of access with consequences for health outcomes also requires, in many instances, a variety of data sources, not only surveys but utilization data with diagnostic information and sometimes other specialized data sets such as disease registries, which contain information on severity. As a result, these types of study are often complicated to design and implement, time-consuming, and expensive.

The Re-emergence of Noneconomic Influences

Although insurance coverage and financing remain at the center of access concerns in the United States, it is clear that even when no financial barriers exist, cultural and behavioral factors influence access. There is some indication these are receiving greater attention, as reflected by discussions of what race conveys, and what lies behind differences by socioeconomic status. These attributes are chiefly viewed as attaching to individuals and influencing their behavior; however, the response of health-care providers and institutions to persons with particular characteristics also may influence access, though these have received less attention. For example, it has been suggested that racism is a factor in lower use of nursing homes among blacks in the United States (Falcone and Broyles 1994), and one study in the UK suggested class differences in the amount of information patients receive from their general practitioners (Cartwright and O'Brien 1976).

Examining access indicators that affect outcomes for individual diseases and conditions may also help questions about the role of psychosocial factors in utilization to resurface. As Andersen has suggested:

> If we examine beliefs about a particular disease, measure need associated with that disease, and observe the services received to deal specifically with the disease, the relationships will probably be much stronger than if we try to relate general health beliefs to global measures of need and a summary measure of all services received. (Andersen 1995: 2)

The Impact of Managed Care

Managed care has elevated concerns about certain organizational aspects of health care as potential barriers. These include financial arrangements with participating physicians which may create incentives for providing less care, organizational policies that require prior authorization or restrict referral to some types of services, and limited recourse for patients to appeal denials of care. There is little empirical data about the prevalence of such policies or their impact on patient access to care. Some of the conceptual, measurement, and data developments needed to address the specific effects of managed care on access are beginning to be addressed (cf. Aday in this volume; Docteur et al. 1996; Gold 1998; Kasper 1998). Rapid changes in the industry and development of new organizational features, for instance point-of-service care, which eases restrictions on specialty access but at a price, make it difficult to study managed care and to generalize from findings. Attention to systematic differences in utilization and selected health outcomes for those who are especially vulnerable (e.g., chronically ill, low income) may prove useful in monitoring access, at least in the short run.

Models and Data

Reformulations of the models of Andersen and Rosenstock have been proposed (cf. Andersen 1995; Institute of Medicine 1993; Strecher and Rosenstock 1997), and the usefulness and durability of each suggests that they will continue to be relied on in access studies. Rosenstock's model highlighted the primacy of decision making by individuals and patients, and Andersen's model emphasized the influence of an individual's place in the social structure. Studies of outcomes and care quality, however, often draw on Donabedian's framework for evaluating quality of care, in which barriers become one of many aspects of the structure or process of care that may influence outcomes (Donabedian 1988). Because this framework emphasizes the behavior of medical organizations and professionals, it risks diminishing the role of patient behavior as a source of variation in health outcomes. On the other hand, applying this framework to treatment outcomes will unavoidably draw attention to some psychosocial aspects of patient behavior that are not included in most studies of barriers to care, such as compliance, attitudes toward treatment, and expectations of treatment. Explanations of these complex behaviors are likely to benefit from the social science perspective that produced the early models.

Pescosolido (1992) has made a compelling case that much can still be learned about using medical care by viewing it through the lens of social science theory, for example, as a type of 'help-seeking strategy' embedded within social networks and influenced by social interaction. Others (cf. Mechanic 1989) have noted the potential contributions of less-used ethnographic or qualitative methods to understanding medical care utilization. Greater interest in the effects of access on health outcomes could lead research in these directions. Analysis of secondary data from large health surveys, which has dominated medical utilization studies in part because of advantages over primary data collection in terms of time and resource constraints (Mechanic 1989), will not meet the objectives of health outcomes research. General population surveys are structured to provide data on the population at large, and sociodemographic subgroups, rather than on people with specific health conditions, who are usually the focus of health outcomes studies. Furthermore, data to address health outcomes must reflect the health-care experience of individuals over time, and draw on multiple sources, including providers, insurers, patients, and possibly family members or caregivers.

There is potential for increased use of qualitative methods in outcomes research. Qualitative data can provide a fuller and more nuanced depiction of the complexities of individual behavior and motivation than is possible from standardized questionnaires. In addition, survey questions and content for outcomes studies cannot be off-the-shelf since they must be sensitive to access issues for individuals in different organized care settings and with disease or condition-specific service needs. Ethnographic studies can provide guidance with regard to meaningful question wording and content. Such methods could be especially useful in instances where little is known about patient or provider behavior and attitudes. Many examples come to mind, such as the impact of culture or religious beliefs in selecting among established treatment alternatives over the course of chronic diseases such as AIDS or schizophrenia, or the growing attraction for both physicians and patients of nontraditional treatments and natural remedies. Because most studies of health outcomes are done within the medical, public health, and health services research communities, the potential contribution of ethnographic studies is not always recognized. At the same time, it is not clear to what extent social scientists with this type of expertise will be attracted to these issues.

Conclusion

Access to care has been a key measure of health system performance. Financial barriers to access, primarily being uninsured, have been a major focus of research and policy in the United States, but even in societies that have eliminated financial barriers to access, research on noneconomic barriers to access continues. A considerable body of research exists that documents barriers related to personal characteristics and organizational aspects of care. There is no question that ability to pay has a major impact on whether people choose to seek care, but research tells us that once this barrier is removed, others remain. Mechanic posed a question 20 years ago that is still relevant:

> Why [do] persons with similar complaints behave so differently and why [does] the same person with comparable symptoms at various times choose to seek medical care on one occasion but not another. (Mechanic 1979: 394)

The effort to generate new access indicators that affect health outcomes in addition to utilization of care, and continued reformulation of access models, indicates that interest in these questions is not waning. Continuing to monitor barriers to access, and who is affected by them, is critical, but a simultaneous effort is needed to understand the mechanisms by which some longstanding and well-documented barriers exert influence. Access research represents the merging of social science research on one aspect of human behavior with health policy and medical concerns about providing care to those in need. The expertise of both will be needed to address the more complex questions that lie ahead.

References

Aday, L. (1975) 'Economic and noneconomic barriers to the use of needed medical services', *Medical Care*, XIII: 447–56.

Aday, L. and Andersen, R.M., (1975) *Development of Indices of Access to Medical Care*. Ann Arbor, MI: Health Administration Press.

Aday, L.A., Andersen, R.M., and Fleming, G.V. (1980) *Health Care in the US: Equitable for Whom?* Beverly Hills, CA: Sage.

Aday, L., Fleming, G., and Andersen, R.M. (1984) *Access to Medical Care in the US: Who Has It, Who Doesn't.* Chicago: Pluribus.

American Association of Retired Persons (1995) *Coming Up Short: Increasing Out-of-Pocket Health Spending by Older Americans*. Washington, DC.

Anderson, O.W. (1990) *Health Services as a Growth Enterprise in the United States since 1875* (2nd edn). Ann Arbor: Health Administration Press.

Andersen, R.M. (1968) *Behavioral Model of Families Use of Health Services.* Research Series No. 25, Chicago IL: Center for Health Administration Studies, University of Chicago.

Andersen, R.M. (1995) 'Revisiting the behavioral model and access to medical care: Does it matter?' *Journal of Health and Social Behavior*, 36: 1–10.

Andersen, R., Lion, J., and Anderson, O.W. (1976) *Two Decades of Health Services: Social Survey Trends in Use and Expenditure.* Cambridge, MA: Ballinger.

Badgley, R. (1991) 'Social and economic disparities under Canadian health care', *International Journal of Health Services*, 21: 659–71.

Becker, M.H., Drachman, R.H., and Kirscht, J.P. (1974) 'A field experiment to evaluate various outcomes of continuity of physician care', *American Journal of Public Health*, 64: 1062–70.

Benzeval, M. and Judge, K. (1996) 'Access to health care in England: Continuing inequalities in the distribution of GPs', *Journal of Public Health Medicine*, 18: 33–40.

Benzeval, M., Judge, K., and Smaje, C. (1995) 'Beyond class, race, and ethnicity: Deprivation and health in Britain', *Health Services Research*, 30: 163–77.

Berk, M. L., Bernstein, A.B., and Taylor, A.K. (1983) 'The use and availability of medical care in health manpower shortage areas', *Inquiry*, (Winter): 369–80.

Berk, M.L., Schur, C.L., and Cantor, J.C. (1995) 'Ability to obtain health care: Recent estimates from the Robert Wood Johnson Foundation National Access to Care Survey', *Health Affairs*, 14: 139–46.

Bindman, A.B., Grumbach, K., Osmond, D., Komaromy, M., Vranizan, K., Lurie, N., Billings, J., and Stewart, A. (1995) 'Preventable hospitalizations and access to health care', *Journal of the American Medical Association*, 274: 305–11.

Birch, S. and Abelson, J. (1993) 'Is reasonable access what we want? Implications of, and challenges to, current Canadian policy on equity in health care', *International Journal of Health Services*, 23: 629–53.

Bloom, B., Simpson, G., Cohen, R.A., and Parsons, P.E. (1997) *Access To Health Care. Part 2. Working-Age Adults.* Vital and Health Statistics, Series 10. Data from the National Health Survey (197): 1–47.

Blumenthal, D., Mort, E., and Edwards, J. (1995) 'The efficacy of primary care for vulnerable population groups', *Health Services Research*, 30: 253–73.

Blustein, J. (1995) 'Medicare coverage, supplemental insurance, and the use of mammography by older women', *New England Journal of Medicine*, 332: 1138–43.

Cartwright, A. and O'Brien, M. (1976) 'Social class variations in health care and in the nature of general practitioner consultations', in M. Stacey (ed.), *The*

Sociology of the National Health Service. Sociology Review Monograph 22, Stoke-on-Trent: Keele University Press.

Chasin, M.R., Kosecoff, J., Park, R.E., Winslow, C.M., Kahn, K.L., Merrick, N.J., Keesey, J., Find, A., Solomon, D.H., and Brook, R.H. (1987) 'Does inappropriate use explain geographic variations in the use of health care services?' *Journal of the American Medical Association,* 258: 2533–42.

Chesney, A.P., Chavira, J.A., Hall, R.P., and Gary, H.E. (1982) 'Barriers to medical care of Mexican Americans: The role of social class, acculturation, and social isolation', *Medical Care,* 20: 883–91.

Cohen, R.A., Bloom, B., Simpson, G., and Parsons, P.E. (1997) *Access to Health Care. Part 3. Older Adults.* Vital and Health Statistics – Series 10. Data from the National Health Survey (198): 1–32.

Committee on the Costs of Medical Care (1932) *Medical Care for the American People: The Final Report of the Committee.* Chicago: University of Chicago Press.

Cornelius, L., Beauregard, K., and Cohen, J. (1991) *Usual Sources of Medical Care and Their Characteristics.* National Medical Expenditure Survey Research Findings 11, Agency for Health Care Policy and Research (Pub. No. 91–0042), Rockville, MD.

Davis, K. (1997) 'Uninsured in an era of managed care', *Health Services Research,* 31: 641–9.

Docteur, E.R., Colby, D.C., and Gold, M. (1996) 'Shifting the paradigm: Monitoring access in Medicare managed care', *Health Care Financing Review,* 17(4): 5–21.

Donabedian, A. (1988) 'The quality of care. How can it be assessed?' *Journal of the American Medical Association,* 260: 1743–8.

Dubos, R. (1959) *Mirage of Health.* Garden City, NY: Doubleday.

Escarce, J.J., Epstein, K.R., Colby, D.C. and Schwartz, J.S. (1993) 'Racial differences in the elderly's use of medical procedures and diagnostic tests', *American Journal of Public Health,* 83: 948–54.

Evans, R.G. and Stoddart, G.L. (1990) 'Producing health, consuming health care', *Social Science and Medicine,* 31: 1347–63.

Eyles, J., Birch, S., and Newbold, K.B. (1995) 'Delivering the goods? Access to family physician services in Canada: A comparison of 1985 and 1991', *Journal of Health and Social Behavior,* 36: 322–32.

Fadiman, A. (1998) *The Spirit Catches You and You Fall Down: A Hmong Child, Her American Doctors, and the Collision of Two Cultures.* New York: Farrar Straus and Giroux.

Falcone, D. and Broyles, R. (1994) 'Access to long-term care: Race as a barrier', *Journal of Health Politics, Policy and Law,* 19: 583–95.

Fiscella, K., Franks, P., and Clancy, C.M. (1998)

'Skepticism toward medical care and health care utilization', *Medical Care,* 36: 180–9.

Ford, E.S. and Cooper, R. S. (1995) 'Racial/ethnic differences in health care utilization of cardiovascular procedures: A review of the evidence', *Health Services Research,* 30: 237–51.

Freeman, H.E., Blendon, R.J., Aiken, L.H., Sudman, S., Mullinix, C.F., and Corey, C.R. (1987) 'Americans report on their access to health care', *Health Affairs,* (Spring): 7–18.

Gold, M. (1998) 'Beyond coverage and supply: Measuring access to healthcare in today's market', *Health Services Research,* 33: 625–52.

Good, B. (1994) *Medicine, Rationality and Experience: An Anthropological Perspective.* Cambridge, New York: Cambridge University Press.

Gray, B.H. and Phillips, S.R. (1995) 'Medical sociology and health policy: Where are the connections?' *Journal of Health and Social Behavior,* Extra Issue: 170–81.

Grumbach, K., Vranizan, K., and Bindman, A.B. (1997) 'Physician supply and access to care in urban communities', *Health Affairs,* 16: 71–86.

Haan, M.N., Kaplan, G.A., and Syme, L. (1989) 'Socioeconomic status and health: Old observations and new thoughts', in J.P. Bunker, D.S. Gomby, and B.H. Kehrer (eds), *Pathways to Health: The Role of Social Factors.* Menlo Park, CA: Henry J. Kaiser Foundation.

Hayward, R.A., Bernard, A.M., Freeman, H.E., and Corey, C.R. (1991) 'Regular source of ambulatory care and access to health services,' *American Journal of Public Health,* 81: 434–8.

Health Care Financing Administration (1996) *1995 Influenza Immunizations Paid for by Medicare.* October, US Department of Health and Human Services.

Hirshowitz, R. and Orkin, M. (1995) *A National Survey of Health Inequalities in South Africa.* Menlo Park, CA: Henry J. Kaiser Family Foundation.

Holahan, J., Winterbottom, C., and Rajan, S. (1995) 'A shifting picture of health insurance coverage', *Health Affairs,* 14: 253–64.

Institute of Medicine (IOM) (1993) in M. Millman (ed.), *Access to Health Care in America.* Washington, DC: National Academy of Sciences.

Janz, N.K. and Becker, M.H. (1984) 'The health belief model: A decade later', *Health Education Quarterly,* 11: 1–47.

Kasper, J.D. (1987) 'The importance of type of usual source of care for children's physician access and expenditures', *Medical Care,* 25: 386–98.

Kasper, J.D. (1998) 'Asking about access: Challenges for surveys in a changing health care environment', *Health Services Research,* 33: 715–39.

Kasper, J.A. and Barrish, G. (1982) *Usual Sources of Medical Care and their Characteristics.* National Health Care Expenditures Study, Pub. No. PHS

82-3324. Washington, DC: Department of Health and Human Services.

Kleinman, J. and Wilson, R. (1977) 'Are "Medically underserved areas" medically underserved?' *Health Services Research*, (Summer): 147–62.

Knickman, J., Hughes, R.G., Taylor, H., Binns, K., and Lyons, M.P. (1996) 'Tracking consumers' reactions to the changing health care system: Early indicators', *Health Affairs*, 15(2): 21–32.

Lambrew, J.M., DeFriese, G.H., Carey T. S., Ricketts, T.C., and Biddle, A.K. (1996) 'The effects of having a regular doctor on access to primary care', *Medical Care*, 34: 138–51.

LaVeist, T. (1994) 'Beyond dummy variables and sample selection: What health services researchers ought to know about race as a variable', *Health Services Research*, 29: 1–16.

LaVeist, T.A., Keith, V., and Gutierrez, M.L. (1995) 'Black/white differences in prenatal care utilization: An assessment of predisposing and enabling factors', *Health Services Research*, 30: 10–58.

Lehman, A.F., Steinwachs, D.M., Buchanan, R., Carpenter, W.T., Dixon, L.B., Fahey, M., Fischer, P., Goldman, H.H., Kasper, J., Levine, J., Lyles, A., McGlynn, E., Osher, F., Postrado, L., Rosenheck, R., Scott, J.C., Skinner, E., Thompson, J., and Zito, J. (1998) 'Translating research into practice: The schizophrenia PORT treatment recommendations', *Schizophrenia Bulletin*, 24: 1–10.

MacIntyre, S. (1997) 'The black report and beyond what are the issues?' *Social Science and Medicine*, 44: 723–45.

Marks, G., Solis, J., Richardson, J.L., Collins, L.M., Birba, L., and Hisserich, J.C. (1987) 'Health behavior of elderly Hispanic women: Does cultural assimilation make a difference?' *American Journal of Public Health*, 77: 1315–19.

Markides, K.S., Levin, J.S., and Ray, L.A. (1985) 'Determinants of physician utilization among Mexican Americans: A three-generation study', *Medical Care*, 23: 236–46.

Marmot, M., Ryff, C.D., Bumpass, L.L., Shipley, M. and Marks, N.F. (1997) 'Social inequalities in health: Next questions and converging evidence', *Social Science and Medicine*, 44: 901–10.

Mechanic, D. (1979) 'Correlates of physician utilization: Why do major multivariate studies of physician utilization find trivial psychosocial and organization effects?' *Journal of Health and Social Behavior*, (20): 387–96.

Mechanic, D. (1989) 'Medical sociology: Some tensions among theory, method and substance', *Journal of Health and Social Behavior*, 30: 147–60.

Mui, A.C. and Burnette, D. (1994) 'Long-term care service use by frail elders: Is ethnicity a factor?' *Gerontologist*, 34: 190–8.

National Center for Health Statistics (NCHS) (1995) *Health United States 1994*. Hyattsville, Md: DHHS Publication No. (PHS) 95-1232.

Newhouse, J.P., Manning, W.G., Morris, C.N., Orr, L.L., Duan, N., Keeler, E.B., Leibowitz, A., Marquis, K.H., Marquis, M.S., Phelps, C.E., and Brook, R.H. (1981) 'Some interim results from a controlled trial of cost sharing in health insurance', *New England Journal of Medicine*, 305: 1501–7.

Nickens, H.W. (1995) 'Race/ethnicity as a factor in health and health care', *Health Services Research*, 30: 151–61.

O'Donnell, O. and Propper, C. (1991) 'Equity and the distribution of National Health Service resources,' *Journal of Health Economics*, 10: 1–19.

Pappas, G., Hadden, W.C., Kozak, L.J., and Fisher, G.F. (1997) 'Potentially avoidable hospitalizations: Inequalities in rates between US socioeconomic groups', *American Journal of Public Health*, 87: 811–16.

Pescosolido, B.A. (1992) 'Beyond Rational choice: The social dynamics of how people seek help', *American Journal of Sociology*, 97: 1096–1138.

Pescosolido, B.A. and Kronenfeld, J.J. (1995) 'Health, illness, and healing in an uncertain era: Challenges from and for medical sociology', *Journal of Health and Social Behavior*, (Extra Issue): 5–33.

Robert Wood Johnson Foundation (RWJ) (1993) *Access to Health Care: Key Indicators for Policy*. Prepared by the Center for Health Economics Research, November.

Roemer, M. (1985) 'I. S. Falk, the committee on the costs of medical care, and the drive for national health insurance', *American Journal of Public Health*, 75: 841–8.

Rosenstock, I.M. (1996) 'Why people use health services', *Milbank Memorial Fund Quarterly*, 44: 94–124.

Schulman, K.A., Rubenstein, L.E., Chesley, F.D., and Eisenberg, J.M. (1995) 'The roles of race and socioeconomic factors in health services research,' *Health Services Research*, 30: 179–95.

Shah-Canning, D., Alpert, J.J., and Bauchner, H. (1996) 'Care-seeking patterns of inner-city families using an emergency room', *Medical Care*, 34: 1171–9.

Shaughnessy, P.W., Schlenker, R.E., and Hittle, D.F. (1994) 'Home health care outcomes under capitated and fee-for-service payment', *Health Care Financing Review*, 16: 187–222.

Short, P.F. and Banthin, J.S. (1995) 'New estimates of the underinsured younger than 65 years,' *Journal of the American Medical Association*, 274: 1302–6.

Simon, G.E., Grothaus, L., Durham, M.L., VonKorff, M., and Pabiniak, C. (1996) 'Impact of visit copayments on outpatient mental health utilization by members of a health maintenance organization', *American Journal of Psychiatry*, 153: 331–8.

Simpson, G., Bloom, B., Cohen, R.A. and Parsons, P.E. (1997) *Access to Health Care. Part 1. Children*. Vital and Health Statistics, Series 10. Data from the National Health Survey (196): 1–46.

Smaje, C. and Le Grand, J. (1997) 'Ethnicity, equity

and the use of health services in the British NHS', *Social Science and Medicine*, 45: 485–96.

Solis, J.M., Marks, G., Garcia, M., and Shelton, D. (1990) 'Acculturation, access to care, and use of preventive services by Hispanics: Findings from HHANES 1982–84' *American Journal of Public Health*, 80 (December): 11–19.

Sox, C.M., Swartz, K., Burstin, H.R., and Brennan, T.A. (1998) 'Insurance or a regular physician: Which is the most powerful predictor of health care?' *American Journal of Public Health*, 88: 364–70.

Stein, J.A., Fox, S.A., and Murata, P.J. (1991) 'The influence of ethnicity, socioeconomic status, and psychological barriers on use of mammography', *Journal of Health and Social Behavior*, 32(June): 101–13.

Strecher, V.J. and Rosenstock, I.M. (1997) 'The health belief model', in K. Glanz, F.M. Lewis, and B.K. Rimer (eds), *Health Behavior and Health Education: Theory Research and Practice* (2nd edn). San Francisco, CA: Jossey-Bass.

Ware, J.E., Bayliss, M.S., Rogers, W.H., Kosinski, M., and Tarlov, A.R. (1996) 'Differences in 4-year health outcomes for elderly and poor, chronically ill patients treated in HMO and fee-for-service systems: Results from the medical outcomes study', *Journal of the American Medical Association*, 276: 1039–47.

Weiner, J.P., Parente, S.T., Garnick, D.W., Fowles, J., Lawthers, A.G., and Palmer, R.H. (1995) 'Variation in office-based quality: A claims-based profile of care provided to Medicare patients with diabetes', *Journal of the American Medical Association*, 273: 1503–8.

Weinick, R.M., Zuvekas, S.H., and Drilea, S.K. (1997) *Access to Health Care: Sources and Barriers 1996.* MEPS Research Findings No. 3, Agency for Health Care Policy and Research, Publication No. 98–0001. Rockville, MD: AHCPR.

Weissert, C.S. and Weissert, W.G. (1996) *The Politics of Health Policy.* Baltimore, MD: Johns Hopkins University Press.

Wells, K.B., Hough, R.L., Golding, J.M., Burnam, M.A., and Karno, M. (1987) 'Which Mexican Americans underutilize health services?' *American Journal of Psychiatry*, 144: 918–22.

White-Means, S.I. (1995) 'Conceptualizing race in economic models of medical utilization: A case study of community-based elders and the emergency room', *Health Services Research*, 30: 207–33.

Williams, D.R. (1990) 'Socioeconomic differentials in health: A review and redirection', *Social Psychology Quarterly*, 53(2): 81–99.

Williams, D.R. (1994) 'The concept of race in health services research', *Health Services Research*, 29: 261–74.

Williams, D.R. and Collins, C. (1995) 'US socioeconomic and racial differences in health: Patterns and explanations', *Annual Review of Sociology*, 21: 349–86.

2.10

Concepts and Measurement of Health Status and Health-Related Quality of Life

COLLEEN A. McHORNEY

INTRODUCTION

The approach of a new century naturally beckons reflections on past, present, and future conditions in science as well as in other domains of life. Over the past 30 years, the field of health status assessment has generated dozens of tools that use patient self-report to measure functional status, emotional well-being, and subjective perceptions of health. These tools can be characterized into three different genres: generic, disease-specific, and preference-based. Generic measures tap a broad spectrum of health concepts and are intended to be appropriate for groups that differ in disease, severity, and comorbidity. Disease-specific tools are applicable to specific patient populations, usually defined by disease pathology. Measurement priorities are focused on aspects of disease-specific health status that are likely to be sensitive to treatment and natural history. Preference-based measures combine a weighted assessment of health state values with life years to yield a single aggregate score of quality-adjusted life years. Applications of all three types of measures have increased dramatically in the past 10 years as a result of the outcomes and accountability movements. Accordingly, the purpose of this chapter is to review the state of the art in health status assessment and accomplishments achieved to date, and to identify outstanding issues for the field in the years ahead.

EVOLUTION OF THE STATE OF THE ART IN HEALTH STATUS ASSESSMENT

Figure 1 presents a timeline depicting the evolution of generic health status measures *vis-à-vis* broader developments in health policy and health measurement paradigms. For brevity's sake, it starts in 1947 with the WHO definition of health. Roughly coincidental with publication of the WHO definition was the emergence of clinically based, 'global' indicators of function whose content extended beyond a physiological conceptualization of health. These measures included Karnofsky's performance status scale (KPS) (Karnofsky et al. 1948) intended to capture the 'therapeutic value' of palliative cancer treatment, and the function scale of the American Rheumatoid Association (ARA), developed to provide a 'common language' of therapeutic effectiveness in rheumatoid arthritis (Steinbrocker et al. 1949). Both the KPS and ARA innovatively recognized that human function is not synonymous with organ function, and both were intended to be used in concert with clinical measures to better understand treatment effectiveness.

In the 1950s, federal efforts to modernize national health indicators were initiated. These ventures began when mortality gains achieved throughout the twentieth century were leveling off and when chronic disease was emerging as the principal threat to population health. The

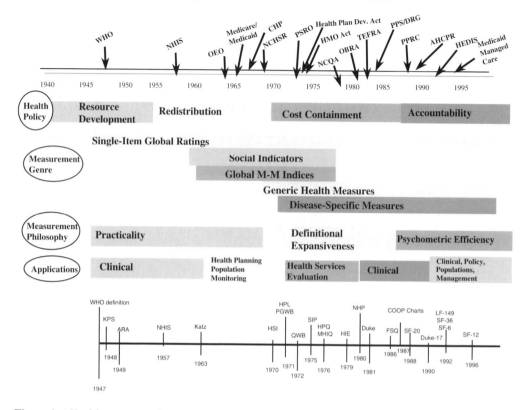

Figure 1   *Health status timeline*

first fielding of the National Health Interview Survey (NHIS) occurred in 1957. The content of the NHIS has reflected the tenets of the medical model insofar as health is conceptualized as the absence of disease or dysfunction, and physical-health constructs, such as morbidity and disability, have clear dominance over mental-health constructs (which signifies body–mind dualism). Even today, there are no items on the NHIS that tap mental health status.

The historic policy initiatives of the 'war on poverty' prompted two breakthroughs in health measurement. First, the social indicators movement ushered in research on the measurement and determinants of general mental health and quality of life (Bradburn and Caplovitz 1965; Campbell et al. 1976; Gurin et al. 1960). Measurement work progressed beyond fiscal accountability to social accountability, and provided indicators of how well we lived to be used with existing indicators of how much we produce and spend (Bauer 1966). These contributions represented a clear break with the dualism intrinsic to the medical model by concentrating measurement advances on well-being, happiness, and life satisfaction.

Second, conceptual and methodological work focused on the derivation of single, 'unified' indices (M–M indices) of population health which combined mortality with morbidity-based data on chronic disease and disability (Chen 1979; Sullivan 1971). These indices were intended to provide more precise measures of population health status for planning and evaluation purposes. Many M–M indices were underutilized for policy and planning purposes, which is attributable in part to their mathematical intricacies as well as their failure to include function in the algorithm. By the early 1970s, functional status assessment was a prolific area of measurement work (Cohen and McHorney in press).

The genesis of generic health assessment can be traced to the Human Population Laboratory (HPL), which initiated measurement work in physical, mental, and social health for general populations (Belloc et al. 1971; Berkman 1971; Renee 1974). Of equal importance, the HPL significantly advanced the state of the art of health survey methods. Up to the early 1970s, considerable skepticism existed about the use of survey methods other than face-to-face interviews.

Important for both the development and use of health status measures, the HPL demonstrated that respondents will complete very long surveys by mail (Hochstim 1970).

Following a 30 per cent increase in national health expenditure over a 15-year period, the 1970s began the era of cost containment in health care. At the same time, the development of generic health status tools proliferated, in part because of extramural support from the National Center for Health Services Research. Definitional expansiveness was the signature of this period, and multi-item scales rapidly replaced single-item scales. The measures developed in this era were diversified in terms of content, source of items, depth and breadth of measured concepts, scaling techniques, and proposed applications. Table 1 provides a content classification for a sampling of these measures.

First off the starting block, the function status index (now the quality of well-being scale [QWB]) represented a breakthrough in measuring the 'value components' of a social indicator of health (Bush et al. 1972; Patrick et al. 1973). Conceived in an era of expansions in the medical work force and private health plans, the QWB was developed for health planning, program evaluation, and population monitoring purposes. The QWB consists of three functional status scales (mobility, physical, and social) and 25 symptoms (e.g., pain, headache, and weakness). Preference weights for the symptoms and function levels were obtained from the general community in order to weight the individual health states differentially by their relative importance. An overall, point-in-time QWB score is the product of the weighted symptom and function levels.

Next, the sickness impact profile (SIP) surfaced (Bergner et al. 1981; Gilson et al. 1975). It was developed for health-care evaluation purposes. The SIP represented a unique approach to health measurement because its items were obtained from open-ended surveys of patients, health-care professionals, and caregivers. Extensive item reduction was performed, and weights were obtained for each item. The SIP also represented an innovative approach to summarizing health information: it yielded twelve individual health profiles, two secondary summary scales (physical and psychosocial), and a total SIP score.

The McMaster health index questionnaire followed on the heels of the SIP. Intended for use in clinical trials and health services research, it measured three health concepts (physical–social–mental) using fifty-nine items obtained from existing surveys and literature (Chambers et al. 1976). Unweighted item aggregation was used to scale items. Psychometric elegance char-

acterized the work of Ware and Karmos (1976) on the health perceptions questionnaire (HPQ). Health perceptions is a domain of health status that cross-cuts physical and mental health, and, in doing so, tries to tap the realm of 'positive health.' The intended uses of the HPQ fell within health planning, administration, and evaluation domains.

In 1979, adult health status measures ensued from the health insurance experiment (HIE) (Brook et al. 1979), a large, randomized experiment of different methods of financing and organizing health-care services (Newhouse 1994). Measurement work was directed toward general populations. The eighty-one items were largely derived from existing literature (e.g., Dupuy's general well-being index) and tapped five domains of health (functional limitations, physical abilities, health perceptions, social health, and mental health) using unweighted item aggregation.

Next, the Nottingham health profile (NHP) emerged (Hunt and McEwen 1980). Like the SIP, items for the NHP were gleaned from hundreds of patient interviews, yielding 2200 statements about ill health that were reduced to thirty-eight items tapping six health concepts. The NHP was developed for use in population-level epidemiological research as well as clinical trials and practice. The final entrant to the flurry of measurement activities in the 1970s was the Duke health profile (DUHP), a sixty-three-item profile that measures physical, social, and mental functioning and symptom status (Parkerson et al. 1981). Items for the DUPH were obtained from the literature and were weighted equally. The DUHP was developed for use in primary care for research and clinical purposes.

Further development of generic measures took a respite in the early 1980s. During this period, however, applications of existing measures grew in clinical and health services research, and interest in methodological issues increased (Deyo and Inui 1984; Patrick et al. 1985). At the same time, development of disease-specific measures was accelerating (Figure 2), in large part due to the growing interest in using health status measures in clinical trials of treatment effectiveness.

Up to the mid-1980s, health status measures were used almost exclusively in group-level research, such as clinical trials and health services evaluation. However, interest in using patient-based health surveys in more microlevel, clinical practice applications arose in the 1980s as a result of several catalysts. First, a growing body of research documented poor correspondence between clinician and patient ratings of function and well-being (Jachuck et al. 1982; Nelson et al. 1983). Second, the clinical and

Table 1   *Summary of content of generic measures*

	HPL	QWB	SIP	HPQ	MHIQ	HIE	NHP	DUKE	FSQ	COOP	SF-20	DUKE-17	EURO-QOL	LF-149	SF-36
Physical functioning	x	x	x		x	x	x	x	x	x	x	x	x	x	x
Mental health	x		x		x	x	x	x	x	x	x	x	x	x	x
Social functioning	x		x		x	x	x		x	x	x	x		x	x
Social/role								x							
Role functioning			x								x			x	x
Symptoms		x						x	x	x	x		x	x	
Cognitive functioning			x					x						x	
Communication			x												
Sleep			x				x							x	
Eating			x												
Recreation			x												
Family/marital			x												
Health perceptions				x		x			x	x	x	x		x	x
Pain							x			x	x	x	x	x	x
Vitality				x		x	x					x		x	x
Disability						x			x			x		x	
Sexual functioning									x					x	
Social support										x					

Adapted from Patrick and Erickson. 1993.

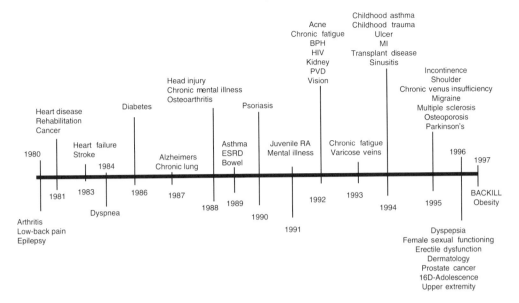

Figure 2	*Health measurement timeline: disease-specific measures*

policy communities grew increasingly cognizant of the challenges represented by an aging population beset with chronic disease. As a result, the medical model was inching toward a biopsychosocial model of health (Engel 1977). Third, health-care delivery was changing from fee-for-service to group practice, and cost containment initiatives were being implemented with increased frequency. All of these stimuli promoted increased recognition that the preservation of patient function and well-being should be a goal of medical care. Health status assessment tools were considered a promising methodology to monitor progress toward these goals on a patient, practice, and population level.

Clinical practice applications ushered in the era of practicality. Shorter tools were developed, with the functional status questionnaire totaling thirty-four items (Jette et al. 1986) and the Dartmouth COOP charts comprising a mere nine items (Nelson et al. 1987). These tools were developed with measurement priorities directed toward 'practical efficiency,' which was achieved at the expense of measurement precision (McHorney and Tarlov 1995; McHorney et al. 1992). The practical considerations that prompted the concern with brevity were more relevant in the mid-1980s, when computers were more expensive and fax machines and optical scanning were less widely used than they are today.

The latest era of health status assessment is that of psychometric efficiency, which has several underpinnings. First, the outcomes movement was gaining momentum following a series of studies on practice variations (Wennberg 1984), Ellwood's Shattuck Lecture on outcomes management (Ellwood 1988), and the establishment of the AHCPR in 1989. Large-scale studies of patient-based outcomes were imminent. Second, applications of health status measures in clinical trials had grown tremendously. Burdened by study costs that spanned pathophysiological adverse events and quality of life outcomes, the clinical trials community longed for more economical measures of quality of life. Third, generic and disease-specific tools were being applied to increasingly diverse groups of patients, including those who were severely ill or undergoing debilitating treatment. Thus, concerns about respondent burden encouraged a desire for shorter surveys. A spate of short-form development ensued.

The medical outcomes study (MOS) SF-20 health survey (Stewart et al. 1988) was the first short form to appear. It was developed for use in large-scale studies of patients in practice settings (Stewart et al. 1989; Wells et al. 1989). SF-20 items were derived largely from the HIE and tapped six health concepts. Next emerged the Duke health profile (Parkerson et al. 1990), a seventeen-item survey intended for research, health promotion, and clinical practice in general and clinical populations. It was a second-generation measure, empirically derived from the DUHP. The SF-36 (Ware and Sherbourne 1992) developed out of practical and empirical experiences with the SF-20 and the 149-item functioning and well-being profile (FWBP). The FWBP measures sixteen different health concepts with excellent depth and precision (Stewart and Ware 1992). The SF-36 was constructed as a compromise between brevity and comprehensiveness and between breadth and depth of measurement. The SF-36 was recommended for use in clinical trials, policy research, population monitoring, and clinical practice. The SF-6 survey uses a single global item to tap six health concepts (Stewart and Ware 1992). The SF-12 survey is an empirically derived short form of the SF-36 (Ware et al. 1996). Other generic measures have undergone measurement compression in recent years (de Bruin et al. 1994).

As Figure 2 shows, measurement of disease-specific health status assessment began with debilitating diseases such as cancer, arthritis, stroke, and heart disease, in which quality of life outcomes were on a par with those of physiological function and survival. In recent years, quality of life assessment has moved beyond incapacitating disease into virtually every medical specialty. Tools currently exist for dozens of clinical conditions, ranging from acne to visual disorders (Bowling 1995). For many diseases (e.g., asthma, arthritis, back pain, and cancer), numerous tools exist that differ in conceptual framework, source of items, scaling techniques, and psychometric properties. This prolific expansion occurred, in part, because generic measures are often less sensitive to treatment effects or the natural history of disease (Guyatt et al. 1987).

DEFINING SIGNATURES: MAJOR WORKS, THEORIES, AND RESEARCH QUESTIONS

Conceptual Frameworks

As Figures 1 and 2 show, an armamentaria of health status assessment tools has been developed in the past 30 years. In general, the assembly of measures can be described as strong in methodologic rigor but weaker in conceptual underpinnings. In other words, the field of health status assessment is regarded more for how it quantifies and validates health status indicators than for how and why it conceptualizes health.

Disease-specific measures have biomedically driven measurement models based upon known or hypothesized manifestations of the underlying pathology. Conceptual frameworks for generic measures can generally be characterized as insubstantial, usually attributing conceptual models to the WHO trinity of physical, social, and mental health. Yet, the WHO definition is just that, only a definition, not a conceptual framework, and one that is at the same time both vague and idealistic (Ahmed and Kolker 1973). There are two principal consequences of over-reliance on the WHO definition as the operational blueprint for health status assessment.

First, across the batteries of available measures, there is a consistent practice to scale physical health separately from mental health, which perpetuates in theory and practice body–mind dualism. The development of superordinate summary scales, like those for the SF-36 (Ware et al. 1995), take this dualism one step further by factor scoring physical and mental health as orthogonal (unrelated) structures. In this scoring scheme, a good (high) 'physical health' summary score is achieved by having high scores on the physical scales (indicating good physical and role functioning and no pain) and low scores on the mental scales (indicating anxiety, depression, and low positive affect). The same applies to the summary mental scale, whereby a high score is achieved by having good mental health status but poor physical health status. This scoring practice has recently been criticized on methodological and conceptual grounds (Simon et al. 1998). An alternative approach to separately scoring and analyzing health status scales is to group together individuals who have similar 'patterns' of scores into 'profile-type' taxonomies. Riley et al. (1998) recently applied this technique to the child health and illness profile – adolescent edition by cross-classifying four multi-item scales to yield thirteen mutually exclusive taxonomies of health.

Second, adherence to the WHO definition has promoted a conceptualization of health that emphasizes medical determinants of health. However, individuals and populations vary greatly in health status scores when they are free of pathological disease as well as when they are matched on pathophysiological disturbance. This occurs because social factors (e.g., socioeconomic status, stress, and environment) exert an important influence on health status (Evans and Stoddart 1992). Figures 3 and 4 show examples of this on an individual level using the SF-36.

Data for Figure 3 were obtained from the 1990 National Survey of Functional Health Status (McHorney et al. 1994). This figure

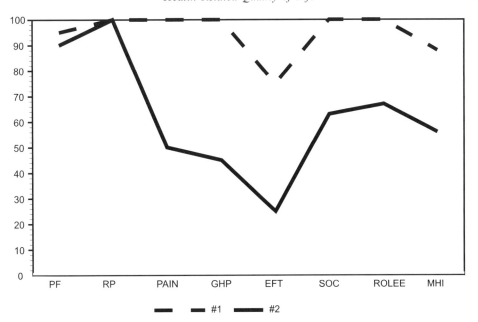

Figure 3   *SF-36 health profiles for two well women. Source: National Survey of Functional Health States*

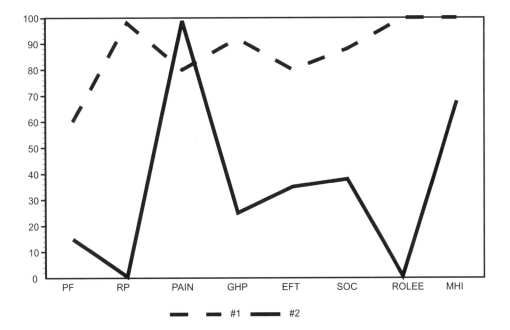

Figure 4   *SF-36 health profiles for two male patients with congestive heart failure. Source: Medical Outcomes Study*

shows SF-36 health profiles for two women of similar demographic make-up (age 45, white, post-high-school education) who did not report any of fourteen diseases on a standardized checklist. Although free of an array of conditions known to impact on functioning and well-being, and although matched on important social characteristics, six of the eight scales span a large range of health, as indicated by differences in scores up to two standard deviations. Clearly, the absence of 'disease' is a necessary, but not sufficient, condition for health-related quality of life. Any number of factors, from social stress to material deprivation, could account for such variations in health among the ostensibly 'well.'

Data from the Medical Outcomes Study were used for Figure 4, which shows SF-36 health profiles for two men of similar demographic make-up (white, high-school education, age within 3 years of one another) who have severe congestive heart failure (McHorney et al. 1993) but no other serious conditions. These profiles also span a large range of scores and reflect variability in the human experience of disease, which could be due to social support or coping strategies or other social psychological variables. As will be discussed, the field of health status assessment, like its forerunners in the medical model, has tended to under-emphasize the role of nonmedical determinants in its prediction and explanatory models. This is an important agenda for both theory building and research for the twentieth century.

Source of Items

The thin conceptual cornerstone that has characterized many health status measures may have impelled instrument developers to use existing items rather than developing them *de novo*. Only two generic measures have obtained their items from consumers themselves – the SIP and the NHP. Otherwise, items have been recycled from the literature, often gleaned from clinically oriented tools (Stewart and Ware 1992). Disease-specific tools derive their items from three main sources: (1) existing generic tools (e.g., Meenan et al. 1980; Roland and Morris 1983; Wu et al. 1991); (2) clinical expertise (Ingersoll and Marrero 1991); (3) patient testimony about the impact of disease and treatment on health status (Hyland et al. 1994; Marks et al. 1992).

Use of existing items to construct health status surveys has both benefits and drawbacks. As to the former, one can select items with known psychometric properties, such as normally distributed score distributions or evidence of con-

vergent and discriminant validity. In practice, however, item characteristics are a combination of the item itself (e.g., its difficulty and discrimination) and the group in which it is tested. In other words, psychometric characteristics of items and scales are invariably group-dependent (McHorney 1994, 1997). For example, an item that taps ability to walk one flight of stairs might be normally distributed in a population 75 years of age and older, but highly skewed in a general population, with a majority reporting perfect ability.

The disadvantages of recycling older items can often outweigh apparent benefits. For example, many older items violate contemporary standards for item writing insofar as they often contain multiple attributions (e.g., do you have difficulty bending, kneeling, or stooping, or how much of the time have you been in firm control of your behavior, thoughts, emotions, feelings?). Cognitive interviewing has revealed the sources of invalidity that these practices can yield (Jobe and Mingay 1990; Lessler 1995). Further, many older items have reading levels that are too high for the 25 per cent of the US adult population that has poor literacy skills (Kirsch et al. 1993). 'Cut and paste' methods also detach the methodologist from the subject matter (e.g., health status as represented from the patient point of view), thereby emphasizing 'technique' over representing the psychological, cognitive, and social components of lay conceptions of health and illness (Saltonstall 1993; van Maanen 1988).

Older, recycled items often have antiquated language, which may require substantial updating for contemporary use. For example, in the SIP, there is an item 'I get sudden frights,' a phrase that is not common today. Similarly, how people express and experience health, illness, and disability is likely to change with the passage of time in terms of societal, cultural, and life-course expectations for health and functioning. For example, life expectancy has increased 3.2 years in the 23 years since the SIP was developed, and the proportion of the population that is elderly has grown from 9.8 per cent to 12.8 per cent in the same period of time. Trends in health-care financing also reflect changing expectations for functioning as more resources are devoted to home care. In short, as people live longer, they have more time to both experience and adapt to acute and chronic disability. This enlargement of the health–illness–disability continuum on both an individual and population level may yield a different configuration of health concepts (or items of different difficulty) than is represented in today's family of measures. These are all empirical questions that have not been adequately addressed to date.

Validity Criteria

If some of the tools in the armamentaria of health status measures are weak conceptually, few can be characterized as so in terms of psychometric testing. A defining signature of health status assessment has been psychometric thoroughness and innovative approaches to instrument validation. Because health status measures have been used largely in clinical applications, such as randomized trials of treatment effectiveness, there has been a great emphasis placed on tests involving clinical criteria. However, validity testing that emphasizes clinical criteria to the exclusion of social and psychological criteria reinforces the 'body as machine' tenet so imbedded in the medical model. Tests of clinical validity are also reductionistic in that they attempt to account for variance in health status scales by biochemical and pathological criteria. Reductionism, however, is a double-edged sword because the often weak correlation between organ-specific biological functioning and self-reported health status (Guyatt 1985; Jette and Downing 1996) makes it problematic to confidently attribute the validity 'independence' to one or the other criteria.

Surprisingly, few investigators have taken complete advantage of some very important, and readily available, validity criteria. Research has long documented social differentials in health as indicated by age, gender, race, and socioeconomic status. These variables are often not used as validity criteria, or if used it is without clear hypotheses or using inefficient psychometric tests, such as bivariate correlations rather than analysis of the differences between means and variances of different known social groups.

Generic measures are intended to be used across populations segments. Thus, one important validity test should be whether they exhibit the same patterns of social differentials as has been observed with mortality and morbidity. Put differently, generic measures should reflect predominant social patterns of inequality in health, especially if they are to be used at the population level for planning and evaluation purposes.

Using data from the National Survey of Functional Health Status (McHorney et al. 1994), Table 2 provides some evidence of 'social' validity for the physical functioning scale from the SF-36 health survey. Consistent with research on mortality and morbidity, increasing

Table 2   *Multivariate deviation scores for SF-36 physical functioning scale*

	Regression coefficient	SE
Sociodemographic[1]		
Age 45–54	−2.46	1.08
Age 55–64	−5.14	1.22
Age 65–74	−10.54	1.38
Age 75 +	−23.39	1.78
Female gender	−2.92	0.72
Black race	−6.65	1.20
Other race	−6.50	1.39
Education < 8	−9.89	1.61
Education 9–11	−7.51	1.25
Education 12	−3.92	0.79
Chronic disease[2]		
Congestive heart failure	−17.81	2.50
Myocardial infarction	−8.05	2.69
Lung disease	−7.54	1.45
Back problems	−5.79	0.96
Angina	−5.44	2.22
Diabetes	−5.07	1.73
Positive screen for depression	−3.12	0.82
Visual impairment	−2.78	1.32
Hypertension	−2.52	0.92
Arthritis	−2.42	0.94

N = 2474
[1] *Holdout groups are age < 45, white race, and education > 12 years.*
[2] *Holdout group is no chronic condition.*
Source: *National Survey of Functional Health Status.*

age is negatively associated with physical functioning, and each consecutive 10 years of age doubles the burden. Also consistent with other research, females, nonwhites, and those with less education have worse physical functioning. Deviation scores for the chronic disease groups indicate large burdens for heart disease and small effects for hypertension. Many of the effects for the social variables exceed those for the clinical indicators. For example, the burden associated with low education (less than 8 years) exceeds that for all the diseases except congestive heart failure. Overall, the co-modeling and co-presentation of social with clinical variables helps to situate the relative importance of both determinants and adds to a deeper and more meaningful understanding of health status determinants.

MAJOR ISSUES AND CONTROVERSIES

Precision

How a problem is initially framed is an important determinant of its consequent operationalization. Health status assessment is a young science, originating only some 40 years ago with the measurement of activities of daily living and single-item measures of functional status. These measures were constructed for use in persons with chronic, debilitating disease; they appropriately tapped functional activities whose nonperformance reflected severe disability. In 1960, the American Public Health Association pronounced that 'we see the United States . . . as ready for Level 3 [measurement] work,' which was to focus on minor morbidity (e.g., illnesses, disturbances, and infections that cause inconvenience, economic loss, tension, annoyance, and impaired social relations) (Kandle 1961). Measurement work on Level 4 – positive health and its expressions of vigor and well-being – was deferred indefinitely. Such official policies had important implications for how investigators conceptualized health because the measurement bar was set in a narrow range.

Nonetheless, over the past 30 years, we have greatly improved our measurement bandwidth or the breadth of health information. As shown in Table 1, as tools were added to the armamentaria, they tapped a broader array of health concepts. However, many measures, even those with excellent bandwidth, suffer from problems of fidelity (thoroughness and precision of measurement). While we can quantify many different domains of health, we often do

so at the expense of exactness. The score distributions obtained are often highly skewed such that a plurality of respondents, particularly those not severely ill, are classified in a state of 'perfect' health at or very near to the ceiling of the measurement scale. Skewed score distributions have been observed across most generic measures (Beaton et al. 1996; Essink-Bot et al. 1996; McHorney and Tarlov 1995; McHorney et al. 1992), and are very problematic in general or primary care samples.

There are two principal effects of score imprecision. First, for cross-sectional studies, it is impossible to differentiate individuals at the ceiling (or floor), even though they likely vary in the underlying construct (McHorney 1997). In other words, ceiling effects paint a more favorable picture of population health than is actually the case. At the group-level, ceiling effects produce Type II errors in hypothesis testing. At the individual-patient level, ceiling effects yield false-negative outcomes in decision making. Second, for longitudinal studies, it is impossible to measure decline in health over time for those at the floor and improvement in health over time for those at the ceiling. As a result, the effects of treatment or the natural history will be underestimated (biased toward zero) with skewed and imprecise measures.

Imprecision can result from several factors: (1) use of a limited number of items to tap a given construct (e.g., single-item measures tend to have higher ceiling effects than multi-item scales, and short-form scales more than long-form measures) (McHorney et al. 1992); (2) use of a narrow rating scale; (3) use of a short recall period; or (4) selection of items that are too homogeneous. Probably the most common source of imprecision is the selection of items whose difficulty is incongruent with the 'ability' of the population of interest. Figure 5 shows the interaction between item difficulty, on the Y-axis, and respondent ability, on the X-axis. Simply put, floor and ceiling effects derive from a poor marriage between the difficulty of an item and the ability of the targeted population. Ceiling effects occur when easy items are administered to high-ability populations (e.g., administering basic activities of daily living to a general population). Floor effects happen when difficult items are administered to low-ability populations (e.g., administering advanced activities of daily living to a long-term care population).

Dupuy's work on the general well-being scale (1973) represented a watershed for the measurement of positive well-being. Even in general populations, few positive well-being scales exhibit ceiling effects (McHorney 1994). This is principally the result of two factors. First, they often

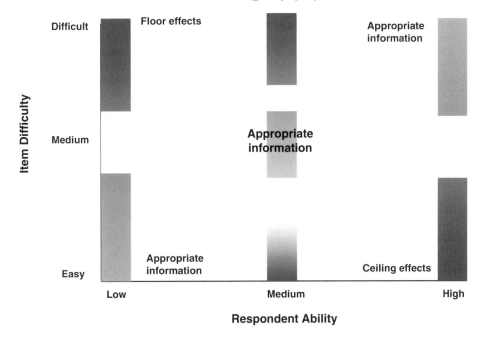

Figure 5   *Sources of floor and ceiling effects*

have five to seven point categorical rating scales, which more precisely differentiates individuals on the underlying construct. Second, they often have balanced items (those tapping both negative and positive health states). Items that tap positive health states have very low ceiling effects (e.g., few individuals report that they are a 'happy person' all of the time).

Thus, problems with precision pertain largely to function – physical, role, and social. Across most generic measures, scales tapping function tend to be composed of few items and have coarse rating scales. How can we 'raise the bar' for the measurement of function? First, it may not be as useful to strive for 'superpositive' indicators of function as it is to refine existing item pools to be more appropriate for longer-living populations. Recent work on calibrating basic and instrumental activities of daily living (Cohen and McHorney, in press; Haley et al. 1994; Spector and Fleishman 1998) have indicated obvious redundancies in measuring lower-level functioning and conspicuous gaps in measuring higher-order functioning. This is a clear beacon for future measurement development. Even for elderly populations, it is not necessary to oversample lower-level functioning because many items are repetitious in terms of item difficulty. The challenge is to sample and distribute the lower-level items more effectively

while concurrently adding items to fill in known gaps at the difficult end of the continuum (e.g., higher-order functioning, productive activities, leisure exercise, and physical fitness). These are activities that will serve to raise the bar while also being consistent with national health objectives and public health recommendations.

Thus, the challenges for future advances in health status assessment are both conceptual and methodological. Methodologically, a better way of matching item difficulty with the ability of the targeted population is needed. If we want to know how well persons are with respect to function, the most efficient procedure is to ask them about activities that are close to their level of ability. What is required is some means of functionally relating performance on each test item to person ability. As will be discussed, item response theory is well-designed for this purpose.

Conceptually, qualitative methods should be used to glean from consumers themselves facets of contemporary functioning. For example, Porter (1995) discovered numerous nuances about ADL performance in the context of qualitative research. The same applies to role and social functioning. The content of these concepts has been fairly narrow to date. For example, many measures of role functioning conceptualize role behavior as unidimensional (with a focus on the employment role), thus excluding consideration of other productive behaviors (Kahn 1983). Also, most measures of role functioning blur the distinction between instrumental and nurturant roles. They also fail to assess role conflict and role transition that often ensues from disease and treatment.

Focus groups with adults differing in age, work status, gender, ethnicity, and socioeconomic status could help to identify components of role and social functioning constructs that have heretofore been eclipsed by professionally driven definitions of function. Information on human values for different health states can help to shape the conceptual blueprint for future measurement work. The practice of medicine today is evolving toward 'patient-centered' care (Laine and Davidoff 1996). Perhaps tools that assess the outcomes of medical care should also be patient-centered and patient-focused. Use of patients and consumers as key informants for new instrument development or construct enhancement has great potential to yield useful information about how illness, disease, treatment, and natural history impacts on the everyday experiences of contemporary functioning and well-being.

Use of Norms

In the medical model, disease is represented by a sufficient pathophysiological deviation from normality. In health status assessment, normality is relative because different groups have different preferences for health states, and preferences change over time as well (Kind and Dolan 1995). Nonetheless, considerable methodological attention has been devoted to calibrating health status scores. For example, some investigators have developed ad hoc health status 'warning zones' (Jette et al. 1986), while others have used more sophisticated methods, such as area-under-the-curve analysis (Parkerson et al. 1996), to define clinically relevant cut-points along with test characteristics of sensitivity and specificity. ROC analyses require an external gold standard, and thus have largely been limited to mental health concepts to date.

A more common practice has been to use norms to define deviations from normality. Likert-scored, multi-item scales have no clear interpretation except for the floor (worst possible score) and the ceiling (best possible score) because scores between the extremes can be achieved by innumerable combinations of item responses (e.g., there are 2850 possible ways to obtain a score of seventy on the SF-36 physical functioning scale). Normative data can facilitate score interpretation by bringing in comparative information about health status relative to scores made by others. However, the adequacy of norms rests upon three attributes of the normative group: (1) size; (2) representativeness; (3) comparability to the analytic sample (Cronbach 1970). The first two features are self-evident: norms based on a small and/or unrepresentative sample may be inaccurate (biased) if there is non-random selection of subjects. The third characteristic is less intuitive: norms are meaningful only to the extent that the individual or group whose score is being interpreted belongs to the normative population (Cronbach 1970; Flanagan 1972). If the normative and analytic sample differ, then norms are of limited value because one is comparing apples with oranges.

In health status assessment, norms have been used in three principal ways. First, norms are used in validity tests to gauge the extent to which scales discriminate between 'sick' and 'well' populations (Langeveld et al. 1996; Sullivan et al. 1990). Many of these tests are psychometrically ineffectual because the comparison groups invariably differ in characteristics other than clinical status, such as age and socioeconomic status. Thus, unless the comparative playing field is leveled, results may not so much reflect 'clinical' as 'social' discriminant validity. In either case, the performance of the scales may be consistent with hypotheses, but the source of the validity attribution is inaccurate.

Norms have also been used at the individual-patient level for decision-making purposes (Bukstein et al. 1995; Meyer et al. 1993). There are two problems with this application. On a philosophical basis, use of norms for individual decision making implies that there is a shared archetype of functioning and well-being to which everyone should aspire. This premise, much like the ones underlying the medical model and the sick role, disregards the diversity that exists in health values and preferences. Further, the desire to raise individuals 'up to the norm' perpetuates the dominance of professional judgements of normality and reinforces clinical indifference to individual values (Leplege and Hunt 1997). On a methodological level, unless a person belongs to the normative group, inappropriate conclusions may be drawn for decision making. To date, most normative groups have been sampled from general populations (Hunt et al. 1986; McHorney et al. 1994; Parkerson 1994), and thus constitute a younger, white, middle-class population with a low burden of disease. The appropriateness of such benchmarks for patients diversified in age, ethnicity, socioeconomic status, and disease is arguable at best and prejudicial at worst.

Finally, norms have been used to garner clinical, social, and political support for vulnerable groups. For example, norms have been used to justify the use of scarce resources, such as organ transplantation (Benedetti et al. 1994), and to call attention to the burden of illness of vulnerable patient groups (Komaroff et al. 1996; Wells et al. 1989; Westlake and George 1994). Use of normative data for these purposes is not inherently problematic; rather, it becomes complex and possibly unfair when health 'deficits' are exaggerated by the failure to adjust for social differences between groups. In short, the line between what should lie in the domain of health and social versus public policy can often be ambiguous, and a given problem can be perceived differently depending on the reference group selected.

Overall, then, norms are potentially very valuable in interpreting scores and in decision making; however, much work remains to be accomplished. As Derogatis and Spencer (1984) noted, while the fundamental concept of a norm is not complicated, use of norms represents 'one of the most misunderstood and misused' aspects of health assessment. Questions that require consensus include the following:

1 What constitutes an appropriate norm?
2 What types of information should be published with norms to increase their practical utility (e.g., variance–covariance matrices)?
3 What sociodemographic variables should be considered as necessary adjusters?
4 What specific quantitative methods should be used for inferential testing?

Resource Allocation

At both micro- and macrolevels, health-care competes with other sectors for scarce resources. To the extent that significant national resources are consumed by health care, investments cannot be made in other sectors that may also produce population health (Evans and Stoddart 1992). It has long been proposed that health status measures, particularly quality-adjusted life years, should be used to allocate resources *vis-à-vis* their costs and benefits. Use of utility measures to determine which interventions realize the greatest population health returns has been a controversial issue. Issues that continue to be debated (Kaplan 1993; Patrick and Erickson 1993) include: (1) how to fairly appraise competing programs with different underlying goals; (2) whose preferences should be used as valuation weights; (3) how to conduct economic evaluations that are not biased against elderly or disabled populations; (4) what utility elicitation method should be used; and (5) how to accommodate subgroup differences in preference valuations.

Soft vs. Hard Science

Professions and specialties often go through a maturation process before they allocate time and resources to studying what some believe is a 'soft' science of quality of life. As Figure 2 shows, over the past 10 years, quality of life assessment has moved beyond debilitating illness into virtually every medical specialty. This occurred, in part, as a result of growing appreciation that some conventional measures were too narrow to fully capture the totality of patients' experiences. Further, clinical researchers raised questions about the sensitivity of generic measures to small, but clinically important, change. (Guyatt et al. 1986). Finally, the psychometric basis of health status assessment had become increasingly accepted in the clinical sciences.

Although clinicians tend to feel most comfortable with physiological outcomes, attitudes are changing as a result of increased reference to quality of life in the literature and at professional meetings. Like any new 'technology,' clinicians need exposure to and experience with quality of life outcomes. Further, quality of life data need to make clinical sense *vis-à-vis* outcome indicators with which clinicians are familiar. A robust finding that has derived from years of research is the significant association between the simplest rating of health status (how do you rate your health: excellent, very good, good, fair, or poor) and subsequent mortality (Idler and Benyamini 1997). This finding has withstood statistical adjustment for sociodemographic characteristics, objective health status, health risk behaviors, and psychosocial factors. It has been suggested that this simple question be used routinely in clinical practice for early risk identification (Schoenfeld et al. 1994).

Other research has also helped to move quality of life from the domain of social scientists to that of clinicians. Appreciation for quality of life outcomes is elevated when they prove to be as or more responsive to treatment effects than clinical measures (Amadio et al. 1996). When published in leading, peer-reviewed clinical journals, such findings go a long way toward legitimizing quality of life measures as tools to include along with familiar clinical measures in research and practice. Additionally, when the covariance between quality of life and clinical outcomes is moderate, it suggests that both types of measures provide independent but complementary information (Mahler and Machowiak 1995; Salek et al. 1993; Stoll et al. 1997), leading clinicians to view the two types of data as mutually contributing toward a complete picture of patient function.

Major Outstanding Questions

Research over the past 40 years has consistently underscored the role of nonmedical factors in determining individual and population health (Evans and Stoddart 1992; McKinlay et al. 1989). It is now well established that social, lifestyle, and psychological factors account for 50 per cent of preventable morbidity and mortality, environmental factors and human biology account for another 20 per cent each, and medical care for only 10 per cent (US DHHS 1979). However, research disproportionately focuses on narrow clinical factors rather than broader determinants. Indeed, the outcomes movement implicitly adopted the medical model's mechanistic and reductionistic view of health because it has focused on what works in 'medicine' – thus, the independent variables are the same ones we have been studying for years. The unique signature of the outcomes movement is that it broadened the scope of the dependent variables to include functioning, well-being, and patient satisfaction, in addition to more traditional indicators of mortality, morbidity, and costs.

The major determinants of health status are biology, medical care, social environment, lifestyle behavior, and psychosocial resources (Bergner 1985; Evans and Stoddart 1992; Tarlov 1992). Biology encompasses genetic constitution and general organ resilience. Medical care includes access, continuity, quality, and the amount of care consumed. Health behavior (exercise and drugs, alcohol, and tobacco use), health attitudes, and health knowledge constitute lifestyle factors. Psychosocial resources entail social support, social networks, coping, mastery, and self-efficacy. Finally, the social environment includes aspects of social location (social class, relative deprivation, and opportunity structure) as well as broader influences of the physical, housing, and work environments. Research has documented the important role of health behavior (Branch 1985), psychosocial resources (House et al. 1994), and the social environment (Smith 1996) on health outcomes.

Most uses of health status measures have focused on clinical factors and to a lesser extent medical care. As a result, our knowledge base is rich in terms of the impact of disease, severity, comorbidity, symptoms, and treatment on health status. However, clinically driven models often have limited explanatory power, as indicated by explained variance estimates that often do not exceed 20 per cent (Dexter et al. 1996). Measurement unreliability accounts for some of the limited predictive power, as does the fact that most explanatory models omit nonmedical determinants of health status.

Since quality of life is the illness-impact iceberg underlying disease, morbidity, and disability, future research needs to expand its explanatory potential by studying other health determinants that are mutable both at the individual-person level as well as at the larger health and social policy level. Further, clinically driven outcome research has tended to view health status in an episodic manner, with most studies being cross-sectional or with limited longitudinal designs. However, health status and health-related quality of life are dynamic phenomenon which change in response to aging, illness adaptation, treatment, and natural history. Thus, future research needs to address the life-course character of health status above and beyond disease and treatment episodes.

Figure 6 suggests a model that accommodates multiple determinants of health status across the life course. Positive health potential characterizes the start of the life course, which is followed by perturbations in functioning and well-being that 'take the top' off of one's health-related quality of life. The development of morbidity from chronic disease, stress, environmental hazards, or material deprivation results in some degree of incipient decline, perhaps first evinced by a deflation of health perceptions (as one observes with uncomplicated hypertension, Stewart et al. 1989). At some point in the natural history, disability in physical or social roles may develop. The end of the life course is characterized by more serious physical or cognitive limitations. Although this trajectory is depicted as linear, considerable fluctuations in health status is likely to occur a result of acuity, rehabilitation, or changes in the physical, social, or economic environment.

This hypothesized model of health status over the life course also recognizes that different health determinants have a greater or lesser influence at different points of the life course. In Figure 6, the relative importance of each of the five determinants is indicated with darker shades for more importance. For example, it is hypothesized that biology and medical care weigh most heavily at the beginning and end of the life course. Psychosocial resources play a more influential role toward the end of the life course, while the social environment exerts a strong influence throughout the life course. The possible benefits of a model of health status as proposed herein are that it explicitly recognizes that health status is dynamic, not static,

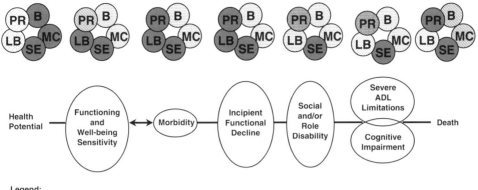

Legend:

B=biology
MC=medical care
SE= social environment
LB= lifestyle behaviors
PR= psychosocial recovery

Figure 6   *Health inputs and outputs across the life course*

that different inputs to health status play relative, not absolute, roles, and that policy efforts
to improve both the quality and quantity of life
may require different investment strategies at
different points in the life course.

METHODS TO ADDRESS OUTSTANDING ISSUES

Paradigm to Achieve Precision

Future instrument development needs to be
acutely attentive to the shape, skewness, and
precision of obtained score distributions in different populations for whom the tools are
recommended or applied. A meaningful goal
for the next era of measurement development
should be to generate *equiprecise* measures,
which yield scores of equal precision at all levels
of the underlying construct (Weiss 1982).
Equiprecise measurement can be achieved
through conjoint use of computerized adaptive
testing as the survey platform and item response
theory as the measurement theory.

A logical extension for health status assessment is to move from pen-and-paper tools to
computerized–adaptive assessment of health status. The technology for computerized testing has
been available for some time, and use of computers is increasingly common in health-care
delivery (Roizen et al. 1992). Computerized
health status assessment could:

1   reduce the human capital involved in admin-
    istering and scoring questionnaires;
2   challenge patients at their targeted level of
    ability instead of boring or discouraging
    them;
3   provide researchers with the exact amount of
    precision they require for each patient sam-
    ple and each specific application;
4   provide 'real-time' scores to clinicians for use
    at the individual-patient level in clinical prac-
    tice.

This vision of a new era of health measurement
is likely some 3–8 years away; however, it can be
achieved.

Development of an adaptive framework
would require three phases of methodological
work. The first task would be to assemble item
banks on different health concepts (concept-
specific banks). An item bank consists of a
substantial number of questionnaire items
that are matched to a given construct or task
(Hambleton and Swaminathan 1985). Items
could be assembled from existing measures.
The language and structure of some items
would have to be modernized, while the reading
level of other items would need to be lowered.
An appropriate rating scale would need to be
selected to maximize reliable variance and minimize respondent burden and response invalidity.

The second task would involve conducting
cognitive interviews with a variety of patient
groups to obtain in-depth information about
respondent understanding and acceptance of
the banked items. The cognitive interviews
could also obtain input from patients/consumers
on gaps in content coverage in each underlying

continuum. Concept-specific focus groups could be conducted to ascertain the relevance of banked items for contemporary conceptions of functioning and well-being.

The third task would be to employ techniques subsumed under item response theory (IRT) to calibrate items and to select a subset of items that comprehensively, and evenly, tap the underlying construct of interest. IRT is a modern measurement theory that is being increasingly embraced as an alternative to classical test theory generally and summative scoring specifically (Hambleton and Swaminathan 1985). IRT is both a theoretical framework and a collection of quantitative techniques used for test construction, scaling, and score equating, as well as for identification of item bias and computerized adaptive testing.

The strengths of IRT for constructing the new era of health status measures are two-fold. First, at the item level, IRT is powerful technique for understanding the structure and order of items *vis à vis* each other and the underlying construct of interest. Data from IRT modeling yield vital information on item performance that can be used to construct more precise and effective tests. Specifically, IRT yields population-independent estimates of item parameters, unlike classical test theory, which can be used to fill in theoretically or empirically identified gaps in item difficulty in the construct of interest, thus both reducing skewed score distributions and making headway toward equiprecise measurement. Second, IRT yields individual ability estimates (of the latent trait) which are 'independent' of the particular set of items administered (assuming the specific test items derive from a larger calibrated item bank). Attainment of item-free ability estimates at the person level has profound implications for using computerized adaptive testing to select the most efficient and targeted set of items for a given ability level.

population health has challenged the ways in which payers, purchasers, and policy makers think about medical care. These key players in the outcomes movement increasingly demand data on both physiological and patient-based outcomes to gauge the quality of care, as well as evaluate 'outcomes performance' at the levels of the provider, the health plan, and health system.

Many health status measures have been developed for use in policy, planning, and evaluation, although few have actually been utilized for these purposes. The emphasis today on population health and managed care, and on the need to balance cost containment with preserving clinical and quality of life outcomes, cries out for health status measures that can be used for planning and evaluation purposes. However, before that can realistically occur, the field needs to make progress on two issues. First, we need to attain a more complete understanding of the determinants of health status – of causality – in order to reliably and confidently attribute changes in policy, delivery, financing, or organization to changes in health status. This requires the design, execution, and support of research that examines the unique and interactive role of biological, medical, social, lifestyle and psychosocial factors on health status. Second, many current measures lack the sensitivity – the precision – for use in program or policy analysis. The fundamental problem with the outcomes and accountability movements has been the underlying assumption that 'one size fits all' – that a given measure can meet the needs of multiple stakeholders. However, different applications in different populations require different health concepts and different degrees of precision. Methodological progress toward dynamic, precise, and conceptually targeted measurement capability will significantly advance our collective opportunity to use health status measures to evaluate treatment effectiveness as well as to set and monitor health and social policies for an aging population.

CONCLUSION

The health-care landscape has changed considerably in the short history of health status assessment. The dramatic rise in health-care expenditure over the past 30 years has focused intense scrutiny on the quality of American health care. Our history of health-care financing and reimbursement has been characterized by paying for what we 'do' (processes of care) rather than for what we 'accomplish' (end results of care). The realization that our high levels of health expenditure have not 'bought us' greater

ACKNOWLEDGMENTS

Preparation of this chapter was supported by the Department of Veterans Affairs (HSR&D HFP #96-001; RR&D C-2016; HSR&D IIR #95-033) and by the Department of Preventive Medicine, University of Wisconsin–Madison Medical School. The author gratefully acknowledges Jody McIntyre and Amy Kramer for their innumerable contributions as research support. Work on this chapter was completed while the author was a Picker/Commmonwealth Scholars Program Finalist.

REFERENCES

Ahmed, P.I. and Kolker, A.K. (1973) 'The role of indigenous medicine in WHO's definition of health', in P. I. Ahmed and G. V. Coelgo (eds), *Toward A New Definition of Health: Psychosocial Dimensions.* New York: Plenum. pp. 113–28.

Amadio, P., Silverstein, M., Ilstrup, D., Schleck, C., and Jensen, L. (1996) 'Outcome assessment for carpal tunnel surgery: The relative responsiveness of generic, arthritis-specific, disease-specific, and physical examination measures', *Journal of Hand Surgery,* 21A: 338–46.

Bauer, R. (1966) *Social Indicators.* Cambridge, MA: MIT Press.

Beaton, D., Bombardier, C., and Hogg-Johnson, S. (1996) 'Measuring health in injured workers: A cross-sectional comparison of five generic health status instruments in workers with musculoskeletal injuries', *American Journal of Industrial Medicine,* 29: 618–31.

Belloc, N.B., Breslow, L., and Hochstein, J.R. (1971) 'Measurement of physical health in a general population survey', *American Journal of Epidemiology,* 93: 328–36.

Benedetti, E., Matas, A.J., Hakim, N., Fasola, C., Gillingham, K., McHugh, L., and Najarian, J.S. (1994) 'Renal transplantation for patients 60 years of age or older', *Annals of Surgery,* 220: 445–60.

Bergner, M. (1985) 'Measurement of Health Status', *Medical Care,* 23: 696–704.

Bergner, M., Bobbitt, R.A., Carter, W.B., and Gilson, B.S. (1981) 'The sickness impact profile: Development and final revision of a health status measure', *Medical Care,* 19: 787–805.

Berkman, P.L. (1971) 'Measurement of mental health in a general population survey', *American Journal of Epidemiology,* 94: 105–11.

Bowling, A. (1995) *Measuring Disease: A Review of Disease-Specific Quality of Life Measurement Scales.* Buckingham,: Open University Press.

Bradburn, N. and Caplovitz, D. (1965) *Reports on Happiness.* Chicago: Aldine.

Branch, L.G. (1985) 'Health practices and incident disability among the elderly', *American Journal of Public Health,* 75: 1436–9.

Brook, R.H., Ware, J.E., Davies-Avery, A., Stewart, A., Donald, C., Rogers, W., Williams, K., and Johnston, S. (1979) 'Overview of adult health status measures fielded in RAND's health insurance study', *Medical Care,* 17(7, Suppl): 1–131.

Bukstein, D., White, E., and Martin, J. (1995) 'The utility of outcomes information at the point of service', *Managed Care Quarterly,* 3(2): 26–32.

Bush, J.W., Chen, M.M., and Patrick, D.L. (1972) 'Social indicators for health based on functional status and prognosis', *Proceedings of the American Statistical Association, Social Statistics Section,* pp. 71–81.

Campbell, A., Converse, P. E., and Rodgers, W. L. (1976) *The Quality of American Life: Perceptions, Evaluations, and Satisfactions.* New York: Russell Sage Foundation.

Chambers, L.W., Sackett, D.L., Goldsmith, C.H., Macpherson, A.S., and Macauley, R.C. (1976) 'Development and application of an index of social function', *Health Services Research,* 11: 430–41.

Chen, M.K. (1979) 'The gross national health product: A proposed population health index', *Public Health Reports,* 94: 119–23.

Cohen, A. S. and McHorney, C. A. (1999) 'Use of item response theory to equate functional health status measures', in R. Campbell, J. McArdle, and F. Wolinsky (eds), *Analysis of Multiple Data Sets in Aging Research.* New York: Springer (in press).

Cronbach, L. J. (1970) *Essentials of Psychological Testing.* New York: Harper and Row.

de Bruin, A.F., Diederiks, J.P.M., de Witte, L.P., Stevens, F.C.J., and Philipsen, H. (1994) 'The development of a short generic version of the sickness impact profile', *Journal of Clinical Epidemiology,* 47: 407–18.

Derogatis, L.R. and Spencer, P.M. (1984) 'Psychometric issues in the psychological assessment of the cancer patient', *Cancer,* 53(10, Suppl): 2228–32.

Dexter, P., Stump, T., Tierney, W., and Wolinsky, F. (1996) 'The psychometric properties of the SF-36 health survey among older adults in a clinical setting', *Journal of Clinical Geropsychology,* 2: 225–37.

Deyo, R.A. and Inui, T.S. (1984) 'Toward clinical applications of health status measures: Sensitivity of scales to clinically important changes', *Health Services Research,* 19: 275–89.

Dupuy, H.J. (1973) *Developmental Rationale, Substantive, Derivative, and Conceptual Relevance of the General Well-Being Schedule.* Fairfax, VA: National Center for Health Statistics.

Ellwood, P.M. (1988) 'Outcomes management: A technology of patient experience', *New England Journal of Medicine,* 318: 1549–56.

Engel, G.L. (1977) 'The need for a new medical model: A challenge for biomedicine', *Science,* 196(4286): 129–36.

Essink-Bot, M., Krabbe, P., vanAgt, H., and Bonsel, G. (1996) 'NHP or SIP – A comparative study in renal insufficiency associated anemia', *Quality of Life Research,* 5: 91–100.

Evans, R. and Stoddart, G. (1992) 'Producing health, consuming health care', *Social Science and Medicine,* 35: 1347–63.

Flanagan, J. C. (1972) 'Units, scores, and norms', in V. R. Fuchs (ed.), *Essays in the Economics of Health and Medical Care.* New York: National Bureau of Economic Research. pp. 695–763.

Gilson, B.S., Gilson, J.S., Bergner, M., Bobbit, R.A., Kressel, S., Pollard, W.E., and Vesselago, M. (1975)

'The sickness impact profile: Development of an outcome measure of health care', *American Journal of Public Health*, 65: 1304–10.

Gurin, G., Veroff, J., and Feld, S. (1960) *Americans View Their Mental Health – A Nationwide Interview Survey*. New York: Basic Books.

Guyatt, G. (1985) 'Methodological problems in clinical trials in heart failure', *Journal of Chronic Disease*, 38: 353–63.

Guyatt, G.H., Bombardier, C., and Tugwell, P.X. (1986) 'Measuring disease-specific quality of life in clinical trials', *Canadian Medical Association Journal*, 134: 889–95.

Guyatt, G.H., Berman, L.B., Townsend, M., Pugsley, S.O., and Chambers, L.W. (1987) 'A measure of quality of life for clinical trials in chronic lung disease', *Thorax*, 42: 773–8.

Haley, S.M., McHorney, C.A., and Ware, J.E. (1994) 'Evaluation of the MOS SF-36 physical functioning scale (PF-10). I. Unidimensionality and reproducibility of the Rasch item scale', *Journal of Clinical Epidemiology*, 47: 671–84.

Hambleton, R. K. and Swaminathan, H. (1985) *Item Response Theory: Principles and Applications*. Boston: Kluwer Nijhoff.

Hochstim, J. R. (1970) 'Health and ways of living', in I. I. Kessler and M. L. Levin (eds), *The Community As an Epidemiologic Laboratory*. Baltimore, MD: Johns Hopkins University Press. pp. 149–76.

House, J.S., Lepkowski, J.M., Kinney, A.M., Mero, R.P., Kessler, R.C., and Herzog, A.R. (1994) 'The social stratification of aging and health', *Journal of Health and Social Behavior*, 35: 213–34.

Hunt, S.M. and McEwen, J. (1980) 'The development of a subjective health indicator', *Sociology of Health and Illness*, 2: 231–46.

Hunt, S.M., McEwen, J., and McKenna, S.P. (1986) *Measuring Health Status*. Dover, NH: Croom Helm.

Hyland, M., Bott, J., Singh, S., and Kenyon, C. (1994) 'Domains, constructs and the development of the breathing problems questionnaire', *Quality of Life Research*, 3: 245–56.

Idler, E.L. and Benyamini, Y. (1997) 'Self-rated health and mortality: A review of twenty-seven community studies', *Journal of Health and Social Behavior*, 38: 21–37.

Ingersoll, G. and Marrero, D. (1991) 'A modified quality-of-life measure for youths: Psychometric properties', *Diabetes Educator*, 17: 114–18.

Jachuck, S.J., Brierly, H., Jachuck, S., and Willcox, P.M. (1982) 'The effect of hypotensive drugs on the quality of life', *Journal of the Royal College of General Practitioners*, 32: 103–5.

Jette, A.M., Davies, A.R., Cleary, P.D., Calkins, D.R., Rubenstein, L.V., Fink, A., Kosecoff, J., Young, R.T., Brook, R.H., and DelBanco, T.L. (1986) 'The functional status questionnaire: Reliability and validity when used in primary care', *Journal of General Internal Medicine*, 1: 143–9.

Jette, D. and Downing, J. (1996) 'The Relationship of cardiovascular and psychological impairments to the health status of patients enrolled in cardiac rehabilitation programs', *Physical Therapy*, 76: 130–9.

Jobe, J.B. and Mingay, D.J. (1990) 'Cognitive laboratory approach to designing questionnaires for surveys of the elderly', *Public Health Reports*, 105: 518–24.

Kahn, R.L. (1983) 'Productive Behavior: Assessment, Determinants, and Effects', *Journal of the American Geriatrics Society*, 31: 750–7.

Kandle, R.P. (1961) 'Report of the Chairman of the Technical Development Board to the Governing Council 1959–1960', *American Journal of Public Health*, 51: 287–94.

Kaplan, R. M. (1993) *The Hippocratic Predicament: Affordability, Access, and Accountability in American Medicine*. San Diego: Academic Press.

Karnofsky, D.A., Abelmann, W.H., Craver, L.F., and Burchenal, J.H. (1948) 'The use of the nitrogen mustards in the palliative treatment of carcinoma', *Cancer*, 634–56.

Kind, P. and Dolan, P. (1995) 'The effect of past and present illness experience on the valuations of health states', *Medical Care*, 33(4 Suppl): AS255–AS263.

Kirsch, I. S., Jungeblut, A., Jenkins, L., and Kolstad, A. (1993) *Adult Literacy in America*. Washington, DC: National Center for Education Statistics.

Komaroff, A., Fagioli, L., Doolittle, T., Gandek, B., Gleit, M., Guerriero, R., Kornish, J., Ware, N., Ware, J., and Bates, D. (1996) 'Health status in patients with chronic fatigue syndrome and in general population and disease comparison groups', *American Journal of Medicine*, 101: 281–90.

Laine, C. and Davidoff, F. (1996) 'Patient-centered medicine', *Journal of the American Medical Association*, 275: 152–6.

Langeveld, J., Koot, H., Loonen, M., Hazebroek-Kampschreur, A., and Passchier, J. (1996) 'A quality of life instrument for adolescents with chronic headache', *Cephalalgia*, 16: 183–96.

Leplege, A. and Hunt, S. (1997) 'The problem of quality of life in medicine', *Journal of the American Medical Association*, 278: 47–50.

Lessler, J. (1995) 'Choosing questions that people can understand and answer', *Medical Care*, 33(4 Suppl): AS203–AS208.

Mahler, D.A. and Machowiak, J.I. (1995) 'Evaluation of the short-form 36-item questionnaire to measure health-related quality of life in patients with COPD', *Chest*, 107(6): 1585–9.

Marks, G.B., Dunn, S.M., and Woolcock, A.J. (1992) 'A scale for the measurement of quality of life in adults with asthma', *Journal of Clinical Epidemiology*, 45: 461–72.

McHorney, C. A. (1994) 'Methodological and psychometric issues in health status assessment across populations and applications', in G. L. Albrecht and R. Fitzpatrick (eds), *Advances in Medical*

Sociology. Vol. 5. Quality of Life in Health Care. Greenwich, CN: JAI Press. pp. 281–304.

McHorney, C.A. (1997) 'Generic health measurement: Past accomplishments and a measurement paradigm for the 21st century', *Annals of Internal Medicine*, 127: 743–50.

McHorney, C.A. and Tarlov, A.R. (1995) 'Individual-patient monitoring in clinical practice: Are available health status surveys adequate?' *Quality of Life Research*, 4: 293–307.

McHorney, C.A., Ware, J.E., Rogers, W., Raczek, A., and Lu, J.F.R. (1992) 'The validity and relative precision of MOS short- and long-form health status scales and Dartmouth COOP charts: Results from the medical outcomes study', *Medical Care*, 30 (Suppl): MS253-MS265.

McHorney, C.A., Ware, J.E., and Raczek, A.E. (1993) 'The MOS 36-item short-form health status survey (SF-36). II. Psychometric and clinical tests of validity in measuring physical and mental health constructs', *Medical Care*, 31: 247–63.

McHorney, C.A., Kosinski, M., and Ware, J.E. (1994) 'Comparisons of the costs and quality of norms for the SF-36 health survey collected by mail versus telephone interview: Results from a national survey', *Medical Care*, 32: 551–67.

McKinlay, J.B., McKinlay, S.M., and Beaglehole, R. (1989) 'A Review of the evidence concerning the impact of medical measures on recent mortality and morbidity in the United States', *International Journal of Health Services*, 19: 181–208.

Meenan, R.F., Gertman, P.M., and Mason, J.H. (1980) 'Measuring health status in arthritis', *Arthritis and Rheumatism*, 23: 146–52.

Meyer, K.B., Espindle, D.M., DeGiacomo, J.M., Jenuleson, C.S., Kurtin, P.S., and Davies, A.R. (1993) 'Monitoring dialysis patients' health status', *American Journal of Kidney Diseases*, 9(42): 267–79.

Nelson, E.C., Conger, B., Douglass, R., Gephart, D., Kirk, J., Page, R., Clark, A., Johnson, K., Stone, K., Wasson, J., and Zubkoff, M. (1983) 'Functional health status levels of primary care patients', *Journal of the American Medical Association*, 249: 3331–8.

Nelson, E.C., Wasson, J., Kirk, J., Keller, A., Clark, D., Dietrich, A., Stewart, A., and Zubkoff, M. (1987) 'Assessment of function in routine clinical practice: Description of the COOP chart method and preliminary findings', *Journal of Chronic Disease*, 40(1 Suppl.): 55S-63S.

Newhouse, J. P. (1994) *Free for All?: Lessons From the Rand Health Insurance Experiment.* Cambridge, MA: Harvard University Press.

Parkerson, G. R. (1994) *User's Guide for the Duke Health Profile (DUKE).* Durham, NC: Duke University Medical Center.

Parkerson, G.R., Gelbach, S.H., Wagner, E.H., James, S.A., Clapp, N.E., and Muhlbaier, L.H. (1981) 'The Duke-UNC health profile: An adult health status

instrument for primary care', *Medical Care*, 19: 806–28.

Parkerson, G.R., Broadhead, W.E., and Tse, C.-K.J. (1990) 'The Duke health profile: A 17-item measure of health and disfunction', *Medical Care*, 28: 1056–72.

Parkerson, G., Broadhead, W., and Tse, C. (1996) 'Anxiety and depressive symptom identification using the Duke health profile', *Journal of Clinical Epidemiology*, 49(2): 85–93.

Patrick, D.L. and Erickson, P. (1993) *Health Status and Health Policy: Allocating Resources to Health Care.* New York: Oxford University Press.

Patrick, D.L., Bush, J.W., and Chen, M.M. (1973) 'Methods for measuring levels of well-being for a health status index', *Health Services Research*, 8: 228–45.

Patrick, D.L., Sittampalam, Y., Somerville, S.M., Carter, W.B., and Bergner, M. (1985) 'A cross-cultural comparison of health status values', *American Journal of Public Health*, 75: 1402–07.

Porter, E. (1995) 'A Phenomenological alternative to the "ADL research tradition" ', *Journal of Aging and Health*, 7: 24–45.

Renee, K.S. (1974) 'Measurement of social health in a general population survey', *Social Science Research*, 3: 25–44.

Riley, A., Green, B., Forrest, C., Starfield, B., Kang, M., and Ensminger, M. (1998) 'A taxonomy of adolescent health: Development of the adolescent health profile-types', *Medical Care*, 36: 1228–36.

Roizen, M.F., Coalson, D., Hayward, R.S.A., Schmittner, J., Thisted, R.A., Apfelbaum, J.L., Stocking, C.B., Cassel, C.K., Pompei, P., Ford, D.E., and Steinberg, E.P. (1992) 'Can patients use an automated questionnaire to define their current health status', *Medical Care*, 30(5, Suppl): MS74-MS84.

Roland, M. and Morris, R. (1983) 'A study of the natural history of back pain: Part II: Development of guidelines for trials of treatment in primary care', *Spine*, 8: 145–50.

Salek, M., Finlay, A., Luscombe, D.K., Allen, B.R., Berth-Jones, J., Camp, R.D., Graham-Brown, R.A., Khan, G.K., Marks, R., and Motley, R.J. (1993) 'Cyclosporin greatly improves the quality of life of adults with severe atopic dermatitis', *British Journal of Dermatology*, 129: 422–30.

Saltonstall, R. (1993) 'Healthy bodies, social bodies: Men's and women's concepts and practices of health in everyday lives', *Social Science and Medicine*, 36: 7–14.

Schoenfeld, D.E., Malmrose, L.C., Blazer, D.G., Gold, D.T., and Seeman, T.E. (1994) 'Self-rated health and mortality in the high-functioning elderly – A closer look at healthy individuals', *Journal of Gerontology*, 49(3): M109–M115.

Simon, G., Revicki, D., Grothaus, L., and VonKorff, M. (1998) 'SF-36 summary scores: Are physical and mental health truly distinct?' *Medical Care*, 36: 567–72.

Smith, G. (1996) 'Income inequality and mortality: Why are they related?' *BMJ*, 312: 987–8.

Spector, W. and Fleishman, J. (1998) 'Combining activities of daily living with instrumental activities of daily living to measure functional disability', *Journal of Gerontology*, 53B (1): S46-S57.

Steinbrocker, O., Traeger, C.H., and Batterman, R.C. (1949) 'Therapeutic criteria in rheumatoid arthritis', *Journal of the American Medical Association*, 140: 659–62.

Stewart, A.L. and Ware, J.E. (1992) *Measuring Functioning and Well-Being: The Medical Outcomes Study Approach*. Durham, NC: Duke University Press.

Stewart, A.L., Hays, R.D., and Ware, J.E. (1988) 'The MOS short-form general health survey: Reliability and validity in a patient population', *Medical Care*, 26: 724–35.

Stewart, A.L., Greenfield, S., Hays, R.D., Wells, K., Rogers, W.H., Berry, S.D., McGlynn, E.A., and Ware, J.E. (1989) 'Functional status and well-being of patients with chronic conditions: Results from the medical outcomes study', *Journal of the American Medical Association*, 262: 907–13.

Stoll, T., Gordon, C., Seifert, B., Richardson, K., Malik, J., Bacon, P., and Isenberg, D. (1997) 'Consistency and validity of patient administered assessment of quality of life by the MOS SF-36', *Journal of Rheumatology*, 24: 1608–14.

Sullivan, D.F. (1971) 'A single index of mortality and morbidity', *HSMHA Health Reports*, 86(4): 347–54.

Sullivan, M., Ahlmen, M., and Bjelle, A. (1990) 'Health status assessment in rheumatoid arthritis. I. Further work on the validity of the sickness impact profile', *Journal of Rheumatology*, 17: 439–47.

Tarlov, A.R. (1992) 'The coming influence of a social sciences perspective on medical education', *Academic Medicine*, 67: 724–31.

US DHHS (Department of Health and Human Services) (1979) *Healthy People – The Surgeon General's Report on Health Promotion and Disease Prevention*. Hyattsville, MD: (PHS) 79–55071.

van Maanen, H. (1988) 'Being old does not always mean being sick: Perspectives on conditions of health as perceived by British and American elderly', *Journal of Advanced Nursing*, 13: 701–9.

Ware, J. E. and Karmos, A. H. (1976) *Development and Validation of Scales to Measure Perceived Health and Patient Role Propensity: Volume II of a Final Report*. Springfield, VA: National Technical Information Services.

Ware, J.E. and Sherbourne, C.D. (1992) 'The MOS 36-item short-form health survey (SF-36). I. Conceptual framework and item selection', *Medical Care*, 30: 473–83.

Ware, J., Kosinski, M., Bayliss, M., McHorney, C., Rogers, W., and Raczek, S. (1995) 'Comparison of methods for the scoring and statistical analysis of SF-36 health profile and summary measures: Summary of results from the MOS', *Medical Care*, 33(4, Suppl): AS264–AS279.

Ware, J., Kosinski, M., and Keller, S. (1996) 'A 12-item short-form health survey: Construction of scales and preliminary tests of reliability and validity', *Medical Care*, 34: 220–33.

Weiss, D.J. (1982) 'Improving measurement quality and efficiency with adaptive testing', *Applied Psychological Testing*, 6: 473–92.

Wells, K.B., Stewart, A., Hays, R.D., Burnam, M.A., Rogers, W., Daniels, M., Berry, S., Greenfield, S., and Ware, J.E. (1989) 'The functioning and well-being of depressed patients: Results from the medical outcomes study', *Journal of the American Medical Association*, 262: 914–19.

Wennberg, J.E. (1984) 'Dealing with medical practice variations: A proposal for action', *Health Affairs*, 3(2): 6–31.

Westlake, L. and George, S.L. (1994) 'Subjective health status of single homeless people in Sheffield', *Public Health*, 108: 111–19.

WHO (World Health Organization) (1947) *Chronicle of the World Health Organization*, 1(1–2): 11.

Wu, A.W., Rubin, H.R., Mathews, W.C., Ware, J.E., Brysk, L.T., Hardy, W.D., Bozzette, S.A., Spector, S.A., and Richman, D.D. (1991) 'A health status questionnaire using 30 items from the medical outcomes study: Preliminary validation in persons with early HIV infection', *Medical Care*, 29: 786–98.

2.11

Health Behavior: From Research to Community Practice

THOMAS R. PROHASKA, KAREN E. PETERS, AND
JAN S. WARREN

INTRODUCTION

The general public is continually being informed of research findings that indicate harmful or beneficial effects of health behaviors such as smoking, exposure to the sun, and physical activity. There are also numerous published reports of health promotion programs that demonstrate success at fostering positive behavior change in the population. However, the translation of scientifically tested research findings to community-based health promotion programs is often slow, fragmented, and subject to speculation by the practitioner community. Similarly, the 'lessons learned' from practitioners who develop and administer health behavior intervention programs for the benefit of their communities are slow to influence subsequent health behavior research. Why is there an apparent gulf between health behavior research and community-based practice? This chapter examines the transition from research to practice in the field of behavioral health promotion to identify and discuss sources that impede the timely and accurate communication of health behavior research findings into useful information for health practitioners. We focus on the process of behavioral health research and on the practice of health promotion in community settings in order to determine what factors contribute to the less than optimal exchange of ideas between research and practice. Finally, we make suggestions for bridging gaps between the practice and research communities.

BACKGROUND

During the past 20 years there has been significant growth in our understanding of health behaviors, behavioral health risk factors, and the impact of health promotion activities through epidemiological and behavioral health research. This research effort has resulted in the development of health education and health promotion programs with documented efficacy and effectiveness (Flay 1986; see also the Combined Health Information Database, CHID, at http://chid.nih.gov – USDHHS 1998a). However, even with the proliferation of empirically tested health behavior research interventions, relatively few of these research programs or their components are adapted to widespread community-based health promotion programs (Glanz et al. 1997; Iverson and Kolbe 1983). Similarly, there are numerous health behavior interventions and programs located throughout the United States which receive considerable attention and dissemination, but which demonstrate minimal effects on health and health behavior change once the program is fully evaluated (e.g., DARE (Drug Abuse Resistance Education) Hansen and McNeal 1998). This situation has led to an increased recognition that a gap exists in the transition between health behavior research and community-based health promotion practice (Altman 1995; Morrissey et al. 1997; Orlandi et al. 1990).

The increasing need to address complex social problems such as violence, drug abuse, and sexually transmitted diseases makes the issue of reciprocal translation between health behavior research and community-based practice timely and significant. This chapter examines the transition between health behavior research and community-based programs to identify factors contributing to the gap between health behavior science and health education/health promotion practice. Recommendations are offered on how to bridge this gap in order to facilitate reciprocal information transfer and interaction between health behavior researchers and practitioners, to disseminate and incorporate behavioral research findings into effective community-based health promotion programs, and to promote the usefulness of community-experience-based 'lessons learned' for informing the future agenda in behavioral health research.

GAPS IN THE TRANSITION FROM RESEARCH TO PRACTICE

The gap in our ability to incorporate research findings on health-risk behavior into health promotion interventions and community-based health promotion practice consists of at least three factors: (1) the timeframes involved in the transition between the development of innovations based on research and the application of these innovations into practice; (2) the loss of theory and content between research and practice; (3) the lack of utility of research methods and findings in their application or in practice.

The time between the publication of research findings demonstrating the value of a government or foundation-sponsored behavioral health research project and its subsequent adoption into community health promotion practice can be a matter of years, or it may never happen. Delays can be lengthy even for effectiveness trials which have already tested treatments, procedures, and interventions under real-world conditions (Morrissey et al. 1997; Portnoy et al. 1989). Another type of delay results from the dynamic nature of the circumstances and events that shape health-risk behavior in community populations and the researcher's ability to incorporate these changes into research designs. While practitioners are likely to recognize and respond to these situations early in the course of program implementation, the time interval may be greater for researchers due to the often inflexible nature of research protocols. The consequences of these time delays are research findings and innovations that are not very useful to the practice community.

The gap in the use of theory between health behavior researchers and health promotion and health education practitioners appears to be the difference between explicit and implicit use of theory (Hochbaum and Lorig 1992). While the explicit use of theory to guide research questions and program interventions is fundamental to the academic research process, the explicit use of theory is not central in the development of community-based programs. Burdine and McLeroy (1992) interviewed practitioners concerning the use of theory in health promotion programs. They found that while practitioners may not be explicitly using social science theory to direct the development of health education interventions, theory is involved in a 'common sense' understanding of how an intervention should work and what the outcomes should be. One reason for the gap in the application of theory in practice settings is the perceived limitation of theory to applied situations.

The third gap between behavioral research and practice pertains to a lack of utility of research-based health promotion intervention components when applied to community-based health promotion programs. Practitioners report that specific intervention components used in health promotion research are often not applicable to the real-world settings of community-based health promotion interventions (Burdine and McLeroy 1992). For example, researchers are often able to justify extensive and costly participant assessments and program evaluations that are not typically possible for community practitioners. Given the priorities of most community-based health promotion programs, the perceived utility of these research components are questionable. Weiss and Bucuvalas (1980) note that decision makers and practitioners apply a 'utility test' in screening social behavioral research for new ideas or application. Research utility is based on two distinct components, application and innovation. Practitioners evaluate application utility in terms of how well it can provide explicit and practical direction on matters they can address. Practitioners also evaluate the utility of behavioral research based on its ability to provide insight for new directions and new goals. Practitioners often screen research for guidance in determining alternatives to current intervention practices and program revisions.

Next, we examine the process of conducting health behavior research in contrast to the activities associated with the development of community-based health promotion programs. The different nature of these processes contributes to an understanding of why gaps occur, resulting in the lack of reciprocal transfer of information between health behavior research and community practice.

HEALTH BEHAVIOR RESEARCH ISSUES

A considerable proportion of the health behavior research that is generated is conducted by academic research faculties in college and university settings. Health behavior researchers come from a variety of disciplines, including communication, psychology, sociology, gerontology, medicine, public health, education, nursing, and anthropology. They have advanced graduate degrees and are trained to look at health behavior from the perspective of their own disciplinary perspectives. This plethora of approaches can cause confusion, as findings are not always presented in a single coherent framework.

Regardless of the perspective taken, the majority of health behavior research typically focuses on addressing one or more of four interrelated questions (Prohaska and Clark 1997).

1 What is the incidence and prevalence of specific health behaviors in populations?
2 What are the health consequences of specific health behaviors on the health and well-being of individuals and populations?
3 What are the antecedents and mechanisms (e.g., cultural, psychosocial, environmental) controlling the initiation, maintenance, and termination of specific health behaviors?
4 Can we intervene in these health-risk behaviors, and if so, under what conditions and settings does this work best?

Behavioral scientists have identified many of the most critical health-risk behaviors, their incidence and prevalence rates, and their health consequences in various populations (for example, see USDHHS 1991, 1996). Researchers in the behavioral sciences assume that the individual has some volitional control over these behaviors, and that the adoption or cessation of behavior is a product of subjective perceptions and rational decision making. There is also recognition that health-risk factors have multiple environmental and contextual determinants. Researchers in the field of health practices have developed a number of cognitive/rational decision-based models of behavior, as well as macro, environmental, and system factors associated with these behaviors in various populations.

Among the more widely utilized theoretical models guiding behavior risk reduction interventions are the health belief model (Janz and Becker 1984; Rosenstock 1974; Rosenstock et al. 1988), Bandura's social cognitive theory (Bandura 1977, 1989; Strecher et al. 1986), the theory of planned behavior (Ajzen 1985), the PRECEDE model (Green and Kreuter 1991; Green et al. 1980), the transtheoretical model of behavior change (Prochaska and DiClemente 1992; Prochaska et al. 1992) and ecological perspectives (Flay and Petraitis 1994; McLeroy et al. 1988). It is this literature and research that guide researchers' decisions for determining health-risk behavior interventions, targeting specific populations, and assessing components of the health promotion intervention. These models focus on the inter-relationship of the individual's knowledge, perceptions, attitudes, and beliefs as well as his or her interpersonal, organizational, and community environments on behavior change. In addition, the role of public policy is also examined in association with health-risk behavior.

The use of theory by behavioral scientists is fundamental to the research process. Theories facilitate our understanding of the array of causal antecedents to behavior and help determine a parsimonious group of variables contributing to behavior change. A goal of health behavior research is to test how well a particular theory (or components of multiple theories), operationalized into an intervention strategy, applies to different health behaviors (e.g., is the health belief model predictive in determining a woman's likelihood of undergoing mammogram screening, joining a smoking cessation program, or starting an exercise class).

Health behavior researchers are encouraged to focus on innovation rather than replication of program interventions. At least two forces, research funding and priorities in research publication, drive this. Academic researchers are encouraged to obtain funding for their research from federal research grants and awards from private foundations. These funding sources typically specify research objectives and criteria that stress experimental control, employment of novel concepts, approaches, and methods and aims that are original and innovative. This funding rarely includes resources for program dissemination or program continuation beyond the grant period (examples of notable exceptions include the Centers for Disease Control and Prevention, the W.K. Kellogg Foundation, and the Robert Wood Johnson Foundation). Published health promotion research in scientific journals share these same values for originality, statistical significance, and innovation. It is unusual for journals to devote space to the reporting of nonsignificant results, or the replication of programs to different age groups, cultures, and settings.

PRACTITIONERS' PROGRAM
IMPLEMENTATION ISSUES

The process used by practitioners in community-based environments can be evaluated on two levels: direct service, practice organizations that deliver health education/health promotion programs, and the field practitioners who direct program implementation such as health educators, program directors, and program evaluators. Practice organizations such as state and local health departments, hospitals and community clinics, social service agencies, not-for-profit organizations, churches, schools, and housing groups have diverse organizational mandates, constituencies, reimbursement mechanisms, material and economic resources, environments, and populations to serve that drive their program development.

Within organizations, health intervention programs may be initiated for a variety of reasons. One reason is to maintain certification as a provider or to meet federal block grant requirements (e.g., local health departments). Other reasons are to improve health status in the surrounding community (local hospitals), to provide a social activity (churches, senior centers), to improve quality of life (nursing homes), to reduce health-care costs (hospitals, clinics, and health maintenance organizations (HMOs)), or to improve relations with the community and generate goodwill. Many organizations implement health intervention programs in partnerships involving multiple community organizations, funders, and networks. For example, Prohaska (1998) noted a trend in health promotion programs for older adults in which there are increasing numbers of community partnerships, such as mall-walking exercise programs sponsored by hospitals and shopping malls. In addition, once practitioner organizations have institutionalized a community health promotion program, it becomes difficult to discontinue or revise it, particularly if it is popular.

Individual field practitioners work within these organizations to implement health education and health promotion programs. The educational training and background of community practitioners varies considerably, ranging from individuals who have little formal training on how to design or implement health promotion programs to persons with graduate degrees in disciplines related to health education and the behavioral sciences. Recent efforts by the National Commission for Health Education Credentialing Inc. to launch a voluntary credentialing system for health education specialists will contribute to assuring quality and standards in the delivery of health education services by practitioners (Wolle et al. 1998).

There is information describing the process by which practitioners choose, adapt, and implement health education/health promotion programs. Morrissey et al. (1997) noted that practitioners use past experience, published research, and other related sources of information when considering implementing health promotion programs. In addition, several practice-based or applied journals such as *Health Education Quarterly* and the *Journal of Health Promotion* regularly publish study results with an emphasis on implementation. Also, computerized databases (e.g., the Computerized Health Information Database, CHID and the Computer Retrieval of Information on Scientific Projects, CRISP, USDHHS 1998b) are continually updated with new health promotion intervention information and health behavior research studies. Research can be helpful in determining the significance of a health problem, targeting at-risk populations, and helping to set health-risk behavior priorities. For example, recommendations provided by the USDHHS (1991) are based on research that has mapped the incidence and prevalence of health-risk behavior in various demographic groups, and has set target objectives for reducing health-risk factors. State and local health departments have mandates to try to meet the objectives issued by their federal funding agencies, and other practitioner organizations use these objectives to determine health promotion program priorities. For example, practitioners within a health department may be asked to implement a health education program for blood pressure control in a targeted area or for a specific population as part of a federal block grant. The concerns of the stakeholders and the priorities of the agency or network in which the practitioner performs his or her activities often determine other types of programs and target populations.

While practitioners may have mandates on what risk factor they address and who they target, they generally have greater latitude on 'how' they address the risk factor. In this regard, it would be expected that research addressing the mechanisms influencing health behavior change and studies documenting the success of interventions on health behavior would be of primary interest to practitioners (research questions 3 and 4). Health educators use research findings in these two content areas to help design intervention programs as well as to provide references for expected success. Ideally, this body of research would be reviewed for pertinent literature and findings, and then be incorporated into the system and the constraints under which the practitioner implements the community-based health promotion programs.

On occasion, practitioners and researchers may collaborate to implement a research intervention as a community-based program through program dissemination. However, even with researcher–practitioner collaboration, there are barriers that make this process problematic and contribute to difficulty in the transition between research and practice.

SOURCES FOR THE LACK OF TRANSITION BETWEEN RESEARCH AND PRACTICE

Diffusion theory, or diffusion and dissemination of innovations, has been used to understand the barriers in transitioning from health behavior research innovation to widespread behavior change (Green et al. 1987; Oldenburg et al. 1997; Rogers 1983). Program dissemination involves the transfer of experimental programs from research environments to community organizations and practitioners who will adapt, implement, and maintain these programs (Manfredi and Warnecke, forthcoming). Application of diffusion theory requires an understanding of the resource innovation attributes (i.e., the research characteristics), the characteristics of the innovation adopter (i.e., the practitioner), and the process by which the transition from research to practice has been implemented (Orlandi et al. 1990). The diffusion process generally involves four phases: awareness, interest, trial, and adoption (Dignan et al. 1994) and can be viewed at two levels or transition points. At one level, diffusion of innovation can be viewed as the transition from the researcher to the practitioner, while at another level, it involves diffusion from the practitioner to widespread use in the community. Our focus is on the diffusion of innovation in research to the practitioner.

Iverson and Kolbe (1983), identified features of successful diffusion of innovation that are applicable to the transition from research to practice. These include compatibility, flexibility, reversibility, relative advantage, complexity, cost-efficiency, and risk. Applying these qualities in successful diffusion, Iverson and Kolbe (1983) and Orlandi et al. (1990) noted that practitioners of community-based health education programs are more likely to adopt innovations in research when they are consistent with the practitioner's (and organization's) value system, have sufficient flexibility to be applied to current circumstances, can be reversed, have advantages over existing programs and innovations, are not overly complex, demonstrate cost efficiency, and do not include significant risk. Unfor-

tunately, these attributes are rarely included in published research. This is often left to the practitioner to determine.

A number of recent articles have focused on possible causes for the difficulty in the transition between health promotion science and health promotion practice. Freudenberg et al. (1995) focused on the lack of interaction between academic researchers and practitioners, and stressed the need for closer collaboration between the two. Others (Morrissey et al. 1997) identified sources for the gap between prevention practice and prevention research, including different theoretical orientations and training, funding procedures, resource constraints, systems-level barriers, and community readiness. In a special issue of *Health Education Quarterly*, D'Onofrio (1992) and others (Burdine and McLeroy 1992; Hochbaum et al. 1992; van Ryn and Heaney 1992) focused on differences in the use of theory in health education research and practice. They concluded that a variety of factors, such as the lack of appropriate teaching of theory to practitioners and differences in explicit and implicit use of theory by researchers and practitioners, have contributed to difficulties in the translation of research and practice.

We believe that the causes for the gap in transition can be categorized into the three previously mentioned areas: the time delay in the transition between research and practice, the loss of theory and content between theory and practice, and the gap in utility between research interventions and community-based programs. Within these three areas we identify six specific reasons for the difficulties found in the transition between research and practice: (1) delay in the research process and transition of research; (2) limitations in the communication of research findings; (3) use of theory; (4) the unidirectional nature of the transition; (5) constraints inherent in program application; (6) different measures of outcomes and success.

Delays in the Research Process

There is a considerable time lag between when funds targeted toward specific areas of research are made available, the development and submission of a proposed research project, the implementation of the research project, and the communication of research results through the publication review process, including the time between acceptance and actual publication. This is most likely a minimum of 3 years. This delay can make even the most 'cutting-edge' behavioral research obsolete in the face of the rapidly changing health behavior issues in the community. Our practical understanding of many health behavior issues changes far more rapidly than the speed with which we can communicate this knowledge, at least through the traditional research publication process. For example, the nature of high-risk behaviors, such as the spread of HIV and other sexually transmitted diseases, the dynamic picture of populations at risk, the factors for risk, and the perceptions held by individuals at risk, all change rapidly. The concerns and problems faced by practitioners who deal with the behavioral risk factors associated with HIV and AIDS frequently outpace the rate of publications on the topic. National and regional topic presentations are often more timely, but may also be subjected to the same delaying process.

Another source of delay is the time between publication and presentation of findings and the awareness, translation, and application of the findings by the practitioner. Even if the initial research has successfully moved from a controlled efficacy trial to an effectiveness trial to a program impact evaluation, delays can occur in terms of the program becoming 'common knowledge' and being perceived as applicable in the context confronted by the practitioner (Flay 1986). Delays can also occur between the time research-based health promotion programs have been adapted and implemented by some practitioners and in the wider dissemination of the program to other agencies, regions, or countries. There appear to be few timely and effective mechanisms in the United States to facilitate the widespread distribution and implementation of successful health education programs. However, some progress has been made through the use of the Internet (e.g., CHID and CRISP), in some peer-reviewed journals that are beginning to feature 'practice'-oriented sections (e.g., Health Education and Behavior *Practice Notes*, American Journal of Public Health *Notes from the Field*), and in the community-based practice field, with its recognition of model programs through award programs.

Critical time is also lost between the point at which field practitioners identify problems with health promotion programs based on research and when the researcher becomes aware of these problems. Changes in the communities where these programs are implemented bring new and important challenges to the practitioner that may not be communicated to the researcher on a timely basis. These challenges may have important implications for revisions in subsequent research that may not even be conducted by the original researcher or author. Finally, emerging health-risk behavior such as the use of new illegal substances are more likely to be observed by community practitioners long

before health behavior researchers and funding agencies discover the problem.

Limitations in the Communication of Research Findings

Probably one of the most fundamental reasons for the difficulty in the transition between research and practice is due to the communication process and channels used by the academic research community. Research is often a required activity in most academic settings, and the primary mechanism for communicating research findings is through peer-reviewed journal articles. Peer-reviewed research articles, based on accepted empirical methods, are considered a quality standard for academic research. Manuscript reviews are subjected to criteria such as documentation of significant findings, extensive use of theory to guide intervention components, and sufficient experimental control to eliminate or minimize alternative explanations or confounds for the findings observed. Researchers review this published literature with the intention of building on their own research. In short, much of the research communication process is directed and evaluated by researchers for other researchers. While there are practitioner-oriented journals where health behavior researchers contribute, these are the exception rather than the rule.

The emphasis in health behavior research publications is on quantitative methods and the presentation of statistically significant differences between study groups participating in the health promotion intervention. While the reporting and usage of rigorous statistical methods may be important to theory development (a primary concern of behavioral science researchers), it is less relevant to practitioners. Practitioners require more information on differences that are *meaningful*, and on the actual implementation process for the intervention. The focus on quantitative data does not always provide sufficient background on the nuts and bolts of how the intervention was implemented and what roadblocks were encountered. More qualitative and observational data could provide the practitioner with relevant facts about the actual implementation issues involved with the intervention, such as recruitment problems, program adherence issues, language or literacy issues in administering measurement instruments, participant beliefs about the intervention or about research in general, and how these barriers were overcome. Qualitative methods, which can be applied with sufficient academic rigor, can provide additional insights into intervention participants' reactions to the program, its materials, the setting, the health educator who conducted the program, and other variables that might not fit into a strictly quantitative evaluation design. Qualitative data of a more descriptive nature may yield the attributes that practitioners need for successful adoption and, ultimately, diffusion. For example, the use of an ethnographic focus group approach with nonparticipants of exercise health promotion programs helped identify factors contributing to attrition during program recruitment and provided useful information for tailoring exercise recruitment strategies (Prohaska and Walcott-McQuigg 1996).

Hand-in-hand with what and how researchers publish is the problem with the research findings that never make it into the communication pipeline. Health behavior research journals rarely publish research that fails to replicate previous intervention successes. Failure to find statistical significance between theoretical constructs and changes in health risk behavior does not get communicated. McGuire (1984) noted that often the researcher will criticize or explain away the insignificance by determining that the design of the intervention was wrong, not that the theory did not work. This problem of nonreplication takes on added importance when interventions targeting a specific community or at-risk population fail to duplicate successful results found with other populations. However, this is important information that may imply that there are theoretical constructs missing that are important to consider for populations other than the original study group. This may result in the unfortunate situation in which considerable time and effort is lost implementing weak or ineffective programs.

While the academic publication process and criteria have been used in health behavior research to increase academic rigor and set standards, it can obscure salient information needed by practitioners. Researchers typically caution the reader on the generalizability of the experimental intervention with respect to populations not included in the study sample and its unknown applicability in other settings. However, it is just this type of information that is critical to the practitioner's decision to adapt and implement the program to their particular circumstances. Also, practitioners, because of their varied background, may lack the critical analysis skills needed when reading published research to discern what is a viable health education/health promotion intervention program which can be adapted for the circumstances within their target community.

Use of Theory

A substantial amount of health behavior research focuses on theory development in order to understand the mechanisms controlling behavior. There are at least four general content areas in health behavior change that require some understanding of theory:

- the mechanisms controlling the behavior (e.g., perceptions of self-efficacy, social support);
- differences between populations (age groups, gender, cultures, and income and education levels);
- the target behavior (e.g., moving from one stage of change to another, exercise versus physical activity, getting a baseline mammogram versus getting annual mammograms);
- the context and environment in which the behavior is performed (e.g., environmental cues, exercise programs conducted at health clubs, at home, in community centers, and group settings versus self-directed).

Discussion of theory in health education research tends to focus on the first of these content areas. That is, a considerable amount of effort has been devoted to the development and refinement of cognitively based theoretical models of behavior change typically examining the psychosocial perspectives of the individual. If practitioners had more exposure to theory relevant to populations, target behaviors, and contextual and environmental influences, it may provide insight on how to tailor the health promotion research to fit their program needs.

Research and theory incorporating an ecological model provides a contextual basis for understanding human behavior within the individual's environment and life circumstances. The ecological approach addresses the need for a deeper understanding of the interaction between individuals, their families, communities, and the environment, so that there is a clearer understanding of how health can be achieved and maintained over time. As a result, multiple types of interventions are required to address the complex issues facing at-risk communities. Using this approach, there is an explicit recognition of the multiple levels of influence that interrelate to impact on the health behavior of individuals and groups including the community, the environment, and public policy (Bronfenbrenner 1979; Garbarino and Abramowitz 1992; McLeroy et al. 1988; Syme 1992). The ecological approach may be more in line with the 'experience'-based understanding that practitioners, who often work and live in the community, bring to an identified problem (Bartholomew et al. 1998).

Researchers often test an individual health behavior theory's generalizability by applying it to a broad array of behaviors to determine its predictive ability. When specific theories in health education interventions are tested, they report significant contributions of theoretical components in predicting behavior change, although only a small to moderate amount of the variance in the behavior may be explained. Subsequent cycles of research build on the previous theoretical application in an effort to explain a greater proportion of the variance through successive refinements of the theory.

In essence, theory *drives* research but theory *guides* practice. Part of the utility of a theory to a practitioner is its commonsense application to intended program activities. If a particular theory is compatible with the practitioner's personal experience or makes intuitive sense (i.e., has face validity), then the program components will more likely be incorporated. Too often, practitioners and researchers alike develop a tendency to use a favorite theoretical model of behavior. While this can limit both groups, practitioners with this perspective can severely limit program development by focusing just on research with their favorite theoretical model. A related problem is the perception by practitioners (and encouraged by researchers) that theories cannot be combined, or that theory must be used in its entirety. This can also severely limit the effectiveness of the practitioner in making full use of the research literature.

Unidirectional Nature of the Transition

Ideally, research and practice should exert a powerful influence on one another, but the reality is that all too often there is an assumed one-way flow from research to practice. However, practitioners have critical information and observations that need to be integrated into the next cycles of research. Unfortunately, there are few resources available for practitioners to communicate their findings back to the research community. Resource constraints often do not allow for program evaluation, and practitioners have neither the time nor the budget to produce manuscripts for publication. The result is that the research community, which operates under its own rigid standards, views program outcomes and 'lessons learned' that do make it into the publication pipeline as suspect.

The relationship between research and its application should move in both directions. Currently, theory and research is perceived as being owned by academics, but we need to demystify theory and theory development so that they become more widely understood and

used by practitioners (D'Onofrio 1992). Knowledge of theoretical perspectives and the ability to apply theory to the population, context, and settings encountered during program implementation should be just another skill in the practitioner's toolbox. In turn, practitioners have significant contributions to make in terms of expanding theory to encompass real-world situations. The application of theory in a particular setting and to specific target populations may uncover additional variables or constructs that need to be incorporated as we look at various cultures within these populations. Individuals sharing a cultural identity hold their own values and priorities in relationship to health, health behavior, and health care. For example, the fatalistic outlook (fatalismo) reported among Latinos has been associated with perceptions of cancer as being incurable, thereby making the use of cancer screening tests unlikely (Perez-Stable et al. 1992). Religious practices, nationality, language, income, gender relations, level of acculturation, and place of residence will all influence behavior and should, in turn, influence theory development. It is not that the researcher is not also aware of these influences, but that the practitioner's hands-on experience with these populations can be a valuable resource for further theory development. In short, practitioners can provide important insights into the realities of applying the health promotion program that would benefit the research process. This is similar to the concept of principles of practice (Freudenberg et al. 1995). They suggest that practitioners have an understanding of the community and the complex environments in which health promotion programs are implemented. This would help researchers better comprehend the context of their own research.

Practitioners' understanding of the community stem from the fact that they are frequently more integrated than researchers into the communities they serve. This occurs in two ways. First, practitioners often come from the communities they serve. For example, it would be expected that Latino health educators and practitioners be from the Latino community and that they live and work in Latin neighborhoods. Practitioners working with the disabled may themselves be disabled, or they may have grown up with a disabled sibling or other relative. In essence, practitioners live and breathe the community because they are part of the community.

Second, practitioners operate in community settings, and they are skilled at community liaison building, a skill that would be a benefit to academic researchers. Community-based health promotion programs are delivered in settings based on partnerships with major stakeholders. There are prerequisites to program implementation in the community that involve building acceptance and trust with community partners and program participants. Academic researchers experience a high level of distrust by the community, especially from disadvantaged populations. These concerns include perceptions from community participants of being exploited by university researchers (Livingston 1994). Seasoned practitioners are acutely aware of community sensitivities and the need for them to build long-term relationships with the community.

Constraints Inherent in Program Application

Health behavior researchers have a higher degree of control over factors that may confound research study findings and the ultimate success of the study than do community-based practitioners. As part of the research activity, university researchers can often provide incentives to study participants, provide transportation to the intervention site, and offer timely feedback and follow-up. Practitioners have fewer resources available and more partners with which to negotiate. This lack of control in community health promotion programs by practitioners is best summarized by Hochbaum et al.

> They [practitioners] cannot often choose a problem, a situation, or a population that happens to fit their interest and allow them to use and test some of their preferred strategies or methods. They are usually expected to assail assigned problems in a given situation and population under conditions over which they have very little control. . . . While academicians generally have a relatively wide range of freedom in designing and conducting their work once it is approved and funded, practitioners do not enjoy such independence. They work constantly with administrators, colleagues and superiors, community leaders, and others whose support or resistance they cannot disregard without paying a price. (Hochbaum et al. 1992: 303)

Given the constraints under which practitioners design and implement health promotion interventions, it is rare that a program developed by researchers will be implemented into the community without revisions.

A health education practitioner frequently cannot incorporate an intervention in its entirety into her community-based program. Rather, a practitioner is looking at the research for a few good jewels to take with her to apply to a specific situation. An obvious problem with this approach is that isolated program components taken from larger intervention strategies may not work the same when applied in a different program context. When practitioners do find a program that can be adopted 'as is,' they may find that it has limited relevance to the environment in which it will be implemented.

Different Measures of Outcomes and Success

Health organizations and community practitioners have articulated specific criteria for determining successful health behavior program interventions and indicators of success. For example, the American Public Health Association (APHA), in collaboration with the Center for Health Promotion and Education of the Center for Disease Control (APHA 1987), has recommended five criteria for the development of health behavior programs. These are listed below.

- A health promotion program should address one or more risk factors that are carefully defined, measurable, modifiable, and prevalent among the members of a chosen target group; factors that constitute a threat to the health status and the quality of life of target group members.
- A health promotion program should reflect a consideration of the special characteristics, needs, and preferences of its target group(s).
- Health promotion programs should include interventions that clearly and effectively reduce a targeted risk factor and are appropriate for a particular setting.
- A health promotion program should identify and implement interventions that make optimum use of available resources.
- From the outset, a health promotion program should be organized, planned, and implemented in such a way that its operation and effects can be evaluated.

The majority of researchers have adopted these criteria when designing and implementing health education promotion interventions. In particular, more research is being targeted to previously neglected at-risk groups. However, with regard to the fourth criteria, the resources available to university researchers often exceed those of the average practitioner, and practitioners are the ones who will ultimately be using the program.

From the practitioner viewpoint, these criteria are consistent with the understanding of what constitutes a successful community-based program. Morrissey et al. (1997) conducted a pilot survey of community health program practitioners (center directors) on the most important characteristics of successful community-based programs. The program characteristics given the highest priorities were: the comprehensiveness of the program in addressing individual, family, and environmental influences (e.g., the desire to design interventions using an ecological approach); a full understanding of the complexity of the target problem (based on research and past experience); sufficient intensity, duration, and dosage of the intervention; a focus on specific target groups and risk factors; appropriateness of the program to fit the needs of the community and the culture of the target group. However, these stated goals and criteria can be in conflict with the realities faced by practitioners as they proceed to design and implement community-based programs.

Even though there may be general agreement between researchers and practitioners on what goes into a successful health education/health promotion program, these two groups frequently have different process and outcome measures. Research projects measure outcomes such as participants' change in behavior, change in attitudes about the behavior, as well as the participants' health status. They also measure process variables such as recruitment rates, retention rates, consistency of participation, and program enjoyment. For practitioners, outcomes are often set by the regulatory agencies and organizations funding the programs and the community partners contributing to the program. Reporting to regulatory agencies can result in outcome and success indicators based on fiscal reporting (e.g., number of unduplicated persons served; number of units of service (time) provided on the intervention) rather than health status or behavior. Practitioners are also faced with pressures to write program objectives that exceed the capacity of the program's impact while having limited access to data relevant to meaningful outcomes (Institute of Medicine 1988). In addition, limited funds may restrict or eliminate program evaluation activity making it difficult accurately to gauge a program's success or failure. While researchers and practitioners have the same goals – improving the populations' health status – they often measure their progress toward the goal in different ways.

SOLUTIONS

Professional organizations and research groups have provided recommendations that are pertinent to solving many of the gaps between behavior research and practice presented in this chapter (Institute of Medicine 1988; Morrissey, et al. 1997; Orlandi et al. 1990). Recent literature on this issue has identified three possible approaches to bridging the gap between research and practice: improving technology transfer, conducting participatory research, and promoting practice-centered prevention. As outlined by Morrissey et al. (1997), the first approach emphasizes education, training, and dissemination through standard academic channels such as journal publications, conferences, and reports. They note that this approach assumes that the gap is the result of a lack of information dissemination between researchers and practitioners. In terms of the flow of information from researchers to practitioners, we have argued that it is not just a lack of information dissemination that is the problem, but also how the information is organized and presented for consumption by practitioners, as well as the speed with which this information is made available to the practitioner. Therefore, the first recommendations focus on the need for researchers to be more responsive to the information needs of the practitioner. This can be accomplished by:

- teaching researchers how to write for both the practitioner and the public consumer;
- increasing publications in journals and magazines read by practitioners and writing articles specific to practitioner needs and concerns;
- providing opportunities for direct communication and interaction between researchers and practitioners;
- utilizing the Internet and related technologies for more timely information dissemination;
- providing incentives in the academic setting to encourage publication and packaging of materials that can be adopted 'off-the-shelf' by practitioners and the public.

Considerable progress has been made with many of these recommendations. The 'Practice Notes' section in the journal *Health Education and Behavior* is an example of a health behavior research journal reaching out and targeting information directly to practitioners. The section focuses on practice notes and innovative programs as well as practice-related issues and solutions. The use of the Internet for more timely dissemination of innovations has also been established. For example, the Health Resources and Services Administration's Bureau of Primary Care established 'Models that Work,' a biannual award that recognizes innovative community health programs. These programs are publicized in a practitioner journal and are made available on the Internet. Since its inception in 1994 fifteen of the award-winning programs have been replicated (Broughton 1998).

While progress is evident in this area, the above recommendations do not address the reciprocal information flow, that is, the information flow from practitioners to researchers.

This can be addressed by:

- encouraging practitioners to communicate important changes observed in their communities, and how health-risk behaviors are expressed that have a bearing on research activities (e.g., practitioners quickly picked up on the dangerous nature of crack cocaine, which was slow to make it into the research pipeline);
- having practitioners provide 'lessons learned' on effective collaboration with community gatekeepers and community liaison building;
- empowering practitioners to become pro-active in asking for the types of research and information they need to be effective in the community.

These recommendations could be addressed by providing opportunities for practitioners to collaborate with academic researchers in the education and training of future community health promotion practitioners (Institute of Medicine 1988). By having practitioners and researchers combine talents and skills in the classroom, students will benefit from timely real-world experiences and will facilitate reciprocal dialogues between practitioners and researchers.

The second approach to bridging the gap focuses on strategies that facilitate participatory research and close collaboration between health behavior researchers and community-based health education/health promotion practitioners. An example of such a strategy is offered by Orlandi et al. (1990), who recommend a linkage approach to diffusion of innovation by developing cooperative exchanges and interaction between the resource system (researcher) and the user system (practitioner). As an approach to scientific inquiry, participatory research integrates three major elements: research, education, and action. A participatory research model also includes the partnering of academic, practitioner, and community representatives who jointly engage in identifying the problem and formulating the solution by selecting the types of activities to address the target issue, analyzing or interpreting the results of the intervention (understanding the effect of the activities), applying the results, and disseminating the results. 'Different actors, each with their own knowledge, techniques and experiences, work together in dialectical process, through which new forms of knowledge are produced' (Cornwall and Jewkes 1995: 1671). While participatory research can advance science through new knowledge and understanding about a social world, it also produces a practical knowledge that can be directly applied to improve the well-being of participants or those whom they represent. The underlying assumption is that in an academic–practitioner–community research partnership, members of a given community are crucial to analyzing and prioritizing their situations, and are necessary partners in designing appropriate solutions. Most importantly, their interpretation of the meaning of the results can contribute to further iterations of the intervention and the research, resulting in a timely flow of information from the practitioner (and community) to the researcher.

Linking researchers and practitioners in participatory research also provides an opportunity to observe theory development in action. It is an opportunity for the practitioner to demystify theory (D'Onofrio 1992) and for researchers to appreciate the contributions of practitioners in terms of expanding theory to encompass real-world situations.

Community participatory research, while conceptually appealing, does have its own set of problems. A fundamental question with participatory research relationships is what are the specific roles and responsibilities of each member (researcher, practitioner, and community representative), and what processes and activities within the partnership facilitate dissemination of innovative research? Participatory research requires a significant amount of flexibility and compromise among all the parties. Researchers usually already have a defined problem that they wish to address in the community. Participants may have an entirely different assessment of priorities and view the researcher's problem as significantly less important. Changing the target of the entire intervention is a major issue, and one that may not be feasible given the constraints imposed by research funding. Also, inclusion of community participants in the design, implementation, data collection, and data analysis will often expand the project time-line because of the need for additional training, accommodation of work schedules, skills, and personalities, as well as the inclusion of another group in the research process. However, the resulting partnership between researchers, practitioners, and the community has the potential for establishing a long-term relationship with the ability to facilitate knowledge acquisition/transfer by all parties. Community participants and community groups also have insight into issues such as effective recruitment strategies, and cultural and regional relevance that are not always known to practitioners. In this scenario, the community participants have project ownership which motivates their ability to recruit participants and to adopt the program once the research has ended. Involving participants and key community groups in community-based health promotion research and program implementation is also compatible with the PRECEDE model (Green and Kreuter 1991) and recommendations by APHA (1987) for effective health promotion programs in that it makes optimum use of available resources.

The participatory research approach has distinct advantages, and should be encouraged by:

- inviting community groups and practitioners to participate in grant proposals, and in responses to requests for proposals (RFPs), and in helping to set agendas and incorporate more real-world issues into intervention recruitment and design;
- choosing community-based settings for interventions even though academic facilities may be more convenient;
- encouraging practitioners and community representatives to participate in problem solving during research and program implementation and to respond to the interpretation of program findings.

The third approach to bridging the gap involves adopting the practice-centered approach, which involves using continuous quality improvement processes in order to improve the effectiveness of community-based prevention programs (Morrissey et al. 1997). In this approach, program evaluators play a key role in bridging the gap between research and practice by providing technical assistance to practitioners, encouraging practitioners to make effective use of behavioral science literature, and facilitating reciprocal transfer of information. This approach has considerable utility in that it recognizes the inherent constraints in program application, takes into account the lack of resources hampering practitioners, and has the potential for correcting the unidirectional nature of information transfer discussed earlier. It also focuses on the need for more and better evaluation of community-based programs. However, this approach of using an intermediary evaluator does not address the benefits of direct practitioner–researcher interaction. Researchers would profit from timely information on changes in the community and direct information on the utility of specific health promotion programs. Practitioners would benefit from education and training on how to abstract information from the research to improve their programs. While evaluators can facilitate practitioner–researcher interactions, direct interactions between the practitioner and the researcher can reinforce the practice-centered

prevention approach. Direct interactions be accomplished by:

- bringing practitioners and researchers together in the classroom to promote reciprocal information exchange and jointly to teach future health practitioners;
- providing training for researchers on how to develop community liaisons and maintain long-term relationships with community partners;
- providing collaborative research opportunities to promote mutual learning experience;
- encouraging joint researcher–practitioner publications that reflect both sound research and relevant health promotion practices.

In a more practical vein, Bartholomew et al. (1998) developed a practice-centered approach based on a framework that helps health education practitioners incorporate academic research into their program planning process. 'Intervention mapping' provides practitioners with specific tasks and ways of analyzing research literature in order to integrate relevant theories and interventions into their schema. Intervention mapping has five steps: (1) create a matrix of proximal program objectives; (2) select theory-based intervention methods and practical strategies; (3) design and organize a program; (4) specify adoption and implementation plans; (5) generate program evaluation plans. While the process of intervention mapping can involve researcher practitioner collaboration, this approach provides sufficient guidelines for individual practitioners to search the literature and determine the utility of the research findings for program development.

CONCLUSION

All three approaches outlined above move us a step closer to bridging the gap between research and community-based practice. However, no one approach or recommendation offered here is sufficient to close the apparent gulf between health behavior research and community-based practice. The transition from research to practice and from practice to research will continue to be an on-going learning process. Both the behavioral science researcher and the health promotion practitioner have a pivotal interest in the development of timely, useful, and reciprocal information transfer systems that include continuous feedback loops between research and practice. A number of recommendations, useful suggestions, and techniques have been offered for researchers and practitioners, each with its own inherent strengths and weaknesses. For example, a collaborative process among the researcher, the practitioner, and the community is contingent upon the goodwill and initiative of all individuals involved. Fortunately, the research and practice communities, along with funding agencies, are recognizing the impetus to encourage collaborative activities. Researchers are frequently asked to serve as consultants on community-based health promotion projects. Practitioners are in demand to serve in advisory capacities on sponsored research projects. These activities provide the practitioner and the researcher with opportunities to gain first-hand knowledge and experience of each others' field. In addition, we have noted that increasingly there exist other activities that promote collegial interaction among professionals in the research and practice fields.

Syme (1992) noted that health education/health promotion research and programs will continue to play a major role in addressing the health needs of society due to the constant influx of successive cohorts who have not been exposed to the health promotion message, the constant evolution of health-risk behavior that impacts on the health of society, and the changing social structure that influences health-risk behavior. To work toward a foundation and structure that facilitates interaction between health behavior research and practice is in the best interests of all of us. We strongly encourage researchers to broaden their academic perspective and to take the lead in working with community-based practitioners and their organizations, thus widening the impact of health behavior research. Similarly, we urge practitioners to take a more active role in integrating research concepts into their field practice, and then communicating their field experiences to influence the research agenda in the behavioral sciences related to health education/health promotion. Direct involvement in collaborative partnerships and a mutual exchange of information can only improve the fields of health behavior research and health promotion practice, and ultimately the nation's health.

References

Ajzen, I. (1985) 'From intention to actions: A theory of planned behavior' in J. Kuhl and J. Bekman (eds), *Action Control: From Cognition to Behavior*. New York: Springer. pp. 11–39.

Altman, D. (1995) 'Sustaining interventions in community systems: On the relationship between researchers and communities', *Health Psychology*, 14: 526–36.

APHA (American Public Health Association) (1987) 'Criteria for the development of health promotion and education programs' (Technical Report), *American Journal of Public Health*, 77: 89–92.

Bandura, A. (1977) *Social Learning Theory*. New Jersey: Prentice Hall.

Bandura, A. (1989) 'Human agency in social cognitive theory', *American Psychologist*, 44, 1175–84.

Bartholomew, L. K., Parcel, G. S., and Kok, G. (1998) 'Intervention mapping: A process for developing theory- and evidence-based health education programs', *Health Education and Behavior*, 25 (5): 545–63.

Bronfenbrenner, U. (1979) *The Ecology of Human Development: Experiments by Nature and Design*. Cambridge, MA: Harvard University Press.

Broughton, B. (1998) 'Models that work', *Healthcare Forum Journal*, July/August: 50–2.

Burdine, J. and McLeroy, K. (1992) 'Practitioners' use of theory: Examples from a work-group', *Health Education Quarterly*, 19(3): 331–40.

Cornwall, A. and Jewkes, R. (1995) 'What is participatory research?' *Social Science and Medicine*, 41: 1667–76.

Dignan, M., Tillgren, P., and Michielutte, R. (1994) 'Developing process evaluation for community-based health education research and practice: A role for the diffusion model', *Health Values*, 18: 56–9.

D'Onofrio, C. (1992) 'Theory and the empowerment of health education practitioners', *Health Education Quarterly*, 19: 385–403.

Flay, B. (1986) 'Efficacy and effectiveness trials (and other phases of research) in the development of health promotion programs', *Preventive Medicine*, 15, 451–74.

Flay, B. and Petraitis, J. (1994) 'The theory of triadic influence: A new theory of health behavior with implications for preventive interventions', in G. Albrecht (ed.), *Advances in Medical Sociology*, Vol. 4. Greenwich, CT: JAI. pp. 19–44.

Freudenberg, N., Eng, E., Flay, B., Parcel, G., Rogers, T., and Wallerstein, N. (1995) 'Strengthening individual and community capacity to prevent disease and promote health: In search of relevant theories and principles', *Health Education Quarterly*, 22: 290–306.

Garbarino, J. and Abramowitz, R.H. (1992) 'The ecology of human development', in J. Garbarino (ed.) *Children and Families in the Social Environment*. (2nd edn.). Hawthorne, NY: Aldine de Gruyter.

Glanz, K., Lewis, F.M. and Rimer, B.K. (eds) (1997) *Health Behavior and Health Education*. San Francisco, CA: Jossey-Bass.

Green, L. and Kreuter, M. (1991) *Health Promotion Planning: An Educational and Environmental Approach*. Mountain View, CA: Mayfield.

Green, L., Kreuter, M., Deeds, S., and Partridge, K.

(1980) *Health Education Planning: A Diagnostic Approach*. Palo Alto, CA: Mayfield.

Green, L.W., Gottlieb, N.H., and Parcel, G.S. (1987) 'Diffusion theory extended and applied', in W.B. Ward (ed.), *Advances in Health Education and Promotion*. Greenwich, CT: JAI.

Hansen, W. and McNeal, R. (1998) 'How DARE works: An examination of program effects on mediating variables', *Health Education Quarterly*, 24: 165–76.

Hochbaum, G. and Lorig, K. (1992) 'Roles and uses of theory in health education practice', *Health Education Quarterly*, 19: 291–4.

Hochbaum, G., Sorenson, J., and Lorig, K. (1992) 'Theory in health education practice', *Health Education Quarterly*, 19: 295–314.

Institute of Medicine (1988) *The Future of Public Health*. Washington, DC: National Academy Press.

Iverson, D. and Kolbe, L. (1983) 'Evolution of the disease prevention and health promotion strategy: Establishing a role for the schools', *Journal of School Health*, 5: 294–302.

Janz, N. and Becker, M. (1984) 'The health belief model: A decade later', *Health Education Quarterly*, 11: 1–47.

Livingston, I. L. (1994) *Handbook of Black American Health: The Mosaic of Conditions, Issues, Policies, and Prospects*. Westport, CT: Greenwood.

Manfredi, C. and Warnecke, R. (forthcoming) Translational research and interfacing with applied health care settings.

McGuire, W. J. (1984) 'Public communication as a strategy for inducing health promoting behavioral change', *Preventive Medicine*, 13: 299–313.

McLeroy, K.R., Bibeau, D., Steckler, A., and Glanz, K. (1988) 'An ecological perspective on health promotion programs', *Health Education Quarterly*, 15: 351–77.

Morrissey, E., Wandersman, A., Seybolt, D., Nation, M., Crusto, C., and Davino, K. (1997) 'Toward a framework for bridging the gap between science and practice in prevention: A focus on evaluator and practitioner perspectives', *Evaluation and Program Planning*, 20: 367–77.

Oldenburg, B., Hardcastle, D.M., and Kok, G. (1997) 'Diffusion of innovations', in K. Glanz, F.M. Lewis, and B. K. Rimer (eds), *Health Behavior and Health Education: Theory, Research and Practice*. San Francisco, CA: Jossey-Bass. pp. 270–86.

Orlandi, M., Landers, C., Weston, R., and Haley, N. (1990) 'Diffusion of health promotion innovations', in K.Glanz, F. M. Lewis, and B. K. Rimer (eds), *Health Behavior and Health Education: Theory, Research and Practice*. San Francisco, CA: Jossey-Bass. pp. 288–313.

Perez-Stable, E.J., Sabogal, F., Otero-Sabogal, R., Hiatt, R.A., and McPhee, S.J. (1992) 'Misconceptions about cancer among Latinos and Anglos', *Journal of the American Medical Association*, 268: 3219–23.

Portnoy, B., Anderson, D., and Ericksen, M. (1989) 'Application of diffusion theory to health promotion research', *Family and Community Health*, 12: 63–71.

Prochaska, J. and DiClemente, C. (1992) 'Stages of change in the modification of problem behaviors', in M. Hersen, R. Eisler, and P. Miller (eds), *Progress in Behavior Modification*. Sycamore, IL: Sycamore Press. pp. 184–214.

Prochaska, J., DiClemente, C., and Norcross, J. (1992) 'In search of how people change: Applications to addictive behaviors', *American Psychologist*, 47: 1102–14.

Prohaska, T. (1998) 'The research basis for the design and implementation of self-care programs', in M. Ory and G. DeFriese (eds), *Self-Care in Later Life*. New York: Springer. pp. 62–84.

Prohaska, T. and Clark, M. (1997) 'Health behavior and the human life cycle', in D. Gotchmen (ed.), *Handbook of Health Behavior Research. III. Demography, Development, and Diversity*. New York: Plenum. pp. 29–48.

Prohaska, T. and Walcott-McQuigg, J. (1996) 'Recruitment of older African-Americans: A focus group approach', *Journal of Aging and Ethnicity*, 1: 33–39.

Rogers, E. M. (1983) *Diffusion of Innovations* (3rd edn.). New York: Free Press.

Rosenstock, I. (1974) 'Historical origins of the health belief model', *Health Education Monograph*, 2: 328–86.

Rosenstock, I., Strecher, V., and Becker, M. (1988) 'Social learning theory and the health belief model', *Health Education Quarterly*, 15: 175–83.

Strecher, V., DeVellis, B., Becker, M., and Rosenstock, I. (1986) 'Theory of self-efficacy in achieving health behavior change', *Health Education Quarterly*, 13: 73–91.

Syme, L. (1992) 'Social determinants of disease', in J.M. Last and R. B. Wallace (eds), *Public Health and Preventive Medicine*. Norwalk, CT: Appleton & Lange.

USDHHS (1991) 'Healthy people 2000: National health promotion and disease prevention objectives', Washington, DC: US Department of Health and Human Services. Public Health Service. DHHS Publication No. (PHS) 91-50212.

USDHHS (1996) *Physical Activity and Health: A Report of the Surgeon General*. Atlanta, GA: US Department of Health and Human Services, Centers for Disease Control and Prevention, National Center for Chronic Disease Prevention and Health Promotion.

USDHHS (1998a) 'The combined health information database', Atlanta, GA: US Department of Health and Human Services, Centers for Disease Control and Prevention, National Center for Chronic Disease Prevention and Health Promotion. Retrieved from the World Wide Web: *http://chid. nih.gov/subfile/contribs/he.html*

USDHHS (1998b) 'The computer retrieval of information on scientific projects', Bethesda, MD: US Department of Health and Human Services, National Institutes of Health. Retrieved from the World Wide Web: http://eos12.dcrt.nih.gov:8002/crisp_pilot/owa/crisp.main

van Ryn, M. and Heaney, C. (1992) 'What's the use of a theory?' *Health Education Quarterly*, 19: 315–30.

Weiss, C. and Bucuvalas, M. (1980) 'Truth tests and utility tests: Decision-makers' frames of reference for social science research', *American Sociological Review*, 45: 302–13.

Wolle, J., Clery, H., and Stone, E. (1998) 'Initiation of a voluntary certification program for health education specialists', *Public Health Reports*, 104: 396–402.

Part Three

HEALTH-CARE SYSTEMS AND PRACTICES

The Medical Profession: Knowledge, Power, and Autonomy

DAVID COBURN AND EVAN WILLIS

INTRODUCTION

Hardly a daily newspaper appears without an article about doctors or about the medical profession. On popular television programs physicians are portrayed either as humanistic healers meeting the complex demands of individual patients, or, more recently, as frantic super-heroes ministering to somewhat anonymous bodies in high-tech emergency rooms. At the same time, there are accounts of strife between governments, insurance companies, or hospitals and medical organizations over fees or costs. Newspapers report on the huge incomes of some doctors, the horrors visited upon patients by malpractice or malfeasance, and complaints by unorthodox healers of being persecuted by the medical profession. An apparently endless procession of new medical discoveries, as well as the much-publicized potential of the 'new' genetics promises much, but the day-to-day reality is less utopian. Whereas medicine at first glance might appear as the self-sacrificing, altruistic, scientific occupation par excellence, the reality is that it contains profound dualities and contradictions.

In what follows, our aim is to cast light on the contradictions noted in the popular press through tracing underlying paths and structures. We will do so, on the one hand, by describing trends in the role of medicine within changing health-care systems, and on the other, by reviewing the ways in which these trends have been analyzed within the sociology of health and illness.

At the broadest level, our argument is as follows. Regarding health-care systems, the chief trend has been towards the development of mass markets, that is, the industrialization of health care. Regarding social theory, there has been an increasing tendency to view medicine less as a unique profession and more as an occupation subject to the same processes faced by many other occupations and professions. These two topics, trends in health care and in social theory, are, of course, related. Physicians are not immune, we argue, to the logic of the capitalist mode of production towards the rationalization and routinization of work. Both the rise of the medical profession to the pinnacle of power, and also the recent decline in this medical hegemony (together the major historical trajectory for medicine), are thus viewed here as a structurally contingent process. Contingent, that is, not simply on the progress of medical knowledge, the actions of the medical profession itself, or even of events within health care, but on the complex changing social structures in the advanced political economies.

At the outset some clarifications are appropriate. First, in this chapter we concentrate on the medical profession. Some of the processes mentioned will have application to all professions, or to other health occupations and professions in the health-care division of labour, and some will not. Second, it should be noted that there are difficulties in analyzing 'the' medical profession as a single entity. The profession has become highly segmented into groups and strata with significantly different interests; generalist and specialists are only the most obvious source of differentiation. Some segments have little in common apart from their shared socialization. Even the relationships between individual physicians and medical organizations are problematic, and these organizations themselves form a terrain of struggle rather than simply 'representing' some form of universal physician interests.

In what follows, we review the state of the field, organizing our discussion chronologically around the notion of the changing nature of medical power. Our analysis is most pertinent to the English-speaking nations, although European examples are mentioned where appropriate.

PROFESSIONS AND POWER

Theory

To paraphrase Johnson (1980) in his comments about work: 'professions are a relation of power.' That is, within the sociology of health, medicine has most often been viewed as being the central node in a network of relationships in which the profession both generates power over other groups or institutions and reflects or is shaped by 'external' factors and forces. In discussing sociological views of medicine we are thus mainly talking about the changing extent, nature, sources, and consequences of, or explanations for, medical power. Put somewhat differently, the focus has been on the social and cultural authority of medicine and its professional autonomy (Elston 1991; Starr 1982). That is, medicine possesses power as expressed in social organization, in the way people think about and act regarding health care, as well as its control over medical work itself. In fact, sociologists are preoccupied with professional power to the neglect, perhaps, of other dimensions of the profession such as the changing nature of actual medical work, or the meaning or implications of illness, caring, and cure for both doctors and patients.

While having its own distinctive history, medicine also shows similarities with other occupations and professions. The historical development of medicine is a part of larger movements of the rise of professions in general, and challenges to medical power are part of broader attacks on the welfare state; hence discussion of medicine alone may conceal as much as it reveals. Both the general and the unique need to be taken into account. Moreover, there is no consensus about how medicine is to be understood, or its social history or current situation explained. Hence, we will illustrate some of the theoretical divergencies; our account is, of necessity, somewhat idiosyncratic.

Social and Health-Care Trends

Just as sociological perspectives on medicine have changed over time, the profession has also inhabited a changing health and health-care context. There has been a major transformation from a situation in which physicians were petty bourgeois entrepreneurs to physicians as part of huge and growing health-care markets. A situation in which health care was given primarily in the domestic sphere has been transformed into one in which most health care is provided 'impersonally' by paid experts within a mass market for care. In the duration of less than a century, medical work has changed from individual healers within a 'cottage industry' to a highly complex health-care division of labour surrounded by huge industries. Health care now dwarfs in size such industrial giants as steel and automobile manufacturing and, in most Western countries, spending on health care is in the range of 8–9 per cent of national GNPs. In this progression, physicians have become involved with large institutions, private and public. The fate of medicine is tied not only to state bureaucracies, but also to the dynamics of both health-care and non-health care businesses and to the transformation of capitalism itself. Medicine relates to other institutions whether medicine still functions mainly within a more market-orientated or a more public-orientated health-care system. The profession itself is composed of a complex series of organizations and groups in which the role of the profession as a corporate entity can, at least analytically, be separated from the actions of individual practitioners.

Current issues regarding medicine thus cannot be fully understood without contextualizing changes in the profession within broader trends towards globalization, a general increase in the power of corporations and the rise of neoconservatism, a decline in the relative autonomy of the state, and subsequent attacks on the 'Keynesian welfare state.' These processes include an increasing tendency to cap the costs of care through attempts to control utilization and to make health care more effective and efficient; that is the rationalization of care 'from above.' This rationalization, whether involving more competition within health care, an increased 'managerialism,' or greater or lesser privatization, or some combination of these, almost always implies intrusion onto territory previously controlled by medicine.

At the same time, medicine is being influenced by various social movements 'from below,' including the women's movement, the patient's rights and consumer's movements, the struggles of other professions to escape from medical dominance, and by changes in the boundaries of medical knowledge. Some of these influences are reflected in changes within medicine itself, particularly regarding the feminization of medicine and the fragmentation of the profession by status and by speciality. Within this conflux of forces the medical profession is actively involved in attempts to control its own destiny. We are confronted with a changing medicine in a changing social context.

In this chapter, although our major focus is on the medical profession, we will unavoidably also be drawn into discussing examples from other health occupations and professions in the 'system of health professions' (Abbott 1988). Medicine has long been at the apex of a whole gamut of health professions in which it gained the power to exclude, limit, or subordinate its potential rivals (Willis 1989). We will argue, however, that this 'system,' and the role of medicine within it, is not simply the consequence of interoccupational struggles, as is often assumed. Medicine, and its relationships with other occupations and institutions, can only be adequately understood in the context of the particular social formation of which it forms a part. For us, this leads to a view of medicine as losing the almost hegemonic control it once had, not only over the context of health care, but even over the content of medical work. While not as powerful as it once was, it still retains a great deal of its professional autonomy although declining somewhat in its social and cultural authority. Our review thus emphasizes the changing nature of medical power and the explanation of these processes.

not only controlled what happened in the medical office, but almost anything that happened in health care. Physicians, it appeared, were not only expert in the application of biological science to particular cases, but also claimed to be, and were so regarded, as public authorities on anything to do with health, including how health care was to be delivered. Medicine had social and cultural authority.

This transformation from the fringes to the centre of the circle of power might be seen as simply a direct reflection of the efficacy of medicine. It could be assumed that medicine rose to power quite rightly on the wave of its increasing ability to improve health or cure or prevent disease. However, sociologists, historians and others have questioned such an explanation. Such questioning of common sense was particularly spurred by the ideas of McKeown and others that improvements in the health of populations in the nineteenth and twentieth centuries were determined more by social conditions generally than by curative medicine (McKeown 1965, 1979). McKeown's writings were one of the first modern critiques of the 'more medical care means more health' thesis (for others see Evans et al. 1994; Illich 1975; McKinlay and McKinlay 1977). McKeown's findings were also supported by historians who claimed that medicine rose to power before it was efficacious (see, e.g., Shortt 1983). While improving efficacy, or in more complex explanations the perception of increasing efficacy, was not irrelevant, the origins and present bases of modern-day medical power cannot rest simply or directly on the base of such explanations.

STATE OF THE FIELD, OR HOW DID WE GET HERE FROM THERE?

Medicine was not particularly well thought of in the eighteenth and nineteenth centuries, yet by the middle of the twentieth century it was at the height of public prestige, power, and authority. From a situation in which many intelligent laypersons thought they knew as much or more than physicians did about how to cure themselves or their families, medical work came to be seen as within the purview of only a highly technically trained few. Medical training, which in the eighteenth and nineteenth centuries consisted of classical training in Greek and the humanities and of apprenticeship, was, in the twentieth century, entirely replaced by rigorous scientific training within a university.

By the end of the Second World War, in all national assessments of occupational prestige, medicine ranked at or near the top. Medicine

THEORIES OF THE PROFESSIONS

Medicine has often been used as an analytical example to advance theories of the professions because medicine is assumed to be the epitome of what 'profession' means. Hence, explanations for medical power are tied to theories of the professions in general.

There is a conventional history of analysis of the professions that moves from Carr-Saunders and Wilson (1933), through Wilensky (1964) and Parsons (1951, 1964), to Johnson (1972) and Freidson (1970), to Larson (1977, 1980), Navarro (1976, 1986), and McKinlay and Arches (1985), to Foucault (1973, 1976), Witz (1992), and the postmodernists. This sequence can be described in terms of a change from trait theories to functionalist theories to neo-Weberian or neo-Marxian 'power' theories. Most recently have come challenges to power theories, particularly from feminism and from Foucault. While we describe this conventional history, we also note that Foucault and, most recently, Krause (1996) note that the professions have their origins much earlier than the Industrial Revolution as some conventional theories seem to assume. In Krause's case, the professions are viewed as forming a continuous line from the Guilds of the Middle Ages to the present.

Trait and Functionalist Theories

In the early 'trait' theories of Carr-Saunders and Wilson (1933), and Greenwood (1957), the professions were said to possess particular traits or attributes, most often including an esoteric body of knowledge, a code of ethics, and an altruistic orientation. Trait theories were followed by process theories in which it was argued that the professions moved through a sequence of the acquisition of particular traits (Wilensky 1964). 'Trait' and 'professionalization' theories, often formed simply by comparing common-sense notions of the professions with the assumed characteristics of other occupations, were superseded by the advent of structural functionalism. Parsons and others in the functionalist tradition explained professional, and particularly medical, power in terms of the potential within the professions to exploit patients (clients, etc.) financially, sexually, or otherwise. Hence an 'implicit contract' between 'society,' and the professions in which the latter were given autonomy in exchange for stringent self-regulation (no substance was given to the notion of 'society', often a convenient abstraction for arguing for a nonexistent convergence of interests or values). However, for both the trait theorists and for the functionalists in the Durkheimian tradition, professionalization was a positive aspect of modernism, in contrast to Marx's view of the degradation of the labour process under capitalism, or to Weber's gloomy analysis of the growth of an 'iron cage' of rationalized bureaucracy. For Durkheim, professionalization, as a system of the organization of work based on self-direction and autonomy, showed an alternative future to that of an ever more pervasive work alienation.

Power Theories

There was an inevitable challenge to the trait and functionalist claims from a number of sources, including some from analysts within the symbolic interactionist tradition (Becker 1962; Hughes 1958) who questioned whether the many positive 'traits' attributed to the professions were enacted in reality. In fact, it soon became clear that medicine and the other professions were far from being as rigorously self-regulating, ethical, or 'community orientated' as some professions, and some analysts, had claimed. Rather rapidly the professions came to be seen, not as altruistic, but as being exploitative monopolies. Medicine, the prime example of what it meant to be a profession, quickly came to be viewed as self-interested and motivated chiefly by the desire to increase the authority and incomes of physicians. Hence, the rise of 'power' theories of the professions and of medicine based on neo-Weberian (focusing on the market and closure theory) or neo-Marxist (focusing on mode of production and class theory) theories.

Most centrally, Freidson (1970) claimed that medicine was dominant in health and health care. Medicine controlled both the content of medical work and also clients, other health-care professions, and the context within which medical care was given (health-care policy). Medicine had social and cultural authority as well as clinical autonomy. Whereas medical knowledge itself was assumed to be relatively untainted by social factors, the application of medical knowledge reflected, not 'pure' medical science, but rather the profession's own practical interests in restricting competition, raising salaries and increasing its control over health and health care. Freidson consequently argued that the 'real' interests of medicine had distorted the application of medical knowledge such that, in the United States, for example, medicine led successful attempts to prevent the introduction of universal or government sponsored health-care insurance because this was viewed as an incursion on medical prerogatives.

In arguing that physician behaviour was more a function of the structure of the situation in which doctors practised, rather than a consequence of how they had been trained or socialized, Freidson redirected attention from the 'socialization' school. The latter, in good functionalist fashion, had assumed that physician behaviour was best explained through their medical training and socialization into the role of 'doctor.' Hence, the many studies at the time of the socialization experiences of medical students (Becker et al. 1961; Merton et al. 1957). The new structural emphasis rapidly eclipsed studies of socialization. At the same time, the questioning of medical authority was supported by changes in the pattern of disease. As infectious and acute disease gave way to the more chronic conditions of an ageing population, physicians, as the major experts in acute care, tended to give way slightly to newly emerging, chronic-care occupations.

At about the same time that Freidson was developing his medical dominance thesis, Terence Johnson, who was later to be central in attempts to develop a 'class' theory of medicine, wrote about professionalism as one stage in a typology of occupation–client relationships (Johnson 1972). Patronage was a type of profession–client relationship in which clients define both their own needs and the way these needs are met. Collegiate control existed when the practitioner defined the needs of the client and the manner in which these needs were met. Mediation is the situation in which a third party, usually the state, mediates the relationship between practitioner and client, defining both needs and the way in which these are filled. The 'ideal type' of a profession was thus collegiate control and was generally associated with a homogeneous occupational community and a heterogeneous client population. If viewed as a historical sequence these types could almost be viewed as describing the history of medicine.

Adherents of the neo-Weberian version of the 'power' school of the professions came to see medicine simply as one of many occupations that used exclusionary strategies to gain and maintain a market monopoly. This monopoly enabled the profession to gain unprecedented control, not only over its own work, but also over health and health care in general.

Neo-Marxist Theories

Freidson's influential formulation was itself criticized, mainly from a Marxian position, for failing to spell out the class basis of the relationships between professions and the capitalist state (see Frankenberg 1974; Johnson 1977; McKinlay 1977). While Freidson felt that 'relationships with an elite, and with the state' were important, he failed to theorize the crucial links between medical power and external forms of power. Marxists (and some Weberians) were led by their perspective, which tends to look at modes of production or social formations as a whole, to take a more holistic view. Beginning in the middle 1970s, a post-Freidson analysis emerged based on a political economy perspective. Although the new political economy cannot be entirely identified with Marxism, many of the writings in the area originate in Marxism or neo-Marxism (Doyal 1979; McKinlay and Arches 1985; Navarro 1976, 1986; Waitzkin 1991). Less traditional writers in the political economy tradition include Derber (1983, 1984) and Larson (1977, 1980). The neo-Marxists 'bring the system back in' by insisting that the func-

tioning of specific types of modes of production (presently capitalism), and the class structure within these, produces or conditions events in every sphere of existence, including that of health. This explains their interests in the class bases of medical power as well as the dynamics of capitalism as a whole, which 'elicited' or 'permitted' a particular kind of medicine to rise at one point but challenged it at another. This approach enabled analysts to escape from the quasi-interest group explanations embodied in some versions of 'occupational imperialism' (Larkin 1983) or 'the system of professions' (Abbott 1988) in which interoccupational competition was simply assumed. While descriptively useful, the 'system of professions' approach failed to explain, as opposed to describe, why there was a hierarchical structure underlying occupational differences and why some occupations rather than others come to be dominant.

A major difference between neo-Marxist writers and others in the health field lies in the neo-Marxist's view that the logic of the capitalist system (the profit imperative, the drive to rationalize, make more efficient and controllable the means of production) and the struggle between social classes, shapes and limits occupational struggles. While medicine is powerful, Navarro and others insist that the profession is an intermediate source of power and not the ultimately determinative one. Within this formulation the state, the major guarantor of professional monopoly, is not simply a 'referee' between competing occupational interest groups, but is structurally constrained by its reliance on a capitalist economy as well as being influenced by class struggle in civil society.

The rise of medicine to a preeminent position within the health division of labour is seen in class terms. Navarro (1976, 1986; see also, Johnson 1977), for example, argues that medical power is partly based on its relationship with a particular class rather than with a 'societal elite.' Medicine emerged as a profession because its appeal to science and the dominance of curative over preventive medicine coincided with, or at least did not contradict, the interests and ideology of a rising class of industrialists – what might be called the 'class congruence' thesis. Brown (1979) for example, pointed to the role of the Rockefeller and Carnegie Foundations in the United States as shaping and 'scientizing' medical education.

Scientific medicine was particularly congruent with the new theories of scientific management in industry. Medicine's individualist and mechanistic orientation obscured the social causes of disease. Capitalists appealed to this 'neutral' new science as a justification for the implementation of mass production methods, that is, new techniques of production were scientific, science was neutral, and therefore the new factory production methods, which many saw as dehumanizing and exploitative, could not be attacked on the grounds of the exploitation of one class by another or as simple profit-making at the expense of others. Medicine appealed to the ideology of science to justify its own market monopoly and its increasing control over the health division of labour (Shortt 1983).

Health itself is an arena for profit making. Through the commodification of health, the production, advertising, and distribution of drugs and hospital and medical supplies and technologies, and the direct ownership of health institutions and commercial health insurance agencies, the corporate class partly defines what medicine does and how it does it. Many analysts, particularly those in the United States, now believe that control of the health sector by corporations leads to the proletarianization of the providers. The rationalization and routinization of health-care work accompanying state and/or corporate drives for efficiency are evidence of this process, which we will discuss later.

The predominance of class over profession is illustrated by the implementation of health policies opposed by medicine, but supported by (or, more weakly, not opposed by) the bourgeoisie or by the state (state policies being a partial reflection of a class struggle in which the working class plays a part). The implementation of health insurance schemes or national health systems and recent state or corporate attempts to 'rationalize' health care are the major instances. The claim is that the profession's input is increasingly more confined to shaping existing decisions in its own interests than to the major decisions (or nondecisions) themselves.

Neo-Weberian Closure Theory

Neo-Marxist approaches have been criticized because they are sometimes restricted to highly abstract analyses. There are few Marxist empirical studies of the linkages between macro-, meso-, and microstructures (the main exception to the latter is the work of Waitzkin 1991), and because of this there are difficulties incorporating nonclass cleavages (e.g., gender, race) into Marxist theory. There is also somewhat of a disjunction between a focus on class and a focus on occupation; these intersect, but are not identical. That is, one can have class-homogeneous and class-heterogeneous professions, as well as occupationally diverse classes.

Although some have criticized specific aspects of Marxist theory, others take issue with the whole Marxian or neo-Marxian schema.

Parkin (1972), for example, builds a theory, loosely based on Weber, which is partly applicable to medicine. The essence of Parkin's position is that relationship to the market (Weber) is much more important than is relationship to the means of production (Marx). Parkin feels that the main class fissure in society is not based on differential relationships to the means of production, but occurs between those groups (based on various criteria) who are attempting to preserve or enhance a dominant market position (through 'exclusion') and those groups who are attempting to encroach on the power and privileges of dominant groups (through 'usurpation').

When applied to the health scene, this Weberian foundation led, not only to the formulation of various forms of 'power' theories of medicine, but to attempts to develop a theory focusing on interoccupational competition, that is, to various forms of 'closure' theory (Collins 1979; Murphy 1988). In this view, various occupations or groups were viewed as using a variety of criteria to exclude others and/or to attempt to usurp the power of others. Sociological studies within this genre, while descriptively interesting, had rather weak explanations for the processes described, that is, why was one group rather than another successful in its strategies? Murphy attempted to remedy this deficiency by postulating principal, derivative, and contingent forms of exclusion. Within capitalism, the legal title to private property was the principal form. Thus, Murphy, like the neo-Marxists, would view medical power within capitalism as partially contingent on its fit within the class structure.

Generally, closure theory seemed useful because it appeared to have the ability to include many 'non-class' factors into the analysis. That is, occupations used various rules of exclusion, whatever seemed available in the social formation at any particular time, e.g., gender, race, religion, to exclude competitors. However, as noted, such formulations also had problems (Manza 1992; Murphy 1988). Not only was the original relationship between closure and class theory often lost sight of but the application of concepts such as exclusion, usurpation, or dual forms of closure sometimes appeared to substitute for analysis or was circular in reasoning (Manza 1992). Closure analyses became little more than a study of 'occupational interest groups.' When closure theory appeared most cogent, as in the work of a sympathetic but critical supporter such as Murphy, it approached neo-Marxist theory even though it was formulated in an attempt to counter Marxist views. Conversely, when neo-Marxist theory seemed most persuasive it was almost neo-Weberian.

Some theorists, such as Larson (1977), were difficult to classify as being in either camp, and there were calls for the greater integration of insights derived from Weber or from Marx. Larson analysed the rise, not only of medicine, but also of the professions in general in the nineteenth and twentieth centuries. She describes the 'professionalization project' as including gaining control over a market for expertise and a collective process of upward mobility. Control over the market involves standardization of the 'production of the producers' and the development of a cognitive base for professional claims. Relating these processes to wider structures, Larson views professional ideology as congruent with a number of facets of liberal ideology in capitalist societies. The professionalization project constituted a justification for new forms of inequality since there is, with the institutionalization of professional education within the university, an apparent matching of rewards with achievement.

The Proletarianization of Medicine Debate

Power theories of medicine did stimulate a body of work on the nature and fate of that power. Historically minded sociologists, such as Larson, noted that medicine had not always been as powerful as it was in contemporary society. Medical power was spatially and historically variant. In the 1980s, almost simultaneously, fairly similar book-length analyses appeared in a number of countries including first the United States (Starr 1982), and then closely followed by Australia (Willis 1989) and the United Kingdom (Larkin 1983). (For a shorter Canadian treatment see Coburn et al. 1983.) All of these studies focused on historical variations in medical power and explanations for such variations. Whereas the initial attention was devoted to how medicine came to rise to a position of dominance, the later focus became whether medicine has experienced declines from its once almost hegemonic position, and how such changes are to be understood. The findings of these studies ranged from claims that, in the latter part of the twentieth century, medicine had declined in power, to those who argued that although medicine had been challenged, it had actually crystallized or maintained its power in the face of various threats, these often emanating from state incursions into the province of health care.

However, the debate was really begun by those writing from a neo-Marxist perspective such as Navarro (1976) and McKinlay and Arches (1985). These authors claim either that medicine had never been dominant because medical power was always contingent on the relationship between medicine and outside sources (Navarro 1988), and/or that recent developments in the 'industrialization' of the medical area has led to the proletarianization of medicine in general (McKinlay and Arches 1985; McKinlay and Stoeckle 1988; Salmon 1994). A debate was thus opened between those who believed that medical power had declined versus those who argued that medical power had simply changed its form or nature. The 'proletarianization of medicine' debate is somewhat clouded because of the use of the term proletarianization in a less than clear-cut manner, and because of the use of differing national examples. To some, the term proletarianization implies a move of medicine to working-class status, a claim which could easily be refuted. Although McKinlay and Arches had insisted that they were only focusing on a trend rather than an end point, others felt the term proletarianization implied too much. The notion that the process of proletarianization refers to developments within a particular domain of labour and not (only) to a single occupation is ignored. The proletarianization of some implies that others are gaining in power and control (Larson 1977).

Contrary to McKinlay and Arches, a number of British writers claim that medical power within the health-care division of labour (itself only one aspect of medical dominance) has been 'crystallized' rather than reduced by state power. That is, state regulation of the health professions (and even of unorthodox 'competitors' to medicine) at this particular point in history embedded in law and statute a situation of medical control over other health occupations (Larkin 1993; Larkin and Saks 1994). Even assuming Larkin and Saks are correct about the crystallizing effect of legislation, however, one might still argue that new legislation creates a new terrain, with newly legitimate 'actors,' on which medicine is challenged. In addition, because of the focus on only the health-care division of labour, this formulation also leaves open the possibility of the decline of medical power in other areas, for example, regarding broader health policy or regarding physicians' relationships with their patients.

While some British writers claim that medicine, while challenged, is still dominant (for example, Elston 1991), others feel that medicine might have declined to a position of 'responsible autonomy' (Dent 1993) or worse (Flynn 1992). Freidson himself at first (1985) argued that medicine had not lost its power even though these arguments were weakened by an implicit move from a contention that medicine was dominant to one in which medicine was still a profession, the latter implying only autonomy rather than dominance, but there is an increasing consensus, from observers in many different countries from Australia to Norway, that medicine is on the defensive (Gabe et al. 1994; Hafferty and McKinlay 1993).

Some of the differences between writers on either side of the 'decline' versus 'maintenance of power' debate rest on whether the glass is viewed as half-full or half-empty. That is, no one would argue that medicine is not still the single most powerful profession in health and health care; the question is, is it as powerful as it once was, and is this trend reversible or not? The notion that professionalization is a strategy of gaining control over a particular work domain implies continual struggles over such control. Certainly, the rise of competing centres of power diluted the centrality of medical interests. The reasons for this lay in changes in the broader political economy rather than with the nature of medical knowledge itself. The authority of medical knowledge, one of the bases of medical authority, was itself said to be the result of political processes (Starr and Immergut 1987). Even so, wider structural changes could be viewed as interacting with internal changes within medicine. Medicine became more fragmented by speciality, in many countries more 'feminized' and, many analysts asserted, more divided between practitioners, scientists, and academic and medico-political elites. Medicine was being internally fragmented or stratified just at the time that it was being externally challenged. Because of their emphasis on social formations as a whole, Marxists were more likely than others to see external challenges as fundamental rather than simply superficial signs of accommodating professional and state/business interests.

There also were differences in emphasis about the major challenges to medicine. Some, such as Haug (1975), emphasized a decline in medical authority over patients (i.e., deprofessionalization). Others focused more on the increasing surveillance of states or corporations over medical work (i.e., proletarianization). Recently, Weiss and Fitzpatrick (1997) have interpreted the concepts of deprofessionalization and proletarianization, not as alternative ways of viewing challenges to medicine, but as referring to distinctly different processes. They argue that proletarianization pertains to occupational control, whereas deprofessionalization is tied to the demystification of medical knowledge.

The increasing specification of what is meant by physician dominance and control, that is medical dominance over what, where, and when, and the different domains in which medical power is exercised, however, has also led to discussions about the meaning of autonomy, said to be the basis of professional power. Even examining the

notion of 'self-regulation,' the measure of professional autonomy, it is clear that one cannot assume a profession is self-regulating simply because of the existence of organizations supposedly embodying self-regulation. Moran and Wood (1993), for example, point to the increasing prevalence of a 'state-constrained' self-regulation. There is a type of meso-corporatist medicine–state relationship (Cawson 1985), but this relationship is heavily state-shaped. Still, few would disagree with the argument that the exertion of power by medicine brings with it countervailing attempts to control or curb that power by others or, conversely, that medicine is now attempting to protect its own privileged position from external attack (Light 1995; Mechanic 1991). We are speaking of a process rather than an 'end-point.'

Given the various dimensions of dominance, and the variety of ways in which dominance or autonomy could be assessed, there is much room for confusion and controversy over the rather crude issue of a possible decline in medical power. Has some crucial threshold been passed? Arguably yes, since the contingent nature of medical power is now more visible. There is, however, more consensus about a decline of medical control over health-care policy, the context of care, than there is about a decline in other domains of medical power.

As noted, the contention of decline is not simply based on changes in the health-care division of labour, but on much wider processes. Not only are states and corporations intruding on medical territory, but within the legal system there is evidence of a broader questioning of medical authority. In Canada, for example, legal rulings have increasingly favoured patients regarding what constitutes adequate information regarding consent to treatment. Legal criteria have shifted from judging adequate consent as being what a reasonable physician would divulge, towards what a reasonable patient would want to know. Some see evidence for the decline in the dominance of the medical profession in the rise of alternatives to, or complements to, medicine and the inability of medicine to prevent this. The question though, as Saks (1995) has argued, is whether these changes are more the result of wider sociopolitical forces rather than anything specific about the alternatives themselves. The nature of these wider sociopolitical changes are encapsulated in debates about the posited historical transformation of the advanced capitalist economies from (late) modernism to postmodernism. One feature of this mooted change is the emergence of what might be called postmodern values, which include a scepticism about the ability of science and technology to provide answers to the problems of humanity, including illness, and the resultant emergence of 'new age' and alternative health-care practices. Challenges to medicine are thus social and cultural, and not only organizational or technical (Hafferty and McKinlay 1993).

Much of the literature on medicine is still embedded in the 'decline or stability' debate to the neglect of other areas of interest. The decline argument has become partially specified into whether individual physicians or the profession as a whole is declining. In the restratification thesis, for example, Freidson (1994) claims that the profession as a corporate identity has retained power, while individual physicians may have become more open to influence from these elites (Annandale 1989). Contra Freidson, however, others assert that the state, in particular countries at particular times, has influenced medicine through coopting or constraining the organized structure of medicine (Coburn et al. 1997). It is true though, that the nature of the relationships between practitioners and the organized profession is always problematic, and that more attention now needs to be devoted to medicine's changing internal structure in interaction with 'external' developments.

The 'rise and fall' debates also tended to ignore national differences. There may be both 'real' and 'theoretical' differences among nations. Much of the 'rise and decline' debate focused on the English-speaking world and on Europe. Even within this restricted range of nations, however, there are striking differences in the role of medicine. In many European countries, in particular, the profession had all along much closer ties with the state than it did in the Anglo-American context even though, in most of these countries, medicine is being challenged by the state or by the possible introduction of state-regulated markets (Wilsford 1991). However, not only do national social structures, health-care systems, and the role of medicine within these vary, but social scientists in these countries adopt particular theoretical perspectives. For example, in Britain, after a period in which Marxism had appeared to be theoretically ascendant, neo-Weberian sociology, viewed as in opposition to, or as a corrective to, Marxism, gained many adherents. In fact, some forms of neo-Weberianism were so 'adapted' to the increasing right-wing political scene in Britain that it sometimes seemed a justification, not only for liberalism, but also for neo-liberalism. More generally, political analyses of health care, or of the role of medicine, seldom mention broader structural forces. The structural determinants of politics disappeared into the analysis of particular political personalities such as Margaret Thatcher or Ronald Reagan.

MEDICAL KNOWLEDGE

A crucial aspect of many views of medical power is the role played by knowledge; for example, the trait theorists' emphasis on the role of esoteric knowledge in leading to, or producing, professional power. This emphasis on knowledge was reinforced by the more recent Foucauldian view of the inseparability of knowledge/power. The control, by a relatively small, homogenous community, over a body of knowledge applied to health care, a vital aspect of human societies, was, many felt, an important, perhaps crucial, underpinning of medical power. This formulation indicated the importance of medical control over the production and application of new medical knowledge. Although much 'medical' knowledge was produced by nonphysicians, it was created within medical schools, health science centres, and hospitals, in which physicians had administrative control, privileged access to research funds and to patients, and whose research was heavily reinforced by the association between medicine and the pharmaceutical industry. Physicians' monopoly of access to patients and to the prescribing of drugs were powerful barriers to research by other professions.

Implicit in the view that knowledge is the basis of the power of medicine is the assumption that only some aspects of medical practice are potentially reproducible. Jamous and Peloille (1970) noted that professional practice embodied a ratio of both a less reproducible tacit form of practice (indeterminacy) and a more reproducible 'science' (technicality), the I/T ratio. The lower the I/T ratio, presumably, the more the profession was open to routinization and proletarianization. Yet, recent developments towards the 'rationalization' of health care undermined the authority of medicine. Planners, managers, and economists were now more expert in health-care systems, or so they claimed, than were physicians. Even at the level of clinical practice, new corps of clinical epidemiologists and others, often at the behest of governments, were busy formulating what worked and what did not, or what were optimal or general 'clinical guidelines' to form the basis for 'evidence-based medicine' (Rappolt 1997). These guidelines can be understood as lowering the I/T ratio by increasing technicality at the expense of indetermination. Medical knowledge had shown itself vulnerable to being nibbled away at the edges. Knowledge boundaries, it seemed, were set politically rather than by any inherent logic of science (Starr and Immergut 1987). Medical knowledge, said to be one of the major sources of medical power, was being undermined. The focus shifted from the assessment of knowledge to study of the determinants of 'claims to knowledge.'

ALTERNATIVE VIEWS

Although neo-Weberian and neo-Marxist power theories of the profession have been the most popular (for a critical view see Saks 1983), there are challenges to both of these paradigms. First came the challenge of feminist theory, then that of a new view embodied in Foucault's writings, and, more generally, postmodernist or relativist views of the human condition. To a very brief consideration of these we now turn.

Medicine and Feminism

The development of 'women-orientated' approaches in sociological theory was, perhaps, more evident in the area of health and health care than in any other. Feminists focused on women as carers and women as patients. Feminists claimed that most healers had been women; and the rise of medical dominance in the eighteenth and nineteenth centuries meant that men appropriated much of the healing that had previously been the task of women. Furthermore, conventional approaches to the professions, it was argued, were gender-blind (Witz 1992). A frequent case study was that of midwifery (Bourgeault and Fynes 1997; Donnison 1977/1988), in which women helping other women were, in the nineteenth century, replaced by male obstetricians. Conversely, the recent revival or 'rise' of midwifery in a number of countries might counter some of the 'continued dominance' thesis. Riska and Wegar (1993), Witz (1992), and others seized on closure theory as a way of explaining female subordination within health care and within medicine. That is, the health occupations were viewed as territories of exclusion and usurpation in which gender was a major exclusionary criterion. However, female-dominated professions themselves attempted to subordinate female alternatives (dual closure).

Within the health-care system most of the 'subordinate' health professions were composed of women. Thus, the health-care division of labour developed into a form characterized by a largely male medicine controlling a largely female group of 'auxiliary' providers. The latter reflected what some had claimed was the 'uniquely' feminine role of caring and housekeeping. The female caring occupations had become part of the official health-care division

of labour at a time when it was generally assumed that women's roles in the public sphere should approximate those in the household (i.e., caring and housework rather than the 'technical' work of curing). Within medicine itself women had first been excluded, then only grudgingly admitted. Since the Second World War, however, women have, in most countries, rapidly risen as a proportion of medical students, although not yet as a large proportion of the practicing profession (apart from in some of the Eastern European countries). Still, it was claimed that, even with the advent of a powerful women's movement, patriarchal ideologies and structures permeated medicine and ensured that women were kept in low-status 'feminine medical enclaves' such as pediatrics and family practice (Riska and Wegar 1993). There are still few female surgeons or women Deans of Medicine. It might also be claimed that those women who are more 'successful' are either in feminine enclaves, or have been 'masculinized.' There is also discussion about the relationship between the 'proletarianization' of medicine and the increasing number of women medical students and physicians. Is medicine becoming proletarianized partly because of the increasing percentage of women in the profession, or is the increasing number of women a sign that medicine had already begun to decline in status and power?

Approaching health care from the viewpoint of women also opened up study of 'unpaid healers.' That is, there is a greater focus than previously on the extent to which health care is given in the home, generally by women. This forced more consideration than previously of the linkage between the 'public' and 'domestic' provision of health care, a topic previously ignored. Much feminist attention, however, was paid to the health of women rather than to the health-care system per se. There was a particular emphasis on the relationship of patriarchy to the topics of women's sexuality and reproduction. The male dominance of medicine or of healing generally had its consequences, feminists assert, in the ignoring of female medical conditions and/or in the examples of various sordid periods of medical history of the late nineteenth and early twentieth centuries of 'sexual surgery.' Medicine, far from being some form of neutral 'science,' rather directly reflected the class and patriarchal nature of society at that time (Ehrenreich and English 1972, 1976).

However, recent decades have witnessed the rise of powerful female social movements aimed at reclaiming health care for women, exemplified by one of the earliest women's health books with mass popularity, the Boston Women's Health Collective's book, *Our Bodies,*

Ourselves. This publication, and the movement underlying it, illustrated the beginning of attempts to re-appropriate what was previously 'women's territory' from the male-dominated profession, often through an emphasis on self-care. Such women's issues as matters of reproduction, childbirth, and the menopause are major foci of attention. The midwifery movement, which in some countries constitutes a challenge to medical hegemony, was reinforced, and elsewhere revived. Still, questions of 'too much' or 'too little' care (versus most appropriate care) arose, and the pronounced longevity of women as compared with men led to an emphasis on illness and care rather than on length of life.

Feminist writers have made a major contribution simply by pointing out how gender had previously been ignored both regarding the functioning of health-care systems and regarding women's health. Medicine is viewed as one vehicle through which patriarchal modes of control are produced and reproduced. There may, however, be a historical difference between forms of male domination. Turner (1995) has made the useful distinction between patriarchy and patrism. The former refers to a situation in which male dominance is embedded in law, statute, and societal norms. In the latter, patrism, there is less legal and open political support for female subordination. Such a formulation might help us understand the changing, yet in some ways unchanging, gendered nature of the medical profession, and of the health-care system generally.

Foucault

Foucault (1973, 1976) also broke with the Marxian/neo-Weberian schools by focusing on the micropractices of power. Not only did Foucault argue that power was both enabling as well as constraining, but also that power and knowledge were inextricably intertwined. Theorizing an area meant constructing it and gaining power over it. Foucault's writings also emphasized the double-edged nature of the move from crime or punishment to medical care (medicalization). Both involved aspects of social control, the latter no less than the former. Thus, the advent of 'public health' or 'health promotion,' for example, could be viewed as an extension of the panoptic 'medical gaze' into lifestyles and the most intimate habits of the general population, and not only as a beneficial strategy in the drive to 'cure or prevent disease' (Petersen and Bunton 1997). As Johnson (1995) notes, the professions, and medicine specifically, form part of the expression or projection of 'governmentality' into civil society.

Most recently, Lupton (1997) believes there is a more complex relationship between doctors and their patients than previous structurally oriented theories seem to permit. Arguing that, following Foucault, power can be viewed as 'power to' and not simply 'power over,' she notes that both patients and doctors might gain in power at the same time, that is, power might not be a zero-sum concept. These findings, along with those of Weiss and Fitzpatrick (1997), suggest that viewing medicine versus the state, versus managerial control, or versus patients might not adequately represent the complex forms of power that emerge from interaction among patients, doctors, and the institutions in which doctors work

Future Possibilities

Of contemporary theories, Foucault and feminist theory have so far had the most influence on theories of the medical profession. Yet it seems unlikely that the current ferment and fragmentation of sociological theory will not have an impact in the future. For example, postmodernist or social constructionist perspectives, with their scepticism of knowledge, including medical knowledge, are relevant to theoretical perspectives on medicine. Similarly, sociological theories characterizing high modernity as 'the risk society' (Beck 1992) may assume importance. Given an emphasis on risk, and the ambiguity of health risks, expert knowledge, including medical expert knowledge, could be central social foci. Certainly, as Turner (1995) points out, there now is an insatiable appetite for things medical, an ever-increasing medicalization. Whether the medical profession is the chief origin of this trend, or is its major beneficiary, is in doubt. However, when particular types of supposedly healthy, everyday foodstuffs can be categorized as 'neutraceuticals,' the role of health-care business and the centrality of 'healthism' are underscored.

There are, however, somewhat more prosaic, but still potentially important, theoretical openings. One of these is the neo-institutionalist view of the professions of Thomas Brante and his colleagues in Sweden (Brante 1998; Castro 1998). These researchers point to the different institutional domains in which medicine (and the other professions) practice, and the effect of these settings on the values, attitudes, and actions of practitioners. For example, physicians in public service or in the private sector develop quite different views about various types of publicly provided health services. The neo-institutionalist view, incidentally, reinforces the notion of the increasing fragmentation of the medical profession.

Yet, as noted, the newer theoretical trends sometimes point in different directions, with postmodernism indicating scepticism of things scientific, medical, or otherwise, while risk theory would tend towards elevating medical knowledge and medical experts to prominence. Although these different visions, and more culturally and phenomenologically orientated viewpoints, are prominent in sociology, their influence on theories of medicine still lie mainly in the future.

Contemporary Changes in Health Care and Theories of Medical Power

Medicine and health care face fundamental changes in the contemporary era. Within the advanced capitalist countries came the rise of neo-liberalism. The Keynesian welfare state, however muted, or however divided into various 'types' (the Anglo-American countries are generally of the market-orientated or 'liberal' variety – see Esping-Andersen 1990), was powerfully attacked by worshippers of market solutions (Stubbs and Underhill 1994).

Although in many ways confined and constrained by various forms of health insurance, medicine benefited financially from the onset of the welfare state and the emergence of mass markets for medical care, whether these had been more state-directed or more market-orientated. While on the one hand physicians gained income or income certainty, on the other hand, their professional prerogatives began to be cribbed and constrained by increasing public or private pressure and regulation. The claim of those who had all along felt that medical power was contingent on the congruence of its interests and ideology with those of dominant classes also received support. When nonhealth corporations saw health-care costs as a problem, their interests were no longer aligned with those of a profession that saw itself as profiting from larger health-care budgets. Physicians no longer controlled state policy making from the inside; they were increasingly 'external' to a state that had its own reasons for gaining control over the health sphere. At the same time, major corporations in the United States, for example, formed an implicit or explicit coalition with state efforts to control health care costs and the work of physicians, although business was divided between those involved in health care and those not (Bergthold 1990; Martin 1993).

Although medicine is currently challenged, might the rise of neo-conservatism and struggles over the role of the state generally, as well as the internationalization of capital, consolidate or even increase medical power? Some physicians still hold to the 'ideal' of private practice in the marketplace, and these might be seen as having common interests with an increasing number of neo-conservative governments, but such interest-congruence is not automatic. Strongly ideological market-orientated governments tend to view the professions as unneeded market monopolies. Strikingly, when the Conservative government under Margaret Thatcher decided to reform health care in Britain (instituting, not a private health-care service but a public service in which there was competition and a clear provider/purchaser distinction), the policy committee that made such recommendations totally excluded physicians. If physicians in some countries benefit from neo-conservative policies or attempt to shape these towards their own interests, this is a highly contingent process. Medicine no longer has the power to define health and health care on its own terms. Which is not to say that medicine is totally unsuccessful or that it is not striving mightily, and sometimes in some instances and in some places for some segments of medicine, successfully, to protect its own interests (Barnett et al. 1998).

More generally, on international differences, it seems no accident that the proletarianization thesis first arose in the United States, where private health service provision is prominent. In the United States, privately owned provider organizations have a direct economic interest in ensuring that physician services are efficient and profitable. Thus arose more microcontrols over physicians in the United States than in countries in which the provision of medical services was more public in nature. Dohler (1989) goes so far as to suggest that physicians' clinical autonomy is more protected in 'state run' health-care systems than in those more entrepreneurial or private in nature. In the publicly run systems, once some form of control over increasing costs had been put in place, the state, it is claimed, tends to leave purely 'clinical' matters in the hands of the profession. This is particularly true, it appears, because politicians do not want to be involved in messy medical matters, easily made the subject of daily newspaper headlines. Such a formulation, however, probably overemphasizes the distinction between microcontrols over medical work and macropolicy (Light 1995). Certainly, in a number of publicly run systems, macrocontrols, such as the almost universal controls over the use of technologies, has an impact on what individual physicians do or are capable of doing at the clinical level. The work of physicians is also influenced, directly and immediately, by the forms and content of payment mechanisms (e.g., fee-for-service versus salary versus capitation). Also, the prospect of real competition promised by some New Right political parties, makes many professional groups nervous. Still, the exact trajectories and nuances of state/business involvement vary across countries, as do the sources, nature, and degree of challenges to medical power. What does seem common, however, is that medicine no longer sets the agenda.

Theories of the rise of supranational trade blocs and globalization brought speculation concerning how various phases of capitalism and changes in medical power might be related. It was suggested that the change from entrepreneurial to monopoly to global capitalism is reflected in the historical rise, maintenance, and then decline of medical power (Coburn 1999; Ross and Trachte 1990). In particular globalization, carrying with it rising business power and unity, produces an increased incongruence between the interests and ideology of business and that of the medical profession.

On a less abstract level, some theorists feel that the rise of supranational organizations, as in the EU, leaves an opening for professional associations, including medicine, to regain some of the power lost under specific national governments. The lack of existing supranational organizations provides leeway for the well-organized medical profession (among other professions) to begin setting its own standards and regulations, free from the constraints it had previously faced when medicine was regulated within national boundaries. Others argue that the state is 'withering away,' or is being replaced by the 'regulative state (Ruggie 1996).' The regulative state is not directly involved in the provision of services, but it still provides the standards and rules for those in the private sector who do. Whether these developments are real or only speculative, and whether or not they can be exploited by medicine to its own advantage are still open questions.

Finally, although we have emphasized the influence of society on medicine, the impact of medicine, and recently medical science, on society is considerable. New diseases such as HIV/AIDS and new methods of diagnosis of 'invisible' defects promote the view of all of us as 'deficient' or 'at risk.' Scientific and technological innovations in the areas of reproduction and genetic manipulation produce, not only new ethical dilemmas, but visions, some utopian, others more Machiavellian, of new forms of social life and organization based on radically different concepts of what were previously taken to be 'natural' human conditions and institutions. These, however, are fairly specula-tive issues and it is uncertain what their implications are for the role of the medical profession and for medical work.

CONCLUSION

The picture that emerges from a focus on the power of medicine is one that increasingly portrays medicine not as a unique occupation, but as one whose work is seen more and more as subject to processes of regulation and codification, similar to those affecting other occupations. While medicine can certainly still claim to possess clinical autonomy, its claims to dominance are less persuasive than they were, although this is true in some areas more than in others. This occurs, ironically, at a time of seemingly ever-increasing medicalization and scientific medical innovation.

It is now difficult to believe that medical knowledge itself has unique properties, which are the main source of medical power. Certainly medicine is a complex occupation, charged with highly emotional tasks associated with birth, illness, and death, but its knowledge is clearly supported by particular social practices, such as its control over the production of new knowledge and its association with the drug industry, rather than being of some 'special' nature. No doubt physicians will never be told what to do in their day-to-day work, although that work will be limited, shaped, and directed by external forces, including payment mechanisms and the nature and source of funding of care. Still, we also do not direct the detailed 'clinical' work of a plumber either. The boundaries of the claims of medicine to control over its own work and knowledge are clearly political in character. While scientific knowledge advances, medical knowledge is now viewed with some postmodernist scepticism.

The rise of neo-liberalism on a worldwide basis has produced a number of strains on the medical profession. On the one hand has come increasing public and private institutional pressure towards the rationalization of care. On the other there are rather ambiguous relationships between medicine and currently dominant neo-liberal governments and ideologies. Given the reliance of the medical monopoly on a mandate from the state, changes in the state, or in those societal institutions influencing state power, have ramifications for the medical profession. While there are some ideological affinities between neo-liberalism and some segments within medicine, even the prospect of privatization is not necessarily appealing to most physicians. Ironically, in some instances physicians are now viewed as defending one of the remaining outposts of the welfare state, that is, the public provision of health care. To protect their own work domain, which in many countries lies in the public sector in national health systems or national health insurance schemes, doctors, if perhaps only coincidentally, defend health care against neo-liberal attacks.

On the theoretical level, neo-Weberian theories appear useful in the description of interoccupational struggles, and in including 'non-class' aspects of social closure, but are less successful in understanding these conflicts or in relating these to wider processes. Neo-Marxist approaches are more adequate regarding understanding interoccupational successes or failures through delineating how these are embedded within broader class structures, while they are not as successful in understanding occupations per se. Perhaps neo-Marxism can more successfully exploit recent changes towards the internationalization of capital to its own explanatory ends than can Weberian theory. In the more sophisticated versions of both approaches, medical power is viewed as contingent on medicine's relationships with dominant elites or classes. However, much more needs to be done to explicate the precise mechanisms and institutions through which medicine is shaped.

Recent theoretical perspectives do not as yet present anything like complete alternatives to the two major approaches noted. Rather, these constitute comments about what is missing in these, or promise much but are as yet undeveloped. Foucaultian perspectives embody a somewhat oppressive view of 'the medical gaze.' Feminist theory has shown the blind spots in existing theory, but it is as yet unclear whether this will demand an entirely new theory of medical power or simply modifications of existing theories. Postmodernist or social constructionist views, as well as attempts to theorize the body or to emphasize the risk society, have focused attention on the 'constructed' nature of medical knowledge and on medicalization, social control, and the perhaps increased status of experts (Turner 1995). Yet the role of medicine, even in the process of 'medicalization,' is unclear. Much medicalization in the modern era reflects the commodification of health as much as the interests of medicine. In the modern era, medicine has thus, never actually been the mistress of its own fate. Ever since it became more attractive to see a physician than to actually avoid one, medicine has been intricately linked to 'external' factors and forces at the same time as its internal composition was itself altered.

We began this chapter by noting the dualities and contradictions surrounding medical work.

We have claimed that the change from cottage industry to mass markets in health care has profoundly influenced the role of medicine. More and more, in its struggles to maintain or increase its control, prestige, or income, medicine seems like many other health, and nonhealth care, occupations. However, viewing medicine in this way, as simply another occupation seeking monopoly and power, surely does injustice both to medicine and to many physicians. In the first place, the actual work of physicians and the role of medicine are more complex than current theories would indicate, and the somewhat cynical views of medicine in the scientific literature or in the public media have, perhaps, had an influence on physicians themselves, who might increasingly come to see themselves as others do. Yet the original premise of the professions was for more. Medicine still appeals to observers as a 'service' occupation, which promises an outlet for altruistic motives. Viewing medicine in 'power' terms is surely as one-sided as the previous view of medicine as actually possessing the traits which its leaders claimed (Brante 1988). Whether the altruism, which many individual physicians feel, can actually be fully expressed within current forms of social organization which emphasize the commodification of all forms of goods and services is another question. The organized medical profession itself seems inevitably to focus on power and money, although many individual practitioners do not. While there has obviously been an overgeneralization of the authority of medicine, some form of 'relative autonomy' is still a minimum condition for the expression of individual creativity and altruism, whether by professionals or by any other worker. An overly regulated medicine directly reflecting state or provider organization goals and aims does not seem an improvement over an overly powerful profession. There is at least an element of truth in some medical politicians' claims that an 'independent' profession is a protector of patients' interests. Certainly, the interests of patients, individually and collectively, vis-a-vis physicians and the organized profession needs more exploration.

Hence, the dualisms or contradictions with which we began. Modern medicine contains the possibility of doctors as servants and healers, yet they are found within an organized profession with specific interests. The profession is part of health-care systems which often contain incentives perverse to doctors' more altruistic orientations, and which hinder the 'rational' application of various types of expertise. Within the current political, social, and economic context such contradictions cannot, perhaps, be escaped; they can be understood and confronted.

Acknowledgments

We would like to thank Lesley Biggs and Susan Rappolt for specific comments. Many others contributed directly and indirectly to this chapter. It was given in draft form to the Conference of the Australian Sociological Association, Wollongong, December 1997.

References

Abbott, A. (1988) *The System of Professions*. Chicago: University of Chicago Press.

Annandale, E. (1989) 'Proletarianization or restratification of the medical profession?' *International Journal of Health Services*, 19: 611–34.

Barnett, J.R., Barnett, P., and Kearns, R.A. (1998) 'Declining professional dominance?: Trends in the proletarianisation of primary care in New Zealand', *Social Science and Medicine*, 46: 193–207.

Beck, U. (1992) *Risk Society. Towards a New Modernity*. London: Sage.

Becker, H. (1962) 'The nature of a profession', in National Society for the Study of Education. *Education for the Professions*. Chicago: University of Chicago Press.

Becker, H., Geer, B., Hughes, E.C., and Strauss, A. (1961) *Boys in White: Student Culture in Medical School*. Chicago: University of Chicago Press.

Bergthold, L.A. (1990) *Purchasing Power in Health: Business, the State, and Health Care Politics*. New Brunswick, NJ: Rutgers University Press.

Bourgeault, I.L. and Fynes, M. (1997) 'Integrating lay and nurse-midwifery into the US and Canadian systems', *Social Science and Medicine*, 44: 1051–63.

Brante, T. (1988) 'Sociological approaches to the professions', *Acta Sociologica*, 31: 119–42.

Brante, T. (1998) 'A theory of professional types and professional waves: The case of Sweden'. Paper presented at the ISA conference on Professional Identities in Transition, Gothenburg.

Brown, E.R. (1979) *Rockefeller Medicine Men: Medicine and Capitalism in America*. Berkeley: University of California Press.

Carr-Saunders, A.M. and Wilson, P.A. (1933) *The Professions*. London: F. Cass.

Castro, F.W. (1998) 'After the wave: The welfare state professionals in Sweden'. Paper presented at the 1998 ISA Conference on Professional Identities in Transition, Gothenburg.

Cawson, A. (ed.) (1985) *Organized Interests and the State: Studies in Meso-Corporatism*. Beverly Hills: Sage.

Coburn, D. (1999) 'Phases of capitalism, welfare states, medical dominance and health care in Ontario', *International Journal of Health Services*, forthcoming.

Coburn, D., Torrance, G., and Kaufert, J. (1983) 'Medical dominance in Canada in historical perspective', *International Journal of Health Services*, 13: 407–32.

Coburn, D., Rappolt, S., and Bourgeault, I. (1997) 'Decline vs. retention of medical power through restratification: The Ontario case', *Sociology of Health and Illness*, 19: 1–22.

Collins, R. (1979) *The Credential Society*. New York: Academic Books.

Dent, M. (1993) 'Professionalism, educated labour and the state: Hospital medicine and the new managerialism', *Sociological Review*, 41: 245–73.

Derber, C. (1983) 'Managing professionals', *Theory and Society*, 12: 309–41.

Derber, C. (1984) 'Physicians and their sponsors: The new medical relations of production', in J.B. McKinlay (ed.), *Issues in the Political Economy of Health Care*. New York: Tavistock.

Dohler, M. (1989) 'Physicians' professional autonomy in the welfare state: Endangered or preserved?' in G. Freddi and B W. Bjorkman (eds), *Controlling Medical Professionals*. London: Gage.

Donnison, J. (1977/1988) *Midwives and Medical Men*. London: Heinemann.

Doyal, L. (1979) *The Political Economy of Health*. London: Pluto.

Ehrenreich, B. and English, D. (1972) *Witches, Midwives and Nurses: A History of Women Healers*. New York: Feminist Press.

Ehrenreich, B. and English, D. (1976). *Complaints and Disorders: The Sexual Politics of Sickness*. London: Writers and Readers Publishing Cooperative.

Elston, M.A. (1991) 'The politics of professional power: Medicine in a changing health service', in J. Gabe, M. Calnan, and M. Bury (eds), *The Sociology of the Health Service*. London: Routledge.

Esping-Andersen, G. (1990) *The Three Worlds of Welfare Capitalism*. Princeton: Princeton University Press.

Evans, R.G., Barer, M.L., and Marmor, T.R. (eds), (1994) *Why are Some People Healthy and Others Not?* New York: Aldine de Gruyter.

Flynn, R. (1992) *Structures of Control in Health Management*. London: Routledge.

Foucault, M. (1973) *Madness and Civilization*. London: Random House.

Foucault, M. (1976) *Birth of the Clinic*. London: Tavistock.

Frankenberg, R. (1974) 'Functionalism and after? Theory and developments in social science as applied to the health field', *International Journal of Health Services*, 4: 411–27.

Freidson, E. (1970) *Profession of Medicine*. New York: Dodd, Mead.

Freidson, E. (1985) 'The reorganization of the medical profession', *Medical Care Review*, 42: 11–35.

Freidson, E. (1994) *Professionalism Reborn: Theory,*

Prophecy, and Policy. Chicago: University of Chicago Press.

Gabe, J., Kelleher, D., and Williams, G. (eds) (1994) *Challenging Medicine.* London: Routledge.

Greenwood, E. (1957) 'Attributes of a profession', *Social Work,* 2(3): 45–55.

Hafferty, F.W. and McKinlay, J.B. (eds) (1993) *The Changing Medical Profession.* New York: Oxford University Press.

Haug, M.R. (1975) 'The erosion of professional authority: A cross-cultural inquiry in the case of the physician', *Milbank Memorial Fund Quarterly,* 54: 83–106.

Hughes, E.C. (1958) *Men and their Work.* Glencoe, IL: Free Press.

Illich, I. (1975) *Medical Nemesis: The Expropriation of Our Health.* New York: Pantheon.

Jamous, H. and Peloille, B. (1970) 'Changes in the French University-Hospital System', in J. Jackson (ed.), *Professions and Professionalization.* Cambridge: Cambridge University Press.

Johnson, T. (1972) *Professions and Power.* London: Macmillan.

Johnson, T. (1977) 'The professions in the class structure', in R. Scase (ed.), *Industrial Society: Class Cleavage and Control.* London: Allen and Unwin.

Johnson, T. (1980) 'Work and power', in G. Esland and G. Salamand (eds), *The Politics of Work and Occupations.* Milton Keynes: Open University Press.

Johnson, T. (1995) 'Governmentality and the institutionalization of expertise', in T. Johnson, G. Larkin, and M. Saks (eds), *Health Professions and the State in Europe.* London: Routledge.

Krause, E. A. (1996) *Death of the Guilds: Professions, States and the Advance of Capitalism 1930 to the Present.* New Haven and London: Yale University Press.

Larkin, G. (1983) *Occupational Monopoly and Modern Medicine.* London: Tavistock.

Larkin, G.V. (1993) 'Continuity in change: Medical dominance in the United Kingdom', in F.W. Hafferty and J.B. McKinlay (eds), *The Changing Medical Profession.* Oxford: Oxford University Press.

Larkin, G. and Saks, M. (1994) 'Revision or renewal in the professional regulation of expertise?' Paper presented at the I.S.A.'s Conference on 'Regulating Expertise', Paris: Carre des Sciences.

Larson, M.S. (1977) *The Rise of Professionalism.* Berkeley: University of California Press.

Larson, M. (1980) 'Proletarianization and educated labor', *Theory and Society,* 9: 131–75.

Light, D. (1995) 'Countervailing powers: A framework for professions in transition', In T. Johnson, G. Larkin and M. Saks (eds), *Health Professions and the State in Europe.* London and New York: Routledge.

Lupton, D. (1997) 'Doctors on the medical profession', *Sociology of Health and Illness,* 19: 480–97.

Manza, J. (1992) 'Classes, status groups, and social closure: A critique of neo-Weberian social theory', *Current Perspectives in Social Theory,* 12: 275–302.

Martin, C.J. (1993) 'Together again: Business, government, and the quest for cost control', *Journal of Health Politics, Policy and Law,* 18: 359–93.

McKeown, T. (1965) *Medicine in Modern Society.* London: Routledge and Kegan Paul.

McKeown, T. (1979) *The Role of Medicine: Dream, Mirage or Nemesis?* Oxford: Basil Blackwell.

McKinlay, J.B. (1977) 'The business of good doctoring or doctoring as good business: Reflections on Freidson's views of the medical game', *International Journal of Health Services,* 7: 459–83.

McKinlay, J.B. and Arches, J. (1985) 'Towards the proletarianization of physicians', *International Journal of Health Services,* 15: 161–95.

McKinlay, J.B. and McKinlay, S.B. (1977) 'Questionable contribution of medical measures to the decline of mortality in the United States in the twentieth century', *Milbank Memorial Fund Quarterly (Health and Society),* 55: 405–28.

McKinlay, J.B. and Stoeckle, J.D. (1988) 'Corporatization and the social transformation of doctoring', *Health Services,* 18: 191–205.

Mechanic, D. (1991) 'Sources of countervailing power in medicine', *Journal of Health Politics, Policy and Law,* 16: 485–98.

Merton, R., Reader, G.G., and Kendall, P.L. (eds), (1957) *The Student-Physician.* Cambridge, MA: Harvard University Press.

Moran, M. and Wood, B. (1993) *States, Regulation and the Medical Profession.* Buckingham: Open University Press.

Murphy, R. (1988) 'Social Closure: The Theory of Monopolization and Exclusion. Oxford: Clarendon.

Navarro, V. (1976) *Medicine Under Capitalism.* New York: Prodist.

Navarro, V. (1986) *Crisis, Health and Medicine: A Social Critique.* New York: Tavistock.

Navarro, V. (1989) 'Why some countries have national health insurance, others have national health services, and the US has neither', *Social Science and Medicine,* 28: 887–98.

Navarro, V. (1988) 'Professional dominance or proletarianization?: Neither', *Milbank Quarterly,* 66, Supplement 2: 57–75.

Parkin, F. (1972) *Marxism and Class Theory: A Bourgeois Critique.* London: Tavistock.

Parsons, T. (1951) *The Social System.* New York: Free Press.

Parsons, T. (1964) *Essays in Sociological Theory* (revised edn). New York: Free Press.

Petersen, A.R. and Bunton, R. (1997) *Foucault, Health and Medicine.* London, New York: Routledge.

Rappolt, S. (1997) 'Clinical guidelines and the fate of medical autonomy in Ontario', *Social Science and Medicine,* 44: 977–87.

Riska, E. and Wegar, K. (1993) *Gender, Work and Medicine: Women and the Medical Division of Labour.* London: Sage.

Ross, R.J.S. and Trachte, K.C. (1990) *Global Capitalism: The New Leviathan*. Albany: State University of New York.

Ruggie, M. (1996) *Realignments in the Welfare State: Health Care Policy in the United States, Britain and Canada*. New York: Columbia University Press.

Saks, M. (1983) 'Removing the blinkers? A critique of recent contributions to the sociology of the professions', *Sociological Review*, 31: 1–21.

Saks, M. (1995) *Professions and the Public Interest: Medical Power, Altruism and Alternative Medicine*. London: Routledge.

Salmon, J.W. (ed.) (1994) *The Corporate Transformation of Health Care*. Amityville, NY: Baywood.

Shortt, S.E.D. (1983) 'Physicians, science, and status: Issues in the professionalization of Anglo-American medicine in the 19th Century', *Medical History*, 27: 51–68.

Starr, P. (1982) *The Social Transformation of American Medicine*. New York: Basic Books.

Starr, P. and Immergut, E. (1987) 'Health care and the boundaries of politics', in C.S. Maier (ed.), *Changing Boundaries of the Political*. Cambridge: Cambridge University Press.

Stubbs, R. and Underhill, G.R.D. (eds) (1994) *Political Economy and the Changing Social Order*. Toronto: McClelland and Stewart.

Turner, B. (1995) *Medical Power and Social Knowledge* (2nd edn). London: Sage.

Waitzkin, H. (1991) *The Politics of Medical Encounters: How Patients and Doctors Deal with Social Problems*. New York: Yale University Press.

Weiss, M. and Fitzpatrick, R. (1997) 'Challenges to medicine: The case of prescribing', *Sociology of Health and Illness*, 19: 297–327.

Wilensky, H.L. (1964) 'The professionalization of everyone?' *American Journal of Sociology*, 70: 137–58.

Willis, E. (1989) *Medical Dominance: The Division of Labour in Australian Health Care* (2nd edn). Sydney: George Allen and Unwin. (1st edn, 1983).

Wilsford, D. (1991). *Doctors and the State: The Politics of Health Care in France and the United States*. Durham, NC: Duke University Press.

Witz, A. (1992) *Professions and Patriarchy*. London: Routledge.

3.2

The Sociological Character of Health-Care Markets

DONALD W. LIGHT

INTRODUCTION

While doctors have been competing amongst themselves and with other providers for centuries over technique, turf, patients, and the organization of work (Abbott 1988; Albrecht 1992: Ch. 6), price competition is a new, largely American, phenomenon that has been aggressively exported and selectively adopted by a number of other countries. Economic arguments have had a dominant influence on health-care policy internationally, but I will argue in this chapter that they do not explain the actual workings of health-care markets, which are described better by sociological studies.

Economic competition and markets in health care, as observed in a review 10 years ago (Light 1989), embody a paradigm shift from the professional dominance that prevailed in most systems, even public ones like Britain's National Health Service (NHS), to buyer dominance, from a doctor-led pressure for more services to a buyer or payer-led pressure for better outcomes, from an emphasis on hospital-based specialized treatments to prevention and primary care. This paradigm shift to buyer dominance promises better health at lower cost. Yet one can separate, as Prime Minister Tony Blair has done (Secretary of State for Health 1997), the results-oriented focus of a purchaser-led paradigm from a competitive strategy. Because price competition in health care is so fraught with dangers of selective marketing, inequalities, worsening care, and ironically higher costs, it is unclear how many countries will employ it and for how long. Already, one of the most sweeping adaptations, the transition of the NHS from the world's largest administered managed care system to the world's largest competitive internal market of contracts between purchasers and providers, has been replaced by reforms that emphasize cooperation and partnership because competition was found to be too disruptive, demoralizing, and costly (Light 1997, 1998a). Competitive markets in health care, then, may be a phase in the historical process of rebalancing relations between the countervailing powers of professions, patients, payers, and states (Light 1995a). Ironically, as states and other payers, counter the dominance of the medical profession, the health-care corporations they use as their agents are coming to dominate both.

Conservative economic theory itself provides as clear a picture as any of the depth to which market failures will plague health-care markets, and thus will lead legislators, doctors, nurses, or patients to limit or eliminate them. We shall start with a review of that theory and the major effort to overcome market failures in health care – managed competition. Because this analysis of competitive health care on its own terms leaves us with more reasons why it should fail than why it should be adopted, we turn to analyzing its proliferation as a social movement with the sponsors, 'moral entrepreneurs,' and agenda found in any social movement. This analysis concludes by identifying the dimensions along which competitive health-care experiments have varied, dimensions that any research on them must attend. Finally, we conclude with some in-depth studies of health-care market behavior, as examples of the many research projects that have yet to be done.

MEDICAL MARKETS AS A THEORETICAL ANOMALY

All markets are social constructions, and customs, norms, and formal rules or laws regulate them all. Politicians, journalists, and business-people talk constantly about 'free markets,' but there are no free markets, except in their fantasies. Even 'black markets,' drug dealing, and organized crime have structure, hierarchy, norms, and rules, whose violation can prove fatal. Moreover, the advocates of 'free markets' would not want to live with the consequences if such markets were allowed, as Etzioni (1988) depicted in his modern classic, *The Moral Dimension*.

Risk and trust are core market issues that concern a given society. Deliberations about how much risk different parties should be allowed to bear and what levels of trust are to be assured reflect a society's values. Societies regulate because they value certain levels of safety, of quality, and of externalities, including protection of the innocent. The key questions are, 'How much risk do different parties bear in a given market?' and 'How much can we trust those whose services or products we buy? Clinical competence is a good example. Licensing and certification requirements reflect certain initial levels of assured quality for patients, although subsequent quality of clinical work can vary a great deal. In the new market-based era, criteria and measurement of quality are becoming more stringent and more focused on actual performance and outcomes, in part reflecting the higher risks and problems of trust that are posed by capitated contracts and strong financial incentives to skimp on quality (Mechanic 1998).

Also, societies sometime regulate because they value access and equity, such as Ireland prohibiting health insurance companies from charging or selecting subscribers by risk in the name of community and solidarity (Light 1998b). They also regulate to avoid political embarrassment, as the British government did when it transformed the National Health Service from publicly administered services to competitive markets, but then clamped so many regulations on contracts with hospitals that it became nearly impossible for them to go bankrupt (Dawson 1995). This last example points to why markets in health care are a theoretical anomaly, because such markets exhibit so many forms of market failure. In order to understand why, one needs to understand the foundations of market theory.

The promise of developing markets in medicine stems from the ability and power of competition to reward promptly those who provide better value for money in terms of efficiency and cost containment. Competition is central to international policy for containing health-care costs. Yet, for competition to benefit society, to reward greater efficiency and service, ten stipulations must be met. Without these ten stipulations to channel people's pursuit of their own self interests so that society benefits, competition rewards collusion, product substitution, favorable selection, monopolization, and other strategies for winning that harm society. These stipulations and conditions are listed below (Abel and Bernanke 1993: 18–21, 316–17; Begg et al. 1987: Ch. 8–9; Ormerod 1994).

1. There must be many buyers and sellers so that no one's actions are large enough to affect the market overall.
2. These buyers and sellers should have no relations with each other that might affect each other's economic behavior.
3. Buyers can purchase from the full array of sellers/providers and products.
4. There are no barriers of entry or exit of sellers, so that failing sellers drop out of the market and sellers with better products or prices can enter the market easily.
5. There is full information about services, products, prices, and quality.
6. This information is free and quickly obtained by sellers and especially buyers.
7. Buyers choose to 'maximize their utilities,' that is, to seek the greatest gain that they can.
8. Market signals are instantaneous, and the market quickly clears differences between supply and demand through price fluctuations.
9. Price conveys all that buyers need to know to buy smart and measure their 'opportunity costs.'
10. There are no externalities to these transactions, so that the buyers directly experience the full benefits and liabilities of their purchases.

If all these stipulations are met, and if people make only rational choices to maximize their predetermined preferences, then the 'invisible hand' of the market will benefit society with greater value.[1] In addition, the model assumes that social welfare is based solely on individual utilities, which in turn are based solely on the goods and services consumed, and that the distribution of wealth is approved of by society (Rice 1998: 5). Even if all these conditions hold, the long-term effect of competition is not to save money but to generate new wealth. In the long run, competition rewards those who develop new products, open new markets, and identify or create new 'needs,' such as cellular phones, fax machines, all-terrain 4-wheel drive vehicles for suburban drivers, or hand-rolled cigars at the zenith of antismoking. Getting people in Beverly Hills to drive a Jeep Cherokee while smoking a $12 cigar and chatting on a cellular phone spurs economic growth. Thus, even aside from problems of market failure, using competition to contain costs in health care would seem to be a fundamentally short-sighted strategy that in fact sets the stage for health care to experience long-term growth as health-care corporations develop new services and create new markets. There are good reasons why Adam Smith's famous book about generating wealth was entitled *The Wealth of Nations*, not *The Cost Containment of Nations*.

However, even if or when health-care services can be defined and priced (such as buying 20 hips or 50 cataracts), or when professionalism works well, many (but not all) aspects of health care fail to meet most or all of the ten requirements for beneficial competition.

1　Often, a few or even just one hospital or provider group dominate a local market, and often a few or even one purchasing unit is buying.
2　These parties almost always have long, entangled relationships, obligations, or rivalries that deeply compromise rational purchasing.
3　A major goal of competition in health care is to restrict and channel choice, and often political pressures limit what services can be purchased from whom.
4　There are high barriers to entry and exit in health care.
5　Market information about quality, service, and price is often incomplete, inaccurate, and fragmented.
6　Market information is very costly, asymmetrical, and largely controlled by the provider; access to it is often blocked (Saltman and Figueras 1996: 26).
7　Buyers, even with good information, do not make choices that maximize their preferences and utilities (Rice 1997).
8　Market signals are slow, or hidden, and markets can take months to 'clear' if at all.
9　Prices are constructed realities that do not convey all a buyer needs to know.
10　There are significant externalities, especially through cost shifting and selection.

Clearly, one would need a great deal of regulation and a rather special structural design to have competition in health care that was beneficial to society. The highly skewed distribution of risk underscores this point. Only 2 per cent of a population require medical care that consumes 41 per cent of the budget, and 10 per cent consume 72 per cent of resources, while 30 per cent

at the other end consume none (Berk and Monheit 1992). The easiest way to 'win' in markets with fixed or capitated contracts is to avoid or undertreat the sickest patients, or get them to disenroll from your plan or practice.

Imagine, for example, the implications of providing cardiac services at a fixed annual rate. The distribution of care and costs over 100 cases tends to be normal. If pay is fairly set, at the mean, *in theory* nothing should change. Suppose that historically these cases cost $500 000, or $5000 each on average, with some costing you $1000 a year at the left tail of the distribution, and others costing you $50 000 at the right tail. However, average pay produces a strong incentive to avoid high-cost cases or to transfer them on to someone else's budget. Often, I find that hospital and clinic administrators set up rules and threaten doctors whose patients stay longer or cost more than the mean. Their viewpoint is quite simple, although not statistical: the patient in room 203 is costing more than our per-case payment and is therefore causing us to lose money. The manager's impulse is to break even or come out ahead on *every* case, but this means that the sickest patients get inadequate care as the manager cuts it to the mean.

Equally worrisome are pressures for providers to price contracts based on capitation below costs in order to gain contracts and market share, especially when combined with pressures to overpay for already-established books of business. Imagine the implications if the going rate for buying patients in the US HMO[2] market is $1500 ('I'll pay you $75 million for your HMO with 50 000 subscribers') and a major insurer (Aetna) buys a huge HMO with a million subscribers (US Healthcare) for twice that price (Given 1997: 186). How will it ever recoup the extra $1.5 billion it paid, except by absorbing large losses or by reducing medical services? Moreover, Ruth Given has demonstrated that there are no economies of scale in HMOs beyond 50 000 enrollees, and US Healthcare is already one of the most efficient, best-run HMOs in the world. Merging with Aetna did not make it more efficient, just bigger. In fact, 2 years later, *The Wall Street Journal* reported that Aetna had much worse service, hundreds of physicians dropping their contracts and services to patients, a 40 per cent drop in profits, and a $300 million per year write-off (Lagnado 1998). The chief executive concluded, nevertheless, that the acquisition had made Aetna more 'vibrant.'

Basic Challenges to Health-Care Markets

A distinguished young health economist, Tom Rice (1997 1998), has recently challenged the foundations of competition theory. Condition 2, for example, requires that no one care about their relative standing or the conditions of others, both of which in fact play important roles in many markets and certainly in health care. Condition 10 means that the concern for others, like the uninsured, is an 'externality.' Rice shows that this affects not only equity, but also efficiency. The belief (or 'preference') that everyone, including the poor, should have access to needed medical care is a principal reason why no country (except the United States) has started with a market system (Rice 1997: 399).

Most important, Condition 7, on utilities, assumes that preferences are inborn or given. Evidence that they are influenced by marketing, or the media, or even by what you are used to having, violates this highly unrealistic condition. Notions of habit, norms, and custom wreak havoc with competition theory. Further, Rice marshals evidence that people often do not bother to get the information they need to max-imize their preferences, and other evidence that even when they do, they often do not use it to their maximum benefit. A special problem in health care is that people cannot predict the con-sequences of their choices. To cover up these problems, economists used 'revealed prefer-ences,' which means that whatever people end up with is by definition what they wanted!

Managed Competition as a Possible Solution

Extensive regulation and a special design char-acterize the most serious attempt to overcome these multiple forms of market failure in health care. In his design for managed competition, Alain Enthoven (1988) attempted to overcome Arrow's problems and to meet several of the stipulations for beneficial competition. His model calls for consumers choosing among com-prehensive, large-volume health-care plans (like American HMOs) that would operate within a set of rules designed to create fair competition. Put theoretically, a given clinical case may be emergent, contingent, and uncertain, but a hun-dred or a thousand cases exhibit regular patterns and distributions that can be costed and priced. Although Enthoven has altered his design many times to suit the audience and politics of the time, at its most complete (Enthoven 1988) his model emphasizes universal access, a common benefits package, excellent information, and a strong system of quality assurance so as to cre-ate a level playing field. Even then, he was so impressed by the ability of hospitals and provi-

ders to exploit any set of regulations that he added an oversight body to actively *manage* this highly regulated market. For '. . . without active collective management on the demand side, the medical plans would be free to pursue profits or survival using numerous competitive strategies that would destroy equity and effi-ciency and that individual consumers would be powerless to counteract' (Enthoven 1988: 11).

Enthoven's theory carries a strong message, namely that competition requires very extensive regulation plus a smart, well-paid watchdog to be sure that the providers do not circumvent or manipulate the regulations. Otherwise, the pro-viders (sellers) have all the advantages, and the stakes are too high to attempt competition. Thus, price competition health care has been accompanied, not by deregulation but by intense talk and action about *more* regulation. In the United States, capitated or fixed-budget con-tracts began with relatively few of Enthoven's safeguards, and soon the easy forms of winning that Enthoven had predicted became evident. A rash of regulations has ensued to protect patients from blocked access, underservice, sup-pression of clinical options and choice ('gag clauses'), and other forms of abuse. Recently, the groundswell of protest led to more than 400 pieces of new legislation being passed in the 50 states to regulate 'managed care' (Brink and Shute 1997). These *post hoc* efforts respond piecemeal to fragments of the problems and satisfy no one.

Managed competition appears to surmount the obstacles to effective markets in health care, and it is uncritically embraced as the model for making health-care services more effi-cient and responsive via competition, but a care-ful analysis shows that the theory is seriously flawed, so that even if managed competition were implemented in its ideal form, it would not work as promised. First, managed competi-tion leads to oligopolies forming in each market, and they would minimize the very competition the model aims to engender (Light 1995b; Sullivan 1995). Second, managed competition assumes that providers cannot be trusted but managers can. That is the key reason why Enthoven did not rest his case with competition framed by regulations to assure a level playing field. Third, it also does not solve the problems of uncertainty or contingency or information asymmetry, but instead puts them inside its basic unit, the HMO, where Enthoven assumes that managers will resolve all these problems better than professionals did in the old market structure. As the inside literature on HMOs indi-cates, many of them remain unresolved or are resolved in disturbing ways (n.a. (no author) 1998a). For example, the broad overlapping networks of providers shared by plans that are supposedly competition means that (a) the providers are in effect competing against themselves, (b) developing good clinical management tools and information is unlikely, (c) providers will be less interested in investing in a given plan's program for clinical re-engineering, and (d) plans can win contracts by paying providers less and limiting services more (Eddy 1998; Ginsberg 1998: 4–5, Sullivan 1997). Managed competition also undermines public health and areawide programs, although many small collaborations are celebrated (Lasker 1997).

Complementing this theoretical analysis of the model is a description of what happened when managed competition was implemented, not for selected parts of health care as in the United States, but for the entire health-care system of the United Kingdom (Light 1997). Briefly, the implementation of managed competition greatly increased market and administrative costs, required extensive new regulations, caused or threatened to cause serious disruptions save for damage control, and raised overall costs. The government that introduced it abandoned it by the fifth year and was subsequently defeated at the polls by a government that promised to end competition and restore cooperation and partnership (Secretary of State for Health 1997). More broadly, an assessment of competition strategies used in Europe in several areas of public service found the results quite mixed (Hollingsworth and Boyer 1997).

The serious flaws of managed competition do not seem to matter much in the political economy of health-care policy because many politicians embrace it as a way to get the pressure of cost containment off their backs and on to providers. It also serves as a political 'front' or front-stage strategy for back-stage reduction of overall coverage and privatization of care for chronic conditions. Harvard economist William Hsiao (1994) reviewed the effects of competition policies in Singapore, South Korea, Chile, and The Philippines. In each case the data showed that it led to privatization, two-tier access, and sharply higher costs.

In the United States, *un*managed competition between HMO-like corporations is credited with halting the upward march of employers' premiums, but backstage, employers have been dropping coverage for dependents and retirees, thinning coverage for mental health and some other areas, making coverage more shallow by limiting how much of given services one can get, and shifting costs back to patients through co-payments (Shearer 1998). The number of uninsured has been rising at about 1.2 million a year since the early 1990s; it then jumped by 1.7 million in 1997 to a total of 43.4 million, or 16 per cent of the US population (Pear 1998). Three-tier care is increasingly evident: stop-gap acute interventions for the poor, good care with hassles for the middle class, and what Reinhardt (1996) calls 'boutique care' for the rich. One example of 'boutique care' is Mt. Sinai's eleven west hospital suites, with views of Central Park, a gourmet chef, a sofa covered in Scalamandre fabric, and dinner parties *en suite* (Bumiller 1997). The Robert Wood Johnson tracking project found that 'few [17 per cent] private employers offer employees a choice of plans, give employees financial incentives to choose economical plans, or provide information so that employees can evaluate the quality of the care they receive – three hallmarks of managed competition' (Long and Marquis 1998: 1).

In conclusion, economic theory provides strong reasons why price competition in health care is unlikely to produce the desired results and may be dangerous, but this does not explain why efforts to create markets in health care have proliferated, and nor does it explain how those markets actually work. We thus turn to a sociological analysis, first of why they have proliferated and then of how they work.

COMPETITIVE HEALTH CARE AS A SOCIAL MOVEMENT

Analyzing competitive health care as a social movement provides a different sociological perspective: one that explains why an unpromising economic theory should gain such a worldwide following. Setting the scene were several background factors. First, for all Western countries, the oil shock of 1973 and the decade of slow growth, together with inflation (stagflation), meant that the cost of health care consumed ever-increasing proportions of countries' gross domestic product and employers' revenue. Second, the dominance of the organized medical profession meant an emphasis on hospital-based and specialty services that kept driving costs up. Whether in a system whose entire structure reflected the values of the organized profession, such as the United States (Light 1997), or in state-run systems, the organized medical profession dominated, and gave us the excesses, costs, and social pathologies of professionalism as a way to allocate resources (Freidson 1970a, 1970b). While fostering impressive advances in technique, the medical profession has emphasized the best clinical treatments for sick patients, downplayed prevention and public health, neglected the growing proportion of chronic conditions, and increased costly hospital and subspecialty care.

Third, the credibility of the medical profession became seriously challenged in the 1970s on three grounds: that very little of the long-term health gain of populations was due to clinical medicine, that large portions of tests and procedures were found by clinical research teams to be unnecessary or not beneficial, and that doctors varied widely in their use of costly procedures after controlling for clinical variables. These studies indicated that while the medical profession was running costs up, it was not making clinically responsible decisions and was not doing much good. These discoveries spawned a new era in which the government as buyer took over from the profession systematic research to assess the outcomes and evidence of different procedures that a profession should be doing (McCormick et al. 1997). This research is providing the basis for externally developed clinical protocols and guidelines (Hafferty and Light 1995). As I argued a decade ago, autonomy is not a defensible foundation for professionalism – accountability is (Light 1988). The era of autonomy came to an end, and the era of accountability began.

Fourth, politicians and policy leaders in most countries declared that health care had become unaffordable and was jeopardizing the economy. This claim of a 'cost crisis,' still present today as a powerful political force, needs to be regarded with the irony of comparative perspective. For it is not clear at what point medical costs might create a crisis. The United States is spending 14 per cent of GDP on health care and has one of the strongest economies in the world. Moreover, each country has its own homegrown sense of when health-care costs are unaffordable. For the British, the real possibility that expenditure for the National Health Service might exceed 5.5 per cent of gross domestic product (GDP) perpetrated a crisis in 1988–9 that spurred Mrs Thatcher (then Prime Minister) to restructure the entire health-care system in order to contain costs. The rest of Europe spent on average nearly 8 per cent of GDP, but British leaders never discussed such a possibility. In Germany, the line not to be crossed for a long time was about 8.5 per cent. When expenditure threatened to exceed that, a grim determination set in to do whatever it took to hold the line. German policy leaders would have been ecstatic if their costs were only 5.5 per cent. The French, on the other hand, would break out champagne if their costs were only 8.5 per cent. Their line in the sand (more like a tire track), however, would be cause for celebration in Canada, whose level of intolerability is about 11 per cent of GDP. Thus, the cost-crisis factor is real and powerful but is also a constructed reality, not grounded in solid evidence or research.

Fifth, there was a worldwide paradigm shift towards portraying the state as inefficient, incompetent, and inflexible, and calling for competition, deregulation, and privatization to replace state functions (Saltman and von Otter 1992: Ch. 1; White and Collyer 1998). Deep forces, which lie beyond the scope of this chapter, underlay this shift and can only be mentioned briefly. They involve inherent contradictions in the roles that the modern state plays as both a promoter of capitalist growth and a provider of social services that take care of the social needs created by, or neglected by, business (O'Connor 1973). In the United Kingdom, for example, the prices that the National Health Service sets for pharmaceuticals aim to support a major industry and export business, but are by that goal an extra burden and drain on the very tight budget for health care. In the United States, where the medical–industrial complex is a huge, profitable, and rapidly growing sector of the economy, one finds states that aim to attract more companies from this booming sector. However, at the same time, states take strong measures to hold down the technologically driven spiral of their own health-care costs.

Competition to the Rescue

When conservative think-tanks throughout Europe and the United States started formulating strategies of competitive markets for containing health-care costs in the early 1980s, they provided a solution to the constellation of problems described above. Nations believe deeply in the benefits of competition in the many markets where it produces better products and services and economic growth, and the appeal to politicians of passing off the political heat from the recession squeeze on financing services to private vendors was very appealing. Economists, as academic entrepreneurs and as staff at the World Bank and international consulting firms, vigorously promoted their diagnosis and solution (Hacker 1997: Ch. 2). Health-care systems, they argued, were steeped in bureaucracy, riddled with perverse incentives, organized around hospitals with their costly brand of subspecialty medicine, and arrogantly insensitive to patients' needs. Competition would align incentives, reward the more cost-effective providers, put prevention and primary care in the driver's seat, and be responsive to patients. In short, competitive health care became a social movement, with its prophets and moral entrepreneurs.

Enthoven played a key role promulgating managed competition for health care, travelling throughout the world and meeting with ministers, politicians, and business leaders. American-based consulting firms took up the cause and created a variety of 'products' and systems for transforming health-care systems into markets like the one that caused the British so much trouble and additional cost. The fees for such transformations ran into millions of dollars. US AID (1996: 7–9) and the World Bank have embraced market approaches to health care and insist that developing countries and poorer countries in the Eastern block of Europe convert their health-care systems as a condition for receiving economic aid and loans. Hsiao (1994 1995) has described the results in several countries or regions: higher cost, reduced access, profiteering, and less control over costs. Twaddle (1999: Ch. 4–7) shows in detail for Sweden the degree to which, despite the economic challenges and weaknesses of the health-care system summarized above, there was neither an economic crisis nor a health-care crisis sufficient to warrant so fundamental a change as the competitive paradigm represented. Rather, one must conclude it was a politically driven social movement.

Fligstein (1985, 1990) has done important historical research on industries, which suggests that when they face a basic crisis, they search for a new 'conception of control' that will enable them to redefine their business and regain a stable, profitable environment. Let me suggest that governments do the same, and that competition policies reconceptualize governmental services and government itself so as to deflect the blame for costly social services away from politicians and on to private contractors, and to make those services more efficient. A large, comparative review of those policies 10 years later finds the evidence very mixed as to whether they saved money or improved services (Hollingsworth and Boyer 1997).

The distinguished health economist Robert Evans (1997: 427) makes a sociological analysis of this social movement in terms of class and power. He marshals evidence that '. . . greater reliance on the market is associated with inferior system performance – inequity, inefficiency, high cost, and public dissatisfaction,' so that one must look to the beneficiaries of this policy bandwagon who are 'going for the gold.' The advocates, and beneficiaries, he concludes are suppliers, providers, insurers, and their political friends, because competition and privatization redistribute national income in their favor, in the name of 'an intellectual framework that makes distributional questions difficult or impossible to ask' (Evans 1997: 432). Evans

unpacks that framework, and also shows that the wealthy gain at the expense of the working class.

Privatization

Ideologically intertwined with competition, yet analytically distinct, is privatization. One can have competition without privatizing public services (as in the NHS), and one can privatize without competition. While this chapter focuses primarily on competition, it is worth mentioning three primary types of privatization: of services, of assets, and of control. Based on the belief that private corporations will be more cost-effective, for example, Australia has privatized some of its health care at all three levels (White and Collyer 1997, 1998). The number of hospital beds and proportion of admissions has been steadily rising since 1980, supported by a growing number of people who buy supplementary health insurance (White 1991). The historically small private hospitals have also been amalgamated into large corporate chains, as they were earlier in the United States (Light 1986). Physicians have also played a central role, as they have in the United States, using their tradition of autonomy and private practice to acquire financial stakes in diagnostic laboratories, ambulatory surgicenters, outpatient clinics, and dialysis centers. Intertwined with these two trends has been contracting-out to private management of emergency rooms, intensive care units, radiological and pathology services, and laboratories (White and Collyer 1998).

In theory, none of these developments necessarily means that access to health-care services as a right has to diminish. Indeed, it should mean that those services are being run more efficiently and are thus more available, but in fact, there is some evidence that 'efficiency' has come to mean raising someone else's costs, as in the case of the Port Macquarie Base Hospital, or increasing costs but shifting them to future generations, as with the hospitals in Mount Gambier and Port Augusta (White and Collyer 1997: 18–20). The Private Financing Initiative in the United Kingdom is becoming the major source of capital for the health service, based on debt financing that costs little now but many times more in interest and operating contracts for the next generation (Light 1998a).

The private sector, through powerful organized lobbying, also begins to control the terms of the market and contractual terms themselves, rather than being competitive sellers in a buyers' market, and the regulatory bodies are relatively weak (Self 1995). The ability to plan equitably and efficiently weakens (Offe 1975), as when private hospitals build next to public ones and siphon off their more affluent clientele (Duckett 1989). While Australian law seems to require that private hospitals build in 'appropriate areas,' the legal framework 'is based on the . . . property rights of entrepreneurs, not the user rights of consumers nor the service responsibilities of government' (White and Collyer 1998: 21). Therefore 'the Health Commission has been unable to prevent the private sector from building hospitals in localities which will maximise revenue for the entrepreneurs and undermine the public system.' In these ways, privatization has effects distinct from competition yet often accompanying it.

The United States is the extreme case of 'anything-goes' private competition. Insurers compete, providers compete, and market makers compete, at all levels, on both the supply side and the demand side, in all combinations of integration and decentralization, using every variety of agency imaginable, on vote-with-your feet volume as well as price, and allowing benefits to vary. Most of this competition and its data are proprietary. This makes it extremely hard for researchers, or even employers as buyers, to know which strategies are cost-effective, or even to know what is going on. To back up their faith in competitive health care to hold down costs, employers have been dropping coverage for children and other dependents, reducing the range of health-care services, or making coverage shallower.

Has Competition Saved Money?

Overall, American-style unmanaged competition between managed care corporations is widely credited with having reduced prices and unnecessary services enough to flatten health-care expenditures at about 13–14 per cent of GDP. However, a number of other factors may explain much or most of the slowdown in rising expenditure. First, general inflation became very low, so even if health-care costs continued to rise at the historic rate of 1.5–2 times inflation, it would drop from 12–15 per cent per year to 4–5 per cent. Second, managed care plans have attracted a healthier population; so by having fewer of the most costly 2 per cent of patients, they appear to be saving a great deal (Morgan et al. 1997). Now, in mature markets where mostly older and sicker patients are left unenrolled, managed care plans are finding their costs rising. Third, managed care plans have largely managed costs by forcing providers to take deep discounts on their historically high charges, and while that is a genuine saving, it is short-lived after two or three rounds of discounting reach a cost floor. Fourth,

many impressive savings by large corporations have resulted from providers and hospitals shifting costs to weaker, less forceful buyers so that overall costs for a region look quite different. Cost-shifting explained the apparent paradox in the 1980s of individual savings and spiraling overall costs, and providers continue to do it as much as they can (Freeman and Reschovsky 1997).

An insightful analysis has been made of the Minnesota market, which was created more than 15 years ago through special enabling legislation sponsored by a coalition of major employers, policy leaders, and government officials (Sullivan 1995). The study found that just as our analysis of the theory would predict, managed competition led to rapid consolidation into bilateral monopolies or oligopolies, and that this concentration gave providers the political power to control the structure of the market itself. Although Minnesota is widely considered the model of managed competition, its costs and beds per thousand remain above the national norm. Nationally, hospitals have been merging to gain market power and, in the process, according to the senior researcher, 'propping up inefficient hospitals that might not have survived if left on their own' (n.a. (no author) 1998b: 1). A national review of large managed-care organizations found evidence that they lowered access, quality, and continuity of care, and they were too large to deal effectively with quality issues (Barr 1995).

In a follow-up study, Sullivan (1997) examined the critical requirement in competitive markets that quality be measured and reported so that consumers can reward high-quality provider groups and leave ones that evidence lower quality. He found that no such measures have been developed, and argues that for technical reasons they never can be, a view supported by the leading national authority (Eddy 1998). This leaves patients vulnerable to the central danger of competition, lower quality, and reduced access to stay under budget. He reviews detailed case evidence that this has happened but will remain the undocumented cost to patients of competition. In 1998, the three major HMOs in the Minneapolis region, in the most mature market in the nation, still had above-average costs and raised their premiums by 12–40 per cent (Winslow 1998).

Europe: Cautious Experimentation

In Europe, the competitive health-care movement has revolutionized thinking but led to more measured, targeted actions. The movement caused people to challenge all the old assumptions. Why *is* the hospital the center of the health-care system, rather than the institution of last resort? Can nurses do many of the things that doctors now do, and primary-care teams handle many of the cases now referred to specialists? How much of what is done is unnecessary? How effective are the procedures and drugs now used? Let's find out, and let's set up evidence-based guidelines to reduce unnecessary variations in practice. Then, why not pay providers based on performance? Services should be audited. Quality should be measured in terms of outcomes, not inputs. As for new technologies and drugs, we need a method by which to see if they are worth adding. Why not educate and mobilize patients and their caregivers to manage a large percentage of their health problems on their own? At the end of the day, let's also calculate firm budgets for all services, or sectors, so that providers have incentives for carrying out all these new ideas.

This paragraph captures the spirit of what European systems are doing (Saltman and Figueras 1996), and much of it does not involve straight competition, like selling cars or computers, but such revolutionary re-thinking was certainly spurred by competitive health care as a social movement. The overall goal, in Hirschman's (1970) terms, is to take a fixed welfare service in which there is loyalty but no exit (a no-choice public system) and introduce voice and exit through choice. Reforms might be regarded as making public services more democratic by giving patients or clients voice and choice (Saltman and von Otter 1992: 97). The intent for providers is to put them on notice as accountable, self-governing entities. The market can be set up within the public sector as an internal market, or be open to competition from the private sector.

A common mistake is not to make private competitors as accountable as public ones, not to require from them full information on quality and service. In the meantime, transaction costs (management, marketing, profit, office overheads) tend to rise, from about 2–4 per cent for state administered systems like the US Medicare or the Finnish systems, to about 8–12 per cent. Ways to link productivity to payment or budgets, forms of capitation, and a higher degree of accountability characterized many reform initiatives (Saltman and von Otter 1992: 15–21). Other themes were to break down organizational and budgetary barriers that protect hospitals and prevent most cost-effective integrated services, to integrate primary care and social services to the same ends, and to devolve planning or even spending to municipal or district levels. Delegation and decentralization can also take political heat off

the central government. Of particular interest were efforts to create consumer-led competition between units only within the publicly planned, financed, and accountable health-care system (Saltman and von Otter 1992: 50–3, 83–5). Patients could choose which primary-care team to join, and expectant mothers could choose which maternity unit they wished to use, resulting in those units receiving proportionately more or less money.

Types of Competitive Health Care

The complex literature and range of experiments involve certain dimensions that can be identified for policy or research (Saltman and von Otter 1992: 85–95).

1 *Provider side competition versus provider and buyer competition.* The market can be set up to limit competition to the provider side or to make insurers compete as well as providers. Many of the former socialist countries in Eastern Europe and the former USSR have wanted to emulate the Bismarkian model of competing insurance funds, and an important review finds that this has increased class discrimination, costs, and overheads (Deppe and Oreskovic 1996). Many other countries have chosen just provider competition because competing insurers can so easily exploit high-risk or sick patients (Chernichovsky 1995; Light 1998b).

2 *A focus on reducing demand versus a focus on reducing supply.* Reducing demand features various kinds of cost sharing and incentives for patients and for doctors. According to an authoritative review, they produce severe equity problems and 'have not worked well' (Saltman and Figueras 1996: 39). The latter include controlling the supply of doctors, beds, and hi-tech equipment, creating substitutes for hospital care, and especially setting firm budgets.

3 *Level of competition.* Some countries set up competitive markets primarily among primary-care providers. Others focus on hospitals and subspecialists, where the stakes and risks are much greater. Still others foster competition among providers of chronic and long-term care services, often in conjunction with privatization, or any combination of the above. Each of these markets has quite different profiles of risk and of providers, so that the implications for fair competition differ considerably.

4 *Degree of decentralization.* Decentralization promises local sensitivity, working partnerships, responsiveness to patients, and inno-

vation. It can also lead to greater inequality, inefficiency, and fragmentation. Self-government and privatization increase as decentralization is extended to smaller and smaller units.

5 *Degree of integration.* Some reforms aim to combine the historically segmented and administratively ensconced governmental services, such as community nursing, community mental health, social services, housing, rehabilitation, and primary care, into horizontally integrated units that coordinate what services are needed from each of these segments for a given subpopulation. Others aim at more strictly medical integration, as implied in disease management and clinical protocols, so that interdisciplinary teams address the array of patient needs that span specialty fiefdoms. A third kind of integration is more vertical, i.e., to combine hospital services with primary care and specialty nursing care. This can only be done with integrated budgets and a forceful purchaser, both of which are largely missing in most national reforms. The United States, while extremely expensive and wasteful, has the advantage of developing markets based on all-service integrated contracts which reward any gains in vertically integrated services, such as fewer admissions and quicker discharge made possible by more extensive outpatient clinical management. These contracts have forced hospitals, specialists and primary-care physicians to combine into all-service, managed-care organizations (Robinson and Casalino 1995, 1996).

6 *Agency.* Reforms vary from having the patient as agent, by choosing which group to sign up with as in the Stockholm experiment, to having the patient's doctor or the area authority or council as the purchasing agent for a population of patients, as in the British 1991–98 NHS reforms.

7 *Price versus volume focused.* The market can be set up so that provider groups compete on price, as in the 1991 NHS reforms (although little price competition actually resulted), or to make provider groups compete for customers (i.e., patients) at the set price of the system. This latter, money-follows-patients, approach has been effective in Stockholm because the size of a clinic's budget varies directly with the number of patients they attract (Twaddle 1999).

8 *Uniform versus variable range of benefits.* The market can be set up with the same, system-wide range of benefits, or competing groups can be allowed to offer differences in range and depth of services. This latter approach is rare outside the United States because it

quickly turns competition into profitable risk selection.

SOCIOLOGICAL STUDIES OF MARKET BEHAVIOR IN HEALTH CARE

Sociologists have barely begun to research the effects of different market arrangements along these eight dimensions on clinical or administrative behavior, or on patients. Yet such research promises to be insightful, and it can draw on broader developments in economic sociology over the past 15 years. A brief review indicates their promise for research into health-care markets. Economic sociology is a burgeoning field, led by Americans, in which the model-driven characterization of market behavior has been replaced with detailed empirical studies. The neoclassical theory of markets was, on the face of it, sociologically deprived, because customs, culture, and roles do not exist, only rational 'buyers' and 'sellers.' Power, influence, and institutions do not exist. Ethnicity, class, and prejudice do not exist. Friendships, networks, trust, and loyalty do not exist (Hirsch et al. 1990; Perrow 1990; Zukin and DiMaggio 1990: 3–13). As Granovetter (1985) pointed out, anonymous social atomization is a prerequisite for perfect competition. Neoclassical theory seems to have persisted for so long because it promotes the interests of the wealthy and powerful, and its simplifications produce elegant, powerful predictions, even if wrong. The Hobbesian problems of order and malfeasance are bypassed.

> The problem is that the assumptions underlying the economic model are not only very simple, they are also very strong and wildly unrealistic. . . .The cost is that economic policy premised on [such] simple assumptions often leads to unintended – and dysfunctional – consequences (Bower 1983: 181).

Even economists began to recognize that the 'neoclassical formulation appears to beg all of the interesting questions' (North 1981: 5). A new institutional economics developed into a major school (Williamson 1975, 1985) that recognized and analyzed institutional forces, but largely as agents of efficiency (Granovetter 1985). However, it is not clear that efficiency is the sole, or even primary, goal of actors in markets, and sociologists have found that the key term, efficiency, is actually used in confusing and contradictory ways (Granovetter 1979; Obershall and Leifer 1986). Likewise, Eccles (1985) found that there is no technically neutral, universal criteria for determining price. This research implies that 'efficiency' and 'price' are socially constructed realities, as are measures of 'performance.' Meyer and Gupta (1994) have identified an ecological dynamic that produces successive cycles of performance measures. Thus, a sociological approach to health-care markets would investigate what terms like price, efficiency, and market mean to the parties involved. It would also investigate how people's relationships and networks affect economic behavior, how power is organized and manifested, how the state and political values frame markets and competition, and what roles institutions play in markets. What follows are just two examples of important work in the sociology of health-care markets.

Disability as a Business

The variability and indeterminancy of health care may be insurmountable sources of market failure, but to the entrepreneur they spell o-p-p-o-r-t-u-n-i-t-y, as Albrecht (1992) amply illustrates in his analysis of the organizational, cultural, and professional dimensions of making disability into a multibillion-dollar business. In an early study of agencies for the blind, Scott (1969) found that these agencies helped the blind but in ways that kept them dependent, and when they ran short of clients, they loosened the definition of 'blind,' thereby doubling their client pool. (At the right tail of a distribution, one does not have to loosen it much to double the area under the curve.) Scott called his book, *The Making of Blind Men*. Albrecht points out that definitions of 'disability' and coverages have also been expanding, that professionals and businessmen share common interests in the expansion, that profit margins are high, that hi-tech interventions predominate, and that large corporations are consolidating the market. Pharmaceutical firms, hospital chains, insurance companies, consulting companies, and managed care corporations are all developing products and programs around the realities and indeterminancies of disabilities. 'The focus of the programs was on providing a modicum of help to individuals who had specific diagnoses and were covered by insurance, not on returning every person with a disability to his or her highest level of functioning regardless of ability to pay or earn income' (Albrecht 1992: 223). For example, National Medical Enterprises, a major for-profit hospital chain, acquired the nation's second largest nursing home chain, then a respiratory home-care chain, then a respiratory equipment manufacturer, and then a rehabilitation services corporation, in order to become 'a major force in the rehabilitation marketplace . . .' (Albrecht 1992: 142). Now the

market has expanded to 'preventive rehabilitation.' 'Rehabilitation organizations further widen their service lines by lobbying for expanded government and private insurance benefits . . ., selling products irrespective of their benefits or risks to the consumer' (Albrecht 1992: 234-9).

Contracting for Health Care

Close observation of market behavior has been largely missing in most research on health services, often leaving the analyst of a large data set on services with little idea as to why a given pattern exists or changes. A revealing example of field research involved interviews and observations on how contracts actually got negotiated in the National Health Service in the mid-1990s (Hughes et al. 1997). Although the regulations imposed on contracting will differ from country to country, studies in economic sociology show that such rules embody values, notions about risk, obligations, and institutional relations that can be used to portray concretely how countries differ in their conceptualization of how the uncertainty, variability, and risk of health services should be addressed. This is an exciting area for future research. Such research can take inspiration from Zelizer's studies (1979, 1985, 1994) of how even babies get commodified and priced, and of how people construct special worlds around different kinds of money. Budgeting and the handling of monies reflect the changing dynamics of social ties, of attempts to control others, of inequalities, of dealing with risk, of managing group identities, of marking rites of passage, of managing conflicts of interest, and of managing clandestine or inadmissible relations (Zelizer 1994: 26).

Hughes and his team found, by sitting in on contract negotiations and interviewing participants in the context of the NHS, that 'prices' were calculated by mechanically dividing total activity in an area by historical cost, and that more than three-quarters of the contracts simply rolled the old pre-market budget forward, with adjustments for inflation and other changes. Thus, the 'market' and 'contracting' largely meant recasting historic administrative budgets in the language and rituals of the market.

Concerning risk, a good deal of contracting work went into bending the official rules about how competitive contracting should be done so that health-care institutions would not be disrupted by the major shifts in historic funding patterns that the rules implied, and so that costs would not go up (Hughes et al. 1997: 266–7; Hughes 1998, personal communication). Does this mean that the parties were betraying the government policy to compete and violating the basic purpose to transform the NHS from a welfare state to competing parties? On the contrary, it would seem, for the government wanted no political embarrassment or disruptions of service, even though its policy of competition pushed the system towards such moments. Thus, the contracting parties were saving the champions of competition from the consequences of their own policies.

Research on contracting in the NHS reveals other gaps between official language and reality. For example, district health authorities (DHAs) were required by the payer (the government) to show they were 'tough' about penalties for hospitals whose waiting lists got too long, and to show they were implementing centrally imposed targets on maximum waiting times, but hospital executives, knowing how little they could control waiting lists without a politically bruising confrontation with surgeons, refused to accept such penalties. Therefore, in five of the nine health authorities in which the research team carried out detailed field studies, the authorities agreed that the sidebar agreements would not in fact be imposed. With these assurances secured, hospital executives signed the official document that included a statement about imposing penalties if waiting list targets were exceeded. Likewise, lists of excluded treatments were written into contracts, but then the monthly statistics on procedures included no detailed breakdown of which treatments were being done by each specialty group, so that no one would know if excluded treatments were in fact performed. 'The significance of exclusion lists appeared to lie more in their presentational value as a public statement of DHA priorities than in the economic savings achieved' (Hughes et al. 1997: 270).

This analysis that the sociological reality of competitive contracting focused on how competitors tried to get along within a very tight budget is supported by the case of a health authority chair from the private sector who played hardball, competitive contracting by the rules. He used incentives, sanctions, and penalties, and built strict monitoring into his contracts. By the third year, the penalties imposed by this neoclassical paragon had become very high, acrimony prevailed, and the senior government office intervened. By the fourth year, 'none of the former executive directors remained in post,' including the chair. The authors concluded that contracting is more sociological and political than economic, like a Rorschach test onto which the various parties project their values, expectations, self-images, and relationships.

CONTRACTING FOR COMMUNITY HEALTH CARE

Other sociological dimensions of health-care markets are illuminated by a detailed field study of community health services (Flynn and Williams 1997). In further research on NHS contracting, Flynn et al. (1996) found that the heterogeneity, local boundedness, and indeterminacy of community health care 'presented fundamental problems for commissioning and contracting . . ., significantly influenced by their willingness to trust the other party in a whole range of circumstances' (Flynn et al. 1996: 136). The variability and uncertainty of services made them difficult to assess and thus required 'substantial amounts of trust in the professional discretion of providers,' but although contracting requires trust, competition and the process of contracting it entails and produces distrust that was not there in pre-market days when community health workers simply set about treating patients. Purchasers asked such questions as how were they to know if providers would do what they said they would? What evidence is there that their services make a difference? The more purchasers asked, the researchers found, the more it undermined the coordination and networking that community health services require. This leads to inefficiencies (because trust is very efficient) even if costs are lowered. A summary of European strategies observes, 'It is entirely possible for cost-containment initiatives to lower total costs while at the same time giving rise to greater inefficiency' (Saltman and Figueras 1996: 15).

Competitive contracting, the researchers found, is exacerbated by other problems as well. Some of the problems stem from the segmented budgets and organization of the NHS and could be overcome through integrated contracting and services (Light 1998a). Many stem from professional rivalries and cultures involved in community or mental health services. While such services may be among the more variable and vague kinds of health care, they highlight practical problems and the negotiated nature of defining products, setting prices, and dealing with risk in all health-care markets.

To conclude, these kinds of study provide valuable evidence of the sociological character of health care that is needed to complement the abstract and often misleading models of neoclassical economic theory. The profound changes in professional power and behavior involved mean that much of the classic research in medical sociology needs to be redone. At both the micro- and macrolevels, market behavior in health care is a fertile area for research and theoretical insight for economic sociology that can particularly benefit from comparative studies.

NOTES

1 Rice (1998), in a major new book that shows why competition does not work well in health care, unpacks this tightly phrased sentence into five further stipulations of neoclassical theory that are worth spelling out. Consumers must know their preferences and they must be predetermined. Consumers must be the best judge of their own welfare, reveal their preferences through their actions, and know with certainty the results of their decisions (so that their rational maximizing of their preferences is realized by their decisions).

2 HMO stands for 'health maintenance organization.' It refers to what was more accurately called for years a 'prepaid group health plan,' in which a group of clinicians and administrators provide for all medical services needed by subscribers, who would pay a fixed annual subscription. This is known as 'capitation,' a given rate per head, or capita. Note that HMOs combine two functions, a finance-insurance function and a health services function. In recent years these two functions have been split, so that a so-called HMO may be no more than a middleman, an executive suite that takes in subscriptions and writes contracts with external groups of providers. When those contracts are also at fixed rates, so that all the risk gets passed on to the providers, it is no longer clear what such an HMO is but a market maker and money maker.

REFERENCES

Abbott, A. (1988) *The System of Professions*. Chicago: University of Chicago Press.

Abel, A.B. and Bernanke, B.S. (1993) *Macroeconomics* (2nd edn). Reading, MA: Addison-Wesley.

Albrecht, G.L. (1992) *The Disability Business: Rehabilitation in America*. Newbury Park, CA: Sage.

Barr, D.A. (1995) 'The effects of organizational structure on primary care outcomes under managed care', *Annals of Internal Medicine*, 122: 353–9.

Begg, D., Fischer, S., and Dornbusch, R. (1987) *Economics* (2nd edn) London: McGraw-Hill.

Berk, M.L. and Monheit, A.C. (1992) 'The concentration of health expenditures: An update', *Health Affairs*, 11(4): 145–9.

Bower, J.L. (1983) *The Two Faces of Management*. Boston: Houghton Mifflin.

Brink, S. and Shute, N. (1997) 'Are HMOs the right prescription?' *US News and World Report*, (13 October): 60–74.

Bumiller, E. (1997) 'Life styles of rich and ailing: In luxury hospitals, high tea to fresh goat', *The New York Times*, (19 October): 37, 42.

Chernichovsky, D. (1995) 'Health system reforms in industrialized democracies: An emerging paradigm', *Milbank Quarterly*, 73: 339–72.

Dawson, D. (1995) *Regulating Competition in the NHS*. York: Centre for Health Economics, University of York.

Deppe, H.-U. and Oreskovic, S. (1996) 'Back to Europe: Back to Bismarck?' *International Journal of Health Services*, 26: 777–802.

Duckett, S.J. (1989) 'Regulating the construction of hospitals or visa versa', *Community Health Studies*, 13: 431–40.

Eccles, R.G. (1985) *The Transfer Pricing Problem: A Theory for Practice*. Lexington, MA: Lexington Books.

Eddy, D.M. (1998) 'Performance measurement: Problems and solutions', *Health Affairs*, 17(4): 7–25.

Enthoven, A.C. (1988) *Theory and Practice of Managed Competition in Health Care Finance*. Amsterdam: North-Holland.

Etzioni, A. (1988) *The Moral Dimension: Toward a New Economics*. New York: Free Press.

Evans, R.G. (1997) 'Going for the gold: The redistributive agenda behind market-based health care reform', *Journal of Health Politics, Policy and Law*, 22: 427–66.

Fligstein, N. (1985) 'The spread of the multidivisional form among large firms: 1919–1979', *American Sociological Review*, 50: 377–91.

Fligstein, N. (1990) *The Transformation of Corporate Control*. Cambridge, MA: Harvard University Press.

Flynn, R. and Williams, G. (eds) (1997) *Contracting for Health*. Oxford: Oxford University Press.

Flynn, R., Williams, G., and Pickard, S. (1996) *Markets and Networks: Contracting in Community Health Services*. Buckingham: Open University Press.

Freeman, V.A. and Reschovsky, J.D. (1997) 'Differences across payors in charges for agency-based home health services', *Health Services Research*, 32: 433–42.

Freidson, E. (1970a) *Profession of Medicine: A Study of the Sociology of Applied Knowledge*. New York: Dodd Mead.

Freidson, E. (1970b) *Professional Dominance: The Social Structure of Medical Care*. New York: Atherton.

Ginsberg, P. (1998) 'A perspective on health system change in 1997', in *Center for Studying Health System Change, Annual Report*. Washington, DC: Center. pp. 1–9.

Given, R.S. (1997) 'Ensuring competition in the market for HMO services', in J.D. Wilkerson, K.J. Devers, and T.S. Given (eds), *Competitive Managed Care*. San Francisco: Jossey-Bass. pp. 167–97.

Grannovetter, M. (1979) 'The idea of "advancement"

in theories of social evolution and development', *American Journal of Sociology*, 85: 489–515.

Grannovetter, M. (1985) 'Economic action and social structure: The problem of embeddedness', *American Journal of Sociology*, 91: 481–510.

Hacker, J.S. (1997) *The Road to Nowhere*. Princeton, NJ: Princeton University Press.

Hafferty, F.W. and Light, D.W. (1995) 'Professional dynamics and the changing nature of medical work', *Journal of Health and Social Behavior*, (extra issue): 132–53.

Hirsch, P., Michaels, S., and Friedman, R. (1990) 'Clean models vs. dirty hands: Why economics is different from sociology', in S. Zukin, and P. DiMaggio (eds), *Structures of Capital: The Social Organization of the Economy*. New York: Cambridge University Press. pp. 39–56.

Hirschman, A.O. (1970) *Exit, Voice and Loyalty*. Cambridge, MA: Harvard University Press.

Hollingsworth, J.R. and Boyer, R. (1997) *Contemporary Capitalism: The Embeddedness of Institutions*. Cambridge: Cambridge University Press.

Hsiao, W.C. (1994) 'Marketization – the illusory magic pill', *Health Economics*, 3: 351–7.

Hsiao, W.C. (1995) 'Medical savings accounts: Lessons from Singapore', *Health Affairs*, 14: 260–6.

Hughes, D., Griffiths, L., and McHale, J.V. (1997) 'Do quasi-markets evolve? Institutional analysis and the NHS', *Cambridge Journal of Economics*, 21: 259–76.

Lagnado, L. (1998) 'Personality change: Old line Aetna adopts managed care tactics and stirs up a backlash', *The Wall Street Journal*, 29 July: A1.

Lasker, R.D. (1997) *Medicine & Public Health: The Power of Collaboration*. New York: New York Academy of Medicine.

Light, D.W. (1986) 'Corporate medicine for profit', *Scientific American*, 225(6): 38–45.

Light, D.W. (1988) 'Turf battles and the theory of professional dominance', *Research in the Sociology of Health Care*, 7: 203–25.

Light, D.W. (1989) 'Towards a new sociology of medical education', *Journal of Health and Social Behavior*, 29: 307–22.

Light, D.W. (1995a) 'Countervailing powers: A framework for professions in transition', in T. Johnson, G. Larkin and M. Saks (eds), *Health Professions and the State in Europe*. London: Routledge. pp. 25–41.

Light, D.W. (1995b) '*Homo economicus*: Escaping the traps of managed competition', *European Journal of Public Health*, 5: 145–54.

Light, D.W. (1997) 'From managed competition to managed cooperation: Theory and lessons from the British experience', *Milbank Quarterly*, 75: 297–341.

Light, D.W. (1998a) *Effective Commissioning*. London: Office of Health Economics.

Light, D.W. (1998b) 'Keeping competition fair for health insurance – how the Irish beat back risk-rated policies', *American Journal of Public Health*, 88: 745–8.

Long, S.H. and Marquis, M.S. (1998) 'How widespread is managed competition?' *Health System Change Data Bulletin*. Washington, DC: Center for Studying Health System Change.

McCormick, K.A., Cummings, M.A., and Kovner, C. (1997) 'The role of the agency for health care policy and research in improving outcomes of care', *Outcomes Measurement and Management*, 32: 521–42.

Mechanic, D. (1998) 'Public trust and initiatives for new health care partnerships', *Milbank Quarterly*, 76: 281–302.

Meyer, M. and Gupta, V. (1994) 'The performance paradox', *Research in Organizational Behavior*, 16: 309–69.

Morgan, R.O., Virnig, B.A., DeVito, C.A., and Persely, N.A. (1997) 'The Medicare–HMO revolving door – the healthy go in and the sick go out', *New England Journal of Medicine*, 337: 169–75.

n.a. (no author) (1998a) 'Managed care challenges', *Health System Change Issue Brief*. Washington, DC: Center for Studying Health Systems Change.

n.a. (1998b) 'A tale of two cities: Hospital mergers in St. Louis and Philadelphia not reducing excess capacity', *Findings Brief*, 2 (2). Washington, DC: Health Care Financing and Organization.

North, D.C. (1981) *Structure and Change in Economic History*. New York: W.W. Norton

Obershall, A. and Leifer, E.M. (1986) 'Efficiency and social institutions: Uses and misuses of economic reasoning in sociology', *Annual Review of Sociology*, 12: 233–53.

O'Connor, J. (1973) *The Fiscal Crisis of the State*. New York: St. Martin's.

Offe, C. (1975) 'The theory of the capitalist state and the problem of policy formation', in L.N. Lindberg, R. Alford, C. Crouch, and C. Offe (eds), *Stress and Contradictions in Modern Capitalism*. Lexington, MA: Lexington Books. pp. 125–37.

Ormerod, P. (1994) *The Death of Economics*. New York: St Martins.

Pear, R. (1998) 'Americans lacking health insurance put at 16 percent', *The New York Times*, 26 September: A1.

Perrow, C. (1990) 'Economic theories of organizations', in S. Zukin and P. DiMaggio (eds), *Structures of Capital: The Social Organization of Economy*. New York: Cambridge University Press. pp. 121–52.

Reinhardt, U. (1996) 'A social contract for 21st century health care: Three-tier health care with bounty hunting', *Health Economics*, 5: 479–99.

Rice, T. (1997) 'Can market forces give us the health care system we want?' *Journal of Health Politics, Policy and Law*, 22: 383–426.

Rice, T. (1998) *The Economics of Health Reconsidered*. Chicago: Health Administration Press.

Robinson, J.C. and Casalino, L.P. (1995) 'The growth

of medical groups paid through capitation in California', *New England Journal of Medicine*, 333: 1684–7.

Robinson, J.C. and Casalino, L.P. (1996) 'Vertical integration and organizational networks in health care', *Health Affairs*, 15: 7–22.

Saltman, R. and Figueras, J. (1996) *European Health Care Reforms: Analysis of Current Strategies, Summary*. Copenhagen: World Health Organization, Regional Office for Europe.

Saltman, R. and von Otter, C. (1992) *Planned Markets and Public Competition*. Buckingham: Open University Press.

Scott, R.A. (1969) *The Making of Blind Men*. New York: Russell Sage.

Secretary of State for Health (1997) *The New NHS: Modern, Dependable*. London: HMSO.

Self, P. (1995) 'The consequences of reorganising government on market lines', *Australian Journal of Public Administration*, 54: 339–45.

Shearer, G. (1998) *Hidden from View: The Growing Burden of Health Care Costs*. Washington, DC: Consumers Union.

Sullivan, K. (1995) *Strangled Competition: A Critique of Minnesota's Experiment with Managed Competition*. St. Paul: COACT Educational Foundation.

Sullivan, K. (1997) *Strangled Competition. II. The Quality of Care under Managed Competition*. St. Paul: COACT Educational Foundation.

Twaddle, A.C. (1999) *Health Care Reform in Sweden 1980–1994*. Westport, CN: Greenword.

US AID (1996) Agency Performance Report 1995. Washington, DC: USAID.

White, K. (1991) 'The sociology of health and illness', *Current Sociology*, 39(2): 1–115.

White, K. and Collyer, F. (1997) 'To market, to market: Corporatisation, privatisation, and hospital costs', *Australian Health Review*, 20(2): 13–25.

White, K. and Collyer, F. (1998) 'Health care markets in Australia: Ownership of the private hospital sector', *International Journal of Health Services*, 28: 487–510.

Williamson, O.E. (1975) *Markets and Hierarchies: Analysis and Antitrust Implications*. New York: Free Press.

Williamson, O.E. (1985) *The Economic Institutions of Capitalism*. New York: Free Press.

Winslow, R. (1998) 'Health-care inflation revives in Minneapolis despite cost-cutting: Failure of efforts to change actual medical practices gets much of the blame', *The Wall Street Journal*, 19 May: A1, A15.

Zelizer, V.A. (1979) *Morals and Markets: The Development of Life Insurance in the United States*. New York: Columbia University Press.

Zelizer, V.A. (1985) *Pricing the Priceless Child*. New York: Basic Books.

Zelizer, V.A. (1994) *The Social Meaning of Money*. New York: Basic Books.

Zukin, S. and DiMaggio, P. (eds) (1990) *Structures of Capital: The Social Organization of the Economy*. New York: Cambridge University Press.

3.3

Medical Uncertainty Revisited

RENÉE C. FOX

INTRODUCTION

Uncertainty is inherent in medicine. Scientific, technological, and clinical advances change the content of medical uncertainty and alter its contours, but they do not drive it away. Furthermore, although medical progress dispels some uncertainties, it uncovers others that were not formerly recognized, and it may even create new areas of uncertainty that did not previously exist.

The theme of medical uncertainty pervades the medical literature. It is also a major motif in the medical sociological literature. In both contexts, uncertainty is not only regarded as a challenging and problematic constant, but also as a matter of serious concern because of the adverse ways it affects the work and role responsibilities of physicians and the fate of patients. Uncertainty complicates and curtails the ability of physicians to prevent, diagnose, and treat disease, illness, and injury, and to predict the evolution and outcome of patients' medical conditions and the results of the medical decisions and actions taken on their behalf. The implications are more than scientific and intellectual. Medical uncertainty raises emotionally and existentially charged questions about the meaningfulness as well as the efficacy of physicians' efforts to safeguard their patients' well-being, relieve their suffering, heal their ills, restore their health, and prolong their lives. It intersects with the risks and limitations and their accompanying ambiguities that medicine and its practice entail, and it evokes the inescapably tragic dimension of medicine: the fact that all patients – and all physicians as well – are mortal.

The primary goal of this chapter is to reconsider the forms of uncertainty that I have previously identified and analyzed (Fox 1957; Fox 1980) in light of the pertinent medical, social, and cultural developments that have occurred during the 1980s and 1990s. My empirical referents are drawn mainly from American milieux.

PREVIOUS SOCIOLOGICAL DISCUSSIONS OF MEDICAL UNCERTAINTY

It was Talcott Parsons who first made medical uncertainty amenable to sociological analysis (Parsons 1951: 428–70). He emphasized 'the great importance of . . . the element of uncertainty' in the role of the physician and 'the situation of medical practice.' He identified some of the sources and forms of medical uncertainty, and he linked them to the 'factors of known [and unknown] impossibility' and the 'limits of control' that physicians continually encounter. 'The remarkable advances of medicine,' he observed, have 'by no means eliminated' these components of medicine from its scientific matrix or its clinical application. Rather, in significant ways, they have 'increased awareness of the vast amount of human ignorance' about health and illness that still exists. This seeming paradox is not unique to medicine, Parsons recognized; it is a generic characteristic of scientific progress. However, what makes medicine special in this and in other regards, he stated, are the distinctive features of medical work: the fact that health, illness, and medicine are associated with basic and intimate aspects of the human body, psyche, and story, and with transcendent and ultimate aspects of the human life cycle, with the privileged and penetrating access to patients' bodies and their private lives that physicians are accorded as part of their work, and with the role that physicians play both in fending off, and in pronouncing, the death of patients. These attributes of physicians' responsibilities, Parsons contended, and 'the magnitude and character' of what they entail augment the meaning and enhance the stress of the medical uncertainties and impossibilities that they face. Invoking anthropologist Bronislaw Malinowski's insights, Parsons pointed out that the 'combination of uncertainty and [the physician's] strong emotional interests' in successfully diagnosing and treating the patient's condition are conducive to magical modes of thought and action. The scientific tradition of modern medicine may 'preclude outright magic,' he went on to say, but the medically 'ritualized optimism' and the 'bias in favor of active intervention' with which many physicians (especially American physicians) are inclined to respond in these conditions contain elements within them that are covertly and functionally magical.

Parsons's perspective on medical uncertainty has had an enduring influence on how sociologists have dealt with this phenomenon in their research and writing. It has been a central source of my own sustained interest in medical uncertainty, my outlook on it, and my first-hand studies of its presence and implications in a variety of medical contexts. These contexts have included a metabolic research ward (Fox 1959), a number of medical schools (Fox 1957, 1978a, 1978b, 1978c, 1989a; Lief and Fox 1963), an array of medical research settings (especially those where patient-oriented clinical research is being conducted) in Belgium, as well as in the United States (Blumberg and Fox 1985; Fox 1959, 1962, 1964, 1976, 1978d, 1996a; Swazey and Fox 1970), and a wide cross section of American and continental European medical centers in which organ transplantation, the artificial kidney, and various models of an artificial heart have been pioneered, developed, and deployed (Fox and Swazey 1974, 1992). My research has consistently focused on the social, cultural, emotional, and moral and spiritual meaning of medical uncertainty for physicians and patients, and on their collective ways of responding to it.

My essay on the 'training for uncertainty' of medical students, published in 1957, appears to have captured and conceptualized a quintessence of becoming a physician. In spite of all the changes in medical knowledge and the reforms in medical school curricula that have occurred during the past four decades, medical students still give spontaneous testimony to the impor-tance of training for uncertainty in the professional education that they undergo. In their 1994 appraisal of the New Pathway curriculum of Harvard Medical School, for example, students affirmed that none of its achievements is 'more impressive . . . [than the] process of wrestling with uncertainty' – the way that it taught them that 'medicine is filled with uncertainty – indeed, that uncertainty rather than certainty tends to be the norm' (Silver 1994: 127–28).

There are three basic types of uncertainty around which the process of 'training for uncertainty' in medical school centers is based. These are the uncertainties that originate in the impossibility of commanding all the vast knowledge and complex skills of continually advancing modern medicine, the uncertainties that stem from the many gaps in medical knowledge and limitations in medical understanding and effectiveness that nonetheless exist, and the uncertainties connected with distinguishing between personal ignorance and ineptitude, and the lacunae and incapacities of the field of medicine itself. The neophyte status of medical students, I found, increases their awareness of these forms of uncertainty in knowledge. In the words of one student, discerning whether the uncertainty they encounter is 'their fault' or 'the fault of the field' is the problem, and the anxieties they experience in medical school are heightened by their anticipatory concern about its implications for how knowledgeably and competently they will be able to care for patients when they graduate into the role of physician, with the responsibilities of clinical practice.

The uncertainty that medical students encounter is not confined to the intellectual, scientific, and technical dimensions of medicine. In the contexts of dissecting a cadaver in the anatomy laboratory, participating in autopsies, assisting at births, and through their contacts with sick children, patients in pain, and those who are terminally ill (among others), students come face to face with what might be termed existential uncertainty. In other words, they are faced with critical problems of meaning, and 'ponderably imponderable' questions about the 'whys' and the mysteries of life and death that are at once integral to medicine and that transcend it.

The collective modes of coming to terms with the multiple uncertainties of medicine that I have watched medical students develop are harbingers of some of the key ways in which many physicians handle uncertainty (Fox 1978c). These include those listed below.

- A process of intellectualization that entails achieving as much cognitive command of the situation as possible through the acquisition of greater knowledge and skill, and increasing mastery of the probability-based logic with which medicine approaches the uncertainties of diagnosis, therapy, and prognosis, and of the clinical judgment that lies at their heart. To a degree, it also involves defining and operationalizing medical problems in strict, scientific terms that siphon off some of their affectivity and reduce some of their complexity.

- The attainment of a more detached kind of concern about uncertainty (Lief and Fox 1963) by muting awareness of its constant presence in medical work, pushing strong feelings about the most emotionally evocative issues it raises below the surface of consciousness not displaying uncertainty, and shrouding it in silence. This complex of responses to uncertainty is influenced and structured by the professional socialization process that medical students undergo. This socialization process consists mainly of the largely latent 'messages' they receive from their teachers and that they reinforce in one another about what medically capable and emotionally mature physicians ought and ought not to admit, exhibit, and discuss with colleagues and with patients.

- The employment of a special genre of medical humor – counterphobic and ironic, infused with bravado and self-mockery, often impious and macabre – that is centered on the uncertainties and limitations of medical knowledge, medical errors, the side effects of medical and surgical interventions, the failure to cure, and death. Ostensibly, the capacity to joke about medical uncertainty in its various guises indicates an attitude of relative ease with its presence. On closer inspection, however, the tightly patterned character of this joking, the fact that it resembles what Sigmund Freud called 'gallows humor' and also front-lines-of-the-battlefield trench humor, and the difficulties that many students and physicians experience in talking *seriously* about medical uncertainty, all suggest that this humor is far from nonchalant. Rather, it seems to be impelled and shaped by a considerable amount of dissembled stress.

Building on my work, sociologist Donald Light set out to discover what kinds of uncertainty newly graduated physicians encounter after their medical school years, and how they deal with the quandaries that these uncertainties present. In the context of his first-hand study of the education and socialization of psychiatrists during their residency training, Light identified a cluster of clinical uncertainties surrounding diagnosis, treatment, and patient responses that cross-cut the uncertainties of knowledge I

delineated (Light 1980). He found that the need of these young physicians to control uncertainty grew as their clinical responsibilities increased, so that progressively, 'training for uncertainty [became] training for control' (Light 1979: 320). He identified two characteristic ways that physicians gained control over their work: through the assertion and exercise of 'individual clinical judgements' based on their personal experience; and by 'acquiring a treatment philosophy' premised on the espousal of a particular 'paradigm' or 'approach.' In adopting these means, Light cautioned, physicians '[ran] the danger of gaining too much control over the uncertainties of their work by becoming insensitive to the complexities of diagnosis, treatment, and client relationships.'

Like Donald Light (on whose writings he drew), psychiatrist Jay Katz contends that some of the mechanisms for coping with uncertainty that physicians learn during their medical school and postgraduate years make it possible for them to 'disregard' uncertainty in clinical situations (Katz 1984). In his view, 'once one leaves the arena of laboratory and clinical experimentation, there is little evidence that physicians ... consciously take uncertainty into account either in their self-reflections or in their interactions with patients.' Their tendency to 'avoid' uncertainty, he alleges, is buttressed by the profession's demand for 'conformity and orthodoxy,' and by specialization that 'narrows diagnostic vision,' and 'fosters belief in the superior effectiveness of treatments prescribed by one's [field]' (Katz 1984: 165–206).

Katz and Light, along with sociologist Paul Atkinson, assert that issues of certainty and uncertainty are intricately entwined (Atkinson 1984: 954). Most importantly, they emphasize how the 'training for uncertainty' trajectory can insulate physicians from medical uncertainty in ways that make them less able to acknowledge it. Thus, an unanticipated and unintended outcome of their professional socialization is that it may inadvertently lead to 'training for certainty,' and beyond that, to 'training for *over*-certainty.'

The article on 'The evolution of medical uncertainty' (Fox 1980) began with a microdynamic account of the cumulative insights that my research on uncertainty in various medical settings had yielded over the course of some 30 years. This provided the background from which I ventured a more macroscopic set of observations and reflections on what appeared to be the growing attention and significance that issues of medical uncertainty were being accorded on the larger American scene.

From the vantage point of a continuous medical uncertainty watcher, I had the impression that a more pervasive societal interest in this phenomenon, and greater professional and public concern about its concomitants and consequences, had been developing throughout the 1960s and 1970s. Health, illness, and medicine seemed to have become foci of heightened anxiety about uncertainty and amplified awareness of it – centering on known and unknown risks, hazards, errors, limitations, and harm that such medical uncertainty could engender. By the end of the 1970s, medical intellectuals as astutely perceptive as physician–essayist Lewis Thomas and Nobel Laureate in Medicine André Cournand were taking note of what they each regarded as this at once notable and perplexing American malaise:

As a people, we have become obsessed with Health. . . . We have lost all confidence in the human body. The new consensus is that we are badly designed, intrinsically fallible, vulnerable to a host of hostile influences inside and around us, and only precariously alive. . . . The new danger to our well-being . . . is in becoming a nation of health hypochondriacs, living gingerly, worrying ourselves half to death. . . . (Thomas 1979: 47–50)

The American public is being swept by a medical epidemic characterized by doubt of certitude, recognition of error, and discovery of hazard. (Cournand 1977: 700)

The expanding professional and public interest in medical uncertainty, and the apprehension that accompanied it, were concentrated both on the human diseases that still elude scientific understanding and clinical control – especially cancer – despite all the medical progress that has been made in the course of the century and despite the potentially dangerous and noxious side effects that advances in the diagnosis, treatment, and prevention of disease and illness have brought in their wake. In addition, research with recombinant DNA (the compound deoxyribonucleic acid) had triggered great worry in the scientific community as well as among the lay public about the 'unexpectedly bad consequences' that this new technology might have for human health and well-being, for example, 'through the creation of new types of organisms never yet subjected to the pressures of evolution and which might have disease-causing potentialities that we do not now have to face' (Watson 1976: 3).

These forms of medical uncertainty had metamedical implications. Cancer was not only portrayed as a set of malignant diseases with which biology and medicine were still unable to deal knowledgeably and effectively, but also as one of the most pernicious and lethal types of suffering to which human beings are subject. The con-

troversy that erupted over DNA technology brought forth feelings of dread over the dangers – even the monsters – that the dawning capacity of humankind to intervene in the evolution of all forms of life on this planet, including and especially its own, might produce. Indignation over the continuing inability of modern medicine to deal with unsolved problems of health and illness coexisted with anxiety about the medical 'hubris' and the 'nemesis'-borne side effects of biomedical attempts to master these problems (Illich 1976). This highly ambivalent outlook was suggestive of a more diffuse societal 'uncertainty about uncertainty,' as if we were culturally unsure about how to approach the kinds of medical uncertainty now before us.

During the two decades that have ensued since 'The evolution of medical uncertainty' (1980), some of the developments that have occurred in medical science and technology, in the practice of medicine, and in the social and cultural conditions surrounding them, have contributed to the appearance of new elements of medical uncertainty. Many of these, however, were foreshadowed by previous manifestations of uncertainty, and all of them are compatible with the uncertainties in medical knowledge that were identified in the original 'Training for uncertainty' essay.

By and large, the new forms of uncertainty that have come into view in the past 20 years have not been extensively described or analyzed by social scientists. Therefore, they will be considered here largely through the medium of scientific and medical literature, and the insights that sociological reflection on that literature yields.

UNCERTAINTY, 'MEDICINE AND MOLECULES'

To begin with, some of the major advances in medicine have done more than produce knowledge and techniques that further enlarge the enormous amount that physicians were already called upon to learn. Cumulatively, they have also resulted in basic changes in some of the underlying assumptions and modes of thought of present-day medicine. Foremost among these are the transformations in the cognitive framework of modern medicine that have occurred since 1953, when Francis Crick and James Watson published articles in which they announced their discovery of the self-complementary, double helix structure of DNA and their hypothesis of 'a possible copying mechanism for the genetic material' (Watson and Crick 1953a, 1953b). This discovery, and Watson and Crick's subsequent work that showed the way toward analysis of the genetic code and understanding of how genetic material directs the synthesis of proteins, ushered in the so-called 'biological revolution' in which the 'new' molecular and cell biology, with its genetic focus, became ascendant. A veritable explosion of information and knowledge has been unleashed, epitomized by the Human Genome Project, a massive, international scientific program to achieve nothing less than mapping and sequencing all the genes in the human body and the noncoding regions of all the DNA contained in the human genes as well.

The nature of this knowledge, however, is highly reductionistic. It disaggregates biological systems by breaking them into smaller and smaller parts. As sociologist Howard Kaye states in his analysis of 'the social meaning of modern biology,' it concentrates attention on genes rather than on individual organisms (Kaye 1986). Medical educators like Daniel Tosteson (the former Dean of Harvard Medical School) point out that there is an unfulfilled need for a conceptual framework within which this kind of micro-knowledge can be synthesized, integrated, and made pertinent to the organismic, pathophysiogical level of clinical medicine. A unifying system does not yet exist, he maintains, that would enable physicians 'to think about their patients in ways that permit appropriate access to molecular detail when such knowledge is crucial for diagnostic, preventive, or therapeutic action, without the burden of such a ponderous accumulation of facts that it will impede analysis and decision' (Tosteson and Goldman 1994: 175).

In this respect, the intellectual gap that exists between 'medicine and molecules'[1] constitutes a paradigmatic source of medical uncertainty and limitation, despite the regnant conviction that the new molecular knowledge will soon transform the practice of medicine by illuminating the etiology and mechanisms of human diseases and providing the basis for more potent and rational therapies. For example, at this stage in the development of somatic gene therapy, 'clinical efficacy in human patients has [still] not been definitively demonstrated,' or even 'clearly established in any gene therapy protocol' (Orkin and Motulsky 1995, non-paginated text). However, as of June 1995, more than 100 clinical protocols involving gene therapy had already been approved and initiated by the US National Institutes of Health (NIH) Recombinant Advisory Committee. Some 597 human subjects had undergone gene transfer experiments under these auspices, approximately $2 million per year for this research was being provided by NIH, and

a larger amount of funding was forthcoming from industrial sources. According to a committee appointed by the Director of NIH, Harold Varmus, to assess the current status and promise of gene therapy, this lack of clinical efficacy in human patients is due to major difficulties in current gene transfer vectors, and in understanding their biological reaction with the host on the one hand, to the inadequacy of attention that has been accorded to studies of disease pathophysiology on the other, and to the challenging problem of bridging the two 'at the interface of frontier science and patient care':

> As the field of gene therapy expands [the committee's report stated], the need for appropriately trained personnel, including basic scientists with familiarity of disease pathophysiology and medical scientists and physicians with an appreciation of the complex basic science issues will become even greater. (Orkin and Motulsky 1995)

The persistence of conceptual, basic scientific, technical, and clinical bases of medical uncertainty notwithstanding, the atmosphere that pervades the field of molecular biology tends to be so exuberant, that the authors of the NIH report on gene therapy believed it important to make the following admonitory observations:

> Expectations of current gene therapy protocols have been oversold. Overzealous representation of gene therapy has obscured the exploratory nature of initial studies, colored the manner in which the findings are portrayed to the scientific press and public and led to the widely held, but mistaken perception that clinical gene therapy is already highly successful . . . We cannot predict when the benefits of gene therapy will be realized. (Orkin and Motulsky 1995)

Nor is such unbridled optimism and certitude confined to the realm of gene therapy. It was conspicuously present, for example, at the workshop on xenotransplantation (animal-to-human organ transplantation) held by the US Institute of Medicine on 17 July 1996 (Fox 1996b: 9–11; Institute of Medicine 1996). The molecular and cell biologists present, and also some of the immunologists, were so enthusiastic about the experiments they were conducting in the laboratory with xenografts of certain animal-to-animal cells and tissues that they were inclined to overestimate the degree of control that currently exists with regard to the transplantation of solid, human-to-human organs, and to underplay the even more vigorous rejection reaction that whole organ grafts between phylogenetically distant species are likely to elicit. Rather ironically, they were more prone to imply that enough is now known to make animal-to-human transplants clinically feasible than the several transplant surgeons participating in the work-shop who had done pioneering clinical trials with baboon to human transplants.

What 'best characterizes molecular biology,' Howard Kaye states, is its 'aggressive, simplify-ing, reductionist approach, . . . attitude, [and] research strategy,' and beyond that, its 'world view,' articulated by its founding practitioners and leading theorists. In this 'aggressively reduc-tionistic' and 'deterministic' perspective, 'culture is reduced to biology; biology, to the laws of physics and chemistry at the molecular level; mind, to matter; behavior, to genes; organism, to program; the origin of species, to macromo-lecules; life, to reproduction' (Kaye 1986: 55–7). Although it is powerfully and brilliantly genera-tive of new biological knowledge, it is also an outlook that greatly simplifies the complexity of the phenomena it observes and analyzes. This attribute accounts in part for the tendency toward hyper-certainty that is visible in newly developing and still experimental areas, such as gene therapy and xenotransplantation, where molecular biology and genetics play a pivotal role. Historians of medicine and science Robert L. Martensen and David S. Jones remind us that, in addition, the fact that '[n]owadays many physicians and researchers believe that "molecular medicine" will satisfy the yearning for medicine to be an "exact science" is part of a much older process of 'searching for medical certainty' ' (Martensen and Jones 1997).

UNCERTAINTY AND THE 'EMERGENCE' AND 'REEMERGENCE' OF INFECTIOUS DISEASES

A second change in the cognitive base of con-temporary medicine that has opened up new areas of uncertainty, and reopened old ones, is related to what is called in the medical literature, 'the emergence and reemergence of infectious diseases.' These terms refer to diseases that have 'newly appeared in the population, or are rapidly expanding their range,' those that are 'already widespread but, while not new in the human population, are newly recognized,' and to the resurgence of old scourges in new, more severe forms (Morse 1993: 10–11). The patho-genic microbes are often viruses, but bacteria and parasites are also involved in these out-breaks of infections. The spectrum of 'new' and 'old' diseases that they cause range from HIV/AIDS, Ebola hemorrhagic fever, Legionnaire's disease, Lyme disease, and bovine spongiform encephalopathy ('mad cow' disease), to cholera, dengue, yellow fever, and tuberculo-sis, among many others.

To a sobering degree, the occurrence of infec-tious diseases and their spread are precipitated by human conditions and behavior, for example, by changes in patterns of agriculture and irriga-tion, massive rural-to-urban population move-ment, increasing population density in cities, global travel and trade, immigration, warfare, refugee migration and internment, economic crises, political upheavals, famine, poverty, and homelessness. Even more humbling, as historian William McNeill points out, is the fact that our human attempts to 'make things the way we want them, and, by skill, organization and knowledge, to insulate ourselves from local and frequent disasters . . . change natural ecological relationships.' In turn, this creates 'new situa-tions that become unstable . . . [and] new vul-nerabili[ties] to some larger disaster' (McNeill 1993: 5–6). Such ecosystem disruptions are as true of medical interventions as of other forms of supposedly ameliorative action. An important and threatening example of this phenomenon is the fact that microbes, such as certain strains of *Staphyloccus aureus*, *Streptococcus pneumoniae*, *Myobacterium tuberculosis*, and *Neisseria gonor-rhea*, have become resistant to a substantial pro-portion of antibiotic drugs considered first-line treatments, partly because they have been exten-sively, often excessively, used in humans and also 'in veterinary medicine, animal husbandry, agriculture, and aquaculture' (Tenoyer and Hughes 1996: 303).

At this historical juncture, most medical and public health professionals have distanced them-selves from the previous certainty (voiced as recently as 1969, by the then US Surgeon General) that 'western scientific medicine can [and/or has] overcome pathogenic agents' (Porter 1998: 491–2). They are poised some-where between a reawakened realization that 'the more we drive infections to the margins of human experience, the wider we open a door for a new catastrophic infection' (McNeill 1993: 36), and the determined conviction that 'because we now understand many of the factors leading to [emerging diseases] . . . we should be in a posi-tion to circumvent [them] at fairly early stages, [through] [s]ophisticated surveillance with clini-cal, diagnostic, and epidemiological components on an international scale' (Morse 1993: 26).

UNCERTAINTY AND PROGNOSIS[2] (CHRISTAKIS 1995, 1999)

Still another conceptual shift occurring in pres-ent-day medicine is the increasing importance that medical prognosis has assumed – a development that has accentuated problems of uncertainty often faced by physicians when they are called upon to make explicit predictions about the outcome of a patient's illness or state. Physician–sociologist Nicholas A. Christakis has shown that 'diagnosis and therapy [have always received] more attention than prognosis in patient care, medical research, and medical education.' In his view, this is partly a consequence of 'the contemporary dominance of an ontological [conception] of disease . . . in which disease is seen as generic and generally independent of its expression in an individual':

> Making a diagnosis has become the central concern of the clinical encounter because prognosis and therapy are seen to follow necessarily and directly from it. The ontological perspective is further reinforced when an effective therapy for a disease exists because effective therapy further narrows the range of possible outcomes a disease might have. Once a diagnosis is made and effective therapy is initiated, the clinical course of a disease is presumed to be relatively fixed, non-individualistic, and standardized. (Christakis 1999)

Even if a patient has a condition that is generally amenable to existing therapy, this does not inevitably mean that his/her medical history will unfold in the usual way, or result in a favorable outcome. Explicit prognostication becomes both more difficult and more necessary in such instances. Although it may be a means of gaining some degree of control over the unfolding clinical situation, prognosticating under these circumstances is likely to be threatening both to the physician and the patient, because it reveals not only medical uncertainty and limitation, but also medical fallibility.

Prognosis comes into special prominence, too, when a patient is facing imminent death in spite of all the means of remedying illness and prolonging life that modern medicine and its practitioners command. Predicting whether a patient will soon die, when, and how, and conveying this information with discernment to the patient and family is one of the physician's most solemn obligations. It is also a way of structuring and managing a situation that challenges the physician's mastery, and that evokes the mortality that he ultimately shares with all patients.

'A close study of physician attitudes and behavior reveals a *dread* of prognostication [Nicholas Christakis writes] – whether accurate or inaccurate . . . favorable or unfavorable. Physicians would rather not formulate or discuss prognosis' (Christakis 1999). This is because they associate prognosis with the limits of their diagnostic and therapeutic powers, and with the grave illnesses and impending deaths of patients. In addition, Christakis has discovered, they have a shared inclination to believe that any negative predictions they make about patients' conditions and their outcomes may have 'self-fulfilling prophecy' effects, whether or not they communicate their somber expectations to patients. For these reasons, physicians not only have a tendency to skew prognosis-setting in a positive, optimistic direction, but also to play down, and if possible avoid, medical forecasting.

Their apprehension notwithstanding, current and pending developments in medical science and technology, and in the social settings in which medicine is practiced, are making overt prognostication more important and more difficult for physicians to eschew than in the past. Christakis has identified a number of such developments. First and foremost, he contends, is the increasing prevalence of chronic disease, in which the diagnosis is already known. Another development is that therapy mainly entails the continuation of previously initiated interventions. In addition, the chief clinical encounters and challenges entail anticipating, forestalling, and mitigating adverse new events stemming from the disease itself, or from cumulative side effects of what is being done to treat it.

The invention and utilization of new forms of medical technology, Christakis avers, is another set of factors contributing to the growing relevance of prognosis. Notable among these are genetic testing methods that can reveal whether an asymptomatic person will or will not develop a genetically based disease such as Huntington's chorea or, through the analysis of both an individual's genes and those of her spouse, testing that can yield a probabilistic prediction about the chances of the couple giving birth to a baby with particular, genetically borne disorders. The emergence of novel reproductive technologies such as prenatal ultrasound and amniocentesis provides information about a pregnancy and the condition and development of the fetus that have postnatal import. As more technologies are invented that either directly or indirectly produce prognostic data, physicians will be under greater pressure to make clinical predictions. In turn, they will be confronted with added problems of uncertainty and limitation, such as what to tell the parents about the future clinical course of a baby diagnosed *in utero* with polycystic kidney disease, or what to offer a person certain to develop in midlife a fatal, degenerative neurological disease such as Huntington's chorea for which no therapy exists.

What Christakis terms 'the increasingly bureaucratic structure of American medical practice' is also focusing more attention on prognostic judgements. In the wake of the accelerating growth of managed care, an expanding percentage of US physicians are becoming salaried employees in large, formal medical organizations. In these milieux, where physicians' practice styles and behavior are reviewed and regulated by others (physician and nonphysician), cost containment, the economic allocation of scarce resources, and efficacy are likely to be emphasized. Within the framework of these structures and norms, physicians are being asked to base clinical decisions, such as the timing of hospitalization, the duration of hospital stay, and the referral of patients for terminal hospice care, on prognostic assessments of the course of the illnesses involved.

Finally, the intensifying interest in ethical (or so-called bioethical) parameters of medical care, and the concern about them that have gained momentum in public as well as professional arenas of American life since the early 1970s, have played a role in accentuating the importance of prognosis. For example, the greater insistence on the ethical imperative of informed, voluntary consent from patients for the diagnostic and therapeutic measures they undergo not only entails explaining to them what these interventions are, but also telling them what they are expected to accomplish and what risks and negative side effects may be involved.

End-of-life medical care is another important area of bioethical deliberation to which prognosis is integral for physicians, patients, and their families. It profoundly affects the tone and the content of the discussion they have with one another about such care, and the decisions that are made about whether to initiate, forego, or terminate the life-sustaining treatment of patients who are critically ill. Making the kinds of forecasts about suffering and pain, and about the quality of life and of death, that this implies carries all the participants in such decisions beyond medicine and into the realm of questions of meaning and of spiritual beliefs and uncertainties.

Uncertainty and the Irony of Iatrogenesis: Side Effects and Error

As the foregoing discussions of prognosis, emerging infectious diseases, and the advent of molecular biology suggest, a continual source of medical uncertainty is the unwanted, sometimes predictable, and frequently unpredictable, side effects of the technology, procedures, and drugs that physicians use to diagnose and treat patients' disorders. Throughout the history of medicine, the actions that physicians have taken on behalf of their patients have always had a mixture of beneficial and harmful consequences. Paradoxically, the impressive advances of modern medicine have in certain ways augmented its iatrogenically induced adverse effects on patients. As the modes of diagnosing and treating disease and illness have become more powerful and efficacious, they have also grown more dangerous, exposing patients to more potential risk, suffering, and harm through their anticipated and unanticipated negative consequences.

The current armamentaria of cancer treatments, for instance, consist of surgical procedures, radiotherapy, and chemotherapy regimens that, however meliorative or curative, are highly invasive, in some cases mutilating, causing physically and psychologically painful symptoms such as fever, infection, anemia, severe fatigue, hair loss, incontinence, impotence, and premature menopause. To cite another instance, the skilled use of various combinations of highly active, antiretroviral drugs, including protease inhibitors, has recently brought about what appears to be a dramatic improvement in the symptoms, daily round, and life span of persons infected with HIV. However, these drug 'cocktails' are so 'expensive and complex, with [such] high pill burdens, numerous adverse effects . . . myriad drug interactions,' and oppressive 'quality of life issues,' that many recipients of the battery of drugs find it difficult to adhere to the regimen necessary for optimal results (Cohen and Fauci 1998: 87). This can cause the HIV virus to mutate into drug-resistant strains, with grave consequences for the patients taking the drug, and in the long run, public health.

Furthermore, whether the drugs are intended for therapy for HIV/AIDS, cancer, or other disease conditions, in spite of all the pharmacological progress that has been made, no satisfactorily encompassing, overall theory of drug action has as yet been developed. This makes it difficult for physicians to foretell how favorable and/or unfavorable an individual patient's responses to particular drugs will be, and to apprise the patient of possible adverse reactions without unduly alarming him or contributing to the occurrence of negative, placebo-like effects.

There is nothing new in medicine about error causing serious injurious consequences, but the increasingly hazardous and intricate character of the instrumentalities that present-day medicine deploys enhances the potential seriousness of the errors that take place. Pediatric cardiac surgeon Marc de Laval depicts the 'high technology' area of medicine in which he works, for example, as 'a complex socio-technical system,' that 'shares many similarities with high hazard enterprises, such as the aviation industry, nuclear power plants, marine and railroad transportation, chemical plants and the like' (de Laval 1996). Using psychologist James Reason's conceptual framework for examining human errors that occur in high-risk systems (Reason 1990), de Laval identifies and analyzes examples of the kinds of error that he has observed or experienced in his own practice. He terms these as active or latent failures: skill-rule-, and knowledge-based mistakes; accidents that may result from 'the combination of high operational hazards (an intramural coronary artery) and human fallibility'; those that emanate from the ever-increasing amount of 'hardware' utilized in high-technology medicine (such as 'diagnostic equipment, anesthetic equipment, perfusion equipment, monitoring equipment, drug delivery systems, [and] cardiomechanical assistance devices'); those that happen at the 'interface' between 'hardware' and what he calls 'liveware.' 'A few months ago, during a repair of tetralogy of Fallot,' de Laval writes illustratively:

> there was a power cut in central London. The hospital generator went on and activated two pumps of the extracorporeal circuit but failed to activate the main head pump. The perfusionist immediately noticed the technical failure and used the handle to activate the pump manually. Unfortunately, he turned it clockwise instead of anticlockwise, and air traveled into the arterial line. This is a good example of technical failure, human error at the hardware/liveware interface, but also a latent failure arising from the company that made the hardware, which should have been equipped with a device preventing such an accidental happening. (de Laval 1996)

He also describes personal examples wherein the physical, administrative, financial, social structural, interpersonal, or cultural 'environment' in which he and his colleagues work can affect surgical performance (its excellence and fallibility) and surgical outcomes, including the way in which errors are dealt with when they occur (de Laval 1996; de Laval et al. 1994).

de Laval is one of a number of physicians who has become sufficiently interested in medical and surgical error, and concerned about it, to try to study its origins, dynamics, and consequences. One of their common conclusions is that if doctors were more open about their fallibility – more able to discuss mistakes both with colleagues and with patients – they would not only be relieved of some of 'the burden of perfection,' and its isolating anguish, they might also be able to establish better communication with patients – especially with regard to their complaints, matters of medical uncertainty, and the

conveying of 'bad news' – and feel more willing to avail themselves of opportunities for improving their knowledge, skill, and performance. Thus, greater physician openness about errors could lead to a reduction in their frequency and in the incidence of malpractice suits as well (Christensen et al. 1992; Levinson et al. 1997; Royal College of Physicians of London 1997).

Uncertainty and Individually Focused versus Collectivity-Oriented Medicine

Reconciling and integrating the one-on-one, doctor–patient relationship of clinical medicine with population-based reasoning and action is a long-standing cognitive problem in modern medicine, fraught with uncertainty, that also evokes strong sentiments about physicians' role responsibilities and value commitments. Although the tensions between these two orientations and modalities of thought are not new, they have been increased by a number of converging factors that include the emergence and reemergence of infectious diseases and the persistent, even mounting, epidemiological tendency of chronic diseases to take their greatest toll on the health and life expectancy of persons in the lowest and poorest strata of advanced modern societies like the United States and the United Kingdom. Other factors include the growing importance of managed care organizations in the United States, and their enrolled patient populations, and the burgeoning emphasis on practicing what is termed 'evidence-based medicine,' with interventions and outcomes that are clinically appropriate, efficacious, and cost-effective. Each of these developments invites a more aggregate-based, collectivity-oriented perspective than is usually characteristic of the individually focused physician–patient dyad of clinical practice. This raises difficult methodological, attitudinal, and professional questions about how the two approaches, and their implications for the handling of medical uncertainty, can be reconciled.

For example, according to what might be called its official definition, 'the practice of evidence-based medicine means integrating individual clinical expertise with the best available external clinical evidence,' derived from the basic sciences of medicine, and from patient-centered clinical research conducted via large, randomized, controlled clinical trials, or from the systematic review (including meta-analysis) of a number of smaller, more disparate published clinical studies (Sackett et al. 1997: 2). David Sackett, one of its founding fathers and chief codifiers, and his co-authors declare that, 'Evidence-based medicine is not "cook-book" medicine. Because it requires a bottom-up approach that integrates the best external evidence and patient choice, it cannot result in slavish cookbook approaches to individual patient care' (Sackett et al. 1997: 3–4).

However, there are numerous thoughtful British and American physicians and some social scientists of medicine who regard evidence-based medicine with skepticism and apprehension. They invoke the very epistemological, philosophical, practicum, and policy concerns that Sackett and colleagues dismiss. Evidence-medicine, they say, is 'bias[ed] toward a narrow scientism' and empiricism and a kind of 'biomedical positivism' whose goal is 'a science-based rationalization of health services research, . . . health care . . . and, by extension, health policy':

> [It] makes a spurious claim to provide certainty in a world of clinical uncertainty. The dilemma facing policy makers, managers and practitioners, as well as the public in general, is that in most cases we are not dealing with a clear-cut question of whether treatment is effective or ineffective. Rather, the questions are how effective, and to what degree of probability? (Hunter 1996: 6)

In the final analysis, what is 'appropriate care'?, a physician asks:

> It depends [he answers], on which clinicians are questioned, where they live and work, what weight is given to different types of evidence and end points, whether one considers the preferences of patients and families, the level of resources in a given health system, and the prevailing values of both the system and the society in which it operates. (Naylor 1998: 1920)

Such physician-critics of evidence-based medicine feel that it may misconstrue clinical expertise by 'reducing the complexity of clinical decision making to the simple matter of following the results of relevant, rigorously controlled trials in its quest for a particular kind of certainty' (Hurwitz 1997a):

> To varying degrees, the judgments required of clinicians in discrete areas of medicine such as diagnosis, the treatment of some chronic conditions, or the management of anticoagulation, can be more or less successfully objectified, but this does not reduce clinical judgment to nothing more than a form of "decisional algebra" that can be encapsulated in expert systems, algorithms, protocols, or guidelines.

> Making judgments about complex individual circumstances in the context of different degrees of

uncertainty, where opinions differ, and where the authority of one's senses, perceptions and intuitions frequently play interacting roles is the routine reality of such medical practice. Opinionated judgments, grounded in clinical experience, counterweighted by knowledge of scientific findings, and modified by respect for patients' wishes are not necessarily simple transductions of input information which result in output decisions. (Hurwitz 1997b)

Physicians who have this perspective on the clinical encounter do not believe that all the variation that exists in medical practice is either surprising or necessarily a state of affairs that can, or should, be remedied through the formulation and application of clinical guidelines derived principally from the results of randomized, controlled clinical trials. It is important to first study these variations, they insist. Soundly based guidelines, they concede, can help to 'focus such variation, especially where there is both considerable certainty about efficacious treatment strategies (based on scientific evidence or expert opinion), and where significant departure from these strategies occurs without valid justification' (Hurwitz 1997b). However, they insist that this is not equally true of clinical situations in which there are 'inherent uncertainties.' Nor is it the case when 'the evidence derived from patients enrolled in published trials is [not] relevant to the patient one is agonizing over – a circumstance that is both frequent and serious in a field like geriatrics; for example, wherein too many RCTs [randomized controlled trials] have excluded older, and particularly older and iller [sic] patients' (Grimley-Evans 1995: 461). In circumstances like these, to place too much credence in evidence-based medicine, standardized clinical guidelines, or average outcomes in the population may eventuate in approaching patients in a pseudo-scientific, 'evidence-*biased*' way that pays insufficient attention to the individual particularities of their states of health, illness, and well-being (Grimley-Evans 1995: 461–2 [italics added]).

Physicians with this intricate view of clinical observation and reasoning are also troubled by the extent to which evidence-based medicine appears to be contributing to the 'fragmenting and shifting away [of] clinical expertise . . . from its previous locus with the practicing physician . . . towards corporate entities such as expert panels, consensus conferences, clinical guideline development groups, and experts in data extraction and analysis [whose] skills are not necessarily similar to those required by the physician' (Hurwitz 1997a).

Other patterns of tension between population-based and individual patient-focused medical reasoning and commitment have arisen in the field of organ transplantation, both with regard to successive retransplants and the transplanting of organs from animals to human (xenotransplants).

Despite advances in the biology of organ and tissue rejection, and the development of new immunosuppressive drugs, which attenuate or retard the immune reactions responsible for the rejection of transplanted organs and that prolong their survival in recipients, the rejection reaction continues to be a major cause of graft failure. This means that virtually all transplant recipients will eventually reject the organ or organs they have received and become potential candidates for retransplants. Their eligibility for repeated transplants is thrown into question by what transplant physicians term the 'shortage' of donated transplantable organs, and consequently the thousands of patients with end-stage diseases waiting for transplants who may never receive them. In addition, the results of retransplants, with regard to graft survival and patient mortality, are generally far less favorable than the outcome of first-time transplants. (This is more true of heart and liver, than of kidney retransplants.)

Transplant clinicians are very reluctant to accept and follow a rule of one organ per recipient. They are also reluctant to concede to bioethicists that because they have a 'moral duty to direct scarce lifesaving resources to those most likely to benefit from them,' primary transplant candidates should be given a better chance of receiving organs than retransplant candidates, and the number of times that transplants are offered to patients should be limited (Ubel et al. 1993). This resistance of transplant clinicians stems from the duration and strength of the relationships they form with these very sick patients, whom they have already wrested from death through organ transplantation. To use their own language, many transplanters feel that they are 'abandoning' their patients if they do not seek a retransplant for them when graft failure takes place (Fox 1997).

Xenotransplantation – the second sphere of transplantation that juxtaposes medical uncertainty, physicians' concerns about the particular patients for whom they care, and physicians' responsibility to a larger collectivity – 'promises great benefit to some patients,' on the one hand, but presents 'the possibility of a new disease entering the human population,' on the other (Bach et al. 1998: 142). There are biomedically sound bases for supposing that the potential for transmission of infectious agents from animal donors to human transplant recipients may be greater than in human-to-human transplants. Some of the organisms carried by a xenograft may be unknown human pathogens, and they may include 'xenotropic' organisms that are not threatening to the animal donor species, but can cause disease in a human recipient. Such infectious diseases may not only have the potential to infect individual organ recipients, but also to spread to the general population. Nobody knows how big this risk is, but all medical scientists and physicians agree that 'it is unequivocally greater than zero' (Institute of Medicine 1996: 92). The ambiguity and possible gravity of the collective risks of xenotransplantation are magnified by the threat to human health posed by emerging viruses and other microorganisms, many of which are thought to be transmissible from animals to humans. In addition, there is the acute realization that some of these diseases – of which the human immunodeficiency virus (HIV) acquired immune deficiency syndrome (AIDS) is the most harrowing example – can become epidemic, even pandemic.

Transplant physicians do not deny that there is a potential risk of infection to organ recipients and to the community at large. They agree with such bodies as the US Public Health Service and Food and Drug Administration (USA Public Health Service 1996), and the UK Xenotransplantation Interim Regulatory Authority and Ministry of Health, that it is advisable to have special guidelines, rules, and comprehensive mechanisms for the close monitoring and continuing surveillance of xenograft recipients, the family members with whom they have intimate contact, and the health professionals who care for them. At the same time, however, transplanters are disposed to playing down the uniqueness and seriousness of the risks associated with xenotransplantation and to minimizing the dangers to the public's health that it might unleash. They are more inclined to dwell on its potential lifesaving benefits, and on what they believe is an obligation to respond to the suffering and need of patients awaiting transplants by augmenting the organs available to them in this way.

EPISTEMOLOGICAL UNCERTAINTY

'These are strange times, when we are healthier than ever but more anxious about our health,' writes social historian of medicine Roy Porter in the introduction to his panoramic 'medical history of humanity,' *The Greatest Benefit to Mankind* (1998). He thereby echoes, at the end of the 1990s, comments that were made by observers like Lewis Thomas and André Cournand twenty years earlier.

In myriad ways [Porter goes on to say], medicine continues to advance, new treatments appear, surgery works marvels, and (partly as a result), people live longer. . . . Yet few people today feel confident about their personal health or about doctors, health-care delivery and the medical profession in general. . . .

Medicine is . . . going through . . . a fundamental crisis, the price of progress and its attendant inflated expectations. . . . [It] has become the prisoner of its success. Having conquered many grave diseases and provided relief from suffering, its mandate has become muddled. What are its aims? Where is it to stop?

'[M]edicine's finest hour is the dawn of its dilemmas,' Roy Porter concludes. 'For centuries medicine was impotent and thus unproblematic. . . . Today, with "mission accomplished", its triumphs are dissolving in disorientation. . . . It is losing its way, or having to redefine its goals' . . . (1998: 3–4, 716-18).

This end-of-the-twentieth-century anxiety, ambivalence, and perplexity about the successes and failures of Western medicine, its progress and impasses, capacities and limits, its sense of direction and of future goals, are subterranean motifs in all the phenomena surrounding medical uncertainty discussed here. This cultural mood is a pervasive, contextual part of the issues associated with the bridging of molecules and medicine, the tenacity of certain chronic diseases, the resurgence of infectious disease, the intellectual and emotional difficulties posed by medical prediction and prognosis, the tensions between individual- and population-oriented medicine, and the iatrogenic effects of the procedures, machines, and pharmacopoeia that are integral to present-day processes of medical diagnosis, therapy, prognosis, and prevention.

I would venture to go several steps further than Roy Porter in interpreting the medicocentric state of 'anomie' that he has identified. In the medical literature published during the 1990s and used as research for this chapter, there are consistent indications that what Porter refers to as the 'disorientation' of medicine at the turn of the millennium not only involves its clinical accomplishments, limitations, liabilities, and overall sense of direction, but also its fundamental way of thought. Whether they deal with phenomena associated with HIV/AIDS, cancer, or inflammatory bowel disease, for example, infectious or chronic syndromes, processes of diagnosis, prevention, treatment, care, or prognosis, or methods of collecting and analyzing medical data, many recent journal articles express concern about current problems of epistemological uncertainty:

. . . Big gaps remain in our knowledge of HIV, and it may be that we need a more complex response in terms of therapeutic approaches. . . . Similarly, prevention has focused largely on fairly simple psychological approaches. . . . The gaps are even bigger in determining how to prevent a million people from becoming infected with AIDS this year . . . and at the same time to care for nearly 30 million people with HIV living in developing countries. . . . (Piot 1998: 1844–5)

In a recent commentary of AIDS therapy, the phrase "Failure isn't what it used to be . . . but neither is success" was coined (Cohen 1998). . . . Failure has generally been defined in virological terms – the inability to achieve complete suppression of viral replication. . . . However, treatment failure is not only viral resistance. In fact, definition of failure or success of treatment is a far more complex phenomenon. (Perrin and Telenti 1998: 1871)

Renal cell carcinoma continues to fool internists and noninternists alike. . . . One source of error [is] the clinicians' overreliance on the use of patterns. . . . Pattern recognition greatly simplifies problem solving. . . . Occasionally, however, we rely on pattern recognition to a fault, trying to fit square pegs into round holes. . . . (Saint et al. 1998: 381)

Diseases like inflammatory bowel disease that have systemic manifestations can pose daunting diagnostic challenges. . . . The focus and training that physicians bring to a clinical case typically create cognitive expectations that determine their attention to and interpretation of events. . . . [T]hese elements can be important to reasoning in the presence of uncertainty while also being a source of error in diagnostic interpretation. (Berkwits and Gluckman 1997: 1683–4)

The National Institutes of Health convened a consensus conference in January 1997 to examine new evidence on the effectiveness of mammographic screening for breast cancer for women ages 40 to 49 years. . . . Critics of the panel stated resoundingly that it had reached the "wrong" conclusion, understating the effectiveness of mammography, exaggerating the potential harms of false-positive results, and raising unnecessary fears about the safety of mammography. The implication that the panel should not have had these concerns or expressed them perpetuates the notion that there is only one correct way to interpret evidence. Who can say when evidence is "good" enough? (Woolf and Lawrence 1997: 2105-6)

Two articles in this issue reach apparently conflicting conclusions regarding the safety of the short postpartum hospital stays that are now . . . standard for apparently well mothers and newborns. . . . [S]cience does not and probably can not supply airtight evidence that longer stays are more effective. . . . In the absence of an adequate base of scientific knowledge about [how] to achieve the best health outcomes, it appears rational and ethical to be guided by a combination of good judgment, caution, and compassion in weighing the best evidence available. (Braveman et al. 1997: 334-46)

It is impossible to say, on the basis of recent evidence alone, whether the results of a large randomized, controlled trial or those of a meta-analysis of many smaller studies are more likely to be close to the truth. . . . We never know as much as we think we know. (Bailar 1997: 559–60)

Embedded in such journal passages are basic questions of epistemology (Hamlyn 1967), involving the nature of medical knowledge, where and how it is generally found and obtained, the role that observation, reason, and experience play in this process, how much of what medical scientists and physicians think they know is real knowledge (certain enough, or based on sufficiently good grounds for this claim to be made), what the connections between medical knowledge, judgment, and belief are, and ought to be, and how errors of cognition, perception, judgment, and belief can be recognized, analyzed, and reduced, if not eliminated. In addition to these classical issues, questions that are more specific to medicine are raised about the intricate relations that exist between scientific and important, nonscientific aspects of medicine and the implications for the "scientificness" of the field. Questions are also raised about the relationship between simplicity and complexity in medical accuracy, understanding, and effectiveness, as well as between the scientific base of medicine, its clinical application to diagnosis, therapy, prognosis, and prevention, and to the formulation and implementation of health policy. These articles also consider the way in which what physician–scientist Ludwik Fleck termed the characteristic 'thought-style' of medicine (Löwy, 1990: 215–27) contributes both to the pattern-recognition and clinical problem-solving capacities of physicians, and to the built-in biases that result from their internalized conceptions and preconceptions. The articles are also concerned with problems of achieving consensus between medical professionals when they disagree in clinical and policy contexts. The articles also deal with how better to join, and more fruitfully integrate patient-, population-, and globally oriented medicine and attention to the disparate health, illness, and medicine conditions and needs in the 'two worlds' of developed and developing countries.

There is an implicit sense in which the evidence-based medicine movement (invoked by a number of the articles I sampled) is as much an indicator of this epistemological uncertainty and searching as a response to it. It implies that a great deal that medicine professes to know is neither strongly supported by reliable and valid scientific evidence, nor clinically efficient and efficacious. Although the ways of determining the effects of medical interventions that the evidence-based medicine approach prescribes (randomized trials, meta-analyses, and systematic reviews) are respected by physicians, they are not viewed as conceptual, methodological, or empirical panaceas for the cognitive challenges, problems, and deficiencies with which modern medicine is presently grappling.

Vocational Uncertainty

The future for US physicians is full of uncertainty – but also full of opportunities. Tomorrow's doctors should not be unemployed; they should be redefined.

(Konner 1998)

Along with the kinds of uncertainty that are associated with the conceptual framework, knowledge base, and technological armamentarium of medicine, physicians are also facing uncertainty in their professional status and roles. The main precipitants of this uncertainty in the United States are the nationwide restructuring of health insurance and reorganization of health-care delivery that are taking place as the country moves rapidly toward a predominantly managed care system. What consequences this will have for the employment of physicians, the fields within medicine that they select and de-select, their conditions of work, their incomes, the scope, continuity, and quality of care they offer to patients, and the relationships they establish with them, the sorts of professional decision-making and autonomy they will and will not be able to exercise, and the meaning, fulfillment, and frustration they will experience in their chosen careers are among the serious vocational questions that doctors, medical students, and 'pre-med' students are mutually facing.

A somewhat anomalous situation exists in the United States in this regard. Although young persons interested in becoming physicians are keenly aware of these uncertainties (*Pulse* 1997, 1998), an unprecedented number of college and university students have been seeking admission to medical schools throughout most of the 1990s. These aspirants include many daughters and sons of physicians who have advised their children not enter the profession under the present circumstances, and have urged them to consider other professional or business fields. We need more knowledge and understanding of the young men and women opting for medical careers at this time of transition and indeterminacy in the profession. What are their conceptions of being a physician? What motivates them to become doctors? How do they see and expect to handle the changing organizational and economic, social and psychological conditions under which they will practice medicine?

'BIOETHICAL' UNCERTAINTY

Finally, medicine is at the center of a larger, more far-reaching form of uncertainty that underlies American bioethics. This area of reflection, inquiry, and action that surfaced at the beginning of the 1970s has grown progressively more prominent ever since (Fox and Swazey 1984; Fox 1989b, 1990, 1994).

'Bioethics is not just bioethics', it pertains to more than medicine and to more than ethics. Using biology and medicine as a metaphorical language and a symbolic medium, concentrating on the problematic consequences of particular biomedical advances, and drawing predominantly on the logico-rational principles of analytic philosophy, US bioethics implicitly deals with uncertainty – fraught questions of value, belief, and meaning that are as religious and metaphysical as they are medical and moral.

What is life? What is death? When does a life begin? When does it end? What is a person? What is a child? What is a parent? What is a family? Who are my brothers and my sisters, my neighbors and my strangers? Is it better not to have been born at all than to have been born with a severe genetic defect? How vigorously should we intervene in the human condition to repair and improve ourselves? And when should we cease and desist? This at once elemental and transcendental questioning, coded into the deep structure of American bioethics, is indicative of the magnitude of foundational change through which not only medicine, but also the society and culture of which it is an integral part, are undergoing.

MEDICAL UNCERTAINTY AND CHANGE: OVERVIEW

The modalities of uncertainty discussed here are closely connected with a variety of changes that are occurring both within and around medicine at this historical juncture. The gamut of these changes is broad; they are scientific and techno-logical, cognitive and ethical, conceptual and empirical, methodological and procedural, and social and cultural in nature, and they have ramifying implications for the way of thought, the value system, and the practice of medicine that affect how it is delivered and experienced by health professionals and patients.

Several general characteristics of these uncertainty-accompanied changes are particularly notable. A number of them – such as mutations and developing drug resistance of certain pathogens – emanate from unintended consequences and iatrogenic side effects of efficacious medical actions. In addition, to an increasing degree, the change-related uncertainties that medicine is currently facing asks physicians to bridge and try to coordinate micro-, macro-, individual, and collective entities that range in size and scope from molecules and genes, organs and organ systems, to embodied patients and large patient populations. This calls for very different angles of vision that not only pose major scientific problems, but also raise important moral issues. For example, within the more corporately organized US system of health care that is unfolding, how can physicians abide by both an 'individual ethic' and a 'distributive ethic' that will enable them to 'provide optimal care for each of their patients and . . . for all patients within a group . . . at the same time?' (Kassirer 1998: 197) As this question suggests, in the changing ethical, social, and scientific situations in which they find themselves, physicians are encountering a considerable amount of uncertainty about how they should practice medicine.

As the grounding of medicine shifts in multidimensional ways, long-standing sources and manifestations of uncertainty have been reactivated, accentuated, or modified and new ones have formed. It is with extensive uncertainty about its state of knowledge and accomplishments, its future directions and limitations, and with a mixture of confidence and insecurity, that modern Western medicine is approaching the twenty-first century.

ACKNOWLEDGMENTS

I wish to express my gratitude to Nicholas A. Christakis, Brian Hurwitz, and Donald Light for their invaluable contributions to this chapter through their ongoing discussions with me about issues of medical uncertainty. I also want to thank my colleagues at Balliol College, University of Oxford, for the opportunity to present an earlier formulation of the chief ideas in this chapter at a research consilium during the

1996–1997 academic year when I was the George Eastman Visiting Professor at Oxford, attached to Balliol as a Supernumerary Fellow.

NOTES

1 The phrase 'medicine and molecules' was suggested by a comment made by Harold Varmus, Director of the US National Institutes of Health, in connection with his voiced concern about the decline of patient-oriented clinical research in recent years. In an *Association of American Medical Colleges Reporter* article, he was quoted as saying that a major reason for this decline was the dearth of young physicians willing to commit themselves to this sort of research career because they were 'choos[ing] molecules over medicine' (Frase-Blunt 1994: 3).

2 Above and beyond my citations to his PhD dissertation, and his forthcoming book *Death Foretold: Prophecy and Prognosis in Medical Care*, I am indebted to Nicholas Christakis for the ideas and insights about prognosis presented in this section of the chapter.

REFERENCES

Atkinson, P. (1984) 'Training for certainty', *Social Science and Medicine*, 19: 949–56.

Bach, F.H., Fishman, J.A., Daniels, N., Proimos, J., Anderson, B., Carpenter, C.B., Forrow, L., Robson, S.C., and Fineberg, H. (1998) 'Uncertainty in xenotransplantation: Individual benefit versus collective risk', *Nature Medicine*, 4: 141–4.

Bailar, J.C. III (1997) 'The promise and problems of meta-analysis', *New England Journal of Medicine*, 337: 559–61.

Berkwits, M. and Gluckman, S.J. (1997) 'Seeking an expert interpretation', *New England Journal of Medicine*, 337: 1682–4.

Blumberg, B. and Fox, R.C. (1985) 'The Daedalus effect: Changes in ethical questions relating to hepatitis B virus', *Annals of Internal Medicine*, 102: 390–4.

Braveman, P., Kessel, W., Egerter, S., and Richmond, J. (1997) 'Early discharge and evidence-based practice: Good science and good judgment', *Journal of the American Medical Association*, 278: 334–6.

Christakis, N.A. (1995) *Prognostication and Death in Medical Thought and Practice*. PhD dissertation, University of Pennsylvania, Philadelphia.

Christakis, N.A. (1999) *Death Foretold: Prophecy and Prognosis in Medical Care*. Chicago: University of Chicago Press.

Christensen, J.F., Levinson, W., and Dunn, P.M. (1992) 'The heart of darkness: The impact of perceived mistakes on physicians', *Journal of General Internal Medicine*, 7: 424–31.

Cohen, J. (1998) 'Failure isn't what it used to be . . . but neither is success', *Science*, 279(5354): 1133–4.

Cohen, O.J. and Fauci, A.S. (1998) 'HIV/AIDS in 1998 – gaining the upper hand?' *Journal of the American Medical Association*, 280: 87–8.

Cournand, A. (1977) 'The code of the scientist and its relationship to ethics', *Science*, 198(4318): 699–705.

de Laval, M.R. (1996) The Edgar Mannheimer Lecture (manuscript).

de Laval, M.R., François, K., Bull, C., Brawn, W., and Spiegehalter, D. (1994) 'Analysis of a cluster of surgical failures: Application to a series of neonatal arterial switch operations', *Journal of Thoracic and Cardiovascular Surgery*, 107: 914–24.

Fox, R.C. (1957) 'Training for uncertainty', in R.K. Merton, G. Reader, and P.L. Kendall (eds), *The Student-Physician: Introductory Studies in the Sociology of Medical Education*. Cambridge, MA: Harvard University Press. pp. 207–41.

Fox, R.C. (1959) *Experiment Perilous: Physicians and Patients Facing the Unknown*. Glencoe, IL: Free Press (republished with a new epilogue, New Brunswick, NJ: Transaction Publishers 1997).

Fox, R.C. (1962) 'Medical scientists in a château', *Science*, 136(3515): 476–83.

Fox, R.C. (1964) 'An American sociologist in the land of Belgian medical research', in P.E. Hammond (ed.), *Sociologists at Work*. New York: Harper and Row. pp. 345–91.

Fox, R.C. (1976) 'The sociology of modern medical research', in C. Leslie (ed.), *Asian Medical Systems: A Comparative Study*, Berkeley: University of California Press. pp. 102–14.

Fox, R.C. (1978a) 'The autopsy: Its place in the attitude-learning of second-year medical students', in R.C. Fox, *Essays in Medical Sociology: Journeys Into the Field*. New Brunswick (USA) and Oxford (UK): Transaction Books. pp. 51–77.

Fox, R.C. (1978b) 'Is there a new medical student?', *Transactions and Studies*, 45: 206–12.

Fox, R.C. (1978c) 'The human condition of health professionals', in R.C. Fox, *Essays in Medical Sociology: Journeys into the Field*. New Brunswick (USA) and Oxford (UK): Transaction Books. pp. 572–87.

Fox, R.C. (1978d) 'Why Belgium?' *European Journal of Sociology*, 19: 205–28.

Fox, R.C. (1980) 'The evolution of medical uncertainty', *Milbank Memorial Fund Quarterly/Health and Society*, 58: 1–49.

Fox, R.C. (1989a) 'The education, training, and socialization of physicians: Medical school', in R.C. Fox, *The Sociology of Medicine: A Participant Observer's View*. Englewood Cliffs, NJ: Prentice-Hall. ch. 3, pp. 72–107.

Fox, R.C. (1989b) 'The sociology of bioethics', in R.C. Fox, *The Sociology of Medicine: A Participant Observer's View*. Englewood Cliffs, NJ: Prentice-Hall. ch. 7, pp. 224–76.

Fox, R.C. (1990) 'The evolution of American bioethics: A sociological perspective', in G. Weisz (ed.), *Social Science Perspectives on Medical Ethics*. Dordrecht/Boston/London: Kluwer. pp. 201–17.

Fox, R.C. (1994) 'The entry of US bioethics into the 1990s: A sociological analysis', in E.R. DuBose, R. Harmel, and L.J. O'Connell (eds), *A Matter of Principles? Ferment in US Bioethics*. Valley Forge, PA: Trinity pp. 21–71.

Fox, R.C. (1996a) 'Experiment perilous: Forty-five years as a participant observer of patient-oriented clinical research', *Perspectives in Biology and Medicine*, 39: 206–26.

Fox, R.C. (1996b) 'The Institute of Medicine's workshop and report on xenotransplantation: A participant observer's account', *Making the Rounds in Health, Faith and Ethics*, 2(2): 8–15.

Fox, R.C. (1997) 'Ethics of retransplantation', *Transplantation and Immnuology Letter*, 8(4): 3, 6.

Fox, R.C. and Swazey, J.P. (1974) *The Courage to Fail: A Social View of Organ Transplants and Dialysis*. (2nd edn, revised 1978). Chicago: University of Chicago Press.

Fox, R.C. and Swazey, J.P. (1984) 'Medical morality is not bioethics: Medical ethics in China and the United States', *Perspectives in Biology and Medicine*, 27: 336–60.

Fox, R.C. and Swazey, J.P. (1992) *Spare Parts: Organ Replacement in American Society*. New York: Oxford University Press.

Frase-Blunt, M.C. (1994) 'Choosing medicine over molecules', *Association of American Medical Colleges Reporter*, 4(1): 1, 3.

Grimley-Evans, J. (1995) 'Evidence-based and evidence-biased medicine', *Age and Aging*, 24: 461–3.

Hamlyn, D.W. (1967) 'Epistemology, history of', in P. Edwards (ed.), *The Encyclopedia of Philosophy*. Vol. 3. New York: Macmillan and Free Press. pp. 8–38.

Hunter, D.J. (1996) 'Rationing and evidence-based medicine', *Journal of Evaluation in Clinical Practice*, 2: 5–8.

Hurwitz, B. (1997a) Personal communication (Letter, 17 June).

Hurwitz, B. (1997b) 'Clinical guidelines: Philosophical, legal, emotional and political considerations' (draft paper commissioned by the *British Medical Journal*).

Illich, I. (1976) *Medical Nemesis: The Expropriation of Health*. New York: Pantheon.

Institute of Medicine USA (1996) *Xenotransplantation: Science, Ethics, and Public Policy*. Washington, DC: National Academy Press.

Kassirer, J.P. (1998) 'Managing care – should we adopt a new ethic?', *New England Journal of Medicine*, 339: 397–8.

Katz, J. (1984) *The Silent World of Doctor and Patient*. New York: Free Press.

Kaye, H.L. (1986) *The Social Meaning of Modern Biology*. New Haven: Yale University Press.

Konner, J.A. (1998) 'Alternative careers for physicians', *Pulse*, the medical student section of the *Journal of the American Medical Association*, 279 (17): 1398.

Levinson, W., Roter, D.L., Mullooly, J.P., Dull, V.T., and Frankel R.M. (1997) 'Physician-patient communication: The relationship with malpractice claims among primary care physicians and surgeons', *Journal of the American Medical Association*, 277: 553–9.

Lief, H.I. and Fox, R.C. (1963) 'Training for "detached concern" in medical students', in H.I. Lief, Victor F. Lief, and N.R. Lief (eds), *The Psychological Basis of Medical Practice*. New York: Harper and Row. pp. 12–35.

Light, D. (1979) 'Uncertainty and control in professional training' *Journal of Health and Social Behavior*, 20: 310–22.

Light, D. (1980) *Becoming Psychiatrists: The Professional Transformation of Self*. New York: W.W. Norton.

Löwy, I. (1990) *The Polish School of Philosophy of Medicine: From Tytus Chalubinski (1820–1889) to Ludwik Fleck (1896–1961)*. Dordrecht, The Netherlands: Kluwer.

Martensen, R.L. and Jones, D.S. (1997) 'Searching for medical certainty: Medical chemistry to molecular medicine', *Journal of the American Medical Association*, 278: 609.

McNeill, W.H. (1993) 'Patterns of disease emergence in history', in S.S. Morse (ed.), *Emerging Viruses*. New York: Oxford University Press. pp. 29–36.

Morse, S.S. (1993) 'Examining the origins of emerging viruses', in S.S. Morse (ed.), *Emerging Viruses*. New York: Oxford University Press. pp. 10–28.

Naylor C. D. (1998) 'What is appropriate care?' *New England Journal of Medicine*, 338: 1918–20.

Orkin, S.H. and Motulsky, A.G. (7 December 1995) 'Report and recommendations of the panel to assess the NIH (National Institutes of Health) investment in research on gene therapy' (unpublished, non-paginated text).

Parsons, T. (1951) 'Social structure and dynamic process: The case of modern medical practice' in T. Parsons, *The Social System*. Glencoe, IL: Free Press. Ch. X, pp. 428–70.

Perrin, L. and Telenti, A. (1998) 'HIV treatment failure: Testing for HIV resistance in clinical practice', *Science*, 280(5371): 1971–3.

Piot, P. (1998) 'The science of AIDS: A tale of two worlds', *Science*, 280(5371): 1844–5.

Porter, R. (1998) *The Greatest Benefit to Mankind: A Medical History of Humanity*. (1st edn, United States). New York: W.W. Norton.

Pulse (1997) The medical student section of the *Journal of the American Medical Association*. 'An uncertain future: Physician jobs in the balance', 277: 68–73.

Pulse (1998) The medical student section of the *Journal of the American Medical Association*. 'Making a living: Alternative careers for physicians', 279: 1398–1403.

Reason, J. (1990) *Human Error*. Cambridge: Cambridge University Press.

Royal College of Physicians of London (1997) *Improving Communication between Doctors and Patients: A Report of a Working Party*.

Sackett, D.L., Richardson, W.S., Rosenberg, W., and Haynes, R.B. (1997) *Evidence-Based Medicine: How to Practice and Teach EBM*. New York, Edinburgh, London, Madrid, Melbourne, San Francisco, Tokyo: Churchill Livingstone.

Saint, S., Saha, S., and Tierney, L.M., Jr. (1998) 'A square peg in a round hole', *New England Journal of Medicine*, 338: 379–83.

Silver, M.T. (1994) 'The student experience', in D.C. Tosteson, A.J. Adelstein, and S.T. Carter (eds), *New Pathways to Medical Education: Learning to Learn at Harvard Medical School*. Cambridge, MA: Harvard University Press. pp. 123–38.

Swazey, J.P. and Fox, R.C. (1970) 'The clinical moratorium: A case study of mitral valve surgery', in P.A. Freund (ed.), *Experimentation with Human Subjects*. New York: George Braziller. pp. 315–57.

Tenoyer, F.C. and Hughes, J.M. (1996) 'The challenge of emerging infectious diseases: Development and spread of multiply resistant bacterial pathogens', *Journal of the American Medical Association*, 275: 300–4.

Thomas, L. (1979) *The Medusa and the Snail*. New York: Viking.

Tosteson, D.C. and Goldman, D.C. (1994) 'Lessons for the future', in D.C. Tosteson, S.J. Adelstein, and S.T. Carver (eds), *New Pathways in Medical Education: Learning to Learn at Harvard Medical School*. Cambridge, MA: Harvard University Press. pp. 173–81.

Ubel, P.A., Arnold, R.N., and Caplan, A.L. (1993) 'Rationing failure: The ethical lessons of the retransplantation of scarce organs', *Journal of the American Medical Association*, 270: 2469–74.

USA Public Health Service (1996) 'Guidelines on infectious disease issues in xenotransplantation' (draft).

Watson, J.D. (1976) 'In defense of DNA', *Annual Report 1976*. Cold Spring Harbor Symposium.

Watson, J.D. and Crick, F.H.C. (1953a) 'A structure for deoxyribose nucleic acid', *Nature*, 171(4356): 737–8.

Watson, J.D. and Crick, F.H.C. (1953b) 'Genetical implications of the structure of deoxyribonucleic acid', *Nature*, 171(4361): 964–7.

Woolf, S.H. and Lawrence, R.S. (1997) 'Preserving scientific debate and patient choice: Lessons from the consensus panel of mammography screening', *Journal of the American Medical Association*, 278(23): 205–7.

3.4

Alternative Health Practices and Systems

SARAH CANT AND URSULA SHARMA

INTRODUCTION

Whilst biomedicine has achieved a position of preeminence in the health-care systems of 'advanced' societies, it has never been the only mode of health care open to sick people in modern times. Biomedicine emerged as the favoured partner of the state in most Western countries in the middle or late nineteenth century. The professional privilege recognized by the state has taken various forms: state registration of the medical profession, along with a high degree of professional autonomy; direct provision or funding of biomedical services for the populace (as in Britain and many other European countries); regulation or organization of insurance schemes covering biomedical but not (until recently) other forms of health care; heavy reliance on the biomedical profession's advice on all public issues relating to health and the body.

This privileging has been associated with what sociologists have called the 'medicalization' of society – referring both to the way in which more and more conditions become defined in terms of medical models of disease, and to the process by which the biomedical profession achieves practical power over patients and over other kinds of health-care professional (see, for example, Stacey 1988). In many Western countries (such as France) the practice of healing by persons without a medical qualification was illegal. In a few (like Britain) the practice of nonbiomedical forms of healing was permitted, but the title of doctor was protected by law from its use by persons not biomedically qualified.

However, even in those countries where biomedicine was most strongly privileged by the state, other forms of healing still flourished.

Rural populations and some of the urban poor never had good access to biomedical care and used folk systems of curing either out of necessity or preference, as also have some ethnic minorities, (see, for instance, Kirkland et al. 1992, Vaskilampi 1993). While biomedicine was beginning to take its modern institutional shape, many other important forms of healing grew in the context of the intellectual and social ferment of the nineteenth century (Cooter 1988; Gevitz 1988). Homoeopathy was one of the earliest, at times rivalling conventional medicine in popularity in some parts of Europe (Faure 1992; Nicholls 1988). Chiropractic and osteopathy developed in, and spread from, the United States in the late nineteenth century (Baer 1984; Wardwell 1992).

Of these modes of healing, many that survived into the twentieth century experienced a period of decline or stagnation during the interwar period, but nonbiomedical healing never actually went away. Many forms have reemerged into greater popularity since the 1960s, becoming the subject of more research and seeing increasing professionalization of their practitioners. This period also saw the emergence or importation of modes such as aromatherapy, reflexology, etc.

Alternative medicine, considered as a category of health care, is therefore not new, although some specific forms may be novel. Increased interest in the 1960s manifested itself first among the educated middle classes (especially women), but is not now confined to those groups. A summary of data from Europe published in 1994 indicates a range between 20 per cent (The Netherlands) and 49 per cent (France) of the population using some form of alternative medicine, with a steady increase during the

1980s being evident where statistics have been available over time (Fisher and Ward 1994: 309).

In the absence of survey data from an earlier period, we cannot easily assess the role which nonbiomedical forms of healing might have played before the 1960s. Evidence of bitter medical opposition to specific therapies suggests that some individual forms presented real threats to biomedicine. However, by the late 1960s a public debate had developed which defined alternative medicine as a generic issue and which focused on the general role and legitimacy of nonbiomedical forms of healing.

This debate has had various forms and levels. At state level, some governments have been moved to reconsider restrictive legislation (as in the case of The Netherlands), provide funds for research into roles and efficacy (United States, The Netherlands, Switzerland, Denmark), or consider state registration for the more professionalized alternative therapies (Great Britain, Australia). Doctors are increasingly asking questions about the possibility of cooperation with alternative practitioners, and many models of collaboration exist in spite of the continued antipathy expressed by many professional medical associations. If the public are voting with their feet in favour of a more diverse system of health care, does this imply a loss of status and legitimacy for biomedicine (even science in general), or perhaps a less disease-orientated revision of popular conceptions of health, well-being, and responsibility for the body? Is medical dominance declining in favour of a more pluralistic provision – does the new role of alternative medicine constitute a significant challenge to biomedicine (Saks 1994)? Or is this apparent pluralism a new dispensation over which biomedicine still exercises a presiding role, keeping the power to define what is and what is not charlatanry? How is the new role for alternative medicine defined in different kinds of health-care systems (market-oriented, state-organized, etc.)?

Much work on alternative medicine has considered the issue principally in terms of 'rejected knowledge' – rejected, that is, by the biomedical and scientific establishment. The relationship between biomedicine and alternative medicines is nowadays very complex. As we shall see, medical attitudes range from outright rejection to incorporation. However, it remains a matter of the utmost political importance and, in any given country, plays a crucial role in shaping the opportunities for alternative medicines to gain greater legitimacy and security.

However, these opportunities are also shaped by patient perceptions. The use of alternative medicines has grown rapidly, and in many Western countries it can be assumed that as much as a third of the population has had some experience of them. Users share their information about, and perceptions of, alternative medicine through patients' self-help groups, consumer groups, and informal local networks. The patient, considered as consumer, cannot be ignored when we consider the present situation and likely outlook for alternative medicines.

The therapies themselves have not stood still. The 'lay' therapy groups that emerged or reemerged in the 1960s look different today. Most have professionalized to some degree and become politically much more sophisticated, and many have engaged with biomedical knowledge in different ways. Within the biomedical camp, doctors who practice alternative medicines have become more confident and vocal in promoting these therapies within medicine, and some have started to enter into closer relationships with 'lay' therapists practising the same therapy.

Such a revolution in health care was bound to have implications for policy and the state. In some countries there has been a demand for a radical reform of the statutory position on non-biomedical therapies. In practice, the changes to the legal position of alternative therapies have usually been very limited, but even where the letter of the law is restrictive with respect to the practice of healing by anyone who is not a doctor, there has been a noticeable relaxation in attitudes. In many countries those responsible for national health policy have shown a degree of interest in integrating some alternative therapies into whatever health-care provision is funded directly or indirectly by the state.

In this chapter we consider the contemporary position of alternative medicines from these four points of view: those of patients, doctors, therapists, and the state. We recognize that this does not exhaust the possible angles from which the debate may be studied. One could, for instance, examine the ways in which insurance companies have increased the number of alternative therapies for which they will reimburse patients, or the attitudes of the pharmaceutical companies to 'natural' medicines. It is unfortunate that there is not space here to deal at length with the relationship between alternative therapies and the nursing profession. However, the four perspectives we discuss are of crucial importance in framing both the opportunities and the problems that alternative medicines face at the present time. We are aware of the problems of a generalizing approach and hope that this overview will do justice to the complexities and diversities of the situation in different 'Western' countries.

The very label 'alternative medicine' is contentious. Some prefer the term 'complementary' medicine, recognizing that many patients and doctors use these forms to complement biomedical health care rather than to replace it. Some healing modes which are 'alternative' or 'complementary' in one country are virtually incorporated into the biomedical canon in another, and where doctors themselves practise nonbiomedical healing, the boundaries between alternative and orthodox medicines are increasingly hard to define. Nonbiomedical healing practices are a highly heterogeneous category everywhere; osteopathy, as practised in Britain today, probably has more in common with biomedicine than it does with spiritual healing or crystal therapy.

Various other terminologies can be used to refer to the healing modes under discussion ('parallel,' 'gentle,' or 'holistic' medicines) and all have their advantages and disadvantages. We have continued to use the term 'alternative medicine(s)' simply because it, or its equivalents in other languages, are the most widely used. We are aware of the conceptual problems in defining and naming nonbiomedical forms of healing, and refer the reader to Fulder (1996) for a helpful discussion.

USERS OF ALTERNATIVE MEDICINE

Alternative medicine can no longer be considered a marginal health-care option. Studies in many countries suggest that increasing numbers of people have consulted alternative practitioners, although it is not always clear whether the survey instruments are quantifying 'one off' consultations or consistent use over a period. Such methodological ambiguities inevitably make comparisons difficult (see Cant and Sharma 1999), but the available evidence suggests that at least 20–25 per cent of populations across the Western world have used an alternative practitioner in the past year (Eisenberg et al. 1993; MacLennan et al. 1996; Menges 1994; Sermeus 1987). Despite the massive growth in the number of available therapies, it is still a relatively small number that attract the greatest support, particularly osteopathy, chiropractic, homoeopathy, herbalism, and acupuncture (Fisher and Ward 1994; NAHAT 1992). In America, relaxation therapy and therapeutic massage are also very popular (Paramore 1997).

What do we know about the characteristics, health beliefs, and practices of those who consult alternative practitioners? Does use of alternative medicine represent a radical alteration in the health behaviour of the lay populace, and do users share demographic and attitudinal characteristics? There is some evidence that middle-aged and middle-class women make up the largest category of users, although this need not surprise us when we note the usage patterns of biomedicine (Verbrugge 1982). The increase in the use of alternative medicine over time has not been matched by an even spatial patterning; for example, there are more practitioners and consequently greater accessibility of services in the south compared with the north of England (Cant and Sharma 1999). Studies in Australia (Lloyd et al. 1993), Britain (Furnham and Bhagrath 1992), and Germany (Furnham and Kirkcaldy 1996) also suggest that users are more health conscious, concerned with healthy living, and sceptical of biomedicine, although such differences can vary according to which therapy group is studied. For example, users of acupuncture were found to be more sceptical of biomedicine than a similar sample of osteopathic patients (Vincent and Furnham 1996).

Evidence of scepticism towards biomedicine does not mean that users of alternative medicine are opting to reject orthodox medical care. On the contrary, the majority of patients see their general practitioner before they seek advice from an alternative practitioner and then rarely abandon biomedicine totally (Ooijendijk et al. 1981; Thomas et al. 1991). It is likely that users of alternative medicine are high consumers of health services generally (not just alternative medicine), especially as many are sufferers of chronic illness. However, more detailed studies (Sharma 1995) have revealed that there are a variety of patterns of usage. Some users are very discerning and knowledgeable in their choice of practitioner. In particular, with increased knowledge about the services that the alternative practitioner can provide (as in the case of those whom Sharma terms 'stable users'), there is evidence that the individual will shop around among practitioners, continuing to use the biomedical practitioner for particular complaints. Similarly, in America it has been shown that as users increase their understanding of chiropractic, they are likely to consult these practitioners as a health-care option of first resort and treat them as primary practitioners (Sawyer and Ramlow 1984). These examples of 'demarcated use' thus show us that patients may undergo trajectories of experience that, in time, enable them to use services selectively, but even this active choice of alternative medical services has not occurred at the expense of biomedicine, as few patients completely reject orthodox care. These patterns of use suggest that we may be seeing the development of plural and complementary medical services.

The Value of Alternative Medicine to Users

These new health practices can tell us an enormous amount about what it is that patients desire from health care. Clearly, patients want efficacious treatment (Sharma 1995), but the decision to use alternative medicine does not appear to be driven by this consideration alone. In the first place, it has been shown that many users of alternative medicine express concerns about the side-effects associated with biomedical interventions (Sharma 1995) and prefer to use what they regard as more 'natural' treatments. (This does not mean that biomedical services are not deemed to be efficacious, nor that alternative medicines should be viewed as 'risk-free.')

Second, qualitative differences in the therapeutic encounter are an attraction to the users of alternative medicine. The amount of time spent by the practitioner is perhaps the most important. Consultations can last more than an hour and provide the opportunity for patients to discuss their medical problem in depth and explore their underlying anxieties. This attention to the holistic nature of health and disease means that a person's spiritual and emotional well-being is as important as their physical symptoms. It necessitates a highly individualistic approach to treatment and the need to extract detailed information from the patient about the nature and personal significance of his illness. Consequently, the patient is treated as 'expert' having valuable knowledge about him/herself, and is afforded a sense of consumer control over the health-care programme. Qualitative studies show that patients respond positively to being treated as an equal and desire a more participatory relationship with their practitioner (Hewer 1993). Of course this more mutual and sharing relationship can bring ambiguities. For example, patients were sometimes confused about how to treat their practitioner – as friend or expert? (see Cant and Sharma 1998.) There may also be limits to the level of expertise the patient is in a position to exercise. All of the patients in Cant's study of users of homoeopathy believed that they had a role to play in the consultation, but the majority were not at all informed about the medication they had been prescribed or indeed about homoeopathy in general. Only one respondent claimed to have tried to read up about the remedy that he had been given.

> I never know what the remedy is – I did read and go to lectures. I got hooked really, but he (the homoeopath) discouraged me and told me to think that it is all magic. (Cant and Sharma 1999: 42)

It appears that patients do not all desire full equality in terms of health knowledge. Certainly it has been shown that practitioners want only to encourage a certain degree of participation and may withhold information, partly no doubt to maintain their own professional distance and boundaries of expertise (see Cant and Sharma 1996a, 1996b). Nevertheless, patients generally feel that they participate more actively in the alternative medical encounter. The fact that most alternative medicine is still only available on the private market means that users are more likely to have made autonomous decisions about whom to consult rather than depending on the advice of a biomedical practitioner. This active participation in the choice of both therapy and practitioner, and the perceived involvement in the consultation itself, suggests a shift in power relations between user and practitioner, the former taking the role of 'consumer' rather than 'patient.'

Alternative medicine may also offer more satisfactory ways of interpreting illness experiences that move beyond reductionist accounts and resonate with ideas held by the patient. We know that the lay public has a wide range of frameworks of meaning which are used to make sense of illness episodes (Stacey 1988), and that these are not generally drawn upon by the biomedical doctor. In contrast, alternative medical practitioners usually spend a long time questioning the patients about their family, their lifestyle, and their environment. Indeed questions can be so probing and wide ranging that new patients may feel perturbed about their relevance. But, there is evidence that some patients do feel that alternative medicine helps them make sense of their situation even if it is by simply linking their health problems to those of their family (Sharma 1995). On the other hand, not all therapists spend extended time with their patients; with chiropractic the average consultation may last no more than 15 minutes (Cant and Sharma 1994). Some patients may consult because they hold particular health ideologies, require a different relationship with their practitioner, or are concerned about the safety of biomedicine, but others may be more pragmatic, desiring no more than the relief of a particular symptom. We should therefore be cautious about giving too much emphasis to the pursuit of meaning.

Use of alternative medicines may be connected with changing understandings of the body. Many alternative practitioners view themselves as educators as well as healers, and try to help patients achieve a better understanding of their bodies and health and well-being. Quantitative data certainly seem to suggest that users themselves are more concerned about preventative health care and are less likely to smoke or drink alcohol than nonusers (Lloyd et al. 1993). It is argued by sociologists that the body has become a 'project' (Shilling 1993), one that is increasingly seen as unfinished, to be shaped by lifestyle choices. Perhaps there is a link between the attraction of alternative therapeutic practice, with its emphasis on holistic health care, and increased concerns about the 'healthy' body. Furnham and Kirkcaldy (1996) showed in their quantitative study that users were more knowledgeable about their body than nonusers, and Cant's qualitative study demonstrated that users were very aware of, and concerned to monitor, bodily changes and to ensure that they worked actively to maintain 'good' health. Such body monitoring was often encouraged by therapists, who asked their patients to keep a diary of how they were feeling and to chart any bodily changes they experienced. Respondents felt that this had transformed their perceptions of themselves.

> It has done something to me – what am I trying to say, my body tells me what is happening all the time. My body leads me now...if the psoriasis starts I know now that I am emotionally stressed...I make the connection between emotional and physical signs. I don't check my body all the time but I do monitor it. (Cant and Sharma 1999: 44)

Others talked about how they had become more preoccupied with their good health and made sure that they did all possible to ensure that a state of such 'good health' was maintained.

Such comments can explain the continued use of alternative therapies by individuals, but they also illustrate the connection between alternative medical practice and what Crawford has called 'healthism' (Crawford 1980) – a belief in the perfectibility of health and the individual's responsibility for maintaining that health. This cultural emphasis can be interpreted as *empowering*, offering individuals the opportunity to know themselves (Busby 1996), or as *disciplining*, placing more responsibility on the individual and operating as a surveillance function (Braathen 1996). Crawford (1980) would favour the latter interpretation, arguing that holism does not empower the individual, for it does not provide effective social and political analysis of the causes of ill health. Alternative medicine seems to de-medicalize personal health by encouraging the individual to be less dependant on biomedicine, but paradoxically it then re-medicalizes life, bringing all areas of a person's emotional and spiritual life under scrutiny (Lowenberg and Davis 1994).

The changes in lay health-seeking practice which we have discussed may signify a change in the power balance within health care generally. Patients appreciate greater equality in their relations with their practitioners, and biomedicine may need to become more patient-orientated if it is to retain support. The greater scepticism towards biomedical knowledge and treatment regimes may also serve to displace trust and question the authority of orthodox doctors. The biomedical profession well aware of such threats, has been concerned to understand the attraction of alternative medicine (BMA 1986), and, as we shall see in the following section, has attempted to exclude, limit, or subordinate alternative medical practice.

RELATIONS WITH THE MEDICAL PROFESSION

Given the social power of biomedicine, the situation of alternative medicine is bound to be influenced by the attitudes of doctors. Whilst alternative therapists have been more conscious of medical hostility than of other dimensions of the relationship, the influence of biomedicine has been positive as well as negative.

Some forms of alternative medicine are widely practised by doctors, and even among doctors who do not claim to practise any form of alternative medicine there is a widespread interest in knowing more about it. According to a study by Goldszmidt et al., 68 per cent of a sample of Canadian general practitioners claimed to refer patients to nonmedical alternative practitioners (Goldszmidt et al. 1995: 31). A British survey found that 93 per cent of a sample of GPs and 70 per cent of hospital doctors claimed to have suggested referral for alternative medical treatment (Perkin et al. 1994: 524). A comparison between Canadian and US survey data also suggests substantial rates of referral (Verhoef 1996), although both this survey and that of Perkin suggest that GPs perceive themselves as under some pressure from patients to refer. Therefore, it is not clear how far any trend towards referral to alternative practitioners is driven by doctors' own conviction of the value of alternative medicines, and how far it is a rather reluctant response to perceived patient demand.

In the United States, Great Britain, and a number of North European countries we are seeing more and more instances of the integration of biomedicine and alternative medicines at various levels. This can take place through various kinds of collaboration between medical and alternative practitioners in the context of local initiatives and the establishment of multidisciplinary, holistic health-care teams. Pietroni (1992) has categorized ways in which alternative medicine could be integrated into general practice. His typology is based on the possibilities contained in the British health-care system, but (with some modification) would be widely applicable elsewhere. The opportunities listed include: (a) appointment of alternative practitioners as ancillary staff funded by the family health service authority; (b) sharing of premises by GPs and privately practising alternative practitioners, with referrals by the GPs; (c) provision of services by alternative practitioners located in the GP practice centre but funded by charities and voluntary contributions; (d) referral centres funded by local health authorities and enabling a group of local GP practices to access the services of alternative practitioners without actually sharing premises. None of these models departs from the 'traditional' relationship between GP and alternative practitioner, in which the GP retains clinical responsibility for the patient. However, Pietroni also proposes a more radical and experimental model in which both doctors and alternative practitioners share ownership of, and jointly manage, health centre premises and resources, share equally in any profits made by the centre, and share medical accountability as a corporate group. Patients would register with the practice and not the GP, and would have the option of going directly to an alternative practitioner within the group rather that through the 'gatekeeper' GP. However, this would require doctors to cede more authority to alternative practitioners than most would probably be prepared to countenance as things are at present.

At the level of research training, we find collaborative schemes like the 'Munich Model,' a university project for the integration of naturopathy into research and training at the Maximilian University in Munich (Melchart 1994). There is increasing inclusion of modules on alternative therapies in the education of undergraduate medical students in the United States, Britain, and other countries where forms of alternative medicine such as homoeopathy, acupuncture, or manipulation had not hitherto been any part of the medical curriculum (Pavek 1995). There is also enormous interest in alternative modes of healing among some other health-care professions, notably nurses and midwives (Rankin-Box 1993).

However, the collective voice of medicine has not always been so kind, and national medical associations have often offered stiff resistance to any move to legitimate alternative medicine. The modern biomedical profession sees itself as practising a form of healing which, in contradistinction to other practices, is based on scientific

enquiry and experimentation, and it legitimates itself largely in these terms. The accusation that nonbiomedical healing lacks scientific proof is the main plank of the modern critique of non-biomedical healing (BMJ Editorial, 1980: 2). Some medical critics have claimed that the re-emergence of alternative medicine represents a return to magic, superstition, and unreason (Glymour and Stalker 1989: 27).

Such negative attitudes cannot be lightly dismissed given the strong influence that the organized medical profession has had on the government policy of individual countries. For instance, the British medical profession managed to block repeated attempts by osteopaths to achieve state registration in the interwar years (Larkin 1992). Of course this influence is very uneven; in Sweden the medical profession has, in spite of a public oppositional stance, been able, at most, only to delay legislation favouring the legitimation of alternative medicine (Eklöf 1996).

The Case of Chiropractic

The case of chiropractic may serve to illustrate some of the different ways in which the medical profession can deal with therapy groups that threaten its privileged position. Chiropractic depends largely on forms of spinal manipulation, and was founded by Daniel David Palmer (1845–1913). It spread very rapidly in the United States and was licensed in almost every state over the 50 years following Palmer's death. Patients evidently regarded it as a form of legitimate medical practice that avoided some of the things they disliked about conventional medicine, especially heavy reliance on drugs, and they seem to have approved of its eclectic practice. They certainly did not share the medical profession's view that chiropractic was a deviant form of healing (Cobb 1977: 18). Conscious of this, legislators were prepared to override medical objections that it had no scientific basis when the inclusion of chiropractic under Medicare was an issue. Paradoxically, in spite of chiropractic's rejection by the medical profession, licensure helped to effect convergence between the knowledge bases of chiropractic and conventional medicine through the requirement for the inclusion of much biomedical knowledge in the curriculum. Legitimation was therefore something of a mixed blessing from the point of view of the chiropractic purist (Baer 1984: 158).

By the 1970s chiropractors had gained enough confidence to bring a lawsuit against the American Medical Association and ten other medical organizations on the grounds that they had breached antitrust laws in conspiring to effect a monopoly over health care and to constrain licensed chiropractors from competing. The court upheld the case of the chiropractors and, in addition to imposing damages, insisted that an interprofessional research institute be set up to promote cooperation between chiropractors and the conventional medical profession. Since this event, the AMA has muted its collective opposition to chiropractic and has attempted containment rather than elimination (Gibbons 1980). It has not yet offered to chiropractors the place within its fold which it extended to American osteopaths.

In some other countries the story was similar. In Australia, chiropractors faced vehement medical opposition, often taking the form of malpractice suits brought against individuals (Fulder 1996: 103). However, when in 1974 the Ministry of Health established a committee to look into the usage of chiropractic, it concluded that chiropractic filled an important gap in the Australian health-care system. Manipulative Therapy Acts have since been passed by individual states offering registration to chiropractors and osteopaths despite continued medical opposition (although some Australian doctors would not object to state licensing for chiropractic if their practice were limited to back pain (Easthope 1993: 294)). On the other hand, in Britain the 1994 Chiropractors Act was passed with active support from the medical profession; the more limited scope of chiropractic practice in Britain meant that it did not constitute a threat to the overall position of medicine, as it had done in the United States. Indeed, it was regarded as helping to relieve back pain, a major issue for both the GP and the orthopaedic specialist. Chiropractors were not asking for parity with the medical profession and could be admitted to a legitimate, although adjunct, role with full medical support.

The case of chiropractic demonstrates that whilst national medical associations have, in general, taken a hostile stance to alternative medicine, their positions have varied over both space and time according to whether they see a particular modality as a major threat to their dominant position or as a possible adjunct to their own practice, capable of being accommodated without major redefinition of their own legitimate and legitimating role in the medical division of labour. But it also shows that doctors can no longer be confident that their objections will be heeded by governments conscious of the popularity which some forms of alternative medicine enjoy with the electorate.

National medical associations will find it harder in the future to maintain blanket opposition to alternative medicine. In some cases the tension between the collective stance and the individual practice of doctors is very evident. In Britain, the 1986 BMA report on Alternative Therapy was generally dismissive of the claims of alternative medicine and stressed the lack of scientific proof in the form of randomized controlled trials for most alternative interventions (BMA 1986). That the tone of this report was generally out of tune with the temper of the public, and indeed the temper of many of its members, became apparent in the debate that followed its publication. A further report was commissioned, and published in 1993. This second report (BMA 1993) took a completely different line, placing much less emphasis on scientific credentials and more on professional training, evidence of competence, and accreditation.

However, if collective medical opposition to alternative medicine is being toned down, it must be recognized that doctors' acceptance of, say, acupuncture or chiropractic in a particular country does not mean that the same doctors are likely to accept the claims of, say, herbalism or kinesiology. There are considerable national variations as to which therapies doctors find acceptable. Homoeopathy, acupuncture, osteopathy, and chiropractic are the most widely accepted by doctors in most countries, but whilst reflexology is taken seriously by doctors in Denmark, in Britain it does not have a high status in the eyes of the medical profession, although the modesty of its practitioners' claims render it unthreatening.

It must also be remembered that conventional biomedicine is not a static system itself. In practice, it is more eclectic than its scientific language and professional rhetoric would suggest. It has always been able to incorporate new ideas, and is probably not immune to the influence of patient demand. Possibly opposition is more explicit and more focused where doctors compete with alternative medicine in something near to an open market situation, but the adaptability of medicine in all kinds of health-care systems is a general feature. It remains to be seen how relations between alternative medicine and biomedicine develop. There is much evidence of cooperation and some convergence of knowledge bases. However, biomedicine is still the most powerful single health-care profession and is unlikely to cease to be so; those forms of alternative medicine that have been most successful in terms of gaining greater public recognition and legitimacy are, on the whole, those which have had the approval of a sizeable section of the medical profession.

THE REJUVENATION OF ALTERNATIVE MEDICINE

In this section we look at the ways in which the therapy groups themselves have changed in the post-war period in terms of their professional organization and therapeutic aspirations. The 1970s saw the revival of alternative medicine across the Western world (Sale 1995; Willis 1989). However, there have been national differences in the types of therapies that have become more favoured in the course of what Baer calls their 'rejuvenation' (Baer 1992). For example, in Denmark alternative therapies became more popular from the 1970s (Staugård 1993), but this was especially the case for reflexology. In contrast, in Iceland (Haraldsson 1993) and The Netherlands (Fisher and Ward 1994) there has been an exponential increase in the use of spiritual healers, and in France acupuncture and homoeopathy have become very popular (Traverso 1993). In the United States therapies such as chiropractic, osteopathy, and naturopathy (Baer 1992) maintained a stronger presence throughout the century but did experience further rejuvenation in the 1970s. Consequently, although we will sketch a general story here, it should be recognized that there are spatial and temporal differences. There are also clear variations across Europe when the training and academic background of the practitioner is examined. In countries with more restrictive legal systems, such as Belgium and France, the expansion of therapies has been confined to doctors or other recognized and biomedically orientated professionals such as physiotherapists.

Even within national boundaries we see that each therapy group has a specific history and distinct perception of their role in the healthcare market. In Britain alone it is estimated that there are at least 160 therapy groups (BMA 1993) which are all different in the way that they are organized and in their views of what they can and cannot treat (see Pietroni, 1992, for a useful typology). Some, more 'radical' therapy groups see themselves as separate from biomedicine, while others prefer a collaborative and complementary position in the health services. Even within therapy groups, the role and scope of the therapy may be the subject of debate, such differences being compounded by the ever-increasing number of therapists. For example, in the United States it has

been projected that the per capita supply of alternative medical clinicians will increase a further 88 per cent by 2010 (Cooper and Stoflet 1996). The number of professional associations is also increasing. Within reflexology in the United Kingdom there are more than 100 schools training practitioners and fourteen professional associations (Cant and Sharma 1994).There are also multiple umbrella associations that purport to represent the therapy groups. Nevertheless, it is possible to outline some general trends.

The 1970s revival of alternative medicine was an unplanned and radical movement, promoted largely by individuals who were not medically qualified. For example, whilst homoeopathy has been practised by some doctors in the United Kingdom since the eighteenth century, the 1970s saw the development of homoeopathy taught and practised by non-medically-qualified practitioners, many of whom also shared spiritual beliefs (i.e., Druidism). Homoeopathic training, in this context, was characterized by a lack of structure, the teaching took place through ad hoc seminars, and there was no curriculum or credentials. The teachings were very radical, proposing that homoeopathy would replace biomedicine in time, and to this end instruction was made available to anyone who was interested, irrespective of their background or qualifications (Cant 1996; Cant and Sharma 1996b).

The initial revitalization of alternative medicine was largely characterized by the direction of energy to the spread of the therapies and defence against the attacks of biomedicine rather than the stringent formulation of syllabi and professional credentials, but the late 1980s were witness to far-reaching changes, at the level of both organization and ideology, which have transformed the 'official' content and practice of alternative medicine, that is, that which is promoted by professional organizations.

In the first place there have been conscious attempts to structure the way that alternative medical knowledge is codified, transmitted, and accredited, with the establishment of formal training colleges. The timing of this process varies by country and depends on where the therapy first became popular. In Canada, for example, colleges of chiropractic emerged in the 1960s (Biggs 1992), whereas in the United Kingdom the shift from apprenticeship and unstructured teaching of chiropractic to a more formalized programme took place later in the late 1970s and 1980s. Even where colleges had a longer history, concerted efforts to achieve accreditation, and particularly degree status, began in the mid-1980s. Elsewhere similar developments took place; the first colleges of naturopathy emerged in the United States (Baer 1992) and Canada (Gort and Coburn 1988) in 1978.

These developments signalled a dramatic growth in student numbers. Baer (1992) shows that within 10 years (by 1988) of the first college of naturopathy opening in the United States, at least 130 students were being trained per year, compared with the original intake of three students. In the United Kingdom, if we take just two of the fourteen professional associations that represent reflexology, we see exponential growth. For example, the Bayley School (albeit one of the largest) estimated in 1994 that it had trained more than 3000 reflexologists. The Association of Reflexologists had 480 full members and 1560 members overall in 1994, and suggested that twenty new members joined every week. This is phenomenal growth when we consider that in 1984, when the Association was inaugurated, there were just ten members.

The 1980s saw the rapid multiplication of colleges for training in various forms of alternative medicine. During this period another nine colleges of naturopathy emerged in the United States. In Britain, although the scale varied by therapy, there was also a significant increase in the number of colleges. For instance, within chiropractic three separate colleges had emerged by the end of the 1980s, in homoeopathy there were twenty by the early 1990s, and in reflexology, at the time of writing, there were more than 100 schools that had been established, with no evidence that the expansion had run its course.

The 'pluralization' of colleges has not simply altered *where* training takes place but has had implications for the *content* of the curricula and the qualifications awarded. Many therapies now require at least 4 years of training in addition to supervised clinical practice. Increasingly, there have been moves to link the courses to nationally approved credentials. At present, in the United Kingdom, it is possible to read for degrees in chiropractic, osteopathy, homoeopathy, and herbalism. Aside from degree status, all colleges in the United Kingdom have made stringent attempts to identify the necessary prerequisites for a competent practitioner and to produce a core curriculum that covers these requirements. In some cases there have been European and International agreements upon what this core curriculum should contain, signifying a serious attempt to codify knowledge so that it can be passed on in a formal and structured way (see Cant and Sharma 1999).

Second, there are many instances where the therapy groups have tempered their original radical ideas. For example, within chiropractic it was believed by a section of the profession that the manipulation of the spine had the potential to cure the whole range of mechanical and organic problems. In Britain, the Druidic homoeopaths stressed the dangers of biomedicine and the capacity of homoeopathy to deal with all medical problems. Yet, the 1980s saw the gradual curtailment of such radical claims. For example, the main associations for the non-medically-qualified homoeopaths have now decided to stop advising patients to reject immunization for infants, although some members still believe that vaccination can account for forms of ill health (Cant and Sharma 1996b). In some cases this curtailment has been accompanied by the expansion of other skills. For example, in the United Sates osteopaths and naturopaths have acquired skills of general practice (Baer 1984).

Significantly, the professional associations that represent the various therapies in Britain publicly state that their practice should not be regarded as 'alternative' but as 'complementary' to biomedicine. This represents a conscious modification to the type of knowledge that is deemed acceptable and the type of public messages that the practitioners wish to convey. Some therapies now define their scope very modestly indeed. For example, in Britain the professional associations that represent reflexology have defined their therapy as supplementary to medical practice, helpful for relaxation and general healing but with no claim to diagnose or even cure (Cant and Sharma 1996a).

Third, we can identify consistent efforts on the part of professional organizations to relate 'complementary' knowledge to the orthodox scientific paradigm, at least in public (notwithstanding the misgivings of many individual members). For example, colleges in Britain and elsewhere (Baer 1992) have incorporated medical science into their curricula and conceive of biology, pathology, and physiology as constituent parts of their knowledge system. Such a move has been recommended by the British Medical Association (BMA 1993), which has argued that such an education will ensure that practitioners know when to refer patients back to a biomedical practitioner. The groups also increasingly make reference to orthodox scientific ideas to explain why their therapy works. This has been attempted in a number of ways, either by drawing directly on biomedical science or by criticising medical science and claiming to use a different scientific paradigm such as a quantum physics (see Sharma 1996). There has also been more openness to the use of scientific research methods, particularly randomized controlled trials, to examine the effectiveness of specific treatments (Meade et al. 1990; Reilly et al. 1986).

Finally, alternative medical groups have attempted to draw boundaries around their therapeutic knowledge in order to support their claims of expertise. This has been effected through higher entry requirements, longer training programmes, and the establishment of registers of qualified practitioners.

In summary, there has been a general shift throughout the alternative medical sector to more professional forms of organization and to a more controlled dissemination of knowledge. This has been accompanied by the inclusion of more biomedical knowledge about health, disease, and the body in training curricula. The expansion of therapy groups has taken place in a context that has required that the teachings and practices conform, to some degree, to an established paradigm and one that still places biomedicine in a position of authority, providing a model to be copied.

THE ROLE OF GOVERNMENT

The preeminence of biomedicine in the health-care systems of the Western world has been a product of the policies of government. In some countries, such as France, healing by nonmedically-qualified therapists is illegal. Elsewhere, alternative medicine has been tolerated but not supported by state funding or licence. For example, in Britain therapists may practice as long as they do not call themselves doctors, and in Germany 'heilpraktiker' may practice if they pass examinations to show certain competencies. Even where (as in India) other systems of healing are recognized and supported by the state, biomedicine still has a privileged position in the medical division of labour (see Last 1990 for a full typology of medical systems). The strength and universality of biomedicine's special relationship with the state has led some to suggest that the biomedical profession is an agent of the state (Navarro 1978). Certainly biomedicine has had an important say in the allocation of public health resources, with the consequence that most state health-care funding has been committed to biomedical provision.

However, the recent and rapid increase in alternative medicine has meant most governments have been called upon to regulate an expanding and diversifying health-care market. The general trend has been towards greater tolerance, even in countries with very strict laws of licensure, particularly for those therapies that have standardized their training and defined an area of competence. We are starting to see divisions in health-care systems not just

between 'legitimate' biomedicine and 'illegitimate' alternative medicine, but between therapies legitimated through state regulation and those without such recognition. On the other hand, greater tolerance cannot always be assumed. For example, three non-medically-qualified homoeopaths were arrested in Belgium in 1996 in a climate of apparent acceptance. Nor does governmental support necessarily lead to greater availability of a given therapy for the general public, especially if funding is not forthcoming.

Where governments have shown greater tolerance, this has taken various forms. For instance, in the United States, the National Institute of Health was instructed by Congress to open an Office for Alternative Medicine and provide funds for research (Pavek 1995). The Labour government in the United Kingdom is exploring a similar possibility, although it is not clear whether funds will follow. The clearest form of support has been through the granting of state registration or, in the United States, licensing laws – although these vary from state to state (Sale 1995). It is important to note that attempts at state registration have been made by therapy groups throughout the twentieth century (Larkin 1992), but have only started to prove successful in more recent years, especially the last decade. Chiropractic has now received state regulation in Switzerland, Norway, Finland, Sweden, the United Kingdom, and the United States.

Why have governments shifted their focus and what are the implications for alternative medicine, biomedicine, and the shape of the health services? In the first place, fiscal crisis and escalating health costs, especially with the increase in chronic and intractable health problems, have prompted governments to re-evaluate their health spending. Second, there is evidence in some countries, especially the United States (Baer 1984), that the support of certain therapies has been in response to shortfalls in the supply of biomedical personnel. Third, it is likely that governments have felt compelled to respond to vocal lay interest. Certainly in the United Kingdom, patient groups have proved to be effective lobbyists. There is also evidence that some governments have become increasingly suspicious of powerful and monopolistic professional groups. For example, in Australia the government has become less likely to offer carte blanche support for the medical profession (Willis 1989). Similarly, in the United Kingdom, since 1979, there has been a general move to curtail professional monopolies, enhance the power of the consumer, and increase competition, in particular through the encouragement of the private sector (Klein 1995).

Whilst governments have appeared more favourably inclined towards alternative medicine there may be limits to how far the support will extend. For example, it is the case that only certain therapies have attracted governmental support, and these are the ones that have undertaken the changes described in the previous section, altering their organizational structures and limiting their medical claims. As a result, it is a small number of therapies that have been able to secure statutory regulation. For example, in Britain only osteopathy and chiropractic have been successful to date. This is not to understate the importance of registration; it signifies that the government is prepared to endorse certain therapies and provide users of these services with some guarantees, but at the present time it appears that only those therapies that have limited their therapeutic claims and practices can hope to gain this endorsement, and only those therapies that are the least threatening to the biomedical paradigm have attracted support. Government support has, on the whole, not included bringing the services of non-medically-qualified alternative practitioners directly into state funded health care. There are few opportunities for patients to receive financial help with fees. Private insurance companies increasingly cover chiropractic and osteopathic services. In the United Kingdom, biomedical GPs have been able to use their budgets to purchase alternative practitioners' services on behalf of their patients. However, a recent study (Thomas et al. 1995) shows that these powers of GPs are under-used. In any case, this arrangement still places the GP in a position of control over both the patient and the alternative medical practitioner.

Overall we have seen some changes to the practices of government in relation to alternative medicine, in particular in making decisions about where the boundaries between legitimate and illegitimate health care lie. There has been some encouragement of a plural medical market, but one where providers have to conform to certain regulative criteria and where biomedicine still holds a dominant position. There has been a restructuring of expertise rather than a radical transformation of the system of health-care delivery.

Conclusion

Nonbiomedical forms of healing, never entirely absent, have come to occupy a more prominent and acknowledged role in the health-care systems of Western countries since the 1960s. As Cobb has shown in the case of chiropractic, the means by which a mode of healing may be legitimated are diverse: licensure or registration laws; government funding for research; academic support; the professionalizing efforts of therapists themselves; social movements, which directly or indirectly support alternative healers; and popular demand, as conveyed through opinion polls or other media to doctors and politicians (Cobb 1977). The process of legitimation has been very uneven and has everywhere taken place in the face of opposition from some quarters. There is much local variation as to which modes are most popular or most readily legitimated. Efforts to integrate alternative health care into the formal health-care system have often been ad hoc and unsystematic, depending on who has been prepared to support which therapies locally.

We have looked at this process of legitimation and acceptance from the point of view of four constituencies, all of which are playing a crucial role in this revision of the social relations of health.

Patients. A major driving force has been the evident popularity of alternative medicine among patients of chronic disease, often associated with a critical stance towards certain aspects of modern biomedicine and a more 'consumerist' approach to health care in general. Some patients clearly find that alternative medicines offer them a more participatory role in their own healing, and that they offer ways of understanding illness in terms of personal meaning rather than impersonal disease categories. Neither doctors nor governments have been able to ignore this. We can see this as a postmodern rejection of the absolute authority of medical science (Easthope 1993: 293). Alternatively, we could regard it as evidence that lay views on health care were never completely medicalized in the first place, and that we are simply seeing a resurgence of health seeking behaviour which was 'normal' before the large-scale provision of biomedical care funded by the state. Without more research the evidence is hard to assess.

The medical profession. It has always been the case that some doctors have practised certain forms of alternative medicine (such as homoeopathy, hypnotherapy, osteopathy), but more and more doctors (especially GPs) are now aware that alternative therapies are popular with many patients and may be helpful in dealing with certain chronic conditions, or at least in providing patients with the emotional support and counselling that GPs are ill-trained to provide. Those who see such scope are, in many countries, still outnumbered by those who perceive only a threat to their monopolistic position from therapists who (from the medical point of view) are not properly trained and who conduct treatments whose efficacy has not yet been demonstrated scientifically. On the whole, outright principled rejection of all kinds of healing which are not biomedical has ceded to acceptance that (whether doctors like it or not) many patients will continue to use alternative medicines. Therefore, a more realistic stance is cautious endorsement of those therapies which seem to be efficacious and cost effective in biomedical terms, or which offer relief from symptoms that biomedicine has not been successful in treating.

Alternative practitioners. Where alternative practitioners have succeeded in gaining professional legitimacy, it has generally been at the cost of a tempering of distinctive theory and practice, and a degree of convergence with biomedical theories of pathology, anatomy, and treatment. In forming their own professional associations, practitioners have had to confront the need to provide clearer ways of delineating their knowledge bases, defining professional competence, and achieving agreement on the claims that they can make for their particular therapies. Patients may reject the meta-narrative of biomedicine, but medical authority creeps in by the back door when homoeopathic or acupuncture colleges are obliged to include much biomedical knowledge in their courses, or when practitioners modify their claims so as to facilitate acceptance by the medical profession and the public at large.

The state. Governments have been unable to ignore the popularity of alternative medicine among the populace, and its increasing use by articulate and vocal members of the public who have pressed for relaxation of the laws against nonbiomedical practice where these have been in force. On the whole, whatever reforms have taken place, governments have not wanted radical disturbance of the relationship between biomedicine and the state, and have permitted the medical profession to act as advisors to government on matters concerning alternative medicines. On the other hand, accommodating some popular and successful forms of alternative medicine is compatible with an agenda (in some countries) of trying to contain the power of a large monopolistic medical profession. Furthermore, the presence of forms of healing which appear less costly than biomedicine and have a less expensive technological base has probably been significant in a period of crisis for public health-care funding.

It is likely that the expansion of alternative medicine will not continue indefinitely, if for no other reason than that it will encounter the same kind of funding constraints as bio-medicine and run up against the same public realization of the limitations to its claims to efficacy. Whilst the demand for health care appears to be boundless in Western countries, the extent to which either governments or insurance companies or individual patients can pay for it is restricted. In the short run, alternative medicine appears to offer treatment that is inexpensive compared with many biomedical treatments and/or to provide the holistic approach, which is the (often unattained) ideal of good biomedical primary health care. As such, it is likely to occupy a limited, but nonetheless important, role in the total health-care systems of Western societies.

REFERENCES

Baer, H. (1984) 'A comparative view of a heterodox health system: Chiropractic in America and Britain', *Medical Anthropology,* 8: 151–68.

Baer, H. (1992) 'The potential rejuvenation of American naturopathy as a consequence of the holistic health movement', *Medical Anthropology,* 13: 369–83.

Biggs, L. (1992) No Bones about Chiropractic. Unpublished PhD Thesis, University of Toronto.

BMA (1986) *Alternative Therapy. Report of the Board of Science and Education.* London: BMA.

BMA (1993) *Complementary Medicine. New Approaches to Good Practice.* Oxford: Oxford University Press/BMA.

Braathen, E. (1996) 'Communicating the individual body and the body politic: The discourse on disease prevention and health promotion in alternative therapies', in S. Cant and U. Sharma (eds), *Complementary and Alternative Medicines: Knowledge in Practice.* London: Free Association Books. pp. 151–62.

Busby, H. (1996) 'Alternative medicines/alternative knowledges: Putting flesh on the bones using traditional Chinese approaches to healing', in S. Cant and U. Sharma (eds), *Complementary and Alternative Medicines. Knowledge in Practice.* London: Free Association Books. pp. 135–51.

Cant, S. (1996) 'From charismatic teaching to professional training', in S. Cant and U. Sharma (eds), *Complementary and Alternative Medicines: Knowledge in Practice.* London: Free Association Press. pp. 44–66.

Cant, S. and Sharma, U. (1994) *The Professionalisation of Complementary Medicine.* Final project report to ESRC.

Cant, S. and Sharma, U. (1996a) 'The professionalisation of complementary medicine in the UK', *Complementary Therapies in Medicine,* 4: 157–62.

Cant, S. and Sharma, U. (1996b) 'The reluctant profession – homoeopathy and the search for legitimacy', *Work, Employment and Society*, 9: 743–62.

Cant, S. and Sharma, U. (1999) *A New Medical Pluralism. Complementary Medicine, Doctors, Patients and the State*. London: Taylor and Francis.

Cobb, A.K. (1977) 'Pluralistic legitimation of an alternative therapy system: The case of chiropractic', *Medical Anthropology*, 4 (Fall): 1–23.

Cooper, R. and Stoflet, S. (1996) 'Trends in the education and practice of alternative medicine clinicians', *Health Affairs*, 15: 226–38.

Cooter, R. (ed.) (1988) *Studies in the History of Alternative Medicine*. Basingstoke: Macmillan.

Crawford, R. (1980) 'Healthism and the medicalization of everyday life', *International Journal of Health Services*, 10: 365–88.

Easthope, G. (1993) 'The response of orthodox medicine to the challenge of alternative medicine in Australia', *The Australian and New Zealand Journal of Sociology*, 29: 289–301.

Editorial (1980) 'The flight from science', *British Medical Journal*, 6202: 1–2.

Eisenberg, D., Kessler, R., Foster, C., Norlock, F., Calkins, M., and Delbanco, T. (1993) 'Unconventional medicine in the United States', *The New England Journal of Medicine*, 328: 246–52.

Eklöf, M. (1996) 'So-called alternative treatment. On the medical profession's views on quackery and alternative medicine in Sweden', in S. Olesen and E. Høg (eds), *Studies in Alternative Therapy. 3. Communication in and about Alternative Therapies*. Odense: Odense University Press. pp. 187–96.

Faure, O. (ed.) (1992) *Praticiens, Patients et Militants de l'Homéopathie (1800–1940)*. Lyon: Presses Universitaires de Lyon.

Fisher, P. and Ward, A. (1994) 'Complementary medicine in Europe', *BMJ*, 309, 9 July: 107–11.

Fulder, S. (1996) *The Handbook of Alternative and Complementary Medicine*. Oxford: Oxford University Press.

Furnham, A. and Bhagrath, R. (1992) 'A comparison of health beliefs and behaviours of clients of orthodox and complementary medicine', *British Journal of Clinical Psychology*, 32: 237–46.

Furnham, A. and Kirkcaldy, B. (1996) 'The health beliefs and behaviours of orthodox and complementary medicine clients', *British Journal of Clinical Psychology*, 35: 49–61.

Gevitz, N. (ed.) (1988) *Other Healers. Unorthodox Medicine in America*. Baltimore: Johns Hopkins University Press.

Gibbons, R. (1980) 'The evolution of chiropractic: Medical and social protest in America. Notes on the survival years and after', in S. Haldeman (ed.), *Modern Developments in the Principles and Practice of Chiropractic*. New York: Appleton-Century Crofts. pp. 5–24.

Glymour, D. and Stalker, C. (1989) 'Engineers, cranks, physicians, magicians' in G. Glymour and D. Stalker (eds), *Examining Holistic Medicine*. Buffalo: Prometheus.

Goldszmidt, M., Levitt, C., Duarte-Franco, E., and Kaczorowski, J. (1995) 'Complementary health care services: A survey of general practitioners' views', *Canadian Medical Association Journal*, 153: 29–35.

Gort, E. and Coburn, D. (1988) 'Naturopathy in Canada: Changing relationships to medicine, Chiropractic and the state', *Social Science and Medicine*, 26: 1061–72.

Haraldsson, E. (1993) Spiritual healing in Iceland', in H. Johannessen, L. Launsø, S. Oleson, and F. Staugård (eds), *Studies in Alternative Therapy. 1. Contributions from the Nordic Countries*. Odense: Odense University Press. pp. 46–51.

Hewer, W. (1993) 'The relationship between the alternative practitioner and his patient', *Psychotherapy and Psychosomatics*, 40: 172.

Kirkland, J., Mathews, H., Sullivan, C., and Baldwin, K. (eds) (1992) *Herbal and Magical Medicine. Traditional Healing Today*. Durham, NC: Duke University Press.

Klein, R. (1995) *The New Politics of the NHS*. London: Longman.

Larkin, G. (1992) 'Orthodox and osteopathic medicine in the inter-war years', in M. Saks (ed.), *Alternative Medicine in Britain*. Oxford: Clarendon. pp. 12–123.

Last, M. (1990) 'Professionalisation of indigenous healers', in T. Johnson and C. Sargent (eds), *Medical Anthropology. Contemporary Theory and Method*. New York: Praeger. pp. 349–66.

Lloyd, P., Lupton, D., Wiesner, D., and Hasleton, S. (1993) 'Choosing alternative therapy: An exploratory study of socio-demographic characteristics and motives of patients resident in Sydney', *Australian Journal of Public Health*, 17: 135–41.

Lowenberg, J. and Davis, F. (1994) 'Beyond medicalisation–demedicalisation: The case of holistic health', *Sociology of Health and Illness*, 16: 579–99.

MacLennan, A., Wilson, D., and Taylor, A. (1996) 'Prevalence and cost of alternative medicine in Australia', *The Lancet*, 347, March 2: 569–73.

Meade, T., Dyer, S., Browne, W., Townsend, J., and Frank, A. (1990) 'Low back pain of mechanical origin: Randomised comparison of Chiropractic and hospital outpatient treatment', *BMJ*, 300 (6737): 1431–7.

Melchart, D. (1994) 'Integration of complementary medicine in research at the University of Munich', in S. Olesen and E. Høg (eds), *Studies in Alternative Therapy. 3. Communication in and about Alternative Therapies*. Odense: Odense University Press. pp. 159–70.

Menges, L. (1994) 'Regular and alternative medicine; The state of affairs in The Netherlands', *Social Science and Medicine*, 39: 871–3.

NAHAT (1992) *Complementary Therapies in the NHS*. Birmingham: NAHAT.

Navarro, V. (1978) *Class Struggle, the State and Medicine*. London: Martin Robertson.

Nicholls, P. (1988) *Homoeopathy and the Medical Profession*. London: Croom Helm.

Ooijendijk, W., Makenbach, H., and Limberger, A. (1981) *What is Better?* Netherlands Institute of Preventative Medicine and The Technical Industrial Organisation, London: Translated and published by the Threshold Foundation.

Paramore, C. (1997) 'Use of alternative therapies: Estimates from the 1994 Robert Wood Johnson Foundation national access to care survey', *Journal of Pain and Symptom Management*, 13(2): 83–89.

Pavek, R. (1995) 'Current status of alternative health practices in the United States', *Contemporary Internal Medicine*, 7(8): 61–71.

Perkin, M., Pearcy, R., and Fraser, J. (1994) 'A comparison of the attitudes shown by general practitioners, hospital doctors and medical students towards alternative medicine', *Journal of the Royal Society of Medicine*, 87: 523–5.

Pietroni, P. (1992) 'Beyond the boundaries: Relationship between general practice and complementary medicine', *BMJ*, 305 (5 September): 564–6.

Rankin-Box, D. (1993) 'Innovation in practice: Complementary therapies in nursing', *Complementary Therapies in Medicine*, 1: 30–3.

Reilly, D.T., Taylor, M.A., McSharry, C., and Aitchison, T. (1986) 'Is homoeopathy a placebo response? Controlled trial of homoeopathic potency, with pollen in hay fever as a model', *Lancet*, 333(2): 881–5.

Saks, M. (1994) 'The alternatives to medicine', in J. Gabe, D. Kelleher, and G. Williams (eds), *Challenging Medicine*. London: Routledge. pp. 84–103.

Sale, D. (1995) *Overview of Legislative Developments Concerning Alternative Health Care in the United States*. Michigan: Fretzer Institute.

Sawyer, C. and Ramlow, J. (1984) 'Attitudes of chiropractic patients: A preliminary survey of patients receiving care in a chiropractic teaching clinic', *Journal of Manipulative and Physiological Therapeutics*, 7 (13): 157–63.

Sermeus, G. (1987) *Alternative Medicine in Europe. A Quantitative Comparison of the Use and Knowledge of Alternative Medicine and Patient Profiles in Nine European Countries*. Brussels: Belgian Consumers' Association.

Sharma, U. (1995) *'Pa ti', Complementary Medicine Today. Practitioners and Patients* revised edn. London: Routledge.

Sharma, U. (1996) 'Situating homoeopathic knowledge: Legitimation and the cultural landscape', in S. Cant and U. Sharma (eds), *Complementary and Alternative Medicines. Knowledge in Practice*. London: Free Association Books. pp. 165–85.

Shilling, C. (1993) *The Body and Social Theory*. London: Sage.

Stacey, M. (1988) *The Sociology of Health and Healing*. London: Unwin Hyman.

Staugård, F. (1993) 'The role of traditional and complementary therapy in primary health care', in H. Johannessen, L. Launso, S. Olesen, and F. Staugård (eds), *Studies in Alternative Therapy. 1. Contributions from the Nordic Countries*. Odense: Odense University Press. pp. 84–93.

Thomas, K., Carr, J., Westlake, L., and Williams, B. (1991) 'Use of non-conventional and orthodox health care in Great Britain', *British Medical Journal*, 302: 207–10.

Thomas, K., Fall, K., Parry, G., and Nicholl, J. (1995) *National Survey of Access to Complementary Health Care via General Practice*. Sheffield University: Medical Care Research Unit.

Traverso, D. (1993) 'La pratique médicale alternative. L'expérience de l'homéopathie et de l'acupuncture', *Sociologie du Travail*, 35: 181–98.

Vaskilampi, T. (1993) 'Alternative medicine in Finland – an overview on the role of alternative medicine and its research in Finland', in H. Johannessen, L. Launsø, S. Olesen, and F. Staugård (eds), *Studies in Alternative Therapy. 1. Contributions from the Nordic Countries*. Odense: Odense University Press. pp. 40–6.

Verbrugge, L.M. (1982) 'Sex differentials in health', *Public Health Reports*, 97: 417.

Verhoef, M.J. (1996) 'Complementary medicine and the general practitioner: Challenges for health policy', *Complementary Medicine International*, May/June: 13–17.

Vincent, C. and Furnham, A. (1996) 'Why do people turn to complementary medicine? An empirical study', *British Journal of Clinical Psychology*, 35: 37–48.

Wardwell, W. (1992) *History and Evolution of a New Profession*. St Louis: Mosby Year Book.

Willis, E. (1989) *Medical Dominance*. Sydney: Allen and Unwin.

3.5

Comparative Health Systems: Emerging Convergences and Globalization

LINDA M. WHITEFORD AND LOIS LACIVITA NIXON

INTRODUCTION

Managed health-care systems in Chile? Preferred provider programs in Bolivia? Herbalists in Indiana? St John's Wort, Cat's Claw, and *Gingko biloba* in Arkansas? Are health-care systems becoming more alike as globalization connects our economic and political systems, e-mail thrusts our communications across continents with speed, accuracy and ease, and people and pathogens fly greater distances with more frequency than ever before? This chapter reviews comparative health system (CHS) research and asks if health systems are converging on a limited number of Western-influenced models of care, or are there new and still emerging 'mosaics' of models stimulated by the conflicting forces of globalization and cultural diversity?

Even a cursory review of the literature on CHS shows a vast array of models, criteria, concepts, and critiques. The lack of standard definitions and comparability of methods in the field of CHS makes cross-cultural comparisons difficult. Some researchers decry the lack of data available for analysis, while others lament the lack of uniform conceptualizations of the units to be measured, the processes to be investigated, and the outcomes to be compared. The field of CHS analysis, traditionally dominated by social scientists such as sociologists, political scientists, anthropologists, economists, and policy and public administration experts, reflects the epistemological and methodological bases of these distinct academic disciplines, as well as the diversity of the subject matter. This very diversity, while difficult to summarize, provides provocative and

challenging analyses suggesting future directions of CHS research in a time of global change.

Interest in health system research has skyrocketed since the 1980s, and in particular, interest in health system reform. Much of the early work in CHS research focused on the developed nations of Europe and North America, with little research on the modern health systems of developing nations and even less written by scientists from other countries. In our review of the current CHS research we found some of the most exciting and challenging analysis being written by Latin American social scientists about their own countries' struggles to reform health systems. To compensate for historical oversight and recognize innovative voices emerging from non-European and non-North American sources, we focus our discussion of current CHS research on health-care reform in Latin America.

The descriptive paradigm of 'systems' that formed the basis for CHS analysis from the 1940s through the 1990s is giving way to an emerging paradigm in which the process of health-care delivery is being redefined, reformed, and re-conceptualized. The new models attempt to include diversity, allow for structural pluralism, and identify health-care methods and evaluations appropriate to their cultural context and articulated goals. To understand those changes it is necessary to review the history of CHS research.

As we explore the field of CHS research, it is helpful to remember how Eurocentric systems came to develop, dominate, and influence approaches to health care throughout the world. Until recently, values, vision, and ethics were viewed as nonessential concerns for corporate managers, who viewed them as tangential to the real work of the enterprise (Wheatley 1992). In health-care sectors strict attention to objectivity, close scrutiny, careful measurement, and prescribed care in the search for absolute answers characterized earlier approaches to health-care concerns and practices. The social science focus of CHS studies, coupled with the conceptual break from industrial age rigidities, provides unprecedented opportunities for innovative reform, multiple routes of access to care, fundamental health status improvements, and a rich array of types of multidisciplinary collaboration.

The formal analysis of health-care systems began in the 1970s with the early work of medical sociologists such as Roemer and the Sidels, and other social scientists such as Navarro, Gish, Elling, Kelman, Kleinman, Mechanic, and Waitzkin. Culminating in a conference on social science and medicine held in Washington, DC in the late 1970s, Charles Leslie stimulated a parallel interest in comparative medical systems (Leslie 1978). The issues they discussed at that time are the same problems that beset CHS analysis today – the lack of shared definitions, methods, concepts, and paradigms. However, the analysis of that period changed the way we think about medical/health-care systems. Social science has contributed to our increasingly sophisticated understanding of how our own knowledge is shaped by cultural experiences, which in turn, shape our definition of data and infuse our interpretations with values. The field of CHS analysis has moved from a reflection of an uncritical and unquestioning dominance of the biomedical paradigm as 'normal' (using Kuhn's 1970 definition) to a greater awareness of values in defining the research process, the role of funding agencies and mass media in giving substance and direction to our perceptions, the inadequacy of extant models, and the need to focus on articulated goals and processes as a means of comparing health systems.

In this chapter we highlight the research of social scientists who have approached CHS as complex social systems, and using health reform as a focus, we incorporate a brief description of Chile as an example of relational analysis in CHS. In our review of David Mechanic's idea of emerging convergences, we move from a discussion of CHS literature in a period of subtly declining but still pervasive Industrial Age influence, to current analysts who step out of traditional disciplinary confinements to explore their subjects in a postmodern view. The transition from a single way of thinking to one that is receptive to change has been described as the struggle 'between those who try to prop up

and preserve industrial society and those who are ready to advance beyond it. This is the super struggle for tomorrow' (Toffler and Toffler 1995: 104). We suggest that CHS analysts are moving beyond the propped up past. Global conditions and trends that stretch beyond national borders increasingly influence the health sector. CHS scientists understand the challenges and opportunities of globalization, and are engaged in cross-national comparisons of health systems, exchanges of information, and provocative debates; their contributions are setting the stage for improved health in a greatly transformed world.

History of Comparative Health Systems Research

Social scientists have long been interested in the organization of health systems: their economic base, structural compartmentalization, service delivery programs, allocation of resources, decision making, and the interactions between physicians, allied health professionals, and the community. Initial research in health systems in the United States began in the 1930s and was motivated by the need to evaluate New Deal social reforms (Roemer 1991). The development of the British National Health Service stimulated comparative research in the 1950s and 1960s, and the health system experiments in Cuba and Nicaragua intrigued social scientists and lay people. The political left in the United States, Europe, and Latin America gave strength and support to social science analyses of the changing structure of health systems. Perhaps in response to the more explicitly polemical writings of the social left, others attempted to write about CHS from a less explicitly political view. Foremost of those writers was Milton Roemer, whose work shaped CHS analysis for 20 years (Roemer 1977, 1985, 1991). Roemer's early work focused particularly on the health systems of Europe and the United States, investigating the relationship between national political structure and health system development. Equally powerful in directing the scope of early CHS analysis were Victor and Ruth Sidel (1974), whose work on non-Western health systems, such as those in China, provided powerful counter-examples to the Western models.

In the late 1960s and early 1970s, the CHS literature focused primarily on the issue of *equity*, concerned with comprehensive health-care availability for entire populations. The writings of the time reflect both an optimistic view of the future and a willingness to challenge past assumptions that economic advantages would trickle down to the poor, that overall prosperity would improve health conditions for all, and that established government programs and policies were designed to make health for all a realistic goal. The *International Journal for Health Services* epitomized the conceptual changes of the time. It provided a way for the influential social health analysts of that era, such as Vincente Navarro, Oscar Gish, Sander Kelman, Ruth and Victor Sidel, Ray Elling, and Howard Waitzkin, to publish research reports, air opinions, and challenge established ideas by focusing on class relations, non-capitalist health models, and world economic system analyses.

The hopeful optimism of the early 1970s changed to more guarded realism in social analysis following the worldwide oil crisis in the mid-1970s. Social scientists engaged in CHS research turned away from structural analyses of equity to analyses of health system *cost containment* (Klein 1991; Sidel 1980–81). The Organization for Economic Cooperation and Development (OECD) published a series of comparative health analyses (OECD 1977, 1985, 1987) as part of their overall research on economic management and public expenditure, which consolidated the shift from equity issues to economic issues. The OECD reports also determined the database that structured the parameters of subsequent research by collecting previously unavailable or inaccessible statistical data on which numerous other studies were based (OECD 1977, 1985, 1987, 1990, as cited in Klein 1991). The nature of the data available and the prevailing interests of the OECD in economic indices ensured a continuing focus on cost containment, moving the center of discussion away from issues of equity toward an emphasis on efficiency.

A review of the CHS literature in the late 1970s and well through the middle 1980s demonstrates a clear shift away from a focus on equity to the new economic indices such as spending levels, administrative costs, number of beds, and recuperative costs. The shift was without doubt influenced by the economic hardships of the times and concomitant emphases on accountability, as well as by the data made available by the OECD. During that decade, economists comparing health inputs in economic terms eclipsed the role of social science analysis from sociologists and anthropologists. Klein (1991), in his excellent discussion of the risks and benefits of comparative studies, forcefully argues that while there was 'an inflation of economists in the field of health research' (1991: 281; see also Fox 1990), there was no conspiracy to

take over the field. Rather, the influence of economists and statisticians reflected both the availability of statistical and economic data, and '...the famine of other data, notably about the impact of different types of health care systems on the *populations* being served' (Klein 1991: 282 [emphasis added]).

As our example of health-care reform in Chile shows, the draconian cuts in health budgets in the 1980s had negative repercussions on the health status of women and children and other at-risk populations. In some cases, this negative consequence precipitated an attempt to mediate between the conflicting goals of cost-cutting and equity in the provision of services. The decade between the middle 1980s and 1990s shows this shift away from cost containment and economic measures to indicators of the 'effectiveness' of various health systems. 'The assumption of the 1990s seems, increasingly, to be that assuring effectiveness – by eliminating unnecessary, redundant, or low-yield forms of treatment – is a necessary condition for reconciling the demands of economy and equity' (Klein 1991: 283). Even the 1990 OECD report moves away from the primacy of economic indices to international comparisons of medical practices and health-care use. However, unlike some economic indices, health service utilization is problematic to define, difficult to measure, and the international data is often unavailable. The lack of internationally shared and mutually understood paradigms and conceptual frameworks complicates and impedes research in this new direction.

This historical review of CHS research highlights how the field has changed in content and focus from system-based comparisons of equity and economic measures, to effectiveness. Concurrently, CHS research has been struggling with questions of methods, models, and conceptual frameworks. While the CHS literature contains examples of many typologies and models, few are explicitly tied to theoretical frameworks. As Klein noted, CHS research tends to be data, not question, driven. As a consequence, there is a proliferation of models, categories, and typologies, with fewer articles that are theory-driven. Too often the data-driven research is difficult to generalize from because of the lack of theory, and the theoretical articles are challenged by lack of cross-cultural data.

Implicit political biases also hamper comparability of CHS research. Roemer (1977, 1985, 1991), perhaps the best known author in the first decades of CHS research, presented a typology in which three types of government planning and control of health systems were tied to three levels of resources in terms of gross national product per capita. According to Roemer, the levels of government planning are as follows: (a) pluralistic or laissez faire, (b) cooperative or welfare states, and (c) socialist or centrally planned. The three resource levels are (a) affluent or industrialized, (b) moderate or developing, and (c) poor or underdeveloped. Thus, nine categories of health systems can be identified by level of government planning and resource base, with the United States representing the affluent pluralistic category, the United Kingdom, the affluent cooperative, the former USSR, the affluent socialist, and China, the socialist and underdeveloped. These early works by Roemer and others (cf. Roemer 1977; Rostow 1971) reflect the dominant 'modernization' framework common to social policy makers in the 1950s through the 1970s. The modernization framework assumes that all societies desire the same end point – to become 'modernized' – and that while they may move at different speeds and through different paths, through time they will become more similar. A related assumption, although not frequently made explicit, is that there is a hierarchy of desirability in health systems, with the US/UK models of affluence setting the standard and the goal for other less developed health systems to emulate. These ideas implicitly deny the validity of alternative directions in health care, denigrate the role of history and culture in shaping national systems, and ignore the value of structured pluralism.

The modernization approach has been thoroughly critiqued by social scientists from a variety of disciplines and fields of concentration. Ray Elling (1981, 1994) points out that while Roemer has made significant, continual and long-lasting contributions to CHS, his early work in particular reflects an assumption that health systems evolve automatically from diversity and variability, to convergence and conformity, to structures and forms modeled on those from highly industrialized nations. These perspectives of convergence of health systems, along with assumptions of modernization, dominate much of the early writing on CHS in the 1970s (see Field 1967; Fuchs 1974; Mechanic 1975). This view abrogates the role of struggle, particularly class struggle, in the development of systems (Elling 1981). The case study of health systems development in Chile that we include in this chapter provides an example of how context and culture challenge modernizationist assumptions of convergence and conformity to *a priori* models.

While many analysts and researchers have made significant contributions to the field of CHS, three classic studies deserve emphasis. Litman and Robins (1971), while sharing the modernization frame, argued that health systems evolve through social, cultural, political,

and economic influences both internal to the country and external (in response to those similar influences from outside of the country). However, they make explicit the need for longitudinal studies that capture change over time. Much of the CHS research, they note, is cross-sectional and fails to demonstrate how variables influence one another. Litman and Robins articulate a previously identified (De Geyndt 1968, cited in Litman and Robins) but often ignored recognition of bias: that research is commissioned and undertaken for political results, providing the appearance but not the reality of 'scientific objectivity.' This watershed article marks the beginning of a serious interest in, and almost domination of, politics in CHS research.

In 1976, Kohn and White brought together population-based surveys from seven countries in an ambitious and problematic study. The study was aimed at addressing problems of '…health services administrators, and investigators, planners and policy makers, as well as scholars in the disciplines of epidemiology, sociology, psychology, economics, and medicine, elements of all of these fields of endeavor combined in the design and execution of the study' (1976: 1). The result was a complex and unwieldy document, difficult to apply to real-life situations. Their contribution brought together data from seven countries for comparison; their failure was the inability to draw meaningful and stimulating conclusions from the research, perhaps due to the unwieldiness and complexity of the data.

The third major study marking these developmental years of CHS research was the examination of 144 studies by van Atteveld et al. (1987). The authors note that the most '…striking conclusions are that there is very little connection between the stated objective of a given study and what is actually described, and that special attention is paid in international comparative research to the organisation and financing of health care, in particular to the subject of cost control' (1987: 105). Atteveld et al. reviewed the literature during the period when economic themes dominated, but concerns about inadequate data and lack of appropriate conceptual frameworks that were sounded then are still resonant throughout CHS research today.

While CHS research remains methodologically and theoretically diverse, and the applications of its results problematic, social scientists continue to make significant contributions to the field. Social scientists are influencing the move away from the modernist paradigm by focusing attention on the validity of data, the methods of analysis appropriate for various applications, identification of observer biases, and the nature, purpose, and most appropriate methods of comparison.

Roemer (1991) identifies six reasons for comparing health systems: (1) for the observers to gain perspective; (2) to learn through observation of other systems, with the intent to improve; (3) to achieve equity; (4) to improve efficiency; (5) to investigate how health-care systems impact health status; (6) to develop generalizations across system types. Other CHS analysts suggest that research can reduce ethnocentrism through the demonstration of similarities across systems (Fox 1986; Klein 1991; Marmor and Thomas 1972) and can sharpen our understanding of problems within our own health systems by providing information to guide constructive change (Sidel 1980-81).

Others argue that comparisons are elusive at best, and fallacious at worse (Hsiao 1992; Illsley 1990). One of the difficulties, as previously noted by Sidel (1980–81), is that too often the nature and purpose of the comparison are not made explicit from the outset. This can result in comparisons between entities that are similar superficially, but whose purpose and function are distinctive. Hsiao (1992) identifies three conceptual struggles in the development of CHS research. The first is the view that a health-care system is a means to an end, and that the ends (and means) must be agreed upon and clearly articulated within the system. This often is not the case; frequently nations fail to reach a consensus about either health system goals or means, let alone a shared, agreed understanding of them both. An additional barrier to effective comparison is the ideological debate between those favoring free enterprise and those who support government health-care planning (demand-side versus supply-side economics). The third obstacle is the lack of empirical data. Klein (1991) disagrees with Hsiao's contention that what CHS lacks is data, and argues instead that the problem with CHS research is that it is driven by the data which are available instead of by research questions. According to Klein, one of the costs of using available data to compare systems is that those data reflect particular national agendas, and may not be the most appropriate basis for cross-cultural comparisons of equity, economy, or efficiency.

The history of CHS is shaped by concern for conceptual and methodological rigor, political sophistication, and application. Social scientists, such as those whose work we have reviewed, have contributed to the struggle to define appropriate measures to be employed in the analysis and comparisons of health systems. The ongoing critiques and challenges to the methodologies, theories, and conceptual frameworks incorporated in CHS research come in large part from social scientists. We turn next to the emerging issues in health-care reform and the effect of globalization on health-care systems.

Emerging Issues in CHS: Health Sector Reform

Findings and determinations of major social trends, such as those just presented, are essential for identifying and clarifying issues for later analysts to incorporate into the next levels of discourse. Concern for methodological and conceptual rigor, political sophistication, and appropriate applications continue to characterize the work done by successive CHS analysts, but the approach and content increasingly correspond to changing epistemological shifts that distinguish modern views from those that are postmodern. Modern theorists devised systems for classifying and compartmentalizing; postmodern theorists tend to veer away from prior patterns of organization and provide open-ended explorations of situations that do not always lead to clear-cut conclusions.

In continuing interrogations of modern systems and limits, globalization or postmodernism calls into question the bases of Western (Eurocentric) modes of thinking, ordering, and constructing. Familiar values are in the process of deconstruction, exploration, and testing as new possibilities emerge. The texts reviewed earlier illustrate a drive toward 'totalization and finite and closed knowledge' (Hutcheon 1988: 75), or what might be described as corporate centralization and the pursuit of the definitive. In both subtle and substantive ways, more recent CHS research demonstrates a change in direction as the impact of globalism has led social scientists to move from past restrictions to new explorations and possibilities concerning the shape and structure of international health care.

Beginning in the 1960s with the social movements accompanying desegregation, the Peace Corps, and the war in Vietnam, increasing in the 1970s with the end of the Cold War, the women's movement, and the collapse of the Berlin Wall, and intensifying in the 1980s and 1990s, with the war in Bosnia, the genocide in Rwanda, and the availability of these images through cable television, inhabitants of Western or Eurocentric societies have come to recognize that old ideologies and views of the world order are undergoing widespread upheaval and transformation. The long-standing and familiar packaging of an industrialized society looming authoritatively over marginalized nations rutted in 'developing' configurations no longer works; it is in the process of entropy.

Worldwide changes in politics, internationalization, civil rights for women and other groups, political correctness, empowerment efforts by marginalized groups, and postmodern art and literature represent a radical departure from modernist views about the world, its people, and societies. These currents of change spread throughout the academic world to generate debates about new conditions, social movements, post-colonial studies, 'orbital' currencies, and speeded-up information sources.

In this section our focus centers on the comparative study of health sector reform within the evolving context of global change. First, we consider why globalism serves as an unavoidable impetus for health system reform, and then we review options for the comparison of health sector reform within the emerging global context.

Globalization as Impetus for Health Systems Reform

The influence of postmodernism can be seen in art and architecture with the debates, for instance, about the Pompidou Museum and the Pei Pyramid in Paris, as well as in the social and natural sciences. The force of postmodernism on academic conceptualizations in the late twentieth century is pervasive. That influence is also reflected in the writings about health-care reform, as social scientists borrow the 'mosaic' concept to discuss how disparate entities form coherent interconnections. A mosaic seems an appropriate image in a time of amorphous boundaries – geopolitical, cultural, personal, and perceptual – and unfamiliar landscapes.

Major transitions or paradigm shifts relating to fundamental ways of seeing and interpreting do not occur without discord and strong reaction; when the dynamics of globalism become local, difficulties relating primarily to power and control produce considerable degrees of tension and conflict. Innovation can occur when different ideas, perceptions, and ways of processing and judging information collide, and so too can dissolution and conflict. The study of comparative health systems, itself a reflection of academic interests, is in the process of reinventing itself in a global context.

Blurring of national borders, another feature of globalism, produces mixed signals for analysts who optimistically envision collaborative improvement of basic human conditions. Concern is expressed about concentrations of power and control by the World Bank and International Monetary Fund, and about trade agreements negotiated under GATT, APEC, and NAFTA that severely limit development of strong national and independent governments. The needs for economic support and cooperation, on the one hand, and for independence and autonomy, on the other, appear to be in conflict (Korten 1995: 87–8). Consolidation of the world's national markets into seamless global economies by powerful mega-corporations, whose view of reality may be dominated by financial incentives (Korten 1995: 37), poses complex social, political, and economic concerns.

Health System Reform as a Result of Globalization

What may have appeared contained and controlled in the past has exploded into strange, unrecognizable formations as a result of electronic simulacra, new technologies, and complex patterns of human migration and dislocation. Old management structures and techniques are increasingly irrelevant.

In the past, health-care workers, for example, under the auspices of bureaucratic organizations, were able to organize immunization campaigns and other programs for fairly static populations in developing countries. However, in recent decades those programs and others have been disrupted by large numbers of people migrating from native homelands to resettle in London, Frankfurt, Miami, Marseilles, Caracas, La Paz, Buenos Aires, and other world cities. Migrations like these overturn traditional assumptions about health-care needs of populations and frustrate established management expectations and norms. Moreover, because migrations bring diverse populations together and raise compelling new concerns about health-care issues, future health-care systems must be prepared to respond quickly and innovatively to global shifts. Continued use of earlier policies and approaches to health care often prove to be outdated, inappropriate, costly, and useless.

An increasingly visualized world reveals financial differences and the concomitant social inequalities that characterize groups in society and increase claims for equity and social redistribution (Kleinman and Kleinman 1997). What might have been unknown, overlooked, or ignored by audiences in industrialized nations before, now becomes an unavoidable reality. Today, the focus is immediate and sustained: the entire world turns on the television set or logs on to the Internet to receive powerfully portrayed accounts of world events. A wired world that has forged connections and links between formerly disparate populations has consequences for social tension and unrest, and also for social improvement.

Emerging Convergences

Through media exposure, the integration of economies in worldwide markets, and technological information resources, globalization's impact on health has been fast-tracked. In an important discussion of comparative health systems, Mechanic and Rochefort (1996: 242) described threads of connection derived from global shifts, or what they call 'emerging convergences,' that are creating cross-national and cross-dependent imperatives for cost containment, expansion of access to care, financing of care, government roles, and patient choice. Underscoring the importance of 'exogenous' or non-health-specific factors contributing to common burdens on systems throughout the world, the authors note that the 'strength of these factors is not identical from one country to another . . . they occur at varying rates and interact in different ways. Nonetheless, they provide an excellent window through which to monitor and evaluate the evolution of medical care in its principal outlines' (1996: 266). The recognition of non-health specific factors becomes a central ingredient for reform collaborators in what is termed 'shared learning experiences' (Gonzalez-Block 1997: 190) and 'networks of communities' (Frenk et al. 1997: 1404), and has set the tone for recent discourse. Intent on promoting meaningful and sustained health sector reform, a critical mass of proponents has begun to assemble overlapping matrices out of diverse and oddly shaped building tool concepts.

Contemporary CHS analysts recognize a trend in health sector reform moving toward goal-related outcomes that include cost containment, while reviving attention to the equity and effectiveness concerns raised by earlier scientists. Within a strengthened environment of collaboration, analysts are proposing a full review of available options in order to imagine and design 'planned, purposeful, and positive health-care transformations and a consistent basis for delivery services, policy, action, and research' (Frenk 1994: 20). Implicit in the identification of options is the need to specify main components of current health systems and their relational elements and structures (Frenk 1994: 24). Having little interest in historical patterns of incremental reform, CHS analysts are calling for re-articulated reform and synthesizing levels of reform, for producing achievable goals, commitment to and support of those agreed-upon

goals, and methods for comparative research and minimum data sets (Gonzalez-Block 1997: 189; Murray 1995: 107). If the processes of health care are to be guided toward equity, quality, cost effectiveness, and sustainability, a 'comprehensive economic and social theory is required that takes account of the peculiar nature and objectives that societies assign to health . . .' (Gonzalez-Block 1997: 188).

Comparative health system research is crucial for shared learning, providing fundamental explanations of current health system structure, function, and change, and generating new health sector models (Gonzalez-Block 1997: 200). Comprehensive research allows analysts to examine *all* key factors rather than just those related to the innately more measurable financial considerations historically central to prior research studies. The emerging relational model signals a shift from bureaucratic and hierarchical structures to more flexible and fluid arrangements that invite new approaches and understandings about multiple perspectives, process, professional discourse, and review. Rather than imposing a single direction or determination, such as cost containment, the emphasis is on complex variables defining multiple dimensions of human beings and their health. Frenk (1994: 23), Nixon (1997: 244), and Wheatley (1992: 10) use the word 'relational' to describe an emerging context in which twentieth century modernism is giving way to postmodernism, its epistemological successor. Frenk (1994: 32) and Gonzalez-Block (1997: 189), for example, argue that traditional comparative health system research has become mired in inflexible, bureaucratic categories generated by past research and financial demands and are encouraged by the opportunities inherent in the evolving context of transformation. In her considerations of change, Wheatley notes the need for 'courage to let go of the old world, to relinquish most of what we have cherished, to abandon interpretations about what does and does not work' (1992: 5).

In a time marked by opportunities for healthcare reform, CHS research needs to remain open to innovation, inclusion, and flexibility so that 'prisoners of the past [can] imagine and design alternative paths to the future' (Frenk 1994: 20). Accordingly, it is necessary, for instance, to 'conduct experiments and demonstrations that introduce, on a small scale, innovations in the financing and delivery of services' (1994: 32), and early evaluations of those efforts before moving to broader implementation. In his advocacy of shared knowledge and 'diffusion of innovations' among health system planners and analysts, Gonzalez-Block proposes a minimum data set to process and compare international information for assessing the advantages and limitations of each situation (Gonzalez-Block 1997: 189). The purpose and scope of health reform, he argues, depends on shared understandings of current conditions, practices, and processes (1997: 205).

Encrusted economies and obsolete institutions symbolized by the banking industry, General Motors, communication networks, and health care are being reshaped by a chaotic kineticism generating an entirely new, relational landscape of complexities in which connections – previously overlooked or ignored in earlier studies – are identified and explored. Health systems have been 'defined as a mere list of the different organizations or persons that participate in producing health services, without requiring that such components be coordinated or integrated' (Frenk et al. 1997: 23). The recent transformations in social, economic, and cultural orientations shift toward an increased recognition of disparate and formerly separated entities, so that current interpretations of 'system' include not only traditionally scrutinized components or units, but also the interrelations that are slippery and not easily packaged into manageable units. For many, the transformed frontier is unfamiliar and strange; others, however, have accepted the challenge of change and are exploring multiple, conflicting, and overlapping spheres of meaning.

Not unlike AT&T, banks, and other large corporations of influence and power, the UN and WHO have been challenged by revisionists who believe that well-intentioned, but mired 'systems' of health care typically have difficulty responding to a new world order comprised of evaporating borders and the commingling of goods, services, people, values, and lifestyles (Frenk et al. 1997: 1404). More than 50 years old, those organizations and others have been constrained by traditional and often paternalistic organizational structures and approaches to problems. Some may be incapable of reinventing themselves and competing with forces seeking a 'code of mutual existence' in which difference is respected and hostilities relating to intolerance and desperation are reduced (Frenk et al. 1997: 1405). Caught between cross-currents of a disappearing past and an alternative future, many reformers (Frenk et al. 1997: 1404) are moving away from established patterns of service to re-articulations of what health can become in the future. 'Current international health agencies ... were designed for a different world, where few problems need global action.... Today the world is a different place.... [Their] efficacy ... has been diminished by lack of coordination, overlapping mandates, and the duplication of efforts' (Frenk et al. 1997: 1405).

Health-care needs are greater than available resources, causing cost-containment and cost-effectiveness measurements to be relevant topics in the general reform dialogue. While reiterating this global concern, discussions by analysts increasingly incorporate wider ranges of more complex factors in their analytical investigations. Hammer and Berman (1995: 30), speaking from a World Bank perspective, suggest that past strategies for health sector reform were molded out of a preference for clear and simple rules (1995: 30). The complexity of health care's varied factors, however, ranging from behavior to risk sharing plans, does not allow for the formation of definitive rules and conclusions. Like other writers in this section, Hammer and Berman propose the development of multiple goals based on community values, and note how information between providers and patients, for example, has become an important area of research in regards to allocation determinations.

In the emerging context of change, many CHS researchers have begun to focus on what Frenk calls 'the repertoire of options' (1994: 19). Given the cost of research, comparative research and policy analysis is crucial for evaluating innovative approaches to health care and recommending broader applications. Other postmodern tools for improving interactive data collection for CHS use are now available through Internet capabilities and the European Union's ability to collect and share cross-national data (Gonzalez-Block 1997: 191). Use of informational-age tools and an exploration of relational configurations suggest a powerful potential for collaborative studies in future phases of CHS research and analysis, one that clearly reflects the passage from modernism to postmodernism – and globalization.

Governments in Transition

With the collapse of authoritarian rule, conditions for the establishment of new, more participatory governmental forms have improved along with the forecast for market development and economic vitality. Advancements in technology, health care, knowledge, and global linkages generate corresponding tensions caused by glaring disparities between the affluent and the poor: internal wars in Eastern Europe and Africa, marginalization of groups of people in Latin America; continued threats to a fragile and seriously damaged environment; intractable corporate powers. Legitimate concerns about threats to developing countries by global powers with self-serving goals challenge the vision posed by social scientists who seek broad social improvements. In an age of neo-liberal reforms, there is grave concern about the potential for consolidation of control by 'consequential institutions of global governance: the United Nations, International Monetary Fund, the World Bank, and the General Agreement on Tariffs and Trade' (Korten 1995: 18). The concern reflects an earlier statement that these institutions are a poor fit for the expanded, cross-boundary mosaic of the future.

Intervention, amelioration, and arrangement of currently disparate health sector pieces into multidimensional entities – without concern for overlaps or extensions beyond traditional framing techniques and expectations – is critical. Because a paradigm shift has revitalized the level of interest and creative momentum, encouraged analysts are focusing on open forums centered around the achievement of productive ends, specifically, how health care can be assembled· so that equity, quality, and efficiency can promote improved health status outcomes.

Analysts acknowledge that government support for the development and funding of a basic health package comprising essential interventions and resources can achieve improved health status (Chernichovsky 1995: 83; Frenk 1995: 270; Hecht and Musgrove 1993: 7). Challenges to this goal are formidable and include various protagonists: providers, financing entities, university and research centers, private corporations, NGOs, governments, and populations served by implementation of the goal. Even though the enormity of resistance is formidable, the following passage by Toffler provides an encouraging outlook:

> In probing the future . . . we must do more than identify major trends. Difficult as it may be, we must resist the temptation to be seduced by straight lines. Most people . . . conceive of tomorrow as a mere extension of today, forgetting that trends, no matter how seemingly powerful, do not merely continue in a linear fashion. They reach tipping points at which they explode into new phenomena. They reverse direction. The future is fluid, not frozen. It is constructed by our shifting and changing daily decisions, and each event influences all others. (Toffler 1990: 145)

In the following section, we briefly review health-care reform in Chile as an example of the type of analysis being called for in current CHS literature. In spite of, or perhaps due to, its tumultuous political history, Chile is beginning to exhibit signs of postmodern relationality in its present struggle for health-care improvements. Such developments correspond to trends discussed by social scientists: the profoundly political process of health-care reform in national and global arenas (Frenk et al. 1997; Reich 1995), historical and cultural structured pluralism (Londono and Frenk 1997), the consequence of changing health-care goals as they affect process (Frenk 1994), and the direction toward the development of a mosaic response to changing conditions.

CASE STUDY OF CHILE

In 1975, David Mechanic introduced the concept of health system convergence. Since then, there has been on-going discussion concerning whether health systems are becoming more similar to one another. According to Mechanic, the convergence in health-care systems is generated by similar conditions such as similar health problems (for instance, the increased number of countries facing populations with chronic health problems such as heart disease, diabetes, stroke). Other contributors include similar international pressures (such as global competition and international monetary policy), and shared analytic models and conceptual trends for health-care systems research (such as the continued emphasis on cost-containment policies).

While some forces exist that cause health-care systems to become more uniform and similar to one another cross-culturally, such as global economic pressures, similar health conditions, and shared health policy goals, there are also important differences that give individuality and identity to the shape and form of health-care systems. Cultural systems, while influenced by global interests, still shape how policy makers, practitioners, and populations view their health-care needs, and how responses to those needs are structured and evaluated. History, which composes a core portion of a country's identity and shapes its external relations with other countries (Whiteford 1990, 1992, 1993, 1998a, 1998b), uniquely structures relations between members of the population and their government, and defines governmental authority and the role of the central government in the provision of health care. Simultaneously, the very definitions of health and illness, disease and sickness are culturally constructed, reflecting the cultural interpretations of what it means to become ill, what courses of treatment are possible, and what are the expected roles of the individual and the government alike during illness, disability, and death.

Allopathic medicine or biomedicine, so dominant in the United States, shares its purview in other countries with more holistic healing systems. Indigenous medical systems relying on naturopathy or other more holistic responses to altered health status find currency in many parts of the world. A perspective that emphasizes the dominance of biomedicine tends to envision health-care systems as undergoing a global transformation toward convergence to models developed in highly industrialized Western countries. Following 20 years of discussion of convergence and divergence, Mechanic and Rochefort (1996) conclude that, in general, there is convergence in health-care delivery systems in response to global politics and concerns. However, they caution that these similarities are difficult to demonstrate because definitions and measures are not always the same and are subject to culturally generated interpretations.

While health-care systems are strongly influenced by international, globalizing factors such as sources and conditions of funding and the education and values of policy makers and practitioners, it is local culture, history, and experience that ultimately determine the efficacy and durability of a health-care system. Responses to globalization can only be understood through the lens of a particular culture and history. To emphasize this point, a brief description of health-care reform in Chile is presented to illustrate the application of what Frenk refers to as relational analysis. The Chile example shows the profoundly political process of health-care reform, in the Chilean experience of 'emerging convergences.'

Several identifiable worldwide trends in health-care reform became clear in the 1990s. In Latin America in general, and in Chile in particular, four reform strategies are notable: (1) privatization (Chile); (2) decentralization and devolution of central government responsibility (Bolivia, Brazil, and Mexico); (3) deconcentration (Cuba); (4) delegation of functions to semiautonomous agencies (Brazil and Mexico) (Frenk and Gonzalez-Block 1992). Latin America is a provocative example of trends in comparative health systems research and health-care reform because of the postmodern approach taken by leading reform analysts in their attempt to create mosaics that combine a recognition of global pressures and a validation of national and indigenous histories.

Reichard (1996) notes that while market forces and the general health status of a population may be fundamentally linked, it is history and societal values that shape a nation's institutions and through which meaning and conflict are interpreted. In his careful account of health reforms in Chile from 1873 to the present, Reichard details how Chile's health-care system grew out of early labor movement reforms generated by nitrate miners and, later, railroad workers. Labor strife led to major redistributive laws by the 1920s, and in 1925 social legislation

mandated sick pay, disability payments, and free medical coverage for all citizens (1996: 83). Reichard's analysis demonstrates how the establishment of the British National Health Service in 1948 influenced the creation of the Chilean National Health Service in 1952. Clearly the enduring support for a distributive health system was rooted in Chile's labor history, but the system also found both popular and political support through the political process. The Chilean National Health Service was established to provide comprehensive health care for all citizens, and in so doing established institutions to meet those needs and developed educational and training programs to provide staff for those institutions. A conservative retrenchment of social programs in the 1950s gave rise to the labor alliance that elected President Eduardo Frei (1964–70), and later the Socialist/Communist alliance of President Salvador Allende (1970–73). The 1973 coup d'etat set the stage for the military dictatorship of General Augusto Pinochet and 'dismemberment' of public sector health programs such as health education, sanitation, occupational health service, medical education, and hospital staffing. Between 1974 and 1983 there was an overall reduction of 10 per cent in public health spending (Reichard 1996: 87) as the Pinochet government brought in economist Milton Friedman and the University of Chicago group of economic theorists to guide Chile's turn toward a market economy.

The Chilean turn toward a market economy has been referred to as the 'Chilean miracle,' a set of economic policies being duplicated throughout Latin America. However, the miracle did not extend to the improvements in Chile's public health system. It is a sad irony that 100 years after the Chilean/Bolivian War of 1873 (when Chile seized lands high in nitrates, initiating nitrate mining and its consequent labor movement which agitated for health care), President Salvador Allende, physician and former Minister of Health, was assassinated in a bloody coup d'etat that marked a turn away from comprehensive health coverage for all Chileans. Privatization began in 1982 with the development of private health insurance modeled on the US health maintenance organizations (HMO) and preferred provider organizations (PPO) systems. The government cut subsidies to the public health system, reduced the University of Chile's Medical School budget by 46 per cent and its personnel by 40 per cent in the decade between 1980 and 1990, and ended the previous governments' redistributed tax policies (Reichard 1996). This reduced the middle class and increased the number of those without access to health insurance.

During and following the Pinochet era, health-care reform turned toward privatization and decentralization, reducing the influence of grass-roots and union organizations. Cost containment became a process as well as an economic goal, which undermined cultural and historical values supporting the state in the delivery of, and access to, health care. Cost containment became a process of social control and marginalization, with far-reaching and long-term health consequences. The turn toward a market economy exacerbated the social, educational, economic, and epidemiological differences within the Chilean population, as exemplified by the disparity of public health services in the rural and urban areas (Montoya-Aguilar and Marchant-Cavieres 1994: 286).

Although the current data show the same trends in health status in Chile as compared with the United States, other social indicators suggest the difficulty of using a system designed for another country without the same social history. The Health-for-All statistics provided by the World Health Organization suggest that Chile was able to eradicate infectious diseases, control malnutrition, reduce the infant mortality rate, and provide proper sanitation for 100 per cent of the population in the urban areas in spite of the economic and political upheavals they endured. On the other hand, the data depict less than one-third of the rural population having access to safe drinking water or adequate human waste disposal. These and other discrepancies also show the likelihood of absent information from the rural areas where infectious diseases, malnutrition, and high infant mortality are rampant. Therefore, although the incorporation of a Western market-driven biomedical model may have improved the health of some citizens, those with the greatest need still are not provided with adequate public health services.

Previous to 1973, the Chilean National Health Service was financed through the central budget (at about 65 per cent) and by compulsory insurance contributions paid by workers and their employers. The overthrow of Allende and the move to neo-liberal and structural adjustment policies led to large direct reductions in the central government contributions, leaving a significant gap in funding to be made up by direct user payments and increased compulsory worker insurance premiums. In 1980, the increased emphasis on market economy policies resulted in the creation of private, for-profit health organizations that marketed health insurance plans against the compulsory contributions (Montoya-Aguilar and Marchant-Cavieres 1994). The result was increased epidemiological polarization.

To resolve the 'epidemiological polarization' (Frenk and Gonzalez-Block 1992: 42) that has defined health conditions in Latin America and much of the rest of the world requires that health-care systems provide for prevention and intervention, maintenance and cure, and programs designed to supplement nutritional needs to children, prevent infectious disease, provide assistance to the elderly, and guarantee access and equity. Instead, what has happened in Chile is increased polarization of society. This has intensified the 'inequalities in health as the dominant causes of death and disease have become different among social and geographical groups' (Frenk and Gonzalez-Block 1992: 42). Health-care systems in Europe and the United States do not face epidemiological polarization to the same degree as in Latin America. Thus, the 'indiscriminate application of economic theories that have shown success in the developed nations of Europe can result in an inequitable social cost in the poor and underdeveloped nations. This has been the experience of Chile' (Alfredo Jadresic, quoted in Reichard 1996: 89).

The Chilean example demonstrates the consequences of borrowing a 'system' or theory from another place and applying it as though the country in which it is being applied has no history, no culture, and no identity of its own. As the emerging CHS research suggests, it would be more advantageous to apply a 'mosaic' of ideas, a range of options that are appropriate to the unique history and cultural context, as well as to the particular sets of alliances and relations within and between countries. In Chile, as in other countries, often the proximate variables and indirect causes provide important information for the comparison of health systems. As various authors have pointed out (Montoya-Aguilar and Marchant-Cavieres 1994; Whiteford 1992, 1993, 1998a, 1998b), public health systems can override radical economic changes – for a while. It takes time for the health indices to reflect the consequences of such changes if populations have had access to basic sanitation, immunization, prenatal care, health education, and nutritional supplements, but they will show up as increased rates of infectious disease, deterioration of health-care infrastructures, reduction of number and quality of health-care personnel, and even more difficult to measure, loss of faith in the government to provide those basic needs for its population (Whiteford 1993, 1998a).

Analysis of health reform in Chile exemplifies some of the difficulties encountered in CHS research. To be meaningful, health-care system comparisons must take into consideration the political, social, and historical context under which they were developed, but to do so often makes the resultant data ungeneralizable to other locations. Without doubt one of the effects of globalization is that ideas from one national context and experience rapidly influence others. In the case of Chile, the diffusion of ideas from other national contexts played an important role in its health reforms. While some consider Chile a model for other Latin American countries, others are less sanguine about the relative success of Chile's health-care reforms. They point out continuing increases in malnutrition among some high-risk populations, continuing increases in chronic disease, and the increasing inequality in health-care services between urban and rural areas. The loss of political and personal freedoms that accompanied the transition to a health-care market economy in Chile must be recognized in any analyses of its health system reform. The health-care reforms undertaken in Chile and touted as part of the Chilean 'economic miracle' were accomplished at great and continuing costs to Chilean citizens. Pinochet's use of 'terror as an element of popular control' (Reichard 1996: 86), and the application of an autochthonous model of laissez-faire capitalism to the Chilean health system, succeeded in generating funds from international lending institutions, such as the World Bank, by disconnecting from Chile's history of national comprehensive health care.

Although it may 'follow' Mechanic's convergence model with similar health problems, international pressures, and health policy goals as other developed nations, the inability to provide basic health services to target populations in the rural areas shows the failure of a single (US) system approach and the need to incorporate a 'mosaic.' In this case, we used only one country (a baseline for any comparison) to suggest how important it is to incorporate ideological (Jimenez de la Jara and Bossert 1995), epidemiological (Frenk and Gonzalez-Block 1992), historical (Reichard 1996), cultural (Montoya-Aguilar and Marchant-Cavieres 1994), and economic indicators in any CHS analysis.

CONCLUSION

Comparative health system research, like its subject matter, is in the process of change. Information is more immediate, whether through the World Wide Web, television, 24-hour news stations, e-mail, fax, or phone, and more available than ever before. Not only can we download data that took years to collect, we can also do it without ever leaving our home. In addition to written data, information is visually available both through the Web and on television, and the images are global – we can see events that occur in England, Rwanda, and Costa Rica. According to some social scientists (Kleinman, for example), this immediacy carries with it responsibilities to step out of disciplinary boxes, destabilize established categories, and collapse old dichotomies. As social scientists challenge the utility of the old categories, they question the need to separate the 'individual from social levels of analysis, health from social problems, representation from experience, suffering from intervention' (Kleinman et al. 1997: x). In CHS research, this means that health systems must be seen as stemming from, and a reflection of, the social fabric.

CHS research has moved from an unquestioning stance where primarily quantitative data were collected and categorized and researchers struggled to compare what in essence are apples and oranges, to an attempt to contextualize health-care research in relational modes, linking attributes in a mosaic whose overall shape is still unclear. Earlier CHS research used a systems metaphor to compare items (policies, practices, indicators, outcomes, economies) that themselves were not comparable because to make them comparable researchers had to remove or ignore underlying cultural and historical differences – thereby making them apparently comparable, but falsely so. The emerging metaphor of a mosaic suggests a myriad of small, self-contained pieces that when placed in relation to one another form a new image. It suggests that both the pieces and their relations are equally important to the whole.

The most exciting new directions in CHS research build on the writings of previous CHS analysts, but incorporate lessons learned from postmodern thought, particularly the importance of identifying biases in research, including those of the researchers, funders, and participants as well as those who use the data. In a time of rapid social and technological change, Mechanic's hypothesis of health system convergence reflects a technological-dependent bias that has generally marked medicine and social science. Mechanic posits that global forces are '...a certain macro process in which a narrowing of the system options takes place, compared with those theoretically possible, due to forces that generally lie beyond the control of particular national actors or institutions and to which more and more societies are being exposed' (Mechanic and Rochefort 1996: 242). According to Frenk, Gonzalez-Block, and Reichard, among other writers, while those unifying global forces do exist and cannot be ignored, diversity arises from the strength of the cultural traditions of a country that also cannot be ignored. A belief in the primacy of technology (and other globalizing influences) is a conceptual box that the relational mosaic metaphor allows the researcher to break out of and consider other variables in relation to one another.

Our example of health-care reform in Chile attempted to show how the incorporation of an autochthonous model results in epidemiological polarization, a disjuncture with the social fabric of previous generations of Chilean health objectives, and was possible only by way of massive social upheaval. To ignore these effects when describing the Chilean health system is to reify the social suffering experienced in Chile and to diminish the power of comparative health system research.

Acknowledgments

We would like to thank the editors for encouraging us to struggle with the materials in this complex study of comparative health systems research. Several people helped us in the process of defining the area and combing the literature, and we want to thank Lori Roscoe, Barbara Szelag, and Alpa Patel for their help in this endeavor. The misinterpretations and omissions remain our responsibilities.

References

Chernichovsky, D. (1995) 'What can developing economies learn from health system reforms of developed economies?' *Health Policy*, 32: 79–91.

Elling, R.H. (1981) 'The capitalist world-system and international health', *International Journal of Health Services*, 11: 21–51.

Elling, R.H. (1994) 'Theory and method for the cross-national study of health systems', *International Journal of Health Services*, 24: 285–309.

Field, M. (1967) *Soviet Socialized Medicine: An Introduction*. New York: Free Press.

Fox, D.M. (1986) *Health Policies and Health Politics*. Princeton: Princeton University Press.

Fox, D.M. (1990) 'Health policy and the politics of research in the United States', *Journal of Health Politics, Policy and Law*, 15: 481–99.

Frenk, J. (1994) 'Dimensions of health system reform', *Health Policy*, 27: 19–34.

Frenk, J. (1995) 'Comprehensive policy analysis for health system reform', *Health Policy*, 32: 257–77.

Frenk, J. and Gonzalez-Block, M.A. (1992) 'Corporatism and health care: A comparison of Sweden and Mexico', *Health Policy*, 21: 167–80.

Frenk, J., Sepulveda, J., Gomez-Dates, O., McGuinness, M.J., and Knaul, F. (1997) 'The future of world health: The new world order and international health', *British Medical Journal*, 314: 1404–7.

Fuchs, V. (1974) 'Who shall live?' in *Health, Economics and Social Issues*. New York: Basic Books.

Gonzalez-Block, M.A. (1997) 'Comparative research and analysis methods for shared learning from health system reforms', *Health Policy*, 42: 187–209.

Hammer, J.S. and Berman, P. (1995) 'Ends and means in public health policy in developing countries', *Health Policy*, 32: 29–45.

Hecht, R. and Musgrove, P. (1993) 'Rethinking the government's role in health', *Finance and Development*, 30: 6–9.

Hsiao, W.C. (1992) 'Comparing health care systems: What nations can learn from one another', *Journal of Health Politics, Policy and Law*, 17: 613–36.

Hutcheon, L. (1988) *A Poetics of Postmodernism: History, Theory, Fiction*. London: Routledge.

Illsley, R. (1990) 'Comparative review of sources, methodology and knowledge', *Social Science and Medicine*, 31: 229–36.

Jimenez de la Jara, J. and Bossert, T. (1995) 'Chile's health sector reform: Lessons from four reform periods', *Health Policy*, 32: 155–66.

Klein, R. (1991) 'Risks and benefits of comparative studies: Notes from another shore', *Milbank Quarterly*, 69: 275–91.

Kleinman, A. and Kleinman, J. (1997) 'The appeal of experience; the dismay of images: Cultural appropriations of suffering in our times', in A. Kleinman, V. Das, and M. Lock (eds), *Social Suffering*. Berkeley: University of California Press.

Kleinman, A., Das, V., and Lock, M. (eds) (1997) *Social Suffering*. Berkeley: University of California Press.

Kohn, R. and White, K.L. (1976) *Health Care: An International Study*. London: Oxford University Press.

Korten, D.S. (1995) *When Corporations Rule the World*. West Hartford: Kumarian Press and San Francisco: Berrett-Koehler (co-publishers).

Kuhn, T.S. (1970) *The Structure of Scientific Revolutions*. (2nd edn). Chicago: University of Chicago Press.

Leslie, C. (ed.) (1978) 'Theoretical foundations for the comparative study of medical systems', *Social Science and Medicine*, 12B: 65–138.

Litman, T.J. and Robins, L. (1971) 'Comparative analysis of health care systems – a socio-political approach', *Social Science and Medicine*, 5: 573–81.

Londono, J.-L. and Frenk, J. (1997) 'Structured pluralism: Towards an innovative model for health system reform in Latin America', *Health Policy*, 41: 1–36.

Marmor, T R. and Thomas, D. (1972) 'Doctors, politics and pay disputes: "Pressure group politics" revisited', *British Journal of Political Science*, 2: 421–42.

Mechanic, D. (1975) 'The comparative study of health care delivery systems', *Annual Review of Sociology*, 1: 43–65.

Mechanic, D. and Rochefort, D.A. (1996) 'Comparative medical systems', *Annual Review of Sociology*, 22: 239–70.

Montoya-Aguilar, C. and Marchant-Cavieres, L. (1994) 'The effect of economic changes on health care and health in Chile', *International Journal of Health Planning and Management*, 9: 279–94.

Murray, C.J.L. (1995) 'Towards an analytical approach to health system reform' *Health Policy*, 32: 93–109.

Nixon, L. La C. (1997) 'Pyramids and rhomboids and the rationalist world of medicine', in H. L. Nelson (ed.), *Stories and Their Limits*. New York: Routledge.

OECD (1977) *Public Expenditure on Health*. Paris: Organisation for Economic Cooperation and Development.

OECD (1985) *Measuring Health Care, 1960–1983*. Paris: Organisation for Economic Cooperation and Development.

OECD (1987) *Financing and Delivering Health Care*. Paris: Organisation for Economic Cooperation and Development.

OECD (1990) *Health Care Systems in Transition*. Paris: Organisation for Economic Cooperation and Development.

Reich, M.R. (1995) 'The politics of health sector reform in developing countries: Three cases of pharmaceutical policy', *Health Policy*, 32: 47–77.

Reichard, S. (1996) 'Ideology drives health care reforms in Chile', *Journal of Public Health Policy*, 17: 80–98.

Roemer, M.I. (1977) *Systems of Health Care*. New York: Springer.

Roemer, M.I. (1985) *National Strategies for Health Care Organization: A World Overview*. Ann Arbor MI: Health Administration Press.

Roemer, M.I. (1991) *National Health Systems of the World. Vol. 1*. New York: Oxford University Press.

Rostow, W. (1971) *The Stages of Economic Growth*. Cambridge: Cambridge University Press.

Sidel, V.W. (1980–81) 'International comparisons of health services: How? who? why?' *Policy Studies Journal*, 9: 300–8.

Sidel, V. and Sidel, R. (1974) *Serve the People: Observations on Medicine in the People's Republic of China*. Boston: Beacon.

Toffler, A. (1990) *The Third Wave*. New York: William Morrow.

Toffler, A. and Toffler, H. (1995) *Creating a New Civilization: The Politics of the Third Wave*. (2nd edn 1990). Atlanta: Turner.

van Atteveld, L., Broeders, C., and Lapre, R. (1987) 'International comparative research in health care. A study of the literature', *Health Policy*, 8: 105–36.

Wheatley, M.J. (1992) *Leadership and the New Science: Learning About Organization from an Orderly Universe*. San Francisco: Berrett-Koehler.

Whiteford, L.M. (1990) 'A question of adequacy: Primary health care in the Dominican republic', *Social Science and Medicine*, 30: 221–6.

Whiteford, L.M. (1992) 'Caribbean colonial history and its contemporary health care consequences: The case of the Dominican Republic', *Social Science and Medicine*, 35: 1215–25.

Whiteford, L.M. (1993) 'International economic Policies and child health', *Social Science and Medicine*, 37: 1391–400.

Whiteford, L.M. (1998a) 'Children's health as accumulated capital: Structural adjustment in the Dominican Republic and Cuba', in N. Scheper-Hughes and C. Sargent (eds), *Small Wars: The Cultural Politics of Childhood*. Berkeley: University of California Press.

Whiteford, L.M. (1998b) 'Sembrando El Futuro: Globalization and the commodification of Health', in M.B. Whiteford and S. Whiteford (eds), *Crossing Currents: Continuity and Change in Latin America*. Upper Saddle River, NJ: Prentice Hall. pp. 264–78.

3.6

The Patient's Perspective Regarding Appropriate Health Care

ANGELA COULTER AND RAY FITZPATRICK

INTRODUCTION

This chapter is concerned with patients' perspectives regarding their health care. Initially, these perspectives were highlighted by a substantial body of research examining patients' satisfaction with the care they received. A number of common themes emerged indicating, for example, universal problems arising from health professionals' failures to communicate effectively with their patients. Research into patient satisfaction, whilst drawing attention to important concerns of patients, has given patients only a limited and passive role in influencing health care. The case is therefore examined for involving patients more actively in decisions about their care. The chapter concludes by speculating about future trends and dilemmas for health care systems arising from increased patient involvement.

ORIGINS OF EMPHASIS UPON PATIENT SATISFACTION

Pressures to pay greater attention to the issue of patient satisfaction have come from many sources and have varied in emphasis from one health-care system to another at different points in time. It is customary to identify the origins of concerns about the patient's views with the growth of consumerism, particularly in the United States in the 1960s. Most strikingly, feminism began to challenge medical professional values and forms of care, whilst various cultural critiques questioned more fundamentally the claims to expertise of the medical profession. Consumerism provided a diffuse range of challenges to the dominant medical model, although analysts at the time held that lay views were invariably coopted by more powerful professional and organizational interests (Alford 1975).

Other more specific reasons why patient satisfaction became an important issue can be identified. First, evidence began to accumulate from the 1960s that patients dissatisfied with their care were less likely to comply with advice and to re-attend (Korsch et al. 1968). Poor communication skills of health professionals were identified as the main reason for such problems. It was possible to show substantial benefits in terms of patient satisfaction from relatively modest efforts to improve communication skills by training (Ley 1983). Second, was the growing application of social science methods to research, both in the clinical context of health care, and also in the use of social survey methodology to obtain the community's views about health care (Davies and Ware 1988). Social research provided an increasingly powerful means of relating the views of patients to specific aspects of their encounters with health care and views of communities about varying types of organization for health-care delivery.

A third specific impetus serving to highlight patient satisfaction was marketing. From the 1970s to date, particularly in the competitive arena of health care in the United States, it was increasingly recognized that patient satisfaction was an essential element in health services.

As evidence increased that patients expressing dissatisfaction in surveys were subsequently more likely to change health-care provider, so it became of growing importance for hospitals, health maintenance organizations, and other large providers to monitor patients' views as a way to maintain or improve levels of satisfaction (Weiss and Senf 1990).

The fourth and most influential factor impelling greater attention to patient satisfaction has been increased external regulation of health services. In both Europe and North America, both public and private bodies funding health care required more evidence of the quality of services provided. Systematic evidence via surveys of public and users' views came to be considered a vital source of evidence regarding quality (Pollitt 1988).

Lessons from Patient Satisfaction Research

Several consistent trends can be detected from the extensive body of evidence now accumulated regarding factors influencing patient satisfaction. In both North American and European health-care systems, patients are critical of poor communication from health professionals. At the simplest level, such criticism focuses on problems of limited or inadequate information. In a United States nationwide, interview-based survey of more than 6000 patients recently discharged from hospital, the most common complaint (45 per cent) was that they had not been told about the daily routines of the hospital (Cleary et al. 1991). The survey also found 32 per cent critical because they had not been told from whom to ask for help if it was needed during their hospital stay. Twenty four per cent of patients were not told about side effects of medicines in ways they could understand, and the same percentage of patients were not given information about resuming normal activities after discharge.

A modified version of the US questionnaire was used in a telephone survey of a random sample of more than 4500 Canadians recently discharged from hospital (Charles et al. 1994). Not being told about daily routines of the hospital again emerged as the most commonly reported problem (41 per cent of respondents). As in the US survey, many problems arose from poor communication about side effects of medication and failures to disclose a variety of simple, but important, matters of concern to patients after discharge from hospital. Another survey conducted using a modified version of the US questionnaire polled more than 5000 patients in England after they had been discharged from National Health Service (NHS)

hospitals (Bruster et al. 1994). The same pattern of problems was reported with difficulties of communication dominating patients' concerns. British patients were even more critical of communication than their North American counterparts. In relation to discharge, 44 per cent reported having no discussion with a doctor about discharge; 62 per cent were not told when they should resume normal activities.

International comparative evidence confirms that communication of information is just as important a determinant of patient satisfaction in primary care as it is in hospital medicine (Calnan et al. 1994). Evidence, therefore, consistently documents failures to convey information to patients in a satisfactory way across types of health-care systems. However, communication in relation to health care is a broader and more complex set of processes than simply the transmission of information. Patients also express widespread dissatisfaction that health professionals fail to allow them to report their concerns fully and in their own terms, do not take full histories of the presenting problem, do not convey reassurance, and do not provide appropriate advice. Crucially, patients also feel that they are not encouraged to share decision making with the doctor.

Whilst such problems have been so widely observed that they may be considered inherent in the provision of modern health care, research has succeeded in demonstrating that communication skills can be improved as judged either by independent observers or from evidence of patient satisfaction. Improvement may be brought about by conventional education training, by use of appropriate hardware and software to facilitate communication of complex information, and indeed by improving the skills and confidence of patients in dealing with health professionals (Fulford et al. 1996).

Interpersonal Skills

As important as communication, and often difficult to disentangle from communication processes, are a diverse range of health professionals' behaviours that influence patient satisfaction, variously referred to as interpersonal skills, rapport, and the ability to instil trust, to demonstrate a sense of caring, and to treat the patient as an individual. The large national surveys referred to above again illustrate the scale of the problem. In the US survey, 20 per cent of all patients felt that hospital staff did not go out of their way to meet their needs as a patient. Thirty nine per cent of patients did not have a relationship of trust with any hospital staff other than the doctor in charge of their care. In the Canadian survey, 12 per cent of all patients experienced the doctors often or sometimes talking in front of the patient as if she was not there.

To some extent impersonal care and poor rapport may be considered difficult to avoid features of relatively brief stays in hospital care. In settings such as primary care where some continuity of contact between patients and their health professionals is more likely, problems in the relationship between parties can have a more deleterious effect on patient satisfaction. Calnan et al. (1994) found from their study of patient satisfaction with primary care in England, Greece, Russia, and Yugoslavia that interpersonal relationships were a major source of dissatisfaction. For example, in each country at least a quarter of patients said their general practitioner did not take their problems seriously enough, and almost a third felt unable to talk to their doctor about personal problems.

From extensive evidence of Israeli primary care, Ben Sira has argued that what he terms the affective behaviour of the doctor toward the patient, indicated by patients' perceptions of being given sufficient time, interest, and attention by their doctor, is the primary determinant of overall satisfaction with their primary care (Sira 1980). Indeed according to such analyses, the patient relies almost entirely on evidence of affective and interpersonal skills to form judgements of health professionals' technical competence that he is otherwise unable to evaluate.

Patients' views have also consistently underlined limitations of continuity, access, and convenience that are increasingly associated with bureaucratic forms of managed care. In British and Norwegian studies, patients registered in primary care practices with no personal doctor or continuity of care were more dissatisfied with overall quality of care (Hjortdahl and Laerum 1992; Baker 1996). In the United States, various studies have shown that patient satisfaction with access and continuity is lower in forms of managed care, such as health maintenance organizations. In the large Medical Outcomes Study of more than 17 000 patients, office waits and difficulties arising from office location gave rise to the highest levels of dissatisfaction across dimensions examined (Rubin et al. 1993). Most importantly, in this study a simple, single-item rating by the patient of their last visit to their doctor was a highly significant predictor of the patient leaving their health-care provider within 6 months. Many basic problems in patients' experiences of health-care can be traced to some aspect of health-care systems that, increasingly compelled to compete in terms of efficiency, resort to impersonal and routinized forms of care.

Critiques of Patient Satisfaction

Despite the substantial body of evidence produced by research into patient satisfaction, work in this field is frequently criticized for failing fully to capture the patient's perspective with regard to health care.

One line of criticism has been that patterns of views about health care obtained in survey research reflect normative values surrounding health care. Patients are reluctant to criticize their health care, at least in part because they risk appearing ungrateful or unappreciative (Fitzpatrick and Hopkins 1983). This is particularly seen as a problem in surveys of patients' views in which respondents are asked fairly simplistic standardized questions about their views regarding aspects of health care experience with minimal opportunity to go beyond basic levels of 'satisfaction' or 'dissatisfaction.' A variant of this critique argues that patient satisfaction research is substantially flawed because of its reliance on insensitive methods of survey research to produce artificially inflated rates of positive satisfaction (Williams 1994). In contrast, it is argued that in-depth qualitative methods are necessary to obtain more valid evidence.

A related criticism is that the evidence obtained via standardized surveys is skewed towards favourable views by the majority of respondents, with the result that uniformly positive data do not permit investigators, managers, and planners to identify sources of poor or substandard care (Carr-Hill 1992). This is especially the case when the variation that is obtained by such methods can be substantially related to patients' demographic characteristics (Fitzpatrick 1997). Thus, older respondents report more positive views about their health care. To the extent that such favourable views are due to diminished expectations, normative values or different response sets in relation to attitudinal questionnaires, the use of information about patients' views to manage and plan patterns of services may be undermined.

At the heart of many critiques of patient satisfaction research is the view that it has given patients only a marginal role in relation to their own health care. To be consulted as a respondent in a survey is to have a very vicarious method of providing feedback to health professionals about the value and appropriateness of care received. The sense of limited involvement would be greater if there were greater awareness of the modest impact such evidence often has on decisions about future provision. More obviously, it is a form of involving patients that can only operate at an aggregate level of feedback to the health-care system as a whole. The health-care system may be expected to shift its pattern of care in the light of accumulating evidence from surveys, but it is inconceivable that individual patients will normally directly benefit by providing their views about care. As a response to pressures towards consumerism, the extensive investment in surveying patients' views in recent years is a very conservative and limited step.

Patients and the Content of Their Health Care

Whilst the patient's viewpoint has received increased attention as a result of patient satisfaction research, it can reasonably be argued to amount to a very limited level of involvement of the patient overall. The most striking evidence of this conservatism, in considering patients' concerns with regard to health care, is to be found in the inability to consider patients' views directly about the content of their health care. Patients are less likely to be asked about the value to them of the treatment they receive than almost any other aspect of their experience of health care. For example, in Hall and Dornan's (1988) meta-analysis of published studies of patient satisfaction, only 6 per cent of studies elicited patients' views about the outcomes of their health care, whereas 65 per cent included items on humaneness and interpersonal relations. Wensing et al. (1994) came to a similar conclusion in their meta-analysis of studies of patients' views regarding primary care; 8 per cent of studies examined any aspect of patients' views regarding effectiveness or outcomes of care, compared with, for example, 65 per cent including assessment of views regarding humaneness, and 48 per cent regarding informativeness. Cleary and McNeil (1988) also note the relative neglect of patients' views about the impact of care on outcomes. They warn that the impression might be gained from the literature on patient satisfaction that health outcomes are actually a secondary or minor concern on the part of patients compared with the need to be treated with courtesy and humanity. However, this apparent pattern may be more an artefact of the tendency of survey research to focus on particular issues such as the humanity of health professionals and neglect areas such as perceptions of outcomes. More generally, the limited attention to patients' views about the content of their care reflects a broader perception of patients as passively and uncritically accepting in their judgements of these areas.

There are several reasons for the neglect of patients' views about the content of their care. First, much of the organizational and political thrust behind involving patients in satisfaction research has come from health service management (Pollitt 1987). This methodology has been seen as a potential form of leverage by management to improve the quality of services. Systematic evidence can be gathered to identify areas of weakness in the performance of services and to monitor efforts made to improve them over time. However, whilst it has been widely considered appropriate that health service management should examine issues such as accessibility, waiting times, and the courtesy shown by staff, there have been clear limits to the domains of health care into which management has felt entitled to enquire. Questions about the content of health and value of treatments received have been treated as an infringement into professional concerns. Whilst health service managers may properly examine the acceptability of 'hotel services,' administrative and interpersonal aspects of health services, obtaining views on medical treatments represents too blunt a challenge to medical dominance. It may also be argued that health service management has mainly chosen to elicit patients' views on those aspects of the quality of services over which managers thought they might have some influence; matters even remotely concerned with clinical judgement have not, to a large extent, become open to managerial intervention.

More generally, it has only recently been accepted by health services that patients can provide reliable judgements about their experiences of health and health care. Slowly, evidence has accumulated to indicate that patients have more understanding of medical knowledge than expected by health professionals (Segall and Roberts 1980). They are capable of making sensible judgements about aspects of the technical quality. Patients' views can be expressed in ways that are highly reproducible and have good construct validity when examined in relation to other evidence of the quality of services. In some circumstances, such as the experience of chronic illness, patients may come to be as knowledgeable about their illness and its treatment as their doctor. However, the implications of the 'patient as expert' have still to be fully recognized.

Perhaps the greatest barriers to overcome in extending patients' involvement in the evaluation of their care has been conceptual. At one extreme, some have viewed the patient as unable to comment sensibly on much at all in relation to health care received other than purely affective behaviour of health professionals. At the other extreme, it is possible to exaggerate the self-confidence and competence of patients in relation to health and illness. Conceptual confusion is only increased by conflating all aspects of the content of health care into the broad category of 'the technical' in the way that some medical sociologists have preferred. Patients may often have only limited capacity to judge the appropriateness to their personal health problems of specific medical interventions, for example, whether a particular drug is likely to be appropriate to, and effective in relation to, their presenting problems. These are the core technical skills of the medical profession in relation to diagnosis and selection of candidate treatments. It is clear that patients, nevertheless, remain uniquely placed to make other relevant judgements about such decisions, particularly regarding two fundamentally important issues: (1) their concerns and priorities in relation to presenting problems, and (2) their personal perceptions of the costs and benefits of alternative interventions to improve the problem.

Thus, patients alone can determine and describe their concerns in relation to presenting problems. For example, among patients presenting to neurological clinics with headache, patients varied enormously in the extent their concerns. Some patients were primarily concerned about possible serious illness; other were seeking symptomatic relief; while others sought lifestyle advice about how to prevent recurrent headaches or simply wanted to understand more about the meaning of their symptoms (Fitzpatrick and Hopkins 1988). History-taking that focused on differential diagnosis alone did not enable neurologists to identify patients' main concerns. Failure to address patients' main concerns resulted in patients feeling disappointed with their specialist's care and less likely to adhere to prescribed treatments, resulting in poorer symptomatic improvement over the following year.

Similarly, in many instances patients alone can make complex judgements about the severity of their health problems and their readiness to undergo risk, discomfort, or other costs from interventions to address their problems. They may also need to make complex judgements to 'trade-off' issues of their survival gained at cost to their quality of life. There are many circumstances where the patient is too ill or too cognitively impaired to participate in determining his or her preferences. A minority of patients also has a strong preference to hand over responsibility to health professionals for such decisions. Nevertheless, it is increasingly clear that the sphere of patients' competence to judge matters in relation to illness is extensive. Our failure has been to confuse and conflate that sphere with the distinct but related role of the doctor to inform and explain from the point of view of epidemiological and clinical evidence; to advise about the options and their probabilities in ways that respond to the patient's concerns and preferences.

The Need to Involve Patients More Directly

As we have seen, the measurement of patient satisfaction has become an important component in the evaluation of health-care interventions and in monitoring the quality of service delivery. However, patient satisfaction is essentially a passive concept. It acknowledges the legitimacy of patients' views on the process and outcomes of care, but says little about their role in decision making. A focus on satisfaction after the event leaves the decision to instigate a particular form of care or treatment unchallenged.

The notion that doctors' decisions may need to be challenged stems from studies of variations in practice patterns. The realization that there are widespread variations in clinical practice, indicative of the fact that doctors disagree among themselves about the appropriate use of particular treatments, has underlined the weakness of the scientific basis of much medical care and heightened awareness that doctors' values and beliefs play a major part in influencing clinical decisions (Andersen and Mooney 1990; Logan and Scott 1996; Mulley and Eagle 1988). In many cases these decisions are based on assumptions about what is best for an individual patient without explicitly determining the patient's values and preferences. Yet, there is evidence that many patients do have strong preferences for particular treatments (Henshaw et al. 1993), that these are not always predictable (Richards et al. 1995), and that doctors often fail to understand them (Coulter et al. 1994).

Patients' views of different treatment options and their attitudes to risk are likely to be influenced by their personal characteristics and social situation as well as by the severity of their symptoms. Benign prostatic hyperplasia (BPH) is an example of a condition that has a detrimental effect on patients' quality of life and which can be treated in a variety of ways using surgical procedures, medical treatments, or simply watchful waiting (careful monitoring without active treatment). Each treatment option involves risks as well as potential benefits. For example, prostatectomy (surgical removal of the prostate) can be very effective, but it involves risks of complications leading to incontinence, impotence, or even death. The goal of treatment in this usually non-life-threatening condition is to improve the patient's quality of life. Outcome probabilities for each of the options can be calculated on the basis of research evidence, but studies of treatment efficacy are often confined to measuring biological markers. These may not be the outcomes most valued by patients, and even if they are, patients are likely to differ in their attitudes to risk and in the extent to which they can tolerate the symptoms (Mulley 1989). When patients with BPH were asked about their preferred treatment outcomes and their attitudes to the symptoms and the risks of treatment, it became clear that doctors could not hope to predict their preferences unless they explicitly asked for them (Wennberg et al. 1993). In situations such as this, where there is a range of treatment options with varying risk/benefit profiles, there would appear to be a strong case for systematically eliciting patients' preferences and involving them in the decision-making process (Deber 1994).

Toward Shared Decision Making

A number of writers have argued that the doctor–patient relationship is undergoing a paradigm-shift away from the traditional paternalistic model towards a new form of decision making, which explicitly recognizes the patient's autonomy (Charles et al. 1997; Emanuel and Emanuel 1992; Laine and Davidoff 1996; Quill 1983). The traditional model assumed that doctors and patients shared the same goals, that only the doctor was sufficiently informed and experienced to decide what should be done, and that patient involvement was limited to giving or withholding consent to treatment. Charles et al. (1997) distinguish three other models of treatment decision making: informed decision making, the professional as agent, and shared decision making. The informed decision-making model is the polar opposite of the paternalistic model, in that it assumes that the patient alone will make the decision once he or she has been provided with all necessary technical information. Thus, the patient's preferences are pre-eminent in this model and the clinician's role is reduced to that of providing technical information to support the patient's decision. The professional-as-agent model is somewhere between these two extremes, in that it recognizes the importance of incorporating the patient's preferences into the process, but still assumes that only the doctor has sufficient technical knowledge to make the final treatment decision. The decision remains with the clinician and is not, therefore, a shared one. In shared decision making, however, the intention is that both the process of decision

making and the outcome – the treatment decision – will be shared. Shared information about values and likely treatment outcomes is an essential prerequisite, but the process also depends on a commitment from both parties to engage in the decision-making process. The clinician has to be prepared to acknowledge the legitimacy of the patient's preferences, and the patient has to accept shared responsibility for the treatment decision.

Patients' Preferences for Participation in Decisions

These are theoretical models or ideal types, but what is the evidence that patients want to participate in decision making? As we have seen, failures in communication of information about illness and treatment are the most frequent source of patient dissatisfaction. There is plenty of evidence that patients want more information, but this does not necessarily mean that they want to participate in decision making. A number of studies have investigated the extent of desire for participation among different groups of patients. In a study of 439 interactions between hospitalized adult cancer patients and oncologists, the majority (92 per cent) preferred to be given all information including bad news, but only 69 per cent said they wanted to participate in treatment decisions (Blanchard et al. 1988). A study of patients with hypertension found that 53 per cent expressed a desire to participate in treatment decisions, but physicians underestimated patients' preferences for discussion about therapy in 29 per cent of cases and overestimated it in 11 per cent (Strull et al. 1984). Although many patients want to participate in decision making, a substantial minority appear to prefer a passive role.

Desire for participation has been found to vary according to age, educational status, disease group, and cultural background. For example, a study of 256 American cancer patients found that younger patients were much more likely to want active participation in decisions about their care: 87 per cent of patients under age 40 expressed a desire to participate, compared wth 62 per cent of those aged 40–59 and 51 per cent of those over 60 (Cassileth et al. 1980). The age differences in decision-making preferences suggest that the desire for involvement may be increasing over time, reflecting greater knowledge of the risks as well as the benefits of medical care and decreased willingness to submit to the authority of clinicians. Preference for an active role in decision making may also vary according to the stage in the course of a disease episode and the severity of the patient's condition. A Canadian study found a much greater desire for active participation among a randomly selected population sample than among a group of newly diagnosed cancer patients, pointing to the difficulty in predicting the level of involvement desired when serious illness strikes (Degner and Sloan 1992). There may also be important cultural differences. A study comparing responses in different countries found that British breast cancer patients were less likely to prefer an active role than Canadian ones (Richards et al. 1995).

There are fears that encouraging patients to choose between competing treatment options places an additional burden on people who are feeling unwell and could cause anxiety and distress (Levy et al. 1989). This is a difficult subject to research, and few methodologically sound studies investigating the effects of patient participation have been published. Retrospective studies face the problem that patients' perceptions of involvement in decision making may have been influenced by the outcomes of the treatment. In a Swedish study of 510 surgical patients, those who were dissatisfied with the results of the surgery were less likely to report that they had participated in the treatment decision (Larsson et al. 1992). Prospective studies involving independent assessments of the extent of participation would be required to overcome this problem.

Shared decision making involves sharing information about the limitations and risks of treatment. Patients with serious disease may prefer an optimistic rather than a realistic account of their chances of recovery. A Canadian study of patients with early stage breast cancer found that patients' desire to adopt a positive approach to fighting their illness resulted in a tendency to want more aggressive interventions, notwithstanding the risks of the treatment (Charles et al. 1996). For example, patients tended to overestimate the possible benefits of chemotherapy and downplay the risks. Attempts to introduce a more evidence-based approach to treatment decision making may serve to invalidate patients' values and beliefs and inadvertently undermine their coping strategies. Most of the cancer patients in this study were said to prefer a shared decision-making style, but they were concerned about how blame for bad outcomes might be apportioned. This illustrates another potential problem with a participatory style of decision making. Active involvement implies accepting responsibility for the outcomes of treatment even when these are adverse. Patients with life-threatening illnesses such as cancer may be less willing to accept shared responsibility than those with less serious condi-

tions. In crisis situations, it is possible that some patients benefit more from a paternalistic than from an egalitarian consultation style.

Involving patients in treatment choices has the potential for harm, therefore, but it could lead to beneficial outcomes. If decision making is to be shared, the information to inform decisions must also be shared. Patients must be given help to obtain the information they need. Kaplan et al. carried out a series of studies in which patients with different conditions (ulcer disease, hypertension, diabetes, and breast cancer) were randomized to an educational intervention in which they were given information about treatment options and coached to ask appropriate questions in the consultation (Kaplan et al. 1989). The control group was given basic information only. The group of patients who had received coaching were more involved in the interaction and had significantly better health outcomes measured physiologically (blood pressure or blood sugar), functionally (activities of daily living), or subjectively (evaluation of overall health status).

Given the short consultation times experienced in most busy clinics, it is often unrealistic to expect clinicians to provide full information about the risks and benefits of all treatment options. This information is not always readily available to clinicians, let alone lay people. If patients are to be able to express their preferences, they require help in the form of user-friendly information packages and decision aids. Ideally this information should come from an independent source and be based on a sound overview of the scientific evidence. Such information is now available for certain diseases in the form of leaflets, videos, and multimedia packages. An evaluation of an interactive video system designed to inform patients about treatment choices for BPH found that use of the video system caused patients to be better informed and more satisfied with the decision-making process and led to improved health and physical functioning, although in this case it had little effect on the choice of treatment (Barry et al. 1997).

Research in situations where patients have been directly offered choice between two options has produced more equivocal results. Three studies in which breast cancer patients were offered a choice between mastectomy or breast-conserving surgery found no ill-effects of involving patients in the decision, but the findings conflicted on whether offering choice led to psychological benefits (Fallowfield et al. 1994; Morris and Royle 1988; Wilson et al. 1988). Having to make a choice between these options led to increased anxiety among some patients. It may be more important to allow patients an opportunity to express their concerns and preferences than to involve them in the decision itself. Despite the lack of evidence of additional benefit of mastectomy, a significant minority of patients opted for the more mutilating surgery, underlining the important role of patients' values and beliefs and the difficulty in predicting these. Decision making in cases of serious illness can be a protracted process. Patients require time to come to terms with the choices facing them and seek a sympathetic hearing from the clinician. In some cases consultation style may have a more important effect on outcome than the decision itself. Real-world decision making may not always conform to the rational tenets of the decision theorists (Dowie 1996), but there is sufficient evidence to suggest that decisions that incorporate patients' values produce more beneficial outcomes than those that ignore them.

Impact on the Health-Care System

At the microlevel of individual doctor–patient interactions, the arguments for giving patients more say in treatment decisions may appear persuasive, but what about the effects on the health system? Is there not a risk that allowing patients more autonomy will increase demand for health care to unaffordable levels? Many clinicians believe that patients will make irrational choices if they are allowed to express a preference. The fear is that patients will want investigations or treatments that are unlikely to do them any good. As well as posing ethical problems for clinicians, this could increase health care costs and lead to greater inequalities in access to care, especially if the demands of the most articulate are acceded to.

To some extent these fears are justified. After all, demand for health care has risen as populations become healthier, better informed, and more empowered. Inequalities in access to health care are a feature of most systems, and the tendency for the most deprived to get the worst deal seems ubiquitous. Better information has not led to an increase in people's willingness to cater for their own health needs without resort to professional help. On the contrary, greater awareness of the potential benefits of medical care makes people want more of it.

Judging by the extensive coverage given to health issues on television and in the popular press and magazines, the public has an insatiable desire for health information. The wider availability of electronic information via the Internet is already having an impact on clinical consultations as patients seek out information on diagnostic tests or treatments and ask their doctors to provide them. The gap between the 'information rich' and the 'information poor' seems set to widen.

This clock cannot be turned back, so strategies will have to be devised for managing demand to ensure that health-care resources are used appropriately. Good quality information, for patients and clinicians, could have a role to play here. There is a need for education about the limits to medical care and the fact that interventions can be harmful as well as beneficial. Some studies have shown that giving patients unbiased information about likely treatment outcomes can lead to a reduction in demand. For example, an interactive video outlining treatment options for patients with benign prostatic hypertrophy led to a reduction in demand for prostatectomy (Wagner et al. 1995). Patients who were better informed about the risks and benefits of screening for prostate cancer were less likely to want the tests (Flood et al. 1996; Wolf et al. 1996), and patients given leaflets about the natural history of lower respiratory tract infections were less likely to re-consult their general practitioners (Macfarlane et al. 1997).

Currently, much of the information patients receive is optimistic about the outcomes of medical interventions. Whether the source is an individual clinician giving verbal advice or published material the patient has acquired, the chances are that the benefits will be emphasised and the risks downplayed. Clinicians are naturally optimistic about the treatments they are trained to provide, and much written material is published by groups with a vested interest in promoting demand for their products or services, for example, pharmaceutical companies, health-care providers, or professional bodies. Dispassionate advice is hard to come by. On the whole, governments or health-care payers have not seen investment in health information as a priority, except for traditional health education topics such as smoking reduction or dietary improvement. Little has been done to encourage a sceptical view of medical care. This may change as governments try to deal with the gap between public expectations and the availability of services, but educating populations about risk or how to access evidence and assess outcome probabilities is a daunting task. Doing this as a response to financial crisis in health-care provision may prove impossible, not least because people will be suspicious of the motive.

Pressures to provide more patient-centred care and to involve patients in decisions about their care lead inevitably in the direction of more individualized forms of care. The health professional will be expected to provide care in ways that more obviously than now respond to each individual patient's concerns, preferences, and circumstances. Increasingly, the patient will come to have a greater voice in relation to the content and direction of consultations with health professionals, which will reinforce the process of increasing individualized care. However, health professionals, like any 'people-processing' occupations, substantially depend on the use of routines and familiar customs in history taking, and the use of investigative tests and treatments to manage the potential complexity of their responsibilities and get through the working day. The routinization of health professional decision making has been considerably reinforced in recent years, in both North America and Europe, by external pressures in the direction of managed care in which clinical autonomy has to be controlled by protocols, guidelines, and professional and external review. It is possible to foresee substantial dilemmas, particularly in the role of doctors as they attempt to meet the conflicting styles of individualized and routinized care in their clinical practice.

A number of developments may be expected to arise from such conflicts in the health professional role. Methods of involving the patient may have to be routinized in order to be incorporated into managed care. Eliciting patients' preferences could be performed by interactive computer facilities supervised by paraprofessional or technical staff and kept out of core clinical contacts of the doctor with the patient. Additionally, issues of involving patients may be expected to be increasingly salient in health professional training, a familiar way in which professional, ethical, and scientific dilemmas can be presented to society as being taken seriously.

Most likely, the availability of high-quality, individualized care will increasingly be a fundamental component of inequality in health services, with more affluent social groups having access to individualized care and the less affluent receiving standardized care.

Conclusion

Increasing the patient's voice has often been considered one of the main sources of potential threat to professional autonomy. The trends discussed in this chapter may appear to imply similar predictions. However, such analyses often require subscribing to a rather simplistic zero-sum game to account for patient–professional relations, where increasing the voice of the patient diminishes the authority of the doctor. Many of the analyses reviewed in this chapter, perhaps optimistically, anticipate mutually

advantageous consequences of shared decision making.

However, whilst increased patient involvement does not necessarily jeopardise professional autonomy, it may challenge professional confidence. Health professionals increasingly feel under threat from diverse forces, including managerial intrusion, cost controls, medico–legal risks, and consumerism. Among other things, these forces expose both the explicit bases for medical decisions and also the enormous range of uncertainty. In numerous ways the traditional doctor–patient relationship left scope for latitude and discretion in decision making that rightly has been questioned as paternalism and professional defensiveness. However, these same elements may sometimes be a necessary resource for coping with contradictory or excessive demands. It will certainly be of vital importance to identify viable forms of practise, for occupations such as medicine, under circumstances when the uncertainties and value judgements involved in decisions about health and illness are more widely visible. The evidence presented in this chapter suggests that there is a substantial momentum behind calls to increase the responsiveness of health care systems to patients' preferences and concerns.

References

Alford, R.R. (1975) *Health Care Politics*. Chicago: University of Chicago Press.

Andersen, T.F. and Mooney, G. (eds) (1990) *The Challenges of Medical Practice Variations*. London: Macmillan.

Baker, R. (1996) 'Characteristics of practices, general practitioners and patients related to levels of patients' satisfaction with consultations', *British Journal of General Practice*, 46: 601–5.

Barry, M.J., Cherkin, D.C., Chang, Y., Fowler, F.J., and Skates, S. (1997) 'A randomized trial of a multimedia shared decision-making program for men facing a treatment decision for benign prostatic hyperplasia', *Disease Management and Clinical Outcomes*, 1: 5–14.

Blanchard, C.G., Labrecque, M.S., Ruckdeschel, J.C., and Blanchard, E.B. (1988) 'Information and decision-making preferences of hospitalized adult cancer patients', *Social Science and Medicine*, 27: 1139–45.

Bruster, S., Jarman, B., Bosanquet, N., Weston, D., Erens, R., and Delbanco, T. (1994) 'National survey of hospital patients', *British Medical Journal*, 309: 1542–9.

Calnan, M., Katsouyiannopoulos, V., Ovcharov, V., Ramic, H., and Williams, S. (1994) 'Major determinants of consumer satisfaction with primary care in different health systems', *Family Practice*, 11: 468–78.

Carr-Hill, R. (1992) 'The measurement of patient satisfaction', *Journal of Public Health*, 14: 236–49.

Cassileth, B.R., Zupkis, R.V., Sutton-Smith, K., and March, V. (1980) 'Information and participation preferences among cancer patients', *Annals of Internal Medicine*, 92: 832–6.

Charles, C., Gauld, M., Chambers, L., O'Brien, B., Haynes, B., and Labelle, R. (1994) 'How was your hospital stay? Patients' reports about their care in Canadian hospitals', *Canadian Medical Association Journal*, 150: 1813–22.

Charles, C., Gafni, A., and Whelan, T. (1997) 'Shared decision-making in the medical encounter: What does it mean? (or it takes at least two to tango)', *Social Science and Medicine*, 44: 681–92.

Charles, C., Redko, C., Whelan, T., Gafni, A., and Reyno, L. (1996) 'Doing nothing is no choice: Lay constructions of treatment decision-making among women with early stage breast cancer', Hamilton McMaster University Centre for Health Economics and Policy Analysis, Working Paper 96-17.

Cleary, P. and McNeil, B. (1988) 'Patient satisfaction as an indicator of quality care', *Inquiry*, 25: 25–36.

Cleary, P. Edgman-Levitan, S., Roberts, M., Moloney, T., McMullen, W., Walker, J. D., and Delbanco, T. (1991) 'Patients evaluate their hospital care: A national survey', *Health Affairs*, 10: 254–67.

Coulter, A., Peto, V., and Doll, H. (1994) 'Patients' preferences and general practitioners' decisions in treatment of menstrual disorders', *Family Practice*, 11: 67–74.

Davies, A.R., and Ware, J.E. (1988) 'Involving consumers in quality of care assessment', *Health Affairs*, 7: 33–48.

Deber, R.B. (1994) 'The patient–physician partnership: Changing roles and the desire for information', *Canadian Medical Association Journal*, 151: 171–6.

Degner, L.F. and Sloan, J.A. (1992) 'Decision making during serious illness: What role do patients really want to play?' *Journal of Clinical Epidemiology*, 45: 941–50.

Dowie, J. (1996) 'Evidence based, cost effective and preference driven medicine: Decision analysis based medical decision making is the pre-requisite', *Journal of Health Services Research and Policy*, 1: 104–13.

Emanuel, E.J. and Emanuel, I.L. (1992) 'Four models of the physician–patient relationship', *Journal of the American Medical Association*, 267: 2221–6.

Fallowfield, L.J., Hall, A., Maguire, P., Baum, M., and A'Hern, R. (1994) 'Psychological effects of being offered choice of surgery for breast cancer', *British Medical Journal*, 309: 448.

Fitzpatrick, R. (1997) 'The assessment of patient satisfaction', in C. Jenkinson (ed.), *Assessment and Evaluation of Health and Medical Care*. Buckingham: Open University Press. pp. 85–101.

Fitzpatrick, R. and Hopkins, A. (1983) 'Problems in the conceptual framework of patient satisfaction research: An empirical exploration', *Sociology of Health and Illness*, 5: 297–311.

Fitzpatrick, R. and Hopkins, A. (1988) 'Illness behaviour and headache, and the sociology of consultations for headache', in A. Hopkins (ed.), *Headache: Problems in Diagnosis and Management*. London: W.B. Saunders. pp. 349–86.

Flood, A.B., Wennberg, J.E., Nease, R.F., Fowler, F.J., Ding, J., and Hynes, L.M. (1996) 'The importance of patient preference in the decision to screen for prostate cancer', *Journal of General Internal Medicine*, 11: 342-9.

Fulford, K.W.M., Ersser, S., and Hope, T. (1996) *Essential Practice in Patient-Centred Care*. Oxford: Blackwell Science.

Hall, J. and Dornan, M. (1988) 'What patients like about their medical care and how often they are asked: A meta-analysis of the satisfaction literature', *Social Science and Medicine*, 27: 935–9.

Henshaw, R.C., Naji, S.A., Russell, I.T., and Templeton, A.A. (1993) 'Comparison of medical abortion with surgical vacuum aspiration: Women's preferences and acceptability of treatment', *British Medical Journal*, 307: 714–17.

Hjortdahl, P. and Laerum, E. (1992) 'Continuity of care in general practice: Effect on patient satisfaction', *British Medical Journal*, 304: 1287–90.

Kaplan, S.H., Greenfield, S., and Ware, J.E. (1989) 'Assessing the effects of physician–patient interactions on the outcomes of chronic disease', *Medical Care*, 27 (suppl): S110–S127.

Korsch, B.M., Gozzi, E.K., and Francis, V. (1968) 'Gaps in doctor–patient communications. 1. Doctor–patient interaction and patient satisfaction', *Paediatrics*, 42: 855–71.

Laine, C. and Davidoff, F. (1996) 'Patient-centred medicine: A professional evolution', *Journal of American Medical Association*, 275: 152–6.

Larsson, U.S., Svardsudd, K., Wedel, H., and Saljo, R. (1992) 'Patient involvement in decision-making in surgical and orthopaedic practice', *Scandinavian Journal of Caring Sciences*, 6: 87–97.

Levy, S.M., Herberman, R.B., Lee, J.K., Lippman, M.E., and d'Angelo, T. (1989) 'Breast conservation versus mastectomy: Distress sequelae as a function of choice', *Journal of Clinical Oncology*, 7: 367–75.

Ley, P. (1983) 'Patients' understanding and recall in clinical communication failure', in D. Pendleton and J. Hasler (eds), *Doctor–Patient Communication*. London: Academic Press. pp. 89–108.

Logan, R.L. and Scott, P.J. (1996) 'Uncertainty in clinical practice: Implications for quality and costs of health care', *Lancet*, 347: 595–8.

Macfarlane, J.T., Holmes, W.F., and Macfarlane, R.M. (1997) 'Reducing reconsultations for acute lower respiratory tract illness with an information leaflet: A randomized controlled study of patients in primary care', *British Journal of General Practice*, 47: 719–22.

Morris, J. and Royle, G.T. (1988) 'Offering patients a choice of surgery for early breast cancer: A reduction in anxiety and depression in patients and their husbands', *Social Science and Medicine*, 26: 583–5.

Mulley, A.G. (1989) 'Assessing patients' utilities: Can the ends justify the means?' *Medical Care*, 27: S269-S281.

Mulley, A.G. and Eagle, K. (1988) 'What is inappropriate care?' *Journal of the American Medical Association*, 260: 540–1.

Pollitt, C. (1987) 'Capturing quality? The quality issue in British and American health policies', *Journal of Public Policy*, 7: 71–92.

Pollitt, C. (1988) 'Bringing consumers into performance measurement: Concepts, consequences and constraints', *Policy and Politics*, 16: 77–87.

Quill, T.E. (1983) 'Partnerships in patient care: A contractual approach', *Annals of Internal Medicine*, 98: 228–34.

Richards, M.A., Ramirez, A.J., Degner, L.F., Fallowfield, L.J., Maher, E.J., and Neuberger, J. (1995) 'Offering choice of treatment to patients with cancers', *European Journal of Cancer*, 31A: 112–16.

Rubin, H., Gandek, B., Rogers, W., Kosinski, M., McHorney, C. A, and Ware, J. E., (1993) 'Patients' ratings of outpatient visits in different practice settings', *Journal of American Medical Association*, 270: 835–40.

Segall, A. and Roberts, L. (1980) 'A comparative analysis of physician estimates and levels of medical knowledge among patients', *Sociology of Health and Illness*, 2: 317–34.

Sira, Z.B. (1980) 'Affective and instrumental components in the physician–patient relationship: An additional component of interaction theory', *Journal of Health and Social Behaviour*, 21: 170–80.

Strull, W.M., Lo, B., and Charles, G. (1984) 'Do patients want to participate in medical decision making?' *Journal of the American Medical Association*, 252: 2990–4.

Wagner, E.H., Barrett, P., Barry, M.J., Barlow, W., and Fowler, F.J. (1995) 'The effect of a shared decision-making program on rates of surgery for benign prostatic hyperplasia', *Medical Care*, 33: 765–70.

Weiss, B. and Senf, J. (1990) 'Patient satisfaction survey instrument for use in health maintenance organisations', *Medical Care*, 28: 434–45.

Wennberg, J.E., Barry, M.J., Fowler, F.J., and Mulley, A. (1993) 'Outcomes research, PORTs and health care reform', *Annals of the New York Academy of Sciences*, 703: 52–62.

Wensing, M., Grol, R., and Smits, A. (1994) 'Quality judgements by patients on general practice care: A literature analysis', *Social Science and Medicine*, 38: 45–53.

Williams, B. (1994) 'Patient satisfaction: A valid concept?' *Social Science and Medicine*, 38: 509–16.

Wilson, R.G., Hart, A., and Dawes, P. (1988) 'Mastectomy or conservation: The patient's choice', *British Medical Journal*, 297: 1167–9.

Wolf, A.M.D., Nasser, J.F., Wolf, A.M., and Schorling, J.B. (1996) 'The impact of informed consent on patient interest in prostate-specific antigen screening', *Archives of Internal Medicine*, 156: 1333–6.

3.7

Consumer and Community Participation: A Reassessment of Process, Impact, and Value

DEENA WHITE

INTRODUCTION

Citizen participation has been a recurrent theme in health-care policy, planning, and organization since the heady days of popular protest and community action in the 1960s. It has advanced in waves, surging with optimism with each new policy endeavor and sinking in disillusionment before the next. It has emerged in a multitude of different of forms: direct participation on decision-making boards and local councils, various levels and forms of public consultation, resource mobilization strategies such as partnerships between lay and public agencies, and indirect forms of participation such as needs or satisfaction surveys. What these diverse activities share in common is not obvious, but they do all involve an invitation to groups with a stake in the health-care system to contribute opinions, information, experience, or other resources to the administration of that system.

The meaning of the term 'participation' is considered so self-evident that it is rarely defined in the abundant literature addressing consumer and community participation in the health field. This same literature, however, often goes on to insist upon the vagueness of the term as it is used in policy, the complex issues it obscures, the misunderstandings it provokes and the pitfalls it conceals. Despite this, its value for health-care decision making and quality assurance is usually taken for granted.

Where 'exit,' or the chance to takes one's health problems elsewhere, is not a viable alternative, due to a public monopoly on health services, 'voice' is typically seen as an equivalent, democratic expression of preferences and expectations that can help ensure accountability to the users or consumers of health-care services (Croft and Beresford 1989). From this perspective, participation is valued in and of itself, as a democratic ideal. The emphasis is on the processes by which stakeholders, such as service users, as well as physicians and other health-care workers contribute to administrative and managerial decisions.

Participatory democracy is not everyone's democratic ideal, however. It is viewed askance by many by who fear that 'popular opinion' is a poor basis on which to make collective health-care decisions, and that the diversity of opinions and interests on health-care issues would quickly degenerate into conflict and instability (Donovan and Coast 1996; Grant 1989). Mainstream political theorists contend that, far more important to democracy than direct participation in decision making is the right to opposition and the assurance of administrative accountability to the public (Pateman 1970). Participation in the health field, however, tends to be more oriented towards consensus and confirmation than debate and opposition, and more concerned with the recruitment and management of participants than with accountability to them or their constituencies (Steckler and Herzog 1979).

If participation in the health field rarely conforms to any democratic ideal, it may still have importance as a means to promote particular objectives that different participants may hold to be of value. For example, participation in priority-setting exercises, or in patient satisfaction or clinical outcome surveys, could lead to substantive effects that would not have been produced if administrators, managers, or physicians simply followed their own counsel. Curiously, however, the vast and eclectic literature on participation displays a common feature: a singular lack of concern with outcomes, or the effectiveness of participation. Now, the organization and management of participation, in any of its diverse forms, is a costly process for governments and administrators in terms of both financial expense and efficiency. In the context of fiscal constraints that have been menacing health systems throughout the West since the early 1980s and the recent surge of interest in evidence-based practice, the absence of any outward preoccupation with the results of participation is odd. It raises the following question: why are governments and other authorities determined to invest and reinvest in consumer and community participation in spite of the relative lack of evidence, one way or another, regarding its impact?

This chapter aims to explore this question by analyzing what we have learned about both the processes and effects of participation over the last 30 years. A previous review of the literature on participation in the health field (Bates 1983) concluded that democratic participation is generally a failure for three principal reasons: because of administrative constraints such as funding and deadlines, because those who participate tend to represent élite interests even within the lay population, and because administrators use participation for their own ends. Before taking up these issues, this chapter will discuss the context within which consumer and community participation emerged as a valued health administration practice, as well as a number of frameworks for analyzing it. The most striking feature of these frameworks is the extent to which they focus on power relations. Themes such as 'empowerment' (Beecker et al. 1998; Croft and Beresford 1989; Watt and Rodmell 1988;), the distinction between 'bottom-up' and 'top-down' participation (Lipsky and Lounds 1976; Lomas and Veenstra 1995; Milewa et al. 1998; White 1993a; White et al. 1994), and citizen or consumer control (Checkoway 1982a, 1982b; Goold 1996; Paap 1978) dominate the analytic literature, reinforcing the concern with process over outcomes.

EXPERT AND LAY PARTICIPATION

In the health field, stakeholders include doctors, nurses, and other health-care workers, politicians, administrators, managers, and researchers, pharmaceutical, insurance, and health maintenance enterprises, and finally, patients, and potential service users. Each has a different perspective from which they view effective health-care strategies. They also have different stakes or interests in the system: some depend on it not only to resolve their health problems but also for their livelihood. Many of these groups are organized into both formal and informal associations that represent their interests, and that play either an up-front or backstage role in their participation in the health system. Because not all social groups are equally well organized and do not all represent or express themselves in similar ways, not all are on an equal footing. Certain participants (or groups of participants) are more likely than others to have their agendas prevail. In this light, the view of participation as the democratic expression of the 'public will' is an overly abstract notion that is inadequate to capture the diversity of participants, and the asymmetry of participation in real world situations.

Metaphorically, we might refer to the relative power of health system 'insiders,' whose livelihood is assured by that system, who circulate in an arena of health-care decisions and actions, and who have some access to the human, financial, informational, and organizational resources that are concentrated there. By comparison, 'outsiders,' or peripheral participants, are those whose participation tends to be more intermittent, passive, and dependent on the resources and structures furnished by insiders, and whose autonomous impact on decisions and actions is limited. The definitions of 'insiders' and 'outsiders' are neither arbitrary nor fixed. Some of those who are decidedly insiders today, such as health administrators, were once considered outsiders, or 'laymen' [sic] with no right or expertise to interfere in the preserve of the medical profession (Horrobin 1977). Physicians themselves once had to compete with all sorts of alternative healers and in no way controlled the medical arena as they do today (Toth 1996). Now, health administrators and health economists have joined physicians in the core arenas of Western health systems. The current outsiders constitute an immensely broad, vague category of people called citizens, consumers, communities, the public or simply 'lay participants,' with nothing in common but the fact that they are not health system insiders.

There are striking contrasts between the simultaneous rise of a discourse on consumer and community participation and the process by which previous 'laymen,' such as administrators, managers, and economists, came to permeate the core arenas of the health-care delivery system. First, when administrators began to surface as the new health system decision makers, physicians resisted their rise to power, considering it an encroachment and interference in an area in which they had no pertinent expertise. In contrast, consumer or community participation has been *invited*, if not *invented* by those very administrators who are now central to the system. This means that insiders determine the rules and structures through which outsiders can approach the decision-making arenas, as well as the resources to which they have access, once there.

Second, the access of physicians, administrators, and other experts to the decision-making arena had been based on the perceived pertinence of their expertise in an increasingly complex, costly, and public health system. In contrast, ordinary citizens or consumers have no *recognized* expertise (Stacey 1994). Their participation always risks descending into the realm of the 'gratuitous,' where it would warrant no more than a polite interest in lay perspectives and beliefs (Popay and Williams 1996). Because their expertise in health matters is not yet established, and because their participation is engineered by administrators and other insiders, lay participants remain firmly ensconced at the periphery of health-care, decision-making arenas. This may explain why the concept of control has been one of the most salient issues for those who have analyzed lay participation in the health-care domain.

WHY LAY PARTICIPATION?

The preceding observations have so far begged the question of why core actors in health systems, including politicians, administrators, managers, and physicians, have decided that lay people ought to be drawn into a more active role in the system. An examination of the history of lay participation suggests three converging factors to explain the phenomenon: the ideology of the community health movement, the consolidation of the welfare state, and the emergence of a populist ethic supporting direct action, all of which emerged during the 1960s and early 1970s. Each provided a motive for encouraging lay participation in health-care decision making at the

political, administrative, and organizational levels.

Social development policies for the Third World have long called for the rational organization of health-care delivery, with a focus on primary care and community involvement. The concept of community involvement came to emphasize the value of lay knowledge and practices and the active participation of local populations in service delivery and organization, as well as the need for health education and community organization to empower communities to handle these responsibilities (Jewkes and Murcott 1998; Midgley 1986). The concept of community empowerment was harnessed to this tradition (Rappaport 1981), but the community health movement was clearly not a grassroots movement. It was inspired and promoted by professional community health organizers, typically from developed countries, as a means of mobilizing indigenous human resources and knowledge necessary to implement effective primary health-care programs on a shoestring budget (Zakus 1998). Nor was the community health approach a plot to exploit lay resources. It rather represented a genuine belief in the socially and medically therapeutic value of participation for the lay participants themselves. It referred to the sense of control that would ostensibly flow from lay people taking active responsibility for their own health at both the individual and community levels (Jewkes and Murcott 1998).

When the community health movement penetrated Western societies, its concern with the mobilization of lay resources and primary health care translated into the promotion of lifestyle changes, self-help, and health advocacy, while its experience with health-care planning was applied to the rationalization of increasingly costly Western health-care systems (Rose 1990; Watt and Rodmell 1988). The inspiration for the movement lay in bodies of knowledge developed and controlled by community health experts who, in many cases, made their way into government, administrative or other public sector positions in expanding welfare states. Indeed, postwar welfare state expansion and consolidation provided a fertile ground for the institutionalization of many community health principles and practices. It was also a second major contributing factor to the promotion of lay participation as one element of a rationalizing triumvirate that included decentralization, health planning, and eventually, prevention and community-based care.

Together, decentralization, health planning, and lay participation framed the establishment of health administration as a distinct area of expertise, and paved the way for the entry of health administrators into the core decision-making arena of health systems during the 1960s and early 1970s. Their mandate, in brief, was the coordination of health systems in the public interest. This meant, amongst other objectives, establishing countervailing forces against the constant pressure towards rising costs that were considered inherent in the professional ambitions of the medical establishment that controlled the domain at the time. In this context, the community health approach was seen to hold promise for a more rational health-care system that valued the expressed interests of patients and potential service users above competing professional interests such high-technology work environments or intensive therapies.

A third impetus for lay participation during the same era was the popular preoccupation with protest and dissent, direct action and anti-establishment sentiment. The medical establishment in particular was severely attacked during this period as an oppressive institution. First targeted was psychiatry, which was reinterpreted as an institutionalized form of social control. Indeed, the very status of mental illness as an 'illness' was challenged by both social scientists and radical psychiatrists (Cooper 1967; Foucault 1961; Goffman 1961; Szasz 1961). This wave was followed by a vast literature which was critical of medicine in general as a form of social control (Doyal 1979; B. Ehrenreich 1970; J. Ehrenreich 1978; Foucault 1975; Freidson 1970; Illich 1976), particularly from a feminist perspective (Ehrenreich and English 1973), and of the medicalization of more and more aspects of Western society (Conrad 1976, 1979; Zola 1972). In this overall context of cultural opposition, the need to legitimate ambitious welfare state reforms and the reorganization of public intervention to a politically engaged public was an important motivation in calling for lay participation, not only in the health arena, but also in economic development, education, and urban renewal. Such exercises in legitimation may well have contributed to the dispersion of radical anti-establishment movements by the end of the 1970s.

In Canada, Québec's CLSCs (local community health and social service centers) provide an instructive example of the convergence of these administrative motives for inviting lay participation in the health field. CLSCs were introduced in 1971 as part of a thoroughly reformed and rationalized system of health delivery, just as universal health insurance and other important welfare policies were also being adopted in the province. The mandate of the CLSCs was to provide primary socio-health care, including both clinical and health promotion services, in small, local, multidisciplinary organizations with a high degree of citizen participation. The network of CLSCs was to be the world prototype of a modern health system built around community health principals. A majority of seats on the board of directors of each CLSC was reserved for local service users, while the rest were reserved for the avant-garde professionals that staffed the organizations.

The CLSC concept had in large part been a response to the emergence of radical community action groups in Quebec that, during the 1960s, were setting up free clinics in working-class and inner-city neighborhoods, raising the consciousness of local populations. These groups had been aggressively advocating greater public investment in health care and greater sensitivity to users' needs. The first CLSCs were established by the government in partnership with existing local community action groups. The roots of the CLSCs, therefore, lay partly in government efforts to appease radical demands by having the grassroots participate in their establishment and operation, and partly in efforts to rationalize health care by substituting local centers of low-tech expertise at the center of the system, in place of the hospital and the medical specialist's office. The user-controlled CLSC clearly represented the intersection of community health ideals, grassroots action, and rational welfare state development and management.

The story of the early years of the CLSCs also illustrates many of the vexing issues intimately associated with lay participation. The CLSC has proven a great disappointment with respect to improving system efficiency, controlling medical power, and increasing grassroots participation. Doctors simply boycotted the CLSCs, with the effect of relegating them, to this very day, to a relatively marginal public health as opposed to primary health role within the system. However, this posed little problem for the avant-garde community health professionals who saw the CLSCs mainly as vehicles for the promotion of their own particular expertise in community mobilization and health promotion. This unfortunately did not coincide with the expectations of CLSC lay board members, who expressed more traditional needs such as improved access to existing services.

The first five years of CLSC development were ridden by internal conflict. On the one side were the militant lay board members who had been instrumental in setting up the CLSCs in their communities and who expected to retain control, especially with their hard-won board majority. On the other side were the idealistic professionals eager to implement their own radically new forms of community health practice. While lay participation was limited to board membership, professional participation permeated the operational level of the CLSCs, and furthermore, created concentrated, material interests for the staff in maintaining control over the organizations. They were able to determine the flow of information to the board, as well as the extent to which board directives were implemented. Furthermore, the professional staff also entered into conflict with CLSC administrators as they undertook the arduous process of union certification during a period characterized by labor unrest. In this climate of conflict and instability, the professionals' position in the CLSCs became increasingly dominant, while lay participation dropped off, leaving board seats empty.

Five years later, community action groups were no longer a feature of Québec's urban landscape; the free clinics had all but disappeared with the introduction of CLSCs. Independent lay participation in the CLSCs was becoming alienated, and professional community organization had become a central feature of CLSC practice. To restore some level of stability and a modicum of legitimacy to its showpiece organizations, the government declared that the role of government-appointed CLSC administrators would be reinforced, that the establishment of future CLSCs would not depend on the grassroots participation of local citizens' groups, and that the provision of primary health and social services would take precedence over community organization. Perhaps most interesting was the government's explanation for retreating from its initial, close partnership with both grassroots groups and ideological community health professionals:

> I don't think you are expecting excuses from me for the government's control over CLSCs. This control is the normal and inseparable counterpart of our responsibilities, which are challenged much less frequently... The state defines the goals of a program like the CLSCs and provides the means for carrying them out. The responsibility delegated by the state concerns the way these means are used to achieve the goals... Participation must be seen in this context. Let there be no confusion: participation does not mean that the state abdicates its role; it merely shares it... (C. Forget, Minister of Social Affairs, 1975, quoted in Lesemann 1984: 260).

Quebec's disappointing experience with participation was not unique. In the United States, the Comprehensive Health Planning Councils instituted in 1966, in which both consumers and providers were represented, and their 1974 replacements the Health Systems Agencies (HSAs), with consumer majorities on their boards, had both been abandoned by the 1980s. In the United Kingdom, Community Health Councils (CHCs), established in 1974 to represent consumer views and interests within the National Health Service, are still a feature of the system, but have never, on the whole, presented a challenge to the traditional health establishment. Despite this discouraging history, support for lay participation has spread and its motives and forms have diversified since the 1980s. It is rapidly becoming an institutionalized feature of Western health organizations and planning bodies.

FRAMEWORKS FOR THE ANALYSIS OF PARTICIPATION

Since the 1980s the spaces and motives for lay participation have broadened and become of increasing interest to policy makers. A whole host of new modes and uses for lay participation have emerged. These range from community needs assessments and patient evaluations of clinical outcomes to national or regional priority-setting and resource allocation decisions. While some empirical evidence of the relative success or failure of different participation strategies has accumulated over the years, usually from single case studies, there is far less than might be expected given the total amount of writing that has been published on the subject. Moreover, it is not clear how to make sense of the research results in such a way as to learn specific lessons from more than three decades of experience.

Diversification makes it difficult to establish a common conceptual or theoretical basis for conducting a meta-analysis of study results on consumer and community participation, one that would be meaningful for all objectives, methods, and degrees of participation. There is no lack of conceptual frameworks suggested in the literature, although they have not often been applied in empirical case studies. Most such conceptual systems have focused on a single issue: the extent of lay control over decision making. Do consumers or communities gain access to core decision-making circles, entailing at least a partial transfer of power from those who already control that arena? Or is participation reduced to a data-collecting exercise, a one-way transfer of information from users to administrators, which further empowers core actors by increasing their knowledge base?

The best-known conceptual framework for the analysis of lay participation is Arnstein's (1969) eight-rung ladder of participation. Arnstein 'rates' participation in terms of the degree of control held by lay actors. For

Arnstein, what sometimes goes by the name of participation is in reality 'therapy' or 'manipulation,' where lay people are encouraged to participate 'for their own good' or because of the resources they can provide in the form of information, services, or public relations. Some community health programs and strategies concerned with consumer satisfaction risk falling into these categories, which Arnstein places at the very bottom of her ladder. The middle rungs consider various two-way communication arrangements between insiders and outsiders, from 'information' and 'consultation,' with little power sharing, to 'placation' and 'partnership,' where some accountability is implied. The top rungs are reserved for 'delegated power' and 'user control.' Arnstein's ladder has inspired other similar approaches such as Feingold's (1977) five-rung version and Brachat's (1994) evolutionary interpretation of the model in which the practices associated with participation are perceived to have moved up the ladder over the years.

Equally concerned with the continuum of control, Webster (1995) suggests an analysis of participation that focuses on the rhetoric of consumerism and empowerment, concepts at the center of Thatcher's reform of the National Health Service in Britain. Webster argues that the logic of the consumer empowerment argument is plagued by confusion over who the 'consumers' of health care are, and therefore, who was empowered by the quasi-market reform. The actual consumers or decision makers are local or regional administrators and groups of general practitioners who purchase hospitals' and specialists' services (or in the American system, private insurance companies and health maintenance organizations, or HMOs). Patients, potential service users, communities, and the public remain entirely outside the realm of consumer-like decisions. Lay access to information is not significantly improved, and experts of various sorts are still making choices on behalf of beneficiaries. Webster concludes that it is not patients who have been empowered by the shift towards consumerism, but health system insiders (see also Milewa et al. 1998).

There are more dimensions to participation than user control or empowerment, however. For example, Charles and DeMaio (1992) devised a three dimensional framework that considers the level of user control and the domain of action (treatment, planning, or policy), as well as 'role perspective' (are participants expected to take the perspective of particular lay groups, or rather of the broader 'public' or 'community' good?). A similar framework was developed by White (1993b) in the context of a study of the 'communitarization' of mental health services.

Here, each domain of action is depicted in the form of a continuum stretching from local, lay control, based on experiential knowledge, to centralized, administrative, and professional control, based on scientific knowledge. However, none of these frameworks is useful for conducting a meta-analysis of existing studies of participation which tend to divide themselves into camps, each treating only one or another dimension of a process that is clearly multidimensional.

One fault line relates to the objectives of lay participation. As we have seen, lay participation is sometimes understood as being an end in itself primarily concerned with democratic process and empowerment, and sometimes as a means to substantive ends related to health-care delivery, such as cost control or improved service access. Usually, only one or the other is addressed, although it becomes apparent that the two are inevitably linked and that this very linkage creates serious tensions around lay participation. A second fault line relates to the question of representation, and how the category of 'participant' is constituted. Lay participants are seen by some to represent some amorphous, undifferentiated 'public' or aggregation of individuals, and by others to represent a collectivity, community, or constituency of lay interests. This issue mirrors Charles and DeMaio's concept of 'role position,' but raises more sharply the question of accountability. Collective representation with accountability to an outside constituency, such as an advocacy group or patients' association, is shown to enhance not only democratic process but also the efficacy of lay participation (Berry 1988; Beeker et al. 1998). On the other hand, it hampers administrative efficiency.

Finally, there is a clear divide in the literature between the perception of participation as a means of drawing lay actors into decision-making arenas, as opposed to a consultation exercise that still excludes lay actors from the inner circles. Overall, it appears that authors who take the perspective of lay actors are more concerned with democracy than efficiency, are more likely to focus on collective rather individual representation, and are more concerned to draw lay actors into a sustained relation with insiders. Those who write from an administrative or managerial perspective are, in contrast, more likely to think of participants as representing their individual opinions and experiences, and to understand participation as a means of gathering data rather than sharing power. Neither group seems to be particularly concerned with the impact of lay participation. The following sections of the chapter address the dynamic relations between the two sides of these fault lines as well as the relation between the questions of objectives, representation, and the relation between insiders and outsiders.

Participation as Democratic Process: What we have Learned

Lay participation as a democratic process empowering service users has received far more attention in the literature than participation as a means for achieving health system outcomes. Most often, however, it is addressed in normative terms, as hopes or expectations that are rarely tested, and even less often fulfilled (Jewkes and Murcott 1998). Thus, Winkler (1987), on the basis of a description of participation strategies used by a Community Health Council, suggests that through participation, users can introduce items onto the council's agenda, force changes in the language used when referring to patients, challenge conventional ways of doing things, and channel information to their constituents. However, the empirically based literature casts considerable doubt on the extent to which these good intentions bear fruit (Checkoway 1982a, 1982b; Fitzpatrick and White 1997; Grant 1989; Lipsky and Lounds 1976; Milewa 1997; Milewa et al. 1998; Pickard et al. 1995; Steckler and Herzog, 1979). Indeed, Winkler herself refers to case study evidence of organized professional resistance to user empowerment.

Researchers have accumulated long and varied lists of methods used by administrators, managers, and physicians to foster lay participation (Checkoway et al. 1984; Donovan and Coast 1996), but the difficulty of any of these methods actually to engage lay participants is a major issue. 'Apathy' is often cited as the principal obstacle to recruiting and maintaining lay participants (Donovan and Coast 1996; Grant 1989). For example, in experiences reported in the United States (Parkum 1980) and Quebec (Godbout 1981), it was found that citizen participation in either management or planning boards dropped off significantly as the organizations in question became institutionalized. In studies of the Oregon experience, one of the most important efforts to date to mobilize public participation around the highly charged issue of health-care rationing, a wide range of means of engagement were implemented, from town hall meetings to telephone interviews. Yet almost 70 per cent of participants in these community consultations were health-care workers, not lay consumers (Lomas and Veenstra 1995).

Indeed, lay actors do not appear to be interested in playing a sustained, decisive role with respect to most health-care issues, although they are more willing to be consulted. In a Canadian study using deliberative polling, a cross-section of randomly selected lay individuals, interested citizens, elected officials, administrators, and health-care experts were asked to identify which of these groups they deemed most appropriate to make decisions regarding a series of health issues (Abelson et al. 1995). For most areas, elected representatives and public administrators were considered the most appropriate groups to take primary responsibility for decision making, with experts included mainly with respect to management issues. Experts were, nonetheless, deemed to have some role to play in all areas, while the role of interested citizens was considered important only with respect to revenue-raising decisions. Randomly selected citizens were overall the least preferred as decision makers, even by their peers. Because the research methodology sought to ensure that participants made informed choices, the results are not likely to reflect 'apathy' on the part of citizens so much as a considered judgement of democratic accountability and administrative competence.

Clearly, drop-outs and poor response to recruitment drives are not always the result of reasoned deliberation on the part of lay actors. In an article analyzing the phenomenon in the context of American Health System Agencies, Marmor and Marone (1980) refer to the effects of 'imbalanced political markets.' Groups of actors lodged close to the active center of the health system, who depend on it for their professional status and effectiveness as well as for their livelihood, have important stakes in the outcome of deliberations and decisions. They are therefore highly likely to mobilize and articulate their preferences and ensure that their agendas are met. In contrast, within the lay public, personal health-care interests tend to be highly diffuse, and the personal benefits of participation are far from clear. Unless an individual or group has a particular interest, such as a neighborhood hospital closing or the availability of home care for the elderly, mobilization is far less likely and less intense than it is for those whose working conditions, professional interests, and paychecks depend on health-care decisions. This explains the more important role accorded concerned citizens as opposed to random citizens in the deliberative polling study by Abelson and colleagues.

Furthermore, research on decision-making processes suggests that members of the general public are unlikely to come to committees or councils with strong, pre-established opinions and preferences on the issues (Hibbard et al. 1997). Opinions are rather constituted through the process of participation, and are therefore relatively unstable and easy to influence. Providing training for lay participants, as some administrators do, may make it easier for them to participate more effectively, but is also likely to reinforce insider control over the agenda, the flow of information, the deliberation process, and the legitimacy of various opinions and orientations. For example, while lay members of the boards in Quebec's CLSCs were highly interested and motivated citizens, the professional staff had far greater stakes in maintaining control over services, and were in a position to 'handle' their boards in such a way as to limit their ability to influence the organizations' activities and overall orientation (Godbout 1981). In this and similar cases, the waning of lay participation can be better attributed to alienation than to apathy.

The existence of concentrated, organized community interests, along with accountability to an outside constituency, emerge in the literature as the most important factors in keeping the process of lay participation alive, even if it provides no guarantee (J. Berry 1981; L. Berry 1988; Bowl 1996; Checkoway et al. 1984; Goold 1996; Grant 1989; Jewkes and Murcott 1998). Insiders, whether professionals or managers, tend to be well-organized in associations of various types which consolidate and sustain their interests or stakes in the health system. Although they rarely participate as official delegates of such associations, they are often taken to represent the perspective of their profession or establishment and, in highly charged situations, can count on the resources of their associations or organizations for support. This type of interested participation on the part of insider groups can be a source of conflict, but such conflicts are typically institutionalized; the positions of the various groups are well known to all, and much of the conflict is resolved backstage.

In contrast, there is a clear reluctance to bring in outsiders representing concentrated, organized, well-articulated interests, and who have access to outside resources to support them (Berry 1988). A study by White et al. (1994) revealed that the possibility of prolonged debates, open conflicts, surprise moves (such as media involvement), and efforts to reset the agenda are seen as a serious threat to decision-making processes, which are geared to achieving consensus, often within a deadline. Thus, many administrators will argue that participation is not about the representation of lay interests, but rather about broadening the forms of expertise and experience that contribute to quality decision making. This suggests that, in the eyes of administrators, lay participation is primarily concerned with efficiency, not democracy.

There is a clear tension between lay participation as a democratic versus an efficiency-enhancing process. Even where there is little danger of disruption and instability, as when participation is solicited through questionnaires, it still represents an administrative burden because of the increased number of people and steps involved and because of participants' uneven awareness and understanding of issues (Donovan and Coast 1996; Lipsky and Lounds 1976). This is why it is a common strategy for insiders to hand-pick or coopt known lay actors (typically, concerned citizens with some experience in the health field) as opposed to requesting outside groups with particular interests to delegate representatives. However, cooption poses a whole host of thorny problems for lay participation as a democratic process (Grant 1989; Rose 1990; Wistow and Barnes 1993).

For example, in contemporary societies where sensitivity to diversity is increasingly valued, it may be expected or required that participants represent the full sociodemographic diversity of the community (Marmor and Marone 1980). Many social groups, such as the mentally ill or physically disabled, ethnocultural minorities, and the economically disadvantaged, are organized in associations that advocate for their interests. Indeed, some planning boards in the United States, and some Community Health Councils in the United Kingdom, have adopted policies so that a number of lay representatives are delegated by such interest groups and are accountable to them, but this is hardly a universal practice. Most administrators try to avoid the disruptive effect that single-interest participants are seen to have on mixed boards and councils (Bowl 1996; Grant 1989; Rose 1990). Indeed, the tendency in the health field is for administrators to nominate familiar, knowledgeable, cooperative individuals who also happen to have the required cultural, racial, demographic, or socioeconomic characteristics. While it has been demonstrated that such characteristics may indeed be predictors of attitudes and opinions (Verba et al. 1993), the individuals who are likely to become representatives are typically part of an élite that has emerged within the social group in question, with attitudes and interests that may well differ from those of the ordinary lay citizen (Jewkes and Murcott 1998).

Strategic recruitment is one of many methods of maintaining efficiency on mixed boards. Others include controlling the flow of information and the rhythm of meetings, burying participants in documentation, bulldozing a committee's way through controversial dossiers, or simply multiplying the number of committees that 'do nothing' (Aronson 1993; Bowl 1996; Lamoureux 1991). Along these lines, Steckler and Herzog (1979) furnish an amusing but accurate compendium of administrative strategies for keeping lay boards 'out of your hair and off your back.' Furthermore, control and efficiency can be maintained by keeping lay actors at a greater distance from core arenas of activity, for example, by reducing participation to the occasional consultation or focus group, or ultimately, by tapping public or local views through remote, one-way, data collection exercises such as surveys or interviews. While surveys are becoming an increasingly popular strategy, they can trivialize the concept of lay participation. For example, patient satisfaction surveys have been criticized for focusing on the 'hotel' aspects of patient care such as food and room decoration at the expense of issues that are known to be of greatest concern to service users, such as the dynamics of staff–patient interaction (Fitzpatrick and Hopkins 1993).

Furthermore, serious questions can be raised about the status of survey data for decision making in complex contexts. For example, the aggregation of individuals' values as expressed in survey results can produce some abstract notion of 'average' values which can be interpreted in either an indiscriminate or a strategic fashion, depending on who is doing the interpreting (Donovan and Coast 1996). Lay respondents to surveys have no control over the manner of interpretation, and concerned individuals may hardly recognize their interests or views in the aggregated results. Moreover, the results are typically taken to represent 'community' views or needs, without any clear definition of the 'community' in question (Jewkes and Murcott 1998). This provides another strong argument in favor of collective representation, where participants are not randomly selected but rather selected or delegated as concerned citizens, representing articulated interests or concerns (Bowl 1996).

In the final analysis, from the perspective of lay participation as a democratic process, the principal issue is that of accountability (Jewkes and Murcott 1998; Marmor and Marone 1980). This involves not only questions of representation, but also mechanisms to ensure that 'voice' is translated into action. Through such mechanisms, democratic process and substantive outcomes are linked. Yet a recent British study of lay participation in a mental health forum found that more than 50 per cent of the issues raised by lay participants were ignored, another 30 per cent were either explained away, rejected, or deferred, and less than 20 per cent were positively addressed (Milewa 1997). The lack of any clear commitment on the part of administrators and other authorities to actually *use* the information pro-

vided or perspectives expressed by lay actors in the context of such forums (even where lay comments are positively received) and the absence of transparent mechanisms for translating lay voices into action are seen to seriously weaken the potential effectiveness of such exercises (Aronson 1993; Fitzpatrick 1994; Milewa 1997; Pickard et al. 1995). To the extent that these failures become obvious to lay actors, alienation or so-called apathy prevails.

However, lay actors do have other choices with respect to the manner of their participation. Unless representing the interests of a particular constituency, they may not have a personal interest in contributing to the efficiency of administrative decision making. Indeed, from the perspective of many advocacy groups, drawing lay actors into administrative decision-making arenas too easily neutralizes their potential input, damages their credibility, and creates a dependency where, in order to participate, they must rely on insiders for pertinent information and cues as to the issues (Grant 1989; Jewkes and Murcott 1998). Their perception is that the centripetal forces of administrative participation can ultimately rob them entirely of their own agenda (Lipsky and Lounds 1976). Many such groups prefer to remain firmly at the periphery, where they retain the capacity for independent, oppositional action based on self-defined goals (Rose 1990). Such independent advocacy is the prototype of participatory democracy. Informal networks, with their broad, loose ties, or direct action involving the press are often seen to be more effective paths into core decision-making arenas than controlled contact within formal administrative structures (Berry 1981; White 1993a). In this case, nonparticipation is a function of neither apathy nor alienation, but rather, strategic choice.

The accumulation of case studies suggests that, for autonomous lay groups, participation as a democratic end in itself is firmly tied to participation as a means of influencing decisions or attaining goals, but efficient administration requires the neutralization of specific interests that are more appropriately defended in the political arena than at the administrative center of the health system. There is, therefore, a constant tension between the political and administrative dimensions of participation (Croft and Beresford 1989; Feingold 1969). To counteract the destabilizing effects of potentially conflictual participation, administrators play it safe: they recruit known individuals who have some link to the health system and who are likely to focus on broad, community, or societywide goals rather than particular lay interests, no matter how loose their status as lay representatives. They choose forms of participation that do not involve sustained interaction, such as occasional consultations or surveys, or where sustained interaction is tolerated, it is strictly controlled. In this light, participation as a democratic end in itself is a contradictory process in which insiders encourage lay actors to participate and provide the resources for them to do so, while at the same time working to ensure that lay participants are largely dependent on insiders for both information and cultural cues and remain firmly tied to the administrative agenda.

IMPACT: WHAT DOES LAY PARTICIPATION ACHIEVE?

Considerably less attention has been paid to the impact of lay participation in the health field, as compared with process. This is partly because of the difficulty of separating out the effects induced by the intervention of lay actors from those that may have occurred without their presence. Yet one of the most prevalent concerns in the literature is the effect of participation *on the participants themselves*. In a community health tradition, many professionals see the prime function of lay participation as therapeutic: it gives people a sense of dignity and self-respect; it increases their self-esteem; it develops their capacities and skills; it enables them 'to discover their own real interests' (Hawker 1989: 289). Professionals may contribute actively to promote these outcomes by offering consciousness raising, training, and other support to lay participants, but on Arnstein's (1969) ladder of participation, this approach lies at the very bottom rung; the principal outcome served by this 'feel good' perspective is the legitimation of the participation process itself. As Bowl points out:

> For those driven by the therapeutic imperative, issues of representation, and whether or not service users have access to real decisions, and indeed ensuring that views that do emerge from user involvement are fed into mainstream decision-making, are secondary to [participants'] development of skills and confidence. (Bowl 1996: 173)

One might presume that concern with the impact of lay input would be most common in the area of patient satisfaction and community needs, where it is clear that results fed back into the system could be useful for improving services in ways that would show an increase in user satisfaction. Yet surveys are typically conducted as isolated, one-off studies that cannot test the

impact of their results on service delivery or clinical outcomes, nor the impact of such changes or the level of patient satisfaction or well-being (Fitzpatrick 1993). The effectiveness of patient surveys may therefore be assumed to lie in the 'human relations' value of the process, with little effective regard for impact.

Interestingly, there have been a greater number of studies concerned with the impact of lay participation on substantive goals more complex than satisfaction or needs, such as regional planning, priority setting and resource distribution. One of the most exhaustive case studies examined over 150 US planning agencies, in which outcome measures were obtained by asking administrators alone to rank the extent to which consumer involvement in regional planning had any of a number of given effects (Checkoway et al. 1984). Most agency officials believed that participation had been instrumental in improving the quality of local health services, increasing their accessibility, increasing the flow of information to and from the agency, and raising public awareness of health issues (Checkoway 1982a). On the other hand, they claimed as well that hospital administrators and physicians were the most influential participants, followed by other health workers, with lay actors the least influential.

Despite the administrative bias of this study, it emerged that the factors having the *least* impact on the perceived effectiveness of participation were those associated with the size of the agency's budget, and with administrative efforts to promote participation such as recruitment, publicity, and training strategies. The variables that had the *greatest* impact on the perceived effectiveness of participation were (a) executive commitment, measured by the number staff dedicated solely to the promotion of lay participation, and (b) community factors, such as a tradition of citizen participation, public awareness, and organized constituencies to which lay participants were accountable (Checkoway et al. 1984). Again, the relation between democratic process, through the representation of lay constituencies, and the effectiveness of participation was clear even to administrators who tended to adopt 'safe' participation methods.

From this and other research, we begin to learn that within fairly similar forms of participation, lay input can have more or less of an impact on different sorts of goals, and that this impact is not always in the direction desired or expected by politicians, administrators, professionals, or social scientists. For example, lay participation is sometimes touted as a valuable instrument for challenging traditional professional practices. An evaluation of the impact of lay participation in Québec's CLSCs, as well as other studies, showed positive effects on service accessibility and responsiveness to local needs, but no impact at all on professional practices (Godbout 1981). Furthermore, Godbout suggests that assertive lay participation was a factor in *blocking* political efforts to transform primary health care in the province. There is little evidence anywhere that lay participation of any type, including independent advocacy, is highly effective for mitigating the effect of professional preferences and institutional ambitions on health-care systems.

This raises the delicate question of the types of impacts that are actually expected of lay participation. Is there any reason to believe that decisions effectively influenced by lay actors would differ from those made by insiders themselves? To address this question, several studies have compared lay and expert priority rankings of health services. In one US study (Fowler et al. 1994) there was substantial convergence in two-thirds of ratings, but where differences did occur, they tended to show victim-blaming tendencies amongst lay respondents: the public was less willing than health-care system insiders to provide treatment for diseases considered to have been brought on by the victims' own behavior or lifestyle, such as lung cancer in a smoker or drug addiction. A UK study (Bowling et al. 1993) that compared the priority rankings of several groups, including random citizens, community groups, general practitioners, specialists, and others, found that the general public ranked high-tech surgery and intervention for life-threatening conditions higher than did physicians. As Bowling and colleagues conclude, priorities based on lay decisions might very well be contrary to 'the spirit of equity and equal access according to need' to which most of our Western health systems aspire. They might also put upward pressure on costs.

This observation takes us back to our original question: Why are governments and other authorities determined to continue investing in lay participation with so little evidence of its impact? If lay participation is costly, if it is not the only option available to lay actors for making their voices heard, if it threatens administrative efficiency, does not appear to be effective but, if made more effective, may destabilize administrative practices, and finally, if effective participation would risk imperiling some of the very objectives that recent policies and reforms throughout the West have been advancing, why do governments and their agencies continue to advocate and support lay participation?

THE TRANSACTION COSTS OF ADMINISTRATIVE AND POLITICAL ACTION

The fact that lay participation is typically neither very democratic nor very effective, in the ways that have been discussed so far, suggests that we may have been looking in the wrong places to determine its value. Lay participation is not about empowering consumers and communities or about turning them into decision makers, but rather, it is about empowering existing decision-makers. This perspective makes it possible to account for the political and administrative investment in participation.

The Oregon experience in rationing health services illustrates this argument (Coast 1996). In a bid to broaden the availability of public health insurance, the state of Oregon had tried and failed to impose service rationing by fiat. It was decided that a second attempt would have to be more transparent and in line with community values. Towards this end, a wide range of formal and less formal consultation procedures were undertaken to determine the public's values, including a telephone survey about the value of certain treatments for given symptoms or conditions. The results were fed into cost–benefit calculations that considered medical effectiveness and cost-effectiveness as well as the community assessment of value, according to an explicit formula. Although the Oregon consultation process has been hotly criticized on numerous methodological and ethical grounds (Coast 1996; Hansson 1994; Lomas and Veenstra 1995; Nelson 1994), and although ultimately, the state itself had to back away from some of the implications of its calculations (Blumstein 1997), the exercise has been hailed by insiders as 'a pioneering attempt...in the context of the state's particular democratic traditions' (Golenski and Thompson 1991).

Be that as it may, the Oregon experience did not significantly empower lay actors; physicians and health economists had the greatest influence on prioritizing services, and tightly controlled the nature and use of lay input. Moreover, the outcome of the exercise was treated with all the necessary flexibility when the unanticipated consequences of its rigid application were revealed, thus overriding a certain number of 'community values' as well as other criteria originally used to prioritize services. Most authors seem to agree that the principal value of the exercise lay in the public dialogue and debate it engendered. This public dialogue gave the appearance of accountability to a government undertaking a politically delicate task, even if the effective role of the public was far more ambiguous than advertised. Nowadays, public dialogue and debate are not to be underrated, and can ultimately influence political decisions. Indeed, therein lies the value of autonomous forms of lay action such as advocacy. However, in the public debate raised in the context of Oregon's formal exercise in lay participation, the objectives were predetermined, the initial consultations remained 'exploratory,' the final survey was strategically designed, and the outcome was defined by insider interpretations. The process served mainly to gage the public acceptability of certain sorts of rationing decisions, and to ensure that the ultimate decisions taken by the government, its administrators, and experts would be politically unassailable.

These uses of lay participation are not to be regarded cynically. The designers of the Oregon experience, like the designers of Quebec's CLSCs and other radical exercises in lay participation throughout the West, took significant administrative and political risks. However, it may be mistaken to understand these actions as an investment in democracy and public choice, as advertised. Rather, they may best be seen as the transaction costs of successful public administration. They empower administrators by reducing the uncertainty of public response and cooperation, by increasing administrators' confidence in the actions they take (Fitzpatrick 1994), and by alleviating authorities of sole responsibility for delicate decisions (Donovan and Coast 1996). Moreover, lay participants have a distinct role to play in comparison with others, such as physicians or staff. Because they can less easily maintain control over their own contribution to decisions, they are useful to administrators either as an ally to counter the interests of more powerful groups, or to control the balance of power between two strong, opposing insider groups (Landsberger 1980; White et al. 1994). In these ways, lay participation also differs significantly from autonomous lay action such as advocacy or participation in social movements in health, which have their own constituencies, agendas, resources, and expertise (Croft and Beresford 1989; Epstein 1995; Popay and Williams 1996; Rogers and Pilgrim 1991; Rose, 1990; Stacey 1994; Williams et al. 1995).

The costs of lay participation in terms of money, time, bureaucratic inefficiency, and political risk thus constitute the transaction costs of setting up and maintaining 'consumers,' 'citizens,' 'communities,' or 'the public' as powerful administrative and political resources. However, those costs are variable, as we have seen. They can be contained by limiting lay participation to one-way transactions, as in surveys and other data-gathering exercises, or by controlling it through recruitment and information management techniques. Thus, the Oregon experience was costly to the extent that it mobilized significant financial and human resources, as well as in terms of the risks involved in fostering public debate. The risk factor was controlled, however, for the debate was carefully structured by administrative means. What is important is that this risk was significantly *less* than that of simply rationing health services for the poor without public consultation, and allowing the public and the press to attack the decision makers freely in the political arena, as had occurred only a few years earlier in Oregon (Coast 1996).

Similarly, when the Quebec government chose to establish the first CLSCs in partnership with grassroots community action groups, and to give them majority status on the boards of directors, it suspected that *not* doing so might be more costly in political terms than doing so. On the other hand, when the CLSCs proved to be a political minefield rather than a triumph, the Minister of Health himself stepped in and redefined the rules of the game. Thatcher's introduction of the quasi-market in the British National Health Service was accompanied by strong consumerist language and a renewed call for health-care administrators to pay attention to 'lay voices.' Ensuring that lay voices are representative of health-care users or potential users, or that a mechanism is in place to translate voices into action, is less pertinent than ensuring that this valuable category of people (consumers or citizens) can be seen to collaborate in health-care decisions. In less politicized forms of lay participation, such as patient satisfaction surveys, the same logic applies. Eisenberg (1997: 20), for example, argues that the justification for such surveys lies in 'the relationship between patient satisfaction and such issues as patient adherence to treatment regimens, predisposition toward litigation, and the tendency to disenroll from a health plan.' For politicians, administrators, managers, and other decision makers, then, lay participation is a valuable strategy for risk management.

Lay participation gains increasing political support with each new wave of health reform. The capacity to claim that reforms either reflect 'public values' or, more often, that they empower 'citizens,' 'consumers,' or 'communities' is valuable protection against the higher political costs of resistance and opposition to radical reforms (Rochefort et al. 1998). Without political support, lay participation would likely have remained a dimension of community health practice rather than an administrative mantra. Administrative bodies would rarely find the resources to implement it, and lay actors seeking to influence their health-care environments would have to engage in independent civic action, including advocacy and social movements in health, a challenge far more formidable for the disadvantaged and marginal than for élites and experts (Williams et al. 1995). It is therefore important to avoid the Manichean conclusion that administrative lay participation is manipulative while independent advocacy is empowering. Advocacy or protest groups and social movements can occupy more than one stage at a time (Rose 1990). They can act simultaneously within the system and beside the system, as well as oppose the system, and if lay participation presents the possibility of manipulation, there is also the possibility of resistance. Regardless of the gap between rhetoric and practice, in the absence of formal exercises in lay participation, those without a voice would likely remain unheard.

Conclusion

The rhetoric of democracy and empowerment that has always surrounded lay participation has, according to the research, almost never been translated into effective practices. Those who participate in formal structures and exercises may contribute to the capacity of administrators to make informed decisions that benefit communities, as certain of the rare outcome studies have suggested. It is evident that the extent to which such outcomes are produced depends on the willingness of administrators to develop mechanisms for translating voice into action, and on the level of autonomous organization of lay participants themselves. These are the two principal factors that might empower lay actors. Studies of the practices of administrators in organizing and managing lay participation processes indicate, however, that lay empowerment is simply not on the agenda. To advance their own agenda, lay actors with particular health-care concerns typically have to empower themselves by organizing, advocating, and taking independent media or political action from their position at the periphery of the health-care system. As outsiders, they can confront insiders in oppositional ways that are not possible when they have been joined in an asymmetrical relation of dependency.

That lay participation in health-care decision making is, to a significant extent, less an investment than a transaction cost of administrative legitimacy and risk management is one conclusion we can draw from what is known about its dynamics and outcomes. This hypothesis should not be seen to disqualify lay participation, however, but rather to distinguish its rhetorical from its practical and political value. Lay participation as it is preached and practiced is clearly about administrative and political efficiency, not democracy, consumer empowerment, or community control. It derives its value principally from its role as an administrative strategy. We may finally learn more about its impact than we have so far by focusing future critical research on public administration, and health-care management and decision making in general, with a view to sorting out the actual and relative roles played by lay participation in its proper context.

References

Abelson, J., Lomas, J., Eyles, J., Birch, S., and Veenstra, G. (1995) 'Does the community want devolved authority? Results from deliberative polling in Ontario', *Canadian Medical Association Journal*, 153: 403–12.

Arnstein, S.R. (1969) 'A ladder of citizen participation', *Journal of the American Institute of Planners*, 35: 216–24.

Aronson, J. (1993) 'Giving consumers a say in policy development: Influencing policy or just being heard?' *Canadian Public Policy*, 19: 367–78.

Bates, E. (1983) *Health Systems and Public Scrutiny*. London: Croom Helm.

Beeker, C., Guenter-Grey, C., and Raj, A. (1998) 'Community empowerment paradigm drift and the primary prevention of HIV/AIDS', *Social Science and Medicine*, 46: 831–42.

Berry, J.M. (1981) 'Beyond citizen participation: Effective advocacy before administrative agencies', *The Journal of Applied Behavioral Science*, 17: 463–78.

Berry, L. (1988) 'The rhetoric of consumerism and exclusion of community', *Community Development Journal*, 23: 266–72.

Blumstein, J.F. (1997) 'The Oregon experiment: The role of cost–benefit analysis in the allocation of Medicaid funds', *Social Science and Medicine*, 45: 545–54.

Bowl, R. (1996) 'Legislating for user involvement in the United Kingdom: Mental health services and the NHS and Community Care Act 1990', *International Journal of Social Psychiatry*, 42: 165–80.

Bowling, A., Jacobson, B., and Southgate, L. (1993) 'Health service priorities. Explorations and consultation of the public and health professionals on priority setting in an inner London health district', *Social Science and Medicine*, 37: 851–7.

Brachat, P. (1994) *Le partenariat de service public*. Paris: Harmattan.

Charles, C. and DeMaio, S. (1992) Lay participation in health care decision making: A conceptual framework. CHEPA working paper series No. 92–16, Hamilton, Ontario: McMaster University.

Checkoway, B. (1982a) 'Public participation in health planning agencies: Promise and practice', *Journal of Health Politics, Policy and Law*, 7: 723–33.

Checkoway, B. (1982b) 'The empire strikes back: More lessons for health care consumers', *Journal of Health Politics, Policy and Law*, 7: 111–24.

Checkoway, B., O'Rourke, T.W., and Bull, D. (1984) 'Correlates of consumer participation in health planning agencies: Findings and implications from a national survey', *Policy Studies Review*, 3: 296–310.

Coast, J. (1996) 'The Oregon plan: Technical priority setting in the USA', in J. Coast, J. Donovan and S. Frankel (eds), *Priority Setting: The Health Care Debate*, Chichester: Wiley.

Conrad, P. (1976) *Identifying Hyperactive Children: The Medicalization of Deviant Behavior*. Toronto: Lexington.

Conrad, P. (1979) 'Types of medical social control', *Sociology of Health and Illness*, 1: 1–11.

Cooper, D.G. (1967) *Psychiatry and Anti-Psychiatry*. Toronto: Tavistock.

Croft, S. and Beresford, P. (1989) 'User-involvement, citizenship and social policy', *Critical Social Policy*, 9(2): 5–18.

Donovan, J. and Coast, J. (1996) 'Public participation in priority setting: Commitment or illusion?' in J. Coast, J. Donovan, and S. Frankel (eds), *Priority Setting: The Health Care Debate*. Chichester: Wiley.

Doyal, L. (1979) *The Political Economy of Health*, London: Pluto.

Ehrenreich, B. (1970) *The American Health Empire: Power, Profits and Politics*. New York: Random House.

Ehrenreich, B. and English, D. (1973) *Complaints and Disorders: The Sexual Politics of Sickness*. New York: Feminist Press.

Ehrenreich, J. (ed.) (1978) *The Cultural Crisis of Modern Medicine*. New York: Monthly Review Press.

Eisenberg, B. (1997) 'Customer service in healthcare: A new era', *Hospital and Health Services Administration*, 42: 17–31.

Epstein, S. (1995) 'The construction of lay expertise: AIDS activism and the forging of credibility in the reform of clinical trials', *Science, Technology, and Human Values*, 20: 408–37.

Feingold, E. (1969) 'The changing political character of health planning', *American Journal of Public Health*, 59: 803–8.

Feingold, E. (1977) 'Citizen participation: A review of the issues', in H. Rosen, J. M. Metsch, and S. Levey (eds), *The Consumer and the Health Care System: Social and Managerial Perspectives*. New York: Spectrum.

Fitzpatrick, R. (1993) 'Assessment of patients' views in primary care', in M. Lawrence and T. Schofield (eds), *Medical Audit in Primary Health Care*. New York: Oxford University Press.

Fitzpatrick, R. (1994) 'Health needs assessment, chronic illness and the social sciences', in J. Popay and G. Williams (eds), *Researching the People's Health*. London: Routledge.

Fitzpatrick, R. and Hopkins, A. (1993) 'Patient satisfaction in relation to clinical care: A neglected contribution', in R. Fitzpatrick and A. Hopkins (eds), *Measurement of Patients' Satisfaction with their Care*. London: Royal College of Physicians.

Fitzpatrick, R. and White, D. (1997) 'Public participation in the evaluation of health care', *Health and Social Care in the Community*, 5: 3–8.

Foucault, M. (1961) *Histoire de la folie*. Paris: Plon.

Foucault, M. (1975) *The Birth of the Clinic: An Archaeology of Medical Perception*. New York: Vintage.

Fowler, F.J., Berwick, D.M., Roman, A., and Massagli, M.P. (1994) 'Measuring public priorities for insurable health care', *Medical Care*, 32: 625–39.

Freidson, E. (1970) *Professional Dominance: The Social Structure of Medical Care*. New York: Altheron.

Godbout, J. (1981) 'Is consumer control possible in health care services?' *International Journal of Health Services*, 11: 151–67.

Goffman, E. (1961) *Asylums: Essays on the Social Situation of Mental Patients and Other Inmates*. Chicago: Aline.

Golenski, J.D. and Thompson, S.J. (1991) 'A history of Oregon's basic health services act: An insider's account', *Quality Review Bulletin*, 17(5): 144–49.

Goold, S.D. (1996) 'Allocating health care: Cost–utility analysis, informed democratic decision making, or the veil of ignorance?' *Journal of Health Politics, Policy and Law*, 21: 69–98.

Grant, J.A. (1989) 'Consumer participation in health planning: Policy and political implications', *Nonprofit and Voluntary Sector Quarterly*, 18: 147–65.

Hansson, L.F. (1994) 'Equality, explicitness, severity, and rigidity: The Oregon plan evaluated from a Scandinavian perspective', *Journal of Medical Philosophy*, 19: 343–66.

Hawker, M. (1989) 'Consumer participation as community development: Action in an ambiguous context', *Community Development Journal*, 24: 283–91.

Hibbard, J.H., Slovic, P., and Jewett, J.J. (1997) 'Informing consumer decisions in health care: Implications from decision-making research', *Milbank Quarterly*, 75: 395–414.

Horrobin, D.F. (1977) *Medical Hubris: A Reply to Ivan Illich.* Montreal: Eden.

Illich, I. (1976) *Limits to Medicine: Medical Nemesis – The Expropriation of Health.* London: Marion Boyars.

Jewkes, R. and Murcott, A. (1998) 'Community representatives: Representing the "community"?' *Social Science and Medicine,* 46: 843–58.

Lamoureux, J. (1991) *Le Choc des cultures: bilan-synthèse de l'expérience de participation aux comités tripartites.* Montreal: Regroupment des ressources alternatives en santé mentale du Québec.

Landsberger, H.A. (1980) 'The trend toward citizens' participation in the welfare state: Countervailing power to the professions, in C. R. Foster (ed.), *Comparative Public Policy and Citizen Participation, Energy, Education, Health and Urban Issues in the US and Germany.* New York: Pergamon.

Lesemann, F. (1984) *Services and Circuses: Community and the Welfare State.* Montreal: Black Rose.

Lipsky, M. and Lounds, M. (1976) 'Citizen participation and health care: Problems of government induced participation', *Journal of Health Politics, Policy and Law,* 1: 85–111.

Lomas, J. and Veenstra, G. (1995) 'If you build it, who will come?' *Policy Options,* November: 37–40.

Marmor, T.R. and Marone, J.A. (1980) 'Representing consumer interests: Imbalanced markets, health planning, and the HSAs', *Health and Society,* 58: 125–65.

Midgley, J. (1986) *Community Participation, Social Development and the State.* London: Methane.

Milewa, T. (1997) 'Community participation and health care priorities: Reflections on policy, theatre and reality in Britain', *Health Promotions International,* 12: 161–7.

Milewa, T., Valentine, J., and Calnan, M. (1998) 'Managerialism and active citizenship in Britain's reformed health service: Power and community in an era of decentralization', *Social Science and Medicine,* 47: 507–17.

Nelson, J.L. (1994) 'Publicity and pricelessness: Grassroots decision making and justice in rationing', *Journal of Medical Philosophy,* 19: 333–42.

Paap, W.R. (1978) 'Consumer-based boards of health centers: Structural problems in achieving effective control', *American Journal of Public Health,* 68: 578–82.

Parkum, V.C. (1980) 'Social planning and citizens' participation: A discussion and empirical analysis, with data drawn from the health planning area', in C.R. Foster (ed.), *Comparative Public Policy and Citizen Participation, Energy, Education, Health and Urban Issues in the US and Germany.* New York: Pergamon.

Pateman, C. (1970) *Participation and Democratic Theory.* London: Cambridge University Press.

Pickard, S., Williams, G., and Flynn, R. (1995) 'Local voices in an internal market: The case of community health services', *Social Policy and Administration,* 29: 135–49.

Popay, J. and Williams, G. (1996) 'Public health research and lay knowledge', *Social Science and Medicine,* 42: 759–68.

Rappaport, J. (1981) 'In praise of paradox: A social policy of empowerment over prevention', *American Journal of Community Psychology,* 9: 1–25.

Rochefort, D., Rosenberg, M., and White, D. (1998) 'Community as a policy instrument: A comparative analysis', *Policy Studies Journal,* 26: 548–68.

Rogers, A. and Pilgrim, D. (1991) '"Pulling down churches": Accounting for the British mental health user's movement', *Sociology of Health and Illness,* 13: 129–48.

Rose, H. (1990) 'Activists, gender and the community health movement', *Health Promotion International,* 5: 209–18.

Stacey, M. (1994) 'The power of lay knowledge: A personal view', in J. Popay and G. Williams (eds), *Researching the Peoples' Health.* London: Routledge.

Steckler, A.B. and Herzog, W.T. (1979) 'How to keep your mandated citizen board out of your hair and off your back: A guide for executive directors', *American Journal of Public Health,* 69: 809–12.

Szasz, T. (1961) *The Myth of Mental Illness.* New York: Free Press.

Toth, B. (1996) 'Public participation: An historical perspective', in J. Coast, J. Donovan, and S. Frankel (eds), *Priority Setting: The Health Care Debate.* Chichester: Wiley.

Verba, S., Schlozman, K.L., Brady, H., and Nie, N.H. (1993) 'Citizen activity: Who participates? What do they say?' *American Political Science Review,* 87: 303–18.

Watt, A. and Rodmell, S. (1988) 'Community involvement in health promotion: Progress or panacea', *Health Promotion,* 2: 359–68.

Webster, G. (1995) 'Public participation in health: Empowerment or control?' in S. Edgell, S. Walklate, and G. Williams (eds), *Debating the Future of the Public Sphere.* Aldershot: Ashgate.

White, D. (1993a) 'Les processus de réforme et la structuration sociale des systèmes. Le cas des réformes dans le domaine de la santé mentale au Québec', *Sociologie et Sociétés,* 25: 77–97.

White, D. (1993b) 'The community-based mental health system: What does it mean', *Canadian Review of Social Policy,* 31: 31–61.

White, D., Mercier, C., Desbiens, F., and Roberge, M.-C. (1994) *The Development of Community Resources in Mental Health: A Study of Reform Processes.* Montreal: Groupe de recherche sur les aspects sociaux de la prévention (GRASP), Université de Montréal.

Williams, G., Popay, J., and Bissell, P. (1995) 'Public health risks in the material world: Barriers to social movements in health', in J. Gabe (ed.), *Medicine, Health and Risk.* Oxford: Blackwell.

Winkler, F. (1987) 'Consumerism in health care: Beyond the supermarket model', *Policy and Politics*, 15: 1–8.

Wistow, G. and Barnes, M. (1993) 'User involvement in community care: Origins, purposes and applications', *Public Administration*, 71: 279–99.

Zakus, J.D. (1998) 'Resource dependency and community participation in primary health care', *Social Science and Medicine*, 46: 475–94.

Zola, I. (1972) 'Medicine as an institution of social control', *Sociological Review*, 20: 487–504.

An Expanded Conceptual Framework of Equity: Implications for Assessing Health Policy

LU ANN ADAY

INTRODUCTION

This chapter will (1) provide a critical review and synthesis of conventional and emerging paradigms for conceptualizing and measuring justice, grounded in contemporary social and political theory, (2) discuss the major conceptual models, empirical indicators, evidence, and new directions for assessing health policy suggested by the respective paradigms, and (3) present an expanded conceptual framework for empirically assessing equity, that integrates the array of dimensions and indicators undergirding these variant conceptualizations of justice.

A number of approaches have been developed and applied in health services research and policy analysis to assess equity. They have focused primarily on potential or realized barriers to access to medical care, the extent to which subgroup variations exist in the utilization of medical care services relative to need, and the conceptual foundations of distributive justice and associated individual rights required to assure equity (Aday and Andersen 1981; Aday et al. 1993).

What these conventional conceptualizations have failed to encompass and accommodate, however, include: the weight of the empirical evidence regarding the limited role of medical care relative to other inputs or sectors for improving health; the corollary concerns with the common good and health of populations and communities; emerging philosophical criticisms of the distributive justice and associated individual rights framework as a basis for judgments of equity; the fairness of the deliberative processes and procedures for deciding who gets what and why in policy debates regarding the allocation of public and private resources.

An implicit assumption underlying this chapter is that the conventional lenses for viewing equity have failed to penetrate the origins of, as well as fully envision other likely remedies for, persistent health and health-care inequalities. An explicit aim is to provide a broader and deeper vision of the foundations of fairness that can explicitly guide the formulation of empirical research to assess equity.

CONTRASTING PARADIGMS OF JUSTICE

Three primary philosophical traditions, that have variously focused primarily on individuals, institutions, or the community in judging justice, may be identified as a foundation for illuminating the correlates and indicators of equity in health and health care (Table 1) (Daly 1994; Habermas 1996; Mulhall and Swift 1992).

The undergirdings for the distinctions between the individual and community perspectives are most deeply lodged in the debate between liberal and communitarian values. The liberal political tradition focuses on the norms of personal well-being and individual freedom. Policies grounded in this tradition have been

Table 1   *Contrasting paradigms of justice*

Focus	Individuals	Institutions	Community
Theory	**LIBERALISM** Person well-being Individual freedom	**DELIBERATIVE DEMOCRACY** Public governance Popular sovereignty	**COMMUNITARIANISM** Common good Social solidarity
Policies	**MINIMALIST STATE** Individual rights	**RESPONSIVE STATE** Civic participation	**RESPONSIBLE STATE** Public welfare
Paradigms	**DISTRIBUTIVE JUSTICE** Why can *I* justly *claim*?	**DELIBERATIVE JUSTICE** *Who decides* and *how*?	**SOCIAL JUSTICE** What's *good* for *us*?

Source: Used with permission from Aday, L.A., Begley, C.E., Lairson, D.R., and Slater, C.H. (1988) *Evaluating the Healthcare System: Effectiveness, Efficiency, and Equality* (2nd edn). Chicago: Health Administration Press. Table 6.1 (p. 175).

concerned with protecting or assuring individual rights, and its underlying distributive justice paradigm. Rights are those benefits to which one has a claim, based on assessing what might be a fair distribution of benefits and burdens. This encompasses a consideration of both negative and positive rights – that is, noninterference and freedom of choice, as well as a positive conferring of specific material or nonmaterial benefits. The question of equity posed from this point of view is, 'What can *I* justly *claim*?'

This framework has guided policy debates regarding universal health insurance and the impact of immigration and welfare reform on the most vulnerable (Chapman 1994). The rising costs of medical care, the increasing corporatization of medical care provision, and the growing dominance of market-oriented care in both the public and private sectors have raised significant questions grounded in the distributive justice paradigm regarding to whom, what, and to what extent the benefits of coverage for medical care might be extended, and how should the burdens or costs be assigned. Increasing emphasis is being placed on consumer choice, personal responsibility, experience rating, actuarial fairness, and free riders. The answer to the question 'What can *I* justly *claim*?' is then more and more sharply focused on the attributes and actions of the *I*.

Communitarian sentiments are based on norms of the common good, social solidarity, and protecting the public welfare. The concept of justice on which this perspective is based is concerned with the underlying social, economic, and environmental underpinnings of inequity. Rather than focusing largely on conferring or assuring positive or negative rights (or benefits) to individuals, this paradigm encompasses a broader consideration of public health and social and economic interventions that may be required to enhance the well-being of groups or communities as a whole. The essential question of justice posed from this perspective is, 'What's *good* for *us*?'

The social justice paradigm is reflected in traditional public health policy and practice, with its emphasis on the public welfare and the use of medical police power (public health regulations, inspections, quarantines, etc.) to protect the population's health (Beauchamp 1985, 1988). However, critics have argued that public health planning and practice have focused less on attending to what communities may say is good for *us*, and more on what public health professionals determine they need, based on agency or administratively driven data gathering or needs assessment activities (Kretzmann and McKnight 1993; Labonte 1993, 1994; Rissel 1994; Robertson and Minkler 1994; Wallerstein and Bernstein 1994). The consequence is, in many communities, that fundamental social, economic, and environmental issues, most determinant of the health of the public in those areas, are not adequately addressed, and the capacities of affected populations to ameliorate them are untapped, or at worst undermined.

These criticisms of the distributive justice paradigm, as applied to medical care and the social justice model underlying public health, mirror the siege of criticisms that have been raised about the liberal and communitarian theories as well (Daly 1994; Habermas 1996; Mulhall and Swift 1992). The dominance of the liberal paradigm in shaping health and social policy has, it is argued, served to weaken communal sentiments, such as civility and mutuality, sacrificed considerations of the public good to serve private interests, promoted self-centeredness, and blamed the victim for what are likely to be circumstances created by society or others. On the other hand, communitarianism is charged with weakening private autonomy, or the ability of the public to make rational, informed choices, due to the increasing bureaucratization of public institutions and attendant shift of individuals served by them into the role of dependent clients.

Contemporary social theorists, most notably the German philosopher Jhrgen Habermas, have addressed the weaknesses of the liberal and communitarian traditions in arguing for a new synthesis for the foundations for fairness, based on a theory of deliberative democracy (Habermas 1995, 1996). Policies attuned to this perspective address the extent to which norms of civic participation appear to guide decision making. The question of justice posed from this point of view is, '*Who decides* and *how*?' The foundation for the enlargement of deliberative justice is the growth and promotion of a public sphere of secondary associations, social movements, and an array of civil and political forums for influencing the formal policy-making process. The deliberative justice paradigm recognizes and attempts to resolve conflicts rooted in the other dominant paradigms of fairness through posing the need for rational discourse on the part of affected groups and individuals. Such discourse is oriented primarily toward mutual understanding. Habermas argues that strategic or technical–rational aims of decision makers at either the macro- or microlevel (such as implementing health-care reform or achieving patient adherence to therapeutic regimens) are unlikely to be orchestrated and achieved unless affected stakeholders (providers, patients, and taxpayers, for example) have the opportunity to present their points of view and have them heard and respected in the process.

The section that follows highlights (a) the major conceptual models, (b) empirical indicators, (c) evidence, and (d) new directions for assessing the equity of health policy suggested by the respective paradigms of justice. The discussion will focus on the prospects for integrating medical care, public health, and broader social and economic policy in enhancing the health of populations. Following this discussion, an expanded framework for the study of equity, incorporating perspectives from the respective paradigms, will be presented.

MODELS, INDICATORS, EVIDENCE, AND NEW DIRECTIONS

National health-care systems can be positioned on a continuum from a market-maximized, demand-based system of health care to a market-minimized, need-based system (Aday et al., 1998). The former, typified most directly by the US health-care system, is characterized by individual choice by consumers, nonuniversal coverage, private insurance, numerous sources of payment, high out-of-pocket payment, the private practice of medicine, and private ownership of health-care facilities, many of which are operated on a for-profit basis. The interaction of supply and demand forces within a market context, however imperfect, guides the allocation of resources within health care and between health care and other sectors. In the United States, market-oriented reforms have been dominated by the growth of an array of forms of managed-care service delivery and financing (Havlicek 1996; Kongstvedt 1995; Reinhardt 1996).

Market-minimized systems are characterized by community need-based determinations, universal and public coverage, relatively few sources of payment, low out-of-pocket payments, public practice or public control of private practice, and public ownership or control of health-care facilities operated on a not-for-profit basis. Professional and bureaucratic determinations of need guides the allocation of resources to and within the health sector. Although the United Kingdom, Canada, and other Organization for Economic Cooperation and Development (OECD) countries lie much more toward the market-minimized end of the continuum, many have undertaken market-oriented reforms in recent years.

An expanded framework for assessing the equity implications of market-dominated reforms in the United States and other countries, that incorporates distributive, social, and deliberative considerations of justice, will be presented in the discussion that follows.

Distributive Justice

Models

A framework developed by Aday and Andersen and their colleagues for the study of access has guided a great deal of research on equity (Aday and Andersen 1981), grounded in the distributive justice paradigm. The relevant characteristics of the health system include the availability, organization, and financing of services. Predisposing characteristics of the population at risk include those that describe the propensity of individuals to use services – including basic demographic characteristics (age, sex), social structural variables (race and ethnicity, education, employment status, and occupation), and beliefs (general beliefs and attitudes about the value of health services, and/or knowledge of disease). Enabling characteristics encompass the means that individuals have available to them for the use of services. Both financial resources (such as family income or insurance coverage), and organizational resources (such as having a regular source or place to go for care) specific to the individuals and their families are relevant here. Need refers to health status or illness as a predictor of health service use. The need for care may be perceived by the individual and reflected in reported disability days or symptoms, for example, or evaluated by a provider in terms of actual diagnoses or complaints.

Realized access refers to objective and subjective indicators of the actual process of care-seeking. These are, in effect, indicators of the extent to which the system and population characteristics predict whether or not, or how much, care is used (or the demand for care) and how satisfied potential or actual consumers are with the health-care system.

Integral to the framework is the value judgment that the system would be deemed fair or equitable if need-based criteria, rather than resources (such as insurance coverage or income), were the main determinants of whether or not, and how much, care is sought (Aday, et al. 1980, 1993).

Indicators

The equity objective in this context focuses on the manner and extent to which care is both provided (made available) and obtained (used). How care is provided is theoretically essential to, and largely determinant of, how care is used. Empirically, the goal recognizes the effect of potential access barriers (a lack of obstetrics providers in rural or inner-city areas) on realized access (the proportion of women who seek prenatal care) for a given population (high-risk mothers). Providers and consumers of care assume benefits and burdens. The intent of the objective is that ultimately people obtain adequate and effective medical care.

Evidence

Managed care by design is fundamentally intended to influence the availability, organization, and financing of care, and the subsequent choice of providers by organizational and financial arrangements limiting consumers' choices to participating network providers, emphasizing primary care gatekeepers and lower use of specialists, and aggressively monitoring and managing the utilization of services. These practices have also led to the reduction or elimination of cross-subsidies to traditional safety net pro-

viders in many communities in the United States, with corollary impacts on the financial viability or sustainability of those institutions (Lipson and Naierman 1996).

Managed care has tended to focus on enrolling employed populations, especially those in large firms. Employers have increasingly sought to restrict enrollment and coverage for employees' dependents, and in partnership with insurers and managed-care providers, limit the risks associated with covering particularly vulnerable or at-risk populations. A major challenge to public policy makers is how to deal with the growing number of individuals without public or private third-party coverage in an increasingly managed-care dominated, health-care environment.

Health services research has documented that patients in health maintenance organization (HMO) arrangements tend to have somewhat lower admission rates, 1–20 per cent lower lengths of hospital stay, the same or higher physician office visit rates, lower use of expensive tests and procedures, and greater use of preventive services (Mark and Mueller 1996; Miller and Luft 1994). There is also evidence, however, that selected health outcomes may be poorer for the poor and elderly under such arrangements (Ware et al. 1996). Overall, managed-care enrollees tend to report lower satisfaction with aspects of care delivery (appointment waiting times, quality, and patient–physician interaction), but greater satisfaction with the cost of care.

New Directions

Docteur et al. (1996) developed an access framework that identifies a variety of components relevant in influencing and assessing individuals' access to managed-care plans. The framework includes the structural, financial, and personal determinants of patients' plan selection, the associated characteristics of the health plan delivery system itself, the influence of these patient and plan characteristics on plan choice and subsequent use of services, the mediators and determinants of the continuity of plan enrollment, and ultimately the clinical and equity outcomes for enrollees and users. This framework then focuses the lenses of distributive justice on the availability, organization, and financing of services within a particular delivery system and the utilization and satisfaction of individuals and their families who chose to enroll in it. This shift may be viewed primarily as one of turning inward in the sense of concentrating on what influences enrollees to want to enter the doors of any particular plan and what transpires once they do.

Social Justice

Models

Aday's (1993) framework for the study of vulnerable populations, which delineates the social and economic factor determinants of health risks, is grounded in the social justice paradigm. Vulnerable populations are defined as those who 'are at risk of poor physical, psychological, and/ or social health' (Aday 1993: 4). An array of social and economic correlates are predictive of who is most likely to be at risk. Vulnerable populations may be identified based on those for whom the risk of poor physical, psychological, or social health has or is likely to become a reality.

- *Physical.* High-risk mothers and infants, the chronically ill and disabled, persons with AIDS.
- *Mental.* The mentally ill and disabled, alcohol or substance abusers, those who are suicide- or homicide-prone.
- *Social.* Abusing families, the homeless, and immigrants and refugees.

There is, of course, overlap among these groups, and the boundaries should be viewed to be diffuse rather than distinct. Poor health along one dimension (physical) is quite likely to be compounded with poor health along others (psychological and/or social, for example). Health needs are greatest for those who have problems along more than one of these dimensions.

Relative risk refers to the differential vulnerability of different groups to poor health. People may be more or less at risk of poor health at different times in their lives, while some individuals and groups are apt to be more at risk than others at any given point in time. The beginning point for understanding the factors that increase the risk of poor health originates in a macrolevel look at the availability and distribution of community resources. Individuals' risks vary as a function of the opportunities and material and nonmaterial resources associated with (1) the personal characteristics (age, sex, and race/ethnicity) of the individuals themselves (social status), (2) the nature of the ties between them (family members, friends, and neighbors, for example) (social capital), and (3) the schools, jobs, incomes, and housing that characterize the neighborhoods in which they live (human capital).

Indicators

Social status differences are associated with the positions individuals occupy in society as a function of age, sex, or race/ethnicity, and the corollary of socially defined opportunities and rewards, such as prestige and power, they have as a result.

Social capital resides in the quantity and quality of interpersonal ties between people. Families provide social capital to members in the form of social networks and support and associated feelings of belonging, psychological well-being, and self-esteem. The value of social capital to individuals (single mothers) is that it provides resources (such as having someone to count on for child care) they can use to achieve other interests (going to school or working).

Human capital refers to investments in people's skills and capabilities (such as vocational or public education) that enable them to act in new ways (master a trade) or enhance their contributions to society (enter the labor force). Social capital can also enhance the generation of human capital through, for example, family and community support for encouraging students to stay in school. Neighborhoods that have poor schools, high rates of unemployment, and substandard housing reflect low levels of investment in the human capital (or productive potential) of the people who live there. Similarly, individuals who are poorly educated, unemployed, and poorly housed are likely to have the fewest resources for coping with illness or other personal or economic adversities.

Those individuals with a combination of statuses (poor, elderly women, those living alone, or minority adolescents) that put them at a high risk of having both poor health and few material and nonmaterial resources are in a highly vulnerable position.

Evidence

Basically, US evidence documents that disparities between groups (particularly racial–ethnic minorities) persist and, in a number of instances, have widened (Aday 1993; NCHS 1997). Very young, minority, and poorly educated mothers are much less likely to have adequate prenatal care and more likely to bear low birth weight or very low birth weight infants. The rates of teenage pregnancy, preterm, and low birth weight babies, inadequate prenatal care, and infant and maternal mortality remain two to three times higher among African–American women compared with white women, and show no sign of diminishing. The prevalence and magnitude of limitation in daily activities, as well as deaths, due to chronic disease increase steadily with age. Men are more likely to die from major chronic illnesses such as heart disease, stroke, and cancer than women at any age, although among those living with it, elderly women have more problems in being able to carry out their normal daily routines. African Americans – particularly African American men – are more likely to experience serious disabilities as well as die from chronic illness than are either white men or women.

Early in the AIDS epidemic, homosexual or bisexual males were most likely to be affected. In recent years, more and more mothers and children are at risk due to women or their sex partners using intravenous drugs. Higher proportions of African Americans and Hispanics, compared with whites, are likely to be HIV-positive, to develop and die of AIDS, and to have contracted the disease through drug use or sexual contact with drug users. Young adults in their late teens and early twenties, particularly men, are more likely to smoke, drink, and use illicit drugs than their younger or older counterparts. Native American youths are much more apt to use alcohol, drugs, and cigarettes than are either white or other minority youths. Minority users are also more likely to develop life-threatening patterns of abuse, as evidenced by higher rates of addiction-related deaths. Death rates for cirrhosis or other alcohol-related causes are greater among Native Americans. Minorities (particularly African Americans) constitute a disproportionate number of medical emergencies and deaths due to cocaine abuse. The health risks and consequences for abusing families, the homeless, and immigrant and refugee populations are likely to be exacerbated due to weak or fractured social and familial ties.

New Directions

Aday's perspective argues for the development of a broader continuum of health services, encompassing prevention-oriented and long-term community-based, as well as acute medical care services, to address the health and health-care needs of the most vulnerable (Aday 1993). The US Public Health Service and World Health Organization Year 2000 Objectives and accompanying empirical and programmatic emphases also provide guidance for identifying and tracking the indicators and predictors of subgroup disparities in health (NCHS 1995; World Health Organization 1994).

In the context of the evolving health-care environment, the new directions suggested by this perspective may be characterized as turning outward. This is reflected in the design of organized delivery systems that integrate and combine an array of providers and services into a population-oriented system of care. Stephen Shortell, based on his and his colleagues' research on organized (or integrated) delivery systems, has argued convincingly for the importance of a population health-oriented perspective in designing and assessing these systems. Health services research has documented the evolution and adoption of this perspective as managed-care markets mature and extend further into the communities they serve (Shortell et al. 1994, 1995, 1996). National health-care systems in other countries have more often had a focus on the health of populations and the integrated array of programs and services needed to address the health needs of the most vulnerable. There is also evidence that selected health outcomes in the OECD countries (life expectancy, infant mortality rates) are better than in the United States, where a much greater percentage of the gross domestic product is spent on health care (Aday et al. 1998; Whitehead 1992).

Deliberative Justice

Models

The deliberative justice paradigm may be seen to undergird commitments to community participation and empowerment as central components of the design of social and health programs in the United States as well as other countries (Green 1986; Labonte 1993, 1994; Robertson and Minkler 1994). Habermas's discourse theory provides an innovative template for examining the nature of these exchanges and the aims and actions of the institutional and individual actors involved in them. For Habermas, communication oriented toward mutual understanding among affected parties can best establish the foundations of trust and collaboration needed for solving the problems with which each is concerned – but perhaps from different points of view (Habermas 1995, 1996). Opportunities for analyzing the form and quality of participation may range from the microcosm of the patient–physician relationship to the design of consumer-oriented health-care programs and services to neighborhood or communitywide needs-assessment and program-development efforts, as well as broader social change-oriented movements that have important impacts for the health of individuals and communities (environmental justice, AIDS advocacy, etc.) (Charles and DeMaio 1993; Labonte 1993, 1994; Waitzkin et al. 1994). The fairness of health-care programs and policies would be judged by the extent to which affected parties are involved in shaping them, assessed through administering qualitative interviews or more structured quantitative scales of participation to key informants.

Indicators

Empirical indicators of deliberative justice attempt to express the type and extent of involvement of affected groups' participation in formulating and implementing policies and programs. A number of different conceptual and empirical approaches for doing so have been developed. Voter turnout rates and public opinion polls regarding levels of perceived confidence in, or ability to influence, public officials provide evidence at the macrolevel of the presence and magnitude of civic participation (Blendon et al. 1995a, 1995b). Attitudinal scales have been developed to measure the extent to which organizational or community members feel a sense of control or influence over the decisions that most directly affect their health and well-being (Israel et al. 1994). Key informant interviews and social network analysis yield data useful for mapping the extent of community activation and involvement in health program design (Wickizer et al. 1993).

Arnstein (1969) conceptualized a ladder of citizen participation, with the respective rungs representing a gradient running from nonparticipation to tokenism to increasing levels of citizen power and control. Charles and DeMaio (1993) incorporated this and other dimensions (reflecting the perspective being adopted – that of a user or broader policy maker – as well as the decision-making domain – individual treatment, overall service provision, or macro policy formulation) in constructing a framework for assessing lay participation in health-care decision making in Canada. Related indicators, of particular relevance in the managed-care context, would focus on the nature and quality of communication between patients and providers, the extent to which norms of 'deliberative democracy' guide the development and organizational policies and procedures, and/or the magnitude of trust of providers or the organization on the part of consumers (Daniels 1996; Mechanic 1996; Waitzkin et al. 1994).

Evidence

The extent to which individuals affected by these initiatives have been fully involved in shaping them has, however, often been less than fully realized in practice. Rissel (1994), Robertson and Minkler (1994), and Wallerstein and Bernstein (1994), for example, documented that public health and health promotion professionals have often imposed interventions they deem that selected target communities or populations need, without necessarily either soliciting or fully taking into account what the affected groups and individuals may want. Program developers may claim that communities have been involved in shaping such interventions when de facto there has been little, or only token, participation on the part of affected groups.

The failure of the Clinton health-care reform initiatives in the United States has been attributed to the dominance of the policy formulation process by technical–rational experts, and the lack of a clear public consensus around, and support for, comprehensive reform (Hacker 1996; Skocpol 1996). Rosenbaum et al. (1997) have documented a number of practices on the part of managed-care organizations that tend to limit the involvement of both patients and providers in influencing decisions that most immediately impact upon them: 'gag rules' that inhibit providers from discussing selected treatment options with patients; 'cram-down rules' that compel providers to participate in a state-mandated managed-care program to receive benefits through other payer arrangements; selective or misleading plan marketing to potential enrollees; time constraints on patient–provider visits or failure to provide cultural competency training that could affect patient–provider communication; and adversarial or obstructionist consumer grievance and dispute resolution procedures.

New Directions

An important new trend, grounded in participation and dialogue among affected parties, is that of forming partnerships with a variety of sectors and providers – particularly to address the needs of the most vulnerable. A historical Medicine and Public Health Initiative, sponsored by the American Medical Association and American Public Health Association, sought to explore the possibilities for fruitful collaboration between medicine and public health in education, research, and health care (Reiser 1996; The Medicine/Public Health Initiative 1997). The World Health Organization has encouraged the promulgation of the Healthy Cities and Healthy Communities model for eliciting and inspiring interest across the array of diverse sectors within a community toward promoting the health of community residents (Ashton 1991). The concept of community empowerment perhaps most directly embodies a perspective and set of approaches mirroring the role that affected populations play in promoting the health of those residing within them. This perspective is manifest in the formulation and implementation of community-based health education and health promotion initiatives (Aday 1997; Wallerstein 1992; Wallerstein and Bernstein 1994). There is evidence that these partnerships are being forged as the public health sector attempts to reinvent and redefine its role in the managed care-dominated market place, and as managed systems increasingly penetrate selected markets and come to acknowledge that some problems that 'hit the doors' of their system (such as victims of violent crimes, child abuse, high-risk pregnancies) are best addressed by broader partnerships with community agencies or sectors that are better equipped to deal with them upstream.

A key access question posed by these emerging partnerships is who is served and who is not? Does it indeed address the equity issues resulting from managed-care systems' turning inward to focus on the population of plan enrollees and not extending their reach far enough in turning outward to address the needs of the most vulnerable? Also, is there effective communication and participation in and among affected parties in forging these partnerships to resolve conflicts that emerge?

The discussion that follows presents an expanded framework of equity incorporating elements of the deliberative, distributive, and social justice paradigms, and the relationships implied between them, as a foundation for guiding health services research on the equity of health-care provision.

An Expanded Conceptual Framework of Equity

Figure 1 shows how an expanded conceptual framework of equity might reflect and integrate the deliberative, distributive, and social justice paradigms. The unshaded boxes in Figure 1, encompassing the delivery system, population at risk, and realized access, define the major components of the conceptual model of equity of access to medical care developed by Ronald Andersen, Lu Ann Aday, and their colleagues, to guide the conduct of national and community surveys of access grounded in the distributive justice paradigm (Aday and Andersen 1981; Aday et al. 1980).

The original Aday and Andersen (1981) access framework begins with the role of health policy

in influencing the characteristics of the health delivery system and the population to be served by it. A new dimension in the expanded model (Figure 1) is the deliberative justice character of health policy that focuses on the institutions and procedures through which policy is formulated and implemented. Placing the governing norm of deliberative justice above health policy in the expanded framework is intended to convey that conflicts between the disparate paradigms of distributive justice and social justice that have tended to guide medical care and public health policy, respectively, must be effectively addressed if the health and well-being of individuals and communities are to be enhanced. Ensuring that those most affected by health policy decisions at both the macro- and microlevels are involved in shaping them constitutes the means for doing so. The deliberative paradigm has not been explicitly explored as a basis for the equity of health policy. It is, however, implicit in the focus on consumer involvement and community participation in the design and implementation of private and public health programs in the United States and other countries (Green 1986; Wallerstein 1992; Wallerstein and Bernstein 1994).

The shaded boxes represent factors that influence the health and health-care needs of vulnerable populations (Aday 1993; Beauchamp 1976). As implied by the shaded boxes in Figure 1, in the expanded social justice component of the model, there is first an explicit acknowledgment of the ultimate outcome of interest that was only implicit or assumed in the original model: the health and well-being of individuals and communities. Second, the model acknowledges that the physical, social, and economic environments in which individuals live and work can also have consequential impacts on their access to health and health care. Third, it delineates that the environment directly influences the likelihood of exposures to significant environmental and behavioral health risks.

The social justice component of the model may be viewed as focusing on the community level of analysis. It primarily examines the characteristics of the physical, social, and economic environment, the population residing within it, and the health risks they experience as a consequence. The distributive justice component of the model relies on individuals as the ultimate unit of analysis. Their attributes and behavior may, however, be aggregated to reflect the characteristics of patients within a given health system or delivery organization, or of the population resident within a designated geographic area. The distributive justice paradigm has guided a look at the equity of the medical-

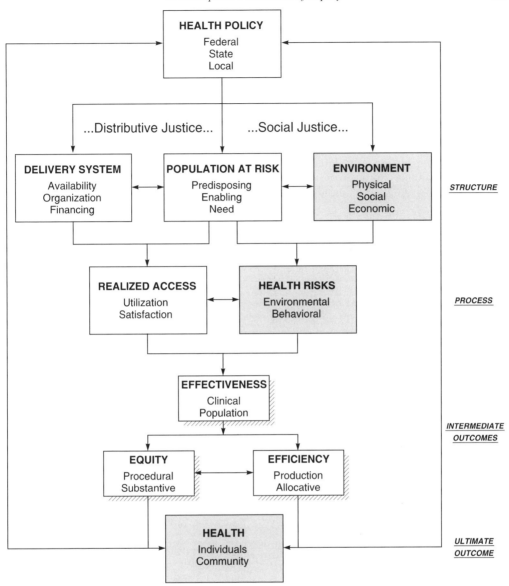

Figure 1   *An expanded conceptual framework of deliberative justice.* Source: Used with permission from Aday, L.A., Begley, C.E., Lairson, D.R., and Slater, C.H. (1998) *Evaluating the Healthcare System: Effectiveness, Efficiency, and Equity* (2nd edn). Chicago: Health Administration Press. Figure 6.1 (p. 179).

care delivery system, while the social justice paradigm is reflected in public health and social and economic policy directly or indirectly related to health.

The explicit addition of the equity, effectiveness, and efficiency concepts to the framework (reflected in the boxes with shadows) points out the importance, as well as the interrelationship, of these factors in ultimately influencing the health of individuals and communities. Equity, efficiency, and effectiveness may be viewed as intermediate outcomes of the health-care delivery process that is ultimately concerned with enhancing the health of individuals and communities. The United States Public Health Service Healthy People and World Health Organization

(WHO) Year 2000 Health Objectives provide reference points for assessing the extent to which the ultimate goal of improving the health of communities has been reached. Effectiveness, efficiency, and equity provide indicators of system performance in achieving this goal. Effectiveness – or the production of health benefits – is arrayed before efficiency and equity in the framework to indicate the central role it plays in assessing the cost of producing health benefits (efficiency), as well as the distribution of these benefits across groups (equity).

Clinical effectiveness, production efficiency, and procedural equity focus on health-care services. Clinical effectiveness addresses the impact of medical care on health improvements for individual patients, production efficiency is concerned with the combination of inputs required to produce these and related services at the lowest costs, and procedural equity assesses the fairness of care delivery.

Population effectiveness, allocative efficiency, and substantive equity focus on the ultimate outcome of interest – communitywide health improvements. Population effectiveness addresses the role of medical and nonmedical factors in influencing the health of populations as a whole, allocative efficiency analysis attempts to address what combination of inputs are required to produce these health improvements at the lowest cost, and substantive equity is judged ultimately by the extent to which those health benefits are shared equally across groups in the community. A comparison of health indicators at the national, state, or local level with desired normative endpoints (such as those defined by the US Public Health Service or WHO) provides an indication of whether the health policy goals of health policy have been achieved. Effectiveness, efficiency, and equity research can assist policy makers in deciding, given constrained resources, how most fairly and effectively to do so.

The ultimate test of the equity of health policy, grounded in the social justice paradigm, is the extent to which disparities or inequalities in health among subgroups of the population are minimized (Whitehead 1992). Substantive equity is reflected in subgroup disparities in health. Procedural equity refers to the extent to which the structure and process (or procedures) for reducing these disparities may be judged to be fair, grounded in norms of deliberative, distributive, and social justice. The normative import of these factors for substantive equity can be judged empirically, based on the extent to which they are predictive of inequalities in health across groups and communities. The expanded framework of equity (Figure 1) is intended to provide normative and empirical guidance for assessing both substantive and procedural equity.

Implicit in the expanded framework is that health policy making must take into account norms of distributive and social justice, and that conflicts between affected stakeholders grounded in these contrasting norms must be resolved through deliberative discourse if the resultant policies are ultimately to contribute to improving health and minimizing health disparities.

CONCLUSION

In summary, approaches to studying equity grounded in the distributive justice paradigm may be seen as primarily turning inward in assessing the fairness of the health-care system for the patients directly served by it. Social justice-oriented frameworks direct attention outward to the community to assess the equity of health and health risks of the population that resides within it. Conceptual approaches to equity grounded in the deliberative justice paradigm attempt to enhance the dialogue between those who design and those who are affected by health policies, for forging partnerships to effectively resolve conflicts. This chapter has provided an integrative conceptual framework for integrating and assessing the evidence regarding the performance of health policy in realizing these objectives in the context of these respective perspectives.

Three primary policy strategies may be identified as a foundation for enhancing the equity of health-care provisions that are lodged in the distributive, social, and deliberative justice paradigms, respectively: (1) enhance access to medical care; (2) reduce health disparities; (3) assure affected parties' participation in policy and program design.

The evidence of the successes of these broad policy strategies for enhancing equity may be viewed as mixed at best, and falling far short of desired equity objectives at worst. The bulk of the evidence regarding the goal of enhancing access to medical care is rooted in the distributive justice paradigm of individual rights to medical care. Although substantial investments in both the organization and financing of medical care services have been made, wide variations in access to care and coverage persist across regions and subgroups, and both the costs and the effectiveness of the care provided continue to present challenges to policy makers in deciding what rights should be assured, and at what cost to whom, within this framework.

The Year 2000 World Health Organization and US Public Health Service Objectives provide templates for examining the extent to which the social justice goals of minimizing health risks and health disparities have been achieved, based on indicators and evidence of subgroup variations in achieving desired health promotion, health protection, and preventive services goals. The data routinely gathered to monitor progress toward these objectives show progress on some and persistent or widening disparities on many others.

Although there is emerging evidence of the importance of the participation of affected parties in health policy and program design, the deliberative justice paradigm has been largely unexamined as a component of the fairness of the policy formulation and implementation process. The challenge to the public health and health services research community is how best to conceptualize and measure norms of deliberative justice, so that both the presence and the impact of this innovative benchmark of fairness can be more explicitly assessed.

The evidence available to date suggests that health policy strategies have, as a whole, fallen short of achieving procedural and substantive equity. The expanded framework presented in this chapter is intended to provide explicit conceptual and methodological guidance for the design and conduct of health services research and policy analysis to assess the equity of health and health care, based on broader conceptualizations of justice that offer greater promise for addressing persistent health and health-care inequities in the United States and other countries.

ACKNOWLEDGMENT

The author acknowledges the granting of copyright permission by Health Administration Press for the use of the following from: Aday, L.A., C.E. Begley, D.R. Lairson, and C.H. Slater (1998) *Evaluating the Healthcare System: Effectiveness, Efficiency, and Equity*. 2nd edn. Chicago: Health Administration Press: Chapters 1, 5, 6, and 7 [selected excerpts]; Table 6.1 (p. 175); Figure 6.1 (p. 179).

REFERENCES

Aday, L.A. (1993) *At Risk in America: The Health and Health Care Needs of Vulnerable Populations in the United States*. San Francisco: Jossey-Bass.

Aday, L.A. (1997) 'Vulnerable populations: A community-oriented perspective', *Family and Community Health*, 19(4): 1–18.

Aday, L.A. and Andersen, R. (1981) 'Equity of access to medical care: A conceptual and empirical overview', *Medical Care*, 19(12, suppl.): 4–27.

Aday, L.A., Andersen, R., and Fleming, G. (1980) *Health Care in the US: Equitable for Whom?* Beverly Hills: Sage.

Aday, L.A., Begley, C.E., Lairson, D.R., and Slater, C.H. (1993) *Evaluating the Medical Care System: Effectiveness, Efficiency, and Equity* (1st edn). Chicago: Health Administration

Aday, L.A., Begley, C.E., Lairson, D.E., and Slater, C.H. (1998) *Evaluating the Healthcare System: Effectiveness, Efficiency, and Equity* (2nd edn). Chicago: Health Administration Press.

Arnstein, S. (1969) 'A ladder of citizen participation', *Journal of the American Institute of Planners* (July): 216–24.

Ashton, J. (1991) 'The healthy cities project: A challenge for health education', *Health Education Quarterly*, 18: 39–48.

Beauchamp, D.E. (1976) 'Public health as social justice', *Inquiry*, 13 (March): 3–14.

Beauchamp, D.E. (1985) 'Community: The neglected tradition of public health', *Hastings Center Report*, 15(6): 28–36.

Beauchamp, D.E. (1988) *The Health of the Republic: Epidemics, Medicine, and Moralism as Challenges to Democracy*. Philadelphia: Temple University Press.

Blendon, R.J., Benson, J., Donelan, K., Leitman, R., Taylor, H., Koeck, C., and Gitterman, D. (1995a) 'Who has the best health care system? A second look', *Health Affairs*, 14: 220–30.

Blendon, R.J., Scheck, A.C., Donelan, K., Hill, C.A., Smith, M., Beatrice, D., and Altman. D. (1995b) 'How white and African Americans view their health and social problems: Different expectations, different experiences', *Journal of the American Medical Association*, 273: 341–6.

Chapman, A.R. (ed.) (1994) *Health Care Reform: A Human Rights Approach*. Washington, DC: Georgetown University Press.

Charles, C. and DeMaio, S. (1993) 'Lay participation in health care decision making: A conceptual framework', *Journal of Health Politics, Policy and Law*, 18: 881–904.

Daly, M. (ed.) (1994) *Communitarianism: A New Public Ethics*. Belmont, CA: Wadsworth.

Daniels, N. (1996) 'Justice, fair procedures, and the goals of medicine', *Hastings Center Report*, 26(6): 10–12.

Docteur, E.R., Colby, D.C., and Gold. M. (1996) 'Shifting the paradigm: Monitoring access in Medicare managed care', *Health Care Financing Review*, 17(4): 5–21.

Green, L.W. (1986) 'The theory of participation: A qualitative analysis of its expression in national and international health policies', in W.B. Ward,

Z.T. Salisbury, S.B. Kar, and J.G. Zapka (eds.), *Advances in Health Education and Promotion*, Vol. 1, Part A. Greenwich, CT: JAI, pp. 215–40.

Habermas, J. (1995) *Moral Consciousness and Communicative Action*. Translated by C. Lenhardt and S. W. Nicholsen. Cambridge, MA: MIT Press.

Habermas, J. (1996) *Between Facts and Norms: Contributions to a Discourse Theory of Law and Democracy*. Translated by W. Rehg. Cambridge, MA: MIT Press.

Hacker, J. (1996) *The Road to Nowhere: The Genesis of President Clinton's Plan for Health Security*. Princeton, NJ: Princeton University Press.

Havlicek, P.L. (1996) *Medical Groups in the US: A Survey of Practice Characteristics*. Chicago: American Medical Association.

Israel, B.A., Checkoway, B., Schulz, A., and Zimmerman, M. (1994) 'Health education and community empowerment: Conceptualizing and measuring perceptions of individual, organizational, and community control', *Health Education Quarterly*, 21: 149–70.

Kongstvedt, P.R. (ed.) (1995) *Essentials of Managed Health Care*. Gaithersburg, MD: Aspen.

Kretzmann, J.P. and McKnight, J.L. (1993) *Building Communities from the Inside Out: A Path Toward Finding and Mobilizing a Community's Assets*. Chicago: ACTA.

Labonte, R. (1993) 'Community development and partnerships', *Canadian Journal of Public Health*, 84: 237–40.

Labonte, R. (1994) 'Health promotion and empowerment: Reflections on professional practice', *Health Education Quarterly*, 21: 253–68.

Lipson, D.J. and Naierman, N. (1996) 'Effects of health system changes on safety-net providers', *Health Affairs*, 15(2): 33–48.

Mark, T. and Mueller, C. (1996) 'Access to care in HMOs and traditional insurance plans', *Health Affairs*, 15(4): 81–7.

Mechanic, D. (1996) 'Changing medical organization and the erosion of trust', *Milbank Quarterly*, 74: 171–89.

Miller, R.H. and Luft, H.S. (1994) 'Managed care plan performance since 1980: A literature analysis', *Journal of the American Medical Association*, 271: 1512–19.

Mulhall, S. and Swift, A. (1992) *Liberals and Communitarians*. Oxford: Blackwell.

NCHS (National Center for Health Statistics) (1995) *Healthy People 2000–Midcourse Review and 1995 Revisions*, Hyattsville, MD: Public Health Service.

NCHS (National Center for Health Statistics) (1997) *Health, United States, 1996–97, and Injury Chartbook*. Hyattsville, MD: Public Health Service.

Reinhardt, U.E. (1996) 'A social contract for the 21st century health care: Three-tier health care with bounty hunting', *Health Economics*, 5: 479–99.

Reiser, S.J. (1996) 'Medicine and public health: Pursuing a common destiny', *Journal of the American Medical Association*, 276: 1429–30.

Rissel, C. (1994) 'Empowerment: The holy grail of health promotion?' *Health Promotion International*, 9: 39–47.

Robertson, A. and Minkler, M. (1994) 'New health promotion movement: A critical examination', *Health Education Quarterly*, 21: 295–312.

Rosenbaum, S., Serrano, R., Magar, M., and Stern, G. (1997) 'Civil rights in a changing health care system', *Health Affairs*, 16: 90–105.

Shortell, S.M, Gillies, R.R., and Anderson, D.A. (1994) 'The new world of managed care: Creating organized delivery systems', *Health Affairs*, 13(5): 46–64.

Shortell, S.M., Gillies, R.R., and Devers, K.J. (1995) 'Reinventing the American hospital', *Milbank Quarterly*, 73: 131–60.

Shortell, S.M., Gillies, R.R., Anderson, D.A., Erickson, K. M., and Mitchell, J.B. (1996) *Remaking Health Care in America: Building Organized Delivery Systems*. San Francisco: Jossey-Bass.

Skocpol, T. (1996) *Boomerang: Clinton's Health Security Effort and the Turn Against Government in US Politics*. New York: W.W. Norton.

The Medicine/Public Health Initiative (1997) 'The Medicine/Public Health Initiative' [Online]. Available: http://www.sph.uth.tmc.edu/mph/ [09/17/97].

Waitzkin, H., Britt, T., and Williams, C. (1994) 'Narratives of aging and social problems in medical encounters with older persons', *Journal of Health and Social Behavior*, 35: 322–48.

Wallerstein, N. (1992) 'Powerlessness, empowerment, and health: Implications for health promotion programs', *American Journal of Health Promotion*, 6: 197–205.

Wallerstein, N. and Bernstein, E. (1994) 'Introduction to community empowerment, participatory education, and health', *Health Education Quarterly*, 21: 141–8.

Ware, J.E., Bayliss, M.S., Rogers, W.H., Kosinski, M., and Tarlov, A.R. (1996) 'Differences in 4-yr health outcomes for elderly and poor, chronically ill patients treated in HMO and fee-for-service systems: Results from the Medical Outcomes Study', *Journal of the American Medical Association*, 276: 1039–47.

Whitehead, M. (1992) 'The concepts and principles of equity and health', *International Journal of Health Services*, 22: 429–45.

Wickizer, T.M., Von Korff, M., Cheadle, A., Maeser, J., Wagner, E.H., Pearson, D., Beery, W., and Psaty, B.M. (1993) 'Activating communities for health promotion: A process evaluation method', *American Journal of Public Health*, 83: 561–7.

World Health Organization (1994) *WHO Progress Towards Health For All: Statistics of Member States 1994*. Albany, NY: WHO.

3.9

Resources and Rationing: Managing Supply and Demand in Health Care

STEPHEN HARRISON AND MICHAEL MORAN

INTRODUCTION

Third-party payment for the health care of individuals is virtually ubiquitous and represents the majority of health-care expenditure in developed countries. Although both the assumptions that underpin such systems and their forms vary, all third-party payment systems function by disconnecting to various degrees the process of health care *consumption* from that of payment. One consequence of this disconnection is the reduction (again, to various degrees) of the disincentive to consume, with the further consequence that demand for health care tends to inflate over time. A still further consequence is that third-party payers must in some way manage the relationship between the demand for and supply of care. The dominance of third-party payment for health care is hardly a new phenomenon, nor is this need to manage supply and demand. Yet there have been two relatively recent developments.

First, discussion about the problem of demand inflation and of possible solutions has increasingly become both explicit and institutionalized. Discussion of 'rationing' in the context of health care is mainly a phenomenon of the 1990s and, although both the terminology and the substantive concept are sometimes contested, the latter has largely been accepted by health policy analysts. Second, there seems to have been a shift in the preferences of third-party payers for the kind of policies to be employed to address demand inflation; such

actors have increasingly lost faith in policies aimed at the supply side and begun to prefer demand-side measures. Of course, neither of these recent developments are themselves *explained* by the basic necessity for the management of supply and demand; nor do third-party payers in specific countries make the actual policy choices.

What follows is divided into eight sections. The first explains the principle of, and rationale for, third-party payment for health care, distinguishing between the rationales for different forms of third-party payment, that is taxation, social insurance, and private insurance.[1] The second explains and justifies the assertion that demand in third-party payment systems can be expected to escalate, whilst the third sets out the broad range of policy options for addressing this, together with the main dimensions of our analysis. In the following four sections we illustrate our analysis with reference to what may be called the 'consumption histories' of four developed countries: the United Kingdom, New Zealand, the United States, and Germany. We conclude, first, that in all of these the former preference for implicit approaches to rationing arose from a conjunction of particular ideas of citizenship with the presence of an established medical profession. Second, and despite important differences, the broad range of pressures on this conjunction and the recent policy trend towards explicit demand-side measures have been similar across these countries. It is far from clear, however, that the new preference is firmly established.

Third-Party Payment and its Rationales

The principle of third-party payment is that financial contributions are collected from population groups, irrespective of the immediate health-care requirements of the individuals who compose them. Such groups may represent a more-or-less complete national population, or narrower groups such as the members (voluntarily or compulsorily) of social or private insurance schemes. These contributions are collected by 'third-party payers,' such as government or quasi-independent agencies or insurance companies, which employ the resources thus obtained to resource or reimburse health-care providers (such as professionals and hospitals) for the care of individuals held to be sick (Figure 1).

Such systems separate payment for care from its immediate consumption by the individual, and to varying degrees separate the financial contribution that the individual makes from the volume of care that she or he actually consumes. In a *tax-financed* system, the government acts as third-party payer by employing resources collected through the tax system (the flow of money across the bottom of Figure 1) to pay for citizens' care in hospitals or by doctors. This does not *necessarily* entail the public ownership of provider institutions because tax revenues can be used for the public funding of private provision. Because the taxation system collects revenues to support public expenditure on services other than health, the share of the

latter may not be hypothecated, thus allowing governments to shift their expenditure priorities. In a *social insurance* system, the third-party payers are social insurance funds, the number of which varies between countries. They may be nongovernmental bodies whose history lies in trade union and voluntary effort, or they may be managed by the state. In either case, their resources will remain 'earmarked' for health care and not merged with other revenues. Membership of a fund may be compulsory for some or all citizens. Typically, members make periodic contributions to the fund (see the flow of money across the bottom of Figure 1) based on a percentage of earnings. Employers may also contribute (although, of course, this can be regarded as money that would otherwise have been paid in wages) and nonearners may have their contributions to the fund met as a social security entitlement. The fund in turn pays the hospital or the doctor (as the case may be) for services provided to members, often at rates negotiated annually between organizations representing the various interests in the health-care industry. A *private insurance* system treats the cost of health care as an insurable risk for an individual. Such coverage is voluntary, although it might be routinely provided as a condition of employment for some workers. In this context, the third-party payer is the insurance company, health maintenance organization, or nonprofit friendly society, and the flow of money shown in Figure 1 takes the form of premiums paid by policy holders, which provide the resources to pay hospitals and clinicians for their care.

The ubiquitousness of third-party payment can be explained in several different ways. From one perspective, it is largely a result of public demand on governments, perhaps coupled with political commitment to some sort of equity. From another perspective, it represents the dominance of provider interest groups such as the professions, who were indeed much implicated in the development of friendly societies and nonprofit insurance organisations such as BUPA in the United Kingdom and Blue Cross/Blue Shield in the United States. From a third, more radical perspective, it is a way in which the capitalist state either assists capital accumulation through the provision of a healthy workforce and/or legitimises its own existence in the eyes of its subjects (O'Connor 1973; Offe 1984). Government action is based on fear of revolutionary activity (as lay behind Bismarck's rudimentary welfare state in nineteenth century Germany). From a fourth perspective, economists' normative arguments explain (in the sense of justifying) third-party payment specifically by governments as a response to market failure: the difficulties cre-

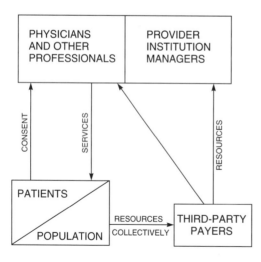

Figure 1   *Third-party payment for health care. Source:* Adapted from S. Harrison (1988) *Managing the NHS.* London: Chapman and Hall.

ated by the special characteristics of health care in treating it just like any other commodity.

Thus, third-party payment systems for health care come in several varieties, but the principle that always underlies them is the detachment of the act of payment for health care from that of receiving it when considered necessary. They therefore separate the financial contribution that the individual makes from the volume of care that she or he actually consumes. This is not the same, however, as saying that there necessarily is no relationship between the amount required to be paid and the volume *predicted* to be used by an individual. They pool resources to smooth out the uncertainties of individuals' health states requiring more expenditure than the individual is able to make. Thus, different as the three types of third-party payment systems that have been outlined may be, it is evident that they all share the fundamental rationale noted above: they all pool (or 'socialize') the financial risks of ill-health across some sort of population, which (as the bottom left-hand corner of Figure 1 shows) is analytically distinct from actual patients. Unlike out-of-pocket payment, third-party payment never limits the value of care provided to an individual to the sum of that individual's contributions.[2] Third-party payment is therefore a partial answer to the problem of the individual's uncertainty about her future health-care needs; a partial answer because any type of third-party payment system might in practice make charges for, and impose access restrictions upon, certain treatments. Thus, rationing attenuates the extent to which (some) individuals' problems are solved.

Third-party payment can also be a partial answer to the problem of equity, that is, to the empirical tendency for the poor and the sick to be the same people. However, the extent to which this occurs will depend on how widely the risks of ill-health are spread, and it is clear from the descriptions above that different variants of third-party payment achieve this to different extents. Tax-financed systems pool the risks across a whole national population and, other things being equal, spread the risk most equitably. Private insurance and any system of social insurance that employs a multiplicity of third-party payers is likely (other things being equal) to be less equitable because there exists the probability that poorer, sicker people will be found in some risk pools and richer, healthier people in others. The former group will therefore receive a poorer range of benefits than the latter.

Although these matters are to some extent technical concerns in health system financing, they are also deeply political for they manifest different normative assumptions about what risks should be pooled. Thus, a tax-financed sys-

tem, in socializing risk across a single national population, might be said to seek to compensate for a broad range of inequalities, such as those resulting from social class, as well as uncertainties about an individual's own future health. In other words, it has a *universalist* rationale, implying a notion of citizenship that includes social rights (Marshall 1950) in which effective participation by individuals in society is to be secured by state action (Flynn 1997). In contrast, a private insurance system seeks to compensate for a much narrower range of uncertainties: those related to the individual's health over his own lifetime and within his own social group, implying a more restricted model of citizenship.

THE UNSOUGHT CONSEQUENCES OF THIRD-PARTY PAYMENT

Third-party payment systems risk the inflation of demand over time. Whilst this is often conceptualized as being 'driven' by variables such as ageing populations, technological drift, and/or rising public expectations, they are not sufficient conditions. Demand increases are more appropriately theorized in terms of two tendencies derived from the economic concept of 'moral hazard' (Arrow 1963: 946) which is not unique to the health-care field.

Provider moral hazard (or 'supplier-induced demand') arises from information asymmetries: the consumer's lack of knowledge of a highly technical service coincides with a provider's interest in increasing provision and allows the latter to affect demand. Whilst patients do, of course, make generalized demands in the sense of arranging a visit to the doctor or being taken to the accident and emergency department, it is typically (though not invariably) the physician or other clinical professional who translates such generalized demand into a specific demand for antibiotics, pathology tests, a specialist appointment, or a surgical operation. Conventional accounts cast such professional motivation in material terms. If the clinician is remunerated on a fee-for-service basis, there are clear incentives to maximize supplier-induced demand unless the total fees are 'capped' in some way. The same incentive may exist if the institution that employs the clinician is itself remunerated by the third-party payer on the basis of its actual costs or on any basis that is volume-sensitive. From such a perspective, a system in which clinicians were salaried would have the opposite effect of 'underprovision,' because there would be no economic incentives to perform beyond the level necessary to retain one's job. However, this seems an unnecessarily narrow perspective on incentives; Donaldson and Gerard (1993: 33) have argued that where providers are salaried and do not have to bear the costs of treatment, simple ignorance of costs may lead to overprovision. We would go beyond this and argue that there may be ethical incentives to provider moral hazard. Even if the hospital's budget is not volume-related and clinicians are remunerated by salary or capitation fees, one might still expect to see such demand increase as a result of the supplier's desire to behave ethically, that is, to do the best possible for her patient. In an out-of-pocket payment system, this might be limited by the patient's inability or unwillingness to pay, but in a third-party payment system such limitations are somewhat attenuated.

Consumer moral hazard arises where some of the third-party payers meet all of the costs of care. It encourages a higher rate of use than would occur if full costs had to be met at the point of use (Pauly 1968) because the demander assumes that the cost of his usage will be spread over a large number of taxpayers, fund members, or policy holders. However, if large numbers of people behave in this way, then total demand (for health care and hence for the resources to provide it) *will* rise. Consumer moral hazard in third-party payment systems for health care is the consequence of divorcing payment for services from their use. Third-party payment makes it easier for many people to obtain care than would otherwise be the case, but at the same time tempts them to increase their demands.

Two points are important to note. First, although analyses often focus on the *price* of services, it seems clear to us that non-money costs of obtaining care can be significant, even where no money charge is made. At the very minimum, the user must take steps such as telephoning for an appointment, rearranging a working day, travelling to the surgery or hospital, and perhaps sitting for some time in a crowded waiting area in order to gain access. Costs can be higher. One may react adversely to the drug that is prescribed, or the needle may hurt as it pierces the flesh; the prospect of gastroendoscopy or sigmoidoscopy is not a pleasant one for most of us, and in the extreme, one may die on the operating table. Second, and irrespective of cost, although people only demand services that they perceive to be good for themselves, such goodness is in the perception of the demander rather than in the reflection of some intrinsic feature. Consequently, consumer moral hazard in health care is not avoided by simply observing that many health-care inter-

ventions have not been properly evaluated by research; unless those who demand the services both know and care about this lack of research, their behaviour will be unchanged.

Thus, demand in a third-party payment system might be expected to increase over time because neither consumers nor providers have the incentive to moderate it. Whilst the two forms of moral hazard provide the immediate basis for the inflation of demand, in third-party payment systems, there are a number of secondary factors that may affect the propensity of patients and clinicians to increase their demands. One obvious candidate is *demographic shift*; many countries have an ageing population in both absolute and relative terms, largely brought about by greater total life expectancy and a falling birth rate. Because older people consume greater amounts of health care *per capita* than do younger people, an increase in the former section of the population implies an increase in demand for health care, all other things being equal.

Another secondary source of demand for health care is the constant invention and development of new medical technologies, many of which are extremely expensive. The pharmaceutical and medical equipment manufacturing industries are important sectors of the economies of the United Kingdom, the United States, and Germany, and significant exporters. It should also be remembered that the term 'technology' carries a broader meaning than simply *high* or 'hard' technology, and encompasses 'drugs, devices, and medical and surgical procedures used in medical care, and the organizational and supportive systems within which such care is provided' (Office of Technology Assessment 1978: 2). New approaches to psychotherapy, new packages of care for the elderly, and new multiprofessional approaches to the care of stroke victims are therefore new technologies, and indeed may carry costs just as high as new drugs. The mere existence of new technologies does not create a demand; their use, or the demand for their use, depends on patients and/or clinicians perceiving that they might be beneficial. Their net financial impact on a health system will depend partly on whether they reduce demand elsewhere in the system, either by substituting for other interventions for the same condition or by helping patients to attain a state of health in which they perceive themselves to need less treatment than would otherwise be the case. Klein has linked the effects of demographic and technological change so as to reach a pessimistic conclusion:

> Even if the limitations of medical technology in curing disease and disability are now becoming appar-

ent, there are no such limitations on the scope of health services for providing care for those who cannot be cured. Even if policies of prevention ... were to be successfully introduced, their very success in extending life expectancy would create new demands for alleviating the chronic degenerative diseases of old age. In other words, no policy can ensure that people will drop dead painlessly at the age of eighty, not having troubled the health services previously. (Klein 1989: 182)

A final secondary factor is *public demand*, which operates against a background in which health care is a prominent public and political issue in the United Kingdom, the USA, and many other countries. One element of this is the much greater public availability of information about health care, with particular emphasis on information about new technologies, the reporting of which is generally high profile in the media. Very recently, the Internet has begun to contribute substantially to the availability of such information (Coiera 1996). Alongside this growth of information, is an apparent increase in the level of activity by patient pressure groups, usually organized around a particular disease or health condition (Wood forthcoming). Such groups (which may also provide advice and other services to their members) are often supported by health professionals from appropriate clinical specialities and, naturally enough, press the appropriate health service bodies for what they perceive to be better services for themselves, including new technologies.

DIMENSIONS OF ANALYSIS

At the heart of the rationing issue is the rise of third-party payment in health care. Although this arrangement has deep historic roots, one of the most striking features of modern health-care systems is the way it has advanced, in part because the cost of care is beyond the resources of all but the super-rich if paid for directly out of pocket. The truth of this can be seen where market-based systems of health-care financing are most deeply entrenched. Even in the United States the proportion of health-care costs accounted for by direct out-of-pocket payments has fallen greatly in the last generation. In 1960 it accounted for 56 per cent of expenditure on care, but by the early 1990s direct out-of-pocket payments had fallen to 20 per cent (Levit et al. 1994: 22). The modern health-care problem can therefore be seen as a reflection of the way health-care financing has been *collectivised* through the sort of risk-pooling arrangements

outlined above and through the way this process of collectivization, by breaking the direct link between consumption and payment, removes or weakens budget constraints on consumers of health-care resources. The problem facing health-care systems is therefore how to reimpose, or reinvent, those constraints in a world where the collectivization of finance has to be taken as a given.

In the remainder of this chapter, we examine how policy makers have addressed the necessary task of managing the demand for, and supply of, health care. In so doing, we have focused on three sets of analytical distinctions. The first relates to the form of collectivization of health-care finance discussed above. These forms can be taken as characterizing different *consumption regimes*: those that rely on tax-based financing; those that rely on social insurance; and those that rest on private insurance markets. Whilst no nation relies solely on one of these financing systems, there are systematic differences in their relative importance between different countries. Our topic can therefore be explored by sketching the *consumption histories* of different nations, and we have chosen four. The United Kingdom stands out as a nation committed in a particularly thoroughgoing way to *tax-based financing*. New Zealand is chosen as a nation that traditionally relied on tax-based financing, but in recent years has tried to revolutionize its financing and delivery system and to confront the rationing problem in a uniquely explicit way. We examine the United States because the sheer volume of consumption has made the rationing problem more acute there than in any other advanced industrial nation. Finally, Germany is selected as one of the largest, and historically better established, examples of social insurance financing.

Convergence of policy attention on a particular problem does not necessarily entail a convergence of the means chosen to address it. Therefore, a second set of distinctions concerns the various (not necessarily mutually exclusive) means of matching supply and demand. These can be roughly classified into *supply-side adjustments*, that is, those which aim to increase the resources available for health care, and *demand-side adjustments,* which aim to reduce or stabilize demand for services. Supply-side adjustments may be in the form of measures to increase the flow of revenue to third-party payers (tax or contribution increases, or co-payments) or to encourage a higher level of out-of-pocket expenditure as an assumed substitute for third-party payment. In publicly funded health-care systems, other supply-side measures include toleration of public sector budget deficits and reallocation of public expenditure priorities so as to increase health-care expenditure at the expense of other public programmes. In any type of system, policy makers may seek to improve the productive efficiency of the sector by a range of management and organizational measures aimed at modifying the incentives facing actors in the system; examples are 'managed competition' (Bruce and Jonsson 1996) and 'managed care' (Robinson and Steiner 1998). In contrast, demand-side adjustments are aimed at *rationing* health care,[3] that is, reducing or containing demand for it.

This relates directly to our third analytical dimension. Some demand-side measures operate *implicitly* so far as the patient is concerned. Examples include the erection of cost barriers that partially offset the effect of consumer moral hazard. Such costs may be financial (thus charges for services are a deterrent[4]), but spatial, psychological, and procedural barriers may also be effective; remote or highly centralized facilities, user-unfriendliness, and strict 'gatekeeping' criteria tend to reduce demand. Other demand-side measures are *explicit*, that is, consist of more-or-less clear rules about patient entitlement; for instance, such rules may exclude certain procedures or drugs. The desirability of implicitness and explicitness are much debated. Some proponents of implicitness (Hoffenberg 1992; Mechanic 1992) have justified their position on the grounds that explicit decisions are too brutal for society to contemplate, whilst others (Hunter 1993: Klein et al. 1996) have concentrated on their conceptual and practical difficulties. Proponents of various degrees of explicitness (Harrison and Hunter 1994; New and LeGrand 1996) often stress the transparency as a prerequisite of fairness. Thus, a central theme in the politics of rationing is the analysis of the consequences of explicitness and implicitness.

Whether implicit or explicit, rationing mechanisms are likely to be underpinned by one or more of a range of *criteria*, of which the following five are perhaps the most widely advocated. First, the *rule of rescue* gives priority to persons in acute or life-threatening conditions and tends to locate moral content in trying rather than in succeeding. This is likely to generate significant opportunity costs, although this is not an analytically fatal flaw (Goodin and Wilenski 1984). Second, *deserts* are sometimes used as the basis of an argument for exclusion, often in the context of a health state that is considered to be self-inflicted (e.g., by smoking). Third, prospective *effectiveness* of a health-care intervention is widely argued to be a commonsensical rationing criterion (Evans 1991) and may be enacted into the policies of third-party payers.[5] The existence of uncertainties about

effectiveness[6] undermines a good deal of the force of arguments that *whatever* is effective should be provided, although the 'prudent insurance principle' (Dworkin 1994) provides a thought experiment for dealing with such difficulties. Fourth, *cost-effectiveness* and *cost-utility* are espoused by those who maintain that the cost, as well as the degree of effectiveness, of interventions should be considered. This position has given rise to a number of artificial measures of health outcome such as quality (or disability)-adjusted life years.[7] In general, the theoretical properties of such appproaches are utilitarian in the sense that they aim at the maximization of health gain in return for any given level of expenditure. Finally, as noted above, third-party payment systems are underpinned by a desire to enhance *equity*, that is, to ameliorate the position of people who cannot afford the care from which they might benefit. *Equity* and *equality* are therefore concerned with the distribution of services or of health status respectively, a criterion that may trade off against cost-effectiveness.

THE UNITED KINGDOM: RATIONING IN A COMMAND-AND-CONTROL STATE[8]

The consumption regime established in the United Kingdom with the foundation of the National Health Service (NHS) in 1948 had several striking characteristics. It combined formally generous entitlements – a system of universal access to almost free health care as a right of citizenship – with, by international standards, low levels of spending on care. Saltman and Von Otter (1992) identify the system that was established as placing Britain (with some Scandinavian countries) in a family of 'command and control' systems, where administrative means are the predominant mechanism for allocating resources. The secret of Britain's success in reconciling universal access with effective cost containment lay in the existence of a powerful, implicit rationing mechanism. The formally generous entitlements offered by the NHS translated, for most citizens, into something more circumscribed: not an automatic entitlement to health care but an entitlement to access to a primary carer, typically the general practice physician (GP) working in the community. The GP system offered a mode of care with little access to modern high-technology medicine. The referral system meant that the GP's surgery was the access route to the more sophisticated – and expensive – care in the hospital. The system turned the GP into a significant gatekeeper regulating access to health-care resources. In the hospitals, specialists dominated most of the history of the NHS decisions about treatment, with substantial control over the waiting lists for access. Thus, although a narrow range of charges (including prescriptions and dental work) was introduced early in its life, rationing was largely based on the exercise of professional authority. The flavour has been well caught by two American observers of the system at a moment when professional authority was still reasonably secure, speaking of one critical set of rationing decisions, those governing access to kidney dialysis:

> Confronted by a person older than the prevailing unofficial age of cut-off for dialysis, the ... GP tells the victim of chronic renal failure or his family that nothing can be done except to make the patient as comfortable as possible in the time remaining. The ... nephrologist tells the family of a patient who is difficult to handle that dialysis would be painful and burdensome and that the patient would be more comfortable without it. (Aaron and Schwarz 1984: 101)

The wider character of the political settlement that underlies this has been vividly described as 'the politics of the double bed'; the setting up of the NHS

> did not mean the triumph of bureaucracy over professionalism or the subordination of doctoring to ministerial diktat. Instead it created a situation of mutual dependency. On the one hand the state became a monopoly employer: effectively, members of the medical profession became dependent on it not only for their own incomes but also for the resources at their command. On the other hand the state became dependent on the medical profession to run the NHS and *to cope with the problems of rationing scarce resources in patient care* (Klein 1990: 700 [italics added]).

This consumption regime might be summarized as involving three partners, one of whom occupied a subordinate position. The two dominant partners were the state and the medical profession, united by the mutual dependency summarised by Klein; the subordinates were the patients. The modern story of rationing as an issue in Britain is the story of the decline of this consumption regime and the struggle, so far unsuccessful, to replace it with anything as stable and successful. The consumption regime established at the foundation of the NHS declined because of the changes in the disposition and the resources of the three partners.

The heart of the implicit system of rationing involved acquiescence by the state in the alloca-

tion decisions of medical professionals, but while health care in the United Kingdom was cheap by international standards, the proportion of national resources was nevertheless rising significantly. In 1960, total health-care spending was 3.9 per cent of GDP; by 1984 the figure was 5.9 per cent (OECD 1987: 55). Because it was overwhelmingly tax-financed, it bulked large in the spending of the central state which, by the 1980s, was struggling with the problem of economic decline by trying to cut back the public sector and squeeze greater efficiency from what remained. The wider political consensus that created high levels of public support for the NHS paradoxically impelled the state to abandon its side of the bargain with the medical profession. The one option closed off even to radical conservative administrations was public abandonment of the universalist principles of the NHS, but in the 1980s that constraint made it even more imperative to invade the sphere of clinical autonomy in order to squeeze efficiency out of the system:

> To secure improvements in efficiency, the government's recent policy has comprised a battery of centre-driven, top-down initiatives, and controls, including a regional review system, performance indicators, policy scrutinies, cost improvement programmes, competitive tendering, and changes in management structures and processes. (Harrison, et al. 1990: 86)

If long-term pressures were making the state a less compliant partner of the profession, long-term social changes were also making patients less compliant subjects of medical authority. The world of the late 1940s, into which the original rationing 'compact' had been born, was one in which (compared with the 1980s) patients were less educated, less aware of their roles as consumers, less exposed to information in the media about clinical decisions and options, and less willing to organize in defence of their interests. Freemantle and Harrison's (1994) study of Interleukin-2 provides a graphic example of the breakdown of the implicit rationing system. In this study, a specialist at a leading cancer clinic, faced with a dispute with managers about access to resources to fund treatment for critically ill patients with an expensive new drug, drew the tabloid press into the issue. The most striking feature of the case is the way in which, in the wake of the collapse of the old system of implicit rationing, all three of the original partners – funders, clinicians, and patients – have been drawn into an increasingly open distributive struggle.

This distributive struggle has as yet failed to result in any settled successor to the traditionally established implicit system based on the exercise of clinician authority. Although purchasers of care in the NHS quasi-market introduced in 1991 could explicitly decide which package of care to fund (and not to fund), Klein and his colleagues found in their study of priority setting that purchasers were not making anything other than marginal exclusions – for instance, of cosmetic services like tattoo removal (Klein et al. 1996). A House of Commons Select Committee investigation of priority setting practices by health authorities showed striking variations in such practices and, more important, in the actual likelihood of patients receiving access to resources (cited in Lenaghan 1997). As Lenaghan remarks: 'Variations in healthcare provision are nothing new, but the purchaser-provider split has made them more explicit and, more importantly, revealed variations in the criteria used to justify these decisions...explicit rationing has not been accompanied by an explicit or shared understanding on how such decisions should be made' (1997: 907).

The effort to reach this 'shared understanding' has involved taking two very different paths. One involves using political mechanisms to create consensus about priorities, without arriving at any view about the substance of decisions in advance. This is the essential rationale of arguments for the introduction of more accountable and representative decision-making institutions into the NHS (Hunter and Harrison 1994). It is likewise the rationale behind mechanisms (such as user panels and citizen juries) that draw on the modes of discursive democracy to try to create conditions for informed consensus among citizens about choices.[9] Two obvious problems arise in taking this road. First, there is the danger that the effect of opening up the process in this way only widens the range of distributive struggle which has been created by the decline of the old rationing system. Commitment to public deliberation involves a trust in what Canovan has called the 'redemptive' capacity of democracy, its ability to produce, where appropriate debate is encouraged, reflective and considered judgements rather than views based on prejudice (Canovan 1999). A more concrete problem is that creating a consensus, and trust in the processes that produce decisional outcomes, is a long-term business whereas time is precisely what is not available because the need to make judgements about priorities presents itself daily, often in circumstances of personal tragedy. At the time of writing, the newly elected Labour government seems to be exhibiting a preference for returning to the use of professional authority as its main rationing device, albeit by emphasising the GP rather than the specialist role.[10]

The alternative path to a shared understanding may be labelled 'technocratic.' It involves employing a rational calculus and using a range of data and analytical techniques to arrive at a judgement about the most effective deployment of resources. Some of the possibilities, and some of the problems, are illustrated by the New Zealand case.

NEW ZEALAND: TECHNOLOGY AND RATIONING[11]

The consumption history of the New Zealand system is unique in two striking ways: it was the first capitalist democracy to commit itself to full universalism (in the late 1930s) and the first (in the 1990s) to try seriously to dismantle that universalism. The reforms introduced in 1938 by the then Labour government were largely funded, as in the system introduced in Britain later, from general revenues (Roemer 1991: 205–8). It came under pressure in the 1980s, more from without than from within the health-care system. New Zealand's exclusion from some of its traditional markets for agricultural goods (especially as the result of the creation of trade barriers around the European Union) created a severe, prolonged economic crisis. This produced immense pressure for economic restructuring, for the dismantling of the historically well-established welfare state, and, by 1993, for the introduction of reforms to the health-care system that both attempted to create a managed market and to define

'core health services' for which government funding would be available although not necessarily fully funded by the state. (OECD 1994: 237)

Many of the key institutional features of the New Zealand reforms are now being rethought (Ham 1997; Hornblow, 1997). One institutional legacy of the reforms, however, arises from the original commitment to identify a set of core services: a National Advisory Committee on Core Health and Disability Services, with the task of advising the Ministry of Health on 'the kinds and relative priorities of public health services, personal health services, and disability services that should, in the committee's opinion, be funded' (cited in Hadorn and Holmes 1997a: 132). The Committee was initially under pressure to develop a single authoritative list of services that would be guaranteed funding, the sort of 'basic benefits' package that has been introduced in some other jurisdictions, such as Israel (Chintz and Israeli 1997):

From the outset, however, the Committee has taken a different approach. It has preferred to define eligibility for services in terms of clinical practice guidelines or explicit assessment criteria which depict the circumstances under which patients are likely to derive substantial health benefit from those services, bearing in mind competing claims on resources. Thus, for example, patients could reasonably expect to receive coronary bypass graft surgery at the taxpayer's expense if (and only if) their clinical circumstances were commensurate with a likelihood of substantial benefit from that procedure. (Hadorn and Holmes 1997a: 132)

The National Criteria project has begun the realization of this process of priority setting. It has developed assessment criteria for five important elective surgery procedures, including hip and knee replacement and coronary bypass surgery. Rankings are determined through a points system based on interval-level measurements, added to form a linear model of priority. Points are assigned for both clinical and social factors. Thus, for joint replacements points are assigned for a range of measures of pain suffered, impact on functional activity, and movement and deformity. Social factors scored include the patient's age, time spent on the waiting list, and the threat to independence from the condition suffered. A critical feature of the scheme is that it is not intended to assign patients to categories that definitively guarantee or exclude entitlement to treatment. It is intended to interact with political judgement about the volume of resources to be allocated to health care. The possibilities are illustrated by the particular case of coronary artery bypass grafts. An audit of patients on waiting lists for surgery in 1996 produced an agreement amongst clinicians that a clinical threshold of 25 points before considering bypass grafting was reasonable. On the other hand, current funding suggested that only those scoring 35 points or above would receive surgery: 'the minister agreed to be held accountable for any gap between what is clinically desirable and what is financially sustainable, reasoning that appropriate funding levels must take into account competing claims on resources – adjudication of which is ultimately up to society to resolve through democratic processes' (Hadorn and Holmes 1997b: 138).

The reference to democratic processes goes to the heart of the issues involved in judging the viability of the approach being piloted in New Zealand. In essence, the New Zealand scheme is yet another variant on a utilitarian approach to solving the problem of rationing. Once the principle is granted that social choice should be based on some additive scheme for balancing utility and disutility, then there is a powerful case for adopting the kind of linear choice model piloted in New Zealand on the grounds that it is more likely to produce decisions that maximize utility than the less systematically informed and more implicit judgements made, for instance, by individual clinicians. Key questions, however, concern not only the normative case for a utilitarian approach, but also the question of whether such an approach is politically manageable. The competing 'rescue principle' is deeply ingrained in the popular mind: witness, for instance, the extent to which it is widespread in popular approval for rescue services that operate on distinctly nonutilitarian principles such as lifeboats and mountain rescue. The attempt to operationalize utilitarian principles means a choice between 'statistical' lives and the lives of 'real' people whose condition can be dramatized in highly affecting terms. Mechanic puts the problem thus:

> studies consistently show that public opinion gives higher priority to saving identifiable lives than to more cost-effective measures to save 'statistical lives'. Any serious cost-effectiveness or rationing policy must come to terms with the rescue principle. (Mechanic 1997: 90)

What this suggests is that the viability of any rationing mechanism is heavily dependent on the cultural setting within which it operates, a point of some importance when we turn to the United States.

The United States: Rationing in a Supply State[12]

The American health-care system is huge, complex, and extraordinarily diverse; so diverse, indeed, that some observers place querying quote marks around 'system' in discussing the United States (Wood 1995). Any sketch of the American consumption regime is likely to be inadequate, but perhaps the single most important fact is that health-care consumers have not, historically, shaped this regime at all. Jacobs has put the point thus in characterizing America as a 'supply state' as far as health care is concerned:

> ...the general sequence and form of health policy in the United States diverge from those of all other industrialized nations. The US government's first and most generous involvement in health care focused on expanding the supply of hospital-centered, technologically sophisticated health care...In contrast to the United States, however, other Western countries have made the expansion

of access their first and primary priority; governments have accelerated the expansion of supply in response to widening access and growing demand for care. (Jacobs 1995: 144–5)

This supply domination helps make sense of three important changes in the American system in the last generation. First, a generation ago the United States was not, by international standards, a remarkably expensive health-care system; more than three decades of more-or-less relentless inflation have left it unique among the advanced capitalist nations in the proportion of national wealth allocated to health care. A second change is in part connected to this. Over the last generation, across the OECD nations, there has developed a common trend to the universalization of access to a range of health-care services. In the United States, by contrast, access has been restricted. As Anderson puts it, summarizing data from twenty-nine leading industrial nations: 'By 1995 the United States was the only country that still had less than half of its population eligible for publicly mandated coverage' (Anderson 1997: 167–8). Finally, despite the enduring importance of private insurance markets, there has been a continuing collectivization of consumption in two distinct senses: third parties (public and private) now dominate payment, and in the delivery of care, the 'liberal' model dominated by solo practitioners is being displaced by various systems of managed care.

The American rationing response to the recent turbulent health-care history has also been highly distinctive and has been well summarized by Grogan:

> ...there are two main strategies that governments can pursue to limit the utilization of medical services.... First, they can limit care by category – by designating either specific groups, such as the elderly, or specific diseases or medical procedures, such as heart transplants, that will not be paid for by the government. This is an explicit form of limitation, because the government creates a set of policies specifying who or what is not covered. The United States is gradually adopting this strategy... The second strategy is not explicit: it limits the supply of medical services through policies for reimbursement... and the acquisition of technology. In general, countries providing universal health care coverage tend to pursue this second strategy. (Grogan 1992: 214)

This sets the famous Oregon experiment[13] in context; although it is an unusually systematic effort at explicit rationing, it is part of the more general drift of policy in the United States. It is therefore ironic that the experiment has gener-ated huge interest outside the United States, mainly in countries whose approach, as we have seen, is rather different. The obvious question is why have US rationing strategies taken this turn?

An answer that presents itself immediately is, quite simply, the depth of the cost containment crisis in the United States. There are numerous measures of the severity of that crisis: the unprecedented (by international standards) rise in the proportion of total national wealth devoted to health care; the extent to which the *Federal* budget has been dominated by the demands of fulfilling Medicare entitlements; the failure, despite all this commitment of resources, to produce either satisfactory health outcomes, or rudimentary access for a substantial section of the population. Yet, a 'crisis as the mother of invention' account can hardly be fully convincing, and the reasons are encapsulated in our earlier account of the range of possible policy responses available to authorities – responses that can be addressed to both the demand and supply sides. The obvious question is why should there have been such a clear tendency for the undoubtedly critical character of the American system to produce such a distinctive response?

An alternative answer draws on the context within which American health-care debates are conducted, in particular the dominant discourse that frames those debates. That context is provided by the commercial insurance market, which has dominated the process by which consumption has been collectivized in the United States in recent decades. Because commercial insurance contracts are written in the language of eligibility, both as far as single entitlements and packages of services are concerned, it is not surprising that such language is retained in framing principles for the rationing of *public* resources. Yet there is another irony here: the attempt to create basic benefit packages *is itself a response to market failure*, notably the failure of occupationally based health insurance schemes organized through commercial markets to deliver access to the whole of the employed population and its dependents.

Another alternative answer has been offered by Morone, who argues that the dominating influence is not an attachment to the market. It is rather that the preference for explicit and automatic policy solutions, and for rationing through openly specified packages, are reflections of a wider cultural characteristic: suspicion of government and a consequent search for policy solutions whose nondiscretionary characteristics limit the freedom of government to intervene in the lives of citizens. In Morone's words:

...because Americans distrust both politics and politicians, they tend to seek solutions which do not rely on either. Rather than empowering political leaders to make political choices.... Americans constantly search for mechanistic, self-enforcing, automatic solutions which might operate without further politics or even self-conscious deliberation at the political center. (Morone 1990: 133)

The search for some rationing 'formula' is indeed part of this search for a 'mechanistic solution.' Yet that raises a question which, in one form or another, is always prompted by such cultural accounts: why should this cultural preference be so strong? The mystery is deepened because it is plainly not a universal feature of American politics and society, nor even of the American health-care system: in the case of the latter, for instance, the story of the last generation is also a story of the growing complexity of regulatory regimes, notably in relation to the exercise of constraints over professional autonomy. This is not to deny that the cultural preference exists; it is to wonder why it manifests itself here when it is suppressed or diverted in other parts of the policy universe.

Making sense of this puzzle takes us back to our opening characterization of the United States as a *supply state*. The United States is unique in that the rationing problem is implicated in two interlocked policy problems: lack of access to care for a substantial section of the population, and the failure to exercise cost containment in a uniquely expensive health-care economy. The expense of the system is closely connected to its supply dominated character, especially to 'hospital-centered, technologically sophisticated health care' (Jacobs 1995: 144). Every important comparative measure shows the United States to be an outlier in its utilization of high-technology medicine (Rublee 1994). That supply domination has also built powerful supplier interests in the American system that span professional communities and industrial sectors (Moran 1997). The forces driving producer interests have been intensified by the development of global markets in expensive medical technology; markets in which the United States is a dominating presence as both consumer and producer. In short, the 'supply state' character of the American system provides powerful disincentives to controlling costs by regulating the production and supply of high-technology medicine and powerful incentives to try to regulate by producing 'non-political' controls over consumers. The *cultural* attractions of 'automatic' rationing mechanisms identified by Morone do exist, but they are triggered by a particular constellation of interests in the American system.

GERMANY: RATIONING IN A CORPORATIST STATE[14]

The German health-care system has been the prototypical example of health-care arrangements organized along *corporatist* lines, involving the attribution of public status and duties to private interests:

> ...a process in which policy-making powers are 'contracted out' to consortia of group representatives who engage in a semi-private type of bargaining, the results of which are then ratified as state policies or state planning. (Offe 1984: 249)

Corporatism in the German health-care system has had three key sets of actors. The first is the state, both at federal level and at the level of individual *Länder* (states of the *Bundesrepublik*). For much of the history of the post-war Federal Republic and before, the state's role was neither to finance the cost of current care directly nor to organize its delivery, but to 'hold the ring' by providing the regulatory framework within which institutions doing the financing and delivering operated. The obligation to finance and deliver was delegated to institutions beyond the core state machine. *Sickness funds* (financed mainly by an obligatory payroll tax) collected the resources needed to pay for current care and negotiated with providers the terms under which it would be delivered. *Doctors' associations*, especially in the ambulatory sector, were the third key set of actors: they agreed with the insurance funds the price for care, assumed an obligation to ensure that it was actually delivered to patients, disbursed to doctors payment for services provided, and, latterly, monitored the claims for payment made by doctors.

In this system, rationing (in the sense both of prioritizing the claims of individual patients and steering the flow of resources in particular directions) took very special forms. In part, outcomes were structurally determined, notably as an outgrowth of the occupational structure. The health-care system, as a subsystem of the wider German welfare state, reflected the features of Esping-Andersen's famous characterization of the German welfare state as one in which entitlements were closely linked to class and status. A striking instance is the way in which the funds for *Beamten* (the most privileged strata of the civil service) offered superior services (Esping-Andersen 1990: 222–4). Prioritization was also moulded by the institutional form of the health service, which has long been distinguished by an unusually clear separation (clearer even than in the United Kingdom) between ambulatory care and hospital care. Access to hospitals (including outpatient services) has been at the discretion of doctors in local practice, who in turn have a monopoly of all ambulatory care.

What is most obvious about these two instances of the process of prioritization is the way they were the outcomes of occupational structures and institutional arrangements, rather than of any debates about priorities. The opaqueness of these processes was sustainable in an era of generous resources and expanding entitlements, an accurate characterization of the West German system until the mid-1970s. By international standards, both the generosity and comprehensiveness of the German post-war entitlement system have been striking; by the mid-1970s, for instance, the German system matched that of the United Kingdom in its universal range, and exceeded it in the range of entitlements and probably in the quality of the services delivered (Knox 1993: 49–50).

The pressure under which German health-care corporatism has come is evident at the macro-, the meso-, and the microlevels. *Macro*-pressures spring from growing doubts about the wider viability of *Modell Deutschland*, in particular the viability of a generous, occupationally based welfare model in a world of global competition, capital mobility, and pressures for labour market flexibility (Leaman 1988). *Meso*-level pressures are illustrated by the destabilizing effect of changes in occupational structure on the institutions of health-care corporatism: the shift to white collar and professional employment, coupled with the development of chronic structural unemployment in some traditional industrial areas has threatened the financial viability of many funds that catered disproportionately for manual workers (Wysong and Abel 1990). The extreme example is the way the collapse of the old East German industrial economy after reunification has forced state intervention to support the insurance funds in the former GDR (Henke 1991). *Micro*-level pressures are illustrated by the effect of the incentive structures created by the established corporatist modes on the behaviour of individual patients and doctors, which resuscitate problems of moral hazard. Since there has been neither a cost nor a limit to the consultations a patient may have with an ambulatory physician, the result has been, by international standards, a high level of utilization, and the fee-for-service payment system has encouraged opportunistic (and occasionally fraudulent) charging by ambulatory physicians (Albritton 1993: 55–7).

Pressures at the three levels are clearly interlocked. They explain why the German system has been in a virtually perpetual state of reform since the end of the 'long boom' in the advanced capitalist world in the middle of the 1970s. These changes have had three particularly important sets of consequences for the prioritization process. They have led to greater *transparency, choice, and hierarchical control*, although not all these changes are readily compatible. The shift to transparency is illustrated by the spread of patient co-payments. Although Germany continues to offer a remarkably generous range of universal, free entitlements, the history of reform in the system since the mid-1970s is one of the unremitting spread of co-payments (Alber 1992: 74). Transparency has also affected providers, notably in the growth of monitoring of the charging practices and treatment patterns of ambulatory doctors by their own associations. Increasing transparency has powerful implications for a system where, historically, rationing was opaquely accomplished by the workings of structural forces and institutional barriers. The same can be said of the growth of choice, especially of choice in finance. The established system had the two characteristic features of German welfare corporatism: it involved compulsion over workers, and it was occupationally stratified. Health-care reforms of 1993, however, included a provision for the introduction in 1996 of 'an almost free choice of sickness fund for the members of the statutory health insurance scheme' (Schwartz and Busse 1997: 116). The change is a response to both meso- and micropressures in the system: to the shifting occupational structure which has diminished the significance of the historical core of the insurance funds, which catered for manual workers, and to pressures for greater incentives for microefficiency.

If these changes are pushing in the direction of greater diversity, the growth of *hierarchical control* is pulling the system in a very different direction. This has involved the strengthening of control within the corporatist institutions themselves, notably by the spread of global budgets within which the partners are obliged both to bargain and to allocate resources (OECD 1992: 61). More important still is a fundamental transformation of the allocation of authority between the state, traditionally only a ringmaster, and the other corporatist partners. Since the mid-1970s the state has reconfigured both itself and many of the most important interests in the system (Döhler 1995). The transformation of the role of the state at Federal level has been substantive, involving, in particular, a historically unprecedented intervention in the previously autonomous domestic economies of the individual funds to redistribute resources between funds according to risk structure and fund resources (Schwartz and Busse 1997: 116). It has also involved a steady augmentation of the state's capacity and inclination actively to steer the system. One sign of this is the succession of fundamental structural reforms sponsored by Federal Government legislation, first in 1989, and then, more radically, in 1993. Another has involved the 'drip feed' effect of 20 years of the institution for Concerted Action in Health Care. Although founded in 1977 as a forum for the corporatist partners, it has developed in two particularly important ways; it has negotiated national targets (not always observed) for the total resources to be allocated to health care, and through its machinery of expert advisers, it has been at the centre of two decades of debate about the allocation of resources to health. The latter is particularly destructive of one of the key features of the established corporatist system of resource allocation, its implicit character, for the debates naturally force to the surface issues that would otherwise remain subterranean. A report of the Advisory Council in 1994 examined the issue of what range of entitlements were sustainable beyond the year 2000. The report raised the issue of whether there should be a 'basic benefits' basket, and discussed a range of medical and social criteria by which decisions about inclusion might be made.[15]

In every democratic political system, rationing is a delicate task, and rationing by explicit criteria is particularly delicate, but there is an obvious added sensitivity in the German case given the nation's history between 1933 and 1945. The old corporatist system of implicit rationing was highly functional in a society where open discussion about life-affecting medical choices called up echoes of the experience of the Nazi years. All democracies find rationing difficult: Germany especially so.

CONCLUSION

In capitalist democracies, the most important socioeconomic configuration in the modern world, the majority of rationing of goods and services of all kinds is achieved through the mechanisms of the market, and there is a widespread consensus supporting direct out-of-pocket payment in the market as a rationing mechanism even for some of the most basic material necessities such as food, clothing, and energy. In such cases, this consensus seems to rest on an economy of comparative historical abundance. Conditions of scarcity often produce widespread public support for the use of some administrative mechanisms to allocate resources: the best documented are the systems of rationing developed in wartime, such as the 'total war'

economy of the United Kingdom during the Second World War.

The rise of the welfare state has also resulted in an array of services that are fundamentally conceived as entitlements of citizenship, even when this language is not itself used. Citizenship entitlements create a second arena, beyond the special and usually temporary circumstances of war-induced scarcity, when the consensus in support of market-based rationing systems is breached, at however minimal a level, there is a presumption of access as a right, rather than depending on the resources to command supply in the marketplace. The scope of such 'welfare citizenship' varies across nations, but across the world of capitalist democracy some form of health care is universally accepted as a citizenship entitlement, thus putting it outside the domain of market rationing. That is true even in the most 'marketized' system, the United States: this is the significance of Medicaid, which is intended as a safety net, albeit a most rudimentary one, for the very poorest. The extent to which health care is conceived in terms of a citizenship entitlement sets a limit to the extent to which rationing can be accomplished on the supply side by imposing new charges (although all the systems that have been considered in this chapter do employ some charges). A consensus supporting charges seems to be achievable only by picturing them as a demand-side solution to the problem of countering moral hazard among patients/consumers of free goods, or by creating a distinction between a 'core' and a 'periphery' of health services. The latter explains the popularity in so many different jurisdictions of the search for a 'basket' of basic services.

The problem of health-care rationing was eased historically by a particular conjunction; the rise of health-care citizenship entitlements was accompanied, or even preceded, by the development of medical professions with substantial authority. This allowed states to shift the rationing process to the sphere of professional competence, that is, to rely on implicit rationing. A combination of political, cultural, and economic changes has both damaged the authority of doctors as arbiters of resource allocation and fractured the compact with states and other third-party payers on which the delegation of the rationing task rested. In general, economic growth has been uncertain. Because government expenditure is an important component of health expenditure, the widespread acceptance by governments of the principles (if not the precise prescriptions) of monetarism and supply-side economics, both macroeconomic paradigms hostile to deficit financing (as inflationary or simply as 'bad housekeeping') and high taxation levels, has entailed a need to restrict supply. In systems where employer contributions (via terms and conditions of employment) are an important source of health-care funds, higher industrial costs are seen as affecting competitiveness.

The decline of implicit, clinician-determined rationing in favour of the more explicit arrangements explored by the countries described above is a comparatively recent development, although it should be noted that the explicitness of the mechanisms proposed has not been entirely matched by the explicitness of the rationing criteria that they generate. These shifts of preference towards both demand-side measures and explicit mechanisms has largely taken place over the last decade, implying that the solutions reviewed in this chapter have a highly provisional character.

NOTES

1 There is a fourth form of third-party payment, which we do not discuss. This is where a state claims direct ownership of marketable resources, such as oil, and resources health care directly from the resultant revenues. Such payments may be regarded as quasi-contributions by the members of the population.

2 Participation in a scheme which limited benefits to contributions already made would be irrational!

3 This term is usually seen as pejorative (hence UK politicians are unwilling to employ it) although it can be represented as implying fairness, as in respect of wartime food rationing. For a discussion, see Harrison and Hunter (1994: 1–13). In this chapter the term is employed neutrally to signify any demand-side adjustment.

4 The introduction of charges may take the form of recategorizing health care as social care, a strategy pursued by recent UK governments.

5 'Evidence-based medicine' in the UK, and the activities of the US Agency for Health Care Policy and Research are examples; see Harrison (1998).

6 As in the case of 'Child B'; see New (1996).

7 For a straightforward account of QALYs, see Gudex (1986), and for a technique critique see Gerard and Mooney (1993). DALYs have been used by the World Bank (1993).

8 For an account of the structure and organisation of the NHS, see Baggott (1998).

9 See, for instance, Coote and Lenaghan (1997), Bowie et al. (1995), and for an overview, Harrison and Mort (1998).

10 Its policy document (Department of Health 1997) retains the *rhetoric* of previous governments in the sense that it purports to reject any need for rationing.

11 For an account of the New Zealand system, see OECD (1994: 227–42).

12 For an account of the US system, see Weissert and Weissert (1996).

13 For a justification of the Oregon scheme, see Kitzhaber (1993), and for the technical details and fate see Crittenden (1995). On its wider national significance, see Brown (1991).

14 For an account of the German system, see Freeman (1998).

15 For a discussion, see Braun (1995).

REFERENCES

Aaron, H.J. and Schwartz, W.B. (1984) *The Painful Prescription: Rationing Hospital Care.* Washington, DC: Brookings Institution.

Alber, J. (1992) 'Bundesrepublik Deutschland', in J. Alber and B. Bernardi-Schenklun (eds), *Westeuropaische Gesundheitssysteme im Vergleich.* Frankfurt: Campus. pp. 31–176.

Albritton, F. (1993) *Health Insurance Reform in the United States: A Market Approach with Application from the Federal Republic of Germany.* London: University Press of America.

Anderson, G. (1997) 'In search of value: An international comparison of cost, access, and outcomes', *Health Affairs,* 16(6): 163–71.

Arrow, K.J. (1963) 'Uncertainty and the welfare economics of medical care', *American Economic Review,* 53: 941–73.

Baggott, R. (1998) *Health and Health Care in Britain* (2nd edn). Basingstoke: Macmillan.

Bowle, C., Richardson, A., and Sykes, W. (1995) 'Consulting the public about health service priorities', *British Medical Journal,* 311: 1155–8.

Braun, B. (1995) 'Health care in Germany – the discovery of managed and solidaristic competition', in S. Iliffe and H. Deppe (eds), *Health Care in Europe: Competition or Solidarity?* Frankfurt-Bockenheim: Verlag für Akademische Schriften. pp. 41–46.

Brown, L. (1991) 'The national politics of Oregon's rationing plan', *Health Affairs,* 10(2): 28–51.

Bruce, A. and Jonsson, E. (1996) *Competition in the Provision of Health Care.* Aldershot: Ashgate.

Canovan, M. (1999) 'Trust the people!: Populism and the two faces of democracy', *Political Studies,* 47(1): 2–16.

Chintz, D. and Israeli, A. (1997) 'Health reform and rationing in Israel', *Health Affairs,* 16(5): 205–10.

Coiera, E. (1996) 'The Internet's challenge to health care provision', *British Medical Journal,* 312: 3–4.

Coote, A. and Lenaghan, J. (1997) *Citizens' Juries: Theory into Practice.* London: Institute for Public Policy Research.

Crittenden, R. (1995) 'Rolling back reform in the Pacific Northwest', *Health Affairs,* 14: 302–5.

Department of Health (1997) *The New NHS: Modern, Dependable.* Cm 3807. London: Her Majesty's Stationery Office.

Döhler, M. (1995) 'The state as architect of political order: Policy dynamics of German health care', *Governance*, 8: 380–404.

Donaldson, C. and Gerard, K. (1993) *Economics of Health Care Financing: The Visible Hand.* London: Macmillan.

Dworkin, R. (1994) 'Will Clinton's plan be fair?' *New York Review of Books.* 13 January: 20–5.

Esping-Andersen, G. (1990) *The Three Worlds of Welfare Capitalism.* Cambridge: Polity.

Evans, R.G. (1991) 'The dog in the night-time: Medical practice variations and health policy', in T.F. Andersen and G. Mooney (eds), *The Challenge of Medical Practice Variations.* Basingstoke: Macmillan.

Flynn, R. (1997) 'Quasi-welfare, associationism and the social division of citizenship', *Citizenship Studies*, 1(3): 17–28.

Freeman, R. (1998) 'The German model: The state and the market in health care reform', in W. Ranade (ed.), *Markets and Health Care.* Harlow: Addison Wesley. pp. 179–93.

Freemantle, N. and Harrison, S. (1994) 'Interleukin-2: The public and professional face of rationing in the NHS', *Critical Social Policy*, 13(3): 94–117.

Gerard, K. and Mooney, G. (1993) 'QALY league tables: Handle with care', *Health Economics*, 2: 59–64.

Goodin, R.E. and Wilenski, P. (1984) 'Rational politicians and rational bureaucrats in Washington and Whitehall', *Public Administration*, 60: 23–41.

Grogan, C. (1992) 'Deciding on access and levels of care: A comparison of Canada, Britain, Germany, and the United States', *Journal of Health Politics, Policy and Law*, 17: 213–32.

Gudex, C. (1986) *QALYs and Their Use by the Health Service.* York: University of York Centre for Health Economics.

Hadorn, D. and Holmes, A. (1997a) 'The New Zealand priority criteria project. Part 1. Overview', *British Medical Journal*, 314: 131–4.

Hadorn, D. and Holmes, A. (1997b) 'The New Zealand priority criteria project. Part 2. Coronary artery bypass graft surgery', *British Medical Journal*, 314: 135–58.

Ham, C. (1997) 'Reforming the New Zealand health reforms', *British Medical Journal*, 314: 1844–5.

Harrison, S. (1998) 'The politics of evidence-based medicine in the UK', *Policy and Politics*, 26: 15–32.

Harrison, S. and Hunter, D.J. (1994) *Rationing Health Care.* London: Institute for Public Policy Research.

Harrison, S. and Mort, M. (1998) 'Which champions, which people? Public and user involvement as a technology of legitimation', *Social Policy and Administration*, 32(1): 60–70.

Harrison, S., Hunter, D.J., and Pollitt, C. (1990) *The Dynamics of British Health Policy.* London: Routledge.

Henke, K.-D. (1991) 'Fiscal problems of German unity – the case of health care', *Staatswissenschaft und Staatspraxis*, 2: 170–8.

Hoffenberg, R. (1992) Letter. *British Medical Journal*, 308: 182.

Hornblow, A. (1997) 'New Zealand's health reforms: A clash of cultures', *British Medical Journal*, 314: 1892–3.

Hunter, D.J. (1993) 'Rationing and health gain', *Critical Public Health*, 4(1): 27–32.

Hunter, D. and Harrison, S. (1994) 'Democracy, accountability and consumerism' in S. Iliffe and J. Munro (eds), *Health Choices: Future Options for the NHS.* London: Lawrence and Wishart. pp. 120–53.

Jacobs, L. (1995) 'Politics of America's supply state: Health reform and technology', *Health Affairs*, 14: 143–57.

Kitzhaber, J. (1993) 'Prioritising health services in an era of limits: The Oregon experience', *British Medical Journal*, 307: 373–7.

Klein, R.E. (1989) *The Politics of the National Health Service.* London: Longman.

Klein, R.E. (1990) 'The state and the profession: The politics of the double bed', *British Medical Journal*, 301: 700–2.

Klein, R.E., Day, P., and Redmayne, S. (1996) *Priority Setting and Rationing in the National Health Service.* Buckingham: Open University Press.

Knox, R. (1993) *Germany: One Nation with Health Care for All.* New York: Faulkner and Gray.

Leaman, J. (1988) *The Political Economy of West Germany 1945–85.* London: Macmillan.

Lenaghan, J. (1997) 'Central government should have a greater say in rationing decisions', *British Medical Journal*, 314: 967–70.

Levit, R., Cowan, C., Lazenby, H., McDonnell, P., Sensenig, A., Stiller, J., and Won, D. (1994) 'National health spending trends, 1960–93', *Health Affairs*, 15(5): 14–31.

Marshall, T.H. (1950) *Citizenship and Social Class and Other Essays.* Cambridge: Cambridge University Press.

Mechanic, D. (1992) 'Professional judgement and the rationing of medical care', *University of Pennsylvania Law Review*, 140: 1713–54.

Mechanic, D. (1997), 'Muddling through elegantly: Finding the proper balance in rationing', *Health Affairs*, 16(5): 83–92.

Moran, M. (1997) 'Technology, American democracy and health care', *British Journal of Political Science*, 27: 573–94.

Morone, J. (1990) 'American political culture and the search for lessons from abroad', *Journal of Health Politics, Policy and Law*, 15: 129–43.

New, B. (1996) 'The rationing agenda in the NHS', *British Medical Journal*, 312: 1593–1601.

New, B. and Le Grand, J. (1996) *Rationing in the NHS: Principles and Pragmatism*. London: King's Fund.

O'Connor, J. (1973) *The Fiscal Crisis of the State*. New York: St Martin's.

OECD (1987) *Financing and Delivering Health Care*. Paris: OECD.

OECD (1992) *The Reform of Health Care: A Comparative Analysis of Seven OECD Countries*. Paris: OECD.

OECD (1994) *The Reform of Health Care Systems: A Review of Seventeen OECD Countries*. Paris: OECD

Offe, C. (1984) *Contradictions of the Welfare State*. London: Hutchinson.

Office of Technology Assessment (1978) *Assessing the Efficacy and Safety of Medical Technologies*. Washington, DC: Government Printing Office.

Pauly, M.V. (1968) 'The economics of moral hazard', *American Economic Review*, 58: 531–57.

Robinson, R. and Steiner, A. (1998) *Managed Health Care*. Buckingham: Open University Press.

Roemer, M. (1991) *National Health Systems of the World: Vol. 1*. New York: Oxford University Press.

Rublee, D. (1994) 'Medical technology in Canada, Germany and the United States', *Health Affairs*, 13(4): 113–26.

Saltman, R. and von Otter, C. (eds) (1992) *Planned Markets and Public Competition: Strategic Reform in Northern European Health Systems*. Buckingham: Open University Press.

Schwartz, F.W. and Busse, R. (1997) 'Germany', in C. Ham (ed.), *Health Care Reform: Learning from International Experience*. Buckingham: Open University Press. pp. 104–18.

Weissert, C. and Weissert, W. (1996) *Governing Health: The Politics of Health Policy*. Baltimore: Johns Hopkins University Press.

Wood, B. (1995) 'Federalism, implementation and equity: The importance of place in American health care reform', *Health and Plac*, 1: 61–4.

Wood, B. (forthcoming) *Patient Power? Patients' Associations in Britain and America*. Buckingham: Open University Press.

World Bank (1993) *World Development Report: Investing in Health*. New York: Oxford University Press.

Wysong, J. and Abel, T. (1990) 'Universal health insurance and high risk groups in West Germany', *Milbank Quarterly*, 68: 527–60.

3.10

Reconfiguring Health Policy: Simple Truths, Complex Solutions

STEVEN LEWIS, MARCEL SAULNIER, AND
MARC RENAUD

INTRODUCTION

Neither health nor health care 'just happens.' To be sure, nature is powerful and the best laid plans gang aft agley, but in developed societies – the context for this chapter – we have considerable latitude to alter our individual and collective states, if not our fates (for in the long run, as Keynes famously put it, we are all dead). Health issues are often at the centre of public debate because health is usually defined more as a public good than a market commodity (particularly outside the United States). As a result, health policy is a powerful instrument that can literally shape destinies.

The title of this chapter implies that health policy should be reconfigured, but that it is tricky business. The premise is that the determinants of health are complex, and producing health is not the same as providing health care to address illness. As our understanding of health deepens, we need to develop health policy responses to problems and issues that are consistent with what we know. Meeting this challenge successfully is made more difficult by its financial and political dimensions. To make sense of these realities, it is important to survey the landscape, identify the barriers to change, and point to opportunities for overcoming the inertia inherent in complex systems. Those are the tasks we have set ourselves. We begin with the known, describe obstacles to change, outline strategies for progress, and conclude with observations on community.

A FEW SIMPLE TRUTHS ABOUT HEALTH AND HEALTH CARE

Public health and social welfare policy emerged mainly in the nineteenth century, but the reach of science remained comparatively limited well into the twentieth century. Particularly since the Second World War, health policy has become a major area of national public policy and economic activity. In this section, we make a number of observations about the experience of industrialized countries during this period, with a particular focus on health care, health promotion, and the so-called broader determinants of health. This sets the stage for a discussion of barriers and strategies to reconfiguring health policy in the following two sections.

HEALTH CARE: A MODERN PREOCCUPATION

The transformation of health policy from a focus on basic public health issues early in the twentieth century to its post-war emphasis on health-care services to individuals can be attributed to a number of factors: advances in medical science, entrenchment of individual rights and entitlements, greater attention to social security, increasing standard of living, and the rise of consumerism, to name only a few. Although data on health expenditures seldom go back farther than

30 or 40 years, it is reasonable to assume that in the early 1900s health spending accounted for a very modest share of national income, and public health outlays were likely as prominent as spending on personal health-care services. Today, health expenditure accounts for anywhere from 7 to 14 per cent of national income in industrialized countries, with an average of about 8 per cent. By far the lion's share of spending is directed to personal health-care services.[1]

Health-care systems are continuously evolving in response to various economic and social pressures, epidemiological patterns, and medical knowledge. The 1980s and 1990s have seen an unprecedented wave of structural reforms in many countries designed to improve the efficiency and effectiveness of health-care services. Amid this inconstant state of affairs, a number of 'simple truths' are emerging from the collective experience of industrialized countries that are highly relevant to the question of reconfiguring health policy.

Simple Truth No. 1: Health-Care Systems Want to Grow

Health-care systems have an inherent tendency towards expansion. The providers of services are often also consumers' agents. Health care is both intrinsically valued, and instrumental to the achievement of a greater goal – better health – that all desire. However, because providers have historically held a virtual monopoly on knowledge, shrouded in the mystique of practice, supplier-induced demand plays a very important role in health care (Evans 1984). If left unchecked, there is no telling how large a share of national income health care would eventually consume. The United States, with roughly 14 per cent of its GDP devoted to health care, has set the high-water mark among industrialized countries – although President Clinton's ill-fated first-term health reform plan envisioned further growth to 17 per cent by early in the new century. In most other countries, cost-containment efforts have limited health care outlays to less than 10 per cent of GDP (Brousselle 1998; Deber and Swan 1998; GRIS 1998); but it is a constant struggle.

At the root of this expansionist dynamic lies a potent interaction among the desires and expectations of recipients and producers of services. We all want to be cured of disease, cared for when we are ill, and live long, healthy lives. We therefore willingly allocate substantial resources to achieving these ends. However, the systems we have put in place to meet our health-care needs – collectively the medical–industrial complex – are not mere instruments of our desires, to be enlarged or curtailed at will. They have become powerful political interests that pursue satisfaction of their own intrinsic needs. As long as there is illness, there will be public pressure to address it and to inject more resources. With so many expansionist forces afoot, governments face a very challenging environment in which to manage health-care resources effectively.

Simple Truth: No. 2: Higher Health Spending does not Necessarily Lead to Higher Health Status

In principle, there would be *prima facie* justification for a continuous growth in real health-care expenditure if the additional outlays could be shown to improve health status. However, beyond a certain threshold of expenditure, long since surpassed by most industrialized countries, one would be hard-pressed to conclude that spending more on health care leads to better health for a population (GRIS 1998). In fact, as shown in Table 1, cross-national comparisons of expenditure and outcome reveal some rather puzzling patterns.

1 Although there is great variation in levels of health-care expenditure, conventional health status indicators for most countries are concentrated within a very narrow band.
2 In several cases, lower-spending countries have better health status than higher-spending countries. The Japan versus the United States example is the most obvious, but there are several other instances where this is true.

Simple Truth No. 3: Universal Access to Health Care does not Lead to Universally Good Health

Despite the enormous progress made over the last few decades in making medically necessary health care a basic entitlement, and despite significant gains in aggregate population health status, health disparities persist. Individuals who are wealthy and well-educated tend to be healthier than those who are poor and illiterate. Universal health care has done little to change the way health status is distributed across groups of the population.

One might argue that it is unreasonable to expect health care to fundamentally affect the distribution of health throughout society. After all, it deals with only a small fraction of the

Table 1   *Health spending and health status indicators in key industrialized countries*

	Health expenditure as a % of GDP		Combined M/F life expectancy at birth		Infant mortality (rate per 1000 live births)	
	1960	1996	1960	1995	1960	1995
Canada	5.5	9.2	71.4	78.3	27.3	6.0
France	4.2	9.6	70.3	77.9	27.4	5.0
Germany	4.3	10.5	69.7	76.3	33.8	5.3
Italy	3.6	7.6	69.8	77.6	43.9	6.2
Japan	—	7.2	67.8	79.6	30.7	4.3
UK	3.9	6.9	71.3	77	22.5	6.0
USA	5.2	14.2	69.9	75.9	26.0	8.0
G-7 average	4.5	9.7	70	77.5	30.2	5.8
OECD average	3.9	7.3	68.6	76	37.5	7.9

Source: OECD Health Data (1997).

population at any given time, and usually comes into play after health problems have occurred. However, if the medical–industrial complex claimed only modest credit for improving population health status, formally recognized the pre-eminence of the socioeconomic, environmental, and other determinants of health, and otherwise acknowledged the limits of its impact, its ability to secure and retain an ever-increasing share of national wealth would be compromised.

Simple Truth No. 4: Public Awareness of Risks to Health has Greatly Improved

The mid-century preoccupation with medical science gave rise, by the 1970s, to a renewed focus on individual risk factors and lifestyle choices. During the 1970s, many countries started turning their attention towards health promotion as a means of addressing the health disparities that universal health care could not tackle effectively. The impact of health care was limited, it was thought, because it was too 'downstream.' Hence the call for a more 'upstream' approach that would prevent health problems by targeting known risk factors such as diet, physical activity, substance abuse, and sexual behaviour, to name only a few (Canada. Health and Welfare Canada 1974).

Upstream approaches to health, of course, are not new; they were about all we had until recent times. The major breakthroughs of the nineteenth and the first half of the twentieth centuries were in public health: improvements in sanitary infrastructure, housing, nutrition and workplace conditions. These advances had widespread population-level effects, as did general improvements in living standards. Depending on whose version of history one favours, life expectancy increased as much as 20 years before the advent of modern and universally accessible medical care (Dubos 1965; McKeown 1979).

Perhaps the greatest contribution of health promotion over the past two decades has been to raise public awareness about individual risk factors. Few people today are ignorant of the dangers of smoking, drug abuse, driving while impaired, fatty diets, risky sexual behaviour, and sedentary living. Further, with some variability across countries due to cultural or political factors, the public is much more ready today to accept state interventions in the marketplace and even curtailment of individual freedoms in the name of protecting or advancing health. Examples of this are many: selective and punitive taxation levels on products deemed injurious to health (tobacco, alcohol); mandatory health warnings on cigarette packages; compulsory seatbelt legislation; and dramatic interventions in food production and distribution to prevent the spread of illnesses such as mad cow disease.

Simple Truth No. 5: Health Care Almost Always Wins Out in the Competition for Resources

In spite of a much greater public awareness of risks to health, there has been no major shift in the allocation of resources away from health care towards health promotion and disease prevention (Canadian Institute for Health Information 1997). This was true in both the 1970s and 1980s, an era of strong economic growth and favourable fiscal conditions, and today in the midst of prolonged fiscal restraint and moderate economic growth.

One intractable reality remains the political cost of shifting resources away from cure towards prevention and promotion. Virtually by definition, health promotion requires a different calculation of costs and benefits because it promises future, not immediate, gains and challenges the status quo. It is the enemy of complacency, the official voice of concern about the future, and a persistent reminder of the perils of our pleasures. In contrast, pouring more resources into health care generates short-term political capital because it responds to highly visible and viscerally felt needs, and expands the domain and security of providers. In addition, perceived motive counts, particularly where cynicism about politics runs high: even the most effective health promotion interventions will gain little public support if thought to be a smokescreen for reductions in health-care expenditure.

Simple Truth No. 6: Changing the Distribution of Health Status through 'Upstream' Strategies Is Extraordinarily Difficult

Whatever the achievements of health promotion in targeting and altering individual behaviour, for example, anti-smoking campaigns, they have, in the main, failed to alter the distribution of health status among groups or classes. On the broader societal front, it is plausible to argue that it is too early to tell, and that health promotion activities have been inadequately funded to make a real difference. However, the evidence suggests that individually targeted health promotion and disease prevention tends to be more effective for higher socioeconomic groups than for lower socioeconomic groups (Lantz et al. 1998). Interventions that are supposed to benefit the disadvantaged benefit the advantaged even more, thus widening disparities.

Personal health practices and behaviours are very much influenced by the social and economic environments in which people live and work. Some face far more barriers to making 'correct' choices than others by virtue of the absence of positive reinforcement, peer values and expectations, and material circumstance. Modifying the distribution of health status is a major societal challenge requiring more than 'upstream' single-sector interventions. The data show that it is far easier to improve population health status differentially than to equalize it.

A Few Less Simple Challenges

So far we have identified features of the health and health-care landscape that suggest that diagnosing the barriers to health is easier than devising effective remedies. Similar and perhaps even more complex challenges confront public policy development.

O What a Tangled Web: The Determinants of Health

Just as the power of medical science exploded in mid-century, researchers began to explore the broader determinants of health in unprecedented depth. It was intuitively obvious prior to social scientific analysis that health and socioeconomic status were correlated. Now we have both data and increasingly persuasive expositions of the nature and extent of these connections (Graubard 1994). After decades of documenting the impact of lifestyle, researchers, most famously Marmot in the Whitehall studies, identified the underlying class-based gradient in health status irrespective of individual risk factors and habits (Marmot 1986). The confirming evidence grows continuously. Moreover, these relationships are inherently plausible: the upper classes tend to be visibly better off on all counts, and it would be peculiar if health status were somehow the exception.

Correlations may in themselves be highly compelling, but the gold standard for evidence is causation. Recently various evidentiary strands have been woven into a conceptual framework that describes how human biology interacts with both the physical and social environments and the health-care system to produce an array of health outcomes within a population (Evans et al. 1994). This analysis has drawn particular attention to the social factors – how individuals are brought up, the coping skills they develop, the degree of support from family and community, educational attainment, employment status, etc. – as crucial determinants of health (Sapolsky 1992; Suomi 1991). For example, we know that adequate nurturing and stimulation during the period from 0 to 6 years of age is critical to the healthy development of a child's brain, and in particular, to building resiliency. The experience with Head Start programs in the United States clearly shows that early childhood interventions significantly improve prospects for a healthy and productive life among the children they serve (Bertrand 1998; Steinhauer 1998). These programs are designed to ensure that children develop the coping skills they require to thrive under very adverse conditions if such conditions cannot be changed.

Community characteristics also appear to influence the health and general welfare of individual citizens. Some communities cope effectively with, and ultimately overcome, adverse conditions – for example, massive unemployment, natural disasters, widespread crime and delinquency – while others barely survive or simply wither away (Hamel 1998). The most resilient communities exhibit good leadership, a sense of common purpose, and an intricate web of relationships among community members through the workplace, leisure, religion, and voluntary organizations (Kaplan et al. 1996). Whether healthy individuals invariably create healthy communities, or vice-versa, is an important question. Even if the influences are bi-directional, it remains essential to ascertain the level at which one would intervene to achieve the best outcomes.

There is also evidence of variations in the slope of both the health status gradient within societies, and of overall health status trends between countries. Japan and Eastern Europe have undergone major transformations linked with changes in overall population health status (Evans et al. 1994; Hertzman et al. 1996). Wilkinson's work (1992) illustrates that overall life expectancy gains over the past 30 or so years have been greater in countries with relatively compressed income differentials. In short, societies have changed, both absolute and relative health indices have changed, and we have some, although incomplete, knowledge of how and why these changes occur. There seems little doubt that societies held genuinely accountable for both reducing health disparities and improving population health status would know roughly how to go about it.

Current realities are sobering. Disparities in market income are widening in most countries, although some have more effective buffers than others through government transfers (Centre for International Statistics 1998; Osberg 1998). Unemployment remains high in Canada and continental Europe. The United States, Japan, and the United Kingdom have been more successful. Some societies, notably the Scandinavian countries, have organized themselves to distribute the determinants of health more equally. Others have countervailing tendencies: the United States has low unemployment and huge inequalities, with the latter apparently responsible for its overall low health status ranking despite enormous health-care expenditure.

These barriers involve, to varying degrees, the classic tensions between ends and means. At times, society does not agree on goals: identifying disparities in health status does not mean there is consensus to eliminate them. Disputes about means are often fundamental: procedural barriers often confound implementation. There are also embedded political and institutional elements – both ends and means – that add to the complexity. If we view health and health care as political rather than rights-based or technical constructs, 'doing the right thing' for health may legitimately not be considered 'doing the right thing' politically.

The Temporal Challenge

People, and their governments, value current over future benefits, all else equal. The immediate and visible usually trumps that which is anticipated and opaque, particularly if posited as mutually exclusive alternatives. It is therefore extraordinarily difficult to withhold resources designed to produce a current benefit in favour of investments designed to produce future – and perhaps greater – benefit. Humans and our governments are, of course, capable of longer range thinking and do make farsighted decisions; we plan, we preserve national parks, education is by definition a future-orientated investment, but we are far less inclined to trade present for future health and health-care states than, say, current consumption for investment in majestic cathedrals that may not be completed in our lifetime.[2]

In light of this, public policy has to establish the appropriate discount rate for future benefits. That health researchers and epidemiologists might accurately project that certain changes and investments would produce better health status in the future does not mean that they ought to be masters of public policy. People may value modest current utilities over far greater future utilities. Psychological rationality may conflict with a more strictly utilitarian long-range accounting. Even when adverse future consequences are quite certain – for example, among smokers – risk-taking behaviour often persists. In a democracy, public policy must win the approval of the same people whose preferences and behaviours may not highly value planning and foresight, and even, in some sense, self-interest.

The Epistemological Dilemma

The evidence for health-orientated social policy is epistemologically less solid than the evidence arising from controlled clinical trials at the heart – in theory – of contemporary medicine.[3] Moreover, the evidence in the social policy sphere is almost always correlational; causality is theoretically inferred, not experimentally demonstrated. Social policy reasoning and 'proofs' do not work like algebra (based on abstract and formal logic) or pharmacotherapy (often based on observable physical phenomena). The mechanisms of action are invariably approximate and often qualitative. This is not normally a problem in the public policy realm, where positivistic social engineering visions have fallen into disrepute, and democracies tend not to hold governments accountable for finely calibrated effects. We seem to have absorbed, however impermanently, the ancient lesson that politics is discussion and persuasion, not calculus.

Yet, the epistemological bar is set higher for health policy. Health care, especially in the latter part of this century, is highly technical and places a premium on controlled experiments. Among insiders and experts, understanding the mechanism of action of interventions is highly valued; the unit of analysis has refined to the molecular level. Much of medicine aspires to the status of a natural science. Its methodological adherents (who are also competitors for public and private resources) often challenge health policy advocates to justify their cases with similarly rigorous and transparent 'proofs.'[4] There is a tendency to expect all policies related to health to adhere to the same concepts of rigour and causation (Mustard 1996). The citizenry demands far greater accountability of health policy because it perceives that diminished levels and quality of health care result from attempts to alter health 'determinants.'

Knowledge and Gridlock

A simple and straightforward understanding of health can be empowering; conversely, knowledge of the complex determinants of health can lead to policy paralysis. If wealth, status, power, and their distribution largely determine the distribution of health, can any health policies, in the end, create effects independent of general economic and political policies? Those who think that astute health policy, rather than more fundamental material and social transformations, can improve absolute or relative population health status may be unduly optimistic. In a sense, the evidence about the determinants of health plays into the hands of those who believe that health policy tinkering is destined to be overwhelmed by broader forces.

The Redistribution Dilemma

Health policy has the potential to alter the distribution of two types of benefits among the population. Providers of health care owe their livelihood and status to the health-care system, and its characteristics at a given time. Rearranging health care rearranges resources and incomes; in a finite world, this creates winners and losers, and one can expect prospective losers to oppose change that may be laudable on wider grounds. If health policy diminishes the emphasis on health care in favour of more social interventions and programs, the health-care constituency – a substantial force in all developed countries – will consider itself under siege and will predictably create or highlight alarmist scenarios designed to create support and nostalgia for the *status quo ante*.

In addition, health status benefits may be redistributed if health policy is successful. If the goal is to reduce health status inequalities, there are four logical options:

1. increase the health status of the worse off more than the health status of the better off;
2. increase the health status of the worse off but hold constant that of the better off;
3. hold constant the health status of the worse off, and lower the health status of the better off;
4. lower the health status of the worse off less than the health status of the better off.

We can dismiss options 3 and 4 as too disheartening to articulate as public policy objectives.[5] Of the two more obviously attractive options, 1 is less disconcerting because it promises something positive for all. In either case, that part of the population with a strong sense of entitlement to be winners in most spheres of life will see its health expectations uncharacteristically subordinated to that of others. The issue is further complicated by the fact that different segments of the population tend to need different kinds of interventions to improve health status. The well off tend to benefit from expensive technological innovations in health care because their nonmedical determinants are typically sound (they are well educated, employed, housed, fed). Those at the bottom end of the spectrum need health care to be sure, but their ticket to durably improved health status is improvement in both their absolute and relative material circumstance. Reducing disparities means precisely that those at the top end will do less well than they would were we indifferent to the magnitude of disparities – regardless of whether their absolute levels of health status continue to improve.

The Power of Belief Systems

People's beliefs about what is important and what is not, and what works and what does not, may influence health policy far more profoundly than research-based reasoning. Belief systems are complex and multifaceted phenomena. They are deep-rooted and inherently stable; they define individuals and populations in the same way that constitutions and jurisprudence define functioning democracies. Yet, although they are fundamental, they need not be rigid; human action and leadership can change them. Policy and belief systems can be mutually reinforcing, but dramatic policy initiatives, to be politically viable, must be compatible with dominant belief systems. Beliefs about health, spirituality, entitlement, hierarchy, fairness, and government set implicit constraints on the nature and scope of policy. Major economic and political policy changes ought therefore to flow from altered understandings and preferences, or at the very least a strong dissatisfaction with existing arrangements.

This suggests that change is likely to be evolutionary, particularly in reconceiving concepts of health, fairness, and collective public action. Belief systems are not easily shaken by data. There is a large and growing use of so-called alternate therapies among educated people (Canadian Medical Association 1997). People are fascinated by, and well disposed towards, sophisticated medical interventions and their impact, but much less so with 'social engineering.' We respond more viscerally to small numbers of dramatically and seriously sick people (those with AIDS, cancer, ALS) than to large numbers of people who are 'merely' unhealthy much of the time (the chronically ill, the undernourished). Societies might have a sophisticated understanding of what creates and diminishes health, but far more volunteer (and government) money goes to medical rather than social services. When declarations in favour of health for all confront the inegalitarian realities of rich societies (let alone desperately poor ones), the cognitive dissonance becomes almost overwhelming.

Redefining much of public policy in health terms is in a sense revolutionary. Given the obstacles to effective, widely supported, and lasting health-orientated policy development, there is a great deal of public intellectual groundwork to lay. It is not enough to persuade a majority of people that economic and social policy should serve health-enhancing ends; one must anticipate and intellectually disarm the critics. The Clinton health reform debacle is here instructive: while a majority of Americans consistently decry the follies of their health-care system, their ostensible desire for change is hostage to a more fundamental antipathy to government-run systems and to the lavishly funded scenarios promulgated by private insurers.

Finally, much current health policy thinking revolves around the assumption that adopting a population health perspective is inherently desirable: to understand it is to hold it. However, there is no reason to believe that the public would prefer a population health perspective, and the policy consequences that flow from it, if they perceive it to endanger the quality or accessibility of health-care services. Perhaps more important, there may be far less support for the goal of maximizing population health if the means are unacceptable. There may be consensus to mitigate, but not eliminate, the disparities inherent in a thriving capitalist economy. There may be implied or explicit limits to the public's desire to maximize population health, particularly if it wishes to maximize other things such as aggregate wealth.[6] If we accept the proposition that most people are utility maximizers most of the time – without denying the capacity for genuine altruism and communitarian sentiments – then both individual and population health will count as only two of many competing utilities.

AGENDAS IN PURSUIT OF A VITAL HEALTH POLICY

All analyses of potential 'solutions' to health policy dilemmas derive from implicit or explicit objectives. The primary assumption of our position is that improving health is a desirable and broadly supported goal. Its organizational corollary is that public policy is instrumental to its achievement, and government has a number of legitimate roles to play, examples being direct interventions, redistribution of resources, regulation, and creation of incentives. Other explicit assumptions and objectives are listed below.

1   Establishing health goals should be a fundamental cornerstone of public policy.
2   Reducing health status inequalities is inherently desirable.
3   Government properly frames social policy objectives and uses its powers and moral authority to advance them.
4   Any initiatives should respect and, if possible, advance democratic processes and participation. That is, good public policy requires public consent. This is not to suggest that public policy cannot provide leadership

and mobilize public support that may not be apparent initially, or that policy-making should be more responsive than initiating, but ultimately, public policy is for the public and good public policy must be supported by the citizenry at large.

Effective and sustainable health policy will, then, involve a good deal of civic groundwork – building an audience for the concepts, creating broad-based support for goals, creating awareness of the linkages between health and other societal constructs, and stimulating intersectoral partnerships. Needless to say, the following strategies are generic, and their success in particular circumstances will depend on a wide variety of factors, including political culture, economic conditions, social capital, leadership, and chance.

THE HEALTH INFORMATION AGENDA

Health information systems have been developed principally to administer health-care systems. As such they are in the main misnamed; they have not been about health, but about sickness and the units of service deployed to address it. These data systems are enormous achievements and sustain important health services utilization and clinical research, but their ore is less rich for the purpose of informing health policy from a broad population or determinants of health perspective.

The problem may be illustrated by two approaches to the health record. The conventional approach would be to apply ever more powerful computing technology to health care, creating a real-time virtual medical record that begins by consolidating existing health data. This 'virtual medical record' would contain basic demographic data (age, sex, residence), and a great deal of utilization data. Plans for expansion would include demographic variables (occupation, family structure), refined utilization data (patient- and doctor-specific diagnostic testing data), and outcomes data associated with major procedures. The expanded record would remain anchored in contacts with the health-care system.

A genuine health record would look much different if the goal were to assemble the data elements essential to understanding individuals' health status over the course of a life (Wolfson 1994). It would include variables such as household income in the formative years, genetic characteristics and risk factors, psychological profile; work history, characteristics of communities lived in (size, industrial profile, income distribu-

tion, environmental factors, etc.), seminal behaviour patterns, and a whole host of items that are known to influence health status. The virtual medical record would be supplanted by a virtual record of health determinants. Certainly one would include the medical record in the personalized profile, but its elements would in essence be dependent rather than independent variables.

There are huge challenges to creating such a database for population health and policy impact studies. Creating a comprehensive, person-specific profile raises profound privacy issues. The spectre of intrusive social engineering, risk-rating, and other unpalatable alternatives is invariably present despite legislative and ethical protections. Nevertheless, if policy is to be informed by good information, and evaluated persuasively, these reconceived databases are prerequisites. A good deal can be done by creatively linking existing data sets (administrative health care data, census files, income data, health survey data), but it may well be that the whole enterprise needs a fresh conceptual examination to overcome constraints imposed by traditional approaches.

These innovations will require years to develop and yield higher-order descriptive and explanatory information. There are short-term options that may produce valuable and compelling insights with the power to shape health policy. Case studies and qualitative investigations trade off breadth for depth, generalizability for understanding. These methods are not new to some disciplines, but they have become valued in health policy and behavioural research quite recently. Health policy has often been made in response to vivid stories and anecdotes; presumably it might also respond to new stories extracted from systematic, in-depth investigations. The definitive explorations and evaluations will have to wait for the reconstruction of health information systems, but meanwhile we are developing a variety of tools to obtain policy-relevant understandings of both need and the impact of various structures and interventions (Fisher et al. 1998; Tranmer et al. 1998).

BUILDING PUBLIC SUPPORT FOR POLICY RENEWAL

Once we have assembled existing research and built powerful new information systems, we must deploy them to good effect. The distribution of health is substantially political, and the adage that knowledge is power is at least partly true. The compelling tales to be told about the accumulating evidence on health, wealth, and social characteristics are all too often confined to the seminar room and the learned journals. While far from being arcane and turgid laboratory accounts, social data and trends have a tough time competing for the attention of a generation weaned on satellites, gigabytes, and cloned sheep. We retain some optimism that civic engagement and the appetite for reflection will grow, but even in the face of significant public indifference to reading and discussion and a sense of political alienation,[7] there are options.

A partial solution is good packaging and careful marketing to important audiences. The public has shown a greater appetite for acutely presented social analysis than researchers often assume. Fictionalized accounts of important social phenomena have often attracted large audiences; Upton Sinclair's *The Jungle*, and Steinbeck's *The Grapes of Wrath* are two famous examples. In Canada, a demographic and economic analysis of historical trends and their implications for the future – David Foot's *Boom, Bust and Echo* – topped nonfiction bestseller lists for two years. It is quite possible to translate scholarly works into essays and articles for the popular press, but there has to be a will and a strategy to reach the larger audiences in various venues.

A crucial message is that health is largely a function of how society organizes itself and the values that underlie it. This is obvious to population health researchers and is not entirely foreign to the thinking of the public (Ekos 1998; National Forum on Health 1997a), but the nature and strength of the linkages need reinforcing and social marketing in the best sense. The health impact of public policy options is, even if properly considered, rarely articulated. Both fiscal and monetary policy influence unemployment rates and income distribution, but as yet health impact analyses are not part of the public policy discourse in the same way that environmental impact assessments are (Lin et al. 1997). Driving home the message may require a central, highly visible focal point. In Canada, the National Forum on Health recommended establishing a Population Health Institute that would have a public education and media penetration agenda, and which, using the best available evidence, would propose policy options for addressing critical health issues (National Forum on Health 1997a, 1997b).

A vital piece of information that should cause some reflection at all levels of society is the connection between income distribution and health status. We have noted that there may be powerful societal divisions on the desirability of reducing material inequalities, but there may be a much stronger consensus in favour of reducing inequalities in health status because it is an argu-

ment that can appeal to both ends of the political spectrum (though for different reasons). The left considers increased equality to be an intrinsic good. Few disagree that health is a precondition for full participation in the economy. Not to caricature conservatives, but let us here assume that they have fewer moral objections to serious inequalities.[8] It would be useful to provide an accounting of the costs of these inequalities in terms of lost productivity, idleness, reduced demand for goods and services, crime and a vast system to protect against it, etc. Appealing to old-fashioned self-interest may be just as effective as appealing to nobler sentiments. Educating the public and politicians on both the disparities in health status and their consequences for economic participation may not in itself create a tidal wave of support for reorganizing the economy, but it should give greater impetus to the view that the level of inequality may be well beyond that which is defensible on either self-interested economic or compassionate grounds.

REACHING THE CORPORATE WORLD

There are three main audiences for the population health policy message. Two are obvious: politicians and the general public. The third may be the key to building support for major changes in health policy. This audience is the workplace, and particularly corporations.

There is a great deal of interest in the health of the workplace and work force. Economic self-interest is here a powerful unifying force. Healthy workers (in both a physical and psychological sense) are more productive, less likely to be injured, less likely to be absent, and reduce current and future liabilities for worker-related health care and rehabilitation. Large employers have long recognized the importance and potential payoffs of programs to improve the health of the work force. Traditional workplace safety standards have given way to more sophisticated and multifaceted programs to improve health. Many employers and unions negotiate health-orientated benefits plans that extend beyond reimbursement for non-publicly-insured health care.

The workplace has an enormous impact on health, and some of the effects may be time-lagged, manifesting fully long after the worker has retired (Avison 1998; Karasek and Theorell 1990; Polanyi et al. 1998a, 1998b; Sullivan et al. 1998). In a sense, the workplace is a population health laboratory where many of the determinants of health come into play. While 'ordinary people' may be indifferent to the effects of current practices and behaviours on future health status because of our psychological make-up, corporations are disciplined by competitive pressures and motivated by the advantages to be gained from treating workers as capital investments rather than expendables. As a result, they should be avid consumers of information that suggest which workplace health policies are likely to pay off over the long term.

Furthermore, as more corporations get the determinants of the health message they will come to realize that progressive policies are just as essential outside their immediate environments. There will be no healthy workers if there are no healthy children. It is to the advantage of corporations to operate in an environment in which they do not have to preoccupy themselves with setting up parallel systems to promote health. Greater awareness of the determinants of health could very well lead to a recognition that a more socially sensitive policy agenda ultimately serves individual and corporate interests better than its absence.

Taking Accountability Seriously

Governments live and die by certain accountability measures: the growth in the GDP, the unemployment rate, fiscal indicators. There is considerable – perhaps excessive – accountability for health care, but not for health. Consequently, policies are almost exclusively orientated towards health care. The means are mistaken for the ends, and most of the 'means' responsible for health status are not included in the accountability framework.

Governments may be disinclined to commit themselves to health goals for several reasons. There may be no consensus on what those goals should be. They may perceive their own powerlessness to change health status. They may be forced to spend money on health care that they know will not improve health status even while it generates political capital. Regardless, the absence of quite precise and widely articulated health goals defines accountability in process terms, which in turn emphasizes health care at the expense of interventions in the determinants of health.

It is therefore important that governments establish health goals, preferably for each important societal sector or subgroup. These goals will not only be targets to reach; they will focus attention on evaluation and effectiveness measures, and will provide a defence against claims for more health-care resources

in areas where the returns will be minimal. The difficulty lies in the secular trends: health status seems to be getting better (at least life expectancy is increasing quite dramatically), and no one knows exactly why. If the trend continues, government may be tempted to claim credit for improvements despite an inability to connect the outcomes with anything the government did. This interesting possibility aside, goal-setting requires deliberation, and adds a dimension to public discourse that shifts attention from anecdote and process. Setting goals is therefore part of the civic educational effort that in our view builds the foundation for health policy reconfiguration (Kushner and Rachlis 1998). If the goals are meaningful and public, based on values and best available evidence, the means revert to the status of means rather than ends.

Saving on Health Care, Investing in Health

Understanding the etiology of, and variations in, health status tends to focus more attention beyond the health-care sector. It remains important to scrutinize the health-care sector for many reasons, not least of which are the enormous resources it consumes. The expansionist tendencies of health care have been noted above. The growth of health services, evaluation, and utilization research has revealed a considerable degree of ineffectiveness and inefficiency. If we are able to jettison those aspects of health care that are obsolete, unnecessary, or harmful, the realized savings could be deployed in the service of creative health-oriented policies and programs.[9]

There is an unusual skew in conventional discourse about the funding of health-care systems. Despite the startling lack of a detectable relationship between health-care expenditure and health status in industrialized nations (GRIS 1998), the possibility that health-care systems are seriously overfunded is rarely raised. There are a number of possible reasons for this silence. As noted above, there is neither general nor system-specific accountability for health status. Population health status and outcomes may be too stringent a measure of the value of health care; the public appears to value accessibility in itself, as well as attempts to defeat illness even if unsuccessful. Health-care providers almost invariably claim that more money would allow them to perform better. Societies may equate their own status and maturity with the presence of a large medical infrastructure and expensive technology, and it is difficult for either individuals or governments (although far easier for the latter) to be prudent purchasers of health care given the asymmetry of knowledge and the understandable tendency to hope for possibilities rather than resign oneself to probabilities.

It remains important to intensify scrutiny of how health-care dollars are spent and subject health care to a stricter accountability. The more health-care is considered both an essential service and a commodity to be consumed in ever-greater quantities by wealthy societies, the harder it is to constrain. Undermining public faith (as opposed to rational and defensible confidence) in the health-care system is in a sense instrumental in creating support for a wider agenda. This could have two principal effects: opportunities to redeploy resources may emerge, and the public will be somewhat less devoted to the notion that health care is the solution to health problems. If skepticism is a prerequisite for transformation, there needs to be greater awareness among the public that the health-care system does not explain very much of the variance in health status.

COMMUNICATING THE CIVIC DIMENSIONS OF HEALTH

Reconfiguring health policy is difficult but achievable. Success requires first the abandonment of comforting assumptions. We should not assume societal consensus that we should invariably act on the determinants of health to improve population health status. If pressed, there will be credible groups that challenge the wisdom of adopting a population health perspective. Achievements the public may reflexively regard as desirable (such as reduced health inequalities) may on further analysis be rejected as too expensive or disruptive of valued social norms. An inability to explain precisely how certain policies will achieve specific goals may cause prospective allies to shift their priorities elsewhere.

The second requirement is sound strategic thinking about health policy in the context of democratic politics. In the end, the public has to support health policy, which means it will have to be persuaded that the ends are just, and the means are essential or at the very least tolerable. Political leadership must be similarly convinced in both absolute (the policies are worthy in themselves) and relative (they are worth pursuing more than the alternatives) terms.

Many broad policy or programmatic interventions have been successful, but the public is not always aware of them. The competition for public allegiance is staged in the media. Health policies are means to an elusive end, products in search of a market. A strategic approach to highlighting the interactions among health determinants and health status, as well as changes attributable to effective policy, would seem essential to generating a widespread public mandate to effect change.

A third element is to focus on smaller, defined, specific initiatives that have made a difference. It is crucial to avoid the impact fallacy: just because everything is ultimately connected to everything else does not mean that smaller actions are futile. Small policy and resource allocation changes can make a big difference for some people. Communicating the results may create a groundswell for larger scale transformations. The microlending phenomenon in developing nations is an example of a seemingly tiny program that may end up fundamentally changing the economies and social hierarchies of millions of people (Robinson 1996). Among the most satisfying aspects of Canada's National Forum on Health was its effort to seek out and communicate concrete success stories about improving health in specific populations (Anisef 1998; Bagley and Thurston 1998; Bennett and Offord 1998, Breen 1998; Caputo and Kelly 1998; Chappell 1998; Dyck et al. 1998; Fralick 1998; Godin and Michaud 1998; Gottlieb 1998a, 1998b; Lord and Hutchison 1998; Marshall and Clarke 1998; McDaniel 1998; Morrongiello 1998; Nahmiash 1998; O-Brien-Cousins 1998; K.A. Scott 1998; Singer and Martin 1998; Sudermann and Jaffe 1998; Tamblyn and Perreault 1998; Wolfe 1998; Zayed and Lefebvre 1998).

Perhaps the most fundamental strategic issue is whether we should regard health policy as logically prior to, or as a product of, broader social and economic policies. Should we address health status inequalities directly, concentrating on health-enhancing programs rather than general economic and social restructuring, or should we focus on the latter on the assumption that better health will follow inevitably? In other words, do we need to concern ourselves with health inequalities in particular if we solve the problem of socioeconomic inequalities in general?

Doubtless the interaction is bi-directional. Good health is a prerequisite to most forms of social and economic participation, while persistent socioeconomic inequalities render the attainment of good health improbable for disadvantaged groups. In light of this, the choices are strategic rather than binary; there is no either/or scenario guaranteed to produce the best results. Nevertheless, if we assume a finite capacity to introduce policy initiatives and mobilize 'civic capital' to effect change, it would appear wise for those who view the world through health lenses to engage in the broader political and economic discussions. There is nothing inherently virtuous about trying to improve health status in isolation from economic and political advancement. Indeed, the synergistic effect of progress on several fronts is almost certain to be more powerful than more narrowly focused policy initiatives.

RECONCILING PARADOXES

Reconfiguring health policy, then, requires thoughtful responses to emerging paradoxes. Healthy people can and do get ahead; but if they get too far ahead, others will be unhealthy because relative rather than absolute circumstances predispose towards good or ill-health after genetic and other luck-of-the-draw factors are controlled for. The loss of faith in 'big government' may have salutary effects on the economy and self-reliance, but if political cynicism translates into detachment from civic activities and community-building, health disparities will persist and new problems may emerge. A sense of remoteness and inability to influence huge organizations – be they governmental or corporate – can create a sense of either alienation or malaise. We do not fully understand the mechanisms by which a sense of powerlessness or disengagement, despite relatively good material conditions, translates into health status outcomes, but the Whitehall data have suggested that the combination of high stress and low control over one's environment are associated with poorer health status, while high stress and high control are not (Syme 1991).

If these relationships are confirmed by further research, the health policy vocabulary will have to include terms such as civicness, power, citizenship, and industrial strategy. Putnam (1993) attributes the comparative vitality of northern Italian regions compared with their southern counterparts to centuries-old differences in civic traditions. Community development theorists argue that the act of acquiring power over one's destiny has more lasting impact than the specific ways in which the power is applied. In Canada, some regional health authorities have established community development teams to address the needs of marginal groups by building their capacity to participate, in addition to ensuring access to services. Conceived in this way, reconfiguring health policy is substantially about extending and enriching democratic participation. While many decry the introduction of politics into matters of health, the web of accumulating evidence suggests that there is no alternative.

ACKNOWLEDGMENTS

The authors thank Denise Kouri, Tom Noseworthy, and Marie Fortier for helpful comments and advice on an earlier draft of this chapter.

NOTES

1 This accounting applies to the formal health system. National accounts do not include informal caregiving and other unpaid transactions. Health care, especially, if broadly defined, has always been a prominent human activity, but the twentieth century brought about both increased capacity to intervene (rather than simply palliate), and an unprecedented division of labour that ushered health care into the formal economy.

2 Universal suffrage and regular elections to some extent reinforce 'official shortsightedness.' A hereditary monarchy could commission the 300-year project without endangering itself politically every 4 years. Needless to say, this is not a refutation of democracy, but an observation about the constraints inherent in what are generally highly desirable political structures and processes.

3 Note, however, that work on the biological pathways is overcoming this gap and had the potential to transform research on population health into a more conventional science.

4 That the epistemological and scientific claims of medicine are often excessive and challengeable is here beside the point. Medicine has successfully marketed itself a 'hard science' and has consequently established a *de facto* methodological standard with which all forms of health interventions are subject to comparison.

5 It is conceivable that societies could find themselves facing an overall reduction in health status due to a severe economic downturn, societal dislocation (as in Eastern Europe), or an unanticipated and difficult-to-control outbreak of disease. In that instance, options 3 and 4 may indeed be relevant to public policy formulation. Nonetheless, in no case would a society deliberately choose to reduce health status; it might have to live with the prospect and decide where to exercise the limits of its control.

6 It would be interesting to discover whether the public generally (and by socioeconomic group) prefers greater aggregate wealth with large disparities in its

distribution, or a smaller GDP with smaller disparities. The inquiry might get even more interesting if one informed respondents of the impact of these alternatives on health status at various places along gradients of varying slope.

7 A full analysis of declining voter turnout, public cynicism about politics, and the impact of modern diversions on civic engagement would require another paper. The point here is simply that it may be prudent to assume that large segments of the public will need to be enticed to engage with certain issues and topics. This will require skilful social marketing.

8 Conservatism is highly nuanced and varied, both within and between nations. Some are economic liberals, others are troubled by unfettered market capitalism because of its disorderliness, disrespect for tradition, and materialism. Other conservatives are genuinely committed to equality of opportunity, but not outcome. One uniting feature of modern conservatism is its distrust of the state, which is a serious challenge for advocates of health-oriented public policy development.

9 Some of the accountability issues are related to the way that governments are organized into segregated departments, with the effects of one department's actions not being accounted for in another department, some departments being accountable in totally different ways than others, with no one taking responsibility for the whole.

REFERENCES

Anisef, P. (1998) 'Making the transition from school to employment', in *Determinants of Health – Settings and Issues* (Papers Commissioned by the National Forum on Health). Ottawa: Éditions MultiMondes.

Avison, W.R. (1998) 'The health consequences of unemployment', in *Determinants of Health – Settings and Issues* (Papers Commissioned by the National Forum on Health). Ottawa: Éditions MultiMondes.

Bagley, C. and Thurston, W.E. (1998) 'Decreasing child sexual abuse', in *Determinants of Health – Children and Youth*. (Papers Commissioned by the National Forum on Health). Ottawa: Éditions MultiMondes.

Bennett, K. and Offord, D.R. (1998) 'Schools, mental health and life quality', in *Determinants of Health – Settings and Issues* (Papers Commissioned by the National Forum on Health). Ottawa: Éditions MultiMondes.

Bertrand, J.E. (1998) 'Enriching the preschool experiences of children', in *Determinants of Health – Children and Youths*. (Papers Commissioned by the National Forum on Health). Ottawa: Éditions MultiMondes.

Breen, M.J. (1998) 'Promoting literacy, improving health', in *Determinants of Health – Settings and Issues*. (Papers Commissioned by the National Forum on Health). Ottawa: Éditions MultiMondes.

Brousselle, A. (1998) 'Controlling health care costs: What matters', in *Striking a Balance – Health Care Systems in Canada and Elsewhere* (Papers Commissioned by the National Forum on Health). Ottawa: Éditions MultiMondes.

Canada. Health and Welfare Canada (1974) *A New Perspective on the Health of Canadians*. (Lalonde Report). Ottawa.

Canadian Institute for Health Information (1997) National Health Expenditure Trends, 1975–77. Ottawa: Canadian Institute for Health Information.

Canadian Medical Association (1997) 'Higher earners seek more alternative care', *CMAJ*, 157: 996.

Caputo, T. and Kelly, K. (1998) 'Improving the health of street/homeless youth', in *Determinants of Health – Settings and Issues*. (Papers Commissioned by the National Forum on Health). Ottawa: Éditions MultiMondes.

Centre for International Statistics (1998) 'Health spending and health status: An international comparison', in *Striking a Balance – Health Care Systems in Canada and Elsewhere* (Papers Commissioned by the National Forum on Health). Ottawa: Éditions MultiMondes.

Chappell, N.L. (1998) 'Maintaining and enhancing independence and well-being in old age', in *Determinants of Health – Adults and Seniors* (Papers Commissioned by the National Forum on Health). Ottawa: Éditions MultiMondes.

Deber, R. and Swan, B. (1998) 'Puzzling issues in health care financing', in *Striking a Balance – Health Care Systems in Canada and Elsewhere* (Papers Commissioned by the National Forum on Health). Ottawa: Éditions MultiMondes.

Dubos, R. (1965). *Man Adapting*. New Haven, CT: Yale University Press.

Dyck, R.J., Mishara, B.L., and White, J. (1998) 'Suicide in children, adolescents and seniors: Key findings and policy implications', in *Determinants of Health – Settings and Issues* (Papers Commissioned by the National Forum on Health). Ottawa: Éditions MultiMondes.

Ekos (1998) Ekos Research Associates and Earnscliffe Research and Communications. 'Research on Canadian values in relation to health and the health care system', in *Making Decisions – Evidence and Information* (Papers commissioned by the National Forum on Health). Ottawa: Éditions MultiMondes.

Evans, R.G. (1984) *Strained Mercy: The Economics of Canadian Health Care*. Toronto: Butterworths.

Evans, R.G., Barer, M.L., and Marmor, T.R. (eds) (1994) *Why are Some People Healthy and Others Not? The Determinants of Health of Populations*. New York: Aldine de Gruyter.

Fisher, P., Hollander, M.J., MacKenzie, T., Kleinstiver, P., Sladecek, I., and Peterson, G. (1998) 'Decision support tools in health care', in *Making Decisions – Evidence and Information* (Papers Commissioned by the National Forum on Health). Ottawa: Éditions MultiMondes.

Fralick, P.C. (1998) 'Youth, substance abuse and the determinants of health' in *Determinants of Health – Children and Youths* (Papers Commissioned by the National Forum on Health). Ottawa: Éditions MultiMondes.

Godin, G. and Michaud, F. (1998) 'STD and AIDS Prevention among young people', in *Determinants of Health – Children and Youths.* (Papers Commissioned by the National Forum on Health). Ottawa: Éditions MultiMondes.

Gottlieb, B.H. (1998a) 'Protecting and promoting the well-being of family caregivers', in *Determinants of Health – Children and Youths.* (Papers Commissioned by the National Forum on Health). Ottawa: Éditions MultiMondes.

Gottlieb, B.H. (1998b) 'Strategies to promote the optimal development of Canada's youth', in *Determinants of Health – Settings and Issues* (Papers Commissioned by the National Forum on Health). Ottawa: Éditions MultiMondes.

Graubard, S. (ed.) (1994) *Health and Wealth. Daedalus,* 123: 4. Cambridge: American Academy of Arts and Sciences.

GRIS (Groupe de Recherche Interdisciplinaire en Santé) (1998) 'How Canada's health care system compares with that of other countries – an overview', in *Striking a Balance – Health Care Systems in Canada and Elsewhere* (Papers Commissioned by the National Forum on Health). Ottawa: Éditions MultiMondes.

Hamel, P. (1998) 'Community solidarity and local development: A new perspective for building socio-political compromise', in *Determinants of Health – Settings and Issues* (Papers Commissioned by the National Forum on Health). Ottawa: Éditions MultiMondes.

Hertzman, C., Kelly, S., and Bobak, M. (eds) (1996) *East-West Life Expectancy Gap in Europe: Environmental and Non-Environmental Determinants.* Dordrecht, The Netherlands: Kluwer, NATO ASI Series.

Kaplan, G.A., Pamuk, E.R., Lynch, J.W., Cohen, R.D., and Balfour, J.L. (1996) 'Inequality in income and mortality in the United States: Analysis of mortality and potential pathways', *British Medical Journal,* 312(7037): 999–1003.

Karasek, R. and Theorell, T. (1990) *Healthy Work: Stress and the Reconstruction of Working Life.* New York: Basic Books.

Kushner, C. and Rachlis, M. (1998) 'Consumer involvement in health policy development', in *Making Decisions – Evidence and Information* (Papers commissioned by the National Forum on Health). Ottawa: Éditions MultiMondes.

Lantz, P.M., House, J.S., Lepkowski, J.M., Williams, D.R., Mero, R.P., and Chen, J. (1998) 'Socioeconomic factors, health behaviours, and mortality', *JAMA,* 279: 1703–8.

Lin, R.J., Shah, C.P., and Svoboda, T.J. (1997) 'The impact of unemployment on health: A review of the evidence', *Journal of Public Health Policy,* 18: 275–301.

Lord, J. and Hutchison, P. (1998) 'Living with a disability in Canada: Toward autonomy and integration', in *Determinants of Health – Settings and Issues.* (Papers Commissioned by the National Forum on Health). Ottawa: Éditions MultiMondes.

Marmot, M.G. (1986) 'Social inequalities in mortality: The social environment', in R. G. Wilkinson (ed.) *Class and Health: Research and Longitudinal Data.* London: Tavistock. pp. 21–33.

Marshall, Victor W. and Clarke, P.J. (1998) 'Facilitating the transition from employment to retirement', in *Determinants of Health – Adults and Seniors* (Papers Commissioned by the National Forum on Health). Ottawa: Éditions MultiMondes.

McDaniel, S.A. (1998) 'Toward healthy families', in *Determinants of Health – Children and Youth* (Papers Commissioned by the National Forum on Health). Ottawa: Éditions MultiMondes.

McKeown, T. (1979) *The Role of Medicine. Dream, Mirage or Nemesis?* (2nd edn) Oxford: Basil Blackwell.

Morrongiello, B.A. (1998) 'Preventing unintentional injuries among children', in *Determinants of Health – Children and Youth.* (Papers Commissioned by the National Forum on Health). Ottawa: Éditions MultiMondes.

Mustard, C.A. (1996) 'Est-il possible de décider d'un ordre de priorité dans nos investissements dans les technologies médicales et autres programmes de santé', in Renaud and Bouchard (eds), *Technologies médicales et changement de valeurs* (Sociologie et Sociétés, vol. XXVIII, numéro 2, automne 1996), 173–88.

Nahmiash, D. (1998) 'Preventing, reducing and stopping the abuse and neglect of older adults in Canadian communities', in *Determinants of Health – Adults and Seniors* (Papers Commissioned by the National Forum on Health). Ottawa: Éditions MultiMondes.

National Forum on Health (1997a) *Canada Health Action: Building the Legacy – Final Report.* Ottawa: Minister of Public Works and government Services.

National Forum on Health (1997b) *Canada Health Action: Building the Legacy* – Synthesis Reports and Issues Papers. Ottawa: Minister of Public Works and Government Services.

O'Brien-Cousins, S. (1998) 'Promoting active living and healthy eating among older Canadians', in *Determinants of Health – Adults and Seniors* (Papers Commissioned by the National Forum on Health). Ottawa: Éditions MultiMondes.

OECD (1997) *Health Data 1997*. Paris.

Osberg, L. (1998) 'Economic policy variables and population health', in *Determinants of Health – Settings and Issues* (Papers Commissioned by the National Forum on Health). Ottawa: Éditions MultiMondes.

Polanyi, M., Eakin, J., Frank, J., Shannon, H., and Sullivan, T. (1998a) 'Creating healthier work environments: A critical review of the health impacts of workplace change', in *Determinants of Health – Settings and Issues*. (Papers Commissioned by the National Forum on Health). Ottawa: Éditions MultiMondes.

Polanyi, M. et al. (1998b) 'Promoting the determinants of health in the workplace', in Poland, Rootman, and Green (eds), *Settings for Health Promotion*, Newbury Park, CA: Sage Publications.

Putnam, R. (1993). *Making Democracy Work: Civic Traditions in Modern Italy*. Princeton, NJ: Princeton University Press.

Robinson, M.S. (1996) 'Addressing some key questions on finance and poverty', *Journal of International Development*, Vol. 8, No. 2, March–April, Special Issue: Sustainable Banking with the Poor (Guest Editors L. Bennett and C. Cuevas).

Sapolsky, R.M. (1992). *Stress, the Aging Brain, and the Mechanisms of Neuron Death*. Cambridge, MA: MIT Press.

Scott, K.A (1998) 'Balance as a method to promote healthy indigenous communities', in *Determinants of Health – Settings and Issues*. (Papers Commissioned by the National Forum on Health). Ottawa: Éditions MultiMondes.

Singer, P. and Martin, D.K. (1998) 'Improving dying in Canada', in *Determinants of Health – Adults and Seniors* (Papers Commissioned by the National Forum on Health). Ottawa: Éditions MultiMondes.

Steinhauer, P.D. (1998) 'Developing resiliency in children from disadvantaged populations', in *Determinants of Health – Children and Youth*. (Papers Commissioned by the National Forum on Health). Ottawa: Éditions MultiMondes.

Sudermann, M. and Jaffe, P.G. (1998) 'Preventing violence: School- and community-based strategies', in *Determinants of Health – Settings and Issues*. (Papers Commissioned by the National Forum on Health). Ottawa: Éditions MultiMondes.

Sullivan, T., Uneke, O., Lavis, J., Hyat, D., and O'Grady, J. (1998) 'Labour adjustment policy and health: Considerations for a changing world', in *Determinants of Health – Settings and Issues* (Papers Commissioned by the National Forum on Health). Ottawa: Éditions MultiMondes.

Suomi, S.J. (1991) 'Primate separation models of affective disorders', in J. Madden (ed.), *Neurobiology of Learning, Emotion and Affect*. New York: Raven. pp. 195–214.

Syme, S.L. (1991) 'Control and health: A personal perspective', *Advances*, 7(2): 16–27.

Tamblyn, R. and Perreault, R. (1998) 'Encouraging the wise use of prescription medication by older adults', in *Determinants of Health – Adults and Seniors* (Papers Commissioned by the National Forum on Health). Ottawa: Éditions MultiMondes.

Tranmer, J.E., Squires, S., Brazil, K., Gerlach, J., Johnson, J., Muisner, D., Swan, B., and Wilson, R. (1998) 'Evidence-based decision making: What works and what doesn't work', in *Making Decisions – Evidence and Information* (Papers commissioned by the National Forum on Health). Ottawa: Éditions MultiMondes.

Wilkinson, R.G. (1992) 'Income distribution and life expectancy', *British Medical Journal*, 304: 165–8.

Wolfe, D.A. (1998) 'Prevention of child abuse and neglect', in *Determinants of Health – Children and Youth* (Papers Commissioned by the National Forum on Health). Ottawa: Éditions MultiMondes.

Wolfson, M. (1994) 'POHEM – a framework for understanding and modelling the health of human populations', *World Health Statistics Quarterly*, 47: 157–76.

Zayed, J. and Lefebvre, L. (1998) 'Environmental health: From concept to reality', in *Determinants of Health – Settings and Issues* (Papers Commissioned by the National Forum on Health). Ottawa: Éditions MultiMondes.

Author Index

Subject Index